# SOCIAL GERONTOLOGY
## A MULTIDISCIPLINARY PERSPECTIVE

FOURTH EDITION

Nancy R. Hooyman

H. Asuman Kiyak

UNIVERSITY OF WASHINGTON

Allyn and Bacon

BOSTON   LONDON   TORONTO   SYDNEY   TOKYO   SINGAPORE

*Executive Editor:* Karen Hanson
*Vice President, Publisher: Social Sciences:* Susan Badger
*Executive Marketing Manager:* Joyce Nilsen
*Production Administrator:* Marjorie Payne
*Cover Administrator:* Linda Knowles
*Composition/Prepress Buyer:* Linda Cox
*Manufacturing Buyer:* Megan Cochran
*Editorial-Production Service:* Chestnut Hill Enterprises, Inc.

*Library of Congress Cataloging-in-Publication Data*

Hooyman, Nancy R.
    Social gerontology : a multidisciplinary perspective / Nancy R.
Hooyman, H. Asuman Kiyak. — 4th ed.
      p.  cm.
    Includes index.
    ISBN 0-205-16776-4 (alk. paper)
    1. Gerontology.  2. Aging.  3. Aged—United States.  I. Kiyak, H.
Asuman.  II. Title.
HQ1061.H583  1995                  95-33032
305.26—dc20                     CIP

Printed in the United States of America

10  9  8  7  6  5  4  3  2       00  99  98  97  96

Photo credits begin on page 591 which is a continuation of this page.

To Gene, Kevin, Christopher and Mani, for their constant support.
To my father, Hugh Runkle, for his 89-year example.

NRH

To my father, who epitomized ego integrity.
To Joe and Lara, for their love and encouragement.

HAK

To our friend and colleague, Naomi R. Gottlieb,
who was a model of successful aging.

NRH
HAK

*Nancy R. Hooyman*

Nancy R. Hooyman is professor and dean at the School of Social Work at the University of Washington in Seattle. Her Ph.D. is in sociology and social work from the University of Michigan. She is nationally recognized for her scholarship in aging, issues related to family caregiving, gender inequities in caregiving, feminist social work practice, and administration. In addition to this textbook, Dean Hooyman is the coauthor of *Taking Care of Aging Family Members*, and *Feminist Perspectives on Family Care: Policies for Gender Justice,* and has edited *Feminist Social Work Practice in Clinical Settings.* She has published over 70 articles and chapters related to gerontology and women's issues. Her research interests are in family caregiving of persons with chronic disabilities, home-based services, feminist practice models, and older women's issues.

*H. Asuman Kiyak*

H. Asuman Kiyak is Director of the Institute on Aging, professor in the School of Dentistry and adjunct professor in the Departments of Architecture and Psychology at the University of Washington. She obtained her Ph.D. in psychology at Wayne State University. Professor Kiyak has been the recipient of major research grants from NIH, AOA, and private foundations in the areas of health promotion and health service utilization by older adults, and in person-environment adaptation to Alzheimer's disease by patients and their caregivers. She has published over 70 articles and 20 chapters in these areas, and is known nationally and internationally for her research on geriatric dental care and the application of psychological theory to health promotion.

# CONTENTS

# PREFACE

Aging is a complex and fascinating process, one which we all experience. It is complex because of its many facets—physiological, emotional, cognitive, economic, and interpersonal—that influence our social functioning and well-being. It is a fascinating process because these changes occur differently in each one of us. There is considerable truth to the statement that, as we grow older, we become more unlike each other.

Aging is also a process that attracts the attention of the media, politicians, business and industry, and the general public, largely because we live in a rapidly aging society. Changes in the numbers and proportion of older people in our population have numerous implications for societal structures, including the family, health and long-term care, pension and retirement practices, political processes, community and recreational services, and housing. In addition, these changes are of growing concern because of the problems of poverty, inadequate housing, and chronic disease faced by some older people, particularly women, ethnic minorities, the oldest-old, and those living alone. Public officials as well as individuals in the private sector are faced with the challenge of planning for a future in which the segment of the population over age 55 will experience the most rapid growth.

These changes have also meant that most colleges and universities now offer courses in gerontology, or the study of aging. The goal of some of these courses is to prepare students to work effectively with older people; most of them seek to enhance students' personal understanding of their own and others' aging. Frequently, students take such a course simply to meet a requirement, discounting the relevance of the aging process to their own lives. Thus, instructors are often faced with the need to help students see the connection between learning about aging and understanding their own behavior, the behavior of their relatives, and often the behavior of their clients.

This book grew out of our experiences in teaching gerontology courses to undergraduate students. In doing so, we were unable to locate a textbook that conveyed the excitement and relevance of understanding the aging process or one that adequately addressed the biological, psychological, and social aspects of aging. For years, we were frustrated by the lack of a text that was comprehensive, thorough, and timely in its review of the rapidly growing research on the elderly. As a sociologist/social worker and psychologist, we have been committed to developing a text that could be useful to a wide range of disciplines, including nursing, social work, sociology, psychology, health education, and the allied health professions.

## AIMS AND FOCUS

The primary focus of this book is social gerontology. As the title implies, however, our goal is to present the diversities of the aging experience and the older population in a multidisciplinary manner. It is our premise that an examination of the social lives of older people requires a basic understanding of the historical, cultural, biological, physiological, psychological, and social contexts of aging. It is important to understand the changes that occur within the aging individual, how these changes influence interactions with social and physical environments, and how the older person is, in turn, affected by such interactions. Throughout this book, the significance of these dynamic interactions between older people and their environments for quality of life is a unifying theme.

Social gerontology is a growing field with numerous salient areas of research. This book does not purport to cover all these areas, but rather to highlight major research findings that illuminate the processes of aging. Through such factual information, we intend to dispel some of the myths and negative attitudes about aging. We also hope to encourage the reader to pursue this field, both academically and for the personal rewards that come from gaining insight into older people's lives. Because the field is so complex and rapidly changing, more recent research findings may appear to contradict earlier studies. We are thorough in presenting a multiplicity of theoretical perspectives and empirical data to insure that the reader has as full and accurate a picture of the field as possible.

## FEATURES

This book begins by reviewing major demographic, historical, and cross-cultural changes and their implications for the development of the field of social gerontology and, in particular, of social theories of aging. We then turn to the major biological and physiological changes that affect older people's daily functioning, as well as their risk of chronic diseases and consequent utilization of health and long term care services. The third section considers psychological changes, particularly in learning and memory, personality, sexuality, and mental health. Given our emphasis on how such physical and psychological changes affect the social aspects of aging, we consider in depth the social context of the family, the community, the economy, living arrangements, and the conditions under which people die. Throughout the book, the differential impacts that these changes have on women and ethnic minorities are identified, with two chapters focusing specifically on such differences. To highlight the application of research findings to everyday situations, each chapter integrates discussions of both the policy and practice implications of the aging process. We conclude by turning to the larger context of social, health, and long-term care policies and future implications for the field.

## NEW TO THIS EDITION

The positive response of students and faculty who have used the first three editions suggests that we have been successful in achieving our goals for this book. Based on the feedback of many students and faculty, the fourth edition represents an update of research in all areas as well as a greater focus on racial, cultural, gender and socioeconomic diversity in aging; the legal and ethical issues surrounding increased life expectancy, including the use of advance directives and the controversies inherent within the right-to-die movement; the growing body of research related to successful and productive aging; and life span changes, including alterations in family relationships, sexuality and intimacy. Given the dramatically changing political arena, the chapters on social, health and long-term care policies have been rewritten to reflect contemporary policy debates, to address the need for home and community-based care alternatives to institutionalization, and to take account of the increasing diversity of the older population.

The fourth edition also elaborates on rapidly changing issues such as new research on the causes of Alzheimer's and other dementias, the prevention of chronic diseases and their potentially debilitating effects among older people, older family members who are caring for younger generations, including those developmentally disabled or chronically mentally ill, and new housing options that allow older people to move in and out of different settings more readily rather than a single trajectory toward dependency. These increased housing alternatives reflect another theme of the book: older persons can improve as well as decline in their physical and functional health. The increased attention given to differences in the aging process by gender, ethnicity and socioeconomic status, and to social, health and long-term policy debates in this edition is a reflection of the dramatic demographic and economic changes facing us as we approach the 21st century.

## ANNENBERG/CPB TELEVISION COURSE

*Social Gerontology* is being offered as part of the Annenberg/CPB college-level television course *Growing Old in a New Age,* broadcast on PBS and used as a telecourse.

*Growing Old in a New Age* is a thirteen-part public television series and college-level course that provides an understanding of the processes of aging, of old age as a stage of life, and the impact of aging on society. The television series and course respond to the demographic wave that is sweeping our nation and world, exploring questions about what roles people will play in their eighth, ninth, and tenth decades, and how institutions may evolve to address their needs. *Growing Old in a New Age* also offers opportunities for the student and viewer to examine personal attitudes toward aging and older people. Material contributed by outstanding social scientists, medical professionals, and clinicians provides a multidisciplinary, multicultural approach. Extensive interviews with older people themselves support this cross-cultural and comprehensive introduction to gerontology.

In addition to *Social Gerontology,* a student *Telecourse Study Guide* is available through the college bookstore. A *Telecourse Faculty Guide* is available without charge to those who license the telecourse. The programs may be purchased on videocassettes by calling the Annenberg/CPB Collection at 1-800-LEARNER. Off-air taping licenses may be acquired from either the Annenberg CPB Collection or the PBS Adult Learning Service. Colleges and universities may license the use of *Growing Old in a New Age* as a telecourse for college credit through the PBS Adult Learning Service (1-800-257-2578; in Virginia, 703-739-5363).

## ACKNOWLEDGMENTS

We are grateful to the many people who have contributed significantly to the successful completion of the fourth edition of *Social Gerontology*. In particular, we thank Alison Beck, Fred Cox, Asantewa DeFrietas, Valerie Higgins (who even violated her doctor's orders to stay home in order to help with the final stages of production), Larry Patrick, and Kim Yelsa for assisting us with library research and the technical aspects of the revisions. Their willingness to "pitch in" and do whatever tasks were necessary was a tremendous support. We also thank Marty Richards for her assistance in preparing "real-life" examples of people's experiences with the diverse aspects of aging. Our families, Gene, Kevin, and Christopher Hooyman, and Joe and Lara Clark, have been the mainstay of support throughout the preparation of all four editions of this book. And Gnanamani Hooyman, who arrived from India to join the Hooyman family in the midst of book preparations, has never known her mother not to be working on THE book. We would also like to thank our editor at Allyn and Bacon, Karen Hanson, for her continued encouragement in completing this edition.

We appreciate the assistance from staff associated with the Center on Aging, University of Hawaii at Manoa, who have chosen our text for the first national telecourse on aging, *Growing Old in a New Age*. We are grateful to Dr. Anthony Lenzer, Telecourse Project Director, for providing us with the opportunity to work with him and his committed, enthusiastic telecourse staff: Dr. Joan Dubanoski, Assistant Project Director; Rebecca Goodman, Project Coordinator; Jay Curlee, Producer/Director for the video series; Dr. Kathryn Braun, Student and Faculty Guides Writer; Ellen Roberts, Field Evaluator; and Floriana Cofman, Researcher. In addition to developing the series, the telecourse staff provided us with detailed, useful feedback on many of our chapters.

We also thank Dr. Hilda Moskowitz, Senior Project Officer at the Annenberg/CPB Project, for the vision and the funding to make the telecourse project possible; and the National Advisory Committee for the Telecourse for their guidance regarding revisions in the text—Mr. Tom MacLachlan, from North Shore Community College in Massachusetts; Mr. Ancil H. Payne, retired President of KING broadcasting in Seattle; Dr. David Peterson, Director of the UCLA Leonard Davis School of Gerontology; Dr. K. Warner Schaie, Director of the Pennsylvania State University Gerontology Center; and Dr. Jeanette Takamura, Director of the Executive Office on Aging, State of Hawaii.

In addition, we would like to thank the following reviewers for their helpful comments: Jeanne E. Bader, California State University; Karen A. Roberto, University of Northern Colorado; Kris Bulcroft, Western Washington University; Perry G. Thompson, University of Arkansas at Little Rock; Donald McTavish, University of Minnesota; Brenda J. Moretta, Our Lady of the Lake University; and Dale A. Lund, The University of Utah.

# INTRODUCTION

# WHAT IS SOCIAL GERONTOLOGY?

## TOWARD UNDERSTANDING AGING

From the perspective of youth and middle age, old age seems a remote and, to some, an undesirable period of life. Throughout history, humans have made attempts to prolong youth and to delay aging. The attempts to discover a substance to rejuvenate the body and mind have driven explorers to far corners of the globe, and have inspired alchemists and scientists to search for ways to restore youth and prolong life. Indeed, the discovery of Florida by Ponce de Leon in 1513 was an accident, as he searched for a fountain in Bimini whose waters were rumored to bring back one's youth. The theme of prolonging or restoring youth is evident today in advertisements for skin creams, soaps, vitamins, and certain foods; in the popularity of cosmetic surgery; in books and movies that feature attractive, youthful-looking older characters; and even in medical research and technology that extends life.

All of these concerns point to underlying fears of aging. Many of our concerns and fears arise from misconceptions about what happens to our bodies, our minds, our status in society,

and our social lives as we reach our seventies, eighties, and beyond. They arise, in part, from negative attitudes toward older people within our own culture. These attitudes are sometimes identified as manifestations of *ageism,* a term that was coined by Robert Butler, the first Director of the National Institute on Aging, to describe stereotypes about old age. As is true for sexism and racism, ageism attributes certain characteristics to all members of a group solely because of a characteristic they share—in this case, their age. In fact, ageism is one prejudice that we are all likely to encounter sooner or later, regardless of our gender, ethnic minority status, social class, or sexual orientation. A frequent result of ageism is discriminatory behavior against the target group (i.e., older persons). For example, some aging advocates have argued that older, experienced workers are encouraged to retire early rather than laying off younger, less experienced workers because of stereotypes about older people's physical and cognitive abilities.

To distinguish the realities of aging from the social stereotypes surrounding this process

1

---

## PONCE DE LEON'S SEARCH FOR THE FOUNTAIN OF YOUTH

The quest for gold and other riches attracted many Spanish adventurers to the New World in the fifteenth and sixteenth centuries. Among these was Ponce de Leon, who landed on Puerto Rico in 1508. He heard from Indians in the area stories of a fountain whose waters were believed to rejuvenate older people and restore their youth. This fountain was said to be located on the island of Bimini in the Bahamas. He set forth in 1512 from Puerto Rico in search of this fountain. By then, word of the magic fountain had spread to Europe; both the Spanish court and the Pope encouraged Ponce de Leon in his efforts. Of course, he never did find the fountain of youth, but his search was not futile; he found Florida instead.

*Source:* From O. Segerberg, *The immortality factor* (New York: E. P. Dutton & Co., 1974).

---

requires an understanding of the "normal" changes that can be expected in the aging body, in mental and emotional functioning, and in social interactions and status. Aging can then be understood as a phase of growth and development—a universal biological phenomenon. Accordingly, the normal processes due to age alone need to be differentiated from pathological changes or disease. As life expectancy increases, as the older proportion of our population grows, and as more of us can look forward to becoming older ourselves, concerns and questions about the aging process continue to attract widespread public and professional attention.

## THE FIELD OF GERONTOLOGY

The growing interest in understanding the process of aging has given rise to the multidisciplinary field of *gerontology*, the study of the biological, psychological, and social aspects of aging. Gerontologists include researchers and practitioners in such diverse fields as biology, medicine, nursing, dentistry, physical and occupational therapy, psychology, psychiatry, sociology, economics, political science, and social work. These individuals are concerned with many aspects of aging, from studying and describing the cellular processes involved, to seeking ways to improve the quality of life for older people. *Geriatrics* is focused on how to prevent or manage the diseases of aging. The field has become a specialty in medicine, nursing, and dentistry, and is receiving more attention with the increase in the number of older people who have long-term health problems.

Gerontologists view aging in terms of four distinct processes, which will be examined throughout this book.

**1.** *Chronological aging* is the definition of aging on the basis of a person's years from birth. Thus, a 75-year-old is chronologically older than a 45-year-old. Chronological age is not necessarily related to a person's biological or physical age, nor to their psychological or social age, as we will emphasize throughout this book.

**2.** *Biological aging* refers to the physical changes that reduce the efficiency of organ systems, such as the lungs, heart, and circulatory system. A major cause of biological aging is the decline in the number of cell replications as an organism becomes chronologically older. Another factor is the loss of certain types of cells that do not replicate. This type of aging can be determined by measuring functioning of an individual's organ systems, as well as physical activity levels.

**3.** *Psychological aging* includes the changes that occur in sensory and perceptual processes, mental functioning (e.g., memory, learning, and intelligence), adaptive capacity, personality, drives, and motives. Thus, an individual who is intellectually active and adapts well to new situations can be considered psychologically young.

4. *Social aging* refers to an individual's changing roles and relationships in the social structure—with family and friends, with the work world, and within organizations such as religious and political groups. As people age chronologically, biologically, and psychologically, their social roles and relationships also alter. The social context, which can vary considerably for different people, determines the meaning of aging for an individual and whether the aging experience will be primarily negative or positive.

Social gerontologists study the impact of changes on both older people and our social structures. They also study social attitudes toward aging and the effects of these attitudes on the older population. For example, as a society, we have tended to undervalue older people and to assume that most elderly are unintelligent, unemployable, nonproductive, uninterested in interacting with younger people, senile, and asexual—assumptions not supported by facts. As a result, the activities open to older people, particularly jobs in fields that require technical skills, have been limited. As Robert Butler has noted, "The tragedy of old age is not that each of us must grow old and die, but that the process of doing so has been made unnecessarily and at times excruciatingly painful, humiliating, debilitating, and isolating" (Butler, 1975, pp. 2–3).

However, since stereotypes of old age are socially constructed, they are capable of undergoing change if society's values alter. Fortunately, such changes are beginning to occur as the public becomes more aware of older people's capabilities and realizes that most elderly are not poor, most do not live in nursing homes, most are not victims of senile dementia, and many are capable of productive activities such as employment, volunteering, and assisting other family members. With the growth in the number and diversity of older persons, societal myths and stereotypes have been challenged. The public has become increasingly aware of older citizens' strengths and contributions. The result of these actions has been to change the status of older people in our society and the way that other groups view them. Contemporary advertising, for example, reflects the changing status of older people, from a group that is viewed as weak, ill, and poor, to one perceived as politically and economically powerful, and, therefore, a growing market.

As older people have become more politically active and as advocacy groups have emerged in support of seniors' rights, they have influenced not only public perceptions, but also laws that govern Social Security and other age-based policies and programs. Organized groups of elderly have helped to bring changes in retirement and pension policies, housing options, community facilities, health and social service organizations, continuing education, and other services. Such political and attitudinal changes, which can profoundly transform the condition of older people, are also important issues in the study of social gerontology.

Equally significant in this area of study are the social and health problems that continue to affect a large percentage of older people. Even though the elderly are financially better off than they were twenty years ago, over 12 percent still fall below our government's official poverty line. Poverty is an even greater problem for women, ethnic minorities, those living alone, and the oldest of the old. Although less than 5 percent of the elderly are in nursing homes, the number who will require long-term care at some point in their lives is increasing. Growing percentages of older people in the community face chronic diseases that may limit their daily activities. One problem that affects an even larger proportion of the older population is escalating health and long-term care costs. In general, older people pay a higher proportion of their income for health care than they have at any time in the past, and often lack access to home and community-based services. Therefore, many gerontologists are also concerned with developing policy and practice interventions to address these problems.

## SOCIAL GERONTOLOGY

The purpose of this book is to introduce you to *social gerontology*. This term was first used by Clark Tibbitts in 1954 to describe the area of gerontology that is concerned with the impact of social and sociocultural conditions on the process of aging and with the social consequences of this process. This field has grown as we have recognized the extent to which aging differs across cultures and societies.

Social gerontologists are interested in how the older population and the varieties of aging experiences both affect and are affected by the social structure. Older people are now the fastest-growing population segment in the United States, with a growth rate much higher than that for younger age groups. The number of people over age 85 will expand rapidly in the coming decades. This fact has far-reaching social implications for the areas of health and long-term care, workplace pension and retirement practices, community facilities, and patterns of government spending. Already, it has led to new specialties in health care and long-term care; the growth of specialized services such as retirement housing, nursing homes, adult day health programs, and a leisure industry aimed at the older population. Changes in the sociopolitical structure, in turn, affect characteristics of the older population. For example, the widespread availability of secondary and higher education, health promotion programs, and employment-based pensions offers hope that future generations of older people will be better educated, healthier, and economically more secure than the current generation.

## WHAT IS OLD AGE?

Contrary to the messages on birthday cards, aging does not start at age 40 or 65. Even though we are less conscious of age-related changes in earlier stages of our lives, we are all aging from the moment of birth. Younger stages are generally referred to as *development* or *maturation*, because the individual develops and matures, both socially and physically, from birth through adolescence. After age 30, additional changes occur that reflect normal declines in all organ systems. This is called *senescence*. Senescence happens gradually throughout the body, ultimately reducing the viability of different bodily systems and increasing their vulnerability to disease. This is the final stage in the development of an organism.

Our place in the social structure also changes throughout our life span. Every society is *age-graded*; that is, it assigns different roles, expectations, opportunities, status, and constraints to people of different ages. For example, there are common social expectations about the appropriate age to attend school, begin work, have children, and retire—even though many people deviate from these expectations, and some of these expectations change over time. To call someone a *toddler, child, young adult,* or *old person* is to imply a full range of social characteristics. As we age, we pass through a sequence of defined stages, each with its own social norms and characteristics. In sum, age is a social construct with social meanings and social implications.

The specific effects of age grading, or age stratification, vary across different cultures and historical time periods. A primitive society, for instance, has very different expectations associated with stages of childhood, adolescence, and old age from our contemporary American cultures. Even within our own culture, those who are old today have different experiences of aging than previous or future groups of elderly. The term *cohort* is used to describe groups of people who were born at approximately the same time and therefore share many common experiences. For example, current cohorts of older persons have experienced the Great Depression and World War II and the Korean War. These experiences have shaped their lives. Its members include large numbers of immigrants who came to the United States in the first third of the twentieth century, and many who have grown up in rural areas. Their average levels of education are lower than those of later generations. Such factors set today's elderly apart from other cohorts and must be taken into account in any studies of the aging process.

## A DIVERSE POPULATION

Throughout this book, we will refer to the phenomenon of aging and the population of older people. These terms are based, to some extent, on chronological criteria, but, more importantly, on individual differences in social, psychological, and biological functioning. In fact, each of us differs somewhat in the way we define old age. You may know an 80-year-old who seems youthful and a 50-year-old whom you consider elderly. Older people also define themselves differently. Some individuals, even in their eighties, do not want to associate with "those old people," whereas others readily join age-based organizations and are proud of the years they have lived. There are significant differences among the "young-old" (ages 65 to 74), the "old-old" (ages 75 to 84), and the "oldest-old" (over age 85) (Riley and Riley, 1986), or, as one of the authors likes to express it, the "frisky, the frail, and the fragile." However, there is diversity even within these divisions.

Older people vary greatly in their health status, their social and work activities, and their family situations. Some are still employed full- or part-time; most are retired. Most are healthy; some are frail, confused, or home-bound. Most still live in a house or apartment; a small percentage are in nursing homes. Some receive large incomes from pensions and investments; many depend primarily on Social Security and have little discretionary income. Most men over age 65 are married, whereas women are more likely to become widowed and live alone as they age. For all these reasons, it is impossible to consider the social aspects of aging without also assessing the impact of individual variables such as physiological changes, health status, psychological well-

being, socioeconomic class, gender, and ethnic minority status. For this reason, many chapters in this book focus on biological, physiological, health, psychological, gender, and ethnic characteristics of older persons that influence their social functioning.

It is likewise impossible to define aging only in chronological terms, since chronological age only partially reflects the biological, psychological, and sociological processes that define life stages. Although the terms *elderly* and *older persons* are often used to mean those over 65 years in chronological age, this book is based on the principle that aging is a complex process that involves many different factors and is unique to each individual. Rather than chronological age, the more important distinctions may be between independent and dependent, or vigorous and frail.

## A PERSON-ENVIRONMENT PERSPECTIVE ON SOCIAL GERONTOLOGY

As we noted at the outset, this text is primarily concerned with social gerontology, and thus with the relationship between older people and society. These social relationships, in turn, are affected by physiological and psychological changes that occur with age. All these domains—the social, the physical, and the psychological—affect older persons' relationships with their environments, including the social world of family, friends, work colleagues, and neighbors, and physical features such as the layout of their homes, neighborhoods, or communities. This textbook will approach topics in social gerontology from a person-environment perspective.

A social environmental (Hendricks and Hendricks, 1981), or person-environment transactional approach (Schwartz, 1974), suggests that the environment is not a static backdrop but changes continually as the older person takes from it what he or she needs, controls what can be manipulated, and adjusts to conditions that cannot be changed. Adaptation thus implies a dual process in which the individual adjusts to some characteristics of the environment (e.g., completing the numerous forms required by Medicare), and brings about changes in others (e.g., lobbying to expand Medicare benefits to cover dental care).

## Environmental Press

One useful way to view the dynamic interactions between the physical and psychological characteristics of the aging individual with the social and physical environment is Lawton and Nahemow's (1973) model of an individual's competence relative to environmental press. *Environment* in this model, which is shown in Figure 1, may refer to the larger society, the community,

the neighborhood, or the home. *Environmental press* refers to the demands that social and physical environments make on the individual to adapt, respond, or change.

The environmental press model can be approached from a variety of disciplinary perspectives. A concept fundamental to social work, for example, is that of person-and-environment and the need to develop practice and policy interventions that achieve a better fit between the person and his or her social environment. Health care providers are increasingly aware of the necessity to take account of social and physical environmental factors in their assessments of health problems. Architects and advocates for persons with disabilities are developing ways to make physical environments more accessible for older

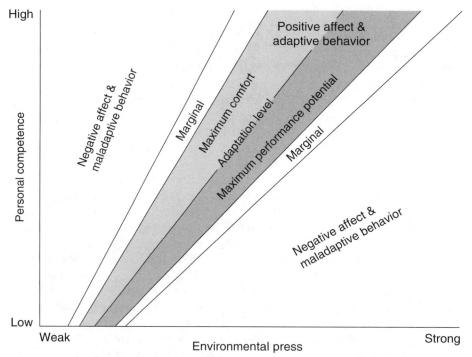

**FIGURE I-I   Diagrammatic Representation of the Behavioral and Affective Outcomes of Person-Environment Transactions**

SOURCE: M. P. Lawton and L. Nahemow, Ecology and the aging process. In C. Eisdorfer and M. P. Lawton (Eds.), *Psychology of adult development and aging* (Washington, D.C.: American Psychological Association, 1973), p. 661. Copyright 1973 by the American Psychological Association. Reprinted by permission of the author and publisher.

people with chronic health care problems. Psychologists are interested in how physical and social environments may be modified to maximize the older person's ability to learn new tasks and perform familiar ones such as driving, taking tests, and self-care. Sociologists study ways that the macro-environment (larger political and economic structures) affects and is affected by an individual's interactions with it. Because the concepts of this model are so basic to understanding the elderly's position in our society and to developing ways to improve the quality of their lives, such environmental interactions will be referred to throughout this text.

We encourage the reader to identify ways to apply this model to diverse settings where older people interact. A concept central to this model is environmental press, which can range from minimal to quite high. For example, very little environmental press is present in an institutional setting where an individual is not responsible for self-care, such as grooming and housekeeping, and has few resources to stimulate the senses or challenge the mind. Other environments can create a great deal of press, for example, a multigenerational household with many members in which the older person plays a pivotal role. Living in a familiar setting with few visitors generates low levels of environmental press. An increase in the number of people sharing the living arrangement or a move to a new home would increase the environmental demands. As the demands change, the individual must adapt to the changes in order to maintain a sense of well-being. Individuals perform at their maximum level when the environmental press slightly exceeds the level at which they adapt. In other words, the environment challenges them to test their limits, but does not overwhelm them. If the level of environmental demand becomes too high, the individual experiences excessive stress or overload. When the environmental press is far below the individual's adaptation level, sensory deprivation, boredom, learned helplessness, and dependence on others may result. However, a situation of mild to moderate stress, just below the

person's adaptation level, results in maximum comfort. It is important to challenge the individual in this situation as well, to prevent a decline to boredom and inadequate stimulation. In either situation—too much or too little environmental press—the person or the environment must change, if the individual's adaptive capacity is to be restored.

Another concept central to this model is *individual competence*. This is defined by Lawton and Nahemow (1973) as the theoretical upper limit of an individual's abilities to function in the areas of health, social behavior, and cognition. Some of the abilities needed to adapt to environmental press include good health, effective problem solving and learning, skills, job performance and the ability to manage the basic activities of daily living such as dressing, grooming, and cooking (Lawton, 1983). As suggested by the model in Figure I-1, the higher a person's competence, the higher the levels of environmental press that can be tolerated. Thus, an older person with multiple physical disabilities and chronic illnesses has reduced physical competence, thereby limiting the level of social and physical demands with which he or she can cope.

## Environmental Interventions

The competence model has numerous implications for identifying interventions to enhance the lives of older individuals. Most services for older people are oriented toward minimizing environmental demands and increasing supports. These services may focus on changing the physical or social environment, or both. Physical environmental modifications, such as ramps and handrails, and community services, such as Meals-on-Wheels and escort vans, are relatively simple ways to reestablish the older person's level of adaptation and to ease the burdens of daily coping. Such arrangements are undoubtedly essential to the well-being of some older people who require supports in the form of environmental adaptations or occasional assistance from family and paid caregivers to enhance their independence. For example, many older people with chronic conditions are able to remain in their own homes because of environmental modifications such as lowered cupboards and countertops, electronic mechanisms that allow them to call for help, and vans equipped for wheelchairs.

A fine line exists, however, between minimizing excessive environmental press and creating an unstimulating or "too easy" environment. Well-intentioned families, for example, may do too much for the older person, assuming responsibility for daily activities, so that their older relative no longer has to exert any effort and may no longer feel he or she is a contributing family member. Likewise, professionals and family members may try to shield the older person from experiencing too many changes. For example, they may presume that an older person is too set in her or his ways to adjust to sharing a residence, thereby denying the person the opportunity to learn about and make an independent decision on home-sharing options. Well-intentioned nursing home staff may not challenge residents to perform such daily tasks as getting out of bed or going to the dining hall. Protective efforts such as these can remove necessary levels of environmental press, with the result that the person's social, psychological, and physical levels of functioning may decline. Understimulating conditions, then, can be as negative in their effects on the elderly as those in which there is excessive environmental press.

Rather than attempting to minimize or prevent changes, a more appropriate intervention is to introduce positive changes and maximize individual options. Effective strategies include both altering environments to be more supportive of older people's changing needs and increasing their competence through activities such as counseling, rehabilitation training, health promotion, or social support groups that emphasize reciprocal exchanges. For example, an environment may be made more supportive by placing handrails along steps of the home, putting textured or colored strips along stairs, raising the level of illumination in the home (without producing glare), and installing automatic timers on irons, stoves, ovens, and toasters. Individual competence may be enhanced by encouraging residents of a retirement community to participate in the landscaping and maintenance of the area, to volunteer as tutors in local schools, or to help in hospitals and nursing homes, or to join exercise and peer counseling groups within the retirement complex. Other examples of both environmental and individual interventions to enhance older people's choices are considered throughout this text.

## ORGANIZATION OF THE TEXT

This book is divided into five parts. Part I is a general introduction to the field of social gerontology and includes a brief history of the field, a discussion of research methods and designs, and a review of several social theories of aging. It also includes information on the demographics (population characteristics) of older people, attitudes toward aging and older people, and aging in other historical periods and cultures.

Part II addresses the physiological changes that influence social aging. It begins with a review of normal age-related changes in the body's major organ systems, followed by a description of sensory changes that frequently occur in old age, and their social/environmental effects. It also discusses the chronic diseases that occur most frequently among older people, factors that influence health care behavior (e.g., when and why older people are likely to seek professional care), and health promotion programs aimed at improving the physical, psychological, and social functioning among older people.

In Part III, we move to the psychological context of aging, including normal and disease-related changes in cognitive functioning (learning, intelligence, and memory), sexuality in the later years, theories of personality development and coping styles, mental health issues of importance to the elderly, and the use of mental health services. The impact of these psychological changes, both normal and secondary to disease, on social functioning is discussed throughout.

The social issues of aging are explored in Part IV, beginning with the importance of family, friends, and neighbors and how the array of housing arrangements for the elderly affects their social interactions. Issues related to income, employment, and retirement are next explored, followed by a review of changing roles in the community, in education, in religious institutions, and in politics, and topics related to death, dying, and the status of widowhood. The last two chapters of Part IV cover two populations at higher risk of problems in old age: ethnic minorities and women.

Part V goes beyond the individual's social context to address societal perspectives, particularly social, health, and long-term care policy issues of importance to the older population, and contemporary policy debates.

Each part begins with an introduction to the key issues of aging that are discussed in that section. In order to emphasize the variations in physiological, psychological, social, and societal aspects of aging, vignettes of older people representing these differences are presented. Throughout each chapter, the diversity of the older population and of the aging process itself is highlighted in terms of chronological age, gender, culture, ethnic minority status and sexual orientation. Where appropriate, the dynamic interaction between older people and their environment is emphasized. How age-related changes are measured and methods for improving measurement in this field are also discussed.

## WHY STUDY AGING?

As you begin this text, you may find it useful to think about your own motivations for learning about older adults and the aging process. Some of you may be in a required course, questioning its relevance, and approaching this text as something you must read to satisfy requirements. Others may have personal reasons for wishing to

learn about aging. You may be concerned about your own age-related changes, wondering whether reduced energy or alterations in physical features are inevitable with age. After all, since middle and old age together encompass a longer time span than any other stage of our lives, it is important that we understand and prepare for these years. Perhaps you are looking forward to the freedom made possible by retirement and the "empty nest." Through increased knowledge about the aging process, you may be hoping to make decisions that can enhance your own positive adaptation to aging and old age. Or perhaps you are interested in assisting aging relatives, friends, and neighbors wanting to know what can be done to help them maintain their independence, what housing options exist for them, and how you can improve your caregiving abilities.

Learning about aging not only gives us insight into our own interpersonal relationships, self-esteem, competence, and meaningful activities as we grow older; it also helps us comprehend the aging process of our parents, grandparents, clients, patients, and friends. It is important to recognize that change and growth take place throughout the life course, and that the concerns of older people are not distinct from those of the young, but represent a continuation of earlier life periods. Such understanding can improve our effectiveness in communicating with relatives, friends, or professionals. In addition, such knowledge can help change any assumptions we may hold about behavior appropriate to various ages.

Perhaps some of you wish to work professionally with older people, but are unsure how your interests can fit in with the needs of the older population. In the final chapter of this book, the Epilogue, you will find an extensive discussion of careers in gerontology. If you are already working with older people, you may genuinely enjoy your work, but at the same time be concerned about the social and economic problems facing some elderly and thus feel a responsibility to work to change these negative social conditions. As professionals or future professionals working with older people, you are probably eager to learn more about policy and practice issues that can enhance their quality of life.

Regardless of your motivations for reading this text, chances are that, like most Americans, you have some misconceptions about older people and the aging process. As products of our youth-oriented society, we have all sensed the pervasiveness of negative attitudes about aging, although our own personal experiences with older people may counter many stereotypes and myths. By studying aging and older people, you will not only become more aware of the older population's competence in many areas, but also be able to differentiate the normal changes that are associated with the aging process from pathological or disease-related changes. Such an understanding may serve to reduce some of your own fears about aging, as well as positively affect your professional and personal interactions with older people. Our challenge as educators and authors is to present you with the facts and the concepts that will give you a more accurate picture of the experience of aging in American society. We also want to convey to you the excitement and importance of learning about the field of aging. We hope that by the time you have completed this text, you will have acquired information that strengthens positive attitudes toward living and working with older people and toward your own experience of aging.

## REFERENCES

Butler, R. *Why survive? Being old in America*. New York: Harper and Row, 1975.

Hendricks, J., and Hendricks, C. D. *Aging in mass society: Myths and realities*. Cambridge, Mass.: Winthrop, 1981.

Lawton, M. P. Environment and other determinants of well-being in older people. *The Gerontologist*, 1983, *23*, 349–357.

Lawton, M. P., and Nahemow, L. Ecology and the aging process. In C. Eisdorfer and M. P. Lawton (Eds.), *Psychology of adult development and aging*. Washington, D.C.: American Psychological Association, 1973, 619–674.

Riley, M. W., and Riley, J. Longevity and social structure: The potential of the added years. In A. Pifer and L. Bronte (Eds.), *Our aging society: Paradox and promise*. New York: W. W. Norton, 1986, 53–77.

Schwartz, A. N. A transactional view of the aging process. In A. N. Schwartz and I. M. Mensh (Eds.), *Professional obligations and approaches to the aged*. Springfield, Ill.: Charles C. Thomas, 1974, 5–29.

Segerberg, O. *The immortality factor*. New York: E. P. Dutton & Co., 1974.

# PART One

# THE FIELD OF SOCIAL GERONTOLOGY

CHAPTER 1

# GROWTH OF THE OLDER POPULATION

A s we noted earlier, the single most important factor affecting current interest in the field of gerontology is the growing size of the older population. In 1900, people over 65 accounted for approximately 4 percent of the United States population—less than one in twenty-five. By 1990, 31.2 million, or 12.6 percent of the population, was 65 or older—a substantial increase (U.S. Bureau of the Census, 1991). During the next 20 years, however, the population over 65 is expected to grow more slowly than it did between 1950 and 1990. After 2010, as the baby boom generation begins to reach old age, the population over 65 will again increase.

## CHANGES IN LIFE EXPECTANCY

Why have these changes in the older population occurred? Chiefly because people are living longer. In 1900, the average life expectancy at birth in the United States (i.e., the average length of time one could expect to live if one were born that year) was 47 years. At that time, there were approximately 772,000 people between the ages of 75 and 84 in this country, and only 123,000 aged 85 and older. In 1990 there were over 3 million in the oldest group. The average life expectancy is now much longer. Females born in 1993 can expect to reach age 79.5, men 72.5. Life expectancy at age 65 was an additional 19.5 years for women and 15.7 years for men (U.S. Bureau of the Census, 1993a). About four out of five individuals can now expect to reach age 65, at which point there is a better than 50 percent chance of living past age 80 (Kingson, Hirshorn, and Cornman, 1986).

According to the Census Bureau (U.S. Bureau of the Census, 1993a), life expectancy at birth is expected to increase from the current 75.9 years to 77.6 in 2005 and to 82.6 in 2050. Sex differences in life expectancy have declined since 1980, when females born that year could expect to live 7.4 years more than men; in 1993, the figure was only seven more years. Projections by the Census Bureau assume a fairly constant seven-year difference in life expectancy well into the future. Therefore, females born in 2005 are

expected to reach age 81; males in that birth cohort will reach age 74. Even in the year 2080, however, male life expectancy will be less than 80 years, whereas women will achieve 84.7 years. Of course, these projections do not take into account potentially new diseases that could differentially increase mortality risks for men and women. For example, if AIDS continues to be a fatal disease that infects younger men more than women, there could be a much greater sex differential in life expectancy. On the other hand, death rates due to hypertension and heart disease have already started to decline. Since both conditions are somewhat more likely to affect men, these factors may narrow the sex differential and increase life expectancy even more. Nevertheless, the trend illustrated in Figure 1–1, where women outnumber men at every age after 55, will continue well into the twenty-first century.

Most of the gains in life expectancy have occurred in the younger ages. For example, during the period from 1900 to 1993, the average life expectancy at birth increased from 47 years to 76 years. In contrast, gains in life expectancy beyond age 65 during this same period have been relatively modest, from about 12.3 to 17.2 years between 1900 and 1993. Gender differences are particularly striking; older men added 3.3 years

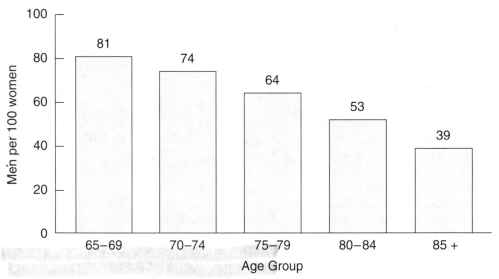

**FIGURE 1–1    Number of Men per 100 Women by older Age-Group: 1990 race, and Hispanic origin data, 1990, Series CPH-L-74.**

and women 6.8 years to their life expectancy from 1900 to 1993. It is not surprising that much of the gain in life expectancy has occurred in the early years of life because of the eradication in this century of many diseases that caused high infant and childhood mortality. On the other hand, we may find significant increases in survival beyond age 65 in future cohorts, when heart disease and cancer become more chronic and less fatal diseases in adulthood.

The reasons for this shift have to do with advances in medicine. A hundred years ago, adults generally died from acute diseases, with influenza and pneumonia as the principal killers. Few people survived these diseases long enough to need care for chronic or long-term conditions. Today, death from acute diseases is rare. Maternal, infant, and early childhood death rates have also declined considerably. The result is a growing number of people who survive to old age, often with one or more health problems requiring long-term care.

## MAXIMUM LIFE SPAN

It is important to distinguish life expectancy from *maximum life span*. While life expectancy is a probability estimate based on environmental conditions such as disease and health care, as described previously, maximum life span is the maximum number of years a given species could expect to live if environmental hazards were eliminated. There appears to be a maximum biologically determined life span for cells that comprise the organism, so that even with the elimination of all diseases, we could not expect to live much beyond 120 years. For these reasons, more and more persons will expect to live longer, but the maximum number of years they can expect to live will not be increased in the foreseeable future unless, of course, some extraordinary and unanticipated biological discoveries occur (Fries, 1980; Fries and Crapo, 1981).

Perhaps the most important goal of health planners and practitioners should be to approach a rectangular survival curve. That is, as seen in the survival curve in Figure 1–2, developments in medicine, public hygiene, and health have already increased the percentage of people surviving into the later years. The ideal situation is one where all people would survive to the maximum life span, creating a "rectangular curve." We are approaching this ideal curve, but it will not be achieved until the diseases of youth and middle age—including cancer, heart disease, diabetes, and kidney diseases—can be prevented altogether, or at least managed as chronic conditions.

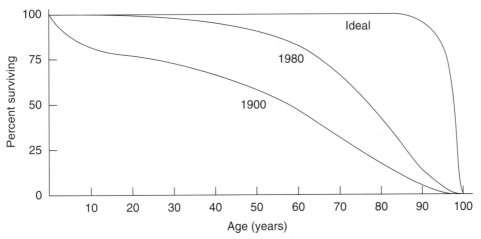

**FIGURE 1–2  Increasing Rectangularization of the Survival Curve**
SOURCE: Adapted from L. Hayflick, The cell biology of human aging. *Scientific American,* 1980, 242, p. 60, by permission of the publisher.

## THE OLDEST-OLD

The population aged 85 and older, also referred to as the "oldest-old," has grown more rapidly than any other age group in our country. In 1990, of the 31.2 million persons aged 65 and over in the United States, 32 percent were age 75 to 84, while another 10 percent were age 85 and over (U.S. Bureau of the Census, 1990). Since World War II, mortality rates in adulthood have declined significantly, resulting in an unprecedented number of people who are reaching advanced old age and who are most likely to require health and social services (Suzman, Willis, and Manton, 1992). For these reasons, the population of "oldest-old" Americans has increased by a factor of 23, compared to a twelvefold growth in the 75–84 age group and an eightfold increase in the population aged 65–74! Those over 85 have increased by 300 percent from 1960 to 1990. Their numbers are expected to reach 4.6 million in 2000, and over 8 million in 2030. Projections vary, depending on predictions about changes in chronic disease morbidity and mortality rates (Suzman et al., 1992).

This tremendous growth in the oldest-old will take place *before* the influx of baby boomers reaches old age, because this latter group will not begin to turn age 85 until after 2030 (i.e., the baby boom generation is generally accepted as those born between 1946 and 1964). By the year 2050, when the survivors of this generation are age 85 and older, they are expected to number to 19 million, or 5 percent of the total U.S. population (Day, 1993). This represents a 500 percent increase within 60 years! The impact of such a surge in the oldest-old on the demand for health services, especially hospitals and long-term care settings, will be dramatic.

It is also important to consider the distribution of selected age groups now and in the future. As noted previously, the young-old (ages 65–74) currently represent 58 percent of the elderly population; those over 85 are slightly less than 10 percent of this population. In contrast, the corresponding proportions in 2050 are projected to be 46 percent young-old and 22 percent oldest-old. (See Figure 1–3).

Projections by the Census Bureau (1993) also suggest a substantial increase in the population aged 100 or older. In 1990 it was estimated that 37,000 Americans were aged 100 or older. These numbers are expected to grow to 75,000 by the year 2000, and to 477,000 by 2030. Even with this twelvefold increase, however, the population over 100 will still represent less than 1 percent of the U.S. population in 2030. Never-

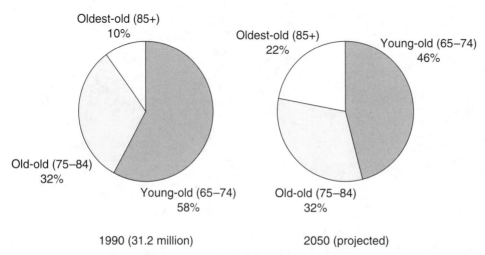

**FIGURE 1–3    Percentage of Older Americans by Age Group**

theless, this group will place increasing demands on the health care system.

Who are the oldest-old? In an analysis of this segment of the population in the 1980 census, Longino (1988) found that the great majority are women (70 percent). Their educational level is lower than for their younger counterparts aged 65 to 74 (8.6 years vs. 12.1), and most are widowed, divorced, or never married (77.2 percent vs. 62 percent). It is not surprising, therefore, that the mean personal income for the oldest-old is lower than for other elderly, and that a high proportion live below or near poverty. The current cohort of oldest-old includes a large number of foreign-born people who immigrated from Italy, Poland, Russia, and other European countries in the early 1900s, as well as later immigrants from China, Japan, the Philippines, and Mexico. The usual problems of aging may be intensified for these nonnative speakers of English as they try to communicate with health care providers. Misdiagnosis of physical, psychological, and cognitive disorders may occur in such cases.

The older population is increasingly diverse.

Because they are more likely to have multiple health problems that often result in physical frailty, and because up to 50 percent of the "oldest-old" may have some form of cognitive impairment (Evans et al., 1989), this group is disproportionately represented in the institutionalized population (nursing homes, group homes, and hospitals). Almost 25 percent live in an institutional setting, and they make up more than half of the population of nursing homes. However, the rate of institutionalization among African Americans aged 85 and older is only about half this rate (12 percent). The oldest-old Blacks are far more likely to be living with relatives other than a spouse (40 percent). Very few of the oldest-old live with a spouse, compared with 50 percent of all elders over age 65 (Bould, Sanborn, and Reif, 1989). Even among those living in the community, functional health is more impaired in the oldest-old.

Given the smaller proportions of younger, more active elderly in the future, in contrast with the increasing proportion of those 85 and older who are most likely to be frail and dependent, one could speculate on changing patterns of employment and leisure activities, as well as on residential arrangements that differ significantly from current patterns (e.g., fewer people employed, more passive activities, and less independent living) among the older population.

## POPULATION PYRAMIDS

The rise in longevity is partly responsible for an unusually rapid rise in the *median age* of the U.S. population—from 28 in 1970 to 33 in 1990—meaning that half the population was older than 33 and half younger in 1990. From an historical perspective, a five-year increase in the median age over a twenty-year period is a noteworthy demographic event (Social Security Administration, 1990). The other key factors contributing to this rise include a dramatic decline in the birth rate after the mid-1960s, high birth rates in the periods from 1890 to 1915 and just after World War II (these "baby boomers" are now all older than the median), and the large number of immigrants who arrived here before the 1920s.

As stated earlier in this chapter, the "baby boom" generation (currently aged 30 to 48) will dominate the age distribution in the United States well into the next century. In fact, by the early part of the twenty-first century, between 2010 and 2030, they will form the "senior boom," and swell the ranks of the 65-plus generation to the point that one in five Americans will be elderly. The projected growth in the older population will raise the median age of the U.S. population from 33 to 36 by the year 2000 and to age 40 by the year 2010. If current fertility and immigration levels remain stable, the only age groups to experience significant growth in the next century will be those older than 55 (Social Security Administration, 1990).

One of the most dramatic examples of the changing age distribution of the American population is the shift in the proportion of elderly in relation to the proportion of young persons, as illustrated in Figure 1–4. In 1900, when approximately 4 percent of the population was age 65 and over, young persons aged 0 to 17 years made up 40 percent of the population. By 1980, reduced birthrates in the 1970s had resulted in a

decrease of young persons to 28 percent of the population. The U.S. Census Bureau predicts that, by 2030, the proportion of young persons and elderly will be almost equal, with persons 0 to 17 years forming 22 percent of the population and the elderly forming 21 percent of the population. Indeed, in 1990, the proportion of people under age 14 was the same as those aged 60 or older (AARP, 1990; U.S. Bureau of the Census, 1992). After the year 2030, if current trends continue, the death rate will be greater than the birth rate.

One way of illustrating the changing proportions of young and old persons in the population is the *population pyramid.* Figure 1–5 contrasts the population pyramid for 1987 and the projected pyramids for the years 2000, 2010, and 2030. Each horizontal bar in these pyramids represents a ten-year *birth cohort* (i.e., people born within the same 10-year period). By comparing these bars, we can determine the relative proportion of each birth cohort. As you can see in the first graph, the distribution of the population in 1987 had already moved from a true pyramid to one with a bulge, represented by the baby-boomers. This pyramid will grow more column-like over the years, as shown in the other

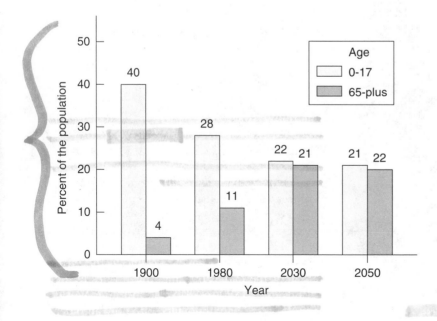

**FIGURE 1–4  Actual and Projected Distribution of Children and Elderly in the Population: 1900–2050**

SOURCE: G. Spencer, U.S. Bureau of the Census, Projections of the population of the United States, by age, sex, and race: 1983–2080. *Current Population Reports,* Series P-25, No. 952 (May 1984).

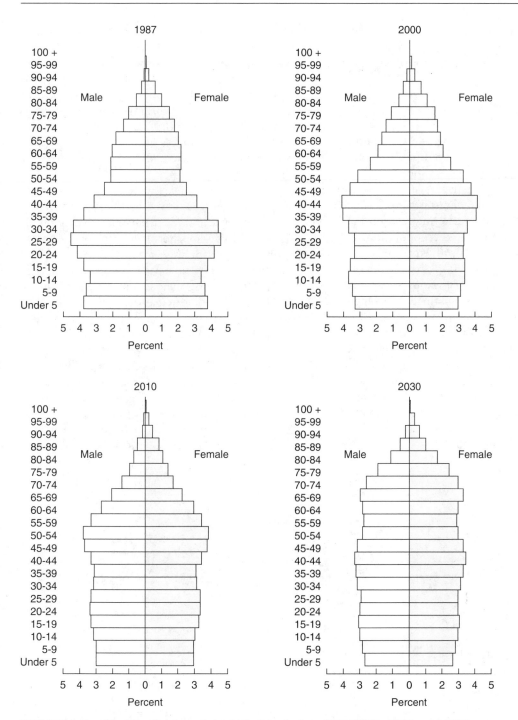

**FIGURE I–5    Age Distribution of the U.S. Population: 1987, 2000, 2010, and 2030**

SOURCE: U.S. Bureau of the Census, Projections of the population of the U.S. by age, sex, and race: 1988–2080. *Current Population Reports,* Series P-25, No. 1018. (Washington, D.C.: U.S. Department of Commerce, 1984).

three graphs. These changes reflect the aging of the baby boomers, combined with declining birth rates and reduced death rates for older cohorts.

## DEPENDENCY RATIOS

One aspect of the changing age distribution in our population that has raised public concern is the so-called *dependency ratio,* or "elderly support ratio" (U.S. Senate Special Committee on Aging, 1990). The way this ratio has generally been used is to indicate the relationship between the proportion of the population that is employed (defined as "productive" members of society) and the proportion that is not in the work force (and is thus viewed as "dependent"). This rough estimate is obtained by comparing the proportion of the population aged 18 to 64 (the working years) to the proportion under age 18 (yielding the childhood dependency ratio) and over 65 (yielding the old age dependency ratio). This ratio has increased steadily, such that there appear to be proportionately fewer employed persons to support older persons today. In 1910, the ratio was less than .10 (i.e., 10 working people per older person), compared

with .18 in 1980 (i.e., 5 or 6 working people per older person). Assuming that the lower birthrate will continue, this trend will continue into the early twenty-first century, as the baby boom cohort reaches old age. By the year 2010, a ratio of .22 (or about 4.5 working people per retired person) is expected (U.S. Bureau of the Census, 1992). These changes since 1960, along with projections through 2050, are illustrated in Figure 1–6.

There are problems with such a crude measure, however. It is flawed by the fact that many of the younger and older persons are actually in the labor force and not dependent, while many people of labor force age may not be employed. A number of analysts have criticized the use of dependency ratios that do not take account of the labor force participation rates of different groups; for example, the labor force participation rates of women aged 16 to 59 are expected to increase from 1985 to 2000, while those of men of all ages are projected to decline. When these variations are taken into account, studies have found that although the total dependency ratio increases as the population ages, even in the year 2050 it will remain lower than recent historical levels. Moreover, despite population aging, those

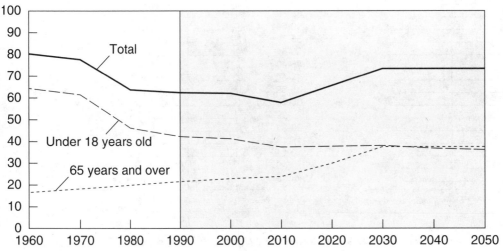

**FIGURE 1–6   Number of Dependents per 100 Persons Aged 18 to 64 Years: Estimates, 1960–1980; Projections, 1990 to 2050**
SOURCE: U.S. Bureau of the Census, *Current Population Reports,* Series P-25, No. 1104, Figure 7, Nov. 1993.

under the age of 16 will continue to constitute the largest "dependent" group well into the twenty-first century. Therefore, we need to be cautious when we hear policy makers predict "burdens" on the younger population and blame rising costs of public pension programs primarily on the changing dependency ratio (Schulz and Myles, 1990; Crown and Schulz, 1987).

## POPULATION TRENDS AMONG ETHNIC MINORITIES

In addition to the proportional growth of the older population in general, there are other demographic trends of interest to gerontologists. These include statistics related to the social, ethnic, gender, and geographic distribution of older populations. In this section, we will review some of these trends, beginning with the demographics of ethnic minorities in the United States.

Today, ethnic minorities comprise 14 percent of the population over age 65; they include

a smaller proportion of elderly and a larger proportion of younger adults than the white population. In 1990, 13 percent of whites, but only 8 percent of African Americans and 5 percent of Hispanics were age 65 and over. The difference results primarily from the higher rates of fertility and higher mortality rates among the nonwhite population under age 65 than among the white population under 65. However, beginning in the early part of the twenty-first century, the proportion of older persons is expected to increase at a *higher* rate for the nonwhite population than for the white population, partly because of the large proportion of children in these groups, who, unlike their parents and especially their grandparents, are expected to reach old age. By 2020, 22 percent of the older population is projected to be nonwhite; by 2050, 36 percent will be nonwhite (U.S. Bureau of the Census, 1992). Figures 1–7 and 1–8 illustrate these differential patterns of growth for whites, African Americans, Hispanics, and other races.

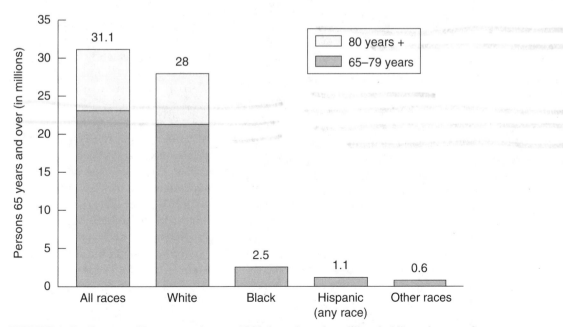

**FIGURE 1–7   Persons 65 years and over: 1990 (numbers in millions). Hispanics are also included in racial group totals.**

SOURCE: U.S. Bureau of the Census, modified and actual age, sex, race and Hispanic origin data, 1990, Series CPH-L-74.

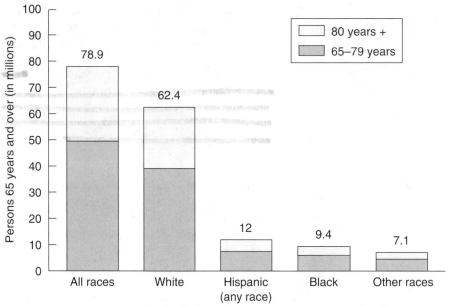

**FIGURE 1–8    Persons 65 Years and Over: 2050 (numbers in millions). Hispanics are also included in racial group totals.**
SOURCE: Bureau of the Census, Middle series projections (1992).

## African American Elders

The percentage of older persons among the African American population is still smaller than among its nonminority counterpart. That is, about 8 percent of the Black population was over 65 years of age in 1992, compared to 13 percent of the white population. The young outnumber the old in the African American population, due primarily to the higher fertility of Black women and blacks' higher mortality at mid-life. The median age of African Americans, 28.4 years, is six years younger than the median age for whites (34.4). Nevertheless, those over age 65 form the fastest growing segment of the African American population. In 1993, the life expectancy for Black men and women was 66 and 74.7 years, respectively, compared with the life expectancy of 73.5 years for white men and 80.1 years for white women (U.S. Bureau of the Census, 1993a). This disparity reflects differences in mortality rates in childhood and youth, because the difference in life expectancy after age 65 is far less dramatic. Black men who make it to age 65

can expect to live another 14 years; Black women 18 years. This is only slightly less than for their white counterparts (15.7 and 19.6 years, respectively). This may be accounted for by the fact that most African Americans who survive to age 65 have overcome the diseases and trauma that struck their peers in the early to middle years. The leading causes of death among African Americans are hypertension, heart disease, and diabetes. On the other hand, the black population is expected to increase by 45.6 percent by 2020. This will raise the proportion of older people in the total African American population from 8 percent to 10.7 percent by the year 2020, and to 13.6 percent by 2050 (U.S. Bureau of the Census, 1993a). It is also noteworthy that the growth among the 85 and older black population has been greater since 1980 than in the white population, although numerically they are less than ten percent of oldest whites (Manuel, 1988; (U.S. Bureau of the Census, 1993a).

The ratio of men to women among African Americans aged 65 and over is slightly lower than among whites, 62 males for every 100 females, compared to 67 males for every 100 females among the white population (U.S. Bureau of the Census, 1990). However, in the population aged 85+, there are 42 African American men for 100 women, compared to 38 among their white counterparts.

The slight relative favorability for the oldest-old African American men compared to whites may be related to the "crossover effect" mentioned earlier, where the mortality differentials between the oldest-old black men and women are less pronounced than among whites (Jackson, 1982). There is also a black/white crossover effect, whereby the mortality rates of blacks and whites are equivalent, then lower for blacks after age 73 for men and after age 85 for women. The 1990 census supports this crossover phenomenon on a national level. In that year the proportion of blacks in the age 85 and older population was about the same as that aged 64 to 74 (7.4 percent and 8.4 percent respectively, according to the U.S. Bureau of the Census, 1991). The African American male aged 85 and over is more "advantaged" in terms of health than his white counterpart because of the greater probability of early death for black men, partly because of homicides in urban areas, relative to the oldest-old black females. Despite this relative "advantage," women age 80 and over are the most rapidly growing group of African American elderly, and they have the longest average remaining lifetime. On the other hand, older black males have a greater probability of being widowed, divorced, or separated than their white counterparts (U.S. Bureau of the Census, 1990).

## Hispanic American Elders

Following African Americans, Hispanic Americans are the largest ethnic minority population, with over 85 percent concentrated in metropolitan areas. They are also the fastest-growing population group in the United States (Torres-Gil, 1986; U.S. Bureau of the Census, 1992). Between 1970 and 1980 the number of older Hispanics in the U.S. increased by 74 percent, compared to a 25 percent increase in the population of all elderly. Hispanic Americans include many groups, each with its own distinct national/cultural heritage: Mexicans, Puerto Ricans, Cubans, Central or South Americans, and the native Mexican American, or Chicano population, whose history in the United States predates settlement by English-speaking groups. Although bonded by a common language, these groups differ substantially in terms of geographic concentration, income, education, and length of residence in the United States. Mexican Americans are the largest but poorest group, constituting 64 percent of the Hispanic population and concentrated in five, primarily rural, southwestern states. Cubans represent the wealthiest and most educated Hispanic group, and have the largest proportion of foreign-born elderly among the three major Hispanic groups. The largest populations of Puerto Ricans and Cubans are in New York City, New Jersey, and Florida. However, the three states with the largest Hispanic population are California, Texas, and Florida (U.S. Bureau of the Census, 1991).

Compared to whites and to other ethnic minorities, the Spanish-speaking population is a youthful group, with a median age of 26.1 years, eight years younger than the norm in the United States. Only 4.9 percent of this population is 65 years of age and over, a figure which has been stable over the past decade (U.S. Bureau of the Census, 1993a). A number of factors underlie the relative youthfulness of the Hispanic American population. One variable is its lower average life expectancy. The most important contributing factor, however, is the generally high fertility rate. The number of children born and the average family size exceed the national average. Immigration and repatriation patterns are secondary factors, with the youngest (and often poorest) people most likely to move to a new country, and some middle-aged and older Mexicans moving back to Mexico (Markides and Martin, 1983; Torres-Gil, 1986). Despite its current relative youthfulness, the Hispanic population has experienced the greatest increase in median age of all ethnic groups from 1960 to 1990. This suggests that the percentage of older Hispanic Americans may rise steeply in the future, as younger cohorts reach old age. By the middle of the 21st century, 15 percent of the Hispanic population is expected to be age 65 or older (U.S. Bureau of the Census, 1992).

Gender patterns of Hispanic Americans are similar to those of other groups of older people. Women live longer and outnumber men, more often remaining widowed and living alone than men do. The ratio of Hispanic men to women aged 65 and over is greater than for whites and blacks, 71 vs. 67 and 62 respectively (U.S. Bureau of the Census, 1990). Older Hispanic American men marry or remarry more often than men in other ethnic minority groups; 83 percent of older Hispanic American males are married, but only 33 percent of older Hispanic women live with a spouse (Lacayo, 1984).

## Pacific Asian Elders

Approximately 6 percent of the Pacific Asian population is 65 years of age and over. The total Asian population in the United States increased rapidly between 1965 and 1975, due to the 1965 repeal of quotas based on race and nationality and the large influx of Southeast Asians in the 1970s (U.S. Bureau of the Census, 1991). Asian Americans represent a diverse group in terms of language, culture, acculturation to the U.S., and socioeconomic status. Because of earlier immigration patterns, many Japanese American and Chinese American elders have lived in this country since their youth. In contrast, older individuals from Vietnam, Cambodia and other Southeast Asian countries came after the Vietnam War, often as parents or grandparents of younger immigrants. For this reason the latter group is generally less acculturated and has lower income than earlier immigrants.

In contrast to other ethnic minority groups and to white older persons, men living alone constitute a larger percentage of the older Pacific Asian population. This reflects the continuing influence of disproportionate male immigration in the early part of the century and past restrictions on female immigration rather than a higher life expectancy for men among Pacific Asians. The overall sex ratio of Pacific Asian elderly was 96 males to 100 females in 1980, whereas the ratio was 68 males to 100 females in the general elderly population (Kii, 1984). In contrast to other subgroups of elderly, the ratio of men to women in the Pacific Asian population *increases* with age, controlling for gender, social class, and levels of functional ability. On the other hand, Asian/Pacific Islander women are much more likely to be married than their white counterparts, with a smaller proportion remaining single in their later years. Chinese and Japanese Americans can expect to live longer than white Americans.

## American Indian Elders

As is the case with other ethnic minorities, the American Indian population (including American Indians, Eskimos, and Aleuts) is younger than the white population. With a median age of 23 years, only 5 percent of this population is 65 years of age and older (U.S. Bureau of the Census, 1991). Nevertheless, the proportion of elderly among the American Indian population has grown faster than in other minority groups. Between 1970 and 1980, their numbers increased by 65 percent, a rate twice that of white or Black elderly. Their current life expectancy at birth is 65 years for both men *and* women, approximately 8 years less than for the white population, and it tends to be even lower in nonreservation areas (American Association of Retired Persons, 1987). With a sex ratio of approximately 64.5 men to every 100 women 65 and over, more than 75 percent of Native American men, but less than 50 percent of their female counterparts, are married (Manson, 1993). The consequences of these demographic patterns on status, social networks, and economic, physical and mental well-being in ethnic minority populations are further discussed in Chapter 17.

## GEOGRAPHIC DISTRIBUTION

Demographic information on the location of older populations is important for a variety of reasons. For example, the differing needs of rural and urban older people may affect research designs as well as local government policy decisions. Statistical information on elderly populations state-to-state is necessary in planning for the distribution of federal funds; comparison of demographic patterns in different nations and cultures may provide insights into various aspects of the aging process. The following are some of the most salient statistics on the geographic distribution of the elderly today. Their implications will be taken up in later chapters, including the impact of these differences on living arrangements, social and health policies affecting older individuals in rural and urban communities, and cross-cultural issues.

Although older adults live in every state and region of the United States, they are not evenly distributed. More live in metropolitan areas; in 1988, 31 percent of the older population lived in cities, 43 percent in suburbs, and 26 percent in rural areas. The Northeast continues to be the region with the oldest population; in 1988 the median age of the region was 34 vs. 33 nationally. Those over 65 represented 13.6 percent of its population, compared to 12.6 percent nationally (U.S. Bureau of the Census, 1989)

Some states have a much higher proportion of residents over 65 than others; for example, in 1990 they represented 18.3 percent of the population in Florida and about 15 percent in Arkansas, Iowa, Pennsylvania, Rhode Island, and South Dakota—compared to just 4 percent of the population in Alaska and 9 percent in Utah (U.S. Bureau of the Census, 1991). It is therefore not surprising that Florida has the highest median age in the United States (36.5 years), and Utah the lowest (26.3 years). In some cases, such as that of Florida, migration of retired persons to the state explains the increase, whereas in others, such as Arkansas and South Dakota, migration of younger persons out of the state leaves a greater proportion of older people. More than 20% of some rural counties in these states are over age 65. Other states may simply reflect the generalized "graying of America." These regional differences are expected to continue into the next

century, when the median age for the Northeast is projected at 37.6 in the year 2000, versus 36.4 nationally. Florida will continue to have the highest median age (41.2), and Utah the lowest (26.0). Utah will also have the distinction of being the only state in the year 2000 that will have more than 50 percent of its population under age 30, due to its continued high birth rate.

Residential relocation is relatively rare for older people in the United States. The movement that occurs tends to be within the same types of environment, that is, people over age 65 generally move from one metropolitan area to another, or from one rural community to another. These trends and their implications for adaptation to aging will be described further in Chapter 13.

## EDUCATIONAL AND ECONOMIC STATUS

In 1960, less than 20 percent of the population over age 65 had finished high school. By 1988, 54 percent had completed high school, with only slight gender differences. However, racial and generational differences are striking. Among whites who were age 65 and older in 1988, the median level of education was 12.2 years, compared with 8.4 years for African Americans and 7.5 years for Hispanic American elderly (AARP, 1990). This represents a disproportionate ratio of older minorities today with less than a high school education. Because educational level is so closely associated with economic well-being, these ethnic differences have a major impact on poverty levels of older members of different ethnic groups. Other implications of these gaps in educational attainment will be discussed further in Chapter 17.

Not surprisingly, the young-old (age 65 to 74) are more educated today than the old-old (75 to 84). More than half of the young-old (59.4 percent) have at least a high school education, while only 45 percent of their older peers have achieved this level of education (U.S. Senate Special Committee on Aging, 1990). For this reason, the median educational level today is

12.1 years for the young-old, 10.5 years for the old-old, and 8.6 years for the oldest-old (age 85+). Women are more likely than men to have completed high school. It is noteworthy that an even greater proportion of people over 25 today (75 percent) have at least a high school education. This suggests that future generations of older people will be better educated, many with college degrees, than their grandparents are today. The implications of this shift for political activism, employment, and expectations from society will be explored in the Epilogue.

Only 16.4 percent of men and 8.7 percent of women over age 65 are in the labor force, largely because of past mandatory retirement practices and a pattern of early retirement. However, part-time work is an increasingly attractive option, with over 50 percent of retired workers employed in a part-time or temporary capacity. Social Security remains the major source of income for old age, not earnings from employment or private pensions. In fact, increases in Social Security benefits along with annual cost of living adjustments are primary factors underlying the improved economic status of the elderly. Currently, approximately 12 percent of older people subsist on incomes below the poverty level, compared to 35 percent in the late 1950s (Radner, 1991). However, this improved economic status masks the growing rates of poverty among older women, ethnic minorities, the old-old, and those living alone, as well as the high percentage who live just above the poverty line. The current and projected economic status of the older population is discussed in detail in Chapters 14 and 19.

## WORLDWIDE TRENDS

All world regions are experiencing an increase in the absolute and relative size of their older populations. The number of persons age 65 or older in the world is expected to increase from 342 million in 1992 to 761 million in 2025. This will result in a world population in which one out of every seven people will be 69 years of age or older by the year 2025 (U.S. Bureau of the Census, 1993b).

There are substantial differences in the current numbers and expected growth of the older population between the industrialized and developing countries, as shown in Figure 1–9. For example, in 1991, 13.7 percent of the population of Western Europe was aged 65 or older; almost 3 percent were 80 or older. The elderly population represented 18 percent in Sweden; 4.5 percent were 80 or older. In contrast, Sub-Saharan Africa and South Asia each counted only 3 percent of their population aged 65 or over. The median age of Western Europe in 1990 was 37, compared with a median age of 23.5 worldwide, 32 in the United States, and about 20 in Latin America (U.S. Bureau of the Census, 1993b). In Africa, with continued high fertility and high mortality rates, the median age will continue to be around 20 in the year 2020.

However, the less developed regions of the world expect to show a nearly fivefold increase in their oldest population, from 3.8 percent in 1975 to 17 percent in 2075. An even greater rise in the proportion of the old-old (ages 75–84) and oldest-old (85+) is expected in these countries, from the current .5 percent to 3.5 percent in 2075. Reasons for this increase in developing countries include improved sanitation, medical care, immunizations, and better nutrition.

An even greater rise in the proportion of the old-old (ages 75–84) and oldest-old (85+) is expected in these countries, from the current .5 percent to 3.5 percent in 2075. By the year 2025, only 28 percent of the world's elderly are expected to reside in industrialized nations, while 72 percent will live in developing countries (United Nations Secretariat, 1989). It is important to note, however, that the less developed regions of the world are currently coping with the tremendous impact of high fertility rates. Even with the continued high infant mortality rates in these countries, children under 15 represent 37 percent of the population in less developed regions, compared with 22 percent of the total

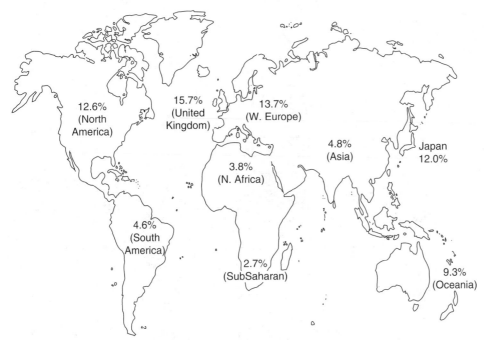

**FIGURE 1–9**  *Proportion of Population over Age 65 in World Regions: 1990.*

population in more developed regions. Figure 1–10 presents a comparison of the age pyramids for these two regions.

Today the fertility rate of industrial nations is less than 2.0 children per woman, or less than the rate necessary to maintain a steady population level.* In fact, the birthrate in Japan is now the lowest of any country at 1.57. In 1990, for example, Japan experienced 11.1 live births per 1,000 population, compared with 15.7 per 1,000 in the United States and much higher rates in less developed countries such as Mexico (29 per 1000) and Egypt (40.7 per 1000). For this reason, Japan is experiencing the most rapid rate of population aging in the world; 7 percent of its population was 65 or older in 1970, and this will reach 14 percent in 1996 (Japan Ministry of Health and Welfare, 1983). Japan also has the

highest life expectancy at birth, 76.4 years for men, 82.1 for women (U.S. Bureau of the Census, 1993b). Combined with the improved life expectancy in industrial nations (which has increased by 6 years for men and 8.5 years for women since 1953), this has resulted in a dramatic increase in the older population. The rate has grown more rapidly over the past 20 years, with a significant impact on the availability of workers to support retired persons. It is evident from the population pyramid for other industrial nations in Figure 1–10 that the problem is even greater for them than for the United States. For example, it is estimated that in the industrialized countries of Europe, there will be a drop from 3.5 workers to support one retiree in 1990 to about 2 in 2030. In Japan, the pyramid will become even more rectangular, with a decline from 4.5 to 2 workers in the next 40 years. In contrast, the ratio in the United States will drop from 4 to 3 workers during this same period (Rauch, 1988). These changes will place

*For purposes of this discussion, "industrial nations" include the United States, Canada, the United Kingdom, France, Germany, Japan, and Australia.

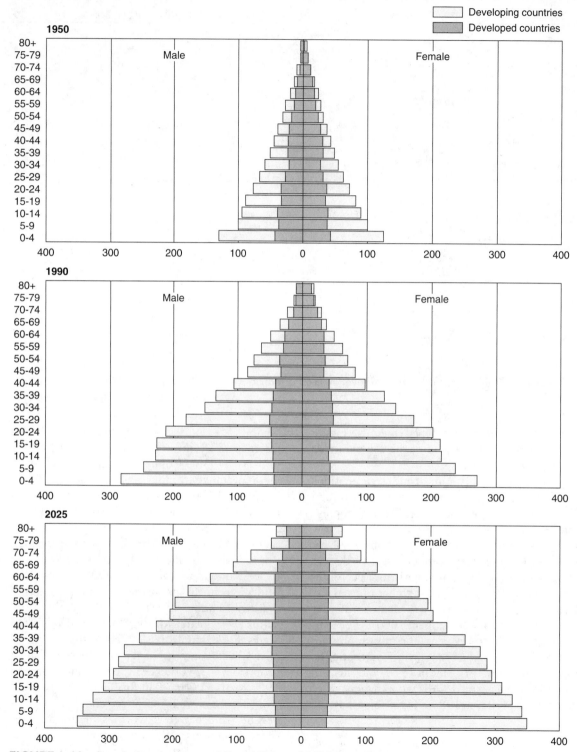

**FIGURE 1–10  Population, by Age and Sex: 1990, and 2025 (In millions)**
SOURCE: U.S. Bureau of the Census, Center for International Research, and UNDIESA, 1991d.

tremendous demands on the social security systems, government-subsidized health care, and pension programs of these nations. They may need to develop incentives for later retirement, which may be difficult, considering the trend toward early retirement in most industrial nations. It may also be necessary for developed countries to permit more immigration of young workers from the developing world and provide training in the technology required by these countries (Rauch, 1988). However, this is a controversial proposal for countries where immigrants often are not easily assimilated because of languages, religions, and cultures divergent from those of the host country.

## IMPACT OF DEMOGRAPHIC TRENDS IN THE UNITED STATES

As will be discussed later in this book, the growth of older populations has wide-ranging implications. The impact of demographic changes in the United States is most striking when we look at patterns of federal spending. The growth in numbers and proportions of older people has already placed pressures on our health and social service systems. Approximately 32 percent of the U.S. federal budget has been allocated to programs which primarily benefit older individuals (U.S. Congress 1994, 1990). Social Security accounts for about half this amount, although it is in a different category than other federal expenditures since Social Security taxes are levied separately. In the early 1980s, there was great concern when projections showed that Social Security reserves were inadequate to meet coming needs. More recent studies predict solvency until approximately the year 2020. However, the Medicare program, the fastest growing program in the federal budget, is less secure. Moreover, as expensive as Medicare has become, it has not adequately protected the elderly from rising health care costs. Even with this federal subsidy, older Americans proportionately pay more for their health care today than before Medicare was enacted in 1965.

In addition, little help is available, either through public programs or through the private sector, to pay the high costs of long-term care (e.g., nursing homes and other community-based in-home services for people with chronic illness).

The increase in life expectancy has brought with it a change in expectations about the quality of life in late adulthood. Increasingly in our society, those facing retirement anticipate living 20 to 30 years in relatively good health, with secure and adequate retirement incomes. When these expectations are not met, because of catastrophic medical costs, widowhood, or a retirement income eroded by inflation, the elderly may not be prepared to manage a change in their lifestyles. For other segments of the older population, particularly women and ethnic minorities, old age may represent a continuation of a lifetime of poverty or near-poverty. Fortunately for most older people, the problems associated with old age, particularly chronic illness and the attendant costs, are forestalled until very old age. As noted, however, the particularly rapid growth of the frail elderly, the majority of whom are women, may severely strain the health and income systems designed to provide resources in old age.

Another consequence of the increase in life expectancy is a growth in the multigenerational family. Already, about 40 percent of persons age 65 and over with children (which comprise 80 percent of all people age 65 and over today) are heads of four-generation families, although very few live in the same household. Another way of understanding the impact of these changing family dynamics is that 10 percent of people over age 65 have a child who is also over age 65 (Brody, 1985). The impact of these demographic changes on caregiving, especially for older women, is discussed further in Chapter 12.

## LONGEVITY IN HEALTH OR DISEASE?

Future cohorts of older people may be healthier and more independent well into their eighties and nineties. A strong argument has been put forth to this effect by Fries (1980), who has suggested that more people will achieve the maximum life span in future years because of healthier lifestyles and better health care during their youth and middle years. Furthermore, Fries argues that future cohorts will have fewer debilitating illnesses and will, in fact, experience "compressed morbidity" (i.e., only a few years of major illness in very old age). These elderly of the future may therefore expect to die a "natural death," or death due to the natural wearing out of all organ systems by approximately age 100. If this process does occur, it will have a significant impact both on the type of health services needed by future generations of older people and on their demand for employment and leisure activities. Long-term care needs may be reduced, with more sub-acute care facilities and short-term home health services being required.

A contrasting perspective to the health of future cohorts of elderly is offered by Verbrugge (1989). Based on her analysis of responses to the National Health Interview Survey (NHIS) from 1958 to 1985, Verbrugge notes that cohorts of middle-aged and older persons in each successive survey reported more short-term disability and days of restricted activity (i.e., morbidity rates) than did previous cohorts. Morbidity rates increased during this 27-year period for major life-threatening diseases (e.g., heart disease, cancer, diabetes, and hypertension), as well as for non-life-threatening diseases (e.g., arthritis), but mortality rates did not. Earlier diagnosis and better health care for these conditions may be responsible for this trend toward survival from major illnesses. Thus, Verbrugge concludes that although medical advances have prevented death from many acute conditions, older people experience more chronic conditions than did previous cohorts. As we will discuss in Chapter 7, chronic conditions cannot be cured, but rather require long-term or custodial care. Verbrugge points out, however, that her findings may not be sensitive to the gradual changes in the health of Americans as a result of improved health habits (e.g., less smoking, less consumption of alcohol and saturated fats, and increased exercise) being adopted by many people. A longer period of healthier lifestyles among people currently in their twenties and thirties may result in fewer chronic health problems when they reach old age.

Others have suggested that the average period of diminished vigor will increase because of the growing number of very old people who are most likely to have multiple chronic illnesses, and because some diseases are more likely to begin in old age (Schneider and Brody, 1983). Another perspective suggests that both phenomena will occur simultaneously (Rice and Feldman, 1983). That is, there will be an increasing number of people reaching advanced old age in very good health, while another segment of equally old people will experience prolonged morbidity.

The concept of "active versus dependent life expectancy" (Katz et al., 1983) may be useful in this debate. These authors distinguish between merely living a long life from living a healthy old age. Instead of death, they define the endpoint of "active" life expectancy as the loss of independence or the need to rely on others for most activities of daily living. For example, a 65-year-old woman today has approximately 18.6 years remaining, 12.6 in active life expectancy, 6 in dependency. In contrast, a 65-year-old man can look forward to living 14.4 more years, 2.4 of these in a dependent state. Thus, life expectancy has increased beyond age 65, but about a quarter of the years lived will be in a dependent state (Manton and Stallard, 1991). Not surprisingly, differences in life conditions of elderly persons with inadequate income and those above the median income in the United States have led to the conclusion that there is a major discrepancy of 1 to 2.5 years in active life expectancy between the poor and nonpoor. Therefore, as Kane, Ouslander, and Abrass (1989) state, there may be a growing bimodal distribution of older people remaining healthier and free of disease (as predicted by Fries), and another, probably larger distribution of elderly surviving diseases that would have been fatal years ago, but living with "battle scars." This latter group may be the segment of the population that is distorting projections for compressed morbidity; as we have seen in the reviews of NHIS findings, this latter group also appears to be increasing in size.

## ATTITUDES TOWARD OLDER PEOPLE

With the growth in the older population, attitudes toward aging and old age have also changed. When older people formed only 4 percent of the population, beliefs and stereotypes about this group were obviously not widespread. But as the older population became more visible, the aging process itself became defined as problematic and misconceptions grew (Estes, 1989). In fact, there are more stereotypes about the causes and outcomes of aging and about the well-being of the older population than about any other period of life. These misconceptions are reinforced by messages on birthday cards, by books on "how to avoid aging," and by pills and creams to eliminate wrinkles and "age spots." The manufacturers of such products, which represent reactions of society against the outcomes of aging, play on the general public's fears and lack of knowledge about aging. The media also create an informational bias toward negative stereotyping of aging by reporting on older adults in need and on the problems of aging instead of its benefits.

It is important to understand the roots of stereotypes and negative values about aging and old age if we are to change these beliefs to benefit both society and older people. The tremendous increase in the population over age 65 makes it imperative that we develop an accurate understanding about older people and about the impact of negative attitudes on intergenerational contacts and social policies affecting older people. For example, societal debates about whether services aimed at the population over age 65 are discriminatory because they are age-based, or benefit the elderly at the expense of younger populations (Torres-Gil, 1993), are an indication of society's ambivalent attitudes toward this segment of the population.

Negative attitudes about aging and about older people often evolve from anxieties about one's own aging and from fears of becoming frail and dependent. With the rapid growth in the population of people over age 80, and their increased needs for health and social services, there is also a growing concern among younger generations about competition for scarce financial resources between the oldest and youngest segments of society. These concerns may lead to heightened negative feelings toward older people in the future, and they have already resulted in a public "backlash" against the elderly who are mistakenly viewed as taking away services from younger generations and contributing to the federal deficit (Torres-Gil, 1993).

### Stereotypes about Older People

Stereotypes are generalized and simplified *beliefs* about a group of people as objects and they may be either positive or negative. A positive stereotype is one that attributes favorable characteristics to all objects or persons in a particular category; for example, "All old people are wise." Conversely, a negative stereotype ascribes unfavorable characteristics to all objects or persons in a certain category; for example, "All older people are cognitively impaired." A review of attitude research reveals a trend toward more positive stereotypes of aging and older individuals among younger persons (Kite and Johnson, 1988).

By forming stereotypes, we simplify reality and attempt to increase the comprehensibility of the world. The danger of stereotyping, however, is that it leads to an oversimplification of reality, often causing us to ignore characteristics that do not fit into a particular stereotype and to minimize individual differences among members of certain groups. Thus, for example, the stereotype that "all elderly persons are lonely" does not take into account the numerous older persons who have active social networks. People who hold such a stereotype tend to view the socially active older person as "atypical," and thus fail to expand their views about the elderly beyond these "exceptions." In fact, throughout this book, there are numerous examples of the tremendous diversity among older people. Perhaps no other segment of the population shows as much variation as the older population, in their biological, functional, cognitive, psychological, and social abilities.

Negative evaluations and stereotypic beliefs are problematic because they can have significant implications for others' behavior toward the elderly, for social and health policies, and for older persons' sense of self. Most importantly, stereotypes can influence the way a younger person interacts with older people, or even whether one chooses to have contact with them. In a study comparing attitudes toward different cohorts among adolescents, middle-aged, and elderly adults, the youngest group held the most stereotypes regarding older persons *and* reported the greatest social distance from and discomfort with older people (Luszcz and Fitzgerald, 1986). Stereotypes may be exaggerated if the individuals who hold them have particular anxieties or fears about their own aging. For example, by defining older persons to be *different* from themselves, people may maintain an image that they will never be like "them," thereby denying their own aging. Stereotypes held by voters and legislators can also lead to ill-conceived and ineffective policies. For example, stereotypes held about cognitive disorders and mental functioning in old age led, until recently, to a proliferation of nursing homes that were no more than warehouses where older people waited to die. Only in the past two decades has there been a movement toward more humane, supportive institutional design and community programs to enhance older people's cognitive functioning. Such shifts in long-term care policy may be traced, in part, to changes in stereotypes about dementia and to the recognition that environmental factors can influence the behavior and well-being of older persons who have cognitive disorders.

As another example, retirement laws were enacted on the basis of beliefs about the ineffi-

ciency and absenteeism of older workers. Discrimination (i.e., a behavior that is based on socially held beliefs) against older workers has resulted from such mistaken beliefs. Despite data about older workers' high productivity and low rates of absenteeism and the elimination of mandatory retirement laws, mistaken beliefs about older workers persist.

Another common stereotype is that older people are socially isolated and that intergenerational caring and interaction were more common in the "good old days." However, the myth of the "good old days" has little empirical support. Most families who historically shared households and caretaking with older generations did so out of economic necessity, and such families were rare even a century ago. Rather, families today provide the majority of in-home care for their older members. Policies and cuts in services that have placed greater demands on families are based on stereotypes that have long been shown to be inaccurate.

On the other hand, "compassionate stereotypes" (Binstock, 1983) about the older population portray them as physically, economically, and socially disadvantaged because of societal factors and therefore needing public support. Some social policy researchers have argued that compassionate stereotypes may promote the development of programs to benefit older people by legitimizing the need for these services. A content analysis of congressmen's statements and voting patterns revealed that most legislators who voted against reductions in programs for the elderly held compassionate stereotypes (82.3 percent), while many who supported program reductions (58.3 percent) held positive stereotypes such as believing that older people are relatively well-off and are a political force (Lubomudrov, 1987).

Stereotypes held about a social group may also influence the self-concept and self-esteem of members of that group. If older people receive messages from individuals around them and from the media that they are perceived to be confused, frail, unattractive, and helpless, they are likely to adopt some of these assumptions about aging into their own self-concepts, and to assume that such characteristics are inevitable. Such stereotypes can also lead to misperceptions about "appropriate role behaviors," such as how the grandparent role or the retired role must be expressed by older people. These definitions of one's identity that are often inconsistent with one's own needs can then lead to self-criticism and loss of self-esteem. One strategy for coping with these stereotypes, adopted by a significant number of elderly persons, is to deny one's own aging, and to define oneself as "middle aged" or "young," even among people over age 70 (Bultena and Powers, 1978). Another strategy is to adopt the socially expected behaviors into one's repertoire and to fulfill societal role expectations, even though the individual's personality or interests may be inconsistent with these stereotyped expectations (e.g., an older woman who feels she must fit the role of nurturing grandmother, even if she has no interest in babysitting her grandchildren).

Maggie Kuhn was an activist who fought to change stereotypes of aging. In a 1989 interview, she said: "The first myth is that old age is a disease, a terrible disease that you never admit you've got, so you lie about your age. Well, it's not a disease. It's a triumph, because you've survived. Failure, disappointment, sickness, loss, you're still here."

Although the examples presented here suggest that unfavorable stereotypes can have negative consequences, positive stereotypes can also result in inappropriate policies or ineffective actions on the part of service providers. One example of such a mistaken generalization is the belief that most people age 65 and over receive private pensions, thereby depicting older persons as being better off than they really are. However, many older retirees today, particularly those who worked in small or family businesses or are widows of men who held such jobs, do not have private pension coverage. Even though 65 percent of the current older cohort have no pensions, some policy makers assume that all older people have adequate income sources so that public support is unnecessary or, at best, is only supplemental income.

## Ageism

Prejudice or rejection and labeling of a particular group of people develops because the individual attributes negative traits to all persons in that group. The societal impact of racial prejudice is widely recognized. But what is the effect of ageism, or prejudice against people merely on the basis of their age? As noted in the Introduction, Robert Butler (1969) coined the word *ageism* to describe the feelings of prejudice that result from misconceptions and myths about older people. This prejudice generally evolves from beliefs that aging makes people senile, unattractive, asexual, weak, and useless. Social discrimination on the basis of age may be a direct result of ageism, just as racism in the United States has reinforced social and political discrimination against ethnic minorities. The past existence of mandatory retirement was a form of societal discrimination on the basis of age alone. Discrimination may be expressed in other ways. For example, older workers generally experience more difficulty finding new jobs or reentering the job market. This is in part due to the prejudices held by employers regarding older people's abilities to learn new tasks or to keep up with the pace, and in part due to the large pool of new job candidates who are willing to work for lower salaries. Even with the passage of legislation that prohibits discrimination on the basis of age, older job applicants still frequently face signs of ageism when they meet many potential employers. Public agencies may also practice subtle forms of age discrimination by excluding older persons from their target populations or by underserving them.

It has also been suggested that some advocates of the elderly, in their zeal to improve the status of the more disadvantaged, have emphasized the need to do more *for* older people (Kalish, 1979). This form of ageism has been labeled "the new ageism." Consistent with the concepts of "compassionate stereotypes," this "new ageism" is characterized by focusing on the least able elderly, who are viewed as powerless, dependent, and victimized, and by encouraging the development of services that do not enhance older people's independence. "New ageism" may be just as detrimental to the self-esteem of older people as is the more typical form of ageism. It is therefore important that advocates of the elderly, service providers, and older people themselves recognize the diversity of this population and work toward maintaining the independence of the many older individuals who are self-sufficient, while assisting those who need help.

The increased number of social, health, and long-term care services for older clients has produced unexpected problems in some cases. The staffs of these services are often young, in many cases decades younger than the older client. This may result in interpersonal tension because the young staff person does not have the empathy to understand the special needs and concerns of older clients (Kahana and Kiyak, 1984). Indeed, some aging advocates have suggested that programs funded through the Older Americans Act should hire only people age 60 and over.

## Changing Attitudes toward Older People

To the extent that intergenerational working or living situations can develop into egalitarian or in-terdependent arrangements, ageist attitudes will be reduced. Such mutually beneficial situations are possible through intergenerational homesharing and Foster Grandparents programs, through neighborhood efforts in which young and old work on community problems, as well as through Phone Pals programs for latchkey children. When younger persons interact with many different older persons under egalitarian conditions and in one-to-one situations, the two groups can come to see each other as individuals with both good and bad traits, not as outsiders who are different from their peers merely because they differ in age.

Another way to develop more accurate perceptions about the elderly is through coursework or other training in gerontology. Some researchers have reported a shift toward more realistic, less stereotypic perceptions among university students who took gerontology courses and nurses' aides who completed inservice training in geriatrics. A review of research in this area, however, found that coursework may improve knowledge and create protective attitudes toward the elderly immediately following the course, but it does not necessarily result in more realistic attitudes about the elderly in the long run (Coccaro and Miles, 1984). It is also important to note that greater knowledge about older people does not necessarily result in more positive evaluations of this group (Michielutte and Diseker, 1985). Various courses that attempt to improve knowledge have been found to result in more positive, more negative, *and* more neutral evaluations of older people as a group (Kosberg, 1983). Although the number of primary and secondary schools that teach gerontological topics has increased, more research is needed on the long-term effects of these programs on children's evaluation of older people.

The study of the influence of legislators' stereotypes on their voting patterns, described above (Lubomudrov, 1987), also found that members of Congressional committees specializing in aging-related issues were less likely to express either positive *or* negative stereotypes about older people. This suggests that involvement in such activities may serve as a form of education for members, or may reflect a self-selection process. Unless the training program includes an opportunity to have contact with a variety of older persons, not just with healthy elderly or with those in institutional settings, genuine attitudinal change is unlikely (Coccaro and Miles, 1984). It is also important to create a learning environment that encourages a view of the older population as a diverse group, and that avoids stereotyping by the nature of the material presented. Many textbooks and films, for example, depict older people in stereotypic roles. Instructors may also reinforce stereotypes by focusing course content on the diseases and losses associated with aging. It is important to portray the older population realistically, with its diverse strengths.

The depiction of the elderly in the media also reflects society's attitudes about old age. There has been a growing effort by the media to draw attention to older persons who are successful and who are continuing to make contributions in art, music, literature, science, and entertainment. Occasional news stories and documentaries about older people who have been exemplary in these areas can reinforce the fact that aging is not a disease or a life stage to be feared. It is also important to present examples of ordinary older people who lead routine, satisfying lives, and with whom most of us can identify.

There have been growing attempts to present more realistic and multi-faceted portrayals of older persons on television and in films (Atchley, 1989). Thanks to the vigorous efforts of the Gray Panthers and the National Council on Aging, stereotypic and offensive portrayals of older persons are less common, while the presentation of older characters in more powerful and attractive roles has increased. Older characters are shown in both a favorable and an unfavorable light, self-sufficient as well as dependent, and in positions of authority as well as lacking in power.

Advertising can also serve to promote stereotypes or to present a more realistic view of aging. Unfortunately, advertisers have been slower than newspaper writers and television producers to integrate positive images of aging into their products. Aging continues to be associated with an unattractive condition to be avoided, stopped, slowed, or ameliorated with products such as skin creams, make-up, vitamins, haircoloring, denture adhesives, and laxatives. To the extent that youth is idealized and old age is demeaned by these advertisers, negative attitudes toward this period in life and toward this segment of the population will be reinforced.

Nevertheless, societal attitudes toward aging and older people appear to have become more positive. This change has been attributed to the increasing visibility of older people in the media and in public roles as well as to the growing positive self-evaluations of older people themselves. A positive shift has been found in college students' attitudes toward older people; in studies where they were asked to rank older people among various ethnic minorities and disabled groups, the elderly were evaluated near the top (Nordby, 1985; Austin, 1985).

## SUMMARY AND IMPLICATIONS

A primary reason for the growing interest in gerontology is the increase in the population over age 65. This growth results from a reduction in infant and child mortality and improved treatment of acute diseases of childhood and adulthood, which in turn increases the proportion of people living to age 65 and beyond. In the United States, average life expectancy from birth has increased from 47 years in 1900 to 76 in 1993, with women continuing to outlive men. The growth in the population over age 85 has been most dramatic, reflecting major achievements in disease prevention and health care since the turn of the century. Ethnic minority groups in the United States and developing nations have had a smaller growth in the proportion of people living beyond age 65 than whites and industrialized nations do, but population projections anticipate a much higher rate of growth for these groups by the early part of the twenty-first century.

The growth in the numbers and proportions of older people, especially the oldest-old, will require that both public and private policies affecting employment and retirement, health and long-term care, and social services be modified to meet the needs and improve the quality of life of those who are living longer. Fundamental issues will have to be resolved about who will receive what societal resources and what will be the roles of the private and public sectors for sharing responsibilities of elder care. Old age and the aging process are surrounded by more misconceptions than any other period of life. These mistaken beliefs grow out of people's fears about their own aging and are reinforced by messages in the media and in advertising that emphasize the adverse effects of aging. Stereotypes can be reduced by gaining more knowledge about aging and by increasing our contact with older people in an egalitarian or mutually interdependent setting. It is becoming more and more evident that all segments of society—educators, employers, social and health service organizations, advertisers, and the media—must actively strive to reduce ageist attitudes toward the elderly and the aging process as we face the challenge of a growing older population. The ways in which our society meets these challenges will determine the quality of life available not only to current generations of elderly but also to those of us for whom old age seems remote.

## REFERENCES

American Association of Retired Persons (AARP). *A portrait of older minorities.* Washington, D.C., 1987.

American Association of Retired Persons (AARP). *A profile of older Americans 1990.* Washington, D.C., 1990.

Atchley, R. C. A continuity theory of normal aging. *The Gerontologist,* 1989, 29, 183–190.

Austin, D. R. Attitudes toward old age: A hierarchical study. *The Gerontologist,* 1985, 25, 431–434.

Bould, S., Sanborn, B., and Reif, L. *Eighty-five plus: The oldest old.* Belmont, Calif.: Wadsworth, 1989.

Brody, E. Parent care as a normative family stress. *The Gerontologist,* 1985, 25, 19–29.

Bultena, G. L., and Powers, E. A. Denial of aging: Age identification and reference group orientations. *Journal of Gerontology,* 1978, 33, 748–754.

Butler, R. N. Ageism: Another form of bigotry. *The Gerontologist,* 1969, 9, 243–246.

Cantor, M. H. The informal support system of New York's inner city elderly: Is ethnicity a factor? In D. E. Gelfand and A. J. Kutzik (Eds.), *Ethnicity and aging: Theory, research and policy.* New York: Springer, 1979.

Coccaro, E. G., and Miles, A. M. The attitudinal impact of training in gerontology/geriatrics in medical school. *Journal of the American Geriatrics Society,* 1984, 32, 762–786.

Crown, W., and Schulz, J. H. *Private expenditures related to the support of younger and older persons not in the labor force.* Washington, D.C.: Public Policy Institute, American Association of Retired Persons, 1987.

Day, J. C. *Population projections of the U.S. by age, sex, and Hispanic origin: 1993–2050.* U.S. Bureau of the Census, Current Population Reports. Washington, D.C., 1993.

Estes, C., and Binney, E. The biomedicalization of aging: Dangers and dilemmas. *The Gerontologist,* 1989, 29, 587–596.

Evans, D. A., Funkenstein, H. H., Albert, M. S., Schett, P. A., Cook, N. R., Chown, M. J., Heibert, L. E., Hennekens, C. H., and Taylor, J. 0. Prevalence of Alzheimer's disease in a community population of older persons: Higher than previously reported. *Journal of the American Medical Association,* 1989, 262, 2551–2556.

Fries, J. F. Aging, natural death, and the compression of morbidity. *New England Journal of Medicine,* 1980, 303, 130–135.

Fries, J. F., and Crapo, L. M. *Vitality and aging.* San Francisco: W. H. Freeman, 1981.

Jackson, J. Death rates of aged Blacks and Whites, 1964–1978. *The Black Scholar,* 1982, 13, 36–48.

Japan Ministry of Health and Welfare. *Annual Report on health and welfare for 1983,* Tokyo, 1983.

Kahana, E. F., and Kiyak, H. A. Attitudes and behavior of staff in facilities for the aged. *Research on Aging,* 1984, 6, 395–416.

Kalish, R. A. The new ageism and the failure models: A polemic. *The Gerontologist,* 1979, 19, 398–402.

Kane, R. L., Ouslander, J. G., and Abrass, I. B. *Essentials of clinical geriatrics,* (2d ed.). New York: McGraw Hill, 1989.

Katz, S., Branch, L. G., Branson, M. H., Papsidero, J. A., Beck, J. C., and Greer, D. S. Active life expectancy. *New England Journal of Medicine,* 1983, *309,* 1218–1224.

Kii, T. Asians. In E. Palmore (Ed.), *Handbook on the aged in the United States.* Westport, Conn.: Greenwood Press, 1984.

Kingson, E. R., Hirshorn, B. A., and Cornman, J. M. *Ties that bind: The interdependence of generations.* Washington, D.C.: Seven Locks Press, 1986.

Kite, M. E., and Johnson, B. T. Attitudes toward older and younger adults: A meta-analysis. *Psychology and Aging,* 1988, *3,* 233–244.

Kosberg, J. J. The importance of attitudes on the interaction between health care providers and geriatric populations. *Interdisciplinary Topics in Gerontology,* 1983, *17,* 132–143.

Lacayo, C. Hispanics. In E. Palmore (Ed.), *Handbook on the aged in the United States.* Westport, Conn.: Greenwood Press, 1984.

Longino, C. F. Who are the oldest Americans? *The Gerontologist,* 1988, *28,* 515–523.

Longino, C. F., Biggar, J. C., Flynn, C. B., and Wiseman, R. F. The retirement migration project. Final report to the National Institute on Aging. University of Miami, 1984.

Lubomudrov, S. Congressional perceptions of the elderly: The use of stereotypes in the legislative process. *The Gerontologist,* 1987, *27,* 77–81.

Luszcz, M. A. and Fitzgerald, K. M. Understanding cohort differences in cross-generational, self and peer perceptions. *Journal of Gerontology,* 1986, *41,* 234–240.

Manson, J. Long-term care of older American Indians: Challenges in the development of institutional services. In C. Barresi and D. Stull (eds.), *Ethnic elderly and long-term care.* NY: Springer, 1993.

Manton, K. G., and Stallard, E. Cross-sectional estimates of active life expectancy for the U.S. elderly and oldest-old populations. *Journals of Gerontology,* 1991, *46,* S170–182.

Manuel, R. C. Demography of older blacks in the United States. In J. S. Jackson (Ed.), *The black American elderly.* New York: Springer, 1988, 25–49.

Markides, K., and Martin, H. *Older Mexican Americans.* Austin: University of Texas at Austin, Center for Mexican American Studies, 1983.

Michielutte, R., and Diseker, R. A. Health care providers' perceptions of the elderly and level of interest in geriatrics as a specialty. *Gerontology and Geriatrics Education,* 1985, *5,* 65–85.

Myers, G. C. Aging and worldwide population change. In R. H. Binstock and E. Shanas (Eds.), *Handbook of aging and the social sciences* (2d ed.). New York: Van Nostrand Reinhold, 1985.

Nordby, N. A. Acceptance of selected disabilities by university graduate students. Unpublished manuscript. Bloomington: Indiana University. Cited in D. R. Austin, Attitudes toward old age: A hierarchical study. *The Gerontologist,* 1985, *25,* 431–434.

Rauch, J. Economic report: Growing old. *National Journal,* December 31, 1988, 3234–3244.

Rice, D. P., and Feldman, J. J. Living longer in the United States: Demographic changes and health needs of the elderly. *Milbank Fund Memorial Quarterly: Health and Society,* 1983, *61,* 362–396.

Rosenwaike, I. A. A demographic portrait of the oldest old. *Milbank Memorial Fund Quarterly: Health and Society,* 1985, *63,* 187–205.

Schneider, E. L., and Brody, J. A. Aging, natural death, and the compression of morbidity: Another view. *New England Journal of Medicine,* 1983, *309,* 854–856.

Schulz, J. H., and Myles, J. Old age pensions: A comparative perspective: In R. Binstock and L. K George (Eds.), *Handbook of Aging and the Social Sciences,* (3d ed.), New York: Academic Press, 1990, 398–414.

Social Security Administration, U.S. Department of Health and Human Services. *Social Security bulletin: Annual statistical supplement.* Washington, D.C.: U.S. Government Printing Office, 1990.

Soldo, B., and Agree, E. America's elderly. *Population Bulletin,* 1988, *43,* 1–46.

*Statistical Abstract of the United States,* "Resident population, male/female ratio," 1990.

Suzman, R. M., Willis, D. P. & Manton, K. G. (eds), *The Oldest Old.* New York: Oxford University Press, 1992.

Taeuber, C. M. Diversity: The dramatic reality. In S. Bass, E. Kutza & F. Torres-Gil (Eds.), *Diversity in aging.* Glenview, Ill: Scott, Foresman & Co., 1990, 1–46.

Tibbitts, C. Can we invalidate negative stereotypes in aging? *The Gerontologist*, 1979, *19*, 10–20.

Torres-Gil, F. Hispanics: A special challenge. In A. Pifer and L. Bronte (Eds.), *Our aging society*. New York: W. W. Norton, 1986.

Torres-Gil, F. M. Interest group politics: generational changes in the politics of aging. In V. L. Bengston & W. A. Achenbaum (eds.), *The changing contract across generations*. NY: Aldene de Gruyter, 1993.

Torrey, B. B. Demographic shifts and projections: The implications for pension systems. Chapter 4 in *Appendices of the report of the President's commission on pension policy*. Washington, D.C.: The Commission, 1980.

United Nations Secretariat. *World population prospects, 1988*. Population Studies No. 106. Department of International Economic and Social Affairs. New York: United Nations, 1989.

U.S. Bureau of the Census. *1980 census of population*. General Population Characteristics, Chapter B, 1980.

U.S. Bureau of the Census. Projections of the population of the U.S. by age, sex, and race: 1983–2080. *Current Population Reports*. Series P-25, No. 952, U.S. Department of Commerce, 1984.

U.S. Bureau of the Census. Estimates of the population of the U.S. by age, sex, and race: 1980 to 1986. *Current Population Reports*. Series P-25, No. 1000, U.S. Department of Commerce, 1987.

U.S. Bureau of the Census. Household Economic Studies. Series P-70, No. 13. Who's helping out? Support networks among American families. *Current Population Reports*. U.S. Department of Commerce, 1988.

U.S. Bureau of the Census. State population and household estimates with age, sex and components of change. 1981–1988. *Current Population Reports*. Special Studies Series P-25, No. 1044, U.S. Department of Commerce, 1989.

U.S. Bureau of the Census. Marital status and living arrangements. *Current Population Reports*, Series P-20, No. 1450, U.S. Department of Commerce, March 1990a.

U.S. Bureau of the Census. *Modified and actual age, sex, race and Hispanic origin data*. Series CPH-L-74. U.S. Department of Commerce, 1990b.

U.S. Bureau of the Census. *Age, sex, race and Hispanic origin information from the 1990 Census*. U.S. Department of Commerce, 1991a.

U.S. Bureau of the Census. 1980 and 1990 Censuses of the population. *General Population Characteristics*. PC80-1-B1. Table 45, 1991b.

U.S. Bureau of the Census. Growth of America's oldest-old population, *Profiles of America's elderly*. U.S. Department of Commerce, 1992.

U.S. Bureau of the Census. Population projections of the U.S., by age, sex, race, and Hispanic origin data: 1993 to 2050. *Current Population Reports*. Series P-25, No. 1104, U.S. Department of Commerce, 1993a.

U.S. Bureau of the Census. *An Aging World II*. International Population Reports. Series P. 95, No. 92-3, 1993b.

U.S. Congress Congressional Budget Office. Reducing the deficit: Spending and revenue options. Washington, DC: U.S. Government Printing Office, 1994.

U.S. Department of Health and Human Services. *Characteristics of the Black elderly—1980*. Administration on Aging, 1980.

U.S. Senate Special Committee on Aging. *Developments in aging: 1984*. Washington, D.C.: U.S. Government Printing Office, 1985.

U.S. Senate Special Committee on Aging. *Aging America: Trends and projections* (1987–1988 edition.) Washington, D.C.: Department of Health and Human Services, 1988.

U.S. Senate Special Committee on Aging. *Developments in Aging: 1989*, Vol. 1. Washington, D.C.: U.S. Government Printing Office, 1990.

Verbrugge, L. Recent, present and future health of American adults. *Annual Review of Public Health*, 1989, *10*, 333–361.

Wing S., Manton, K. G., Stallard, E., Hames, C. G., and Tryoler, H. A. The black/white mortality crossover: Investigation in a community-based study. *Journal of Gerontology*, 1985 *40*, 78–84.

# CHAPTER 2

---

# THE OLDER POPULATION AND HOW IT IS STUDIED

You are undoubtedly aware that more researchers are studying older people and the process of aging now than at any time in the past. Some of the concerns that have motivated this increasing professional interest in the field have probably influenced your own decision to study gerontology. As we noted in Chapter 1, the single most important reason is the rapid current growth in the older population. This in turn has numerous effects. It influences social, health and long-term care policies and marketing and manufacturing decisions, and it has a profound effect on service providers and relatives of older people, on the elderly themselves, and ultimately on all of us as we look forward to longer lives than those normally experienced by past generations.

This chapter turns to the question of how the older population is studied: What are the particular challenges of social gerontological research, and how are they addressed? Methods of conducting research in this field will be described. The net effect of this information is to give you a basic orientation to the field of aging,

how it has developed, and methods of studying the older population.

## DEVELOPMENT OF THE FIELD

Although the scientific study of social gerontology is relatively recent, it has its roots in biological studies of the aging processes and in the psychology of human development. Biologists have long explored the reasons for aging in living organisms. Several key publications and research studies can be identified as milestones in the history of the field.

One of the first textbooks on aging, *The History of Life and Death,* was written in the thirteenth century by Roger Bacon. Focusing on the potential causes of aging, Bacon suggested that life expectancy could be extended if health practices, such as personal and public hygiene, were improved. The first scientist to explain aging as a developmental process, rather than as stagnation or deterioration, was a nineteenth-century Belgian mathematician-statistician named Adolph Quetelet. His interest in age and creative achievement preceded the study of these issues by social scientists by 100 years (Elias, Elias, and Elias, 1977). His training in the field of statistics also led him to consider the problems of *cross-sectional research;* that is, the collection of data on people of different ages at one time, instead of the study of the same person over a period of months or years *(longitudinal research)*. These problems will be examined in greater detail in the next section of this chapter.

## Early Community-based and Laboratory Studies

Later in the nineteenth century, Russian scientist S. P. Botkin provided some of the earliest data on the differences between normal and *pathological aging* (i.e., diseases that may speed the process of aging, but are not a normal part of the process), sex differences in atherosclerosis, and the link between alcohol abuse and longevity (Birren and Clayton, 1975). He derived his data from a large community-based study, conducting extensive physiological analyses and comparing these with the social characteristics of nearly 3,000 older residents of St. Petersburg in Russia.

One of the first laboratory studies of aging was undertaken in the 1920s by another Russian physiologist, Ivan Pavlov, and his students. Pavlov is best known for his research with animals, which has provided the foundation for stimulus-response theories of behavior. Recognizing that the ability of older animals to learn and distinguish a response differed from that of younger animals, Pavlov explored the reasons for these differences in the brains of these animals (Birren, 1961). The work of Raymond Pearl and colleagues in the 1920s established the insect species *Drosophila* as an ideal animal model for studying biological aging and longevity. During this era, in 1922, American psychologist G. Stanley Hall published one of the first books on the social-psychological aspects of aging in the United States. Titled *Senescence, the Last Half of*

*Life,* it remains a landmark text in gerontology because it provided the experimental framework for examining changes in cognitive processes and social and personality functions.

## Historical Forces of the Late Nineteenth and Early Twentieth Centuries

Two important forces led to the expansion of research in social gerontology in the late nineteenth and early twentieth centuries: the growth of the population over age 65 and the emergence of retirement policies in industrial settings. Changes in policies toward the elderly were first evident in many European countries (e.g., Germany) where social services and health insurance programs were developed specifically for older citizens. In the United States, these changes came somewhat later. At the turn of the century, the focus on economic growth and the immediate problems of establishing workers' rights and child welfare laws took precedence over interest in the welfare of older people. The prevailing belief in this country had been that families should be responsible for their aging members. However, the Great Depression of the 1930s brought to policy makers the stark realization that families struck by unemployment and homelessness could not be responsible for their elders. The older segments of society suffered a disproportionate share of the economic blight of the Depression. New concern for the special needs of the aging population was exemplified by the Social Security system, established in 1935 to help people maintain a minimal level of economic security after retirement. Early work in social gerontology dealt largely with social and economic problems of aging. For example, E. V. Cowdry's *Problems of Aging,* published in 1939, focused on society's treatment of older people and on their particular needs.

## Formal Development of the Field

As society grew more aware of issues facing the older population, the formal study of aging emerged in the 1940s. In 1945, the Gerontological Society of America (GSA) was founded, bringing together the small group of researchers and practitioners who were interested in gerontology and geriatrics. Today, this organization numbers its membership between 6,000 and 7,000, and it is the major professional association for people in diverse disciplines who are working in the field of aging. Gerontology became a division of the American Psychological Association in 1945 and, later, of the American Sociological Association.

The *Journal of Gerontology,* which the GSA began publishing in 1946, served as the first vehicle for transmitting new knowledge in this growing field.[*] Although it remains a major journal, today numerous others are devoted to the study of aging and to the concerns of those who work with older people, some of which are listed in Table 2–1. An indicator of the knowledge explosion in the field is that the literature on aging published between 1950 and 1960 equalled that of the previous 115 years (Birren

### TABLE 2–1    Some Representative Journals Devoted to Gerontology

*Aging and Society*
*Experimental Aging Research*
*Geriatrics*
*The Gerontologist*
*Gerontology and Geriatrics Education*
*International Journal of Aging and Human Development*
*Journal of the American Geriatrics Society*
*Journals of Gerontology*
*Journal of Geriatric Nursing*
*Journal of Geriatric Psychiatry*
*Journal of Gerontological Social Work*
*Research on Aging*
*Psychology and Aging*
*Women and Aging*

[*]The title of this journal was changed in 1988 to "The Journals of Gerontology," reflecting the four sections of GSA: Biological Sciences, Clinical Medicine, Psychological Sciences, and Social Sciences.

and Clayton, 1975). An effort to compile a bibliography of biomedical and social research from 1954 to 1974 produced 50,000 titles (Woodruff, 1975). Today, the burgeoning periodicals in diverse disciplines focused on gerontology have resulted in a proliferation of research publications in this field.

## Major Research Centers Founded

Research in gerontology took on growing significance after these developments, and an interest in the social factors associated with aging grew in the late 1950s and early 1960s. In 1946, a national gerontology research center, headed by the late Nathan Shock, a leader in geriatric medicine, was established at Baltimore City Hospital by the National Institutes of Health. This federally funded research center undertook several studies of physiological aspects of aging, using a *cross-sectional approach.*

In 1958, Dr. Shock and his colleagues began a *longitudinal* study of physiological changes in healthy, middle-aged and older men living in the community, by testing them annually, or less often, on numerous physiological parameters. They later started to examine the cognitive, personality, and social-psychological characteristics of these men. Much later, in 1978, older women were included in their samples. Known as the Baltimore Longitudinal Studies, these assessments of changes associated with healthy aging are still continuing, now under the direction of the National Institute on Aging. The results of this ongoing research effort continue to provide valuable information about normal age-related changes in physiological and psychological functions.

Concurrently with the Baltimore Longitudinal Studies, several university-based centers were developed to study the aging process and the needs of older adults. One of the first, the Duke University Center on Aging, focused initially on the mental health of older people but also conducted pioneering research on the social issues of aging. The University of Chicago, under the direction of Robert Havighurst, developed the first research center devoted exclusively to the social aspects of aging. The Kansas City studies of adult development, discussed in Chapters 4 and 9, represent the first major social-psychological studies of adult development, and were conducted by researchers from the Chicago center. Research and training centers on aging have since evolved at many other universities, generally stimulated by government sponsorship of gerontological research through the National Institute on Aging (established in 1975), the Center for Studies of the Mental Health of the Aging through the National Institute of Mental Health (1976), and the Administration on Aging (1965).

## HOW IS AGING STUDIED?

Before moving on to an examination of the issues and areas of special concern to social gerontologists, let us first consider the ways in which such information about the aging process is gathered. The topic of research methodologies in gerontology may seem an advanced one to introduce in a basic text, but in fact, it is essential to understanding the meaning and validity of information presented throughout this book.

The study of aging presents particular conceptual and methodological difficulties. A major one is how research is designed and data interpreted regarding age changes. A point that complicates research in aging and also produces some misleading interpretations of data is how to distinguish *age changes* from *age differences*. This differentiation is necessary if we are to understand the process of aging and the conditions under which age differences occur. If we wish to determine what changes or effects are experienced as an individual moves from middle age to old age and to advanced old age, we must examine the same individual over a period of years, or at least months. In order to understand age changes, longitudinal research is necessary; that

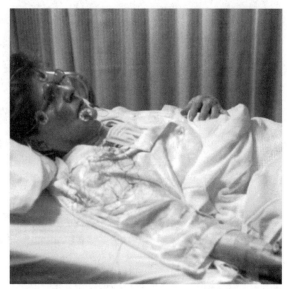

Increased research attention has been focused on sleep changes with normal aging.

is, the repeated measurement of the same person over a specified period of time.

Unfortunately, the time and cost of such studies prevent many researchers from undertaking longitudinal research. Instead, much of the research in this field focuses on age differences, by comparing people of different chronological ages at the same measurement period. These studies, cross-sectional in nature, are the most common ones in gerontology.

The unique problems inherent in how gerontological research is designed and how data are interpreted are evident in the following question: Given that aging in humans is a complex process that proceeds quite differently among individuals in varied geographic, cultural, and historic settings, and that it takes place over a time span as long as 100 to 120 years, how does one study it? Obviously, scientists cannot follow successive generations—or even a single generation of subjects—throughout their life span. Nor can they be expected to address the entire range of variables that affect aging—including lifestyle, social class, cultural beliefs, public policies, and so on—in a single study.

## The Age/Period/Cohort Problem

The problem in each case is that of distinguishing *age differences* (ways that one generation differs from another) from *age changes* (ways that people normally change over time). This has been referred to as the "age/period/cohort" problem (Maddox, 1979). (The word *cohort*, you will recall, refers to those people born at roughly the same time. *Period* refers to the effects of the specific historical period involved.) The concept of cohort is an important one in gerontology because historical events differentiate one cohort from another in attitudes and behaviors. Those people in the same cohort are likely to be more similar to each other because of comparable social forces acting on them during a given era (Maddox and Campbell, 1985).

## Cross-sectional Studies

As noted earlier, the most common approach to studying aging is cross-sectional; that is, researchers compare a number of subjects of different ages on the same characteristics in order to determine age-related differences. One reason that cross-sectional studies are frequently used is that, compared to other designs, data can be readily gathered. Some examples might include a comparison of the lung capacity of men aged 30 with those who are aged 40, 50, 60, 70, and 80, or a study comparing church attendance by American adults under age 65 with those over age 65. The average differences among different age groups in each study might suggest conclusions about the changes that come with age.

The danger with such cross-sectional studies is that these differences might not be due to the process of aging, but rather to particular cultural and historical conditions that shaped each group of subjects being studied. For example, a higher rate of church attendance among today's elderly

than among younger adults might (and indeed probably does) reflect a change in social attitudes during this century toward attending church, as opposed to, say, an increased need for spiritual and religious life as one grows older.

Even in studies of biological factors, such as lung capacity, there may be many intervening variables that threaten the validity of comparative results. In this case, they include the effects of exercise, smoking, and other lifestyle factors, genetic inheritance, and exposure to pollution (this, in turn, might be a product of work environments and social class) on relevant outcome variables.

The major limitation of cross-sectional studies has been when differences among younger and older respondents were erroneously attributed to growing old; for example, some researchers have found that the older the respondent, the lower his or her score on intelligence tests. As a result, cognitive abilities have been misinterpreted as declining with age. In fact, such differences may be due to the lower educational levels and higher test anxiety of this cohort of elderly compared to younger adults, not to age. This is an example of *confounding*, or a joint effect of two variables on an outcome of interest. In this case, age and cohort effects are confounded.

Similarly, in studying individuals' values about the meaning of money and personal savings, for example, it is important to know whether differences between age groups are due to chronological age per se (e.g., whether the younger respondents would eventually think like the older ones as they reached that age), or to differences arising from the historical periods in which the different age groups have lived (known as environmental factors or *period effects*). It is difficult to distinguish period effects from age differences in a cross-sectional research design. As an example, the current cohort of elderly have all lived through and been affected by the Great Depression. The financial burdens imposed by this period in American history probably have affected their values about frugality in saving. In contrast, people whose childhood years occurred during the post–World War II economic boom in this country have adopted less cautious values about saving and investing their earnings. A cross-sectional study would not capture the reasons for these differences. Because many issues in social gerontology center on distinguishing age from cohort effects, a number of research designs have emerged that attempt to do this. They include longitudinal and sequential designs.

## Longitudinal Studies: Design and Limitations

Longitudinal designs permit inferences about age *changes*. They eliminate cohort effects by studying the same people over time. Each row in Table 2–2 represents a separate longitudinal study in which a given cohort (e.g., A, B, or C) is measured once every ten years. Despite the advantages of longitudinal designs over the cross-sectional approach, it still has limitations. First, the longitudinal method does not allow a distinc-

tion between age and time of testing. For example, if a sample of 55-year-old workers had been interviewed regarding retirement policies in 1975, before the mandatory retirement age was changed to age 70, and again in 1995, long after mandatory retirement was eliminated, it would be difficult to determine whether the changes found in their attitudes toward retirement came about as a result of their increased age and proximity to retirement, or as a result of the modifications in retirement laws during this period. Longitudinal designs cannot separate the effects of events extraneous to the study that influence people's responses in a particular measurement period.

Another problem with longitudinal studies is the potential for practice effects. This problem occurs in studies that administer aptitude or knowledge tests, where repeated measurement with the same test improves the test-taker's performance because of familiarity or practice. For example, a psychologist who is interested in age-related changes in intelligence could expect to obtain improvements in people's scores if the same test is administered several times, with a brief interval (e.g., less than one year) between tests. In such cases, it is difficult to relate the changes to maturation unless the tests can be

### TABLE 2–2   Alternative Research Designs in Aging

| Cohort Born In | TIME OF MEASUREMENT | | | |
|---|---|---|---|---|
|  | 1950 | 1960 | 1970 | 1980 |
| 1900 | $A_1$ | $A_2$ | | |
| 1910 | | $B_1$ | $B_2$ | |
| 1920 | | $C_1$ | $C_2$ | $C_3$ |
| 1930 | | | | $D_4$ |

Cross-sectional: Cohorts A, B, and C are measured in 1960. Longitudinal: Cohort A is measured in 1950 and 1960; or Cohort B is measured in 1960 and 1970; or Cohort C is measured in 1960, 1970, and 1980. Cohort-sequential: Cohort A is measured in 1950 and 1960; Cohort B is measured in 1960 and 1970. Time-sequential: Cohorts B and C are measured in 1970; Cohorts C and D are measured in 1980. Cross-sequential: Cohorts B and C are both measured in 1960 and 1970.

SOURCE: Adapted from K. W. Schaie (Ed.), *Longitudinal studies of adult psychological development* (New York: Guilford Press, 1983).

An interview with an older adult participant in a research study.

varied or parallel forms of the same tests can be used.

Longitudinal studies also present the problem of *attrition,* or dropout. Individuals in experimental studies and respondents in surveys that are administered repeatedly may drop out for many reasons—death, illness, loss of interest, or frustration with poor performance. To the extent that people who drop out are not different from the original sample in terms of demographic characteristics, health status, and intelligence, the researcher can still generalize from the results obtained with the remaining sample. However, more often it is the case that dropouts differ significantly from those who stay until the end. As we shall see in Chapter 8, those who drop out of longitudinal studies tend to be in poorer health, score lower on intelligence tests, and are more socially isolated. In contrast, those who remain are the more educated, healthy, successful, and motivated elderly participants.

This is known as the problem of *selective dropout.* While many researchers have pointed to the potential bias introduced by selective dropout, others have suggested that the results of such longitudinal data provide a positive developmental image about a significant proportion of older adults (Cooney, Schaie, and Willis, 1988; Schaie and Willis, 1986).

## Sequential Designs

Some newer research designs have emerged in response to the problems of cross-sectional and longitudinal methods. One is the category of sequential designs (Schaie, 1967, 1973, 1977, 1983). These include the cohort-sequential, time-sequential, and cross-sequential methods, which are illustrated in Table 2–2.

A *cohort-sequential* design is an extension of the longitudinal design, whereby two or more cohorts are followed for a period of time, so that measurements are taken of different age groups at different points in time. Thus, for example, an investigator may wish to compare changing attitudes toward federal policies among the cohort born in 1900 and the cohort born in 1910 and follow each one for 10 years, from 1950 to 1960 for the first cohort, and from 1960 to 1970 for the second. This approach is useful for many social gerontological studies in which age and cohort must be distinguished. However, it still does not separate the effects of cohort from historical effects or time of measurement. As a result, historical events that occurred just before one cohort entered a study but later than another cohort entered may influence each cohort's attitude scores differently.

The *time-sequential* design is useful for distinguishing between age and time of measurement or historical factors. It can be used to determine if changes obtained are due to aging or to historical factors. The researcher using this design would compare two or more cross-sectional samples at two or more measurement periods. For example, a group of 70-year-olds and a group of 60-year-olds might be compared in 1970; the latter could be compared with a new group of 60-year-olds in 1980. Time-sequential designs do not prevent the confounding of age and cohort effects, but it is acceptable to use this method where one would not expect age differences to be confused with cohort differences.

The third technique proposed by Schaie (1983) is the *cross-sequential* design, which combines cross-sectional and longitudinal designs. Thus, for example, the researcher could compare people who were age 40 and 50 in 1960, and again in 1970 when they were age 50 and 60 respectively. This would permit the assessment of cohort and historical factors, because the same cohorts are being compared at two different times, with one providing information on changes from age 40 to 50, and the other representing changes from age 50 to 60. This approach is an improvement over both the traditional cross-sectional and longitudinal designs, but it still confounds age and time of measurement effects. These three sequential designs are becoming more widely used by gerontological researchers, especially in studies of intelligence. Table 2–3 summarizes

**TABLE 2–3   Potential Confounding Effects in Developmental Studies**

| Design | CONFOUNDING EFFECT | | |
|---|---|---|---|
| | Age × Cohort Confounded | Age × Time of Measurement Confounded | Cohort × Time of Measurement Confounded |
| Cross-sectional | Yes | No | No |
| Longitudinal | No | Yes | No |
| Cohort-sequential | No | No | Yes |
| Time-sequential | Yes | No | No |
| Cross-sequential | No | Yes | No |

SOURCE: Adapted from M. F. Elias, P. K. Elias, and J. W. Elias, *Basic processes in adult developmental psychology* (St. Louis: C. V. Mosby, 1977).

potential confounding effects in each of these methods.

Despite the growth of new research methods, much of social gerontology is based on cross-sectional studies. For this reason, it is important to read carefully the description of a study and its results in order to make accurate inferences about age changes as opposed to age differences, and to determine whether the differences found between groups of different ages are due to cohort effects or to true effects of aging.

## Measuring Attitudes toward Older People

Aside from these problems unique to gerontology, the basic research tools are similar to those used in sociology and psychology, and include psychological tests, observations, interviews, questionnaires, and case histories. As in all research studies, the measures used must be valid (accurately reflecting the concepts that they are intended to measure) and reliable (yielding the same results from repeated measurements of the same phenomenon).

Efforts to measure attitudes and stereotypes about the elderly represent one example of social gerontological research that has used basic research methods borrowed from social psychology and sociology. Questionnaires with rating scales and open-ended items have been developed

to assess the components of attitudes described in Chapter 1. Other methods, such as behavioral observation techniques, have been used to assess how younger persons interact with older people in diverse settings. Most paper-and-pencil methods ask the respondent to agree or disagree with a series of statements that describe the "typical" older person. These methods often rely on factual information; thus it is difficult to distinguish stereotyped responses from simply not knowing the information precisely.

The most frequently used measure of beliefs about old age and elderly persons is the "Facts on Aging Quiz," developed by Palmore (1977). Using information derived from large national studies and from census data, Palmore prepared 25 statements describing the psychological, physiological, and demographic characteristics of persons age 65 and over. Slightly more than one-half of these items are factually true; the remainder are false. In a review of the research using this scale, Lutsky (1980) points out the consistency with which some items are missed by diverse respondent groups. It appears that many respondents are misinformed about the percentage of older persons in the general population and in long-term care settings as well as the extent of poverty and religiosity among the elderly; there is a tendency to overestimate the total number of elderly and those in institutions. With media attention often focused on improvements in the economic well-being of the older population, some people may stereotype *all* elders as being financially more secure than younger families. As a result, respondents who, for example, do not know the percentage of older people in nursing homes are assumed to be stereotyping the elderly when, in fact, they do not *know* if the figures given in a statement are an overestimate or an underestimate.

Other methods of measuring stereotypes include open-ended questions (e.g., the respondent is asked to describe characteristics of older people in his or her own words), word association techniques, adjective pairs, and projective techniques such as interpreting the meaning that a picture of a stimulus object has for the respondent (e.g., a picture of an older person engaged in "atypical" behavior). Since none of these methods has been tested widely in the area of attitudes toward the elderly, it is difficult to compare their relative merits.

More recently, attitude researchers in gerontology have provided subjects with hypothetical persons of varying ages, sometimes accompanied by a photograph, and have asked them to describe the characteristics of the older or younger stimulus person with an adjective checklist, a visual analogue scale, or open-ended questions (Kite, Deaux, and Miele, 1991; Miller, Oppenheimer, and Melcher, 1990; Revenson 1989).

## Measuring Feelings toward Older People

*Affect* is the evaluative dimension of attitudes that demonstrates liking or disliking, acceptance or rejection of a target group. The affect component of attitudes has been assessed by asking respondents to rate older people on a series of adjective pairs such as "friendly–hostile," or "good–bad." Most studies have revealed neutral affect toward older persons, with college students expressing fewer positive responses than children or middle-aged adults. Research on children's affect toward the elderly has shown that they respond positively to photos of older persons. At the same time, however, many children associate old age with poor health and helplessness, and hold negative stereotypes about older people.

Many educators have bemoaned the lack of widespread interest among students in geriatric medicine, nursing, and dentistry, as well as the low priority given to treatment of older patients by psychiatrists, clinical psychologists, and social workers. These problems have often been attributed to the existence of negative attitudes toward older persons by the young. Despite these hypothesized associations between attitudes and behavior, few studies have been undertaken to test these relationships.

Most researchers who have focused on health care providers' attitudes have found that most groups hold neutral to positive feelings about the elderly (Chandler, Rachel, and Kazelskis, 1986). In general, level of education has been found to be associated with knowledge about older people, but to have no impact on affect or stereotypes. It appears that the *quality* of one's previous experiences with the elderly strongly influences subsequent perceptions. To the extent that their prior experiences have been positive, most respondents will offer more favorable evaluations of older people in general.

Studies of elderly persons' evaluations of their peers are rare. Somewhat surprisingly, respondents in their seventies are more likely than younger respondents to agree with stereotypic statements about the elderly. Studies that seek to determine respondents' preferences for people of various age groups have found that older respondents express greater preference for middle-aged persons than for older persons (Kogan, 1979). Such attitudes can be a significant barrier to recruiting older persons to age-based activities such as senior centers.

One problem with research on evaluations of older people is the use of generalized stimuli such as "old people" or "young people" rather than a specific hypothetical person. Such general stimuli force the respondent to evaluate a whole class of people with no opportunity to indicate perceived variations among people within that group. A study of attitudes of staff in facilities serving aged clients showed differences in evaluations of the stimuli "older persons in general," "my older clients," and "my own aging" (Kahana and Kiyak, 1982). On the other hand, recent studies that have used specific hypothetical young and old stimulus persons have found more stereotypes (both positive *and* negative) of the latter (Kite, Deaux, and Miele, 1991; Revenson, 1989).

## Measuring Behavioral Intentions

One component of attitudes which has not been explored widely in gerontology is *behavioral intentions.* This term refers to the individual's preconceived notion of what he or she would do in certain situations with older persons. Knowledge about such behavioral intentions is helpful in developing educational and community programs for younger people who will be interacting with older people.

One method of measuring behavioral intentions is through the use of *social distance scales,* in which respondents are asked to indicate how comfortable they would feel with a stimulus person in various interpersonal situations (e.g., one distance scale has been designed specifically to ascertain how respondents would feel with persons of different ages in situations of increasing intimacy (e.g., "would sit next to the person on a bus" represents low intimacy; "would consider as a close friend" indicates high intimacy) (Kidwell and Booth, 1977). Increased age differences between the respondent and the stimulus person have been found to lead to greater social distance, indicating less desirability of interacting with older persons. Older respondents expressed greater social distance from their age peers when compared with younger respondents.

Another method of measuring behavioral intentions is to ask respondents to rate their preference for working with the elderly. Studies of students in the health professions have revealed a generally low desire to work with older persons (Geiger, 1978), even though evaluations of older persons may be just as positive as respondents' ratings of younger stimulus persons. This raises the issue of potential inconsistency among the three dimensions of attitudes. As we have already noted, positive affect toward older persons does not necessarily imply fewer stereotypes and a desire to interact with people in this age group. Furthermore, actual behavior toward older persons may not be related to any particular situation (Kahana and Kiyak, 1982, 1984). For example, a staff person in a nursing home with an institutional philosophy that older people should be encouraged to be independent may demonstrate such independence-oriented behavior in an effort to fit with the organization's values, even though he or she believes that elderly in nursing homes are dependent.

## Measuring Behavior toward Older People

Few studies have examined the relationship between attitudes and actual behavior toward older persons. This may be due to the difficulties of conducting the necessary longitudinal research, or of identifying behaviors that may be linked to specific attitudes. In one study, staff in facilities for the elderly were found to display affect and behaviors that encouraged *both* dependence and independence (Kahana and Kiyak, 1984). This study provided an opportunity to observe staff interacting with elderly clients within a few weeks after they completed questionnaires describing their stereotypes, affect, and behavioral intentions toward older persons. There was very little association between the staff person's self-reported affect and stereotypes and their observed behavior. In fact, the majority of behaviors were neutral, with few overtly positive or negative behaviors toward older clients. Behavioral intentions were most closely related to actual behaviors. That is, staff members who believed that older persons should be encouraged to take care of themselves were more likely to encourage independence-inducing behaviors than were staff who had endorsed behavioral intentions of encouraging dependency.

Further research is needed to determine the impact of social attitudes on behavior toward older persons, on policies aimed at this population, and on the development of older persons' self-esteem. Both cross-sectional and longitudinal studies are necessary. In particular, it is important to assess the effect of interventions aimed at changing attitudes. For example, what is the long-term influence of intergenerational programs that aim to develop more positive attitudes about the elderly in young children? How can the reduction of stereotypes influence a professional person's desire or willingness to work with older clients? These and other attitude-behavior associations must be examined if we are to gain a deeper understanding of the effect of attitudes on the lives of older persons, and on their social interactions with the young.

## Selecting Older Persons as Research Subjects

Accurate sampling can be difficult with older populations. If the sample is not representative, the results are of questionable validity. However, comprehensive lists of older people are not readily available. Membership lists from organizations, such as the American Association of Retired Persons, tend to overrepresent those who are healthy and financially secure. Studies in institutions, such as nursing homes and adult day centers, tend to overrepresent those with chronic impairments. Reaching ethnic minority elderly through organizational lists can be especially difficult.

The problem of selective survival affects all samples of older people. Over time, the birth cohort loses members, so that those who remain are not necessarily representative of all in the original group. Those who survive, for example, probably were healthiest at birth, and maintained their good health throughout their lives— all variables that tend to be associated with higher socioeconomic status.

Even when an adequate sample is located, older respondents may vary in their memories or attention spans; such variations can interfere with conducting interviews or tests. Ethical issues and unique difficulties arise in interviewing the frail elderly. Currently there are no ethical guidelines specifically aimed at research with the elderly. The issue of informed consent becomes meaningless when dealing with a confused or a severely medically compromised older person. In such cases, family members or guardians must take an active role in judging the risks and benefits of research for frail elderly persons (Ratzan, 1980). Streib (1983) has urged the use of qualitative methods to gather information about this population that has been neglected in gerontological research. An additional problem is that studies of the old-old may be influenced by *terminal drop,* a decline in some tests of intelligence shortly before death (Botwinick, 1984; White and Cunningham, 1988). Since death becomes increasingly likely with age, terminal drop will manifest as a gradual decline in performance test scores with age in cross-sectional designs. In longitudinal studies, this problem may result in an overestimation of performance abilities in the later years because those who survive are likely to represent the physically and cognitively most capable elderly. This problem will be explored further in Chapter 8.

Further refinement of research methodologies is a challenging task for social gerontologists. As progress is made in this area, the quality of data with which to study aging will continually improve.

## SUMMARY AND IMPLICATIONS

Gerontology has grown as a field since early philosophers and scientists first explored the reasons for changes experienced with advancing age. Roger Bacon in the thirteenth century, Adolph Quetelet in the early nineteenth century, Botkin in the late nineteenth century, and Ivan Pavlov and G. Stanley Hall in the early twentieth century made pioneering contributions to this field. During the early 1900s, in Europe and the United States, the impact of an increasing aging population on social and health resources began to be felt. Social gerontological research has expanded since the 1940s, paralleling the rapid growth of the older population and its needs.

The growing older population, and associated social concerns, have stimulated great interest in gerontological research. However, existing research methodologies are limited in their ability to distinguish the process of aging per se from cohort, time, and measurement effects. Cross-sectional research designs are most often used in this field, but these can provide information only on age differences, not on age changes. Longitudinal designs are necessary for understanding age changes, but suffer from the possibility of subject attrition and the effects of measuring the same individual numerous times. Newer methods in social gerontology, known as cohort-sequential, time-sequential, and cross-sequential designs, test multiple cohorts, or age groups, over time. They also are limited by possible confounding effects, but represent considerable improvement over traditional research designs.

Research on attitudes toward older people represents a focus of social gerontology, one that has borrowed methods from social psychology and sociology. Our understanding of individual and environmental factors that influence attitudes can aid in the development of research and educational interventions to improve the quality of interactions between young and old, and potentially on older people's quality of life. Because research methods in gerontology have improved, today there is a better understanding of many aspects of aging. Research findings to date provide the empirical background for the theories and topics to be covered in the remaining chapters. Despite the recent explosion of knowledge in gerontology, there are many gaps in what is known about older people and the aging process. Throughout the text, we will call attention to areas in which additional research is needed.

## REFERENCES

Birren, J. E. A brief history of the psychology of aging. *The Gerontologist*, 1961, *1*, 69–77, 127–134.

Birren, J. E., and Clayton, V. History of gerontology. In D. S. Woodruff and J. E. Birren (Eds.), *Aging: Scientific perspectives and social issues*. New York: Van Nostrand, 1975.

Botwinick, J. *Cognitive processes in maturity and old age* (3d ed.). New York: Springer, 1984.

Brody, E. Parent care as a normative family stress. *The Gerontologist*, 1985, *25*, 19–29.

Cameron, P., and Cromer, A. Generational homophyly. *Journal of Gerontology*, 1974, *29*, 232–236.

Chandler, J. T., Rachel, J. R., and Kazelskis, R. Attitudes of long-term care nursing personnel toward the elderly. *The Gerontologist*, 1986, *26*, 551–555.

Cooney, T. M., Schaie, K. W. and Willis, S. L. The relationship between prior functioning on cognitive and personality dimensions and subject attrition in longitudinal research. *Journals of Gerontology*, 1988, *43*, P12–17.

Cowdry, E. V. (Ed.), *Problems of aging*. Baltimore, Md.: The Williams & Wilkins Co., 1939.

Crown, W. Some thoughts on reformulating the dependency ratio. *The Gerontologist*, 1985, *25*, 166–171.

Elias, M. F., Elias, P. K., and Elias, J. W. *Basic processes in adult developmental psychology*. St. Louis: C.V. Mosby, 1977.

Geiger, D. L. How future professionals view the elderly: A comparative analysis of social work, law, and medical students' perceptions. *The Gerontologist*, 1978, *18*, 591–594.

Greene, R. L., and Siegler, I. C. Ethnic groups: Blacks. In E. Palmore (Ed.), *Handbook on the aged in the United States*. Westport, Conn.: Greenwood Press, 1984, 219–233.

Kahana, E. F., and Kiyak, H. A. Attitudes and behavior of staff in facilities for the aged. *Research on Aging*, 1984, *6*, 395–416.

Kahana, E. F., and Kiyak, H. A. *Attitudes toward the elderly: antecedents, content and outcome*. Final report submitted to the National Institute on Aging. 1982.

Kidwell, I. J., and Booth, A. Social distance and intergenerational relations. *The Gerontologist*, 1977, *17*, 412–420.

Kite, M. E., Deaux, K., and Miele, M. Stereotypes of young and old: Does age outweigh gender? *Psychology and Aging*, 1991, *6*, 19–27.

Kogan, N. A. A study of age categorization. *Journal of Gerontology*, 1979, *34*, 358–367.

Lutsky, N. S. Attitudes toward old age and elderly persons. In C. Eisdorfer (Ed.), *Annual review of gerontology and geriatrics* (Vol. 1). New York: Springer, 1980.

Maddox, G. Sociology of later life. *Annual Review of Sociology*, 1979, *5*, 113–135.

Maddox, G. L., and Campbell, R. T. Scope, concepts and methods in the study of aging. In R. H. Binstock and E. Shanas (Eds.), *Handbook of aging and the social sciences* (2d ed.). New York: Van Nostrand Reinhold, 1985, 3–34.

Manton, K. G., and Stallard, E. Cross-sectional estimates of active life expectancy for the U.S. elderly and oldest-old populations. *Journals of Gerontology*, 1991 *46*, S170–182.

Miller, M. D., Oppenheimer, K. C., and Melcher, R. Medical student attitudes toward elderly patients: Effects of social attractiveness. *Family Medicine*, 1990, *22*, 29–32.

Myers, G. C. Aging and worldwide population change. In R. H. Binstock and E. Shanas (Eds.), *Handbook of aging and the social sciences* (2d ed.). New York: Van Nostrand Reinhold, 1985, 173–198.

NRTA-AARP (National Retired Teachers Association-American Association of Retired Persons) (1981). National survey of older Americans.

Ratzan, R. M. "Being old makes you different": The ethics of research with elderly subjects. *Hastings Center Report*, October 1980.

Revenson, T. A. Compassionate stereotyping of elderly patients by physicians: Revising the social contact hypothesis. *Psychology and Aging*, 1989, *4*, 230–234.

Schaie, K. W. Age changes and age differences. *The Gerontologist*, 1967, *7*, 128–132.

Schaie, K. W. Methodological problems in descriptive developmental research on adulthood and aging. In J. R. Nesselroade and H. W. Reese (Eds.), *Lifespan developmental psychology: Methodological issues*. New York: Academic Press, 1973.

Schaie, K. W. Quasi-experimental research designs in the psychology of aging. In J. E. Birren and K. W. Schaie (Eds.), *Handbook of the psychology of aging*. New York: Van Nostrand Reinhold, 1977.

Schaie, K. W. (Ed.), *Longitudinal studies of adult psychological development*. New York: Guilford Press, 1983.

Schaie, K. W., and Willis, S. L. Can adult intellectual decline be reversed? *Developmental Psychology*, 1986, *22*, 223–232.

Schulz, J. H. *The economics of aging*. Belmont, Calif: Wadsworth, 1984

Streib, G. F. The frail elderly: Research dilemmas and research opportunities. *The Gerontologist*, 1983, *23*, 40–44.

Ward, R. A. The impact of subjective age and stigma on older persons. *Journal of Gerontology*, 1977, *32*, 227–232.

Weinberger, L. E., and Millham, J. A. Multidimensional, multiple method analysis of attitudes toward the elderly. *Journal of Gerontology*, 1975, *30*, 343–348.

White, N., and Cunningham, W. R. Is terminal drop pervasive or specific? *Journals of Gerontology*, 1988, *44*, 141–144.

Woodruff, D. Introduction: Multidisciplinary perspectives of aging. In D. Woodruff and J. Birren (Eds.), *Aging: Scientific perspectives and social issues*. New York: Van Nostrand, 1975.

# CHAPTER 3

# HISTORICAL AND CROSS-CULTURAL ISSUES IN AGING

The experience of aging is not the same today as it was in earlier historical periods. The social and economic roles of older persons, their expectations of the social system, as well as what society expects of them, are in many ways profoundly different today from previous generations. Until relatively recently, only a minority of people lived long enough to be considered old. As the number of older people has grown and as social values have changed, the authority and power of the elderly in society have also shifted.

The experience of aging differs cross-culturally as well as historically. That is, in addition to historical changes, there are significant cultural variations that affect the social position of older persons. Perhaps the greatest differences in the elderly's status are between traditional societies and those of the modern Western world, with its rapidly changing values and norms. Examining the different ways that other societies, both historical and contemporary, have dealt with issues affecting the elderly can shed light on the process of aging in our society. The emergence of "comparative sociocultural gerontol-

ogy" or an "anthropology of aging" has served to refute some of the myths of the "good old days" presumed to exist in historical times and in contemporary nonindustrial societies. It begins to differentiate what aspects of aging are universal or biological as opposed to factors largely shaped by the sociocultural system (Sokolovsky, 1987, 1990). Understanding how aging in contemporary American society differs from that experienced elsewhere, and which factors are socioculturally determined, can also suggest strategies for developing better environments in which to grow old.

This chapter briefly examines the extent to which older people were valued in stable, pre-literate, or primitive societies and in some other nonwestern cultures. Changes in the social roles of older persons, society's expectations of them, and their expectations of society are considered. In addition, contrasting perspectives are reviewed regarding the impact of modernization on the relationship between older persons and the larger society. These influences are examined first historically and then cross-culturally. Within the constraints of this one chapter, we can only glance at a few other cultures. For a more complete view, we urge you to turn to the developing anthropological works on aging (Cowgill, 1986; Fry and Keith, 1986; Keith, 1982, 1985; Sokolovsky, 1987, 1990). While this chapter explores aging cross-culturally and historically, Chapter 17 focuses on the cultural diversity represented by older ethnic minorities within contemporary American society.

## OLD AGE HISTORICALLY

### Old Age in Ancient Cultures

Although our knowledge of the elderly in prehistoric and primitive societies is limited, we do know that people of advanced age were rare, with most dying before the age of 35. Nevertheless, there were always a few people perceived to be old, although they were probably chronologically relatively young, since maturity and death came quickly in the lives of people struggling to survive in harsh environments. Those few elders were treated with respect, in a manner that reflected a sense of sacred obligation. During ceremonial occasions, elders were seated in positions of high honor and served as the clan's memory. The belief that an older person was a mediator between this world and the next gave added prestige to elders by conferring on them the role of witch-doctors or priests (Minois, 1989; Simmons, 1945).

Even though positive attitudes toward the young-old were widespread, nonsupportive or death-hastening behavior was shown toward those who survived beyond an "intact" stage of life. This stage of old-old age was often referred to as the "sleeping period." No longer able to contribute to the common welfare and look after themselves, the elderly were then viewed as useless, "overaged," or "already dead," and were sometimes treated brutally. Those who outlived their usefulness were a heavy burden in societies that existed close to the edge of subsistence, particularly those in harsh climates or with little

agriculture (Glascock, 1990; Glascock and Feinman, 1986; Minois, 1989; Simmons, 1945). In some rural areas of ancient Japan, for example, older people were carried into the mountains and left there to die. It was not unusual for aged Eskimos to walk off into the snow when famine and disease placed great burdens on the tribe. This practice of *geronticide* or *senecide*—the deliberate destruction of aged community members—was viewed as functional and, for many traditional societies, often performed with great reverence or ceremony. In a minority of primitive tribes, the frail were killed outright; in most, they were abandoned, neglected, or encouraged to commit suicide, and the burial place was converted into some sort of shrine. Ritual sacrifice was used to kill the oldest members perceived to be a burden among the Ojibwa Indians of Lake Winnipeg and the Siriono of the Bolivian rain forest. Consistent with the coexistence of positive attitudes toward the old along with their nonsupportive treatment, geronticide in many societies often occurred under the older person's direction and by a close relative, usually a son. Examples of geronticide, abandonment, and forsaking support to the oldest-old have been reported in persons in remote cultures even in the twentieth century (Glascock, 1990).

### Old Age in Greek and Roman Cultures

In Greek and Roman classical cultures, 80 percent of the population perished before reaching the stage of life that we now consider to be middle-age. Nevertheless, our chronological conception of age, with *old* defined as age 60 and over, began during this period. Age implied power in the ancient cities, which were ruled by councils of elders who derived their authority from their years. Within the family, the eldest male's authority was nearly absolute, and the young were dependent on the old by custom and by law. However, only the elite members of society, not the peasants, benefited from the respect accorded age by the community.

Some idea of the changing status of older people in ancient Greek society can be obtained by analyzing how old and young were depicted in Greek tragedy. In her book, *Time in Greek Tragedy,* de Romilly (1968) points to an evolution of views about age from Aeschylus in the late sixth and early fifth centuries B.C., to Euripides in the mid- to late fifth century B.C. For Aeschylus, age brought with it wisdom, especially about justice and prudence. Although he refers to the destructive influences of age, particularly loss of physical strength, Aeschylus insists that such physical decline has no impact on the older person's mind or spirit. In contrast, Sophocles' tragedies, which were written during the middle of the fifth century, depict old age as distasteful, a time of decline in physical and mental functioning. For Sophocles, youth is the only period of life of true happiness. Later, in Euripides' plays, older people are both wise and weak. Older characters of Euripides long for eternal youth; old age is described as miserable, bitter, and painful. The shift from Aeschylus' admiration of old age to the exaltation of youth and denigration of old age by Sophocles and Euripides may be a reflection of the growth of democracy in fifth-century Greece (and, consequently, a growing belief in social equality) as well as the heroism of young men in the wars of that era.

This coincided with the Classical period, when beauty, youth, and strength were idealized in the visual arts. Greek mythology also depicts the old as tyrannical and wicked, the ultimate enemy in many myths. The gift of immortality was cherished only if it meant rejuvenation or eternal youth. Greek and later Roman mythology contrasted the eternal youthfulness of the gods with the gradual deterioration of mortals. In the myth of Eos and Tithonus, Eos (or Aurora), the goddess of dawn, fell in love with Tithonus, a mortal. She prevailed on Zeus to grant him immortality but forgot to ask that he remain eternally young like her. She left him when he became very old and frail, and eventually turned him into a grasshopper. Presumably this was a better fate for the ancient Greeks and Romans than remaining a feeble old man.

During the Hellenistic era (third and second centuries B.C.), the old regained political power; their increased prestige was reflected by more flattering depictions of elders in art and mythology. The Roman world continued this tradition of greater authority vested in old men; older women were far less powerful than men in both Roman and Greek society (Minois, 1989).

## Old Age in Medieval Europe

Little is known about the role of older people during the medieval period, except that life expectancy was even shorter than in the Greek and Roman eras. To a large extent, increasing urbanization and related problems of sanitation and disease were responsible for the high death rates before people reached old age. Nevertheless, older people were more likely than the young to survive the Black Plague and other epidemics, creating a disproportionate population of elders in many communities and arousing bitterness among the young. This also resulted in more extended family living arrangements (Minois, 1989).

The nobility lived longer than the common people during the Middle Ages, mostly because of better standards of living. Furthermore, the general populace was more likely to die of war or the numerous diseases that plagued this era. The nobility had the freedom to flee such conditions. For the small proportion of poor who did manage to survive, old age was a cruel period of life.

To the extent that the prevailing attitudes toward older persons in that historical period can be inferred from art, one would have to conclude that old age was depicted as ugly, weak, and deceptive. During the Renaissance, artists and poets reestablished links with classical Greece, contrasting the beauty of youth with the unattractiveness and weakness they, like the ancient Greeks, saw in old age. Even later, Shakespeare's description of the seven ages of man in his play *As You Like It* also portrays such a contrast. Youth evolves from an impulsive boy to soldier, to the fifth age "full of wise saws and modern instances." The sixth age is depicted as weak, with "his big manly voice, turning again toward childish treble." The seventh and final stage "is second childishness and mere oblivion, sans teeth, sans eyes, sans taste, sans everything." Thus, Shakespeare's view of old age is that of decline and uselessness; this may reflect the attitude of sixteenth-century Europe that the old were a burden to a community struggling with food shortages and high death rates among its infants and young soldiers. Perhaps most striking is Shakespeare's attribution of wisdom and perspective to middle age, in contrast to the beliefs of pre-Classical and Hellenistic Greek playwrights and philosophers that old age is the time of greatest wisdom.

## Old Age in Colonial America

In seventeenth- and eighteenth-century America, old age was treated with deference and respect, in part because it was so rare. This attitude has been described as one of veneration, an emotion closer to awe than affection and a form of worship deeply embedded in the Judeo-Christian ethic of early America (Fischer, 1978). The Puritans, for example, viewed old age as a sign of God's favor and assumed that youth would inevitably defer to age. Old men occupied the highest public offices, as well as positions of authority within the family, until they died; fathers waited until their sixties before giving their land to their eldest son. Church seats were given to the old. The primary basis of the power enjoyed by the elderly in colonial times was their control of property, especially productive property in farmland. In this agricultural society, such control amounted to the ability to dominate all key institutions—the family, the church, the economy, and the polity (Achenbaum, 1985).

Even though the old were exalted by law and custom in colonial times, they received little affection or love from younger people; in fact, most were kept at an emotional distance. In re-

serving power and prestige for the elderly, society in many ways created this separation between young and old. Elders frequently complained that they had lived to become strangers in their communities. Old age was not a time of serenity, but rather anxiety about adequately fulfilling social obligations and keeping faith with God (Fischer, 1978; Stearns, 1982).

This pattern persisted until about 1770, when attitudes toward the elderly began to change and the relative status of youth was elevated. There are a number of indications of this change: church-seating arrangements that had favored the old were abolished; the first mandatory retirement laws for legislators were passed; and the eldest son no longer automatically inherited the family property. New fashions were introduced that flattered youth rather than the white wigs and broadwaisted coats that favored older men. Words that negatively portrayed elders, such as *codger* and *fuddy-duddy*, appeared in dictionaries in the nineteenth century. In family portraits, all members of the family were placed on the

Older people in traditional societies symbolize power and wisdom.

same horizontal plane rather than positioning the oldest male members to stand over women and children (Fischer, 1978).

A major demographic change occurred in approximately 1810, when the median age began to rise, creating a greater percentage of the population older than the typical "old" age of 40 or 50. This was due primarily to a declining birth rate, not a falling death rate. After 1810, the median age advanced at a constant annual rate, approximately 0.4 percent per year, until about 1950 (Fischer, 1978); this has been attributed to reductions in the impact of diseases. A dramatic change was that parents began to live beyond the period of their children's dependency, for the first time historically experiencing health at the time their children left the home.

## The Effects of Modernization

As the foregoing historical examples suggest, definitions of old age, as well as the authority that older people exercised, largely rested on the material and political resources controlled by the elderly. Examples of these resources are traditional skills and knowledge, security from property rights, civil and political power, food from communal sharing, information control, and general welfare from routine services performed by older people such as child care. Within the constraints set by the social environment and its ideology, the elderly's social rank was generally determined by the balance between the cost of maintaining them and the societal contributions they were perceived to make. As age became a less important criterion for determining access to and control of valued resources, the elderly's status and authority tended to decline.

A number of explanations have been advanced for the declining status of the old in our society. One major explanation is modernization theory. One of the first comparative analyses that raised this issue was reported by Leo Simmons in *The Role of the Aged in Primitive Society* (1945). He noted that the status of older persons, as reflected in their resources and the honor bestowed upon them, varied inversely with the degree of technology, social and economic diversity, and occupational specialization (or modernization) in a given society. As society becomes more modernized, according to this theory, older people lose political and social power, influence, and leadership. These social changes also may lead to disengagement of aging persons from community life. In addition, younger and older generations become increasingly separated socially, morally, and intellectually. Youth is glorified as the embodiment of progress and achievement, as well as the means to attain such progress.

Modernization theory has been advanced primarily by Cowgill and Holmes (1972; Cowgill, 1974a; 1974b, 1986). Modernization is defined by Cowgill (1974a) as:

> The transformation of a total society from a relatively rural way of life based on animate power, limited technology, relatively undifferentiated institutions, parochial and traditional outlook and values, toward a predominantly urban way of life, based on inanimate sources of power, highly differentiated institutions, matched by segmented individual roles, and a cosmopolitan outlook which emphasizes efficiency and progress (p. 127).

The characteristics of modernization that contribute to lower status for the elderly were identified by Cowgill and Holmes as (1) health technology, (2) scientific technology as applied in economic production and distribution, (3) urbanization, and (4) literacy and mass education.

According to Cowgill and Holmes, the application of *health technology* has reduced infant mortality and maternal deaths, and prolonged adult life, thereby increasing the number of older persons in the population. With more older people in the labor market, competition for jobs between generations has intensified, and retirement has developed as a means of forcing older people out of the labor market.

*Scientific technology* creates new jobs primarily for the young, with the elderly more likely to remain in traditional occupations that become obsolete. The rapid development of industries that rely on high technology in the twentieth century and the gap between generations in using computers illustrate this phenomenon. Unable to perform the socially valued role of contributors to the workforce, many retirees feel marginal and alienated.

In the early stages of modernization, when the society is relatively rural, young people are attracted to urban areas, whereas older parents and grandparents remain on the family farm or in rural communities. The resulting residential segregation of the generations has a dramatic impact on family interactions. The geographical and occupational mobility of the young, in turn, leads to increased social distance between generations and to a reduced status of the aged.

Finally, modernization is characterized by efforts to promote *literacy and education,* which tend to be targeted toward the young. As younger generations acquire more education than their parents, they begin to occupy higher status positions. Intellectual and moral differences between the generations increase, with the elderly experiencing reduced leadership roles and influence (Cowgill, 1974a, 1974b).

This theory has received some empirical support. Using a series of socioeconomic measures, Palmore and Whittington (1971) found that the status of the older population, compared to the younger, had generally declined in the United States from 1940 to 1969. Watson and Maxwell (1977), in their study of the ethnographic records of 26 different societies in Europe and Asia, reported that as the use of technology increased, the elderly's control of important information and the esteem and deference accorded them declined. In a cross-cultural study of 31 countries at different stages of modernization, Palmore and Manton (1974) found that the elderly's relative employment status was lower in the more modernized societies, due primarily to the increased education of the young and a shift away from agriculture as an economic base.

Occupation and education, however, had a reversed J-shaped relationship to modernization; that is, in the early phases of rapid social change (illustrated by nations such as Turkey and the Philippines), the occupational and educational status of the elderly declined, but then later improved (exemplified by New Zealand, Canada, and the United States). This suggests that as societies move beyond an initial state of rapid modernization, status differences between generations decrease and the relative status of older people may rise, particularly when reinforced by social policies such as Social Security. Similarly, Pampel (1981) documented improvement in the relative financial status of the elderly in the United States since World War II. Pampel maintains that societies in advanced stages of modernization become more aware of the older population's devalued status. Thus, through public education, social policies, and the media, they attempt to create more opportunities and positive images of the elderly. This has already begun in the United States, with advertising and television programs increasingly portraying older persons as vital, active, and involved, with many local governments encouraging employers to hire older workers, and with colleges opening their doors to older students.

## Alternatives to Modernization Theory

More recent analyses of older people's status in nonindustrial societies have found that conditions for high status did not always apply. For example, differences often existed between the prestige of the old and the way they were actually treated; over 80 percent of the 60 nonindustrial societies in Glascock and Feinman's (1986; 1990) sample had some form of nonsupportive treatment (ranging from insults to killing) for the old, even though older members were also respected. Most societies have some norms of favorable treatment toward the elderly, but considerable variability in practice. For example, filial piety in China and Taiwan was not always manifest, but affected by family resources and number of living children (Ikels, 1980). The coexistence of high status and bad treatment in many traditional societies can be partially explained in terms of differential behavior toward the young-old versus old-old, noted in our earlier discussion of traditional societies that abandoned or murdered their frail elders (Keith, 1985).

Class and sex differences also come into play. For instance, the norms of filial piety were more often practiced by the well-to-do in traditional rural China. Despite the Confucian reverence for age, older people in lower class families had fewer resources to give them status (Cherry and Magnuson-Martinson, 1981). The importance of women's household responsibilities throughout life may explain their relatively higher status in old age than men's (Cool and McCabe, 1987).

Turning to contemporary China, there has been a transformation of life for the elderly in that country. The "political economy" has had an impact on elders' status as government policies have been altered. For example, women have benefited from changes such as not having to submit to arranged marriages or having their feet bound. Their work opportunities have expanded by opening up more jobs to women. National social insurance has also been developed to benefit the elderly. But not all changes have had positive effects. Rules limiting family size and the breaking up of communes have had negative consequences for the childless elderly in particular; these effects are expected to continue as future cohorts of elderly contend with fewer children to care for them in times of need (Olson, 1990).

## Ideal of Equality Versus Status of Age in America

Fischer (1978) has formulated reasons other than modernization for explaining changes between generations in American society. He argues that these changes cannot be attributed to modernization, because the decline in older people's status occurred before industrialization and urbanization. He also contends that the increase in numbers of older people does not fully explain the shifts in attitudes toward the old. Instead, he suggests that the emphasis on youthfulness that characterizes our society can be partially attributed to our cultural values of liberty and equality. Both of these values run counter to a hierarchy of authority based on age.

According to Fischer, the elevated status of older persons in earlier historical periods gradually became supplanted in the late eighteenth and early nineteenth centuries by an emerging ideal of age equality. The fundamental change was caused by the social and intellectual forces unleashed by revolutions in America and France. The spirit of equality was dramatically expressed in public fetes borrowed from the French Revolution, where a symbolic harmony of youth and age was celebrated in elaborate rituals of young and old exchanging food (Fischer, 1978).

However, although our society's ideology was egalitarian, economic inequalities actually grew in the nineteenth century. For example, economic status became the basis of seating arrangements in public meetings. Individualistic pursuits of wealth created countervailing forces to a sense of community that had previously been founded on the power of elders (Fischer, 1978). Thus, the age equality that had initially replaced veneration of elders was later supplanted by a celebration of youthfulness and a derogation of age. Inequalities based on age reemerged, but this time to the advantage of youth. Growing contempt toward the elderly in the mid-1800s is vividly illustrated by Thoreau's (1856) conclusion, "Age is no better, hardly so well qualified for an instructor of youth, for it has not profited as much as it has lost." Heroes and legends centered on younger men, such as Daniel Boone. Social trends in the early twentieth century, such as the development of retirement policies, mass education, and residential segregation of generations, furthered perceptions of the elderly as useless, with the cult of youth reaching its peak in the 1960s. One irony was that as the economic and social conditions of many elderly declined in modern America, their ties of family affection, especially between grandparents and grandchildren, often grew stronger (Fischer, 1978).

## Other Perspectives on Historical Change

Historians and gerontologists have questioned whether a "revolution" in age relations occurred between 1770 and 1830 (Achenbaum, 1985). Achenbaum (1978), for example, has taken a position somewhere between Fischer's view and modernization theory regarding the change in status of the elderly in the United States. He has identified social trends similar to those documented by Fischer, stating that prior to the middle of the nineteenth century, the elderly were venerated because of their experiences and were actively involved in socially useful roles. A decline in the status of the elderly, Achenbaum asserts, occurred during the post-Civil War era. The growing emphasis on efficiency and impersonality in bureaucracies, along with increased misperceptions about senility, furthered a perception of old age as obsolescence. Both Fischer and Achenbaum suggest that it is not possible to establish a firm relationship between modernization and the elderly's status; rather, they maintain that Americans have always been ambivalent about old age. Shifting beliefs and values are viewed as more salient in accounting for loss in status than changes in the economic and political structures that occurred with modernization.

These contrasting perspectives of social gerontologists and anthropologists suggest that there is not a simple "before and after" relationship in the meaning and significance of old age between pre-industrial and modern societies (Achenbaum, 1985). People in pre-industrial societies who, by reason of social class, lacked property and power undoubtedly suffered from loss of status, regardless of their age. For such persons, modernization brought less improvement in status than for the elderly who were better educated and of higher socioeconomic background. Such inequities continue to be problematic, particularly among ethnic minorities within our society. Achenbaum and Stearns (1978) have emphasized

that modernization is not a linear process, but proceeds at different rates and through varied stages, each of which may have a different impact on older people's status.

In addition, cross-cultural evidence shows that cultural values can mitigate many of the negative effects of modernization on older people. This is illustrated in modern, industrialized, and urban Japanese society where Confucian values of filial piety and ancestor worship have helped to maintain the relatively high status of older persons and their integration in family life, as well as their leadership in national politics. Traditional values of exchange and lifelong indebtedness to one's parents are a major reason for continued three-generational households in Japan (Akiyama, Antonucci and Campbell, 1990; Palmore and Maeda, 1985).

Political ideology may also be an intervening variable, as illustrated by the effect of Communist party policies in Maoist China which at first villified the elderly but eventually sought them to work with the young to promote the Cultural Revolution. Despite their emphasis on collectivization, the Communist leaders did not provide a comprehensive welfare program for older people, especially those in rural China. Families were expected to provide care for their elders, except for

Many older women in China continue in self-employed positions.

those who were childless in their old age. However, as modernization and especially urbanization continued in China after the 1950s, societal views of and governmental benefits to older persons improved (Olson, 1990).

In sum, the effects of modernization historically do not appear to be uniform nor unidirectional. As shown in the next section, many contemporary cultures are still struggling to define satisfying roles for their rapidly increasing populations of older people. Changing values and declining resources result in conflicting attitudes toward the elderly in many transitional societies.

## A CROSS-CULTURAL VIEW OF OLD AGE IN CONTEMPORARY SOCIETIES

As we have discussed, every society defines people as old on some basis, whether chronological, functional, or generational, and assigns that group a particular set of rights, privileges, and duties that differ from those of its younger members. For example, older persons in our society today qualify for Social Security and Medicare on the basis of their age. In some religious groups, only the oldest members are permitted to perform the most sacred rituals. Societies generally distinguish two classes of elders: (1) those who are no longer fully productive economically, but are physically and mentally able to attend to their daily needs; and (2) those who are totally dependent, who require custodial care, and who are regarded as social burdens and thus may be negatively treated. A third group of older people exists in many societies: those who continue to participate actively in the economy of the social system, through farming or self-employment, through care of grandchildren, or through household maintenance while younger adults work outside the home.

Older people who can no longer work but who control resources essential to fulfill the needs of younger group members generally offset the societal costs incurred in maintaining them.

In some social systems, political, judicial, or ritual power and privileges are vested in older people as a group, and this serves to mediate social costs. For instance, in societies such as those of East Africa, politically powerful positions are automatically assigned to men who reach a certain age (Keith, 1990). In other societies, the old do not inherently have privileges, but gain power as individuals, often through diplomatic skills and contacts with powerful others. The following examples from other cultures illustrate the balance between the costs and contributions made by the elderly.

In the subsistence society of the Chipewyan Indians of Canada, older men are accorded low status, and old age is despised and feared; this is primarily because older men, who are no longer able to hunt, are perceived as unproductive, costing society more than they contribute. Dependent on the contributions of each tribal member, the Chipewyans have sometimes been forced to abandon their old when faced with a choice between the death of older men and that of the entire tribe. Unlike the older men, Chipewyan older women are still able to perform customary domestic and gathering tasks that do not require physical vigor. As a result, aging does not produce as substantial a decline in the status of older women as in that of older men (Sharp, 1981).

Unlike Chipewyan men, older men among the Asmats of coastal New Guinea are able to assert political leadership in kinship and local groups even after their hunting skills have deteriorated. The primary reason for this difference is that the Asmat economy is less precarious, so that older men can still acquire resources to protect their position in old age (Amoss and Harrell, 1981).

In other cultures, respect toward intact elders may be promoted, but a subtle acceptance of benign neglect may result in the demise of elderly persons who are physically and/or cognitively impaired. An ethnographic analysis of Niue, an independent Polynesian island, revealed significant discrepancies between the status of older people who were in good health and had important social and political functions, and those who were too frail to care for themselves. Although medical services are free on Niue, families and neighbors did not summon visiting doctors and public health nurses even for infected sores, painful joints, and other treatable conditions in these frail elders. The basic needs of cognitively impaired elders were even more frequently ignored. This may stem from values of reciprocity. Like other societies where reciprocity is crucial for intergenerational exchanges, the frail elders of Niue can no longer contribute to the group's well-being (Barker, 1990). Therefore, such neglect may be seen as a way of merely hastening the inevitable death of these frail elders (Glascock, 1990).

## Importance of Social Position and the Control of Property

The control of property is a means of achieving power in most societies. Both in past and present times, the elderly have used their rights over property to guarantee their security by compelling others to support them or to provide them with goods and services. For example, among the Etal Islanders in Micronesia, the old try to keep enough property to ensure continued care by younger members who hope to inherit it (Nason, 1981). In the Gwembe Tonga tribe in Zambia, males were formerly able to secure their position by accumulating land and livestock. As their lineage land became covered by water, however, forced relocation cost many older people their exclusive control of property, and the old became dependent on sons and nephews, who acquired better land at the time of flooding (Colson and Scudder, 1981).

In other societies, the leadership of males derives from their positions within the family. The traditional Chinese extended household is an example. The position of the aging father in the Chinese family depends almost entirely on the political and economic power he wields (Harrell, 1981). Elders in wealthy Chinese households and those with substantial pensions to contribute to family expenses enjoy higher status within the family and are better able to control the lives of their adult children than those in poor households (Olson, 1990). Both China and India illustrate substantial class differences in the elders' power, as well as the persistence of the extended family structure that confers status on older members, even in the face of modernization. As economic resources decline and class differences disappear in these cultures with increasing modernization, the traditions of filial piety may become undermined. For example, the growing pressures of limited housing and low income in China appear to be having a negative effect on younger generations' attitudes toward old people. In such instances, increased provision of public housing, health care, an old age pension plan, and policies that support family care of elders may serve to reduce tensions between generations (Chow, 1983).

Older persons from traditional cultures who immigrate to Western countries face even more problems adjusting to the loss of power. In the past 20 years, waves of Indochinese refugees have come to the United States from countries experiencing political strife and unrest. Elders who arrived with younger family members have had more difficulties in becoming part of the culture. Property and other resources in their native lands which afforded them importance and power have been stripped from them. Being in the United States has brought them a different life than the one they might have expected for their later years. These elderly refugees do not have the ability to provide material goods, land, or other financial support which has traditionally given them status (Yee, 1992). Traditional power has been eroded as families have started new lives in this culture. Indeed, financial self-sufficiency has been found to be the major determinant of adjustment to life in the United States among older Indochinese refugees, regardless of education, gender, and English proficiency (Tran, 1992). Recent refugees from Eastern Europe are also struggling with the adjustment to the loss of property and status in their host country.

## Knowledge as a Source of Power

Control over knowledge, especially ritual and religious knowledge, is another source of power. The aged Shaman is an example, revered in many societies for knowledge or wisdom. The importance of the elderly in maintaining cultural values is illustrated in India, where traditional Hindu law prescribes a four-stage life cycle for high-caste men: student, householder, ascetic, and mendicant. In the last two stages, older religious men are expected to renounce worldly attachments to seek enlightenment in isolated retreats. This practice ensures that the pursuit of the highest form of knowledge is limited to older men of higher castes (Sokolovsky, 1987). As another example, the !Kung Bushmen value the storytelling ability of people age 45 and over, because the stories are considered to contain the accumulated knowledge of the people. Information and stories are the elderly's resource which can be

Native American elders are frequently respected members of their community.

exchanged for food and security (Biesele and Howell, 1981).

Knowledge as the basis of the elders' power has been challenged in many traditional societies by Western technological and scientific expertise (Cowgill, 1974a). For example, the aged farmer who passes on to his children traditional methods of growing crops may be dismayed to find that they ignore this advice and rely on new agricultural methods and products. Examples in which the relevance of traditional knowledge declines with modernization abound in many fields: farming, fishing, construction, housekeeping, even childrearing. They include the Tong elderly of Zambia who lost status due to the flooding of their old habitat and the outmoding of their specialized knowledge (Colson and Scudder, 1981), the elderly in Taiwan who are less knowledgeable in new commercial and industrial contexts (Harrell, 1981), and many native North American groups faced with changing patterns of production and consumption. Among Western Irish peasants, the once dignified movement of the older couple to the sacred "west room" of the house, which signified high esteem, has been replaced by "warehousing" of the elderly in institutions (Scheper-Hughes, 1987).

Women in Ganga in Papua, New Guinea have assumed a larger role in local coffee production. However, these changes in their work lives have affected their control over the rituals of education and initiation for younger girls, traditionally an important part of their knowledge base and power. What was once provided by a group of older women is now acted out by a young girl's closest relatives. Consequently the power base of older women in shaping the lives of young women has eroded (Dickerson-Putman, 1994).

Among some cultural groups, however, such as the Coast Salish Indians of Washington, a revival of interest and pride in native identity and religion has occurred, thus raising the esteem of elders who possess ritual knowledge (e.g., they are the only ones who know the words and dance steps) (Amoss and Harrell, 1981; Keith, 1990).

Knowledge of the group's culture, particularly traditional arts and handicrafts, and of native songs and epics has enhanced the social status of older persons in these societies; furthermore, the traditions of reverence for old age and wisdom remain strong, overriding the impact of modernization on older people's roles. The timing of such a revival is critical, however. A similar revival among Plains Indians did not have comparable positive consequences for the tribe's older members who were no longer expert in traditional ways (Keith, 1990).

The growing desire for ethnic or tribal identity among many Native Americans, which has led to a conscious restoration of old forms, illustrates that modernization does not automatically erode the status of the elders. Similarly, the search for one's heritage or roots has led to increased contacts between younger generations seeking this information from older persons who often are a great repository of family histories.

Cultural and historical factors can also mitigate the presumed negative consequences of modernization for the elderly. For example, in Samoa, despite the influx of U.S. aid, industries, and educational programs designed to promote modernization, the cultural system has been flexible enough to maintain the elderly as a viable part of society. This has largely been due to the persistence of the traditional *matai* family system, which involves the elders in leadership roles within large bilateral kinship groups, and a village council that accords the elders respect and power (Holmes and Rhoads, 1987). The traditional family system has combined with Samoan values of reciprocity in social relationships and an acceptance of dependency in old age to retain high status among Samoan elders (Rhoads, 1984).

Indeed, modernization has not resulted in the disintegration of extended families in most non-Western societies, including the rapidly developing Asian and Third World countries. Extended families in rural Thailand and Zimbabwe have adapted to the need for adult chil-

Older grandparents in rural China serve a vital role as full-time caregivers for their grandchildren.

dren to migrate to the cities for jobs by creating "skip-generation households," where grandparents remain in their rural homes, caring for grandchildren while their adult children work in urban settings. This reciprocal dependency has also proved useful for many Asians and Eastern European refugee families in the United States where grandparents have immigrated with their adult children in order to provide regular child care to grandchildren in the extended family (Hashimoto, 1991, 1993; Martin, 1989).

The way that older people react to change can serve to maintain or improve their position. Among the Sherpa in Tibet, for example, as younger sons move away from the community, and are not available to share households and care for the old, the old resist the traditional division of property and tend to keep the younger sons' shares for themselves. The elderly Sherpa are also becoming proponents of birth control; since they cannot count on sons to take care of them as they wish, they prefer to share their property among fewer children, keeping more for themselves (Keith, 1990).

## Effects of Culture and Modernization Are Still Changing

In other situations, the buffering effects of culture on modernization are less distinct. There are contrasting views, for example, on the issue of modernization and aging in contemporary Japan. As noted earlier, Palmore (1975b; 1985) has described the high status and prestige of the elderly in Japan. Values adopted from Confucianism have been viewed as linking the aged to a family system that emphasizes filial devotion, in which the dependence of elders in this "second privileged period" is accepted (Kiefer, 1990; Palmore and Maeda, 1985). More recently, demographic and economic changes appear to have altered traditional conceptions of old age and reduced the positive influences of cultural values. For instance, the modernization of Japanese society has resulted in increased economic demands on the nuclear family; accordingly, the old-old, becoming more dependent on family who have fewer resources to care for them, have sometimes prayed for a quick death in Buddhist temples (Plath, 1983). The unprecedented higher percentage of older people has increased the societal costs of maintaining elders and has created dilemmas for younger family members responsible for their support.

The majority of middle-aged persons still believe that care of older parents is the children's responsibility. Indeed, negligence toward one's parents is still a source of great public shame in Japan. Society also assumes responsibility for the care of Japan's elders; all those over 70 receive free basic medical services.

For these reasons, the proportion of older parents living in multigenerational households is higher than in any other industrialized nation (approximately 2/3, according to Hashimoto, 1993). Nevertheless, the number of nursing homes and long-stay hospitals in Japan has grown rapidly. These trends suggest that tradi-

tional customs of caring for aging parents in adult children's homes are slowly changing in Japan, while the percentage of parents living with children has declined, due to urbanization, industrialization, the growing numbers of employed women, and the declining number of children since 1950 (Tobin, 1987). As more elderly live longer, they may increasingly require goods and services at the perceived expense of younger members of society.

The negative consequences of social change are not inevitable, however, and there are conditions under which the old may benefit even from rapid social change. For example, with modernization, men are more vulnerable to changes in the public domain, but women can more easily retain favorable positions in the domestic arena (Keith, 1990).

## SUMMARY AND IMPLICATIONS

These brief examples from diverse cultures around the world illustrate how each society responds to its aging members within the constraints set by both the natural environment and the larger human environment of social and technological change. A basic principle governing the status of the elderly appears to be the effort to achieve a balance between older people's contributions to the society and the costs of supporting them. As will be discussed in detail in Chapter 12, however, the family plays an important role in supporting the old in most societies. Historical and cross-cultural evidence also suggests that maximum social participation of the elderly results in greater acceptance and respect of elders by the young in most cultures.

The extent to which the elderly are engaged in society appears to vary with the nature of their power resources, such as their material possessions, knowledge, and social authority (Dowd, 1980). In most of their exchanges, older people seek to maintain reciprocity and to be active, independent agents in the management of their own lives. That is, they prefer to give money, time, or other resources in exchange for services or materials. This theoretical perspective, which will be described in more detail as social exchange theory in Chapter 4, suggests that modern society should seek ways of increasing the elderly's exchange resources so that they are valued by society. For example, maximizing the social value of the old in our society might include retraining and educational programs and part-time employment. (See Chapter 14.)

Control of resources as a basis for social interactions between members of a society is important throughout the life cycle. However, it becomes even more crucial in old age, because retirement generally results in a decline in one's level of control over material and social resources. As their physical strength diminishes and their social world correspondingly shrinks, many older people face the challenge of altering their environments and using their capacities in ways that will help them to maintain reciprocal exchanges and to protect their competence and independence. This is also a problem for older refugees who may still have full physical and cognitive functions, but have lost material resources in their homeland that would have given them power and prestige.

These attempts to maintain control over one's environment in the face of changing personal capacities and resources, consistent with the person-environment model presented in the Introduction, will be discussed in detail in subsequent chapters on biological, psychological, and social changes with aging. The next chapter reviews social theories of aging that offer some explanation of the various ways in which people interact with the larger society as well as their immediate social environments as they age.

# REFERENCES

Achenbaum, W. A. *Old age in the new land: The American experience since 1790*. Baltimore: The Johns Hopkins Press, 1978.

Achenbaum, W. A. Societal perceptions of aging and the aged. In E. Shanas and R. Binstock, *Handbook of aging and the social sciences* (2d ed.). New York: Van Nostrand, 1985, 129–148.

Achenbaum, W. A., and Stearns, P. Old age and modernization. *The Gerontologist, 1978, 18*, 307–312.

Akiyama, H., Antonucci, T. C., and Campbell, R. Exchange and reciprocity among two generations of Japanese and American women. In J. Sokolovsky (Ed.), *The Cultural Context of Aging*. New York: Bergin and Garvey, 1990.

Amoss, P., and Harrell, S. (Eds.), *Other ways of growing old*. Stanford, Calif: Stanford University Press, 1981.

Barker, J. C. Between humans and ghosts: The decrepit elderly in a Polynesian society. In J. Sokolovsky (Ed.), *The Cultural Context of Aging*. New York: Bergin and Garvey, 1990.

Biesele, M., and Howell, N. The old people give you life: Aging among !Kung hunters-gatherers. In P. Amoss and S. Harrell (Eds.), *Other ways of growing old*. Stanford, Calif.: Stanford University Press, 1981, 77–99.

Brown, J. K., and Kerns, V. (Eds.) *In her prime: A new view of middle-aged women*. South Hadley, Mass.: Bergin and Garvey, 1985, 21–64.

Cherry, R., and Magnuson-Martinson, S. Modernization and the status of the aged in China: Decline or equalization? *Sociological Quarterly, 1981, 22*, 253–261.

Chow, N. The Chinese family and support of the elderly in Hong Kong. *The Gerontologist, 1983, 23*, 584–588.

Colson, E., and Scudder, T. Old age in Gwemba District, Zambia. In P. Amoss and S. Harrell (Eds.), *Other ways of growing old*. Stanford, Calif.: Stanford University Press, 1981, 125–154.

Cool, L., and McCabe, J. The "scheming hag" and the "dear old thing." The anthropology of aging women. In J. Sokolovsky (Ed.), *Growing old in different cultures*. Acton, Mass.: Copley, 1987.

Cowgill, D. Aging and modernization: A revision of the theory. In J. F. Gubrium (Ed.)., *Late life communities and environmental policy*. Springfield, Ill.: Charles C. Thomas, 1974a, 123–146.

Cowgill, D. The aging of populations and societies. In F. Eisele (Ed.), *Political consequences of aging. The annals of the American Academy of Political and Social Science*, 1974b, 415, 1–18.

Cowgill, D. *Aging around the world*. Belmont, Calif.: Wadsworth, 1986.

Cowgill, D., and Holmes, L. *Aging and modernization.* New York: Appleton-Century-Crofts, 1972.

de Romilly, J. *Time in Greek tragedy.* Ithaca, N.Y.: Cornell University Press, 1968.

Dickerson-Putnam, Jeanette. Old Women at the Top: An exploration of age stratification among Bena Bena women. *The Journal of Cross-Cultural Gerontology,* 1994, *9,* 193–205.

Dowd, J. J. Social exchange: Class and old people. In J. Dowd (Ed.), *Stratification among the aged.* Monterey, Calif.: Brooks Cole, 1980.

Fischer, D. H. *Growing old in America.* Oxford: Oxford University Press, 1978.

Fry, C., and Keith, J. (Eds.). *New methods for old age research: Strategies for studying diversity.* South Hadley, Mass.: Bergin and Garvey, 1986.

Glascock, A. P. By any other name, it is still killing: A comparison of the treatment of the elderly in America and other societies. In J. Sokolovsky (Ed.), *The Cultural Context of Aging.* New York: Bergin and Garvey, 1990.

Glascock, A. P., and Feinman, S. Treatment of the aged in non-industrial societies. In C. Fry and J. Keith (Eds.), *New methods for old age research: Strategies for studying diversity.* South Hadley, Mass.: Bergin and Garvey, 1986.

Harrell, S. Growing old in rural Taiwan. In P. Amoss and S. Harrell (Eds.), *Other ways of growing old.* Stanford, Calif: Stanford University Press, 1981, 193–210.

Hashimoto, A. Family relations in later life: A cross-cultural perspective. *Generations,* 1993, *17,* 24–26.

Hashimoto, A. Living arrangements of the aged in seven developing countries. *Journal of Cross-Cultural Gerontology,* 1991, *6,* 359–381.

Hendricks, J., and Hendricks, C. D. *Aging in mass society: Myths and realities.* Cambridge, Mass.: Winthrop, 1981.

Holmes, L., and Rhoads, E. Aging and change in Samoa. In J. Sokolovsky (Ed.), *Growing old in different societies.* Acton, Mass.: Copley, 1987.

Keith, J. *Old people as people: Social and cultural influences on aging and old age.* Boston: Little, Brown, 1982.

Keith, J. Age in anthropological research. In R. H. Binstock and E. Shanas (Eds.), *Handbook of aging and the social sciences* (2d ed.). New York: Van Nostrand, 1985, 231–263.

Keith, J. Age in social and cultural context: Anthropological perspectives. In R. Binstock and L. George (Eds.), *Handbook of aging and the social sciences* (3d ed.). New York: Academic Press, 1990, 91–111.

Kiefer, C. The elderly in modern Japan: Elite, victims, or plural players. In J. Sokolovsky (Ed.), *The Cultural Context of Aging.* New York: Bergin and Garvey, 1990.

Maeda, D. Family care in Japan. *The Gerontologist,* 1983, *23,* 579–583.

Martin, L. Living arrangements of the elderly in Fiji, Korea, Malaysia and the Philippines. *Demography,* 1989, *4,* 627–633.

Maxwell, R., and Silverman, P. Information and esteem. *Aging and Human Development,* 1970, *1,* 361–392.

Minois, G. *History of old age.* Cambridge, England: Polity Press, 1989.

Nason, J. D. Respected elder or old person: Aging in a Micronesian community. In P. Amoss and S. Harrell (Eds.), *Other ways of growing old.* Stanford, Calif: Stanford University Press, 1981, 155–175.

Olson, P. The elderly in the People's Republic of China. In J. Sokolovsky (Ed.), *The Cultural Context of Aging.* New York: Bergin and Garvey, 1990.

Palmore, E. *The honorable elders.* Durham, N.C.: Duke University Press, 1975a.

Palmore, E. The status and integration of the aged in Japanese society. *Journal of Gerontology,* 1975b, *30,* 199–208.

Palmore, E., and Maeda, D. *The honorable elders revisited.* Durham, N.C.: Duke University Press, 1985.

Palmore, E., and Manton, K. Modernization and the status of the aged: International comparisons. *Journal of Gerontology,* 1974, *29,* 205–210.

Palmore, E., and Whittington, F. Trends in the relative status of the aged. *Social forces,* 1971, *50,* 84–91.

Pampel, F. *Social change and the aged: Recent trends in the United States.* Lexington, Mass.: Lexington Books, 1981.

Plath, D. Ecstasy years—Old age in Japan. In J. Sokolovsky (Ed.), *Growing old in different societies.* Belmont, Calif.: Wadsworth, 1983, 147–154.

Rhoads, E. Reevaluation of the aging and modernization theory: The Samoan evidence. *The Gerontologist,* 1984, *24,* 243–250.

Scheper-Hughes, N. Deposed kings: The demise of the rural Irish gerontocracy. In J. Sokolovsky (Ed.), *Growing old in different societies.* Acton, Mass.: Copley, 1987.

Sharp, H. Old age among the Chipewyan. In P. Amoss and S. Harrell (Eds.), *Other ways of growing old.* Stanford, Calif.: Stanford University Press, 1981, 99–110.

Sokolovsky, J. (Ed.). *Growing old in different societies.* Acton, Mass.: Copley, 1987.

Stearns, P. *Old age in preindustrial societies.* New York: Holmes & Meier, 1982.

Thoreau, H. D. *Walden.* New York: New American Library, 1856, Chapter 1, p. 8.

Tobin, J. J. The American idealization of old age in Japan. *The Gerontologist,* 1987, 27, 53–38.

Tran, T. V. Adjustment among different age and ethnic groups of Indochinese in the United States. *The Gerontologist,* 1992, 32, 508–518.

Waring, J. Social replenishment and social change: The problems of disordered cohort flow. *American Behavioral Scientist,* 1975, 19, 237–256.

Watson, W. H., and Maxwell, R. J. (Eds.). *Human aging and dying: A study in sociocultural gerontology.* New York: St. Martin's Press, 1977.

Yee, Barbara, W. Elders in Southeast Asian Refugee Families. *Generations,* 1992, 17(3), 24–27.

# C H A P T E R 4

# SOCIAL THEORIES OF AGING

## WHY STUDY SOCIAL THEORIES OF AGING?

The notion of developing and verifying a *theory* of aging may seem unnecessary or overly academic. We all grow older. Our bodies change with age, and so do our interests and lifestyles—not just theoretically, but in fact. Yet in a very informal and often unconscious way, we all develop theories from our own experiences. We observe older people in our families and communities and make generalizations about them. In a sense, the stereotypes of older people, sometimes labeled *ageist,* are the result of unconscious theorizing about the meaning of growing old.

The scientific approach to theory development is different in that it is a conscious and methodical attempt to explain why an event or set of events occurs. A scientific theory is based on a logically related set of statements, called *propositions* or *hypotheses,* each of which is subjected to testing through empirical research.

Propositions may be either statements of existing knowledge or predictions based on that knowledge. Each theory is based on not one but on a series of such propositions, any one of which may be partially in error. Scientists never entirely prove or disprove a theory. Instead, through empirical research, they gather evidence that may strengthen their confidence in it or move them closer to rejecting the theory by proving that parts of it are untrue. The possibility always exists that with the next empirical test, the theory will not be supported.

Such scientific theories are valuable because they allow us to accumulate knowledge and make sense of the world, to see more coherently and logically what we might otherwise only vaguely perceive, and thus they serve as guides to further research. They may predict what might happen in the future as well as point to unanswered questions or potential changes.

This chapter focuses on social theories—explanations of the changes in social relationships that occur in late adulthood. In effect, these theories attempt to answer questions we all wonder about: What makes for successful aging? What should the elderly do? What should our society be doing with regard to older people?

Should we force older people to retire or will they be more satisfied if they continue to be employed? What enhances older people's life satisfaction and well-being? What explains different levels of productive activity? Is it beneficial for the elderly to be active in the community? All of these theories address the basic issue of determining the optimal way for older people to relate to their environments.

As noted in Chapter 2, early research in the field of social gerontology tended to be applied rather than theoretical in nature, primarily because many older people were facing problems requiring immediate solutions. Since the 1950s and 1960s, however, researchers have been addressing broader theoretical questions regarding how people adapt to the changes characteristically associated with aging. Because the resulting proliferation of theoretical perspectives is relatively recent, the theories advanced by sociologists and psychologists tend to be more descriptive than explanatory; most are unable to explain how and why associations occur among the concepts being studied. None of the theories discussed in this chapter has been sufficiently tested to be rejected or to provide accurate predictions about the behavior of individuals. However, each theory suggests some important factors that may be related to aging and thus serves as a guide for further inquiry and possible intervention in the aging process. The theoretical perspectives examined in this chapter with reference to their gerontological applications are: role, life span, activity, disengagement, and continuity theories; patterned differentiation, the elderly as a subculture, age stratification, interactionist perspectives, social exchange theory, and the political economy framework. All of these have their foundations in basic sociological and psychological models.

## ROLE THEORY

One of the earliest attempts by social gerontologists to explain how individuals adjust to aging involved an application of role theory (Cottrell, 1942). People play a variety of social roles in their lifetimes, such as student, mother, wife, daughter, businesswoman, consultant, grandmother, and so on. Such roles identify and describe a person as a social being and are the basis of self-concept. They are organized sequentially into a life course; each social role is associated with a certain age or stage of life. In most societies, particularly Western ones, chronological age is used to determine eligibility for various positions, to evaluate the suitability of different roles, and to shape expectations of people in social situations. Some roles have a reasonable biological basis related to age (e.g., the role of mother), but many could be filled by individuals of a wide age range (e.g., the role of volunteer). Age alters not only the roles expected of people, but also the manner in which they are expected to play them. For example, a family's expectations of a 32-year-old mother are quite different from their expectations of her at age 62. How well individuals adjust to aging is assumed to depend on how well they accept the role changes typical of the later years.

Age norms serve to open up or close off the roles that people of a given chronological age can play. Age norms are assumptions of age-related capacities and limitations—beliefs that a person of a given age can and ought to do certain things. As an illustration, an older widower who starts dating and staying out late at night may be told by a disapproving family member that he should "act his age." Norms may be formally expressed through social policies and laws (e.g., laws against discrimination and mandatory retirement policies). More often, however, they operate informally. For example, even though employers cannot legally refuse to hire a 55-year-old woman because of her age, they can assume that she is too old to train for a new position. Their business norm is to hire younger workers. In such instances, age norms seem unjust and often have detrimental psychological consequences for older persons, causing them to feel worthless, angry, and depressed. In addition, such norms reinforce ageist stereotypes among younger people who are then more likely to assume that older workers are less productive and unreliable. Individuals also hold norms about the appropriateness of their own behavior at any particular age, so that "social clocks become internalized and age norms operate to keep people on the time track" (Hagestad and Neugarten, 1985). Most men in our society, for example, have expectations about the appropriate age at which to graduate from school, start working, marry, have a family, reach the peak of their career, and retire. These expectations have been shifting among younger cohorts, however. For instance, more men in their forties and fifties are entering second or third careers, rather than assuming they must work at their first jobs until they retire.

Every society conveys age norms through socialization, a lifelong process by which individuals learn how to perform new roles, adjust to changing roles, relinquish old ones, and thereby become integrated into society. We tend to think of socialization as occurring primarily in childhood, but we are constantly adjusting to new roles throughout our lives; older adults become socialized to numerous roles that accompany old age.

## Role Dilemmas of Late Adulthood

Older adults face a number of role dilemmas. With age, people are more likely to lose roles they have filled in the past than to acquire new ones; in addition, the most common role losses are largely irreversible, for example, the loss of the spouse role with widowhood or of the worker role with retirement. Although some older widows remarry and some retirees return to work that they find satisfying, the majority do neither, nor do they develop new roles to replace those they have lost. Since roles are the basis of an individual's self-concept, role loss can lead to an erosion of social identity and self-esteem (Rosow, 1985). Some early research found that the role losses of retirement and widowhood were related to maladjustment, as measured by self-reports about the amount of time devoted to

daydreaming about the past, thinking about death, and being absent-minded (Phillips, 1957). Later research provided less support for this conclusion (Lemon, Bengtson, and Peterson, 1972). In fact, older people often display a considerable degree of role creation, substitution, and flexibility in altering the social structure of their lives in the face of major changes in life circumstances (Rice, 1989).

With age, roles also tend to become more ambiguous. Guidelines or expectations about the requirements of roles, such as that of family authority or nurturing parent, become less clear to the elderly themselves as well as to others (Rosow, 1985). Burgess (1960) maintained that the role of the retired person is "roleless." This means that older individuals lack a consensus about societal rules to guide their behavior, which serves to exclude them from socially meaningful activity. Norms that do exist for older adults in our society tend to reflect "middle-aged" standards related to independence and social activity (Bengtson, 1973; Rosow, 1985). This can actually hinder socialization to old age.

Without clear-cut norms to measure conformity to or deviation from a role, there are few rewards for performing a role successfully. This, in turn, can deprive older people of the motivation to master new roles (e.g., role of volunteer) or maintain existing ones (e.g., role of helpful neighbor). Furthermore, the many older people who are unwilling to take on the diminished status and "uselessness" of the retiree role face a lack of desirable role options and models. Others, particularly women and ethnic minorities, may lack the resources to move into new roles or to emulate younger, more physically attractive role models.

The lack of appropriate role models is partially due to the fact that, until this century, most people did not live to old age. Not only did few role models exist, but also those in the media and the public realm tended to be youthful in appearance and behavior, maintaining middle-age standards which can actually hinder socialization to old age. With the growing numbers and visibility of older people, middle-aged persons today have more role models to emulate than they did in the past. In addition, more attention has recently been paid to alternative roles that older people can play in our society—trends that may serve to reduce role ambiguity for future cohorts of older people.

Another dilemma is that the transition from the worker role to the retiree role is characterized by role discontinuity, whereby what is learned at one age level may be useless or conflicting at the next age level. For example, learning to be highly productive in the workplace may be antithetical to adjusting to leisure time in retirement. Most workers have few opportunities to prepare for the new, more leisurely lifestyle of retiree, either through retirement planning programs or through interactions with retirees while in occupational roles. Institutions or situations that help people prepare for role changes with age have been limited in our society. However, more recent research has identified a process of role-exit, which occurs when individuals disengage from roles to which they have had a major commitment and which have been central to their identity, such as the work role. Interventions during the preretirement stage can encourage a process of gradually ceasing identification with the worker role and its demands and preparing for leisure roles (Ekerdt and De Viney, 1993).

## Changes on the Horizon?

Although the framework of role theory can help us understand why some older people have difficulties adjusting to aging, the rapid increase in the number of elderly may change this. In the future, roles appropriate to old age may become clearer, more continuous with past roles, and more satisfying. Future cohorts of older people may be better prepared for the role changes that often accompany the aging process; a growing number of interventions, such as preretirement counseling and widows' support groups, may help to smooth role transitions, particularly if the older person feels that she or he has the freedom

and autonomy to choose particular roles after retirement.

As the number of active, healthy, older people grows, our perception of the role changes that accompany old age and what may be considered productivity in old age may also be altered. Although old age is a time of role loss, it can also encompass role gains, such as volunteer, part-time worker, grandparent, and so on. In fact, recent studies suggest that older people participate in a variety of productive roles and activities comparable to those of middle-aged and younger Americans—volunteer work, informal help to others, maintenance and repair of their homes and possessions, and housework—even though they are not being paid for their activity (Herzog, Kahn, Morgan, Jackson, and Antonucci, 1989; Herzog and House, 1991).

Roles such as neighbor, friend, or parent generally continue throughout life, although the particular individuals involved and the conception of the roles may shift over time. The role of neighbor, for example, may assume greater importance to the older retiree in good health who now has more time to help others by watching over neighborhood children, assisting less healthy neighbors, or participating in community crime watch programs.

There is also growing recognition that the role of "dependent person" is not inevitable with age. Rather, the life course is characterized by varying periods of greater or lesser dependency in social relationships, with most people being emotionally dependent on others regardless of age. Even a physically impaired older person may still continue to support others emotionally (e.g., through a telephone reassurance program), and may be able to devise creative adaptations to ensure competence at home. Current efforts to maintain older people in their own homes as alternatives to institutionalization reflect an awareness of the need to preserve autonomous roles as long as possible.

Many of the concepts of role theory, particularly the concepts of age norms and non-normative life events, are central to a *life-span perspective* on aging. However, the life-span approach takes account of the diversity of roles and role changes throughout life, including old age, since it suggests that development is not restricted to any one part of the life span, but rather is a lifelong process. According to this perspective, development cannot be solely equated with steady incremental growth or change. Instead, development is characterized by the simultaneous appearance of role gain and role loss, continuity and discontinuity since later life achievements often depend upon earlier ones (Baltes, 1987). Development is multidirectional, with stability in some functions, decline in others, and improvement in others. For example, an older person may experience some decrement in memory, but still be very creative. In addition, these patterns of development are not the same in all individuals, as reflected by the considerable heterogeneity among the older population. In contrast with role theory per se, life span theory gives greater recognition to the historical-cultural conditions within which development occurs. Age changes in individual development and adaptation can be examined within a larger framework that takes into account changing social structures and contexts. While the life-span perspective is not explicitly articulated throughout this text, our multidisciplinary person-in-environment approach encompassing biological, psychological, physiological, and social changes draws upon many of the concepts of intra-individual change, inter-individual variability, and historical-cultural context.

Two of the most widely debated theories of successful aging examine the role changes experienced by older people: activity and disengagement theory. Both were based on the Kansas City Studies of Adult Life, which were formally launched in 1952 at the University of Chicago to pursue questions about middle age and aging. To some extent, these two theoretical perspectives of the social psychology of aging during the 1960s and 1970s have served to legitimize various social policies and programs with the elderly (Minkler and Estes, 1984).

## ACTIVITY THEORY

Activity theory is a dominant theoretical perspective in social gerontology; to a large extent, it is a commonsense theory. It was developed from Robert Havighurst's (1963, 1968) analyses of the Kansas City Study of 300 people—primarily white, middle class, healthy, ranging from 40 to 85 years of age—who were interviewed at regular intervals over a six-year period. It assumes that older people who are active will be more satisfied and better adjusted than less active elderly. Since activity theory presumes that a person's self-concept is validated through participation in roles characteristic of middle age, it is seen as desirable for older people to maintain as many middle-age activities as possible, and to substitute new roles for those that are lost through widowhood or retirement. In order to minimize society's withdrawal from the elderly, which occurs against older people's will or desire, older people must deny the existence of old age by maintaining middle-age lifestyles as long as possible: remain active, keep busy, and stay young! Behavior inappropriate to middle age is considered to be maladaptive. In fact, data from a 1964 cross-national study of patterns in retirement suggest a consistent and moderate relationship between role activity and life satisfaction (Bengtson, 1969).

To a large extent, this perspective is consistent with our society's value system, which emphasizes work and productivity. It has resulted in policies that stress continued social activities as a way to assist the elderly's social integration. Such a perspective is reflected in gerontological practitioners' efforts to develop new roles for older people that involve responsibilities and obligations. The activity perspective is perhaps most strikingly apparent in the numerous recreation events, travel tours, and classes sponsored by retirement communities and senior centers. Many older persons themselves have adopted this perspective and believe it helps them maintain life satisfaction, as illustrated by the following vignettes.

---

**AN OLDER PERSON PURSUING LEISURE ACTIVITIES**

Bob lives in the Northeast region of the United States. He retired at age 62 after thirty years of work in a management position for an aerospace company. He and his wife of forty years carefully saved money so that they could be very active in their retirement. They now spend their winters as "snowbirds," traveling in their mobile home to the "sun belt." Now at age 69, they have spent seven years in the same community in Arizona where they are well-known and have made many friends. In the summer, they usually take one extended trip to the mountains. They enjoy good health and believe that keeping active is the key to their zest for life.

---

**AN OLDER PERSON PURSUING EDUCATION AND LEISURE ACTIVITIES**

Rose was a nurse for thirty years. In her career in direct patient care and teaching, she has held positions of authority. She has always liked learning new things. Now 74 and retired, she is very active in her church and directs the adult education program. She has participated in Elderhostel four times, and has had the opportunity to visit several foreign countries. She has taken two trips with her teenage grandchildren as well. Staying active means learning to her and she has shared slide shows of her journeys with her retired friends and the women's group at her church.

---

## Critique of Activity Theory

Empirical support for activity theory is mixed. Informal social activity with friends has been found to be somewhat related to well-being (Lemon, Bengtson, and Peterson, 1972). The Second Duke Longitudinal Study found that being active in organizations and physical activity were two major predictors of successful aging (Palmore, 1979). Other studies, however, identified a negative association between formal group activity and life satisfaction (Longino and Kart, 1982), which suggests that variables other than level of activity, such as opportunities to interact intimately with others, are needed to explain life satisfaction. Although some studies found that active people have better physical and mental health and take greater satisfaction in life than do the inactive, such people are generally better educated and have more money and options than those less active (Havighurst et al., 1969; Palmore, 1974; Thurmond and Belcher, 1980–81). In fact, the individual resources that older people possess affect their ability to continue in their social roles (Covey, 1981). Therefore, socioeconomic, lifestyle, and generational variables may be more important than maturational ones in the associations found between activity and life satisfaction, health, and well-being.

Activity level also does not appear to predict death rates when age and health status are controlled. In an eight-year follow-up of older Mexican Americans and whites, informal activity levels (as defined by attendance at movies, sports events, and museums; hunting and fishing; social visits) of elders who had died was not significantly different four and eight years previously from those who were still alive (Lee and Markides, 1990).

Activity theory tells us little about what happens to people who cannot maintain the standards of middle age. By failing to acknowledge a personality dimension, it does not explain the fact that some older persons are passive and happy while others are highly active and unhappy. Another limitation is its assumption that people want to continue their same pattern of activity. Many elderly who were active during middle age may no longer want to sustain their activity level and, in fact, may value the opportunity to curtail their social involvements. Some older people may simply want to have time to "do nothing," to "sit and rock," and to engage in solitary pursuits. The value placed by older people on being active probably varies with their lifelong experiences, personality, and needs. Havighurst himself (1968) later acknowledged the importance of personality in predicting the association between activity levels and life satisfaction; thus, people who have been active, achieving, and outward-directed in middle age will probably be satisfied to continue this into old age, whereas those who have been passive, dependent, and home-centered may be content to sustain this contrasting pattern later in life. This perspective has led other sociologists to argue that, rather than remaining active, good adjustment to the aging process involves disengagement.

## DISENGAGEMENT THEORY

Disengagement theory was the first comprehensive, explicit, and multidisciplinary theory advanced by social and behavioral scientists in gerontology (Achenbaum and Bengtson, 1994). One of the most widely known and controversial theories of social gerontology, it was first formulated by Elaine Cumming and William Henry in 1961. Their book, *Growing Old*, challenges the assumption that older people have to be active in

order to be well-adjusted. Instead, the process whereby older people decrease their activity levels, seek more passive roles, interact less frequently with others, and become increasingly preoccupied with their inner lives is viewed as normal, inevitable, and personally satisfying, and may begin the phase of life review (discussed in more detail in Chapter 9). Disengagement has its basis in the assumption of an inevitable decline in abilities with age and the universal expectation of death. The process of disengagement may be started either by the older person or by society. Regardless of how the withdrawal process is initiated, it is presumed to be mutual, having positive consequences for both society and the individual.

According to this theory, older people, experiencing losses of roles and energy, want to be released from societal expectations that they be productive and competitive. Disengagement is thus viewed as adaptive behavior, allowing the elderly to maintain a sense of worth and tranquility while performing more peripheral social roles. For example, Cumming and Henry argued that disengaged older people, freed from the demands of employment roles, are better able to participate in satisfying family relationships than those who remain occupied with work. For men, the process of disengagement tends to be abrupt, as they forfeit their occupational roles. For women, the transition from what is often their central role as parent is more gradual and smooth; however, future cohorts of employed women may experience this transition period differently.

---

**AN OLDER PERSON REPRESENTING DISENGAGEMENT THEORY**

Inga was an executive secretary to a highly successful businessman. She has never married. When she retired at age 62, she took a creative writing class, something she had dreamed of all her life, but had not had the time. At 75 she is very content to sit in her rent-controlled apartment which overlooks a park. She has lived there for fifteen years. She finds much inspiration in watching life pass before her in the park. Writing poetry and short stories gives her an outlet for her thoughts. She feels that her writing has developed greater depth as she has contemplated the meaning of her life.

**VIGNETTE FOR DISENGAGEMENT THEORY**

John worked for forty years on the assembly line at a factory making cars. He believed that it was a good job which supported his family well, but he had worked many overtime hours and had had little time for leisure. Now at age 70, he sits in the chair in his living room and watches TV and reads the paper. This has been his pattern since his retirement five years ago. Occasionally, he and his wife of forty-five years will go out to dinner. John is glad not to have to go to the "rat race" of work every day.

Disengagement is presumed not only to be adaptive for older people, but also to be functional or useful to society. According to Cumming and Henry, all societies need orderly ways to transfer power from older to younger generations. Retirement policies, for example, are assumed to be a way to ensure that younger people with new energy and skills will move into occupational roles. Some blue collar workers may choose to disengage after a lifetime of tedious, repetitive work, as the retired auto worker described above illustrates. When the elderly have disengaged from the mainstream of society, their deaths are also thought to be less disruptive to society's optimal functioning. Thus, disengagement theory holds that social services, if provided at all, should not seek to revitalize the aged, but rather to encourage their withdrawal.

## Critique of Disengagement Theory

This theoretical perspective has been widely criticized for assuming that disengagement is inevitable, functional, and universal. Critics point to other cultures where the elderly move into new roles of prestige and power. Likewise, not everyone in our culture disengages, as evidenced by the growing numbers of older people, many in their eighties, who are employed, healthy, and politically and socially active. As with activity theory, disengagement theory fails to account for variability in individual preferences and for differences in the sociocultural setting (Achenbaum and Bengtson, 1994; Hochschild, 1975; Marshall, 1994).

Yet the extent to which a person disengages may vary with the individual's position in the social structure and with their culture. A retired college professor, for example, has more opportunities to remain professionally involved than a retired steel worker. On the other hand, a low-income person of color may not have the option of disengaging from the job setting, but must continue to work in order to survive economically. Disengagement also does not appear to be uniform within the individual. A person may disengage socially (e.g., attend fewer social events), but remain fully engaged psychologically (e.g., continue to read about and discuss current events). In addition, what may appear to be disengaged behavior to an outsider may have a very different meaning for the aging person. An older person who sits by a window for hours may not necessarily be disengaged, but may fully enjoy the changing street scenes.

Disengagement theory has also tended to ignore the part that personality plays in the way a person adjusts to aging. People who have always been active, assertive, and socially involved probably will not retreat as they age, but rather will maintain typical ways of adapting to their environments. Similarly, some people always have been withdrawn or passive; hence, disengagement may represent for them a natural transition or continuation of their previous lives rather than the culmination of a process characteristic of all aging individuals. When older people have disengaged, this may not represent personal preference but rather the failure of our society to provide opportunities for continued engagement. For instance, the lack of meaningful part-time jobs is a better explanation of the decline in employment among the elderly than is their personal preference not to work part-time; it makes a difference whether disengagement is forced or freely chosen.

Lastly, it cannot be assumed that older people's withdrawal from useful roles is necessarily good for society. For example, disengagement theory may be seen as legitimizing the earlier mandatory retirement laws and other policies that foster the separation of the elderly from others in society (Minkler and Estes, 1984). Yet policies that have encouraged early retirement have had negative societal consequences. For example, as more people have retired earlier, proportionately fewer workers are available to support those retired persons, thereby straining pension systems. Likewise, the workplace has been deprived of older workers' skills and knowledge. At the same time, a number of social trends are counteracting forces that previously might have led to disengagement, including advances in preventive medicine, growing economic security for older people, and the expansion of leisure roles and options for retirees.

In response to such criticisms, Cumming (1963) reformulated the theory to give more consideration to the relationship between personality and disengagement. This reformulation acknowledged that not everyone disengages; rather, adaptive behavior in old age varies widely. Two modes of interacting with the environment were distinguished: impinging and selecting. Impingers were defined as assertive and active in their interactions, whereas selectors tend to be more passive and restrained in their social relations, waiting for others to confirm preexisting assumptions about themselves. Both assertive and passive coping styles were viewed as ways for older people to protect themselves from contradictory or negative social messages, and thus to preserve their self-worth. Cumming (1975) also maintained that misinterpretations of disengagement as isolation, loneliness, and passivity overlook ways that disengaged behavior can be adaptive.

Disengagement is a broad theory encompassing many elements, yet it has been tested only in parts. It has generally not been supported by empirical research (Prasad, 1964; Youmans, 1967; Palmore, 1968; Tallmer and Kutner, 1970), although some researchers have found differential disengagement (occurring in some older individuals at different rates and in different aspects of behavior) to be useful (Williams and Wirth, 1965; Streib and Schneider, 1971; Cumming, 1975). Several studies have shown disengagement to be linked to a variety of individual and environmental variables. Differences in environmental opportunities have been found to produce different patterns of engagement and disengagement. It has been suggested that the increased physical and social stress that often accompanies aging, not age per se, may produce disengagement (Carp, 1968; Tallmer and Kutner, 1970). It also makes intuitive sense that some people will disengage from unsatisfying contacts and maintain satisfying ones; they may also put up with less than satisfying relationships in order to remain engaged (Brown, 1974). Thirty years later, disengagement theory has largely disappeared from the empirical literature and has been widely discredited (Achenbaum and Bengtson, 1994). Yet, as the first attempt to define an explicitly multidisciplinary theory of aging, it has had a profound impact upon the field.

Clearly, neither activity nor disengagement theory fully explains successful or well-adjusted aging. Neither adequately addresses the social structure or cultural and historical contexts in which the aging process occurs. Minkler and Estes (1984) maintain that theories that focus only on what older people do, without considering the social conditions and policies that cause them to act as they do, are inadequate. For example, rather than study individual adjustment in retirement, researchers might explore the possible association between the larger political and economic context and unemployment among older people. These theories have also been criticized as blaming the older people for their condition and legitimizing incrementalist, individualistic approaches to social policy (Levin and Levin, 1980).

A potential danger of both theories is that society, as well as older individuals, may interpret them as prescriptive; for example, older people may believe that they are supposed to behave in certain ways. Both theories may be described more appropriately as philosophical recommendations about how to live during the later years rather than explanations of the aging process. More variables need to be examined before we can explain why some people are happy in an active old age while others are content to narrow their activities and involvement.

## CONTINUITY THEORY

The evident shortcomings of and skepticism about disengagement and activity theories led to the emergence of a third social-psychological theory of adaptation in old age. Bernice Neugarten, who was associated with the Kansas City Studies, urged that gerontologists examine the entire life course in addressing the processes of aging to take account of different pathways to old age (Neugarten, Havighurst, and Tobin, 1968; Havighurst, Neugarten and Tobin, 1968).

According to continuity theory, the aging person substitutes similar types of roles for lost ones, and continues to maintain typical ways of adapting to the environment in order to maintain inner psychological continuity as well as the outward continuity of social behavior and circumstances (Neugarten, Havighurst, and Tobin, 1968). Its basic tenets are that people, whether young or old, have different personalities and lifestyles, and that personality plays a major role in adjusting to aging. This results in diversity in the patterns of aging, based on probable continuities with earlier personality styles.

People who have always been passive or withdrawn are unlikely to become activists upon retirement. Similarly, those who have always been active, assertive, and socially involved are unlikely to sit quietly at home in their old age. Changes are integrated into one's prior history without necessarily causing upheaval or disequilibrium (Atchley, 1989). Basically, this perspective states that, with age, we become more of what we already were when younger. Central personality characteristics become even more pronounced and core values even more salient with age. An individual ages successfully if she or he maintains a mature, integrated personality while growing old. This, according to continuity theory, is the basis of life satisfaction (Neugarten, Havighurst, and Tobin, 1968).

As the two vignettes below illustrate, continuity of social roles and activities can help maintain self-esteem and life satisfaction for older persons who have always cherished these roles. These valued roles may be occupational or social. Individuals, therefore, provide their own standards for successful aging rather than try to adjust to a common norm. This subject will be discussed further in Chapter 9.

### Critique of Continuity Theory

Although continuity theory has some intuitive appeal and appears to overcome the weaknesses of activity and disengagement theories, it also has limitations. One is that it may not have ecologi-

---

### AN OLDER MAN REPRESENTING CONTINUITY THEORY

At age 80, Rabbi Green, who has taught rabbinical students for forty years, still makes the trip from his suburban home into the city to work with students one day per week. He speaks with considerable excitement about the reciprocal relationship between him and his students. When students talk about their relationship with him, it becomes clear how much they value him as a mentor. Being a "teacher" is who he is now and who he has always been.

---

### AN OLDER WOMAN REPRESENTING CONTINUITY THEORY

Mary, 90, has always been the "cookie jar" mother to her children and their friends. She was there to offer goodies and a listening ear. Now her children and the generation of young persons who were their friends live far away. But a new generation of younger persons has moved into the neighborhood in the small town where she lives. She has become acquainted with many of them and their parents as they stop to talk with her as she works in her beloved yard. Now many will stop by for a cookie and a glass of milk after school. She is fondly called the "cookie jar grandma." Along with giving them cookies, the children say that she always listens to them.

---

cal validity. That is, it places earlier stages of development as the criteria for successful aging and assumes that individuals seek to maintain a particular pattern of behavior throughout life. It can only be inferred that the lifestyles observed in old age were developed earlier in life and continued into old age. Lifestyles observed in old age may be a response to growing old, rather than reflections of lifelong patterns.

The need for continuity may reduce an individual's self-esteem in the later years when poor health or limited finances may require modifications in one's earlier lifestyle. In fact, maintaining previous patterns can be maladaptive (Fox, 1981–82). There is evidence that the need for continuity may also interfere with an individual's desire to remove himself or herself from disliked roles and behaviors. Research shows that freeing oneself from former roles may have positive effects (Gutmann, 1974; Gutmann, Grunes, and Griffin, 1980). For example, many women adopt more typically "masculine" personality traits as they age; and some aging men act on tendencies in themselves that are generally identified as "feminine." It appears that older individuals most satisfied with their lives are those who have not rigidly conformed to traditional sex roles, but have integrated traits culturally defined as masculine with those culturally defined as feminine (Sinnott, 1977).

The complexity of continuity theory makes it difficult to test empirically, since an individual's reaction to aging is explained through the interrelationships among biological and psychological changes, the continuation of lifelong patterns, and so on. Because it focuses primarily on the individual as the unit of analysis, overlooking the role of external social factors in modifying the aging process, policies based on continuity theory could rationalize a laissez-faire or "live and let live" approach to solving individual problems facing the elderly. The multiple variations in the aging processes of different individuals could be assumed to make concerted policy interventions unfeasible.

Part-time work in his son's upholstery shop is a major source of satisfaction for this 90-year-old man.

## PATTERNED INTERACTION AND DIFFERENTIATION

Also growing out of the Kansas City Studies of Adult Life was the sociological theory of patterned differentiation of the aging process and of the interaction of "successful" older adults as "active agents" within the social contexts in which they live and work (Williams and Wirths, 1965). Williams and Wirths' basic argument was that active agents develop their lives over time in socially structured environments, which result in various lifestyles that are differentially successful (Maddox, 1994). Their capstone concept is a pattern of aging, a judgment based on a synthesis of three factors—a reasonably clear and salient personality type, life satisfaction, and apparent social integration. These three factors produce an assessment of maturity of the older individual and four dominant lifestyles—familism, living alone, easing through, and living fully—which vary along two dimensions: autonomy/dependence and persistence/precariousness. In their review of 168 biographies, they found that the majority of lifestyles were autonomous and persistent, which they defined as "success" in later life (and which did not provide support for disengagement theory). Their sociological focus on the interaction of the person in his or her environment recognized the value of longitudinal studies in order to document differential strategies and outcomes in aging processes, and that no single lifestyle is inevitably successful for all older adults (Maddox, 1994).

Overall, the Kansas City Studies of Adult Life lead to a strong emphasis on the social-psychological aspects of aging in contrast to the sociological or social-structural aspects. This emphasis on the individual set the tone for most of social gerontology in the 1960s and early 1970s with its emphasis on the social-psychological aspects of aging, such as personality and life satisfaction (Achenbaum and Bengtson, 1994; Marshall, 1994). The factors found to be associated with optimal aging were individualistic—autonomy, persistence, keeping active, and so on. When macro-level phenomena were considered, they were not conceptualized as structurally linked between the individual and society. Nor were race and class identified as social structural variables. Even Williams and Wirths' work,

which was more sociological than others associated with the Kansas City Studies, set forth a micro notion of structure, in which the "structural properties are located in the social systems of individual actors" (1965, p. 6)

In contrast to this psychological focus are later more sociological theories: the elderly as a subculture, age stratification, social interaction, social exchange, and political economy.

## THE ELDERLY AS A SUBCULTURE

In contrast to activity theorists, proponents of a subculture of aging believe that older people maintain their self-concepts and social identities through their membership in a subculture (Rose, 1965). A subculture is formed when particular members within a society interact more with each other than they do with others in the society. Such interaction is presumed to occur when persons within a group develop an affinity for each other through shared backgrounds, problems, and interests, and are simultaneously excluded from interacting with other members of the population.

A number of social and demographic trends are viewed as increasing the opportunities for older people to identify with each other and to separate them from the mainstream of American society. These trends include: the increasing numbers of older people; their self-segregation within retirement communities; their "involuntary" segregation in inner cities and rural areas, due primarily to younger people leaving these areas; and their growing dependence on social services and on other people as they withdraw from occupational roles. The formation of an aging subculture is viewed as having two significant consequences for older people: an identification of themselves as old, and thus socially and culturally distant from the rest of our youth-oriented society; and a growing group consciousness that creates the potential for political power and social action. The example below illustrates one type of subculture of older persons in a large community.

---

**AN OLDER PERSON REPRESENTING SUBCULTURE THEORY**

Roy, 63, has resided in a downtown SRO hotel in the Pacific Northwest for the past four years. A logger for many years, he never married, living alone in the woods for most of his work life and coming into town only when he needed supplies. When logging was curtailed, he "retired" early.

Now he lives with many other elderly men downtown, having only a nodding acquaintance with them. He is able to make use of a low income clinic for health care, and goes once a week to a downtown church where they serve lunch to older adults in the area.

---

### Critique of the Subculture Perspective

Although the concept of the elderly as a subculture provides descriptive guides for understanding the role and status of older people in our society, it has limited power to predict behavior and has been widely criticized. Clearly, the concept of a disadvantaged subculture does not apply to all situations nor to all older people. In some settings, older people have high status; the seniority system in Congress, for example, favors age. In addition, many older people are financially well off; most still live in age-integrated neighborhoods; and most interact across generations within their families—forces contrary to the formation of a cohesive subculture. Partially as a result of such contacts with people of other ages, the elderly have not organized in a single, unified way to advance their own interests. Instead, a variety of groups are formed around aging interests, ranging from the age-integrated Gray Panthers to large organizations such as the American Association of Retired Persons (AARP), which attracts members, in part, through its financial benefits. As will be seen in Chapter 15, the question of whether older people form a subculture with a collective age identity is closely related to debates about the political influence of age-based organizations and voting blocs. This perspective also views older people as a status group similar to other such groups in our society, a concept discussed below in terms of the theory of age stratification.

### AGE STRATIFICATION THEORY

Age stratification is less a formal theory than a conceptual framework for viewing societal processes and changes that affect aging. Proponents Matilda White Riley (1971, 1972, 1985) and Ann Foner (1975) maintain that an approach similar to that used in sociological analyses of class stratification is useful to understanding the position of age groups and the meaning of age within a particular social context. Just as societies are stratified in terms of socioeconomic class, gender and race, every society divides people into categories or strata according to age—"young," "middle-aged," and "old." That is, people are defined in terms of social roles and responsibilities, not just chronologically (Riley, Johnson, and Foner, 1972).

The sociology of age stratification is concerned with the relationships within and across all age strata, not only the older ones. The basic assumption is that age is a universal criterion by which people's roles, rights, and privileges are distributed as they move from one stratum to the next. Age may be linked directly to social roles (e.g., through legal criteria for voting or retirement) or indirectly, when socially prescribed parameters exist for given roles (e.g., the appropriate ages for dating and marriage).

Each age stratum can be evaluated according to the roles its members typically play and the extent to which these roles are valued by society. Some age strata have more valued qualities than others. Therefore, inequality is a central aspect of age systems (Foner, 1984). Such age grading commonly occurs in the workplace, for example, where younger workers are viewed as more productive and desirable than older employees. The fact that social roles are age-graded within an age stratification system produces structured inequalities between age groups, such as between younger and older workers. Age stratification of roles both frees and limits the elderly in modern society. Older retirees, for instance, are freed from many obligatory adult roles. However, norms for age-appropriate behavior also discourage them from choosing such options as returning to school or working part-time.

Because of the variety of physical, social, or psychological factors that affect the aging process, age strata differ in age-related capacities. As we observe daily, people of different ages tend to behave differently and are assigned dissimilar roles; they may be motivated by diverse political and social attitudes, generally have varied organizational attachments, and may be treated differently by other age strata (Riley and Foner, 1968).

Such differences between strata partially result from the processes of allocation and socialization. *Allocation* is the process of assigning and reassigning people of various ages to suitable roles as a way to meet society's needs. For example, age as a criterion for retirement is related to overall employment patterns in the society. *Socialization,* the other intervening process, serves to smooth the transition of individuals from one age status to the next. Age stratification necessitates socialization throughout a lifetime, because, as noted in our discussion of role theory, people move into and out of a succession of roles as they age.

## Cohort and Life Course Effects

The members of one strata differ from each other in both their stage of life (young, middle-aged, or old), and in the historical periods they have experienced. The two factors, the life course dimension and the historical dimension, explain many differences in how people behave, think, and, in turn, contribute to society. According to the life course dimension, age strata may be defined by chronological age or by stages in the life cycle (e.g., infancy, childhood, adolescence, early adulthood, etc.). Chronological age is important not in an absolute sense, but as an approximate indicator of an individual's personal experiences (biological, psychological, and social) and the varying probabilities of resultant behavior and attitudes. Individuals in the same stage of the life course have much in common: their biological development, the kinds of roles they have experienced (e.g., worker, spouse, or parent), the number of years behind them, and the potential years ahead. Likewise, people at different life stages differ in these respects.

Other differences between age strata are due to the historical dimension, to what is termed *cohort flow.* As we saw in our discussion of research designs (Chapter 2), people who were born at the same time period (cohort) share a common historical and environmental past, present, and future. They have been exposed to similar events, conditions, and changes. Think about some of the major events of this century, such as the two World Wars, the Depression, the Civil Rights Movement, the Vietnam War, human explorations into space, and technological developments that have had a differential impact on different cohorts, often creating wide variations in values, attitudes, and behaviors (the so-called "generation gap"). Riley (1971) referred to the behavior and attitudes that developed from a particular intersection of the life course and historical dimension as "cohort-centric." What this means is that people who are in a similar place on the life course dimension (in the same age stratum) experience historical events similarly and may come to see the world in a like fashion. For example, older people who were at the early stages of their occupational and child-rearing careers during the Depression tend to value economic self-sufficiency and "saving for a rainy day," compared to younger cohorts who experienced periods of economic prosperity during early adulthood. Cohort-centrism solidifies age strata by encouraging the selection of friends from among age-mates who have similar values and behaviors as a result of common experiences.

The metaphor of people stepping on an escalator at birth has been used to illustrate the process of cohort flow (Riley, Johnson, and Foner, 1972). How many and what types of people step on are never identical, although those who begin at the bottom at the same time move up collectively. The number of people stepping on (i.e., the size of any age stratum) is determined by rates of fertility, age-specific mortality, and migration in and out of a country. The age group does not remain stable as they move along, however. Instead, people acquire distinctive social attributes that enhance or impede the likelihood of their staying on the escalator for the full ride. Some get off, particularly men, by dying. Eventually, fewer people are left in the cohort, until all those who began together are dead.

## A Dynamic Process

The complex, dynamic nature of the system of age stratification is illustrated by how it influences and is influenced by the changing social-political-economic fabric of society. For example, the trend toward early retirement among the age 55 to 65 cohort has had an impact on Social Security, on our pension systems, and on the "leisure industry." As more people have chosen early retirement, they have faced living on lower, fixed incomes, at a time when health, long-term care, housing, and food costs have rapidly risen. In turn, some elderly have worked through age-based organizations to try to influence retirement policies, which has led to some public perceptions that the older population is financially secure. In sum, socioeconomic factors assure that different cohorts grow old in different ways as they "move up the escalator."

Another illustration of the dynamic nature of age strata involves individual mobility across the strata. In contrast to class mobility, age mobility is universal, inevitable, and irreversible. In other words, although people age in different ways and at different rates, no one can become younger, stop the flow of time, or achieve downward age mobility. All people shift to different age strata with advancing age.

As cohorts "move up the escalator," they may collectively influence age stratification (Waring, 1975). When there is a lack of fit in terms of the roles available to them, cohort members may challenge the existing patterns of age stratification. For example, successive cohorts in this century have experienced increased longevity and formal education levels, which, in turn, have changed the nature of how they age, how they view aging, and the age stratification system itself. Because of their particular relationship to historical events, the people in the old age stratum today are very different from older persons in the past or in the future, and they experience the aging process differently. The cohort retiring in the 1980s tends to be oriented more positively toward retirement and leisure than the cohort that retired in the early 1950s. They have also been more likely to challenge restrictions on their roles as workers and community participants through age discrimination suits, legislative action, and political organization than cohorts 10 or 20 years their senior. These variations, in turn, will affect the experiences and expectations of future cohorts as they age. In other words, as successive cohorts move through the age strata or "up the escalator," they alter conditions to such a degree that later groups never encounter the world in exactly the same way, and therefore age in different ways.

Age stratification also interacts with socio-economic, ethnic, and sex stratification to determine differences in roles. Just as women and men generally play different roles throughout the life cycle, the nature of their aging experience tends to differ, with women undergoing fewer abrupt transitions in their roles. The timing of life events has been found to vary by social class, with middle- and upper-class individuals tending to marry and have children later than working-class persons. Indeed, there are many ways in which different status or social classes cause people to age differently. For example, older people who have lifelong wealth or who were politically influential have higher status than younger persons without wealth or political power.

## Critique of Age Stratification Theory

Age stratification theory has been criticized for too narrowly assessing age primarily in terms of chronology or life stage, while giving little consideration to the importance of physical appearance, length of time that a person has been in a given position, and level of physical, mental, and social functioning. As will be shown throughout this text, functional differences in physiological, psychological, and social aging must be taken into account in any theory of aging. These different ways of assessing age make it harder to defend the concept that birth cohorts remain cohesive. Because the diversity of levels of physical appearance and functioning increases with age, cohorts probably become less cohesive as they grow older, not more unified. Another limitation of this theoretical perspective is that family background, gender, ethnic minority status, social class, and the political and economic structure may all be more salient in defining people's roles than age stratification itself (Minkler and Estes, 1984). In fact, some social gerontologists contend that we are moving toward an "age-irrelevant" society, with age-based constraints weakening and socioeconomic status becoming more salient (Hagestad and Neugarten, 1985).

Age strata, cohort succession, historical time, and the life course are all somewhat abstract, global concepts, which thus far have yielded few empirical studies. Because of its focus on structural, demographic, and historical characteristics, age stratification theory is not useful in explaining an individual's behavior as he or she ages. But it can help us understand the ways in which society uses age to fit people into structural niches in the social world, and to observe that this age structure changes with the passage of time. By viewing age groups as members of status groups within a social system, as well as active participants in a changing society, strat-

ification theory is conducive to sociological explanations of age cohorts' behaviors and values, and as such, it deserves further empirical testing.

## INTERACTIONIST PERSPECTIVES

Consistent with the person-environment perspective outlined in the Introduction, recent efforts among social gerontologists have focused on the person-environment transactional process. In particular, symbolic interaction, labeling, and social breakdown theories all emphasize the dynamic interaction between older individuals and their social world. These theories implicitly assume that older people must adjust to ongoing societal requirements. When confronted with change, whether relocation to a nursing home or learning to use a computer, older individuals are expected to try to master the changing situation while extracting from the larger environment what they need to retain a positive self-concept.

The *symbolic interactionist* view of aging argues that the interaction of such factors as the environment, individuals, and their encounters in it can significantly affect the kind of aging process people experience (Gubrium, 1973). Changes in these interactional variables may produce results that are erroneously attributed to inherent maturational changes. For example, the older person who becomes confused following a move to a new apartment may mistakenly be labeled as *senile*. Efforts to ease the stress of moving could minimize resulting confusion. Similarly, apparent disengagement, low self-esteem, and dissatisfaction may result from how other people interpret the elderly's behavior. For instance, the older person who sits and reads may be defined by others as disengaged, yet he or she may actually be very involved in reading about and discussing current events.

Both the self and society are viewed by symbolic interactionists as able to create new alternatives. Therefore, low morale and withdrawal from social involvement are not inevitable with aging, but are one possible outcome of an individual's interactions that can be altered. Policies based on the symbolic interactionist framework optimistically assume that both environmental constraints and individual needs can be changed. An environmental intervention, for example, is the elimination of age discrimination in employment, whereas the individual's decision to pursue leisure rather than paid employment is an attempt to modify personal needs.

*Labeling theory*, derived from symbolic interaction theory, states that people derive their self-concepts from interacting with others in their social milieu. In other words, we all tend to think of ourselves in terms of how others define us and react to us. Once others have defined us into distinct categories, they react to us on the basis of these categorizations, and as a result, our self-concept and behavior change. For example, this labeling process occurs when someone who is about to retire starts to behave as others have defined retirees: nonproductive, useless, and inactive. Or the older person who forgets to turn off the stove burner is likely to be labeled by concerned relatives as "senile," yet a younger person's forgetfulness will be explained as being busy and preoccupied. You can probably think of numerous other examples where older persons' behaviors depended largely on the reactions of significant others.

The theories of *social breakdown* and *social reconstruction* are outgrowths of the labeling perspective. The social breakdown syndrome initially referred to the negative feedback generated by a person already susceptible to psychological problems. For example, friends of a person who was once hospitalized for depression may overreact to the slightest indication of another depressive episode, so that what might be a normal grief reaction to a loss becomes labeled as "depression." Once the cycle is initiated, it reinforces others' perception of incompetence, which then ensures even more difficulties (Zusman, 1966). A similar process is assumed to occur among older people who are experiencing role loss and ambiguity; as discussed under role theories, older people faced with changes such as retirement or

widowhood reach out for specific cues for how they should act. Should they sell their house? Should they move in with their children? Others, frequently well-intentioned children, react to their reaching out as a sign of their failing capacities. Thus, an adult child who is accustomed to his or her father decisively handling finances may interpret his indecision following his wife's death as a cause for concern rather than as a normal part of grieving. The father may react to such concern by greater indecisiveness, eventually perceiving himself as less competent and turning all decision making over to others. In other words, older persons who accept negative labeling are then inducted into a negative, dependent position. As they learn to behave in ways that older people are "supposed" to act in our society, previous skills of independence atrophy. They perceive themselves as inadequate, and a negative spiral is set into motion.

The social reconstruction model suggests ways to intervene in this negative cycle (Kuypers and Bengtson, 1973). This model asserts that even small changes in restructuring the environment can provide a more satisfying life among older people. One way to improve the larger society is to furnish older people with frames for self-judgment that are more humanitarian than the work ethic that prevails in our society. Another intervention is to provide publicly funded services to address problems of inadequate housing, poor health care, and poverty. Older persons could also be provided with opportunities to develop greater self-confidence and autonomy by involving them in the planning and delivery of such services. These suggestions for altering the environment are consistent with the concept of environmental press, as discussed in the Introduction.

An underlying assumption of the social reconstruction model is that resources which allow older people to exert control over their physical and social environments are not distributed equally across all social classes. Socioeconomic class imposes a structured inequality which limits an individual's mastery over life

(Tindale and Marshall, 1980). For example, individuals from lower socioeconomic classes pass from young to middle to old age at a younger chronological age than those from higher socioeconomic backgrounds. Lacking the valued resources that are required for upward mobility, lower income individuals tend to be less healthy, have less access to health care, have children and grandchildren earlier in the life cycle, and so on—all factors that may make them appear older than they are chronologically.

The interactionist perspective has been criticized for focusing on how individuals react to aging rather than on the broader sociostructural factors that shape the experience and management of aging in our society (Minkler and Estes, 1984). This critique is further developed by the political economy theorists, described later in this chapter.

## SOCIAL EXCHANGE THEORY

With roots in behavioral psychology and utilitarian economics, social exchange theory attempts to explain the structured inequality that exists among different age strata. Simone de Beauvoir (1972) asserted that aging is a struggle between classes. Taking this further, Dowd (1980) maintains that definitions of age stratification are incomplete without reference to power, since unequal access to resources as a basis of power determines social status and opportunities. According to social exchange theory, a key factor in defining older people's status is the balance between their contributions to society, which are determined by their control of power resources, and the costs of supporting them. Social class predetermines the elderly's possession or absence of valued resources and thus is central to understanding one's power (Denigelis and McIntosh, 1993).

Through the possession of material goods, abilities, achievements, and other qualities defined by society as desirable, individuals are able to exert power in their social relationships. Be-

cause some older people in our society possess fewer power resources than younger people, their status has declined accordingly. Public attitudes about the costs of supporting the older population are illustrated by those who misperceive older people as the underlying cause of rising health, social service, and long-term care costs. Yet, Dowd would argue that the dominant groups within a society attempt to sustain their own interests by perpetuating institutional arrangements. From this perspective, scapegoating of the elderly for "breaking the federal budget" serves the dominant groups' interests.

Exchange theory was not originally formulated by gerontologists, but as a sociological theory first advanced by Homans (1961) and Blau (1964). It includes four basic premises:

1. Individuals and groups act rationally to maximize rewards and minimize costs to themselves, including those of time, energy, effort, and wealth. These transactions are not only economic, but also encompass intrinsic psychological satisfaction. Individuals attempt to choose interactions from which they "profit" in some way. Profit can be in the form of increased social opportunities, enhanced sense of self-worth, or accomplishment. The principle of reciprocity is

Older persons often volunteer as tutors for school-aged children.

implicit in these interactions: people should help those who have assisted them, and should not injure them or retaliation may result.

2.   Individuals use their past experiences to predict the outcomes of similar exchanges in the present. An assessment of the benefits and costs involved includes appraising alternatives for reaching the same goal.

3.   An individual will maintain an interaction as long as it continues to be more rewarding than costly. If the rewards become devalued relative to their cost (what must be done or forfeited in order to attain them), social interactions will cease.

4.   When one individual is dependent on another, the latter accrues power. In other words, power is derived from imbalances in the social exchange, with the individual who values the rewards more highly losing power as the other participant gains power.

Research on family visiting patterns was one of the first applications of social exchange theory to the study of older people (Martin, 1971). Older family members whose only source of power is to remind others of their obligation to visit are put in a dependent and deferent position. Visitors experience little pleasure and satisfaction when faced only with the older person's complaints about their not visiting enough. On the other hand, older family members who have other sources of power, such as a potential inheritance or interesting anecdotes to tell, actually hold the power position, placing the relatives in a dependent position.

The most general and extensive application of exchange theory to explain the status of the elderly has been made by Dowd (1975). He began by criticizing disengagement and activity theories for not addressing the question of why social interaction and activity often decrease with age.

Exchange theory, like activity or disengagement theory, predicts that with increasing age, there is decreasing participation in major social interactions. The basis of this prediction, however, is distinct from the other theoretical approaches. First, the explanation of decreasing social integration of the aged is located in the social system via major social institutions as older people are systematically deprived of valued resources needed for favorable social exchanges. Second, the explanation at the level of individual behaviors does not rely on categorizing the elderly as a unique group. Rather, the processes and outcomes identified could be relevant to any individual experiencing comparable changes in resources. Finally, exchange theory suggests possible remedies to ameliorate the existing low resource condition for many older people.

According to Dowd, reciprocal benefits cannot be assumed in social exchanges; rather, both parties to a social transaction must be examined to determine who is benefiting more and why. Loss of power or the ability to control one's environment is offered as the explanation of why older people, left only with the capacity for compliance, disengage. Older people disengage not because it is mutually satisfying, but because society enjoys a distinct advantage in the power relationship. This power advantage is reflected in the economic and social dependency of older people who have outmoded skills. With little to exchange that is of value, they are forced to accept the retirement role in exchange for limited social services, retirement pensions, and Medicare. Unable to participate in labor markets, they are limited in their access to two valued power resources: material possessions and positions of authority.

The other power resources identified by Dowd are personal characteristics, such as beauty, strength, and intelligence; relational characteristics, such as influential friends or caring children; and generalized reinforcers, such as respect, approval, recognition, and support. All these power resources tend to favor the young. For example, aging generally results in a decline of strength and beauty, as defined by the larger society, reducing older people's power in intergenerational interactions. Dowd maintains that the only major source of power left untouched by the aging process is the category of generalized reinforcers. However, because generalized reinforcers such as respect and approval are more readily available, they are also less valued than other resources, permitting older individuals only minimal ability to influence exchange rates. Dowd (1980) has emphasized the concepts of dependence and deference as indicators of power: power is acquired through the ability to satisfy one's needs without having to depend on or become indebted to other people. For many older people without resources as a basis of power, deference predominates in their interactions.

Despite their limited resources, most older people seek to maintain some degree of reciprocity and to be active, independent agents in the management of their own lives. Dowd suggests that a principle for the development of policies and services for older people should be a quest for strategies to maximize their resources that are valued by our society. In this model, adaptability is a dual process of influencing one's environment as well as adjusting to it. Older individuals are presumed to be able to maximize their power through withholding anticipated rewards and developing their sense of political efficacy and age consciousness. More empirical research is essential to attempt to determine the value of exchange theory as an explanation of the aging process. In particular, research is needed to quantify the somewhat abstract concepts that form this theoretical perspective.

## POLITICAL ECONOMY OF AGING

The argument that social class is a structural barrier to older people's access to valued resources and that dominant groups within society try to sustain their own interests by perpetuating class inequities is basic to the formulation of the political economy of aging (Minkler and Estes, 1984; Walker, 1981). This perspective is less a theory of individual attributes and processes than a macro analysis of structural properties that determine how people adapt in old age. Estes argues that social, political, and economic conditions affect how social problems, including those of the elderly, are defined and treated. Therefore, the major problems faced by older people are socially constructed as a result of our societal conceptions of aging and the aged. These social constructions then take on an objective quality because people act as if they point to concrete realities. The process of aging itself is not the problem; the problems are societal conditions facing older people without adequate income, health and long-term care, or housing—needs that a capitalist society has created. Second, national social and economic policies are the key determinants of the elderly's life conditions. These policies, in turn, reflect the dominance of certain values and normative conceptions of social problems and of how benefits and privileges are distributed. "Solutions," such as Social Security, Medicare, and Medicaid, are viewed as a means of social control designed to meet the dominant needs of the economy (Minkler and Estes, 1984). Social policies are also directly influenced by the state of the economy. In a time of shrinking resources, for example, the federal government has reduced its role in addressing problems faced by older adults. Instead, local responsibility has been emphasized, and problems have been defined as the need for more efficient coordination of fewer resources.

According to Estes, our society's view of older people has tended to set them apart to be a dependent group with needs requiring special policies and programs. The fact that most gerontological research has focused on individual biological and psychological changes to be treated with medical strategies has resulted in the characterization of old age as a time of inevitable physical decline. Estes and Binney (1989) refer to this as the "biomedicalization of aging." This characterization, in turn, justifies the stigmatization and continuing marginality of the elderly. This process, whereby gerontologists stereotype the elderly in terms of the least capable and healthy, has also been referred to as the "New Ageism" (Kalish, 1979). The marginality of the older population is furthered by the development of the "Aging Enterprise," a service industry of agencies, providers, and planners that reaffirms the outgroup status of the elderly in order to maintain their own jobs (Estes, 1979; Kalish, 1979). Policy solutions tend to focus on integrating and socializing older people to adapt to their status, rather than efforts to fundamentally alter social and economic conditions. Such policies also serve to maintain social harmony; for example, services such as senior centers are viewed by Estes (1979) as benefiting middle- and upper-income groups and thus preserving social class differences. Similarly, policies such as Social Security, Medicare, and tax credits do not benefit all older people but only the "deserving" elderly—upper-income and downwardly mobile middle-income groups—and thus perpetuate class inequities (Crystal, 1982; Minkler and Estes, 1984; Nelson, 1982).

The problems of old age have been defined as a crisis that is the result of declining birth rates, increased longevity, and earlier retirement, not the outcome of prior social inaction or economic policy. This definition has resulted in a "scapegoating" of the older population, blaming them for rising health care and Social Security costs (Kalish, 1979). Estes argues that fundamental policy changes are necessary in order to shift perceptions and structural alignments. For example, policies are needed that would not separate the elderly because of their age. Instead, policies should alter both the older population's objective conditions, as well as the social processes by which policies are made and implemented. For instance, the status of older people can be understood within the context of the labor market and the social relations it produces, and how these change with age. Policy interventions from this perspective would be directed toward institutionalized structures, particularly the labor market. The major contribution of Estes's work has been her critical analysis of the larger sociopolitical conditions that generate the necessity for separate social policies for groups such as older adults. The major limitation of her radical critique to date is the lack of empirical research.

## SUMMARY AND IMPLICATIONS

These theoretical perspectives, often drawing on shared concepts such as role loss, all aim to explain the aging process and why some people age more successfully than others. Role theory suggests that the ease with which individuals adjust to aging depends on how they adapt to role changes, such as role ambiguity and discontinuity, that frequently characterize the later years. Activity theory predicts that older people who maintain active roles characteristic of middle age will be more satisfied than less involved older people. In contrast, disengagement theory contends that withdrawal from such active roles is conducive to satisfaction in old age, as well as beneficial for society.

Continuity theory emphasizes the continuity of roles, personality, and relationships, while the life course perspective acknowledges both role gain and loss, continuity and discontinuity across life, and patterned differentiation identified as different effective life styles. The viewpoint that the elderly form a subculture is focused less on the types of roles performed by older people than on their frequent interaction with one another, which forms the basis for a homogeneous subculture of the aged.

Age stratification theory builds on the basic sociological constructs of role, status, norms, and socialization to provide a framework for understanding the position of older people in society. Age is viewed as one criterion for assigning roles to individuals, with the result that people are divided into age strata. Within the age stratification system, both individual lives and social structures are subject to change. Since age strata have differential access to rewards, structured inequality exists among different age strata.

Interactionist perspectives emphasize the interrelationship of individuals with their physical and social environments. Labeling and social breakdown theories describe a cycle in which the older person, who is defined in a negative or limiting way by society, begins to internalize and to act on those definitions, and thus reinforces the initial stereotype. An interactionist approach to intervention, such as the social reconstruction model, involves altering the environment to make adaptation easier.

The concept that unequal access to power resources determines social status and life changes is fundamental to social exchange theory. From this perspective, lesser access to power resources underlies the elderly's declining status, rather than their desire to disengage or their inability to remain active in roles characteristic of middle age.

The political economy theory attributes problems of aging to social constructs and public policies. It argues that current academic and governmental approaches to aging tend to preserve, rather than challenge, underlying social and economic inequities. Solutions must involve fundamental policy changes to alter both social perceptions and objective conditions of the aged.

Thus far, none of these theories adequately explains social aging, but rather describes different aspects of older people's roles in our society. None of these theories is universal. As we have noted, there is no one course of "normal" aging; not all older people disengage or lose power as they age. Nor do any of these theoretical perspectives fully account for the wide variations or multiple dimensions in aging experiences. Instead, as noted by Marshall in a 1994 review of the legacy of the Kansas City Studies, aging is a set of processes occurring at different levels, from the personality to passages through social structure; the relationships between aging processes at these different levels are not straightforward, so that social aging cannot be predicted from psychological aging and so on (p. 773). The development of one "grand theory" of aging is unlikely, as shown by the failure of disengagement theory to meet this goal (Marshall, 1994). Yet the growth of these theoretical models has laid the framework for future research directions. As the social, economic, and political conditions affecting older people change, new theoretical perspectives must be developed or former ones revised through the process of empirical research in a variety of sociocultural contexts.

We now turn to reviewing age-related physical and psychological changes that may create both constraints and opportunities for how people age socially.

## REFERENCES

Achenbaum, W. A., and Bengtson, V. C. "Re-engaging the disengagement theory of aging: Or the history and assessment of theory development in gerontology." *The Gerontologist*, 1994, *34*(6), 756–763.

Atchley, R. C. A continuity theory of normal aging. *The Gerontologist*, 1989, *29*, 183–190.

Baltes, P. B. "Theoretical propositions of life-span developmental psychology: On the dynamics between growth and decline," Baltes, P. B. (Ed.). *Developmental Psychology*, 1987, *23*, 611–626.

Bengtson, V. C. "Cultural and occupational differences in level of present role activity in retirement." In *Adjustments to retirement: A cross-national study*, R. J. Havinghurst, J. M. A. Munnicks, B. C. Neugarten, and H. Thomas (Eds.), 35–53. Assen, The Netherlands: Van Gorkum, 1969.

Bengtson, V. *The social psychology of aging*. Indianapolis, Ind.: Bobbs-Merrill, 1973.

Blau, P. *Exchange and power in social life*. New York: John Wiley & Sons, 1964.

Brown, A. S. Satisfying relationships for elderly and their patterns of disengagement. *The Gerontologist*, 1974, *14*, 258–262.

Burgess, E. W. *Aging in western societies*. Chicago: University of Chicago Press, 1960, 20.

Carp, F. M. Some components of disengagement. *Journal of Gerontology*, 1968, *23*, 382–386.

Cottrell, L. The adjustment of the individual to his age and sex roles. *American Sociological Review*, 1942, *7*, 617–620.

Covey, H. "A reconceptualization of continuity theory: Some preliminary thoughts." *The Gerontologist*, 1981, *21*, 628–633.

Crystal, S. *America's old age crisis*. New York: Basic Books, 1982.

Cumming, E. Further thought on the theory of disengagement. *International Social Science Journal*, 1963, *15*, 377–393.

Cumming, E. Engagement with an old theory. *Aging and Human Development*, 1975, *6*, 187–191.

Cumming, E., and Henry, W. E. *Growing old*. New York: Basic Books, 1961.

Danigelis, N., and McIntosh, B. "Resources and the productive activity of elders: Race and gender as contexts." *Journals of Gerontology*, 1993, *48*(4), S192-S203.

DeBeauvoir, S. *The coming of age*. New York: Putnam and Sons, 1972.

Dowd, J. J. Aging as exchange: A preface to theory. *Journal of Gerontology*, 1975, *30*, 584–594.

Dowd, J. J. *Stratification among the aged*. Monterey, Calif: Brooks Cole, 1980.

Ekerdt, D. J., and DeViney, S. "Evidence for a preretirement process among older male workers." *Journals of Gerontology*, 1993, *48*(2), S35-S43.

Estes, C. *The aging enterprise*. San Francisco: Jossey Bass, 1979.

Estes, C., and Binney, E. The biomedicalization of aging: Dangers and dilemmas. *The Gerontologist*, 1989, *29*, 587–596.

Foner, A. Age in society: Structures and change. *American Behavioral Scientist*, 1975, *19*, 289–312.

Foner, A., and Kertzer, D. Transitions over the life course: Lessons from age-set societies. *American Journal of Sociology*, 1978, *83*, 1081–1104.

Foner, N. *Ages in conflict: A cross-cultural perspective on inequality between old and young*. NY: Columbia University Press, 1984.

Fox, J. H. Perspectives on the continuity perspective. *International Journal of Aging and Human Development*, 1981–82, *14*, 97–115.

Gibson, R. "Minority aging research: Opportunity and challenge." *The Gerontologist*, 1988, *28*, 559–560.

Gubrium, J. F. *The myth of the golden years*. Springfield, Ill.: Charles C. Thomas, 1973.

Gutmann, D. L. Alternatives to disengagement: Aging among the Highland Druze. In R. LaVine (Ed.), *Culture and personality: Contemporary readings*. Chicago: Aldine, 1974.

Gutmann, D. L., Grunes, J., and Griffin, B. The clinical psychology of later life: Developmental paradigm. In N. Datan and N. Lohman (Eds.), *Life span developmental psychology: Transitions of aging*. New York: Academic Press, 1980.

Hagestad, G., and Neugarten, B. Age and the life course. In R. H. Binstock and E. Shanas (Eds.), *Handbook of aging and the social sciences* (2d ed.). New York: Van Nostrand, 1985.

Havighurst, R. J. Successful aging. In R. Williams, C. Tibbits, and W. Donahue (Eds.), *Processes of aging* (Vol. 1). New York: Atherton Press, 1963.

Havighurst, R. J. Personality and patterns of aging. *The Gerontologist*, 1968, *8*, 20–23.

Havighurst, R. J., Munnichs, J.M.A., Neugarten, B. L., and Thomae, H. *Adjustment to retirement*. The Netherlands: Van Goreum and Company, N.V., 1969.

Havighurst, R. J., Neugarten, B. L., and Tobin, S. S. Disengagement and patterns of aging. In B. L. Neugarten (Ed.), *Middle age and aging*. Chicago: University of Chicago Press, 1968, 161.

Herzog, A. R., and House, J. S. "Productive activities and aging well." *Generations*, 1991, XV 49–54.

Herzog, A.; Kahn, R.; Morgan, J.; Jackson, J., and Antonucci, T. "Age differences in productive activities." *Journals of Gerontology*, 1989, *44*(4), S129-S138.

Hochschild, A. Disengagement theory: A critique and proposal. *American Sociological Review*, 1975, *40*, 553–569.

Homans, G. *Social behavior: Its elementary forms*. New York: Harcourt, Brace and World, 1961.

Kalish, R. The new ageism and the failure models: A polemic. *The Gerontologist*, 1979, *19*, 398–402.

Kuypers, J. A., and Bengtson, V. L. Social breakdown and competence: A model of normal aging. *Human Development*, 1973, *16*, 181–201.

Lee, D. J. and Markides, K. S. Activity and mortality among aged persons over an eight year period. *Journals of Gerontology*, 1990, *45*, S39–S42.

Lemon, B., Bengtson, V., and Peterson, J. Activity types and life satisfaction in a retirement community. *Journal of Gerontology*, 1972, *27*, 511–523.

Levin, J., and Levin, W. C. *Ageism: Prejudice and discrimination against the elderly*. Belmont, Calif.: Wadsworth, 1980.

Longino, C. F., and Kart, C. S. Explicating activity theory: A formal replication. *Journal of Gerontology*, 1982, *37*, 713–722.

Maddox, G. L. "Lives through the years revisited." *The Gerontologist*, 1994, *34*(6), 764–767.

Marshall, V. W. "Sociology, psychology in the theoretical legacy of the Kansas City studies." *The Gerontologist*, 1994, *34*(6), 768–774.

Martin, J. D. Power, dependence, and the complaints of the elderly: A social exchange perspective. *Aging and Human Development*, 1971, *2*, 108–112.

Minkler, M., and Estes, C. *Readings in the political economy of aging.* Farmingdale, N.Y.: Baywood, 1984.

Nelson, G. Social class and public policy for the elderly. *Social Science Review,* 1982, *56,* 85–107.

Neugarten, B., Havighurst, R. J., and Tobin, S. S. In B. L. Neugarten (Ed.), *Personality and patterns of aging in middle age and aging.* Chicago: University of Chicago Press, 1968, 173–177.

Neugarten, B., and Moore, J. The changing age-status system. In B. Neugarten (Ed.), *Middle age and aging.* Chicago: University of Chicago Press, 1968.

Palmore, E. The effects of aging on activities and attitudes. *The Gerontologist,* 1968, *8,* 259–263.

Palmore, E. (Ed.). *Normal aging II: Reports from the Duke longitudinal study.* Durham, N.C.: Duke University Press, 1974.

Palmore, E. Predictors of successful aging. *The Gerontologist,* 1979, *19,* 427–431.

Phillips, B. A role theory approach to adjustment in old age. *American Sociological Review,* 1957, *22,* 212–217.

Prasad, S. B. The retirement postulate of the disengagement theory. *The Gerontologist,* 1964, *4,* 20–23.

Rice, S. "Single, older childless women: Differences between never-married and widowed women in life satisfaction and social support." *Journal of Gerontological Social Work,* 1989, *13*(3/4), 35–47.

Riley, M. W. Social gerontology and the age stratification of society. *The Gerontologist,* 1971, *11,* 79–87.

Riley, M. W. Age strata in social systems. In R. H. Binstock and E. Shanas (Eds.), *Handbook of aging and the social sciences* (2d ed.). New York: Van Nostrand, 1985, 369–414.

Riley, M. W., and Foner, A. *Aging and society: An inventory of research findings.* New York: Russell Sage Foundation, 1968.

Riley, M. W., Johnson, J., and Foner, A. *Aging and society* (Vol. 3): *A sociology of age stratification.* New York: Russell Sage Foundation, 1972.

Rose, A. M. A current theoretical issue in social gerontology. In A. M. Rose and W. A. Peterson (Eds.), *Older people and their social worlds.* Philadelphia: F. A. Davis, 1965.

Rosow, I. Status and role change through the life cycle. In R. H. Binstock and E. Shanas (Eds.), *Handbook of aging and the social sciences* (2d ed.). New York: Van Nostrand, 1985, 62–93.

Sinnott, J. D. Sex-role inconstancy, biology, and successful aging: A dialectical model. *The Gerontologist,* 1977, *17,* 459–463.

Streib, G. F., and Schneider, C. J. *Retirement in American society.* Ithaca, N.Y.: Cornell University Press, 1971.

Tallmer, M., and Kutner, B. Disengagement and morale. *The Gerontologist,* 1970, *10,* 317–320.

Thurmond, G., and Belcher, J. Dimensions of disengagement among black and white rural elderly. *International Journal of Aging and Human Development.* 1980–81, *12,* 245–265.

Tindale, J. A., and Marshall, V. W. A generational conflict perspective for gerontology. In V. W. Marshall (Ed.), *Aging in Canada: Social perspectives.* Don Mills, Ontario: Fitzhenry and Whiteside, 1980, 43–50.

Walker, A. Toward a political economy of old age. *Aging and Society,* 1981, *1,* 73–94.

Waring, J. M. Social replenishment and social change. The problems of disordered cohort flow. *American Behavioral Science,* 1975, *19,* 237–256.

Williams, R. H. and Wirths, C. G. *Lives through the years.* New York: Atherton Press, 1965.

Youmans, E. G. Disengagement among older rural and urban men. In E. G. Youmans (Ed.), *Older rural Americans.* Lexington: University of Kentucky Press, 1967.

Zusman, J. Some explanations of the changing appearance of psychotic patients: Antecedents of the Social Breakdown Syndrome Concept. *The Milbank Memorial Fund Quarterly,* 1966, *44,* 363–394.

# PART Two

# THE BIOLOGICAL AND PHYSIOLOGICAL CONTEXT OF SOCIAL AGING

If we are to understand how older people differ from younger age groups, and why the field of gerontology has evolved as a separate discipline, we must first review the normal changes in biological and physiological structures as well as diseases that impair these systems and affect the day-to-day functioning of older persons. Part II provides this necessary background. Normal changes in major organ systems and how they influence the older person's ability to perform activities of daily living and to interact with their social and physical environments are described in Chapter 5. This area of research has received considerable attention as scientists have explored the basic processes of aging. Numerous theories have been developed to explain observable changes such as wrinkles, gray hair, stooped shoulders, and slower response time, as well as other biological functions that can only be inferred from tests of physiologic function. These include changes in the heart, lungs, kidneys, and bones. There are many normal changes in these organ systems within the same person that do not imply disease, but in fact may slow down the older person. Furthermore,

significant differences have been observed among people and among organ systems within the same person in the degree of change experienced. The implications of these changes for the maximum life span of humans are discussed.

Age-related changes in the five major senses are the focus of Chapter 6. Because sensory functions are so critical for our daily interactions with our social and physical environments, and because many of the normal declines observed in sensory systems are a model of changes throughout the body, it is useful to focus on each sensory system and its role in linking individuals with their environments. The implications of biological changes in each system for older individuals' abilities to adapt to and interact with the world around them are also discussed in Chapter 6. Recommendations are made for modifying the environment and for communicating with older people who are experiencing significant declines in vision, hearing, taste, smell, touch, and even in their kinesthetic sense.

Chapter 7 focuses on secondary aging, i.e., diseases of the organ systems described in Chapters 5 and 6, and how these diseases can affect older people's social functioning. Acute and chronic diseases are differentiated, and the impact of these diseases on the demand for health and social services is presented. The growing problem of AIDS among older persons and implications for long-term care are discussed. Moreover, since automobile accidents among older people often result because of psychomotor changes associated with aging, methods to reduce auto fatalities through new programs in driver training and through better environmental design are considered in this chapter. Chapter 7 also provides some striking statistics on older people's use of health services, barriers to their use, and recommendations for enhancing utilization. Most existing medical, dental, and mental health services do not adequately address the special needs of the older population. As a result, older people who could benefit most from the services fail to use them. The dynamic interactions between older people and their environments are acknowledged in a theoretical model that explains differences in the use of health and long-term care services. According to this model, some segments of the older population are unable or unlikely to use existing services because the services are not appropriate for their physical and economic needs and abilities. As a result, it is important to design health and long-term care services that fulfill the needs of frail, low-income, and ethnic minority elderly in order to maximize use among these groups, who have traditionally underutilized formal services. Health promotion has proven successful in maintaining and even improving older people's health in many areas, including exercise, prevention of falls and osteoporosis, and nutrition. Chapter 7 describes some of these programs and the diversity of people who have benefited from them.

Throughout Part II, the tremendous variations in how people age physically are emphasized. Because of genetic, lifestyle, and environmental factors, some people will show dramatic declines in all of their organ systems at a relatively early age. Most older people, however, will experience varied rates of decline in different systems. For example, some people may suffer from chronic heart disease, yet at the same time maintain strong bones and muscle strength. In contrast, others may require medications for painful osteoarthritis, but their heart and lungs remain in excellent condition. The following vignettes illustrate these variations:

### A Healthy Older Person

Mrs. Hill is an 84-year-old widow. She has been slightly deaf all her life, has some recent loss of vision, and has to watch her blood pressure, primarily by paying attention to her diet. Despite her minor physical limitations, Mrs. Hill is able to get around to visit her many friends, neighbors, and family in the community. She is still able to drive, walk to the local grocery store almost daily, and take bus trips to visit her grandchildren. Active in the local senior center, she was one of the first participants in a health promotion project for older adults at the center. Now she exercises at the center three times a week and tries not to miss the lunches on Mondays and Wednesdays. She rarely visits the doctor except for an annual check-up. She does admit to getting frustrated by her reduced energy and the need to slow down, but, for the most part, she accepts these changes and adjusts her physical activities accordingly. Her son-in-law has made some minor modifications in her home, especially in the height and location of kitchen shelves, so that her daily routine is an easy one for her. Friends and relatives are frequently telling her how she does not look her age; she, in turn, becomes impatient with older people who stay home all the time, watch TV, and complain. She is usually optimistic about her situation, believing that throughout life a person has to accept the bad with the good.

### An Older Person with Chronic Illness

Mr. Jones, age 69, had a stroke at age 64 and is paralyzed on his left side, so he is unable to walk. The stroke has also left him with slightly slurred speech and some personality changes. His wife states that he is not the kind, gentle man she used to know. He has to be lifted from bed to chair and recently became incontinent. His wife first tried to care for him at home, but after he became incontinent, she felt she could no longer handle the responsibility and made the difficult decision to institutionalize him. Both Mr. and Mrs. Jones are having difficulty adjusting to the nursing home placement. Since Mr. Jones remains mentally alert and aware of all the changes, he continually expresses his frustration with his physical limitations and with his forced retirement and reduced income. Their children live in another state and have been unable to help their mother with the daily care or the financial burden of the nursing home. In fact, the children are critical of their mother's decision to institutionalize their father because they think she should have kept him at home, no matter what. As their financial resources dwindle, Mr. and Mrs. Jones are facing the need to apply for Medicaid to cover nursing home costs. Mr. Jones starts to cry easily, sobbing that he is losing control of his life and that his life was never meant to be like this. Mrs. Jones feels angry that her caregiving efforts have not been appreciated and that her husband is so difficult.

These two vignettes point to the complexity of physiological aging. Chronological age is often a poor predictor of health and functional status, as illustrated by Mrs. Hill's excellent functional and emotional health, and Mr. Jones's situation of physical dependency, even though he is 15 years younger than Mrs. Hill. Part II describes these variations in physical health and sensory function that are related to normal aging, contrasts these with changes due to disease, and presents factors that influence older people's health care behavior.

# CHAPTER 5

# THE SOCIAL CONSEQUENCES OF BIOLOGICAL AGING

When asked to describe the physical aspects of aging, most people think only of the visible signs—graying hair, balding among some men, wrinkled skin, stooped shoulders, and a slower walk or shuffling gait. Although these are the most visible signs of old age among humans, there are numerous other changes that occur in our internal organs—the heart, lungs, kidneys, stomach, bladder, and central nervous system. These changes are not as easy to detect because they are not visible. In fact, x-rays and computer-assisted images of organ systems are not very useful for showing most changes that take place. It is primarily by measuring the functional capacity of these systems (i.e., the performance capacity of the heart, lungs, kidneys, and other organs) that their relative efficiency across the life span can be determined.

Biological aging, or *senescence,* can be defined as the normal process of changes over time in the body and its components, a process that eventually affects an individual's functioning vis-à-vis the environment but does not necessarily result in disease or death. As noted in the Introduction, this process is gradual and common to all living organisms. It is not, in itself, a disease, but aging and disease are often linked in most people's minds, since declines in organ capacity and internal protective mechanisms do make us more vulnerable to sickness. Because certain diseases such as Alzheimer's, arthritis, and heart conditions have a higher incidence with age, we may erroneously equate age with disease. However, a more appropriate conception of the aging process is a gradual accumulation of irreversible functional losses to which the average person tries to accommodate in some socially acceptable manner. Conversely, people may attempt to alter their physical and social environments by reducing the demands placed on their remaining functional capacity (e.g., relocating to a one-story home or apartment to avoid stairs; selecting a larger, safer car; avoiding crowds). Individual differences are evident in the rate and severity of physical changes, as illustrated by the vignettes of Mrs. Hill and Mr. Jones. Not all people show the same degree of change in any given organ system, nor do all the systems change at the same rate and at the same time. Individual aging depends largely on genetic inheritance, nutrition and diet, physical activity, and environment.

In this chapter, normal age-related changes in major organs of the human body are reviewed. The implications of these changes for older people's ability to interact with their social and physical environments, and the impact of system deterioration and disease on life expectancy, are examined within the context of personal competence vis-à-vis the environment. In the next chapter, the diseases of aging that may impair organ functions more than would be expected from normal aging will be discussed. First, it is useful to examine the major theories of biological aging that have been advanced to explain the changes in all living organisms over time.

## BIOLOGICAL THEORIES OF AGING

The process of aging is complex and multi-dimensional, involving significant loss and decline in some physiological functions, and minimal change in others. Scientists have long attempted to find the causes for this process. A theme of some theories is that aging is a process that is programmed into the genetic structure of each species. Other theories state that aging represents an accumulation of stimuli from the environment that produce stress on the organism. Any theory of aging must be based on the scientific method, using systematic tests of hypotheses and empirical observations; in addition, biological theories must meet the following three criteria (Rockstein and Sussman, 1979):

1. The aging phenomenon described must be evident in all members of a given species.
2. The process must progress with time.
3. The process must have a deteriorating effect on the organism, leading finally to organ or system failure.

Each of the following theories meets these criteria, although the evidence to support them is not always clear. Even though these theories help our understanding of aging, none of them is totally adequate for explaining what *causes* aging.

*The Wear and Tear Theory* suggests that, with time, the organism simply wears out (Wilson, 1974). In this model, aging is a pre-programmed process; that is, each species has a biological clock that determines its maximum life span and the rate at which each organ system will deteriorate. This process is compounded by the effects of external stress on the organism (e.g., nutrient deficiencies). Cells continually wear out, and existing cells cannot repair damaged components within themselves. This is particularly true in tissues that are located in the striated skeletal and heart muscle and throughout the nervous system; these tissues are composed of cells that cannot undergo cell division. As we will see later, these systems are most likely to experience significant decline in their ability to function effectively with age.

*The Autoimmune Theory* proposes that aging is a function of the body's immune system becoming defective and attacking not just foreign proteins, bacteria, and viruses, but also producing antibodies against itself. This explanation of the immune system is consistent with the process of many diseases that increase with age, such as cancer, diabetes, and rheumatoid arthritis (Walford, 1969). Nevertheless, this theory does not explain why the immune system becomes defective with age; only the *effects* of this change are described. For example, the thymus gland, which controls production of disease-fighting white blood cells, shrinks with aging, but the reasons for both this reduction in size and why *more* older people do not suffer from autoimmune diseases are unclear.

*The Cross-Linkage Theory* (Bjorksten, 1974) focuses on the changes in collagen with age. Collagen is an important connective tissue found in most organ systems. As a person ages, there are clearly observable changes in collagen, for instance, wrinkling of the skin. These changes lead to a loss of elasticity in blood vessels, muscle tissue, skin, the lens of the eye, and other organs, and to slower wound healing. Another visible effect of changes in collagen is that the nose and ears tend to increase in size. These changes are due to the binding of essential molecules in the cells through the accumulation of cross-linking compounds, which in turn slows the process of normal cell functions.

A special case of the cross-linkage theory is the *Free Radical Theory* of aging (Harman, 1956, 1981). Free radicals are highly reactive chemical compounds possessing an unpaired electron. Produced normally by the use of oxygen within the cell, they interact with other cell molecules and may cause DNA mutations, cross-linking of connective tissue, changes in protein behavior, and other damage. Such reactions continue until one free radical pairs with another or meets an *antioxidant,* which can safely absorb the extra electron. It has been proposed that the ingestion of antioxidants such as vitamin E and beta carotene can inhibit free radical damage; this can then slow the aging process by delaying the loss of immune function and reducing the incidence of many diseases associated with aging (Cutler and Cutler, 1983; Harman, 1981).

Nevertheless, it appears that free radicals are not totally destroyed. Those that survive in the organism damage the proteins needed to make cells in the body by interacting with the oxygen used to produce protein. As a result, free radicals may destroy the fragile process of cell-building and the DNA strands that transmit messages of genes. Some have argued that this continuous pounding by dangerous oxidants wears away the organism over time, not just by interfering with cell-building but also by requiring antioxidants to be ever-vigilant. This damage to cell tissue by free radicals has been implicated in normal aging, as well as in the development of some cancers, heart disease, Alzheimer's disease, and Parkinson's disease.

Molecular biologists have explored this theory further by splicing genes to measure the cumulative effects of free radicals in cells, with the goal of developing ways to counter these effects. It may be that synthetic antioxidants can be developed and administered to older people as the body's natural supply is depleted. Animal studies have shown dramatic enhancements of memory and physical activity with high doses of antioxidants. It may be that the free radical theory holds the greatest promise for reversing the aging process in the future.

*The Cellular Aging Theory* suggests that aging occurs as cells slow their number of replications. Hayflick (1970) reported that cells grown in culture (i.e., in controlled laboratory environments) undergo a finite number of replications, approaching 50 doublings. Cells from older subjects replicate even fewer times, as do cells derived from individuals with *progeria,* a rare condition in which aging is accelerated and death may occur by age 15 to 20. In addition, proponents of this theory point out that each cell has a given level of DNA that is eventually depleted. This in turn reduces the production of RNA, which is essential for producing enzymes necessary for cellular functioning. Hence, the loss of DNA and subsequent reduction of RNA eventually results in cell death (Goldstein and Reis, 1984).

Of all the theories of physiological aging, the *cellular* theory appears to explain best the causes and processes of aging. The role of cell replication and RNA production in aging is widely accepted in the scientific community. It should not be assumed, however, that the step from understanding to reversing the process of aging will be achieved soon. It is often erroneously assumed that scientific discoveries of the *cause* of a particular physiological process or disease can immediately lead to *changing* or reversing that condition. Unfortunately, that step is a difficult one to make, as evidenced by research progress in cancer. Scientists have long observed the structural changes in cancer cells, but the reasons for these changes are far from being understood. Without a clear understanding of why a particular biological process takes place, it is impossible to move toward reversing that process.

## CAN AGING BE REVERSED OR DELAYED?

Nevertheless, genetic researchers have made great strides in the past 30 years in their understanding of the aging process. Indeed, contrary to our long-held assumptions about aging, many scientists have become convinced that aging is *reversible*. This may be achieved by introducing new hormones into the body to replace the depleted hormones in genes that serve as chemical messengers. Researchers at the National Institute on Aging, VA centers, and universities around the country are testing the effects of injecting growth hormones into aging animals and humans. So far many startling discoveries have been made, such as increased lean muscle mass and vertebral bone density, and reduced fat levels. These changes in turn led to increased activity and vigor. While these effects are short-lived, it may not be long before a human growth hormone is marketed that can safely be administered on a regular basis, like daily doses of vitamins.

One promising compound that is being tested by U.S. and French researchers is the molecule dehydroepiandrosterone, or DHEA. This molecule is secreted by the adrenal glands after age 7 and declines significantly by age 70. Preliminary studies in which DHEA was given orally have shown improved sleep, greater energy, and greater tolerance of stress. The effects were sustained up to three months (Morales, et al, 1994; Mortola & Yen, 1990). While these and other experiments with growth hormones and other compounds are still in their infancy, they offer promise of extending active life expectancy for future cohorts of older adults. That is, they may not add years to the human life span, but will more likely add life to the years.

Several studies using animal models (fruit flies, rodents, rhesus monkeys) have demonstrated that reducing caloric intake by 65 percent increased the life span of experimental animals by as much as 35 percent. Dietary restriction did not, however, include limiting nutrients in these studies. Indeed, the only beneficial effects have been found with fat intake. Caloric restriction that was accomplished mostly through reducing fat intake has been found to be most successful in extending the life of experimental animals. These studies have also found that caloric restriction reduces the growth of tumors, delays kidney dysfunction, decreases loss of muscle mass, and slows other age-related changes ordinarily found in these animals (Ausman & Russell, 1990; Masoro, 1990; Walford, Harris & Weindruch, 1987). While this area of research is

### STUDIES OF VITAMIN E AND AGING

Vitamin E is a fat-soluble substance that has long been known to be important for membrane structure and metabolism, and more recently as a natural antioxidant. It has been suggested that antioxidants can slow cellular aging, and thereby extend the life span through the process of depressing appetite and reducing food intake, in this manner delaying growth and maturation. Antioxidants have also been hypothesized to suppress tumor growth and slow the decline of immune processes. Animal studies that have tested the addition of vitamin E to mice diets have found some increases in survival. It has been found to reduce the levels of lipofuscin in the heart, liver, and testes of mice. Well-controlled studies with human populations are lacking; therefore, it is too early to conclude that antioxidants such as vitamin E can slow the aging process in humans. However, consumption of very high levels of vitamin E (greater than 1,000 international units per day) has been associated with increased mortality in some groups of people over age 65 (Schneider and Reed, 1985).

not yet ready for clinical trials in humans, it is noteworthy that obesity among participants in the Baltimore Longitudinal Studies of Aging was associated with an average age of death that was 2–3 years younger than older persons within the normal weight range. These studies offer further support for improving active life expectancy rather than merely extending life span.

## RESEARCH ON PHYSIOLOGICAL CHANGES WITH AGE

It is difficult to distinguish normal, age-related changes in many human functions from changes that are secondary to disease or other factors. Until the late 1950s, much of our knowledge about aging came from cross-sectional comparisons of healthy, young persons with institutionalized or community-dwelling elderly who had multiple health problems. These comparisons led to the not surprising conclusion that the organ systems of older persons function less efficiently than those of younger persons.

Since the 1950s, a series of longitudinal studies have been undertaken with healthy younger and middle-aged persons who have been followed for several years to determine changes in various physiological parameters. The first of these studies began in 1958 at the Gerontology Research Center in Baltimore, as described in Chapter 2. The initial sample of 600 healthy males between the ages of 20 and 96 was expanded in 1978 to include females. Today, many of the people in the original sample are still participating in the study. Another longitudinal study was undertaken in 1955 at Duke University's Center for the Study of Aging, with a sample composed entirely of older adults. Some of these individuals were followed every two years for more than 20 years (Palmore, 1974, 1985). Many other researchers around the country are now examining physiological functions longitudinally. The information in this chapter is derived from their work.

## Aging in Body Composition

Although individuals vary greatly in body weight and composition, there is a general decline in the proportion of body weight contributed by water for both men and women: on the average, from 60 percent to 54 percent in men, and from 52 percent to 46 percent in women (Kenney, 1982). Lean body mass in muscle tissue is lost, whereas the proportion of fat increases (see Figure 5–1). Because of an increase in fibrous material, there is a loss of elasticity and flexibility in muscle tissue. After age 50, the number of muscle fibers steadily decreases, although exercise can still increase muscle tone. These changes in body composition have a significant effect on older people's ability to metabolize many medications.

With advanced old age, there is a tendency toward weight loss. This is why we rarely see people in their eighties and nineties who are obese. The balance of sodium and potassium also changes, with the ratio of sodium increasing by 20 percent from age 30 to 70. Changes in body composition also have implications for the diets of older people; although older people generally need fewer total calories per day than active younger people, it is important for them to consume a higher proportion of protein, calcium, and vitamin D (Guigoz and Munro, 1985). However, many older individuals do not change their diet during the later years unless advised specifically by a physician. Others, especially those living alone, eat poorly balanced meals.

## Changes in the Skin

As stated at the beginning of this chapter, changes in the appearance and texture of skin and hair are often the most visible signs of aging. These also tend to have deleterious consequences on how older people view themselves and are perceived by others. The human skin is unique among all other mammals in that it is exposed directly to the elements, with no protective fur or feathers to shield it from the direct effects of sunlight. In fact, ultraviolet light from the sun, which

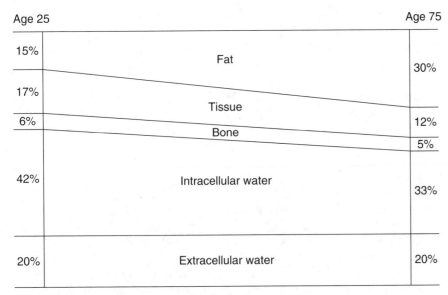

**FIGURE 5–1** **Distribution of Major Body Components**
SOURCE: Reprinted with permission from the American Geriatrics Society. Speculations on vascular changes with age, by R. J. Goldman (*Journal of the American Geriatrics Society,* Vol. 18, p. 766, 1970).

damages the elastic fibers beneath the skin's surface, is probably most directly responsible for the wrinkled, dried, and tougher texture of older people's skin. This is evident when one compares the appearance of the skin of two 75-year-olds: one a retired farmer who has worked under the sun most of his life, the other a retired office worker who has spent most of his years indoors. The farmer generally will have more wrinkles; darker pigmentation known as *melanin,* which has been produced by the body to protect it from ultraviolet rays; and drier skin with a leathery texture. He is also more likely to have so-called *age spots* or *liver spots*—harmless from a health standpoint but of concern sometimes for their appearance. As one might expect, people who spend most of their lives in sunny climates are more prone to these changes. There is now growing concern about the negative consequences of extensive exposure to the sun, such as premature wrinkling and the disease state of skin cancers.

Besides these environmental factors, the human body itself is responsible for some of the changes in the skin with age. The outermost layer of skin, the epidermis, constantly replenishes itself by shedding dead cells and replacing them with new cells. As the person gets older, the process of cell replacement is slowed, up to 50 percent between ages 30 and 70 (Leyden, McGinley, and Grove, 1978). More importantly, the connective tissue that makes up the second layer of skin, the *dermis,* becomes less elastic with age. This results in reduced elasticity and thickness of the outer skin layer, longer time for the skin to spring back into shape, and increased sagging and wrinkling. Women often experience these problems earlier than men, sometimes in their twenties and thirties. This is because women tend to have less oil in the sebaceous glands. However, there is considerable variation in the process of skin change, depending on the relative amount of oil in the glands, exposure to the sun, and heredity. Despite its changing appearance, the skin can still perform its protective function throughout old age.

Wound healing is also slower in older persons. Thus, people over age 65 require 50 percent more time than those under age 35 to form blisters as a means of closing a wound, and more time to form new epithelial tissue to replace blistered skin (Gilchrest, 1982).

The sebaceous and sweat glands, located in the dermis, generally deteriorate with age. Changes also occur in the deepest, or *subcutaneous,* skin layers, which tend to lose fat and water. This can damage the effectiveness of the skin's temperature regulatory mechanism and make older people more sensitive to hot and cold temperatures. As a result, older persons' comfort zone for ambient temperature is generally three to five degrees warmer than that for younger persons. It also takes longer for an older person to adjust after being exposed to either hot or cold extreme temperatures. This leaves the older individual much more vulnerable to hypothermia (low body temperature, sometimes resulting in brain damage and death) and hyperthermia (heat stroke), as evidenced by reports of increased accidental deaths among the elderly during periods of extremely cold winter weather

and during prolonged heat spells. It is recommended that indoor temperatures be set above 68°F in older people's homes, and that humidity be minimized; even though some older people are concerned about conserving energy and money by lowering their thermostats below 68°F, especially at night (Collins, 1986; Kolanowski and Gunter, 1981; Macey, 1989; Macey & Schneider, 1993).

## Changes in the Hair

As we age, we also experience changes in the appearance and texture of our hair. Hair is thickest in early adulthood and decreases by as much as 20 percent in diameter by age 70. This is why so many older people appear to have fine, limp-looking hair. This change is compounded by the increased loss of hair with age. Although we lose up to 60 strands of hair daily during youth and early adulthood, the hair is replaced regularly through the action of estrogen and testosterone. As we age, however, more hairs are lost than

---

### SYMPTOMS OF HYPOTHERMIA AND HYPERTHERMIA

*Hypothermia* is defined as body temperatures below 95°F over a long period. It occurs when an individual's shivering response cannot be activated because of systemic changes or because it is ineffective after prolonged exposure to cold. Symptoms of hypothermia can appear in just a few hours, or over several days. These include confusion and forgetfulness, problems with speaking or breathing, shivering, sleepiness, poor coordination, a puffy face, and a stomach that is cold to touch in the early stages. In the late stages, the skin becomes very cold, pupils become fixed, and the body becomes more rigid. Body heat is lost faster than it can be replaced, resulting in an inability to raise one's body heat, loss of functional capacities, confusion, disorientation, and, in extreme cases, death. Older people who cannot afford to keep their homes heated above 68°F in the winter are at higher risk for hypothermia (Avery, 1984).

*Hyperthermia,* on the other hand, occurs when body temperature rises above normal and cannot be relieved by sweating, which results in heat exhaustion, heat stroke, heart failure, and stroke. Dizziness, nausea, vomiting, dry skin, cramps, fainting, and confusion may be initial symptoms. The problem is aggravated in older persons because of a reduced efficiency in their sweating response. Those who are overweight or have kidney problems, high blood pressure, poor circulation, diabetes, or emphysema are more vulnerable to hyperthermia than healthy older people. Older people with low income levels who live in houses with no air conditioning are at great risk for hyperthermia in climates where temperatures exceed 90°F with high humidity for several days in a row (Macey and Schneider, 1993).

replaced, especially in men. Some men experience rapid hair loss, leading to a receding hairline or even complete baldness by their mid-forties. Reasons for the observed variation in hair loss are not clear, but genetic factors appear to play a role.

Gray hair is a result of loss of pigment in the hair follicles. As we age, there is less pigment produced at the roots, so that eventually all the hair becomes colorless, or white in appearance. The gray color of some people's hair is an intermediate stage of pigment loss. In fact, some people may never experience a total loss of pigment production, but will live into an advanced old age with relatively dark hair. Others may experience graying in their twenties. In our society, graying of hair tends to have more stigma associated with it for women than for men.

## Changes in the Musculo-skeletal System

Stature or height declines an average of three inches with age, although the total loss varies across individuals and between men and women. We reach our maximum size and strength at about age 25, after which our cells decrease steadily in number and size. This decline occurs in both the trunk and the extremities, and may be attributable to the loss of bone mineral. The spine becomes more curved, and discs in the vertebrae become compacted. Such loss of height is intensified for individuals with *osteoporosis,* a disease that makes the bones less dense, more porous, and hence more prone to fractures following even a minor stress. For older people who have no natural teeth remaining, it is not unusual to lose a considerable volume of bone in the jaw or alveolar bone. This results in a poor fit of dentures and a painful feeling when chewing or biting with dentures. The loss of bone mass characteristic of osteoporosis is *not* a normal process of aging, but a disease that occurs with more frequency among older women, as will be discussed in Chapters 7 and 18.

Another normal change with aging is that shoulder width decreases as a result of bone loss, weakened muscles, and loss of elasticity in the ligaments. Crush fractures of the spine cause the vertebrae to collapse, such that over time, some older people (especially women) appear to be stoop-shouldered or hunched—a condition known as *kyphosis.* Stiffness in the joints is also characteristic of old age; this occurs because cartilage between the joints wears thin and fluid that lubricates them decreases. Strength and stamina also decline with aging. Maximum strength at age 70 has been found to be 65 to 85 percent of the maximum capacity of a 25-year-old. This drops to 50 percent by age 80, although older persons who maintain an active physical fitness program show much less decline in strength.

These musculo-skeletal changes make it difficult for older people to perform some tasks of daily living, such as getting out of a chair or bed, or reaching up or deep inside a cabinet located overhead. The older person may attempt to accommodate to the latter situation by climbing on a chair or footstool in the kitchen to reach objects on top shelves. This is a dangerous way to solve the problem, because of the loss of balance and the increased brittleness of bones that some older people experience. These changes contribute to a higher incidence of falls and hip fractures in older people, which in turn may produce long-term disability and even death. In fact, falls are the leading cause of accidental death among people 65 and older (Morse, 1985). This may indicate a growing incongruence between aging

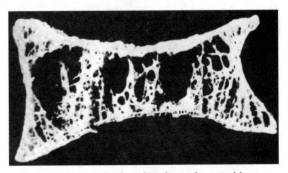

With osteoporosis, both trabecular and cortical bones become more brittle and lace-like.

individuals and their physical environment: Poor lighting, uneven stairs and ground surfaces, and slippery bathroom floors are often found in older people's homes. Minor modifications around the home can reduce the risk of falls, for instance, installing handrails and grab bars, and making sure that surfaces are smooth but not slippery.

## Aging in the Respiratory System

Almost every organ system shows some decline in functional or reserve capacity with age, as illustrated by several physiological indices in Figure 5–2. It is important to keep in mind that this graph is based on *cross-sectional* data collected from healthy men in these age groups; results may vary when longitudinal data for each cohort are examined. Complex functions that require the integration of multiple systems experience the most rapid decline. For example, maximum breathing capacity—which requires coordination of the respiratory, nervous, and muscular systems—is greatly decreased. Accordingly, normal changes in the respiratory and cardiovascular system become most evident with age. These changes are responsible for an individual's declining ability to maintain physical activity for long periods and the increasing tendency to fatigue easily. With aging, the muscles that operate the lungs lose elasticity so that respiratory efficiency is reduced. Vital capacity, or the maximum amount of oxygen that can be brought into the lungs with a deep breath, declines. In fact, it has been estimated that the average decline for men is 50 percent at age 70 from age 25, the peak of a healthy man's lung function, or a decline from six

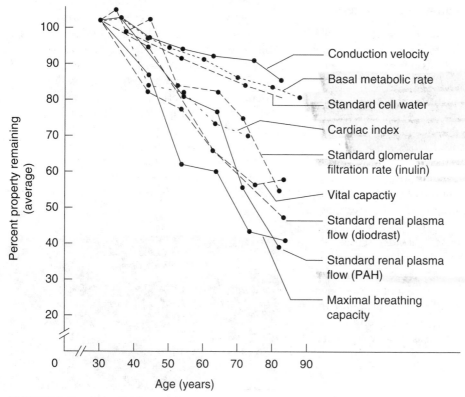

**FIGURE 5–2 Aging in Organ Systems**
SOURCE: N. W. Shock, The physiology of aging. *Scientific American, 206,* 110.

quarts of air to three quarts. Breathing may become more difficult after strenuous exercise or after climbing up several flights of stairs, but it does not necessarily impair the older person's daily functions. It may simply mean that the person has to move more slowly or rest on the stairway landing. However, the rate of decline in vital capacity has been found to be slower in physically active men than in sedentary healthy men. Indeed, longitudinal studies have consistently found the former to have twice the vital capacity of the latter in middle-age (Dehn and Bruce, 1972; Bruce, 1984).

Of all the body systems, the respiratory system suffers the most punishment from environmental pollutants and infections (Rockstein and Sussman, 1979). For this reason, it is difficult to distinguish normal, age-related changes from pathological or environmentally induced diseases. *Cilia,* which are hairlike structures in the airways, are reduced in number and are less effective in removing foreign matter; this diminishes the amount of oxygen available. This, combined with declining muscle strength in the chest that impairs cough efficiency, makes the older person more susceptible to chronic bronchitis, emphysema, and pneumonia. Older people can avoid serious loss of lung function by remaining active, pacing their tasks, and taking part in activities that do not demand too much exertion. Avoiding strenuous activity on days when the air quality is poor can also reduce the load on an older person's lungs.

## Cardiovascular Changes and the Effects of Exercise

Structural changes in the heart and blood vessels include a reduction in bulk, a replacement of heart muscle with fat, a loss of elastic tissue, and an increase in collagen. Within the muscle fibers, an age pigment composed of fat and protein, known as *lipofuscin,* may take up 5 to 10 percent of the fiber structure (Pearson and Shaw, 1982). These changes produce a loss of elasticity in the arteries, weakened vessel walls, and varicosities,

Group walking provides opportunities for aerobic exercise and socializing.

or abnormal swelling, in veins that are under high pressure (e.g., in the legs). In addition to loss of elasticity, the arterial and vessel walls become increasingly lined with lipids (fats), creating the condition of *atherosclerosis,* which makes it more difficult for blood to be pumped through the vessels and arteries. It should be noted that this buildup of fats and lipids occurs to some extent with normal aging, but it is exacerbated in some individuals whose diet includes large quantities of saturated fats. In Chapter 7, such lifestyle risk factors for heart disease are reviewed.

Blood pressure is expressed as the ratio of systolic to diastolic pressure. The former refers to the level of blood pressure (in mm.) during the contraction phase (systole), whereas the latter refers to the stage when the chambers of the heart are filling with blood. For example, a blood pressure of 120/80 indicates that the pressure created by the heart to expel blood can raise a column of mercury 120 mm. During diastole, in this example, the pressure produced by blood rushing into the heart chambers can raise a column of mercury 80 mm. Both systolic and diastolic blood pressure increase somewhat with normal aging, but the elevation of the former is greater (see Figure 5–3). As with changes in the heart, extreme elevation of blood pressure is not normal and is

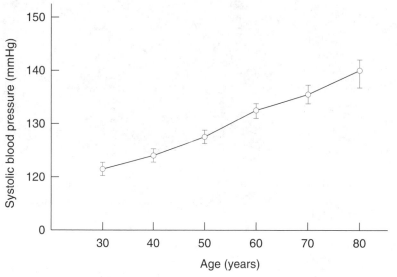

**FIGURE 5–3    Effect of Age on Systolic Blood Pressure**

SOURCE: J. D. Tobin, Physiological indices of aging. In D. Danon, N. W. Shock, and M. Marois (Eds.), *Aging: A challenge in science and society*, Vol. 1 (New York: Oxford University Press, 1981).

associated with diet, obesity, and lifestyle, all of which have cumulative effects over the years. The negative effects of abnormally high or low blood pressure are examined in Chapter 7.

The maximum heart rate achievable by sustained exercise is directly associated with age; an easy way to calculate this is: 220 minus age in years. For example, a 25-year-old could expect a maximum heart rate of 195 (220–25), whereas a 70-year-old could achieve 150 (220–70) beats per minute. However, there is some variation across individuals, with the heart rate remaining relatively high in physically active older persons. Resting heart rates also decrease with aging, although physically well-conditioned older people tend to have heart rates more similar to the average younger person.

These changes in the heart and lungs result in less efficient utilization of oxygen. This, in turn, reduces an individual's capacity to maintain physical activity for long periods. Nevertheless, physical training for older persons can significantly reduce blood pressure and increase their aerobic capacity (O'Brien and Vertinsky, 1991).

Studies of older persons described as "master athletes"—individuals who have continued to participate in competitive, aerobic exercise (running, bicycling, swimming) into the later years—have shown that physical training results in a greater volume of oxygen, more lean body weight, and lower percent of fat than is found in untrained older persons. However, these levels were found to be poorer than in younger athletes, underscoring the reality that normal changes in the body's physiology and its operation cannot be eliminated completely. (Pollock et al., 1987).

Nevertheless, the positive effects of moderate exercise, such as a brisk walk three to four times per week, on slowing these changes are becoming widely recognized. Researchers have found a significant increase in aerobic capacity, as measured by maximum volume of oxygen intake, and a reduction in fat composition among sedentary older persons after six months of low-intensity exercise training (e.g., walking for 20 to 30 minutes), followed by six months of high-intensity training (e.g., jogging for 20 to 30 minutes) (Seals et al., 1984). High-intensity exercise resulted in significant weight loss, but low-intensity exercise did not. However, high-intensity training resulted in more orthopedic injuries than did low-intensity training among older participants. For this reason, walking is often the best exercise. Both high- and low-intensity programs have been found to increase significantly the volume of oxygen consumed and to reduce blood pressure among women aged 67 to 89 (Foster et al., 1989; O'Brien and Vertinsky, 1991). These studies, however, suggest that exercise may not be sufficient for reducing cholesterol and triglyceride* levels in the blood, both of which have been associated with heart disease. Instead, reduced intake of animal fats, tropical oils, and refined carbohydrates appears to be essential. Although there are limitations, such findings justify optimism that physical health can be considerably improved through lifestyle changes, even after age 65.

These findings regarding the benefits of regular exercise for older people raise the concept of *active life expectancy* discussed in Chapter 1. This is the portion of remaining life during which one is independent and not living a disabled existence. Thus, for a sedentary 65-year-old, *active* life expectancy has been calculated to be 10 years of the remaining 16.5 years life expectancy for that age (Katz et al., 1983). Aerobic exercise and a healthy lifestyle can significantly increase active life expectancy by postponing and shortening the period of morbidity (e.g., days of sickness) that one can expect in the later years. The significance of certain lifestyle habits for maintaining good health in old age is discussed further in Chapter 7.

## Changes in the Urinary System

Both kidney and bladder functions change with age. The kidneys play an important role in regulating the body's internal chemistry by filtering blood and urine through an extraordinary system of tubes and capillaries, known as glomeruli. As blood passes through these filters, it is cleaned,

and the necessary balance of ions and minerals is restored. In the process, urea (e.g., water and waste materials) is collected and passed through the ureter and the bladder, where it is excreted in the form of urine. With age, the kidneys decrease in volume and weight, and the total number of glomeruli correspondingly decreases by 30 percent from age 30 to age 65. As a result, renal function, defined by the rate at which blood is filtered through the kidneys, declines by up to 50 percent with age. These changes have significant implications for an older person's tolerance for certain medications such as penicillin, tetracycline, digoxin, and others that are cleared by glomerular filtration. These drugs remain active longer in an older person's system and may be more potent, indicating a need to reduce drug dosage and frequency of administration.

The kidneys also lose their capacity to absorb glucose, as well as their concentrating and diluting ability, contributing to increased problems with dehydration and hyponetremia (i.e., a loss of salt in the blood). Of any organ system, renal function deteriorates most dramatically with age, irrespective of disease.

Compounding this problem, bladder function also deteriorates with age. The capacity of the bladder may be reduced by as much as 50 percent in some persons older than age 65. At the same time, however, the sensation of needing to empty the bladder is delayed. The latter condition may be more a function of central nervous system dysfunction than changes in the bladder. As a result, urinary incontinence is common in the elderly. It has been estimated that as many as 15 to 30 percent of older people living in the community and at least half of those in nursing homes suffer from difficulties with bladder control. The problem may be made worse by a stroke, dementia, or other diseases associated with the nervous system, such as Parkinson's (Cramer, 1993).

Because of these changes in the kidney and the bladder, older people may be more sensitive to the effects of alcohol and caffeine. Both of these substances inhibit the production of a hormone that regulates urine production. Ordinarily, this

---

*Triglyceride is a molecular compound made up of three fatty acids synthesized from carbohydrates.

hormone, known as antidiuretic hormone (ADH), signals to the kidneys when to produce urine in order to keep the body's chemistry balanced. When it is temporarily inhibited by the consumption of alcohol, coffee, or tea, the kidneys no longer receive messages and, as a result, produce urine constantly. This, in turn, dehydrates the body. It appears that ADH production is slowed with aging, so substances that inhibit its production increase the load on the kidneys and the bladder. Because of these changes, older people may start to avoid social outings, even a trip to the grocery store, out of fear that they may not have access to a bathroom. Possible treatments for urinary incontinence, as well as ways that older people can alter their daily habits to accommodate bladder problems, are discussed more fully in Chapter 7.

## Sexual Changes

Men and women experience changes in their sexual organs as they age, but these do not necessarily lead to sexual incapacity. The normal physiological changes that characterize aging alter the nature of the sexual response, but do not interfere with sexual pleasure. These changes are discussed in detail in Chapter 10.

## Changes in the Gastrointestinal System

The gastrointestinal system includes the esophagus, stomach, intestines, colon, liver, and biliary tract. Although the esophagus does not show age-related changes in appearance, there are some changes in its function in older people. These may include a decrease in contraction of the muscles and more time for the cardiac sphincter (a valvelike structure that allows food to pass into the stomach) to open, thus taking more time for food to be transmitted to the stomach. The result of these changes may be a sensation of being full before having consumed a full meal. This in turn may reduce the pleasure a person derives from eating, and result in inadequate nutrient intake. This sensation also explains why

older people may appear to eat such small quantities of food at mealtimes.

Secretion of digestive juices in the stomach apparently diminishes after age 50, especially among men. As a result, older people are more likely to experience the condition of atrophic gastritis, or a chronic inflammation of the stomach lining. Gastric ulcers are more likely to occur in middle age than in old age, but older people are at greater risk for colon and stomach cancer. Because of this risk, older people who complain of gastrointestinal discomfort should be urged to seek medical attention for the problem, instead of relying on home remedies or over-the-counter medications.

As with many other organs in the human body, the small and large intestines decrease in weight after age 40. There are also functional changes in the small intestine, where the number of enzymes is reduced, and simple sugars are absorbed more slowly, resulting in diminished efficiency with age. The smooth muscle content and muscle tone in the wall of the colon also decrease. Anatomical changes in the large intestine are associated with the increased incidence of chronic constipation in older persons.

However, behavioral factors are probably more important than organic factors in the development of constipation, as will be discussed in more detail in Chapter 7. Spasms of the lower intestinal tract are an example of the interaction of physiological with behavioral factors. Although they may occur at any age, such spasms are more common among older persons. These spasms are a form of functional disorder, that is, a condition without any organic basis, often due to psychological factors. Many gastrointestinal conditions that afflict older people are unrelated to the anatomical changes described previously. Nevertheless, they are very real problems to an older person who experiences them.

The liver also grows smaller with age, by about 20 percent, although this does not appear to have much influence on its functions. However, there is a deterioration in the ability to process medications that are dependent on liver function. Jaundice occurs more frequently in older people, and may be due to changes in the liver or to the obstruction of bile in the gall bladder. In addition, high alcohol consumption may put excessive strain on the older person's liver.

## Changes in the Nervous System

The brain is composed of billions of neurons, or nerve cells, which are lost as we grow older. Neuronal loss begins at age 30, well before the period termed *old*. It is compounded by alcohol consumption, cigarette smoking, and breathing polluted air. The frontal lobe has been found to experience a greater loss of cells than other parts of the brain (Brody, 1973). A moderate degree of neuronal loss does not create a major decline in brain function, however. In fact, contrary to popular belief, we can function with fewer neurons than we have, so their loss is not the reason for mild forgetfulness in old age. Even in the case of Alzheimer's disease and other dementias, severe loss of neurons may be less significant than changes in brain tissue, blood flow, and receptor organs.

Other aging-related changes in the brain include a reduction in its weight by 10 percent, an accumulation of lipofuscin (e.g., an age pigment composed of fat and protein), and slower transmission of information from one neuron to another. The reduction in brain mass occurs in all species, and is probably due to loss of fluids. The gradual buildup of lipofuscin, which has a yellowish color, causes the outer cortex of the brain to take on a yellow-beige color with age. As with the moderate loss of neurons, these changes do not appear to alter brain function in old age. That is, difficulties in solving problems or remembering dates and names cannot be attributed to these slight changes in the size and appearance of the brain.

In contrast, the change in neurotransmitters and in the structure of the synapse (the junction between any two neurons) does affect cognitive and motor function. Electroencephalograms, or readings of the electrical activity of the brain,

show a slower response in older brains than in the young. These changes may be at least partially responsible for the increase in reaction time with age. Other hypotheses include neuronal loss and reduced blood flow; however, available data are inconclusive. Reaction time is a complex product of multiple factors, primarily the speed of conduction and motor function, both of which are slowed by the increased time needed to transmit messages at the synapses.

The reduced speed with which the nervous system can process information or send signals for action is a fairly widespread problem, even in middle age when people begin to notice lagging reflexes and reaction time. As a result, such tasks as responding to a telephone or doorbell, crossing the street, completing a paper and pencil test, or deciding among several alternatives generally take longer for older people than for the young. Most people adjust to these changes by modifying their physical environment or personal habits, such as taking more time to do a task and avoiding rush situations; for example, an older person may compensate by leaving the house one hour before an appointment instead of the usual 15 minutes, shopping for groceries during times when stores are not crowded, or shopping in smaller stores. Such adaptations are perhaps most pronounced in the tasks associated with driving. The older driver tends to be more cautious, to slow down well in advance of a traffic signal, to stay in the slower lane, and to avoid freeways during rush hour. Many choose to drive larger cars that can survive collisions better than compact cars. Despite this increased cautiousness, accident rates are high among older drivers, as will be discussed in Chapter 7.

Changes in the central nervous system that accompany aging also affect the senses of hearing, taste, smell, and touch. Despite these changes, intellectual and motor function apparently do not deteriorate significantly with age. The brain has tremendous reserve capacity that takes over as losses begin. It is only when neuronal loss, inadequate function of neurotransmitters, and other structural changes are severe that the older person experiences significant loss of function. The changes in the brain that appear to be associated with Alzheimer's disease will be discussed in Chapter 11.

## Changes in Sleep Patterns with Aging

One of the most common complaints of older people is that they can no longer sleep well, with 25 to 40 percent of older persons in community surveys complaining of sleep problems (Vitiello and Prinz, 1991). These complaints have a basis in biological changes that occur with aging. Results of laboratory studies of sleep-wake patterns of adults have consistently revealed age-related changes in EEG patterns, sleep stages, and circadian rhythms.

Sleep occurs in five stages; the first four stages occur when no rapid eye movements take place (non-REM sleep), the fifth stage is that of rapid eye movements (REM sleep). Stage 4 is when deep sleep takes place. Sleep stages occur in a linear pattern from stage 1 through stage 4, then REM sleep, stage 5. Each cycle is repeated four or five times through the night. Brain wave activity differs in a characteristic pattern for each stage.

With normal aging, even in the absence of any predisposing diseases, there is a slowing down of many of these brain waves; the length of time in each stage changes. In particular, lab tests have shown a decline in total sleep time in stages 3, 4, and 5, and sleep is lighter. Older people have shorter cycles from stages 1 to 4 and REM sleep, with the latter stage occurring earlier in the cycle. During these stages older people, more so than the young, are easily awakened, apparently by environmental stimuli that would not disturb a younger person (Vitiello and Prinz, 1991).

Changes in circadian rhythms, or the individual's cycle of sleeping and waking within a 24-hour period, are characterized by a movement from a two-phase pattern of sleep (awake during the day, asleep during the night) to a multiphasic rhythm that is more common in infants, i.e. daytime napping and shorter sleep cycles at night.

These changes may be associated with changes in core body temperatures in older people (Weitzman et al., 1982).

The older person may compensate by taking more daytime naps, which can lead to further disruptions in night sleep. More often, older people who report sleep disturbances to their primary physician are prescribed sleeping pills or sedative hypnotic medications; this age group represents the highest users of such medications (Institute of Medicine, 1979). Both the incidence of sleeping difficulties and the use of sleeping pills is more common in older women than in older men. In fact, these normal, age-related changes in sleep patterns need not be disruptive to the older person's well-being. It may be disturbing for people accustomed to normal sleep in their youth to have a lighter, shorter, and more disrupted sleep pattern as they age, but individuals can adjust to these changes just as they do to other normal physiological changes without resorting to medications. Many hypnotics used to treat sleep disorders can produce a paradoxical effect by resulting in insomnia if used for a long time (NIH, 1984). Sleep disturbances can be alleviated somewhat by an increase in physical exercise and a reduction in the intake of caffeine and other medications and hours spent napping during the day, as well as improving the sleeping environment (e.g., a quieter bedroom with heavy curtains to block out the light).

There are a few true *disorders of sleep* that can occur with aging; these include respiratory problems, sleep apnea, which is defined as a 5- to 10-second cessation of breathing, and nocturnal myoclonus, which is a neuromuscular disturbance affecting the legs during sleep. These must be treated with medications.

## SUMMARY AND IMPLICATIONS

As shown by this review of the major biological systems, the aging process is gradual, beginning in some organ systems as early as the twenties and thirties, and progressing more rapidly after age 70, or even 80, in others. Even with 50 percent deterioration in many organ systems, an individual can still function adequately. The ability of human beings to compensate for age-related changes attests to their significant amount of excess reserve capacity. In most instances, the normal physical changes of aging need not diminish a person's quality of life if person-environment congruence can be maintained. Since many of the decrements are gradual and slight, older people can learn to modify their activities to adapt to their environments—for example, by pacing the amount of physical exertion throughout the day. Family members and professionals can be supportive by encouraging modifications in the home, such as minimizing the use of stairs, moving the focus of the older person's daily activities to the main floor of the home, and reinforcing the older person's efforts to cope creatively with common physical changes.

There are significant differences in the rate and severity of decline in various organ systems, with the greatest deterioration in functions that require coordination among multiple systems, muscles, and nerves. Similarly, there are wide variations across individuals in the aging process, springing from differences in heredity, diet, exercise, and living conditions. Many of the physiological functions that were once assumed to deteriorate and to be irreversible with normal aging are being reevaluated by researchers in basic and clinical physiology, as well as by health educators. Even people who begin a regular exercise program late in life have experienced significant improvements in their heart and lung capacity. The role of preventive maintenance and health promotion in the aging process will be discussed in Chapter 7.

Sleep patterns do, however, change with normal aging. Lab studies have revealed changes in EEG patterns, sleep stages, and circadian rhythms with advancing years, even in the absence of disease. Sleeping pills are widely used by older people who complain of sleep disturbance. However, physical exercise, and reduced intake of alcohol, caffeine, and some medications are generally more effective than sleeping pills for long-term use. Only in the case of true sleep disorders, such as sleep apnea and twitching legs during sleep, are medications useful.

## REFERENCES

Ausman, L. M., and Russell, R. M. Nutrition and aging. In E. L. Schneider and J. W. Rowe (Eds.), *Handbook of the Biology of Aging* (3rd ed.). San Diego: Academic Press, 1990.

Avery, W. M. Hypothermia and heat illness. *Aging,* 1984, *8,* 43–47.

Bjorksten, J. Crosslinkage and the aging process. In M. Rockstein, M. L. Sussman, and J. Chesky (Eds.), *Theoretical aspects of aging.* New York: Academic Press, 1974.

Brody, H. Aging of the vertebrate brain. In M. Rockstein (Ed.), *Development and aging in the nervous system.* New York: Academic Press, 1973, 121–134.

Bruce, R. A. Exercise, functional capacity and aging— Another viewpoint. *Medical Science Sports Exercise,* 1984, *16,* 8–13.

Collins, K. J. Low indoor temperatures and morbidity in the elderly. *Age and Ageing,* 1986, *15,* 212–220.

Cramer, D. Promoting continence: Strategies for success. *Perspectives in Health Promotion and Aging,* 1993, *1,* 1–3.

Cutler, E. D., and Cutler, R. G. Tissue auto-oxidation, antioxidants, and life span potential. *The Gerontologist,* 1983, *23* (Special Issue), 194.

Dehn, M. M., and Bruce, R. A. Longitudinal variations in maximal oxygen intake with age and activity. *Journal of Applied Physiology,* 1972, *33,* 805–807.

Foster, V. L, Hume, G.J.E., Byrnes, W. C., Dickinson, A. L., and Chatfield, S. J. Endurance training for elderly women: Moderate vs. low intensity. *Journals of Gerontology,* 1989, *44,* M184–M188.

Fries, J. F. Aging, natural death, and the compression of morbidity. *New England Journal of Medicine,* 1980, *303,* 130–135.

Fries, J. F., and Crapo, L. M. *Vitality and aging.* San Francisco: W. H. Freeman, 1981.

Gilchrest, B. A. Skin. In J. W. Rowe and R. W. Besdine (Eds.), *Health and disease in old age.* Boston: Little, Brown, 1982, 381–392.

Goldstein, S., and Reis, R.J.S. Genetic modifications during cellular aging. *Molecular and Cellular Biochemical,* 1984, *64,* 15–30.

Guigoz, Y., and Munro, H. N. Nutrition and aging. In C. E. Finch and E. L. Schneider (Eds.), *Handbook of the biology of aging* (2d ed.). New York: Van Nostrand, 1985, 878–893.

Harman, D. A theory based on free radical and radiation chemistry. *Journal of Gerontology,* 1956, *11,* 298.

Harman, D. The aging process. *Proceedings of the National Academy of Science,* 1981, *78,* 7124–7128.

Hayflick, L. Aging under glass. *Experimental Gerontology,* 1970, *5,* 291–303.

Institute of Medicine. *Report of a study: Sleeping pills, insomnia and medical practice.* Washington, D.C.: National Academy of Science, 1979.

Katz, S., Branch, L. G., Branson, M. H., Papsidero, J. A., Beck, J. C., and Greer, D. S. Active life expectancy. *New England Journal of Medicine,* 1983, *309,* 1218–1224.

Kenney, R. A. *Physiology of aging: A synopsis.* Chicago: Year Book Medical Publishers, 1982.

Kirkwood, T.B.L. Comparative and evolutionary aspects of longevity. In C. E. Finch and E. L. Schneider (Eds.), *Handbook of the biology of aging* (2d ed.). New York: Van Nostrand, 1985, 27–44.

Kolanowski, A., and Gunter, L. Hypothermia in the elderly. *Geriatric Nursing,* 1981, *2,* 362–376.

Leyden, J. J., McGinley, K. J., and Grove, G. L. Age-related differences in the rate of desquamation of skin surface cells. In R. D. Adelman, J. Roberts, and V. J. Christafalo (Eds.), *Pharmacological interventions in the aging process.* New York: Plenum Press, 1978.

Macey, S. M. Hypothermia and energy conservation: A tradeoff for elderly persons? *International Journal of Aging and Human Development,* 1989, *29,* 151–161.

Macey, S., and Schneider, D. Deaths from excessive heat and excessive cold among the elderly. *The Gerontologist,* 1993, *33*(4) 497–500.

Masoro, E. J. Animal models in aging research. In E. L. Schneider and J. W. Rowe (Eds.), *Handbook of the Biology of Aging* (3rd ed.). San Diego: Academic Press, 1990.

Morales, A. J., Nolan, J. J., Nelson, J. C., and Yen, S. S. Effects of replacement dose of dehydroepiandrosterone in men and women of advancing age. *Journal of Clinical Endocrinology and Metabolism,* 1994, *78,* 1260–1367.

Morse, J. M., Prowse, M. D., and Morrow, N. A retrospective analysis of patient falls. *Canadian Journal of Public Health,* 1985, *76,* 116–118.

Mortola, J., and Yen, S. S. The effects of oral dehydroepiandrosterone on endocrine-metabolic parameters in postmenopausal women. *Journal of Clinical Endocrinology and Metabolism,* 1990, *71,* 696–704.

National Institutes of Health (NIH). Consensus Development Conference Summary: *Drugs and Insomnia,* 1983, *4.*

O'Brien, S., and Vertinsky, P. Unfit survivors: Exercise as a resource for aging women. *The Gerontologist,* 1991, *31,* 347–357.

Palmore, E. (Ed.). *Normal aging: Reports from the Duke Longitudinal Study, 1955–1969.* Durham, N.C.: Duke University Press, 1970.

Palmore, E. (Ed.). *Normal aging II: Reports from the Duke Longitudinal Study, 1970–1973.* Durham, N.C.: Duke University Press, 1974.

Palmore, E. (Ed.). *Normal aging III: Reports from the Duke Longitudinal Study.* Durham, N.C.: Duke University Press, 1985.

Pearson, D., and Shaw, S. *Life extension.* New York: Warner Books, 1982.

Pollock, M. L., Foster, C., Knapp, D., Rod, J. L., and Schmidt, D. H. Effect of age and training on aerobic capacity and body composition of master athletes. *Journal of Applied Physiology,* 1987, *62,* 725–731.

Rockstein, M., and Sussman, M. *Biology of aging.* Belmont, Calif: Wadsworth, 1979.

Schneider, E. L., and Reed, J. D. Modulations of aging processes. In C. E. Finch and E. L. Schneider (Eds.), *Handbook of the biology of aging* (2d ed.). New York: Van Nostrand, 1985, 45–78.

Seals, D. R., Hagberg, J. M., Hurley, B. F., Ehsani, A. A., and Holloszy, J. O. Endurance training in older men and women. *Journal of Applied Physiology,* 1984, *57,* 1024–1029.

Shephard, R. J. *Physical activity and aging.* Chicago: Croon Helm, 1978.

Shock, N. W. The physiology of aging. *Scientific American,* 1962, *206,* 100–110.

Vitiello, M. V., and Prinz, P. N. Sleep and sleep disorders in normal aging. In M. J. Thorpy (Ed.), *Handbook of sleep disorders.* New York: Marcell Decker, 1991, 139–151.

Walford, R. L. *The immunological theory of aging.* Baltimore: Williams and Wilkins, 1969.

Walford, R. L., Harris, S. B., and Weindruch, R. Dietary restriction and aging: Historical phases, mechanisms & current directions. *Journal of Nutrition,* 1987, *117,* 1650–1654.

Weitzman, E. D., Moline, M. L., Czeisler, C. A., and Zimmerman, J. C. Chronobiology of aging: Tem- perature, sleep/wake rhythms and entertainment. *Neurobiology of Aging,* 1982, *3,* 299–309.

Wilson, D. L. The programmed theory of aging. In M. Rockstein, M. L. Sussman, and J. Chesky (Eds.), *Theoretical aspects of aging.* New York: Academic Press, 1974, 11–21.

# 6

# SENSORY CHANGES AND THEIR SOCIAL CONSEQUENCES

Our ability to see, hear, touch, taste, and smell has a profound influence on our interactions with the social and physical environment. Recognizing this relationship between our sensory and social functioning, and the gradual decline in our sensory abilities with aging, it is critical that we understand these changes and how they can influence our social capabilities as we age. There is a popular belief that, as we get older, we cannot see, hear, touch, taste, or smell as well as we did when we were younger, and it appears to be true. The decline in all our sensory receptors with aging is normal; in fact, it begins relatively early. We reach our optimum capacities in our twenties, maintain this peak for a few years, and gradually experience a decline, with a more rapid rate of decline after the ages of 45 to 55. Having said this, we should note that there is tremendous diversity among individuals in the rate and severity of sensory decline, as illustrated earlier by Mrs. Hill and Mr. Jones. Some older persons may have better visual acuity than most 25-year-olds; there are many 75-year-olds who can hear better than most younger persons. Think

about the wine taster who, in old age, may still be considered the master of his trade, performing a job that requires excellent taste discrimination.

Although age per se does not determine deterioration in sensory functioning, it is clear that many internal changes do occur. (The older person who has better visual or hearing acuity than a 25-year-old probably had even better sensory capacities in the earlier years.) It is important to focus on *intraindividual* changes with age, not *interindividual* differences, when studying sensory and perceptual functions. Unfortunately, most of the research on sensory changes with age is cross-sectional, that is, based on comparing different persons who are older and younger. For this reason, the reader needs to be aware that there are tremendous individual differences in how much and how severely sensory functions deteriorate with age.

This chapter examines changes that occur with aging in the structure and function of all the sensory organs. Both normal and disease-related changes in the eye, the ear, the taste and smell receptors, as well as in the skin and the temperature-regulating system, are reviewed. Some implications of these changes for older people's social functioning and quality of life are discussed. Finally, the importance of recognizing these sensory changes in designing appropriate environments for older persons is considered.

## NORMAL CHANGES WITH AGE

Changes in different senses occur at varied rates and degrees. Thus, the person who experiences an early and severe decline in hearing acuity may not have any deterioration in visual functioning. Some sensory functions, such as hearing, may show an early decline, yet others, such as taste and touch, change little until well into advanced old age. Over time, however, sensory changes affect an older person's interactions with the social and physical environments.

Because these changes are usually gradual, people adapt and compensate by using other, still-intact sensory systems. For example, they may compensate by standing closer to objects and persons in order to hear or see, by using nonverbal cues such as touch and different body orientations, or by utilizing technical devices such as bifocals or hearing aids. To the extent that people can control their environment and make it conform to their changing needs, sensory decline need not be incapacitating. However, if the environment does not allow for modification to suit individual needs, if the decline in any one system is severe, or if several sensory systems deteriorate at the same time, it becomes much more difficult for individuals to use compensatory mechanisms. Such problems are more likely to occur in advanced old age.

Before reviewing the major changes in sensory processes that accompany aging, it is helpful to clarify some terminology. *Sensation* is the process of taking in information through the sense organs. *Perception* is a higher function in which the information received through the senses is processed in the brain. *Sensory threshold* is the minimum intensity of a stimulus that a person requires in order to detect the stimulus. This differs for each sensory system. *Recognition threshold* is the intensity of a stimulus needed in order for an individual to identify or recognize it. As might be expected, a greater intensity of a stimulus is necessary to recognize than to detect it. *Sensory discrimination* is defined as the minimum difference necessary between two or more stimuli in order for a person to distinguish between them. There is considerable evidence that, with normal aging, a decline occurs in all sensory systems (Ordy and Brizzee, 1979). That is, sensory and recognition thresholds increase, and discrimination between multiple stimuli demands greater distinctions between them.

## CHANGES IN VISION

Although the proportion of blind persons in old age is not significantly higher than among younger persons, the rates of impairments that affect some aspects of visual functioning increase with age. Vision problems increase with age; when we compare 55–64-year-olds with those over age 85, there is a fourfold increase in the rate of visual impairments, from 55 per 1,000 people to 225 per 1,000 (Adams and Collins, 1987). As a result, older persons are more likely to experience problems with daily tasks that require good visual skills, such as reading small print or signs on moving vehicles, locating signs, or adapting to sudden changes in light level. In addition, impaired vision caused by untreated cataracts or glaucoma is much more likely to result in problems with activities of daily living than is hearing impairment (Rudberg et al., 1993).

### Anatomy and Physiology of the Eye

Before reviewing the changes in visual function that occur with age, it is useful first to describe how the eye works. As shown in Figure 6–1, the eye is composed of several elements that work in harmony to transmit visual images from the external world to the brain, which in turn translates them into meaningful stimuli for understanding the environment. The process of seeing begins when light enters through the cornea and passes the pupil and the lens, which refracts light rays into angles that then reach the retina. The lens is shaped in such a way as to allow refraction, or scattering of light at specific angles to form an image on the retina; many age-related changes affect the shape of the lens, as will be noted later. Images formed on the retina, which covers more than two-thirds of the eye, are transformed into messages that can be carried by the optic nerve to the brain. The richest concentration of blood vessels in the retina is in the macula. This part of the eye allows us to see fine detail and provides central vision. Located in the retina are the rods and cones, visual receptors that allow us to see at low light levels and to discern colors respectively. As the person moves from a dimly lit situation to bright light, there is a shift in the retina from rod to cone vision. This change, undetected by the individual, allows a person to see under different conditions of light and dark. Note also that there are chambers in front of and behind the lens, filled with a clear viscous fluid that regulates the amount of pressure on the optic nerve. The fluid in the front of

the lens is known as *aqueous humour;* that behind the lens is *vitreous humour.*

Most age-related problems in vision are attributable to changes in parts of the eye. However, these problems are aggravated by changes in the central nervous system which block the transmission of stimuli from the sensory organs. Changes in the visual pathways of the brain and in the visual cortex may be a possible source of some of the alterations that take place in visual sensation and perception with age.

## Effects of Structural Changes in the Cornea and Pupil

The cornea is usually the first part of the eye to be affected by age-related changes. The surface of the cornea thickens with aging, and the blood vessels become more prominent. The smooth, rounded surface of the cornea becomes flatter and less smooth, and may take on an irregular shape. The older person's eye appears to lose its luster and is less translucent than it was in youth. In some cases, a fatty yellow ring, known as the *arcus senilis,* may form around the cornea. This is not a sign of impending vision loss; in fact, it has no impact on

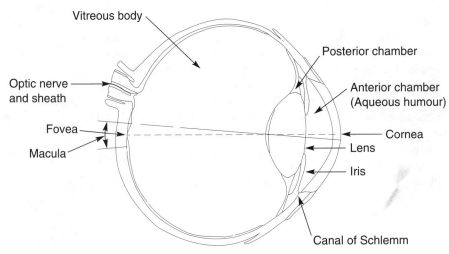

**FIGURE 6–1   The Eye**

vision. It is sometimes associated with increased lipid deposits in the blood vessels.

At its optimal functioning, the pupil is sensitive to light levels in the environment, widening in response to low light levels and contracting when light levels are high. With aging, the pupil appears to become smaller and more fixed in size. The maximum opening of the pupil is reduced in old age, commonly to about two-thirds the original maximum. That is, the older person's pupil is less able to respond to low light levels by dilating or opening to the extent needed. The eye also responds more slowly to changes in light conditions. This problem is compounded by a slower shift from cones to rods under low-light conditions. As a result, the older person may have considerable difficulty functioning in low-light situations, or in adjusting to significant changes in ambient light. In fact, older people may need three times more light than younger persons to function effectively. Studies of older drivers have found that highway signs must be 65–75 percent closer than for younger drivers to be readable at night (Sivak, Olson, and Pastalan, 1981). These changes may also reduce the older person's ability to discern images in conditions of poor light contrast (e.g., driving at twilight or under foggy or rainy conditions), and to detect details in moving objects (Sekuler, Owsley, and Hutman, 1982). Even among healthy older persons who are still driving, age-related visual changes may significantly alter their abilities under marginal conditions. For example, a survey of participants aged 22 to 92 in the Baltimore Longitudinal Study of Aging (described in Chapter 2) revealed that age was highly correlated with reports of problems with sudden merging of other vehicles, judging their own and other vehicles' speed, driving under glare and hazy conditions, and reading street signs while driving (Kline et al., 1992).

For these reasons, older people may choose to avoid such activities, especially driving among fast-moving traffic on freeways at night when bright headlights create glare against asphalt surfaces, and in rain. Although this is a safe approach for coping with age-related difficulties in low-light situations, older people must be encouraged to maintain their activity level and not become isolated because of declines in visual function. In such instances, families and professionals may have to encourage older people to use other forms of transportation, such as buses and taxis, thereby avoiding the problem of too little environmental stimulation relative to the person's competence.

As another illustration, many older people may feel frustrated when they go to a special restaurant for an evening dinner, only to find that the tables are lit by candles. This makes it difficult to read the menu, to see the way to the table, and even to have eye contact with companions. Family and friends may be frustrated in such situations if they do not understand that the older person's complaints about the restaurant stem from these changes in vision, not from their lack of appreciation for their efforts. Some older people cope with these problems by avoiding such restaurants altogether or going there only during daylight hours.

## Problems Related to Oxygen and Fluid Levels

Problems in rod and cone function may be related to a reduced supply of oxygen to the retina; oxygen is necessary for the production of rhodopsin, which is a critical element in the functioning of rods. Some researchers have suggested that the slowing of rhodopsin production may be due to a deficiency of vitamin A. However, there is little research evidence to suggest that increased intake of vitamin A in old age can improve visual functioning under low-light conditions.

As stated earlier, there are two fluid-filled chambers in the eye; aqueous humour fills the anterior or front portion of the eye, and vitreous humour is found in the posterior chamber, behind the lens. The aqueous humour drains through the Canal of Schlemm. In the disease state known as *glaucoma*, there may be less efficient drainage, or perhaps excessive production of the aqueous humour. Glaucoma occurs more frequently after middle age and can be managed with regular medications. More severe cases may require surgery or, more recently, the use of laser treatment. In its later stages, glaucoma may result in tunnel vision, which is a gradual narrowing of an individual's field of vision, such that peripheral vision is lost and the individual can focus only in the center. Untreated glaucoma is the third leading cause of blindness in the United States, the United Kingdom, and Canada (Leibowitz et al., 1980; Accardi, Gombos, and Gombos, 1985), and increases in frequency with age (see Table 6–1). Among African Americans, glaucoma is the leading cause of blindness, with a prevalence rate in middle-class blacks 15 times that of whites. Even when socioeconomic differences and access to health care are controlled, glaucoma is both more prevalent and more difficult to treat in Blacks (Wilson, 1989).

Unlike the aqueous humour, which drains and is replenished throughout life in healthy persons, the vitreous humour remains constant. With aging, it may thicken and shrink. Lumps of collagen, the primary content in this fluid, may be formed. Older persons who complain of "floaters" in the eye are responding to these free-floating formations in the front chamber of the eye. These changes, which cannot be prevented or stopped, are often upsetting to individuals. Those who experience them should be assured that floaters do not cause blindness. Frequent examinations by an ophthalmologist are useful in the later years to check for such conditions and to determine if they may be caused by other diseases.

## Effects of Aging on the Lens

Perhaps the greatest age-related changes in the eye occur in the lens. In fact, it has been suggested that the lens is a model system for studying aging because it contains some of the oldest cells in the body, formed during the earliest stages of the development of the embryo (Vaughan, Schmitz, and Fatt, 1979). Furthermore, the lens is a relatively simple structure biochemically; all of its cells are of the same type, composed of protein.

Collagen is the primary protein in the lens, and makes up 70 to 80 percent of the total tissue composition of the entire body. As with collagen in other parts of the body, the lens tissue thickens and hardens with age. This makes the lens less elastic, thereby reducing its ability to change form (i.e., from rounded to elongated and flat) as it focuses from near to far. Muscles that help stretch the lens also deteriorate with age, thereby compounding the problem of changing the shape of the lens. This process, known as *accommodation*, begins to deteriorate in middle age and is manifested in increasing problems with close vision. (We all are familiar with people even in their forties and fifties who need to hold their

**TABLE 6–1  Framingham Eye Study: Prevalence of Major Diseases of the Eye**

|  | SENILE CATARACT (%)* | SENILE MACULAR DEGENERATION (%)* | DIABETIC RETINOPATHY (%)* | OPEN–ANGLE GLAUCOMA (%)* |
|---|---|---|---|---|
| Total | 15.5 | 8.8 | 3.1 | 3.3 |
| Age 52 to 64 | 4.5 | 1.6 | 2.1 | 1.4 |
| Age 65 to 74 | 18.0 | 11.0 | 2.9 | 5.1 |
| Age 75 to 85 | 45.9 | 27.9 | 7.0 | 7.2 |

*Statistically significant increase with age (P < .01)

SOURCE: M. M. Kini, H. M. Leibowitz, T. Colton, R. J. Nickerson, J. Ganley, and T. R. Dawber, Prevalence of senile cataract, diabetic retinopathy, senile macular degeneration and open–angle glaucoma in the Framingham Eye Study. *American Journal of Ophthalmology 85* (1978): 31. Published with permission from *The American Journal of Ophthalmology*. Copyright by The Ophthalmic Publishing Company.

reading material at arm's length.) As a result, many persons in their forties may need to use reading glasses or bifocals. By age 60, accommodative ability is significantly deteriorated. Decrements in accommodation may cause difficulties for the older person when shifting from near to far vision; for example, when looking across a room, walking up or down stairs, reading and looking up, and writing notes while looking up at a blackboard or a lecturer.

The hardening of the lens due to changes in collagen tissue does not occur uniformly. Rather, there is differential hardening, with some surfaces allowing more light to enter than others. This results in uneven refraction of light through the lens and onto the retina. When combined with the poor refraction of light through the uneven, flattened surface of the cornea, extreme sensitivity to glare often results. This problem becomes particularly acute in environments with a single source of light aimed at a shiny surface, such as a large window at the end of a long, dark corridor with highly polished floors, occasional street lights on a rain-slicked highway, or a bright, single, overhead incandescent light shining on a linoleum floor. These conditions may contribute to older people's greater caution and anxiety, while driving or walking.

From childhood through early adulthood, the lens is a transparent system through which light can easily enter. With normal aging, the lens becomes more opaque, and less light passes through (especially shorter wavelengths of lights), compounding the problems of poor vision in low light that were described earlier. Some older persons experience a more severe opacification (clouding of the lens) to the point that the lens prevents light from entering. This condition, known as a *cataract*, is the second leading cause of blindness in the United States. Its incidence increases tenfold between ages 60 and 80. (see Table 6–1).

A cataract may occur in any part of the lens, in the center, the peripheral regions, or scattered throughout. A scattered cataract produces extreme opacity in various parts of the lens and causes light to refract at varying densities, resulting in severe problems with glare. If the lens becomes totally opaque, cataract surgery may be required to extract the lens; one of the most frequently performed types of eye surgery, it carries relatively little risk, even for very old persons, and can significantly enhance quality of life. Indeed this is the most common surgical procedure performed on people over age 65 and can often be performed as an outpatient procedure (Straatsma, Foos, and Horwitz, 1985). A lens implant in place of the extracted lens capsule is the most common treatment, but a contact lens or special cataract glasses are alternative treatments. The advantage of the implant is that it does not require the older person to have good finger dexterity to put the lens in the eye and take it out. The implant is particularly useful for the person who still has one natural lens, because it allows an image to form at the same distance from the retina in both eyes. When the older person first obtains a substitute lens, it takes some time to adjust to performing daily activities, especially if the artificial lens is not an implant, and the images form on different planes for the two eyes. Researchers have found that patients who receive a lens implant show improvement not just in visual function, but also in objective assessments of activities of daily living and manual function within 4 to 12 months (Applegate et al., 1987).

In addition to getting harder and more opaque, the lens becomes yellower with age. This is also due to changes in the collagen tissue that makes up the lens. The increasingly more opaque and yellowing lens acts as a filter to screen out wavelengths of light, thus reducing the individual's color sensitivity and ability to discriminate among colors that are close together in the blue-green range. Changes in the lens are especially noticeable after age 60 (Cooper, Ward, Gowland and McIntosh, 1991; Weale, 1988). Older people may have problems selecting clothing in this color range, sometimes resulting in their wearing poorly coordinated outfits. Deterioration in color discrimination may also be due to age-related changes in the visual and neural pathways.

The physical environment can be redesigned to accommodate the older person's competence in this area. For example, older people can benefit from rooms and hallways that use widely contrasting colors on opposite ends of the color spectrum, such as red and yellow, green and orange. Generally, blue and green should not be used to define adjoining spaces, such as stairs and stair landings, floors and ramps, and curbs and curbcuts. This is particularly important when the junction of those spaces represents different levels, so that not seeing these color distinctions leaves a person at risk of an accident.

## Other Changes in Vision

Depth and distance perception also deteriorate with aging, because of a loss of convergence of images formed in the two eyes. This is caused by differential rates of hardening and opacification in the two lenses, uneven refraction of light onto the retina, and reduced visual acuity in aging eyes. (The problem of depth perception becomes compounded for people who have had cataract surgery and must use contact lenses or cataract glasses.) As a result, there is a rapid decline after age 75 in the ability to judge distances and depths, particularly in low-light situations and in the absence of orienting cues. Examples of situations with inadequate cues include stairs with no color distinctions at the edges and pedestrian ramps or curbcuts with varying slopes and no cues to guide the user. The older driver who is undergoing changes in depth perception experiences increased problems when driving behind others, approaching a stop sign, or parking between other cars.

Another change in the visual system that normally occurs with age is narrower peripheral vision (the ability to see on either side without moving the eyes or the head). The field of vision may be as wide as 270° in some young persons, and as narrow as 120° in some older adults. This is because the fovea (or blind spot) increases in size between ages 60 and 90, and retinal metabolism deteriorates, especially in the peripheral

region where there are fewer nerve endings. The problem of reduced peripheral vision becomes particularly acute when driving. An older person may not see cars approaching from the left or right at an intersection. Combined with reduced reaction time and age-related musculo-skeletal changes that make turning the neck difficult, older drivers experience greater risks. These changes are often of great concern to family and friends who worry about whether and how to convince an older person to stop driving.

Some elderly persons experiencing senile macular degeneration may have the opposite problem: loss of the central visual field. The macula is that point in the retina with the best visual acuity, because it has the highest concentration of cones. *Macular degeneration,* the fourth major cause of blindness in the United States, occurs if the macula receives less oxygen than it needs, resulting in destruction of the existing nerve endings in this region. The incidence of macular degeneration, like cataracts, increases with age, but even more dramatically. People over age 80 have 15 times the likelihood of developing macular degeneration than people aged 60.

The early stages of macular degeneration may begin with a loss of detail vision; then central vision gradually becomes worse, so that in severe cases, the older person has poor central vision, but adequate peripheral vision. Total blindness rarely occurs. Older persons with this condition may compensate by using their remaining peripheral vision. They may then appear to be looking at the shoulder of someone they are addressing, but actually be relying on peripheral vision to see the person's face. Laser treatment in the early stages of this disease has been effective in preventing the loss of central vision in many cases.

Some older people experience reduced secretion of tears, often associated with diseases such as Sjögren's Syndrome. These individuals, most often post-menopausal women, complain of "dry eyes" that cause irritation and discomfort. Unfortunately, this condition has no known cure, but it does not cause blindness and it can be managed with artificial tears to prevent redness and irritation. Artificial tears can be purchased at most drugstores.

The muscles that support the eyes, similar to those in other parts of the body, deteriorate with age. In particular, two key muscles atrophy. These are the elevator muscles, which move the eyeball up and down within its socket, and the ciliary muscle, which aids the lens in changing its shape. Deterioration of the elevator muscles results in a reduced range of upward gaze. This may cause problems with reading overhead signs and seeing objects that are placed above eye level, such as on high kitchen shelves. Weakening of the ciliary muscles contributes to the problem of poor accommodation in the later years.

## Assisting Adaptation and Quality of Life through Environmental Modifications

Many older adults report significant impairments in their activities of daily living, including reading small print, functioning in and adjusting to dimly lit environments, tracking moving targets, and locating a sign in a cluttered background (Kosnick et al., 1988). This may mean that an older person feels compelled to give up valued social activities, such as playing cards, participating in reading clubs, driving, cooking, and hobbies such as sewing, leathercrafts, and stamp collecting. Abandoning these activities often produces a sense of loss and isolation. Furthermore, the environment outside the home can become too demanding and difficult to negotiate safely. Family and friends can assist by providing encouragement and by improving the physical environment to support rather than hinder an older person who is experiencing these changes.

In terms of maintaining person-environment congruence and psychological well-being, an aging person should be encouraged to maintain social contacts, even if new activities must be substituted for old. Older people can take advantage of large-print newspapers and books, "talking books" that are available in many community libraries, and, more recently, larger fonts on flat-screen computer monitors that are designed to reduce glare. Playing cards with large letters also allow the person to continue participating in bridge club activities. Local agencies serving the visually impaired often provide low-vision aids at minimal cost. These include needle threaders for sewing; templates for rotary telephones, irons, and other appliances; large-print phone books, clocks, and calendars; and magnifying glasses for situations where large-print substitutes are unavailable.

Family and friends also can help by improving the physical environment inside and around an older person's home. These changes may be as simple as replacing existing lightbulbs with higher wattage and 3-way bulbs, rearranging furniture so that low tables and footstools are outside the traffic flow, and putting large-print labels on prescription bottles, spices, and cooking supplies. Other environmental modifications may be more costly or require the use of a professional architect. Contrasting color strips on stairs, especially on carpeted or slippery linoleum stairs, aid the older person's depth perception.

A magnifying glass helps older people read small print.

Color and light coding of ramps and other changes in elevation also can be valuable. To the extent possible, changes in floor surfaces such as door sills should be removed or well demarcated. Increasing the number of light sources, installing nonslip and nonglossy floor coverings, and using a flat paint instead of glossy finishes can reduce the problem of glare. Venetian and vertical blinds can also help the older person control glare throughout the day. An even better architectural solution is to use indirect or task lighting (e.g., reading lamps, countertop lamps) rather than ceiling fixtures, and adding dimmer switches to the rooms used most by older people.

All these solutions can enhance the competence of a person who is experiencing gradual declines in visual functions. Age-related changes in vision need not handicap people if they can be encouraged to adapt their usual activities and their environment to fit their current level of visual functioning and their needs. An older person who is having difficulty adjusting to losses produced by vision decrements may initially resist such changes. One way to address this resistance is for family members and service providers to involve the older person in decisions about environmental modifications and alternative activities.

## CHANGES IN HEARING

In terms of survival, vision and hearing are perhaps our most critical links to the world. Although vision is important for negotiating the physical environment, hearing is vital for communication. Because hearing is closely associated with speech, its loss disrupts a person's understanding of others and even the recognition of one's own speech. Consider some ways in which we rely on our hearing ability in everyday life: in conversations with family, friends, and coworkers; in localizing the sound of approaching automobiles as we cross the street or drive; and in interpreting other people's emotions through their tone of voice and use of language.

How does a person function if these abilities gradually deteriorate? Clearly, an older person who is experiencing hearing loss learns to adapt and make changes in behavior and in social interactions, so as to reduce the detrimental social impact of hearing loss. Many younger hearing-impaired persons learn sign language or lip reading. But these are complex skills requiring extensive training and practice, and are less likely to be learned by those who experience gradual hearing loss late in life.

### The Anatomy and Physiology of the Ear

It is useful to review the anatomy of the ear in order to understand where and how auditory function deteriorates with age. The auditory system has three components, as illustrated in Figure 6–2. The outer ear begins at the pinna, that visible portion that is identified as the ear. The auditory canal is also part of the outer ear. Note the shape of the pinna and auditory canal; it is a most efficient design for localizing sounds.

The eardrum, or tympanic membrane, is a thin membrane that separates the outer ear from the middle ear. This membrane is sensitive to air pressure of varying degrees and vibrates in response to a range of loud and soft sounds. In the middle ear are located three bones: the malleus, the incus, and the stapes, more commonly known as the hammer, the anvil, and the stirrup (so named because of their shapes). These very finely positioned and interrelated bones carry sound vibrations from the middle ear to the inner ear—that snail-shaped circular structure called the cochlea. Amplified sounds are converted in the cochlea to nerve impulses, which are then sent through the internal auditory canal and the cochlear nerve to the brain, where they are translated into meaningful sounds. The cochlea is a fluid-filled chamber with thousands of hair cells that vibrate two parallel membranes to move sound waves. High-pitched sounds stimulate hair cells at the base of the cochlea; low-pitched sounds stimulate hair cells at the apex. The vibration of these hair cells is one of several factors

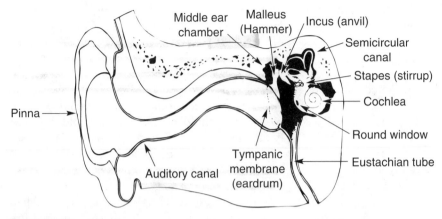

**FIGURE 6–2    The Ear**

## HEARING LOSS AND PERSONALITY CHANGE

Some researchers have suggested that hearing problems lead to social isolation and reduced intellectual functioning (Granick, Kleban, and Weiss, 1976; Gilhome-Herbst and Humphrey, 1980). Based on your own personal and professional experiences with the elderly, this may initially seem to be the case. However, it is difficult to distinguish the effect of hearing acuity from true intellectual functioning, since most tests of cognitive function demand some hearing ability. Elderly with hearing loss have been found to perform worse on verbal tests of cognition than older persons with no hearing loss. However, the researchers found no differences in nonverbal tests (Thomas et al., 1983). Emotional stability and social integration were also found to be unaffected by hearing loss. In another study, 50 older persons with high-frequency hearing loss were questioned about their social interactions and organizational involvement; there was no association between hearing loss and social involvement (Norris and Cunningham, 1981). These findings support the results of an earlier study which found that hearing loss does not significantly affect older people's social involvement (Powers and Powers, 1978).

There is some clinical evidence that older persons with a diagnosis of paranoia are more likely to have severe hearing problems than are normal elderly, especially among paranoid persons who have had the hearing loss since middle age. Some research with hospitalized aged psychiatric patients supports these clinical observations (Cooper and Curry, 1976). In contrast, Moore's (1981) study of elderly psychiatric patients in the United Kingdom revealed no association between deafness and paranoid disorders. However, this latter study did not obtain information on the duration of the deafness or the psychiatric disorder. A study of community elderly also confirmed the lack of association between hearing disorders and emotional distress (Thomas et al., 1983).

It is important to note that these are *correlational* findings; that is, the finding that some elderly who have psychiatric symptoms are also hearing impaired does not provide sufficient evidence to conclude that hearing impairments that begin in middle age will cause paranoid reactions in old age. Other reports of the co-existence of hearing loss and psychiatric disorders in older populations (Gilhome-Herbst and Humphrey, 1980; Eastwood et al., 1985) must also be interpreted with caution because the data are correlational. In summary, we cannot conclude that there is a causal relationship between hearing loss and cognitive or affective disorders in old age.

involved in the perception of pitch (or frequency) and loudness (intensity) of a sound.

## Age-related Changes

The pinna appears somewhat elongated and rigid in some elderly. These changes in the outer ear, however, have no impact on hearing acuity. The supporting walls of the external auditory canals also deteriorate with age, as is true for many muscular structures in the human body, including, as we have seen, the muscles of the eye. Arthritic conditions may affect the joints between the malleus and stapes, making it more difficult for these bones to perform their vibratory function. Otosclerosis is a condition in which the stapes becomes fixed and cannot vibrate. It is sometimes found in young persons, but more frequently occurs in the later years.

The greatest decline with age occurs in the cochlea, where structural changes result in *presbycusis,* or age-related hearing loss. Changes in auditory thresholds can be detected by age 30 or even younger, but the degeneration of hair cells and membranes in the cochlea is not observed until much later. Tests of pure tone thresholds (i.e., the level at which a tone of a single frequency can be detected) have revealed a steady decline in longitudinal studies over 15 years. Changes in the high-frequency range were found to be about 1dB per year. In the range of speech, changes were slow until age 60, then accelerated to a rate of 1.3dB per year after age 80 (Brant and Fozard, 1990). These declines may be even worse for the general population, since this study excluded people with diseases of the ear and with self-reported hearing difficulties. It is estimated that 13 percent of the population age 65 and older in the United States suffer from advanced presbycusis. Up to 75 percent have mild to moderate loss of hearing (Corso, 1987; Olsho, Harkins, and Lenhardt, 1985).

As with studies regarding changes in the visual system, researchers in the area of auditory perception have suggested that changes in the brain are responsible for the deterioration in auditory functioning. These may include cellular deterioration and vascular changes in the major auditory pathways to the brain (Corso, 1987).

*Tinnitus* is another problem that affects hearing in old age. This is a high-pitched "ringing" that is particularly acute at night or in quiet surroundings. It may occur bilaterally or in one ear only. The incidence increases threefold between youth and middle age, and fourfold between youth and old age. Tinnitus is generally not associated with other types of hearing impairments; it cannot be cured, but people suffering from tinnitus can learn to manage it.

In contrast to visual changes, hearing loss appears to be significantly affected by environmental causes. People who have been exposed to high-volume and high-frequency noise throughout their lives (e.g., urban dwellers and factory workers) experience more hearing decrements in old age than do those from rural, low-noise environments. Women generally show less decline than men (see Figure 6–3). It is interesting to speculate why these sex differences appear. Are they due to variations in noise exposure or to hormonal differences between men and women? The fact that severe hearing loss is found in some women suggests that the former hypothesis may be more likely.

Hearing loss may also be caused by excess ear wax, which seems to accumulate more rapidly in some older people. A thorough audiology exam should be done after a physician removes the ear wax in these cases.

## Compensation and Adaptation

Hearing loss can be of several types, involving limited volume and range or distortion of sounds perceived. Older persons who have lost hearing acuity in the range of speech (250–3,000 Hz.) have particular difficulties distinguishing the sibilants or high-frequency consonants such as *z, s, sh, f, p, k, t,* and *g.* Their speech comprehension deteriorates as a result, which may be the first sign of hearing loss. In contrast, low-frequency hearing loss has minimal impact on speech comprehension. As Figure 6–3 illustrates, higher

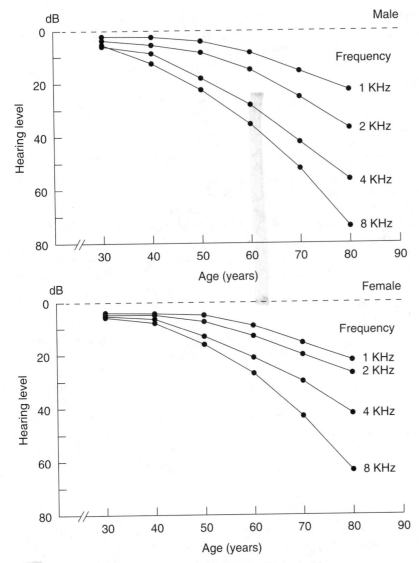

**FIGURE 6–3**   **Gender Differences in Hearing Thresholds**
SOURCE: J. M. Ordy, K. R. Brizzee, T. Beavers, and P. Medart. Age differences in the functional
and structural organization of the auditory system in man. In J. M. Ordy and K. R. Brizzee
(Eds.), *Sensory systems and communication in the elderly* (New York: Raven Press, 1979), p. 156.
Reprinted with permission of the author and publisher.

frequency sounds can be heard better by raising
the intensity. Studies of speech perception have
increased the recognition of consonants (p, t, k,
b, d, g) by 50–90 percent among older persons by
raising their intensity (Guelke, 1987).

Thus, an individual experiencing increased
problems with hearing may compensate by raising the volume of the TV and radio, moving
closer to the TV, or even listening to other types
of music made by lower pitched instruments such

as an organ. When this occurs, it is imperative to determine whether a hearing loss exists, to identify the cause, and to fit the individual with an appropriate hearing aid, if that is possible. A hearing aid increases the volume of sound. This may compensate for loss of higher-frequency sounds, but hearing aids cannot completely obliterate the problem of presbycusis. In fact, they often result in such major adaptation problems that many older persons stop wearing them after several months of frustrated attempts to adjust to the device. A major difficulty with hearing aids is that the volume of background noise is raised, in addition to the sound that the user of the device is trying to hear. There is also a greater social stigma associated with wearing a hearing aid than with wearing glasses. These are undoubtedly some of the reasons why relatively few older people who are hearing impaired use them.

If an older person feels stigmatized by the hearing aid, emotional support from others can be useful in easing the adjustment. If the hearing aid does not appear to fit an older person's needs, a replacement should be sought. Fortunately, developments in hearing aid technology are resulting in custom-made designs that amplify only those frequencies that an individual user has trouble hearing, without magnifying background noises. These newer designs also are less obtrusive and fit well inside the ear.

Other means of compensating for hearing loss are to design environments that dampen background noises or to select such settings for communicating with older persons. Sound levels should not exceed 80 decibels in settings where older persons are found. Soundproof rooms are beneficial, particularly if housing for older people is built on busy streets or near freeways, but this is a costly alternative. Clinics and offices of health professionals should have at least one quiet area where an older patient can communicate with professionals without being distracted by background noises. Older people who are experiencing auditory decline can also benefit from new designs in telephones with volume adjusters and lights that blink when the phone rings.

When conversing with people who are experiencing age-related hearing loss, the following hints can help both younger and older persons enjoy their communication:

1. Face an older person directly.
2. Sit somewhat close.
3. Do not cover the face with hands or objects when speaking.
4. Speak slowly and clearly, but without exaggerating speech.
5. Do not shout.
6. Avoid distracting background noises by selecting an appropriate place away from other people, machines, and traffic sounds.
7. Speak in a lower, but not monotonic, tone of voice.
8. Repeat key points in different ways.

One of the most frustrating experiences for some older people is the simultaneous deterioration of both hearing and vision. Although it is relatively rare for aging to result in significant declines in both these functions, family members, friends, and professionals must be especially sensitive to the communication techniques described earlier. When talking with an older person who is impaired in both hearing and vision, touching his or her hand, arm, or shoulder may aid communication.

## CHANGES IN TASTE AND SMELL

Although older people may complain that food does not taste as good as it once did, these complaints are probably not due to an age-associated generalized loss of taste sensitivity. It was once thought that age brought dramatic decreases in the number of taste buds on the tongue, that this loss of receptor elements led to functional loss that was experienced as a dulling of taste sensation, and that these changes accounted for older people's reduced enjoyment of food (Mistretta, 1984). Recent studies, however, have challenged each link in this chain of reasoning.

Early research on taste anatomy reported taste bud loss (Arey, Tremaine, and Monzingo, 1935), but more recent studies show that the number of taste buds does not decline with age (Miller, 1988). Early studies of taste function found large age-related changes in taste thresholds (Murphy, 1979). However, more recent research has found much smaller age-related declines in threshold sensitivity (Bartoshuk, 1986; Cowart, 1989). Moreover, there are improved measurement techniques in this field that control for differences between generations in the way they respond to demand characteristics of the task. This has led to the conclusion in more recent studies that threshold loss almost never involves more than one of the four basic taste qualities.

Thresholds reflect the ability of the sensory system to detect weak stimuli, but this aspect of taste function may be less relevant to the enjoyment of food than the ability to appreciate taste intensity. For example, older people with decreased taste threshold sensitivity will require more salt to know if there is any salt on their vegetables. But to determine *how* salty the vegetables are requires a different taste mechanism that may still be functioning. This ability to appreciate the strength of a taste stimulus can be assessed by modern direct scaling techniques. Studies using these techniques have demonstrated that taste intensity perception is remarkably robust with age (Tylenda and Baum, 1988).

The notion that various functions decline differentially has replaced the belief that older people experience a generalized taste loss. The research task now is to specify *which* aspects of taste function remain intact and which decline with normal aging or disease. Although the taste function of older people does not undergo a general decline in strength, it demonstrates changes that are specific in a variety of ways (Weiffenbach, 1990). For example, although the relationship between taste intensity and stimulus strength is age-stable, judgments of taste intensity become less reliable with age. Even this change in reliability is specific. It affects salt but

not sugar judgments (Weiffenbach, Cowart, and Baum, 1986). It is also important to note that in studies where the average performance of the older individuals is poorer, some older persons perform as well as, or better, than many younger persons.

Appreciation of food does not depend on taste alone. The sense of smell clearly is involved. We have all experienced changes in the way food "tastes" while ill with a head cold and a stuffy nose. These changes, which you can mimic by holding your nose, suggest that sensitivity to airborne stimuli plays a key role in the perception of foods. There is considerable evidence for age-related decline in the sense of smell. Older people perceive airborne stimuli as less intense than younger persons, and do less well on odor identification. External factors such as smoking and medications contribute to these differences, but even after accounting for these factors, age differences are dominant (Ship and Weiffenbach, 1993; Doty et al., 1984). When parallel assessments are made in the same subject, age-related declines for smell are greater than for taste. This suggests that

Cooking with fresh ingredients and spices stimulates olfactory and taste sensitivity.

one way to increase older people's enjoyment of eating is to provide them with enhanced food odors (Schiffman and Warwick, 1988).

Certain problems are associated with reduced sensitivity to taste and smell. For example, declines in the recognition and identification of odors, especially the odor of gas, are observed in people over age 80. This raises an important safety concern with this age group. Some older people compensate for losses in taste sensitivity by increasing their salt intake. This is not only harmful for individuals with hypertension, but it is also ineffective if the lack of taste is really due to reduced sensitivity to the smell of food. Other older people may find that food is so unappetizing that they lose interest in it, and eat only when they are very hungry. This is risky because it may result in poor nutrition. A better approach is to enhance the flavor of foods with herbs and spices, and with pleasant aromas (e.g., basil, tarragon, and cinnamon) that do not disturb the older person's digestive system, and may actually enhance the digestive process. Classes in cooking with herbs and spices can be valuable for older people who are experiencing changes in their taste and olfactory abilities. Along with cooking techniques, the nutritional value of each ingredient, and the benefits and potential harm of each spice and herb should be reviewed in these classes. These activities can also help older people in sharpening their sensitivity to tastes and odors, and enhancing quality of life.

## CHANGES IN THE SENSE OF TOUCH

*Somesthetic* or touch sensitivity also deteriorates with age. This is partially due to changes in the skin (see Chapter 5) and partially to a loss with age in the number of nerve endings. Reduced touch sensitivity is especially prevalent in the fingertips and palms, and in the lower extremities. Age differences in touch sensitivity of the fingertips have been found to be much more dramatic than in the forearm. Using two-point discrimination tests (i.e., the minimum distance

at which the subject detects the two points of a caliper), researchers have found that older persons need two to four times the separation of two points as do younger persons. This has significant implications for daily tasks that require sensitivity of the fingertips, such as the use of Braille by older blind persons (Stevens, 1992; Verillo, 1980).

An important aspect of touch sensitivity is pain perception. Older people are less able to discriminate among levels of perceived pain than young respondents. Studies of age differences in threshold levels of pain, however, have produced mixed results (Harkins and Warner, 1980).

It is important to distinguish between pain perception and pain behavior. Tolerance for pain is a subjective experience, which may be related to cultural and personality factors. In older people, increased complaints of pain may be a function of depression and psychosomatic needs. On the other hand, some people may attempt to minimize their pain by not reporting above-threshold levels of unpleasant stimuli. This is consistent with a frequently observed attitude among many older persons that pain, illness, and discomfort are necessary corollaries of aging. In fact, most elderly probably underreport actual pain experienced. For example, an older person may not report symptoms of a heart attack unless or until it is severe. This has significant implications for health-seeking behaviors, as in Chapter 7.

## CHANGES IN MOBILITY AND THE KINESTHETIC SENSE

Although the incidence of mobility problems is greater among older people, aging per se is not the cause of motor disabilities. Disease states such as arthritis, stroke, some cardiac disorders, and damage to the kinesthetic sense may affect both the peripheral and central mechanisms responsible for mobility. Other factors limiting mobility include stiffness of joints, reduced ability to raise or turn the neck, and difficulty in gait

## AN OLDER PERSON WITH MULTIPLE SENSORY IMPAIRMENTS

Mrs. Wilson is an 82-year-old widow who has lived on her own for the past 20 years since her husband died. She had cataract surgery 12 years ago in her left eye, and began wearing a hearing aid 10 years ago. She has adjusted quite well to these changes in her vision and hearing, and maintains her quality of life by remaining active. The only situations she avoids are large gatherings, such as lunch at the senior center where it always seems to be too noisy for her to enjoy conversations with her friends. More recently, Mrs. Wilson has stopped driving at night because of increasing sensitivity to glare and problems with finding her way on the poorly lit rural roads near her home. She enjoys gardening and is proud of her rose garden with its varied fragrances in the summer. Recently she has noticed a slight loss of her well-honed skills in

telling apart one variety of rose from another by their fragrances, but she remains better at it than her children and grandchildren! She also plants aromatic herbs in her garden so she can use them to perk up her cooking. The medications she has been taking over the past several years seem to have affected her taste sensitivity, so she enjoys cooking with herbs and spices for herself and her friends. Mrs. Wilson realizes that her vision, hearing, taste, and smell have all declined as she has aged, but she is determined to make the best use of her remaining abilities in these senses. The changes she has made in her environment, such as avoiding night driving and using more herbs in cooking, are examples of Mrs. Wilson's attempts to maintain person-environment congruence.

and posture. Arthritis is a common chronic disease in older people that has a major impact on daily functioning, as will be discussed in Chapter 7. Simple tasks, such as reaching cupboards and overhead shelves, may become more difficult for an older person with arthritis or *kyphosis* (i.e., curvature of the spine due to osteoporosis). These conditions occur more frequently in older women. Combined with declines in the visual system that limit peripheral vision and upward gaze, an older person experiencing stiffness of neck joints and kyphosis must make adjustments while driving. Environmental modifications, such as a driver's seat that tilts back and raises to fit an older driver's special needs, can be useful.

The kinesthetic system lets an individual know his or her position in space; adjustments in body position become known through kinesthetic cues. Because of age-related changes in the central nervous system, which controls the kinesthetic mechanism, as well as in muscles, older people demonstrate a decreased ability to orient their bodies in space and to detect externally induced changes in body position. Other physiological and disease-related changes, such as dam-

age to the inner ear, may exacerbate this problem. Researchers who have compared old and young subjects have found that older persons need more external cues to orient themselves in space, and can be incorrect by 5 to 20 degrees in estimating their position. If both visual and surface cues of position are lost, older people experience postural sway or inability to maintain a vertical stance (Teasdale, Stelmach, and Breunig, 1991).

Not surprisingly, these changes in motor functioning and in the kinesthetic system result in greater caution among older persons, who then tend to take slower, shuffling, and more deliberate steps. Older people are more likely to seek external spatial cues and supports while walking. As a result, they are less likely to go outside in inclement weather for fear of slipping or falling. Some may complain of dizziness and vertigo. These normal, age-related changes combine with the problems of slower reaction time, muscle weakness, and reduced visual acuity to make it far more likely for older people to fall and injure themselves. However, recent attempts to improve balance through general and aerobic exercise, and through systematic programs to increase visual cues have been successful in enhancing the postural stability of healthy older persons (Hu and Woollacott, 1994). Other advantages of exercise programs for older adults will be discussed in Chapter 7.

## Summary and Implications

Changes in sensory function with age do not occur at a consistent rate in all senses and for all people. Some people show rapid declines in vision while maintaining their hearing and other sensory abilities. Others experience an early deterioration in olfactory sensation, but not in other areas. All of us experience some loss in these functions with age, but interindividual differences are quite pronounced.

Normal age-related declines in vision reduce the ability to respond to differing light levels; to function in low-light situations; to see in places with high levels of glare; to discern color tones, especially in the green-blue-violet range; and to judge distances and depth. Peripheral vision becomes somewhat narrowed with age, as does upward and downward gaze. Older people have more diseases of the eye, including glaucoma, cataracts, and macular degeneration; if these diseases are not treated, blindness can result. Visual impairments generally result in more problems with activities of daily living than do hearing impairments. Therefore, older persons who experience significant declines in visual function with age should be encouraged to maintain former levels of activity, either by adapting the environment to fit changing needs or by substituting new activities for those that have become more difficult. Some older people prefer to withdraw from previous activities, thereby becoming more isolated and at risk of depression and declining quality of life.

Decline in auditory function generally starts earlier than visual problems, and affects more people. Significant impairments in speech comprehension often result. Although hearing aids can frequently improve hearing in the speech range by raising the intensity of speech that is in the high frequency range, many older people feel uncomfortable and even stigmatized when using them. Hence, the solutions to communicating with hearing-impaired older people may lie mostly within the environment, not within older persons themselves. These include changes in communication styles, such as speaking directly at an older person in a clear voice, but not shouting; speaking in a lower tone; repeating key points; and sitting closer to a hearing-impaired person. Environmental aids such as soundproof or quiet rooms and modified telephones can also be invaluable for older people who are experiencing significant hearing declines.

Although many older people complain that food does not taste as good as it once did, there are only minimal changes with age in taste acuity. The decline in olfactory receptors with age is more significant than in taste receptors, and may be responsible for the perception of reduced taste acuity. These changes are more pronounced in people who smoke or drink heavily, but the use of medications has only modest effects. There is less change in people who have sharpened their taste and olfactory sensitivity, such as professional winemakers and perfumers. This pattern suggests that older people should be encouraged to participate in activities that enhance their taste and olfactory functions.

Age-related changes in touch sensitivity can affect pain perception and produce reduced sensitivity in the extremities (e.g., fingertips, palms, and toes). This could place an older person at greater risk of scalding because of an inability to detect hot water and surface temperatures. Slower reaction times and poorer kinesthetic responses with aging often result in slower movement and greater caution in older people, especially in unfamiliar environments or where surfaces are slippery or wet.

As we have seen in previous chapters, normal aging does not lead to disability. However, the changes that occur with normal aging, as noted here and elsewhere, are likely to result in a slowing of functions, increased caution, and a reduction of physical activity. This should not be considered a sign of disease but a recognition of the older person's sensory and physical limitations and capabilities.

Older people should be encouraged to maximize use of all their functions, so that deterioration does not occur more rapidly than necessary. Unfortunately, the fear of not being able to hear, see, or maintain their balance keeps many older people tied to their homes and increases the risk of social isolation. It is important for people of all ages to maintain and perhaps even increase their activity levels because those who use their neuromuscular functions, sensory capacities, and cognitive skills regularly can prevent premature deterioration of these functions. Hence, the recognition of and use of one's capacities to the fullest should begin early in life and continue into advanced old age.

As we learn more from studies of sensory changes with aging, reports that once appeared definitive are found to be less so, and a complete understanding of some areas is shown to be lacking. This is particularly true in the areas of taste, smell, and pain perception. Research is needed to distinguish normal changes in these areas from those that are related to disease, and those that can be prevented. Longitudinal research would help to answer many of these questions. Finally, research that examines the impact of sensory deterioration on the older person's interactions with the environment is also needed.

# REFERENCES

Accardi, F. E., Gombos, M. M., and Gombos, G. M. Common causes of blindness: A pilot survey in Brooklyn, New York. *Annals of Ophthalmology,* 1985, *17,* 289–294.

Adams, P. F., and Collins, G. Measures of health among older persons living in the community. In R. J. Havlik, M. G. Liu and M. G. Kovar (Eds.). *Health statistics on older persons, United States, 1986. Vital and Health Statistics,* Series 3, No. 25, DHHS Publ. No. PHS 87–1409. Washington, D.C.: U.S. Government Printing Office, 1987.

Anand, M. P. Accidents in the home. In W. F. Anderson and B. Isaacs (Eds.), *Current achievements in geriatrics.* London: Cassell, 1964.

Applegate, W. B., Miller, J. T., Elam, J. T., Freeman, J. M., Wood, T. O., and Gettlefinger, T. C. Impact of cataract surgery with lens implantation on vision and physical function in elderly patients. *Journal of the American Medical Association,* 1987, *257,* 1064–1066.

Applegate, W. B., Runyan, J. W., Brasfield, L., Williams, M. L., Konigsberg, C., and Fouche, C. Analysis of the 1980 heat wave in Memphis. *Journal of the American Geriatrics Society,* 1981, *29,* 337–342.

Arey, L., Tremaine, M., and Monzingo, F. The numerical and topographical relations of taste buds to human circumvallate papillae throughout the life span. *Anatomical Record,* 1935, *64,* 9–25.

Avery, W. M. Hypothermia and heat illness. *Aging,* 1984, *344,* 43–47.

Bartoshuk, L. B., Riflein, B., Marks, L. C., and Barns, P. Taste and aging. *Journal of Gerontology,* 1986, *41,* 51–57.

Borish, J. M. *Clinical refraction* (3d ed.). Chicago: Professional Press, 1970.

Bradley, R. M., Stedman, H. M., and Mistretta, C. M. A quantitative study of lingual taste buds and papillae in the aging rhesus monkey tongue. In R. T. Davis and Charles W. Leathers (Eds.), *Behavioral pathology of aging in rhesus monkeys.* New York: A. R. Liss, 1985.

Brant, L. J., and Fozard, J. Age changes in pure-tone hearing thresholds in a longitudinal study of normal human aging. *Journal of the Acoustical Society of America,* 1990, *88,* 813–820.

Cooper, A. F., and Curry, A. R. The pathology of deafness in the paranoid and affective psychoses of later life. *Journal of Psychosomatic Research,* 1976, *20,* 97–105.

Cooper, B. A., Ward, M., Gowland, C. A., and McIntosh, J. M. The use of the Lanthony New Color Test in determining the effects of aging on color vision. *Journals of Gerontology,* 1991, *46,* 320–324.

Corso, J. F. Sensory-perceptual processes and aging. *Annual Review of Gerontology and Geriatrics,* 1987, *7,* 29–55.

Cowart, B. J. Relationships between taste and smell across the life span. In C. Murphy, W. S. Cain, and D. M. Hegsted (Eds.), Nutrition and the chemical senses in aging: Recent advances and current research needs. *Annals of the New York Academy of Sciences, 561,* 39–55. New York: New York Academy of Sciences, 1989.

Doty, R. L., Shaman, P., Applebaum, S. L., Giberson, R., Siksorski, L., and Rosenberg, L. Smell identification ability: Changes with age. *Science,* 1984, *226,* 1441–1443.

Eastwood, M. R., Corbin, S. L., Reed, M., Nobbs, H., and Kedward, H. B. Acquired hearing loss and psychiatric illness: An estimate of prevalence and co-morbidity in a geriatric setting. *British Journal of Psychiatry,* 1985, *147,* 552–556.

Foster, K. G., Ellis, F. P., Doré, C., Exton-Smith, A. N., and Weiner, J. S. Sweat responses in the aged. *Age and Ageing,* 1976, *5,* 91–101.

Gilhome-Herbst, K., and Humphrey, C. Hearing impairment and mental state in the elderly living at home. *British Medical Journal,* 1980, *281,* 903–905.

Granick, S., Kleban, M. H., and Weiss, A. D. Relationships between hearing loss and cognition in normally hearing aged persons. *Journal of Gerontology,* 1976, *31,* 434–440.

Guelke, R. W. Consonant burst enhancement: A possible means to improve intelligibility for the hard of hearing. *Journal of Rehabilitation Research and Development,* 1987, *24,* 217–220.

Harkins, S. W., and Warner, M. H. Age and pain. In C. Eisdorfer (Ed.), *Annual review of gerontology and geriatrics* (vol. 1). New York: Springer, 1980.

Hu, M. H., and Woollacott, M. H. Multisensory training of standing balance in older adults. *Journals of Gerontology,* 1994, *49,* M52–M71.

Kenshalo, D. R. Changes in the vestibuler and somesthetic systems as a function of age. In J. M. Ordy and K. R. Brizzee (Eds.), *Sensory systems and communication in the elderly.* New York: Raven Press, 1979.

Kini, M. M., Leibowitz, H. M., Colton, T., Nickerson, R. J., Ganley, J., and Dawber, T. R. Prevalence of senile cataract, diabetic retinopathy, senile macular degeneration and open-angle glaucoma in the Framingham Eye Study. *American Journal of Ophthalmology,* 1978, *85,* 28–34.

Kline, D. W., Kline, T. J. B., Fozard, J. L., Kosnik, W., Schieber, F., and Sekuler, R. Vision, aging, and driving: The problems of older drivers. *Journals of Gerontology,* 1992, *47,* 27–34.

Kolanowski, A., and Gunter, L. Hypothermia in the elderly. *Geriatric Nursing,* 1981, *2,* 362–365.

Kosnick, W., Winslow, L., Kline, D., Rasinski, K. and Sekuler, R. Visual changes in daily life throughout adulthood. *Journals of Gerontology,* 1988, *43,* 63–70.

Leibowitz, H. M., Krueger, D. E., Maunder, L. R., Milton, R. C, Kini, M. M., Kahn, H. A., Nickerson, R. J., Pool, J., Colton, T. L., and Ganley, J. P. The Framingham Eye Study Monograph. *Survey of Ophthalmology Supplement,* 1980, *24,* 335–610.

McFarland, R. A., and Fisher, M. B. Alterations in dark adaptation as a function of age. *Journal of Gerontology,* 1955, *10,* 424–428.

Miller, I. J. Human taste bud density across adult age groups. *Journals of Gerontology,* 1988, *43,* B26–30.

Mistretta, C. M. Aging effects on anatomy and neurophysiology of taste and smell. *Gerodontology,* 1984, *3,* 131–136.

Moore, N. C. Is paranoid illness associated with sensory defects in the elderly? *Journal of Psychosomatic Research,* 1981, *25,* 69–74.

Murphy, C. The effect of age on taste sensitivity. In S. Han and D. Coons (Eds.), *Special senses in aging.* Ann Arbor: Institute of Gerontology, University of Michigan, 1979.

National Center for Health Statistics. Current estimates from the national health interview survey. *Vital and Health Statistics,* 1975, Series 10, No. 115.

Norris, M. L., and Cunningham, D. S. Social impact of hearing loss in the aged. *Journal of Gerontology,* 1981, *36,* 727–729.

Olsho, L. W., Harkins, S. W., and Lenhardt, M. L. Aging and the auditory system. In J. E. Birren and K. W. Schaie (Eds.). *Handbook of the psychology of aging* (2d ed). New York: Van Nostrand Reinhold, 1985.

Ordy, J. M., and Brizzee, K. R. (Eds.). *Sensory system and communication in the elderly.* New York: Raven Press, 1979.

Pastalan, L. *Age-related vision and hearing changes: An empathic approach.* Slide-tape program developed at the University of Michigan, Ann Arbor, 1976.

Powers, J. K., and Powers, E. A. Hearing problems of elderly persons: Social consequences and prevalence. *Journal of the American Speech and Hearing Association (ASHA),* 1978, *20,* 79–83.

Rudberg, M. A., Furner, S. E., Dunn, J. E., and Cassel, C. K. The relationship of visual and hearing impairments to disability. *Journals of Gerontology*, 1993, *48*, M261–M265.

Schiffman, S. S., and Warwick, Z. S. Flavor enhancement of foods for the elderly can reverse anorexia. *Neurobiology of Aging*, 1988, *9*, 24–26.

Sekuler, R., Owsley, C., and Hutman, L. Assessing spatial vision of older people. *American Journal of Optometry and Physiological Optics*, 1982, *59*, 961–968.

Ship, J. A., and Weiffenbach, J. M. Age, gender, medical treatment, and medication effects on smell identification. *Journals of Gerontology*, 1993, *48*, M26–M32.

Sivak, M., Olson, P. L., and Pastalan, L. A. Effect of driver's age on nighttime legibility of highway signs. *Human Factors*, 1981, *23*, 59–64.

Spetzer, M. E. Taste acuity in institutionalized and noninstitutionalized elderly men. *Journals of Gerontology*, 1988, *43*, 71–74.

Stevens, J. C. Aging and spatial acuity of touch. *Journals of Gerontology*, 1992, *47*, 35–40.

Stevens, J. C., Plantinga, A., and Cain, W. S. Reduction of odor and nasal pungency associated with aging. *Neurobiology of Aging*, 1982, *3*, 125–132.

Straatsma, B. R., Foos, R. X., and Horwitz, J. Aging-related cataracts: Laboratory investigation and clinical management. *Annals of Internal Medicine*, 1985, *102*, 82–92.

Teasdale, N., Stelmach, G. E., and Breunig, A. Postural sway characteristics of the elderly under normal and altered visual and support surface conditions. *Journals of Gerontology*, 1991, *46*, B238–B244.

Thomas, P. D., Hunt, W. C., Garry, P. J., Hood, R. B., Goodwin, J. M., and Goodwin, J. S. Hearing acuity in a healthy elderly population: Effects on emotional, cognitive and social status. *Journal of Gerontology*, 1983, *38*, 321–325.

Tylenda, C. A., and Baum, B. J. Oral physiology and the Baltimore Longitudinal Study of Aging. *Gerodontology*, 1988, *7*, 5–9.

Vaughan, W. J., Schmitz, P., and Fatt, J. The human lens: A model system for the study of aging. In J. M. Ordy and K. R. Brizzee (Eds.), *Sensory systems and communication in the elderly*. New York: Raven Press, 1979.

Venstrom, D., and Amoore, J. E. Olfactory threshold in relation to age, sex or smoking. *Journal of Food Science*, 1968, *33*, 264–265.

Verillo, R. T. Age-related changes in the sensitivity to vibration. *Journal of Gerontology*, 1980, *35*, 185–193.

Weale, R. A. Senescence and color vision. *Journal of Gerontology*, 1988, *41*, 635–640.

Weiffenbach, J. M. Assessment of chemosensory functioning in aging: Subjective and objective procedures. In E. L. Schneider and J. W. Rowe (Eds.), *Handbook of the biology of aging*. San Diego: Academic Press, 1990.

Weiffenbach, J. M., Cowart, B. J., and Baum, B. J. Taste intensity perception in aging. *Journal of Gerontology*, 1986, *41*, 460–468.

Wilson, M. R. Glaucoma in Blacks: Where do we go from here? *Journal of the American Medical Association*, 1989, *261*, 281–282.

# CHAPTER 7

# HEALTH, CHRONIC DISEASES, AND USE OF HEALTH SERVICES

No aspect of old age is more alarming to many of us than the thought of losing our health. Our fears center not only on the pain and inconvenience of illness, but also on its social-psychological consequences, such as loss of personal autonomy and economic security. Poor health, more than other changes commonly associated with aging, can reduce a person's competence in dealing with his or her environment.

This chapter examines social and psychological factors that affect perceptions of health and use of health services, looking first at definitions of good health and how the social context, especially stress, affects it. Chronic and acute health problems are then differentiated, followed by a discussion of the most common chronic diseases experienced by older people and some of their social consequences. The remainder of the chapter is devoted to utilization of health care by the elderly, including descriptions of three models for predicting and analyzing health behavior. Health promotion programs are described as a way to reduce the incidence of chronic diseases, primarily through altering health behaviors.

## DEFINING HEALTH

It is not necessary to argue that good health is valued, but what do we mean by *good health?* Most people would agree that health is something more than the mere absence of disease or infirmity. As defined by the World Health Organization in 1947, health is a state of complete physical, mental, and social well-being. Thus, health implies an interaction and integration of body, mind, and spirit, a perspective that is reflected in the growth of health promotion programs with the elderly.

As used by health care workers and researchers, the term *health status* refers to: (1) the presence or absence of disease, and (2) the degree of disability in an individual's level of functioning (Branch, 1980; Kane and Kane, 1981). Thus, activities that older people can do, or think they can do, are useful indicators of both how healthy they are and the services and environmental changes they need in order to cope with their impairments. Older people's ability to function independently at home is of primary concern.

The most commonly used measure of *functional health*, termed the *Activities of Daily Living (ADL)*, summarizes an individual's performance in personal care tasks such as bathing, dressing, using the toilet, eating, getting in or out of a bed or chair, caring for a bowel control device, as well as such home management activities as managing money, shopping, light housework, meal preparation, making a phone call, and taking medications (Jette and Branch, 1981; National Center for Health Statistics, 1987).

The World Health Organization defines "disability" as impairments in the ability to complete multiple daily tasks. Slightly more than 20 percent of older people are estimated to have a mild degree of disability in their ADL. Only a small proportion—approximately 4 percent—are severely disabled. The more disabled elderly are limited in their amounts and types of major activities and mobility, such as eating, dressing, bathing, or toiletry. Severely disabled persons are often unable to carry on major activities without the assistance of family or professionals. The extent of disabilities and need for help in personal care activities increase with age, as shown in Figure 7–1. Those aged 85 and older are four to five times more likely to be disabled and to require assistance than those aged 65 to 74. About 46 percent of persons over age 85 are disabled, compared to about 13 percent of those aged 65 to 74, and 25 percent aged 75 to 84 (McBride, 1989).

Loss of function among 65 to 74 year-olds tends to be associated with life-threatening diseases, such as cancer, but among those 75 or older, disability is usually related to chronic degenerative diseases, such as arteriosclerosis and cerebrovascular accidents (Longino and Soldo, 1987).

In 1987, approximately 5.2 million persons 65 years or older needed assistance in order to remain in the community. This figure is expected to reach 7.2 million by the year 2000, 10.1 million by 2020, and 14.4 million by 2050 (U.S. Senate Special Committee on Aging, 1988). Another way to describe these projections is to state that the proportion of persons over age 65 with one or more activity limitations will increase from the current 18 percent to 22 percent by the year 2030. Two-thirds of this group will have severe limitations in ADLs (McBride, 1989).

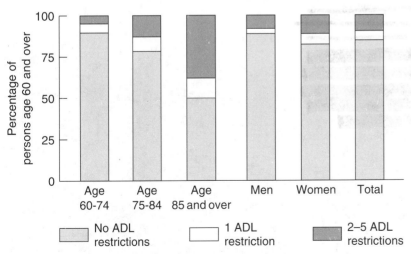

**FIGURE 7–1   Disability of the Elderly: ADL Limitations by Age and Sex**
SOURCE: T. D. McBride, Measuring the disability of the elderly: Empirical analysis and projections into the 21st century. Paper presented at the Population Association of America meeting, Baltimore, March 1989.

## Quality of Life in Health and Illness

Societal values affect our attitudes toward loss of health. In our own culture, the attitudes tend to be negative. The importance placed by our culture on being independent and highly active may underlie our relative inability to accept illness graciously. Such values may also partially explain why healthy older people often do not want to share housing or recreational activities with those who have mental or physical disabilities.

Yet the fear of declining health may trouble us more than the actual experience of it. Although younger people assume that health issues are older people's greatest preoccupation, most elders appear to be fairly positive about their health. A 1989 survey by the National Center for Health Statistics indicated that 70 percent of older respondents in the community described their health as excellent, very good, or good compared to their age peers, while only 30 percent reported their health as fair or poor (National Center for Health Statistics, 1990). Even institutionalized older persons tend to rate their health positively. These positive ratings, despite health problems, have been explained in terms of a comparison with peers, a sense of accomplishment from having survived to old age, a perception of competence to meet environmental demands, and a broad definition of quality of life to include social and economic factors. A reliable evaluation of health takes into account not only a physician's assessment of a patient's physical condition, but also the older person's self-perceptions, observable behavior, and life circumstances. Most older people appear to adjust their perceptions of their health in response to the aging process (Cockerham, Sharp, and Wilcox, 1983). Perceived health is influenced mostly by limitations in activities of daily living and the number of medications an older person consumes, especially among older women (Kaplan et al., 1988; Johnson and Wolinsky, 1994).

Older people who must take multiple medications, those who are experiencing limitations in their ADLs and in their interpersonal relations, as well as chronic pain, are more likely to report lower quality of life. On the other hand, those who have recently had a successful medical or surgical intervention to *alleviate* the symptoms of their chronic conditions are more likely to report improved quality of life (Kaplan et al., 1988; Pearlman and Uhlmann, 1988). It is noteworthy that physicians rate the quality of life of older persons with diabetes, arthritis, or even ischemic heart disease lower than do these elders themselves. This may indicate greater adaptation to disabling conditions among patients than physicians expect, or may suggest that medical professionals' definitions of quality of life are more constrained by health factors than are definitions by patients themselves. However, a national survey of 9,000 adults with chronic diseases revealed that people with arthritis, heart disease, and chronic lung disease reported the greatest impairments in quality of life; those with hypertension reported the least (Stewart et al., 1989).

Social and psychological factors also influence people's assessments of their physical well-being. An older person's position in the social structure—for example, whether one is male or female, Black or white, high or low income—affects perceptions of health. Thus, while more

Participation in sports can enhance physiological and psychological well-being.

than 70 percent of white persons age 65 and older rate their health as good or excellent, only 52 percent of Blacks and less than 50 percent of Hispanics that age do so. About 26 percent of persons aged 65 and older with incomes over $25,000 rate their health as excellent, compared with 10 percent of their age counterparts with incomes less than $10,000 (AARP, 1991). Similarly, older women are more likely to rate their health more poorly than men (Schick, 1986). In most cases, these self-assessments are fairly accurate, since women, ethnic minority and lower-income elderly do, in fact, have poorer health, as is discussed later in this chapter.

Perceptions of good health tend to be associated with other measures of well-being, particularly life satisfaction. Older persons who view themselves as reasonably healthy tend to be happier, more satisfied, more involved in social activities, and less tense and lonely. In turn, lower life satisfaction is associated with lower levels of self-perceived health (Cockerham, Sharp, and Wilcox, 1983). It has also been found that self-ratings of health are correlated with mortality. That is, older people who report poorer health are more likely to die in the next five years than those who perceive their health to be good (Kaplan et al., 1988).

## EFFECTS OF STRESS ON HEALTH

As the previous discussions suggest, health status involves the dynamic interplay among physical, social, and psychological forces. Environmental factors affect both perceptions of and actual degree of physical well-being. One of the most significant environmental factors is stress.

Individuals are subject to different degrees of stress from their environments, with diverse consequences for their overall physical and mental health. In this context, *stress* can be defined as the gamut of social-psychological stimuli that produce physiological responses of shallow, rapid breathing, muscle tension, increased blood pressure, and accelerated heart rate. The litera-

ture on social stress and health emphasizes that stress has broad physiological effects on the body, thereby predisposing people to a wide range of diseases (Maes, Fingerhoets and Vanheck, 1987; Vogt, 1992). How people cope with stress, however, affects the likelihood of deleterious consequences, as will be seen in the discussion of adaptation in Chapter 9. Hypertension, cardiovascular disease, and cancer have been correlated with particular risk factors, such as stressful lifestyles, cigarette smoking, drinking, and being overweight. Health risk factor analyses move beyond assessments of possible differences in genetics and in health care to variations in health behaviors and lifestyles that can affect the outcome of stressful life events. Although definitive proof from large-scale controlled studies is not available, considerable evidence suggests that the control of multiple risk factors can reduce such potentially fatal conditions as cardiovascular disease (Multiple Risk Factor Intervention Trial Research Group, 1982). Possible health promotion interventions to minimize stress are discussed later in this chapter.

Studies concerning stressful life events and health are especially relevant to older people. As people age, they are more likely to experience events involving loss, especially loss of health and income. In addition, the cumulative amount of stress they have experienced may increase. This can tax their declining physiological and psychological capacities to the limit, leading to illness, disease, and death. On the other hand, older persons have been found to perceive less stress in every important life domain except health, and to report greater life satisfaction than do their younger counterparts (House and Robbins, 1983). The old-old, in particular, are "survivors" who have coped with multiple stressful social changes, including the Great Depression and two World Wars.

The impact of stress on the health of older people is as yet unclear. Although the psychological resources gained through older people's life experiences may have important mediating effects, more research is needed to determine whether the findings of reduced stress with age reflect cohort differences or the effects of aging over the life course.

## CHRONIC AND ACUTE DISEASES

As noted in Chapter 5, the risk of disease and impairment increases with age; however, the extreme variability in older people's health status, as illustrated by Mrs. Hill and Mr. Jones in the vignettes in Chapter 6, shows that poor health is not necessarily a concomitant of aging (Fries and Crapo, 1981). The incidence of acute or temporary conditions, such as infections or the common cold, decreases with age. Those acute conditions that occur, however, are more debilitating and require more care, especially for older women. The average number of days of restricted activity due to acute conditions is nearly three times greater for people age 65 and over than it is for those 17 to 44 years old. Among the elderly, 33 days per year are restricted activity days, of which 14 are spent in bed. (National Center for Health Statistics, 1984; Jack and Ries, 1981). An older person who gets a cold, for example, faces a greater risk of pneumonia or bronchitis because of changes in organ systems (described in Chapter 5) which reduce his or her resistance and recuperative capacities. Thus, older people are more likely to suffer restrictions on their social activities as a result of temporary health problems.

In some cases, an acute condition that merely inconveniences a younger person may result in death for an older person. For example, respiratory infection rates are similar in young and old people, but death rates from such infections for the latter are 30 percent higher. This is why it is important for older people to get a flu vaccine at the start of each flu season.

They are also much more likely than the young to suffer from chronic conditions. Chronic health conditions are defined as long term (more than three months), often permanent, and leaving a residual disability that may require long-term management or care rather than cure. More than 80 percent of persons age 65 and over have

at least one of these, with multiple conditions being common in the elderly (National Center for Health Statistics, 1990). Chronic problems are often accompanied by continuous pain and/or distress; at the very least, the individual is inconvenienced by the need to monitor health and activities. National surveys have found that almost 40 percent of older persons with chronic diseases report limitations in their ability to perform basic ADLs (German and Fried, 1989; Guralnick and Simonsick, 1993).

The pattern of illness and disease has changed in the past 80 years. With advances in medical technology and the growth in the percentage of people surviving infectious diseases and accidents and reaching old age, chronic conditions have replaced acute diseases as a major health risk for older people and have increased the need for long-term care services, especially for those over age 80. The societal consequences of this change, especially the effects on health and long-term care financing, are discussed at length in Chapter 20.

The most frequently reported chronic conditions causing limitation of activity in persons age 65 and over are arthritis (49 percent), hypertension (37 percent), hearing impairment (32 percent), and heart disease (30 percent). Not surprisingly, most chronic conditions increase in prevalence with age (AARP, 1991; National Center for Health Statistics, 1989).

For example, people age 65 and over are almost twice as likely to suffer from arthritis as those age 45 to 64 (National Center for Health Statistics, 1989). Other conditions, such as heart disease and diabetes, show lower rates in the oldest-old, probably because of the higher mortality associated with these diseases. The difference in morbidity, or days of sickness, from the top ten chronic conditions for older and middle-aged individuals per 1,000 persons are shown in Figure 7–2.

Although the nature and the severity of any chronic condition varies with the individual, most older persons are capable of carrying out their normal daily routines, as noted in our earlier discussion of ADL. For example, chronic

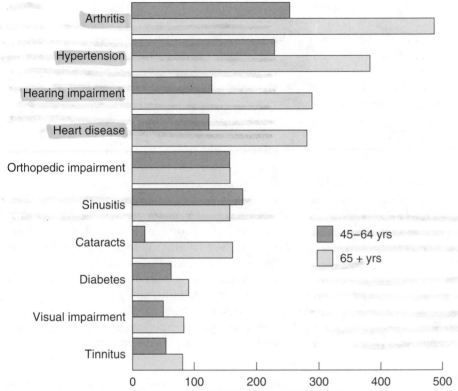

**FIGURE 7–2   Morbidity from the Top 10 Chronic Conditions: 1989 (rates per 1,000 persons)**

SOURCE: National Center for Health Statistics, Current Estimates from the National Health Interview Survey: 1989. *Vital & Health Statistics,* Series 10, #176, 1990.

heart problems may limit an older person's capacity to jog five miles a day, but he or she may still be able to live at home, visit with friends, and take a daily walk. Only about 2 percent of those age 65 and over are confined to bed by their chronic conditions, and most older people with chronic conditions are not dependent on others for managing their daily routines. On the other hand, the small percentage who do need assistance with care have placed enormous pressures on formal health and long-term care services as well as on informal caregivers.

## Interactive Effects

Even though the majority of chronic conditions are not severely limiting, they can nevertheless make life difficult and lower older people's resistance to other illnesses. The functional limits imposed by a chronic illness interact with the social limits set by others' perceptions of the illness to influence an older person's daily functioning. Therefore, it is important to look beyond the statistics on the frequency of chronic conditions to the nature of chronic illnesses, the interaction of physical changes with emotional and sociocultural factors, and the physiological differences between younger and older people.

Certain types of chronic diseases (e.g., cancer, anemia, and toxic conditions) may be related to older people's declining immunity, that is, reduced resistance to environmental carcinogens, viruses, and bacteria (Hickey, 1980). The accumulation of long-term, degenerative diseases may mean that a chronic condition, such as bronchitis, can have different and more negative complications than the same disease would have in a younger person. With reduced resistance to physical stress, an older individual may be less able to respond to treatment for any acute disease, such as a cold or flu, than a younger person would. The cumulative effect of chronic illness and an acute condition may become the crisis point where the older person becomes dependent on others for care.

Sociocultural factors also are apparently related to the incidence and severity of chronic conditions; the prevalence of disability is higher among nonwhites, people with low socioeconomic and education status, and those in nonfarm rural areas (Kickbush, 1989). Disabling chronic illnesses tend to occur earlier among African Americans, Mexican Americans, and American Indians than among whites, resulting in higher rates of hospitalization, longer hospital stays, and a shorter life expectancy (Cantor,

1991; Ferraro, 1987; Markides, 1983). Poorer self-assessments of health and lower life expectancies have been explained as products of discriminatory policies, where nonwhites have had lower incomes and inadequate nutrition throughout their lifetimes. An additional factor is that ethnic minorities, because of their cultural values and negative experiences with formal services, are less likely to utilize the health care system. (The effects of ethnic minority status on the incidence and treatment of chronic conditions are further discussed in Chapter 17.)

Psychological factors also influence how a person reacts to chronic physical problems. For example, people with a pessimistic outlook toward their health and aging tend to have less physiological reserve capacity, as illustrated by comments such as, "She lost her will to live," or "He stopped fighting and gave up." There are numerous examples of the impact of an optimistic attitude on the outcome of disease, perhaps best exemplified by Norman Cousins'

---

### CHRONIC DISEASES OF AGING

Our society's technological ability to keep alive people with multiple chronic illnesses—individuals who in earlier years would have died of these same conditions—means that many older people survive into advanced old age with some loss of quality of life. As each of these illnesses progresses, the older person adjusts his or her lifestyle and environment accordingly. Consider the case of 82-year-old Mrs. Fox. She is proud that she has run the household of her son and his two children for the past 20 years. Today, as her grandchildren reach adulthood, Mrs. Fox realizes that she can no longer maintain the household and do the shopping and cooking for her family as she once did. Her diabetes, which was first detected 25 years ago, has become more bothersome, depleting her of the energy and stamina that she needs for keeping up her activities. High blood pressure and two heart attacks have placed her in the hospital four times during the past five years. A recent fall in her son's home revealed fractures in her hip and wrist bones that were attributed to osteoporosis. She has recovered from the fall, but now walks slowly with the aid of a cane.

Her doctors suspect that Mrs. Fox's tendency to fall may be due to her heart condition that occasionally leads to blackouts. They have suggested that she may benefit from a pacemaker, and have proposed that she undergo surgery to implant one soon. They have also recommended to Mrs. Fox and her son that she give up her housekeeping functions and move to a retirement apartment. Mrs. Fox has adamantly refused surgery, saying that she is fine now and does not want any artificial extension of her life. She is also determined to maintain her role as the manager of her son's home. In an attempt to accommodate these needs, he has decided to move to a small, one-story home where Mrs. Fox can still run the household, thereby re-establishing P-E congruence, but it will not be so large as to tax her diminishing physical capacities.

(1979) accounts of the positive effects of humor on curing his potentially fatal disease. Thus, the impact of any chronic condition appears to be mediated by the physiological changes that occur with age, the sociocultural context, and the person's mental and emotional outlook.

Unfortunately, well-intentioned family members and health care professionals may assume that all chronic conditions are disabling or that a certain degree of disability is inevitable with aging. As a result, they may prematurely restrict a person's independence or not use the same treatments that they might administer to younger adults. The following anecdote illustrates how others' perceptions of health typical of old age can be unnecessarily limiting.

A 101-year-old man went to see a doctor about a pain in his left leg. The doctor said, "It is just a sign of aging," to which the man replied, "But my right leg is the same age, and it feels just fine."

In sum, disabling health changes occur at different rates in different individuals and are not inevitable with age. We turn now to an examination of the most common chronic health problems faced by older people.

## Types of Chronic Conditions

Heart disease, cancer, and strokes account for over three-quarters of all deaths among people over age 65, as shown in Table 7–1 (National Center for Health Statistics, 1990). Even though there have been rapid declines since 1968, heart disease remains the major cause of death. It is the number-one risk factor among adults age 65 and over, killing twice as many people as do all

**TABLE 7–1    Mortality Rates for Older Women and Older Men, from All Causes and the Four Leading Causes**

|  | DEATHS PER 100,000 POPULATION PER YEAR, 1987 | | |
|---|---|---|---|
|  | 65–74 | 75–84 | 85+ |
| All Causes |  |  |  |
| Females | 2,091 | 5,152 | 14,298 |
| Males | 3,701 | 8,353 | 18,187 |
| Diseases of heart |  |  |  |
| Females | 724 | 2,197 | 6,889 |
| Males | 1,447 | 3,376 | 7,912 |
| Malignant neoplasms (cancer) |  |  |  |
| Females | 658 | 954 | 1,277 |
| Males | 1,087 | 1,846 | 2,460 |
| Cerebrovascular diseases (strokes) |  |  |  |
| Females | 148 | 541 | 1,805 |
| Males | 185 | 629 | 1,656 |
| Chronic obstructive pulmonary disease |  |  |  |
| Females | 100 | 171 | 212 |
| Males | 211 | 502 | 745 |

SOURCE: *Statistical Abstracts of the United States,* 1990, 110th ed., p. 81.

forms of cancer combined, and accounting for 20 percent of adult disabilities. Heart disease accounts for 18 percent of hospital admissions, and over 45 percent of deaths that occur among older people. Although death rates from cancer, especially lung cancer, continue to rise, it is estimated that eliminating cancer as a cause of death would extend the average life span by less than two to three years. Eliminating deaths due to major cardiovascular diseases, however, would add an average of 5 years to life expectancy at age 65 and would lead to a sharp increase in the proportion of older persons in the total population (U.S. Senate Special Committee on Aging, 1990). Stroke has been decreasing as a leading cause of death among the older population over the past 30 years (National Center on Health Statistics, 1990).

Men have higher rates of heart disease and cancer than women. In fact, gender differences in mortality are due mainly to the greater incidence of the principal fatal chronic diseases among men (U.S. Senate Special Committee on Aging, 1990). However, women experience more acute and nonfatal chronic conditions than men, and they have higher rates of arthritis, high blood pressure, strokes, diverticular disease of the colon, hiatus hernia, incontinence, osteoporosis, and senile macular degeneration (Verbrugge, 1989; *Women's Health,* 1985). These diseases are less likely to result in death than cancer and heart disease, but they may lead to nearly as many days spent in bed. In other words, older women are more likely to be bothered by chronic conditions and to be functionally disabled, but they are less likely to be seriously sick, to be hospitalized, or to face life-threatening diseases than are older men (Verbrugge, 1987; Lewis, 1985). These differences imply a reduction in the quality of life for women who live to advanced old age.

## Heart Disease and the Cardiovascular System

Heart disease is a condition in which blood to the heart is deficient because of a narrowing or constricting of the cardiac vessels that supply it. This narrowing may be due to *atherosclerosis,** in which fatty streaks or plaque formation begins early in life and accumulates to reduce the size of the passageway of the large arteries. A number of factors have been found to increase the risk of atherosclerosis. These include: hypertension or high blood pressure, elevated blood lipids (resulting from a dietary intake of animal products high in cholesterol), cigarette smoking, diabetes mellitus, obesity, inactivity, stress, and family history of heart attack. People in industrialized nations have higher levels of atherosclerosis, but the extent to which this is due to lifestyle factors in developed countries is unknown.

As the reduced blood flow caused by atherosclerosis becomes significant, angina pectoris may result. The symptoms are shortness of breath and pain from beneath the breastbone, in the neck, and down the left arm. For older individuals, these symptoms may be absent or may be confused with signs of other disorders, such as indigestion or gallbladder diseases. Treatment includes rest and nitroglycerine, which serves to dilate the blood vessels.

If deficient blood supply to the heart persists, heart tissue will die, producing a dead area known as an *infarct.* In other words, coronary artery disease can lead to a myocardial infarction, or heart attack. Acute myocardial infarction results from blockage of an artery supplying blood to a portion of the heart muscle. The extent of heart tissue involved determines the severity of the episode. Heart attacks may be

---

*The terms *atherosclerosis* and *arteriosclerosis* are often used interchangeably, causing confusion regarding their distinction. Arteriosclerosis, a generic term, sometimes called hardening of the arteries, refers to the loss of elasticity of the arterial walls. This condition occurs in all populations, and can contribute to reduced blood flow to an area. In atherosclerosis, the passageway of the large arteries narrows as a result of the development of plaques on their interior walls; atherosclerosis has been found to be age-related and of higher incidence in industrialized populations. Arteriosclerosis and atherosclerosis can be superimposed, but there is not a causative relationship between the degree of atherosclerosis and the loss of elasticity (arteriosclerosis) (Kart, Metress, and Metress, 1978; Boss and Seegmiller, 1981).

more difficult to diagnose in older people, since the symptoms in the elderly are often a generalized state of weakness, dizziness, confusion, or shortness of breath rather than the chest and back pains or numbness in the arms that characterize heart attacks in younger people. Symptoms in older people may also merge with other problems, so that a heart attack may not be reported or treated until it is too late for effective help. Although women are less likely to have heart attacks than men prior to menopause, their rates are similar after age 65. Even at younger ages, women who develop a myocardial infarction fare less well than men, as evidenced by their higher mortality within the first year (Cantor, 1991; Kannel and Brand, 1983).

The term *congestive heart failure,* or heart failure, indicates a set of symptoms related to the impaired pumping performance of the heart, so that one or more chambers of the heart do not empty adequately during the heart's contractions. Heart failure does not mean that the heart has stopped beating, but that its pumping efficiency has decreased. This results in shortness of breath, reduced blood flow to vital body parts, including the kidneys, and a greater volume of blood accumulating in the body tissues, causing edema (swelling). Treatment involves drugs, dietary modifications (e.g., salt reduction), and rest.

Most cardiovascular problems can be treated with rest, drugs, and appropriate diet, and thus do not prevent older people from carrying out modified daily routines. Preventive steps are most important, however. For example, hypertension, or high blood pressure, has been found to be the major risk factor in the development of cardiovascular complications and can be affected by preventive actions (Kannel, 1985). The risk of hypertension is greater for women than men aged 55 and over, with the difference becoming more pronounced with age (Kannel and Brand, 1983). This may partially explain why the incidence of coronary heart disease and strokes increases with age among women, although women on the average still live longer than men.

As noted in Chapter 5, blood pressure often increases with age, from an average of 120/70 to 130–140/80, but increases greater than this represent a definite hazard. Among the elderly, the risk of coronary heart disease, stroke, and death rises progressively with increasing blood pressure (Kannel, 1985). The rates of high blood pressure, or *hypertension,* are higher among African Americans than whites.

Significant increases in blood pressure should never be considered normal. In some isolated, primitive populations, a rise in pressure with age does not occur. Although genetic factors may come into play, this difference suggests that individuals can make lifestyle changes that may reduce their vulnerability to high blood pressure. The preventive measures most likely to reduce cardiovascular risk are weight control; physical activity; treatment of diabetes; reduced intake of salt, saturated fats, and cholesterol; and avoidance of cigarette smoking and excessive alcohol intake. For most people, hypertension can be controlled by medications and/or changes in the health habits described previously (Borham, 1986; Kirkendall, 1986; U.S. Preventive Services Task Force, 1989).

Another cardiovascular problem, which is less frequently addressed than hypertension, is *hypotension,* or low blood pressure. Yet hypotension, characterized by dizziness and faintness from exertion after a period of inactivity and frequently related to anemia, is actually very common among the elderly. Problems with hypotension may be more pronounced for an older person after sitting or lying down for a long time (postural hypotension) or suddenly standing, after which a person may appear to lose balance and sway. Hypotension is not in itself dangerous, but can increase the risk of falls. Older people who have a history of low blood pressure or who are taking some types of antihypertensive medications need to move more slowly.

**Strokes and Other Cerebrovascular Problems**  We have seen how heart tissue can be denied adequate nourishment because of changes in the blood vessels that supply it. Similarly, arteriosclerotic and atherosclerotic changes in blood vessels that serve the brain can reduce its nourishment and result in the disruption of blood flow to brain tissue and malfunction or death of brain cells. This impaired brain tissue circulation is called *cerebrovascular disease.* When a portion of the brain is completely denied blood, a cerebrovascular accident (CVA), or stroke, occurs. The severity of the stroke depends on the particular areas as well as the total amount of brain tissue involved. Many elderly who have heart problems also are at risk for cerebrovascular disease.

CVAs represent the fourth leading cause of death following accidents. Of the 200,000 deaths from strokes each year, 80 percent occur among persons aged 65 and over (National Center for Health Statistics, 1987). African American elderly are at greater risk for strokes than whites or other minority groups. In 1987, for example, older Blacks had twice the death rate due to strokes than did whites (*Statistical Abstracts,* 1990).

Atherosclerotic changes, in which fatty deposits gradually obstruct an artery in the brain or neck, are a common underlying condition. The most frequent cause of strokes in older persons is a cerebral thrombosis, a blood clot that either diminishes or closes off the blood flow in an artery of the brain or neck. Another cause of stroke is cerebral hemorrhage, in which a weak spot in a blood vessel of the brain bursts. Cerebral hemorrhage is less common in the elderly, although more likely to cause death when it does occur. The risks of stroke appear to be related to social and personal factors, most prominently hypertension, but also age, previous lifestyle, diet, and activity patterns. Regular, sustained exercise and lowfat diets are associated with the reduction of fatty particles that clog the blood stream. New findings about the benefits of common drugs like aspirin and warfarin in preventing blood clots are also reducing the risk of strokes. Indeed, the death rate from strokes has dropped by 40 percent in the last 20 years because of these preventive measures, and because of improved and immediate treatment of strokes.

The area of the brain that is damaged by a stroke dictates which body functions may be affected. For instance, if the speech center of the brain dies, then the stroke victim may be unable to speak or understand speech (aphasia). Another possible effect is paralysis of one side of the body (hemiplegia), which also may be associated with blindness in half of the victim's visual field (heminanopsia).

The treatment for strokes is similar to that for heart attacks and hypertension: modulated activity and supervised schedules of exercise and drugs. Stroke victims often require physical, occupational, and speech therapy, and their recovery process can be slow, frustrating, and emotionally draining for the victim and his or her family. Rehabilitation must address not only physical conditions, but also the psychosocial needs for support and respite of stroke victims and their families. The recognition of this wider range of rehabilitation has led to the creation of stroke support groups in many communities, organized by stroke victims and their families, or by local hospitals and senior centers.

**Cancer** Among those 65 years old and over, 21 percent of deaths are due to cancer, especially cancers of the stomach, lungs, intestines, and pancreas. In fact, these malignancies in old age are the second leading cause of death, and 50 percent of all cancer occurs and is diagnosed after age 65. Cancer of the bowel is the most common malignancy in those age 70 and over, and is second to lung cancer in cancer-related deaths. Lung cancer has its highest incidence in men age 65 and over, but appears to be associated more with smoking than with age. Cancer of the colon is more common in women, whereas rectal cancer is more frequent in men. Women also face increasing risks of breast and cervical cancers with age (National Center for Health Statistics, 1990). Both the incidence and mortality rates due to cervical cancer are greater in older African American women than in older white women (Baquet and Ringen, 1986).

The greater risk of cancer with age may be due to a number of factors, such as the effects of a slow-acting carcinogen, prolonged "development time" necessary for growth to be observable, extended pre-exposure time, and failing immune capacity that is characteristic of increased age (Weg, 1983). Certain diet and lifestyle factors may also be related to cancer. Diagnosing cancer in old age is often more difficult than at earlier life stages, because of the existence of other chronic diseases and because symptoms of cancer, such as weight loss, weakness, or fatigue, may be inaccurately attributed to aging, depression, or dementia. In addition, the current older generation's fear of cancer may be so great that they do not seek medical help to address their suspicions and fears.

**Arthritis**  Although not a leading cause of death, arthritis is the most common chronic condition affecting older people and is a major cause of limited activity. In fact, all persons over age 60 have been estimated to have some physical evidence of arthritis, with over 70 percent having some musculoskeletal complaint (National Center for Health Statistics, 1990). Because arthritis is so common and the symptoms are so closely identified with the normal aging process, older people may accept arthritis as an inevitable accompaniment of a long life. If so, they may fail to seek treatment or to learn strategies to reduce pain and support their independent functioning. Although many treatments are used to control arthritic symptoms, little is known about ways to postpone or eliminate these disorders.

Arthritis is not a single entity, but includes over 100 different conditions of inflammations and degenerative changes of bones and joints. *Rheumatoid arthritis* is a chronic inflammation of the membranes lining joints and tendons, and is characterized by pain, swelling, bone dislocation, and limitation of motion. It afflicts two to three times more women than men and can cause severe crippling. Rheumatoid arthritis is not associated with aging per se; many young people also have this condition, with initial symptoms most commonly appearing between 20 and 50 years of age. Symptoms of rheumatoid arthritis include malaise, fatigue, loss of weight, fever, joint pain, redness, swelling, and stiffness affecting many joints. The disease is characterized by acute episodes followed by periods of relative inactivity. The cause of rheumatoid arthritis is unknown; treatment includes a balance of rest, exercise, and use of aspirin, which provides relief from pain, fever, and inflammation. Use of other antiinflammatory agents, antimalarials, and corticosteroids, as well as surgical procedures to repair joints and correct various deformities, have been found to be effective for some people.

*Osteoarthritis,* which is presumed to be a universal corollary of aging, is a gradual degeneration of the joints that are most subject to stress—those of the hands, knees, hips, and shoulders. Pain and disfigurement in the fingers are manifestations of osteoarthritis, but are generally not disabling. Osteoarthritis of the lower limbs, however, can limit mobility. Heredity, as well as environmental or lifestyle factors—particularly obesity, occupational stresses, and wear and tear on the joints—have been identified as causes of osteoarthritis. Some progress has been made in minimizing inflammation and pain through the use of antiinflammatory drugs, mild exercise, heat and cold, and reduction of strain on weight-bearing joints through weight loss and the use of weight-bearing appliances. Surgical procedures may restore function to the hips and knees, but cannot cure the arthritic condition. In addition, long-range effects are unknown since the surgery is usually performed on people over age 70.

The pervasive and unpredictable nature of the pain of arthritis can dominate a person's life and result in frustration and depression. Even on "good days" when pain subsides, an older arthritic may live with the fear of the inevitable "bad day," and may structure daily activities in order to avoid pain. Each day may seem to consist of a succession of obstacles, from getting out of bed and fastening clothing, to opening mail, dialing the phone, and handling dishes for meals.

Concentrating on coping with one obstacle after another in the completion of tasks can be exhausting, even when minimal physical exertion is involved in each task.

The prime danger for people with arthritis is reducing their physical activity in response to pain. Movement stimulates the secretion of synovial fluid, the substance that lubricates the surfaces between joints and increases blood flow to joint areas. Movement also tones the muscles that hold joints in place and that shield joints from excessive stress. When someone tries to avoid pain by sitting still as much as possible, the losses in lubricating fluid and muscular protection make movement still more painful. Eventually, the muscles surrounding immobilized areas lose their flexibility, and affected joints freeze into rigid positions called *contractures*. For these reasons, older people need to be encouraged to maintain physical activity in spite of pain. The adage "use it or lose it" has special meaning to an arthritis victim! The environment may need to be restructured in these cases, so that a person with arthritis is able to walk around and keep up with daily activities, but is not burdened by extreme press or demands. For example, a smaller home on one level, such as that selected by Mrs. Fox in our earlier description of multiple chronic diseases, can reduce the environmental press for older people with arthritis.

**Osteoporosis** The human body is constantly forming and losing bone through the metabolism of calcium. As noted in Chapter 5, osteoporosis involves a more dramatic loss in bone mass. The increased brittleness of the bones associated with this condition can result in diminished height, slumped posture, backache, and a reduction in the structural strength of bones, making them susceptible to fracture. Compressed or collapsed vertebrae are the major cause of kyphosis, or "dowager's hump," the stooped look that many of us associate with aging.

The primary risk posed by osteoporosis is a fracture of the neck of the femur, or thigh. Many of the falls and associated hip fractures of old age

actually represent an osteoporotic femoral neck that broke from bearing weight, causing the individual to fall. Osteoporosis results in 1.5 million fractures per year; 40 percent are spinal, 25 percent are hip, and 15 percent are wrist fractures (OWL, 1994). Many older people have undiagnosed osteoporosis, often showing no symptoms until a fall or fracture occurs. Typically, no immediate preceding event can be identified as the cause of the fracture.

Some 20 percent of white women experience fractures by age 65, increasing to more than 30 percent by age 90. Although both sexes lose bone mass with aging, it is rare for men to develop symptomatic osteoporosis before age 70. White men are far less likely than white women to experience hip fractures; African American men and women have even lower rates of fractures than white men (Marcus, 1989). Hip fractures are of concern because of their impact on mortality; it is estimated that 15 percent of people with a hip fracture die from it or from surgical complications (Gambrell, 1987; Riggs and Melton, 1986). Those who survive hip surgery face reduced mobility and loss of independence, as well as a fear of further falls and fractures, all factors that may constrict their social worlds. (However, not all falls and fractures among older people result from osteoporosis. Cardiovascular disease underlies approximately one-half of them. Others are due to a decline in postural control, produced by impairments of the senses and the central nervous system, changes previously discussed in Chapter 5 [Kerzner, 1983].)

Osteoporosis apparently starts well before old age (perhaps as young as age 35) and is more than four times more common in women than in men. The causes of osteoporosis are unclear, although it may be associated with loss of calcium and estrogen in menopausal women, a sedentary lifestyle, cigarette smoking, excessive alcohol consumption, or a genetic factor that determines bone density. For example, Caucasian women are more likely to develop this condition than African American women (Exton-Smith, 1985; Goldberg, 1988).

The goal in treatment is to prevent further bone loss. Increased intake of dietary calcium, vitamin D, fluoride, moderate weight-bearing exercise such as vigorous walking and strength-training to help retain calcium, and estrogen have been used as therapies (Goldberg, 1988; Nelson, Fiatarone, Morganti, Trice, Greenberg, and Evans, 1994). In the years immediately following menopause, the rate of bone loss can be as high as 5 percent compared to a normal rate of one or two percent. For women entering menopause, reduced estrogen, not calcium, is the primary cause of bone loss in the first five years after menopause. Hormone replacement therapy can decrease the risk of hip fractures by 25 to 50 percent, and of spinal crush fractures by 50 to 75 percent. Since estrogen blocks the process of bone reabsorption, it can increase bone density 3 to 5 percent in the first year, but the effects are not long-term (OWL, 1994). Although hormone replacement therapy is the best medical means of preventing osteoporosis and bone fractures, especially when started soon after menopause, and continued for several years, it has been found in some cases to be associated with endometrial, breast, and uterine cancer (Gambrell, 1987; Peck et al., 1984). Hormone replacement therapy is far less effective if begun long after the menopause than immediately after it. Small, short-stature women who are postmenopausal, have high caffeine intake, smoke cigarettes, and have a family history of osteoporosis appear to be most at risk of cancer associated with hormone treatments. An additional problem is that when hormone replacement therapy is discontinued, bone loss is more rapid than prior to treatment. On the other hand, hormone replacement therapy actually reduces the incidence of coronary heart disease and has no effect on the risk of strokes, according to a large-scale, 10-year study of nurses and in studies of women over age 70 (Stampfer et al., 1991; Henderson et al., 1991; Stampfer and Colditz, 1991). For women who cannot or choose not to undergo hormone replacement therapy, only one other medication—synthetic salmon calcitonin—has been approved. Administered daily or three times weekly by injection, it has been found to slow the rate of bone loss and help relieve bone pain (Older Women's League, 1994). Fluoride treatments have also been given, but may have negative side effects of gastrointestinal and rheumatic complaints.

Certain dietary and exercise habits may help prevent osteoporosis, especially increasing the amount of calcium after age 40 (Gambrell, 1987). Physicians recommend increasing daily calcium intake from 800 mg to 1,200 mg or more among postmenopausal women (i.e., by drinking three or more eight-ounce glasses of milk daily, or by using calcium supplements). However, low dietary calcium appears to be only partly responsible for osteoporosis (Arnaud and Sanchez, 1990). Therefore increasing calcium intake may not prevent fracturing after bone loss has occurred. One reason is that an estimated 40 percent of osteoporotic women have a deficiency of the enzyme that is needed to metabolize calcium (lactose), thus making calcium less easily absorbed (Kerzner, 1983). An additional problem is that once one fracture is present, a patient has a 70 to 80 percent chance of developing another (Lindsay, 1981).

A combination of calcium and exercise (twice-weekly brisk walks and once-weekly aerobics) appears to reduce bone loss over a two-year period more than exercise alone. This combined regimen is not as effective as moderate exercise combined with hormone replacement therapy, which actually *increases* bone density almost 3 percent per year (Prince et al., 1991). The fracture rate may be reduced by estrogen combined with fluoride and calcium in women who already have osteoporosis (Gambrell, 1987). Two longitudinal studies have shown that high-intensity strength-training using exercise machines for one year can significantly *increase* bone mineral density in postmenopausal women (Notelovitz, Martin, and Tesar, 1991; Nelson, et al, 1994). The strength-training program was combined with estrogen therapy in the former study, but not in the latter study. These recent clinical experiments demonstrate that high-intensity (i.e., twice weekly), strenuous exercise not only maintains, but also *increases* bone mineral density in older women (up to age 70 in both studies). The research by Nelson and colleagues also resulted in increased muscle mass, muscle strength, balance, and spontaneous physical activity.

**Chronic Obstructive Pulmonary Disease or Respiratory Problems:** *Chronic bronchitis, fibrosis, asthma,* and *emphysema* are manifestations of chronic obstructive pulmonary diseases (COPD) that damage lung tissue. They increase with age, develop slowly and insidiously, and are progressive and debilitating, often resulting in frequent hospitalizations, major lifestyle changes, and death. In fact, by age 90, most people are likely to have some signs of emphysema, with shortness of breath and prolonged and difficult exhalation. Getting through daily activities can be extremely exhausting under such conditions. Causes of COPD are both genetic and environmental, especially prolonged exposure to various dusts, fumes, or cigarette smoke. Three to four times as many men as women have these diseases (Shepard, 1982), probably due to a combination of normal age changes in the lung and a greater likelihood of smoking and exposure to airborne pollutants. This is especially true in old-old cohorts, as shown in Table 7–1. Treatment is usually continuous, and includes drugs, respiratory therapy, breathing exercises to compensate for damage, and the avoidance of respiratory infections, smoking, pollution, and other irritants.

Allergic reactions to bacterial products, drugs, and pollutants also increase with age. The greater incidence of drug allergies may be a function of both decreases in physiological capacities and the increased use of many drugs, such as sedatives, tranquilizers, antidepressants, and antibiotics.

**Diabetes** Compared with other systems of the body, the endocrine glands do not show consistent and predictable age-related changes, other than the gradual slowing of functioning. However, insufficient insulin, produced and secreted by the pancreas, can lead to *diabetes mellitus*. Diabetes mellitus is characterized by above-normal amounts of sugar (glucose) in the blood and urine, resulting from an inability to use carbohydrates. Diabetics may go into a coma when their blood sugar levels get very high. Low blood sugar (hypoglycemia) can also lead to unconsciousness.

Older diabetics include: (1) those who have had the disease since youth; (2) those who develop it in late middle age and incur related cardiovascular problems; and (3) those who develop it late in life and generally show mild pathologic conditions. The last type is most common in older persons, and can often be managed without medication. The incidence of newly diagnosed adult onset diabetes is highest in the 60- to 80-year-old category (National Center for Health Statistics, 1990). Although diabetes can occur at any age, diabetic problems related to the body's lessened capability to metabolize carbohydrates can be particularly severe in the elderly. In fact, adult-onset diabetes is estimated to affect 79.7 per 1,000 older persons. Many cases in the elderly are associated with being overweight, especially due to changes in fat/muscle ratio and slower metabolism with aging (Marchesseault, 1983). This is particularly true among older African American women, who have a higher rate of obesity and diabetes than do elderly white women (National Center for Health Statistics, 1989). Glucose tolerance and the action of insulin are often compromised by poor diet, physical inactivity, and coexistent diseases.

Symptoms of diabetes include excessive thirst, increased appetite and urination, fatigue, weakness, loss of weight, and decreased wound healing. These symptoms may not be present in older people, however. Instead, diabetes among the elderly is generally detected incidentally through eye examinations, hospitalization, and testing for other disorders. Since blood glucose may be temporarily elevated under the stress of illnesses such as stroke, myocardial infarction, or infection, people should not be labeled as diabetic unless the high glucose level persists under conditions of reduced stress (Marchesseault, 1983; Levin, 1982).

The cumulative effect of high blood glucose levels can lead to complications in advanced stages of diabetes. These include infections, nerve damage, blindness, renal disorders, stroke, harm to the coronary arteries, skin problems, and poor circulation in the extremities, leading to gangrene. The interaction of diabetes with ordinary age-related physical problems such as hypertension can result in serious health difficulties and consequent limitations on daily activities. Atherosclerosis and coronary heart disease, for example, are more common in diabetics than in nondiabetics.

Diabetes cannot be cured, but it can generally be managed at home through a diet of reduced carbohydrates and calories; regular exercise; proper care of feet, skin, teeth, and gums; and monitored insulin intake for those who require it. To minimize forgetfulness and treatment errors, older people, especially those who acquire diabetes late in life, may need instruction regarding the importance of diet, daily examination of their bodies, urine testing, and the correct dosage of insulin or other drugs. With proper management, diabetics can live long and useful lives. Some promising results from studies with rhesus monkeys offer potential approaches to preventing diabetes in humans. A diet that provided 30 percent fewer calories but the same level of nutrition resulted in *lowered* blood glucose and insulin levels compared to an age-related increase in these markers of diabetes in a control group of rhesus monkeys (Kemnitz et al., 1994).

**Problems with the Kidneys and Urinary Tract**   The various diseases and disorders of the urinary system characteristic of old age tend to be either acute infections or chronic problems resulting from the gradual deterioration of the structure and function of the excretory system with age. As we have seen in Chapter 5, the kidneys shrink in size, and their capacity to perform basic filtration tasks decreases, leading to a higher probability of disease or infection. One of the most common age-related problems for women is inability of the bladder to empty completely. This often results in cystitis, an acute inflammatory state accompanied by pain and irritation. Cystitis can generally be treated by antibiotics. Older men face an increased risk of diseases of the prostate gland, with cancer of the prostate being the most frequent malignancy of older men. Cancer of the prostate frequently spreads to the bones, but surgery is rarely recommended for men over age 70.

*Incontinence*   A more difficult, noninfectious, and chronic urinary problem is incontinence (inability to control urine and feces), which has been estimated to occur in 5 to 19 percent of men and 7 to 38 percent of women over age 65 and living in the community (Ouslander, 1989; Ouslander and Abelson, 1990; Teasdale, et al., 1988; Cramer, 1993). Since older people and their families consider incontinence a taboo topic, they tend to be unaware of methods to cope with and treat it. Most elderly do not discuss the problem with their doctors, and only a small percentage use any protective devices. This widespread reluctance to acknowledge incontinence as a problem can have serious psychological and social implications, particularly on the decision to institutionalize an older person. Accordingly, about half of the elderly living in nursing homes experience at least one episode of incontinence daily.

There are two types of incontinence: (1) *urge incontinence*, where the person has a strong urge to urinate and is unable to hold urine long enough to reach a toilet, and (2) *stress incontinence*, where leakage occurs during physical exertion or when sneezing or coughing, a phenomenon that can also occur among younger women. Incontinence sometimes results from a specific precipitating factor, such as acute illness, infection, or even a change in residence. It can be treated if the cause is known. Temporary incontinence can be caused by bladder or urinary tract infections which may be treated with antibiotics. Prescribed medications can also cause urgent and frequent urination. If informed of the detrimental effects of medication on an older person, a physician may reduce the drug dosage. With age, the bladder and urethra in women commonly descend, resulting in stress incontinence; leaking then occurs with the increased abdominal pressure brought on by coughing, sneezing, lifting, or physical exercise. Chronic functional incontinence often results from neurological changes and accompanies other problems, such as Parkinson's disease and organic brain syndrome. Other physical causes that should be investigated medically are prostate problems, pernicious anemia, diabetic neuropathy, and various cancers.

Since the types and causes of incontinence vary widely, thorough diagnosis and individualized treatment programs are critical. Even habitual incontinence should not be assumed to be irreversible; it may be treated or partially controlled through drugs, dietary changes, exercises, surgical procedures, or behavioral management techniques, such as reducing fluid intake when bathroom access is limited. Even incurable problems can be managed through protective products (e.g., absorbent pads) and catheters (tubes draining the bladder) to reduce complications, anxiety, and embarrassment. In fact, only about 25 percent of older persons with incontinence are so severely disabled that they are unlikely to regain continence and require a catheter or other external appliances to cope with the conditions (Cramer, 1993). Physical exercise designed to promote and maintain sphincter muscle tone can also be a means to prevent or reduce age-related incontinence, particularly among older women. All possible treatments, including behavioral techniques and biofeedback, should be explored, since older people's embarrassment and humiliation over their difficulties may result in their avoiding social gatherings out of fear of having their incontinence detected. Support groups, such as "Help for Incontinent People," have chapters nationwide.

**Problems with the Intestinal System**   Many older people experience problems in digestion and continuing gastrointestinal distress, due particularly to age-related slowing down of the digestive process. Most intestinal problems are, in fact, related to unbalanced diets or diets with limited fiber content. Diverticulitis is one of the most common difficulties, affecting up to 50 percent of persons aged 80 and over, and especially women (Almy and Howell, 1980). It is a condition in which pouches or sacs (diverticula) in the intestines (especially in the colon) result from weakness of the intestinal wall; these sacs become inflamed and infected, leading to symptoms of nausea, abdominal discomfort, bleeding, and changes in bowel function. Management includes a high-fiber diet and antibiotic therapy. Diverticulitis is increasing in industrialized nations, and may be associated with a highly refined diet lacking in fiber.

Many older people worry about constipation, but this is not an inevitable outcome of aging, as noted in Chapter 5. Causes of constipation include overuse of cathartics, lack of exercise, psychological stress, gastrointestinal disease, and an unbalanced diet with respect to bulk. Constipation may be a symptom of an underlying disease or obstruction. If this is not the case, treatment commonly includes physical activity, dietary modification, and increased fluid intake. Because many older people are overly concerned about having regular bowel movements, they may become dependent on laxatives, which can, over time, cause problems, such as irritating the colon and decreasing the absorption of certain vitamins. Some older people may become preoccupied with bodily functions, often boring or frustrating family members with detailed accounts.

Hiatus hernia appears to be increasing in incidence, especially among obese women; this occurs when a small portion of the stomach slides up through the diaphragm. Symptoms include indigestion, difficulty in swallowing, and chest pain that may be confused with a heart attack. Medical management includes weight reduction, elevation of the upper body when sleeping, changes in the size and frequency of meals, and medication. Although hiatus hernia in itself is not especially severe, it may mask the symptoms of more serious intestinal disorders, such as cancer of the stomach.

The incidence of gall bladder disease, especially with gallstones, also increases with age and is indicated by pain, nausea, and vomiting, with attacks increasing in number and severity. Most cases in the elderly are asymptomatic, and physicians debate whether to perform surgery or follow a more conservative course of medical management. Medical treatment usually involves a program of weight reduction, avoidance of fatty foods, and use of antacids.

Oral Diseases   The current oral health status of older people in the United States is largely unknown, but there is evidence that several types of oral diseases increase with age. The most visible condition is edentulism, or loss of teeth. A nationwide epidemiological study showed that 42 percent of adults over age 65 were edentulous (Brunelle, 1987), a rate much lower than that reported in previous years for the U.S. (U.S. Public Health Service, 1974), or the rates for other industrialized countries such as Scotland and the Netherlands (Manderson and Ettinger, 1975; Swallow, 1978). As might be expected, the rate increases with age from about one-third of the young-old to almost one-half of the oldest-old. This is due entirely to historical differences in dental care delivery, *not* because of the aging process.

The common problems of dental caries and gum disease also appear to increase with age, although the evidence is limited and less clear. In the Baltimore Longitudinal Study, the rate of root caries (cavities that develop on exposed root surfaces) was found to be four times greater among subjects over age 60 than in those under age 40 (Baum, 1981). The rate of secondary coronal caries (cavities that develop in the exposed enamel of teeth that were restored many years before) relative to the number of remaining

natural teeth seems to be higher among older persons (Brunelle, 1987). To what extent the higher rates in adults reflect changes over time in preventive dental care, such as the widespread use of water fluoridation, is unclear. Many studies show an age-related increase in the incidence of periodontitis (or gum disease), although evidence of substantial increases after age 54 is lacking (Beck, 1984).

In contrast, cancers of the lip, tongue, mouth, gum, pharynx, and salivary glands increase with aging, regardless of ethnic minority status or sex. In North America and Western Europe, cancer of the lip is the most frequent and has the highest survival rates among those listed previously (between 65 and 90 percent over a five-year period). Presently, very little is known about lifestyle characteristics associated with the development of this disease.

AIDS in the Older Population   While it cannot be classified as a chronic disease in the same way as diabetes or COPD is, the growing number of older adults with AIDS (Acquired Immune Deficiency Syndrome) and the increasing time between infection, diagnosis, and death make this an important public health issue in gerontology. Over the next few years, AIDS will place greater demands on long-term care, especially home-based services. Because reporting AIDS cases is mandatory, the Centers for Disease Control (CDC) receive reports from all state and territorial health departments on all diagnosed cases of AIDS. Between 1981 and 1989, there were 115,786 patients with AIDS[*] aged 13 and older in the United States. During this period 10.4 percent of the patients were aged 50 and older at diagnosis; the majority of these were 50 to 59 (7.3 percent), 2.4 percent were 60 to 69, and .7 percent were 70 and older (Ship, Wolff, and Selik, 1991). Although this represents only a small proportion of the total AIDS cases, the incidence of AIDS in older adults has increased dramatically,

[*]This does not include the much larger number of persons with ARC (AIDS-Related Complex).

from 6.9 percent of all AIDS cases in 1981 to a peak of 10.9 percent in 1987.

The greatest growth has been in the group aged 60 to 69, from a low of .7 percent in 1982 to 3.2 percent in 1987. This may be accounted for by the long latency period (4 to 7 years) between transfusions with contaminated blood and the onset of full-blown AIDS symptoms. Transfusion-related AIDS increases with age, from 5.8 percent of all AIDS cases in 50- to 59-year-olds, to 27.6 percent in those aged 60 to 69, and 64.2 percent of cases over age 70. The greatest proportion of AIDS in those aged 50 to 69 continues to be through male homosexual contact (67.5 percent of those 50 to 59, 48.9 percent of those 60 to 69) (Ship, Wolff and Selik, 1991).

However, there is a growing incidence of heterosexual transmission of the virus in older adults by partners who were first infected by a blood transfusion. Because of the large number of blood transfusions received by then-middle-aged adults between 1978 and 1985 (after which time greater efforts have been made to screen blood supplies), and because of the long latency between transfusions and diagnosis, even more cases of newly diagnosed older adults are likely in the next few years, both through recipients of transfusions themselves or through sexual contact with a transfusion-infected partner (Peterman et al., 1988; Catania, et al., 1989). In a study of families of transfusion-infected AIDS patients, slightly more wives (18 percent) than husbands (8 percent) of AIDS patients were seropositive (i.e., the HIV antibody was detected in their blood); seropositive wives were older than seronegative wives (median age 62 versus 54 respectively) (Peterman et al., 1988). These results lend support to the argument that older persons are more vulnerable to infection with the AIDS virus because their immune system deteriorates with aging, as described earlier in this chapter (Catania et al., 1989). Another reason why older women may be more likely to become infected are the vaginal changes after the menopause. In particular, there is a thinning of the vaginal walls, as described in Chapter 10; this

leads to mucosal disruption and tearing of the vaginal wall, and thus easier access for the HIV into the bloodstream.

For these reasons, it is important to educate older adults about *their* risk for AIDS. Even those who know something about this disease may feel that it cannot affect them if they are not engaging in homosexual activity or IV drug use. Most older people have relied on the media for their knowledge in this area. Unfortunately, there have been few reports in the media of *older* adults contracting AIDS through blood transfusions compared to the focus on young hemophiliacs who have contracted AIDS in this manner. It is therefore not surprising that many older people who received transfusions before 1985 are unaware that they may be infected, and that in the survey by Peterman et al., (1988), none of these people had used a condom during intercourse. This is in stark contrast to the increased rate of condom use among gay men, both young and old, and among younger heterosexuals.

**Accidents among Older People**    Although mortality statistics suggest that older people are less likely than the young to die of accidents (only 7 per 10,000 deaths), these numbers mask the true incidence of deaths due to accident-related injuries. For example, if an older person breaks a hip after falling down a flight of stairs or breaks a leg in an auto accident, she enters a hospital, often is discharged to a nursing home, and soon after may die from pneumonia. Pneumonia is then listed as the cause of death, when in fact this acute condition was brought on by the patient's problems in recovering from the accident.

Despite this underestimate, people over age 65 have the highest rates of auto injury-related hospitalization and death of any age group except teenagers. The risk of death for similar physical injuries is about 4 times greater for 80-year-olds than for 20-year-olds, due probably to their greater physical vulnerability (Evans, 1991; Maher, 1990). In 1989, for example, more than 6,000 elderly persons died as drivers, passengers, or pedestrians in traffic accidents. In a retrospective study of accident victims of all ages in an urban trauma hospital, patients over age 70 were most likely to have had pedestrian accidents and least likely to have been assaulted. The older group was also most likely to die as a result of their injuries (Haymond et al., 1988).

Older drivers are less likely to drive in bad weather, at night, in freeway traffic, or in rush hour. In fact, they drive fewer miles per year than younger drivers. Nevertheless, they have more accidents per mile driven. This higher rate of accidents may be attributed to changes in eye-hand coordination, slower reaction time, impaired vision (especially diminished night vision and sensitivity to glare), and hearing impairments, as described in Chapter 6. Changes in cognitive function that may impair driving abilities are described in Chapter 8. Even though most accidents by older drivers occur at low speeds, age-related declines in organ systems and brittle bones (see Chapter 5) make the older person more vulnerable to injuries as a result of accidents. Because the extent to which people experience these changes varies across individuals, it may be useful for state licensing departments to test all adults annually on some of the relevant physiological and cognitive abilities, and to retrain older drivers who are experiencing significant declines in these areas. The American Association of Retired Persons, National Safety Council, and the Automobile Association of America have developed such courses. For example, AARP estimates that some 500,000 older drivers enroll in their "55 Alive/Mature Driving" program each year. This 8-hour course is offered through retirement homes, senior centers, shopping malls, libraries, and churches throughout the United States. Older persons can obtain discounts of 5–10 percent on their auto insurance in many states after completing such courses.

Older drivers also can be assisted by improved environmental design. For example, older people have more accidents while making left turns; these could be avoided by designing better left-turn intersections with special lanes and left arrow lights. Road signs that are clearer and redundant could reduce the high number of violations obtained by older drivers for improperly changing lanes, entering and exiting highways. Automobiles with right sideview mirrors, enlarged rearview mirrors, less complicated dashboards, airbags, and better protection on doors could also go a long way to reduce accident rates among older individuals.

## FALLS AND THEIR PREVENTION

Older people are at a greater risk of falls than the young. Up to 30 percent of older adults in the community, and even more in long-term care settings, experience a fall in a given year. This can result in hip fractures, especially among women with osteoporosis. Of the annual rate of 200,000 Americans who fracture a hip each year, less than half are able to return to full functioning even many months later. Many enter a long-term care facility as a result of the fall. Mortality rates have been estimated to be as high as 20 percent within six months (Josephson et al., 1991; Kennedy and Coppart, 1987; Tinetti, 1989).

A less obvious but serious outcome is that many older people who fall become more fearful of falling and therefore restrict their activity levels further. They may also become more rigid or overly cautious in walking. This may in turn increase the likelihood of subsequent falls. Therefore it is important to identify risk factors for falls, and to help older persons prevent falls.

Risk factors for falls include inactivity, visual impairment, multiple diseases and medications (e.g. cardiac conditions and medications that cause postural hypertension), and gait disorders that are common among older persons. Lighting levels and hazards in the environment such as slippery floors, loose area rugs, and poorly demarcated stairs can also precipitate a fall.

Many interventions to prevent falls have been successful. In one study, environmental modifications of the homes of older people who had experienced multiple falls in the past resulted in a 72 percent decrease in falls (Tideiksaar,

1990). In another study, elderly persons who had not fallen in the past year visited a nurse to identify and reduce their risk factors (e.g., to increase exercise, reduce home safety risks), and received follow-up calls from the nurse. After one year, this group experienced a lower incidence of falls than did older persons without such nurse visits (Wagner et al., 1994).

## Use of Physician Services by Older People

The increased incidence of many chronic and acute diseases among the older population would seem to predict a striking growth with age in the use of health care services. As shown in Table 7–2, there is some support for a differential pattern of utilization. The probability of seeing a doctor at least once in the previous year increases with age; 75 percent of those aged 45 to 64 reported doing so in 1987, compared with 82.2 percent of those aged 65 to 74 and 87.2 percent of those persons 75 years or older. (National Center for Health Statistics, 1990; U.S. Senate Special Committee on Aging, 1990). When they do visit physicians, both younger and older people do so primarily for acute symptoms and to receive similar diagnostic and therapeutic services. It appears, however, that older persons underutilize physician services for chronic conditions and preventive health care, although women seek medical care more readily than do

men (Haug, 1984; Schick, 1986). It is noteworthy that only a small proportion of the elderly are high users of all health services. In a Canadian study, for example, less than one-third of the elderly accounted for over 70 percent of all physician visits (Roos and Shapiro, 1981). In a longitudinal study of a U. S. national sample of over 2000 older adults, only 3 percent were consistently high users of physician services over a six-year period, while 40.5 percent were consistently low to medium users, i.e., six or fewer annual physician visits. (Stump, Johnson, and Wolinsky, 1995).

Although a variety of medical and dental services aimed specifically at the elderly have developed in recent years and increasing numbers of specialists are trained in geriatric health care, there are several possible explanations for older people's relatively low rates of seeking medical help for chronic conditions. One may be the belief among older persons that these conditions are natural concomitants of aging, and that a physician can do little to relieve or cure them. In addition, older people may not report symptoms nor seek help for health problems because they fear the possibility of a serious illness and they are concerned about the expense of physician visits, diagnostic tests, and hospitalization (Rowe, 1985). Another barrier may be the negative attitudes of health professionals, some of whom may believe that older patients are difficult to manage and that the diseases associated with aging cannot be reversed. Clearly, such perceptions by

**TABLE 7–2  Interval Since Last Physician Visit**

| AGE | LESS THAN 1 YEAR | 1 TO 2 YEARS | 2 TO 5 YEARS | 5 PLUS YEARS |
|---|---|---|---|---|
| | (Percentage) | | | |
| All ages | 76.0 | 10.1 | 10.0 | 3.9 |
| 25 to 44 | 71.5 | 11.4 | 12.6 | 4.5 |
| 45 to 64 | 75.0 | 8.6 | 10.6 | 5.8 |
| 65 to 74 | 82.2 | 5.5 | 7.1 | 5.2 |
| 75 + | 87.2 | 4.4 | 4.6 | 3.8 |

SOURCE: National Center for Health Statistics, Health Interview Survey, 1987

physicians interact with older patients' attitudes in ways that do not enhance the likelihood that the elderly will receive adequate care for serious chronic diseases.

Inadequate health service utilization can be fatal. These differential patterns of health service utilization may account for the fact that five-year survival rates for cancer of the cervix, uterus, and esophagus are lower in blacks than in any other racial group (Baquet and Ringen, 1986). Similarly, African American women are less likely to seek health care than white women. As a result, they are more likely to die of breast cancer, even though the rates for this disease are higher among whites. This is attributed to the fact that the average size of a tumor is much larger at diagnosis in African American women, reflecting the lack of regular medical check-ups.

## Use of Other Health Services

Hospital utilization apparently reflects older people's need for health care more accurately than do elective visits to a physician's office. Older people are more frequently hospitalized and for longer

Home health aides are a vital source of assistance for frail elderly.

periods of time than younger populations, accounting for about 30 percent of all short-stay hospital days of care. However, the average length of stay has been reduced since the introduction of Diagnostic Related Groupings (DRGs) for Medicare patients in 1983 (see Chapter 20)—from 14.1 days in 1981 to 8.9 days in 1988; but those aged 85 and older continue to be hospitalized longer (U.S. Senate Special Committee on Aging, 1990). While DRGs prompted a transfer of care from inpatient hospital settings to outpatient settings, home health utilization by older people has decreased overall since 1985, reflecting more stringent eligibility and reimbursement criteria rather than a diminishing need for care.

The use of prescription medications may also be an indication of the elderly's real needs for health care. Although representing only 12 percent of the population, older people purchased approximately 30 percent of all prescription drugs and 40 percent of all over-the-counter drugs (Kusserow, 1989). About 25 percent of the elderly take three or more prescription drugs a day, compared to 9 percent of younger people (AARP, 1986). It has been estimated that some older people take as many as ten different medications simultaneously (Wolfe, 1988). The problem is more acute in nursing homes. Not surprisingly, because of the higher likelihood of their having many chronic conditions, the nursing home residents take an average of 6.1 prescription drugs (Kidder, 1987). As might be expected, most of these drugs are for the chronic health problems that occur with greater frequency in old age (e.g., hypertension, cardiovascular disease, and arthritis). In many instances, however, older people may be taking either too many medications or inappropriate drugs. Overmedication is a concern for older people because the less efficient excretion of drugs by the kidney and liver, and the changing proportions of fat and muscle tissue throughout the older person's body, as discussed in Chapter 5, may prolong the effects of some drugs.

The higher rate of medication use among older persons also may result in reporting errors and in incorrect use of these drugs. A recent study of older people admitted to a hospital found significant inconsistencies in medication reporting. For example, medication histories provided by elderly patients at admission differed from their reports to a research assistant within two days in 83 percent of the cases; 46 percent had three or more inconsistencies. Fully 22 percent of the drugs included in the medication history were denied by older patients in the subsequent interviews (Beers, Munekata, and Storrie, 1990). Problems of incorrect use of medications are discussed in Chapter 11.

An area of elective health care, ignored even more than routine medical care, is the use of professional dental services. Although the rate of preventive dental service utilization in the United States has risen significantly over the past 20 years among younger cohorts, the use of dental services by the elderly has increased only slightly. In the latest national survey, older persons continued to be the lowest utilizers of professional dental care; 26.5 percent had not seen a dentist in more than five years in 1985–86, in contrast to 2 percent among the youngest age group and 11.5 percent of those aged 45 to 64 (Brunelle, 1987). This rate is incongruent with the level of oral diseases that require professional attention in older persons. Yet, once older persons enter the dental care system, their average number of visits is similar to that of younger people. The current state of Medicare reimbursement, where physician visits are covered but dental care is not, plays an important role in this differential pattern of utilization.

The use of mental health services is even lower than that of dental care in the older population. Some reasons for this low level of utilization will be discussed in Chapter 11.

## MODELS OF HEALTH BEHAVIOR

Some older persons do seek regular medical and dental health services. What distinguishes them from the underutilizers? Numerous studies have shown that it is not the severity of the older person's health problems (Wolinsky, 1978; Krout,

1983; Holtzman and Akiyama, 1985). Sometimes an older person with the most serious problems is the least likely to seek care. Researchers who have explored this question have developed a number of predictive models. The most widely used frameworks are the behavioral model and the health belief model.

### The Behavioral Model

The behavioral model suggests that three sets of variables can account for differences in the use of health services These are predisposing, enabling, and need variables. (Aday and Andersen, 1974; Aday, Fleming, and Andersen, 1984). The first consists of demographic characteristics, such as age, sex, ethnic minority status, education, and occupation of the head of a household, which will be discussed next. Age differences already have been noted.

**Predisposing Variables: Age, Gender, Ethnic Minority Status, and Education** Although frequency of physician utilization does not increase with age, the number of visits in a given year *doubles,* from 4.4 visits by 17 to 24-year-olds, to 8.9 by those 65 and older. Dentist utilization shows little change, despite increased disease rates. Turning to gender differences, females are more likely than males to use medical and dental services at all ages. As noted previously, however, females at all ages are less likely to be hospitalized and stay fewer days than males do.

Nursing homes are more than twice as likely to be occupied by older women than by men. Two reasons may be cited for this: A greater proportion of women live to be 75 years and older, and there is a greater availability of family members, especially wives, to care for chronically ill older men at home. As a result of smaller family size during the Depression, many women today have outlived a spouse or adult child who could provide help in times of health crises.

This relative availability of family supports may explain differences in the use of nursing home and hospital services by ethnic minority groups. Thus, for example, American Indians,

**Table 7–3   Number of Medical and Dental Visits per Person per Year, by Age: United States, 1987**

| ALL AGES | 17 TO 24 YEARS | 25 TO 44 YEARS | 45 TO 64 YEARS | 65 YEARS AND OVER |
|---|---|---|---|---|
| | | Number of Physician Visits per Person per Year | | |
| 5.8 | 4.4 | 4.8 | 6.4 | 8.9 |
| | | Number of Dental Visits per Person per Year | | |
| 2.0 | 1.7 | 2.0 | 2.2 | 2.1 |

SOURCE: National Center for Health Statistics, *Vital & Health Statistics,* Series 10, No. 158, 1988.

African Americans, and Hispanics, who tend to have more extensive family networks than many Caucasian ethnic groups, are less likely to use these professional services. However, the differential use of health services may be due to factors other than ethnicity per se. This situation illustrates one of the problems with the behavioral model of health service utilization. It is likely that ethnic minority status interacts with the older person's income, occupation, and perceptions of the health care system; availability of third-party payments (i.e., private and government funded insurance plans) for health care; and professional attitudes toward treating ethnic minorities. Unfortunately, the behavioral model does not consider interactions among the predisposing, enabling, and need variables.

Education is another predisposing variable that predicts differential use of health services. Like ethnicity, however, it probably interacts with occupation, income, availability of health insurance, attitudes, and knowledge about health care. Nowhere is the difference in utilization associated with educational levels more dramatic than in the use of dental services. Across all age groups, families headed by college graduates are two to three times more likely to seek dental services than are those headed by an individual with eight years of education or less (Kiyak, 1984).

Enabling Variables   The second category, enabling variables, includes family income, the ability to

pay for services, the availability of third-party payments, and community resources. These reflect the fact that while an individual may be predisposed to use health services, he or she will not do so unless able to use them. Not surprisingly, family income plays a critical role in the use of all health services. It appears that Medicare and Medicaid can reduce some of the differential effects of income for older persons, but because some health expenses must still be paid out-of-pocket, the poorest elderly remain the least likely to obtain health services. And it is precisely the poorest among the older population who are the most vulnerable to the diseases that increase with age.

The individual's own perception of the ability to pay may be even more important than actual costs in determining use of health services. Regardless of income level, older people who feel that they cannot afford health care (often because they have an exaggerated concept of the expense) will not seek care. Although this may also be true among the younger population, the latter are more likely to be knowledgeable about ways to obtain low-cost health services. As a result, younger people may be less likely to report avoiding health services because of high costs.

Another factor that may affect utilization of health services is their accessibility. It is generally assumed that the relatively fewer services available in rural and nonmetropolitan areas, combined with the greater transportation difficulties, result in lower utilization rates in these areas. However, older persons' utilization of general health services does not differ significantly by community size, although hospital admissions are greater among rural elderly (Krout, 1983; Shapiro and Roos, 1984, 1985).

Information about the availability of services, their costs, and criteria for enrolling in special programs is a critical determinant of access to services, especially the utilization of services supported by public funds for special populations. To the extent that older persons have strong informal networks, or are integrated into the community's formal support systems, they are more likely to know about services and to seek additional information. Such knowledge is the first step in entering the health care system. The challenge for health care providers is to understand the factors that determine how older persons enter the health care system and how they make regular use of health services.

**Need Variables** The third set of variables in the behavioral model, and perhaps the most important for motivating older persons to use health services, is the need factor. This includes symptoms of health and illness, perceived need for health care, and functional health problems. Studying these variables systematically is difficult, particularly in large-scale national surveys where a detailed assessment of physical symptoms and perceived need for various services is prohibitively expensive. Yet need variables are often the best predictors and the primary determinant of utilization. For example, an older person who is reluctant to admit to any pain associated with a physical health condition will not seek health care.

Because of the widespread acceptance by older people of poor health as a concomitant of aging, the physical symptoms of a disease must be accompanied by a perceived need for treatment. Depression is one example of a condition with numerous physical and psychological symptoms (e.g., sleeplessness, loss of appetite, crying spells) that an older person may define as normal, or as something to adapt to; worse yet, an older person may assume that nothing can be done about the problem.

Health care providers and health educators must encourage consistency between older persons' perceptions and actual symptoms of disease. Perceived need depends on the individual's "health IQ," that is, an understanding of the processes of disease and health, an ability to distinguish normal aging from disease, and a psychological willingness to deal with one's health problems. Many older people may deny that they need health care because they are unwilling to view themselves as ill, helpless, or dependent. It is therefore critical to disassociate the need for health care from dependency in the minds of older people, and to reinforce the belief that they can improve their health. These concepts of self-responsibility should be a part of any health education and health promotion program aimed at the elderly, as discussed later in this chapter.

## The Health Belief Model

Another model of health services utilization is the *health belief model* (Rosenstock 1966, 1974; Becker et al., 1977). This model hypothesizes that people will not seek health services unless they (1) view themselves as vulnerable or susceptible to a disease which they (2) perceive as having severe consequences. In addition, individuals must (3) see an association between performing particular behaviors and outcomes, and must (4) be convinced that the benefits to seeking health care outweigh the barriers. Many older people, for example, believe that a doctor cannot help them or that their illness is not severe enough to require medical attention (Shanas and Maddox, 1985).

This model would predict that an older woman will be more likely to practice preventive health behaviors related to breast cancer if she sees herself *susceptible* to breast cancer and if she believes that the disease can be fatal, and that monthly breast self-examinations are *effective* for preventing it. The older woman who does not think she is at risk, or believes that preventive behaviors make no difference because she will get the disease anyway, will be less likely to practice such behaviors. Thus, all four elements of the health belief model must operate simultaneously.

An important distinction between this model and the behavioral model described earlier is that the former focuses on the individual's internal state, that is, motives and self-reported likelihood of taking action, not on demographic and social conditions that differentially affect groups of people.

The health belief model has been used to examine retrospectively numerous health behaviors among subjects of varying ages (Eve, Watson, and Reiss, 1980; Ferraro and Mutran, 1983). It is less useful for predicting health behavior. Some components of the model, particularly the belief that preventive behaviors are effective, are more closely related to actual health service utilization than are other components.

The health belief model appears potentially valuable for changing health behaviors. Attempts to use it in behavior change programs, however, have met with mixed success, and there are no reports of research on its application to older persons' health behaviors specifically. This area deserves further study, considering the significance of perceived need in both the health belief and behavioral models of health care utilization.

## The Congruence Model

An alternative approach to examining health service utilization among older people is the person-environment (P-E) congruence model. As briefly described in the Introduction, this model (Lawton and Nahemow, 1973; Kahana, Liang, and Felton, 1980) has been applied to the integration of older persons with their physical and social environments. Health behavior is proposed to be a function of the "fit" or congruence between an individual's perceived and objective health needs, cognitive and physical capacities to deal with the health care system, informal support systems, and the health care

delivery system's characteristics, constraints, and opportunities.

On Lok Senior Health Services in San Francisco is an example of modifying health care services to be responsive to the particular needs of Chinese, Filipino, and Italian older people who do not speak English, and whose health beliefs are often incongruent with the prevailing medical model in the United States. On Lok has utilized informal neighborhood networks, altered traditional methods of financing through the use of waivers and health maintenance organizations, and made services accessible in order to maintain frail older persons in the community. Without the usual fee-for-service limitation, On Lok has the flexibility to provide any service, from meals to acute hospitalization, based on the individual participants' needs. The On Lok model has been able to cut health care costs by reducing the need to use expensive institutional care, while simultaneously providing high-quality services (Van Steenberg, Ansak, and Chin-Hansen, 1993).

The congruence model has not been widely tested, but it holds promise for planning alternative health care delivery systems that are most likely to fit the needs of older persons. The greatest strength of a person-environment approach to evaluating health service utilization is that it avoids the pitfall of viewing the environment as static; that is, it suggests that the health care system cannot remain as it has always been, or as it was designed to serve younger people's needs, but that it must be modified if older persons are to utilize services effectively. The other two models focus primarily on characteristics of the person, not on the nature of the service delivery system. This alternative model also minimizes the danger of assuming that some older people just cannot be helped because of demographic and historical characteristics that affect their use of health services. Instead, the emphasis of the congruence model is on developing services that fit the needs of all types of older adults. This model predicts that utilization can be made most effective if two conditions change: (1) patients' attitudes, values, and knowledge about health care can be enhanced; and (2) health care settings can be designed to be more sensitive to the older patients' needs. Only by effecting changes in both of these areas can health practitioners and gerontologists expect to improve older persons' use of all health care services: ambulatory, acute, chronic, and dental.

## HEALTH PROMOTION WITH OLDER PEOPLE

Another intervention to impact older people's health behavior and utilization of health services is health promotion. Health promotion includes ". . . any combination of health education and related organizational, political, and economic changes conducive to health" (Green et al., 1980). This emphasis on the variety of interventions acknowledges the complex social, biological, cultural, and economic factors that influence health and health behavior. Accordingly, this definition includes altering individual health practices, such as diet and exercise, as well as trying to create healthier environments and to change cultural attitudes and expectations toward health (*Healthy People,* 1979; U.S. Public Health Service, 1991). Health promotion represents a shift from a biomedical model that emphasizes the physician's responsibility to treat disease, to a model where individuals are responsible for and feel more in control of their own health and can optimize their quality of life. Health promotion thus makes explicit the importance of people's environments and lifestyles as determinants of their health status.

The primary rationale for health promotion programs for adults is to reduce the incidence of disabling *chronic* diseases, and thereby to enhance the elderly's functional independence and overall quality of life, not merely to prolong life. Health promotion is also a recognition that chronic conditions cannot be "cured," but can be prevented from causing disability. As Dychtwald (1983), one of the leading proponents of health promotion for the elderly, has noted, "If we are

to survive the aging of America, we must first find ways to make our older citizens well" (p. 5). As suggested in our earlier discussion of disease, as many as 80 percent of the chronic illnesses that afflict older individuals are estimated to be related to social, environmental, and behavioral factors, particularly poor health habits. In addition, 90 percent of fatal and near-fatal episodes of strokes and heart attacks are believed to be preventable. For example, heart disease has been linked to daily stress, sedentary living, weight gain, smoking, and high-cholesterol diets. Yet all of these risk factors can be reduced, even in later life, through changes in health habits (e.g., controlling blood pressure and weight, stopping cigarette smoking, reducing cholesterol levels, and engaging in regular, moderate exercise) (Farquhar, 1978; U.S. Public Health Service, 1989; Surgeon General's Workshop, 1988). A viable health care goal, as noted in Chapter 1, is therefore the "compression of morbidity," delaying the age at which chronic illness and the infirm period of life begins (Fries, 1983; 1984; Berg and Cassells, 1990). This goal translates into helping people to live as much of the normal life span as possible—that is, to die of some acute disease in old age—and to enjoy the highest possible quality of life in their later years. This goal of improvement seems feasible, given the evidence that individuals over age 75 who followed seven health-enhancing behaviors achieved the same health index ratings as those 30 years younger who followed few or none of these behaviors (Paffenberger et al., 1986). Other evidence is shown by master athletes who steadily improve their times, become more fit and physically stronger, and who, even as they grow older, achieve a maximum capacity comparable to their younger counterparts (Vaccaro et al., 1984).

As stated succinctly by the 1988 Surgeon General's Report on Health Promotion and Aging, prevention not only improves the quality of life, but also may save dollars in the long run, although recent findings on the cost-effectiveness of health promotion are mixed (Vogt, 1994). Growing awareness of these benefits is not reflected in the allocation of health dollars, however, since only 6 percent of the national health care dollar is spent on prevention and early detection services (Brown, 1991). Medicare and most private health insurance plans do not pay for preventive services. Most health promotion efforts have been funded through short-term publicly funded demonstration projects or by private foundations. An encouraging sign, however, is the number of health maintenance organizations, health care clinics, universities, and work sites that are offering health promotion programs. Some of these programs have been carried into senior centers, assisted living and retirement homes. They include blood pressure and cholesterol screenings sponsored by local hospitals and businesses.

## The Relationship of Health Practices to Health Outcomes

Considerable research demonstrates the relationship of personal health habits to health status and life satisfaction, although more longitudinal research is needed (Berkman and Breslow, 1983; Branch and Jette, 1984; Green, 1984; Heckler, 1985; Kane, Kane, and Arnold, 1985). The following factors have been identified to be related to good health status: not smoking, limiting alcohol consumption, controlling one's weight near the ideal level, sleeping seven to eight hours per night, and maintaining moderate levels of aerobic exercise. These relationships have been found to be cumulative and independent of age, sex, and economic status (Rakowski, 1994).

Additional epidemiological evidence demonstrates links between specific health habits and decreased longevity and/or increased health risks. These specific lifestyle factors, discussed briefly next, include alcohol consumption, cigarette smoking, diet, and exercise.

The relationship between drinking alcohol and physical health is U-shaped, with the least healthy tending to be those who drink heavily and those who abstain, although abstainers may include former heavy drinkers who have damaged their systems. Excessive drinking (five or more drinks at a single sitting) has been found to contribute to poorer than average physical health and to hasten death (Williams, 1988).

The effects of cigarette smoking, especially in interaction with other risk factors, on heart disease, emphysema, and lung cancer have been extensively documented (Harris, 1994). Smokers who use oral contraceptives, are exposed to asbestos, have excessive alcohol consumption, or are at risk for hypertension have a greater chance of experiencing nonfatal myocardial infarction and are at significant risk for cancers of the oral cavity and lung and for osteoporosis (Goldberg, 1988). Even those who have smoked for years can benefit from smoking cessation (Rimer, 1988).

Poor diet has been determined to be related to obesity, cancer, and heart disease. Obesity carries an increased risk of cardiovascular and pulmonary difficulties, aggravates other conditions such as hypertension, arthritis, and diabetes, and adds risk to surgery. Interpretation of the relationship between obesity and morbidity and mortality is difficult, however, since obesity is correlated with other risk factors, such as high blood pressure.

The relationship between diet, blood cholesterol, coronary heart disease, and stroke has also been suggested in numerous studies. As noted earlier, diets high in fat, sugar, and salt and low in fiber have been found to be associated with a high incidence of coronary heart disease, hypertension, diabetes, obesity, tooth decay, and certain cancers common among older people. Most of such evidence, however, is from epidemiologic studies that demonstrate an association between diet and disease, but do not necessarily prove causation. For example, some environmental factors that influence the likelihood of disease are also linked to poor nutrition. These include low socioeconomic status, ill-fitting dentures, eating alone, or a sedentary way of life.

There is considerable evidence of the relationship between regular, moderate exercise and reduction in a person's chances of dying from heart disease and cancer, which may, in fact, add up to two years to a person's life (Blair et al.,

1989). Up to 50 percent of physical changes in older people that are mistakenly attributed to aging may be due to being physically unfit. Physically inactive people age faster and look older than physically fit persons of the same age, in part because of what has been termed *hypokinesia,* a disease of "disuse," or the degeneration and functional loss of muscle and bone tissue (Drinkwater, 1988; O'Brien and Vertinsky, 1991).

The goal of remaining physically active with advancing age is to delay the declines in functional capacity with aging. Because the body's adaptability to exercise remains unimpaired by aging, exercise can slow the decline of physiological functions. In particular, cross-training that includes aerobic exercises three times per week, as well as stretching and weight training can maintain cardiovascular and respiratory functioning; it can restore and maintain muscular strength and joint flexibility; reduce the risk of hypothermia, osteoporosis, and accidents; and enhance cognitive ability. It appears to benefit even those with coronary artery disease, diabetes, hypertension, and pulmonary disorders by causing weight loss; reducing blood sugar, blood fat, and high blood pressure; and improving circulation (Goldberg, 1988; Clarkson-Smith, and Hartley, 1989; Stones and Komza, 1989).

In 1990, the federal government facilitated the collaboration of numerous expert working groups representing 300 national organizations, the health departments of all states, and the Institute of Medicine of the National Academy of Sciences, to develop health goals for the nation. Based on the successes and failures of a similar report in 1979 (Healthy People, 1979), this report established several health objectives that Americans should attempt to achieve by the year 2000. Labeled *Healthy People 2000,* this document has been used widely by policy makers and practitioners as a blueprint for health promotion programs. Three broad goals of this report are relevant for older adults: (1) increase the span of *healthy* life (i.e. compressed morbidity); (2) reduce health disparities among Americans; (3) improve access to preventive services for all Americans (U. S. Department of Health & Human Services, 1991).

Despite the known benefits of exercise, a major goal of *Healthy People 2000,* i.e. 50-percent participation by individuals 65 years and older in "appropriate" physical activity, is far from being met. It has been estimated that less than 30 percent have achieved this goal. New activity objectives of 30 percent of older adults exercising have now been established, but current activity levels among most older adults are so low that meeting objectives for the year 2000 will mean behavioral changes among the general public of up to 200 percent (Dishman, 1990).

Psychosocial conditions, particularly a loss of control, excessive stress, and the absence of social supports, have also been linked to decreased longevity and/or poor health. There is relatively strong epidemiologic evidence that persons who are married, have close contacts with friends and relatives, and share common religious, ethnic, or cultural interests with others experience lower morbidity and greater longevity than those without such ties. Social networks apparently act to buffer the negative effects of stress (Berkman, 1986; Cohen, Teresi, and Holmes, 1985). Translating the results of research on social supports into health services has been slow, partly because they do not fit the traditional biomedical model of disease and treatment.

## Health Promotion Guidelines

Given the growing evidence about the relation of health practices to health status, most health promotion programs include components on injury prevention, nutrition, exercise, and stress management. Oral health promotion has also been implemented in geriatric dentistry. An underlying theme is taking responsibility for one's own health, rather than relying on medical professionals. Some programs also include educating participants to change the larger social environment, perhaps through collective action. Several components of health promotion programs are briefly described.

1. *Nutrition.* Although information on older people's dietary needs is incomplete and often contradictory, the basic principles are:

(a) Consume a wide variety of foods.

(b) Increase consumption of unprocessed foods containing complex carbohydrates (starch and fiber), such as whole grains and legumes.

(c) Restrict intake of sugar, fat, cholesterol (less than 10 percent of the total calories consumed should be derived from saturated fat) (Surgeon General's Workshop, 1988; USDHHS, 1991).

Unfortunately, there are a number of barriers to adequate nutrition. Some of these result from physiological and social changes common to aging and include an inability to chew and swallow due to no teeth, missing teeth, or loose-fitting dentures; problems with taste or smell; poor digestion of certain foods; and emotional barriers, such as loneliness, that deprive mealtime of its social satisfactions and may diminish appetite. Others result from societal conditions, such as the expense of particular foods or lack of access to them. Any nutritional assessment of an older person must take account of such factors that can affect the amount and type of food consumed.

2. *Exercise.* Exercise programs need to be tailored to take account of variability in physical function and fitness levels. There is growing recognition that past exercise programs for older people may have been overly cautious and that the elderly need to be individually challenged to obtain the full benefits of an appropriate exercise level (Frontera and Meredith, 1989). Beyond the benefits of aerobic fitness, a variety of physical activities are important to maintain other needs of the body for overall muscle strength and endurance, joint mobility, balance and upright posture (Teague, 1987).

Prior to beginning an exercise program, older people should have a thorough medical examination, including a treadmill or other exercise tolerance test, to determine their baseline for physical fitness. An ideal exercise program begins with a low level of activity and includes an initial warm-up, with stretching, light calisthenics, and leisurely walking, more strenuous exercise for 20 minutes or more, and a relaxing cool-down period of five to 10 minutes of light exercise, at least three times each week. Brisk walking is the safest and best exercise for older people. Most ambulatory older persons, even those at a lower level of fitness, can build up their walking to one or more miles daily, and at a speed of three or four miles per hour. There is evidence that greater physiological benefits, such as fat loss and cardiovascular change, require more intense and vigorous exercise, such as jogging or bicycling, which can be safely undertaken by healthy older people (Blair et al., 1989; O'Brien and Vertinsky, 1991).

3. *Stress Management.* Stress-related disorders include emotional disturbances, psychosomatic complaints, headaches, insomnia, hypertension, and certain types of rheumatic or allergic afflictions as well as cardiovascular and kidney diseases. As noted earlier, older people may be more susceptible to such negative effects because of the body's decreased ability to adapt to stress and increased vulnerability to physiological changes induced by the stress response itself. This means that the aging process may be accelerated by repeated exposure to stress at a time of diminished adaptability (Vogt, 1992). Health care

Thorough medical assessments are a necessary part of health promotion.

professionals have shown increasing interest in ways to reduce such potential negative effects through stress management techniques, such as stress alleviation, progressive muscle relaxation, and clinical biofeedback.

When using techniques to regulate stress, a person focuses on a constant stimulus, such as the repetition of a word or phrase, or fixed gazing at an object. Another self-regulatory approach is progressive muscle relaxation, in which various muscle groups are systematically tensed and then released to achieve a state of deep relaxation. When used with a group of widows, these techniques were found to reduce stress-related psychosomatic symptoms of headaches, insomnia, and nightly awakenings, as well as self-reported tension and anxiety levels (De-Berry, 1981–82). Biofeedback training aims to increase awareness of specific muscle tension, to control that tension through the use of biofeedback equipment in the laboratory, and to transfer that ability from the laboratory to real-life situations. Clinical biofeedback has been used to treat high blood pressure, migraine, and tension headaches. Underlying all these relaxation techniques is an emphasis on quiet attentiveness to one's own bodily sensations.

Another important outcome of physical activities is stress reduction, which is linked to other benefits such as better sleep, muscle relaxation, positive mood, and improved self-image and self-concept. Overall, exercise appears to act as a buffer in many stress-illness relationships, possibly through biochemical interactions linking mind and body (Haug, Ford, and Sheafor, 1985). More research is needed, however, on which particular modalities of stress reduction are most helpful to older people.

## Oral Health Promotion

Only a few health promotion programs include preventive dentistry. One reason for this is that dental disease and tooth loss are frequently assumed to be natural concomitants of aging.

Once an individual has lost many teeth from poor oral health in the middle years, it is presumed there is little to promote and maintain. Despite this skeptical attitude, held by professionals and older people alike, some oral health promotion efforts have been found to be successful (Kiyak and Mulligan, 1987; Kiyak and Grayston, 1989).

With increased preventive dentistry in youth and middle-age, tooth loss has become less prevalent in the later years (Brunelle, 1987). This means that individuals with teeth remaining must perform regular oral health care, including brushing, flossing, and regular visits to a dentist or hygienist. As noted earlier, older people are not only less inclined to use professional dental services, but also less likely to know and value techniques of preventive dentistry (Gilmore and Kiyak, 1984). Instead, prevention must be defined differently by age: In younger persons, the initiation of dental disease and tooth loss can be prevented; in the elderly, the goal is to prevent *further* disease, particularly disease caused by poorly fitting dentures and by regimens prescribed for other medical conditions.

## Health Promotion for Frail Older People

Although preventive efforts have focused on healthy older people in the community, health promotion principles have been implemented in institutional settings. For example, the concepts of self-responsibility and control have been promoted through giving nursing home residents the care of plants, pets, or bird feeders (Banziger and Roush, 1983). Range-of-motion exercise for institutionalized older persons has been found under certain conditions to improve muscle tone and enhance feelings of well-being (Allen, 1985). Many chair exercises can be adapted for impaired, even bed-bound, older persons. Even the slowest pace of walking has been shown to provide significant benefits to extremely frail individuals who rarely leave the sitting position (Gueldner and Spradley, 1988). More work is needed to adapt health promotion materials and techniques to take account of differing incidences of specific conditions, risk factors, or living situations of frail older people.

## Limitations of Health Promotion

Health promotion programs have been criticized for their emphasis on individual responsibility for change, which minimizes the societal factors that underlie individual health practices and use of services, such as income and access to affordable health care (O'Donnell and Harris, 1994; Walker, 1994). Likewise, some educational efforts ignore the roles of policy makers, health care providers, food manufacturers, and the mass media in creating social and economic environments that may counter health promotion interventions. In addition to educating individuals to adopt healthy habits, the broader social environment must be changed, for example, through training older people in advocacy and political action (U. S. Department of Health and Human Services, 1991).

Another limitation of health promotion is that, although the value of such efforts is widely publicized, individuals often do not act on this information. Think about the number of people who continue to smoke despite the empirical evidence linking smoking to lung cancer, or the small proportion of women over age 45 who have a Pap smear and breast exam on a regular basis even though such tests are important in detecting cancer (Thornsberry, Wilson, and Golden, 1986). As another example, despite the widely known benefits of exercise, only 10 percent of Americans are regularly and vigorously active, and only about 5 percent of those over age 65 engage in appropriate levels of physical activity (Dishman, 1990; Blair, Brill, and Kohl, 1989).

As we are all aware, people do not always engage in healthy behaviors, even when they know that they should! The gap between health knowledge and health practices can be large. On the other hand, some studies indicate that, when educated about health habits, older people have higher levels of compliance and behavior change than those in other age groups (Green, 1985).

To the extent that interventions focus primarily on individual change, their relevance is questionable for low-income and ethnic minority populations, whose health problems often stem from situational factors such as poverty over which individuals have little control. Accordingly, low-income populations, preoccupied with meeting basic needs, may view exercise and healthy foods as luxuries. Few health promotion efforts have been effectively implemented with low-income or ethnic minority groups. The programs that have been tried have had problems with recruitment and retention (Yee and Weaver, 1994).

In general, organized health promotion programs have difficulty recruiting more than 50 percent of the target population; even those focused on rehabilitation of post-myocardial infarct patients and managing high blood pressure through exercise have had difficulties with recruitment. Attrition is also high, with rates of 30 to 60 percent. Older people most likely to participate in organized health promotion are those with a preventive attitude (e.g., regular users of physicians and dentists for check-ups, nonsmokers, exercisers, and users of seat belts and smoke alarms), and those with higher participation rates in community services (Carter et al., 1991; Wagner et al., 1991).

Even when individual behavioral change is a legitimate goal, sustaining health practices over time is difficult in the face of years of habit. In fact, little is known about the long-term changes resulting from many health promotion interventions, because most evaluations have been conducted soon after program completion, with no long-term follow-up. Health promotion demonstration programs have not been long-lasting or widely replicated. Thus, at present, there is no strong evidence for the long-term effectiveness of health promotion for older people (Warshaw, 1988). Longitudinal research is needed to assess the long-range consequences of health promotion interventions for individuals and for health care costs, especially since programs to modify health-related behaviors may initially be very costly before they achieve long-run savings.

On the other hand, it is encouraging that short-term educational programs aimed at improving older participants' knowledge and preventive health behaviors in the areas of cancer, heart disease, and oral diseases have shown significant improvements at their termination (Keintz et al., 1988; Clark et al., 1988; Kiyak and Mulligan, 1987). The most effective prevention appears to come from two approaches: eliminating iatrogenic disease that is induced in the patient by medical care, especially with regard to the side effects of medications, and preventing the transformation from disease to disability (Fried and Bush, 1988). Health promotion is clearly a growing area, especially in light of societal pressures to reduce rising health care costs, and it raises numerous opportunities for policy and program development and research. One of the major conclusions of the 1995 White House Conference on Aging is that preventive health care and exercise among older people can save $260 billion in health care costs.

## SUMMARY AND IMPLICATIONS

Although older persons are at risk of more diseases than younger people, most older people rate their own health as satisfactory. Health status refers not only to an individual's physical condition, but also to her or his functional level in various social and psychological domains. It is affected by a person's social surroundings, especially the degree of environmental stress and social support available. Although stress has been found to increase the risk of certain illnesses, such as cardiovascular disease, older people are generally less negatively affected by stress; this may reflect maturity, self-control, or a lifetime of developing coping skills.

Older people are more likely to suffer from chronic or long-term diseases than from temporary or acute illnesses. The majority of older persons, however, are not limited in their daily activities by chronic conditions. The impact of such conditions apparently varies with the physiological changes that occur with age, the individual's adaptive resources, and his or her mental and emotional perspective. The type and incidence of chronic conditions also vary by gender.

The leading causes of death among persons over age 65 are heart disease, cancer, accidents, and stroke. Diseases of the heart and blood vessels are the most prevalent. Since hypertension or high blood pressure is a major risk in the development of cardiovascular problems, preventive actions are critical, especially weight control, dietary changes, appropriate exercise, and avoidance of cigarette smoking. Cancers, especially lung, bowel, and colon cancers, are the second most frequent cause of death among older persons; the risk of cancer increases with age. Cerebrovascular disease, or stroke, is the third leading cause of death among older persons. It may be caused by cerebral thrombosis, or blood clots, and by cerebral hemorrhage. Healthy lifestyle practices are important in stroke prevention.

Arthritis, although not fatal, is a major cause of limited daily activity and is extremely common among older persons. Osteoporosis, or loss of bone mass and the resultant increased brittleness of the bones, is most common among older women, and may result in fractures of the hip, spine, and wrist. Chronic respiratory problems, particularly emphysema, increase with age, especially among men. Diabetes mellitus is a frequent problem in old age, and is particularly troubling because of the many related illnesses that may result. Problems with the intestinal tract include diverticulitis, constipation, and hiatus hernia. Cystitis and incontinence are frequently occurring problems of the kidneys and urinary system. Although the majority of older persons have some type of incontinence, many kinds can be treated and controlled.

The growth of the older population, combined with the increase in major chronic illnesses, has placed greater demands on the health care system in this country. Nevertheless, older people seek outpatient medical, dental, and mental health services at a slightly lower rate than their incidence of chronic illnesses would predict. Like younger people, the older population is most likely to seek health services for acute problems, not for check-ups on chronic conditions or for preventive care. Beliefs that physicians, dentists, and mental health professionals cannot cure their chronic problems may deter many older people from seeking needed care. The problem may be compounded by some health care professionals' attitudes that older people are poor candidates for health services because many of their health conditions cannot be cured. More university and continuing education classes are needed to provide training in geriatrics and gerontology for staff in health care settings and to address their attitudes toward older people.

Three theoretical models identify reasons for utilization and nonutilization of health services by older people. The behavioral model suggests that utilization differs as a function of predisposing variables such as age, sex, race, and occupation; enabling variables such as family income and perceived ability to pay; and need variables (actual and perceived need). This model is useful in describing why some people use health services and others do not, but it does not explain differences within subgroups such as the elderly.

The health belief model predicts that people are more likely to seek health services if they view themselves as susceptible to a disease, believe that it has severe consequences, and are convinced that the benefits of treatment outweigh the barriers. Although this model has been tested mostly in retrospective studies and rarely with older populations, it holds promise for evaluating different interventions to increase older people's use of health services.

A third approach, the person-environment congruence model, postulates that utilization is a function of the "fit," or integration, between individual needs and capacities and the opportunities and constraints of the health care system. Thus, the availability of nearby and physically accessible services with staff who are sensitive to the needs of ethnic minority elderly is critical if utilization rates are to increase dramatically among traditionally underserved populations. As the number of people with more education and experience with the health care system increases, designing specialized health services may be less important. Nevertheless, it is essential that health planners consider the special needs of the aging population in designing appropriate services that fit them.

The elimination or postponement of the chronic diseases that are associated with old age appears to be the major task for future biomedical researchers as well as health promotion specialists. Treatment methods for all these diseases are changing rapidly with the growth in medical technology and the increasing recognition given to such environmental factors as stress, nutrition, and exercise in disease prevention. If health promotion efforts to modify lifestyles are successful, and if aging research progresses substantially, the chronic illnesses that we have discussed will undoubtedly be postponed and disability or loss of functional status will be delayed.

## REFERENCES

Aday, L. A., and Andersen, R. A framework for the study of access to medical care. *Health Services Research*, 1974, 9, 208–220.

Aday, L. A., Andersen, R., and Fleming, G. *Health care in the U.S.: Equitable for whom?* Beverly Hills: Russell Sage Foundation, 1980.

Aday, L. A., Fleming, G., and Andersen, R. *Access to health care in the U.S.: Who has it, who doesn't.* Chicago: Pluribus Press, 1984.

Allen, J. The use of isometric exercises in a geriatrics treatment program. *Geriatrics*, 1985, 20, 346–347.

Almy, T. P., and Howell, D. A. Diverticular disease of the colon. *New England Journal of Medicine*, 1980, 202, 324–331.

American Association of Retired Persons (AARP). *A profile of older Americans 1990.* Washington, D.C.: AARP, 1991.

American Association of Retired Persons. *Survey of 1,000 persons 45 and older.* Washington, D.C.: AARP, 1986.

Anda, R. F. Elevated blood cholesterol. In R. Brownson, P. Remington, & J. Davis (eds.), *Chronic disease epidemiology and control.* Washington D. C.: American Public Health Association, 1994.

Arnaud, C. D., and Sanchez, S. D. The role of calcium in osteoporosis. *Annual Review of Nutrition,* 1990, *10,* 397–414.

Avorn, J. Medicine: The life and death of Oliver Shay. In A. Pifer and L. Bronte (Eds.), *Our aging society.* New York: Norton, 1986.

Banziger, G., and Roush, S. Nursing homes for the birds: A control-relevant intervention with bird feeders. *The Gerontologist,* 1983, *23,* 527–532.

Baquet, C. R., and Ringen, K. *Cancer among Blacks and other minorities: Statistical profiles.* NCI Publication No. 86–2785, Washington, D.C.: Department of Health and Human Services, 1986.

Baum, B. J. Characteristics of participants in the oral physiology component of the Baltimore Longitudinal Study of Aging. *Community Dentistry and Oral Epidemiology,* 1981, *9,* 128–134.

Beck, J. D. The epidemiology of oral diseases in the elderly. *Gerodontology,* 1984, *3,* 5–116.

Becker, M., Maiman, L., Kirscht, J., Haefner, D., and Drachman, R. The health belief model and prediction of dietary compliance: A field experiment. *Journal of Health and Social Behavior,* 1977, *18,* 348–366.

Beers, M. H., Munekata, M., and Storrie, M. The accuracy of medication histories in the hospital medical records of elderly persons. *Journal of the American Geriatrics Society,* 1990, *38,* 1183–1187.

Berg, R. L. and Cassells, J. S. *The second fifty years: Promoting health and preventing disability.* Washington D. C.: National Academy Press, 1990.

Berkman, L. Social networks, support and health: Taking the next step forward. *American Journal of Epidemiology,* 1986, *123,* 559–562.

Berkman, L., and Breslow, L. *Health and ways of living: The Alameda County study.* New York: Oxford University Press, 1983.

Blair, S. N., Brill, P. A., and Kohl, H. W. Physical activity patterns in older individuals. In W. W. Spirdieso and H. M. Eckert (Eds.), *The academy papers: Physical activity and aging.* Champaign, Ill.: Human Kinetics Publishers, 1989, 120–139.

Blair, S. N., Kohl, H. W., Paffenbarger, R., Clark, D., Cooper, K., and Gibbons, L. Physical fitness and age-cause mortality: A prospective study of healthy men and women. *Journal of the American Medical Association,* 1989, *262,* 2395–2401.

Borham, N. O. Prevalence and prognostic significance of hypertension in the elderly. *Journal of the American Geriatrics Society,* 1986, *34,* 112–114.

Branch, L. Functional abilities of the elderly: An update on the Massachusetts health care panel study. In S. G. Haynes and M. Feinleib (Eds.), *Epidemiology of aging.* NIH Publication No. 80–969, Washington, D.C.: U.S. Government Printing Office, 1980.

Branch, L., and Jette, A. Personal health practices and mortality among the elderly. *American Journal of Public Health,* 1984, *74,* 1126–1129.

Brown, R. E. *National expenditures for the health promotion and disease prevention and activities in the United States.* Washington D. C. : The Medical Technology Assessment & Policy Research Center, 1994.

Brunelle, J. A. Coronal and root surface caries and tooth mortality of U.S. adults. Presented at symposium on NIDR Adult Dental Health Survey, Meetings of the International Association for Dental Research, Chicago, March 1987.

Cantor, M. Family and community: Changing roles in an aging society. *The Gerontologist,* 1991, *31,* 337–346.

Carter, W. B., Elward, K., Malmgren, J., Martin, M. L., and Larson, E. Participation of older adults in health programs and research: A critical review of the literature. *The Gerontologist,* 1991 *31,* 584–592.

Cassel, J. The contribution of the social environment to host resistance. *American Journal of Epidemiology,* 1976, *104* (2), 107–123.

Catania, J. A., Turner, H., Kegeles, S. M., Stall, R., Pollack, L., and Coates, T. J. Older Americans and AIDS: Transmission risks and primary prevention research needs. *The Gerontologist,* 1989, *29,* 373–381.

Clark, N. M., Rakowski, W., Wheeler, J.R.C., Ostrander, L. D., Oden, S., and Keteyian, S. Development of self-management education for the elderly heart patients. *The Gerontologist,* 1988, *28,* 491–494.

Clarkson-Smith, L., and Hartley, A. A. Relationship between physical exercise and cognitive abilities in older adults. *Psychology and Aging,* 1989, *4,* 183–189.

Cockerham, W. C., Sharp, K., and Wilcox, J. Aging and perceived health status. *Journal of Gerontology,* 1983, *38,* (3), 349–355.

Cohen, C., Teresi, J., and Holmes, D. Social networks, stress and physical health: A longitudinal study of an inner-city elderly population. *Journal of Gerontology,* 1985, *40,* 478–486.

Cousins, N. *Anatomy of an illness.* New York: Bantam Books, 1979.

Cramer, D. Promoting continence: Strategies for success. In, *Perspectives in Health Promotion and Aging,* 1993, *1,* 1–3.

Cunningham, D. A., Rechinitzer, P. A., Howard, J. H., and Donner, A. P. Exercise training of men at retirement: A clinical trial. *Journal of Gerontology,* 1987, *42,* 17–23.

Cutler, S. J., and Young, J. L. (Eds.), *Third national cancer survey: Incidence data.* National Cancer Institute Monograph E1:1–454, 1975.

DeBerry, S. An evaluation of progressive muscle relaxation on stress related symptoms in a geriatric population. *International Journal of Aging and Human Development,* 1981–82, *14,* 255–269.

deVries, H. A. Physiology of physical conditioning for the elderly. In R. Harris and L. J. Frankel (Eds.), *Guide to fitness after 50.* New York: Plenum Press, 1977.

Dishman, R. K. Determinants of physical activity and exercise for persons 65 years of age and older. In W. W. Spirduso and H. M. Eckert (Eds.), *The Academy Papers: Physical activity and aging.* Champaign, Ill.: Human Kinetics Publishers, 1990, 75–102.

Drinkwater, B. Exercise and aging: The female master athlete. In J. L. Puhl and R. G. Voy, (Eds.), *Sport science perspectives for women.* Champaign, Ill.: Human Kinetics Publishers, 1988.

Dychtwald, K. Overview: Health promotion and disease prevention for elders. *Generations,* 1983, *7,* 5–7.

Evans, L. *Traffic safety and the driver.* New York: Van Nostrand Reinhold, 1991.

Evashwick, C., Rowe, G., Diehr, P., and Branch, L. Factors explaining the use of health care services by the elderly. *Health Services Research,* 1984, *19,* 357–382.

Eve, S. B., Watson, J. B., and Reiss, E. M. Use of health care services among older adults. Paper presented at meetings of the Gerontological Society of America, San Diego, Nov. 1980.

Exton-Smith, A. N. Mineral metabolism. In C. Finch and E. Schneider (Eds.), *Handbook of the biology of aging* (2d ed.). New York: Van Nostrand, 1985.

Farquhar, J. W. *The American way of life need not be hazardous to your health.* New York: W. W. Norton, 1978.

Federal Council on the Aging. *The need for long-term care: Information and issues.* DHHS Publication Number OHDS81–20704, Washington, D.C., U.S. Department of Health and Human Services, 1981.

Ferraro, K. F. Double jeopardy to health in Black older adults. *Journal of Gerontology,* 1987, *42,* 528–533.

Ferraro, K. F., and Mutran, E. Differences in health care utilization of older men and women. Paper presented at meetings of the Gerontological Society of America, San Francisco, Nov. 1983.

Fried, L. R., and Bush, T. L. Morbidity as a focus of preventive health care in the elderly. *Epidemiologic Review,* 1988, *10,* 48–64.

Fries, J. F. Aging, natural death, and the compression of morbidity. *New England Journal of Medicine,* 1980, *303,* 130–135.

Fries, J. F. Aging, natural death, and the compression of morbidity. *Generations,* 1983, Spring, 16–18.

Fries, J. F. The compression of morbidity: Miscellaneous comments about a theme. *The Gerontologist,* 1984, *24,* 354–359.

Fries, J. F., and Crapo, L. M. *Vitality and aging.* San Francisco: W. H. Freeman, 1981.

Frontera, W. R. and Meredith, C. N. Strength training in the elderly. In R. Harris and S. Harris (Eds.), *Physical activity, aging and sports.* Albany, N.Y.: Center for the Study of Aging, 319–331.

Gambrell, R. D. Estrogen replacement therapy for the elderly woman. *Medical Aspects of Human Sexuality,* 1987, *21*(5), 81–93.

German, P. S., and Fried, L. P. Prevention and the elderly. *Annual Review of Public Health,* 1989, *10,* 319–332.

Gilmore, S. S., and Kiyak, H. A. Predictors of dental behavior among the elderly. *Special Care in Dentistry.* 1984, *5,* 169–173.

Goldberg, A. Health promotion and aging: Physical exercise, Surgeon General's Workshop. *Health Promotion and Aging,* March 1988.

Green, L. W. Modifying and developing health behavior. In L. Breslow, (Ed.), *Annual Review of Public Health,* 1984, *5,* 215–236.

Green, L. W. Some challenges to health services research on children and the elderly. *Health Services Research*, 1985, *19*, 793–878.

Green, L. W., et al. *Health education planning: A diagnostic approach.* Palo Alto, Calif: Mayfield, 1980.

Gueldner, S. H., and Spradley, J. Outdoor walking lowers fatigue. *Journal of Gerontological Nursing*, 1988, *14*, 6–12.

Guralnik, J. M. and Simonsick, E. M. Physical disability in older Americans. *Journals of Gerontology*, 1993, *48*, 3–10.

Hamburg, D. A. An outlook on stress research and health. In G. R. Elliott and C. Eisdorfer (Eds.), *Stress and human health: An analysis and implications of research.* New York: Springer, 1982.

Harris, J. The health benefits of health promotion. In M. P. O'Donnell, and J. Harris (eds.), *Health Promotion in The Workplace.* Albany, NY: Delmar, 1994.

Harris, L., et al. *Aging in the 80's: America in transition.* Washington, D.C.: National Council on Aging, 1981.

Harris, R. Fitness and exercise: A day in the life of Dr. H. *Generations,* Spring 1983, 23–26.

Haug, M. Doctor and elderly patient relationships and their impact on self-care. Paper presented at meetings of the Gerontological Society, San Antonio, Nov., 1984.

Haug, M. R., Ford, A. V., and Sheafor, M. (1985). *The physical and mental health of aged women.* New York: Springer, 1985.

Haymond, C., Nicholson, C., Kiyak, H. A., and Trimble, D. Age differences in response to facial trauma. *Special Care in Dentistry*, 1988. *8*, 115–118.

*Healthy people. The surgeon general's report on health promotion and disease prevention.* Washington, D. C.: U. S. Government Printing Office, Department of Health, Education and Welfare, 1979.

Heckler, M. Health promotion for older Americans. *Public Health Report,* 1985, *100*, 225–230.

Henderson, B. E., Paganini-Hill, A., and Ross, R. K. Decreased mortality in users of estrogen replacement therapy. *Archives of Internal Medicine,* 1991, *151*, 75–78.

Hickey, T. *Health and aging.* Belmont, Calif.: Wadsworth, 1980.

Holmes, T. H., and Masuda, M. Life change and illness susceptibility. In B. S. Dohrenwend and B. P. Dohrenwend (Eds.), *Stressful life events: Their nature and effects.* New York: Wiley, 1974.

Holtzman, J. M., and Akiyama, H. Symptoms and the decision to seek professional care. *Gerodontics,* 1985, *1*, 44–49.

House, J., and Robbins, C. Age, psychosocial stress, and health. In M. W. Riley, B. Hess, and K. Bond, (Eds.), *Aging in society: Selected reviews.* Hillsdale, N.J.: Erlbaum, 1983.

Jack, S., and Ries, P. Current estimates from the National Health Interview Survey: United States, 1979. *Data from the National Health Interview Survey. Series 10, No. 136.* Rockville, Md.: NCHS, 1981.

Jette, A., and Branch, L. The Framingham disability study, II: Physical disability among the aging. *American Journal of Public Health,* 1981, *71*, 1211–1216.

Johnson, R. J., and Wolinsky, F. D. Gender, race, and health: The structure of health status among older adults. *The Gerontologist,* 1994, *34*, 24–35.

Josephson, K. R., Fabacher, D. A., and Rubenstein, L. Z. Home safety and fall prevention. *Clinics in Geriatric Medicine,* 1991, *7*, 707–731.

Kahana, E., Liang, J., and Felton, B. Alternative models of P-E fit: Prediction of morale in three homes for the aged. *Journal of Gerontology,* 1980, *35*, 584–595.

Kane, R., Kane, L., and Arnold, S. Prevention and the elderly: Risk factors. *Health Services Research,* 1985, *19*, 945–1006.

Kane, R., and Kane R. *Assessing the elderly: A practical guide for measurement.* Lexington, Mass.: Lexington Books, 1981.

Kannel, W. B. Habitual level of physical activity and risk of coronary heart disease: The Framingham study. *Canadian Medical Association Journal,* 1967, *96*, 811–812.

Kannel, W. B. Hypertension and aging. In C. Finch and E. Schneider (Eds.), *Handbook of the biology of aging (2d ed.).* New York: Van Nostrand, 1985.

Kannel, W. B., and Brand, F. N. Cardiovascular risk factors in the elderly woman. In E. Markson (Ed.), *Older Women.* Lexington, Mass.: Lexington Books, 1983, 315–327.

Kaplan, G., Barell, V., and Lusky, A. Subjective state of health and survival among elderly adults. *Journals of Gerontology,* 1988, *43*, S114–S120.

Keintz, M. K., Rimer, B., Fleisher, L., and Engstrom, P. Educating older adults about their increased cancer risk. *The Gerontologist,* 1988, *28*, 487–490.

Kemnitz, J. W., Roccer, E. B., and Weindruch, R. Dietary restriction increases insulin sensitivity and lowers blood glucose in rhesus monkeys. *American Journal of Physiology*, 1994, *266*, E540–E547.

Kennedy, T. E., and Coppart, L. C. (Eds.), The prevention of falls in late life. *Danish Medical Bulletin* (Supplement 14), 1987, *34*, 1–24.

Kerzner, L. Physical changes after menopause. In E. Markson (Ed.), *Older women*. Lexington, Mass.: Lexington Books, 1983.

Kickbush, I. Healthy cities: A working project and a growing movement. *Health Promotion*, 1989, *4*, 77–82.

Kidder, S. W. Cost-benefit of pharmacist-conducted drug regimen reviews. *The Consultant Pharmacist*, 1987, *2*, 394–398.

Kirkendall, W. M. Treatment of hypertension in the elderly. *American Journal of Cardiology*, 1986, *57*, 63–68.

Kiyak, H. A. Utilization of dental services by the elderly. *Gerodontology*, 1984, *3*, 17–26.

Kiyak, H. A., and Grayston, N. A statewide oral health promotion program for Washington's elderly. Final report submitted to the Administration on Aging, 1989.

Kiyak, H. A., and Mulligan, K. Studies of the relationship between oral health and psychological well-being. *Gerodontics*, 1987, *3*, 109–112.

Kosberg, J., and Harris, A. Attitudes toward elderly clients. *Health and Social Work*, 1978, *3*, 68–90.

Krout, J. A. Knowledge and use of services by the elderly: A critical review of the literature. *International Journal of Aging and Human Development*, 1983, *17*, 153–167.

Kusserow, R. P. *Medicine drug utilization review*. Office of the Inspector General, Department of Health and Human Services, April 1989.

Lawton, M. P., and Nahemow, L. Ecology and the aging process. In C. Eisdorfer and M. P. Lawton (Eds.), *The psychology of adult development and aging*. Washington, D. C.: American Psychological Association, 1973.

Lewis, M. Older women and health. *Women and Health*, 1985, *10*, 1–16.

Lindsay, R. Osteoporosis. In *Health issues of older women*. State University of New York at Stony Brook, 1981.

Longino, C., and Soldo, B. The graying of America: Implications of life extension for quality of life. In R. Ward and S. Tobin (Eds.), *Health in aging: Sociological issues and policy directions*. New York: Springer, 1987.

Lopez-Aqueres, W., Kemp, B., Staples, F., and Brummel-Smith, K. Use of health care services of older Hispanics. *Journal of the American Geriatrics Society*, 1984, *32*, 435–440.

Maes, S., Fingerhoets, A., and Vanheck, G. The study of stress and disease: Some developments and requirements, *Social Science and Medicine*, 1987, *25*, 567–578.

Maher, M. C. "Driving difficulties increase with age," *Washington Post*, Oct. 30, 1990.

Manderson, R. D., and Ettinger, R. L. Dental status of the institutionalized elderly population of Edinburgh. *Community Dentistry and Oral Epidemiology*, 1975, *3*, 29–32.

Marchesseault, L. C. Diabetes mellitus and the elderly. *Nursing Clinics of North America*, 1983, *19*, 791–798.

Marcus, R. Understanding and preventing osteoporosis. *Hospital Practice*, 1989, *24*, 189–215.

Markides, K. Minority aging. In M. W. Riley, B. Hess, and K. Bond (Eds.), *Aging in society*. Hillsdale, N.J.: Erlbaum, 1983.

Masuda, M., and Holmes, T. H. Life events: Perceptions and frequencies, *Psychosomatic Medicine*, 1978, *40*, 236–361.

McBride, T. D. Measuring the disability of the elderly: Empirical analysis and projections into the 21st century. Paper presented at the Population Association of America meetings, Baltimore, March 1989.

Multiple Risk Factor Intervention Trial Research Group. Multiple risk factor intervention trial. *The Journal of the American Medical Association*, 1982, *248*, 1465.

National Center for Health Statistics. Summary of the national health interview survey. Unpublished tabulation, 1983.

National Center for Health Statistics. Changes in mortality among the elderly, United States, 1940–78 supplement to 1980. *Vital and health statistics, Series 3*. DHHS Publication No. (PHS) 82–1406a, Washington, D.C.: Department of Health and Human Services, 1984.

National Center for Health Statistics. Current estimates from the national health interview survey: U.S. 1986. *Vital and Health Statistics*, Series 10, #164, 1987.

National Center for Health Statistics, Current estimates from the National Health Interview Survey: U.S. 1989. *Vital and Health Statistics*, Series 10, 176, 1990.

National Pacific/Asian Resource Center on Aging. On Lok senior health services. *Update*, 1986, *7*, 1–3.

Nelson, M. E., Fiatarone, M. A., Morganti, C. M., Trice, I., Greenberg, R. A., and Evans, W. J. Effects of high intensity strength training on multiple risk factors for osteoporotic fractures. *Journal of the American Medical Association*, 1994, *272*, 1909–1914.

Notelovitz, M., Martin, D., and Tesar, R. Estrogen therapy and variable resistance weight training increase bone mineral in surgically menopausal women. *Journal of Bone Mineral Research*, 1991, *6*, 583–590.

O'Brien, S. J., and Vertinsky, P. A. Unfit survivors: Exercise as a recourse for aging women. *Gerontologist*, 1991, *31*, 347–357.

Ouslander, J. G. Urinary incontinence in the elderly. *The Western Journal of Medicine*, 1981, *135*, 482–483.

Ouslander, J. G. Urinary incontinence: Out of the closet. *Journal of the American Medical Association*, 1989, *261*, 2695–2696.

Ouslander, J. G., and Abelson, S. Perceptions of urinary incontinence among elderly outpatients. *The Gerontologist*, 1990, *30*, 369–372.

OWL (Older Women's League). *A status report on osteoporosis: The challenge to midlife and older women.* Washington D. C., 1994.

Paffenberger, R., Hyde, R., Wing, A., and Hsied, C. Physical activity, all-cause mortality and longevity of college alumni. *The New England Journal of Medicine*, 1986, *314*, 605–613.

Palmore, E. Health practices and illness among the aged. *The Gerontologist*, Winter, 1970, Part I, 313–316.

Pearlman, R. A., and Uhlmann, R. F. Quality of life in chronic disease: Perceptions of elderly patients. *Journals of Gerontology*, 1988, *43*, M25–M30.

Peck, W. A., Barrett-Conner, E., Buckevalten, J. A., Gambrell, R. D., Jr., et al. Consensus conference: Osteoporosis. *Journal of the American Medical Association*, 1984, *252*, 799.

Peterman, T. A., Stoneburner, R. L., Allen J. R., Jaffe, H. W., and Curran, J. W. Risk of human immunodeficiency virus transmission from heterosexual adults with transfusion-associated infections. *Journal of the American Medical Association*, 1988, *259*, 55–58.

Pfeiffer, S. The evolution of human longevity: Distinctive mechanisms? 1990, *9*, 95–103.

Prince, R. L., Smith, M., Dick, I. M., Price, R. I., Webb, P. G., Henderson, K., and Harris, M. P. Prevention of postmenopausal osteoporosis. *New England Journal of Medicine*, 1991, *325*, 1189–1195.

Rakowski, W. The definition and measurement of prevention, preventative health care, and health promotion. *Generations*, 1994, *18*, 18–23.

Rice, D., and LaPlante, M. Chronic illness, disability and increased longevity. In S. Sullivan and M. Ein Lewin (Eds.). *The economics and ethics of long term care and disability.* Washington, D.C.: American Enterprise Institute for Public Policy, 1988, 9–55.

Riggs, B. L., and Melton, L. J. Involutional osteoporosis. *New England Journal of Medicine*, 1986, *314*, 1676–1684.

Rimer, B. Health promotion and aging. Smoking among older adults: The problems, consequences and possible solutions. In *Surgeon General's Workshop, Health Promotion and Aging,* March 1988.

Roos, N. P., and Shapiro, E. The Manitoba longitudinal study on aging: Preliminary findings on health care utilization by the elderly. *Medical Care,* 1981, *19*, 644–657.

Roos, N. P., Shapiro, E., and Roos, L. L. Aging and the demand for health services: Which aged and whose demand? *The Gerontologist*, 1984, *24*, 31–36.

Rosenstock, J. M. Why people use health services. *Milbank Memorial Fund Quarterly,* 1966, *44*, 94–127.

Rosenstock, J. M. The health belief model and preventive health behavior. *Health Education Monographs*, 1974, *2*, 354–386.

Rothman, K. J. Alcohol. In J. Fraumeni (Ed.), *Persons at high risk of cancer: An approach to cancer etiology and control.* New York: Academic Press, 1975.

Rowe, J. W. Health care of the elderly. *New England Journal of Medicine*, 1985, *312*, 827–835.

Schick, F. L. *Statistical handbook on aging Americans.* New York: Oryx Press, 1986.

Shanas, E. *The health of older people: A social survey.* Cambridge, Mass.: Harvard University Press, 1982.

Shanas, E., and Maddox, G. Health, health resources and the utilization of care. In E. Shanas and R. Binstock (Eds.), *Handbook of aging and the social sciences* (2d ed.) New York: Van Nostrand, 1985.

Shanas, E., Townsend, P., Wedderburn, D., Friis, H., Milhoj, P., and Stehouwen, J. *Old people in three industrial societies.* New York: Atherton, 1968.

Shapiro, E., and Roos, L. Using health care: Rural/urban differences among the Manitoba elderly. *The Gerontologist,* 1984, *24,* 270–274.

Shapiro, E., and Roos, N. P. Elderly nonusers of health care services. *Medical Care,* 1985, *23,* 247–257.

Sharpe, W. D. Age changes in human bone: An overview. *Bulletin of the New York Academy of Medicine,* 1979, *55,* 757–773.

Ship, J. A., Wolff, A., and Selik, R. M. Epidemiology of acquired immune deficiency syndrome in persons aged 50 and older. *Journal of Acquired Immune Deficiency Syndromes,* 1991, *4,* 84–88.

Stampfer, M. J., and Colditz, G. A. Estrogen replacement therapy and coronary heart disease: A quantitative assessment of the epidemiologic evidence. *Preventive Medicine,* 1991, *20,* 47–63.

Stampfer, M. J., Colditz, G. A., Willett, W. C., Manson, J. E., Rosner, B., Speizer, F. E., and Heinnekens, C. H. Postmenopausal estrogen therapy and cardiovascular disease: Ten-year follow-up from the Nurses' Health Study. *New England Journal of Medicine,* 1991, *325,* 756–762.

*Statistical Abstracts of the United States,* 1990, (110th ed.), 81.

Stewart, A. L., Greenfield, S., Hays, R. D., Wells, K., Rogers, W. H., Berry, S. D., McGlynn, E. A., and Ware, J. E. Functional status and well-being of patients with chronic conditions. *Journal of the American Medical Association,* 1989, *262,* 907–913.

Stewart, A., King, A., and Haskell, W. Endurance exercise and health-related quality of life in 50–65 year-old adults. *The Gerontologist,* 1993, 782–789.

Stones, M. J., and Komza, A. Age, exercise and coding performance. *Psychology and Aging,* 1989, *4,* 190–194.

Stump, T. E., Johnson, R. J., and Wolinsky, F. D. Changes in physician utilization over time among older adults. *Journals of Gerontology,* 1995, *50B,* S45–S58.

Surgeon General's Workshop: *Health Promotion and Aging: Proceedings.* Washington, D.C.: U.S. Government Printing Office, 1988.

Swallow, J. N. A survey of edentulous individuals in a district in Amsterdam. *Community Dentistry and Oral Epidemiology,* 1978, *6,* 210–216.

Teague, M. L. *Health promotion: Achieving high level wellness in the later years.* Indianapolis, Ind.: Benchmark Press, 1987.

Teasdale, T., Taffet, G., Luchi, R., and Adam, E. Urinary incontinence in a community-residing elderly population. *Journal of the American Geriatrics Society,* 1988, *36,* 606–606.

Thornsberry, O., Wilson, R., and Golden, P. Health promotion and disease prevention: Professional data from the National Health Interview Survey, United States, January–June 1985. *NCHS Advance Data,* 119(5/14), 1986.

Tideiksaar, R. Environmental adaptions to preserve balance and prevent falls. *Topics in Geriatric Rehabilitation,* 1990, *5,* 78–84.

Tinetti, M. E. Instability and falling in elderly patients. *Seminars in Neurology,* 1989, *9,* 39–45.

Tucker, R. M. Is hypertension different in the elderly? *Geriatrics,* 1980, *35* (5), 28–32.

U.S. Department of Health and Human Services, *Healthy People 2000: National Health Promotion and Disease Prevention Activities.* Washington, D. C.: DHHS Publication No. (PHS)91–50213, 1991.

U.S. Public Health Service, National Center for Health Statistics. *Edentulous persons, United States,* 1971. Washington, D.C.: Department of Health, Education, and Welfare, 1974.

U.S. Public Health Service. *Promoting health/preventing disease: Year 2000 objectives for the nation.* Washington, D.C.: U.S. Department of Health and Human Services, 1989.

U. S. Preventive Task Force. *Guide to Clinical Preventive Services.* Baltimore, Md.: Williams and Wilkins, 1989.

U.S. Senate. *Dietary goals for the U.S.* (2d ed.). Washington, D.C.: U.S. Government Printing Office, 1977.

U.S. Senate Special Committee on Aging. *America in transition: An aging society,* 1984–85 edition. Washington, D.C.: U.S. Government Printing Office, 1985.

U.S. Senate Special Committee on Aging. *Developments in Aging: 1989.* Washington, D.C.: U.S. Government Printing Office, 1990.

U. S. Surgeon General. *The Health Benefits of Smoking Cessation: A Report of the Surgeon General.* Washington D.C.: U. S. Department of Health and Human Services, 1990.

Vaccaro, P., Ostrove, S. M., Vandervelder, L., Goldfarb, A. H., and Clarke, D. H. Body composition and physiological responses of masters female swimmers 20 to 70 years of age. *Research Quarterly for Exercise & Sport,* 1984, *55,* 278–284.

Van Steenberg, C., Ansak, M., Chin-Hansen, J. On Lok's model L Managed long-term care. In Barresi, C., and Stull, D., (eds.), *Ethnic elderly and long-term care.* N.T.: Springer, 1993, 178–190.

Verbrugge, L. From sneezes to adieux: Stages of health for American men and women. In R. Ward and S. Tobin (Eds.), *Health in Aging: Sociological issues and policy directions.* New York: Springer, 1987.

Verbrugge, L. The twain meet: Empirical explanations of sex differences in health and mortality. *Journal of Health and Social Behavior,* 1989, *30,* 282–304.

Vogt, T. Aging, stress and illness: Psychobiological linkage. In M. Ory, R. Abales, & P. Lysman, *Aging, Health and Behavior.* Newbury Park, CA: Sage, 1992.

Vogt, T. Cost-effectiveness of prevention programs for older people. *Generations,* 1994, *18,* 63–68.

Wagner, E. H., Grothaus, L. C., Hecht, J. A., and LaCroix, A. Z. Factors associated with participation in a senior health promotion program. *The Gerontologist,* 1991, *31,* 598–602.

Wagner, E. H., LaCroix, A. Z., Grothaus, L., Leveille, S. G., Hecht, J. A., et al. Preventing disability and falls in older adults: A population-based randomized trial. *American Journal of Public Health,* 1994, *84,* 1800–1806.

Waldron, I. Why do women live longer than men? Parts I and II. *Social Science and Medicine,* 1976, *10,* 340–362.

Walker, S. Health promotion and prevention of disease and disability. *Generations,* 1994, *18,* 45–49.

Waller, J. B. Challenges to the provision of health care to minority aged. *First Annual Summer Symposium—Geriatric Education Center of Michigan,* 1989.

Warshaw, G. Health promotion and aging "Preventive Health Services," *Surgeon General's Workshop: Health promotion and aging.* Washington, D.C.: U.S. Government Printing Office, 1988.

Weg, R. Changing physiology of aging: Normal and pathological. In D. S. Woodruff and J. E. Birren (Eds.), *Aging: Scientific perspectives and social issues.* New York: Van Nostrand, 1983.

Weiss, B. D. Unstable bladder in elderly patients. *American Family Physician,* 1983, *4,* 243–247.

Weiss, N. S. Decreased risk of fractures of the hip and lower forearm with postmenopausal use of estrogen. *New England Journal of Medicine,* 1980, *303,* 1195–1198.

Wheeler, M. Osteoporosis. *Medical Clinics of North America,* 1976, *60* (6), 1213–1223.

Wiley, J., and Camacho, T. Life-style and future health: Evidence from the Alameda county study. *Preventive Medicine,* 1980, *9,* 1–21.

Williams, E. Health promotion and aging: Alcohol. In Surgeon General's Workshop, *Health Promotion and Aging.* Washington, D.C.: U.S. Government Printing Office, 1988.

Williams, T. F. Diabetes mellitus in older people. In W. Reichel (Ed.), *Clinical aspects of aging.* Baltimore, Md.: Williams and Witkin, 1978.

Wolfe, S. *Worst pills, best pills.* New York: Random House, 1988.

Wolinsky, F. D. Assessing the effects of predisposing, enabling, and illness-morbidity characteristics on health services utilization. *Journal of Health and Social Behavior,* 1978, *19,* 384–396.

Wolinsky, F. D., Coe, R., and Mosely, R. The use of health services by elderly Americans: Implications from a regression-based cohort analysis. In R. Ward and S. Tobin (Eds.), *Health in aging: Sociological issues and policy directions.* New York: Springer, 1987.

Women's Health. Report of the Public Health Service Task Force on Women's Health Issues. *Public Health Reports,* 1985, *100,* 73–92.

World Health Organization. *Planning and organization of geriatric services.* Technical Report, Series 548. Geneva, 1974.

Yee, B., and Weaver, G. Ethnic minorities and health promotion: Developing a culturally competent agenda. *Generations,* 194, *18,* 39–44.

# PART Three

# Three

# THE PSYCHOLOGICAL CONTEXT OF SOCIAL AGING

T he dynamic interactions between people and their environments as they age, the population trends that have made gerontology such an important concern in the late twentieth century, and the historical background of social gerontology were discussed in Part I. Part II focused on the normal and the pathological, physiological, and sensory changes that take place with aging. The types of chronic and acute health problems that afflict older people and influence their social functioning were presented. The older population's demands on the health care system and their reasons for using or not using health services were reviewed. Part II concluded with a discussion of the growing field of health promotion, and how improved health behaviors can affect older people's social interactions.

In this section, the focus is on psychological changes with aging—both normal and abnormal—that influence older people's social behavior and dynamic relationships with their physical and social environments. As we have already seen, many changes take place in the aging organism that make it more difficult to perform

activities of daily living and to respond as quickly and easily to external demands as in youth. Many older people have chronic health problems, such as arthritis, diabetes, or heart disease, that compound the normal changes that cause people to slow down. In a similar manner, some changes in cognitive functioning, personality, and sexuality are a function of normal aging. Other psychological changes may be due to the secondary effects of diseases.

Many researchers have examined changes in intelligence, learning, and memory with aging. The literature in this area, reviewed in Chapter 8, suggests that normal aging does not result in significant declines. Although older subjects in the studies described do not perform as well as younger subjects, their scores are not so poor as to indicate significant impairments in social functioning. Laboratory tests also may be less than ideal as indicators of cognitive function in older people. Suggestions for improving memory in the later years are discussed in Chapter 8.

Chapter 9 describes personality in old age, psychological models of personality development, the importance of maintaining self-esteem in the later years, and threats to self-esteem that result from changes in social roles. This chapter also focuses on coping and successful adaptation to the changes associated with aging. Given the normal age-related changes in physiological, sensory, and cognitive functions, in personality styles, and in older individuals' social networks, some gerontologists have argued that older people experience more stress in a given time period than the young. Furthermore, there has been considerable debate about whether aging results in the use of different types of coping strategies. Older people appear to perceive life events differently from the young, and to attribute less stress to events that they have already experienced. However, there is insufficient longitudinal research in this area to conclude with any certainty that aging is associated with more stressful life events than youth. Coping strategies also appear to remain consistent throughout adulthood and old age. Chapter 9 concludes with a discussion of qualities that define "successful aging."

An important aspect of personality is sexuality, the individual's ability to express intimate feelings through a wide range of love and pleasurable experiences. Chapter 10 addresses the influence of social attitudes and beliefs, normal physiological changes, and diseases on older people's sexuality. Contrary to popular belief, aging need not reduce sexual pleasure and capacity. More often, older people withdraw from sexual activity because of societal expectations and stereotypes. As societal attitudes become more enlightened and sexual taboos are reduced, older people will express their sexuality more easily.

Some forms of psychopathology, such as manic antisocial behavior, are more common in youth than in old age. However, as described in Chapter 11, some older people are at high risk for major depressive episodes, paranoia, and some forms of dementia. In the case of dementia, such as Alzheimer's disease, memory and problem-solving abilities decline quite dramatically,

sometimes within a few years, other times over many years. Older individuals with a diagnosis of dementia experience significant impairments in their ability to interact with other people, and to control their physical and social environments. To the extent that such people do not seek mental health services for treatable disorders such as depression or paranoia, their social interactions will deteriorate. Some may become reclusive and, in the case of severely depressed older persons, at greater risk of suicide. Despite the growing number of studies that support the benefits of therapeutic interventions for older people, the older population (especially ethnic minorities) underutilizes mental health services. Most of the mental health care provided to older people takes place in hospitals, not in community mental health centers or in private practice. And most therapy is provided by family doctors who often are not specialists in geriatrics.

Perhaps the most important knowledge to be gained in Part III is that aging does not affect all people's psychological functions in the same way. Normal cognitive changes generally are not so dramatic as to impair older people's social functions. However, some people report mild forgetfulness, a condition known as "benign senescent forgetfulness." A relatively small segment of the older population experiences Alzheimer's disease or other types of dementia. Personality and patterns of coping also do not change so dramatically as to impair social functioning, although some sex-typed behaviors become less pronounced with age. Coping and adaptation skills do not become impaired with normal aging; styles of coping vary widely among older people. Indeed, aging results in increasing differences in psychological functioning among people, not greater similarity. Some older people age successfully despite chronic diseases and deterioration in cognitive function, while others experience poor adaptation to these normal and secondary changes of aging. The following vignettes illustrate the contrasts in psychological aging:

## An Older Person with Intact Cognitive Abilities

Mr. Wallace, age 75, is a retired professor in a midwestern community. He retired 10 years ago, after teaching history in a large state university for 40 years. He remains active by doing volunteer work in the local historical society, teaching part-time at the university, and traveling to Europe with his wife for three months every summer, occasionally leading groups of other retirees in tours of medieval European towns. Mr. Wallace's major project that he wishes to complete before he dies is an historical novel about Charlemagne. This is a topic about which he has lectured and read extensively, and one he enjoys investigating in detail during his trips to Europe. Mrs. Wallace often remarks that he is busier these days than he was before his retirement. During the first few months after retirement, Professor Wallace experienced a mild bout of depression; it was relieved as he became involved in group therapy with other retirees. Mr. Wallace enjoys intellectual challenges today as much as he did when he was employed, in fact, more so, because he is pursuing these activities without the pressures of a day-to-day job. He vows to keep up his level of activity until he "runs out of energy."

## An Older Person with Good Coping Skills

Mrs. Johnson, age 83, has suffered numerous tragedies throughout her life. Born to a poor farming family in Mississippi, she moved North with her mother and eight older sisters and brothers as a child, after her father died and the family farm was lost. The family supported itself through hard work in the factories. Mrs. Johnson married young; she and her husband struggled through the years to own their home and raise their three children. Her husband died 20 years ago, leaving her with a small pension. She worked at a manual labor job until she was 70 years old, when her arthritis made it painful for her to do the heavy work needed on the job. During the past three years, Mrs. Johnson has experienced a series of losses: her son and daughter-in-law died in an auto accident; her last surviving sister died; and her oldest granddaughter, the one on whom she could most depend, moved West to attend medical school. Mrs. Johnson admits these losses are painful, but that it is "God's will" that she experience them. Her strong faith in God helps her accept these changes in her life and her deteriorating health as part of a "Master Plan." When she becomes too distraught, she turns to the Bible, and looks forward to visits from her grandchildren and great-grandchildren to keep her busy.

## An Older Person with Severe Cognitive Impairment

Mr. Adams is age 68. Several years ago he started showing signs of confusion and disorientation. He was diagnosed as having Alzheimer's disease at age 64, one year before his retirement. He and his wife had purchased a large motor home in anticipation of traveling during retirement; now all their plans have completely changed. While there have been some brief periods during the past four years where he has seemed to be better, Mr. Adams now is extremely agitated and disoriented, wanders during the night, and is occasionally abusive to people near him. He often does not know who his wife and children are. The slightest change in routine will upset him. In his lucid moments, Mr. Adams cries and wonders what has happened to his life; at some points, he can also carry on short conversations. His wife is determined to keep him at home, even though he often verbally abuses her and does not recognize or appreciate all that she does for him. She is able to take him to an adult day-care center during the day, where the staff try to keep him active and stimulated. He and his wife also attend meetings of a support group for Alzheimer's patients and their families. The group has been especially helpful to his wife, where she can often ventilate about how hard things are and then be supported for her efforts. Mr. Adams expresses great fear at the thought of a nursing home, but his wife worries about how long she can manage him at home.

The next four chapters describe how the aging process influences cognitive abilities, personality styles, and intimacy and sexuality, as well as responses to major life events. They emphasize the wide variations in these processes with aging. Mental health and illness also occur in older people, but sometimes take on different features than in youth. The vastly different psychological states of Mr. Wallace, Mrs. Johnson, and Mr. Adams result in significant variations in the social aspects of their lives.

# CHAPTER 8

## COGNITIVE CHANGES WITH AGING

One of the most important and most studied aspects of aging is cognitive functioning; that is, intelligence, learning, and memory. These are critical to an individual's performance in every aspect of life, including work and leisure activities, relationships with family and friends, and roles in the community. Older people who have problems in cognitive functioning will eventually experience stress in these other areas as well, along with an increasing incongruence between their competence levels and the demands of their environments. Researchers have attempted to determine whether normal aging is associated with a decline in the three areas of cognitive functioning and, if so, to what extent such a decline is due to age-related physiological changes. Much of the research on these issues has evolved from studies of cognitive development across the life span. Other studies have been undertaken in response to concerns expressed by many older persons or their families that they cannot learn as easily as they used to, or that they have more trouble remembering names, dates, and places than previously.

This chapter reviews the research on cognition and normal aging, the problems of determining why observed changes occur, some of the social consequences of age-related cognitive changes, and some techniques that older persons can use to improve their learning and memory. We examine the three key elements of intellectual processes: intelligence, learning, and memory, and briefly discuss the issue of creativity.

### INTELLIGENCE AND AGING

The first of the three components of cognition, intelligence, is difficult both to define and to measure. Of all of the elements of cognition, it is the least verifiable. We can only infer its existence and can only indirectly measure individual levels. Intelligence has been defined as the "theoretical limit of an individual's performance" (Jones, 1959, p. 700). The limit is determined by biological and genetic factors; however, the ability to achieve the limit is influenced by environmental opportunities, such as a challenging educational experience, as well as by environmental constraints, such as the absence of books or other intellectual stimulation. Intelligence has been defined as a range of abilities, including the ability to deal with symbols and abstractions, to acquire and comprehend new information, to adapt to new situations, and to appreciate and/or create new ideas (Huyck and Hoyer, 1982). Intelligence quotient (or IQ) refers to an individual's relative abilities in some of these areas compared to others of the same chronological age. Unfortunately, most tests of intelligence (IQ tests) do not measure all the components of intelligence. For example, how can a person's creativity be determined and evaluated with sufficient validity? How can criteria of successful adaptation be established that can be measured in paper and pencil form?

Most theorists agree that intelligence is composed of many different components. Perhaps the most complex model is Guilford's (1966, 1967) three-dimensional structure of intellect (see Figure 8–1). The three dimensions represent the content of knowledge (e.g., figures, symbols, and words), the operations that an individual must perform with this knowledge (e.g., memorize, evaluate, and come up with single or multiple solutions), and the products that are derived from these operations (e.g., relations, systems, and implications). This is probably the most complete model, yielding 120 separate components. Such a model is difficult to test. Nevertheless, a multidimensional structure of intelligence, although not identical to Guilford's model, is assumed by most contemporary measures of intelligence.

In contrast, the general factor theory (or "General Capacity") of intelligence, which was first proposed by Spearman in 1927, suggests that there is a general ability that is required for all intellectual tasks, as well as a set of specific

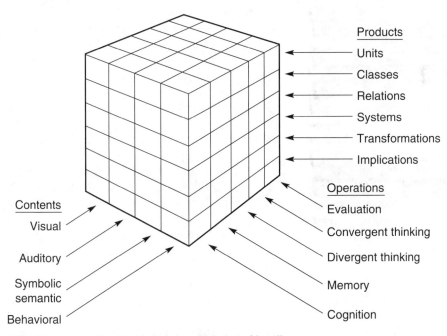

**FIGURE 8–1  A Three-Dimensional Model of Intellect**

SOURCE: J. P. Guilford, *The nature of human intelligence* (New York: McGraw-Hill, 1967) and J. P. Guilford, *Way beyond the IQ* (Buffalo, N. Y.: Creative Education Foundation, 1977). Reprinted by permission of the author, McGraw-Hill, and the Creative Education Foundation.

abilities that are necessary for some tasks, but not for others. This concept of a general ability that determines an individual's performance on *all* tasks was reflected in early tests of intelligence, for example, the one developed by Binet in 1906. Such a general aspect of intelligence may exist, but it is difficult to measure it independently of the specific abilities that are associated with it.

The work of Thurstone and Thurstone (1941, 1958) gives credence to both positions. They proposed a *primary mental abilities* model that includes a general intelligence factor and is composed of five primary and independent abilities: number, word fluency, verbal meaning, reasoning, and space. Although this model was initially developed with young adults, subsequent work by Schaie and colleagues provided support for this multi-ability model in older adults (Schaie, 1979, 1983). A useful distinction has been made between *fluid intelligence* and *crystallized intelligence* (Cattell, 1963; Horn, 1970, 1982; Horn and Donaldson, 1980). Fluid intelligence consists of skills that are biologically determined, independent of experience or learning, and may be similar to what is popularly called "native intelligence." It involves processing information that is not embedded in a context of existing information for the individual. These skills may be measured by tests of spatial orientation, abstract reasoning, and perceptual speed. Crystallized intelligence refers to the knowledge and abilities that the individual acquires through education and lifelong experiences. Some indicators are verbal comprehension, word association, and social judgment. These two types of intelligence have been found to show different patterns with aging, as we will see in the next section.

There has been considerable controversy regarding intelligence in the later years (Botwinick, 1984). Many researchers have found significant differences between young and old persons on intelligence tests, with older persons performing at a much lower level. Even when the same cohort is followed longitudinally, there is a decline in some intelligence tests that is independent of generational differences (Schaie and Hertzog, 1988). Others have concluded that aging is not really associated with a decline in intelligence, but that the particular IQ tests and the time pressures on test-takers are more detrimental to older persons than to the young. Still others have pointed to methodological problems in conducting research in this area. Unfortunately, these mixed research findings have served to perpetuate the stereotype that older people are less intelligent than the young.

Many older persons are concerned that their intelligence has declined from when they were young. This concern may loom so large for them that merely taking part in a study intended to "test their intelligence" may provoke sufficient anxiety to affect their performance on the test. Such anxieties may also influence the older person's daily functioning. Research with children has shown that false information given to them about their IQ scores or test performance, whether the information shows that they scored very well or very poorly, leads to future behavior that is consistent with the false test scores. This situation represents a confirmation of expectations or a "self-fulfilling prophecy." In the same way, people who are told by friends, family, test-givers or society in general that they should not expect to perform as well on intellectual tasks because aging causes a decline in intelligence may, in fact, come to perform more poorly.

The most widely used measure of adult intelligence is the Wechsler Adult Intelligence Scale (WAIS). It consists of 11 subtests, 6 of which are described as Verbal Scales (which measure, to some extent, crystallized intelligence), and 5 as Performance Scales (providing some measure of fluid intelligence). Verbal scores are obtained by measuring an individual's ability to define the meaning of words, to explain why such things as social and legal laws are established, to interpret proverbs, and to explain similarities between words and concepts. In this way, accumulated knowledge and abstract reasoning can be tested. Performance tests focus on an individual's ability to manipulate unfamiliar objects and words, often in unusual ways. These include tests of spatial relations and abstract reasoning, and may require an individual to put puzzles together to match a picture, match pictures with symbols or numbers, or arrange pictures in a particular pattern. Both psychomotor and perceptual skills are needed in performing these tasks. In addition, the performance tests on the WAIS are generally timed; the verbal tests are not.

A consistent pattern of scores on these two components of the WAIS has emerged in numerous studies; it has been labeled the *Classic Aging Pattern*. People beyond the age of 65 in some studies, and even earlier in other studies, perform significantly worse on Performance Scales (i.e., fluid intelligence), but their scores on Verbal Scales (i.e., crystallized intelligence) remain stable. The tendency to do worse on the performance tasks with aging may reflect age-related changes in noncognitive functions, such as sensory and perceptual abilities, and in psychomotor skills. As we have seen in Chapters 4 and 6, aging results in a slowing down of the neural pathways and of the visual and auditory functions. This slower reaction time, and the delay in receiving and transmitting messages through the sense organs, explain poorer performance on subtests requiring such capabilities. Some researchers have therefore argued for the elimination of time constraints in performance tasks. Studies that have not measured speed of performance have still found significant age differences in these subtests (Botwinick, 1984). Furthermore, when motor speed (i.e., the time to physically perform a task) was measured separately from cognitive components of the task (e.g., visual search, memory, and coding), older persons did worse than young test-takers in both components (Storandt, 1976). These results suggest that there is a decline in performance-related aspects of intellectual function, independent of psychomotor or sensory factors. Speed of cognitive processing may also decline with age and, in turn, slow an individual's responses on tests of performance.

Turning to verbal skills, the Classic Aging Pattern suggests that the ability to recall stored verbal information and to use abstract reasoning tends to remain constant throughout life. Declines, where they exist, tend not to show up until advanced old age, or, in the case of cognitive impairment such as the dementias, to begin early in the course of the disease.

Some researchers have argued that this age-related decline in tests of intelligence may reflect a deterioration in complex, formal-logical, and integrative thinking (Denney, 1981, Craik, 1977). That is, older people may be using more concrete, less abstract thought processes than in youth. In contrast, there is some evidence that, when given logically inconsistent statements, older subjects have been found to analyze these inconsistencies on the basis of their own knowledge, whereas younger adults tend to ignore the logic and attempt to reach conclusions (Labouvie-Vief and Blanchard-Fields, 1982). Older subjects have also been found to reject simplified solutions and to prefer a complex analysis of the problem. This finding from laboratory-based research is supported by surveys of attitudes and beliefs among respondents of varying ages. Younger respondents are more willing to provide a direct response, whereas many older persons attempt to analyze the questions and give more contingency responses; that is, analyzing the question and stating that the answer could be $x$ in one situation and $y$ in another, rather than an all-encompassing response. For example, on a measure of environmental preference, the respondent may be asked, "How much privacy do you generally prefer?" A younger respondent is more likely to focus on the "general" situation, whereas the older respondent will be more likely to consider both situations in which privacy is preferred and where it is not. It thus appears important to review older persons' responses to tests of problem solving and abstract reasoning from other perspectives beyond the traditional approaches that are grounded in cognitive theories developed with younger populations.

## Problems in Measurement of Cognitive Function

A major shortcoming of many studies of intelligence in aging is their use of cross-sectional research designs rather than longitudinal approaches. As we saw in Chapter 2, the former method is used to compare at a single point in time, two or more groups defined by age or other characteristics. The latter approach is used to examine the same group (or groups) several times over a period of weeks, months, or years. Age differences that are obtained in cross-sectional studies may be a reflection of cohort or generational differences rather than actual age changes. In particular, changes in educational systems and the development of television, computers, and high-speed travel have had a profound impact on the experiences of today's youth when compared with those of people who grew up in the early twentieth century. These historical factors may then have a greater effect on intelligence scores than age per se.

Critics of cross-sectional methods have pointed to the advantages of following the same individual in longitudinal studies. However, the length of time and cost to complete longitudinal studies may make them impossible in many situations. Another problem is subject attrition, or dropout from such studies. Researchers who have conducted longitudinal research on intelligence have found a pattern of selective attrition, whereby the people who drop out tend to be those who have performed less well, who perceive their performance to be poor, or whose health status and ambulatory abilities are worse than average (Riegel and Riegel, 1972; Siegler, 1975; Botwinick, 1977). The people who stay in the study (i.e., "the survivors") performed better in the initial tests than did dropouts. This is consistent with our earlier observation that older persons often become unduly anxious about poor performance on tests of intellectual function. Hence, the results become biased in favor of the superior performers, indicating stability or improvement over time, and do not represent the wider population of older adults, whose performance might have shown a decline in intelligence.

## Longitudinal Studies of Intelligence

Several major longitudinal studies have examined changes in intellectual function from youth to old age (Schaie, 1983). The Iowa State Study of intellectual development began as a cross-sectional assessment of 363 male college freshmen in 1919. The first longitudinal follow-up took place in 1950 with 127 of the men who could be located. In 1961, 96 men were retested (Owens, 1953, 1966; Cunningham and Owens, 1983). Using the Army Alpha Test of intelligence, the researchers found general stability in intellectual functioning through middle age, with a peak in the ages of late forties and fifties. Declines were observed after age 60 in many men, but the degree of change varied widely among the men and across variables. The Iowa State Study is significant as the first major longitudinal assessment of adult intelligence. However, the loss of 75 percent of the original sample by the third follow-up and the selection of college-educated men limit the generalizability of these findings.

The New York State Study of Aging Twins began in 1946 with the goal of examining heredity and aging. Of the original sample of 268 twins (or 134 pairs) over age 60 initially tested between 1947 and 1949 (Kallmann and Sander, 1949), 61 were available for the final follow-up in 1973. This study tested twins five times over this 26-year period on two measures of intelli-

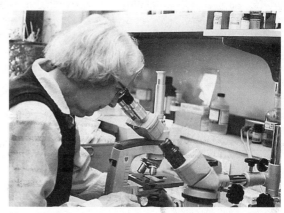

Many people practice higher-level cognitive skills throughout their lives.

gence and a test of hand-eye coordination. Average performance declined significantly on timed tests, but, as with the Iowa State Study, individual differences were pronounced. Among the individuals who were healthy enough to complete the final follow-up, performance on nonspeeded intelligence tests remained stable until they reached their ninth decade. The greatest declines were observed in the test of hand-eye coordination and in a measure of fluid intelligence. The Aging Twins Study provides valuable information about intellectual function from age 60 to 90. It offers unique insights into the differential effects of heredity and environment on the intellectual function of identical and fraternal twins, and about the intellectual strength of the old-old (Jarvik and Bank, 1983).

The Seattle Longitudinal Study began in 1956, and collected data on Thurstone's primary mental abilities every 7 years over 28 years (Schaie, 1983; Schaie and Hertzog, 1986; Hertzog and Schaie, 1988). At each follow-up assessment, individuals who were still available from the original sample were retested, along with a new, randomly selected sample from the same population. The 1984 cycle included a test of some older people who had previously participated in a cognitive retraining program (Willis and Schaie, 1986). This study has provided the basis for the development of sequential research models, described in Chapter 2. Peak performance varied across tests and between men and women, ranging from age 32 on the test of Numbers for men and age 39 on the test of Reasoning for women, to age 53 for Educational Aptitude. A review of age changes for the 128 people who were observed over the entire course of this study reveals age decrements after age 60 on tests of word-fluency, space, and numbers that became progressively worse in later years. Tests of spatial abilities and inductive reasoning, both indicators of fluid intelligence, showed greater decline with age. However, other primary mental abilities, such as verbal meaning and reasoning, showed no declines until the mid-seventies. These results are consistent with cross-sectional results using the WAIS, as we have seen earlier. They suggest

that the Classic Aging Pattern holds up in both cross-sectional and longitudinal studies, and that some performance aspects of intelligence may begin to deteriorate after age 60, although major changes are generally rare until the mid-seventies.

In their analysis of changes for each cohort over the 21-year life of this study, Hertzog and Schaie (1988) concluded that the changes observed were indicative of a normative developmental transition from stability in general intelligence in the middle years, to a gradual decline that begins around age 60. It is noteworthy, however, that less than half the participants experienced significant declines by age 81, and even fewer showed decline in all areas. Most people maintained their abilities in one or more areas well into their advanced years, as shown in Figure 8–2. However, Schaie and colleagues found no linear decline in all five primary mental abilities for any participants over the course of 28 years, which suggests that changes in intelligence are gradual and demonstrate long plateaus and periods of decline (Schaie, 1989; Willis and Schaie, 1986).

The cognitive retraining component of this longitudinal study was based on the premise of maximizing one's remaining potential, a widely accepted concept in physical aging but only recently applied to cognitive aging. Intellectual activities that involve problem solving and creativity, such as Scrabble, are described by these researchers as effective ways for older people to maximize their intellectual abilities. Cognitive performance improved in about 65 percent of participants, and 40 percent who had declined in the preceding 14 years showed a return to their predecline levels (Schaie and Hertzog, 1986; Willis and Schaie, 1986, 1988).

The Duke Longitudinal Studies, described in Chapters 2 and 5, assessed intelligence and memory, in addition to many health variables. This series of three longitudinal samples, each measured several times, provides useful information about the relationship between intellectual function and health status, especially cardiovascular disease (Palmore, 1974, 1985; Siegler,

1983). The findings regarding age changes generally are consistent with the other longitudinal studies described in this section; declines in cognitive function were not observed until individuals reached their seventies. Scores on performance tests were found to decline earlier than scores on verbal measures. Another longitudinal study in Sweden has examined cognitive functioning among the oldest old (ages 84–90 in this study). A two-year follow-up revealed that participants who had scored high on tests of memory, attention, orientation, and ability to follow instructions continued to perform well at follow-up. However, average performance declined slightly on all these tests. Another 10 percent met the criteria for significant cognitive decline at the second assessment (Johansson, Zarit, and Berg, 1992).

## Factors that May Influence Intelligence in Adulthood

Researchers who have compared intelligence test scores of older and younger persons have found wide variations in scores of both groups. As described earlier, older test-takers generally have obtained poorer scores, but age per se is only one factor in explaining intellectual functioning.

As mentioned, there is also a biological factor in intelligence, such that some people are innately more intelligent than others. However, it is difficult to determine the relative influence of biological factors, because it is impossible to measure the specific mechanisms of the brain that account for intelligence. There are structural changes in the brain and in neural pathways with aging, as we have seen in Chapter 5; however, these changes are generally diffuse and not focused in a particular region of the brain. It is therefore impossible to determine what specific changes in the brain and its pathways may account for the age-related deterioration that is observed.

Several other factors may be measured that appear to explain some of the observed differences in intelligence tests between older and younger persons. These include initial level of intelligence, education, occupation, chronic dis-

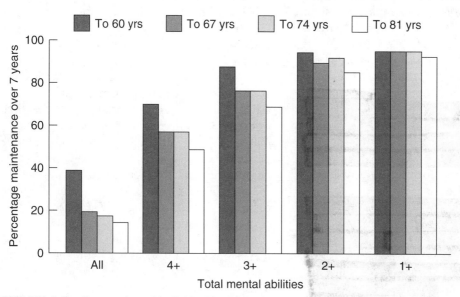

**FIGURE 8–2   Proportion of individuals who maintain scores on multiple abilities**
SOURCE: Schaie, K. W. The hazards of cognitive aging. *The Gerontologist,* 1989, *29,* 484–493. Reprinted with permission.

eases (especially cardiovascular conditions), involvement in intellectually stimulating activities, sensory functions, and test anxiety. It is important to control statistically for educational differences when analyzing the relationship between age and intelligence. A recent study of healthy, cognitively intact adults aged 70–79 found significant effects of education on all tests of cognitive function. In particular, participants with the highest level of education (12+ years) did three times better on a test of abstract thinking than did people with seven or fewer years of education (Inouye et al., 1993).

In an earlier study, WAIS results of four age groups—25–29, 35–39, 45–49, and 55–64—were compared. Consistent with other studies, the Classic Aging Pattern emerged (i.e., verbal scores did not differ across age groups, whereas performance scores consistently declined). However, when age groups were matched on the basis of educational level, there was a significant *increase* in verbal scores with age, and no differences in performance scores, except on the Digit Symbol, where even in groups with comparable educational achievement, older persons performed more poorly (Green, 1969).

Similarly, occupational level, which is generally correlated with educational level, has an impact on a person's intelligence test scores. Older people who still use their cognitive abilities in jobs that require thinking and problem-solving (such as Mr. Wallace in the introductory vignette) show less decline on cognitive tests than those who do not keep working. In addition, people whose occupations demand more verbal skills (e.g., lawyers and teachers) may continue to perform very well on these aspects of the intelligence tests, whereas those who use more abstract and fluid skills in their occupations (e.g., architects and engineers) may do well on the performance tests of the WAIS, even into their seventies and eighties. (Dutta, Schulenberg, and Lair, 1986; Inouye et al., 1993).

The effects of declining physical health and sensory losses on intelligence become more severe in the later years, and these factors may displace any positive influence due to education and occupation for people who are 75 years and older. Several studies have identified poorer performance on intelligence tests by older people in poor health and by those who do not participate in cognitively demanding activities (e. g., playing a musical instrument, bridge or Scrabble).

Older people with cardiovascular problems tend to do worse on tests of intelligence than those without such disorders, particularly in tests that demand psychomotor speed (Hultsch, Hammer, and Small, 1993). In a landmark study, changes in WAIS scores were analyzed over a 10-year period among older people whose blood pressure was judged to be normal, borderline, or high. Those who were aged 60 to 69 at the start of the study and had high blood pressure throughout the 10 years declined the most in performance subtests of the WAIS. Those with borderline blood pressure showed the least decline. This may be because mild elevations of blood pressure in older persons are useful for maintaining sufficient blood circulation to the brain (Wilkie and Eisdorfer, 1971). In both cross-sectional and longitudinal studies that separated hypertension status from age, sex, and education, at least some cognitive tests were found to be adversely affected by high blood pressure. (Elias et al., 1990; Sands and Meredith, 1992).

Another physical health factor that appears to be related to intelligence test scores is an apparent and rapid decline in cognitive function within five years of death. This phenomenon is known as the *terminal drop hypothesis* (Kleemeier, 1962; White and Cunningham, 1988). Older subjects whose test scores are in the lower range have been found to die sooner than good performers, especially on tests of vocabulary and word fluency (Cooney, Schaie, and Willis, 1988; White and Cunningham, 1988). This suggests that time since birth (i.e., age) is not as significant in intellectual decline as is proximity to death.

As we noted in Chapter 6, hearing loss is common in older persons, especially moderate levels of loss that affect their ability to comprehend speech. The effect of hearing loss on verbal communication may explain findings of poorer scores on verbal subtests of the WAIS among older persons with moderate to high hearing loss. However, there is less association between test scores on performance scales and hearing loss (Botwinick, 1984).

Finally, anxiety may negatively affect older people's intelligence test scores. As shown in the following section, older people in laboratory tests of learning and memory are more likely than the young to express high test anxiety and cautiousness in responding. These same reactions may occur in older people taking intelligence tests, especially if they think that the test really measures how "intelligent" they are. Anxieties about cognitive decline and concerns about becoming cognitively impaired may make older people even more cautious, and hence result in poorer performance on intelligence tests.

## THE PROCESS OF LEARNING AND MEMORY

Learning and memory are two cognitive processes that must be considered together. That is, learning is assumed to have occurred when an individual is able statistically to retrieve information from his or her memory store. Conversely, if an individual cannot retrieve information from memory, it is assumed that learning has not adequately taken place. Thus, learning is the process by which new information (verbal or nonverbal) or skills are encoded, or put into one's memory. Memory is the process of retrieving or recalling the information stored in the brain when needed. Memory also refers to a part of the brain that retains what has been learned throughout a person's lifetime. For example, a person may have learned many years ago how to ride a bicycle. If this skill has been encoded well through practice, the person can retrieve it many years later from his or her memory store, even if he or she has not ridden a bicycle in many years. Although most neuroscientists today agree that the process of encoding memories begins in the hippocampus, the exact location in the brain where memories

are stored has not been identified. Researchers have attempted to distinguish three separate types of memory: sensory, primary or short-term, and secondary or long-term.

Sensory memory, as its name implies, is the first step in receiving information through the sense organs and passing it on to primary or secondary memory. It is stored for only a few tenths of a second, although there is some evidence that it lasts longer in older persons because of slower reaction times of the senses (Abel, 1972). Sensory memory has been further subdivided into iconic (or visual) and echoic (or auditory) memory. Examples of iconic memory are words or letters that we see, faces of people with whom we have contact, and landscapes that we experience through our eyes. Of course, words can be received through echoic memory as well, such as when we hear others say a specific word, or when we repeat words aloud to ourselves. A landscape can also enter our sensory memory through our ears (e.g., the sound of the ocean), our skin (e.g., the feel of a cold spray from the ocean), and our nose (e.g., the smell of salt water). To the extent that we focus on or rehearse any information that we receive from our sense organs, it is more likely to be passed into our primary and secondary memories.

Despite significant changes in the visual system with aging (as described in Chapter 6), studies of iconic memory have found only small age differences in the ability to identify stimuli presented briefly. Older people have been found to take longer to identify a single letter or icon (Walsh, Till, and Williams, 1978). In another study, when old and young individuals were tested with seven-letter strings, the former were slower by a factor of 1.3, a rate similar to that found with single letters (Cerella, Poon, and Fozard, 1982). Such modest declines in iconic memory would not be expected to influence observed decrements in secondary or long-term memory. Thus, iconic memory may have little effect on secondary memory.

Although research on iconic memory is limited, there has been even less with echoic memory and less still that has compared older persons with younger. We have all experienced the long-term storage of memories gained through touch, taste, or smell. For example, the odor of freshly baked bread evokes memories in many older people of their early childhood. However, these sensory memories are more difficult to test. As a result, very little is known about any changes experienced with these other modes of sensory memory.

Primary memory is a temporary stage of holding and organizing information, and does not necessarily refer to a storage area in the brain. Despite its temporary nature, primary memory is critical for our ability to process new information. We have all experienced situations where we hear or read a bit of information such as a phone number or someone's name, use that name or number immediately, then forget it. In fact, most adults can recall seven, plus or minus two, pieces of information (e.g., digits, letters, or words) for 60 seconds or less. It is not surprising, therefore, that local phone numbers in most countries are seven digits or less! In order to retain this information in our permanent memory store (secondary memory), it must be rehearsed actively. This is why primary memory has been described as a form of "working memory" that decides what information should be attended to or ignored, which is most important, and how best to store it (Baddeley, 1986). If we are distracted while trying to retain the information for the 60 seconds that it can last in short-term memory, we immediately forget it, even if it consists of only two or three bits of information. This happens because the rehearsal of such material is interrupted by the reception of newer information in our sensory memory.

Most studies of primary memory have found minimal age differences in its storage capacity. For example, people aged 20 to 30 have been found to recall 6 or 7 letters presented auditorily, compared with 5.5 letters by subjects in their seventies (Botwinick and Storandt, 1974). Differences that exist may be due more to increased reaction time with age than to a reduced capacity of primary memory. However, recent studies have

demonstrated some age-related decline in the ability to sort out information that was acquired in a specific order (Dobbs and Rule, 1989).

True learning implies that the material we have acquired through our sensory and primary memories has been stored in secondary memory. Thus, for example, looking up a telephone number and immediately dialing it does not guarantee that the number will be learned. In fact, only with considerable rehearsal can information from primary memory be passed into secondary memory. This is the part of the memory store in which everything we have learned throughout our lives is kept; unlike primary memory, it has an unlimited capacity.

Age differences in secondary memory appear to be more pronounced than in sensory or primary memory and are often frustrating to older people and their families. Indeed, there appears to be a widespread concern among middle-aged and older people that they cannot remember and retrieve information from secondary memory (Poon, 1985). This perception that one has poor memory can seriously harm older people's self-concepts, their performance on many tasks, and may even result in depression (O'Hara et al., 1986). Such concern is generally out of proportion to the actual level of decline. These concerns often stem from the fear of dementia, a relatively rare set of conditions that dramatically impair cognitive functions, as described in Chapter 11. Older people consistently recall less information than younger people in paired associate tests with retention intervals as brief as one hour or as long as eight months. However, older individuals can benefit significantly from methods to help organize their learning, such as imagery and the use of mnemonics. Examples of such techniques to improve learning and memory are discussed later in this chapter.

## THE INFORMATION PROCESSING MODEL

Figure 8–3 presents the information processing model of memory. This is a conceptual model;

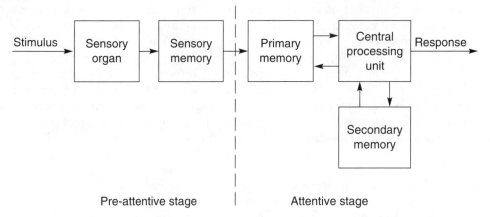

**FIGURE 8–3  Schematic Representation of the Information Processing Model**

that is, it provides a framework for understanding how the processes of learning and memory take place. It is not necessarily what goes on in the neural pathways between the sense organs and the secondary memory store. Having described each of the components in this model, let us review the steps involved in processing some information that we want to retain. One example is the experience of learning new names at a social gathering. Sensory memory aids in hearing the name spoken, preferably several times by other people, and seeing the face that is associated with that name. Primary memory is used to store that information temporarily, so that a person can speak to others and address them by name (an excellent method of rehearsing this information), or manipulate the information in other ways in order to pass it on to secondary memory. This may include repeating the name several times to oneself, trying to isolate some aspect of the person's physical features and relating it to the name, and associating the name with other people one has known in the past who have similar names. In the last type of mental manipulation, information from secondary memory (i.e., names of other people) is linked with the new information. This is a useful method because the material in secondary memory is permanent, and associating the new information with well-

learned information aids in its storage and subsequent recall.

During any stage of this cognitive processing, the newly obtained information can be lost. This may occur if the sensory memory is flooded with similar information; in this case, if a person is being introduced to multiple new names and faces at a party, it is almost impossible to distinguish the names or to associate each name with a face. Information may also be lost during the primary memory stage. In our example, if a person is trying to use the newly heard name and is distracted by other names and faces, or receives unrelated but relevant information (e.g., a telephone call) while rehearsing the new name, the name has not been sufficiently processed to pass into secondary memory.

The learning process may also be disrupted because of inability to retrieve information efficiently from secondary memory. For example, a person may associate the newly heard name with someone known in the past; if he or she has difficulty retrieving the stored name from secondary memory, however, this may be so frustrating as to redirect the individual's attention from the new name to the old name. How often have you ignored everything around you to concentrate on remembering a name that is "on the tip of the tongue" (i.e., in secondary memory) but not easily retrievable? As noted above, aging appears to reduce the efficiency of *processing* information in sensory and primary memories, and retrieval from secondary memory (i.e., working memory). It does *not* influence the storage capacity of primary or secondary memories. That is, contrary to popular opinion, these memory stores are not physical spaces that become overloaded with information as we age.

## Factors that Affect Learning in Old Age

One problem with assessing learning ability is that it is not possible to measure the process that occurs in the brain while an individual is acquiring new information. Instead, we must rely on an individual's performance on tests that presumably measure what was learned. This may be particularly disadvantageous to older persons, whose performance on a test of learning may be poor because of inadequate or inappropriate conditions for expressing what was learned (Botwinick, 1984). For example, an older person may in fact have learned many new concepts in reading a passage from a novel, but not necessarily the specific concepts that are called for on a test of learning. Certain physical conditions, such as lighting levels, size of print, tone and loudness of the test-giver's voice in an oral exam,

Computer classes provide opportunities for active learning.

and the time constraints placed on the test-taker, may affect performance and thus lead to underestimates of what the older person has actually learned. Consistent with the P-E model, to the extent that the learning environment can be improved with glare-free and direct lighting, lettering of good quality, size, and contrast, a comfortable test-taking situation with minimal background noise, and a relaxed and articulate test-giver, the older learner will learn and recall more on subsequent tests of learning.

Time constraints are particularly detrimental to older people. Although the ability to encode new information quickly is a sign of learning ability, it is difficult to measure this ability. Instead, response time is generally measured. As we have already seen, psychomotor and sensory slowing with age has a significant impact on the older person's speed in responding. One of the first researchers to test the effect of these conditions on learning was Canestrari (1963). Using a common test of learning, the paired associates task (i.e., linking two unrelated words, letters, digits, or symbols, such as *cat* and *82*, and asking subjects to respond with the second when the first is mentioned), Canestrari presented the paired associates at varying rates, or allowed individuals to pace the task by controlling the visual apparatus themselves. In comparing people aged 60–69 with those aged 17–35, he found striking differences between old and young individuals' performance when the task was paced fast, fewer differences in moderate pacing, and the fewest differences in self-paced conditions. Young persons did well in all conditions, but older persons in this study benefited the most from self-pacing. Similar results have been reported by Monge and Hultsch (1971), Arenberg (1973), and Smith (1976).

The study by Canestrari and a later study by Botwinick (1978) have shown that older persons make more *errors of omission* than *errors of commission*. That is, older persons are more likely not to give an answer than to guess and risk being wrong. This phenomenon was first recognized in middle-aged and older adults in tests of psychomotor functioning (Welford, 1951). The older the respondent, the more likely he or she was to work for accuracy at the expense of speed. This occurs even when the older learner is encouraged to guess and is told that it is acceptable to give wrong answers (i.e., commission errors). Errors of omission may be reduced somewhat by giving rewards for both right and wrong answers.

This tendency toward errors of omission is consistent with studies of cautiousness in older persons, which have yielded some evidence of less risk-taking with age. Some studies have used a vocabulary test in which individuals could earn points for defining words, with more points for difficult words. In situations of uncertainty, older persons chose easier words, but did not differ from the young in situations of certainty (Okun and DiVesta, 1976). In a subsequent study, individuals were provided with a rational basis on which they could choose easy or difficult words. In this case, older persons were no more cautious than younger subjects (Okun and Elias, 1977).

These results suggest that in conditions of uncertainty and high risk, older persons are more cautious than the young. Low-risk situations elicit less caution from older people and greater willingness to give responses in a learning task. Results of these studies suggest also that the aging process creates an increased need to review multiple aspects of a problem, probably because of past experiences with similar dilemmas.

Verbal ability and educational level are important factors in learning verbal information (Hultsch and Dixon, 1984). Studies that entail learning prose passages have shown age deficits among those with average vocabulary abilities and minimal or no college education. In contrast, older persons with high verbal ability and a college education perform as well as younger subjects in such experiments. This may be due to greater practice and facility with such tasks on the part of more educated persons and those with good vocabulary skills. It may also reflect differences in the ability to organize new information,

a skill that is honed through years of education and one that assists in the learning of large quantities of new material (Ratner et al., 1987). In fact, education and vocabulary skills are generally correlated, and emerge as better predictors of performance in studies of prose learning than does chronological age (Rice and Meyer, 1985, 1986).

Similarly, older people who have developed manual skills in a particular area have been found to perform just as well on perceptual-motor tests as do younger persons with skills. Two studies examined choice reaction time, tapping rate, and accuracy by testing people aged 19 to 72 who varied in typing speed (Salthouse, 1984). These well-designed experiments measured age differences in real-life studies where typists were asked to type prose passages as well as random letter series. While the older typists had more years of relevant employment, there were no differences between old and young in the *recency* of this experience (i.e., older typists were just as likely to be using their skills currently). This research demonstrated that typing time remains stable with increasing age, even though choice reaction time increases and tapping rate declines. These findings are consistent with other studies of the basic components of perceptual-motor abilities (McDowd and Craik, 1988).

The apparent inconsistency between typing time and choice reaction time/typing rate may be explained by the added finding that older typists apparently compensate for their declining perceptual-motor speed by anticipating impending keystrokes. Perhaps this is one of the greatest benefits of increased skill—the accomplished performer makes more efficient moves in completing a task than does a less skilled person. Such differences are evident in many areas demanding skill, from typing and driving (Salthouse and Somberg, 1982) to playing a musical instrument or operating a lathe.

The conditions under which learning takes place affect older persons more than the young, just as test conditions are more critical. Older persons respond differently to varied testing situations; people tested under challenging conditions ("this is a test of your intelligence") are likely to do worse than those in supportive conditions ("the researcher needs your help"). Positive feedback appears to be a valuable tool for eliciting responses from older adults in both learning and test situations.

It is helpful to pace the information so that it is presented at a rate suitable to the older learner and to give him or her opportunities to practice the new information (e.g., writing down or spelling aloud newly learned words). Another condition that supports learning is the presentation of familiar and relevant material compared to material perceived by the older learner to be unimportant. Recall of recently acquired information has been found to be worse in older persons than in younger when the new information is unfamiliar or confusing (Hoyer and Plude, 1980; Barrett and Wright, 1981). Similarly, greater age differences have been identified when the material to be learned was low in meaning and personal significance (Fozard, 1980). Laboratory studies of cognitive functioning often seem artificial and meaningless to older people who are unaccustomed to such research methods, and even more so to those with little academic experience. Many people will complain that such tests are trivial, nonsense, or that these tasks have no connection to the "real world." Indeed, it may appear odd to anyone to be learning meaningless words and symbols on a tachistoscope (a screen that is timed to present visual stimuli at a specific pace) or other laboratory device. But for those older people who are unfamiliar with test-taking situations, it may appear particularly foolish and not worth the effort required. This may also serve a useful ego-defensive function for people who feel uncomfortable or threatened by a test-taking situation. It is generally easier for people to blame the environment or the test situation for their poor performance than to accept it as a sign of a decline in their intelligence or their ability to learn.

The use of words familiar to older persons actually results in better performance by them than by the young. For example, when words such as *fedora* (a term with which older persons are more likely than the young to be familiar) were used in one study, older people could recall more words. In contrast, words with which older individuals were less familiar (e.g., *ripoff*) resulted in worse recall (Barrett and Wright, 1981).

Most studies of learning focus on verbal information. It is generally assumed that nonverbal information is learned in the same way. In the few studies that have compared the ability of older and younger adults to recognize facial photos, recall has consistently been worse among the former. For example, Ferris and colleagues (1980) showed two age groups (17–39 and 60–88) black and white slides of individual faces. When shown the same slides later, together with other pictures, the elderly recognized fewer faces than did the younger people. In an attempt to compare verbal and nonverbal learning, old and young people were shown black and white drawings of objects and their verbal labels. The ability to recall pictures was better than that for words for both groups. However, age differences again emerged, such that older adults recalled fewer drawings and verbal labels (Winograd, Smith, and Simon, 1982).

*Spatial memory,* that is, the ability to recall where objects are in relationship to each other in space (e.g., when finding one's way around a community or using a map), also appears to decline with aging. It is unclear, however, if older people do worse than the young because they have difficulty encoding and processing the information, or if the problem is in retrieval. The possibility of encoding problems as the cause was tested in one study where 48 women aged 60 to 70 were compared with 48 women aged 20 to 30 in their ability to view a three-dimensional model of a town, and then to reconstruct the town from memory (Bruce and Herman, 1986). Older women needed two trials to do as well as the young did with one trial. They also did better when the buildings and roads were clearly labeled and made distinct with different roof forms and colors than when there were no labels.

This study provides support for an age-related decline in encoding ability for spatial information. Further support for this explanation comes from another study in which spatial recall was tested following the presentation of a two-dimensional black and white map versus a colored map or a three-dimensional model. Older subjects in this study recalled fewer items than the young did under the condition of no visual cues, but no age differences were found when color or 3-D representations were used. (Sharps and Gollin, 1988). Similarly, older people have more difficulty than younger persons in reading maps that are misaligned relative to the user. For example, when older people stand in front of a "You are here" map that is aligned 180° away from themselves, they take up to 50 percent more time and make 30 percent more errors than younger persons in the same condition. However, when the map is aligned directly with the user, no age differences are observed. This may be attributable to increased problems with mental rotation of external images and with perspective-taking as we age (Aubrey and Dobbs, 1990; Aubrey, Li, and Dobbs, 1994).

## AGE-RELATED CHANGES IN MEMORY

As we have seen, learning involves encoding information and storing it into secondary or long-term memory, so that it can be retrieved and used later. Studies of this process have focused on two types of retrieval: recall and recognition. *Recall* is the process of searching through the vast store of information in secondary memory, perhaps with a cue or a specific, orienting question (e.g., "List the capitals of each state." "Describe how to repair a bicycle." "Give the dates when the U.S. Constitution was signed, when the U.N. Charter was signed," etc.). *Recognition* requires less search. The information in secondary memory must be matched with the stimulus information in the environment (e.g., "Which of these three cities is the capital of New York?"). Recall is demanded in essay exams, recognition in multiple-choice tests.

Not surprisingly, most researchers have found age-related deficiencies in recall, but few, if any, differences in recognition (Inman and Parkinson, 1983). However, in studies that have tested for recognition ability with multiple response categories, older people do worse when many words or numbers have to be recognized from a large list, or when the word to be identified is included in a list of four rather than just two words (Botwinick and Storandt, 1974; Kausler and Kleim, 1978). Recall tasks have been further divided into *free recall* and *cued recall* situations. In the former, no aids or hints are provided for retrieving information from secondary memory. In the latter case, the individual is given some information to aid in the search (e.g., category labels and first letter of a word). Older people tend to do much worse than the young in tests of free recall, but are aided significantly by cueing. In particular, use of category labels (semantic cues) at the learning stage has been found to be more helpful to older persons than the use of structural cues—for example, giving the respondent the first letter of a word to be recalled (Smith, 1977). However, cued recall tests are not as helpful as recognition tests for older learners.

An area of considerable controversy in aging and memory function is the question of whether older people have better recall of events that occurred in the distant past than recent situations. Many events are firmly embedded in secondary memory because they are unique or so important that subsequent experiences do not interfere with the ability to recall them. The birth of a child, one's wedding ceremony, or the death of a parent, spouse, or sibling are events that most people can recall in detail 40 to 50 years later. This may be because the situation had great private significance or, in the case of world events, such as the bombing of Hiroshima or John F. Kennedy's assassination, had a profound impact on world history. Some distant events may be better recalled because they had greater personal relevance for the individual's social development than recent experiences, or because they have been rehearsed or thought about more.

Another possibility is that cues that helped the older person recall events in the past are less effective with recalling recent occasions because of "cue-overload" (Schonfield and Stones, 1979). That is, the same cues that were once helpful in remembering certain information are also used to recall many recent events. But the cues are so strongly associated with one's earlier life experiences that the newer information becomes more difficult to retrieve. For example, older people may have difficulty memorizing new phone numbers because the cues that helped them recall phone numbers in the past may be so closely associated with previous ones that they confuse recent phone numbers with old ones.

One problem in determining whether recall of distant situations is really better than recall of recent events is the difficulty in validating an older person's memories. In many cases, there are no sources that can be checked to determine the accuracy of an older person's recollections. We can all identify with this process of asking an old friend or family member, "Do you remember the time when . . .?" If others have no recollection of the event, it may make us wonder if the situation really took place or it may mean that the event was so obscure that it made no impact on other people. Hence, such memories are difficult to measure accurately.

Some researchers who have tested older persons' recall of historical facts, such as world events that occurred during their youth and middle years, have found that distant events could not be remembered as well as recent ones (Warrington and Saunders, 1971; Squire, 1974). However, other researchers have found the opposite (Botwinick and Storandt, 1974, 1980). Indeed, Poon and colleagues (1979) observed that older persons demonstrated better recognition performance than did young subjects when presented with historical events that took place between 1920 and the 1970s. In a study of personally relevant remote events, high-school graduates aged 17 to 74 were shown yearbook pictures and asked to match the photos with names. The researchers controlled statistically for class size and attendance at reunions. Recognition memory was as high as 90 percent in middle-aged subjects; free recall of names was generally worse for all age groups, but even those who had graduated 48 years earlier could remember 20 percent of the names (Bahrick, Bahrick, and Wittlinger, 1975).

Several theories have been offered to explain why older people may have problems with retrieving information from secondary memory. One explanation is that not using the information results in its loss (the disuse theory). This theory suggests that information can fade away or decay unless it is exercised, as in the adage, "Use it or lose it." However, this explanation fails to account for the many facts that are deeply embedded in a person's memory store and that can be retrieved even after years of disuse.

A more widely accepted explanation is that new information interferes with the material that has been stored over a period of many years. As we have noted earlier, interference is a problem in the learning or encoding stage. When the older person is distracted while trying to learn new information, this information does not become stored in memory. Poor retrieval may be due to a combination of such distraction during the learning stage and interference by similar or new information with the material being searched in the retrieval stage. Although researchers in this area have not conclusively agreed on any of these explanations, the interference theory appears to hold more promise than others for explaining observed problems with retrieval.

Researchers have begun to examine older people's feelings about their memory failures and how they cope with these. For example, participants in one longitudinal study kept diaries of their experiences with memory. Older adults described more incidents in which they forgot names, objects, locations, and appointments, especially in nonroutine tasks. They also reported feeling more frustrated with a memory failure than did younger people (Cavanaugh, Grady, and Perlmutter, 1983). This may impair the older person's confidence in a learning or test situation, thereby negatively affecting performance in these cases. Indeed, older persons have been found to express less confidence in their responses than the young do in tests of recognition and recall (Bahrick, Bahrick, and Wittlinger, 1975).

## IMPROVING MEMORY IN THE LATER YEARS

There has been considerable experimentation with techniques for improving memory. Some of the most exciting research in this field focuses on developing new drugs that enhance the chemical messengers in neurons or improve the function of neural receptors. Within the next ten years there may be some approved memory-enhancing drugs for older adults. Other researchers have examined practical methods such as cognitive aids. Although useful at any age, cognitive aids may be particularly helpful for an older person who is experiencing increased problems with day-to-day cognitive functions, such as recalling names, words, phone numbers, and daily chores. Older persons are more likely to use external aids such as notes and lists than they are to use cognitive aids such as imagery and word association. That is, they are more likely to reduce environmental press than to enhance their competence in learning as a means of improving P-E congruence. Many techniques for remembering are acquired as part of a person's formal educational experiences; as a result an older person who has had minimal educational opportunities will have had less exposure to such techniques. There are a number of excellent guides for training older people to improve their memory (AARP, 1990).

Most memory improvement techniques are based on the concept of mediators, that is, the use of visual and verbal links between information to be encoded and information that is already in secondary memory. Mediators may be visual (e.g., the method of locations) or verbal (i.e., the use of mnemonics). The method of locations (or loci) is useful for learning a list of new words, names, or concepts. Each word is associated with a specific location in a familiar environment. For example, the individual is instructed to "walk through" his or her own home mentally. As the person walks through the rooms in succession, each item on the list is associated with a particular space along the way. Older persons using this technique have been found to recall more words on a list than when they used no mediators (Robertson-Tchabo, Hausman, and Arenberg, 1976). One advantage of the method of loci is that learners can visualize the new information within a familiar setting, and can decide for themselves what new concept should be linked with what specific part of the environment. Older learners have been found to recall more information when given the time to develop their own mediators than if the experimenter provides the links for them (Treat and Reese, 1976). Imaging is a useful technique in everyday recall situations as well. For example, an older person can remember what he or she needs to buy at the grocery story by visualizing using these items while preparing dinner.

Another way of organizing material to be learned and to ensure its storage in secondary memory is to use mnemonics, or verbal riddles, rhymes, and codes associated with the new information. Many teachers use such rhymes to teach their students multiplication, spelling (e.g., "*i* before *e* except after *c*"), and the calendar ("30 days hath September, April, June, and November/ all the rest have 31, except February alone, and that has 28 days clear/ except every leap year"). One of the first mnemonics a music student learns is in conjunction with memorizing the scales (*Every Good Boy Does Fine*). Sailors learn that *r*ed lights in the harbor signify *r*ight and *r*eturn. There are many other mnemonics that we acquire through experience as well as our own efforts to devise ways to learn a new concept. Both cognitively intact and impaired older people have shown improved memory function with the use of mnemonics (Poon et al., 1980).

Other mediators include using the new word or concept in a sentence, associating the digits in a phone number with symbols or putting them into a mathematical formula (e.g., "the first digit is 4, the second and third are multiplied to produce the first"), placing the information into categories, using multiple sensory memories, and even combining sensory with motor function. In this last technique, one may write the word (iconic memory), repeat it aloud to oneself (echoic memory), or "feel" the letters or digits by outlining them with one's hand.

Unfortunately, many older persons do not practice the use of newly learned memory techniques. They may not be motivated to use the techniques, which often seem awkward, or they may forget and need to be reminded. Perhaps the major problem is that these are unfamiliar approaches to the current generation of older people. As future cohorts become more practiced in these memory techniques through their educational experiences, the use of such strategies in old age should increase.

The most important aspect of memory enhancement may be the ability to relax and to avoid feeling anxious or stressed during the learning stage. As noted earlier, many older people become overly concerned about occasional memory lapses, viewing them as a sign of deterioration and possible onset of senile dementia. Thus, a young person may be annoyed when a familiar name is forgotten, but will probably not interpret the memory lapse as loss of cognitive function, as an older person is likely to do. Unfortunately, society reinforces this belief. How often are we told that we are "getting old" when we forget a trivial matter? How often do adult children become concerned that their parent sometimes forgets to turn off the stove, when in fact they may frequently do this themselves?

In addition to mediators, simple devices or *external aids* are often used by older people to keep track of the time or dates, or to remember to turn the stove on or off. For example, placing several large-print calendars around the house or, better yet, using digital clocks that also display the day of the week and the date can be helpful. Older people can develop the habit of associating medication regimens with specific activities of daily living, such as using marked pill boxes and taking the first pill in the morning before their daily shower, or just before or after breakfast, taking the second pill with lunch or before their noontime walk, and so on. These behaviors need to be associated with activities that occur every day at a particular time, so that the pill-taking becomes linked with that routine. Charts listing an individual's daily or weekly routine can be posted throughout the house. Alarm clocks and kitchen timers also can be placed wherever an older person will be while the oven or stove is in operation. This will help in remembering that the appliance is on without having to stay in the kitchen. The stove could be connected to a red signal light in the older person's bedroom or front entryway. This light would go on every time the oven or stove was turned on, so that the person would be reminded of this when going to bed or leaving the house. A fire alarm or smoke detector is essential for every older person's home, preferably one for every floor or wing of the house. Finally, for older people who have serious memory problems and a tendency to get lost while walking outdoors, a bracelet or necklace imprinted with the person's name, address, phone number, and relevant medical information can be a lifesaver.

## WISDOM AND CREATIVITY

Wisdom and creativity are more difficult to define and measure. Most people have an image of what it means to be wise or creative, but it is impossible to quantify an individual's level of wisdom or creativity. It has been suggested that *wisdom* requires the cognitive development and mastery over a person's emotions that come with age (Clayton and Birren, 1980; Butler and Gleason, 1985). It is a combination of experience, introspection, reflection, intuition, and empathy; these are qualities that are honed over many years and that can be integrated in people's interactions with their world. Thus, younger people may have any one of these skills, but their integration requires more maturity. Wisdom also implies that the individual does not act on impulse and can review all aspects of a given situation objectively. In many cultures, older persons are respected for their years of experience, and the role of "wise elder" is a desired status. Not all elderly have achieved wisdom, however. Indeed, Butler and Gleason (1985) suggest that wisdom requires the ability to transcend the limitations of basic needs such as health, income, and housing, and that the individual must have continued opportunities for growth and creativity. Such older people could play a useful role as "wise elder" in many businesses and government agencies, where their years of experience and ability to move beyond the constraints presumed by others could help such organizations succeed.

*Creativity* refers to the ability to apply unique and feasible solutions to new situations, to come up with original ideas or material products. A person may be creative in science, the arts, or technology. Although we can point to creative people in each of these areas (e.g., Albert Einstein in science, Wolfgang Amadeus Mozart and Georgia O'Keeffe in the arts, and Thomas Edison in technology), it is difficult to determine the specific characteristics that make such persons creative. As with intelligence in general, creativity is inferred from the individual's output, but cannot really be quantified or predicted. One measure of creativity is a test of *divergent thinking,* which is part of Guilford's (1967) structural model of intelligence. This is measured by asking a person to devise multiple solutions to an unfamiliar mental task (e.g., name some different uses for a flower). Unfortunately, there is no way to know if such a test actually predicts creativity.

Divergent thinking may be only one component of creativity, however. It has been suggested that a creative person must also know much about a particular body of knowledge such as music or art before he or she can make creative contributions to it (Rebok, 1987). However, this neglects the contributions to scientific problem-solving or the arts by people who may have expertise in one area and bring a fresh perspective to a different field. To date, very few researchers have administered a test of divergent thinking to people who are generally considered to be creative. Much of the research on creativity has been performed as analyses of the products of artists and writers, not on their creative process directly. Indeed, no studies have been conducted to compare the cognitive functioning of artists, scientists, technologists, and others who are widely regarded as creative with that of persons not similarly endowed. Researchers who have examined the *quantity* of creative output by artists, poets, and scientists have found that the average rate of output at age 70–80 drops to approximately half that of age 30–40. However, a secondary peak of productivity often occurs in the 60s, although not as high as the first peak (Simonton, 1988). Indeed, an analysis of the last works of 172 classical composers in their final years revealed compositions that were judged highly by musicologists in terms of esthetics, melody, and comprehensibility (Simonton, 1989). There are numerous examples of late-life creativity in the arts (e. g., Georgia O'Keeffe, who painted some of her most highly acclaimed pieces in her 80s), in the sciences (e. g., Humboldt's last volume of

In many cultures, old age is viewed as a time of wisdom.

*Cosmos* was completed at age 89), and in gerontology (e. g., Chevreul, who moved from his profession as a chemist to the study of gerontology at age 90 and continued to publish scientific papers at age 100).

## SUMMARY AND IMPLICATIONS

This chapter presented an overview of the major studies on cognitive functioning in the later years. Researchers have examined age-related changes in intelligence, learning, and memory, and what factors in the individual and the environment affect the degree of change in these three areas of cognitive functioning.

Of all the cognitive functions in aging, intelligence has received the greatest attention and controversy. It is also the area of most concern for many older persons. One problem with this area of research is the difficulty of defining and measuring what is generally agreed to be intelligence. In examining the components of intelligence measured by the Wechsler Adult Intelligence Scale (WAIS), fluid intelligence (as measured by performance scales) has been shown to decline more with aging than verbal, or crystallized, intelligence. This may be due partly to the fact that the former tests are generally timed, while the latter are not. However, age differences emerge even when tests are not timed, and when variations in motor and sensory function are taken into account. This decline in fluid intelligence and maintenance of verbal intelligence is known as the Classic Aging Pattern. To the extent that older persons practice their fluid intelligence by using their problem-solving skills, they will experience less decline in this area. In contrast, aging does not appear to impair the ability for remembering word and symbol meanings. This does not imply that the ability to recall words is unimpaired, but when asked for definitions of words, older people can remember their meanings quite readily.

One problem with studying intelligence in aging is that of distinguishing age changes from age differences. To determine changes with age, people must be examined longitudinally. The problems of selective attrition and terminal drop make it difficult to interpret the findings of longitudinal studies of intelligence. These factors may result in an underestimate of the decline in intelligence with aging. The problem of cross-sectional studies of intelligence is primarily that of cohort differences. Even if subjects are matched on educational level, older persons have not had the exposure to computers and early childhood learning opportunities that have become available to recent cohorts. Other factors, such as occupation, sensory decline, poor physical health, and severe hypertension, have been found to have a significant impact on intelligence test scores.

Learning and memory are cognitive functions that are usually examined because tests of memory are actually tests of what a person has learned. According to the information-processing model, learning begins when information reaches sensory memory, and then is directed via one or more sensory stores to primary memory. It is in primary memory that information must be organized and processed if it is to be retained and passed into secondary memory. Information is permanently stored in this latter region. Studies of recall and recognition provide evidence that aging does not affect the capacity of either primary or secondary memory. Instead, it appears that the aging process makes us less efficient in "reaching into" our secondary memory and retrieving material that was stored years ago. Recognition tasks, in which a person is provided with a cue to associate with an item in secondary memory, are easier than pure recall for most people, but especially for older individuals.

The learning process can be enhanced for older people by reducing time constraints, making the learning task more relevant for them, improving the physical conditions by using bright but glare-free lights and large letters, and providing visual and verbal mediators for learning new information. These include mnemonics and the method of loci. Helping the older learner to relax and not feel threatened by the learning task also ensures better learning. Such modifications are consistent with the goal of achieving greater congruence between older people and their environment.

This review of the research in cognitive functioning with aging provides considerable evidence of relatively small declines in intelligence, learning, and memory with aging. The declines that do occur begin later in life than generally assumed, and are less dramatic than popularly believed. To the extent that an older person remains healthy and intellectually active, decline in cognitive function is slight, and does not seriously impair an individual's ability to enjoy life in the later years.

Although there is some agreement that wisdom is enhanced by age and that creativity reaches a second peak for some people in old age, there has been less research emphasis in these areas. Indeed, these concepts are more difficult to measure in young and old persons. These and other issues in cognition must be studied more fully with measures that have good construct validity before gerontologists can describe with certainty cognitive changes that are attributable to normal aging.

## REFERENCES

Abel, M. *The visual trace in relation to aging.* Unpublished doctoral dissertation. Washington University, St. Louis, Missouri, 1972.

American Association of Retired Persons (AARP), *Memory: The long and short of it.* Washington, D.C.: AARP, Social Outreach and Support Section, 1990.

Arenberg, D. Cognition and aging: Verbal learning, memory, and problem solving. In C. Eisdorfer and M. P. Lawton (Eds.), *Psychology of adult development and aging.* Washington, D.C.: American Psychological Association, 1973.

Aubrey, J. B., and Dobbs, A. R. Age and sex differences in the mental realignment of maps. *Experimental Aging Research,* 1990, *16,* 133–139.

Aubrey, J. B., Li, K. Z. H., and Dobbs, A. R. Age and sex differences in the interpretation of misaligned "You-are-Here" maps. *Journals of Gerontology,* 1994, *49,* P29–P31.

Baddeley, A. *Working memory.* New York: Oxford University Press, 1986.

Bahrick, H. P., Bahrick, P. P., and Wittlinger, R. P. Fifty years of memory for names and faces: A cross-sectional approach. *Journal of Experimental Psychology,* 1975, *104,* 54–75.

Barrett, T. R., and Wright, M. Age-related facilitation in recall following semantic processing. *Journal of Gerontology,* 1981, *2,* 194–199.

Botwinick, J. Intellectual abilities. In J. E. Birren and K. W. Schaie (Eds.), *Handbook of the psychology of aging* (1st ed.). New York: Van Nostrand Reinhold, 1977, 580–605.

Botwinick, J. *Aging and behavior.* New York: Springer, 1978.

Botwinick, J. *Aging and behavior: A comprehensive integration of research findings* (3d ed.). New York: Springer, 1984.

Botwinick, J., and Storandt, M. *Memory related functions and age.* Springfield, Ill.: Charles C. Thomas, 1974.

Botwinick, J., and Storandt, M. Recall and recognition of old information in relation to age and sex. *Journal of Gerontology,* 1980, *35,* 70–76.

Bruce, P. R., and Herman, J. F. Adult age differences in spatial memory. *Journal of Gerontology,* 1986, *41,* 774–777.

Butler, R. N., and Gleason, H. *Productive aging: Enhancing vitality in later life.* New York: Springer, 1985.

Canestrari, R. E. Paced and self-paced learning in young and elderly adults. *Journal of Gerontology,* 1963, *18,* 165–168.

Cattell, R. B. Theory of fluid and crystallized intelligence: A critical experiment. *Journal of Educational Psychology,* 1963, *54,* 1–22.

Cavanaugh, J. C., Grady, J. G., and Perlmutter, M. P. Forgetting and use of memory aids in 20 and 70-year-olds' everyday life. *International Journal of Aging and Human Development,* 1983, *17,* 113–122.

Cerella, J., Poon, L. W., and Fozard, J. L. Age and iconic read-out. *Journal of Gerontology,* 1982, *37,* 197–202.

Clayton, V., and Birren, J. E. Age and wisdom across the life span: Theoretical perspectives. In P. B. Baltes and O. G. Brim, Jr. (Eds.), *Life-span development and behavior* (Vol. 3). New York: Academic Press, 1980.

Cooney, T. M., Schaie, K. W., and Willis, S. L. The relationship between prior functioning on cognitive and personality dimensions and subject attrition in longitudinal research. *Journals of Gerontology,* 1988, *43,* P12–P17.

Craik, F. I. M. Age differences in human memory. In J. E. Birren and K. W. Schaie (Eds.), *Handbook of the psychology of aging* (1st ed.). New York: Van Nostrand Reinhold, 1977.

Cunningham, W. R., and Owens, W. A. The Iowa state study of the adult development of intellectual abilities. In K. W. Schaie (Ed.), *Longitudinal studies of adult psychological development.* New York: Guilford Press, 1983.

Denney, N. W. Adult cognitive development. In D. S. Beasley and G. A. Davis (Eds.), *Aging: Communication processes and disorders.* New York: Grune and Stratton, 1981.

Dobbs, A. R., and Rule, B. G. Adult age differences in working memory. *Psychology and Aging,* 1989, *4,* 500–503.

Dutta, R., Schulenberg, E., and Lair, T. J. The effect of job characteristics on cognitive abilities and intellectual flexibility. Paper presented at the annual meeting of the Eastern Psychological Association, New York, 1986.

Elias, M. F., Robbins, M. A., Schultz, N. R., and Pierce, T. W. Is blood pressure an important variable in research on aging and neuropsychological test performance? *Journals of Gerontology* 1990, *45,* P128–P135.

Ferris, S. H., Crook, T., Clark, E., McCarthy, M., and Rae, D. Facial recognition memory deficits in normal aging and senile dementia. *Journal of Gerontology,* 1980, *35,* 707–714.

Fozard, J. L. The time for remembering. In L. W. Poon (Ed.), *Aging in the 1980's: Psychological issues.* Washington, D.C.: American Psychological Association, 1980.

Green, R. F. Age-intelligence relationship between ages sixteen and sixty-four. *Developmental Psychology,* 1969, *1,* 618–627.

Guilford, J. P. Intelligence: 1965 model. *American Psychologist,* 1966, *21,* 20–26.

Guilford, J. P. *The nature of human intelligence.* New York: McGraw-Hill, 1967.

Hertzog, C. K., and Schaie, K. W. Stability and change in adult intelligence: 2. Simultaneous analysis of longitudinal means and covariance structures. *Psychology and Aging,* 1988, *3,* 122–130.

Horn, J. L. Organization of data on life-span development of human abilities. In L. R. Goulet and P. B. Baltes (Eds.), *Life-span developmental psychology: Research and theory.* New York: Academic Press, 1970.

Horn, J. L. The aging of human abilities. In B. B. Wolman (Ed.), *Handbook of developmental psychology.* Englewood Cliffs, N.J.: Prentice-Hall, 1982.

Horn, J. L., and Donaldson, G. Cognitive development in adulthood. In O. G. Brim and J. Kagan (Eds.), *Constancy and change in human development.* Cambridge, Mass.: Harvard University Press, 1980.

Hoyer, W. J., and Plude, D. J. Attentional and perceptual processes in the study of cognitive aging. In L. W. Poon (Ed.), *Aging in the 1980's: Psychological issues.* Washington, D.C.: American Psychological Association, 1980.

Hultsch, D. F., and Dixon, R. A. Memory for text materials in adulthood. In P. B. Baltes and O. G. Brim, Jr. (Eds.), *Lifespan development and behavior* (Vol. 6). New York: Academic Press, 1984.

Hultsch, D. F., Hammer, M., and Small, B. J. Age differences in cognitive performance in later life: Relationships to self-reported health and activity lifestyle. *Journals of Gerontology,* 1993 *48,* P1–P11.

Huyck, M. H., and Hoyer, W. J. *Adult development and aging.* Belmont, Calif.: Wadsworth, 1982.

Inman, V. W., and Parkinson, S. R. Differences in Brown-Peterson recall as a function of age and retention interval. *Journal of Gerontology,* 1983, *38,* 58–64.

Inouye, S. K., Albert, M. S., Mohs, R., and Sun-Kolie, R. Cognitive performance in a high-functioning, community-dwelling elderly population. *Journals of Gerontology,* 1993, *48,* M146–M151.

Jarvik, L. F., and Bank, L. Aging twins: Longitudinal psychometric data. In K. W. Schaie (Ed.), *Longitudinal studies of adult psychological development.* New York: Guilford Press, 1983.

Jarvik, L. F., and Falek, A. Intellectual stability and survival in the aged. *Journal of Gerontology,* 1963, *18,* 173–176.

Johansson, B., Zarit, S. H., and Bergh, S. Changes in cognitive functioning of the oldest old. *Journals of Gerontology,* 1992, *47,* P75–P80.

Jones, H. E. Intelligence and problem-solving. In J. E. Birren (Ed.), *Handbook of aging and the individual: Psychological and biological aspects.* Chicago: University of Chicago Press, 1959.

Kallmann, F. J., and Sander, G. Twin studies on senescence. *American Journal of Psychiatry,* 1949, *106,* 29–36.

Kausler, D. H., and Kleim, D. M. Age differences in processing relevant versus irrelevant stimuli in multiple item recognition learning. *Journal of Gerontology,* 1978, *33,* 87–93.

Kleemeier, R. W. Intellectual change in the senium, or death and the IQ. Presidential Address, American Psychological Association, New York, August 1961.

Kleemeier, R. W. Intellectual change in the senium. *Proceedings of the Social Statistics Section of the American Statistical Association,* 1962, *1,* 290–295.

Labouvie-Vief, G., and Blanchard-Fields, F. Cognitive aging and psychological growth. *Aging and Society,* 1982, *2,* 183–209.

McDowd, J. M., and Craik, F. I. M. Effects of aging and task difficulty on divided attention performance. *Journal of Experimental Psychology: Human Perception and Performance,* 1988, *14,* 267–280.

Monge, R. H., and Hultsch, D. Paired-associate learning as a function of adult age and the length of the anticipation and inspection intervals. *Journal of Gerontology,* 1971, *26,* 157–162.

O'Hara, M. W., Hinrichs, J. W., Kohout, F. J., Wallace, R. B., and Lemke, J. Memory complaint and memory performance in depressed elderly. *Psychology and Aging,* 1986, *1,* 208–214.

Okun, M. A., and DiVesta, F. J. Cautiousness in adulthood as a function of age and instructions. *Journal of Gerontology,* 1976, *31,* 571–576.

Okun, M. A., and Elias, C. S. Cautiousness in adulthood as a function of age and payoff structure. *Journal of Gerontology,* 1977, *32,* 451–455.

Owens, W. A. Age and mental abilities: A longitudinal study. *Genetic Psychology Monographs,* 1953, *48,* 3–54.

Owens, W. A. Age and mental ability: A second adult follow-up. *Journal of Educational Psychology,* 1966, *57,* 311–325.

Palmore, E. (Ed.). *Normal aging II: Reports from the Duke longitudinal study.* Durham, N.C.: Duke University Press, 1974.

Palmore, E. (Ed.). *Normal aging III: Reports from the Duke longitudinal study.* Durham, N.C.: Duke University Press, 1985.

Poon, L. W. Differences in human memory with aging: Nature, causes, and clinical implications. In J. E. Birren and K. W. Schaie (Eds.), *Handbook of the psychology of aging* (2d ed.). New York: Van Nostrand Reinhold, 1985, 427–462.

Poon, L. W., Fozard, J. L., Cermak, L. S., Arenberg, D., and Thompson, L. W. (Eds.). *New directions in memory and aging: Proceedings of the George A. Talland Memorial Conference.* Hillsdale, N.J.: Erlbaum, 1980.

Poon, L. W., Fozard, J. L., Paulshock, D. R., and Thomas, J. C. A questionnaire assessment of age differences in retention of recent and remote events. *Experimental Aging Research,* 1979, *5,* 401–411.

Ratner, H. H., Schell, D. A., Crimmins, A., Mittleman, D., and Baldinelli, L. Changes in adults' prose recall: Aging or cognitive demands. *Developmental Psychology,* 1987, *23,* 521–525.

Rebok, G. W. *Life-span cognitive development.* New York: Holt, Rinehart and Winston, 1987.

Reese, H. W. Models of memory development. *Human Development,* 1976, *19,* 291–303.

Rice, G. E., and Meyer, B. J. F. Reading behavior and prose recall performance of young and older adults with high and average verbal ability. *Educational Gerontology,* 1985, *11,* 57–72.

Rice, G. E., and Meyer, B. J. F. Prose recall: Effects of aging, verbal ability, and reading behavior. *Journal of Gerontology,* 1986, *41,* 469–480.

Riegel, K. F., and Riegel, R. M. Development, drop, and death. *Developmental Psychology,* 1972, *6,* 306–319.

Robertson-Tchabo, E. A., Hausman, C. P., and Arenberg, D. A classical mnemonic for old learners: A trip that works. *Educational Gerontology,* 1976, *1,* 215–226.

Ross, E. Effects of challenging and supportive instructions on verbal learning in older persons. *Journal of Educational Psychology,* 1968, *59,* 261–266.

Salthouse, T. A., Effects of age and skill in typing. *Journal of Experimental Psychology: General,* 1984, *113,* 345–371.

Salthouse, T. A., and Somberg, B. L. Skilled performance: Effects of adult age and experience on elementary processes. *Journal of Experimental Psychology: General,* 1982, *111,* 176–207.

Sands, L. P., and Meredith, W. Blood pressure and intellectual functioning in late midlife. *Journals of Gerontology,* 1992, *47,* P81–P84.

Schaie, K. W. Age changes and age differences. *The Gerontologist,* 1967, *7,* 128–132.

Schaie, K. W. Quasi-experimental research designs in the psychology of aging. In J. E. Birren and K. W. Schaie (Eds.), *Handbook of the psychology of aging.* New York: Van Nostrand Reinhold, 1977.

Schaie, K. W. The primary mental abilities in adulthood: An exploration in the development of psychometric intelligence. In P. B. Baltes and O. G. Brim, Jr. (Eds.), *Life-span development and behavior* (Vol. 2). New York: Academic Press, 1979.

Schaie, K. W. The hazards of cognitive aging. *The Gerontologist*, 1989, *29*, 484–493.

Schaie, K. W. The Seattle longitudinal study: A 21-year exploration of psychometric intelligence in adulthood. In K. W. Schaie (Ed.), *Longitudinal studies of adult psychological development*. New York: Guilford Press, 1983.

Schaie, K. W., and Hertzog, C. Toward a comprehensive model of adult intellectual development: Contributions of the Seattle longitudinal study. In R. J. Sternberg (Ed.), *Advances in human intelligence* (Vol. 3). Hillsdale, N.J.: Erlbaum, 1986.

Schaie, K. W., and Labouvie-Vief, G. V. Generational versus ontogenetic components of change in adult cognitive behavior: A fourteen-year cross-sequential study. *Developmental Psychology*, 1974, *10*, 305–320.

Schonfield, D., and Stones, M. J. Remembering and aging. In J. F. Kihlstrom and F. J. Evans (Eds.), *Functional disorders of memory*. Hillsdale, N.J.: Erlbaum, 1979.

Sharps, M. J., and Gollin, E. S. Aging and free recall for objects located in space. *Journals of Gerontology*, 1988, *43*, P8–P11.

Siegler, I. C. The terminal drop hypothesis: Fact or artifact. *Experimental Aging Research*, 1975, *1*, 169–185.

Siegler, I. C. Psychological aspects of the Duke longitudinal studies. In K. W. Schaie (Ed.), *Longitudinal studies of adult psychological development*. New York: Guilford Press, 1983.

Simonton, D. K. Age ad outstanding achievement; What do we know after a century of research? *Psychological Bulletin*, 1988, *104*, 215–267.

Simonton, D. K. The swan-song phenomenon: Last works effects for 172 classical composers. *Psychology & Aging*, 1989, *4*, 42–47.

Smith, A. D. Aging and the total presentation time hypothesis. *Developmental Psychology*, 1976, *12*, 87–88.

Smith, A. D. Adult age differences in cued recall. *Developmental Psychology*, 1977, *13*, 326–331.

Spearman, C. *The abilities of man: Their nature and measurement*. New York: Macmillan, 1927.

Squire, L. R. Remote memory as affected by aging. *Neuropsychologia*, 1974, *12*, 429–435.

Storandt, M. Speed and coding effects in relation to age and ability level. *Developmental Psychology*, 1976, *12*, 177–178.

Thurstone, L. L., and Thurstone, T. G. *Factorial studies of intelligence*. Chicago: University of Chicago Press, 1941.

Thurstone, L. L., and Thurstone, T. G. *SRA primary mental abilities* (3d ed.). Chicago: Science Research Associates, 1958.

Treat, N. J., and Reese, H. W. Age, pacing, and imagery in paired-associate learning. *Developmental Psychology*, 1976, *12*, 119–124.

Warrington, E. K., and Saunders, H. I. The fate of old memories. *Quarterly Journal of Experimental Psychology*, 1971, *23*, 432–442.

Welford, A. T. *Skill and age: An experimental approach*. London: Oxford University Press, 1951.

White, N., and Cunningham, W. R. Is terminal drop pervasive or specific? *Journals of Gerontology*, 1988, *43*, P141–P144.

Wilkie, F., and Eisdorfer, C. Intelligence and blood pressure of the aged. *Science*, 1971, *172*, 959–962.

Willis, S. L., and Schaie, K. W. Training the elderly on the ability factors of spatial orientation and inductive reasoning. *Psychology and Aging*, 1986, *2*, 239–247.

Willis, S. L., and Schaie, K. W. Gender differences in spatial ability in old age: Longitudinal and intervention findings. *Sex Roles*, 1988, *18*, 189–203.

Winograd, E., Smith, A. D., and Simon, E. W. Aging and the picture superiority effect in recall. *Journal of Gerontology*, 1982, *37*, 70–75.

# CHAPTER 9

# PERSONALITY AND SOCIAL ADAPTATION IN OLD AGE

We have all had the experience of watching different people respond to the same event in different ways. For example, you probably know some students who are extremely anxious about test-taking while others are calm, and some students who express their opinions strongly and confidently while others rarely speak in class at all. All of these characteristics are part of an individual's personality.

Personality may be defined as a unique pattern of innate and learned traits that influence the manner in which each person responds and interacts with the environment. An individual may be described in terms of several personality traits, such as passive or aggressive, introverted or extroverted, independent or dependent. Personality may be evaluated with regard to particular standards of behavior; for example, an individual may be described as adapted or maladapted, adjusted or maladjusted. Personality characteristics affect people's interactions with their environments. This chapter examines changes in personality that influence these interactions.

The chapter reviews the research on personality and discusses how changes with aging influence interactions with the environment. Theories of personality that have considered age-related changes are examined. The manner in which personality characteristics may change or remain stable are discussed. The following questions are considered: Are personality characteristics both innate and capable of developing throughout life? To what extent do an individual's interactions with the environment change his or her personality or reveal the individual's "true self" that may have been concealed because of social pressures to conform to particular norms? The ways in which self-concept and self-esteem are affected by these normal changes in personality with aging are also reviewed.

Personality styles influence how we cope with and adapt to the changes we experience as we age. The process of aging involves numerous stressful life experiences. How an older person responds to these experiences in an attempt to alleviate such stress has an influence on that individual's long-term well-being. This chapter also examines the life events that occur more frequently in old age, and how older people have been found to cope with them.

Finally, characteristics of people who have aged successfully or have been able to adapt readily to the numerous physiological and social changes brought about by aging are examined.

# INNATE AND ENVIRONMENTAL FACTORS

For many generations, psychologists have considered the issue of nature versus nurture; that is, whether we are born with specific personality traits or whether the environment in which we are raised plus our experiences determine our personality. Studies of twins reared apart and newborn babies suggest that some traits are in fact innate. In spite of differences in the environment in which each twin is raised, they often display behavioral tendencies that are more similar to each other than to siblings raised in the same environment. Furthermore, anyone who has seen a nursery full of infants has seen individual differences in dependency, passivity, and other traits that cannot be attributed solely to environmental influences. Still, personality is shaped by experiences throughout a person's life; in this sense, personality development is mediated by the environment.

The person-environment congruence model presented in this book's Introduction suggests that our behavior is influenced and modified by the environment, and that we shape the environment around us. This relationship was first proposed by Lewin (1935): $B = f(P,E)$; that is, behavior is a function of the person and his or her environment. An individual's behavior is often quite different from one situation to another, and depends both on the social norms and expectations of each situation and on that person's needs and motives. Unfortunately, few researchers have examined this reciprocal relationship in adult development.

# PERSONALITY DEVELOPMENT IN ADULTHOOD

## Erikson's Psychosocial Model

Most theories of personality have emphasized the developmental *stages* of personality and imply that the social environment influences development. As we focus on stages of adult development, however, it is important to avoid the image of rigid, immutable stages and transitions that are inevitable, with no room for individual differences (Neugarten, 1985; Troll, 1985). In fact, people *do* make choices regarding their specific responses to common life changes. This results in numerous expressions of behavior under similar life experiences such as adolescence, parenting, retirement, and even the management of chronic diseases. There has been disagreement about whether this development continues through adulthood. Sigmund Freud's focus on psychosexual stages of development through adolescence has had a major influence on developmental psychology. In most of his writings, Freud suggests that personality achieves stability by adolescence. Accordingly, adult behavior is a reflection of unconscious motives and unsuccessful resolution of early childhood stages. Some personality theorists have agreed that personality traits remain stable after these years (see Worchel and Byrne, 1964).

In contrast, Erik Erikson, who was trained in psychoanalytic theory, moved away from this approach and focused on psychosocial development throughout the life cycle. According to his model (Erikson, 1963, 1968, 1982; 1986), the individual undergoes eight stages of development of the ego. Three of these are beyond adolescence, with the final stage occurring in mature adulthood. At each stage the individual experiences a major task to be accomplished and a conflict; the conflicts of each stage of development are the foundations of successive stages. Depending on the outcome of the crisis associated with a particular stage, the individual proceeds to the next stage of development in alternative ways.

Erikson also emphasized the interactions between genetics and the environment in determining personality development. His concept of the *epigenetic principle* assumed an innate plan of development in which people proceed through stages as they become cognitively and emotionally more capable of interacting within a wider social radius (Erikson, 1963).

As shown in Table 9–1, the individual in the last stage of life is confronted with the task of ego integrity versus despair. According to Erikson, the individual at this stage accepts the inevitability of mortality, achieves wisdom and perspective, or despairs because he or she has not come to grips with death and lacks ego integrity. A major task associated with this last stage is to integrate the experiences of earlier stages and to realize that one's life has had meaning, whether or not it was "successful" in a socially defined sense. Older people who achieve ego integrity feel a sense of connectedness with younger generations, and need to share their experiences and wisdom with them. This may take the form of face-to-face interactions with younger people, counseling, sponsoring an individual or group of younger people, or writing memoirs or letters. This latter has been described as *life review,* and has been found to be a useful mode of therapy with older adults, as we will discuss in Chapter 11.

Life satisfaction, or the feeling that life is worth living, may be achieved through these tasks of adopting a wider historical perspective upon one's life, accepting one's mortality, sharing experiences with the young, and leaving a legacy to future generations.[*] Erikson's theory provides

---

[*]Researchers have found that health, marital, and financial status, as well as the availability of a confidant, are also significant predictors of life satisfaction.

## Table 9–1   Erikson's Psychosocial Stages

| | STAGE | GOAL |
|---|---|---|
| I | Basic trust vs. mistrust | To establish basic trust in the world through trust in the parent. |
| II | Autonomy vs. shame and doubt | To establish a sense of autonomy and self as distinct from the parent; to establish self-control vs. doubt in one's abilities. |
| III | Initiative vs. guilt | To establish a sense of initiative within parental limits without feeling guilty about emotional needs. |
| IV | Industry vs. inferiority | To establish a sense of industry within the school setting; to learn necessary skills without feelings of inferiority or fear of failure. |
| V | Ego identity vs. role diffusion | To establish identity, self-concept, and role within the larger community, without confusion about the self and about social roles. |
| VI | Intimacy vs. isolation | To establish intimacy and affiliation with one or more others, without fearing loss of identity in the process that may result in isolation. |
| VII | Generativity vs. stagnation | To establish a sense of care and concern for the well-being of future generations; to look toward the future and not stagnate in the past. |
| VIII | Ego integrity vs. despair | To establish a sense of meaning in one's life, rather than feeling despair or bitterness that life was wasted; to accept oneself and one's life without despair. |

a framework for studying personality in late life because it suggests that personality is dynamic throughout the life cycle. Indeed, this theory fits the person-environment model presented in the Introduction; we interact with a variety of other people in different settings, and our personality is affected accordingly.

## Jung's Psychoanalytic Perspective

Carl Jung's model of personality also assumes changes throughout life, as expressed in the following statement from one of his early writings:

> We cannot live the afternoon of life according to the program of life's morning, for what was great in morning will be little at evening, and what in the morning was true will at evening have become a lie (1933, p. 108).

The model emphasizes stages in the development of consciousness and the ego, from the narrow focus of the child to the other-worldliness of the older person. But the development of personality need not always imply maturation and increased wisdom. As Jung (1933) suggests, "the wine of youth does not always clear with advancing years; oftentimes it grows turbid" (p. 105).

Like Erikson, Jung examined the individual's confrontation with death in the last stage of life. He suggested that life for the aging person must naturally contract, that the individual in this stage must find meaning in inner exploration and in an afterlife. In contrast to the young, older persons have "a duty and a necessity to devote serious attention to (themselves). After having lavished its light upon the world, the sun withdraws its rays in order to illuminate itself" (Jung, 1933, p. 109). Jung also focused on changes in archetypes with age. That is, according to Jung, all humans have both a feminine and a masculine side. An archetype is the feminine side of a man's personality (the anima) and the masculine side of a woman's personality (the animus). Both biological and social conditioning have produced these archetypes (Jung, 1959). As they age, peo-

High life satisfaction is apparent in an older person with ego integrity.

ple begin to adopt psychological traits more commonly associated with the opposite sex. For example, older men may show more signs of passivity while women may become more assertive as they age, a change that is referred to throughout this text in discussions of gender differences.

## Experimental Testing of These Perspectives

In testing the validity of these theories, subsequent research has contributed to our understanding of personality development in late adulthood. Many of these studies are cross-sectional; that is, they derive information on age differences, not age changes. There are notable exceptions to this approach, including the Baltimore Longitudinal Study (described in Chapter 2) and the Kansas City Studies (described in Chapter 4 and in the following section), which have examined changes in physiological, cognitive, and personality functions in the same individuals over a period of several years. Research by Costa and McCrae (1986; 1988) in the Baltimore Longitudinal Study is related to Erikson's work in that it has emphasized changes in personal *adjustment*, but not in traits, with age. Costa, McCrae, and Norris (1981) tested Erikson's formulation of the last stage of psychosocial development and noted that personal adjustment should be defined in old age as "subjective well-being," or individuals' reports that they are satisfied with their life's accomplishments and have high morale. However, Costa and McCrae found no evidence for changes in basic personality traits with age, specifically in the five dimensions they examined as the primary components of personality: neuroticism, extroversion, openness to experience, agreeableness, and conscientiousness. Other studies support the lifelong stability, and even the possible heritability of some personality traits. A study of middle-aged identical and fraternal twins in Sweden found high correlations between twins, whether they were reared together or apart, in five traits: emotionality, activity, sociability, extroversion, and neuroticism (Plomin et al., 1988; Pederson et al., 1988). Some personality dimensions, such as extroversion, are correlated with subjective well-being in old age (McCrae and Costa, 1987).

Researchers who have systematically examined personality in middle and old age have found support for Jung's observations regarding decreased sex-typed behavior in old age. David Gutmann (1974a, b; 1980), who has studied personality across the life span in diverse cultures from a psychoanalytic perspective, has found a shift from active mastery to passive mastery as men age. In contrast, women appear to move from passive to active mastery. That is, in most cultures examined by Gutmann, young adult males tend to be more achievement-oriented and concerned with controlling their environments, whereas young adult women tend to be more affiliative and expressive. Gutmann found greater expressiveness, nurturance, and need for affiliation among older males than in younger men, whereas older women tended to be more instrumental and to express more achievement-oriented responses than young women. Gutmann's research also suggests that people may

vary with age in their use of magical mastery styles (maladaptive ego responses to stressful situations). He found a smaller proportion of middle-aged persons with this ego style than with active or passive mastery styles. However, magical mastery styles were more frequently observed in men and women beyond age 60. A later analysis of ego styles in other cultures by Gutmann (1977) suggests that this shift toward magical mastery may be more likely to take place among men than women.

## The Kansas City Studies

Longitudinal research by Neugarten and her associates (1968) among community-dwelling older people in Kansas City is consistent with Gutmann's findings and has contributed to our understanding of many other age-related changes in personality and coping. Neugarten found that older men became more accepting of their affiliative, nurturant, and sensual side, while women learned to display the egocentric and aggressive impulses that they had always possessed but had not displayed during their younger years. Neugarten, similar to Jung, has suggested that these characteristics always exist in both sexes, but social pressure and societal values encourage the expression of more sex-typed traits in youth.

The Kansas City studies represented the first major attempt to examine personality longitudinally and provided the empirical basis for activity and differentiation theories described in Chapter 4. In this landmark study of adaptation to aging, Neugarten and her associates interviewed 700 residents of Kansas City in the 1950s who were aged 40 to 70, living independently in the community, and relatively healthy; this was then followed with a six-year longitudinal study of 300 persons aged 50 to 90. They found changes in such personality characteristics as nurturance, introversion, and aggressiveness in the later years. Contrary to popular stereotypes, aging was also associated with greater differences (individuation) among individuals; as the people aged, they developed more unique styles of interaction. Neugarten and colleagues (1968) suggested that people do not resemble each other more in old age, but in fact become more differentiated because they grow less concerned about societal expectations.

Other age-related changes observed in the Kansas City studies included shifts toward greater cautiousness and interiority; that is, a preoccupation with one's inner life and less extroversion. The movement toward interiority does *not* mean, however, that older persons become more religious, as noted in our discussion of cross-sectional research in Chapter 2. There is very little research evidence that we become more religious as we age. It may be that the current cohort of people over age 70 have always been more religious than younger cohorts (see Chapter 15).

The Kansas City researchers also observed decreased impulsiveness and a movement toward using more sophisticated ego defense mechanisms with age. For example, older persons tended to use less denial and more sublimation. Attitudes toward the world were also likely to change with age, but these were found to relate closely to personal experiences. For instance, people do not necessarily become more conservative as they age. Based on generational (cohort) differences and personal experiences, some persons become more liberal in their social perspective during the later years. Others have been more conservative than younger cohorts throughout their lives. These age-related changes in impulsiveness, types of defense mechanisms used, and attitudes have been supported in studies of personality by researchers examining a diverse variety of cultural and ethnic groups (Thomae, 1980; Shanan, 1978).

Neugarten and colleagues (1968) categorized the personalities that were observed in the Kansas City studies into four major types:

1. *The Integrated Type.* These are self-actualized older people who are most satisfied with their lives, and who have complex inner lives and competent egos. They are flexible, real-

istic, and possess high self-esteem. These persons have come to grips with their mortality and accept death as inevitable. Some integrated elders may have voluntarily "disengaged" from society and are now concerned about their inner lives. Others, similar to Mr. Wallace in the introductory vignette, are "focused" retirees, or "reorganizers," who shift their energy and interest in retirement to other activities. The first of these may be illustrated by a teacher who retires at age 60, is not involved in many professional or social activities, but is happy with a quiet retirement. The focused retiree may be illustrated by another teacher who retires at age 65, but continues to volunteer for several community organizations and legislative efforts of the local Retired Teachers' Association. Both are happy with their lives because they have chosen to spend their retirement years in a particular style consistent with their needs. Measures of life satisfaction in this group in the Kansas City studies revealed high satisfaction regardless of activity levels.

2. *The Armored-Defensive Type.* These are individuals who are still ambitious and aggressive. Some appear to be fighting an internal battle against aging and death. Such persons often are not introspective and lack insight into their actions. Usually this is not a very successful adaptation to old age but rather expressed in a "holding-on" pattern (i.e., forcing themselves to remain active for fear of becoming dependent). Another expression of this style is the constricted personality, or individuals who are preoccupied with the losses of aging, thereby shutting out new experiences. They often feel angry and resentful toward others. Older persons who refuse to stop working despite poor health and/or problems with psychomotor and intellectual functioning illustrate these aspects of the armored-defensive type.

3. *The Passive-Dependent Type.* Older persons in this category may achieve moderate to high life satisfaction if their dependency needs are met. Included are individuals who relegate all their important tasks to others, let others take care of them, and participate in very few social

activities. Neugarten has labeled such persons the "succorance seeking type." This category includes older persons who are apathetic, withdrawn, and isolated (the "rocking chair" type). Unlike the constricted-defensive individuals described previously, this personality type is generally not bitter or resentful toward the rest of the world. Mrs. Johnson in the introductory vignette has some of these characteristics.

4. *The Disorganized (or Unintegrated) Type.* Older persons who fit into this personality category often have a gross deterioration in their cognitive and emotional functions as a result of adult-onset dementia or a personality disorder that has existed since youth (as illustrated by Mr. Adams in the introductory vignette). These individuals generally have poor coping abilities, are only marginally adjusted to their environment, and express little satisfaction with their lives. Contrary to many stereotypes about aging, this group represents a minority of all older persons.

The personality types just described do not encompass all older persons. Many possess characteristics of more than one category; others do not fit into any of the types. Yet these categories are effective in describing widely varying ways in which people age and the effects of poor adaptation. Other researchers have described similar personality types, even in widely divergent cultures (Thomae, 1980; Gaber, 1983; Shanan and Jacobowitz, 1982).

## Dialectical Models of Adult Personality

A more recent model of adult personality development has been proposed by Levinson (1977, 1986) and his colleagues (Levinson et al., 1978). This model is based on secondary analyses of American men described in published biographies and in interviews with working-class men. It has also been found to apply equally well to women (Roberts and Newton, 1987). In contrast to Erikson, who focused on stages of ego development, Levinson and colleagues have examined developmental stages in terms of life structures,

or the underlying characteristics of a person's life at a particular period of time. Of all stage theories of adult development, this model is the most explicit in linking each stage with a specific range of chronological age.

These life structures include sociocultural features (e.g., social class, ethnic group membership, and occupation), one's personal self (e.g., conflicts, fantasies, and anxieties), and participation in society (e.g., interaction between the self and society). The choices that individuals make in this participation or interaction with the outside world determine what structure their lives will take. Thus, for example, a man who has anxieties about his role in society and his identity as a male will select a different occupation and intimate relationships than one who has no such ego conflicts. Each period in the life structure (defined as "eras" by Levinson) represents developmental stages. Levinson defines four eras, each one lasting about 20 years. These are separated by *transitions* of about five years each which generally occur as the individual perceives changes in the self, or as external events such as childbirth and retirement create new demands on one's relationships with others. (See Table 9–2.)

Levinson's model represents an example of a dialectical approach to personality development; it proposes that change occurs because of interactions between a dynamic person (one who is biologically *and* psychologically changing) and a dynamic environment. To the extent that an individual is sensitive to the changing self, he or she can respond to changing environmental or societal conditions by altering something within the self or by modifying some expectations from the environment. This process thereby reestablishes equilibrium with the environment. In previous chapters, we have seen how some normal, age-related changes in physiological functions can slow down older people and affect their activities of daily living. Older persons who deny these biological and physiological changes are more likely to experience problems in modifying their lifestyles and moving into a different developmental phase.

**TABLE 9–2  Levinson's "Seasons" of Life**

Era I  Preadulthood (Age 0–22)
(An era when the family provides protection, socialization, and support of personal growth)
Early Adult Transition (Age 17–22)[*]

Era II  Early Adulthood (Age 17–45)
(An era of peak biological functioning, development of adult identity)
Entering the adult world, entry life structure for early adulthood.
Age 30 transition[*]
Settling down, culminating life structure for early adulthood.
Mid-life transition (Age 40–45)[*]

Era III  Middle Adulthood (Age 40–65)
(Goals become more other–oriented, compassionate roles, mentor roles assumed; peak effectiveness as a leader)
Entering life structure for middle adulthood
Age 50 transition[*]
Culmination of middle adulthood
Late adulthood Transition (Age 60–65)[*]

Era IV  Late Adulthood (Age 60+)
(An era when declining capacities are recognized, anxieties about aging, loss of power and status begin)
Acceptance of death's inevitability

[*]Indicates major transitions to a new developmental era.

SOURCE: D. Levinson, C. M. Darrow, E. B. Klein, M. H. Levinson, and B. McKee, *The seasons of a man's life* (New York: Alfred A. Knopf, 1978). Reprinted with permission of the author and publisher.

The first researcher to emphasize the importance of the dialectical perspective for adult development was Klaus Riegel (1976). Riegel viewed personality development as a necessary consequence of the conflicts that arise between changing personal needs and abilities and the demands of the social environment. Indeed, growth is defined by Riegel as the resolution of such conflicts and movement to the next stage of greater fit. This approach is quite similar to the person-environment model first presented in the

Introduction to this book. Proponents of this model (Lawton and Nahemow, 1973; Kahana, 1975; Kahana, Liang, and Felton, 1980) argue for the continuing need to maintain congruence between changing personal competence and the demands of the physical and social environment. The dialectical approach to personality development has received little research attention (except from an environmental design perspective, as we will see in Chapter 13), compared to other theories described earlier.

## Kohlberg's Model of Moral Development

In contrast to models of personality development that focus on growth of the ego across the life span, the work of Lawrence Kohlberg (1969, 1973, 1987) and his colleagues (Snarey, Reimer, and Kohlberg, 1985) emphasizes the development of the conscience, or superego, through the acquisition of moral values. By presenting hypothetical moral dilemmas to people and asking them to describe how they would resolve the problem and why, Kohlberg observed six stages of moral development that are different from the others. The first stage is defined by obedience to authority, regardless of the circumstances (e.g., a starving person who has no money and steals food would be perceived as guilty of disobeying the law by the respondent in this stage of moral development). In the second stage, respondents perceive a need for exchange and reciprocity; for example, they believe that one can obtain favors from others if one initiates a favor *for* others. The third stage, described by Kohlberg (1969) as the "good boy orientation," is defined by a need to meet others' expectations (e.g., completing a job because that is what the teacher or employer expects). Those in the fourth stage focus on the need to maintain social order and to respect authority, and those in the fifth stage expand beyond this to the need to involve all members of society in the maintenance of social order. An individual in this stage recognizes that there must be an arbitrary starting point for rules and expectations of people's behavior, and that one must avoid violating others' contractual or legal rights.

According to Kohlberg, few people reach the sixth stage, which is characterized by a belief in universal logic and ethical principles (e.g., the use of civil disobedience in order to reverse unjust social practices such as discrimination). People at this stage of moral development are directed by their conscience and by the trust and respect of others. Martin Luther King and South African President Nelson Mandela are individuals who have achieved this ultimate stage of moral development.

Unlike other theories of personality development, Kohlberg's approach is less chronologically oriented. That is, some middle-aged and older people may remain in stage two or three (such as an older person who feels he must seek revenge anytime he is mistreated), whereas a few young persons achieve stage four or five of moral development (such as youths who risk their freedom by protesting against nuclear warfare and injustice). Furthermore, Kohlberg's theory does not consider the possibility that some people may be in different stages of moral development simultaneously; for example, an individual may believe that stealing should be punished no matter what (stage one), yet at the same time claim that all people in a democratic society should play a role in devising a social order (stage five). Many moral values held by people may also be contradictory, suggesting that a smooth progression through stages should not be expected in moral development, unlike the development of cognitive abilities and the ego.

## SELF-CONCEPT AND SELF-ESTEEM

A major adjustment required in old age is the ability to redefine one's self-concept or one's image of the self as social roles shift and as new roles are assumed. For example, how does a retired teacher identify himself or herself upon giving up the work that has been that individual's central focus for the past 40 to 50 years? How

does a woman whose self-concept is closely associated with her role as a wife express her identity after her husband dies?

As noted in Chapter 4, many older persons continue to identify with the role that they have lost (think of those who continue to introduce themselves as "teacher" or "doctor" long after retiring from those careers). Others experience role confusion, particularly in the early stages, when cues from other people are inconsistent with an individual's self-concept. Still others may undergo a period of depression and major readjustment to the changes associated with role loss. These persons generally have not established independent self-concepts. To the extent that a person's self-concept is defined independently of particular social roles, one adapts more readily to the role losses that may accompany old age.

In a study of self-concept across the life span, 4,540 persons aged 9 to 89 were measured on four dimensions: achievement-leadership, congeniality-sociability, adjustment, and masculinity-femininity (Monge, 1975). Both age and sex differences emerged on all four components of self-concept. Women in the oldest group (65–89) tended to report more achievement-leadership than women of any other age, except those aged 20 to 34. No significant differences emerged among men of various age groups. Both older men and women had the highest scores on the congeniality-sociability dimension. Adjustment scores remained high in the oldest group. Consistent with Jung's model of adult personality development and the findings of the Kansas City studies, there was a significant decline in self-reported masculinity among men beyond age 50, with a corresponding increase in self-definitions of masculinity among women in midlife.

For an older person whose self-concept is based on social roles and others' expectations, role losses have a particularly significant impact on that individual's self-esteem—that is, evaluation or feeling about his or her identity relative to some ideal or standard. *Self-esteem* is based on an emotional assessment of the self, whereas *self-concept* is the cognitive definition of one's identity. The affective quality of self-esteem makes it more dynamic and more easily influenced by such external forces as retirement, widowhood, health status, and reinforcements (both positive and negative) from others (e.g., respect, deference, or ostracism). As a result, alterations in social roles and the loss of status that accompanies some of these changes often have a negative impact on an older person's self-esteem. Think, for example, of an older person whose "ideal self" is as an independent individual. If this person is forced to rely on others for care because of a major debilitating illness such as a stroke or dementia, he or she is unwittingly robbed of this ideal, and self-esteem may suffer.

An individual who experiences multiple role losses must not only adapt to the lifestyle changes associated with aging (e.g., financial insecurity or shrinking social networks), but must also integrate the new roles with his or her "ideal self" or learn to modify this definition of "ideal." Older persons who are experiencing major physical and cognitive disabilities simultaneously with role losses, or worse yet, whose role losses are precipitated by an illness (e.g., early retirement due to stroke or institutionalization because of Alzheimer's disease), must cope with multiple problems at a time in their lives when they have the fewest resources to resolve them successfully. Depression is not an uncommon reaction in these cases (see Chapter 11). Other older persons may not experience such major emotional upheavals; nevertheless, their self-esteem may be affected. Some studies have shown a generalized decrease in self-esteem from age 50 to 80, although others have found considerable variability in patterns of self-esteem. Stressful life events and severe hearing loss can impair self-esteem among older people (Chen, 1994, Tran, Wright, and Chatters, 1991). Older people who are socially isolated and have significant physical disabilities have been found to have the poorest self-esteem (Pinquart, 1991).

The following personality factors have been suggested as important to maintaining self-esteem in the later years (Morgan, 1979):

1. Reinterpretation of the meaning of self, such that an individual's self-concept and self-worth are independent of any roles he or she has played ("I am a unique individual" rather than "I am a doctor/teacher/wife"). To the extent that an older person can focus more on internal realities such as personality characteristics, skills, and abilities, and less on external sources of reinforcement, the ego is strengthened and free of environmental influences.

2. Acceptance of the aging process, its limitations, and possibilities. That is, individuals who realize that they have less energy and respond more slowly than in the past, but that they can still participate in life, will adapt more readily to the social and health losses of old age. It is critical to achieve this level of awareness without giving up on life, as some older persons do. Unfortunately, socialization into old age is not as easy as socialization into other stages, because most people have few appropriate role models that they can emulate (Rosow, 1974). As a result, environmental feedback in the form of television advertising and negative remarks of family and friends may reinforce an individual's internal slowing process and suggest that the older person must withdraw. It therefore appears important for the media and society to provide role models of older people who have adapted successfully to their aging, and how they have done so. (All too often, however, the images of "successful" aging are persons who have unusual athletic, intellectual, or artistic powers, or who have achieved extreme longevity in isolated societies. The typical older person often cannot identify with such people; hence, these "exceptional" people are not used by most individuals as role models of how *they* can adapt to old age.)

3. Reevaluation of one's goals and expectations throughout life. Too often people establish life goals at an early age and can be constantly disappointed as circumstances change. The ability to respond to internal and external pressures by modifying life goals appropriately reflects flexibility and harmony with one's environment. An older person who has these skills is most

Senior centers provide opportunities to try new activities and enhance self-esteem.

likely to adapt successfully to the changes associated with aging.

4. The ability to look back objectively on one's past and to review one's failures and successes. *Life review,* as its name implies, entails an objective review and evaluation of one's life. The individual takes an historical perspective of past experiences and how these have influenced subsequent personality development, behavior, and interpersonal relationships. An older person who has, or who can develop, this ability can call upon coping strategies that have been most effective in the past and adapt them to changed circumstances. We will see in Chapter 11 how life review or reminiscence therapy has been used successfully as a form of psychotherapy with depressed and chronically ill older adults.

## STRESS, COPING, AND ADAPTATION

The process of aging entails numerous life changes, as noted in this and previous chapters. These changes, both positive and negative, place demands on the aging person's abilities to cope with and adapt to new life situations. Together with health and cognitive functioning, personality characteristics influence coping responses.

Self-concept and self-esteem are two important elements that play a role in coping styles, and may help explain why some older people adjust readily to major life changes, while others have difficulty with such transitions. Indeed, self-esteem, health, and cognitive skills all contribute to an individual's sense of competence. Major life events and situations represent environmental stressors that place demands on an individual's competence. These and other factors that influence adaptation in old age are discussed in this section.

## Some Useful Definitions

Before examining coping and adaptation in old age, it is important to clarify and define some key concepts. The concept of *life events* or *life experiences* forms the basis for this section. These terms refer to internal or external stimuli that cause some change in an individual's daily life. They may be positive or negative, gains or losses, discrete or continuous. Examples of internally created events include changes in eating or sleeping habits and the effects of a chronic disease such as arthritis or diabetes. Externally initiated events might include starting a new job, losing one's job, or retirement.

Improvement in one's own health or in a family member's health are examples of positive life events, whereas deteriorating health and death are negative events. Life experiences that represent gains include the birth of a grandchild or promotions that lead to increased responsibility and a higher salary. Life events that are losses include the death of a family member or friend, the loss of a spouse through divorce or death, or the loss of the driver role because of declining vision. Some life experiences may have both positive *and* negative aspects. For example, older workers may view their pending retirement with great joy and make numerous plans for the post-retirement years; however, there are some negative consequences as well, including reduced income, unstructured time, and loss of the worker role. Other events with both positive and negative aspects are purchasing a new home, taking a vacation, and even attending a long-awaited family reunion.

One of the problems in assessing the impact of life events is variability in duration. Some events are discrete, such as a vacation or an accident. Others last for long periods, with no distinctive starting and end points. These include changes in eating and sleeping patterns and in health status. Still other events may be discrete but may have long-term antecedents or consequences. Many events experienced by older persons typically have this feature, including retirement, death of spouse, and "the empty nest." Since stress produced by such events is generally ongoing, an individual experiencing them must cope with their diverse aspects over a period of time.

Another distinction to be made is that between *on-time* and *off-time* events (Neugarten, 1979, 1989). This concept distinguishes life experiences that a person can anticipate because of one's stage in the life cycle (on-time) from those that are unexpected at a given stage (off-time). Other researchers have used the terms *normative* and *non-normative* events, suggesting that an individual anticipates some life experiences because they are the norm for most people of a given age (Pearlin, 1975; Pearlin and Lieberman, 1979). Thus, for example, a man married to a 75-year-old woman is more likely to expect the death of his wife than is the husband of a 35-year-old woman. A 50-year-old woman is more likely than a 35-year-old to anticipate the onset of menopause and its accompanying physiological and psychological changes. As we will see later in this chapter, researchers have found differences in how people respond to on-time and off-time events.

The concept of stress is also important for this chapter. Since Selye's (1946) introduction of this term, many researchers have explored the antecedents, components, and consequences of stress. One problem in understanding this concept has been the diverse definitions given for it. Selye's original definition of stress (which he also

calls the "general adaptation syndrome") is the "nonspecific response of the body to any demand made upon it," the goal of which is to prepare the organism for "fight or flight" (Selye, 1946). Fight or flight reactions are the simplest means by which organisms respond to stressful situations. Later in this chapter, we review more complex coping responses used by humans who are experiencing stress. In his early research with rats, Selye found that animals subjected to constant negative external stimuli (e.g., crowding or frustration in finding food) were more likely to develop enlarged adrenal glands and to show physical signs of aging earlier than animals who were not subjected to unpleasant stimuli. In fact, Selye (1970) defined aging as the sum of stresses experienced across one's lifetime.

One recurring problem with the definition of stress is that it has been used to describe both a response (as in Selye's description of perceived tension, enlarged adrenal glands, heightened blood pressure) and a stimulus (labeling a particular event as a stress). In this chapter, the term *stressor* is used to identify stimuli that cause stress or a state of imbalance in the organism, and result in physiological or psychological demands on the person to adapt or escape from the situation (i.e., fight or flight). Such stimuli may also be described as *stressful*.

It is important to note that not everyone perceives the same events to be stressful. Lazarus and DeLongis (1983) have introduced the concept of *cognitive appraisal*—the way in which a person perceives the significance of an encounter for his or her well-being. Cognitive appraisal serves to minimize or magnify the importance or stressfulness of an event by attaching some meaning to it. If a situation is construed as benign or irrelevant by an individual, it does not elicit coping responses. On the other hand, if a person appraises a situation as challenging, harmful, or threatening, it becomes a stressor, and calls upon the individual's adaptation responses.

It is useful to distinguish between positive and negative stressors such as life events. The concept of cognitive appraisal suggests that a person who perceives a particular situation as a challenge (i.e., a positive stressor) copes differently with it than one who views it as a threat (i.e., a negative stressor). For example, a student who views a final exam as a challenge will prepare for it differently than one who feels threatened by it. The first student will anticipate it as a positive and exciting situation, whereas the second may avoid thinking about, preparing for, or even taking the exam. On the other hand, a student who perceives the exam as irrelevant may do poorly because the situation has not generated enough of a stress response to induce him or her to prepare for or cope with it.

Older people experience similar reactions. An older woman who moves voluntarily to a retirement home may view it as an exciting and much-needed change in her lifestyle, or she may resent the change as too demanding and disruptive. In the former case, she will adapt more readily and will experience less negative stress than in the latter. On the other hand, if this person views the move as totally benign and does not expect it to place any demands on her, she will probably be unpleasantly surprised by the level of stress that she eventually encounters, no matter how minimal.

A certain level of stress is needed in order to stimulate us to perform. Moderate levels of stress are indeed necessary, but too much or too little stress appears to be harmful to emotional and physical well-being. Let us now examine what happens to our stress responses as we age.

## Aging and Life Events

There has been much discussion among researchers about the nature of life events in the later years, the older person's ability to cope with them, and whether old age is associated with more or fewer life events than youth. Admittedly, many significant life events tend to occur more often in old age, such as widowhood, retirement, and relocation to a nursing home. Numerous other events generally take place in people's lives during youth and middle age. As noted earlier,

many of these represent role gains or replacement, such as the role of student, voter, homeowner, marital partner, and worker. Both the nature of such roles and the novelty associated with assuming a social role for the first time result in major changes in an individual's daily functioning and demand adaptation to the new situation. Table 9–3, adapted from the work of Pastalan (1977), illustrates the ages when many social roles are generally gained or lost. Note that many social roles are rarely lost (e.g., the voter role, the parent role), and some roles, especially those associated with aging, are extensions of others (e.g., becoming a grandparent or parent-

**TABLE 9–3  Continuum of Role Gains and Losses**

| AGE | EVENT |
| --- | --- |
| 0 | Student +[*] |
| 10 | Consumer + |
| | Driver + |
| | Adult + |
| 20 | Voter + |
| | Worker + |
| | Marital partner + |
| 30 | Parent + |
| | Home owner + |
| 40 | Auditory decline −[*] |
| | Empty nest − |
| 50 | Visual decline − |
| | Grandparent + |
| 60 | Widowhood − |
| | Tactile decline − |
| | Taste decline − |
| | Retirement − |
| 70 | Olfactory decline − |
| | Motor function − |
| 80 | Give up driving − |
| | Health − |
| | Institutionalization − |
| 90 | |

[*]+ indicates role gain;  − indicates loss.

SOURCE: Adapted from L. A. Pastalan, Designing housing environments for the elderly. *Journal of Architectural Education 31* (1977).

in-law). On the other hand, some of the role losses that may occur with aging, such as retirement, are associated with a decline in social status. Few studies have compared the relative stressfulness of role losses, role gains or replacements, and role extensions in old age, although there is extensive research on life stress among younger populations.

Thomas Holmes and his colleagues undertook the first studies of the physiological and psychological impact of increased sources and amounts of stress on humans (Holmes and Rahe, 1967; Rahe, 1972; Holmes and Masuda, 1974). They introduced the concept of life change units, a numerical score indicating the typical level of change or stress that a particular event produces in an individual's day-to-day life. Based on interviews with hundreds of people, Holmes and Rahe derived the Social Readjustment Rating Scale (SRRS). This instrument consists of 43 events, each with an associated change score. The greatest change score is 100, for death of spouse. This is the event that was used as an "anchor point" in the development of the SRRS. That is, respondents were asked to assign life change scores to all other life events, comparing each one with death of spouse, which had been preassigned a score of 100. A copy of the SRRS is presented in Table 9–4. The studies by Holmes and colleagues on young and middle-aged adults revealed that people who experienced multiple events with life change units totaling more than

**TABLE 9–4   The Social Readjustment Rating Scale**

| EVENTS | VALUE |
|---|---|
| 1.   Marriage | 50 |
| 2.   Troubles with the boss | 23 |
| 3.   Detention in jail or other institution | 63 |
| 4.   Death of spouse | 100 |
| 5.   Major change in sleeping habits (a lot more or a lot less sleep, or change in part of day when asleep) | 16 |
| 6.   Death of a close family member | 63 |
| 7.   Major change in eating habits (a lot more or a lot less food intake, or very different meal hours or surroundings) | 15 |
| 8.   Foreclosure on a mortgage or loan | 30 |
| 9.   Revision of personal habits (dress, manners, associations) | 24 |
| 10.  Death of a close friend | 37 |
| 11.  Minor violations of the law (e.g., traffic tickets, jaywalking, disturbing the peace, etc.) | 11 |
| 12.  Outstanding personal achievement | 28 |
| 13.  Pregnancy | 40 |
| 14.  Major change in the health or behavior of a family member | 44 |
| 15.  Sexual difficulties | 39 |
| 16.  In-law troubles | 29 |
| 17.  Major change in number of family get-togethers (e.g., a lot more or a lot less than usual) | 15 |
| 18.  Major change in financial state (e.g., a lot worse off or a lot better off than usual) | 38 |

*continued*

**TABLE 9–4** *Continued*

| EVENTS | VALUE |
|---|---|
| 19. Gaining a new family member (e.g., through birth, adoption, older relative moving in, etc.) | 39 |
| 20. Change in residence | 20 |
| 21. Son or daughter leaving home (e.g., marriage, attending college, etc.) | 29 |
| 22. Marital separation from mate | 65 |
| 23. Major change in church activities (e.g., a lot more or a lot less than usual) | 19 |
| 24. Marital reconciliation with mate | 45 |
| 25. Being fired from work | 47 |
| 26. Divorce | 73 |
| 27. Changing to a different line of work | 36 |
| 28. Major change in the number of arguments with spouse (e.g., either a lot more or a lot less than usual regarding childrearing, personal habits, etc.) | 35 |
| 29. Major change in responsibilities at work (e.g., promotion, demotion, lateral transfer) | 29 |
| 30. Wife beginning or ceasing work outside the home | 26 |
| 31. Major change in working hours or conditions | 20 |
| 32. Major change in usual type and/or amount of recreation | 19 |
| 33. Taking on a mortgage greater than $10,000 (e.g., purchasing a home) | 31 |
| 34. Taking on a mortgage or loan less than $10,000 (e.g., purchasing a car, TV, freezer, etc.) | 17 |
| 35. Major personal injury or illness | 53 |
| 36. Major business readjustment (e.g., merger, reorganization, bankruptcy, etc.) | 39 |
| 37. Major change in social activities (e.g., clubs, dancing, movies, visiting, etc.) | 18 |
| 38. Major change in living conditions (e.g., building a new home, remodeling, deterioration of home or neighborhood) | 25 |
| 39. Retirement from work | 45 |
| 40. Vacation | 13 |
| 41. Christmas | 12 |
| 42. Changing to a new school | 20 |
| 43. Beginning or ceasing formal schooling | 26 |

SOURCE: Reprinted with permission from *Journal of Psychosomatic Research, volume 11,* by T. H. Holmes and R. Rahe, "The Social Readjustment Rating Scale," copyright 1967, Pergamon Journals, Ltd.

200 points within a two-year period were more susceptible to physical illnesses.

## Potential Problems in Measurement

It is unclear whether these same life events produce the same level of stress in older persons as they do in younger people. As shown in Table 9–4, many of them are less likely to be experienced in old age (e.g., jail term, marriage, assuming a new mortgage, or beginning or ending school). Furthermore, the life change units assigned to some events by the young respondents in Holmes and Rahe's sample may not reflect the degree of stress actually produced by events that they have not yet experienced (e.g., death of spouse).

Eisdorfer and Wilkie (1977) discussed the need to develop appropriate methods for assessing life events in older persons. Efforts by Amster and Krauss (1974), Muhlenkamp, Gress, and Flood (1975), and Kiyak and Kahana (1975) have led to the development and testing of life event scales that are more relevant to the elderly. Whereas the first two studies eliminated many items from the SRRS that were not applicable to older persons, Kiyak and Kahana kept many of the original SRRS items but also added some items that were appropriate for older persons. Comparisons were made between weights assigned to these events by older persons and by college students (the median age was 70 and 20, respectively).

Table 9–5 presents comparisons across some items that were common to all four scales. The wide variation in life change scores across these four scales illustrates the problem of relying on absolute scores to determine the stressfulness of an event. However, the relative stress of some items remains constant across the studies; for example, death of spouse received the highest readjustment score in all four. Young and old respondents appear to perceive the stressfulness of an event differently, as illustrated by the significant differences between these groups in Table 9–5; note how marital reconciliation and

death of a close friend were perceived to be more stressful by younger respondents. These findings highlight the need for caution in administering to older persons life events measures that were originally developed with younger samples.

Another problem with such measures is the implicit assumption that positive and negative life events produce equal levels of stress. When events such as "change in financial status" were split into "problems with finances" versus "improvements in finances," both young and old respondents assigned higher stress scores (life change units) to negative events (Kiyak and Kahana, 1975).

Most researchers have not explored the impact of previous experience on the life change score assigned by each respondent. In the study by Kiyak and Kahana, scores assigned to three events that had been experienced by older respondents (menopause, retirement, death of spouse) but not by college students were compared. In all three cases, older persons assigned lower readjustment scores than did young students. Other researchers have provided similar evidence. For example, voluntary retirement was not perceived to be highly stressful by older men who had already experienced it (Haynes, McMichael, and Tyroler, 1978). Nor is menopause generally recalled as a traumatic event by older women (Neugarten, Havighurst, and Tobin, 1968). Likewise, the event of the "empty nest" has not received high readjustment scores

**TABLE 9–5  Comparison of Life Change Units**

| EVENT | SRRS | KIYAK AND KAHANA | | AMSTER AND KRAUS | MUHLENKAMP, GRESS, AND FLOOD |
|---|---|---|---|---|---|
| | | Young | Old | | |
| Death of spouse | 100 | 88 * | 79 | 125 | 73 |
| Marriage | 50 | 78 * | 64 | 50 | 50 |
| Marital Reconciliation | 45 | 65 * | 47 | 39 | 35 |
| Death of a close friend | 37 | 67 * | 47 | 50 | 52 |
| Change in residence | 20 | 59 * | 51 | 43 | 39 |
| Financial problems | 38 | 68 * | 59 | 56 | 43 |
| Improved financial status | 38 | 59 * | 48 | 56 | 43 |

by older parents. These findings support the work of researchers who have argued that the anticipation of an event is more stressful than the actual experience (Lundberg, Theorell, and Lind, 1975). Previous experiences may also predict an individual's response to subsequent life events. As a result, an older person who has already experienced the death of many friends and relatives may be less stressed by the death of another close friend than an individual, young or old, who has never experienced such an event. This is not to say that an older person will not need to cope with new events as they occur, but the duration and intensity of the stress may be less, thereby alleviating the person's adaptation to a new situation. Thus, research evidence suggests that past experience with similar events enables the older person to cope with a new event.

## Historical, Life Cycle, and Daily Living Factors

As noted earlier, the degree to which a person can anticipate an event may influence the stress produced by it and the ability to cope with it. Life events that are on-time or are expected (e.g., death of spouse following a long illness) are less stressful than unexpected events (Neugarten, 1979). On the other hand, the loss of a spouse following a long illness has been found to result in more medical problems of the widowed spouse than sudden death or chronic illness of shorter duration (Gerber et al., 1975). This may be due to the cumulative effects of other stressors (e.g., the demands of caregiving) associated with the terminal illness that the surviving spouse could not resolve during the caregiving and anticipatory grieving stages. Thus, the evidence is mixed regarding older people's ability to cope with on-time events. It may be that anticipatory coping does not take the place of coping with an event *after* it occurs. In addition, an individual must cope with other stressors that were not part of the anticipated event.

It has been argued that the cohort of people aged 65 and older today have experienced more

traumatic life events than have younger age groups because they lived through the Depression, World War II, and the Korean and Vietnam Wars. In the Duke Longitudinal Study, such sociohistorical events were probed. Respondents who had lived in the era of such events did not report any trauma associated specifically with them, but many personal and family experiences were influenced by these major occurrences (Siegler and George, 1983). Thus, sociohistorical events form the background for many personal life events, and may even influence an individual's own life (e.g., a war injury or loss of a job during the Depression). These events, however, do not necessarily have long-term effects on a person's adaptation and psychological well-being, unless an individual has experienced them directly (e.g., post-traumatic stress disorder has been identified in veterans of the Vietnam War).

Although researchers have focused on the stress produced by major life events, Lazarus and Cohen (1977) have suggested that most people experience stress as a result of "chronic daily hassles." Their "hassles scale" measures such day-to-day problems as feelings of loneliness, lack of energy, regrets over past decisions, and concerns about one's current situation. Other emotions that may produce stress for an individual include feelings of powerlessness, normlessness, and social isolation (Seeman, 1976). These are generally not specific events with a beginning or end point, but are chronic and may occur simultaneously with other "hassles." An individual must cope with these emotions, just as with discrete life events. To the extent that an older person feels powerless, lonely, and regretful, feelings of stress will increase, with a corresponding need to adapt to the situation in some way. Lazarus and Cohen have not reported differences in the frequency with which older persons experience such chronic feelings in comparison to younger persons.

One aspect of life events that has not been explored with the elderly, but which may influence psychological well-being, is the impact of anticipated events that do not materialize. That is, how do older persons respond after anticipating a major event and then discovering that it will not take place? One can list many such events, both positive and negative, that may result in stress if they do not occur. For example, anticipating relocation to a nursing home from the hospital, an older person may direct family members to sell his or her home and its furnishings. What happens if a suitable nursing home is not found, and family members put pressure on the person to move in with them? What is the impact of learning just a few days before a major holiday that a family gathering anticipated eagerly by an older person must be canceled? Variables such as an individual's level of anticipation and availability of optional outcomes undoubtedly play a role in reactions to these situations. Research on how people of different ages cope with such "non-events" is needed.

## What Determines Stress Responses in Old Age?

The manner in which we respond to life events, role changes, and chronic daily hassles depends on many personal and environmental factors. The cognitive appraisal of a situation by an individual as being stressful or not has already been noted to be important. In addition, an event's relative desirability or undesirability, whether or not it is anticipated, and a person's previous experiences with similar events may determine how he or she responds to the situation. The availability of a strong social network that can provide emotional support also has an effect. A person who must face all challenges alone may use different coping strategies than one who has family and friends to turn to in times of crisis.

Both situational and personal factors affect the process of coping with stressful events, sometimes in different ways (Dohrenwend and Dohrenwend, 1980). The former consist of external mediators, such as social and material resources (e.g., friendships and family support, or financial adequacy). The latter include the individual's level of functional health and cognitive status,

aspirations, values, vulnerabilities, and needs that mediate between a particular stressful situation and its outcomes. For example, an older woman whose husband has recently died after a long illness will be more likely to rely on others if she has a strong need for dependency (e.g., Neugarten's passive-dependent type), and if she has family and friends who have previously supported her in crises. If, on the other hand, she is highly independent and/or has no strong social network on which she has relied for past help, she will be more likely to use instrumental, self-initiated coping strategies (e.g., find out more about the problem or learn new skills to solve it), and less likely to ask others to assist her during her grieving. According to these researchers, the outcomes of coping responses may be personal growth, decline, or no change. The type of coping response rarely determines what outcomes will emerge; more often, the outcome varies with the interaction between the nature of the problem and the quality and quantity of internal and external mediators.

Personality styles also may influence how people respond to stress. Earlier in this chapter, Gutmann's (1974a, 1974b, 1977) research on active and passive mastery styles was described. A person with a passive style does not feel powerful enough to directly influence his or her fate, whereas one with an active style tends to rely more on personal abilities and less on others. Differences in responses to stress by older people with these different styles would be expected; however, research has not provided sufficient evidence for such hypothesized variations.

Another personality characteristic that may influence how successfully people respond to stress is *locus of control*. This is the belief by an individual that events in his or her life result from personal actions (internal locus), or are determined by fate or powerful others (external locus). Internal locus of control has been found to be related to successful coping in both young and old (Thomae, 1980). Studies on the stress of relocation have provided additional support for this relationship. Older persons with internal locus of control were found to adjust better to institutional living than those with external locus (Kivett, 1976; Baker, 1976). These studies have examined the outcomes of reactions to stress; successful adjustment has been defined as survival, satisfaction with living arrangements, and the maintenance of personal identity. In contrast, research on mastery styles has emphasized differences in how persons with active and passive mastery styles respond to stress, without predetermining criteria for success or failure.

## Coping

As noted earlier in this chapter, a critical personality feature in the later years is an individual's ability to adapt to major changes in life circumstances, in health and social status, and in social and physical environments. In fact, successful aging requires considerable flexibility in adaptation. This, in turn, requires awareness of the aging process, acceptance of the limitations that aging places on a person's activities, and an ability to reevaluate life goals and search for alternative means of satisfying needs. An important aspect of adaptation is the ability to use appropriate coping mechanisms when faced with a

stressful event, or when personal needs are incongruent with environmental needs.

Does coping change with age? Before answering, we must first define and consider the functions of *coping*. Coping is the manner in which a person responds to stress. It includes cognitive, emotional, and behavioral responses made in the face of internally and externally created events. It differs from defense mechanisms in that people are generally conscious of how they have coped in a particular situation and, if asked, can describe specific coping responses to a given stressor. Indeed, Birren (1969) has emphasized the concept of coping strategy to denote "planful behavior" in response to a stressful situation. *Defense mechanisms,* in contrast, are unconscious reactions that a person adopts to defend or protect the self from impulses and memories that threaten one's identity. Defense mechanisms also have an underlying evaluative quality; some defenses are more primitive or less mature than others (see Table 9–6). Thus, for example, a young child is more likely to use the defense mechanisms of denial and projection, or to need to view threatening impulses as present in others, not in the self. As people mature, so do the defense mechanisms that they use. Vaillant's (1977) longitudinal study of men who were

### TABLE 9–6 Major Ego Defense Mechanisms

| DEFENSE MECHANISM | EXAMPLE |
|---|---|
| 1. Denial (a premature defense mechanism) | Denying what one really feels to avoid punishment by the super-ego and rejection by others. |
| 2. Projection | Feeling that others are untrustworthy when one feels unsure about one's own trustworthiness. |
| 3. Repression | Forgetting an event that could disturb the feeling of well-being if brought into consciousness. |
| 4. Reaction formation | Extreme display of love and affection toward someone who is actually hated. |
| 5. Regression and fixation | Returning to a comfortable stage of life and/or way of behaving under conditions of anxiety and stress. |
| 6. Displacement | Taking out one's anger and hostility on family because one is afraid of expressing anger toward one's supervisor at work who has humiliated the individual. |

Harvard graduates provides support for this conclusion. As the men reached middle age, they used fewer primitive mechanisms, such as projection, and more mature mechanisms, such as sublimation (e.g., finding more socially acceptable ways of expressing hostility than through physically threatening behavior). Vaillant includes humor and altruism among mature defense mechanisms. He suggests that health behaviors such as smoking and alcoholism can limit the development of mature ego defenses (Vaillant, 1994).

Unlike defense mechanisms, coping styles cannot easily be categorized as primitive or mature. Some forms of coping, however, are aimed not at resolving the problem, but at providing psychological escape, as illustrated by the categories of coping defined by some researchers (see Table 9–7). For example, an older man who is confronted with the news that he has lung cancer may cope by eating or sleeping more, or by taking a vacation to "get away from it all." This response may alleviate the stressful feeling, but it does not aid in the treatment of the cancer. Pfeiffer (1977) has suggested that older persons are more rigid in their thinking than are younger persons, and are therefore prone to use more passive and ineffective coping mechanisms, such as withdrawal, denial, and anxiety. Pfeiffer's description may apply only to a small segment of older persons who are experiencing emotional and cognitive deterioration, however. Other researchers have not found such differences in studies of normal older people and have not made a distinction between mature and immature coping (McCrae and Costa, 1985).

## Functions of Coping

Coping reactions generally serve two functions: to solve a problem that has produced stress for the individual (e.g., a life event, a role loss or gain, or a chronic "hassle"), and to reduce the emotional and physiological discomfort that accompanies the stressful situation. These have been defined as problem-focused and emotion-

**TABLE 9–7    Classification of Coping Responses**

### GENERAL STRATEGIES OF COPING
(Lazarus, 1975a, 1975b; Lazarus and Folkman, 1984; Lazarus and Launier, 1978)

1. Information search in an attempt to understand the situation
2. Direct action to change the situation
3. Inhibition of action
4. Psychological responses to the emotional arousal created by the situation

### COPING RESPONSES TO TERMINAL ILLNESS
(Moos, 1977)

1. Searching for information
2. Setting goals
3. Denying or minimizing the problem
4. Seeking emotional support
5. Rehearsing alternative outcomes

### DIMENSIONS OF COPING
(Kahana and Kahana, 1982)

1. Instrumental (taking action, alone or with the assistance of others)
2. Intrapsychic (cognitive approaches, acceptance of the situation)
3. Affective (releasing tensions, expressing emotions)
4. Escape (avoiding or denying the problem, displacement activities such as increased exercise, eating, and smoking)
5. Resigned helplessness (feeling impotent, unable to cope)

focused coping (Folkman and Lazarus, 1980; Lazarus and Folkman, 1984). In some cases, an individual may focus only on solving the problem *or* on dealing with the emotional distress that it creates. In the earlier example, the older man who responds to the diagnosis of lung cancer by taking a vacation to get away may address the emotional distress but not the problem per se. Such reactions tend to be incomplete and do not resolve the problem that is producing stress. In other situations, people may need to deal first with the anxiety produced by a stressful situation, then with the problem itself. For example, upon learning that a close friend has a terminal illness, a person must first cope with shock and helplessness. Only then can rational decisions be made about what to do to help the dying friend through the last months or weeks of life. In most situations, however, emotion-focused coping and problem-focused coping take place simultaneously. An individual must deal with his or her emotions throughout the course of trying to solve the problem. It has been suggested that coping must fulfill both emotion-regulating and problem-solving functions in order to alleviate stress (Folkman and Lazarus, 1980).

## Consistency versus Variability in Coping

Although some researchers have suggested that certain personalities are associated with specific coping styles, there is little evidence for consistency of coping responses in different situations. Indeed, it is difficult to imagine that many situations are similar enough in the types of stress they produce that an individual could use the same responses in all cases. Furthermore, most problems produce multiple demands on a person and evoke diverse emotional reactions. For example, upon learning of a close friend's impending death, a person must cope with the grief, anger, hopelessness, and guilt that such news evokes. The individual may also have to cope with comforting and easing the friend's pain, aiding in financial and funeral plans, and notifying others. How an older person copes with this situation may be somewhat similar to the way he or she copes with an event such as taking a trip to visit children and grandchildren, but the events are so dissimilar that the individual must select appropriate coping strategies for each specific situation.

People may have different repertoires of coping strategies, so that one person is more likely to use a particular set of strategies while another avoids those strategies and uses others. That is, people generally do not cope in just one way, such as only by crying, talking to others or consulting with a professional. We generally express multiple coping responses, sometimes simultaneously, other times in sequence. As stated earlier, we must cope with the emotional stress produced by the problem *and* with the problem itself.

Many studies have found that certain situations evoke particular coping responses. Loss of loved ones and illness result in more emotion-focused coping and less instrumental coping. Consistencies have been identified in how people deal with spinal cord injury (Bulman and Wortman, 1977) and cancer (Weisman and Worden, 1976–77) and with a terminal illness (Kübler-Ross, 1969). Other researchers have noted considerable flexibility in older people's selection of coping responses, based on what is "appropriate" or potentially effective in a given situation. For example, studies of self-reported coping in response to multiple stressful events support the concept of situational variability (Kahana and Kahana, 1982; Thomae, 1978).

## Aging and Coping Styles

The question of whether coping styles change with age has not been extensively researched. Some studies of coping among young and middle-aged persons have reported few significant differences (Billings and Moos, 1981; Folkman and Lazarus, 1980; Folkman et al., 1987), although these groups have generally not been compared with older persons. Older (ages 65 to 91) and middle-aged (ages 50 to 64) respondents in McCrae's (1982) study used more mature coping styles (e.g., problem-solving, and seeking the advice of family, friends, and professionals) and fewer escapist strategies than did younger (ages 24 to 49) respondents. Other cross-sectional studies have also found age differences. For example, older persons are less likely than the young to use confrontive coping, especially when the stressor could be defined as a threat. They are more likely to use distancing techniques and to reappraise the situation in a positive light (Folkman et al., 1987; Irion and Blanchard-Fields, 1987). However, in a 1989 report of a seven-year longitudinal study of coping among 113 persons who were ages 24 to 91 when they were first interviewed, cross-sectional differences again emerged, but individual stability in coping responses was also observed over this seven-year period (McCrae, 1989). As in the earlier study (McCrae, 1982), both older men and women were *less* likely to use hostile reactions and escapist fantasy, and *more* likely to use faith, whereas younger persons were more likely to express their feelings and to use positive thinking and neurotic coping styles. Nevertheless, when the responses of people who completed both coping assessments were compared, there was considerable stability in coping. In particular, coping mechanisms related to the personality characteristic of neuroticism remained stable over seven years, even though cross-sectional comparisons had revealed older respondents in general to use *less* neurotic coping. These results highlight the importance of examining the same individual over time in order to determine if coping styles are in fact stable or if they are related to age. Indeed, there may be some support for the hypothesis that at least some coping styles are part of an individual's basic personality.

Studies by Kahana and Kahana of older people who move to institutions and by Kiyak and colleagues (1985) of older people who must cope with Alzheimer's disease suggest that older people use a diverse range of coping styles. Similarly, women aged 55 to 65 in stressful situations were likely to use a variety of coping responses, including turning to work or religion or ignoring the problem (Griffith, 1983). It is important to note that religious coping has been found to be an important coping strategy in several studies of older persons, especially in African Americans (McCrae, 1984, 1989; Koenig, George, and Siegler, 1988). Indeed, in the second Duke Longitudinal Study, 45 percent of the respondents aged 55 to 80 mentioned trust and faith in God, prayer, and seeking help from God as a coping

strategy for at least one of the three major life events they had experienced. McCrae reports that over 70 percent of adults used religion in coping with major life events. Taking this one step further, Pargament and colleagues (1990) found in a sample of 586 adult members of ten churches that religious coping significantly predicted three outcomes: recent mental health, perceived general health, and religious outcomes of the stressors.

In most cases, these styles are appropriate for the problem at hand and result in successful adaptation. Only in the case of significant cognitive deterioration is there a restriction in the range of an individual's coping responses and a tendency to resort to more primitive reactions, such as denying or ignoring the problem. This small segment of the elderly population may fit Pfeiffer's (1977) description of restricted coping abilities. Nevertheless, the majority of older people appear capable of using a wide repertoire of coping responses and can call upon the most effective ones for a given situation. In sum, the available research suggests that most people maintain their coping styles into old age, and use appropriate responses for the problem at hand.

Even less is known about how gender affects coping. In an eight-year follow-up of older adults in the Duke Longitudinal Study, gender differences were found in the types of life events experienced but not in the coping styles used (Siegler and George, 1983). Older men reported more work and health-related events; women identified more events affecting family members and health problems of significant others. The majority of men and women stated that instrumental strategies (i.e., acting to solve the problem) resulted in better outcomes for most events that occurred to them personally, while palliative coping (i.e., dealing with the emotions created by events) was more helpful for responding to events that affected their families, work, and financial situations. On the other hand, researchers in the Baltimore Longitudinal Study have found that women at all ages are more likely than their male counterparts to express their feelings and to use distraction, wishful thinking, sedation, and neurotic coping responses (McCrae, 1989).

## SUCCESSFUL AGING

Researchers and clinicians have become increasingly interested in the concept of "successful aging" (Rowe and Kahn, 1987; Seeman et al., 1994; Roos and Havens, 1991). This interest has been sparked by the growing number of older people who have avoided the chronic health problems and declining cognitive skills that afflict other elderly, and have managed to cope effectively in their daily lives. What are the characteristics of such elders who age successfully that distinguish them from their less hearty peers? A major longitudinal study of older people in Manitoba, Canada, who were interviewed in 1971 and again in 1984, found that the 583 respondents who were classified as having aged successfully (i.e., not residing in a nursing home, receiving fewer than 60 days of home care services in the past year, independent in activities of daily living and high on a mental status test) differed from the 666 who were alive but dependent, and from another group of 1,694 who had died since 1971. The 20 percent who could be described as "successful agers" in 1984 had been young-old and had reported excellent or good health in 1971, had made fewer demands on the health care system (although it is difficult to determine if this was a cause or an effect of successful aging), had not retired due to poor health, and their spouse had not died or become institutionalized during this 13-year interval (Roos and Havens, 1991).

The MacArthur Studies of Successful Aging have examined longitudinally a cohort of men and women (aged 70 to 79 at baseline) in three Eastern U.S. communities. These 1192 people were selected because they represented the top third of their age group in several areas of cognitive and physical function. Within this selective group of "robust" older persons, more specific

Gerontologists have recently focused on identifying the characteristics of people who age successfully.

tests of function were conducted in 1988 and 1991. Those with the highest performance scores in this group had fewer chronic conditions (especially cardiovascular diseases), better self-rated health (similar to the successful older people in the Manitoba study), and were more likely to have higher educational and income levels. The majority of these robust elderly reported no problems with activities of daily living such as walking ¼ mile without stopping, lifting a ten-pound weight, and crouching and stooping without help. Three year follow-ups revealed that the majority (55 percent) maintained their 1988 performance levels. Another 23 percent showed a decline on the performance tests, while 22 percent actually *improved* on these tests. Those who declined were older, had lower income levels, and had reported diabetes and high blood pressure at baseline (Seeman et al., 1994; Suzman et al., 1992).

The Oregon Brain Aging Study, a longitudinal assessment of a smaller number of optimally healthy persons aged 65 to 74 and 84 to 100, has measured many more physical, cognitive, neurologic, and sensory functions than the Manitoba and MacArthur studies of successful aging (Howieson et al., 1993). This group of older adults was selected because they had no history of diseases affecting brain function, no psychiatric disorders, and medications that could impair cognition. The researchers found very few areas of decline in this group of healthy elders; the oldest-old differed from the youngest-old only on tests requiring visual perception and constructional skills, *not* on tests of memory or reasoning.

To conclude this section, it is important to discuss the implications of older persons' coping responses for their long-term adaptation. *Adaptation* refers to the adjustments that people make in response to changes in themselves and/or their environments, in order to fit themselves to the new conditions. Given older people's numerous experiences with life events, role loss, and environmental changes throughout life, it would appear that adaptation in old age should occur with relative ease. Indeed, in one sense, an individual who has reached age 75 or 80 has proved to be the most adaptable of his or her generation, since the ultimate proof of adaptation is survival. As we have seen thus far, older people continue to face challenges to their well-being in the form of personal and family illnesses, age-related declines in sensory and physiological functions, and changes in their social and physical environments. To the extent that older people are capable of using coping skills that were effective in youth and middle age, they will continue to adapt to change successfully, thereby maintaining life satisfaction and morale.

## SUMMARY AND IMPLICATIONS

Personality development in adulthood and old age has received increasing attention over the past 25 years. Earlier theories of personality suggested that development takes place only during childhood and adolescence, and stabilizes by early adulthood. Beginning with Erik Erikson, however, several theorists have suggested that personality continues to change and evolve into old age. According to Erikson's theory of psychosocial development, the individual experiences stages of development, with crises or conflicts at each stage, and the outcome of each has an impact on ego development in the next stage. The eighth and last stage of personality development occurs in old age and poses the conflict of ego integrity versus despair in dealing with one's impending death.

The work of Carl Jung also emphasizes the growth of personality across the life span, but does not specify stages of development. Jung's model, like Erikson's, focuses on the individual's confrontation with death in this last stage. In addition, Jung described a decrease in sex-typed behavior with aging. This has been supported in cross-cultural studies by Gutmann (1974a, 1974b, 1980) and in the longitudinal Kansas City studies by Neugarten and colleagues (1968). These investigators found that men become more accepting of their nurturant and affiliative characteristics as they age, whereas women learn to accept their egocentric and aggressive impulses.

The Kansas City studies have provided other important insights into normal personality development from middle to old age. With aging, people in the sample were found to become more unlike each other. However, some changes in personality were shared by a majority of those studied: increased preoccupation with their inner lives, less extroversion, and a movement toward less impulsiveness and more sophisticated ego defenses. Based on the large number of people interviewed both cross-sectionally and longitudinally in the Kansas City studies, Neugarten described four major personality types in old age: integrated, armored-defensive, passive-dependent, and unintegrated. The majority of people fell into the first two categories and expressed high life satisfaction. Contrary to popular stereotypes, very few older persons could be described as unintegrated. Research by Costa and McCrae (1986) with adults in the Baltimore Longitudinal Study has provided support for the stability of some personality traits across the life span. These findings are strengthened by the Swedish twins study (Pederson et al., 1988; Plomin et al., 1988), which reported high correlations between pairs of twins, even those reared apart, on five traits.

Other models of adult personality development have been proposed but have received less research attention. Levinson's life structures model is an extension of Riegel's dialectical theory of personality. These approaches emphasize the interaction between an individual and his or her environment as the impetus for development from one level to the next. In Kohlberg's model of moral development (based on theories of cognitive development), the basis for movement from one stage to the next is not specified.

The development of self-concept and self-esteem in old age has been researched even less. It is recognized that older persons' self-concepts must be redefined as they move from traditional roles of worker, spouse, and parent to less well-differentiated roles such as retiree or widow. But the process by which such changes take place and, more important, how they influence life satisfaction and self-esteem in old age is unclear.

Somewhat more research has been devoted to age-related changes in the nature of life events and the stress associated with them. Neugarten and others have compared the impact of on-time (or normative) versus off-time (or non-normative) events in terms of older people's ability to cope; anticipating an event such as retirement or menopause may make it less stressful than a situation that is completely unanticipated. However, little is known about how older people cope with an event that is anticipated but fails to occur.

Cognitive appraisal is also an important consideration in understanding people's reactions to life events. To the extent that people perceive a situation as a positive challenge, they experience more positive stress and adapt more readily. If the situation is viewed as a threat, or as a negative stressor, the response may be avoidance or ineffective coping. If a particular life event is viewed as benign or unimportant, coping responses will not be activated. This is fine if the event does not place any demands on an individual, but if it proves to be more stressful than anticipated, an older person will be unprepared to cope with these demands.

The evidence is mixed regarding the question of whether older people experience more major life events in a given period than younger people. The majority of studies have found a similar distribution of stressful events in the lives of young, middle-aged, and aged persons, but more longitudinal studies are needed in this area in order to conclude this with more certainty. The effects of sociohistorical events, such as wars and the Depression, on the current aged cohort's adaptive responses have been found to be relatively minor.

Coping responses are influenced by an individual's access to a support network, cognitive skills, and personality traits such as active versus passive "mastery style" and "locus of control." Although ego defense mechanisms have been observed to become more mature in middle age and old age, it is difficult to describe coping styles in a similar manner. Age differences in the use of coping styles have been observed in cross-sectional studies, but longitudinal comparisons reveal considerable stability in coping. Successful aging may be defined as the ability to cope effectively with both major life events and chronic hassles, and to adapt to new situations. An individual who has survived to the age of 75 or older has proved to be adaptable to new situations. Hence, older people who continue to use coping strategies that have proved successful in the past will be likely to maintain their life satisfaction and well-being throughout the later years.

# REFERENCES

Amster, L. E., and Krauss, H. The relationship between life crises and mental deterioration in old age. *International Journal of Aging and Human Development*, 1974, *5*, 51–55.

Baker, E. K. Relationship of retirement and satisfaction with life events to locus of control. *Dissertation Abstracts International*, 1976, *37*, (9B), 4748.

Billings, A. G., and Moos, R. H. The role of coping responses and social resources in attenuating the stress of life events. *Journal of Behavioral Medicine*, 1981, *4*, 139.

Birren, J. E. Age and decision strategies. In A. T. Welford and J. E. Birren (Eds.), *Decision making and age*. New York: S. Karger, 1969, 23–36.

Bulman, R. J., and Wortman, C. B. Attributions of blame and coping in the "Real World": Severe accident victims react to their lot. *Journal of Personality and Social Psychology*, 1977, *35*, 351–363.

Butler, R. N. *Why survive? Being old in America*. New York: Harper and Row, 1975.

Butler, R. N., and Lewis, M. I. *Aging and mental health* (3d ed.). St. Louis: Mosby, 1983.

Chen, H. L. Hearing loss in the elderly: Relation to loneliness and self-esteem. *Journal of Gerontological Nursing*, 1994, *20*, 22–28.

Costa, P. T., and McCrae, R. R. Cross-sectional studies of personality in a national sample. Development and validation of survey measures. *Psychology and Aging*, 1986, *1*, 140–143.

Costa, P. T., McCrae, R. R., and Norris, A. H. Personal adjustment to aging: Longitudinal prediction from neuroticism and extroversion. *Journal of Gerontology*, 1981, *36*, 78–85.

Cumming, E., and Henry, W. E. *Growing old*. New York: Basic Books, 1961.

Dohrenwood, B. S., and Dohrenwood, B. P. What is a stressful life event? In H. Selye (Ed.), *Selye's guide to stress research, Volume 1*. New York: Van Nostrand Reinhold, 1980.

Eisdorfer, C., and Wilkie, F. Stress, disease, aging, and behavior. In J. E. Birren and K. W. Schaie (Eds.), *Handbook of the psychology of aging*. New York: Van Nostrand Reinhold, 1977, 251–275.

Erikson, E. H. *Childhood and society* (2d ed.). New York: Norton, 1963.

Erikson, E. H. *Identity, youth and crisis*. New York: Norton, 1968.

Erikson, E. H. *The life cycle completed: A review*. New York: Norton, 1982.

Erikson, E. H., Erikson, J. M. and Kivnick, H. Q. *Vital involvement in old age*. New York: Norton, 1986.

Folkman, S., and Lazarus, R. S. An analysis of coping in a middle-aged community sample. *Journal of Health and Social Behavior*, 1980, *21*, 219–239.

Folkman, S., Lazarus, R. S., Pimley, S., and Novacek, J. Age differences in stress and coping processes. *Psychology and Aging*, 1987, *2*, 171–184.

Gaber, L. B. Activity/disengagement revisited: Personality types in the aged. *British Journal of Psychiatry*, 1983, *143*, 490–497.

Gerber, I., Rusalem, R., Hannon, N., Battin, D., and Arkin, A. Anticipatory grief and aged widows and widowers. *Journal of Gerontology*, 1975, *30*, 225–229.

Griffith, J. W. Women's stress responses and coping: Patterns according to age groups. *Issues in Health Care of Women*, 1983, *4*, 327–340.

Gutmann, D. L. Alternatives to disengagement: Aging among the highland Druze. In R. A. LeVine (Ed.), *Culture and personality: Contemporary readings*. Chicago: Aldine, 1974a.

Gutmann, D. L. The country of old men: Cross-cultural studies in the psychology of later life. In R. A. LeVine (Ed.), *Culture and personality: Contemporary readings*. Chicago: Aldine, 1974b.

Gutmann, D. L. The cross-cultural perspective: Notes toward a comparative psychology of aging. In J. E. Birren and K. W. Schaie (Eds.), *Handbook of the psychology of aging*. New York: Van Nostrand Reinhold, 1977.

Gutmann, D. L. Psychoanalysis and aging: A developmental view. In S. I. Greenspan and G. H. Pollock (Eds.), *The course of life: Psychoanalytic contributions toward understanding personality development. Vol. 3: Adulthood and the aging process*. Washington, D.C.: U.S. Government Printing Office, 1980.

Havighurst, R. J., Neugarten, B. L., and Tobin, S. S. Disengagement and patterns of aging. In J. E. Birren (Ed.), *Relations of development and aging*. Springfield, Ill.: Charles C. Thomas, 1964.

Havighurst, R. J., Neugarten, B. L., and Tobin, S. S. Disengagement and patterns of aging. In B. L.

Neugarten (Ed.), *Middle age and aging.* Chicago: University of Chicago Press, 1968.

Haynes, S. G., McMichael, A. J., and Tyroler, H. A. Survival after early and normal retirement. *Journal of Gerontology,* 1978, *33,* 269–278.

Holmes, T. H., and Masuda, M. Life change and illness susceptibility. In B. S. Dohrenwend and B. P. Dohrenwend (Eds.), *Stressful life events: Their nature and effects.* New York: Wiley, 1974.

Holmes, T. H., and Rahe, R. The social readjustment rating scale. *Journal of Psychosomatic Research,* 1967, *11,* 213–218.

Howieson, D. B., Holm, L. A., Kaye, J. A., Oken, B. S., and Howieson, J. Neurological function in the optimally healthy oldest old. *Neurology,* 1993, *43,* 1882–1886.

Irion, J. C., and Blanchard-Fields, F. A cross-sectional comparison of adaptive coping in adulthood. *Journal of Gerontology,* 1987, *42,* 502–504.

Jung, C. G. *Modern man in search of a soul.* San Diego: Harcourt Brace and World, 1933.

Jung, C. G. Concerning the archetypes, with special reference to the anima concept. In *C. G. Jung, Collected Works,* Vol. 9, Part I. Princeton, N.J.: Princeton University Press, 1959.

Kahana, E. F. *Matching environments to needs of the aged.* Final Progress Report submitted to NICHD, Fall, 1973.

Kahana, E. F. A congruence model of person-environment interaction. In M. P. Lawton (Ed.), *Theory development in environments and aging.* New York: Wiley, 1975.

Kahana, E. F., and Kahana, B. Environmental continuity, discontinuity, futurity, and adaptation of the aged. In G. Rowles and R. Ohta (Eds.), *Aging and milieu: Environmental perspectives on growing old.* New York: Academic Press, 1982.

Kahana, E. F., Liang, J., and Felton, B. Alternative models of P-E fit; Prediction of morale in three homes for the aged. *Journal of Gerontology,* 1980, *35,* 584–595.

Kahana, R. J. Strategies of dynamic psychotherapy with the wide range of older individuals. *Journal of Geriatric Psychiatry,* 1979, *12,* 71–99.

Kivett, V. A. Physical, psychological and social predictors of locus of control among middle aged adults. *Dissertation Abstracts International,* 1976, *37* (5B), 2481.

Kiyak, H. A., and Kahana, E. F. Life events scaling by college students and the elderly. Paper presented at meetings of the American Psychological Association, New York, 1975.

Kiyak, H. A., Montgomery, R., Borson, S., and Teri, L. Coping patterns among patients with Alzheimer's disease and non-demented elderly. Paper presented at meetings of the Gerontological Society, New Orleans, November, 1985.

Koenig, H. G., George, L. K., and Siegler, I. C. The use of religion and other emotion-regulating coping strategies among older adults. *The Gerontologist,* 1988, *28,* 303–310.

Kohlberg, L. *Stages in the development of moral thought and action.* New York: Holt, Rinehart and Winston, 1969.

Kohlberg, L. Continuities in childhood and adult moral development revisited. In P. B. Baltes and K. W. Schaie (Eds.), *Life-span developmental psychology* (2d ed.). New York: Academic Press, 1973.

Kohlberg, L. The development of moral judgment and moral action. In L. Kohlberg (Ed.), *Child development and childhood education: A cognitive-developmental view.* New York: Longman Press, 1987.

Kübler-Ross, E. *On death and dying.* New York: Macmillan, 1969.

Lawton, M. P., and Nahemow, L. Ecology and the aging process. In C. Eisdorfer and M. P. Lawton (Eds.), *Psychology of adult development and aging.* Washington, D.C.: American Psychological Association, 1973.

Lazarus, R. S. The self-regulation of emotions. In L. Levi (Ed.), *Emotions—Their parameters and measurement.* New York: Raven Press, 1975a, 47–67.

Lazarus, R. S. Psychological stress and coping in adaptation and illness. In S. M. Weiss (Ed.), *Proceedings of the National Heart and Lung Institute working conference on health behavior.* DHEW Pub. No. (NIH) 76–868,1975b, 199–214.

Lazarus, R. S., and Cohen, J. B. *The hassles scale, stress and coping project.* Berkeley: University of California, 1977.

Lazarus, R. S., and Folkman, S. *Stress, appraisal and coping.* New York: Springer, 1984.

Lazarus, R. S., and Launier, R. Stress-related transactions between person and environment. In L. A. Pervin and M. Lewis (Eds.), *Perspectives in interactional psychology.* New York: Plenum, 1978, 287–327.

Levinson, D. J. Middle adulthood in modern society: A sociopsychological view. In G. DiRenzo (Ed.), *We the people: Social change and social character.* Westport, Conn.: Greenwood Press, 1977.

Levinson, D. J. A conception of adult development. *American Psychologist*, 1986, *41*, 3–13.

Levinson, D. J., Darrow, C. M., Klein, E. B., Levinson, M. H., and McKee, B. *The seasons of a man's life.* New York: Knopf, 1978.

Lewin, K. *A dynamic theory of personality.* New York: McGraw-Hill, 1935.

Lundberg, U., Theorell, T., and Lind, E. Life changes and myocardial infarction: Individual differences in life change scaling. *Journal of Psychosomatic Research*, 1975, *19*, 27–32.

McCrae, R. R. Age differences in the use of coping mechanisms. *Journal of Gerontology*, 1982, *37*, 454.

McCrae, R. R. Age differences and changes in the use of coping mechanisms. *Journals of Gerontology*, 1989, *44*, P161–Pl64.

McCrae, R. R. Situational determinants of coping responses: Loss, threat and challenge. *Journal of Personality and Social Psychology*, 1984, *46*, 919–928.

McCrae, R. R., and Costa, P. T., Jr. Personality, stress, and coping processes in aging men and women. In R. Andres, E. L. Bierman, and W. R. Hazzard (Eds.), *Principles of geriatric medicine.* New York: McGraw-Hill, 1985.

McCrae, R. R., and Costa, P. T. Validation of the five factor model of personality across instruments and observers. *Journal of Personality & Social Psychology*, 1987, *52*, 81–90.

Monge, R. H. Structure of the self-concept from adolescence through old age. *Experimental Aging Research*, 1975, *1*, 281–291.

Moos, R. *Coping with physical illness.* New York: Plenum, 1977.

Morgan, J. C. *Becoming old.* New York: Springer, 1979.

Muhlenkamp, A., Gress, L. D., and Flood, M. A. Perception of life change events by the elderly. *Nursing Research*, 1975, *24*, 109–113.

National Center for Health Statistics. Advance report of final mortality statistics, 1980. *Monthly Vital Statistics Report*, 32 (4, supplement), 1983.

Neugarten, B. L. Personality change in late life: A developmental perspective. In C. Eisdorfer and M. P. Lawton (Eds.), *The psychology of adult development and aging.* Washington, D.C.: American Psychological Association, 1973.

Neugarten, B. L. Time, age and the life cycle. *American Journal of Psychiatry*, 1979, *136*, 887–894.

Neugarten, B. L. Time, age and the life cycle. In M. Bloom (Ed.), *Life span development.* New York: Macmillan, 1985.

Neugarten, B. L., Havighurst, R. J., and Tobin, S. S. Personality and patterns of aging. In B. L. Neugarten (Ed.), *Middle age and aging.* Chicago: University of Chicago Press, 1968.

Neugarten, B. L., Wood, V., Kraines, R. J., and Loomis, B. Women's attitudes towards the menopause. In B. L. Neugarten (Ed.), *Middle age and aging.* Chicago: University of Chicago Press, 1968.

Palmore, E., Cleveland, W. P., Nowlin, J. B., Ramm, D., and Siegler, I. C. Stress and adaptation in late life. *Journal of Gerontology*, 1979, *34*, 841–851.

Pargament, K. I., Ensing, D. S., Falgout, K., Olsen, H., Reilly, B., Van Haitsma, K., and Warren, R. Religious coping efforts as predictors of outcomes to significant negative life events. *American Journal of Community Psychology*, 1990, *18*, 793–824.

Pastalan, L. A. Designing housing environments for the elderly. *Journal of Architectural Education*, 1977, *31*, 11–14.

Pearlin, L. Sex roles and depression. In N. Datan and L. Ginsberg (Eds.), *Life-span developmental psychology: Normative life crises.* New York: Academic Press, 1975.

Pearlin, L., and Lieberman, M. Social sources of emotional distress. In R. Simmons (Ed.), *Research in community and mental health.* Greenwich, Conn.: JAI Press, 1979.

Pederson, N. L., Plomin, R., McClearn, G. E., and Friberg, L. Neuroticism, extroversion, and related traits in adult twins reared apart and reared together. *Journal of Personality & Social Psychology*, 1988, *55*, 950–957.

Pfeiffer, E. Psychopathology and social pathology. In J. E. Birren and K. W. Schaie (Eds.), *Handbook of the psychology of aging.* New York: Van Nostrand Reinhold, 1977.

Pinquart, M. Analysis of the self-concept of independently living senior citizens. *Zeitschrift für Gerontologie*, 1991, *24*, 98–104.

Pinsky, J. L., Leaverton, P. E., and Stokes, J. Predictors of good function: The Framingham Study. *Journal of Chronic Diseases*, 1987, *40* (Supplement), 159S–167S.

Plomin, R., Pederson, N. L., McClearn, G. E., Nesselroade, J. R., and Bergeman, C. S. EAS temperaments during the last half of the lifespan: Twins reared apart and twins reared together. *Psychology and Aging*, 1988, *3*, 43–50.

Rahe, R. H. Subjects' recent life changes and their near future illness reports: A review. *Annual Clinical Research*, 1972, *4*, 393.

Reigel, K. The dialectics of human development. *American Psychologist*, 1976, *31*, 689–700.

Roberts, P., and Newton, P. M. Levinsonian studies of women's adult development. *Psychology and Aging*, 1987, *2*, 154–163.

Roos, N. P., and Havens, B. Predictors of successful aging: A 12-year study of Manitoba elderly. *American Journal of Public Health*, 1991, *81*, 63–68.

Rosow, I. *Socialization to old age*. University of California Press, 1974.

Rowe, J. W., and Kahn, R. L. Human aging: Usual and successful. *Science*, 1987, *237*, 143–149.

Seeman, M. Empirical alienation studies: An overview. In R. F. Geyer and D. R. Schweitzer (Eds.), *Theories of alienation*. Leiden: Martinus Nijhoff, Social Services Division, 1976.

Seeman, T. A., Charpentier, P. A., Berkman, L. F., Tinetti, M. E., Guralnick, J. M., Albert, M., Blazer, D., and Rowe, J. W. Predicting changes in physical performance in a high functioning elderly cohort: MacArthur Studies of Successful Aging. *Journals of Gerontology*, 1994, *49*, M97–M108.

Selye, H. The general adaptation syndrome and the diseases of adaptation. *Journal of Clinical Endocrinology*, 1946, *6*, 117–230.

Selye, H. Stress and aging. *Journal of the American Geriatrics Society*, 1970, *18*, 660–681.

Shanan, J. The Jerusalem study of mid-adulthood and aging. *Israel Journal of Gerontology*, 1978, *2*, 37–49.

Shanan, J., and Jacobowitz, J. Personality and aging. In C. Eisdorfer (Ed.), *Annual Review of Gerontology and Geriatrics*, 1982, *3*, 148–180.

Siegler, J. C., George, L. K. The normal psychology of the aging male: Sex differences in coping and perception of life events. *Journal of Geriatric Psychiatry*, 1983, *16*, 197–209.

Snarey, J. R., Reimer, J., and Kohlberg, L. Development of social-moral reasoning among Kibbutz adolescents: A longitudinal cross-cultural study. *Developmental Psychology*, 1985, *21*, 3–17.

Suzman, R. M., Harris, T., Hadley, E. C., Kovar, M. G., and Weindruch, R. The robust oldest old: Optimistic perspectives for increasing healthy life expectancy. In R. M. Suzman, D. P. Willis, and K. G. Manton (Eds.), *The Oldest Old*. New York: Oxford Press, 1992.

Thomae, H. Reactions to life stress. Paper presented at 11th International Congress of Gerontology, Tokyo, 1978.

Thomae, H. Personality and adjustment to aging. In J. E. Birren and B. Sloane (Eds.), *Handbook on mental health and aging*. Englewood Cliffs, N.J.: Prentice-Hall, 1980.

Tran, T. V., Wright, R., and Chatters, L. Health, stress, psychological resources, and subjective well-being among older blacks. *Psychology and Aging*, 1991, *6*, 100–108.

Troll, L. *Turning points: Stability and change*. Paper presented at Brookdale Institute On Aging, New York, 1985.

Vaillant, G. E. *Adaptation to life*. Boston: Little, Brown, 1977.

Vaillant, G. E. Ego mechanisms of defense and personality psychopathology. *Journal of Abnormal Psychology*, 1994, *103*, 44–50.

Weisman, A., and Worden, J. W. The existential plight in cancer: Significance of the first 100 days. *International Journal of Psychiatry in Medicine*, 1976–77, *7*, 1–15.

Worchel, P., and Byrne, D. (Eds.). *Personality change*. Wiley, 1964.

# CHAPTER 10

# LOVE, INTIMACY, AND SEXUALITY IN OLD AGE

The previous chapter focused on personality: who one is and how one feels about oneself. An important aspect of one's personality is sexuality. In fact, sexuality encompasses many aspects of one's being as a man or a woman. As defined by Starr and Weiner (1981), sexuality is a quality of the person, an energy force that is expressed in every aspect of being. A person's speech and movement, vitality, and ability to enjoy life are all parts of sexuality. Sex is not just a biological function involving genital intercourse or orgasm, but also includes the expression of feelings and self in an intimate way through a wide-ranging language of love and pleasure in relationships.

Because of the importance of sexuality in individuals' lives, both older people and professionals who work with them need to understand the normal physiological changes that may affect sexual functioning with age and the centrality of intimacy across the life span. As noted by Dr. Alex Comfort (1976), "The first step in preserving your sexuality, which for many people is deeply important in preserving personhood, is to realize that, if cultivated, sexuality can be and

normally is lifelong for both sexes" (p. 194). Since our sexual nature goes far beyond whether we are sexually active at any particular point in life, older individuals need to be comfortable with whatever decisions they make regarding their sexuality. Although most older individuals can and do engage in intercourse, some older adults genuinely have no desire to engage in the physical aspects of sexual behavior—just as varying patterns of sexual expression are present at all ages (Walz and Blum, 1987).

This chapter begins by examining the prevalent attitudes and beliefs about sex and love in old age that frequently affect an older person's sexuality. It then reviews the age-related physiological changes that may alter the nature of older men and women's sexual response and performance but do not necessarily interfere with their overall experience of sexuality. Other factors that affect sexual activity—chronic illness, psychosocial conditions, and professionals' attitudes—are identified. In many instances, these dynamic contextual factors may exert greater influence than physiological changes as such. Sexual behavior, because of the powerful role it plays in the lives of most people, is especially likely to be affected by the interactions of physiological changes, the larger physical and social environment, the individual's personal learning history, self-concept, and the psychological meaning attached to one's experiences (Corby and Solnick, 1980). These factors are examined in terms of both male-female and same-gender relationships, as well as within the larger context of the importance of late-life affection, love, and intimacy. The chapter concludes by identifying implications for professionals who work with older people.

## ATTITUDES AND BELIEFS ABOUT SEXUALITY IN LATER LIFE

Widespread stereotypes, misconceptions, and jokes about old age and sexuality can powerfully and negatively affect older people's sexual experience. Many of these attitudes and beliefs stem from ageism generally, such as the perceptions of older people as physically unattractive and therefore as asexual. Another example of ageism is the perspective that all older people are the same, lifeless and devoid of human feeling, and therefore are not interested in sex. Since sexuality in our society tends to be equated with youthful standards of attractiveness, definitions of older people as asexual are heightened for older women and for individuals with chronic illness and disability.

Other attitudes and beliefs may stem from misinformation, such as the perception that sexual activity and drive do and should decline with old age. Accordingly, older people who speak of enjoying sexuality may be viewed as sinful, exaggerating, or deviant—for example, the "dirty old man." Alternatively, older people who express caring and physical affection for one another may be infantilized, defined as "cute" and ridiculed by professionals, their age peers, and family members. Such public scrutiny and teasing frequently occur among residents and staff of long-term care facilities. The current cohort of

older people grew up in periods of restrictive guidelines regarding appropriate sexual behavior and taboos relating to other forms of sexual activity, such as masturbation. Many of these attitudes and beliefs of both older people and their families may reflect a Victorian morality that views sex only as intercourse and intercourse only as appropriate for conception; sex for communication, intimacy or pleasure is considered unnecessary and immoral.

Unfortunately, the widely accepted attitude in our society that sexual interaction between older persons is both socially unacceptable and physically harmful may have negative consequences for older people. Surrounded by those with such beliefs and fearing ridicule or censure, many older people may unnecessarily withdraw from all forms of sexual expression long before they need to, thereby depriving themselves of the energy and vitality inherent in sexuality. Older respondents in a study by Starr and Weiner (1981) emphasized that sexual activity, in the broadest sense of encompassing both physical and emotional interaction, is necessary for them to feel alive, to reaffirm their identity, and to communicate with their partners. Yet, by accepting society's stereotypes, some older individuals may be barring themselves from sexual and intimate experiences that could benefit their overall physical and mental well-being (Teitelman, 1990). Understanding the natural physiological alterations in sexual response associated with the aging process is an essential first step toward dispelling such myths. In future years, those myths may change, as the media, gerontologists, and other professionals convey the message that sex is permissible and desirable in old age.

### Myths and Reality about Physiological Changes and Frequency of Sexual Activity

One of the most prevalent societal myths is that age-related physiological changes detrimentally affect sexual functioning. Such misconceptions have been created by some of the early research on sexuality. In part because of researchers' assumptions that older people do not engage in sex or would be embarrassed to talk about it, many early surveys of sexual attitudes did not even question older people about their sexuality. Such avoidance of the topic fostered further misinformation and misconceptions. Yet, in later studies, most older people have shown little embarrassment or anxiety in discussing sex, particularly as cultural norms regarding sexuality have changed (Starr and Weiner, 1981).

Other early studies included questions about sexuality, but focused on changes only in the frequency of sexual activities—intercourse. These researchers thereby overlooked the subjective experience or more qualitative aspects of sexuality in old age. For example, from 1938 to 1948 Kinsey and his colleagues studied primarily 16- to 55-year-olds, but their discussion of respondents over age 60 focused almost exclusively on the frequency of sexual intercourse. Using numbers of orgasm or ejaculation as the measure of good sex, they found that by age 70, 25 percent of men were impotent. Women were portrayed as reaching the peak of their sexual activity in their late twenties or thirties, then remaining on that plateau through their sixties, after which they showed a slight decline in sexual response capability (Kinsey, Pomeroy, and Martin, 1948, 1953). Because Kinsey and his colleagues overlooked the broader psychological aspects of sexuality, they failed to address the subjective experience, meaning, and importance of sex at different ages. Older individuals may have sexual intercourse less often, but it is not necessarily less meaningful than at a younger age. In fact, few age-related physiological changes are prohibitive of continued sexual enjoyment and activity in old age.

In addition to the emphasis on frequency of sexual intercourse, early research on sexuality was limited by the nonrandom and therefore nonrepresentative nature of the sample and by comparing younger and older cohorts at one point in time. For example, the 1954 Duke Longitudinal Study, which examined the frequency of sexual intercourse and interest in sex, found declining frequencies of sexual activity for older adults (approximately 50 percent reported being sexually active) compared to their young and middle-aged counterparts, especially for women and unmarried individuals. Older women were found to be less interested in sex than older men. The median age for stopping intercourse was 68 in men and 60 in women. Although it was found that 38 percent of respondents remained sexually active, this finding was downplayed against the observation of overall decline (Newman and Nichols, 1960). Other limitations were that the cohort effect was not identified. The definition of sexual activity was limited to heterosexual intercourse, and the respondents constituted a cohort of individuals raised during a period of strict sexual conservatism. We now know that such cross-sectional data fail to give a lifetime picture of an individual's sexual activity. The low levels of sexual activity reported at the time (the survey was conducted in 1954) may have reflected the attitudes and behaviors, including reluctance to report on their activity, of that cohort of elders, who grew up in the late 1890s to early 1900s, rather than any age-related physiological changes in sexual functioning (Starr, 1985; Traupmann, 1984).

A subsequent reanalysis of the 1954 Duke Longitudinal Study data to control for a possible cohort effect and the second Duke Longitudinal Study over a six-year period revealed a stability of sexual activity patterns from mid- to late life (George and Weiler, 1981). In other words, those who were sexually conservative and inactive in young adulthood and midlife, perhaps because of their social upbringing, carried that pattern through their later years. Similarly, those who were more sexually active in young adulthood and middle age continued to remain active in old age. A later analysis of the Duke data also found older women to be more interested in sex than older men, although the rate of sexual activity among older women declined, partly because of the absence of partners and because the husband tended to be the one responsible for curtailing or discontinuing sexual activities.

Other studies have found that, although the frequencies of reported sexual activity tend to decline with age, many older respondents continue to have active sexual experiences. For example, Comfort (1980) found that, among individuals 60 to 71 years of age, almost 50 percent had intercourse regularly, while 15 percent of those over 78 years regularly engage in intercourse. Despite the apparent decline, young-old individuals perceived their sexuality to be an exciting, enjoyable, pleasurable, and important part of their lives (Adams and Turner, 1985; Brecher, 1984; Kaplan, 1990; Starr, 1985). In their study of sexual responsivity across the life span, Masters and Johnson (1981) determined that, while physiological changes occur with age, the capacity for both functioning and fulfillment does not disappear. They concluded that there are no known limits to sexual activity.

In an open-ended questionnaire completed by 800 participants in senior centers, Starr and Weiner (1981) found the majority of respondents to be sexually active. For all the subjects who reported a frequency of sexual relations, almost 80 percent were sexually active; among this group, 50 percent reported the frequency of sexual intercourse to be once a week or more, 13 percent twice a week, and 12 percent three times a week. In fact, 99 percent desired sexual relations with varying frequencies if they could engage in sexual activity whenever they wanted. Sexual inactivity appeared to be based upon life circumstances, not lack of interest or desire. Contrary to earlier findings from the 1954 Duke study, sexual frequency did not decline sharply with age, but ranged instead from 1.5 times a week for 60- to 69-year-olds, 1.4 times a week for 70- to 79-year-olds to 1.2 times a week for the group over age 80. Starr and Weiner concluded that older people who remain sexually active do not differ significantly in the frequency of sexual relations compared with when they were younger (longitudinal data). Rather, sexual activity appears to decrease significantly when older people are compared with younger people at the same point in time (cross-sectional data).

When a partner is available, the rate of sexual behavior is fairly stable throughout life. And sexually active older people perceive their sex lives as remaining much the same as they grow older. A 1991 analysis of cross-sectional data from the National Survey of Families and Households found that more than 50 percent of married persons 60 years of age and older reported having had sex within the past month, with an average of slightly more than four times a month. The respondents' sense of self-worth/competence and their partners' health status significantly and positively related to the incidence of sex within the past month (Marsiglio and Donnelly, 1991).

In sum, as our biological clocks change with age, it is not necessarily for the better or the worse in terms of either the frequency of activity or the nature of the sexual experience. Individuals who have been sexually responsive all their lives will still be sexual in later years, but their experience may differ subjectively from their earlier years. Yet this difference can be positive. For example, 75 percent of the respondents in the Starr and Weiner (1981) study said that sex is the same or better compared with when they were younger. While the majority of female respondents considered orgasm essential to a good sexual experience, they also emphasized mutuality, love, and caring as central to a satisfying sexual relationship and willingly varied their sexual practices to achieve satisfaction. Male respondents emphasized that it is not only the physical stimulation of sex that is important, but also that sex is necessary for them to feel alive, to reaffirm their identity, and to communicate with a person they care about. Nevertheless, a number of physiological, age-related changes can affect the *nature* of the sexual response (Kaplan, 1990).

## Women and Age-Related Physiological Changes

Increasing attention is being given to menopause, given the growing numbers of woman in the 45- to 54-year-old age group. The major changes for women as they grow older are associated with the reduction in estrogen and progesterone, the predominant hormones produced by the ovaries, during menopause. The *climacteric*—loss of reproductive ability—takes place in three phases: premenopause, menopause, and postmenopause, and may extend over many years. Premenopause is marked by a decline in ovarian function in which a woman's ovaries stop producing eggs and significantly decrease their monthly production of estrogen. Menopause, in the strictest sense as one event during the climacteric, is a period in a woman's life when there is generally a gradual cessation of the menstrual cycle, including irregular cycles and menses, which are related to the loss of ovarian function. Menopause is considered to have occurred when 12 consecutive months have passed without a menstrual period. The average age of menopause is 50 or 51 years across most cultures, although it can begin as early as age 40 and as late as age 58. Surgical removal of the uterus or hysterectomy also brings an end to menstruation.

The major physiological changes related to the decrease in estrogen in menopausal and postmenopausal women are hot flashes, genital atrophy, urinary tract changes, and bone changes. Hot flashes are caused by vasomotor instability, when the nerves overrespond to decreases in hormone levels. This affects the hypothalamus (the part of the brain that regulates body temperature), causing the blood vessels to dilate or constrict. When the blood vessels dilate, blood rushes to the skin surface, causing perspiration, flushing, and increased pulse rate and temperature. Hot flashes are characterized by a sudden sensation of heat in the upper body, often accompanied by a drenching sweat and sometimes followed by chills. Gradually diminishing in frequency, hot flashes generally disappear within a year or two (Harmon and Talbert, 1985). Sleep disturbances can also result from hormonal changes, with sleep deprivation leading to irritability and moodiness often associated with menopause. Although 80 percent of women aged 45 through 55 experience some discomfort such as hot flashes and sweats during menopause, most find that these physiological changes do not interfere with their daily activities or sexual functioning, nor do they cause psychological difficulties, although vasomotor instability does disrupt and reduce sleep (Porcino, 1983).

Estrogen loss combined with the normal biological changes of aging leads to genital atrophy—a reduction in the elasticity and lubricating abilities of the vagina approximately five years after the menopause. As the vagina becomes drier and the layer of cell walls thinner, the amount of lubricants secreted during sexual arousal is reduced. Although vaginal lubrication takes longer, these changes have little impact on the orgasm as such and do not result in an appreciable loss in sensation or feeling. Any discomfort associated with these changes during intercourse can be minimized by using artificial lubricants such as KY jellies and vaginal creams. In addition, regular and consistent sexual activity, including masturbation, maintains vaginal lubricating ability and vaginal muscle tone, thereby reducing discomfort during intercourse (Corbett, 1987; Gambert, 1987).

Because of thinning vaginal walls, which result from estrogen degeneration and which offer less protection to the bladder and the urethra, lower urinary tract infections such as cystitis and burning urination may occur more frequently. These problems can be treated and often reversed with hormone replacement therapy most often estrogen combined with progesterone (Gambrell, 1987; Older Women's League, 1984).

As discussed in Chapter 7, osteoporosis, which is related to the loss of estrogen during menopause, is caused by a woman's inability to absorb sufficient calcium to strengthen her bones. The reduction in quantity of bone mass predisposes older women to fractures. Hormone replacement therapy combined with regular exercise has been found to prevent osteoporosis and may actually increase bone mass by promoting new bone formation (Gambert, 1987; Jarvik and Small, 1988).

Contrary to stereotypes and taboos regarding menopause, approximately 20 percent of women go through menopause with no intense symptoms such as hot flashes, while 15 percent experience symptoms sufficiently severe to warrant treatment, and 65 percent experience only mild symptoms that do not require any medical intervention. The primary medical response to the symptoms of hot flashes and vaginal atrophy has been hormone replacement therapy (HRT) which restores body hormones to levels similar to those before menopause. In 1992, the National Institutes of Health began a study of 70,000 post menopausal women ages 50 to 79 to study the long-term benefits and risks of hormone replacement therapy. Estrogen does alleviate hot flashes and vaginal changes, including atrophy, dryness, itching, pain during intercourse, lower urinary tract problems, and frequent urination, and appears to be a major factor in the prevention of osteoporosis and cardiovascular diseases (Gambert, 1987; Lewis, 1989; Karagos, 1990). The average amount of time spent on hormone therapy by most women is nearly 10 years. However, estrogen may merely postpone menopausal symptoms. When estrogen is stopped, even 20 years later, symptoms may recur (Gambert, 1987; Older Women's League, 1994).

In addition, hormone replacement therapy is controversial because of the slight increase in the risk of endometrial or uterine cancer among women receiving estrogen for a long period, although this risk is reduced when estrogen is combined with progesterone. However, recent findings regarding the risks of estrogen are mixed, with some data suggesting that long-term estrogen use may be protective against breast cancer and that judicious use is safe, effective, and even desirable, particularly in terms of preventing osteoporosis (Gambert, 1987; Lewis et al., 1989). Given these contradictory findings, women should be fully informed of the potential risks of estrogen and treatment should be at low doses, generally combined with progesterone, for short periods and continuously monitored. In instances of a strong family history of cancer, estrogen should not be given, despite its potential benefits in relieving discomforts associated with menopause and in preventing osteoporosis. In

addition, women who have had a stroke, recent heart attack, blood clots, liver, gallbladder or pancreatic disease, or undiagnosed vaginal bleeding should be cautioned against hormone replacement therapy. A newly developed patch system for delivering hormones through the skin and thus bypassing the stomach, digestive system and liver may be a safer form of hormone replacement therapy. It is clear that estrogen at any dose does not alter the aging process, depression, or insomnia (Jarvik and Small, 1988; National Institutes of Health, 1983).

Other symptoms reported by menopausal women, such as headaches, dizziness, palpitations, depression, and weight increase, are not caused by menopause itself. Increasingly, nutrition, exercise, and herbal or naturopathic treatments have been found useful in moderating symptoms associated with menopause. Although our cultural view is that women are expected to have difficulty at this period of life, the incidence of insomnia, depression, and anxiety may be traced to the meaning or psychosocial significance that individuals attach to menopause. For example, women who greatly value their roles as mothers and their capacity to bear children, or who have personality characteristics such as low self-confidence, tend to have a higher incidence than those who see themselves differently. (Newman, 1982; Polit and LaRocco, 1980). The findings on whether menopause is more distressing to employed women or to housewives are mixed. Increasingly, however, women are viewing menopause as a potentially positive transition rather than as a loss of fertility or the role of mother or as a cause of depression (Datan, 1986; Lennon, 1987). In sum, menopause, like other transitions that women experience, is affected by physiological and sociocultural factors, personality, and cultural influences, such as whether women are employed.

Despite some of the uncomfortable symptoms, menopause, from a physiological point of view, does not impede full sexual activity. In fact many women, freed of worries about pregnancy and birth control, report greater sexual satisfaction after menopause (Katchadourian, 1987; Starr and Weiner, 1981). Generally, an older woman's sexual response cycle has all the dimensions of her younger response, but the time it takes for her to respond to sexual stimulation gradually increases. The subjective levels of sexual tension initiated or elaborated by clitoral stimulation do not differ for older and younger women. The preorgasmic plateau phase, during which sexual tension is at its height, is extended in duration. Contrary to stereotypes, most older women experience and enjoy orgasm (Cutler and Garcia, 1984). For example, in the Starr and Weiner study (1981), 69 percent of women aged 60 to 69 years were orgasmic always or most of the time, 76 percent of those 70 to 79 years of age, and 68 percent of the group over age 80. These and other data suggest that an older woman's capacity for orgasms may be slowed, but not impaired. The orgasm is experienced more rapidly, somewhat less intensely, and more spasmodically; the resolution phase, during which the body returns to its baseline prearousal state, occurs more rapidly than in younger women.

From a physiological point of view, no impediment exists to full sexual activity for women after menopause. In fact, women experience only a slight decline in their capacity for sexual pleasure throughout their lives. Changes such as the thinning of vaginal walls and loss of vaginal elasticity may render intercourse somewhat less pleasurable, but they can be minimized by sexual regularity. Instead, older women's sexuality tends to be influenced more by sociocultural expectations than by physiological changes—primarily by the limited number of male partners and the common cultural definition of older women as asexual and unattractive. These psychosocial barriers will be discussed more fully subsequently.

## MEN AND AGE-RELATED PHYSIOLOGICAL CHANGES

The *male climacteric* differs from menopause in two significant ways; it comes later, generally after age 50, and progresses at a much slower rate, since the loss of testosterone (approximately 1 percent) is not as dramatic nor as abrupt as the estrogen depletion for menopausal women. Recent research suggests that the testosterone level beyond a minimal threshold is less important for sexual potency than is commonly believed. Since men maintain their fertility and generally do not lose the capacity to father children, there is little evidence that men experience changes sufficient to constitute a male menopause or to reduce their sexual enjoyment and desire (Teitelman, 1990). It has been suggested that the male climacteric has less to do with hormonal changes than with the psychological adjustments that men face as they age, such as declining physical energy, increasing economic pressures, loss of status with retirement, or depression (Katchadourian, 1987). Some changes in secondary sexual characteristics occur during the climacteric; a man's voice may become higher pitched, his facial hair may grow more slowly, and muscularity may give way to flabbiness (Whitbourne, 1985).

The normal physiological changes that characterize men's aging alter the nature of the sexual response, but do not interfere with sexual performance. The preorgasmic plateau phase, or excitement stage, increases in length, so that there is a slower response to sexual stimulation. An erection may take longer to achieve and may require more direct stimulation. For example, in 18-year-old males, full erection is achieved on stimulation on an average of three seconds; at age 45, the average time is 18 to 20 seconds, while a 75-year-old man requires 5 minutes or more (Thienhaus, 1988). Erections tend to be less full with age and the firmness of the erect penis may be somewhat reduced. But these erective changes do not necessarily alter a man's sexual enjoyment and satisfaction (Schiovi et al., 1990). The frequency and degree of erections can be studied while a man is sleeping by measuring nocturnal penile tumescence. The recording of sleep-related erections offers an opportunity to evaluate objectively sexual functioning under relatively controlled conditions. Such studies have found that the volume and force of the ejaculation are decreased in older men as they sleep (Masters and Johnson, 1981). The two-stage orgasm—the sense of ejaculation inevitably followed by actual semen expulsion that is experienced by younger males—often blurs into a one-stage ejaculation for older men (Thienhaus, 1988).

Accordingly, orgasm is experienced more rapidly, somewhat less intensely, and more spasmodically, occurring every second or third act of intercourse rather than every time. The length of time between orgasm and subsequent erections increases; in other words, the refractory period after ejaculation, before a second ejaculation is possible, is longer (Masters and Johnson, 1981; Katchadourian, 1987). However, although these changes may alter the nature of the sexual experience, none of them causes sexual inactivity or impotence, and the subjectively appreciated levels of sensual pleasure may not diminish (Masters and Johnson, 1981).

Nevertheless, impotence is the chief cause of older men's withdrawing from sexual activity. Unfortunately, an older man may be particularly at risk of impotence when he faces the combination of the unexpected onset of involuntary alterations in his established sexual patterning and the negative conditioning of cultural stereotypes related to sexual function and aging. There are mixed findings about the extent to which impotence is psychological in origin, however (Starr and Weiner, 1981; Brecher, 1984). Therefore, health care providers must be sure to rule out the physical basis of impotence, such as the effects of drugs (especially antihypertensives, antidepressants, and tranquilizers), diabetes, vascular disease, alcohol, or prostate disorders. Most prostate operations do not cause impotence, as will be discussed in more detail in the next section, "Disease and Sexual Activity." Health care providers must also be sensitive to providing older patients with as much information as possible about the implications of surgery and disease for sexual functioning. In some instances, a man's postoperative "impotence" may be a convenient excuse for not engaging in sexual activity, or may represent fears of additional illness. Whether impotence is real or imagined, the concept of sexuality in old age needs to be expanded to include more than erection and ejaculation during inter-

course. For example, health care providers must encourage couples to communicate their fears about impotence and suggest ways that they can enjoy openly fulfilling sexual experiences without an erection (Masters and Johnson, 1981; Starr and Weiner, 1981).

In summary, the normal physiological changes that characterize men's aging alter the nature of the sexual response, but do not interfere with men's sexual performance. These include (1) slower response to sexual stimulation, with a longer time needed for an erection, (2) less full erections, (3) decreased volume and force of ejaculation, (4) occasional lack of orgasm during intercourse, and (5) increased length of time between orgasm and subsequent erections. Impotence, the most common sexual disorder among older men, is influenced by both physiological and psychosocial factors.

Table 10-1 describes the physiological changes that affect sexual activities in older women and men.

## DISEASE AND SEXUAL ACTIVITY

Although normal physiological changes do not inevitably reduce sexual enjoyment, physical well-being does appear to be associated with sexual responsiveness and activity (Pfeiffer, 1972: Brecher, 1984). Not surprisingly, physical health problems, of one's own and/or one's partner, are a frequently cited reason for refraining from sexual activity (Walz and Blum, 1987; Kaplan, 1990). Even when an illness does not directly affect the sexual organs themselves, disease can affect sexual function because of physical decline, associated pain, iatrogenic complications of medication, and partner's fears about causing further injuries to health (Gambert, 1987). Since sexual response depends on the cooperation of multiple systems of the body—hormonal, circulatory, and nervous systems—if any of these are disrupted, sexual functioning can be adversely affected. And because sexual response also depends upon an individual's mental well-being, the distraction

## TABLE 10–1  Age-Related Physiological Changes in Genital Function

*Normal changes in aging women that do not interfere with full sexual activity:*

Reduction in vaginal elasticity and lubrication

Thinning of vaginal walls

Slower response to sexual stimulation

Preorgasmic plateau phase is longer

Fewer and less intense orgasmic contractions

After orgasm, rapid return to pre-arousal state

*Normal changes in aging men that alter the nature of the sexual response, but do not interfere with performance:*

Erection may require more direct stimulation

Erection is slower, less full, disappears quickly after orgasm

Orgasm experienced more rapidly, less intensely, and more spasmodically; decreased volume and force of ejaculation

Increased length of time between orgasm and subsequent erections (longer refractory period)

Occasional lack of orgasm during intercourse

More seepage or retrograde ejaculation

---

of illness may be all-consuming and deplete the psychic energy needed for sexual interest and response (Walz and Blum, 1987). On the other hand, sexual activity can be an important component of treatment following a major illness or surgery and is minimally risky to a person's health (Gambert, 1987). In this section, the chronic illnesses that commonly affect sexual functioning—heart disease and strokes, prostate disease, diabetes, and degenerative and rheumatoid arthritis—are briefly discussed.

Older people who have experienced a heart attack or heart surgery may erroneously assume that sexual activity will endanger their lives; therefore, they give it up. Unfortunately, many health care providers are not sensitive to such fears and fail to reassure individuals that sexual activity can be resumed within 8 to 12 weeks after hospitalization. A common guideline is that an individual who can perform moderate exercise, such as brisk walking or ascending two flights of stairs, can resume sexual activity. For those unable to engage in such exercise, taking their usual dose of nitroglycerin fifteen minutes to a half hour before engaging in sex reduces any health risks (Gambert, 1987; Thienhaus, 1988). Similarly, stroke patients may feel compelled to abstain from sexual activity because of an unfounded fear that sex after a stroke could cause another cerebrovascular accident. In the majority of cases, strokes do not harm the physiology of sexual functioning or the ability to experience arousal (Thienhaus, 1988). However, hypertensive drugs to control high blood pressure can cause impotence or inhibit ejaculation, with the exception of diuretics. Fortunately, a new class of drugs, called ACE inhibitors, has been reported to cause fewer side effects on sexual function.

Changes in prostatic cells with age result in an enlargement of the prostate in more than 90 percent of men over the age of 80; by age 40, 10 percent of men already have enlarged prostates (Silber, 1981). One out of every three men over age 65 will experience prostate difficulties, usually inflammation or enlargement of the prostate gland. Although most prostate problems are treatable through simple interventions such as warm baths and gentle massage, almost half of these will require surgery. After surgery, semen is no longer ejaculated through the penis, but is pushed back into the bladder and is later discharged in the urine. After healing occurs, the capacity to ejaculate and fertility may return in some men. The feeling of orgasm or climax can still be present, and sexual pleasure is not inevitably lessened (Walz and Blum, 1987). It is only when radical perineal prostatectomy is performed, generally for prostate cancer, and nerves are cut, that irreversible impotence results (Corbett, 1981). Fortunately, there are an increasing number of alternatives to radical prostatectomy for early prostate cancer, such as radioactive pellet implantation or some other form of radiation therapy (Brecher, 1984). However, in instances where impotence is irreversible, partners need to be encouraged to pursue alternate means of sexual pleasure or consider a penile implant.

Despite the fact that prostate surgery does not cause impotence in the majority of instances, between 5 percent and 40 percent of men who have undergone such surgery say that they can no longer achieve an erection (Thienhaus, 1988). In such instances, psychological factors need to be addressed through counseling, and couples need to be encouraged to try alternate methods of sexual satisfaction until the man can achieve an erection. Masturbation, more leisurely precoital stimulation, and use of artificial lubricants can all provide satisfying sexual experiences (Brecher, 1984). Another alternative in instances of irreversible impotence is a penile implant.

While most older men fear that prostate surgery will interfere with their sexual functioning and satisfaction, women may fear that a hysterectomy (surgical removal of the uterus), an ovariectomy (surgical removal of both ovaries), or a mastectomy (surgical removal of one or both breasts) will negatively affect their sexual functioning. However, in most instances, women's sexual satisfaction and long-term functioning are not affected by these surgeries, particularly if their partners are sensitive and supportive. However, some hormonal changes associated with a complete hysterectomy may affect sex drive. When women experience menopause as a result of a hysterectomy, perhaps earlier than the average age of onset for menopause, hormone replacement therapy is advisable (Brecher, 1984), except when the hysterectomy was due to cancer.

A more common medical cause of male impotence than prostate surgery is diabetes, particularly for those who have been diabetic most of their lives. Impotence in life-long diabetics occurs because diabetes interferes with the circulatory and neurologic mechanisms responsible for the supply of blood flowing to the penis for erection. In such instances, a penile implant may be an option. In instances of late-onset diabetes, impotence may be the first observable symptom (Brecher, 1984). However, when the diabetes is under control, potency generally returns. The sexual functioning of women diabetics appears to be relatively unimpaired. When diabetes is controlled through balanced blood chemistry, sexual problems other than impotence that are attributable to the disease should disappear or become less severe (Walz and Blum, 1987). Other less common diseases that may cause impotence are illnesses that affect the vascular and endocrine systems, kidney diseases, and neurological lesions in the brain or spinal cord (Gambert, 1987).

Arthritis does not directly interfere with sexual functioning, but can make sexual activity painful. Some of the medications used to control arthritic pain may also affect sexual desire and performance. Yet sexual activity can serve to maintain some range and motion of the limbs and joints and thereby help sore joints; it can also stimulate the body's production of cortisone, which is one of the substances used to treat the symptoms of rheumatoid arthritis (Cochrane, 1989). Pain during sexual intercourse can also be minimized by experimenting with alternative positions. A warm bath, massage of painful joints, and timing the use of pain-killing medications approximately thirty minutes prior to intercourse may also help to control some of the pain associated with arthritis. As with most chronic diseases, communication with the partner about what is comfortable and pleasurable is essential (Walz and Blum, 1987).

Closely related to the effects of chronic illness upon sexuality are those of drugs, including alcohol. Diagnosing the effects of drugs on sexuality may be particularly difficult, since drugs affect individuals differently, and drug interactions frequently occur. Drugs that inhibit or otherwise alter the performance of any one of the systems of the body can alter sexual response. For men, drug treatments may cause impotence, decrease sexual drive, delay ejaculation, or result in an inability to ejaculate. Psychotropic drugs used to treat depression and psychosis are particularly likely to impair erectile functioning (Corbett, 1981). Of patients taking thioridazine, 49 percent will experience impaired ejaculation, and 44 percent impotence. Yet this is one of the first drugs that a physician will prescribe for an older person who is agitated, depressed, schizophrenic, or anxious. Similarly, in 40 percent of the cases involving the drug amoxapine for treatment of depression, comparable impotence occurred (Lewis et al., 1989). Other types of drugs likely to affect sexual functioning are antihypertensive medications used to treat high blood pressure, drugs to control diabetes, and those that employ steroids.

For women, drugs may be associated with decreased vaginal lubrication, reduced sexual drive, and a delay or inability to achieve orgasm (Walz and Blum, 1987). Fortunately, physicians as well as older people are becoming more aware of potential negative effects of drug regimes on sexual functioning. Likewise, more drugs are now available that do not have negative side-effects on sexual desire and/or ability. These include ACE inhibitors among the antihypertensives; fluoxetine, trazodone, and maprotiline among the antidepressants; desipramine among the tricyclic antidepressants; and lorazepam, alprazolam, and buspirone among antianxiety agents (Lewis, et al., 1989).

Alcohol, when used excessively, can act as a depressant on sexual ability and desire. Alcohol consumption affects male sexual performance by making both erection and ejaculation difficult to attain; consequently, a man's anxiety about performance may increase and result in temporary impotence. Prolonged alcoholism may lead to impotence as a result of irreversible damage to the nervous system. Although the effects of alcohol on women's sexual performance have not been extensively researched, some women who abuse alcohol appear to experience less sexual desire and the absence of orgasm (Friedeman, 1978).

## GAY AND LESBIAN PARTNERS IN OLD AGE

Although most examples of sexual activity in this chapter are presented in terms of heterosexual or marital relationships, this should not be assumed to always be the case. Older people, their family members, and health and social service professionals must be sensitive to heterosexual relationships outside of marriage as well as same-gender relationships. Such sensitivity includes the discarding of stereotypical views of the nature of gay and lesbian relationships. Contrary to commonly held images, the varieties of gay and lesbian bonding are similar to those within heterosexual communities—ranging from monogamous life partners and nonmonogamous primary relationships to serial monogamy and episodic liaisons. Gay and lesbian life partners face many of the same issues that confront long-term heterosexual spouses, such as fears about the loss of sexual attractiveness, the death or illness of a sexual partner, or diminished interest or capacity for sex because of chronic disease. On the other hand, after a lifetime of discrimination or ostracism from family members, coworkers, or society generally, homosexual couples face additional issues regarding intimacy and sexuality, which are discussed in this chapter and in Chapter 12.

Although there is as much diversity of sexual activity for gay and lesbian older people as for heterosexuals, there is also a consistent pattern of relatively good adjustment to old age and ongoing sexual interest and activity. Older lesbians have generally practiced serial monogamy throughout their lives and continue in later life to expect to find a new partner, although many remain closeted about their sexual orientation

Most older gay men are sexually active and satisfied with their lives.

(Blumstein and Schwartz, 1983; Raphael and Robinson, 1980, 1981). They usually report positive self-image and feelings about being identified as a lesbian (Kehoe, 1986; Deevey, 1990). Older lesbians generally do not fear changes in physical appearance, loneliness, or isolation in old age as much as some heterosexual women do, perhaps because of the strong friendship networks that characterize many lesbian relationships (Laner, 1979). Most lesbians remain sexually active, although sexual frequency generally declines (Raphael and Robinson, 1980; Robinson, 1979). The extent to which sexual activity is considered to be an integral part of a lesbian relationship varies, although sexuality in a broader sense continues to play an important role in their lives (Kehoe, 1986; 1989). For some, lesbianism is a wider female interdependence rather than a sexual relationship as such.

The number of gay men with partners increases with age and peaks at 59 percent of those 46 to 55 years old. After age 60, the percent of gay couples decreases because of death, illness, cautiousness, or rejection of the notion of having a single, lifelong partner (Berger, 1982; Kelly, 1977). Older gay men are more likely to be in long-term relationships (with an average length of 10 years) or none at all, with only about 10 percent in short-term relationships of one year or less (Bennett and Thompson, 1980). Gay men tend to be more concerned about age-related changes in physical appearance than are lesbians, although perhaps no more so than their heterosexual peers, and they generally maintain positive feelings about their looks in old age (Gray and Dresser, 1985). Compared with their younger counterparts, older gay men have been found to be similarly involved in the homosexual world, satisfied with their social lives and sexual orientation, and confident in their popularity with other homosexuals (Bennett and Thompson, 1980). Consistent with the continuity theory of aging, sex appears to be equally important at all phases of a gay man's life (Vacha, 1985). Contrary to the myth of lonely, rejected, depressed older gay men, most gay men are generally sexually active, and satisfied with their partners and their sex lives; they report a positive sense of self-

esteem, well-being, and contentment and adapt fairly well to the aging process (Bennett and Thompson, 1980; Gray and Dressel, 1985; Lee, 1988; Kimmel, 1978, 1979). Despite fears of loneliness, most gay men have closer friendships in old age than do heterosexual men, and these friends and confidants may serve to resolve their fear of aging (Friend, 1990; Quam and Whitford, 1992). For many gay men, friendships may replace family ties disrupted by declaration of their homosexuality.

On the other hand, compared with their younger counterparts, older gay men are more likely to fear exposure of their homosexuality, to hide their sexual orientation, to view their relatives, friends, and employers as less accepting of their homosexuality, and to see their sexual orientation as outside of their personal control. However, these differences reflect cohort effects, rather than the aging process per se (Bennett and Thompson, 1980). The social support function of gay and lesbian relationships is discussed further in Chapter 12.

As noted in Chapter 7, there is growing concern about the increase in AIDS among older homosexual and bisexual males. In 1987, older gay and bisexual men represented 65.8 percent of all older persons who had AIDS, although the total number of older people with AIDS remains relatively small compared to other age groups (Stall, Catania, and Pollack, 1988). Despite the risks, most older gay men remain sexually active, although they less frequently engage in one-night encounters and are more knowledgeable about safe sex than comparably aged heterosexual males (Catania, Turner, Kegeles, Stall, Pollack, and Coates, 1989). With the growing public awareness about the importance of safe sex, future cohorts of gay men will probably be less likely to engage in high-risk sexual behavior.

## LATE-LIFE AFFECTION, LOVE, AND INTIMACY

In addition to the effects of normal physiological changes and chronic disease upon sexual activity and enjoyment, a number of psychosocial factors affect the ways in which older people express their sexuality.

1. Past history of sexual activity. Those who were most sexually active in middle age generally remain so in old age; this finding suggests that sexuality is a stable and continuous function across the life span (George and Weiler, 1981; Martin, 1981).

2. Attitudes toward sexual activities other than intercourse. Older people should recognize that partners can enjoy close, warm sexual activities without an erection through kissing, petting, holding and being held, dancing, massage, and masturbation.

3. Reactions to physiological changes and to illness-induced or doctor-induced changes. For example, if older men subscribe to the myth that in sex, as elsewhere, performance counts (how many orgasms, how long an erection) rather than focusing on pleasuring and closeness, they are likely to experience performance anxiety. Since anxiety tends to block sexual interest and response, such older men may be caught in a bind. The more they are concerned about performing well, the harder they try and the more difficult it becomes. In such instances, older men need to be reminded that there is no right way. Rather, sex can be whatever they and their partners find satisfying at the moment.

4. Reactions to the attitudes of others, including the larger society. Societal misconceptions regarding sexuality in later life can have a powerful effect on one's self-concept and perception of oneself as still sexually attractive and interesting. For example, Masters and Johnson (1981) note that when an older person says, "I'm too old for sex," this usually means "I'm too anxious about the effectiveness of my current level of sexual performance as judged against remembered functional facility in my twenties rather than realistically from the perspective of my sixties."

A primary psychosocial factor, especially for women, is the availability of a partner. Although the nature of sexual relationships is becoming increasingly varied in our society, most sexual activity occurs, for the current cohort of older people, within the context of a marital relationship (Teitelman, 1990). For women in heterosexual relationships, a central problem is differential life expectancy and the fact that most women have married men older than themselves. Because of older women's lower marriage rates, the opportunity for sexual activity within heterosexual relationships is dramatically reduced with age, but the capacity for sexual enjoyment is not altered.

The current cohort of older women, for whom sexual activity was tied to marriage, have relatively few options for sexual relationships. Unfortunately, these options are made more difficult because of the lack of socially approved models of sexuality for older women. For many women, their only models for sexuality may be the young. In addition, the pairing of older women with younger men is still rare, largely because of the double standard of aging in which older men are often viewed as distinguished while older women are perceived as unattractive and asexual. Women are also more likely than men to face socioeconomic barriers to meeting new partners, given the higher incidence of poverty among women compared to men. If a woman is preoccupied with financial or health worries, sexual activity may become a low priority.

Although an increasing number of women may discover that they prefer relationships with other women in their later years, it is currently difficult to estimate how frequently such shifts in sexual orientation occur in later life. In some instances, developing a close relationship with another woman may not be overtly sexual, but rather a preference for the companionship of the same sex. In addition, fearing isolation from family and friends, some older lesbians may not feel comfortable with being open about their sexual orientation. On the positive side, there is growing acceptance of masturbation by older women without partners as an alternative to a sexual relationship. However, older women may experience some defensiveness or guilt about masturbating, in large part because of the Victorian morality under which most of the current generation of older persons was raised. (Ludeman, 1981; Starr and Weiner, 1981). As noted by Comfort (1972), masturbation is not a substitute for being valued by someone else.

In contrast, marital status has little or no effect on men's sexual behavior or interest. Rather, the central issue for men appears to be understanding the physiology of impotence and possible treatments or prevention (Corby and Solnick, 1980). However, sexual functioning in both men and women is affected by the presence of a partner. Accordingly, a man who has not had sexual intercourse for a lengthy period of time following the loss or illness of a partner may experience what has been called *widower's syndrome.* He may have both the desire and new opportunities for sexual activity, but his physiological system may not respond and he cannot maintain an erection. If he becomes anxious and fearful about his performance, partial or incomplete impotence may result. A similar condition has been reported among husbands whose wives have Alzheimer's disease (Litz, Zeiss, and Davies, 1990). Fortunately, this syndrome can be resolved through unhurried, nondemanding sexual interaction with an understanding partner (Masters and Johnson, 1981).

Similarly, women may face *widow's syndrome.* After a year or more of sexual withdrawal, women are likely to experience a reduction in the elasticity of the vaginal walls. With the woman less likely to respond to sexual excitement, vaginal lubrication is slowed and reduced. Although these are all symptoms that arise from estrogen deficiency, they become more severe when there is a long period of no sexual contact. For men and women, frequency of contact is important to ensure sexual responsiveness and comfort (Masters and Johnson, 1981). Both men and women who are grieving the loss of a partner are unlikely to have the energy, sensitivity, and interest in someone beyond themselves that are essential to successful sexual activity.

Another critical factor in the physical and social environment is whether living arrangements provide opportunities for privacy. Such opportunities are most likely to be limited for those in long-term care facilities. Lack of privacy, negative staff attitudes, administrative difficulties, and the unromantic atmosphere of institutional environments all reduce the incentive of residents to be sexually interested or involved. On the other hand, when conjugal rooms are set aside, residents may be too embarrassed to use them.

Staff attitudes, which tend to reflect those of the larger society, may be the greatest barrier. Staff of such facilities tend to assume that frail residents no longer have needs for sexual intimacy. If older residents express a desire for sexual activity, staff may ignore them, infantilize, tease, or ridicule them, or report it to administrators, thereby adding to a sense of embarrassment experienced by this current cohort (Solnick and Corby, 1983; Blackwell and Hunt, 1980). Other staff may believe that chronic illness makes sexual activities impossible or harmful. Despite such obstacles, some residents in such settings are sexually active, and others would be if the opportunity allowed (White, 1981). The institutionalization of older persons does not necessarily mean the end of their sexual interest. Even institutionalized elders with dementia may maintain the competency to initiate sexual relationships (Lichtenberg and Strzepek, 1990; McCartney, Izeman, Rogers, and Cohen, 1987). Long-term care facilities need to develop policies to assure privacy, establish conjugal rooms, provide more romantic social programming, and offer sex education and sensitization for both staff and residents (Walz and Blum, 1987; Burnside, 1981).

Table 10-2 summarizes the psychological and social factors that may affect sexual activity among older people.

As noted throughout this chapter, sex encompasses more than intercourse. It is also important to recognize and to convey to older individuals that affection may be expressed in a wide variety of ways other than through sex. Intimacy, love, attachment, and friendship are cherished aspects of life, vital to an older person's sense of well-being. When older persons are experiencing

**TABLE 10–2 Psychosocial Factors That Influence Sexual Activity in the Elderly**

Past history of sexual activity

Attitudes toward sexual activities other than intercourse

Reactions to physiological changes or to illness-induced changes

Reactions to attitudes of others

Availability of a partner, especially for women

Performance anxiety; widower's/widow's syndrome

Opportunities for privacy

Staff attitudes toward those in institutional settings

assaults on their self-esteem, the need for affection may become even more intense. Without such affection, older individuals may feel lonely, even though they may be surrounded by other people and not physically alone.

Intimacy and attachment can be conveyed through mutuality, openness, commitment, sharing, respect, and enjoyment (Davis, 1985). With age, long-term relationships frequently move toward deeper levels of intimacy expressed in terms of loyalty, security, and mutual emotional interest, although this is not the case in relationships characterized by conflict, emotional distance, and emotional or physical abuse throughout the years (Reedy, Birren, and Schaie, 1981). On the other hand, many older people dealing with the feelings of loss and loneliness occasioned by the divorce or death of a spouse may find it difficult to invest the energy needed to develop intimate relationships.

An important aspect of most intimate relationships is touch. The need to be touched is lifelong; physical contact through touching and caressing is as powerful in the sixties, seventies, and eighties as in infancy, childhood, and early adulthood (Starr and Weiner, 1981). As the sense of touch is the most basic sense, older individuals may rely upon the sense of touch to a greater extent in interactions than other age groups (Hollinger, 1986). Just below an older person's expres-

sion of loneliness or of missing a former partner may lie the desire for someone to touch them. A handclasp or hand laid gently on the shoulder or arm, a child's hug, or a back massage can all be vital to addressing an older person's needs for affection and can increase their responsiveness. Staff in long-term care facilities especially need to be sensitive to the life-affirming role of touch for most older people, including those with dementia and those who are withdrawn or disoriented (Moses, 1985). As discussed in Chapter 12, pets can provide companionship and physical contact. On the other hand, helping professionals must be sensitive to cultural differences regarding the meaning and appropriateness of touch.

Friends are often important sources of intimacy, especially after a major role transition such as death of a spouse, divorce or retirement. For example, an intimate friendship with a confidant has been found to be as effective as several less intimate relationships in preventing the demoralization often produced by widowhood (Lowenthal and Haven, 1968). The presence of a close confidant also appears to be related to life satisfaction and a sense of belonging, worth, and identity (Lowenthal, Thurnher, and Chiriboga, 1975). In any senior center or congregate meal site, gatherings of highly valued same-sex companions are frequent. Among women especially, same-sex companions frequently greet each other warmly with a hug and kiss, may join arms while walking, and spend valued time together. These contacts are nonsexual in the narrow definitions of the term, but can be important to sexual health and to a person's psychological adaptation to aging (Walz and Blum, 1987). The importance of friendship in old age is discussed further in Chapter 12.

## FACILITATING OLDER ADULTS' SEXUAL FUNCTIONING

Unfortunately, most professionals who work with older people have been taught little or nothing about sexuality and intimacy in late adult-

FOR BETTER OR FOR WORSE © 1991 Lynn Johnston Prod., Inc. Reprinted with permission of Universal Press Syndicate.

hood. Many professionals may be uncomfortable or intimidated when asked to respond to the life-long intimacy needs of people as old as their own parents or grandparents. Physicians are often in a central position to respond to an older person's concerns about sexuality, yet they may be more likely to prescribe treatment for physical symptoms, such as vaginal dryness, than to respond to the older person's emotional concerns or need for information (Genevay, 1990). Often the topic of sexuality or intimacy is just below the surface when an older person is reminiscing or discussing losses and loneliness, such as the death of a partner. The loss of intimacy may underlie other disorders that the physician is treating, such as depression.

When an older person raises concerns about sexual functioning, such as impotence, it is important that the physician first differentiate potential physical causes from psychological ones through a careful medical and social history, a thorough physical assessment, and basic hormone tests. Such an approach can help to distinguish short-term problems that many individuals experience at various times, such as transitory impotence, from problems that persist under all circumstances with different sexual partners over a prolonged time period. These techniques have been described earlier in this chapter.

Other health and social service providers also can encourage and assure continuity of sexual expression for those for whom this has been an important part of their lives. As noted by Comfort (1980), sexual responsiveness should be fostered but not preached. What an older person may want most when he or she raises sexual concerns is support, acceptance, and listening. Older people who are concerned about their sexual functioning should be encouraged to focus on pleasuring rather than on genital sex. Professionals should convey that intercourse is only one way of relating sexually and that there is no normal or natural way for sex to proceed. Rather, many choices can be made regarding sexuality.

When a partner is not available, masturbation should be viewed as an acceptable release of sexual tension. Explicit discussion of masturbation with older people may relieve anxiety caused by earlier prohibitions during adolescence and young adulthood. Alternatively, professionals need to be sensitive to the fact that some older people do not want to engage in any sexual activity and must not put undue pressure upon them to be sexually active. What is important is for practitioners to take account of an older person's values and life experiences and support them in making their own choices about sexual behavior and sexuality.

Many older people need to be encouraged to develop alternative definitions of sexual activity that are not performance oriented (e.g., broader than genital intercourse) in order to gain intimacy, joy, and fulfillment through a broad spectrum of sensual interactions. Sex education in general can increase their sexual awareness, knowledge, interest, enjoyment, and range of activities. As noted above, sex education is also important for staff who work with older people. For example, nursing home staff need to avoid the stereotype of dirty old men and must recognize that the desire for intimacy and closeness continues throughout life. When working with older people who are experiencing memory loss or disorientation, staff need to assess the competencies of the older person to engage in intimate relationships. Lichtenberg and Strzepek (1990) have set forth guidelines for assessing the older person's awareness of the relationship, ability to avoid exploitation, and awareness of potential risks.

In the past, sex therapists have focused on working with younger people. Fortunately, this bias is changing, and various therapies for older people who report sexual difficulties have been found to be effective (White and Catania, 1982; Kaplan, 1990). Sex therapy with older persons should include the following elements: The first step is to eliminate or control medical problems, including drug interference, that may directly impair genital functions or indirectly affect sexual functioning. Sex training therapy and psychotherapy should include practical behavioral techniques in the form of specifically structured sexual interactions that the couple can conduct in the privacy of their home (Kaplan, 1990). These activities should emphasize intimacy, giving pleasure, communicating with the partner, and letting the partner know when pleasure is experienced. Opportunities should be provided to discuss problems encountered as well as concerns about performance (Thienhaus, 1988).

## SUMMARY AND IMPLICATIONS

As we have seen throughout this chapter, the normal physiological changes that men and women experience in their sexual organs as they age do not necessarily affect their sexual pleasure or lead to sexual incapacity. Even chronic disease does not necessarily eliminate sexual capacity. For example, many older persons, after adequate medical consultation, can resume sexual activity following a heart attack. Contrary to the myths about sexuality in old age, many people in their seventies and eighties participate in and enjoy sexual activities.

Older couples can adapt to age-related changes in sexual functioning in a variety of ways. Simply knowing that such changes are normal may help older people maintain their sexual self-esteem. For both older men and women, long leisurely foreplay can enhance sexual response. Avoiding alcohol use prior to sexual activity can be helpful, since alcohol increases desire, but decreases sexual ability. Health professionals need to be alert to medications that adversely affect sexual functioning, such as antihypertensives, tranquilizers, and antidepressants.

This chapter emphasizes how social factors also can influence an older person's sexual behavior. Myths, stereotypes, and jokes pervade the area of sexuality in old age. Unfortunately, societal expectations of reduced sexual interest may mean that older people stop sexual activity long before they need to. In future years, these myths may change as the media, gerontologists, and other professionals convey the message that sex is not only permissible but desirable in old age.

In professional work with older partners, definitions of sexuality need to be broadened beyond sexual intercourse. A variety of behaviors, such as touching, kissing, hugging, and lying side by side, can contribute to sexual intimacy and satisfaction, even for institutionalized older persons. Touching older people—a handclasp or back rub, for example—is especially important in home-bound and institutional settings.

Practitioners need to be sensitive to their clients' values and life experiences and to support them in making their own choices about sexual behavior and sexuality. Many of the current cohort of older persons grew up with taboos relating not only to intercourse but to other forms of sexual activity, such as masturbation. Hence, older individuals may need encouragement from professional counselors or others if they are to be free to affirm their sexuality and to experience intimacy with others.

## REFERENCES

Adams, C. G., and Turner, B. F. Reported change in sexuality from young adulthood to old age. *The Journal of Sex Research*, 1985, *21*,(2) 126–141.

Banzinger, G., and Roush, J. Nursing homes to the birds: A control-relevant intervention with bird feeders. *The Gerontologist*, 1983, *23*, 527–536.

Barbar, H., Lewis, M., Long, J., Whitehead, E., and Butler, R. Sexual problems in the elderly, I: The use and abuse of medication. *Geriatrics*, 1989, *44*,(3), 61–75.

Bennett, K., and Thompson, N. Social and psychological functioning of the aging male homosexual. *British Journal of Psychiatry*, 1980, *137*, 361–370.

Berg, W. B., and Garcia, C. *The medical management of menopause and premenopause*. New York: J. B. Lippincott, 1984.

Berger, R. M. *Gay and gray: The older homosexual man*. Urbana, IL: University of Illinois Press, 1982.

Blackewell, L., and Hunt, S. S. Sexuality and aging: Staff attitudes toward sexual expression among aged nursing home residents. *Journal of Minority Aging*, 1980, *5*(3), 273–277.

Blumstein, P., and Schwartz, P. *American couples*. New York: Franklin Watts, 1983.

Brecher, E. M. *Life, sex and aging: A consumer's union report*. Boston: Little, Brown, 1984.

Brickel, C. M. Initiation and maintenance of the human-animal bond: Familial roles from a learning perspective. *Marriage and the Family Review*, 1985, *8*, 31–48.

Burnside, I. M. Sexuality in nursing homes: A need for sensitivity and compassion. *Generations*, 1981, *6*(1), 22–23, 41.

Catania, J. A., Turner, H., Kegeles, S. M., Stall, R., Pollack, L., and Coates, T. J. Older Americans and AIDS transmission risks and primary prevention research needs. *The Gerontologist*, 1989, *29*, 373–381.

Cochrane, M. Immaculate infection. *Nursing Times*, 1989, *26*, 31–32.

Comfort, A. *A good age*. New York: Crown, 1976.

Comfort, A. *The joy of sex*. New York: Crown, 1972.

Comfort, A. Sexuality in later life. In J. E. Birren and R. B. Sloane. (Eds.), *Handbook of mental health and aging*. New York: Van Nostrand Reinhold, 1980.

Corbett, L. The last sexual taboo: Sex in old age. *Medical Aspects of Human Sexuality*, 1987, *15*(4), 117–131.

Corby, N., and Solnick, R. Psychosocial and physiological influences on sexuality in the older adult. In J. E. Birren and R. B. Sloane (Eds.), *Handbook of mental health and aging*. Englewood Cliffs, NJ: Prentice Hall, 1980.

Cormack, B. J. The effects on family members and functioning after the death of a pet. In M. B. Sussman (Ed.), *Pets and Family*. New York: Haworth Press, 1985.

Datan, N. Corpses, lepers and menstruating women: Tradition, transition and the sociology of knowledge. *Sex Roles*, 1986, *14*, 693–703.

Davis, K. E. Near and dear: Friendship and love compared. *Psychology Today*, 1985, *19*, 22–30.

Deevey, S. Older lesbian women: An invisible minority. *Journal of Gerontological Nursing*, 1990, *16*(5), 35–39.

Friedeman, J. S. Factors influencing sexual expression in aging persons: A review of the literature. *Journal of Practiced Nursing: Mental Health Services*, 1978, 34–47.

Friend, R. A. Gaying: Adjustment and the older gay male. *Alternative Lifestyles,* 1990, *3,* 231–248.

Futterwheit, W., Molitch, M. E., Morley, J. E., and Cherlin, R. S. Is there a male climacteric? *Medical Aspects of Human Sexuality,* 1984, *18,* 147–171.

Gambert, S. R. (Ed.). *Handbook of geriatrics.* New York: Plenum Medical Book Company, 1987.

Gambrell, D. Estrogen replacement therapy for the elderly woman. *Medical Aspects of Human Sexuality,* 1987, *21,* 81–92.

Genevay, B. Being old, sexual and intimate: A threat or a gift? In B. Genevay and C. Katz (Eds.), *Countertransference and older clients.* Newbury Park, CA: Sage, 1990, 148–167.

George, L. K., and Weiler, S. J. Sexuality in middle and late life: The effects of age, cohort and gender. *Archives of General Psychiatry,* 1981, *38,* 919–923.

Gray, H., and Dressel, P. Alternative interpretations of aging among gay males. *The Gerontologist,* 1985, *25,* 83–87.

Griggs, W. Sex and the elderly. *American Journal of Nursing,* 1978, *78,* 1352–1354.

Gwenwald, M. The Sage model for serving older lesbians and gay men. *Homosexuality and Social Work,* 1984, *2,* 53–61.

Harman, S. M., and Talbert, G. Reproductive aging. In C. E. Finch and E. L. Schneider (Eds.), *Handbook of the biology of aging* (2d ed.). New York: Van Nostrand Reinhold, 1985.

Hays, A. M. Intimacy and sexuality in the elderly: Discussion. *Journal of Geriatric Psychiatry,* 1984, *17,* 161–165.

Hollinger, L. Communicating with the elderly. *Journal of Gerontological Nursing,* 1986, *12,* 9–13.

Jarvik, L., and Small, G. *Parent care: A common sense guide for adult children.* New York: Crown, 1988.

Kaplan, H. Sex, intimacy and the aging process. *Journal of the American Academy of Psychoanalysis,* 1990, *18,* 185–205.

Karagos, M. *Reproductive history, menopausal factors and noncontraceptive hormone use in relation to the risk of coronary heart disease in women.* University of Washington, doctoral dissertation, 1990.

Katchadourian, H. *Fundamentals of human sexuality* (4th ed.). New York: Holt, Rinehart, and Winston, 1987.

Kehoe, M. Lesbians over 65: A triply invisible minority. *Journal of Homosexuality,* 1986, *12,* 139–152.

Kehoe, M. *Lesbians over 60 speak for themselves.* New York: Harrington Pore Press, 1989.

Kelly, J. The aging male homosexual: Myth and reality. *The Gerontologist,* 1977, *17,* 328–332.

Kidd, A. H., and Feldman, B. M. Pet ownership and self-perceptions of older people. *Psychological Reports,* 1981, *48,* 867–875.

Kimmel, D. C. Adult development and aging: A gay perspective. *Journal of Social Issues,* 1978, *34,* 113–130.

Kimmel, D. C. Gay people grow old too: Life history interviews of aging gay men. *The International Journal of Aging and Human Development,* 1979, *10,* 239–248.

Kinsey, A., Pomeroy, B., and Martin E. *Sexual behavior in the human female.* Philadelphia, PA: W. B. Saunders, 1953.

Kinsey, A. C., Pomeroy, B., and Martin, E. *Sexual behavior in the human male.* Philadelphia, PA: W. B. Saunders, 1948.

Laner, M. Growing older female: Heterosexual and homosexual. *Journal of Homosexuality,* 1979, 219–230, 267–275.

Lee, J. A. Invisible lives of Canada's gray gays. In V. Marshall (Ed.), *Aging in Canada.* Toronto: Fitzhenry and Whiteside, 1988, 138–155.

Lennon, M. Is menopause depressing? An investigation of three perspectives. *Sex Roles: A Journal of Research,* 1987, *17,* 1–16.

Lewis, M. Sexual problems in the elderly: Men's vs. women's; A geriatric panel discussion, *Geriatrics,* 1989, *44,* 75–86.

Lichtenberg, P. A., and Strzepek, D. M. Assessments of institutionalized dementia patient's competences to participate in intimate relationships. *The Gerontologist,* 1990, *30,* 117–120.

Litz, B. T., Zeiss, A. M., and Davies, H. T. Sexual concerns of male spouses of female Alzheimer's Disease patients. *The Gerontologist,* 1990, *30,* 113–116.

Long, J. W. Many common medications can affect sexual expression. *Generations,* 1980, 6, 32–33.

Lowenthal, M., and Haven, C. Interaction and adaptation. *American Sociological Review,* 1968, *33,* 20–30.

Lowenthal, M., Thurnher, M., and Chiriboga, D. *Four stages of life: A comparative study of women and men facing transitions.* San Francisco: Jossey-Bass, 1975.

Ludeman, K. The sexuality of the older person: Review of the literature. *The Gerontologist,* 1981, *21,* 203–208.

Marsiglio, W., and Donnelley, D. Sexual relations in later life: A national study of married persons. *Journal of Gerontology,* 1991, *46,* 338–344.

Martin, C. E. Factors affecting sexual functioning in 60–79 year old married males. *Archives of Sexual Behavior,* 1981, *10,* 399–420.

Masters, W. H., and Johnson, V. E. Sex and the aging process. *Journal of the American Geriatrics Society,* 1981, *29,* 385–390.

McCartney, J., Izemen, H., Rogers, D., and Cohen, N. Sexuality in the institutionalized elderly. *Journal of the American Geriatrics Society,* 1987, *35,* 331–333.

Molligan, T., Retchin, S. M., and Chinchilli, V. The role of aging and chronic disease in sexual dysfunction. *Journal of the American Geriatrics Society,* 1988, *36,* 520–524.

Moses, S. Stroking the child in withdrawn and disoriented elders. *Transactional Analysis Journal,* 1985, *15,* 152–158.

Myers, W. A. Sexuality in the older individual. *Journal of the American Academy of Psychoanalysis,* 1985, *13,* 511–520.

National Institute of Health. *Health benefits of pets.* Washington, DC: U.S. Department of Health and Human Services. 1988.

National Institute of Health. *The menopause time of life.* Washington, DC: U.S. Department of Health and Human Services, 1983.

Newman, B. M. Midlife development. In B. B. Wolman. (Ed.), *Handbook of developmental psychology.* Englewood Cliffs, NJ: Prentice Hall, 1982.

Newman, G. and Nichols, C. R. Sexual activities and attitudes in older persons, *Journal of the American Medical Association,* 1960, *173,* 33–35.

Older Women's League. *Status Report on Osteoporosis.* Washington, DC: Older Women's League, 1994.

Ory, M. G., and Goldberg, E. L. Pet possession and well-being in elderly women. *Research on Aging,* 1983, *5,* 389–409.

Pfeiffer, E., and Davis, G. C. Determinants of sexual behavior in middle and old age. *Journal of the American Geriatrics Society,* 1972, *20,* 151–158.

Polit, D., and LaRocco, S. Social and psychological correlates of menopausal symptoms. *Psychosomatic Medicine,* 1980, *42,* 335–345.

Pope, M., and Schulz, R. Sexual attitudes and behavior in midlife and aging homosexual roles. *Journal of Homosexuality,* 1991, *20,* 169–177.

Porcino, J. *Growing older, getting better: A handbook for women in the second half of life.* Reading, MA: Addison-Wesley, 1983.

Quam, J., and Whitford, G. Adaptation and age-related expectations of older gay and lesbian adults. *The Gerontologist,* 1992, *32,* 367–374.

Raphael, S., and Robinson, M. Lesbians and gay men in later life. *Generations,* 1981, *6,* 16–18.

Raphael, S., and Robinson, M. The older lesbian: Love relationships and friendship patterns. *Alternative Lifestyles,* 1980, *3,* 207–229.

Reedy, M. N., Birren, J. E., and Schaie, K. W. Age and sex differences in satisfying love relationships across the adult life span. *Human Development,* 1981, *24,* 52–66.

Robb, S. S., Boyd, M., and Pritash, C. C. A wine bottle, plant and puppy. *Journal of Gerontology Nursing,* 1980, *6,* 721–728.

Robinson, M. *The older lesbian,* Masters thesis, California State University, Dominiquez Hills, Carson, Calif, 1979.

Salamon, M. J., and Charytan, P. A sexuality workshop program for the elderly. *Clinical Gerontologist,* 1984, *2,* 25–35.

Schiavi, R., Schreiner-Engal, P., Mandati, J., Schanzen, H., and Cohen, E. Healthy aging and male sexual function. *American Journal of Psychiatry,* 1990, *147,* 766–771.

Schmall, V. L., and Staton, M. Sex education for older adults. *Generations,* 1981, *6,* 24–26.

Silber, S. J. *The male: From infancy to old age.* New York: Charles Scribner and Sons, 1981.

Soares, C. J. The companion animal in the context of the family system. *Marriage and the Family Review,* 1985, *8,* 49–62.

Solnick. R. E., and Corby, N. Human sexuality and aging. In D. S. Woodruff and J. E. Birren (Eds.), *Aging: Scientific perspectives and social issues* (2d ed.). Monterey, CA: Brooks-Cole, 1983.

Stall, R., Catania, J., and Pollack, L. AIDS as an age-defined epidemic: The social epidemiology of HIV infection among older Americans. *Report to the National Institute of Aging.* Unpublished document, 1988.

Starr, B. D. Sexuality and aging. In M. P. Lawton and G. C. Maddox (Eds.), *Annual Review of Geri-*

*atrics and Gerontology,* Vol. 5. New York: Springer, 1985.

Starr, B. D., and Weiner, M. B. *The Starr-Weiner report on sex and sexuality in the mature years.* New York: Stein and Day, 1981.

Teitelman, J. Sexuality and aging. In I. Parham, L. Poon, and I. Siegler (Eds.), *Aging curriculum content for education in the social-behavioral sciences,* New York: Springer, 1990.

Thienhaus, J. Practical overview of sexual functions and advancing age. *Geriatrics,* 1988, *43,* 63–65.

Traupmann, J. Does sexuality fade over time? A look at the question and the answer. *Journal of Geriatic Psychiatry,* 1984, *17,* 149–159.

Vacha, K. *Quiet fire: Memoirs of older gay men.* Trumansburg, NY: The Crossey Press, 1985.

Walz, T., and Blum, N. *Sexual health in later life.* Lexington, MA: Lexington Books, 1987.

Whitbourne, S. *The aging body.* New York: Springer-Verlag, 1985.

Whitbourne, S. "Sexuality in the aging male." *Generations,* 1990, *14*(3), 28–30.

White, C. B. Sexual interest, attitudes, knowledge and history in relation to sexual behavior in the institutionalized aged. *Archives of Sexual Behavior,* 1982, *11,* 11–21.

White, C. B., and Catania, J. Psychoeducational intervention for sexuality with the aged, family members of the aged, and people who work with the aged. *International Journal of Aging and Human Development,* 1982, *13,* 121–138.

Whitehead, E. D. Penile prostheses and papaverine: Current concepts. *Geratrics,* 1989, *44,* 77.

Women's Medical Center. *Menopause.* Washington, DC: Women's Medical Center, 1977.

# 11

# MENTAL DISORDERS AND THE USE OF MENTAL HEALTH SERVICES

As shown in previous chapters, old age is usually accompanied by some deterioration in sensory and cognitive functions, but personality remains relatively stable in normal aging. Nevertheless, personality disorders and psychiatric symptoms may emerge among some older persons who showed no signs of psychopathology earlier in their lives. Although such conditions are not a normal process of aging, in some individuals the stresses of old age may compound any existing predisposition to psychopathology. These stresses may be internal, resulting from the physiological and psychological processes described earlier, or external, that is, a function of role losses and the deaths of spouse, friends, and especially one's children. These conditions significantly impact older people's competence, so that they become more vulnerable to environmental press.

The primary affective or emotional disorder of old age is depression, accounting for a significant number of suicides, especially among older men. Alzheimer's disease and other dementias are cognitive disorders that are far more likely to affect the old than the young. Alcoholism and drug abuse are less common in older individuals, although their effect on the physical health and cognitive functioning of older people is more detrimental than on younger persons. Paranoid disorders and schizophrenia are even less likely to begin in old age; the majority of individuals who have either of these conditions were first diagnosed in youth or middle age. Each of these conditions is reviewed in this chapter.

## EPIDEMIOLOGY OF MENTAL DISORDERS

The prevalence of psychiatric disorders among older persons who are living in the community ranges from 15 to 25 percent, depending on the population studied and the categories of disorders examined. Even higher rates can be expected in institutionalized elderly, with estimates of 10 to 40 percent of people with mild to moderate impairments, and another 5 to 10 percent with significant impairments (Blazer, 1980; American Psychiatric Association, 1987).

Twenty percent of all first admissions to psychiatric hospitals are persons over age 65 (Brody and Kleban, 1983). Older psychiatric patients are more likely to have chronic conditions and to require longer periods of inpatient treatment than are younger patients, as evidenced by the fact that 25 percent of all beds in these hospitals are occupied by older persons. Note the discrepancy between this proportion and the proportion over age 65 in the U.S. population—12.6 percent in 1990. It has been estimated that 100,000 older chronic psychiatric patients live in state mental hospitals, 500,000 in nursing homes, and the remainder (over 1 million) in the community, where they often receive inadequate treatment for their psychiatric condition (Butler, Lewis, & Sunderland, 1991). As discussed later in this chapter, older persons are less likely to use community mental health services. Older patients comprise only four percent of the load of psychiatric outpatient clinics and less than 2 percent of those served by private practitioners (Butler et al, 1991; Roybal, 1988).

Older African Americans are twice as likely as whites to enter mental hospitals, but are far less likely to use nursing home services (National Center for Health Statistics, 1988). Older Mexican Americans and American Indians are less likely to use psychiatric facilities. These lower rates of institutionalization do not necessarily reflect differences among ethnic minority groups in the incidence of psychiatric disorders; indeed, prevalence data are extremely difficult to obtain for these conditions in older ethnic minorities (Markides, 1986). Few epidemiological studies of late-life psychopathology have examined ethnic minority differences. In one such study, no differences in the rates of psychiatric disorders were found among older individuals of different ethnic minority backgrounds (Romaniuk, McAuley, and Arling, 1983).

One problem with describing the prevalence of mental disorders of older people is the lack of criteria distinguishing conditions that emerge in old age from those that continue throughout adulthood. In fact, the major classification system for psychiatric disorders, the *Diagnostic and Statistical Manual,* fourth edition, (DSM-IV, 1994), of the American Psychiatric Association, makes such a distinction only for dementias that begin in late life. No other mental disorders are distinguished for old age, although other diagnostic categories are described specifically for adulthood as separate from childhood or adolescence. The problem of inadequate criteria for late-life psychopathology is compounded by the lack of age-appropriate psychological tests for diagnosing these conditions. An increasing number of researchers, however, are developing such measures, especially for diagnosing depression and dementia in older people.

## DEPRESSION

The three most prevalent forms of late-life psychopathology are depression, dementia, and paranoia. Of these, depression is the most frequently diagnosed. Epidemiologic surveys have found that 15 to 22 percent of community-dwelling older persons report depressed moods; 10 to 15 percent have depressions that require clinical interventions (Blazer and Williams, 1980; Gurland and Cross, 1982). A more recent epidemiologic survey of five communities (the Epidemiological Catchment Area, or ECA study) reported a much lower prevalence of depressive disorders—2.8 percent of a sample of 1,351 community-dwelling persons age 60 and older (Blazer, George, and Landerman, 1986). This may be due to differences in criteria for depression in these studies. Women tend to report more symptoms of depression in middle age and early old age, but it may be that more men have clinically diagnosable depression at age 80 and beyond (Gurland et al., 1980). Studies of depression in nursing homes have found rates as high as 25 percent of major depression, and 20 percent for minor depression (Parmelee, Katz, and Lawton, 1992; NIH, 1991).

It is important to distinguish *unipolar* depression from *bipolar* disorders (that is, ranging from a depressed to a manic state), as well as severe conditions such as sadness, grief reactions, and other affective disorders. Most of the depressions of old age are unipolar; manic-depressive disorders are rare. Still other cases in late life are *secondary* or *reactive depressions,* which arise in response to a significant life event with which the individual cannot cope. For example, physical illness and the loss of loved ones through death and relocation may trigger depressive reactions in the older people (Phifer and Murrell, 1986). The vegetative signs, suicidal thoughts, weight loss, and mood variations from morning to night that are observed in major depression are not found in reactive depression. Studies of older individuals in community settings and in nursing homes suggest that the prevalence of major depression is generally lower than the rates of secondary depression (Blazer, Hughes, and George, 1987; Parmelee, Katz, and Lawton, 1989).

As described in Chapters 4 and 9, most role *gains* (e.g., worker, driver, voter, spouse, or parent) occur in the earlier years, whereas many role *losses* come one after another in the later years, although many older people do experience some role gains. As we have seen, loss of roles may be compounded by decrements in sensory abilities, physical strength, and health. Although depression usually does not result from any one of these alone, the combination of several losses in close sequence may trigger a reactive depressive episode. Other older people at risk include those with major physical conditions (e.g. stroke, cancer), as well as widowed elders who do not have a supportive social network (NIH, 1991).

If the psychiatric symptoms persist beyond six months in these patients, this may indicate the development of a major depressive episode (Nacoste and Wise, 1991; Neshkes and Jarvik, 1987). Consistent with the approach of a better fit between the older person and the environment, environmental and social interventions, as well as psychotherapy, are more effective than antidepressant medications for secondary depression, as will be seen later in this chapter.

Death rates appear to be greater among older persons with a diagnosis of depression. Some specialists have suggested that older persons with depression are more apathetic, less interested in their environments, and more likely to entertain thoughts of suicide than younger depressives (Blazer, George, and Landerman, 1986; Mignogna, 1986).

The most obvious signs of depression are reports or evidence of sadness and feelings of emptiness or detachment. Also common are expressions of anxiety or panic for no apparent cause, loss of interest in the environment, and neglect of self-care, as well as changes in eating and sleeping patterns. The depressed person may complain of vague aches and pains, either generally or in a specific part of the body. Occasional symptoms are not problematic, however. Only when multiple symptoms appear together and persist *for at least two weeks* should an individual and his or her family suspect a depressive episode, especially if an older person speaks frequently of death or suicide. The symptoms of a major depression are listed in Table 11–1.

One problem with detecting depression in older people is that they may be more successful than their younger counterparts at masking or hiding symptoms of depression. In fact, many cases of depression in older persons are not diagnosed because the patient either does not express changes in mood or denies them in the clinical interview. A *masked depression* is one in which few mood changes are reported. Instead, the patient complains of atypical pain, bodily discomfort, pain, and sleep disturbance; reports problems with memory; is apathetic; and withdraws from others (Gallo, Anthony, and Muthen, 1994; Lichtenberg, Ross, Millis, and Manning, 1994; Mignogna, 1986; Neshkes and Jarvik, 1987). This is a common condition in older generations because many of these people were raised in an environment that discouraged the expression of feelings.

Health care professionals and family members need to distinguish depression from medical conditions and changes due to normal aging. For

## TABLE 11–1  Summary of DSM-IV Criteria for Major Depressive Episode

At least five of the following symptoms are present during the same 2-week period and represent a change from previous function:

1. Depressed mood most of day, nearly every day[*]

2. Markedly diminished interest or pleasure in activities, apathy[*]

3. Significant weight loss or weight gain, or appetite change

4. Sleep disturbance (insomnia or hypersomnia) nearly every day

5. Agitation or retardation of activity nearly every day

6. Low energy level or fatigue nearly every day

7. Self-blame, guilt, worthlessness

8. Poor concentration, indecisiveness

9. Recurrent thoughts of death, suicide

[*]At least one of the symptoms should be these.

SOURCE: Adapted with permission from the *Diagnostic and Statistical Manual of Mental Disorders,* 4th Ed. Copyright 1994 American Psychiatric Association, 327.

example, an older woman with arthritis who complains of increasing pain may actually be seeking a reason for vague physical discomfort that is related to a depressive episode. People with masked depression are more likely to complain of problems with memory or problem-solving. Their denial or masking of symptoms may lead the physician to assume that the individual is experiencing dementia, a condition that is generally irreversible. It is for this reason that depression in older persons is often labeled *pseudo-dementia.*

Because of such likelihood of denial, a physician's first goal with an older patient who has vague somatic and memory complaints should be to conduct a thorough physical exam and lab tests, in order to determine if an individual is depressed or has a physical disorder or symptoms of dementia. If the cognitive dysfunction is due to depression, this will improve when the depres-sion is treated. On the other hand, some medical conditions, including Parkinson's, rheumatoid arthritis, thyroid dysfunction, and diseases of the adrenal glands, may produce depressive symptoms. In some cases, depression can co-exist with medical conditions such as heart disease and stroke, compounding the dysfunction associated with these medical problems and delaying the recovery process. Certain medications may also produce feelings of depression; these include antihypertensives, digoxin, corticosteroids, estrogens, some antipsychotic drugs, and antiparkinsonism drugs such as L-dopa. In fact, any medication that has a depressant effect on the central nervous system can produce depressive symptoms in older patients, specifically lethargy and loss of interest in the environment (Schmidt, 1983). For these reasons, it is important for older persons to be examined thoroughly for underlying physical illness and reactions to medications. Physicians must frequently conduct medication reviews to determine if their older patients begin to show side effects to a drug, even after using it for several months or years.

## Therapeutic Interventions

It is important to treat both major and secondary depressions in older people as soon as they are diagnosed, because the older depressed patient is at higher risk of self-destructive behavior and suicide. Several researchers have tested the efficacy of alternative therapies for depression in older persons. There is some disagreement, however, about the value of such therapies. Although short-term improvements may be achieved through treatment, the long-range prognosis is often not very good. If the onset of depression occurs before age 70, therapy is generally more successful. Indeed, depression has been described as the most treatable psychiatric disorder in late life (Blazer, 1989; Gallagher and Thompson, 1983; Sholomskas et al., 1983).

The most common therapeutic intervention with depressed older individuals is pharmacological, which is particularly useful for those experi-

---

**SEEKING A DIAGNOSIS**

Often, older people who show symptoms of depression may deny any problems. Family, friends, and professionals who interact with the older person can help get an accurate diagnosis and appropriate treatment. The following actions are recommended:

  1. If the symptoms shown in Table 11–1 have persisted long after a negative life event, it is probably not a reaction to the loss. Seek out a medical evaluation by a specialist in geriatric psychiatry or psychology.
  2. If the older person resists the initial or subsequent visits to the geriatric mental health specialist, emphasize to the person that depression is *not* a normal process of aging and can be treated.
  3. Explore the most appropriate treatment for each patient; antidepressant medications may be the treatment of choice for one older person, but group psychotherapy may be best for another.
  4. Whatever treatment is selected, give it time to work. The patient should not be discouraged if medications do not improve moods immediately, or if they have side effects initially. It may require changing the dosage several times before an ideal level is found for that particular patient.

---

encing a major depression (NIH, 1991). Therapy with antidepressants is generally long term. Although antidepressants work well for some older persons, many others cannot use these drugs because of other medications they are taking, or because the side effects are more detrimental than the depression itself. These effects include postural hypotension (i.e., a sudden drop in blood pressure when rising from a prone position), increased vulnerability to falls and fractures, cardiac arrhythmias, urinary retention, constipation, disorientation, skin rash, and dry mouth (Salzman, 1984; Neshkes and Jarvik, 1987). Because of these potentially dangerous reactions, it is important to start antidepressant therapy at a much lower dose in older than in younger patients, perhaps doses 50 percent lower for some types of antidepressants (Mignogna, 1986). For these reasons, more and more physicians are, quite appropriately, reluctant to prescribe antidepressants to older persons. Many prefer to try short-term psychotherapy and behavioral therapies first. Unfortunately, however, many older persons who turn to a general practitioner for treatment of depression often receive antidepressants as a first line of attack rather than psychotherapy, which may be more appropriate for many of them.

Despite past controversy about its use, electroshock or electroconvulsive therapy (ECT) is sometimes used in cases of severe depression. ECT is regarded as a quick method for major depression in patients who have not responded to medications, who have a higher risk of suicide, and/or who refuse to eat. Older patients with severe agitation, vegetative symptoms, or feelings of hopelessness, helplessness, worthlessness, and delusions often respond well to ECT (Mignogna, 1986). Clinical reports cite the effectiveness of ECT for patients as old as 94 years (O'Shea et al., 1987). On the other hand, some psychiatrists have avoided using ECT with older patients because of its potentially harmful effects on memory. It also poses risks for patients with a recent myocardial infarction, stroke, or severe hypertension. Risks to memory function apply in particular when bilateral ECT (i.e., shock to both sides of the brain) is administered. Unilateral nondominant hemisphere ECT is often preferred because it is capable of alleviating depression without impairing cognitive functioning (Fraser and Glass, 1980; Weeks, Freeman, and Kendall, 1980). However, it has been suggested that bilateral ECT results in greater clinical success for most patients than does unilateral, especially if the technique of brief pulse waves rather than

Psychotherapy can be effective with many older people.

sine wave forms is used (Abrams and Fink, 1984; Kramer, 1987). The long-term effectiveness of ECT for older depressed persons, as well as what type of maintenance therapy works best following ECT, is unclear.

There have been fewer studies examining the usefulness of psychotherapy with older people. Clinicians have reported that it is an effective approach for older people, even those with dementia. Older people are just as likely as younger persons to benefit from the insight and empathy provided by a therapist trained in geriatric psychotherapy (Butler et al., 1991). In particular, secondary depression responds well to supportive psychotherapy that allows the patient to review and come to terms with the stresses of late life. Supportive psychotherapy is useful with older patients because it allows them to reestablish control and emotional stability. Older depressed persons appear to benefit from short-term, client-centered, directive therapy more than from therapy that is nondirective or uses free association to uncover long-standing personality conflicts (Gallagher and Thompson, 1983; Sholomskas et al., 1983). These methods can help depressed older patients understand the source of their anxieties, fears, guilt, and apathy that are

so detrimental to their interpersonal functioning. The success of a particular treatment strategy may be related to the duration and severity of the depression. Alternative approaches to psychotherapy with older people are discussed later in this chapter.

## Suicide among Older People

It has been estimated that 17 to 25 percent of all reported suicides occur in persons aged 65 and older (Koenig and Blazer, 1992). In 1986, the national rate was 12 suicides per 100,000 population. The rate for persons over age 65 was over 21.5 per 100,000, ranging from 18 for those aged 65–69 to 25 per 100,000 among those over age 85 (NCHS, 1988; Meehan, Saltzman and Sattin, 1991). It is noteworthy that the highest suicide rates in the United States are found among older white males. The prevalence of suicide in this population rises linearly after age 65; almost three times as many suicides occur in white males aged 85 and over as in all other subgroups of older people combined (Belsky, 1984). According to the National Center for Health Statistics (Meehan, Saltzman, and Sattin, 1991), white males over age 85 completed 61 suicides per 100,000 in 1986. In contrast, white females completed 7.5; nonwhite females 2; and nonwhite males 18 suicides per 100,000 in the same year. Since there are probably a significant number of suicides that appear to be accidents or natural deaths (e.g., starvation or gas poisoning), these statistics may underrepresent the actual incidence of the problem.

One explanation for the higher rates of suicide among older white males is that they generally experience the greatest incongruence between their ideal self-image (that of worker, decision-maker, or holder of relatively high status in society) and the realities of advancing age (Miller, 1979; Butler and Lewis, 1982). With age, the role of worker is generally lost, chronic illness may diminish one's sense of control, and an individual may feel a loss of status. Social isolation may have an additive effect on the incidence of suicide, which is an important factor in the lives of older white widowed males, who are most likely to lack strong social support networks (Holinger and Offer, 1982; Manton, Blazer, and Woodbury, 1987). Older males in minority populations such as African American, Chinese, and Filipino are less likely to commit suicide because of more extensive family support systems (McIntosh and Santos, 1981). However, recent statistics show increased rates among older black men, from 11 to 16 suicides per 100,000 in 1986 (Meehan, Saltzman, and Sattin, 1991). Suicide rates declined among the older population from 1940 to 1980, but rose again from 1980 to 1986, especially among men over age 70. It is difficult to explain this reversal in trends; the growing availability of firearms, greater acceptance of suicide by society, and lack of strong social supports among unmarried older men have been suggested as reasons for the increase. Risk factors for suicide in this population include being a white male, as noted above, a history or current diagnosis of psychiatric problems, coexisting medical problems (especially congestive heart failure, or chronic pain), and social isolation (Frierson, 1991).

There are fewer nonfatal suicide attempts in older men compared to the young. That is, the rate of completed suicides is far greater among older men—4:1 versus 200:1 in the young (Stenback, 1980; McIntire and Angle, 1981). This difference may be due to the use of more lethal methods of suicide such as shotguns (73 percent of suicides among older men in 1986 involved firearms) and a lower likelihood of survival from serious injury.

Because attempts at suicide are more likely to be successful in older men, it is important for family members and professional service providers to be sensitive to clues of an impending suicide. In one study of older persons who had committed suicide, 75 percent had seen a primary care physician in the preceding month, but their psychiatric disturbances had not been detected or were inadequately treated. In most cases, these older persons had not sought psychiatric care. This study reported that less than 14 percent of older men who committed suicide had seen a mental health care provider (Conwell and Caine, 1991). Risk factors include a serious physical illness with severe pain, the sudden death of a loved one, a major loss of independence, or financial inadequacy. Statements that indicate frustration with life and a desire to end it, a sudden decision to give away one's most important possessions, and a general loss of interest in one's social and physical environment must be attended to closely by those who are familiar with the older person. Since older people are less likely to make threats or to announce their intentions than are young people who intend to commit suicide, it is even more important to watch for subtle cues. Clearly, not all older people displaying such symptoms will attempt suicide, but the recognition of changes in an older family member's or client's behavior and moods can alleviate a potential disaster.[*]

## DEMENTIA

As stated in Chapter 8, normal aging does not result in significant declines in intelligence, memory, and learning ability. Mild impairments do not necessarily signal a major loss but often represent a mild form of memory dysfunction known as benign senescent forgetfulness. Only in the case of the diseases known collectively as the dementias does cognitive function show marked deterioration. Dementia, also referred to as organic brain syndrome or senile dementia, actually includes a variety of conditions that are

---

[*] As will be described in Chapter 16, some people believe that suicide for terminally ill older people allows them to maintain control over their death. Groups who adhere to this viewpoint, particularly the Hemlock Society, would be opposed to interventions to stop an older person from choosing suicide.

caused by or associated with damage of brain tissue, resulting in impaired cognitive function and, in more advanced stages, impaired behavior and personality. Such changes in the brain result in progressive deterioration of an individual's ability to learn and recall items from the past. Until recently, it was assumed that all these syndromes were associated with cerebral arteriosclerosis ("hardening of the arteries"). Although it is now known that a number of these conditions occur independently of arteriosclerosis, research on the causes of the deterioration in brain tissue is at an early stage. Some features are unique to each type of dementia, but all dementias have in common a change in an individual's ability to recall events in recent memory, and problems with comprehension, attention span, judgment, and orientation to time, place, and person. The individual with dementia may experience increased concreteness of thought (i.e., be unable to understand abstract thought or symbolic language; for example, he or she cannot interpret a proverb), particularly in the later stages of the disease.

Although not part of normal aging, the likelihood of experiencing dementia does increase with advancing age. Approximately three million persons over age 65 experience some degree of cognitive loss (Ringler, 1981), and up to 50 percent of institutionalized older people are estimated to have mild to moderate levels of dementia. As more people live to be over age 70, the number of persons with dementia is expected to increase by 44 percent in whites and 72 percent in African Americans between 1980 and 2005 (Kramer, 1983). This difference by ethnic minority status is attributed to the more rapid growth of African Americans living beyond age 70. However, just as aging and disease are not synonymous, dementia is not inevitable with age.

The major types of dementias are shown in Table 11–2. Note the distinction between *reversible* and *irreversible* dementias. The first refers to cognitive decline, which may be caused

**Table 11–2  Major Dementias of Late Life**

| REVERSIBLE | IRREVERSIBLE |
|---|---|
| Drugs | Alzheimer's |
| Alcohol | Multi-infarct |
| Nutritional deficiencies | Huntington's Chorea |
| Normal pressure hydrocephalus | Pick's disease |
| Brain tumors | Creutzfeldt-Jacob |
| Hypothyroidism/Hyperthyroidism | Kuru |
| Neurosyphilis | Korsakoff |
| Depression (pseudo–dementia) | |

by drug toxicity, hormonal or nutritional disorders, and other diseases that may be reversible. Sources of potentially reversible dementias include tumors in and trauma to the brain, toxins, metabolic disorders such as hypo- or hyperthyroidism, diabetes, hypo- or hypercalcemia, infections, vascular lesions, and hydrocephalus. Severe depression may produce confusion and memory problems in some older people. Some medications may also cause dementia-like symptoms. This problem is aggravated if the individual is taking multiple medications or is on a dosage that is higher than can be metabolized by the older kidney or liver. An individual who appears to be suffering from such reactions should be referred promptly for medical screening.

Irreversible dementias are those that have no discernible environmental cause and cannot yet be cured. Although there is considerable research on the causes and treatments for these conditions, they must be labeled irreversible at the present time. Some of these are more common than others; some have identifiable causes while others do not. Pick's disease is one of the rarest; in this type, the frontal lobes of the brain atrophy. Of all the dementias, it is most likely to occur in younger persons and to result in significant personality changes. Creutzfeldt-Jacob and Kuru diseases have been traced to a slow-acting virus. In the former type of dementia, decline in cognitive abilities occurs quite rapidly. The latter type is quite rare. Huntington's Chorea is a genetically transmitted condition that usually appears in people in their thirties and forties. It results in more neuromuscular changes than do the other dementias.

Multi-infarct dementia has been estimated to represent 15 to 20 percent of all nonreversible dementias (Terry and Wisniewski, 1977). This is the form of dementia that in the past was identified as "senility." In this type, several areas of the brain show infarcts or small strokes that result in damage to one or more blood vessels feeding those areas of the brain. Older people with this condition often have a history of hypertension, strokes, and blackouts. Although multi-infarct dementia may be diagnosed without such a history, such cases are relatively rare and may indicate another type of dementia, most likely Alzheimer's disease.

## Alzheimer's Disease

The most common irreversible dementia in late life, accounting for 50 to 70 percent of all dementias, is senile dementia of the Alzheimer's type (Alzheimer's disease or AD). Prevalence rates are difficult to obtain, but it has been estimated that 5 to 15 percent of all persons over age 65 and over 25 percent in nursing homes have symptoms of AD. The prevalence of Alzheimer's disease appears to increase with age; less than 2 percent of the general population under age 60 are affected, whereas rates of 20 percent and higher have been estimated for the population over age 80 (Evans, et al., 1989; Rocca, Amaducci, and Schoenberg, 1986). A survey of 467 community-dwelling elderly in East Boston revealed much higher rates. Using a battery of neurological, neuropsychological, and laboratory tests, the team of researchers estimated a prevalence rate of 10.3 percent in all persons over age 65 in this survey. There was a dramatic increase with age, such that 3 percent among the 65–74-year-old group were diagnosed with Alzheimer's

disease, compared with 18.7 percent of the 75–84-year-olds, and 47.2 percent of those 85 and older (Evans et al., 1989). However, because of selective survival, it appears that men who survive into their nineties become less likely to develop AD after this age (Perls, 1995). Although a distinction was made in the past between presenile (i.e., before age 65) and senile dementia, there is now common agreement that these are the same disease. Recent analyses also suggest that AD now ranks third in health care costs, just after cancer and heart disease. It has been estimated that the average AD patient requires over $47,000 annually for care and treatment. The national costs for direct care in 1991 for AD patients was more than $20 billion (Ernst and Hay, 1994).

Several hypotheses have been proposed to explain the causes of Alzheimer's disease. Some researchers have suggested that it may result from a slow virus, or a virus-like agent called a prion, as in Kuru and Creutzfeldt-Jacob disease (Wurtman, 1985). Others have identified its link with Down syndrome (i.e., a greater frequency in families where Down syndrome has occurred, and a high prevalence in people with Down syndrome by age 40). Multiple occurrences have been found in some families (e.g., two siblings or a parent and child both develop AD), which suggests that chromosomal or other genetic factors may play a role in its etiology (Heston et al., 1981). There is increasing evidence for a hereditary type of Alzheimer's disease. Still others have argued that the disease is caused by the accumulation of heavy metals (such as aluminum) in the brain. The abnormal tangles (a web of dead brain cells) found in the neurons of the brain of Alzheimer's victims have been observed to contain 10 to 50 times more aluminum than is found in normal neurons. However, it is difficult to determine if such accumulation of aluminum is a cause or outcome of the disease (Perl and Brody, 1980). To date, none of these hypotheses has received conclusive support.

More recently, emphasis has been placed on the finding of a biochemical imbalance in the brains of AD patients, specifically a reduction in the number of cholinergic cells in the brain (up to 80 percent loss in some key areas). These brain cells are important for learning and memory because they release an important chemical "messenger," *acetylcholine,* that transfers information from one cell to another. Their loss reduces the acetylcholine available for this important function. The noradrenergic system is another chemical messenger system that becomes impaired with Alzheimer's disease, further complicating our understanding of why and how these neurochemical systems appear to break down in this disease (Katzman and Jackson, 1991). Still another neurochemical change observed in Alzheimer brains is the accumulation of *amyloid,* a protein. It appears that there may a genetic defect in one of the normal proteins located in brain regions responsible for memory, emotions, and thinking. Amyloid is actually a group of proteins found in the neurofibrillary tangles that characterize an Alzheimer brain. The precursor protein to amyloid (Beta-amyloid) is coded by a gene located in chromosome 21, which is also the chromosome responsible for Down syndrome. Researchers have found deposits of amyloid or its precursor Beta-amyloid in the brains of Down patients who die at a younger age with Alzheimer's disease, which provides further evidence of the link between these two conditions. Beta-amyloid may be responsible for the death of brain cells in these patients. As with other changes observed in the brains of AD patients, it is not yet clear whether these beta-amyloid deposits are the *cause* of AD or secondary to other structural or biochemical changes.

Recent genetic research has centered on a protein called apolipoprotein, or *apo-E,* which is responsible for transporting cholesterol in the blood. Of the three common types of apo-E proteins, *E2, E3, E4,* those who inherit an E4 gene from *each* parent have 8 times the risk of developing AD than the general population. Those who acquire an E3 gene from each parent also have a greater risk of developing AD, but at a later age than those with two E4 genes (at an average age of 75 versus 68). The role of E2 in Alzheimer's disease is not yet understood (Perls, 1995). Other proteins that may be associated with Alzheimer's disease are being targeted for study as researchers observe high levels of abnormal intraneuronal proteins in the Alzheimer brain, such as tau, ubiquitin, and Alz-68 (Katzman and Jackson, 1991).

As illustrated by Mr. Adams in the introductory vignette, Alzheimer's disease is characterized by deficits in attention, learning, memory, and language skills. An individual with this condition may also have problems in judgment, abstraction, and orientation. These changes in cognitive function appear to be related to structural changes in the brain. For example, the hippocampus is a region in the limbic system deep inside the brain that is involved in learning new information and retrieving old information. It is one of the first regions where plaques and tangles occur, so it is not surprising that patients in the earlier stages of the disease often have difficulties with attention span and with orientation to the environment, increased anxiety and restlessness, and unpredictable changes in mood. Family members may complain that the older person has become more aggressive or, in some cases, more passive than in the past. Depression may set in as the individual realizes that he or she is experiencing these problems. This depression may also be associated with deterioration in the locus ceruleus, a part of the brain that produces a mood-regulating chemical. In the more advanced stages of the disease, as it spreads to the cerebral cortex, which controls language and movement, there may be marked aphasia (i.e., problems recalling appropriate words and labels), perseveration (i.e., continual repeating of the same phrase and thoughts), apathy, and problems with comprehension, such that Alzheimer's victims may not recognize their spouses, children, and longtime friends. However, it is not unusual for some patients in the moderate stages of AD to describe quite articulately and vividly events that took place many years ago. In the advanced phases, as the neurons in the motor cortex die, the patient may need assistance with bodily functions such as eating and toileting. At autopsy, there is a generalized deterioration of cortical tissue, which appears to be tangled and covered with plaque.

Further evidence for the association between deterioration of brain regions and progression of the disease comes from recent studies measuring the density or number of synapses (quantified by antibodies to synaptophysin, a chemical located in the synapse) and scores on a cognitive test of dementia. By testing patients diagnosed with Alzheimer's disease, the researchers in these studies found correlations greater than .70 between synapse density and scores on a dementia rating scale (Masliah et al., 1989; Terry et al., 1990).

There have been some attempts to determine if AD proceeds through a series of stages, such that symptoms become more prevalent and severe. This is a difficult task because the course of AD varies so widely. Some patients may experience a rapid decline in memory while their orientation to time, place, and people may remain relatively intact. Other patients may experience mood and personality changes early, whereas still others maintain their pre-morbid personality for many years after the symptoms first appear.

A broad distinction is often made among early, middle, and advanced stages of AD. These categories are based on the patient's levels of decline in memory, orientation, and activities of daily living. Some psychologists have provided guidelines with the use of assessment tools such as the Mini-Mental Status Exam and the Dementia Rating Scale (Folstein, Folstein, and McHugh, 1975; Mattis, 1976), which give clues to the patients' levels of deterioration on the basis of their test scores. Perhaps the most extensive research to determine the stages of AD has been conducted by Reisberg et al. (1982). Based on their observations of functional and cognitive declines in AD patients, they have developed a Global Deterioration Scale that delineates seven stages of the disease. See Table 11–3.

Because of recent attention by the media and by researchers on Alzheimer's disease, there is

**TABLE 11–3  Global Deterioration Scale**

Stage 1:  No cognitive or functional decrements

Stage 2:  Complaints of very mild forgetfulness and some work difficulties

Stage 3:  Mild cognitive impairment on cognitive battery; concentration problems; some difficulty at work and in traveling alone

Stage 4:  Late confusional stage; increased problems in planning, handling finances; increased denial of symptoms; withdrawal

Stage 5:  Poor recall of recent events; may need to be reminded about proper clothing and bathing

Stage 6:  More advanced memory orientation problems; needs assistance with activities of daily living; more personality changes

Stage 7:  Late dementia with loss of verbal abilities; incontinent; loss of ability to walk; may become comatose

SOURCE: B. Reisberg, S. H. Ferris, M. J. De Leon, and T. Crook, The Global Deterioration Scale for assessment of primary degenerative dementia. *American Journal of Psychiatry, 139,* pp. 1136–1139, 1982. Copyright 1982, the American Psychiatric Association. Reprinted by permission.

some tendency to overestimate its occurrence and to assume that it is the cause of all dementias. It has even created what one neurologist has called "Alzheimer's phobia" in many older people (Fox, 1991). In many ways, it has taken on the role that multi-infarct dementia had several years ago; that is, the label has been given without a thorough diagnosis. Unfortunately, the most confirmatory diagnosis of Alzheimer's disease may be made only at autopsy, when the areas and nature of damaged brain tissue can be identified. However, several psychological measures of cognitive functioning and a thorough physical exam can provide clues to its existence in the earlier stages, or may indicate that the observed changes in behavior and/or personality are due to a reversible condition. Early diagnosis can be made with some certainty with an extensive patient work-up. These include a medical and nutritional history; laboratory tests of blood, urine, and stool; tests for thyroid function; a thorough physical and psychological examination; and, in some cases, extensive radiological studies, including a CAT (computerized axial tomography) scan or MRI (magnetic resonance imaging) (Eisdorfer, Cohen, and Veith, 1980; Small, Liston, and Jarvik, 1981). In fact, it is primarily through a process of elimination of other conditions that some dementias such as AD may be diagnosed. In such diagnoses, it is particularly important to detect depression, drug toxicity, and nutritional deficiencies because, as stated earlier, these conditions may be reversed.

## Therapy for Patients with Dementia

Unfortunately, no completely successful treatment for dementia is yet available. If the evidence for high levels of certain abnormal proteins in Alzheimer brains proves correct, future treatment might involve the use of drugs that interrupt the production of those proteins and their precursors so they cannot accumulate in brain tissue (Katzman and Jackson, 1991). Some researchers have focused on nerve growth factor, a naturally occurring protein that replenishes and maintains the health of nerve cells. Animal studies have shown remarkable success in repairing damaged brain cells.

Currently, many researchers are testing medications that may improve the cognitive functioning of victims of dementia. These medications include some drugs that restore the activity of neurotransmitters in the brain and some that even replace lost neurochemicals. As yet, no medication effectively restores cognitive function in the severely impaired older person for any significant period of time. Nevertheless, researchers have made dramatic strides toward understanding the neurochemical basis of this disease and are rapidly moving toward its treatment.

Medications are often prescribed to manage behavioral problems such as agitation, hallucinations, physical aggressiveness, and wandering.

Because of their potential side effects, however, it is important to weigh the severity, frequency, and harm caused by these behaviors to the patient and caregivers, against the possible side effects of medications. Furthermore, the prescribing physician must regularly re-evaluate the need to continue or reduce the dosage of any drugs used for behavior management, perhaps as frequently as every 3 to 4 months.

The cognitive functions that are lost with most irreversible forms of dementia cannot be restored through psychotherapy. However, many older persons can benefit from memory retraining and environmental modifications. That is, individual competence can be enhanced somewhat and the environment simplified considerably in an effort to maintain P-E congruence. The individual's social and home environments can be changed in order to encourage independent functioning. Research has shown, however, that most caregivers of AD patients do not make the necessary environmental changes unless professionals or other friends and family encourage or initiate such changes (Kiyak, 1991). Written schedules of activities, simplified routes from room to room, and written directions for cooking, bathing, and taking medications can aid a person in finding his or her way around and prevent the frustration that results from getting lost or not recognizing once familiar people and places. It is also important to maintain a regular schedule, to keep the patient active, and to prevent withdrawal from daily interactions. But it is also important to encourage activities without overstimulation or exposure to new situations.

Ultimately, the goal of managing these dementias is to slow the rate of deterioration and to prevent institutionalization for as long as possible. For the AD patient who does enter a nursing home, there are a growing number of facilities with special care units (SCUs) for elderly with Alzheimer's disease. These units provide a higher staff-to-resident ratio, a safe environment where patients can explore without getting lost, and special services aimed at maintaining the patients' remaining cognitive capacities.

However, SCUs are faced with the problems of establishing criteria for selecting residents, recruiting and retaining staff trained in dementia, and dealing with the cost of maintaining the necessary staff-to-patient ratio (Gold et al., 1991; Rabins, 1986).

## Caregiver Needs

One of the most important considerations with Alzheimer's disease and other dementias is to provide social and emotional support to the family as well as the patient. Half of all people with Alzheimer's disease remain in the community, cared for by a spouse or child. In recent years, there has been a significant growth in family support groups, which now exist in almost every major city and even in smaller communities. The national Alzheimer's Disease and Related Disorders Association (ADRDA) serves as a major coordinating body for many of these local groups and also spearheads attempts to increase research funds to understand and treat this most common form of dementia. The local support groups provide a network of help for families who are faced

with the often devastating impact of this disease. The stress of caring for this population often results in deterioration of family members' physical and psychological health. Many caregivers feel they must shoulder this responsibility alone, resulting in increasing levels of depression and burden (Reese et al., 1994).

Support groups aid their members in coping with the inevitable losses faced by the victims of AD, problems such as forgetting where they are when they go for a walk in the neighborhood, not recognizing their own children, agitation and aggressive behavior, and, in more advanced cases, needing assistance with dressing, eating, bathing, and toileting. These groups also provide caregivers with emotional support and respite. In a systematic study of the effects of a support group that included education about AD and how to manage behavioral disturbance in dementia patients, participating caregivers expressed increased knowledge and competence in managing and coping with the day-to-day problems of caring for a dementia patient (Chiverton and Caine, 1989). The growth of adult day centers has been one response to the need to keep persons

---

**CAREGIVER STRESS IN ALZHEIMER'S DISEASE.**

It is often said that caregivers of AD patients are "the second victims" of this disease. The following vignette illustrates the dilemma faced by these caregivers.

John Jones has had Alzheimer's Disease for five years and is cared for by his wife, Mary. Married for 60 years, by all accounts they have had mutual sharing and caring throughout those years. Now Mary does all personal care for John, and it is getting to the point where he does not recognize her. It saddens her when he asks "Where is Mary?" The mutuality of the past relationship is fast disappearing. Yet she takes very seriously the marriage vow to care for him until death. And it is the love and caring of the past that sustains her now.

They have four children, all of whom live out of state. When her children telephone weekly, Mary

assures them that all is going well. However, a neighbor called the oldest daughter to inform her that her mother is not doing well. Mary has lost a good deal of weight; she looks at least ten years older and seems to have "the weight of the world on her shoulders." Mary has a known history of heart troubles. The daughter plans to come home to insist that her mother take care of herself, by enlisting home health or institutional care for John. When she mentioned this to her mother on the last phone call, Mary adamantly insisted that it is her responsibility to care for her husband. The daughter is afraid that she will be caring for two patients in the future, as she is most concerned that her mother's health will fail.

with dementia in the community, to help them remain active and retain learned skills, and to provide respite for their family caregivers. As noted in Chapter 20, however, the need for publicly funded respite and support is greater than the availability of services.

## ALCOHOLISM

It is difficult to obtain accurate statistics on the prevalence of alcoholism in older people because of the stigma associated with this condition among this cohort. Estimates vary, from 2 to 15 percent of all older people living in the community (Adams, et al., 1993; Blazer, 1990; Whittington, 1988). Surveys of older outpatients in general medical hospitals estimate that 15 to 30 percent show symptoms of alcoholism (Schuckit and Miller, 1976). A review of national surveys conducted between 1971 and 1982 of drinking patterns among women concluded that women over age 65 report the lowest incidence of alcohol consumption in general, and the lowest incidence of heavy drinking, with 26 to 40 percent stating that they consume some alcohol and less than 5 percent indicating high consumption (Wilsnack, Wilsnack, and Klassen, 1984). In contrast, older men are four times more likely to have alcohol problems than are older women, with widowers and men who have never married at greatest risk (Blazer, 1990; Maddox, 1988).

Alcoholics are less likely to be found among the ranks of persons over age 60 because of higher death rates at a young age among alcoholics (Miller et al., 1991). Nevertheless, surveys of alcoholism rates among older persons have revealed approximately equal proportions of those who began to drink heavily before age 40 and those who began in old age, often in response to age-related stressful events and isolation.

It is important to distinguish lifelong abusers of alcohol from those who began drinking later in life. Some older persons who are diagnosed as alcoholics have had this problem since middle age, but increasing age may exacerbate the condition for two reasons. First, the central nervous system, liver, and kidneys become less tolerant of alcohol with age because of the physiological changes described in Chapter 5 (e.g., loss of muscle tissue, reduction in body mass, and reduced efficiency of liver and kidney functions). For this reason, a smaller dose of alcohol can be more deleterious in the later years. Second, an individual who has been drinking heavily for many years has already produced irreversible damage to the central nervous system, liver, and kidneys, creating more problems than those due to normal aging alone. It is difficult to determine the incidence of alcoholism among older persons who have no previous history of alcoholism. Physiological evidence is lacking, and drinking is often hidden from friends, relatives, and physicians. The older person may justify overconsumption of alcohol on the grounds that it relieves sadness and isolation. Even in cases where family members are aware of the situation, they may minimize it by rationalizing that it is one of the older person's few remaining pleasures. Denial is a problem of many alcoholics, especially older alcoholics, in whom the influence of Prohibition in the 1920s may have instilled the belief that alcoholism is a moral problem and not a disease. There is also the issue of self-reliance in many older people who feel that they personally should be able to cope with their alcoholism and not have to rely on health professionals or even on support groups such as Alcoholics Anonymous.

Physicians may overlook the possibility that alcohol is creating a health problem for the older person because the adverse effects of alcohol resemble some physical diseases or psychiatric and cognitive disorders that are associated with old age. For example, older alcoholics may complain of confusion, disorientation, irritability, insomnia or restless sleep patterns, heart palpitations, or a dry cough. Beliefs held by health care providers that alcoholism does not occur in older people may also prevent its detection.

In a survey of male patients in Veterans Administration hospitals, social disruption such as aggressive behavior toward staff and other patients was found more frequently among long-term alcoholics, but physical health problems were more severe among men who commenced heavy drinking late in life (Schuckit and Miller, 1976). This same survey revealed greater mental deterioration and more attempts at suicide among older alcoholics compared with age-matched men who had no history of alcohol abuse. However, older women alcoholics have been found to make fewer suicide attempts and to undergo fewer hospitalizations for psychiatric care than older male alcoholics (Schuckit and Morrissey, 1976). It is noteworthy that older alcoholics are less likely than young alcoholics to demonstrate a serious personality disorder, but are more likely to have symptoms of dementia. Indeed, middle-aged alcoholics have been found to show significant impairments in learning and memory that are more common in advanced old age, suggesting a premature aging phenomenon due to long-term alcohol abuse (Ryan and Butters, 1980). Korsakoff's syndrome is a form of dementia that is sometimes found in long-term alcoholics. Alcoholism and depression may occur together in the same individual. Heavy drinkers in all age groups have been found to report more depressive symptoms (Wilsnack et al., 1984).

Therapy for geriatric alcoholics has not been differentiated from that for younger alcoholics. However, it is probably more important to focus on older alcoholics' medical conditions because of physical declines that make them more vulnerable to the secondary effects of alcohol. As with younger alcoholics, psychotherapy and occupational and recreational therapy are important for treating older people experiencing alcoholism. Recovery rates for older alcoholics are just as high as for younger alcoholics.

## DRUG ABUSE

As noted in Chapter 7, older persons use a disproportionately large number of prescription and over-the-counter (OTC) drugs, representing approximately 30 percent of prescription expenditures. In particular, older people are more likely than the young to be using tranquilizers, sedatives, and hypnotics, all of which have potentially dangerous side effects. In a survey of elderly persons residing in the community, 83 percent of the respondents were using two or more medications; the average was 3.8 per person (Chien, Townsend, and Townsend, 1978). Older persons have been found to abuse aspirin compounds, laxatives, and sleeping pills, often because of misinformation about the adverse effects of too high a dosage or too many pills. It is not unusual to hear older patients state that they took twice or three times as much aspirin as they were prescribed because they did not feel their pain was being alleviated with the lower dose. Yet, changes in body composition, renal, and liver functions that occur with age, combined with the use of multiple medications, make older persons more likely to experience adverse drug reactions. Noncompliance with therapeutic drug regimens is often unintentional; older patients may take too much or too little of a drug because of nonspecific or complicated instructions by the physician, and they may use OTC drugs without reading warning labels about their side effects and interactions with other drugs they are using (Shimp and Ascione, 1988). Intentional noncompliance generally takes the form of older patients' deciding for themselves that they no longer need the medication or that it is not working for them. Such noncompliance has been found to be responsible for 10 percent of all hospital admissions among the older population (Col, Fanale, and Kronholm, 1990; Stewart, 1988).

Fortunately, there is growing awareness of the effects of "polypharmacy" among health care providers and among older people themselves. There is very little evidence that older persons abuse drugs to the extent that younger populations do, or use illicit drugs such as heroin, cocaine, and marijuana. Nor do they use hallucinogens, amphetamines, or mood-enhancing inhalants (Whanger, 1984).

## PARANOID DISORDERS AND SCHIZOPHRENIA

Paranoia, defined as an irrational suspiciousness of other people, actually takes several forms. In older persons, paranoia may be due to social isolation, a sense of powerlessness, progressive sensory decline, and problems with the normal "checks and balances" of daily life (Eisdorfer, Cohen, and Veith, 1980). Hearing loss may also be a risk factor in paranoia, although research evidence for this is mixed (see Chapter 6). Still other changes in the aging individual, such as problems with memory, may result in paranoid reactions.

Although the foregoing conditions may produce a genuine paranoid state, some of the suspicious attitudes of older persons may represent accurate readings of their experiences. For example, an older person's children may in fact be trying to institutionalize him or her in order to take over an estate; a nurse's aide may really be stealing from an older patient; and neighborhood children may truly be making fun of the older person. It is therefore important to distinguish actual threats to the individual from unfounded suspicions. To the extent that the individual has some control over his or her environment, again consistent with the P-E model, the older person's perception of a threatening situation will be reduced. The diagnosis of paranoid disorders in older people is similar to that in younger patients; the symptoms should have a duration of at least one week, with no signs of schizophrenia, no prominent hallucinations, and no association to an organic mental disorder (APA, 1987).

Schizophrenia is much less prevalent than depression or dementia in old age. It has been estimated that about 7 percent of the population over age 60 living in the community have some schizophrenic symptoms. Most older persons with this condition were first diagnosed in adolescence or in middle age and continue to display behavior symptomatic of schizophrenia, although the severity of symptoms appears to decrease with age (Blazer, George, and Hughes,

1988). Late onset schizophrenia with paranoid features has been labeled *paraphrenia* by some psychiatrists, especially in Europe and in Great Britain (Butler et al., 1991).

Many of the current cohort of older chronic schizophrenics residing in the community were deinstitutionalized during the early 1960s as part of the national Community Mental Health Services Act of 1963. After spending much of their youth and middle age in state hospitals, these patients were released with the anticipation that they could function independently in the community with medications to control their hallucinations and psychotic behavior. Although this approach has proven effective for many former schizophrenic inpatients, some have not adjusted successfully to deinstitutionalization, as witnessed by the number of homeless older schizophrenics seen on the streets in most major cities.

### Therapeutic Interventions

As with depression, psychotherapy can be useful for paranoid older persons. In particular, cognitive behavioral approaches, in which an individual focuses on changing specific problem areas or misconceptions, may be useful in treating paranoid older persons, because these individuals often attribute causality to external factors (e.g., the belief that someone took their pocketbook, that they themselves did not misplace it). Psychotherapy with paranoid older individuals may be effective in redirecting beliefs about causality to the individuals themselves. On the other hand, pharmacotherapy with antipsychotic medications is generally more effective than psychotherapy for older schizophrenic patients.

## ANXIETY

Anxiety disorders are another type of functional disorder or emotional problem with no obvious organic cause. Although more common than schizophrenia and paranoid disorders, anxiety disorders are much rarer in older populations than in the young. This may be because the older person develops more tolerance and better ability to manage stressful events. More likely, however, those who have anxiety disorders in middle age may be less likely to survive to old age (Belsky, 1984). Data from the Epidemiological Catchment Area study revealed a prevalence rate of 5.5 percent among those 65 and older (Regier et al., 1988).

## THE CHRONICALLY MENTALLY ILL

The plight of older persons who are chronically mentally ill has recently been addressed by mental health advocates. This population is defined as people who suffer mental or emotional disorders that erode or prevent the development of their functional capacities in ADL, self-direction, interpersonal relations, social transactions, learning, and recreation (Light and Lebowitz, 1991). Many chronically mentally ill older persons were institutionalized in their young adult years and released into the community after the deinstitutionalization movement began in 1963, but since then they have been in and out of hospitals as their conditions have become exacerbated. These people have survived major upheavals in their lives under marginally functional conditions.

As noted by Quam and Abramson (1991), who have examined the well-being of chronically mentally ill adults, "it is remarkable that members of this population survive into middle age and old age" despite the social neglect they have experienced. Of course, the social disruption and years of treatment with psychotropic drugs take their toll on many of these people, who are physiologically old in their fifties and sixties. It often becomes difficult for chronically mentally ill persons to obtain medical care for purely physical symptoms because primary care providers may dismiss a complaint as hypochondriasis and/or attribute it to the patient's psychiatric disorder, rather than perform a thorough exam to exclude conditions caused by the mental disorder or by aging per se.

An alarming number of older chronically mentally ill people are homeless.

### Therapeutic Interventions

Taking an adult developmental perspective, specifically Erikson's (1968) stages of development (described in Chapter 9), Quam (1986) proposes three treatment approaches to helping chronically mentally ill older people work toward ego integrity. These include *reminiscence or life review* through movement therapy, music, art, and occupational therapy; separate *men's and women's support groups,* which are particularly useful for working through unresolved psychosexual issues; and *therapy to reframe or redefine* the older chronically mentally ill person's life so that his or her strengths and successes can be highlighted even after a life of emotional struggle.

## PSYCHOTHERAPY WITH OLDER PERSONS

Despite early doubts by Freud (1924) and others about the value of psychotherapy for older patients, many researchers and therapists have proposed and developed psychotherapeutic intervention strategies specifically for this population, or have modified existing approaches. One problem in working with older individuals may be overcoming the misconceptions held by some older persons about psychotherapy. For this reason, short-term, goal-oriented therapies may be more effective with older patients (Brink, 1979; Zarit, 1980) because these patients can begin to experience benefits immediately. On the other hand, older patients who are reluctant and unwilling to open up to a therapist may benefit more from long-term treatment in which rapport and trust between the therapist and the client can be established gradually (Mintz, Steuer, and Jarvik, 1981). Several different types of therapy have been explored with this population.

*Life review* is one therapeutic approach that has been successfully used with older persons. Such therapy encourages introspection through active reminiscence of past achievements and failures, and may reestablish ego integrity in depressed older persons (Lewis and Butler, 1974). This method may also be used effectively by social service providers who are not extensively trained in psychotherapy.

*Group therapy* has been advocated for older patients experiencing mental disorders, especially depression (Ingersoll and Silverman, 1978; Hartford, 1980). Groups offer the opportunity for peer support, social interaction, and role modeling. Life review may be used effectively as part of group therapy. The opportunity to share life experiences and to learn that others have had similar stresses in their lives appears to enhance insight, self-esteem, and a feeling of catharsis. This was found in a study of a therapy group with older persons who wrote their autobiographies and read them aloud to each other (Birren, 1982).

Groups have also been established for improving memory and enhancing cognitive skills. They are an ideal setting for teaching memory skills with the use of games and puzzles, as well as reminiscence exercises. Both reminiscence and learning exercises have been found to improve scores on a test of intelligence; social contact groups showed no change on these tests (Hughston and Merriam, 1982).

Empirical studies have been conducted to compare the efficacy of alternative therapeutic interventions. For example, short-term behav-

ioral (i.e., changing maladaptive behavior with operant techniques) and supportive group therapy (i.e., helping the patient to develop ego strength and feelings of control) were found to be equally effective in alleviating secondary depression. The positive impact of treatment continued at the five-week follow-up study (Gallagher, 1981). The effects of a nine-month course of cognitive-behavioral therapy were compared with a psychodynamic approach with depressed persons aged 55 to 78 (Steuer et al., 1984). The former approach consists of active, directive, structured, and time-limited therapeutic modes. Its goal is to change behavior *and* self-defeating thought processes. Psychodynamic group therapy uses psychoanalytic concepts such as insight, transference, and the unconscious to relieve symptoms of depression and to prevent its recurrence by understanding why the individual behaves in self-defeating ways. In general, the researchers found that both approaches reduced depression, but that cognitive-behavioral strategies resulted in greater improvements on one of the depression measures. In comparisons of cognitive therapy with behavioral and supportive psychotherapy among depressed older persons, all three approaches were effective in reducing symptoms of depression. However, cognitive and behavioral approaches resulted in continued improvement (i.e., up to one year later), while supportive therapy had less long-term impact (Gallagher and Thompson, 1981). This may be because cognitive and behavioral therapies, alone or in combination, teach skills that the patient may practice outside the clinical setting.

The therapeutic interventions just described are more frequently used in community settings than with older people in nursing homes. The latter setting lends itself to more intense, long-term therapies: behavior-change programs, milieu therapy, reality orientation, and remotivation therapy. Behavior-change techniques using operant reinforcement and token economies have been successfully used in long-term care settings with psychiatrically impaired young and old patients. These methods have been found to increase self-feeding and self-care, and have been effective in reducing dependency in older persons (Kiyak and Mulligan, 1987). Milieu therapy is consistent with Lawton and Nahemow's competence model described earlier in this book. This approach focuses on improving the therapeutic environment of the nursing home or enhancing an individual's sense of control over some important aspects of life. One application of principles of milieu therapy has been to encourage older residents to make decisions for themselves in specific domains, such as caring for a pet bird. These elders were found to remain more active, sociable, and alert than older residents who were given no control over their environment (Langer and Rodin, 1976; Langer et al., 1979). In another study aimed at enhancing the perception of control and encouraging cognitive activity among nursing home residents, contingency reinforcement was used to encourage residents to seek out information about their environment and historical events. Memory improvement was found among those in the contingent conditions (Beck, 1982).

Reality orientation was developed by Folsom (1968) to aid confused and disoriented patients in hospital settings. Signs and "reality orientation boards" are used to denote the current date, place, and special events. Staff members are encouraged to remind residents of these facts constantly and to use the residents' names during their daily interactions. Unfortunately, studies of reality orientation have provided mixed results. It has not been found to be a valuable therapeutic mode for severely demented older persons. As a result, it is used less frequently today than in the 1970's and 1980's.

Remotivation therapy has been used successfully with less confused elders. Groups of older persons with some cognitive impairment but, more important, who are withdrawn from social activities, meet together under the guidance of a trained group leader. The purpose is to discuss events and experiences by bringing all group members into the discussion, emphasizing the event's relevance for each member, and encour-aging them to share what they have gained from the session. This approach has been found to be effective in psychiatric hospitals and nursing homes as well as in adult day centers.

There are few systematic comparative studies on the long-term effects of these therapeutic approaches in nursing homes; likewise, the feasibility of instituting such programs within the constraints of nursing homes' policies and procedures has not been examined. Without a commitment to using these therapeutic modes on a long-term basis following successful experimental interventions, nursing home staff cannot expect lasting therapeutic benefits from any of these methods.

## USE OF MENTAL HEALTH SERVICES

As noted in Chapter 7, older persons use physician services somewhat more than the young do, and are hospitalized at a much higher rate. In contrast, mental health services are significantly underutilized by older people, especially ethnic minorities. Community-based care is used at a far lower rate than inpatient hospital treatment by older people.

It has been estimated that only 4 to 6 percent of patients using community mental health centers are age 65 or older (Butler et al., 1991; Flemming et al., 1986), far below their representation in the U.S. population and less than the estimated prevalence of mental disorders among the elderly. An even smaller percentage of users are ethnic minority elderly. A 1986 survey of community mental health centers revealed that only 30 percent were making any effort to meet the needs of minority elders in their communities (Flemming et al., 1986). These findings were supported by a later survey, which revealed that mental health services for older adults in general had increased at a much faster rate than for minority elders (Fellin and Powell, 1988). The problem is compounded by poor coordination of activities between mental health centers and senior centers or other programs directed specifically at older persons. Furthermore, a significant portion (44 percent) of community mental health centers reported having no clinical staff trained in geriatrics and no programs specifically for the older population; an even greater proportion (73 percent) stated that they had no special programs or staff skilled in working with ethnic minority elders.

The incidence of older people seeking professional help for mental disorders has been found to range from 3 to 13 percent (Evashwick et al., 1984; Butler et al., 1991). An epidemiological survey in Baltimore revealed that 4.2 percent of the population aged 65 to 74 and 1.4 percent of those over 75 had sought treatment for mental disorders during the preceding six months compared with 8.7 percent of the population under age 65 (German, Shapiro, and Skinner, 1985). These statistics are particularly striking when compared to the proportion of older respondents in that survey who had sought medical treatment during the same six-month period; over 66 percent of the group aged 65 and older had received medical care at least once, compared to slightly more than 50 percent of the population under age 65.

Older persons may be more likely to seek help from their primary physicians and to be hospitalized for mental disorders than to seek community mental health services, possibly because such health care does not carry the stigma of mental health services, especially for older persons from other cultural backgrounds. A disproportionate number of older persons represent the population of patients in state mental hospitals that house the chronically mentally ill. Despite the deinstitutionalization movement of the 1960s, the great majority of all psychiatric services to older people are in hospital settings.

## Barriers to Older Persons' Use of Mental Health Services

In a small sample of senior center participants, older persons perceived a general physician to be more effective in treating psychiatric symptoms than mental health professionals (Waxman, Carner, and Klein, 1984). Of this sample, 79 percent would choose general physicians for treatment of depression, and 90 percent would do so for dementia. Less than 10 percent thought that a mental health professional would be able to treat the latter condition effectively. Older adults are generally unwilling to interpret their problems as psychological, preferring instead to attribute them to physical or social conditions or to normal aging. In addition, the current cohort of older persons may be less oriented to the use of mental health services because of societal stigmas, limited knowledge about mental disorders, and a lack of confidence in mental health workers. This requires a good "psychological ear" on the part of the older person's primary care physician. Because the patient may complain of physical symptoms rather than focus on psychological concerns, the physician must be attuned to the underlying emotional distress the patient presents.

Attitudes of physicians and mental health professionals, especially the belief that older persons cannot benefit from therapy simply because of their age, also have been cited as barriers to obtaining psychiatric services. Butler and Lewis (1982) have labeled such attitudes "professional ageism." These attitudes may partially explain the results of a study in which vignettes of old versus young patients with obvious psychiatric symptoms were presented to 60 general physicians. Whether a general physician referred patients for professional psychiatric treatment depended on the patient's age and the perceived severity of the symptoms (Kucharski, White, and Schratz, 1979). A similar approach was used with psychologists (Dye, 1978) and with psychiatrists (Ford and Sbordonne, 1980). In both studies, these mental health professionals were not optimistic about the effectiveness of psychotherapy with older patients. This belief, in turn, may affect the decision to use psychotherapy alone or as an adjunct to pharmacotherapy with older patients. However, as more mental health professionals receive specialized training in geriatrics, these stereotypes are expected to be reduced in the future.

Perhaps the greatest barrier to older individuals' obtaining mental health services is accessibility. In addition to the physical access issues of transportation and architectural barriers, there are significant problems of fragmented services and older people's lack of knowledge about seeking mental health services on their own or obtaining appropriate referrals from physicians or social service providers. Fortunately, many new and innovative programs have arisen to overcome these barriers and respond to the mental health needs of older Americans. For example, home visits by a psychiatrist, social worker, and a nurse are made to the homes of low-income, isolated elderly in Baltimore through the "Psychogeriatric Assessment and Treatment in City Housing" (or PATCH) program. Rural elders in Iowa are served by mental health professionals through the Elderly Outreach Program (or EOP) of the community mental health system. The Family Services Program of greater Boston offers a community mental health program aimed especially at minority elderly, entitled Services for Older People (or SOP). In an effort to overcome cultural barriers, this program has focused on training mental health workers to recognize cultural differences in the expression of mental disorders. In Seattle, a mental health team from the community mental health network provides on-site evaluation and therapy to area nursing homes on a regular basis. In many communities, "gatekeepers" (nontraditional referral sources such as meter readers, postal carriers, and apartment and mobile home managers who have contact with isolated older people in the community) are trained to identify older persons who may require psychiatric care. They refer these elders to the in-home case management component of the local community mental health center. These isolated elders currently account for over 40 percent of admissions to this program, and represent primarily the chronically mentally ill (Raschko, 1991).

Many senior centers employ social workers trained in geriatrics to conduct support groups, education programs, and individualized sessions on coping with grief, loss, loneliness, and on methods to improve memory. Such programs reduce the stigma of psychotherapy by their informal structure in a familiar environment.

Reimbursement for psychological services is also a problem. For example, Medicare Part A pays no outpatient mental health expenditures, but pays for a limited number of days for inpatient treatment. Furthermore, co-payment by the subscriber for mental health services is greater than for physical health services (Roybal, 1988). It should be noted that this discrepancy occurs in many health insurance programs used by younger persons as well. Because of attitudes held by older patients toward mental disorders and by therapists toward older clients, however, these reimbursement issues are greater barriers to older persons' use of mental health services than they are for the young. Future cohorts of older people may be more likely to seek such services in community mental health centers, because of increasing awareness of mental disorders and treatment modalities.

## SUMMARY AND IMPLICATIONS

The prevalence of mental disorders in old age is difficult to determine, although estimates range from 5 to 45 percent of the older population. Research in acute and long-term care institutional settings provides higher estimates than epidemiological studies conducted in the community. This is because many older persons with mental disorders are treated in institutional settings rather than through community mental health services.

The most common mental disorder in late life is depression, although estimates of its prevalence also vary widely, from 2.8 to 22 percent, depending on the criteria used to diagnose depression. Manic-depressive disorders are rare in old age; unipolar depression is more common. Reactive depression that is secondary to major life changes is found frequently in older persons;

this condition responds well to environmental and social interventions, whereas antidepressant therapy is more effective for major depression and electroconvulsive therapy for severe depression in older people who do not respond to other forms of therapy. Diagnosing depression in older people is often difficult. Many deny it, while others attribute it to medical conditions. On the other hand, it is important to screen for medical conditions and medications that may produce depressive symptoms as a side effect.

Depression is a risk factor for suicide in older people, particularly for white men over age 85. Life changes that result in a loss of social status and increased isolation may explain why this group is more likely to commit suicide. The increased risk of suicide in the older population highlights the need for family members and service providers to be sensitized to clues of an impending suicide.

Dementia includes numerous reversible and irreversible conditions that result in impaired cognitive function, especially recall of recent events, comprehension, learning, attention, and orientation to time, place, and person. These conditions differ from "benign senescent forgetfulness," which is a mild form of memory dysfunction that generally does not become worse with time. It is essential to perform a complete diagnostic work-up of older people who have symptoms of dementia. A medical history, physical examination, assessment of medications, lab tests, psychological and cognitive testing, as well as neurological testing, will aid in distinguishing "reversible" dementias that can be treated from the "irreversible" dementias such as Alzheimer's disease that currently can be managed but not cured. The biological basis of Alzheimer's disease is being examined in numerous studies; future treatments may involve medications that replace or prevent the loss of brain chemicals. Family members and service providers should be aware of changes in the older person's cognitive functioning and behavior that may signal dementia, and must avoid labeling such changes as normal aging or as—the catchall phrase—"senility."

Although cognitive functioning cannot be restored in irreversible dementias, older persons in the early stages of these conditions often benefit from memory retraining and from psychotherapy to cope with the changes they are experiencing. Environmental modifications that simplify tasks and aid in orienting the patient may slow the rate of deterioration and postpone institutionalization. It is also important to provide emotional and social support to family caregivers of elders with Alzheimer's disease and other dementias. Adult day care and other such respite programs are valuable for spouses and other caregivers who assume fulltime care for these patients at home, although they are limited by funding constraints.

Alcoholism and drug abuse are less common in older persons than in the young, although accurate estimates of prevalence are difficult to obtain. Physical health and cognitive function are significantly impaired in older alcoholics. Older men with a history of alcohol abuse also have a greater risk of suicide than do younger men or young and old women who are alcoholics. There are few studies of the efficacy of alternative treatments for older alcoholics. Drug abuse in older persons is rarely associated with illicit drugs, but often takes the form of inappropriate use or overuse of some prescription and over-the-counter drugs. Adverse reactions are more likely to occur in older persons because of age-related physiological changes that impair the ability to metabolize many medications and because of the greater likelihood of polypharmacy.

Paranoia and schizophrenia are far less common than depression and dementia in older persons. Most people with these conditions first developed them in middle age; life changes such as relocation and confusion that result from dementia may trigger paranoid reactions in old age. Psychotherapy, especially using cognitive behavior strategies, may be effective in treating paranoia, although it is important first to determine and to verify the underlying causes of the condition.

The chronically mentally ill, who age physiologically faster because of disruptions throughout their lives, have long been ignored by health care providers and society. These older persons can benefit from reminiscence and support groups.

Many researchers have explored the feasibility of psychotherapy with older patients. Both short-term, goal-oriented therapy and long-term approaches have been advocated. Specific modes of therapy with older patients include life review and group therapy using cognitive-behavioral and supportive techniques. These interventions have been particularly effective with depressed older people in community settings. Nursing homes are ideal settings for long-term, intense therapies using groups, but staff may not have the time or training to implement them. Behavior change and milieu therapy have resulted in significant improvements in short-term experimental interventions. Unfortunately, there are few reports on the success of such programs as part of the day-to-day activities of a nursing home.

Despite the demonstrated efficacy of many forms of psychotherapy with older persons, they significantly underutilize mental health services. Most treatments for mental disorders in this population take place in hospitals. Many older people prefer to seek treatment for depression and other mental disorders from a general physician. This may result in an overreliance on pharmacological treatment and an underutilization of psychotherapy in cases where the latter may be more effective. Such behavior may be attributed to reluctance among the current cohort of elders to admit they have a psychiatric problem, a lack of knowledge about such conditions and their treatment, as well as problems with accessibility. Attitudes of mental health providers and social service providers about the value of psychotherapy for older persons and, perhaps most important, the lack of effective links between mental health and social services to the older people, have been barriers in the past. As more programs evolve that integrate services, and as future cohorts become aware of mental disorders and their treatment, there will be greater acceptance and use of mental health services by older people.

## REFERENCES

Abrams, R., and Fink, M. The present status of unilateral ECT: Some recommendations. *Journal of Affective Disorders,* 1984, 7, 245–247.

Adams, W. L., Zhong, Y., Barboriak, J. J., and Rimm, A. A. Alcohol-related hospitalizations of elderly people. *Journal of the American Medical Association* 1993, 270, 6–9.

American Psychiatric Association (APA). *Diagnostic and statistical manual of mental disorders* (4th ed.). Washington, D.C.: APA, 1994.

Beck, P. Two successful interventions in nursing homes: The therapeutic effects of cognitive activity. *The Gerontologist,* 1982, 22, 378–383.

Belsky, J. K. *The psychology of aging: Theory, research and practice.* Monterey, Calif.: Brooks-Cole, 1984.

Birren, J. E. A review of the development of the self. Paper presented at the annual meeting of the Gerontological Society of America, 1982.

Blazer, D. Alcohol abuse and dependence. *Merck Manual of Geriatrics.* Rahway, N.J.: Merck & Co., 1990, p. 1018–1021.

Blazer, D. Depression in the elderly. *New England Journal of Medicine,* 1989, 320, 164–166.

Blazer, D. The epidemiology of mental illness in late life. In E. Busse and D. Blazer (Eds.), *Handbook of geriatric psychiatry.* New York: Van Nostrand Reinhold, 1980.

Blazer, D., George, L. K., and Hughes, D. Schizophrenic symptoms in an elderly community population. In J. A. Brody and G. L. Maddox (Eds.). *Epidemiology and aging: An international perspective.* New York: Springer, 1988.

Blazer, D., George, L. K., and Landerman, R. The phenomenology of late life depression. In P. E. Bebbington and R. Jacoby (Eds.), *Psychiatric disorders in the elderly.* London: Mental Health Foundation, 1986.

Blazer, D., Hughes, D. C., and George, L. K. The epidemiology of depression in an elderly community population. *The Gerontologist,* 1987, 27, 281–287.

Blazer, D., and Williams, C. D. Epidemiology of dysphoria and depression in an elderly population. *American Journal of Psychiatry,* 1980, 137, 439–444.

Brink, T. L. *Geriatric psychotherapy.* New York: Human Sciences Press, 1979.

Brody, E. M., and Kleban, M. H. Day-to-day mental and physical health symptoms of older people: A report on health logs. *The Gerontologist,* 1983, *23,* 75–85.

Busse, E. W., and Pfeiffer, E. *Behavior and adaptation in late life.* Boston: Little, Brown, 1975.

Butler, R. N. Psychiatry and the elderly: An overview. *American Journal of Psychiatry,* 1975, *132,* 893–900.

Butler, R. N., Lewis, M., and Sunderland, T. *Aging and mental health* (4th ed.). New York: Macmillan, 1991.

Chien, C. P., Townsend, E. J., and Townsend, A. R. Substance use and abuse among the community elderly: The medical aspect. *Addictive Diseases: An International Journal,* 1978, *3,* 357–372.

Chiverton, P., and Caine, E. D. Education to assist spouses in coping with Alzheimer's disease. *Journal of the American Geriatrics Society,* 1989, *37,* 593–598.

Coblentz, J. M., Mattis, S., Zingesser, L. H., Kasoff, S. S., Wisniewski, H. M., and Katzman, R. Presenile dementia: Clinical evaluation of cerebrospinal fluid dynamics. *Archives of Neurology,* 1973, *29,* 299–308.

Col, N., Fanale, J. E. and Kronholm, P. The role of medication noncompliance and adverse drug reactions in hospitalizations of the elderly. *Archives of Internal Medicine,* 1990, *150,* 841–845.

Conwell, Y., and Caine, E. D. Suicide in the elderly chronic patient population. In E. Light and B. D. Lebowitz (Eds.) *The elderly with chronic mental illness.* New York: Springer, 1991.

Crapper, D. R., Karlik, S., and de Boni, U. Aluminum and other metals in senile dementia. In R. Katzman, R. D. Terry, and K. L. Bick (Eds.), *Aging, Vol. 7. Alzheimer's disease, senile dementia and related disorders.* New York: Raven Press, 1978.

Dye, C. J. Psychologist's role in the provision of mental health care for the elderly. *Professional Psychology,* 1978, *9,* 38–49.

Eisdorfer, C., Cohen, D., and Veith, R. The psychopathology of aging. *Current concepts.* The Upjohn Co., 1980.

Epstein, L. J. Depression in the elderly. *Journal of Gerontology,* 1976, *31,* 278–282.

Erickson, E. *Identity, youth and crisis.* New York: Norton, 1968.

Ernst, R. L., and Hay, J. W. The U.S. economic and social costs of Alzheimer's disease revisited. *American Journal of Public Health,* 1994, *84,* 1261–1264.

Evans, D. A., Funkenstein, H. H., Albert, M. S., Scherr, P. A., Crook, N. R., Chown, M. J., Hebert, L. E., Hennakens, C. H., and Taylor, J. D. Prevalence of Alzheimer's disease in a community population of older persons: Higher than previously reported. *Journal of the American Medical Association,* 1989, *262,* 2551–2556.

Evashwick, C., Rowe, G., Diehr, P., and Branch, L. Factors explaining the use of health care services by the elderly. *Health Services Research,* 1984, *19,* 357–382.

Fellin, P. A., and Powell, T. J. Mental health services and older adult minorities. *The Gerontologist,* 1988, *28,* 442–447.

Flemming, A. S., Richards, L. D., Santos, J. F., and West, P. R. Mental health services for the elderly. *Action Committee to Implement the Mental Health Recommendations of the 1981 White House Conference on Aging* (Vol. 3). Washington, D.C.: American Psychological Association, 1986.

Folsom, J. C. Reality orientation for the elderly mental patient *Journal of Geriatric Psychiatry,* 1968, *1,* 291–307.

Folstein, M., Folstein, S., and McHugh, P. R. Minimental state: A practical method for grading the cognitive state of patients for the clinician. *Journal of Psychiatric Research,* 1975, *12,* 189–198.

Ford, C. V., and Sbordonne, R. J. Attitudes of psychiatrists toward elderly patients. *American Journal of Psychiatry,* 1980, *137, 571–575.*

Fox, J. "Broken connections, missing memories." Interviewed in *Time,* April 15, 1991, 10–12.

Fraser, R. M., and Glass, I. B. Unilateral and bilateral ECT in elderly patients. *Acta Psychiatrica Scandinavia,* 1980, *52,* 13–31.

Freud, S. *Collected papers, Volume I.* London: Hogarth Press, 1924.

Frierson, R. L. Suicide attempts by the old and the very old. *Archives of Internal Medicine,* 1991, *151,* 141–144.

Gaitz, C. M., and Baer, P. E. Characteristics of elderly patients with alcoholism. *Archives of General Psychiatry,* 1971, 24, 372–378.

Gallagher, D. Behavioral group therapy with elderly depressives: An experimental study. In D. Upper and S. Rose (Eds.), *Behavioral group therapy.* Champaign, Ill.: Research Press, 1981.

Gallagher, D. E., and Thompson, L. W. *Depression in the elderly: A behavioral treatment manual.* Los

Angeles: University of Southern California Press, 1981.

Gallagher, D. E., and Thompson, L. W. Effectiveness of psychotherapy for both endogenous and nonendogenous depression in older adult outpatients. *Journal of Gerontology,* 1983, *38,* 707–712.

Gallo, J. J., Anthony, J. C., and Muthen, B. O. Age differences in the symptoms of depression: A latent trait analysis. *Journals of Gerontology,* 1994, *49,* 251–264.

Geriscope. *Geriatrics,* 1972, *27,* 120–125.

German, P. S., Shapiro, S., and Skinner, E. A. Mental health of the elderly. *Journal of the American Geriatrics Society,* 1985, *33,* 246–252.

Gold, D. T., Sloane, P. D., Mathew, L. J., Bledsoe, M. M., and Konane, D. A. Special care units: A typology of care settings for memory-impaired older adults. *The Gerontologist,* 1991, *31,* 467–475.

Gurin, G., Veroff, J., and Feld, S. *Americans view their mental health.* New York: Basic Books, 1960.

Gurland, B. J., and Cross, P. S. Epidemiology of psychopathology in old age. In L. F. Jarvik and G. W. Small (Eds.), *Psychiatric clinics of North America.* Philadelphia: W. B. Saunders, 1982.

Gurland, B., Dean, L., Cross, P., and Golden, R. The epidemiology of depression and dementia in the elderly: The use of multiple indicators of these conditions. In J. O. Cole and J. E. Barrett (Eds.), *Psychopathology in the aged.* New York: Raven Press, 1980.

Hartford, M. E. The use of group methods for work with the aged. In J. E. Birren and R. B. Sloane (Eds.), *Handbook of mental health and aging.* Englewood Cliffs, N. J.: Prentice-Hall, 1980.

Heston, L. L., Mastri, A. R., Anderson, V. E., and White, J. Dementia of the Alzheimer's type: Clinical genetics, natural history and associated conditions. *Archives of General Psychiatry,* 1981, *38,* 1085–1090.

Holinger, P. C., and Offer, D. Prediction of adolescent suicide: A population model. *American Journal of Psychiatry,* 1982, *139,* 302–307.

Hughston, G. A., and Merriam, S. B. Reminiscence: A nonformal technique for improving cognitive functioning in the aged. *International Journal of Aging and Human Development,* 1982, *15,* 139–149.

Ingersoll, B., and Silverman, A. Comparative group psychotherapy for the aged. *The Gerontologist,* 1978, *18,* 201–206.

Katzman, R., and Jackson, J. E. Alzheimer's disease: Basic and clinical advances. *Journal of the American Geriatrics Society,* 1991, *39,* 516–525.

Kiyak, H. A. *Adaptation among elderly with Alzheimer's disease.* Final report submitted to the National Institute of Aging, (Grant No. RO1 AG04070), 1991.

Kiyak, H. A., and Mulligan, K. Studies of the relationship between oral health and psychological well-being. *Gerodontics,* 1987, *3,* 109–112.

Kleinman, M. B., and Clemente, F. Support for the medical profession among the aged. *International Journal of Health Services,* 1976, *6,* 295–299.

Koenig, H., and Blazer, D. Mood disorders and suicide. In J. E. Birren, R. B. Sloan, and G. Cohen (Eds). *Handbook of mental health and aging.* San Diego: Academic Press, 1992.

Kramer, B. A. Electroconvulsive therapy use in geriatric depression. *Journal of Nervous and Mental Disease,* 1987, *175,* 233–235.

Kramer, M. The increasing prevalence of mental disorders: A pandemic threat. *Psychiatric Quarterly,* 1983, *55,* 115–145.

Langer, E. J., and Rodin, J. The effects of choices and enhanced personal responsibility for the aged: A field experiment in an institutional setting. *Journal of Personality and Social Psychology,* 1976, *34,* 191–198.

Langer, E. J., Rodin, J., Beck, P., Weinman, C., and Spitzer, L. Environmental determinants of memory improvement in late adulthood. *Journal of Personality and Social Psychology,* 1979, *37,* 2003–2013.

Lawton, M. P. Clinical geropsychology: Problems and prospects. In *Master lectures on the psychology of aging.* Washington, D.C.: American Psychological Association, 1979.

Lewis, M. I., and Butler, R. N. Life review therapy: Putting memories to work in individual and group psychotherapy. *Geriatrics,* 1974, *29,* 165–173.

Lichtenberg, P. A., Ross, T., Millis, S. R., and Manning, C. A. The relationship between depression and cognition in older adults: A cross-validation study. *Journals of Gerontology,* 1995, *50,* P25–P32.

Light, E., and Lebowitz, B. D. (Eds.) *The elderly with chronic mental illness.* New York: Springer, 1991.

McIntire, M., and Angle, C. The taxonomy of suicide and self-poisoning. In C. Wells and J. Stuart (Eds.), *Self-destructive behavior in children and adolescents.* New York: Van Nostrand Reinhold, 1981.

McIntosh, J. L. Suicide among the elderly: Levels and trends. *American Journal of Orthopsychiatry,* 1985, *55,* 288–293.

McIntosh, J. L., and Santos, J. F. Suicide among minority elderly: A preliminary investigation. *Suicide and life threatening behavior,* 1981, *11,* 151–166.

Maddox, G. L. Aging, drinking, and alcohol abuse. *Generations,* 1988, *12,* 14–16.

Manton, K. G., Blazer, D. G., and Woodbury, M. A. Suicide in middle age and later life. *Journal of Gerontology,* 1987, *42,* 219–227.

Markides, K. S. Minority status, aging, and mental health. *International Journal of Aging and Human Development,* 1986, *23,* 285–300.

Masliah, E., Terry, R. D., DeTeresa, R., and Hansen, L. A. Immunohistochemical quantification of the synapse-related protein synaptophysin in Alzheimer's disease. *Neuroscience Letters,* 1989, *103,* 234–238.

Mattis, S. Mental status examination for organic mental syndrome in the elderly patient. In R. Bellack and B. Karasu (Eds.), *Geriatric psychiatry.* New York: Grune and Stratton, 1976.

Meehan, P. J., Saltzman, L. E., and Sattin, R. W. Suicides among older U.S. residents: Epidemiologic characteristics and trends. *American Journal of Public Health,* 1991, *81,* 1198–1200.

Mignogna, M. J. Integrity versus despair: The treatment of depression in the elderly. *Clinical Therapeutics,* 1986, *8,* 248–260.

Miller, M. *Suicide after sixty: The final alternative.* New York: Springer, 1979.

Miller, N. S., Belkin, B. M., and Gold, M. S. Alcohol and drug dependence among the elderly. *Comprehensive Psychiatry,* 1991, *32,* 153–165.

Mintz, J., Steuer, J., and Jarvik, L. Psychotherapy with depressed elderly patients: Research considerations. *Journal of Consulting and Clinical Psychology,* 1981, *49,* 542–548.

Nacoste, D., and Wise, W. The relationship among negative life events, cognitions and depression within three generations. *The Gerontologist,* 1991, *31,* 397–403.

National Center for Health Statistics. Advance report of final mortality statistics: 1980. *Monthly Vital Statistics Report,* 1983, *32* (Supplement).

National Center for Health Statistics, Public Health Service. *Monthly Vital Statistics Report,* 1988, *36,* 25–30.

Neshkes, R. E., and Jarvik, L. F. Affective disorders in the elderly. *Annual Review of Medicine,* 1987, *38,* 445–456.

NIH (National Institutes of Health) Consensus Development Conference. *Diagnosis and Treatment of Depression.* Washington D.C.: November 1991.

O'Shea, B., Lynch, T., Falvey, J., O'Mahoney, G. Electroconvulsive therapy and cognitive improvement in a very elderly depressed patient. *British Journal of Psychiatry,* 1987, *150,* 255–257.

Parmelee, P. A., Katz, I. R., and Lawton, M. P. Incidence of Depression in long-term care settings. *Journals of Gerontology,* 1992, *47,* M189–M196.

Perl, D. P., and Brody, A. R. Alzheimer's disease: X-ray spectrometric evidence of aluminum accumulation in neurofibrillary tangle-bearing neurons. *Science,* 1980, *208,* 297–299.

Perls, T. T. The oldest-old. *Scientific American,* 1995, *272,* 70–75.

Pfeiffer, E. Psychotherapy with elderly patients. *Postgraduate Medicine,* 1971, *50,* 254–258.

Phifer, J. E., and Murrell, S. A. Etiologic factors in the outset of depressive symptoms in older adults. *Journal of Abnormal Psychology,* 1986, *95,* 282–291.

Quam, J. K. Life tasks and developmental issues of the chronically mentally ill elderly. In N. S. Abramson, J. K. Quam, and M. Wasow (Eds.), *The elderly and chronic mental illness.* San Francisco: Jossey-Bass, 1986.

Quam, J. K., and Abramson, N. S. The use of time lines and life lines in work with chronically mentally ill people. *Health and Social Work,* 1991, *16,* 27–33.

Rabins, P. V. Establishing Alzheimer's disease units in nursing homes: Pros and cons. *Hospital and Community Psychiatry,* 1986, *37,* 120–121.

Raschko, R. Spokane community mental health center elderly services. In E. Light, and B. D. Lebowitz

(Eds.) *The elderly with chronic mental illness.* New York: Springer, 1991.

Reese, D. R., Gross, A. M., Smalley, D. L., and Messer, S. C. Caregivers of Alzheimer's disease and stroke patients: Immunological & psychological considerations. *The Gerontologist,* 1994, *34,* 534–540.

Regier, D. A., Boyd, J. H., Burke, J. D., Rae, D. S., Myers, J. K., Kramer, M., Robins, L. N., George, L. K., Karno, M., and Locke, B. Z. One month prevalence of mental disorders in the United States: Based on five epidemiologic catchment area sites. *Archives of General Psychiatry,* 1988, *45,* 977–986.

Reisberg, B., Ferris, S. H., De Leon, M. J., and Crook, T. The Global Deterioration Scale for assessment of primary degenerative dementia. *American Journal of Psychiatry,* 1982, *139,* 1136–1139.

Rickards, L. R. Mental health services for the elderly: Block grant impact. Paper presented at meetings of the American Psychological Association, 1985.

Ringler, R. L. Aging perspectives. In N. E. Miller and G. D. Cohen (Eds.), *Clinical aspects of Alzheimer's disease and senile dementia.* New York: Raven Press, 1981.

Rocca, W. A., Amaducci, L. A., and Schoenberg, B. S. Epidemiology of clinically diagnosed Alzheimer's disease. *Annals of Neurology,* 1986, *19,* 415–424.

Romaniuk, M., McAuley, W. J., and Arling, G. An examination of the prevalence of mental disorders among elderly in the community. *Journal of Abnormal Psychology,* 1983, *92,* 458–467.

Roybal, E. R. Mental health and aging: The need for an expanded federal response. *American Psychologist,* 1988, *43,* 189–194.

Ryan, C., and Butters, N. Further evidence for a continuum of impairment encompassing male alcoholic Korsakoff patients and chronic alcoholic men. *Alcholism: Clinical and Experimental Research,* 1980, *4,* 190–198.

Salzman, C. (Ed.). *Clinical geriatric psychopharmacology.* New York: McGraw-Hill, 1984.

Schuckit, M. A., and Miller, P. L. Alcoholism in elderly men: A survey of a general medical ward. *Annals of the New York Academy of Sciences,* 1976, *273,* 558–571.

Schuckit, M. A., and Morrissey, E. R. Alcoholism in women: Some clinical and social perspectives with an emphasis on possible subtypes. In M. Greenblatt and M. A. Schuckit (Eds.), *Alcoholism problems in women and children.* New York: Grune and Stratton, 1976.

Shimp, L. A., and Ascione, F. J. Causes of medication misuse and error. *Generations* 1988, *12,* 17–21.

Sholomskas, A. J., Chevron, E. S., Prusoff, B. A., and Berry, C. Short-term interpersonal therapy (IPT) with the depressed elderly: Case reports and discussion. *American Journal of Psychotherapy,* 1983, *37,* 552–560.

Small, G. W., Liston, E. H., and Jarvik, L. F. Diagnosis and treatment of dementia in the aged. *Western Journal of Medicine,* 1981, *135,* 469–481.

Stenback, A. Depression and suicidal behavior in old age. In J. E. Birren and R. B. Sloane (Eds.), *Handbook of mental health and aging.* Englewood Cliffs, N. J.: Prentice-Hall, 1980.

Steuer, J. L., Mintz, J., Hammen, C. L., Hill, M. A., Jarvik, L. F., McCarley, T., Motoike, P., and Rosen, R. Cognitive-behavioral and psychodynamic group psychotherapy in treatment of geriatric depression. *Journal of Consulting and Clinical Psychology,* 1984, *52,* 180–189.

Stewart, R. B. Drug use in the elderly. In J. C. Delafuente and R. B. Stewart (Eds.), *Therapeutics in the elderly.* Baltimore: Williams and Wilkins, 1988.

Talbott, J. A. A special population: The elderly deinstitutionalized chronically mentally ill patient. *Psychiatric Quarterly,* 1983, *55,* 90–105.

Terry, R. D., Masliah, E., Salmon, D., and Butters, N. Structure-function correlations in Alzheimer's disease. *Journal of Neuropathology and Experimental Neurology,* 1990, *49,* 335.

Terry, R. D., and Wisniewski, H. Structural aspects of aging of the brain. In C. Eisdorfer and R. O. Friedal (Eds.), *Cognitive and emotional disturbance in the elderly.* Chicago: Yearbook Medical Publishers, 1977.

Waxman, H. M., Carner, E. A., and Klein, M. Underutilization of mental health professionals by community elderly. *The Gerontologist,* 1984, *24,* 23–30.

Weeks, D., Freeman, C. P. L., and Kendall, R. E. Enduring cognitive defects. *British Journal of Psychiatry,* 1980, *137,* 26–37.

Whanger, A. D. Substance use disorders. In A. D. Whanger and A. C. Meyers (Eds.), *Mental health assessment and therapeutic intervention with older adults.* Rockville, Md: Aspen, 1984.

Whittington, F. J. Making it better: Drinking and drugging in old age. *Geriatrics*, 1988, *12*, 5–7.

Wilsnack, R. W., Wilsnack, S. C., and Klassen, A. D. Women's drinking and drinking problems: Patterns from a 1981 national survey. *American Journal of Public Health*, 1984, *74*, 1231–1238.

Wurtman, R. J. Alzheimer's disease. *Scientific American*, 1985, *252*, 62–74.

Zarit, S. H. *Aging and mental disorders*. New York: Free Press. 1980.

# THE SOCIAL CONTEXT OF AGING

Throughout the previous three sections, we have identified how changes in the physical and psychological aspects of aging have diverse consequences for older people's cognitive and personality functioning, sexuality, and mental health. We have also seen how social factors (e.g., the presence of strong family and friendship ties) can affect physical changes (e.g., being at-risk for certain chronic illnesses) as well as psychological experiences (e.g., the likelihood of suicide). Within this framework of the dynamic interactions among physical, psychological, and social factors, we turn now to a more detailed discussion of the social context of aging and its congruence with older people's level of functioning.

Chapter 12 begins by examining the importance of informal social supports, particularly family, neighbors, and friends, to quality of life. In the Introduction, we saw how longer life expectancies, combined with earlier marriages and childbearing, which have reduced the average span in years between generations, have also increased the number of three- and four-generation families. The growth of the multigenerational family has numerous ramifications for relationships between spouses, between grandparents and grandchildren, between adult children and older relatives, and among siblings and other extended family members. Generally, these relationships are characterized by reciprocity, with older family members trying to remain as independent as possible. The normal physical and psychological changes of aging usually are not detrimental to family relationships, although caring for an older relative with a long-term illness can burden family members. Compared to the earlier years, late-life family relationships are more often characterized by losses that demand role shifts and adjustments. A widower may cope with the loss of his wife by remarrying, whereas a widow tends to turn to adult children and friends.

Although there are some older people living alone—including a growing number who are homeless—friends, neighbors, and even acquaintances often perform family-like functions for them. More conducive to reciprocal exchanges, they may be an even more important source of support for an older person than one's family members. As gerontologists have recognized the importance of informal social networks for older people's well-being, programmatic interventions have been developed specifically to strengthen these ties. Some of these interventions, such as the use of mutual help groups, are briefly described in Chapter 12.

Where people live—the type of housing, age homogeneity of the neighborhood and community, and rural-urban location—affects their social interactions. Chapter 13 illustrates the importance of achieving congruence between older people's social, psychological, and physical needs and their physical environment. Relocation is an example of a disruption of this congruence or fit between the environment and the older person. Another illustration of a physical environment that no longer fits a person's social needs is when older residents in high-crime neighborhoods become so fearful of victimization that they dare not leave their homes. The extent of age homogeneity of a neighborhood can enhance older persons' social interactions and, in some instances, their feelings of safety. Planned housing, homesharing, congregate housing, assisted living facilities with multiple levels of care, and nursing homes are ways to modify the physical environment to support older people's changing and diverse needs. Chapter 13 includes a discussion of housing policies that affect older people, as well as an analysis of the problems of homelessness among the older population.

Throughout our discussion of the social context for aging, the effects of socioeconomic status on types of interactions and activities are readily apparent. Economic status is largely determined by past and current employment patterns and by the resulting retirement benefits. Chapter 14 shows declining rates of labor force participation among both men and women age 65 and over, due largely to the trend toward early retirement. Most people choose to retire early, provided their public or private pensions will enable them to enjoy economic security. Although most older people apparently do not want to work full-time, many would like the option of flexible part-time

jobs. For most people, retirement is not a crisis, although for people without good health, adequate finances, or prior planning, retirement can be a difficult transition. Accordingly, women, ethnic minorities, and low-status workers are most vulnerable to experiencing poverty or near-poverty in old age. The pressures on public financial assistance programs, created in part by the trend toward early retirement and the barriers to finding employment in old age, are further discussed in Chapter 14.

Chapter 15 examines how people's interactions change with age in terms of their leisure time, involvement in community, organizational and religious activities, and political participation. The extent and type of involvement is influenced not only by age, but also by gender, ethnic minority status, health, socioeconomic status, and educational level. Therefore, declines in participation may not necessarily be caused by age-related changes but instead represent the influence of other variables. Generally, involvement tends to be fairly stable across the life course; leisure, volunteer and community activities and interests formed in early and middle adulthood are maintained into later life. This does not mean, however, that older people cannot develop new interests and skills. Many people form new roles and interests through senior centers, volunteering, clubs, political activism, and continuing education programs.

Chapter 16 examines attitudes toward death and dying, with an emphasis on age differences in these attitudes. The process of dying, from both a theoretical and an empirical perspective, is considered. The impact of social and cultural values, as well as individual factors such as the relationship between the dying person and care-givers, are discussed in reviewing grief and mourning. Recent trends in an individual's right to die and the debates about active and passive euthanasia also are reviewed in this chapter.

Because of the predominance of social problems faced by older women and ethnic minorities, their special needs and some practice and policy interventions are discussed in Chapters 17 and 18. Economic difficulties experienced in young and middle adulthood by these groups tend to be perpetuated in old age. These are not isolated problems, but rather of increasing concern to gerontologists and policy-makers, since women over age 65 form the majority of older people, and older ethnic minorities, although a small percentage of the total older population today, are growing rapidly.

The following vignettes illustrate the diversity of social interactions experienced by older people and set the stage for our discussion of the social context of aging.

### An Older Person with Limited Social Resources

Mr. Valdres, age 73, has been separated from his wife for 20 years. He lives in a small room in an inner-city hotel. Since he worked odd jobs all his life, often performing migrant farm labor, he collects only the minimum amount of Social Security. Some months he finds it very hard to get by and has only one meal a day. Although he is not in contact with his former wife or his six children, he does have a group of buddies in the area who watch out for one another and who get together at night to have a beer and watch TV in the hotel lobby. Although he has smoked all his life and suffers from emphysema, he refuses to see a doctor or any other staff at the downtown medical clinic. He also will not apply for any public assistance, such as SSI or food stamps, in part because he does not understand what these programs are, but also because he does not want government "handouts." The hotel manager keeps track of his activities and will occasionally slip him some extra money or food.

### An Older Person with Extensive Social Resources

Mrs. Howard, age 78, lives with her husband in a small town. Most of her relatives, including three of her children and eight grandchildren, live in the area, and there are large family gatherings on Sundays and holidays. She is a retired teacher; her husband was a successful local realtor until he retired. Both retired in their early seventies. They have considerable savings; in addition, they always lived simply and frugally, saving for their retirement. They have lived in the same house for the past 42 years, and their home is well maintained and recently modernized. Mrs. Howard enjoys gardening, doing housework, reading, and visiting. In addition, she is very active in her church, serves on the Advisory Board to the Area Agency on Aging, and is involved in the town's politics.

She also tutors children with learning disabilities. Her days are filled with housework, talking to friends, neighbors, or relatives, or helping someone out, whether a grandchild or neighbor. Despite all her activity, she occasionally complains of being lonely and useless.

### An Older Person Coping with Multiple Losses

Mr. Mansfield is 87 years old. He and his wife had six children. After having been a successful businessman in the Chicago area, he retired to the south when he turned 66. Mr. Mansfield and his wife were active in their church, enjoyed going to plays and keeping up with their children who had interesting careers all over the United States.

He enjoyed his retirement until his wife of 50 years died when he was 80. Mr. Mansfield was heartbroken and thought that his life had ended. He then became involved in a support group offered through his church and started teaching adult education classes. Through that experience he became involved in the ecumenical life of the small southern town and was very active in putting on an annual conference. Although he still speaks with tears when talking about his relationship with his deceased wife, it has become clear that his life has found new meaning and purpose in his church work, and in becoming a volunteer for the Area Agency on Aging. However, Mr. Mansfield recently faced a new challenge. His youngest and his oldest child have both died. The oldest died in her early 50's of a drug overdose of pills she was taking for chronic pain. The youngest, a son, died six months later after a long battle with AIDS. Although these were wrenching experiences for him, he is now facing these bereavements with a different support network. The pain is still there, but he is able to share it with others. And he continues to be an active volunteer. His own health is beginning to deteriorate, however, and he has started to talk about his own death. He is concerned about his ability to drive, as his eyesight is diminished. His faith and belief system are integral to his dealing with these concerns about death and dying.

These vignettes show the importance of informal social support networks, both for an apparently isolated person in a low-income hotel and for an older person coping with multiple social losses. We turn now to examining the role of family, friends, neighbors, and acquaintances in the quality of older people's daily lives.

# CHAPTER 12

# THE IMPORTANCE OF SOCIAL SUPPORTS: FAMILY, FRIENDS, AND NEIGHBORS

As people age, the nature of their social roles and relationships changes. Earlier chapters have noted and the introductory vignettes have illustrated that the way older people interact in their social world of family, friends, and neighbors is affected by physiological, social, and psychological changes. For example, with children gone from the home and without daily contacts with co-workers, older people lose a critical context for social involvement. At the same time, their need for social support may increase because of changes in health, cognitive, and emotional status. Such incongruence between needs and environmental opportunities can result in stress for some older people. In previous chapters, formal support systems characteristic of the larger environment, particularly the health care system, have been described. This chapter focuses on the informal social support systems of family, friends, neighbors, and acquaintances, how these networks can buffer some of the stress and losses of aging, and policy and practice issues posed by the use of social networks to deliver services.

## THE NATURE AND FUNCTION OF INFORMAL SUPPORTS

The importance of informal social supports in older people's lives has been extensively documented (Mor-Barak, Miller & Syme, 1991; Sussman, 1985; Ward, Sherman, and LeGory, 1984; Shanas, 1979; Rosow, 1967). Informal reciprocal relationships are, in fact, a crucial concomitant of an older person's well-being, morale and autonomy (Matthews, 1991). A common myth is that older people are lonely and alienated from family and friends. Yet, even the most apparently isolated and vulnerable older person may be able to turn to some informal network for information, financial advice, emotional reassurance, or concrete services (Cantor, 1994). Consistent with social exchange theory discussed in Chapter 4, most older people try to maintain reciprocity in their interactions with each other and with younger people. Older individuals first use informal social supports to meet their emotional needs, and move to more formal relationships only when necessary. As suggested by the person-environment model, they draw upon these informal supports as a way to enhance their competence.

With cutbacks in formal services in the past decade, gerontologists have become more aware of the critical roles played by informal relationships. Families, friends, neighbors, and even acquaintances, such as grocery clerks and postal carriers, can be powerful antidotes to some of the negative consequences of the aging process, as in the description of Mr. Mansfield on p. 281. For example, informal networks have been found to be associated with health and to reduce the adverse effects of stressful life events, such as bereavement and widowhood, although it is unclear whether an older person's social networks act as buffers against the negative impacts of life events on health, or whether they have a more direct effect, independent of the presence or absence of major life events (Mor-Barak, et al., 1991).

Alternatively, loss of social support, through divorce or death of a spouse, can contribute to health problems (Cohen and Syme, 1985; Asher, 1984; Berkman and Syme, 1979; Cossell, 1974). For example, for older people who live alone and are not tied into informal networks, the use of formal services and the likelihood of institutionalization are generally higher; their personally reported well-being tends to be lower; and their burdens of adjusting to widowhood are greater than for those with strong social supports (Lopata, 1979; Kasper, 1988; Wallston et al., 1983). Having an intimate friend, for example, has been found to be related to high morale and less likelihood of depression, even during major role losses, such as a spouse's death (Blau, 1981). While informal networks are vital to well-being, support for older people must be shared between formal and informal systems, which raises policy, practice, and ethical issues.

The family—the basic unit of social relationships—is the first topic considered here. We examine the rapid growth of the multigenerational family and how relationships with spouses, adult children, parents, grandparents,

siblings, and gay and lesbian partners change with age.

## THE CHANGING CONCEPT OF THE AGING FAMILY

Contrary to the myth of alienation, the family is the primary source of social support for older people. Nearly 94 percent of people over age 65, similar to Mrs. Howard in the introductory vignette, have living family members, although this proportion decreases with age. In fact, 67 percent live in a family setting, although older men (82 percent) are more likely to do so than are older women (57 percent) (U.S. Senate Special Committee on Aging, 1992). Likewise, older African American women, especially widows, are more likely to live in extended family households than are older white women (Choi, 1991). Even when family members live apart, the emotional bonds between them tend to be strong, creating what has been termed "intimacy at a distance" (Rosenmayr, 1977).

Families provide approximately 80 percent of the in-home care to older people with chronic illness, even when formal services are used selectively (U.S. Senate Special Committee on Aging, 1992; Leutz, Capitman, MacAdams, and Abrahams, 1992). The family not only helps directly, but also provides information and advocates for services for their older members. As an illustration of the importance of family support, nearly 10 percent of older people would require nursing home placement if family members were not providing care in home settings. For every older person in a nursing home, two or more equally impaired older individuals live with and are cared for by family. If these elders were institutionalized, the number of nursing home residents would triple (Brody, 1985). The assistance of family members is thus often a major determinant of whether an older person lives in a nursing home or in the community. Persons without family ties, primarily widowed women and the very old who have outlived other family members, are those most likely to be institutionalized.

## The Multigenerational Family

As noted in Chapter 1, the rapid growth of the multigenerational family is one of the most significant demographic changes affecting family members' interactions with their older relatives. Along with the increase in life expectancy, patterns of earlier remarriage and child-bearing in some generations have resulted in the growth of families spanning four, and sometimes five, generations. Among adult children, over 80 percent of middle-aged couples have at least one living parent, compared to fewer than 50 percent at the turn of the century. Even those who are among the young-old, and facing their own declines in finances, energy and health, may have surviving parents and grandparents who require some assistance. It has been estimated that 40 percent of adult children in their late fifties have a surviving parent, 20 percent in their early sixties, 10 percent in their late sixties, and 3 percent in their seventies. The changing multigenerational dynamics are reflected in the fact that 10 percent of people over age 65 have a child who is also over 65, so that they may be both a child and a grandparent at the same time (U.S. Senate Special Committee on Aging, 1992). Given

continuing technological and medical advances, these trends will undoubtedly continue.

Another change is that the demographic structure of many family lineages has gone from a pyramid to a narrow beanpole, with more relationships that cross generational lines, more time spent in intergenerational roles, and fewer siblings and other age peers within a single generation (Bengtson, Rosenthal, and Burton, 1990). Accordingly, the lines of demarcation between generations are sharper. Only rarely nowadays do we hear of aunts and uncles the same age or younger than their nieces and nephews, which was a common phenomenon at the turn of the century (Cantor, 1991), although, as a result of remarriage, there may be some blended families in which an aunt-in-law or uncle-in-law or step-relatives are younger.

The multigenerational family is, in turn, influenced by a number of social trends that affect interactions of family members across generations. Women's labor force participation has increased. Rates of divorce and remarriage and the consequent number of "blended families" have escalated. New and diverse family structures, such as communal living, cohabitation by unmarried couples, and gay and lesbian partnerships, have grown. Whether these various family forms will result in more or less obligation, commitment, or resources to meet the needs of older dependents is still unknown.

## The Role of Culture

Cultural values also affect family interactions. American culture places a high value on the family's privacy and independence. What occurs within it is generally viewed as its private affair, not to be interfered with by government or other outside sources. Similarly, family members' independence from each other is emphasized. Offspring are expected to move away from childhood dependency and toward the independence of adulthood. As a result of this emphasis, family members' emotional interdependence tends to be overlooked. These values affect not

Assistance across generations is a common pattern.

only commonly held views of adult child-parent relationships, but also the right of the state to intervene in high-risk family situations, for example, cases of suspected elder abuse and/or neglect. They also partially underlie the relative infrequency of multigenerational family households in our society. This contrasts with developing countries where three- and four-generation families, although a small percentage of the total population, are more likely to live together under one roof. The extended family is stronger within different ethnic groups, especially Hispanics and African Americans, within our increasingly diverse society (Brubaker, 1990). It is within this context—the relatively recent growth of the multigenerational family, the Western cultural emphasis on family privacy, and the increasing cultural and economic diversity within our society—that we examine the range of family relationships in old age.

## Older Couples

The marital relationship plays a crucial support function in most older people's lives, especially men's. As parental and employment responsibil-

ities decline, having a spouse provides built-in companionship. Of all family members, spouses are most likely to serve as confidants and to provide support. More than half of the population over age 65 is married and lives with a spouse in independent households (U.S. Senate Special Committee on Aging, 1992). Significant differences exist, however, in the living arrangements of older men and women. Because of women's longer life expectancy and fewer options for remarriage, 40 percent of women age 65 and older are married, as compared to 74 percent of men (see Figure 12-1). Accordingly, women represent 80 percent of the older individuals who live alone (see Figure 12-2). Among noninstitutionalized older men, only about 18 percent are living by themselves, compared to 43 percent of their female counterparts (U.S. Bureau of the Census, 1991). There are some variations among different ethnic minority groups. For example, compared with whites, a larger proportion of African Americans and Hispanics over age 65 live without a spouse because of widowhood, divorce, or separation. Other ethnic minority differences are discussed in Chapter 17.

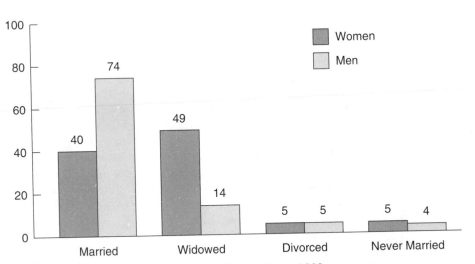

**FIGURE 12-1  Marital Status of Persons 65 and Over: 1990**
SOURCE: U.S. Bureau of the Census. *Marital Status and Living Arrangements,* Current Population Reports, Series P-20, No. 450, 1991.

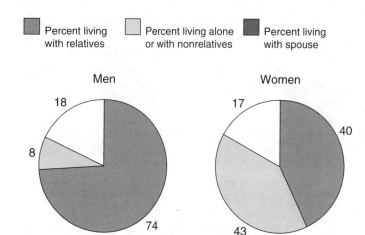

■ Percent living with relatives  □ Percent living alone or with nonrelatives  ■ Percent living with spouse

Men

18
8
74

Women

17
40
43

**FIGURE 12–2  Living Arrangements of Noninstitutionalized Persons 65 and Over: 1990**

SOURCE: U.S. Bureau of the Census. *Marital Status and Living Arrangements*, Current Population Reports, Series P-20, No. 450, 1991.

Couples are faced with learning to adapt to changing roles and expectations throughout marriage. Family life is characterized by a continual tension between maintaining individual autonomy and negotiating issues of equitable exchange and dependence. Such tensions may be heightened in old age. As partners change roles through retirement, post-parenthood, or illness, they face the strain of relinquishing previous roles and adapting to new ones. Couples today experience a post-childrearing period of perhaps 30 to 40 years, ranging from late maturity to frailty, and must renegotiate their marital expectations and roles in light of their changed family structure. Failure to negotiate role expectations and the consequent disagreements and divergent paths tend to be associated with feelings of inequity and depression in older spouses (Holahan, 1984). One of the most difficult transitions can be retirement, particularly when wives consider it their responsibility to plan for their husbands' retirement or when couples have difficulty working out time to be apart from one another (Long and Mancini, 1990; Gilford, 1986; Szinovacz, 1989).

Such strains tend to be heightened by the fact that long-lived relationships are a contemporary phenomenon. At the end of the nineteenth century, the average length of marriage at the time one spouse died was about 28 years; now it is over 43 years (Troll, 1986). Never before in

history have the lives of so many couples remained interwoven long enough to encounter the variety of life-changing events that later stages of marriage now bring. Most older couples were not socialized for handling the associated stresses. Yet they are more likely than younger cohorts to view marriage as a lifetime commitment governed by obligation.

## Marital Satisfaction

Despite these potential tensions, most older partners appear satisfied, with men tending to be more satisfied with marriage and the degree to which their emotional needs are fulfilled than are women (Chappell, 1990). Marital satisfaction has been found to be high among those recently married, lower among those in the childrearing period—especially in middle age—and higher in the later stages[*] (Brecher, 1984; Robinson, 1990). Many older spouses report improvement in their marriages over time as well as more positive interactions with less conflict and negative

---

[*]A word of caution is necessary in interpreting data on the increase in marital satisfaction in later age. Because most studies of marital satisfaction are cross-sectional, the higher prevalence of happily married couples in later life could be a result of greater divorce or separation at earlier stages among those who are unhappily married or of older cohorts' being brought up to be satisfied with less.

sentiment such as sarcasm, disagreement, and criticisms than do younger couples (Levenson, Cartensen, and Gottman, 1993; Treas and Bengtson, 1987).

Increases in marital satisfaction among the young-old may be partially due to children leaving home. Contrary to stereotypes, most women are not depressed when their children leave home, but rather view the "empty nest" as newfound freedom and an opportunity for new activities, although both fathers and mothers may initially be unhappy and dissatisfied (Barber, 1989). In fact, rigid sex-role expectations and behaviors are often relaxed in old age, with men becoming more affectionate and less career-oriented and women becoming more achievement-oriented and both men and women sharing more sources of pleasure (Levenson et al., 1993), as illustrated in the discussion of personality styles in Chapter 9. This tendency for men to turn away from occupational interests and women to focus outward on employment will probably increase in the future. Successful negotiation of such role changes appears to be related to marital satisfaction. Happy marriages have been found to be characterized by more equality and joint decision making through a gradual relaxation of boundaries between sex roles and a decreasing division of household labor according to traditional male/female sex roles. Nevertheless, some areas (e.g., dependent care and family finances) often remain gender-differentiated (Miller and Cafasso, 1992; Szinovacz, 1989). Freed from issues of control over children and with more opportunities for companionship, partners may discover or develop common interests and interdependence. As a consequence, expressive aspects of the marriage—affection and companionship—may emerge more fully (Dobson, 1983).

Older partners' ability to negotiate these role transitions depends, in large part, on their prior adaptability and satisfaction in their relationship. Studies of marital longevity have found that couples celebrating golden anniversaries (who form approximately 3 percent of all marriages) were characterized by intimacy, autonomy, commitment, congruence of values, religious faith, communication, and an ability to accommodate one another (Robinson, 1990; Robinson and Blanton, 1993).

For happily married older couples, their relationship is central to a "good life." Married persons appear to be happier, healthier, experience higher levels of self-esteem, and live longer than widowed or divorced persons of the same age (Lee and Shehan, 1988; Brubaker, 1985; Gove, Hughes, and Style, 1983). In fact, marital satisfaction may be more important than age, health, education, or retirement in predicting life satisfaction and quality of life for older women, and second only to good health for older men. These positive effects appear to emanate from three major functions that marriage performs for older couples: intimacy, interdependence, and a sense of belonging (Atchley, 1985; Gilford, 1986). Not surprisingly, dissatisfied marriages tend to negatively affect health, especially for women (Levenson et al., 1993).

Although most older couples have been together since young adulthood, a small proportion remarry after widowhood or divorce later in life. Women have fewer options to remarry, since they generally outlive their male peers, and men tend to marry women younger than themselves. The likelihood that widowed men will remarry is seven times greater than that for widowed women (Longino, Soldo, and Manton, 1990). Moreover, the divorced are more likely to remarry than are the widowed. Having sufficient economic resources is an important consideration in remarrying. The major reason for remarriage for both men and women, however, is a desire for companionship. Having a confidante and wanting someone to care for them appear to be more important to men than to women (Wright, 1994). Most older people who remarry choose someone they have previously known, with a similar background and interests. Factors that appear to be related to successful late-life remarriages are long prior friendship, family and friends' approval, adequate pooled financial resources, and personal adaptability to life changes. Remarriage is an especially complex event since both partners have a long prior family history (Brubaker, 1985). Some older couples choose to live together but not to marry, generally for economic and inheritance reasons (Sussman, 1985).

## Spouses as Caregivers

With the increase in life expectancy, more older partners may end up caring for each other, frequently for long periods of time. Spouses are generally the primary caregivers, with children predominating as secondary caregivers. Reflecting the fact that women outlive men by an average of seven years, more wives than husbands provide care. In fact 60 percent of primary caregivers to older people are wives of disabled, often older husbands. Of these caregivers, 73 percent are age 65 or older (Cantor, 1994; Stone, Cafferata, and Sangl, 1987). Caregiving wives are referred to as "hidden victims," experiencing isolation, loneliness, and role overload (Fengler and Goodrich, 1979). Older caregivers face not only the 24-hour responsibilities associated with care, but also may be coping with their own aging, physical illnesses, or financial and legal burdens. These stresses may be even greater for recently married older couples who cannot draw upon a lifetime of shared experiences and for spouses who are caring for those with cognitive impairment and personality changes (Wright, 1991). The quality of the marital relationship (e.g., high levels of spousal interaction and commitment) undoubtedly affects the continuation of the caregiving relationship, along with the caregiver's health (Wright, 1992).

## Divorce in Old Age

Even though most older marriages are reasonably happy, a small percentage are not, and an increasing proportion of older couples are choosing divorce rather than tolerate an unhappy marriage. While only 4 percent of older persons are divorced, the numbers have increased twice as fast as the older population as a whole since 1980, and rates are even higher among ethnic minority elderly (U.S. Bureau of the Census, 1989). Although late-life divorce is still relatively uncommon, 10 to 13 percent of persons age 65 and over have experienced a divorce at some time, with the highest rates among African American older women (Brubaker, 1985; Uhlenberg and Myers, 1981). What appears to be happening is that the frequency of divorce has changed, not the age profile, with more people of every age seeing divorce as an option (Hennon, 1983).

The number of divorced older persons is predicted to increase in the future; nearly half of the people currently marrying (and entering old age around the year 2020) will divorce (Brubaker, 1990; Glick, 1984; Goldman and Lord, 1983). This increase may be partially explained by successive generations' acceptance of divorce as a solution to a bad marriage, and by an accompanying increase in remarriages. Across all groups, three out of four divorced persons remarry within five years; however, 44 percent of these remarriages are estimated to end with divorce (Hennon, 1983). For older individuals, however, the likelihood of remarriage after widowhood or divorce is relatively small, with more men likely to remarry than women (Brubaker, 1990). These trends clearly affect economic and social status. Being divorced in old age often means economic hardships, especially for women, as well as diminished socioemotional support at a stage when other supports are also weakened. In general, divorced older persons are less satisfied with their lives than married or widowed persons (Glick, 1984; Hennon, 1983; Uhlenberg and Myers, 1981).

## Lesbian and Gay Partners

As we have seen in Chapter 10, the concept of couples in old age needs to be broadened to include gay men and lesbians. Older gay men and lesbians share concerns similar to those of most older adults—loneliness, health, and income, but what is unique to them is that they have lived the majority of their lives through historical periods that have been actively hostile and oppressive toward homosexuality (Friend, 1990). Many older lesbians and gays have faced discrimination from family, friends, and professionals, so their later life development is not affected by sexual orientation per se, but rather by how they cope with the social stigma and low status attached to a gay identity (Adelman, 1990; Cruikshank, 1990). Recent research indicates that discrimination and stigma profoundly affect the older gay and lesbian's aging experience, life satisfaction, and quality of life (Friend, 1990).

Although some older gay men and lesbians are concerned with "passing" or "being invisible" in a heterosexual society and only marginally accept some aspects of their homosexuality, the majority, especially the young-old, are able to reconstruct into something positive what it means to be gay or lesbian and aging (Friend, 1990; Quam and Whitford, 1992). By doing so, they generally experience greater self-acceptance and self-esteem (Adelman, 1990). Through the painful process of "coming out," they often become stronger and more competent in adjusting to changes associated with aging, thereby buffering losses, such as friends and family moving away or dying. Experiencing greater flexibility,

freedom, and differentiation in gender role definitions throughout their lives, gay men and lesbians tend to be more independent, non-traditional, and self-affirming, and to adapt more readily to the role changes associated with aging (Quam and Whitford, 1992). For example, role flexibility may ease an individual's adjustment when a partner dies or leaves (Gwenwald, 1984).

By having confronted real or imagined loss of family support earlier in life, gays and lesbians are less likely to assume that families will provide for them in old age and more likely to plan for their own future security. Accordingly, they tend to build a "surrogate family" through a strong network of friends, which either replaces or reinforces family supports. Some older gay men and lesbians share innovative housing arrangements and are a part of an empowering community that may include social and advocacy organizations, such as Senior Action in a Gay Environment (SAGE) based in New York City, the Lavender Panthers, and the National Association of Lesbian and Gay Gerontologists. Those who have the support of other gay men and lesbians as friends and confidants, in social organizations and in housing alternatives tend to be characterized by high self-esteem and life satisfaction, less fear of aging, and greater effectiveness in managing the societal aspects of aging, such as rejection (Friend, 1990; Quam and Whitford, 1992).

Despite the fact that most gay men and lesbians have acquired certain skills and attitudes that facilitate their adjustment to aging, they nevertheless face more structural and legal barriers than heterosexual couples do. The partners of those who are hospitalized or in a nursing home may be denied access to intensive care units and to medical records, and staff may be insensitive to and ignore partners, even limiting their visits and discouraging any expression of affection (Friend, 1990). Private space for conjugal visits for gay or lesbian couples in nursing homes is limited, and some institutions may admit only one member of a homosexual couple. Moreover, families may contest a gay or lesbian partner's right to an inheritance. Service barriers and

Recent research suggests that lesbians adjust positively to age-related changes.

research areas specific to older homosexual partners need to be better addressed.

## SIBLING RELATIONSHIPS

Research on sibling relationships in later life is limited compared to that on such relationships in childhood and adolescence, even though they represent the one family bond with the potential to last a lifetime. The sibling relationship in old age is characterized by a shared history, egalitarianism, and increasing closeness, particularly among sisters (Scott, 1990; Brubaker, 1990; Gold, 1989; Avioli, 1989). Most older people, even those over age 80, have at least one sibling (Cicirelli, 1991). As with other kin-keeping responsibilities, sisters are more likely than brothers to maintain frequent contact with same-sex siblings, generally by phone or face-to-face interaction rather than by letter writing (Scott, 1990).

Studies based on the criterion of feelings of closeness and affection suggest that, with age, siblings often renew past ties, forgive past conflict and rivalry, and become closer, frequently through shared reminiscence (Cicirelli, 1991; Scott, 1990; Brubaker, 1990). Siblings are particularly important sources of support in the lives of never-married older persons and those without children. Such support generally increases after a spouse's death, at which time siblings, concerned about each other's welfare, may share households; in such instances, the widowed person's psychological well-being tends to be enhanced (Cicirelli, Coward, and Dwyer, 1992; Scott, 1990).

Although siblings are less frequently caregivers to each other than are spouses and adult children, they do supplement the efforts of other family caregivers during times of crisis or special need. The very existence of siblings as a possible source of help may be important, even if such assistance is rarely used. Siblings can also perform a socialization function in later life, acting as positive role models or as motivators to try new activities, thereby enhancing adaptations to late-life changes.

Current demographic trends will affect these relationships in future decades. As more couples remain childless or have only one or two children, siblings will become even more important supports. Greater longevity and better health among the current middle-aged cohort imply greater availability of living siblings in the future, with sibling relationships expected to strengthen. However, reduced fertility rates in the current period will mean that later cohorts will have fewer siblings on whom to rely and will need to be flexible in efforts to more equitably share caregiving tasks (Scott, 1990).

The steadily increasing rate of divorce and remarriage will undoubtedly affect sibling relationships. With the increase in "blended" families through remarriage, there will be more half-siblings and step-siblings. For divorced older people who do not remarry, sibling interaction may become more important than when they were married. The degree of commitment to these new and varied relationships is unknown at this time.

## OTHER KIN

Interaction with secondary kin—cousins, aunts, uncles, nieces, and nephews—appears to depend on geographic proximity, availability of closer relatives, and preference. Shanas (1980) found that about three out of every ten persons age 65 and over had seen a relative who was not a child, grandchild, brother, or sister during the previous week. Extended kin can replace or substitute for missing or lost relatives, especially during family rituals and holidays. For example, compared to their white counterparts, black childless elders often turn to nieces and nephews when siblings are not available. Personal or historical connections that allow for remembering pleasurable events may be more important than closeness of kinship in determining interactions.

# RELATIONSHIPS WITH ADULT CHILDREN

After spouses, adult children are the most important source of support and social contact in old age. Nearly 80 percent of persons age 65 and over have surviving children, although the number of children in a family has decreased—a trend expected to continue. The majority of older adults live near at least one adult child, sharing a social life but not their homes (Brubaker, 1990). Most older people state that they prefer not to live with their children, generally for reasons of privacy and a sense of autonomy. This stated preference may, at times, represent a socially acceptable response, consistent with our cultural value of independence (Rosenthal, 1986). Although less than 20 percent of older persons live in their children's households, this percentage increases with advancing age and for widowed, separated, and divorced elderly. Approximately 33 percent of all men, and 50 percent of all women age 65 and over who are widowed, separated, or divorced share a home with their children or other family members. When older parents do live with their children, they usually live with a daughter (Brubaker, 1990). However, less than 3 percent of older people live in multigenerational households composed of parents, children, and grandchildren (U.S. Senate Special Committee on Aging, 1992), although African American elders are more likely than their white counterparts to reside in extended households (Taylor and Chatters, 1991).

While most older parents and adult children do not live together, they nevertheless see each other frequently. Studies over the past two decades have consistently found that approximately 80 percent of older people with children live less than an hour away from at least one child; 40 percent have at least one child within ten minutes of their home; 40 percent see an adult child at least once a week; and more than 75 percent talk on the phone at least weekly (AARP, 1991; Crimmins and Ingegneri, 1990; Shanas, 1979; 1980). In a study of older persons living in rural or urban communities, the best predictor of regular visits with children was the proximity of children, regardless of community type (Krout, 1988). Although older children, especially daughters, were more likely to maintain contact with their parents, these factors were less important than proximity. More research is needed on the quality of interactions between older parents and their adult children across a geographic distance.

Geographic separation of family members is generally due to mobility of the adult children, not of the older relatives. Future cohorts of older persons may have an increasing proportion of distant children because of the growing trend toward greater residential separation between adult children and older parents (Treas, 1981). However, proximity does not appear to affect the quality of parent-child relationships (Lee and Ellithorpe, 1982). Instead, socioemotional distance seems more important than geographic distance, and most adult children feel "close" to their older parents despite geographic separation (Cicirelli, 1981; Litwak, 1981). Such emotional bonds tend to be strongest among female family members (Gallup, 1989).

In sum, studies have repeatedly found that most people over age 65 are integral members of family networks, see their adult children frequently, and interact regularly by telephone or letter with relatives who live at a geographic distance. Although most parents and children report positive feelings for each other, feelings of obligation and sense of duty often underlie intergenerational relationships (Hagestad, 1984; Finley, Roberts and Banahan, 1988).

## Patterns of Intergenerational Assistance

Generally, families establish a pattern of reciprocal support between older and younger members that continues throughout an individual's lifetime. Consistent with social exchange theory discussed in Chapter 4, the rule of exchange is from those with more valued resources (e.g., money or good health) to those with less. Not only concrete assistance is exchanged, but also emotional and social support (Rossi and Rossi, 1990; Dowd, 1980; Sussman, 1985). At various points, older parents provide substantial support, especially financial assistance to their children and grandchildren, oftentimes at a geographic distance (Aldous, 1987; Brubaker, 1990; Greenberg and Becker, 1988; Bengtson, Rosenthal, and Burton, 1990). Parents, for example, are the most important source of support in coping with adult children's early widowhood and grief (Bankoff, 1983).

## Never-Married Older People

Approximately 5 to 6 percent of the older population have never married (Rubenstein, Alexander, Goodman, and Luborsky, 1991). Contrary to a commonly held image of lonely social isolates, the majority of never-married older persons have typically developed reciprocal relationships with other kin, especially siblings, and with friends and neighbors (Baresi and Hunt, 1990). They may actually be more socially active and resourceful, with more diversity in their social networks, especially with younger persons, than their married counterparts (Stull and Scarisbrick-Hauser, 1989; Rubenstein, 1987). Compared to widowed peers, they tend to be more satisfied with their lives, to be self-reliant, and to be oriented to the present (Rice, 1984; Keith and Lorenz, 1989). Whites, Asians, and Hispanics who are young-old have higher rates of never married than the middle and old-old among these ethnic groups, with this pattern reversed for African Americans and American Indians. Among Asian and American Indian populations, there are considerably more never married males than females (Baresi and Hunt, 1990).

An increasing number of organizations specifically for single people have formed, although many of these are for younger singles. Alternative living arrangements, such as multigenerational share-a-home programs, may also appeal to some single elderly who choose not to continue to live alone.

In some instances, parents continue to provide care to adult children beyond normative expectations of "launching" one's adult children to be more independent. For example, parents of adult children who are developmentally disabled or chronically mentally ill may be perpetual parents, for whom parental care remains a central role even late in life. Yet many parental caregivers of adults with disabilities are facing their own age-related health changes, which can limit their ability to provide care; in addition, they worry about how their child will be cared for after their own death or illness. The history of and the cumulative nature of care demands can make their situation particularly stressful (Kelly and Kropf, 1995; Jennings, 1987). However, both the aging and developmentally disabled service networks have tended to be unresponsive to the needs for support of older parents (Seltzer and Kraus, 1989; Smith and Tobin, 1993; Kropf and Greene, 1993; Kelly and Kropf, 1995).

As parents age, the normative pattern is for adult children to provide assistance to their parents, particularly those who have chronic health problems and are widowed or divorced. Norms of filial responsibility—that adult children should help their parents—thus become operationalized in daily caregiving behavior (Walker and Pratt, 1991). As noted earlier, families provide nearly 80 percent of the in-home care for older relatives with chronic impairments (U.S. Senate Special Committee on Aging, 1992).

A common myth in our society is that families do not care for their older members as well as they did in the "good old days." As we saw in Chapter 3, older relatives at the turn of the century were rare and valued because of their economic contributions to the family. Today, however, adult children provide more difficult care to parents over much longer periods of time than they did when life expectancy was 47 years and elders comprised only 4 percent of the population. This is the first time in history that American couples have had more parents than children. In fact, today the average American woman can expect to spend 18 years caring for an older family member compared to 17 years for her children, while in 1900, she spent an average of 8 years for elder care (Stone, Cafferata, and Sangl, 1987). Adult children are the primary caregivers of older widowed women and older unmarried men, and they are the secondary caregivers in situations where spouses of the older person are still alive. The age cohort most affected by caregiving responsibilities is the 45–54-year-olds, with 17 percent of them caring for a disabled elder (Cantor, 1991). With five million adult children estimated to be caring for parents at any one time, parent care is a predictable and nearly universal experience. Yet most people are not prepared for it (Scanlon, 1988; Brody, 1985).

The primary forms of assistance to older parents are emotional support, financial aid, instrumental activities inside and outside the home (e.g., transportation, meal preparation, shopping, and housework), personal care (e.g., bathing, feeding, and dressing), and mediating with agencies to obtain services. Such a social care system begins with opportunities for socialization, moves to assistance with tasks of daily living, and progresses to help with personal care needs that arise out of severe disability. Basic to the concept of social care is that such assistance augments the older person's competence and mastery of the environment, rather than his or her increasing dependence. The type of familial assistance given is largely determined by the older member's functional level, co-residence and the caregiver's gender, with personal care most often performed by wives or daughters (Cantor, 1991; Stoller, 1990; Tennstedt, Crawford, and McKinlay, 1993).

Responsibilities are usually differentiated by gender, such that women comprise over 80 percent of the family caregivers to chronically ill elders. Nearly 29 percent of both primary and secondary caregivers are daughters, 23 percent wives, and 20 percent more distant female relatives or female nonrelatives, although wives and husbands constitute the majority of the sole or primary caregivers (Older Women's League,

1989; Stone, Cafferata, and Sangl, 1987; Brody, 1985). Within the female kin network, a hierarchy of preference exists, based on the centrality of the caregiver's relationship to the older person and on geographic proximity (Coward and Dwyer, 1990; Matthews, 1987). Wives are favored over all others. If the older person is unmarried, widowed, or has an ill spouse, then an adult daughter or daughter-in-law is commonly the primary caregiver. If a spouse or child is unavailable, then a sister is primarily responsible, and if none of these are available, a female member of the extended family—such as a niece or a granddaughter—assumes responsibility. Even when older persons move in with the eldest son, as in East Indian, Korean, and Japanese culture, the daughter-in-law is generally still the caregiver (Qureshi and Walker, 1989). The predominance of women as caregivers of older relatives seems to be as true in developing countries as in industrialized nations.

The prominence of women in the caregiving role should not obscure the efforts of men who are primary caregivers, or what Brody (1985) calls the "unsung heroes." But studies consistently show that men rarely provide the primary personal care that is frequently time-consuming and emotionally demanding; rather, they tend to assist indirectly, such as with financial management. Men generally become involved in personal care and instrumental tasks of cooking and cleaning only when no female relative is available (Stoller, 1988; Tennstedt, McKinlay, and Sullivan, 1988; Finley, 1989; Foster and Brizius, 1993; Kaye and Applegate, 1990; Miller and Cafasso, 1992). Similarly, sons are less likely than daughters to share their households with a dependent parent. Even when sons are involved in tasks similar to those daughters perform, they experience less stress from caregiving experiences than do daughters, in part because men tend to maintain more emotional distance from the care receiver, focusing primarily on economic and concrete assistance. In contrast, women frequently feel responsible for their older relative's psychological well being (Barusch and Spaid,

1989; Biegel, Sales, and Schulz, 1991; Coward and Dwyer, 1990; Pruchno and Resch, 1989; Young and Kahana, 1989; Wethington, McLeod, and Kessler, 1988).

The extent to which ethnicity rather than socioeconomic status influences intergenerational relationships is unclear. As noted earlier, in western European cultures, both young and old view maintaining independence as a high priority. This value on individual independence is believed to underlie the lack of respect accorded to many older people of Western European descent (Weeks and Cueller, 1981). In contrast to Caucasian families, multigenerational households are more prevalent among African American, Latino and Asian American families (Beck and Beck, 1989; Tennstedt, Crawford, and McKinlay, 1993). The greater prevalence of co-residence in communities of color may underlie the higher levels of assistance to frail elders and the generally positive parent-adult child

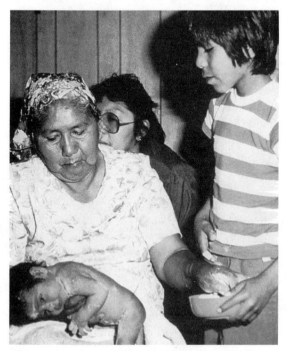

Older persons play a significant role in cultural and family rituals.

relationships reported by Hispanic American, African American, or Asian American families (Luben and Becerra, 1987). Even when controlling for need, racial and ethnic minorities have been found to be more likely to live in extended families, which provide both social support and instrumental assistance with finances and activities of daily living, especially for unmarried children and unmarried parents (Silverstein and Waite, 1993; Speare and Avery, 1993).

Others have argued that the role of the extended family is over-exaggerated or disintegrating in populations of color (Purdy and Arguello, 1992). Similarly, some studies of ethnic minority families document a growing adherence to the majority culture's norm of "mutuality at a distance" (Tobin and Kulys, 1981). In some ethnic minority groups, endorsements for norms of filial obligation and multigenerational households, for example, are stronger among young and middle-aged adults than among older adults (Hanson, Sauer, and Seelbach, 1983). This suggests the tempering of idealism, as adult children and older parents face the realities of impending caregiving and dependency.

Considerable variability exists within as well as among ethnic minority groups. In traditional Asian American families, the value system emphasizes the importance of the family unit rather than individual gain and independence. However, such values of family obligation are increasingly difficult to implement in a competitive, mobile society, particularly when adult children move into a higher social class than their parents. Many Hispanics have developed strong intergenerational ties mandated by both their cultural heritage and economic realities. But urbanization and modernization appear to have weakened patterns of intergenerational cohesion and support characteristic of Hispanic families in the past (Torres-Gil, 1976; Maldonado, 1975). The effects of changing societal conditions and of socioeconomic class on ethnic minority families are explored further in Chapter 17.

## DEMOGRAPHIC TRENDS AND ADULT CHILD-PARENT RELATIONSHIPS

A number of social and demographic trends are affecting adult child-parent relationships, particularly caregiving. One trend is the increasing proportion of older relatives compared to younger family members. The current cohort of frail elders, who raised children during the Great Depression, had a low birth rate, which resulted in a smaller number of adult children as potential caregivers. Yet, children more than any other group are caregivers of older widowed women (Cantor, 1994).

Another trend is the longer economic dependence of young adults combined with parents who are living longer. As a result, many contemporary middle-aged individuals, described as the "sandwiched generation" (illustrated in the box below) are faced with a dilemma that is relatively new historically—the competing responsibilities of caring for parents and children. The "empty nest" is thus frequently filled by frail elders and by grown children who cannot afford to leave home, or who return home because of divorce, economic need or substance abuse problems (Brody, 1985; Cantor, 1994). In fact, the percentage of unmarried adults age 18 to 24 living at home has increased from 43 percent in 1960 to 55 percent in 1987 (U.S. Bureau of the Census, 1988). Women especially face multiple, cross-generational demands along with employment responsibilities. More women are employed than in the past: 62 percent between the ages of 45 and 54, and 42 percent between the ages of 55 and 64 (U.S. Bureau of the Census, 1988). Forty-three percent of the daughters and wives and 69 percent of the sons and husbands of the disabled older population are employed full time. Yet women employed full-time are four times as likely to be the primary caregivers as are men (Stone and Kemper, 1989). Moreover, employed daughters provide nearly equal amounts of care as nonemployed daughters do, either directly or through purchased services (Brody and Schoon-over, 1986). In addition, 90 percent of today's middle-aged married women have children of their own to attend to, compared to 66 percent of those born before the turn of the century. These "women in the middle" (Brody, 1981), the traditional caregivers to older relatives, may thus be juggling extensive family responsibilities in addition to employment and their own age-related transitions. Given the in-

---

### WOMEN IN THE MIDDLE

A woman in her mid-fifties with teenage children and a full-time job, Annette had cared for both her parents. Her mother, crippled with rheumatoid arthritis, lived with Annette's family for five years before she died. Within a year, Annette's father suffered a stroke and lived with the family for three years before his death. Annette's teenagers had resented the amount of time she gave to her parents, and her husband became impatient with how little time they had alone together. They had not had a vacation in five years. Since family and friends were not interested in helping her with the care of her parents, Annette and her husband rarely even had a night out alone together. As an employed caregiver, Annette frequently missed work and was distracted on the job whenever she had to consult doctors or take her parents for therapy during normal business hours. She felt alone, isolated, and overwhelmed by the stress. She was physically and mentally exhausted from trying to meet too many demands, not knowing that some support services were available in her community, and feeling that she had to be capable of handling these responsibilities on her own. When her mother-in-law became too frail to live alone, Annette knew her family and job would suffer once again if she tried to balance household duties, a full-time job, and the care of both older and younger relatives.

creasing mobility of our society, they also may be providing care at a geographic distance.

However, given the increases in life expectancy and the consequent likelihood that middle-aged young-old grandmothers will be caring for old-old parents, conflicts between caregiving and employment are more frequent than between care of young children and care of aging parents (Stone and Kemper, 1989). In fact, only about seven percent of all women are potentially faced with simultaneously caring for children under 15 years of age and older persons (Cantor, 1991). Regardless of their particular configuration of responsibilities, such women generally do not reduce the amount of assistance given, but manage their multiple responsibilities by maintaining rigid schedules, negotiating care tasks around their employment, and giving up their own free time. Despite the inordinate amounts of care provided, many female caregivers still feel guilty for not doing more (Brody, 1985).

Another social trend that affects the adult child-parent relationship is the growth of "blended" or "reconstituted families" as a consequence of divorce and remarriage. Adult children may thus be caring not only for their biological parents and for current parents-in-law, but, if previously divorced, may be emotionally tied to their former spouse's parents, especially through their children of the earlier marriage. Such ties may lead to caregiving responsibilities for former parents-in-law as well. Difficult definitions of family membership and loyalties may complicate the distribution of time, attention, and financial resources across generations.

More older parents are experiencing the divorce of one of their adult children. It is estimated that over 50 percent of all marriages that occurred during the 1970s will end in divorce, and it is this cohort of individuals who are likely to be faced with caregiving responsibilities. Of the high proportion who will remarry, 44 percent are estimated to divorce again (Martin and Bumpass, 1989; Pratt and Kethley, 1988), creating the phenomenon of "serial monogamy"— persons having a series of divorces and

remarriages throughout their lives. While undergoing the stresses of divorce, adult children may not have the emotional stamina or the time to assist their older parents. Their divorce can also affect their older parents' life satisfaction. For example, older parents have been found to react with feelings of loss and sadness to the stress of their adult child's divorce (Eckles, 1986; Pearson, 1986; Smyer and Hofland, 1982).

## THE STRESSES OF CAREGIVING

Most women are willing to assume primary caregiving responsibility, despite the physical, financial, and emotional costs. For some women, caregiving can be a rich and rewarding experience, characterized by greater closeness with family members (Cicirelli, 1990). For many, however, their health, employment, personal freedom, privacy, and social relationships can all be negatively affected by providing care. The literature on caregiving differentiates objective from subjective burden or stress. Objective burden refers to the reality demands that confront the caregiver, such as symptomatic behaviors of the illness, disruptions in family relationships, income, and social life, and problems with service systems. Subjective burden refers to feelings aroused in caregivers as they fulfill their functions, such as worry, sadness, resentment, anger, or guilt (Braithwaite, 1992). This distinction recognizes that burden is a subjective phenomenon: what is difficult for one caregiver need not be difficult for another (Poulshock and Diemling, 1984).

The physical demands of providing daily personal assistance, such as frequently changing the bedding of an incontinent elder, are experienced most frequently by caregivers who live with the care recipient. Physical stress often manifests itself in health problems, including headaches, stomach disturbances, and weight changes. Caregivers also use prescription drugs more than the rest of the population (Biegel, Sales, and Schulz, 1991; Haley et al, 1987).

Financial burdens include not only direct costs of medical care, adaptive equipment, or hired help, but also indirect opportunity costs of lost income or missed promotions. Not surprisingly, caregiving employees report greater job-family conflicts than non-caregiving employees (Scharlach and Boyd, 1989), and financial concerns tend to be greater for female caregivers than for males (Barusch and Spaid, 1989). Compared to male caregivers, instead of limiting the amount of care provided, women are more likely to quit their jobs, reduce their hours, or miss opportunities for career development or job promotion, in part because women earn less than men and therefore their jobs are viewed by other family members as less important (Anastas, Gibeau and Larson, 1990; Scharlach and Boyd, 1989; Scheyett, 1988; Stone et al., 1987). As will be discussed in Chapter 14, those who interrupt employment to be caregivers generally receive fewer retirement benefits than those who have a continuous work history (Kingston and O'Grady-LeShane, 1993; Older Women's League, 1990).

The emotional burdens of feeling alone, isolated, and without time for oneself appear to be the greatest costs, and they are experienced more frequently by women than men. Rates of depression increase, especially among female caregivers, and relationships with other family members are frequently disrupted by other care demands (Abel, 1986; Haley, et al., 1987; Gallagher et al., 1989). While the number of educational programs, support groups, and services for caregivers has grown in the past decade, funds for public services to reduce caregivers' strains are limited (Estes, Swan, and Associates, 1993).

About 50 percent of families provide care without any outside assistance (Stone, Cafferata and Sangl, 1987), and this lack of formal support resources heightens caregivers' feelings of isolation, and, in turn, of stress. In fact, feelings of burden have been found to be related primarily to the availability of external helping resources and social support, not to the severity of the illness (Zarit, Reeves, and Bach-Peterson, 1980; Morycz, 1985). Accordingly, positive social interaction with friends and other family members can reduce the burden (Thompson, Futterman, Gallagher-Thompson, Rose, and Lovett, 1993).

In some cases, caregiving stress may become severe enough to lead to family conflict, breakdown and/or neglect or abuse of the older person (Strawbridge and Wallhagen, 1991). Abuse can be psychological (e.g., verbal aggression), financial, or involve physical violence. Spouses and sons are most often the abusers (Finkelhor and Pillemer, 1988). In some instances, elder abuse may be an inevitable outcome of stressful situations combined with inadequate caregiving skills (Steinmetz, 1990; Quinn and Tomita, 1986). A growing number of states have passed laws re-

---

**WHAT IS ELDER ABUSE?**

Five commonly defined types of maltreatment, often together referred to as abuse, are:

*Physical or sexual abuse:* Malnutrition or injuries such as bruises, welts, sprains, dislocations, abrasions, or lacerations

*Psychological abuse:* Verbal assault, threat, fear, or isolation

*Exploitation:* Theft or misuse of the person or the person's money or property for another person's profit or advantage

*Medical abuse:* Withholding or improper administration of needed medications, or withholding of aids such as dentures, glasses, or hearing aids

*Neglect:* Conduct by the vulnerable adult or others resulting in the deprivation of care necessary to maintain physical and mental health.

quiring professionals to report familial abuse of older relatives.

Adult Protective Services is the state or county service system that becomes involved in instances of abuse or neglect, including self-neglect. Since mandatory reporting laws require that APS workers must accept all reports of abuse or neglect, their caseloads are often filled with the most troubled elderly with whom other agencies are unwilling or unable to work. An additional barrier that APS workers face is that few community-based alternatives exist for older people who are removed from abusive situations. Although APS workers frequently deal with older people who are no longer competent to make decisions, they need to assess the individual's level of competence and therefore the older person's right to refuse professional assistance.

The myth of family abandonment may be replaced by a new countermyth—that all families are able and willing to provide adequate care for older relatives (Cicirelli, 1990). This assumption has led to government policies that place greater responsibility on family caregivers, especially for marginally poor older persons who are excluded from many low-cost or free services. In some ways, this is a return to the attitude of pre-Depression days, when families were expected to financially support aging relatives. In fact, some lawmakers fear that families will overutilize services or neglect their care responsibilities if more support services are made available. Although men are more likely than women to utilize formal services, most families do not use them and continue to provide primary care even when assistance is available (Montgomery and Borgatta, 1989). It is thus estimated that the cost of replacing the care provided "free" by family members ould be as high as $17 billion (Paringer, 1983). In some cases, such as those involving elder abuse or inadequate financial and social supports, the family should not be expected to assume all caregiving functions; in many instances, the caregivers themselves are vulnerable, since nearly 30 percent of caregivers are over age 74, over 30 percent rate their own health as fair or poor, and 30 percent

are low income (Wilson, 1990). Unless family care efforts are strengthened by formal support services, emotional, financial and physical problems may be perpetuated across generations.

## Institutionalization: A Painful Decision for Family Members

The strain on caregivers, especially high levels of subjective burden, may cause them to seek relief through institutionalization of their older relatives (McFall and Miller, 1992). Most families first attempt to provide care on their own, without utilizing alternative community-based services, even though use of such services could perhaps prevent caregiver stress and burnout as well as nursing home admission (Collins, King, and Kokinakis, 1994; Gwyther, 1989; Hendricks and Rosenthal, 1993; Kammer, 1994; Office of Technology Assessment, 1990; Tennstedt, et al., 1993). Cultural differences in service utilization exist. African Americans, for example, are more likely to turn to informal supports and religious faith and to use cognitive strategies to reframe the situation in positive terms than are whites, who are more likely to seek help from professionals and use problem-solving methods (Leutz, et al., 1992; Wood and Parham, 1990).

Although older persons without families are more likely to be in nursing homes, 55 percent of those in institutions do have children. In most cases, children and spouses resort to institutionalization only after exhausting their own resources, but husbands tend to turn to nursing home placement earlier than do wives. In approximately 25 percent of nursing home applications, the decision to seek institutionalization has been precipitated by the family caregiver's illness or death, or by severe family strain (Tennstedt et al., 1993). For example, the characteristics of the caregiver and of the caregiving context, especially perceived burden, are better predictors of whether an Alzheimer's patient will be institutionalized than are the illness characteristics or symptoms of the care receiver (Poulshock and Diemling, 1984; Zarit, Todd, and Zarit, 1986).

Most older people and their caregivers hold negative attitudes toward nursing homes, and prefer home health care even though the quality of care in many nursing homes is good (Hatch and Franken, 1984). Placing an older relative in a nursing home is a stressful life event for the family, once referred to as the "nadir of life" for adult children (Cath, 1972; Johnson, 1990). Characterized by moral dilemmas, the placement decision may arouse feelings of grief, guilt, and fear, and renew past family conflicts. As a result of reduced burden, however, most families experience improvements in their relationship with institutionalized members and continue to visit their older relatives and assist with their care (Brown, Potter, and Foster, 1990). With the growth of the oldest-old, nursing home placement may come to be viewed as a step in a normal life cycle. To ease the transition to the post-placement phase, many nursing homes develop support and educational groups for families (Gwyther, 1985; Richards et al., 1984; Schneewind, 1990).

## Legal and Policy Questions Regarding Caregiving

The role of adult children in caring for older relatives is an increasingly important policy and practice issue, given the trends identified earlier. The issue of family responsibility has long been a topic of debate. Many states have had filial responsibility laws that require financially able children to contribute to their aging parents' support, but the laws are rarely enforced. Policies have been organized on the premise that the family has first responsibility for dependent older persons, and that the state should intervene only after the family's resources are exhausted. For example, ours is the only Western industrialized society without a caregiver allowance as part of the Social Security system. Instead, policy makers often fear that formal services would be overutilized and substitute for families, and some programs limit services when a family caregiver is available. Yet, as noted above, most families,

particularly minority families, provide care without formal assistance. When they do use services, it is in addition to their own care, not to replace it, even though such services can serve to reduce caregiver stress and burnout and prevent nursing home admission (Gwyther, 1989; Hendricks and Rosenthal, 1993; Noelker and Bass, 1994; Office of Technology Assessment, 1990; Montgomery and Borgatta, 1989; Tennstedt et al., 1993).

Since 1975, legislation has been introduced in Congress that either requires adult children to financially support their older parents or, alternatively, supports family care through tax credits and limited cash benefits, oftentimes as a cost-effective way to reduce institutionalization (Keigher and Murphy, 1992; Stone and Keigher, 1994). Recently, there has been growing recognition that the costs of caregiving are too great for either the family or the state to bear alone, and more policies and programs are being developed to complement the family's efforts. However, these policy changes are limited in their impact. For example, the Family Caregiver Support Act, which would provide an entitlement of $2400 a year for supportive services for caregivers of individuals with functional disabilities, was introduced in Congress in 1993 but not passed. After a lengthy political battle and compromise, the Family and Medical Leave Act was signed into law by President Clinton in 1993. This act offers job protection to workers requiring short-term leaves from their jobs for the care of a dependent parent or seriously ill, newborn, or adopted child. However, this legislation does not cover temporary or part-time workers or those in small firms, even though 50 percent of all employees in the private sector work for small businesses. In contrast, many Western European countries, particularly in Scandinavia, provide more public social and health services to older people, pay relatives to stay home to provide care and offer special pensions for those who have spent many years caring (Chappel, 1990).

In our country, some corporations have developed family leave policies, and over 34 states provide some type of economic supports through tax credits or direct payments, although these tax supports are underutilized by caregivers of the elderly (Biegel et al., 1988; Stone and Keigher, 1994). In addition, a growing number of localities have initiated services to support families, decreasing the older person's needs for care (e.g., adult day care programs and in-home chore services) or by increasing the family's resources (e.g., educational programs, support groups, respite care and clinical or direct service interventions). Local area agencies on aging are often the best place for families to begin to access such services. Corporations are also beginning to provide elder care information and referral and education, often through employee assistance programs (Scharlach, 1990). More services, however, are needed for those with the greatest needs: low-income and those just above the poverty line, ethnic minority, and unmarried elders, and caregivers still caring for children at home (AARP and Travelers Companies Foundation, 1988).

The growth of the multigenerational family and the consequent responsibilities of caregiving also have implications for practitioners. For example, family therapy has often been based on a theoretical foundation that applies primarily to the nuclear family and considers the life cycle only through adolescence. In order to correspond to the reality that family life is no longer limited to the nuclear two-generation family, practitioners need to take account of the older person within the total family system, the effects of long-term family interactions, and each generation's developmental concerns.

## CHILDLESS ELDERLY

Although the majority of older people have living children, approximately 20 percent are childless, and thus lack the natural support system of children and grandchildren. The adage that "children will take care of you in your old age" contains some degree of truth. A study of the interactions of childless older people found they had fewer social contacts than their counterparts with living children, yet they are not necessarily unhappy and dissatisfied (Beckman, 1985; Houser, 1984). When faced with health problems, childless elders turn first to their spouses for support, then to siblings, then nieces and nephews. Childless older individuals also have a higher probability of illness and living alone. Given these factors, it is not surprising that the unmarried childless utilize social services and nursing homes more than the married childless (Choi-Namkea, 1994).

On the other hand, some childless unmarried older people, particularly women, develop kin-like or "sisterly" nonkin relations and may be quite satisfied with their lives. Yet they do not want these relationships to be a source of care, fearing the change of voluntary mutuality into dependency (Rubenstein et al, 1991). If the number of childless and unmarried older individuals continues to grow, so too will the proportion of older people who will need the assistance of service providers in the future.

## GRANDPARENTHOOD AND GREAT-GRANDPARENTHOOD

At the turn of the century, families with grandparents were rare. Now, with the increase in life expectancy, more older people are experiencing the role of grandparenthood and, increasingly, of great-grandparenthood, although they have proportionately fewer grandchildren. Of the 80 percent of older people with children, 94 percent are grandparents and nearly 50 percent are great-grandparents. Approximately 75 percent of these grandparents see some of their grandchildren every week or two, and nearly 50 percent see a grandchild every day or so, although only about 5 percent of the households headed by older people include grandchildren (Smyer and Hofland, 1982). Geographic proximity appears to be more important than whether the grandparents get along with their own children in determining frequency of visits (Cherlin and Furstenberg, 1986).

Grandparents provide a sense of continuity for grandchildren.

In recent years, the topic of grandparenthood has emerged as a growing area of study within the family and gerontological literature (Roberto, 1990). While the early research suggested that one style of interacting with grandchildren may predominate, later studies have identified multiple roles and meanings. These meanings and functions of grandparenthood must be viewed within the social context described previously: increases in geographic mobility, divorce, reconstituted families, and employed middle-aged women who are also grandmothers.

Research findings on satisfaction derived from the grandparent role are inconsistent. Age, proximity, and parental influences all affect grandparents' extent of satisfaction from the role (Roberto, 1990). Some studies have found the role to be peripheral and not a primary source of identity, interaction or satisfaction. Instead, friendships and organizational activities appear to be related to life satisfaction more than the status of grandparenthood (Wood and Robertson, 1976). Other research has found that grandparents, especially grandmothers, derive great emotional satisfaction from frequent interaction with their grandchildren (Kivnick, 1982; Barranti, 1985) and from relatively high levels of responsibilities for helping grandchildren (Ro-

berto, 1990). In the absence of a family crisis, grandparents play a role that emphasizes emotional gratification from their grandchildren, and serve as a symbol of family continuity (Cherlin and Furstenberg, 1986). Geographic distance is not necessarily a barrier; grandparents who have close ties with their children may be important to their grandchildren even when they do not see each other often, especially when a close relationship is established early in a child's life (Kornhober and Woodward, 1981).

In a classic study by Neugarten and Weinstein (1964), elders were categorized by the meaning given to the role and by the style of grandparenting. The prime significance of grandparenthood was reported to be (1) biological renewal and/or continuity (i.e., seeing oneself extended into the future); (2) emotional self-fulfillment, especially the opportunity to be a better grandparent than parent; and (3) distance from grandchildren, with little effect on the grandparents' lives. In terms of style, older grandparents were more apt to be formal or distant, whereas younger ones emphasized mutuality, informality, and playfulness.

Regardless of age, grandparents generally offer grandchildren unconditional love that their parents, because of other responsibilities, may be less able to offer (Kornhober and Woodward, 1981). A later study identified grandparenthood as providing opportunities for older people to experience feelings of immortality, to relive their lives through grandchildren, to indulge grandchildren, and to develop an increased sense of well-being and morale (Kivnick, 1982, 1986). Grandparent-grandchild relationships change over time, with less contact and expectation of closeness as grandchildren become older (Cherlin and Fur-stenberg, 1986).

The grandparenthood relationship appears to differ by gender, with grandfathers most closely linked to sons of sons, and grandmothers to daughters of daughters. Grandmothers have more influence than grandfathers on how their grandchildren relate to family and friends. However, it is unclear whether fathers who are more directly involved in parenting than only as providers will become more invested in the roles of grandfather and great-grandfather in the future.

Even less is known about how the grandparenthood role and its meaning vary by ethnic minority status. Some studies suggest greater interactions through an extended kin network and more grandparent responsibility for child-rearing among ethnic minorities. When the child's mother is a single parent, the grandmother may have responsibilities essential to the child's care, especially in the black urban community (Mutran and Skinner, 1981). Grandparent involvement in childrearing may be a consequence of teen pregnancy coupled with limited financial resources. It should be noted that these situations reflect differential opportunities of socioeconomic class, not ethnic minority status per se. In a growing number of instances, as illustrated by Mr. and Mrs. Smith, grandparents are solely responsible for the care of grandchildren, with their parents unable to provide care because of poverty, drugs, or other problems (Brookdale, 1992).

Approximately 3 million children now live with grandparents, and in a third of these cases,

neither parent is present. In fact, the incidence of grandparents as the sole caregivers of grandchildren has doubled in the last decade and has been found to be associated with the mother's ability to pursue her education or employment (Unger and Cooley, 1992). This cross-generation parenting may also benefit the child; for example, studies of low birth weight infants have found that coresidence with the infant's grandmother was associated with improved cognitive and health outcomes (Pope, Whiteside, Brooks, Kelleher, Rickert, Bradley, and Casey, 1993). Although it occurs in all racial minority groups, it is especially pronounced in the African American community, where 13 percent of children are cared for by grandparents, compared to 3 percent of Hispanic and 2 percent of Caucasian children (Minkler and Roe, 1993). Many older people who had looked forward to retirement and the "empty nest," and who must often cope with their own health and financial problems, now may instead be faced with the problems of sleepless nights, childhood illness, and locating child care. Recognizing the need of grandparents for support and information, national organizations

---

### CASE VIGNETTE: GRANDPARENTHOOD

Mr. and Mrs. Smith are both 69 years old. After successful careers as teachers, they retired seven years ago with anticipation of a retirement of travel and continued learning through ElderHostel.

They have a daughter, 36, who lives about 50 miles away. After leaving home at 17, she lived a life of traveling from place to place and never settling down. She has one daughter who is now 10. Her husband left her when the baby was six months old and has not been heard from since. Four years ago, the daughter was taken from the custody of her mother by the courts because of severe problems with addiction and unwillingness to get treatment. It was felt that she could not care for the daughter's needs.

Mr. and Mrs. Smith could not bear the thought of their granddaughter being raised by strangers in

the foster care system, so they decided to bring her to live with them. Now their days have been filled with PTA meetings, Scouts, and helping with homework. Their daughter has only contacted them twice in the past four years and the Smiths have begun proceedings to legally adopt their grandchild.

It has been a very difficult adjustment for the Smiths. Many of their friends from before have dropped away, as they have more freedom to "take off and do things." They also struggle with much guilt about their daughter and her situation. But they feel they would do it again if needed. A support group for grandparents raising grandchildren meets in their city and they attend on a regular basis. They love their granddaughter and enjoy her company, so they also feel great rewards.

have formed and developed newsletters, including ROCKING (Raising Our Children's Kids: An Intergenerational Network of Grandparenting, Inc.) and the National Coalition of Grandparents (NCOG).

Rather than focusing on the role of grandparenthood as an individual attribute, recent research suggests that a systems perspective better accounts for the complexity of the grandparent-grandchild relationship. This perspective takes account of the relationships that exist between persons in a common kinship system, and recognizes that although nuclear families are becoming smaller, more members of more generations are alive at one time who share a greater part of each others' life spans. The grandparent-grandchild bond is initially mediated by parents, but this bond becomes more direct as time passes, and can be substantially altered by events such as divorce. The potential for direct voluntary interaction between young adult children and their grandparents contributes not only to the individuals involved, but also to the total kinship system. As noted in Chapter 1, direct involvement with grandparents also prevents the development of ageist stereotypes.

More recently, the role of great-grandparent has emerged with increasing frequency among the older population. There appear to be two predominant styles of performing this role. The most common, which tends to characterize generations separated by physical distance, is remote, involving only occasional and somewhat ritualistic contact on special occasions such as holidays and birthdays. Despite the remote nature of contacts, however, great-grandparents derive considerable emotional satisfaction and a sense of personal and familial renewal from seeing a fourth generation as representing family immortality. Living long enough to be a great-grandparent is viewed as a positive sign of successful aging or longevity (Roberto, 1990; Wentowski, 1985; Doka and Mentz, 1988). The other common great-grandparenting style occurs when great-grandparents are geographically close (within 25 miles) to the fourth generation, and thus have opportunities

for emotional closeness to great-grandchildren as well. Even great-grandparents who are in their seventies and eighties may serve as babysitters, go shopping, and take trips with their great-grandchildren, activities which provide diversions in their lives and can lead to renewed zeal (Roberto, 1990). Such positive interactions will undoubtedly be more common in the future, when great-grandparenthood is the norm and the oldest-old generations are healthier than current cohorts. Consistent with the reciprocity characteristic of most intergenerational relationships, growing numbers of grandchildren care for great-grandparents (Roberto, 1990).

## The Effects of Divorce

The growing divorce rate, discussed earlier, is a social trend that is affecting the meaning of grandparenthood. At least 50 percent of all persons marrying today will face divorce, and slightly more than 40 percent of all current marriages are second and third marriages (Furstenberg, 1990; U.S. Bureau of the Census, 1992). The consequences of these for younger generations—over 15 million children living in one-parent families and 10 million in blended families, with less than 50 percent of all young people in nuclear families—clearly influence the nature of the grandchild-grandparent relationship (U.S. Bureau of the Census, 1991). Since the tie between young grandchildren and their grandparents is mediated by the grandchildren's parents, divorce disrupts these links, changes the balance of resources within the extended family, and requires a renegotiation of existing bonds. Who is awarded custody primarily affects the frequency of interaction with grandchildren; the grandparents whose child is awarded custody have more contact (Matthews and Sprey, 1984). Recent media coverage of grandparents' visiting rights and proposed state legislation to ensure such rights highlight the issues faced by grandparents when the in-law is awarded custody and controls the amount of child-grandparent interactions. Groups such as Grandparents Anonymous, the Foundation for Grandparenting, and Grandparents'-Children's Rights are pressing for grandparents' visitation rights legislation in several states.

During the last decade, most states have passed laws granting grandparents the right to petition a court to legally obtain visitation privileges with their grandchildren. In 1983, a uniform nationwide statute was passed that ensures grandparents visitation rights even if parents object. These laws raise complex issues for the involved generations, however. For example, because of court-enforced visitation against the parents' wishes, a young child may unwittingly become involved in intergenerational conflict. The benefits for grandchildren from visiting non-custodial grandparents over the objections of a parent are as yet unclear. What is apparent is that factors outside the family, such as the courts, may play a larger role in how families resolve conflicts and thus in a child's development (Thompson et al., 1989).

Conversely, complex issues are also emerging concerning the liability of grandparents and step-grandparents for support of grandchildren in the absence of responsible parents. When divorce in the parent generation occurs, the norm of noninterference by grandparents generally disappears. Instead, grandparents, especially those on the side of the custodial parent, provide substantial assistance to their grandchildren, function as surrogate parents, and mediate tensions. Grandparents have been referred to as "the family watchdogs," who are in the background during tranquil times, but are ready to step in during an emergency (Roberto, 1990; Troll, 1983).

Despite the fact that blended families constitute about 50 percent of all households with children (National Academy on Aging, 1994), little is known about stepgrandparenting relationships. From a grandparent's perspective, the growing phenomenon of divorce-remarriage means sharing grandchildren with their newly acquired relatives under conditions in which grandchildren will be scarcer because of the declining birth rates. Grandchildren, in turn,

may find themselves with four or more sets of grandparents. Kinship systems are further complicated by the fact that with the increased divorce rate, members of a grandparental couple may no longer be married to one another when they become grandparents. It is difficult to predict the magnitude of the effects—positive and negative—of these trends on intergenerational relations because of the limited research in this area.

In summary, the grandparent role is idiosyncratic and subject to negotiation. The role of valued grandparent is earned, and for some, it can bring considerable satisfaction. Furthermore, grandparents can play a major role within the extended family system during a family crisis such as divorce.

## FRIENDS AND NEIGHBORS AS SOCIAL SUPPORTS

Although the majority of older people live with others, 30 percent of those over 65 and 45 percent of those 85 and over live alone. In fact, the rate of older persons living alone increased by one and a half times the growth rate for older people in general from 1970 to 1987 (U.S. Bureau of the Census, 1988). Those living alone are most likely to be women, ethnic minorities, the oldest-old, and people of low socioeconomic status. They tend to rely on community services more than on support from friends and neighbors in their efforts to continue living independently in the community. They also report less satisfaction with the quality of their lives than married people (Kasper, 1988).

As noted in Chapter 13, among those living alone, the most vulnerable are the homeless. While 27 percent of the homeless are estimated to be age 60 and over (including those who live in missions on skid row), their absolute number appears to be increasing. Characterized by higher rates of physical impairment, economic deprivation, and alcohol misuse than the older population in general, homeless elders tend not to be tied into senior programs and services (Cohen et al., 1988).

These individuals living alone and the estimated 5 percent of the older population who are without family ties are dependent upon friends, neighbors, and acquaintances to create family-like relationships. Men, the widowed, and the childless are the most vulnerable to being without support in times of need, often experiencing exacerbated health problems and institutionalization as a result. A small percent of older persons living alone do not even have phone conversations with friends and neighbors (Kasper, 1988).

However, most elders who live alone, such as Mr. Valdres in our introductory vignette, have some friends and acquaintances to whom they can turn in emergencies. Such non-kin informal helpers are especially common among the oldest-old in ethnic minority communities (Taylor and Chatters, 1991).

In fact, older persons who have kin may turn more to friends and neighbors for immediate assistance than to family, in part because friendship involves more voluntary and reciprocal exchanges between equals, consistent with social exchange theory described in Chapter 4 (Hatch and Bulcroft, 1992). Whether family, friends, or neighbors become involved appears to vary with the type of task to be performed as well as the helper's characteristics, such as proximity, extent of long-term commitment, and degree of interaction. Friends and neighbors are well-suited to provide emotional support and to perform predictable tasks, such as transportation, while families are best equipped for personal care (Antonucci, 1990). Among ethnic minorities, friends often link older persons to needed community services (Taylor, 1988). In fact, African American peers have been found more likely than whites to provide and receive both instrumental and emotional support (Silverstein and Waite, 1993). Friends also often link older people, particularly ethnic minority elders, to needed community services (Taylor, 1988). For the most part, however, friends and neighbors play smaller roles in the long-term helping network; although

they are important resources when children are absent or unavailable, their efforts usually do not approach those of family members in duration or intensity and do not compensate for the loss of spouse or children (Kivett, 1985; Spivak, Haskin, and Capitman, 1984; Stoller and Stoller, 1983).

Nevertheless, friends and neighbors can contribute to morale. For example, older people who are part of well-defined friendship groups tend to have more positive self-concepts and higher morale than those not part of such groups (Blau, 1981). There are three explanations for these findings: (1) people have more in common with age peers, (2) friendship is more rewarding because it is not obligatory, and (3) friendship involves older people in the larger society more than family relationships do (Adams, 1986).

Friends are often important sources of intimacy, while relatives other than marital partners usually are not (Wright, 1994). This is especially the case after major role transitions such as widowhood or retirement; for example, an older widow generally prefers help from confidants because relatives may reinforce her loss of identity as "wife." Peer interaction can be an effective alternative to the marital, occupational, or grandparent role (Blau, 1981; Wood and Robertson, 1978; Rosow, 1967). The role of friend can be maintained long after the role of worker, organization member, or spouse is lost. The extent of reciprocity and quality of interaction, not the quantity, appear to be the critical factors in the maintenance of friendship networks. For instance, one intimate friendship with a confidant has been found to be as effective as several less intimate ones in preventing the demoralization often produced by widowhood and retirement (Lowenthal and Haven, 1968).

Older people who refuse to leave their own homes and communities in order to live with or near their adult children may recognize that friends are important sources of companionship, and that replacing lost friends can be difficult in old age. Although mortality in the short run reduces the number of friends, most older people are steadily making new friends from acquaintances and neighbors, and close relationships generally get closer with age (Adams, 1989; Bleiszner, 1989).

Types of social interaction vary by gender. Women in general, such as Mrs. Howard in the introductory vignette, have more intimate, diverse, and intensive friendships than men, who tend to have more acquaintances and who place a higher value on career-oriented activities (Reisman, 1988; Wright, 1994). For many men, their wives are their only confidants, a circumstance that may make widowhood devastating for them (Chappell, 1990). In contrast, women tend to satisfy their needs for intimacy throughout their lives by establishing close friendships with other women and therefore are less dependent emotionally on the marital relationship. When faced with widowhood, divorce, or separation, they can turn to these friends. Accordingly, widowed older women tend to receive more help and emotional support from friends than married older women. The resilience of some older women, in fact, may be rooted in their ability to form close reciprocal friendships (Litwak, 1985; Riley and Riley, 1986). On the other hand, some recent research suggests that as women respond to others for support, their caregiving networks may inadvertently increase their exposure to

stress, foster conflicts, and produce unhappiness (Antonucci, 1990).

Both men and women tend to select friends from among people they consider their social peers—those who are similar in age, sex, marital status, sexual orientation, and socioeconomic class. Most choose age peers as their friends, even though common sense would suggest that age-integrated friendship networks can reduce their vulnerability to losses as they age. A person's adult children are not likely to be chosen as confidants, primarily because of their being from different cohorts who are at different places in the life cycle and more likely to produce an inequality of exchange. Age homogeneity plays a strong role in facilitating friendships in later life, in part because of shared life transitions, reduced cross-generational ties with children and work associates, and possible parity of exchange. Age as a basis for friendship may be most pronounced at those stages where the individual's ties to other networks are loosened (Hess, 1972).

Type of living environment clearly affects the quality and quantity of informal exchanges, as will be discussed in Chapter 13. Although the findings were mixed, early studies found that age-segregated environments tend to lead to more peer group interaction, helping networks, and satisfaction with one's environment (Blau, 1981; Hochschild, 1973; Jonas and Wellin, 1980; Longino and Lipman, 1981). Age segregation, however, may not always be by choice but may result when younger people leave an area. In such cases, older people's length of residence rather than the homogeneity of the living situation may be more strongly related to extensive social ties.

## Interventions to Strengthen or Build Social Supports

Because of the importance of peer group ties for well-being, there have been an increasing number of professionally planned interventions to strengthen existing community ties, or to create new ties if networks are nonexistent. Consistent

Postal carriers can act as gatekeepers, regularly checking on an older person's safety.

with the person-environment model, such interventions are ways to alter the environment to be supportive of the older person. They can be categorized as personal network building, volunteer linking, mutual help networks, and neighborhood and community development. Such interventions aim to build upon the strengths and resources of local communities, including communities of color (Meyers and Souflee, 1990–91).

Personal network building aims to strengthen existing ties, often through "natural helpers"—people turned to because of their concern, interest, and innate understanding. Such natural helpers can provide emotional support, assist with problem solving, offer concrete services, and act as advocates. Neighbors often perform natural helping roles, and may strengthen these activities through organized block programs and block watches. Even people in service positions, often referred to as "gatekeepers," can fulfill natural helping functions, because of the visibility of their position and the regularity of their interactions with the elderly. For example, postal alert systems, whereby postal carriers observe whether an older person is taking in the mail each day, build upon routine everyday interactions. In some communities, fuel oil dealers and meter readers, who have occasional access to an older person's home, have been trained to watch for signs that indicate needs for services and to refer the older person to the local information and assistance program. Beauticians, pharmacists, ministers, bus drivers, local merchants and managers of housing for older people, as in the case of Mr. Valdres in the introductory vignette, are frequently in situations to provide companionship, advice, and referrals. In high-crime areas, local businesses, bars, and restaurants may have a "safehouse" decal in their windows, indicating where residents can go in times of danger or medical emergencies.

Churches may also serve to strengthen and build personal networks, in some cases providing a surrogate family for older people. National initiatives affiliated with churches and synagogues, such as the Shepherds Centers, emphasize empowering older people through caring for each other. Church members can provide help with housework, home repair, transportation, and meal preparation, as well as psychological assurance. At the same time, older members may take on many leadership and teaching roles within the church, thereby enhancing their sense of belonging and self-worth, as in the example of Mr. Mansfield on p. 281. In many private and

---

## GATEKEEPERS

Mrs. Jones, 80, shuffled down the sidewalk with the aid of a cane. A boy delivering newspapers from his bicycle zoomed past, nearly hitting her. Mrs. Jones wasn't fazed. She moved on, staring straight ahead, as if she hadn't seen the youngster. Other incidents could have alerted a trained observer that Mrs. Jones was having serious trouble. She had difficulty signing her name on the back of her Social Security check when she cashed it at the bank. She couldn't count out change to pay for a cup of coffee at a local diner. When Mrs. Jones picked up her prescription at the local drug store, she had difficulty conversing with the pharmacist she had known for many years.

The Gatekeeper Project tries to address the needs of people like Mrs. Jones. The program identifies and trains Gatekeepers, people who are in contact with the public during the course of their regular work activities. In Mrs. Jones' case, they could be the bank teller, the newspaper carrier, or the pharmacist. They are called Gatekeepers because they "open the gates" between isolated older people and sources of assistance, oftentimes by turning to Senior Information and Assistance lines.

*Source:* Washington State Aging and Adult Services Administration and Puget Sound Power and Light Company, 1986.

public programs, volunteers are commonly used to develop new or expand existing networks for older persons. For example, volunteers provide chore services in older people's homes, peer counseling and senior center outreach activities, and serve as Friendly Visitors (Morrow-Howell and Ozawa, 1987).

Another approach aims to create or promote the supportive capacities of mutual help networks, especially through joint problem solving and reciprocal exchange of resources. Mutual help efforts may occur spontaneously, as neighbors watch out for each other, or may be facilitated by professionals. They may also be formed on the basis of neighborhood ties or around shared problems, such as widow-to-widow programs, stroke clubs, and support groups for caregivers of family members with Alzheimer's or other types of chronic impairments (Greene and Monahan, 1989; Gwyther and Brooks, 1984; Silverman, Brahce, and Zielinski, 1981; Mellon, 1982). Mutual help groups can provide participants with new skills and roles, expand their social networks, and increase their problem-solving capacities. Both volunteer and mutual help efforts are frequently found in communities of color; for example, projects in Hispanic neighborhoods in California train "natural" helpers to broker services and to be gatekeepers to facilitate the flow of information into and out of the neighborhood (Meyers and Souflee, 1990–91). The Mutual Aid Self-Help Program (MASH) through Centro del Barrio in Texas trains volunteers to assist with homecare, shopping, gardening, phone reassurance, and transportation.

Another approach is neighborhood and community development, which attempts to strengthen a community's self-help and problem-solving capabilities, and may involve social action through lobbying and legislative activities. An example is the Neighborhood Family in Miami, Florida, where older people in a low-income neighborhood worked together as a "family" to solve personal and community problems. This model combined social action with the provision of medical services (Ross, 1983). The Tenderloin Project, in a low-income area of single-room occupants in San Francisco, is another example of neighborhood development. Nearby residents acted on the immediate problem of crime and victimization of older people and then moved on to deal with issues such as nutrition and health promotion. In the process, social networks were strengthened and weekly support groups were formed (Minkler, 1986). Project LINC (Living Independently through Neighborhood Cooperation) utilized a combination of neighborhood-based intergenerational helping networks connected to the formal service system as a method to provide personal care services to frail elders (Pynoos, Hade-Kaplan, and Fleisher, 1984).

## RELATIONSHIPS WITH PETS

Pets are another source of affection and touch, and may offer the most significant relationship in some older people's lives. Many elderly talk to their pets as if they were people, confide in them, and believe that they are sensitive to their moods and feelings. Having a pet to feed, groom or walk can provide structure and a sense of purpose to the day of an otherwise isolated older person (Soares, 1985), and caring for it can provide an anchor for those whose lives have undergone major change or loss. A pet may even serve as a family substitute (Akiyama, Holtzman, and Britz, 1986; Brickel, 1985). Pet owners tend to score higher on measures of happiness, self-confidence, responsiveness, and dependability than non-pet owners (Ory and Goldberg, 1983; Kidd and Feldman, 1981). These measures of well-being may be partially due to the fact that an older person's caring for pets, rather than his or her only being taken care of by others, can give meaning, purpose, and a sense of control over his or her environment. On the other hand, the loss of a pet can result in grief as intense as that precipitated by the death of a family member or friend (Carmack, 1985).

Pets are another source of affection for the elderly.

The recognition that animals fulfill many human needs has led to an increase in pet-facilitated programs for older people living in senior housing and long-term care facilities, as well as in loan-a-pet programs for those individuals in their own homes. In fact, animals, even tropical fish and wild birds attracted to feeders, have been found to evoke responses such as care and stroking from persons who were previously non-responsive (Robb, Boyd, and Pritash, 1980; Banzinger and Roush, 1983; Brickel, 1985). Older people participating in pet therapy programs have been found to become less depressed and more communicative, and to experience higher rates of survival than do controls who do not participate in such programs (National Institutes of Health, 1988). Although a pet should never be viewed as a substitute for human relationships, gerontologists are increasingly aware that pet ownership can enhance well-being and enrich the quality of older people's lives, particularly in institutional environments.

## SUMMARY AND IMPLICATIONS

The importance of informal social relationships for older people's physical and mental well-being has been widely documented. Contrary to stereotypes, very few older people are socially isolated. The majority have family members with whom they are in contact, although they are unlikely to live with them. Their families serve as a critical source of support, especially when older members become impaired by chronic illness or accidents. The marital relationship is most important, with more than half of all persons age 65 and over married and living with a partner in independent households. Most older couples are satisfied with their marriages, which influences their life satisfaction generally. The older couple, freed from childrearing demands, has more opportunities to pursue new roles and types of relationships. The sexual relationship of older couples is limited less by physiological changes than by psychosocial factors, such as cultural definitions of unattractiveness and fear of failure. In general, most older people are able to enjoy sexual relationships, particularly when they are defined in terms of intimacy.

Less is known about sibling, grandparent, and other types of family interactions in old age, although the importance of their support is likely to increase in the future. Also, comparatively little research has been conducted on lesbian and gay relationships in old age and on never-married older persons who may rely primarily on friendship networks to cope. Siblings can be crucial in providing emotional support, physical care, and a home. Interaction with secondary kin tends to depend on geographic proximity and whether or not more immediate family members are available.

Contrary to the myth that adult children are alienated from their parents, the majority of older persons are in frequent contact with their children, either face-to-face or by phone or letter. Filial relationships are characterized by patterns of reciprocal aid throughout the life course, until the older generation becomes physically or mentally disabled. At that point, adult children—generally women—are faced with providing financial, emotional, and physical assistance to older relatives, oftentimes with little support from others for their caregiving responsibilities. In ethnic minority and lower income families, older relatives are most likely to receive daily care from younger relatives, and to be involved themselves in caring for grandchildren.

Most families, regardless of socioeconomic class or ethnic minority status, attempt to provide care for their dependent members for as long as possible, and seek institutionalization only when they have exhausted other resources. Such caregiving responsibilities are affected by a number of social trends, most notable among them the increasing percentage of middle-aged women—traditionally the caregivers—who are more likely to be employed, and the number of reconstituted families resulting from divorce and remarriage. The needs of caregivers are clearly a growing concern for health practitioners and policy makers.

With the growth of three- and four-generation families, more older persons are experiencing the status of grandparenthood. Although most grandparents are in relatively frequent contact with their grandchildren, the grandparent role does not appear salient in terms of life satisfaction or identity. The demands of grandparenthood are changing, however, as a result of divorce and remarriages.

For many older persons, friends and neighbors can be even more critical than family members to maintaining morale and a quality of life. Generally, women have more interaction with friends than do men. Age-segregated settings appear to facilitate friendships rather than isolate older persons. In recognition of the importance of peer group interaction to physical and mental well-being, an increasing number of neighborhood and community-based interventions have

been developed to strengthen friendship and neighborhood ties. In sum, the majority of older persons continue to play a variety of social roles—partner, parent, grandparent, friend, and neighbor—and to derive feelings of satisfaction and self-worth from these interactions.

## REFERENCES

Abel, E. Adult daughters and care for the elderly. *Feminist Studies*, 1986, *12*, 479–497.

Adams, B. N. *Kinship in an urban setting*. Chicago: Markham, 1968.

Adams, R. Conceptual and methodological issues in studying friendships of older adults. In *Older adult friendships*, R. Adams and R. Bleiszner (Eds.), 17–41. Newbury Park, Calif.: Sage, 1989.

Adams, R. G. A look at friendship and aging. *Generations*, 1986, *10*, 40–43.

Adelman, M. Stigma, gay lifestyles and adjustment to aging: A study of later-life gay men and lesbians. In *Journal of Homosexuality*, 1990, *20*, 7–32.

Akiyama, H., Holtzman, J. M., and Britz, W. E. Pet ownership and health status during bereavements. *Omega*, 1986, *17*, 187–193.

Aldous, J. New views on the family life of the elderly and new elderly. *Journal of Marriage and the Family*, 1987, *49*, 227–234.

American Association of Retired Persons (AARP) and the Travelers Companies Foundation. *National Survey of Caregivers*. October 1988.

Anastas, J., Gibeau, J., and Larson, P. Working families and eldercare: A national perspective in an aging America. *Social Work*, 1990, *35*, 405–411.

Antonucci, T. C. Social supports and social relationships. In R. H. Binstock and L. K. George (Eds.), *The handbook of aging and the social sciences* (3d Ed.). New York: Academic Press, 1990, 205–227.

Asher, C. C. The impact of social support networks on adult health. *Medical Care*, 1984, *22*, 349–359.

Atchley, R. *Social forces and aging* (4th ed.). Belmont, Calif.: Wadsworth, 1985.

Avioli, P. S. The social support functions of siblings in later life. *American Behavioral Scientist*, 1989, *22*, 45–57.

Bachrach, C. A. Childlessness and social isolation among the elderly. *Journal of Marriage and the Family*, 1980, *42*, 627–637.

Bankoff, E. A. Aged parents and their widowed daughters: A support relationship. *Journal of Gerontology*, 1983, *38*, 226–230.

Banzinger, G., and Roush, J. Nursing homes to the birds: A control relevant intervention with bird feeders. *The Gerontologist*, 1983, *23*, 527–536.

Baresi, C., and Hunt, K. The unmarried elderly: Age, sex and ethnicity. In *Family relationships in later life* (2nd Ed.), T. Brubaker, (Ed.), 169–192. Newbury Park, Calif.: Sage, 1990.

Barranti, C. C. R. The grandparent/grandchild relationship: Family resource in an era of voluntary bonds. *Family Relations*, 1985, *34*, 343–352.

Barusch, A., and Spaid, W. Gender differences in caregiving: Why do wives report greater burden? *The Gerontologist*, 1989, *29*, 667–676.

Beckman, L. *Childlessness, family composition and well-being of older men*. Presented at the Annual Convention of the American Psychological Association, Los Angeles, Calif., August 1985.

Bengtson, V. C., Rosenthal, C. J., and Burton, C. Families and aging: diversity and heterogeneity. In R. H. Binstock and L. K. George, (Eds.), *Handbook of aging and the social sciences* (3d ed.). New York: Academic Press, 1990, 263–287.

Berger, R. M. *Gay and gray: The older homosexual man*. Urbana: Ill.: University of Illinois Press, 1982.

Berger, R. M. Realities of gay and lesbian aging. *Social Work*, 1984, *29*, 57–62.

Berkman, L. F., and Syme, S. L. Social networks, host resistance, and morality: A nine-year follow-up study of Alameda County residents. *American Journal of Epidemiology*, 1979, *109*, 186–204.

Biegel, D., Sales, E., and Schulz, R. *Family caregiving in chronic illness*. Newbury Park, Calif.: Sage, 1991.

Biegel, D., Schulz, R., Shore, B., and Morycz, R. *Economic supports for family caregivers of the elderly: Tax policies and direct payment programs*. Cleveland, OH.: Case Western Reserve University, School of Applied Social Sciences, 1988.

Blau, Z. S. *Aging in a changing society* (2d ed.). New York: Franklin Watts, 1981.

Bleiszner, R. Developmental processes of friendship. In R. Adams and R. Bleiszner (Eds.), *Older adult friendships*. Newbury Park, Calif.: Sage, 1989, 108–126.

Blumstein, P., and Schwartz, P. *American couples*. New York: William Morrison, 1983.

Braithwaite, V. Caregiver burden: Making the concept scientifically useful and policy relevant. *Research on Aging*, 1992, *14*, 3–27.

Brecher, E. *Love, sex and aging*. Boston: Little Brown, 1984.

Brickel, C. M. Initiation and maintenance of the human-animal bond: Familial roles from a learning perspective. *Menopause and the Family Review*, 1958, *8*, 31–48.

Brody, E. Women in the middle and family help to older people. *The Gerontologist*, 1981, *25*, 471–480.

Brody, E. Parent care as a normative family stress. *The Gerontologist*, 1985, *25*, 19–30.

Brody, E., and Schoonover, C. Patterns of parent-care when adult children work and when they do not. *The Gerontologist*, 1986, *26*, 372–381.

Brody, S. J., Poulshock, S. W., and Masciocchi, C. F. The family caring unit: A major consideration in the long-term support system. *The Gerontologist*, 1978, *18*, 556–561.

Brookdale. Grandparent caregiver information project, focus on research. *Newsletter*, 1992(Oct.), 1,3, 5–6. University of California Berkeley.

Browne, L. J., Potter, J. F., and Foster, B. C. Caregiver burden should be evaluated during geriatric assessment. *Journal of the American Geriatrics Society*, 1990, *38*(4), 455–460.

Brubaker, T. H. Families in later life: A burgeoning research area. *Journal of Marriage and the Family*, 1990, *52*, 959–981.

Brubaker, T. Family relationships in later life (2nd Ed.). In T. Brubaker (Ed.), *An overview of family relationships in later life*. Newbury Park, Calif.: Sage, 1990, 13–26.

Brubaker, T. H. *Later life families*. Beverly Hills,Calif.: Sage, 1985.

Bulcroft, K. A., and Bulcroft, R. A. The timing of divorce: Effects on parent-child relationships in later life. *Research on Aging*, 1991, *13*, 226–243.

Bureau of National Affairs. Employers and eldercare: A new benefit coming of age. In *The National Report on Work and Family*, Washington, D.C.: Bureau of National Affairs, 1988.

Cantor, M. Family caregiving: Social care. In M. Cantor (Ed.), *Family caregiving: Agenda for the future*. San Francisco, Calif.: American Society on Aging, 1994, 1–9.

Cantor, M. Family and community: Changing roles in an aging society. *The Gerontologist*, 1991, *31*, 337–340.

Carmack, B. J. The effects of family members and functioning after the death of a pet. In M. B. Sussman (Ed.), *Pets and the family*. New York: Haworth Press, 1985.

Cassell, J. Psychological processes and "stress": Theoretical formulations. *International Journal of Health Services*, 1974, *41*, 471–482.

Cath, S. H. The institutionalization of a parent: A nadir of life. *Journal of Geriatric Psychiatry*, 1972, *5*, 25–46.

Chappell, N. C. Aging and social care. In R. B. Binstock and L. K. George, (Eds.), *The handbook of aging and the social sciences* (3d ed.). New York: Academic Press, 1990.

Cherlin, A., and Furstenberg, F. *The new American grandparent*. New York: Basic Books, 1986.

Cherlin, A. J. *Marriage, divorce, remarriage: Changing patterns in the postwar United States*. Cambridge, Mass.: Harvard University Press, 1981.

Cherlin, A. J., and Furstenberg, F. Grandparents and family crisis. *Generation*, 1986, *10*, 26–28.

Choi, N. K. Racial differences in the determinants of living arrangements of widowed and divorced elderly women. *The Gerontologist*, 1991, *31*, 496–504.

Choi-Namkea, G. Patterns and determinants of social service utilization: Comparison of the childless elderly and elderly parents living with or apart from their children. *The Gerontologist*, 1994, *34* (3), 353.

Cicirelli, V. Family support in relation to health problems of the elderly. In T. Brubaker (Ed.), *Family relationships in later life* (2nd Ed.). Newbury Park, Calif.: Sage, 1990, 212–228.

Cicirelli, V. G. *Helping elderly parents: The role of adult children*. Boston: Auburn House, 1981.

Cicirelli, V. G. Siblings as caregivers in middle and old age. In J. Dwyer and R. Coward, (Eds.), *Gender, families and elder care*. Newbury Park, Calif.: Sage, 1991.

Cicirelli, V., Coward, R., and Dwyer, J. Siblings as caregivers for impaired elders. *Research on Aging*, 1992, *14*(3), 331.

Cleveland, W. P., and Gianturco, P. T. Remarriage probability after widowhood: A retrospective method. *Journal of Gerontology*, 1976, *31*, 99–103.

Cobb, S. Social support as a moderator of life stress. *Psychosomatic Medicine*, 1976, *38*, 300–314.

Cohen, C., Teresi, J., and Holmes, D. The physical well-being of old homeless men. *Journals of Gerontology*, 1988, *43*, S121–128.

Cohen, C., Teresi, J., Holmes, D., and Roth, E. Survival strategies of older homeless men. *The Gerontologist*, 1988, *28*, 58–64.

Cohen, S., and Syme, S. L. (Eds.), *Social support and health*. Orlando, Fla.: Academic Press, 1985.

Collins, C., King, S., and Kokinakis, C. Community service issues before nursing home placement of persons with dementia. *Western Journal of Nursing Research*, 1994, *16*(2), 40–52.

Comptroller General of the United States. *Report to Congress: The well-being of older people in Cleveland, Ohio*. Washington, D.C.: United States General Accounting Office, 1977.

Condie, S. J. Older married couples. In S. J. Bahr and E. T. Peterson, (Eds.), *Aging and the family*. Lexington, Mass.: Lexington Books, 1989.

Coward, R. T., and Dwyer, J. W. The association of gender, sibling network composition, and patterns of parent care of adult children, *Research on Aging*, 1990, *14*, 331–350.

Crimmins, E. M., and Ingegneri, D. G. Interaction and living arrangements of older parents and their children: Past trends, present determinants, future implications. *Research on Aging*, 1990, *2*, 3–35.

Crossman, L., London, C., and Barry, C. Older women caring for disabled spouses: A model for supportive services. *The Gerontologist*, 1981, *21*, 464–470.

Cruikshank, M. Lavender and gray: A brief survey of lesbian and gay aging studies. *Journal of Homosexuality*, 1990, *20*, 77–87.

Cumming, E., and Schneider, D. Sibling solidarity: A property of American kinship. *American Anthropologist*, 1961, *63*, 498–507.

Dawson, K. Serving the older gay community. *SEICUV Report*, 1982, 5–6.

Deevey, S. Older lesbian women: An invisible minority. *Journal of Gerontological Nursing*, 1990, *16*, 35–39.

Diamond, L. M. *Financial support for family care: A review of current policies and programs*. Working paper No. 23. Waltham, Mass.: Brandeis University, Policy Center on Aging, 1985.

Dobson, C. Sex-role and marital expectations. In T. H. Brubaker (Ed.), *Family relationships in later life*. Beverly Hills, Calif.: Sage, 1983.

Doka, K. J., and Mentz, M. E. The meaning and significance of great-grandparenthood. *The Gerontologist*, 1988, *28*, 192–197.

Doty, P. Family care of the elderly: The role of public policy. *Milbank Quarterly*, 1986, *64*, 34–75.

Dowd, J. *Stratification among the aged*. Monterey, Calif.: Brooks/Cole, 1980.

Dowd, J., and Bengtson, V. C. Aging in minority populations: An examination of the double-jeopardy hypothesis. *Journal of Gerontology*, 1978, *33*, 427–436.

Dwyer, J. W., and Coward, R. T. Gender, family and long-term care of the elderly. In J. W. Dwyer and R. T. Coward, *Gender, families and elder care*. Newbury Park, Calif.: Sage, 1992, 3–17.

Eckles, E. T. Negative aspects of family relationships for older women. Paper presented at the Joint Annual Meetings of the Gerontological Society of America and the Canadian Association on Gerontology, Toronto, Canada, 1986.

Ehrlich, P. *The mutual help model: Handbook for developing a neighborhood group program*. Washington, D.C.: Administration on Aging, 1979.

Essex, M. J., and Nam, S. Mental status and loneliness among older women: The differential impact of close family ties and friends. *Journal of Marriage and the Family*, 1987, *49*, 93–106.

Estes, C., Swan, J. and Associates. *The Long Term Care Crisis: Elders Trapped in the No-Care Zone*. Newbury Park, Calif.: Sage, 1993.

Fengler, A., and Goodrich, N. Wives of elderly disabled men: The hidden patients. *The Gerontologist*, 1979, *19*, 175–183.

Finkelhor, D., and Pillemer, K. The prevalence of elder abuse: A random sample survey. *The Gerontologist*, 1988, *28*, 51–57.

Finley, N. J. Theories of family labor as applied to gender differences in caregiving for elderly parents. *Journal of Marriage and the Family*, 1989, *51*, 79.

Finley, N., Roberts, D., and Banahan, B. Motivators and inhibitors of attitudes of filial obligation toward aging parents. *The Gerontologist*, 1988, *28*, 73–83.

Foster, S. E., and Brizius, J. A. Caring too much? American women and the nation's caregiving crisis. In J. Allen and A. Pifer (Eds.), *Women on the front lines: Meeting the challenge of an aging America*. Washington, D.C.: The Urban Institute Press, 1993, 47–73.

Friend, R. A. GAYing: Adjustment and the older gay male. *Alternative Lifestyles*, 1980, *3*, 231–248.

Friend, R. A. Older lesbian and gay people: A theory of successful aging. *Journal of Homosexuality*, 1991, *20*, 99–118.

Furstenberg, F. F., Jr. Divorce and the American family. *American Review of Sociology*, 1990, *16*, 379–403.

Gallagher, D., Rose, J., Rivera, P., Lovett, S., and Thompson, L. W. Prevalence of depression in family caregivers. *The Gerontologist*, 1989, *4*, 449–456.

Gallup Poll News Service. *Mirror of America*. Los Angeles, Calif.: Gallop Poll News Service, 1989.

Garcia, C. What do we mean by extended family: A closer look at Hispanic multigenerational families. *Journal of Cross-Cultural Gerontology*, 1993, *8*(1), 137–146.

George, L. *Role transition in later life*. Belmont, Calif.: Wadsworth, 1980.

Gilford, R. Contrasts in marital satisfaction throughout old age: An exchange theory analysis. *Journal of Gerontology*, 1984, *39*, 325–333.

Gilford, R. Marriages in later life. *Generations*, 1986, *10*(4), 16–20.

Glick, P. C. Marriage, divorce, and living arrangements: Prospective changes. *Journal of Family Issues*, 1980, *5*, 7–26.

Gold, D. T. Sibling relationships in old age: A typology. *International Journal of Aging and Human Development*, 1989, *28*, 53–66.

Gold, D. T. Late-life sibling relationships: Does race affect typological distribution? *The Gerontologist*, 1990, *30*, 741–748.

Goldman, N., and Lord, G. Sex differences in life cycle measures of widowhood. *Demography*, 1983, *20*, 177–195.

Gove, W., Hughes, M., and Style, C. Does marriage have positive effects on the psychological well-being of the individual? *Journal of Health and Social Behavior*, 1983, *24*, 122–131.

Gray, H., and Dressel, P. Alternative interpretations of aging among gay males. *The Gerontologist*, 1985, *25*, 83–87.

Greenberg, J., and Becker, M. Aging parents as family resources. *The Gerontologist*, 1988, *28*(6), 786–791.

Greene, V. L., and Monahan, D. J. The effect of a support and education program on stress and burden among family caregivers to frail elderly persons. *The Gerontologist*, 1989, *4*, 472–477.

Gubrium, J. F. Being single in old age. *International Journal of Aging and Human Development*, 1975, *6*, 29–41.

Gwenwald, M. The SAGE model for serving older lesbians and gay men. *Homosexuality and Social Work*, 1984, *2*, 53–61.

Gwyther, L. *Care of Alzheimer's patients: A manual for nursing home staff*. Washington, D.C.: American Health Care Association and the Alzheimer's Disease and Related Disorders Assoc., 1985.

Gwyther, L. P. Overcoming barriers: Home care for dementia patients. *Caring*, 1989, *8*, 12–16.

Gwyther, L., and Brooks, B. *Mobilizing networks of mutual support: How to develop Alzheimer caregiver support groups*. Durham, N.C.: Duke University, Duke Family Support Network Chapter, 1984.

Hagestad, G. The continuous bond: A dynamic multigenerational perspective on parent-child relations between adults. In M. Perlmutter (Ed.), *Minnesota Symposium on Child Psychology*. Hillsdale, N.J.: Erlbaum, 1984.

Haley, W. E., Levine, E., Lane-Brown, S., Berry, J., and Hughes, G. Psychological, social, and health consequences of caring for a relative with senile dementia. *Journal of the American Geriatrics Society*, 1987, *35*, 405–411.

Hanson, S., Sauer, W., and Seelbach, W. Racial and cohort variations in filial responsibility norms. *The Gerontologist*, 1983, *23*, 626–631.

Harris, L., and Associates. *The myth and reality of aging in America*. Washington, D.C.: The National Council on the Aging, 1975.

Hatch, L., and Bulcroft, K. Contact with friends in later life: Disentangling the effects of gender and marital status. *Journal of Marriage and the Family*, 1992, *54*, 222–232.

Hatch, R. C., and Franken, M. C. Concerns of children with parents in nursing homes. *Journal of Gerontological Social Work*, 1984, *7*, 19–30.

Heinemann, G., and Evans, P. Widowhood: Loss, change and adaptation. In T. Brubaker (Ed.), *Family relationships in later life* (2nd Edition). Newbury Park, Calif.: Sage, 1990, 142–168.

Hendricks, J., and Rosenthal, C. *The remainder of their days: Domestic policy in older families in the United States and Canada*. New York: Garland Publishing, 1993.

Hennon, C. Divorce and the elderly: A neglected area of research. In T. Brubaker (Ed.), *Family relationships in later life*. Beverly Hills, Calif.: Sage, 1983.

Hess, B. Friendship. In M. W. Riley, M. Johnson, and A. Foner (Eds.), *Aging and society, Vol. III: A sociology of age stratification*. New York: Russell Sage Foundation, 1972.

Hess, B., and Waring, J. M. Divorce and the elderly: A neglected area of research. In T. Brubaker (Ed.), *Family relationships in later life*. Beverly Hills, Calif.: Sage, 1982.

Heyman, D., and Gianturco, D. Long-term adaptation by the elderly to bereavement. *Journal of Gerontology*, 1973, *28*, 359–362.

Hochschild, A. L. *The unexpected community*. Englewood Cliffs, N.J.: Prentice-Hall, 1973.

Holahan, C. Marital attitudes over 40 years: A longitudinal and cohort analysis. *Journal of Gerontology*, 1984, *39*, 49–57.

Horowitz, A. Sons and daughters as caregivers to older parents: Differences in role performance and consequences. *The Gerontologist*, 1985, *25*, 612–623.

Houser, B. The relative rewards and costs of childlessness for older women. *Psychology of Women Quarterly*, 1984, *8*(4), 395–398.

Jennings, J. Elderly parents as caregivers for their adult dependent children. *Social Work*, 1987, *32*, 430–433.

Johnson, E. S., and Bursk, B. J. Relationships between the elderly and their adult children. *The Gerontologist*, 1977, *17*, 90–96.

Johnson, M. A. Nursing home placement: The daughter's perspective. *Journal of Gerontological Nursing*, 1990, *16*(11), 6–11

Jonas, K., and Wellin, E. Dependency and reciprocity: Home health in an elderly population. In C. Fry (Ed.), *Aging in culture and society*. New York: Bergin, 1980.

Kammer, C. Stress and coping of family members responsible for nursing home placement. *Research in Nursing and Health*, 1994, *17*(2), 89–98.

Kammeyer, K., and Bolton, C. Community and family factors related to the use of a family service agency. *Journal of Marriage and the Family*, 1968, *30*, 488–498.

Kaplan, J. Planning the future of institutional care: The true costs. *The Gerontologist*, 1983, *23*, 411–415.

Kasper, J. *Aging alone: Profile and projections.* Baltimore, Md.: Commonwealth Fund Commission, 1988.

Kaye, L. W., and Applegate, J. S. *Men as caregivers to the elderly: Understanding and aiding unrecognized family support.* Lexington, Mass.: Lexington Books, 1990.

Kehoe, M. *Lesbians over 60 speak for themselves.* New York: Harrington Pore Press, 1989.

Keigher, S., and Murphy, C. A consumer view of a family care compensation program for the elderly. *Social Services Review,* 1992, 66, 256–277.

Keith, P. Isolation of the unmarried in later life. *Family Relations,* 1986, 35(4), 389–395.

Keith, P., and Lorenz, F. Financial strain and health of unmarried older people. *The Gerontologist,* 1989, 29(5), 684–688.

Kelly, T., and Kropf, N. Stigmatized and perpetual parents: Older parents caring for adult children with lifelong disabilities. *Journal of Gerontological Social Work,* 1995.

Kidd, A. H., and Feldman, B. M. Pet ownership and self-perceptions of older people. *Psychological Reports,* 1981, 48, 867–875.

Kingston, E., and O'Grady-LeShane, R. The effects of caregiving on women's social security benefits. *The Gerontologist,* 1993, 33, 230–239.

Kivett, V. R. Consanguinity and kin level: Their relative importance to the helping network of older adults. *Journal of Gerontology,* 1985, 40, 228–234.

Kivnick, H. *The meaning of grandparenthood.* Ann Arbor: University of Michigan Press, 1982.

Kivnick, H. Grandparents and the life cycle. *Journal of Geriatric Psychiatry,* 1986, 19, 39–55.

Kleeson, M. H., Brody, E. M., Schoonover, E. B., and Hoffman, C. Family help to the elderly: Perceptions of sons-in-law regarding parent care. *Journal of Marriage and the Family,* 1989, 51, 303–312.

Kornhober, A., and Woodward, K. L. *Grandparents/grandchildren: The vital connection.* Garden City, N.Y.: Anchor Press/Doubleday, 1981.

Korte, C., and Gupta, V. A program of friendly visitors as network builders. *The Gerontologist,* 1991, 31, 404–407.

Koser, G. *Enhancing and sustaining informal support networks for the elderly and disabled.* Albany: New York State Health Planning Commission, 1981.

Kraus, A. S., Spasoff, R. A., Beattie, E. J., Holden, D. E. W., Lawson, J. S., Rodenburg, M., and Woodcock, G. M. Elderly application process: Placement and care needs. *Journal of the American Geriatrics Society,* 1976, 24, 165–172.

Krout, J. A. Rural vs. urban differences in elderly parents' contact with their children. *The Gerontologist,* 1988, 28, 198–203.

Laner, M. Growing older female: Heterosexual and homosexual. *Journal of Homosexuality,* 1979, Spring, 219–235, 267–275.

Lang, A., and Brody, E. Characteristics of middle-aged daughters and help to their elderly mothers. *Journal of Marriage and the Family,* 1983, 45, 193–202.

Larson, P. C. Gay male relationships. In W. Paul, J. D. Weinrich, and J. C. Gonsioreh (Eds.), *Homosexuality: Social, psychological, and biological issues.* Beverly Hills, Calif.: Sage, 1982.

Lee, G. R. Marriage and morale in later life. *Journal of Marriage and the Family,* 1978, 40, 131–139.

Lee, G. R., and Ellithorpe, E. Intergenerational exchange and subjective well-being among the elderly. *Journal of Marriage and the Family,* 1982, 44, 217–224.

Lee, G., and Shehan, C. *Family relations and the self-esteem of older persons.* Presented at the Annual Meeting of the National Council on Family Relations. Philadelphia, Penn.: November 1988.

Leigh, G. Kinship interaction over the family life span. *Journal of Marriage and the Family,* 1982, 44, 197–208.

Leutz, W. N., Capitman, J., Mac Adams, M. and Abrahams, R. *Care for frail elders: Developing community solutions.* Westport, Conn.: Auburn House, 1993.

Levenson, R., Cartensen, L., and Gottman, J. Long-term marriage: Age, gender and satisfaction. *Psychology and Aging,* 1993, 8(2), 301–313.

Levkoff, S., Pratt, C., Esperanza, R., and Tomine, S. *Minority elderly: A historical and cultural perspective.* Corvallis: Oregon State University, 1979.

Lieberman, G. L. Children of the elderly as natural helpers: Some demographic differences. *American Journal of Community Psychology,* 1978, 6, 489–498.

Litwak, E. *The modified extended family, social networks, and research continuities in aging.* New

York: Center for Social Sciences at Columbia University, 1981.

Litwak, E. *Helping the elderly.* New York: The Guilford Press, 1985.

Livson, F. B. Gender identity: A life span view of sex role development. In R. B. Weg (Ed.), *Sexuality in the later years.* New York: Academic Press, 1983.

Long, J., and Mancini, J. Aging couples and the family system. In T. Brubaker (Ed.), *Family relationships in later life* (2nd Ed.). Newbury Park, Calif.: Sage, 1990.

Longino, C., and Lipman, A. Married and spouseless men and women in planned retirement communities: Support network differentials. *Journal of Marriage and the Family,* 1981, *43,* 169–177.

Longino, C., and Lipman, A. The married, the formerly married, and the never married: Support system differentials of older women in planned retirement communities. *International Journal of Aging and Human Development,* 1982, *15,* 285–297.

Longino, C., Soldo, B. J., and Manton, K. G. Demography of aging in the United States. In K. Ferraro (Ed.), *Gerontology issues and perspectives.* New York: Springer, 1990.

Lopata, H. *Women and widows.* New York: Elsevier, 1979.

Lowenthal, M. F., and Haven, C. Interaction and adaptation. *American Sociological Review,* 1968, *33,* 20–30.

Luben, J., and Becerra, R. M. Mexican and Chinese elderly. In D. E. Gelford and C. H. Barreri (Eds.), *Ethnic dimensions of aging.* New York: Springer, 1987, 130–144.

Maddox, G. L. Families as a context and resource in chronic illness. In S. Sherwood (Ed.), *Long term care: A handbook for researchers, planners, and providers.* New York: Spectrum, 1976.

Maldonado, D. The Chicano aged. *Social Work,* 1975, *20,* 213–216.

Maracek, J., Finn, S. E., and Cardell, M. Gender roles in the relationships of lesbians and gay men. *Journal of Homosexuality,* 1982–83, *8,* 45–50.

Martin, T., and Bumpass, L. Recent trends in marital disruption. *Demography,* 1989, *26,* 37–51.

Matthews, A. The relationship between social support and morale: Comparisons of the widowed and never married in later life. *Canadian Journal of Community Mental Health,* 1991, *10*(2), 47–63.

Matthews, S. H. Provision of care to old parents: Division of responsibility among adult children. *Research on Aging,* 1987, *9,* 45–60.

Matthews, D. H., and Sprey, J. The impact of divorce on grandparenthood: An exploratory study. *The Gerontologist,* 1984, *24,* 41–47.

McAdoo, H. P. Stress-absorbing systems in Black families. *Family Relations,* 1982, *31,* 479–488.

McFall, S., and Miller, B. H. Caregiver burden and nursing home admission of frail elderly persons. *Journals of Gerontology,* 1992, *47,* 573–679.

Mellon, J. *Support groups for caregivers of the aged: A training manual for facilitators.* New York: The Natural Supports Program, Community Service Society, 1982.

Meyers, R., and Souflee, F. Utilizing social support systems in the delivery of social services to the Mexican-American elderly. *The Journal of Applied Social Sciences,* 1990–91, *15*(1), 31–50.

Miller, B., and Cafasso, L. Gender differences in caregiving: Fact or artifact? *The Gerontologist,* 1992, *32,* 498–507.

Miller, D. The "Sandwich" generation: Adult children of the aging. *Social Work,* 1981, *26,* 419–423.

Minkler, M. Building support networks from social isolation. *Generations,* 1986, *10,* 46–49.

Minkler, M., and Roe, K. *Grandmothers as caregivers: Raising children of the crack cocaine epidemic.* Newbury Park, Calif.: Sage, 1993.

Minkler, M., and Roe, K. *Preliminary findings from the grandmother caregiver study of Oakland, California.* Berkeley, Calif.: University of California, 1991.

Minkler, M., and Stone R. The feminization of poverty and older women. *The Gerontologist,* 1985, *25,* 351–357.

Minnigerode, F., and Adelman, M. Elderly homosexual women and men. *Family Coordinator,* October 1978, 451–456.

Mitchell, J., and Register, J. C. An exploration of family interaction with the elderly by race, socioeconomic status and residence. *The Gerontologist,* 1984, *24,* 48–54.

Montgomery, R., and Borgatta, E. F. The effects of alternative support strategies on family caregiving. *The Gerontologist,* 1989, *29,* 457–464.

Mor-Barak, M., Miller, L., and Syme, L. Social networks, life events and the health of the poor, frail elderly: A longitudinal study of the buffering versus the direct effect. *Family Community Health*, 1991, *14*(2), 1–13.

Morrow-Howell, N., and Ozawa, M. Helping network: Seniors to seniors. *The Gerontologist*, 1987, *27*(1), 17–20.

Morycz, R. Caregiving strain and the desire to institutionalize family members with Alzheimer's disease. *Research on Aging*, 1985, *7*, 329–361.

Mutran, E., and Skinner, G. Family support and the well-being of widowed: Black-white comparison. Paper presented at meetings of the Gerontological Society, Nov., Toronto (Ont.), 1981.

Mutschler, P. H. From executive suite to productive lives: How employees in different occupations manage elder care responsibilities. *Research on Aging*, 1994, *16*, 7–26.

National Academy on Aging. *Old Age in the 21st Century.* Syracuse, NY: Syracuse University, The Maxwell School, 1994.

National Institutes of Health. *Health benefits of pets.* Washington, D.C.: U.S. Department of Health and Human Services, U. S. Government Printing Office, 1988.

Neugarten, B., and Weinstein, K. The changing American grandparent. *Journal of Marriage and the Family*, 1964, *26*, 199–204.

Noelker, L., and Bass, D. Relationships between the frail elderly and informal and formal helpers. In E. Kahana, D. Biegel and M. Wykle (Eds.), *Family caregiving across the lifespan.* Thousand Oaks, Calif.: Sage, 1994, 356–386.

Nydegger, C. N. Family ties of the aged in cross-cultural perspective. *The Gerontologist*, 1983, *23*, 26–32.

O'Brian, J., and Whitelaw, N. *Planning options for the elderly.* Portland, Ore.: Institute on Aging, Portland State University, 1978.

Office of Technology Assessment, U.S. Congress. *Confused minds, burdened families: Finding help for people with Alzheimer's Disease and other dementia.* OTA-BA-403, Washington, D.C.: U.S. Government Printing Office, 1990.

Older Women's League. *Report on the status of midlife and older women.* Washington, D.C.: Older Women's League, May 1986.

Older Women's League. *Failing America's caregivers: A status report on women who care.* Washington, D.C.: Older Women's League, May 1989.

Older Women's League. *Heading for hardship: Retirement income for American women in the next century.* Washington, D.C.: Older Women's League, 1990.

Ory, M. G., and Goldberg, E. C. Pet possession and well-being in elderly women. *Research on Aging*, 1983, *5*, 389–409.

Paringer, L. *The forgotten costs of long-term care.* Washington, D.C.: The Urban Institute, 1983.

Pearson, J. L. *Older parents' reactions and adjustment to their child's marital separation.* Unpublished doctoral dissertation, East Lansing: Michigan State University, 1986.

Peplau, L., Cochran, S., Rook, K., and Pedesky, C. Loving women: Attachment and autonomy in lesbian relationships. *Journal of Social Issues*, 1978, *34*, 7–27.

Peplau, L. A., and Gordon, S. L. The intimate relationships of lesbians and gay men. In E. R. Allgeirer and N. B. McCormick (Eds.), *Gender roles and sexual behavior.* Palo Alto, Calif: Mayfield, 1982.

Pope, S., Whiteside, L., Brooke, G., Kelleher, K., Rickert, V., Bradley, R., and Cossey, P. Low birthweight infants born to adolescent mothers: Effects of co-residency with grandmother on child development. *Journal of the American Medical Association*, 1993, *269*(11), 1396–1400.

Poulshock, S. W., and Diemling, G. T. Families caring for elders in residence: Issues in the measurement of burden. *The Gerontologist*, 1984, *24*, 230–239.

Pratt, C., and Kethley, A. Aging and family caregiving in the future: Implications for education and policy. *Educational Gerontology*, 1988, *14*, 657–576.

Pruchno, R. A., and Resch, N. Husbands and wives as caregivers: Antecedents of depression and burden. *The Gerontologist*, 1989, *29*, 159–165.

Purdy, J. K., and Arguello, D. Hispanic familism in caretaking of older adults: Is it functional? *Journal of Gerontological Social Work*, 1992, *19*, 29–43.

Pynoos, J., Hade-Kaplan, B., and Fleisher, D. Intergenerational neighborhood networks: A basis for aiding the frail elderly. *The Gerontologist,* 1984, *24,* 233–237.

Quam, J. K., and Whitford, G. Adaptation and age-related expectations of older gay and lesbian adults. *The Gerontologist,* 1992, *32,* 367–374.

Quinn, M. J., and Tomita, S. K. *Elder abuse and neglect: Assessment and intervention.* New York: Springer, 1986.

Qureshi, H., and Walker, A. *The caring relationship: Elderly people and their families.* London: MacMillan, 1989.

Raphael, S., and Robinson, M. The older lesbian: Love relationships and friendship patterns. *Alternative Life Styles,* 1980, *3,* 207–229.

Raphael, S., and Robinson, M. Lesbians and gay men in later life. *Generations,* 1981, *6,* 16–18.

Reisman, J. M. An indirect measure of the value of friendship for aging men. *Journal of Gerontology,* 1988, *43,* 109–110.

Rhyne, C. Bases of marital satisfaction among men and women. *Journal of Marriage and the Family,* 1981, *43,* 941–955.

Rice, S. *Support groups for a specialized population—Single, elderly, childless women.* Presented at the Annual Meeting of the Western Gerontological Society, Anaheim, Calif., 1984.

Richards, M., Hooyman, N., Hansen, M., Brandts, W., Smith-DiJulio, K., and Dahm, L. *Nursing home placement: A guidebook for families.* Seattle: University of Washington Press, 1984.

Riddick, C., Cohen, J., Fleshner, E., and Kraft, G. Caregiver adaptation to having a relative with dementia admitted to a nursing home. *Journal of Gerontological Social Work,* 1992, *19*(1), 51–76.

Riley, M. W., and Riley, J. Longevity and social structure: The potential of the adult years. In A. Pifer and L. Bronte (Eds.), *Our aging society.* New York: W. W. Norton, 1986.

Robb, S. S., Boyd, M., and Pritash, C. L. A wine bottle, plant, and puppy. *Journal of Gerontological Nursing,* 1980, *6,* 721–728.

Roberto, K., and Scott, J. P. Friendship patterns among older women. *International Journal of Aging and Human Development,* 1984–85, *19,* 1–11.

Roberto, K. Grandparent and grandchild relationships. In T. Brubaker (Ed.), *Family relationships in later life.* Newbury Park, Calif.: Sage, 1990, 100–112.

Robinson, B., and Thurnher, M. Taking care of aged parents: A family cycle transition. *The Gerontologist,* 1979, *19,* 587–593.

Robinson, L. *A qualitative study of marital strengths in enduring marriages.* Paper presented at the Annual Conference of the National Council on Family Relations, Seattle, Wash., 1990.

Robinson, L., and Blanton, P. Marital strengths in enduring marriages. *Family Relations,* 1993, *42*(1), 38–45.

Robinson, M. *The older lesbian.* Master's Thesis, California State University, Carson, California, 1979.

Rosenmayr, L. The family—A source of hope for the elderly. In E. Shanas and M. Sussman (Eds.), *Family, bureaucracy and the elderly.* Durham, N.C.: Duke University Press, 1977.

Rosenthal, C J. Family supports in later life: Does ethnicity make a difference? *The Gerontologist,* 1986, *26,* 19–24.

Rosow, I. *Social integration of the aged.* New York: Free Press, 1967.

Ross, H. The neighborhood family: Community mental health for the elderly. *The Gerontologist,* 1983, *23,* 243–247.

Ross, H. G., and Milgram, J. I. Important variables in adult sibling relationships: A qualitative study. In M. E. Lamb and B. Sutton-Smith (Eds.), *Sibling relationships: Their nature and significance across the lifespan.* Hillsdale, N.J.: Lawrence Erlbaum, 1982.

Rossi, A. S., and Rossi, P. M. *Of human bonding: Parent-child relations across the life course.* New York: Aldine, 1990.

Rubenstein, R. Never married elderly as a social type: Reevaluating some images. *The Gerontologist,* 1987, *27*(1), 108–113.

Rubinstein, R. L., Alexander, B. B., Goodman, M. and Luborsky, M. Key relationships of never married, childless older women: A cultural analysis. *The Journals of Gerontology,* 1991, *5,* S270–277.

Scanlon, W. J. A perspective on long term care for the elderly. *Health Care Financing Review, Annual Supplement,* 1988, 7–15.

Scharlach, A., and Boyd, S. C. Caregiving and employment: Results of an employee survey. *The Gerontologist,* 1989, *29,* 382–387.

Scharlach, A., Lowe, B., and Schneider, E. C. *Elder care and the work force.* Lexington, Mass.: D.C. Heath, 1991.

Schneewind, E. The reaction of the family to the institutionalization of an elderly member: Factors influencing adjustment and suggestions for easing the transition to a new life phase. *Journal of Gerontological Social Work*, 1990, *15*(1–2), 121–136.

Schooler, K. K. *National senior citizens survey, 1968.* Ann Arbor: Inter-University Consortium for Political Social Research, 1979.

Scott, J. P. Sibling interaction in later life. In T. Brubaker (Ed.), *Family relationships in later life.* Newbury Park, Calif.: Sage, 1990, 89–99.

Seltzer, M. N., and Kraus, M. W. Aging parents with adult mentally retarded children: Family risk factors and sources of support. *American Journal on Mental Retardation*, 1989, *94*, 303–312.

Shanas, E. The family as social support in old age. *The Gerontologist*, 1979, *19*, 169–174.

Shanas, E. Older people and their families: The new pioneers. *Journal of Marriage and the Family, 1980, 42*, 9–14.

Shanas, E., Townsend, P., Wedderburn, D., Friis, H., Milhhoj, P., and Stehouver, J. *Older people in three industrial societies.* New York: Atherton, 1968.

Shimkin, D. B., Shimkin, E. M., and Frate, D. A. *The extended family in Black societies.* Manton: The Hague, 1975.

Silverman, A., Brahce, C., and Zielinski, C. *As parents grow older. A manual for program replication.* Ann Arbor: Institute of Gerontology, The University of Michigan, 1981.

Silverstein, M., and Waite, L. Are blacks more likely than whites to receive and provide social support in middle and old age? Yes, no and maybe so. *Journals of Gerontology*, 1993, *48*(4), 5212–5222.

Skolnick, A. Married lives: Longitudinal perspectives on marriage. In D. Eicharn, J. Clausen, N. Haan, M. Honzik, and P. Mussen (Eds.), *Present and past on middle life.* New York: Academic Press, 1981.

Smith, G. C., and Tobin, S. S. Case managers' perceptions of practice with older parents of adults with developmental disabilities. In K. A. Roberto (Ed.), *The elderly caregiver: Caring for adults with developmental disabilities.* Newbury Park, Calif.: Sage, 1993, 146–169.

Smyer, M., and Hofland, B. F. Divorce and family support in later life. *Journal of Family Issues*, 1982, *3*, 61–77.

Soares, C. J. The companion animal in the context of the family system. *Marriage and Family Review*, 1985, *8*, 49–62.

Sommers, T. *Til death do us part: Caregiving wives of severely disabled husbands.* Washington, D.C.: Older Women's League, 1982.

Speare, A., and Avery, R. Who helps whom in older parent-child families? *Journals of Gerontology*, 1993, *48*(2), 564–573.

Spitze, G., and Logan, J. Sons, daughters and intergenerational social support. *Journal of Marriage and the Family*, 1990, *52*, 420–430.

Spitze, G., Logan, J., Joseph, G., and Lee, E. Middle generation roles and the well-being of men and women. *Journals of Gerontology*, 1994, *49*(3), S107–S116.

Spivak, S., Haskin, B., and Capitman, J. A review of research on informal support systems. Appendix F of *Evaluation of coordinated community oriented long-term care demonstration projects.* Final Report, Contract No. 400-80-0073. Washington, D.C.: Department of Health and Human Services, 1984.

Steinitz, L. The church as family surrogate for the elderly. Paper presented at meetings of the Gerontological Society, San Diego, Calif., November 1980.

Steinmetz, S. Elder abuse: Myth and reality. In T. Brubaker (Ed.), *Family relationships in later life* (2nd Ed.). Newbury Park, Calif.: Sage, 1990, 193–211.

Stoller, E. P. Male caregivers in a community setting: Changing contributions over time. Paper presented at the Annual Meeting of the Gerontological Society, San Francisco, Calif., 1988.

Stoller, E., and Stoller, E. P. Help with activities of everyday life: Sources of support for the noninstitutionalized elderly. *The Gerontologist*, 1983, *23*, 64–70.

Stone, R., Cafferata, G., and Sangl, J. *Caregivers of the frail elderly: A national profile.* Washington, D.C.: U.S. Department of Health and Human Services, 1987.

Stone, R., and Keigher, S. Toward equitable universal caregiver policy: The potential of financial supports for family caregivers. *Aging and Social Policy*, 1994, *6*, 57–76.

Stone, R. I., and Kemper, P. Spouses and children of disabled elderly: How large a constituency for long-term reform? *The Milbank Quarterly*, 1989, *67*, 485–506.

Strawbridge, W., and Wallhagen, M. Impact of family conflict on adult child caregivers. *The Gerontologist*, 1991, *31*, 770–777.

Stull, D., and Scarisbrick-Hauser, A. Never married elderly: A reassessment with implications for long-term care policy. *Research on Aging*, 1989, *11*(1), 124–139.

Sussman, M. The family life of old people. In R. Binstock and E. Shanas (Eds.), *Handbook of aging in the social sciences* (2d ed.). New York: Van Nostrand Reinhold, 1985.

Sussman, M. D., and Burchinol, L. Parental aid to married children: Implications for family functioning. *Marriage and Family Living*, 1962, *24*, 320–332.

Szinovacz, M. Retirement, couples and household work. In S. J. Bahr and E. T. Peterson, (Eds.), *Aging and the family*. Lexington, Mass.: Lexington Press, 1989.

Taylor, R. J. *Aging and supportive relationships among Black Americans: Research on physical and psychosocial health*. New York: Springer, 1988.

Taylor, R., and Chatters, L. Extended family networks of older black adults. *Journal of Gerontology*, 1991, *46*, S210–218.

Tannenbaum, D. *People with problems: Seeking help in an urban community*. Toronto: University of Toronto, Center for Women and Community Studies, 1975.

Tennstedt, S. L., Crawford, S., and McKinley, J. Determining the pattern of community care: Is coresidence more important than caregiver relationship? *Journals of Gerontology*, 1993, *48*(2), 574–583.

Tennstedt, S., McKinley, J., and Sullivan, L. Informal care for frail elders: The role of secondary characteristics. Presented at the Annual Meeting of the Gerontological Society, San Francisco, Calif., 1988.

Thompson, E., Futterman, A. Gallagher-Thompson, D., Rose, J., and Lovett, S. Social support and caregiving burden in family caregivers of frail elders. *Journals of Gerontology*, 1993, *48*(5), S245–S254.

Thompson, R. A., Tinsley, B. R., Scalora, M. J., and Parke, R. D. Grandparents' visitation rights. *American Psychologist*, 1989, *44*, 1217–1222.

Tobin, S. S., and Kulys, R. The family in the institutionalization of the elderly. *Journal of Social Issues*, 1981, *37*, 145–157.

Torres-Gil, F. M. Age, health and culture: An examination of health among Spanish-speaking elderly. Paper presented to the First National Hispanic Conference on Health and Human Services, Los Angeles, 1976.

Treas, J. Family support systems for the aged: Some social and demographic considerations. *The Gerontologist*, 1977, *17*, 486–491.

Treas, J. The great American fertility debate: Generational balance and support of the aged. *The Gerontologist*, 1981, *21*, 98–103.

Treas, J., and Bengtson, V. The family in later years. In M. B. Sussman and S. K. Steinmetz (Eds.), *Handbook on Marriage and the Family*. New York: Plenum Press, 1987, 625–648.

Treas, J., and Van Hilst, A. Marriage and remarriage rates among older Americans. *The Gerontologist*, 1976, *16*, 132–136.

Troll, L. E. The family of later life: A decade review. *Journal of Marriage and the Family*, 1971, *33*, 263–290.

Troll, L. E. Grandparents: The family watchdogs. In T. Brubaker (Ed.), *Family relationships in later life*. Beverly Hills, Calif: Sage, 1983.

Troll, L. E. (Ed.). *Family issues in current gerontology*. New York: Springer, 1986.

Troll, L. E., Miller, S., and Atchley, R. *Families in later life*. Belmont, Calif: Wadsworth, 1979.

Uhlenberg, P., and Myers, M. A. Divorce and the elderly. *The Gerontologist*, 1981, *21*, 276–282.

Unger, D., and Cooley, M. Partner and grandmother contact in black and white teen parent families. *Journal of Adolescent Health*, 1992, *13*(7), 546–552.

U.S. Bureau of the Census. *Current Population Survey*, unpublished data, March 1986.

U.S. Bureau of the Census. *Statistical abstract of the United States: 1988* (10th ed.). Washington, D.C.: U.S. Government Printing Office, 1988.

U.S. Bureau of the Census. *Marital status and living arrangements*. Washington, D.C.: U.S. Government Printing Office, March 1989.

U.S. Bureau of the Census. *The diverse living arrangements of children*. Washington, D.C.: U.S. Government Printing Office, Summer 1991.

U.S. Bureau of the Census. *Marital Status and Living Arrangements*, Current Population Reports, Series P-20, No. 450, Washington, D.C.: U.S. Government Printing Office, 1991.

U.S. Bureau of the Census. *Population projections of the United States by age, sex, race and Hispanic origin, 1992 to 2050,* Current Population Reports, P-25, No. 1092. Washington, D.C.: U.S. Government Printing Office, 1992.

U.S. Department of Labor, Bureau of Labor Statistics. *Employment and earnings: Table 3.* Washington, D.C.: U.S. Department of Labor, January 1984.

U.S. House of Representatives, Select Committee on Aging. *Exploding the myths: Caregiving in America.* Washington, D.C.: U.S. Government Printing Office, 1987.

U.S. Public Health Service, C.D.C., National Center for Health Statistics. *Health/United States.* Washington, D.C.: U.S. Public Health Service, 1987.

U.S. Senate Special Committee on Aging. *America in transition: An aging society,* 1984–85 Edition. Washington, D.C.: U.S. Government Printing Office, 1985.

U.S. Senate Special Committee on Aging. *Developments in aging: 1985.* Washington, D.C.: U.S. Government Printing Office, 1986.

U.S. Senate Special Committee on Aging. *Aging America: Trends and projections,* Washington, D.C.: U.S. Government Printing Office, 1992.

Vincente, L., Wiley, J. A., and Carrington, R. A. The risk of institutionalization before death. *The Gerontologist,* 1979, *19,* 361–367.

Wales, C. T., and Zarit, S. Informal support from Black churches and the well-being of elderly Blacks. *The Gerontologist,* 1991, *31,* 490–495.

Wallston, B., Alagna, S., DeVellis, B., and DeVellis, R. Social support and physical health. *Health Psychology,* 1983, 2, 367–391.

Ward, R. Informal networks and well-being in later life: A research agenda. *The Gerontologist,* 1985, *25,* 55–61.

Ward, R., Sherman, S., and LeGory, M. Subjective network assessments and subjective well-being. *Journal of Gerontology,* 1984, *39,* 93–101.

Washington State Aging and Adult Services Administration and Puget Sound Power and Light Company. *Gatekeeper program.* Seattle, Wash., 1986.

Weeks, J. R., and Cueller, J. B. The role of family members in the helping networks of older people. *The Gerontologist,* 1981, *21,* 388–394.

Wentowski, G. Older women's perceptions of great-grandparenthood: A research note. *The Gerontologist,* 1985, *25,* 293–296.

Wethington, E., McLeod, J., and Kessler, R. The importance of life events for explaining sex differences in psychological distress. In R. Barnett, L. Biener, and G. Baruch (Eds.), *Gender and stress.* New York: Free Press, 1988.

White House Conference on Aging. *Chartbook on aging in America,* Washington, D.C.: U.S. Government Printing Office, 1981.

Wilson, K. B., and DeShane, M. R. The legal rights of grandparents: A preliminary discussion. *The Gerontologist,* 1982, 22, 67–71.

Wilson, V. The consequences of elderly wives caring for disabled husbands. *Social Work,* 1990, *35,* 417–421.

Wolf, D. C. *Growing older: Lesbians and gay men.* Berkeley: University of California Press, 1982.

Wood, J., and Parham, I. Coping with perceived burden: Ethnic and cultural issues in Alzheimer's family caregiving. *Journal of Applied Gerontology,* 1990, *9*(3), 325–339.

Wood, V., and Robertson, J. The significance of grandparenthood. In J. Gubruim (Ed.), *Time, roles and self in old age.* New York: Human Sciences Press, 1976.

Wright, L. K. Alzheimer's disease afflicted spouses who remain at home: Can human dialectics explain the findings? *Social Science and Medicare,* 1994, *38*(8), 1037–1046.

Wright, L. K. The impact of Alzheimer's disease on the marital relationship. *The Gerontologist,* 1991, *31*(2), 224–237.

Wright, P. Gender differences in adults same and cross-gender friendships. In R. Adams and R. Bleiszner (Eds.), *Older adult friendship.* Newbury Park, Calif.: Sage, 1989, 197–221.

Wykle, M., and Segal, M. A comparison of black and white family caregivers experiences with dementia. *Journal of National Black Nurses Association,* 1991, *5*(1), 29–41.

Young, R., and Kahana, E. Specifying caregiver outcomes: Gender and relationship aspects of caregiving strain. *The Gerontologist,* 1989, *29,* 660–666.

Zarit, S. H., Reeves, K. E., and Bach-Peterson, J. Relatives of the impaired elderly: Correlates of feelings of burden. *The Gerontologist,* 1980, *20,* 649–655.

Zarit, S., Todd, P., and Zarit, J. Subjective burden of husbands and wives as caregivers: A longitudinal study. *The Gerontologist,* 1986, *26*(3), 260–266.

# CHAPTER 13

# LIVING ARRANGEMENTS AND SOCIAL INTERACTIONS

As we have seen in previous chapters, successful aging depends on physical health, cognitive and emotional well-being, and a level of activity that is congruent with an individual's abilities and needs. Another important element in the aging process is the environment, both social and physical, which serves as the context for activities as well as the stimulus with which an individual interacts. According to person-environment theories of aging, an individual is more likely to experience life satisfaction in an environment that is congruent with his or her physical, cognitive, and emotional needs and abilities.

Previous chapters have examined the relationships between older persons and their social settings. In this chapter, the focus is on diverse *physical* environments and their social and psychological consequences. We examine the impact of the natural and built environment on older persons' social functioning, the influence of a growing older population on community planning and housing, and the interaction between older persons and their physical environments. Many of the age-related changes in physiological status, sensory function, and cognitive

abilities, as well as the diseases and cognitive disorders associated with aging that have been discussed in previous chapters, are affected in important ways by the environment. These age-related changes and disease conditions make the average older person sensitive to characteristics of the setting that may have no effect on the typical younger person. They may impair the older person's ability to adapt to and interact with complex and novel environments. On the other hand, there are many older people who function as well as younger persons do in a wide range of physical surroundings. Observation of these differences in individual responses has led to the concept of *congruence* or *fit* between the environment and the individual. This concept, briefly reviewed in the Introduction of this book, forms the basis of the discussion in this chapter.

## PERSON-ENVIRONMENT THEORIES OF AGING

The impact of the environment on human behavior and well-being is widely recognized in diverse disciplines. It was in the early work of psychologist Kurt Lewin and his associates (Lewin, 1935; Lewin, Lippitt, and White, 1939; Barker, Dembo, and Lewin, 1941) that the environment as a complex variable entered the realm of psychology. Lewin's field theory (1935, 1951) emphasizes that any event is the result of multiple factors, individual and environmental; or more simply stated, B = f(P,E) (i.e., behavior is a function of personal and environmental characteristics). A change in either the person or the environment produces a change in behavior.

Murray's theory of personality (1938), known as *personology,* provides the earliest framework for a person-environment congruence model. This theory depicts the individual in dynamic interaction with his or her setting, the type of interaction that we have portrayed throughout this book. Murray viewed humans as "motile, discriminating, valuating, assimilating, integrating beings who attempt to produce temporal unity within a changing environmental matrix" (Murray, 1938, p. 36). Thus, the individual attempts to maintain equilibrium as the environment changes. Murray's concepts of *need* and *press* are relevant for theories of person-environment congruence. In Murray's personology, need is viewed as a force in the individual that works to maintain equilibrium by attending and responding to, or avoiding, certain environmental demands (e.g., the concept of press in the P-E model).

According to Murray's and other theories of person-environment congruence, the individual experiences optimal well-being when his or her needs are in equilibrium with characteristics of the environment (Kahana, 1973; Holland, 1961; Stern, 1965). Thus, for example, an older woman who has spent most of her life on a farm will adjust more readily to a small nursing home in a rural area than to a large facility in an urban center. In contrast, an older couple who have always lived in a large city may be dissatisfied if they decide to spend their retirement years on a small farm far from town; adaptation may be more difficult and perhaps never fully achieved. To the extent that individual needs are not satisfied because of existing environmental characteristics and level of "press," it is hypothesized that the individual will experience frustration and strain.

The impact of the physical setting on the aging person, and the dynamic interaction between the two, has only recently been considered by gerontologists. Yet the environment plays a more dominant role for older than for younger people, because the older person's ability to control his or her surroundings (e.g., to leave an undesirable setting) is considerably reduced. The individual's range of adaptive behaviors to a stressful environment becomes constrained because of changes in physical, social, and psychological functioning. Therefore, this perspective may be even more useful for understanding older people's behavior than for understanding the behavior of other populations.

The socioenvironmental theory, developed as a sociological perspective on aging and briefly described in Chapter 4, suggests that both the social and physical environments influence the activities of older people (Gubrium, 1973). Accordingly, social interactions occur as a function of the age homogeneity of an environment and the extent to which people are living in physical proximity to each other. Gubrium developed a matrix of social contexts that reinforce or discourage friendship formation among the older population. (See Table 13-1.) The four environmental contexts are: (1) high age homogeneity and close proximity, (2) age homogeneity and low proximity, (3) age heterogeneity and close proximity, and (4) age heterogeneity and low proximity. The first context is typical of high-rise residences for older people and generally conducive to friendship formation. The second may be a retirement community of detached housing or townhouses that are spread out over several acres; this situation is less conducive to interactions unless the community plans activities to encourage residents to get to know each other. The third context is found in urban housing or apartments that have residents of diverse ages living near each other, thereby encouraging facial

**TABLE 13–1   Social Contexts in Aging**

| | | AGE HOMOGENEITY | |
|---|---|---|---|
| | | Homogeneous | Heterogeneous |
| Physical Proximity: | Close | Type I | Type III |
| | Distant | Type II | Type IV |

SOURCE: J. Gubrium, *The Myth of the Golden Years* (Springfield, Ill.: Charles C. Thomas, 1973). Courtesy of Charles C. Thomas, Publisher, Springfield, Illinois.

recognition of neighbors but providing less chance of friendship formation than do the first two contexts. The final category of residential environment is represented by suburban neighborhoods with housing spaced far apart and residents of diverse ages. Compared to the other types, this social context results in different activity norms and demands on older people than do the others. To the extent that an older person's resources and personal needs are consistent with the needs of a given environment, a particular social context may result in greater social interaction than another one does. This may be one reason why research on the impact of age-homogeneous housing on social interaction and life satisfaction among older people has led to mixed findings, as we will see later in this chapter.

## P-E Congruence Models in Gerontology

Kahana's theory of P-E fit (1973, 1975) is the first congruence model developed and empirically tested with older individuals. Kahana hypothesized that incongruence between specific individual needs and environmental press along parallel dimensions produces stress, which in turn requires adaptation, and ultimately affects the older person's well-being. For example, an older person who has a high need for privacy would experience discomfort in a nursing home that offered no opportunities for physical privacy or solitude, although, as noted next, too much privacy is generally not stressful. Adaptation may

consist of modifying this environmental press or the individual's deciding to leave the setting, if circumstances permit. Further stress and discomfort result if the individual's response does not improve the situation (Kahana, Liang, and Felton, 1980). Such stress is compounded for older people whose cognitive and functional capacities are severely impaired, because they are less likely to be able to modify the environment or to leave the situation.

It has been suggested that a deficiency in environmental press relative to individual needs ("undersupply") has a negative effect, while an "oversupply" of press (i.e., more environmental demands than the individual prefers or is able to manage) is assumed to have no effect (French, Rodgers, and Cobb, 1974). Kahana's theory does not make a priori assumptions in this regard. However, empirical tests of this model suggest that the relative effects of undersupply and oversupply depend on the specific aspects of environmental press that are examined. For example, oversupply has been found to be as beneficial as congruence in the areas of privacy, organization, and order, whereas an undersupply of stimulation in the individual's immediate environment results in greater well-being than either congruence or an oversupply of stimulation (Kahana, Liang, and Felton, 1980; Kiyak, 1977, 1978). That is, older people who have as much privacy and order in their lives as they prefer, and those with more privacy and order than they prefer, are equally satisfied with their situation. In contrast, older people whose home environments are less physically stimulating (i.e., in terms of noise, lights, and colors) than they prefer tend to be more satisfied with their environments and with their lives than older people whose home environments are more stimulating than they prefer.

Examples of the differential benefits of oversupply, undersupply, and congruence abound in daily situations. An older woman who lives alone and keeps her home as tidy as she likes may be experiencing more privacy and order than she ordinarily prefers, but she is likely to be just as satisfied as she would be if she had as much privacy and order as she wished. If this level of homeostasis between her preference and the environment is disrupted in the direction of less privacy and order than this older woman prefers (e.g., grandchildren visiting for several weeks, playing with their toys in all the rooms), a situation of undersupply in these two preferences is created. Similar to the older woman in the nursing home described previously, she is then likely to experience frustration, dissatisfaction, and a desire to leave the situation.

The advantage of an environment that provides less stimulation than an individual prefers is that the person can create a preferred level of stimulation; in contrast, the overly stimulating environment does not permit an individual to manipulate the situation or to impose a chosen level of stimulation on the environment. An older man who lives with his daughter and teenage grandchildren in a small home may feel overwhelmed and unable to control the high level of activity (and choice of music!) by the younger family and their friends. In contrast, an older man who lives alone in a quiet neighborhood has greater control over the level of activity in his home, even though the house may seem too quiet and unstimulating at times.

## The Competence Model

Another theory of person-environment transactions is the competence model that was described in the Introduction. This model assumes that the impact of the environment is mediated by the individual's competence level. Competence is defined as "the theoretical upper limit of capacity of the individual to function in areas of biological health, sensation-perception, motives, behavior and cognition" (Lawton, 1975, p. 7). This definition focuses on different aspects of the individual than does Kahana's model. The competence model is more concerned with cognitive and physical capacities; Kahana's model emphasizes the individual's perceived needs and preferences. Environment is also defined somewhat differently by these theorists. In the competence model, "environmental press" refers to the potential of a given environmental feature to influence behavior (for example, the level of stimulation, physical barriers, and lack of privacy).

Lawton and Nahemow's model may be a useful one with which to follow changes in an older person's ability to negotiate the physical setting. As competence in cognition, physical strength and stamina, health and sensory functioning decline over time, the individual would be expected to experience increased problems with high environmental press. Thus, for example, grocery shopping in a large supermarket on a busy Saturday morning may become an overwhelming task for an older person who is having increasing difficulty with hearing and walking. To the extent that the aging person can reduce the level of environmental press, adaptation occurs, and the individual maintains his or her level of well-being. In this example, the older person might decide to shop in a smaller supermarket at nonpeak hours, or to avoid supermarkets altogether and use a neighborhood grocery store or order groceries by phone.

For the older person with Alzheimer's disease or other forms of dementia, it can be difficult to reestablish P-E congruence or to adapt to incongruence. This is a population that has not been examined widely within a P-E framework, but severe cognitive deterioration may result in an inability to recognize the incongruence experienced between one's needs and the external world. The dementia patient may become behaviorally disturbed unless others intervene to re-establish congruence. This may be accomplished by simplifying the environment in order to make it fit the individual's cognitive competence; for example, by providing cues and orienting devices in the home to help the individual find his or her way without becoming lost or disoriented. The ultimate goal of any modification should be to maximize the older person's ability to negotiate and control the situation, and to minimize the likelihood that the environment will overwhelm the person's competence.

## RELOCATION

Relocation, or moving from one setting to another, represents a special case of P-E incongruence or discontinuity between the individual's physical, cognitive, and emotional competence, and the demands of the environment. Anyone who has moved from one city to another, or even from one house to another, has experienced the problems of adjusting to new surroundings and to different orientations, floor plans, and designs of specific features in the home. A healthy person can usually adjust quite easily. An older person who has lived in his or her home for many years will require more time to adapt, even if the move is perceived as an improvement to a better, safer, more comfortable home. This is because the individual has adjusted to a particular configuration of P-E fit over a long period of time. The greater the change (e.g., moving from a private house in the suburbs to a small apartment in an urban center), the longer it will take to adapt. A relocation that entails extensive changes in lifestyle, such as a move to a retirement community or to a nursing home with its rules and policies governing the residents, requires even greater adjustments.

The majority of older homeowners (60 percent) have lived in the same house for at least 20 years, often longer (Redfoot and Gaberlavage, 1991). In general, older people are less likely to move to a different community than are younger families, but are more likely to move to a different type of housing within the same community. A survey of members of the American Association of Retired Persons revealed an overwhelming desire by people aged 55 and older to remain in their own homes; 86 percent stated that their preference was to remain in the same community. Among those who had moved in the past ten years, most had moved within the same county (AARP, 1990). Between 1986 and 1987, less than 5 percent of people over age 65 had moved (U.S. Bureau of the Census, 1989).

Among those who moved out of state, almost 50 percent went to Florida, California, Arizona, Texas, or New Jersey. This is part of a continuing trend that has resulted in a significant increase in the over age 65 population in sunbelt states. A study of more than 4,000 people over age 65 found that unmarried persons and married couples in which both spouses retire at the same time are more likely to move to another region than are other elders (Henretta, 1986).

The problem of relocation is compounded for the person who is experiencing multiple or severe physical disabilities and cognitive dysfunction. As we have seen in Chapter 9, these individuals have more difficulty coping with stressful life events than healthy older people. Unfortunately, they are often the very people who must relocate to hospitals and skilled nursing facilities, environments that are most incongruent with the homes of most older people. Indeed, the oldest-old are most likely to relocate, often to their children's home or to a location near their children (Rosenwaike, 1985). Such moves are precipitated by widowhood, significant deterioration in health, or a disability.

Concern about adapting to a new setting is one reason that many frail older people who can no longer maintain their own homes are reluctant to move to congregate housing, even though they may recognize that they "should" move to a safer environment. Among 85 residents of a deteriorating neighborhood, those who were least competent in terms of psychological and social resources were least satisfied with their current housing but also were least active in attempting to find a better situation (Lawton, Kleban, and Carlson, 1973). That is, these people probably recognized that their neighborhoods no longer fit their needs, but the same characteristics that made it difficult to function independently in these settings (e.g., impaired motor and cognitive abilities, or a loss of social supports) impeded them in seeking a better fit. As anyone who has searched for a new home can attest, it requires considerable stamina and determination to find housing and a neighborhood that best fits one's needs and preferences. To the extent that one is frail and unable to muster the energy to search for such housing, it becomes even more difficult to make the transition.

For many years, gerontologists have argued about the detrimental effects of residential relocation for frail elders. Concern has been especially great for those forced to move en masse from one nursing home to another, when, for example, a facility has to be closed for safety reasons. One of the first studies that stimulated the controversy was a longitudinal examination of older persons who had applied for admission to a nursing home. Death rates were higher after relocation than before (Lieberman, 1961). Subsequent studies of older people moving from one institution to another confirmed these results (Bourestom, Tars, and Pastalan, 1973; Lieberman and Tobin, 1983), and raised serious concerns about the mortality risks associated with relocating. This led to descriptions of relocation as transplantation shock, transfer trauma, and relocation stress.

Subsequent research has suggested that the early studies had methodological flaws that resulted in overestimates of mortality risks (Lieberman, 1974; Wittels and Botwinick, 1974; Schulz and Brenner, 1977; Borup, Gallego, and Heffernan, 1979). Such factors as age, health status, radical versus moderate environmental change, and personal involvement in the move had not been considered by previous investigators. These variables have been noted to influence both morbidity and mortality. A review of 26 studies of institutional relocation concluded that relocations that disrupt an older person's perceived or actual support system are more traumatic and more likely to increase the risk of mortality than are relocations that involve intact groups of elders or that move an individual from one intact group to another (Coffman, 1981). Furthermore, relocation to facilities that foster independence rather than dependency often results in improved physical and cognitive functioning (Marlowe, 1974). Positive results were also noted in a study of 78 residents of a nursing home who were transferred to a new skilled-care facility and followed for three months post-relocation. Improved morale and increased satisfaction with their living situation were found within one month among some older persons, those who had wanted to move enjoyed positive outcomes, whereas those who experienced disruption in the relocation process faced more negative outcomes (Mirotznik and Ruskin, 1985). The negative effects of relocation can generally be reduced by extensively preparing older people for a move, such as having them make several visits to the new facility, seeing the rooms to which they have been assigned, and meeting the staff. Even greater involvement in the move, such as older people deciding whether to move, choosing their room or unit in the facility, and deciding on the timing of the move, is beneficial to those who must relocate for any reason.

## URBAN-RURAL DIFFERENCES

With the trend toward urbanization in the Western world, a smaller proportion of all population subgroups, including those aged 65 and over, currently reside in rural farm communities. The great majority of older persons (74 percent) lived in metropolitan areas (i.e., urban and suburban communities) in 1990 (U.S. Bureau of the Census, 1991), compared with only 5 percent in communities with fewer than 2,500 residents. Ethnic minority differences are particularly pronounced in the proportion of older persons in urban centers. Thus, although only 29 percent of white elders live in central cities, 55 percent of all older African Americans and 53 percent of older persons with Spanish surnames reside in these settings. This distribution of older minorities in central cities places them at greater risk for victimization and poor quality housing. Moreover, 24 percent of the white population, as opposed to only 11 percent of Hispanics, live in medium (2,500–10,000) nonmetropolitan communities (see Figure 13-1).

There is also a "graying of the suburbs"; that is, a greater proportion of people who moved into suburban developments in the 1950s have now raised their children and have remained in these communities after retirement (Logan, 1983; Golant, 1990). Since 1977, more older people have lived in the suburbs than in central cities (12 million versus 9 million, respectively, in 1988). Compared to their counterparts living in urban settings, elders in suburban communities tend to have higher incomes, are less likely to live alone, and report themselves to be in better functional health (Logan and Spitze, 1988). On the average, the suburbs where older people live tend to have more rental housing, lower home values, and higher population densities. These demo-

Farming communities can provide a support network for older people.

graphic changes in suburbs raise the issue of changing needs for services and businesses, as well as greater dependence on public transportation in comparison to the time when the residents were young parents.

Older persons who live in non-metropolitan areas have lower incomes (near the poverty level) and poorer health than those in urban areas. A greater proportion rely on Social Security benefits for their primary source of income. This is particularly true for African Americans who reside in small towns and rural areas, where 41.5 percent have incomes near the poverty level, compared with 28 percent of Black elders in metropolitan areas (Lichter, 1989; McLaughlin and Jensen, 1993). Consistent with these findings, limitations in mobility and activity are greater among those in nonmetropolitan nonfarm areas and least among suburban elders. This may be a function of income differences, but also may be related to the greater availability of medical and social services (e.g., hospitals, clinics, senior centers, private physicians, transportation) in urban and suburban communities. Despite attempts to offset urban-rural differences in human services, significant gaps remain in terms of service delivery and availability, so that rural services for

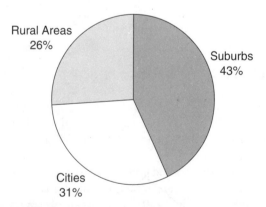

**FIGURE 13–1 Population of Older Americans Living in Urban, Suburban, and Rural Areas**
SOURCE: U.S. Bureau of the Census, *Population Profile of the United States: 1987. Current Population Reports*, Series P-23, No. 159, 1989.

seniors do not have the quality and diversity of metropolitan areas. Transportation remains a critical problem for rural elderly, both to transport them for medical and social services and to bring service providers to the homes of frail and homebound elders. Nevertheless, as noted in Chapter 7, there is little difference in health service utilization rates between rural and urban older people, suggesting that the former do seek medical services when necessary, although they may need to travel farther to find them.

Despite their lower income and poorer health, older persons in small communities have been found to interact more with neighbors and friends and with people of the same and younger ages than do those in urban settings. Mr. and Mrs. Howard in the introductory vignette illustrate the positive aspects of smaller communities for older people. These include the greater proximity of neighbors, stability of residents, and shared values and lifestyles. On the other hand, some researchers have found evidence to contradict the stereotype of greater family integration in rural communities. For example, a survey of older people in Iowa found that only 19 percent of rural persons lived near their children, compared with 34 percent of urban elders (Bultena et al., 1971). Although proportionately fewer rural elders have been found to live near their children and to receive financial and social support from them, friendship ties appear to be stronger and more numerous among rural older people (Lozier and Althouse, 1974; Lawton, Nahemow, and Teaff, 1975).

Studies of life satisfaction among older residents of small towns and metropolitan areas yield mixed reports. Metropolitan residents were found to have greater life satisfaction in two national surveys (Schooler, 1975; Hynson, 1975), but when individual circumstances, such as health and income, were controlled in a reanalysis of earlier data, no significant differences emerged in life satisfaction by community size (Sauer et al., 1976).

In sum, the data suggest that older persons in rural areas and small towns are more disadvantaged in terms of income, health, and service availability than are those in urban centers, who are in turn more disadvantaged than older people in metropolitan areas. Rural elders in general also live farther from their children than do older persons in urban settings. However, it appears that interactions with neighbors occur more frequently in smaller communities, and life satisfaction is affected less by community size than by individual differences. Based on the earlier discussion about the importance of P-E fit for older persons, we would predict that older persons who have a high need for social interaction and have lived most of their lives in rural settings would be most satisfied in such settings, and would experience severe adaptation problems in more anonymous urban environments.

## THE IMPACT OF THE NEIGHBORHOOD

All of us live in a neighborhood, whether a college campus, a nursing home, a retirement park, an apartment complex, or the several blocks surrounding our homes. Because of its smaller scale, the neighborhood represents a closer level of interaction and identification than does the community. Results of the American Housing Survey by the U.S. Bureau of the Census reveal that most older people (76 percent) are satisfied with their neighborhoods, even those in poorer neighborhoods (71 percent). Among those who reported problems, noise and traffic concerns topped the list, followed by complaints of people and crime in the neighborhood (U.S. Bureau of the Census, 1991).

When asked to draw a neighborhood map, older persons tend to include smaller areas and more limited boundaries than do younger individuals. Nearby resources such as a shopping area or park are included. Relatively large neighborhood maps have been drawn by older males, people who drive a car, those in better health, and those with higher incomes (Regnier, Eribes, and Hansen, 1973). According to P-E theories, individuals with better health and higher incomes are the most "competent" elderly.

Given these findings, it is not surprising that the closer a resource is to an individual's home (i.e., within his or her definition of neighborhood), the more likely the older person is to use it. Older tenants of public housing and those in neighborhoods with many older residents have been found to use proximal services (i.e., those on the housing site or within walking distance) with greater frequency than those farther away (Chapman and Beaudet-Walters, 1978). For example, a laundromat, grocery store, or senior center that is on-site or nearby is more popular with tenants than the same service that requires the use of an automobile or bus. Older people are willing to travel farther for physician services, entertainment, family visits (although friends need to be nearby for regular visiting to occur), and club meetings, probably because these activities occur less frequently than grocery shopping and laundry. Visits to family members may occur more often, but many older persons are less concerned with proximity than with the chance to maintain family ties. Distance is less important if family members assume responsibility for driving older persons to various places, including their homes. In some cases, family members may prefer visits in the older person's home.

Proximity and frequent contact with families may not be as critical if neighbors and nearby friends can provide the necessary social support for older persons. As discussed in Chapter 12, neighbors play an important role in older people's social networks, especially for those who have lived in the same homes for many years. Particularly for older people with children at a geographic distance, neighbors are more readily available to help in emergencies and on a short-term basis, such as contacting an ambulance when needed by the older person. It is often more convenient for neighbors than family to drive an older individual to stores and doctors' offices when they are going in that direction anyway. In addition, neighbors can provide a "security net," as partners in a "Neighborhood Watch" crime prevention program or in informally arranged systems of signaling to each other (e.g., pulling open the living room drapes everyday by 9:00 A.M. to signal that all is well). This does not mean that neighbors can or should replace family support systems because, as we have seen, families play a central role in assisting their older members, especially those with chronic illnesses or disabilities.

## AGE HOMOGENEITY-HETEROGENEITY

As mentioned earlier, one factor that influences social interactions in a neighborhood is its age mix. Greater interaction rates and satisfaction with one's neighborhood have been found in settings that are predominantly occupied by older persons (Hinrichson, 1985; Teaff, Lawton, and Carlson, 1973). Residents of age-segregated neighborhoods, for example, may establish informational and helping networks that can compensate for weak or nonexistent family ties. Age homogeneity can facilitate friendships because of shared life situations and the parity of exchange among peers (Blau, 1981).

In contrast, another study found that older people living in areas with mixed age groups expressed *greater* satisfaction with their housing (Chapman and Beaudet-Walters, 1978) Still another study comparing elderly residents in mixed age communities with those in age-segregated housing identified no differences in life satisfaction, but the latter group of communities had larger and more supportive social networks (Poulin, 1984). Other studies have found little evidence of social interaction or mutual support among older residents of age-segregated housing (Ehrlich, Ehrlich, and Woehlke, 1982; Stephens and Bernstein, 1984; Sheehan, 1986).

## VICTIMIZATION AND FEAR OF CRIME

Other characteristics of one's neighbors, such as socioeconomic status, may be more important determinants of social interaction than age per se. For example, age dissimilarity may be compounded by social class differences in a public housing project. Many older persons in such settings have not experienced a lifetime of poverty, whereas the youth who live in these projects often have grown up poor. Older persons in age-mixed public housing projects may be more vulnerable to victimization than those in age-homogeneous settings. Problems of drug traffic may not affect the older tenants directly, but the youth who are openly buying and selling drugs in public housing facilities can create the perception of vulnerability in older residents. This perception may result in fewer attempts at social interaction and more isolation.

To some extent, older people's fears of youth and their unwillingness to interact with them in these settings are due to a lack of intergenerational experiences and to their stereotypes about teenagers. It is true that the perpetrators of crimes against older persons tend to be teenage youths. This is often the case with crimes to which older people are most vulnerable: purse snatchings and pickpocketing.

A commonly held stereotype is that crime affects the older population much more than other age groups. However, both national and local surveys (U.S. Department of Justice, 1981, 1987; Skogan and Maxfield, 1981; Russell, 1980) have revealed that people over age 65 have lower rates of overall victimization than other age groups, especially when compared with the 12- to 25-year-old group. Violent crime against the older population (i.e., assault, robbery, or rape) was only one-fifth the rate against younger groups between 1973 and 1980. Older persons in urban areas have the highest rates of all age groups as victims of personal larceny with contact (i.e., purse snatchings and pickpocketing). They are just as likely as other adults to be robbed, although burglaries occur with less frequency in older households: 50 per 1,000 versus 89 per 1,000 in the homes of younger families. Approximately 82 percent of all personal crimes against older people consist of such predatory crimes as personal larceny with and without contact and robbery with injury (Lawton, 1980–81).

In general, older African Americans have a higher rate of victimization by violent crimes than older whites; older women are at greater risk of predatory crimes than older men (U.S. Department of Justice, 1981, 1987). In fact, a low actual victimization ratio occurs along with high levels of fear, creating a fear-victimization paradox (Linquist and Duke, 1982). On the other hand, the lower proportion of crimes against older people may be a fallacy, reflecting a significant underreporting of crimes by this age group. Older people may be more reluctant to report crimes than are younger people because they believe it would not help solve the crime. They may also think that admitting they have been victimized reveals their vulnerability and an inability to take care of themselves.

The conditions under which crimes are committed against older people differ from those of other age groups. For example, they are more likely to be victimized during the day, by strangers, in or near their homes, and with less use of weapons (Hochstedler, 1981). This suggests that perpetrators of crimes feel they can easily overtake the older victim without a struggle. The sense of helplessness against an attacker may make many older persons more conscious of their need to protect themselves, and may produce levels of fear that are incongruent with the statistics about their relative vulnerability to violent crimes. It is true, however, that even a purse snatching can be traumatic for older women, because of the potential for injury and hip fractures during a struggle and because of the economic consequences for women on limited incomes. It can also disrupt the victim's sense of competence and trust. (O'Keefe and Reid-Nash, 1985).

Fear of crime is not much higher for the group aged 65 and older when compared with the young. But those living alone, with low income, in multiple-unit housing, and in central areas of cities express greater fears than do other older respondents in one survey. Older respondents report feeling less confident about protecting themselves against crime, and believe that they know less than other citizens do about how to make themselves and their homes less vulnerable (O'Keefe and Reid-Nash, 1985).

Variations in the levels of fear reported by older people may be due to residence in an urban, suburban, or rural community, to living in an age-homogeneous or age-heterogeneous neighborhood, or to personal characteristics of the older person interviewed (e.g., gender, ethnic minority status, income, or previous victimization). The fear may even result from hearing about crimes perpetrated against other elders (Yin, 1980). The media often overemphasize the level of such incidents, thereby perpetuating the myth that this age group is most vulnerable to all types of crime. As a result, fear of crime among older people is disproportionate to the actual incidence, although it may be that differences in survey methods and specific questions asked to determine level of fear are more likely to distinguish older individuals with high fear of crime from those with low fear levels (Yin, 1980). In sum, the significance of the fear of crime is not whether or not it is warranted, but the effect it has on older people's psychological well-being.

Whether or not it is based on objective grounds, fear of crime compromises satisfaction with the neighborhood (Lawton and Hoover, 1979). Annual housing surveys of older people have revealed that fear of crime is a more serious personal concern for many older people than are worries about income, health, or housing (Harris, 1981; House Select Committee on Aging, 1977). Neighborhood attributes mentioned most frequently by older people dissatisfied with their housing were crime, poorly maintained housing, abandoned structures, and inadequate police protection (note that these last two variables contribute to the incidence of crime). Older persons of higher socioeconomic levels who resided in non-metropolitan areas and owned their own homes (especially those in single-family structures) expressed greater satisfaction with their housing. All these characteristics are related to the likelihood of crime; that is, smaller communities and those with higher income residents

have lower crime rates and better police protection than do larger urban centers.

In response to the problems of crime, "Neighborhood Watch" and other programs encourage neighbors to become acquainted and to look out for signs of burglaries and other crimes against neighbors and their homes. Such neighborhood crime prevention programs allow older people to have access to their neighbors; they break down the perception of neighbors as strangers and the fear of being isolated in a community, both of which foster fear of crime. Some large communities, such as Milwaukee, have established special police units to investigate and prevent crimes against older people; these units have been found to improve the satisfaction and confidence of older crime victims (Zevitz and Gurnack, 1991). Improvements in the built environment can also create a sense of security. For example, brighter and more uniform street lighting, especially above sidewalks and in alleys, can deter many would-be crimes.

Older people also have been found to be more susceptible to economically devastating crimes such as fraud, confidence games, and medical quackery (Malinchak and Wright, 1978; Elmore, 1981). Police departments in major cities have reported higher rates of victimization against older people by con-game artists and high-pressure salesmen. Medical quackery and insurance fraud are also more common, perhaps because many older people feel desperate for quick cures or are overwhelmed by the costs of traditional medical care. They therefore become easy prey for unscrupulous people who exploit them by offering the "ultimate medical cure" or the cheapest and most comprehensive insurance coverage available. Older people are also more vulnerable to commercial fraud by funeral homes, real estate brokers, and investment salespeople. Door-to-door salespeople of hearing aids have been investigated for fraud, often because the "hearing tests" they offer are inadequate and costly. Perhaps more important than the financial consequences of fraud, such salespeople prevent the older person from seeking appropriate professional services for hearing problems, medical conditions, investments, and other transactions.

## Housing Patterns of Older People

In this section, we review the residential arrangements of older persons, including private homes, planned housing and retirement communities, congregate housing, and nursing homes. We will also discuss a recent model of housing for older people who have physical and cognitive impairments, the assisted living option for residential care. Policies that have been implemented and that govern long-term care options are discussed in Chapter 20.

Older people are more likely than any other age group to occupy housing that they own free and clear of a mortgage. Over 76 percent of all dwelling units in which older persons reside are owned by them. These include condominiums, mobile homes, and even congregate facilities that offer "life care" for retired persons; but by far the greatest proportion of owned units (84 percent) are single-family homes. In 1989, 79 percent of people aged 65 to 74, and 69.5 percent of those 75 and older were homeowners. The proportion of older people owning their homes increases as one moves from urban to rural areas. Older whites are significantly more likely than African Americans or Hispanics to own their own homes (77.7 percent, 63.4 percent, and 61 percent respectively). There is evidence that older homeowners have greater life satisfaction than renters, perhaps to some extent because their financial status is better with lower monthly costs of housing (Fengler, Danigelis and Little, 1983; Atchley, 1985). However, the cost of utilities, taxes, insurance, and repair and maintenance can be prohibitive (U.S. Bureau of the Census, 1991; U.S. Senate Special Committee on Aging, 1992). Not surprisingly, older people living alone are much less likely to own their homes than are older married couples.

### Independent Housing

The majority of older homeowners have occupied their homes for many years. According to the 1987 Annual Housing Survey, 43 percent of older homeowners lived in houses built before 1950, and 15 percent in structures built before 1920. This compared to 25 percent and 8 percent for younger homeowners, respectively (U.S. Senate Special Committee on Aging, 1992).

These statistics have some important implications. First, older persons who have resided in one place for many years are more likely to experience problems with deciding to move and adjusting to a new residence than those who have moved frequently throughout life and have not become attached to a particular residence. It may seem odd to family, friends, and service providers that an older person does not wish to leave a home that is too large and too difficult to negotiate physically, especially if he or she is frail and mobility-impaired. The problem is compounded if the home needs extensive repairs that an older person cannot afford. Despite such seemingly obvious needs for relocating, it is essential to consider older people's preferences before encouraging them to sell a home that appears to be incongruent with their needs. The emotional meaning of home, in terms of personal identity, history of family life (e.g., marriage, childrearing, and grandparenting), and associations with friends and neighbors, cannot be ignored. As discussed in the section on relocation, older people who have lived in one place for many years will experience more problems adjusting to a new residence because they have adapted to a particular level of P-E fit over a long time.

At the same time, however, the older person's current level of competence may be incongruent with the physical environment, and may require a more appropriate housing situation. One solution to this dilemma is the growing number of homesharing programs around the country. These are community-based programs that are operated out of the Area Agency on Aging or other governmental or voluntary service agency.

Their goal is to assist older persons who own their own homes and wish to rent rooms to others in exchange for rental income or services, such as housekeeping and assistance with other chores. The role of a homesharing agency is to serve as a "matchmaker," selecting appropriate homesharers for each older person with a home. These services have been especially popular near universities and colleges, where students can find low-cost or free living arrangements and can benefit from intergenerational contacts. The disadvantage of such programs is that, like any other living situation where dissimilar and unrelated persons share housing, differences in values and lifestyles may be too great to bridge. This is particularly true when a younger person moves into an older person's home. The success of such programs depends on appropriate matches between potential homesharers. Generally, there are more older people with homes to share than younger people wanting rooms. In some instances, such as the Miami, Florida, share-a-home program, a group of older people live together.

The second implication of prolonged home ownership among older persons is that many of

Low-cost housing for older persons is often run down.

these houses are old, with inadequate weather-proofing and other energy-saving features and more deficiencies with respect to construction and maintenance. Exposed wiring, lack of sufficient outlets, and worn-out furnaces can be hazards. Older persons in metropolitan areas, especially older African Americans, are more likely to live in housing with physical defects (Taeuber, 1992).

It is not unusual to hear news stories during winter months of fires starting in older homes due to faulty wiring, overloaded circuits, and the use of space heaters because of an inadequate furnace. The latter situation is particularly troublesome for older persons who have difficulties in maintaining body heat and prefer warmer ambient temperatures (see Chapter 4). Many communities have attempted to prevent these problems by providing free or low-cost home repairs for low-income elders and special assistance to all senior citizens to make their homes more energy efficient (for example, providing no-interest loans for weatherproofing and installing storm windows). Major cities that have experienced sudden increases in their electricity and natural gas rates have also developed programs to aid low-income people of all ages. These services can be invaluable for helping older people to maintain their independence in their own homes.

Home equity conversion mortgages, or reverse mortgages, are becoming increasingly available as another means of helping older homeowners stay in their homes. These programs are offered by mortgage banks, with some backing from the federal government, to older people who are "house-rich but cash-poor." It has been estimated that 83 percent of homeowners over age 65 have paid off their mortgages, and the average amount of equity exceeds $55,000 for these homes. This is true for older persons of all income levels, with 22 percent of the poorest oldest homeowners and 32 percent of the near-poor having more than $50,000 in net home equity (Jacobs and Weissert, 1987). In effect, such programs provide a reverse mortgage, whereby the title is retained by the lender or the lender owns part of the home; the older person receives a monthly payment (or annuity) from the lender and still lives in the house. This can mean an additional $1,000 or more for many older homeowners. When the older person dies and the house is sold, the lender generally deducts the portion of the mortgage that has been paid, including interest, as well as a portion of the home's appreciated value.

Since 1989, HUD has had the authority to offer insurance for reverse mortgages, available to homeowners age 62 and older with little or no mortgage debt remaining. With insurance from the FHA, numerous lenders across the country have been selected to provide reverse mortgages for older persons. Thirty states currently have such programs for older homeowners, and the expectation is that this program will need to be expanded as more older persons learn about its benefits for their economic well-being (Smith-Sloan, 1989). There is some concern about the long-term risks of reverse mortgages for the lender; currently, there are no guidelines for the duration of such mortgage plans. For example, what if the older homeowner outlives the home's equity? Lenders do not want to evict such a person, but at the same time they do not want to lose their investment. In addition, homeowners must consider the initial costs of such a mortgage. These include a two-percent mandatory mortgage insurance fee, a loan origination fee, and standard closing costs. These expenses may require $5,000–10,000 up front in order to borrow a few hundred dollars per month. For older people with other assets to use as collateral, others types of loans may be more cost-effective than a reverse mortgage.

## Planned Housing

During the past 30 years, federal and local government agencies and some private organizations (such as religious groups) have developed planned housing projects specifically for older persons, either as subsidized housing for low-income elders or as age-segregated housing for middle- and upper-income older persons. Gerontologists have attempted to understand the effects of the quality and type of housing on older persons' satisfaction level and behavior following relocation to such housing environments. In one of the first such studies, Frances Carp (1966) followed for one year 204 new occupants of Victoria Plaza, a public housing project for low-income persons in San Antonio, and a control sample of 148 comparable older people who had also applied to live in Victoria Plaza but were not selected to live there. Comparisons before and one year after the move revealed that the Victoria Plaza sample felt greater satisfaction with their housing and neighborhoods, and also experienced better health, improved morale, and more participation in community activities. A follow-up of surviving residents eight years later revealed continuing satisfaction and well-being. No significant changes were found among the nonmovers (Carp, 1974). A major benefit of this study is its use of a comparable control group that also desired to move. Its weakness lies in the reliance on self-report measures. One explanation for the difference is that the novelty of new and safer surroundings produced a "halo effect" for the movers; that is, they perceived all other aspects of their lives (morale, health, and social participation) to have improved as a result of the new environment. This study and others that examine the impact of environmental change would be strengthened by interviewing "significant others" (e.g., spouses or roommates) to determine their evaluations of the older persons' functional and emotional status following the move.

Subsequent studies have supported the positive impact of relocation to planned housing on housing satisfaction, self-assessed health, and activity levels among low-income older people. But no changes were observed by these researchers in functional health, hospitalization rates, and morale (Lawton and Cohen, 1974; Sherwood et al., 1972). It appears that planned housing can indeed improve the quality of life for low-income elders, but it is difficult to generalize to other older populations, particularly those of higher income status. These research results also provide some support for the need to use objectively verifiable measures in housing studies, such as rates of hospitalization and physician visits (which, in turn, are an indicator of functional health).

The problem of where to locate planned housing projects for older persons has no simple solution. As stated earlier in the discussion of neighborhood characteristics, older people are most likely to use services such as a senior center or laundromat if they are on site. Medical and meal services would also undoubtedly be more heavily utilized if they were included on the housing site, but these services are costly to establish and maintain. Moreover, their inclusion cuts down on the space available for residential units. As a result, planners of housing projects for senior citizens usually do not include such services in the building. Instead, they rely on existing organizations, such as local churches and Area Agencies on Aging, to provide these programs. Given the increasing tendency of planners and developers to exclude such services from housing plans, it is critical to locate housing projects for senior citizens near preexisting amenities, including supermarkets and shopping centers. Public transportation should also be easily accessible. If a particular site is not already near a bus stop, this convenience should be arranged with the local public transportation authority well in advance of the completion of the housing project.

Planning must also take into account such factors as whether the area is zoned for residential, commercial, or industrial use. The topography of this site, crime rates, and security of the community are important considerations, as is the need to integrate the housing project into the neighborhood. The last item is especially crucial. In a housing project that is architecturally distinct from the rest of the neighborhood (e.g., a tall, multilevel structure in the midst of single-family homes, or a sprawling "retirement community" on the edge of an industrial area), residents are likely to experience a lack of fit with their environment and to feel isolated from the larger neighborhood. The lack of fit may also be felt by the residents of the larger neighborhood, who often reject the presence of an entire community of older people in their midst, no matter how architecturally consistent the housing project is with other neighborhood buildings. Both physical and psychological barriers are created by walls, vegetation, and architectural features that clearly distinguish a housing project from its surroundings, adding to the older residents' sense of separation from the neighborhood.

## Congregate Housing

Congregate housing differs from planned housing and single-family residences in its provision of communal services, at the very least a central kitchen and a dining room for all residents. Some congregate facilities also provide housekeeping, social, and health services. Others may have space for such services, but do not have established services on site, including congregate meals, home health care, and transportation services. In 1970, when the first federally supported congregate housing act was passed, these services could not be paid through HUD programs that financed the construction, but space for such services was provided. Developers and planners assumed that tenants would be charged for these additional services if they became available, or that the services would be subsidized by local agencies. Recent evidence suggests that such services have indeed become necessary, as the residents of congregate housing have reached advanced old age. To the extent that a housing site has the space and resources to plan for such needs in the future, people are more likely to remain in such settings and to avoid or delay relocation to a skilled care facility.

Congregate housing is a desirable option for many older persons who do not need skilled nursing care but prefer having meals and some personal care services provided if they are to give

Congregate housing offers older people opportunities for social interaction.

up their homes. Probably the most important feature of congregate housing is the availability of prepared meals, which not only provide a·balanced and nutritional diet but also offer regular opportunities for socializing. Usually, residents also have the choice of eating some meals in their own units, because many congregate buildings provide each unit with a small kitchen (often a small refrigerator, a range, and a few kitchen cabinets). The opportunity to eat in a congregate dining facility *or* to cook in their own kitchen was cited as a desirable option by 71 percent of older Texans in a study of housing preferences (Curry and Shroyer, 1989).

The growth of congregate housing is due in great part to the interest shown by private non-profit and profit-making corporations. However, despite their increased numbers, congregate sites are inadequate in many regions of the country and for specific segments of the aging population. Federal and local governments have significantly reduced their construction of new congregate facilities for low-income seniors since 1980. As a result, the number of congregate housing units for middle- and upper-income older persons has increased, but low-income elders who need housing subsidies have not benefited from this increase.

There has been a growth in the number of *multilevel facilities* or continuous care retirement communities (CCRCs) for older persons, that is, housing projects that offer a range from independent to congregate living arrangements and intermediate to skilled care facilities. Such options are more widely available in housing that is purchased, less so for rental housing. As the number of oldest-old persons has increased (as noted in Chapter 1), owners and administrators of facilities that do not provide extensive nursing services have become increasingly concerned. They realize that some of their residents will eventually need to move to other facilities; they are also more aware that potential buyers of units in these facilities would prefer to have a range of services and housing options on site. Such alternatives are often of particular concern for couples, who face the likelihood that one partner will require skilled nursing care eventually. When several levels of care are available at one site, older couples can feel assured that they will be able to remain near each other, even if one becomes institutionalized.

Many housing plans for older people that offer options in living arrangements have *lifecare contracts, life lease contracts,* or *founders' fees.* That is, the older person must pay an initial entry fee, often quite substantial, based on projections of life expectancy and on the size of his or her living quarters. In the case of a lifecare contract, the individual who eventually needs increased care is provided nursing home care without paying more for these services. This is a form of self-insurance for small groups of older adults that provides them with institutional and home-based care as needed. There are over 700 such retirement communities in the United States that house over 200,000 elderly (Hull, 1987). With a life lease contract or a founders' fee, the individual is guaranteed lifetime occupancy in the apartment. However, in the case of life lease contracts, if more expensive care is required, such services are generally not provided by the facility, and the older person must give up the apartment and find a nursing home. Lifecare, life lease, and founders' fees contracts also charge monthly fees, but the monthly costs are generally not as high as those charged in facilities that rely only on month-to-month payments. The advantage of lifecare contracts and founders' fees is that the individual is guaranteed lifetime care; this is important given the actuarial tables of life expectancy for those who reach age 65 (another 17 years) and those who reach 70 (another 13 years). The older person who pays month-to-month may use up all of his or her life savings long before dying if skilled care is needed. In contrast, the option of a lifecare contract may provide a sense of security for the older person who can pay a large lump sum. The individual is taking the chance that he or she will eventually need higher levels of care, so the costs are averaged out over a long period. For those who die soon after moving in, some facilities refund part of the entry fee to the family, but in many cases there is a policy of not refunding any portion of this fee. Obviously, the ability to purchase these contracts is limited to the small percentage of older people who have considerable cash assets. Indeed, older persons in these facilities are better educated and have greater financial resources than the general population of elders. Nonetheless, the number of CCRCs is expected to double before the next century (Tell et al., 1987).

Considering the high cost of CCRCs with lifecare contracts or founders' fees, it is useful to understand the motivations of older people who enter into these contracts. In a survey of almost 1,500 residents of CCRCs and those on a waiting list, the most frequently cited reasons for joining were access to services that permitted independent living and, for married respondents, the opportunity to continue to live together if one spouse needed institutionalization (Cohen et al., 1988).

A potential risk for older people who enter into a lifecare contract is that the facility will declare bankruptcy. In an attempt to avoid this, many states that license lifecare housing projects require providers to establish a trust fund for long-term expenses.

## Institutional Living for Older People

Many people who are unfamiliar with the residential patterns of older people mistakenly assume that the majority live in nursing homes. The actual proportion of older persons living in all institutions (nursing homes, boarding homes, psychiatric hospitals) is only 5 percent, although approximately 25 percent of all people over age 65 will spend some time in a long-term care facility at some point during later life. Estimates of an older person's risk of admission to a nursing home run as high as 50 percent and range from 30 percent for men to 50 percent for women, especially with the trend toward early discharge from hospitals. Each year more than 1 million older persons leave long-term care institutions, almost evenly divided among discharges to the community, transfers to other health facilities, and death. Therefore, the statistic of 5 percent is a cross-sectional snapshot of the institutional population that does not take account of movement into and out of long-term care facilities. Although there was a decline in the proportion of institutionalized older persons between 1985 and 1989, there has been a growth in the *absolute numbers* of people entering long-term care facilities, due mostly to population increases among the oldest-old. People aged 80 and older are far more likely than the young-old to become institutionalized (Manton, Corder and Stallard, 1993; McConnell, 1984; NCHS, 1987; Wiener, Illston and Hanley, 1994).

The U.S. actually has lower rates of institutionalization than other developed countries have. The smallest proportion is in Germany and Japan (about 4 percent each); the highest is in Canada (8.7 percent), Sweden (9.6 percent), and Switzerland (9 percent) (Doty, 1988). In contrast, less developed countries such as Greece, Turkey, and Argentina have fewer than 1 percent of their elderly population in long-term care facilities. This may be because fewer facilities are available in these countries, the costs are too high for families and\or governments, or social attitudes deter potentially needed institutionalization. In some countries, such as Japan and Germany, hospitals provide both long-term and acute care, so the total number of institutionalized older persons is much higher.

It appears that the number of older persons in U.S. nursing homes will increase as the population of oldest-old increases; a 58 percent increase has been estimated between 1978 and 2003 if constant mortality rates are assumed, and by more than 115 percent if mortality rates decline (NCHS, 1987). Institutions are home for the oldest, most frail, and most dependent of the aged population. Among all persons aged 65 to 74, only 1.2 percent live in nursing homes, compared with 23.7 percent among those who are aged 85 and above. The average age of nursing home residents is 82, and, as illustrated by Figure 13-2, women are disproportionately represented (NCHS, 1987, 1989). It has been estimated that the proportion of residents aged 85 and older will increase further, from 42 per-

cent to 51 percent in the next 25 years (Rivlin and Wiener, 1988).

The primary factors that determine institutionalization appear to be age (85 or older), being female, a recent hospital admission, living in retirement housing rather than being a homeowner, having no spouse at home, having some degree of cognitive impairment and having one or more problems with instrumental activities of daily living. (Greene and Ondrich, 1990). In one study, these risk factors in combination resulted in a 62 percent chance of institutionalization within 30 months and a 75 percent chance within seven years (Shapiro and Tate, 1988). Older persons in nursing homes are more likely to have major long-term impairments in activities of daily living, some form of dementia, and multiple major chronic diseases.

The typical resident has lived in a nursing home for more than one year. Nursing home stays of 90 days or less account for only 15 per-

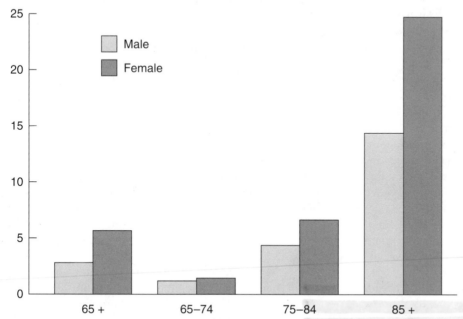

**FIGURE 13–2   Percentage of Nursing Home Residents among the 65 and Over Population, by Sex and Age in the U.S.: 1985**

SOURCE: National Center for Health Statistics. The national nursing home survey: 1985. *Vital & Health Statistics.* Series 13 #97, 1989.

cent of all nursing home days nationally, whereas almost 45 percent of nursing home days are represented by people who have stayed more than two years. Indeed, it has been estimated that 66 percent of all nursing home expenditures are accounted for by people who stay more than two years (Rivlin and Wiener, 1988; Pawlson, 1989). Nevertheless, daily costs for long-term care are considerably less than for acute health care. Even with the expected increase in the older population peaking in the year 2040, it is expected that costs of long-term care will be less than one-third of acute care expenditures and account for less than 3 percent of the GNP (Rivlin and Wiener, 1988).

Nursing homes are relatively new living arrangements. Until the late 1930s and early 1940s, few existed in the United States. The enactment of Medicare and Medicaid in 1965 provided the largest impetus to their development; the rate of nursing home use by older people almost doubled between 1966 and 1980, from 2.5 to 5.0 percent of the population age 65 and over (George, 1984). The growth of the nursing home industry has also been fueled by some of the trends described in Chapters 1 and 12, specifically declining family size, the growth in the numbers and proportion of the older population, particularly women over age 75, and the increase in employed women who were traditionally the family caregivers.

Although the majority of nursing home residents are functionally impaired and unable to live independently in the community, it is noteworthy that for every impaired older person in a long-term care facility, there are at least two—and perhaps as many as five—equally impaired older persons residing in the community (Rivlin and Wiener, 1992). Poor physical health and medical need do not, by themselves, sufficiently explain institutionalization. Instead, the factor that appears to distinguish long-term nursing home residents from equally impaired older community residents is the absence of a caregiver or social support network among the institutionalized. In fact, as mentioned in Chapter 12, up to

25 percent of nursing home placements are precipitated by the caregiver's illness or death (Colerick and George, 1986; Morycz, 1985).

The gender differential in nursing homes is due to women's longer life expectancy, their greater risk of multiple chronic illnesses, and their greater likelihood of being unmarried. The last factor is a critical one, given that the absence of a spouse or other caregiver is a major predictor of institutionalization. For example, in 1985, 80 percent of the nursing home population was without a spouse; the majority were widowed (NCHS, 1989). This compares with 30 percent of men and 76 percent of women over age 75 in the noninstitutional population who were unmarried in that period (U.S. Senate Special Committee on Aging, 1992).

Over 90 percent of nursing home residents are white, compared to 7 percent who are African American, 2.5 percent who are Hispanic, and less than 0.5 percent who are American Indian or Asian Americans. This underrepresentation of ethnic minority groups appears to reflect cultural differences in the willingness to institutionalize older persons, greater availability of family supports, or discrimination in admission policies (generally unofficial) against minorities (Kart, 1993; NCHS, 1989). It may also reflect the dearth of facilities that address the unique needs of these ethnic minorities, thereby forcing older persons of these ethnic backgrounds to enter nursing homes that are incongruent with their cultural needs.

Most nursing homes (75 percent) are *proprietary* or *for-profit,* and thus operate as a business that has a goal of making a profit for the owners. The number of nursing homes owned by large multifacility chains is increasing dramatically. *Nonprofit* homes (20 percent of the total) are generally sponsored by religious or fraternal groups; although making a profit is not their goal, they must be self-supporting. These are governed by a board or advisory group, rather than owners or investors as in the case of proprietary homes. Although instances of reimbursement fraud by proprietary homes have been highly publicized, the terms *proprietary* and *non-profit* do not designate type or quality of care, but rather how the home is governed and how its earnings are distributed. The type of ownership affects who makes major decisions regarding the facility's staff, policies, and programs, but not necessarily the standards of care.

Nursing homes must follow a number of federal guidelines to become certified by Medicare and to meet regulations that are imposed by each state. Most nursing homes are not certified for Medicare, however, primarily because this program does not reimburse for long-term care or maintenance, but only for short-term care (i.e., rehabilitation following hospitalization). Medicaid is widely applied to nursing home care, however, and pays for over 40 percent of all nursing home expenditures (U.S.

Senate Special Committee on Aging, 1990). Many older people with incomes below a specified level (varying across states) would not be able to afford nursing home care without Medicaid assistance. Under this program, nursing homes are reimbursed according to the level of care required by each resident. For example, residents who need more hands-on care by diverse staff are billed at a higher rate. Nursing personnel within the facility determine the level of care required on the basis of the older person's abilities to perform various ADLs and depending on their mental status. Many who enter nursing homes as private pay residents eventually seek public assistance (e.g., Medicaid).

The decision to enter a nursing home is often a hurried one, in reaction to a crisis, such as the older person's imminent discharge from the

---

## GUIDELINES FOR SELECTING A NURSING HOME

**1.** Is the nursing home operated as a nonprofit or as a proprietary business?
- If nonprofit, with which organization is it affiliated?
- If proprietary, is the facility part of a chain or is it independent?

**2.** Does the nursing home participate in the Medicaid program?

**3.** What are the rates for each level of care, and what level will this particular older person require?

**4.** What services are included and excluded from the daily rate?

**5.** What types of patients are refused admission?

**6.** What is the staff-resident ratio during each work shift; more specifically, what is the ratio of nurses and nurses' aides to residents?

**7.** Does the nursing home have a rehabilitation program?
- If yes, is there a registered physical therapist on staff, or therapy aides only?

**8.** What professional services besides nurses and physicians are provided? For example, is there a

staff social worker? How often does a dentist, pharmacist, or member of the clergy visit the facility? What services do they provide residents?

**9.** Is there a residents' council in the home?
- If yes, what are its roles and rights?

**10.** What are the home's rules and regulations regarding meals, snacks, or keeping food in the room?

**11.** Are private rooms available for residents?
- If yes, what is the price differential between private and shared rooms?

**12.** What provisions are made to assure privacy; for example, what are the rules and regulations regarding private, locked storage units? What types of personal furniture may be brought in by residents?

**13.** How far is the facility from the homes of family members and close friends?

*Source:* Adapted with permission from the authors and publisher. W. Lustbader and N. R. Hooyman, *Taking Care of Aging Family Members: A Practical Guide* (New York: The Free Press, 1994.)

*Note:* These are guidelines only, not criteria or a prescriptive listing.

hospital. Hospital staff who work with patients and families to plan the patient's discharge frequently pressure family members to make their decision after physicians and other hospital staff press them to "get those hospital beds open." This may mean that the discharge planner accepts the first available nursing home bed rather than wait for the best possible placement. Unfortunately, this disruption in a frail older person's life may occur repeatedly; over half of those admitted to a nursing home are discharged within three months, and many of them are transferred to a hospital (just 33 percent return to the community), only to die there or return to the same or another nursing home (Kane and Kane, 1990). In instances where families have more time to make a decision, it is desirable for them and their older relative to visit a number of homes. The box on page 341 offers some guidelines for selecting a nursing home.

Even when there is time to plan for placement, few older people willingly choose to live in a nursing home, and most families arrive at this decision only after exhausting their home care resources. As noted in Chapter 12, however, it is important for older people and their relatives to realize that nursing home life does offer some benefits. These include increased social contact, accessible social activities, and intensive rehabilitation services, as well as relief from the stress of caregiving on family members. Although the media tend to publicize instances of abuse and violation of regulations, there are many excellent nursing homes, especially with the growing awareness of the need to improve nursing homes and the development of special care units (SCUs) for residents with cognitive or severe physical impairments. Increasingly, residents and their families are having more influence over their lives, through resident councils, patients' bills of rights, nursing home ombudsmen, and the advocacy of groups such as the National Citizens Coalition for Nursing Home Reform (NCCNHR). In its resident surveys, this organization has found that a major concern of residents is to be involved in decisions about their daily lives in the facility.

Even such basic choices as what to eat, when to wake up, and the level of privacy in their own rooms are not provided to residents of many nursing homes. Through such efforts and through increased gerontological training, health care professionals are also becoming more sensitive about ways to involve family members, friends, and members from the larger community in the care of nursing home residents.

## ASSISTED LIVING: A NEW LONG-TERM CARE OPTION

Since the late 1980s, in response to perceived needs for more cost-effective, long-term care options, there has been a dramatic growth in home care, respite care, adult day care, and assisted living. In particular, assisted living is seen by its advocates as a new, more humane model of housing that is aimed at elders who need assistance with personal care (e.g., bathing and taking medications) and with some ADLs, but who are not so severely impaired physically or cognitively that they need 24-hour attention (Kane and Wilson, 1993). These facilities are generally smaller than the average nursing home. Most provide congregate meals in a common dining room, as well as housekeeping, laundry, and help with some activities of daily living. Staff often include at least one nurse, a social worker, and one or more people to provide case management services. Access to health care is provided for specific tenants as needed (often contracting the services of physicians, physical therapists, mental health specialists). As a result, staffing costs are lower than in nursing homes, thereby keeping the average cost of assisted living lower.

It is important not to place assisted living in a "continuum of care," since this type of facility can generally serve older people with a wide range of disabilities, many of whom are now in nursing homes. Although many states are exploring the option of Medicaid waivers for assisted living, it is currently implemented only in

Oregon. As a result, most people in assisted living facilities (including 75 percent of Oregon's assisted living population) are private pay residents. Many who move out do so because they have run out of funds and must turn to nursing homes that are covered by Medicaid, even though they might benefit from the greater autonomy and self-care encouraged by assisted living facilities (Kane and Wilson, 1993). As more states provide Medicaid waivers, it is anticipated that greater congruence can be achieved between needs of specific elders and their housing needs.

In an analysis of existing facilities in the United States, Scandinavia, and northern Europe, Regnier (1994) illustrates the tremendous variety of assisted living options. Assisted living has been provided for many years in Scandinavian and some European countries, especially for less frail elders. Many of these homes have moved from a medical model of care, which is typical of nursing homes, to a residential model. Residents are often provided with private rooms or apartments with their own baths and kitchenettes, individual control over temperature, personal furnishings, and schedules. These countries provide excellent models of assisted living that can be implemented in the U.S.

## Services to Aid Older People in the Community

In recent years, the term *long-term care* has evolved from an emphasis on purely institutional care to a broad range of services to impaired older adults in both institutional and community settings. Under this broader definition, homemaker services, nutrition programs, adult day care, and visiting nurse services are all part of long-term care. Nursing homes and the newly emerging assisted-living programs represent one component of long-term care options. Indeed, for every person 65 and older residing in a nursing home, there are nearly four times as many living in the community who need some form of long-term care (U.S. Senate Special Committee, 1992).

Over the last decades, there has been an increase in the number of federal, state, and local services to help older people maintain their independence for as long as possible, and in the least restrictive environment feasible, thereby helping the older person to maintain P-E congruence. Such support services include visiting nurses, housecleaning, assistance with personal care, hot meals delivered to the home, and occasional or daily trips to an adult day health program. Some adult day centers include memory retraining programs, physical therapy, scheduled medications, and regular checkups by a nurse. Some centers provide intensive rehabilitative services, but most serve a social integration function. Equally important, day health programs provide respite for family members who may be caring for the older person. Clearly, such services are not suitable for the most impaired or bedbound older person, but they have been an invaluable resource for elders with moderate levels of dementia or with serious physical impairments and chronic illnesses who can still benefit from living in more familiar non-institutional settings. A statewide study comparing participants in adult day health centers with nursing home residents in Virginia found that the latter had more physical disabilities, more sensory impairments, and fewer social supports (Arling et al., 1984). Older people living alone, especially those who are poor and over age 75, use community services, such as transportation and meals, more than do those who are living with others. The latter are more likely to utilize home health services and to rely on family members, especially a spouse, daughter, or daughter-in-law (Reschovsky and Newman, 1990; Kasper, 1988).

These newly emerging community services appear to help delay institutionalization and to minimize the stress of community living for older people and their families. It is important to note, however, that most older individuals with activity limitations who live alone do *not* receive any outside help (Kasper, 1988).

Perhaps the greatest impetus to the development of community services to the older population was the Older Americans Act (described in detail in Chapter 19). It was passed in 1965 and amended significantly in 1969, 1973, 1978, and 1981 to include a broader range of elders who should receive services, and to expand the types of services available. These amendments to the Older Americans Act have resulted in programs to coordinate services within the community, a special emphasis on frail and vulnerable elders, and efforts to maintain older persons in the "least restrictive environment." Unfortunately, while the intent of this policy is laudable, funding to support the services specified by OAA has been limited. In 1990, for example, only $800 million of the $37.4 billion budget for the federal government's share of Medicaid funding was allocated for OAA (Kutza, 1990).

Funding to local planning units, such as Area Agencies on Aging, through this Act can be used in the following categories of preventive, supportive, and restorative services:

1. *Access services.* Information and referral, case management, and transportation.

2. *Health services.* Home health aides, physical therapists and visiting nurse services, health education, rehabilitation therapy, and specialized health services at a local center, such as foot care, dental care, and blood pressure screening.

3. *Nutrition services.* These can be provided at a congregate meal site such as a senior center or hot lunch program site, or in the form of home-delivered hot meals (meals-on-wheels). This category also includes nutrition education and food co-ops that purchase food at reduced prices in some senior centers.

4. *Employment and volunteer services.* These range from employment opportunity listings, such as through a job bank for older workers, to community and federal service employment programs aimed specifically at older people. The Retired Senior Volunteer Program (RSVP) emerged as an amendment to the Older Americans Act in 1969; it has since helped thousands of communities benefit from the expertise and experience of older persons while at the same time enabling them to contribute to society.

5. *Social and recreational services.* The growth of senior centers in most communities has provided a significant focal point of services (e.g., social and recreational activities, education, health assessment, monitoring, and counseling) to older people, while recent developments in adult day care and respite programs for cognitively and physically impaired elders have allowed many families to keep at home their older relatives who would have been institutionalized in the past.

6. *Personal support services.* These include companion services, choreworkers and homemakers, home repair services, and telephone reassurance programs. These services assist older people who cannot manage all their home maintenance or personal activities of daily living because of a short-term illness or who are recuperating from surgery or injury, and those who have become too frail to perform these tasks but are not so impaired as to move to a congregate living situation.

Medicare covers limited home health care services provided by specially licensed agencies through visiting nurses, home health aides, and choreworkers, but only under specific guidelines. These include (1) the approval of a physician for each service to be obtained, (2) the requirement that the older person be homebound and unable to obtain services outside the home, and (3) the requirement that the services be for an acute or rehabilitative situation, not for a chronic health problem. Unfortunately, however, under current reimbursement regulations, Medicare generally cannot be used for community services such as homemaker and nutrition services without prior hospitalization or for extended periods of time. Of all older people who received long-term care in the community in the 1980s, almost 41 percent paid for all services out of their own pocket. Medicare covered all costs for only 8.4 percent and Medicaid for 6 percent of older adults requiring such care. Private insurance paid only 1 percent of the nation's long-term care bill (NCHS, 1987). If a "continuum of long-term care" is to be successfully implemented, reim-

Transportation and other community-based services can enable older people to remain in their homes.

bursement regulations will have to be substantially altered from current practices that provide incentives for institutional rather than community-based care and assisted living. These regulations will be discussed in more detail in the next section and in Chapter 20.

A diversity of social and health services has evolved in many communities, but urban areas are more likely than rural communities to provide the variety described previously. Such diversity can be a blessing for many elders who choose to live in the community, but the lack of a coordinated service delivery system has, in the past, precluded access by those who were most in need. The recent expansion of information and referral, as well as case management programs through Area Agencies on Aging, has led to greater coordination and selection of appropriate services for the most needy elders residing in the community.

As the number and variety of community-based services have grown, so too have questions regarding their cost-effectiveness for severely impaired older persons. That is, should such services be considered a valid alternative to institutionalization for the most vulnerable elderly, or is it more psychologically, socially, and econom-ically advantageous for these older persons to relocate to a nursing home? Despite the loss of independence associated with institutionalization, such a move may result in a greater sense of security for the impaired older person who needs round-the-clock care.

### Emergency Aids for Independent Older Persons

In recent years, several products and services have come into the marketplace to assist older people in emergency situations, especially those who are living alone. Some of these are simply pullcords in the bathroom or bedroom that are connected to a hospital or to the local emergency medical service. Others, such as the Life Safety System and Lifeline Service, are more sophisticated communication systems that use a portable medical alert device or an alarm unit to transmit specific signals for a fire, or a medical emergency, or for "no activity" through telephone lines or computers. These systems have been found to be cost-effective in reducing the need for nursing home care and enhancing the older person's sense of security about living alone (Sherwood and Morris, 1981; Brenner, 1981; Dibner, Lowry, and Morris, 1982). Such electronic services are becoming more widely available with advances in computer technology. Indeed, computers have already been developed to turn appliances on and off; diagnose malfunctions in appliances; control light, noise, temperature and air quality; sense fire or smoke; and convert information from one medium to another (e.g., sound to light). These advances in computer technology will aid older persons who choose to live independently (AARP, 1987).

## HOUSING POLICY AND GOVERNMENT PROGRAMS

Housing policy for older people has received less attention than has income security and health care. One reason for this is that housing policy has been influenced by well-organized interest groups, such as builders and real estate developers, rather than by an aging constituency. As a result, only about 3 percent of older people have benefited from federally funded housing assistance programs (Pynoos, 1984). In addition, housing in the United States has generally received less public financial support than in many other countries. Great Britain, for example, provides publicly funded housing for one-third of its older population (Rubenstein, 1979). The cultural value placed on individual home ownership in the United States may partially explain this difference.

The major housing programs that have benefited older people involve subsidies to suppliers of housing to enable them to sell or rent housing for less than the prevailing market price. The Section 202 Direct Loan Program of the Housing Act of 1959 has provided housing for moderate-income older persons and for the disabled whose incomes are too high to qualify for public housing but too low to obtain housing in the private market. Under Section 202, low-interest loans are made to nonprofit corporations or to nonprofit consumer cooperatives.

Section 236 and Section 8 housing programs provide private enterprise with additional means of developing quality rental and cooperative housing for low- and moderate-income persons, regardless of age, by lowering their housing costs through interest-reduction payments (Section 236) and rent supplements (Section 8). In the latter case, landlords receive from federal and state governments the difference between the rental cost of a housing unit and 30 percent of the tenants' income available for rent. Older people form an important segment of users of this rent supplement program (Kutza, 1981).

Until 1983, in return for tax advantages, developers of large scale housing projects could contract with the Department of Housing and Urban Development (HUD) to house a specified number of low-income persons who met federal eligibility standards. As of 1989, 48 percent of these subsidized housing units were occupied by older people. As these contracts expire, owners convert their units into market-rate properties, so

it is estimated that as many as 10 percent to 15 percent of the subsidized units have not been available since 1991, resulting in a further shortage of low-cost housing for older persons (National Low Income Housing Information Service, 1990). According to a 1986 report of the National Low Income Housing Coalition, federal housing efforts have fallen far short of meeting elders' housing needs. In 1984 there were 1.1 million older renter households with incomes below the poverty level, and less than 40 percent of them (or 2 percent of all older persons) lived in subsidized housing. The remainder either lived in substandard housing or paid more for housing than they could afford, or both. The coalition estimates that at least 700,000 older persons need housing assistance (U.S. Senate Special Committee on Aging, 1990).

Other policies that indirectly affect older homeowners are property tax relief, energy assistance, and home equity conversion. Energy assistance for low-income homeowners to offset air conditioning and heating costs is provided under the federal government's allocation of block grant money to cities and states. As noted earlier, home equity conversions provide long-term homeowners with some discretionary income.

Most recent federal activity in the housing arena has been to maintain what exists, modifying programs only incrementally to serve larger numbers of older people. The policy focus has been to make better use of existing housing resources through homesharing, accessory apartments, and home equity conversions, rather than to increase the overall housing supply for the aging. Indeed, concern over the growing budget deficit has resulted in reductions in federally subsidized housing. Another major need, especially for low-income older persons, is for more congregate housing services. As described earlier, congregate housing is an important link in the long-term care continuum enabling older people to remain in the community and thereby maintain P-E congruence. The best way to achieve this may be innovations that modify existing communities and neighborhoods to meet the older population's housing needs rather than expensive housing supply programs. (Newcomer, Lawton, and Byerts, 1986).

## ENVIRONMENTAL QUALITY

Regardless of the type of housing in which older persons reside, numerous elements of environmental quality need to be taken into account. These include fire safety, security from crime, accessibility, privacy, territoriality, legibility or negotiability (i.e., the extent to which an environment is easy or difficult to orient oneself to), social activity, and stimulation. We have already reviewed security from crime in relation to specific housing types. In this section, housing characteristics that offer or fail to offer other aspects of environmental quality are discussed.

*Accessibility* refers to the reduction of physical barriers that impede an individual's ability to enter a building and to move from one area of a building or site to another, as well as features that enable the disabled to use buildings. We are all familiar with the international symbol of accessibility that denotes widened parking places, building entrances with ramps, and toilet stalls that are wider than average and include grab bars. These features are important for both younger and older persons who use wheelchairs. Regulations on accessible features in public buildings were established by the federal government in the early 1960s; specific standards for the slopes of ramps, width of doors, and other accessibility codes have been set by the American National Standards Institute (ANSI), and the Americans with Disabilities Act (ADA), passed in 1993.

These standards have made previously inaccessible facilities open to a much broader segment of the population, including older people. Unfortunately, however, many physical and sensory changes experienced by older persons (discussed in previous chapters) have not been considered in establishing federal or state accessibility codes. For example, older persons generally have more difficulty traversing long distances, but many congregate housing projects require long walks from individual units to the dining and recreational facilities. Older people who do not use wheelchairs may nevertheless have difficulty walking up and down stairs due to arthritis or stamina problems, but their homes may require this. Many such people "move" to the main level of their home, so that all their activities can take place on one floor. In an attempt to maximize the use of space, designers of housing and nursing homes often build cabinets and cupboards high above or below the reach of many older persons. This ignores the special problems of many older people with kyphosis or curvature of the spine, and of others whose upward reach has become limited. It also creates serious difficulties for those with arthritis and other motor disorders who cannot bend down to search in floor-level cabinets. Numerous other problems are created by designers who ignore age-related changes in vision, hearing, and tactile sensations. Recommendations for designing environments to counter these problems have been offered in Chapter 6.

*Physical safety* and age-related changes in mobility and sensory functioning are important considerations in the design of facilities for the elderly. Prosthetic aids such as handrails in bathtubs and showers, lift bars adjacent to the toilet, front door access, and reserved parking areas for handicapped persons are essential for maintaining an adequate quality of life for older residents. Good lighting on stairs and at entrances, and non-skid surfaces on steps and bathroom floors are important for preventing accidents. These have all been noted by older persons and designers alike as the most important physical features of housing for the older population (Brennan, Moos, and Lemke, 1988).

*Privacy* is a concept that is often ignored in designing facilities for elders. It is especially lacking in nursing homes, where access to residents' most personal activities (sleeping, dressing, bathing, grooming, and sexual needs) are open even to the passing stranger. The principles of protection of nursing home residents from risks often supersedes the respect for individual privacy. Yet, privacy is a basic need for individuals across the life span, essential for maintaining autonomy, self-reflection, and identity. Institutionalized elders may be even more acutely aware of the need for privacy than older persons who reside in the community and college students. In response to a questionnaire on privacy needs, the latter two groups perceived a need for privacy along two dimensions (physical privacy, connoting physical separation from others, and solitude, the opportunity to reflect and introspect). However, older people in institutions expressed needs for isolation as well; that is, they perceived a need for being physically distant from others and controlling others' access to themselves (Kiyak, 1977). It is important to return to the concept of congruence; for example, a subsequent study revealed that personal needs for privacy vary widely among elders in nursing homes, indicating that the level of physical privacy and solitude provided must be congruent with the older person's individual needs (Kiyak, 1978). Unfortunately, most housing facilities either provide a uniform level of privacy for all residents, or offer greater privacy (e.g., single rooms) only for those who can afford it.

*Territoriality* is a basic human need, in fact one that is shared by most animal species (Ardrey, 1966; Sommer, 1969). Individuals and social groups have a strong need to identify a given space as their own. The more a person loses control over physical space and conditions of life, the greater the need may be to identify available space as one's own. It is not uncommon for people sharing a room (e.g., college roommates, nursing home roommates, or even spouses) to draw an invisible line in the middle of the room; access to the other side must be approved first by the "owner" of that side. Such behavior may include the need to ask the permission of the person who "owns" the room's only window or thermostat for access to it. Older people with dementia in institutions have been found to show less need for identifying spaces and objects as their own after being given private rooms (De-

Long, 1970). Long-term care facilities that encourage older residents to furnish and decorate their rooms as they wish are more likely to reduce residents' territorial needs than those with many built-in features and predecorated units. Unfortunately, there is little research testing the association between levels of privacy and control and the psychological well-being of older persons.

*Legibility* refers to the degree to which an environmental setting facilitates or impairs users' understanding and identification of a place, and the ease with which people can orient themselves in it. A home built on several levels, with a complicated system of hallways and many barriers that interfere with an understanding of the home's layout, may be interesting and challenging, but it has poor legibility and makes it difficult for a newcomer or a confused resident to negotiate the environment. This is a particularly important consideration for facilities that are designed for cognitively impaired older persons. Maps and signs, while useful, cannot make up for a poorly designed home. It is therefore not surprising that, in a survey of 435 older persons living in the community and 44 designers, orientation aids were considered to be important features of housing for elders by more than two-thirds of all respondents (Brennan, Moos, and Lemke, 1988). Items as simple as maps throughout a facility to orient users, color coding, and design features to guide people through the building were perceived to be very important in such facilities.

*Stimulation*, or the ability of a given setting to encourage expression and activity, has long been assumed essential in psychology (Wohlwill, 1966; Pincus, 1968) and is implicit in the competence model. That is, environments with minimal press create a situation of stimulus deprivation and are not beneficial for even the least competent older person. Environments that stimulate the older person's cognitive, physical, and sensory capacities without overwhelming him or her can prevent an undesirable state of apathy. In the study by Kiyak (1978), described earlier, high levels of stimulation in the older person's immediate environment, together with low to moderate levels of stimulation in the larger institutional setting, resulted in greater satisfaction and improved morale. This contrasting need for high stimulation in the immediate environment and low stimulation in the larger environment may be attributable to the greater controllability of the immediate environment, where individuals can reduce the impact of high stimulation, but are helpless to control the larger institutional environment.

## SRO HOUSING

Single Room Occupancy (SRO) hotels in urban centers have traditionally served as minimal housing for the urban poor, particularly the single elderly poor who make up the largest group of SRO residents. Indeed, the typical SRO resident has been characterized as a white older male with 8.7 percent years of education and an income level 20 percent lower than that of his non-SRO peers, who reports multiple chronic conditions, and who has lived in his room (often with incomplete kitchens and with shared bathrooms) for at least five years. Increasing numbers of deinstitutionalized mental hospital patients have become SRO tenants as well (Dear and Wolch, 1987; Haley, Pearson and Hull; Rollinson, 1991). A survey in New York found that because of their longer tenancy, older SRO residents paid less for their SRO unit than did younger tenants, but because of lower income levels, they paid a higher proportion of their income (44 percent) than did younger tenants (25 percent) in the same buildings (Crystal and Beck, 1992). Although overall satisfaction with SRO housing was not high, this survey found that older residents liked the opportunity to have their own room and the physical safety afforded by such a building in an otherwise hostile city core. The lack of services such as congregate meals and counseling was not considered a disadvantage by these elders.

Yet this housing option is rapidly disappearing. For example, 89 percent of SRO units and other lower-price, substandard housing in New York City was lost to development between 1970 and 1983, while San Francisco (which still has proportionately more SRO hotel rooms than any other U.S. city) lost 40 percent of its SRO units between 1975 and 1982 (Ovrebo, Minkler, and Liljestrand, 1991). As the process of "gentrification" of urban cores becomes more popular across the country, and as more and more upper-income people discover the advantages of living downtown, the trend of demolishing SRO hotels and using this valuable land for upscale condominiums and office and retail space will continue. Already we are seeing the result of this—a dramatic increase in the homeless population in urban centers.

## THE PROBLEMS OF HOMELESSNESS

While this chapter has focused on housing and community service options for older people, there is a growing older segment who are homeless, often unable to afford basic housing or unaware of services to which they are entitled. A survey of homeless shelters in eight cities estimated that about 27 percent of their occupants are age 60 and older, but this may actually be an underestimate, since many older homeless persons avoid shelters out of fear both of victimization by younger tenants and institutionalization (Aging Health Policy Center, 1985; Coalition for the Homeless, 1984). In the mid 1960s many homeless elders had recently been released from long-term psychiatric facilities as a result of the 1963 Community Mental Health Act. Today's homeless elders are largely the chronic homeless who have lived on the streets for many years and have lost any contact with their families. As noted above, still others have been displaced from low-cost housing and SRO hotels in central cities as these buildings have been demolished and replaced by expensive new housing and office developments.

Not only do homeless people have no place to live, but they also lack food, clothing, medical care, and a social support system. Such a disorganized lifestyle can magnify the usual age-related declines in biological and psychological processes described in earlier chapters. A life at the edge, in which the individual is constantly trying to fulfill basic human needs (food, shelter, safety from predators), does not leave much energy for these elders to maintain even a modicum of health and well-being, and their problems are compounded by chronic psychiatric disorders, alcoholism, drug abuse, and cognitive impairment (often a result of long-term alcohol abuse). Homeless older persons with chronic health problems often do not have the physical, social, or psychological resources to seek regular medical care for these conditions, or even to follow the necessary medication schedules and dietary restrictions. They obtain most of their health care through the emergency rooms of public hospitals, and even necessary clinical appointments and follow-up visits are not kept (Doolin, 1986; Filardo, 1985). Thus, they often die unnecessarily because of diseases that are neglected and as a result of accidents and victimization in the streets.

In a study of 281 men residing in the Bowery, New York's skid row, researchers were able to assess homeless elders' physical and psychiatric well-being and to compare these findings with a community sample of men in the same age range (Cohen, Teresi, and Holmes, 1988; Cohen et al., 1988). Although the majority had annual incomes far below poverty levels—which should have qualified them for some social service assistance—only 45 percent of the men living in the street and 33 percent living in flophouses or apartments received some form of social service aid. Not surprisingly, physical illness among this population was much higher than among men in the general community, with the most common health problems being respiratory disorders, high blood pressure, dizziness or weakness, edema, and gastrointestinal complaints. The primary source of medical care for these men was local hospitals (73 percent) or clinics (26 percent).

Although 26 percent reported being hospitalized for psychiatric disorders, only 3 percent were currently using medications for these conditions.

This study provides a disturbing portrait of the plight of homeless elders. The prevalence of chronic diseases in this group is higher than for other segments of the older population, yet their access to health services is inadequate and sporadic at best. Health maintenance and maintenance of medication regimens are limited by the unstable nature of their lifestyles and frequent disruptions in psychological well-being. These critical needs for housing, health care, and social services may increase in the next few decades, given growing poverty, chronic mental illness, and homelessness among younger cohorts.

## SUMMARY AND IMPLICATIONS

This chapter presented ways in which environmental factors affect the physical and psychological well-being of older people. Perhaps the most important lesson to be gained from this discussion is that a given environment is not inherently good or bad. Some environments are more conducive to the optimal functioning of *some* older people, while other older people need an entirely different set of features. For example, the older person who has a high need for activity and stimulation, and who has always lived in an urban setting, will be more satisfied with a large nursing home in a metropolitan center than will the individual from a rural community who has always lived in a single-family dwelling. Both Lawton's competence model and Kahana's congruence model point to the necessity of examining each older person's specific needs, preferences, and abilities, and of designing environments that can both meet the needs of this broad cross-section and, more important, flexibly respond to individual differences. To the degree that environmental press can be reduced to accommodate personal abilities and needs, the aging person can function more effectively and maintain his or her level of well-being.

Relocation represents a special case of P-E incongruence that can disturb the well-being of an impaired older person by raising the level of environmental press. Early studies emphasized the high mortality and morbidity associated with relocation of nursing home residents from one facility to another and among older people who recently moved into a nursing home. More recent studies have concluded that health status, degree of environmental change imposed by the move, and disruption of personal support systems moderate the extent of trauma produced by the relocation. Furthermore, researchers who have attempted to increase relocatees' control over and preparation for the move have identified beneficial effects on older people who must move.

There has been some concern with differences in housing quality and services for rural older residents. Although current cohorts are much less likely than previous cohorts to live in farm and nonfarm rural communities, those who do tend to have lower incomes and poorer health, with more limitations in activities of daily living. This is particularly true for African Americans in rural communities. The recognition of these disparities has led to the growth of state and federally funded services for rural elders, but more are needed. Older persons in rural communities appear to have more frequent social interactions with neighbors and friends than do urban elders, but at the same time they need more formal health and social services.

The neighborhood and neighbors play a significant role in the well-being of older people. With retirement and declining health, the older person's physical lifespace becomes more constricted. The neighborhood takes on greater significance as a source of social interactions, health and social services, grocery shopping, banking, and postal services. Those who have good health and high incomes are less limited in their definition of neighborhood or lifespace. Those in public housing and especially in housing for older people are more likely to prefer resources in the immediate vicinity. Older people are generally satisfied with their neighborhoods, even those in poorer areas. This may be due to their sense of environmental competence in these familiar surroundings. Neighbors represent an important component of older people's social and emotional network, especially where family members are not available.

Research on older people's preferences for and ability to function in age-segregated versus age-integrated neighborhoods has yielded mixed results. Although some studies have shown greater preference for and more social interaction in the former, it appears that social class similarity and a feeling of invulnerability to victimization by teenage neighbors can improve interaction levels in age-integrated communities. Both types of community options are important for diverse elders.

Fear of crime among older persons is widespread and is justified on the basis of victimization rates for petty larceny but not violent crimes. Older people experience one-fifth the rates that younger people do for violent crimes, but are more vulnerable to petty larceny than any other age group. The potential danger of injury and long-term disability, as well as the fear of economic loss, may contribute to this incongruence between actual victimization rates and older people's fear of crime.

The high rate of home ownership and long-term residence in their homes makes it difficult for older people to relocate to new housing, even when the new situation represents a significant improvement over the old. The poor condition of many older people's homes and the high costs of renovating and maintaining them sometimes makes relocation necessary, even when the older homeowner is reluctant. Better living conditions and a safer neighborhood in which several other elders reside have been found to improve older people's morale and sense of well-being, especially following a move to a planned housing project from substandard housing. The growth of planned and congregate housing programs for seniors has raised the issue of site selection and service provision. It is especially important when designing housing for low-income older people and for those who do not drive that public transportation be located nearby and that facilities such as medical and social services, banks, and food shopping be within easy access of the housing facility. As people live longer and healthier lives beyond retirement, the need for multilevel housing (providing a range of care options) will continue to grow. Several alternative methods of purchasing such housing are available—some guarantee lifetime care, others do not provide personal and health services. Considering the high likelihood of using a nursing home facility at some time in old age, many retirees prefer to select the more comprehensive options.

The proportion of older people in a nursing home at any one time is very low, but approximately 25 percent will spend some time in such settings, especially during the last year of life. Because of the greater likelihood of physical and cognitive impairments among residents of nursing homes, it is critical to enhance the environmental quality of these facilities either at the design stage or, if the facility has already been built, by modifying features that increase privacy and control and allow for the expression of territoriality and other personal needs. Aging and institutionalization do not reduce the individual's needs for identity and self-expression.

Assisted living is rapidly becoming a cost-effective option for many older people who need help with ADLs but do not necessarily need 24-hour care. Many assisted-living facilities provide greater independence, more options for privacy, and less direct supervision for their older tenants. Funding for such housing is not covered by Medicaid in the great majority of states, making it a viable option only for those elders with adequate personal financial resources.

The problems of homelessness in the United States have affected the older population as well. Many older homeless people have chronic medical, psychiatric, and cognitive disorders that often go unattended because of lack of access to health services. As a result, these homeless elders grow physiologically older more rapidly than do their more stable peers.

## REFERENCES

Aging Health Policy Center. *The homeless mentally ill elderly.* Working paper, University of California at San Francisco, 1985.

Altman, I. *The environment and social behavior.* Monterey, Calif: Brooks Cole, 1975.

American Association of Retired Persons (AARP). *The gadget book: Ingenious devices for easier living.* Washington, D.C., 1987.

American Association of Retired Persons (AARP). *Understanding senior housing.* Washington, D.C.: AARP, 1990.

Ardrey, R. *The territorial imperative.* New York: Atheneum, 1966.

Arling, G., Harkins, E. B., and Romaniuk, M. Adult day care and the nursing home. *Research on Aging,* 1984, 6, 225–242.

Ashley, M. J., Olin, J. S., Le Riche, W. H., Kornaczewski, A., and Rankin, J. G. Skid row alcoholism: A distinct sociomedical entity. *Archives of Internal Medicine,* 1976, 136, 272–278.

Atchley, R. C. *Social forces and aging: An introduction to social gerontology.* Belmont, Calif.: Wadsworth, 1985.

Auerbach, A. J. The elderly in rural areas. In L. H. Ginsberg (Ed.), *Social work in rural communities.* New York: Council on Social Work Education, 1976.

Barker, R. G., Dembo, T., and Lewin, K. Frustration and regression: An experiment with young children. *University of Iowa Studies in Child Welfare,* 1941, 18.

Blau, Z. S. *Aging in a changing society* (2d ed.). New York: New Viewpoints, 1981.

Borup, J. H., Gallego, D. T., and Heffernan, P. G. Relocation and its effect on mortality. *The Gerontologist,* 1979, 19, 135–140.

Bourestom, N., Tars, S., and Pastalan, L. Alterations in life patterns following nursing home relocation. Paper presented at meetings of the Gerontological Society, November 1973. Printed in *The Congressional Record—Senate,* 1974, July, 25697–25699.

Brennan, P. L., Moos, R. H., and Lemke, S. Preferences of older adults and experts for physical and architectural features of group living facilities. *The Gerontologist,* 1988, 28, 84–90.

Brenner, D. A Southwark community alarm partnership scheme. In A. Buter and C. Oldman (Eds.), *Alarm systems for the elderly.* Proceedings of a conference held at the University of Leeds, England, 1981.

Bultena, G. L., Powers, E., Falkman, P., and Frederick, D. *Life after 70 in Iowa.* Sociology Report No. 95. Ames: Iowa State University, 1971.

Carp, F. M. *A future for the aged: The residents of Victoria Plaza.* Austin: University of Texas Press, 1966.

Carp, F. M. Short-term and long-term prediction of adjustment to a new environment. *Journal of Gerontology,* 1974, *29,* 444–453.

Cath, S. H. The institutionalization of a parent: A nadir of life. *Journal of Geriatric Psychology,* 1972, *5,* 25–46.

Chapman, N. J., and Beaudet-Walters, M. Predictors of environmental well-being for older adults. Paper presented at meetings of the Gerontological Society, Dallas, November 1978.

Chevan, A. Homeownership in the older population. *Research on Aging,* 1987, *9,* 226–235.

Coalition for the Homeless. *Crowded Out: Homelessness and the elderly poor in New York City.* New York: Coalition for the Homeless, 1984.

Coffman, T. L. Relocation and survival of institutionalized aged: A re-examination of the evidence. *The Gerontologist,* 1981, *21,* 483–500.

Cohen, M. A., Tell, E. J., Batten, H. L., and Larson, M. J. Attitudes toward continuing care retirement communities. *The Gerontologist,* 1988, *28,* 637–643.

Cohen, C. I., Teresi, J. A., and Holmes, D. The physical well-being of old homeless men. *Journals of Gerontology,* 1988, *43,* S121–S128.

Cohen, C. I., Teresi, J. A., Holmes, D., and Roth, E. Survival strategies of older homeless men. *The Gerontologist,* 1988, *28,* 58–65.

Colerick, E. J., and George, L. K. Predictors of institutionalization among caregivers of patients with Alzheimer's disease. *Journal of the American Geriatrics Society,* 1986, *34,* 493–498.

Crystal, S., and Beck, P. A room of one's own: The SRO and the single elderly. *The Gerontologist,* 1992, *32,* 684–692.

Curry, Z. D. and Shroyer, J. Alternative housing designed for the rural elderly. *The Southwestern,* 1989, *5,* 47–60.

Dear, M. and Wolch, J. *Landscapes of despair: From deinstitutionalization to homelessness.* Princeton, N.J.: Princeton Univ. Press, 1987.

DeLong, A. J. The microspatial structure of the older person. In L. A. Pastalan and D. H. Carson (Eds.), *The spatial behavior of older people.* Ann Arbor: Institute of Gerontology, University of Michigan, 1970.

Dibner, A. S., Lowry, L., and Morris, J. N. Usage and acceptance of an emergency alarm system by the frail elderly. *The Gerontologist,* 1982, *22,* 538–539.

Doolin, J. Planning for the special needs of the homeless elderly. *The Gerontologist,* 1986, *26,* 229–231.

Doty, P. Long-term care in international perspective. *Health Care Financing Review,* 1988, Annual supplement, 145–155.

Duke Center for the Study of Aging and Human Development. *Multidimensional functional assessment: The OARS methodology* (2d ed.). Durham, N.C.: Duke University Center for the Study of Aging and Human Development, 1978.

Ehrlich, P., Ehrlich, I., and Woehlke, P. Congregate housing for the elderly: Thirteen years later. *The Gerontologist,* 1982, *22,* 399–403.

Elmore, E. Consumer fraud and the elderly. In D. Lester (Ed.), *The elderly victim of crime.* Springfield, Ill.: C. C. Thomas, 1981.

Fengler, A. P., Danigelis, N., and Little, V. C. Later life satisfaction and household structure. *Aging and Society,* 1983, *3,* 357–377.

Filardo, T. Chronic disease management in the homeless. In P. W. Brickner, L. K. Scharer, and B. Conanen (Eds.), *Health care of homeless people.* New York: Springer, 1985.

French, M.P.R., Rodgers, W., and Cobb, S. Adjustment as person-environment fit. In D. Coehlo, A. Hamburg, and D. Adams (Eds.), *Coping and adaptation.* New York: Basic Books, 1974.

General Accounting Office. *The well-being of older people in Cleveland, Ohio.* Washington, D.C.: General Accounting Office, 1977.

George, L. The institutionalized. In E. Palmore (Ed.), *Handbook on the aged in the United States.* Westport, Conn.: Greenwood Press, 1984.

Goffman, E. *Asylums.* Garden City, N.Y.: Anchor Books, 1961.

Golant, S. M. The metropolitanization and suburbanization of the U.S. elderly population: 1970–1988. *The Gerontologist,* 1990, *30,* 80–85.

Goldsmith, J., and Tomas, N. E. Crime against the elderly: A continuing national crisis. *Aging,* 1974, No. 236–237, 10–13.

Greene, V. L., and Ondrich, J. I. Risk factors for nursing home admissions and exits. *Journals of Gerontology,* 1990, *45,* S250–S258.

Gubrium, J. *The myth of the golden years: A socio-environmental theory of aging.* Springfield, Ill.: Charles C. Thomas, 1973.

Haley, B. A., Pearson, M., and Hull, D. A. Primary individuals in single room occupancy (SRO) housing in metropolitan areas aged 20 to 61: 1976–1980. Paper presented at meetings of the American Sociological Association, San Francisco, August 1982.

Harris, L. *Aging in the eighties: America in transition.* Washington, D.C.: National Council on the Aging, 1981.

Henretta, J. C. Retirement and residential moves by elderly households. *Research on Aging,* 1986, 8, 23–37.

Hing, E. Use of nursing homes by the elderly: Preliminary data from the 1985 National Nursing Home Survey *(Advance data from Vital and Health Statistics,* No. 135, DHHS Pub. No. PHS 87-1250). Hyattsville, Md.: U.S. Public Health Service, 1987.

Hinrichson, G. The impact of age-concentrated, publicly assisted housing on older people's social and emotional well-being. *Journal of Gerontology,* 1985, 40, 758–760.

Hochschild, A. L. *The unexpected community.* Englewood Cliffs, N.J.: Prentice-Hall, 1973.

Hochstedler, E. *Crime against the elderly in 26 cities.* Washington, D.C.: Bureau of Justice Statistics, 1981.

Holland, J. L. Creative and academic performance among talented adolescents. *Journal of Educational Psychology,* 1961, 52, 136–147.

House Select Committee on Aging, U.S. Congress. *In search of security: A national perspective on elderly crime victimization.* Washington, D.C.: U.S. Government Printing Office, 1977.

Hull, J. D. Insurance for the twilight years. *Time,* April 6, 1987, 53.

Hynson, L. M. Rural-urban differences in satisfaction among the elderly. *Rural Sociology,* 1975, 40, 64–66.

Jacobs, B., and Weissert, W. Using home equity to finance long-term care. *Journal of Health Politics, Policy and Law,* 1987, 12, 77–94.

Kahana, E. *Matching environments to needs of the aged.* Final Progress Report submitted to NICHD, Fall, 1973. 1R01 HD 03850.

Kahana, E. F. A congruence model of person-environment interaction. In M. P. Lawton (Ed.), *Theory development in environments and aging.* New York: Wiley, 1975.

Kahana, E. F., Liang, J., and Felton, B. Alternative models of P-E fit: Prediction of morale in three homes for the aged. *Journal of Gerontology,* 1980, 35, 584–595.

Kane, R., and Kane, R. Health care for older people: Organizational and policy issues. In R. Binstock and L. George (Eds.), *Handbook of aging and the social sciences.* (3d ed.) New York: Academic Press, 1990, 415–438.

Kane, R. A., and Wilson, K. B. *Assisted living in the United States: A new paradigm for residential care for frail older persons?* Washington D.C.: AARP, 1993.

Kart, C. S. Community-based, noninstitutional long-term care service utilization by aged Blacks: Facts and issues. In C. M. Barresi and D. E. Stull (Eds.), *Ethnic elderly and long-term care.* New York: Springer, 1993.

Kasper, J. *Aging alone: Profiles and projections.* Baltimore: The Commonwealth Fund Commission, 1988.

Kastenbaum, R., and Candy, S. The 4% fallacy. *International Journal of Aging and Human Development,* 1973, 4, 15–21.

Killian, E. C. Effect of geriatric transfers on mortality rates. *Social Work,* 1970, 15, 19–26.

Kiyak, H. A. Person-environment congruence models as determinants of environmental satisfaction and well-being. Unpublished doctoral dissertation. Wayne, Ind.: Wayne State University, 1977.

Kiyak, H. A. A multidimensional perspective on privacy preferences of institutionalized elderly. In W. E. Rogers and W. H. Ittelson (Eds.), *New directions in environmental design research.* Tempe: University of Arizona Press, 1978.

Kraus, A. S., Spasoff, R. A., Beattie, E. J., Holden, D. E. W., Lawson, J. S., Rodenburg, M., and Woodcock, G. M. Elderly application process: Placement and care needs. *Journal of the American Geriatrics Society,* 1976, 24, 165–172.

Kutza, E. *The benefits of old age: Social welfare policy for the elderly.* Chicago: University of Chicago Press, 1981.

Lawton, M. P. Competence, environmental press, and the adaptation of older people. In P. G. Windley and G. Ernst (Eds.), *Theory development in environment and aging.* Washington, D.C.: Gerontological Society, 1975.

Lawton, M. P. *Environment and aging.* Monterey, Calif: Brooks Cole, 1980.

Lawton, M. P. Crime, victimization, and the fortitude of the aged. *Aged Care and Services Review.* 1980–1981, 2, 1–31.

Lawton, M. P., and Cohen, J. The generality of housing impact on the well-being of older people. *Journal of Gerontology*, 1974, *29*, 194–204.

Lawton, M. P., and Hoover, S. L. *Housing and neighborhood: Objective and subjective quality*. Philadelphia: Philadelphia Geriatric Center, 1979.

Lawton, M. P., Kleban, M., and Carlson, D. The inner city resident: To move or not to move. *The Gerontologist*, 1973, *13*, 443–448.

Lawton, M. P., Moss, M., and Grimes, M. The changing service needs of older tenants in planned housing. *The Gerontologist*, 1985, *25*, 258–264.

Lawton, M. P., and Nahemow, L. Ecology and the aging process. In C. Eisdorfer and M. P. Lawton (Eds.), *Psychology of adult development and aging*. Washington, D.C.: American Psychological Association, 1973.

Lawton, M. P., and Nahemow, L. *Cost, structure and social aspects of housing for the aged*. Final report to the Administration on Aging. Philadelphia: Philadelphia Geriatric Center, 1975.

Lawton, M. P., Nahemow, L., and Teaff, J. Housing characteristics and the well-being of elderly tenants in federally assisted housing. *Journal of Gerontology*, 1975, *30*, 601–607.

Lewin, K. *Dynamic theory of personality*. New York: McGraw-Hill, 1935.

Lewin, K. *Field theory in social science*. New York: Harper and Row, 1951.

Lewin, K., Lippitt, R., and White, R. Patterns of aggressive behavior in experimentally created social climates. *Journal of Social Psychology*, 1939, *10*, 271–299.

Lichter, D. T. Race, employment hardship, and inequality in the American nonmetropolitan South. *American Sociological Review*, 1989, *54*, 436–446.

Lieberman, M. A. Relationship of mortality rates to entrance to a home for the aged. *Geriatrics*, 1961, *16*, 515–519.

Lieberman, M. A. Relocation research and social policy. *The Gerontologist*, 1974, *14*, 494–501.

Lieberman, M. A., and Tobin, S. *The experience of old age: Stress, coping and survival*. New York: Basic Books, 1983.

Linquist, J. H., and Duke, J. M. The elderly victim at risk. *Criminology*, 1982, *20*, 1–10.

Logan, J. R. The graying of the suburbs, *Aging*, 1983, *345*, 4–8.

Logan, J. R., and Spitze, G. Suburbanization and public services for the aging. *The Gerontologist*, 1988, *28*, 644–647.

Longino, C. F., Biggar, J. C., Flynn, C. B., and Wiseman, R. F. The retirement migration project. Final Report to the National Institute on Aging, University of Miami, 1984.

Longino, C., and Lipman, C. Married and spouseless men and women in planned retirement communities: Support network differential. *Journal of Marriage and the Family*, 1981, *43*, 169–177.

Lozier, J., and Althouse, R. Social enforcement of behavior toward elders in an Appalachian mountain settlement. *The Gerontologist*, 1974, *14*, 69–80.

Malinchak, A. A., and Wright, D. Older Americans and crime: The scope of elderly victimization, *Aging*, 1978, *281*, 10–16.

Manton, K. G., Corder, L. S., and Stallard, E. Estimates of change in chronic disability and institutional incidence and prevalence rates in the U.S. Elderly population from the 1982, 1984, and 1989 National Long-Term Care Survey. *Journals of Gerontology*, 1993, *48*, S153–S166.

Marlowe, R. E. When they closed the doors at Modesto. Paper presented at NIMH conference on closure of state hospitals, Scottsdale, Arizona, February 1974.

McConnell, C. E. A note on the lifetime work of nursing home residency. *The Gerontologist*, 1984, *24*, 193–198.

McLaughlin, D. K., and Jensen, l. Poverty among older Americans: The plight of nonmetropolitan elders. *Journals of Gerontology*, 1993, S44–S54.

Merry, S. The management of danger in a high crime urban neighborhood. Paper presented at meetings of the American Anthropological Association, Washington, D.C., 1976.

Mirotznik, J., and Ruskin, A. P. Inter-institutional relocation and its effects on psychosocial status. *The Gerontologist*, 1985, *25*, 265–270.

Morycz, R. Caregiving strain and the desire to institutionalize family members with Alzheimer's disease. *Research on Aging*, 1985, *7*, 329–361.

Murray, H. A. *Explorations in personality*. New York: Oxford University Press, 1938.

National Center for Health Statistics (NCHS). Use of nursing homes by the elderly: Preliminary data from the 1985 National Nursing Home Survey. *Vital and Health Statistics*, No. 134. Washington,

D.C.: DHHS, U.S. Public Health Service, May 1987.

National Center for Health Statistics (NCHS). The national nursing home survey 1985: Summary for the United States. *Vital and Health Statistics,* Ser. 13, No. 97. Washington, D. C.: DHHS, U.S. Public Health Service, 1989.

National Low Income Housing Information Service. *The fiscal year 1991 budget and low income housing* (SM-290). Washington, D.C.: National Low Income Housing Information Service, 1990.

Neugarten, B. L., Havighurst, R. J., and Tobin, S. S. The measurement of life satisfaction. *Journal of Gerontology,* 1961, *16,* 134–143.

Newcomer, R. J. An evaluation of neighborhood service convenience for elderly housing project residents. In P. Suedfeld and J. A. Russell (Eds.), *The behavioral basis of design* (Vol. 1). Stroudsburg, Penn.: Dowden, Hutchinson and Ross, 1976.

Newcomer, R. J., Lawton, M. P., and Byerts, T. O. *Housing an aging society.* New York: Van Nostrand Reinhold, 1986.

Newman, 0. *Defensible space.* New York: Macmillan, 1972.

O'Keefe, G. J., and Reid-Nash, K. Fear of crime and crime prevention competence among the elderly. Paper presented at meetings of the American Psychological Association, Los Angeles, 1985.

Ovrebo, B., Minkler, M., and Liljestrand, P. No room in the inn: The disappearance of SRO housing in the United States. In S. Keigher (Ed.), *Housing risks and homelessness among the urban elderly.* Chicago: Haworth Press, 1991, p. 77–92.

Pawlson, L. G. Financing long-term care: The growing dilemma. *Journal of the American Geriatrics Society,* 1989, *37,* 631–638.

Pihlblad, C. T., and Rosencranz, H. A. *Social adjustment of older people in the small town.* Columbia: University of Missouri Department of Sociology, 1969.

Pincus, A. The definition and measurement of the institutional environment in homes for the aged. *The Gerontologist,* 1968, *8,* 207–210.

Poulin, J. E. Age segregation and the interpersonal involvement and morale of the aged. *The Gerontologist,* 1984, *24,* 266–269.

Pynoos, J. Elderly housing politics and policy. *Generations,* 1984, *9,* 26–31.

Redfoot, D., and Gaberlavage, G. Housing for older Americans: Sustaining the dream. *Generations,* 1991, *15,* 35–38.

Regnier, V. *Assisted living housing for the elderly.* New York: Van Nostrand Reinhold, 1994.

Regnier, V. A. Neighborhoods as service systems. In M. P. Lawton, R. J. Newcomer, and T. O. Byerts (Eds.), *Planning for an aging society.* Stroudsburg, Penn.: Dowden, Hutchinson and Ross, 1976.

Regnier, V. A., Eribes, R. A., and Hansen, W. Cognitive mapping as a concept for establishing neighborhood service delivery locations for older people. Paper presented at the Association for Computing Machinery symposium, New York City, 1973.

Reschovksy, J. D., and Newman, S. J. Adaptations for independent living by older frail households. *The Gerontologist,* 1990, *30,* 543–552.

Rivlin, A. M., and Wiener, J. M. *Caring for the disabled elderly: Who will pay?* Washington, D.C.: The Brookings Institute, 1988.

Rollinson, P. A. Elderly single room occupancy (SRO) hotel tenants: Still alone. *Social Work,* 1991, *36,* 303–308.

Rosenberg, G. S. *The worker grows old.* San Francisco: Jossey-Bass, 1970.

Rosenwaike, I. A demographic portrait of the oldest old. *Milbank Memorial Fund Quarterly/Health and Society,* 1985, *63,* 187–205.

Rubenstein, J. Housing policy issues in three European countries. Paper presented at meetings of the Gerontological Society of America, Washington, D.C., 1979.

Russell, C. The elderly: Myths and facts. *American Demographics,* 1980, *2,* 30–31.

Sauer, W. J., Shehan, C., and Boymel, C. Rural-urban differences in satisfaction among the elderly: A reconsideration. *Rural Sociology,* 1976, *41,* 269–275.

Schulz, R., and Brenner, G. F. Relocation of the aged: A review and theoretical analysis. *Journal of Gerontology,* 1977, *32,* 323–333.

Seligman, M.E.P. *Helplessness: On depression, development and death.* San Francisco: W. H. Freeman, 1975.

Shapiro, E., and Tate, R. Who is really at risk of institutionalization? *The Gerontologist,* 1988, *28,* 237–245.

Sheehan, N. W. Informal support among the elderly in public senior housing. *The Gerontologist,* 1986, *26,* 171–175.

Sherwood, S., Greer, D. S., Morris, J. N., and Sherwood, C. C. *The Highland Heights experiment.*

Washington, D.C.: U.S. Department of Housing and Urban Development, 1972.

Sherwood, S., and Morris, J. N. *A study of the effects of an emergency alarm and response system for the aged: Final report.* Grant No. HS01788, NCHSR, 1981.

Skogan, W. G., and Maxfield, M. E. *Coping with crime.* Beverly Hills: Sage, 1981.

Smith-Sloan, K. Home equity conversion: A promising alternative. *The Southwestern,* 1989, *5,* 31–36.

Sommer, R. *Personal space.* New York: Prentice-Hall, 1969.

Stephens, M., and Bernstein, M. Social support and well-being among residents of planned housing. *The Gerontologist,* 1984, *24,* 144–148.

Stern, G. Student ecology and the college environment. *Journal of Medical Education,* 1965, *40,* 132–154.

Struyk, R. J. The housing situation of elderly Americans. *The Gerontologist,* 1977, *17,* 130–139.

Taeuber, C. M. *Sixty-five plus in America.* U.S. Bureau of the Census, Current Population Reports, P23-178. Washington, D.C.: U.S. Government Printing Office, 1992.

Teaff, J. D., Lawton, M. P., and Carlson, D. Impact of age integration of public housing projects upon elderly tenant well-being. Paper presented at meetings of the Gerontological Society, Washington, D.C., November 1973.

Tell, E. J., Cohen, M. A., Larson, M. J., and Batten, H. L. Assessing the elderly's preferences for life-care retirement options. *The Gerontologist,* 1985, *27,* 503–509.

U.S. Bureau of the Census. Geographic mobility: March 1986 to March 1987. Current Population Reports, Series P-20, No. 430. U.S. Government Printing Office, 1989.

U.S. Bureau of the Census. Housing of the elderly. *Current Housing Reports,* Series H-121, Washington, D.C.: U.S. Government Printing Office, 1991a.

U.S. Bureau of the Census, *Statistical Abstract of the United States, 1990.,* 110th ed. Washington D.C.: U.S. Government Printing Office, 1991b.

U.S. Bureau of the Census. *1990 Census of population and housing,* Summary Tape File 1A. Washington, D.C.: U.S. Government Printing Office 1990.

U.S. Bureau of the Census. Households, families, marital status and living arrangements: March 1988. *Current Population Reports,* Series P-20, No. 432, Advance Report, Sept. 1988.

U.S. Bureau of the Census. State population estimates, by age and components of change: 1980–1984. *Current Population Reports,* Series P-25, No. 970. Washington, D. C.: U.S. Department of Commerce, 1984.

U.S. Bureau of the Census. Population profile of the United States: 1987. *Current Population Reports,* Series P–23, No. 159. Washington, D.C.: U.S. Department of Commerce, 1989.

U.S. Department of Justice. Crime and the elderly. *Special Report, Bureau of Justice Statistics Bulletin.* Washington, D.C.: U.S. Government Printing Office, December, 1981.

U.S. Department of Justice. *Criminal victimization in the United States: 1985.* National Crime Survey (NCJ 194278). Washington, D.C.: U.S. Government Printing Office, 1987.

U.S. Senate Special Committee on Aging. *Aging America: Trends and Projections,* Washington, D.C.: U.S. Government Printing Office, 1992.

U.S. Senate Special Committee on Aging. *Developments in Aging: 1989 (Vol. I).* Washington, D.C.: U.S. Government Printing Office, 1990.

Wiener, J. M., Illston, L. H., and Hanley, R. J. *Sharing the burden: Strategies for public and private long-term care insurance.* Brookings Institute: Washington, D.C., 1994.

Wittels, I., and Botwinick, J. Survival in relocation. *Journal of Gerontology,* 1974, *36,* 440–443.

Wohlwill, J. The physical environment: A problem for a psychology of stimulation. *Journal of Social Issues,* 1966, *22,* 29–38.

Yin, P. P. Fear of crime among the elderly: Some issues and suggestions. *Social Problems,* 1980, *27,* 492–504.

Zevitz, R. G., and Gurnack, A. M. Factors related to elderly crime victims' satisfaction with police service. *The Gerontologist,* 1991, *31,* 92–101.

# CHAPTER 14

# ECONOMIC STATUS, WORK, AND RETIREMENT

Economic status has a powerful effect on many aspects of older people's lives—their health, social relationships, living arrangements, community activities, and political participation. Patterns of employment, retirement, and income are major components of the larger environment that shape older people's daily opportunities and competence in numerous ways. Although economic resources in themselves do not guarantee satisfaction, they do determine many of the options available to older people to lead satisfying lives.

Economic status in old age is largely influenced by environmental conditions, especially past and current employment patterns and resultant retirement benefits. For many people, economic status is consistent across the life course. For example, ethnic minorities in low-paying jobs in young and middle adulthood generally face a continuation of poverty in old age. Other older people, including widowed or divorced women who depended on their husbands' income, or retirees with only Social Security as income, may face poverty or near-poverty for the first time in their lives. Alternatively, those in higher-paying careers with private pensions and assets continue to enjoy economic advantages in old age.

This chapter begins by reviewing the employment status of the older population and then focuses on retirement, both as a social institution and a social process. Since one of the primary consequences of retirement is reduced income, we conclude by examining the extent of poverty and near-poverty among the older population.

## EMPLOYMENT STATUS

Work and work-related values influence the life course in many ways. Men in particular, but increasingly women among younger cohorts, develop age-related expectations about the rhythm of their careers—when to start working, when to be at the peak of their careers, and when to retire; and they assess whether they are "on time" according to these socially defined schedules. In American society, the value placed on work and productivity also shapes how individuals approach employment and retirement. The current cohort of older people, in particular, was socialized to a traditional view of hard work, job loyalty, and occupational stability.

However, current demographic trends and social policies are having an impact on these values and expectations. Changing work patterns and increased longevity mean that both men and women are spending more years in employment and enjoying a longer retirement. As men live longer, a smaller proportion of their lifetime is devoted to paid employment, even though the number of years they work is longer. For example, a man born in 1900 could expect to live about 47 years. He would work for 32 years (70 percent of his lifetime) and be retired for about one year (2 percent of his lifetime). In contrast, a man born today can anticipate living about 75 years, working for about 55 percent of his life, and being retired for over 26 percent. Women, too, are living longer past the age of retirement and are devoting a smaller portion of their lives to childbearing and rearing. A woman born in 1900 could expect that 6 years of her 48-year life span (or 12 percent) would be spent in the labor force, whereas the comparable figure for a woman born in 1987 is nearly 40 percent of her 78-year lifespan (U.S. Senate Special Committee on Aging, 1992).

Before we begin our discussion of paid work, it is important to recognize that there are a variety of ways in which older people can be productive, without being employed. A definition of productivity that is broader than paid work includes any activity that produces goods and services, including housework, child care, volunteer work, and help to family and friends (Caro, Bass, and Chen, 1993; Herzog et al., 1989, S130). Participation in such activities, many of which are discretionary rather than obligatory, has been found to be related to physical and psychological health and well-being and is contrary to the common image of retirement as a "nonproductive" period of life. Instead, consistent with the person-environment framework that undergirds this book, productive older people appear to choose and adjust their behavior and aspirations in order to maintain a sense of competence in a changing environment (Herzog and House, 1991).

## What Kinds of Jobs Do Older Workers Hold?

Among those over age 65, only 16.4 percent of men and 8.7 percent of women are in the labor force (Parnes and Sommers, 1994). As illustrated in Figure 14-1, these percentages represent a decline

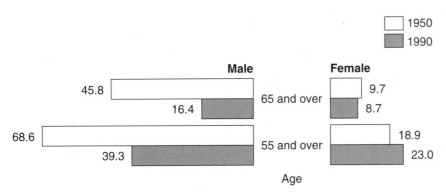

**FIGURE 14–1 Percentage of Civilian Noninstitutional Population in the Labor Force, by Age and Sex: 1950 and 1990**
SOURCE: U.S. Bureau of Labor Statistics. Data for 1990, Employment and Earnings, Vol. 38. No. 1, January 1991, Table 3; data for 1950, unpublished tabulations from 1950 Current Population Survey, available from the Bureau of Labor Statistics.

from 1950, when nearly 46 percent of older men and 10 percent of older women were employed, and a shift from "near-universal" work for older people to near-universal retirement (Quinn and Burkhauser, 1993). This phenomenon of low employment is described as the "graying of America's population, but not of its work force" (McConnell, 1983, p. 347). Older workers, who comprise less than 3 percent of the total labor force, are concentrated in jobs that initially require considerable education and a long training process (e.g., managerial and professional positions or self-employment) or those with flexible retirement policies (U.S. Senate Special Committee on Aging, 1992). Compared with their younger counterparts, older workers are less likely to be in jobs that are physically demanding, low or entry level, or high-tech. This shift from physically demanding or hazardous jobs to those in which skills or knowledge are the important requirements may increase the potential for older workers to remain in the labor force longer.

Although the trend toward early retirement from full-time employment has increased, part-time work among older people, especially among women, has expanded to over 50 percent of retired workers. In fact, part-time work is perceived by the working public of all ages as a desirable alternative, especially when a flexible work schedule is combined with the ability to draw partial pensions and therefore allows gradual retirement (Burkhauser and Quinn, 1989; AARP, 1991; Quinn and Burkhauser, 1993). Most older workers would like to retire gradually, with periods of part-time work before complete retirement. Among those employed, 21 percent of men and 54 percent of women wanted to be working part-time. Accordingly, 10 percent of men and 13 percent of women indicate that they expect to stop working earlier than they want, and would prefer to work another three to five years (Quinn and Burkhauser, 1993). More than 50 percent of all workers age 50 to 64 would continue working, typically on a part-time basis, if their employer were willing to retrain them for a new job, to continue making pension contributions after age 65, or to transfer them to a job with less responsibility, fewer hours and less pay as a transition to full retirement (Quinn and Burkhauser, 1993; Commonwealth Fund, 1993; National Institute on Aging, 1993). Although the number of older people working part-time is smaller than the number who report they would like to do so, the proportion of workers on part-time schedules does increase with age, as illustrated in Table 14-1. Similarly, more older

**Table 14–1  Persons 45 Years and Over on Part– and Full–Time Work Schedules***
**(Percent Distribution)**

| Sex and Age | 1960 | | 1970 | | 1982 | | 1989 | |
|---|---|---|---|---|---|---|---|---|
| | Full Time | Part Time | Full Time | Part Time | Full Time | Part Time | Full Time | Part Time |
| Males: | | | | | | | | |
| 45 to 64 | 94 | 6 | 96 | 4 | 93 | 7 | 93 | 7 |
| 65 plus | 70 | 30 | 62 | 38 | 52 | 48 | 52 | 48 |
| Females: | | | | | | | | |
| 45 to 64 | 78 | 22 | 77 | 23 | 76 | 27 | 75 | 24 |
| 65 plus | 57 | 43 | 51 | 49 | 40 | 60 | 39 | 59 |

SOURCE: U.S. Department of Labor, Bureau of Labor Statistics, *Employment and Earnings,* 37, 1990.

*Figures may not total 100 percent due to rounding.

Some older people continue to work full or part time.

workers (25 percent) are self-employed compared to younger workers (8 percent) (AARP, 1991). The growth in part-time workers therefore does not fit the stereotypical pattern of retirement from full-time work to full-time leisure. Depending upon one's definition of career, 25 to 50 percent of all Americans, especially those who are self-employed, remain in the labor force after they leave their career job.

## Unemployment among Older People

The number of older workers who experience unemployment has been rising as a result of plant closures, downswings, and restructuring. Even though the unemployment rate (approximately 3 percent) is lower among older workers compared to younger workers, they stay out of work longer than younger workers, suffer a greater loss of earnings in subsequent jobs, and are more likely to become discouraged and stop looking for work. For those needing to work for economic reasons or wanting to stay active, unemployment has been found to be associated with dissatisfaction with their lives (Commonwealth Fund, 1993; Quinn and Burkhauser, 1993). Those who do find jobs often experience downward mobil-

ity to low pay, temporary or part-time work with fewer benefits.

Unemployed older workers have a difficult time with their job search for a number of reasons. They may have been in one occupation for many years and therefore lack experience in job-hunting techniques. In addition, they are more vulnerable to skill obsolescence with changes in the economy, including the shift away from product manufacturing and medium-wage jobs in manufacturing toward low-wage positions in the service industries and high-wage services in high-tech fields (Hall and Mirvis, 1993; Mor-Barak and Tynan, 1993; National Academy on Aging, 1994) To prepare older workers for the rapidly changing workplace, a growing number of cities and corporations are forming job referral and training services, including the Experience Plus Program that provides training in computer processing, the retired Senior Executives Program and counseling services through the American Association of Retired Persons.

Although more older Americans are retiring at increasingly younger ages, many older workers feel forced out of their jobs because of technological and workplace changes, and have difficulty finding other work with comparable wages and salaries. Up to 12 percent of older Americans not currently working report that they are willing and able to work, but cannot find a job. Two factors may partially explain why, despite a growing number of early retirements, more older people, especially among the young-old, are seeking employment.

One factor is that many people choose to retire and then find it harder to live on their retirement income than they had anticipated (Calasanti and Borianno, 1993). In fact, some studies have found that over 52 percent of retired workers return to work within four years, largely for economic reasons, moving back and forth from full or partial retirement into non-retirement, accepting jobs at substantially lower pay in order to get by financially (Butler, Anderson, and Burkhauser, 1989; Myers 1991; Quinn and Burkhauser, 1993). Others are forced out of work because of company closures, mergers or reorganization. For example, of the 9.5 million workers displaced between 1986 and 1987, 24 percent were age 55 or older (Markey and Parks, 1989). In the past decade, more employers have tried to reduce the costs of wages and employee benefits and to create labor force structures that can be readily altered at management discretion. This has also resulted in the growth of a contingent or temporary work force, even for highly skilled professional positions, which allows firms flexibility, but does not provide security and benefits based on workers' seniority or skills (National Academy on Aging, 1994). Workers displaced by these market changes may be too old to have good job prospects, but nevertheless need to work to make ends meet.

Others want to continue working after retirement in order to feel productive and share expertise. While 37 percent of respondents in a 1992 Harris Survey cited financial need as the most important reason for seeking employment, an additional 21 percent were bored with retirement, and 14 percent wanted to do something useful but could not find suitable jobs (Taylor and Bass, 1992). In such instances, retirees are often more willing to work in lower status positions (Achenbaum and Morrison, 1993). Continued employment into old age has been found to be associated with higher morale, happiness, adjustment and longevity, in part because of the friendship networks with coworkers (Mor-Barak and Tynan 1993; Mor-Barak, Scharlach, Birba, and Sokolar, 1992) For some older people, a job can be a new career, a continuation of earlier work, or a way to learn new skills and form friendships.

## BARRIERS TO EMPLOYMENT

The extent to which declining labor force participation by older people reflects age-based employment discrimination is a topic of considerable debate. The American public has been nearly unanimous in opposing mandatory retirement policies as discriminatory. The Age Discrimination in Employment Act (ADEA) was passed in 1967 to protect workers age 45 and over from denial of employment strictly because of age, to eliminate obstacles to prolonged employment, and thus to allow a later retirement age. This act was amended in 1978 to prohibit the use of pension plans as justification for not hiring older workers and to raise the mandatory retirement age to 70. In 1986, mandatory retirement was eliminated for businesses with more than 20 employees. (State and local public safety officers and tenured college faculty were exempt from the new provisions until 1994.) Despite such legislation, age discrimination alleged as the basis for loss of employment is the fastest growing form of unfair dismissal litigation.

The Americans with Disabilities Act, passed in 1990, also offers protection to older adults. Employers are expected to make work-related adjustments and job redesign for workers with disabilities, including impairments in sensory, manual or speaking skills. Although the most blatant forms of age discrimination, such as newspaper ads restricting jobs to younger people, have declined since the passage of the ADEA, more subtle forms persist, such as norms of attractiveness in dress and hairstyle. Employers can make a job situation undesirable to older workers by stopping raises and promotions and removing responsibilities to downgrade workers' jobs. Perceptions that most employers discriminate against older people remain widespread despite antidiscrimination legislation, and can make it difficult for older people to find employment.

One reason that discrimination persists is the pervasiveness of negative stereotypes about aging and productivity, as described in Chapter 1. Many employers still assume that older workers will not perform as well as younger workers because of poor health, declining energy, diminished intellectual ability, or different work styles (Stern and McDaniel, 1994). Employers express concerns about older workers in terms of cost effectiveness, given their proximity to retirement;

---

## BARRIERS TO EMPLOYMENT

Mr. Lewis is a 60-year-old with no car, no savings, and no relatives nearby. He works two part-time jobs and finds it difficult to make ends meet. One of his jobs is under a government program with a local agency that signed an agreement to hire him full-time when an opening arose. That was over 2 years ago. In that time, they have hired 15 to 20 people without experience or training in the field to do the job he would like. They are all people under age 40. Mr. Lewis has a background of 20 years in large organizations, so he assumes that he has the appropriate experience.

At first, Mr. Lewis was told he had to "go through the system" to be hired full-time. Much later, after he had been through the system time and time again, it became obvious he would never be hired full-time. Eventually, he was told that "the agency feels it wants to give younger employees a chance to come up the career ladder." He is resentful at seeing these younger workers move ahead so quickly. He is beginning to wonder if he is a victim of age discrimination, but he does not know what he can do about his situation.

---

their flexibility with the changing workplace; their comfort with new technology; and their suitability for training (American Association of Retired Persons, 1989; Barth et al., 1993; Rix, 1994; Straka, 1992). These attitudes endure despite the growth of research findings that older workers are characterized by lower turnover, incidence of voluntary absenteeism, and rate of injuries (Sterns and McDaniel, 1994; Commonwealth Fund, 1993). In fact, in spite of their concerns, most employers rate older workers highly on loyalty, dependability, emotional stability, and ability to get along with coworkers (Barth et al., 1993). Another major institutional barrier is rising health care costs, since it is estimated that older workers cost 15 percent more to insure than younger employees (Quinn and Burkhauser, 1993). A few companies have made innovative use of retirees, such as the Travelers Insurance Company's hiring of temporary workers and Days Inn's employment of older workers in national reservation centers, where they effectively utilize modern technical equipment. However, these are isolated instances, and relatively few companies have implemented skills training programs or educated managers about ways to involve older workers, even though labor market productivity has been found to decline little as workers age. This means that the resources and expertise of older workers are not being fully uti-

lized, a pattern which will need to change in the future with the aging of the "baby boomers."

In addition to these barriers to employment generally, numerous obstacles exist to part-time employment. Even when an older person indicates an interest in working part-time, he or she may not be able to find such employment at the same wage level that full-time work offers, although an increasing number of older workers indicate that they are willing to move into new industries and occupations, work fewer hours, and take pay cuts (Quinn and Burkhauser, 1993). The greatest obstacles are employer policies against part-time workers' drawing partial pensions (e.g., defined benefit pension plans do not permit a worker to stay on the job and collect a pension) and Social Security limits on the amount that can be earned at a given age before full benefits are reduced (Social Security benefits are currently reduced $1.00 for every $3.00 earned above a fixed minimum of $11,104 for workers age 65–69). Employers may resist the additional administrative work and health insurance costs entailed in hiring part-time or temporary older workers, but this may be tempered by the advantage of fewer employer-paid benefits for dependents among older workers. The obstacles to part-time employment are not insurmountable, however. For example, some countries, such as Sweden, allow part-time employees to receive reduced pensions and to adjust their working time gradually, at their own pace.

## CREATING NEW OPPORTUNITIES FOR WORK

Findings about older workers' job performance have been cited by advocacy organizations for older people, such as the Gray Panthers, in their arguments for policies to extend the period of labor force participation. These groups maintain that judging a person's job qualifications solely on the basis of age, without regard to suitability for a job, is inequitable, and that chronological age alone is a poor predictor of job performance. Not hiring older workers deprives society of their skills and capacities. In most cases, work environments may be modified and technical training provided to compensate for any drawbacks associated with older workers, if employers are willing to do so.

Many ways have been suggested to restructure work to enable older people to have the option of longer work lives. These include:

1. Changes in federal policy, such as modifying Social Security and pension restrictions against earnings and giving tax credits or other tax incentives to employers who hire older workers
2. Programs to link older adults and potential employees with job referrals, training and counseling
3. Programs to accommodate the older workers' needs in the job environment, such as part-time work, job sharing, flex time, and incremental retirement though reduced work weeks or "gliding out" plans of staged retirement that permit a gradual shift to a part-time schedule (Mor-Barak and Tynan, 1993).

However, most businesses have not made changes in the work environment to support such options for older workers. In the Labor Force 2000 Survey, only 35 percent of the participating firms offer opportunities to transfer to jobs with reduced pay and responsibility and only 21 percent a program of phased retirement through a gradual decrease in hours worked (The Commonwealth Fund, 1993). Similarly, only about 4 percent of U.S. corporations provide retraining programs as incentives for older workers to return to active labor force participation while 62 percent encourage early retirement through inducement programs (Ramirez, 1989). Another institutional barrier is that only a few programs, such as the federal Senior Community Service Employment, specifically target low-income elderly through retraining and subsidized employment. To address potential labor shortages in the future, changes in government and corporate policies are needed both to extend employment opportunities for older workers and to modify the financial incentives for work via changes in Social Security and pensions.

The need for new opportunities for older workers will increase early in the 21st century, when a majority of the older population is likely to seek employment, a trend counter to the current situation where most older adults are retired. Reasons for this shift include a decreasing pool of younger workers, a healthier and better educated cohort of older persons who are oriented toward lifelong careers, economic expectations to continue a similar lifestyle, and increasingly expensive health and long-term care (Mor-Barak et al., 1992; Parnes and Sommers, 1994). Already, older people are moving into jobs traditionally filled by youth (e.g., providing service at fast food restaurants), in part because of the decline among young people willing to work in such positions. Opportunities in higher paying positions must also be created for older workers, particularly for aging "baby boomers" accustomed to challenging jobs.

## RETIREMENT

With increased longevity and changing work patterns, retirement has become as much an expected part of the life course as having a family, completing school, or working. This is a relatively recent phenomenon in Western society, however. Retirement developed as a twentieth-century social institution, along with industrialization, surplus labor, and a rising standard of living. Social Security legislation, passed in 1935, established the right to financial protection in old age and thus served to institutionalize retirement. Based on income deferred during the worker's years of employment, Social Security was viewed as a reward for past economic contributions to society, which entitled the worker to a share of the country's wealth. At the same time, Social Security served to create jobs (or technically, the redistribution of existing jobs) by removing people from the labor market when they reached age 65 (Schulz, 1985).

Retirement serves a variety of institutional functions in an industrialized society. It can stimulate and reward worker loyalty. In addition, it is a way to remove older, presumably more expensive, workers, and replace them with younger employees, assumed to be more productive. It thereby serves as a way to reduce the number of people holding or seeking jobs. For many individuals, retirement is not a fixed, abrupt point. Rather, there are a diversity of exit patterns, among them partial employment and moving into another career in late adulthood.

Although Social Security was presented to the public as a means to support people physically unable to maintain jobs, retirement has become associated in the public mind with the chronological age of 65 (the age of eligibility for full Social Security benefits) and, in turn, with being old, physically disabled, and no longer capable of full-time employment—an association that has had deleterious consequences for older people (Johnson and Williamson, 1987). In fact, society has come to associate aging with decreased work and training capacity, with little or no regard for the heterogeneity of the older population and little or no knowledge of new and special work arrangements and retraining techniques (Mor-Barak and Tynan, 1993).

## Factors Supporting Early Retirement

Despite our society's work-oriented values and the importance of income derived from work, employment and retirement policies since the 1900s have been directed toward encouraging early retirement. Early retirement has thus become the norm. For example, nine out of ten pension plans, particularly for white-collar workers, provide financial incentives for early retirement. Even employees who were not planning on retirement often feel they cannot turn down attractive retirement benefits. Public and employer pension plans, combined with mandatory retirement policies that were in effect until 1987, a highly competitive work force, and rapidly changing technologies, result in few older persons being employed, as illustrated in Table 14-2 (Myers, 1991). This trend may be compounded by a growing emphasis on leisure as an alternative to the work ethic, particularly among the middle-aged and young-old. Furthermore, many older persons retire early because of poor health, even though they may wish to continue working. (These issues will be discussed in more detail later in this chapter.) The trend toward early retirement is consistent with patterns in most other industrialized countries, reflecting the increased availability of retirement pensions.

The pattern of more men retiring early and more middle-aged and young-old women entering the labor force has meant that the labor force activity of older Americans is becoming similar for men and women. Overall, both men and women are choosing early retirement, although both express a preference for part-time work. The retirement process for minorities, particularly African Americans and Mexican Americans, is likely to be very different from the traditional pattern for white males. Their lifetime work patterns tend to yield an unclear line between work and nonwork, to lack access to private pensions as well as adequate public pensions, and to have lengthy periods of nonwork at an early age (Gibson, 1987; Zsembik and Singer, 1990). A study comparing African American and

**TABLE 14–2   Labor Force Status by Age, Sex, and Ethnic Minority Status, 1990 (Not Seasonally Adjusted)**

| | AGE | | | | | |
|---|---|---|---|---|---|---|
| | 50 to 54 | 55 to 59 | 60 to 64 | 65 to 69 | 70 to 74 | 75 Plus |
| Percent in labor force: | | | | | | |
| Total male | 83.6 | 79.5 | 52.4 | 26.0 | 15.8 | 7.6 |
| Total female | 68.6 | 57.2 | 37.6 | 17.6 | 7.8 | 3.5 |
| White male | 85.1 | 75.0 | 53.5 | 26.6 | 16.5 | 7.9 |
| White female | 69.5 | 48.4 | 38.3 | 18.6 | 8.0 | 3.3 |
| Black male | 70.4 | 67.1 | 39.3 | 20.0 | 10.9 | 3.8 |
| Black female | 62.9 | 52.2 | 32.4 | 11.3 | 6.7 | 5.8 |

SOURCE: U.S. Department of Labor, Bureau of Labor Statistics, *Employment and Earnings,* Vol. 41, No. 11, November 1994.

Caucasian men and women found that white men were the most likely to be retired, African American and white women least likely, even if they were in poor health (Belgrave, 1988; Belgrave, Haug, and Gomez, 1987).

## The Timing of Retirement

The arbitrary nature of any particular age for retirement is shown by the fact that most people retire between the ages of 62 and 64, and very few continue to work past age 70, even though 1986 legislation eliminated mandatory retirement for most occupations. Financial incentives have a greater effect on the decision to retire than do any mandatory retirement policies (Quinn and Burkhauser, 1990, 1993). In fact, it can hardly be said that age 65 is the "normal" retirement age. Instead, 60.6 years is the median age for retirement. Three-quarters of all new Social Security beneficiaries each year retire before their sixty-fifth birthday, and most begin collecting reduced benefits at age 62, the minimum age for eligibility (U.S. Senate Special Committee on Aging, 1990). The 1983 amendments to the Social Security Act delayed the age of eligibility for full benefits and increased the financial penalty for retiring at age 62. However, it is unclear how much this will prolong the older population's working life. Federal workers, who

may retire after 25 years of service, do so at an average age of 62, even though there has never been a mandatory retirement age for federal employees (U.S. Department of Labor, 1989).

The average retirement age in heavy industries, such as steel and auto manufacturing, is even lower than age 62, because of private pension inducements. These plans provide supplemental pension payments at an adequate level, thereby allowing employees to retire before the age of Social Security eligibility. The "30 years and out" pension provisions of labor contracts in the auto industry have been widely supported by union members. Those who retire from the military after the minimum required 20 years often move on to other careers that enable them to draw double pensions after age 65. With longer life expectancies, some may even move into a third career during their post-military years.

The timing of retirement is influenced by several factors. Certainly, one element is the minimum age of eligibility for an adequate retirement income, provided either through Social Security or a private pension. Economic factors (e.g., expected level of pensions, income, net assets and availability of health insurance) are central in influencing attitudes toward retirement, inasmuch as they directly affect decisions about the feasibility of retirement and indirectly contribute to worker health and job satisfaction. When given a choice and assuming financial security and adequate health insurance, most people elect to retire as soon as they can (Clark, Ghent, and Heeden, 1994; U.S. Department of Labor, 1989). Mandatory retirement was probably not a salient factor in influencing the age of retirement, since less than 10 percent of employees were forced to retire because of such requirements in the past (Ruhm, 1989).

Issues other than economics clearly affect the retirement decision. While the majority of young-old express interest in paid work after retirement, most retirees seem not to want the constraints inherent in full-time employment; rather, they want the option of retiring gradually or early from regular employment, as well as opportunities for new career directions or for part-time and other flexible work to meet their economic and social needs. Even delays in Social Security benefits and reductions in the early retirement benefits of private pensions would probably have little effect on significantly delaying the retirement age (National Academy on Aging, 1994).

In addition to income, the timing of retirement may be determined by health, families' preferences, informal norms of the work situation, and long-range plans. Some workers retire to escape boring, repetitive jobs, such as assembly line and office work. Workers who have a positive attitude toward retirement but a negative view of their jobs, often because of undesirable and stressful working conditions, are likely to retire early. In contrast, workers with high satisfaction in interesting jobs are less likely to retire early. Higher status professional or managerial workers and those who are self-employed tend to be highly committed to their work and to want to remain employed for as long as possible. Well-educated employees are less likely to retire early than those with a high-school education or less, as illustrated by Mr. and Mrs. Howard in the introductory vignette (Quinn and Burkhauser, 1993).

The effects of gender on the retirement decision are not clear-cut, in part because of the limited research on women and retirement (Haug, Belgrave, and Jones, 1992). In general, women of retirement age have been found to be less likely to be fully retired and more likely to be employed part-time than their male counterparts (Belgrave, 1989; Szinovacz, 1989). For women who entered the labor force in middle age or later, they may need to continue working for economic reasons (Hatch, 1992). Economic factors are especially salient for women who are divorced, widowed or have a discontinuous employment history. Not surprisingly, current income and receipt of a pension other than Social Security are primary factors in women's decisions whether to continue to work beyond normal retirement age (Belgrave, 1989; U.S. Department of Labor, 1989). Accordingly, career women, particularly those never married, are more likely to retire early and be better adjusted than reentry women (Feuerbach and Erdwins, 1994; Keith, 1985). In other instances, women continue employment roles because of the satisfaction they derive, with employed women typically reporting higher levels of life satisfaction than homemakers or retirees (Mor-Barak et al., 1993; Riddick, 1985). In general, for both men and women, degree of satisfaction in retirement appears to be related to similar factors, particularly income and health (Belgrave, 1989). The slightly lower levels of retirement satisfaction found among women seem to be due primarily to their lower retirement incomes, typically because of the lack of a private pension (Campione, 1987; Hayward, Grady, and McLaughlin, 1988).

In sum, the most important factors for the timing of retirement appear to be financial security and health status. Self-reports of poor health as the motivation for retirement need to be interpreted cautiously, however. Retirees may report poor health as the reason, despite their actual health status, because they perceive this to be a socially acceptable response. Two categories of people who retire early have been identified: those with good health and adequate financial resources who desire additional leisure time, and those with low incomes and health problems that make their work burdensome. Poor health, when combined with an adequate retirement income, usually results in early retirement. In contrast, poor health and an inadequate income generally delay retirement by reason of necessity. The extent to which poor health influences retirement also varies with the job, with health problems being a greater motivation for retirement from physically demanding and stressful jobs and for ethnic minority elders (Colsher et al., 1988; Johnson and Williamson, 1987). Conversely, good health, a strong psychological commitment to work and a corresponding distaste for retirement are all associated with continued employment (Parnes and Sommers, 1994).

The complexity of variables discussed thus far, in terms of the causes, timing, and consequences of retirement, suggest several distinct types of retirement situations. These can be summarized as follows:

- Strong preference for retirement as soon as financially feasible
- Retirement due to health problems
- Retirement following unemployment and inability to find a job

These various circumstances of retirement have different consequences for satisfaction with retirement.

## Satisfaction with Retirement

The importance of factors other than policies that set retirement age and benefits suggests the value of examining retirement as a *process* or transition that affects people's lives in multiple ways. This concept encompasses not only the timing and type of retirement situation as a life stage, but also the phases after the event of retirement (Bossé et al., 1991). Atchley (1983) has suggested that an initial euphoric, busy honeymoon phase is followed by a letdown or disenchantment phase due to loss of status, income, or purpose, which, in turn, is followed by a reorientation to the realities of retired life (Jacobs, 1990). This sequence leads to a subsequent stable phase, when the retiree has settled in a predictable routine. Individuals for whom work was not their primary source of meaning adjust to a satisfying routine more readily than do those who did not develop leisure activities during their working years. These phases are presented as a "typical progression of processes" (Atchley, 1983), although not every individual will experience all the phases or in the order described. Atchley did not offer empirical evidence to support his framework. A more recent conceptualization of retirement as a process of role exit found that as individuals approach retirement, they express increasing discontent and fatigue with the job as a way of withdrawing from their current role commitments (Ekerdt and DeViney, 1993).

The early gerontological literature emphasized retirement as a life crisis due to loss (Atchley, 1976; Streib and Schneider, 1971). As described in Chapter 9, it is included in many lists of stressful life events that require some adjustment. Although it is a major transition, 60 to 79 percent of retirees experience minimal stress and are relatively satisfied with their life circumstances (Bosse, Aldwin, Levenson, and Workman-Daniels, 1991; US. Senate Special Committee on Aging, 1990). For most American workers, retirement is desired, and their decision is not *whether* to retire but *when*. A variety of factors affect the degree of satisfaction. Retirement in itself does not directly affect levels of social activity, life satisfaction, morale, or self-esteem (Palmore, Fillenbaum, and George, 1984). Rather, satisfaction in retirement depends more on factors such as health, the voluntary nature of retirement, income, type of occupation, work values, job history, perceptions of daily activities as useful, education, one's partner's happiness with retirement, and level of social support (Bosse, Aldwin, Levenson, Spiro, and Mroczek, 1993; Haug, Belgrave, and Jones, 1992). Retirees who do not adjust well have been found to have poor health, inadequate family finances, marital problems, and difficulties making transitions throughout the life span (Bosse et al., 1991). Those who retire early because of poor health or lack of job opportunities or who are experiencing other stressful events in their life are less satisfied with being retired, but they are also less pleased with other aspects of their lives, such as their housing, standard of living, and leisure (Matthews and Brown, 1987; Bossé et al., 1991).

Occupational status is also an important predictor of the likelihood of retirement satisfaction, with lower status workers having more health and financial problems, and therefore less satisfaction, than higher level white-collar workers. The more meaningful work characteristics of higher status occupations may "spill over" to a greater variety of satisfying nonwork pursuits throughout life, which are conducive to more social contacts and more structured opportunities during retirement (Calasanti, 1988). For example, a college professor may have a work and social routine that is more readily transferable to retirement than that of a construction worker. Some research suggests that retirees with strong traditional work values are not as satisfied as retirees with weaker work values (Hooker and Ventis, 1984). Differences between retirees in upper and lower status occupations do not develop with retirement, but rather reflect variations in social and personal resources throughout the life course (Ward, 1982). This view of retirement as a long-term process that presents continual challenges as retirees adapt is consistent with continuity theory.

Less is known about the effect of occupational status on retirement satisfaction among ethnic minorities, or about gender differences in the antecedents, consequences, and decision-making processes of retirement (George, Fillenbaum, and Palmore, 1984). For men in some racial minority groups, the negative economic impact of retirement can be somewhat ameliorated by income maintenance subsidies and programs. On the other hand, African Americans, who have had a lifetime of discontinuous work patterns and continue to experience economic need, are unlikely to even define themselves as retired (Gib-

son, 1991). As noted earlier, women's retirement plans, like men's, appear to be strongly influenced by their own pension and Social Security eligibility, not by their husbands' (Johnson and Williamson, 1987). However, adjusting to a full-time housewife role during retirement can be difficult for women used to the routine, rewards, and sociability of paid employment (Szinovacz, 1989). In such instances, women's role transition may not be in synchrony with their husbands (Ekerdt and Vinick, 1991).

More recent literature portrays retirement not as a single transition in a person's life course but as a dynamic process with several stages, including that of "unretirement." This stage reflects the increasing numbers of older people who are dissatisfied with retirement and are returning to work typically on a part-time or part-year basis (Achenbaum and Morris, 1993). The propensity to work appears to be generalized, not specific to a particular job. Those who change jobs shortly before retirement are the most likely to work afterward, suggesting that "unretirement" is part of a repertoire of adaptive behavior in the later years.

In general, health and financial security appear to be the major determinants of retirees' satisfaction with life, rather than retirement status per se (Atchley and Miller, 1983; Ekerdt, 1987; Ekerdt, Bossé, and LaCastro, 1983). Retirement does not *cause* poor health, as is commonly assumed. Although some people's functional health does deteriorate after retirement, other people's functional health frequently improves after retirement because they are no longer subject to stressful, unhealthy, or dangerous work conditions (Minkler, 1981). Contrary to stereotypes about the negative health effects of retirement, people who die shortly after retirement were probably in poor health before they retired. In fact, deterioration in health is more likely to cause the retirement than vice versa (Bossé et al., 1991; Johnson and Williamson, 1987; Palmore et al., 1984). Accordingly, retirement has not been found to increase the incidence of mental health problems, and in some instances, has improved mental health (Bossé, Aldwin, Levinson, and Ekerdt, 1987; Crowley, 1985; Howard, 1986; Palmore et al., 1985). Studies that have found that retirees have more physical and mental illness than nonretirees have relied on cross-sectional data, so that it remains uncertain whether retirees had these disabilities prior to retirement (Mor-Barak, Scharlach, and Sokolov, 1992). The misconception that people become ill and die as a consequence of retirement undoubtedly persists on the basis of findings from cross-sectional data, as well as reports of isolated instances of such deaths. In addition, the traditional American ideology that life's meaning is derived from paid work may reinforce the stereotype that retirement has negative consequences. Another factor is that retirees may be motivated to exaggerate their health limitations in order to justify their retirement. Leaving the labor force because of health problems or, in earlier instances, because of mandatory retirement may later be associated with dissatisfaction in retirement, however.

## LEISURE ACTIVITIES AND THE IMPORTANCE OF PLANNING

Community involvement is another important predictor of well-being in retirement. Most retirees do not miss their jobs per se, but rather the income, associations with fellow employees, and activity levels related to work. Retirement affects identity, self-esteem, and feelings of competence to the extent that it influences such involvement. As we will see in Chapter 15, leisure and community activities during retirement vary by economic status, but do not differ significantly between retirees and workers of the same age. Retirement tends to be characterized by a continuity of preretirement activities, such as social interactions, church attendance, or community and volunteer participation (Kunkel, 1989).

The continuity of leisure activities from working years through retirement suggests the importance of preparation and planning prior to retirement. In fact, preparation has been found to

be associated with a more positive retirement experience. People who have focused only on work all their lives cannot expect suddenly to develop leisure interests and skills upon their retirement. Most preretirees weave fantasies about the trips they will take or the household projects they will complete. After a "honeymoon period" of enjoying new pursuits for about six months, they often find that these activities will not meaningfully fill every day for the next 20 or 30 years. As will be discussed in the next chapter, if nonwork interests are not developed prior to retirement, they are unlikely to be cultivated after retirement. Instead, people need to develop activities outside of the worker role during their employed lives.

Comprehensive retirement planning programs that address social activities, health promotion, and family relationships are one way of encouraging this development. Unfortunately, existing retirement preparation programs often include only information about pension benefits, not health and lifestyle planning. Because such programs are not widespread, only about 10 percent of the labor force benefits from any kind of retirement planning (American Association of Retired Persons, 1986). Older men with more years of education, higher occupational status, and private pensions have greater access to these programs, as do government employees. Accordingly, the group of older workers who might benefit the most from retirement preparation—single people, women, and those facing the probability of lower retirement incomes—are the least likely to have access to or utilize such services (Keith, 1985; Perkins, 1992).

Another approach to preparation is to restructure work patterns, gradually allowing longer vacations, shorter work days, job-sharing, and more opportunities for community involvement during the preretirement working years, thereby easing the transition to more leisure time.

In sum, most people do not have a problem with retirement as a transition, provided they have sufficient preparation for it and an adequate income, enjoy good health, were not forced to retire, and were not wedded to their work. When people are unhappy in retirement, it is more often

Musical skills can be continued into advanced old age.

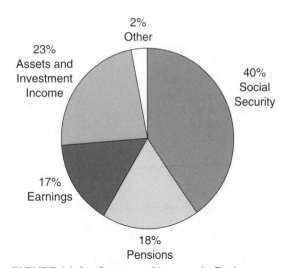

**FIGURE 14–2  Sources of Income in Retirement**
SOURCE: American Association of Retired People, A profile of older Americans, 1994 (Washington, D.C.: AARP, 1994).

because of health or income problems than because of the loss of worker role per se. Retirement policies, labor market conditions, and individual characteristics all converge on the decision to retire. Collectively, these individual decisions translate into a rate of retirement for our society. The rate or level of retirement, in turn, has an impact on businesses, communities, and society at large. Thus, while the individual's experience of retirement as a process is not necessarily painful, our society is increasingly confronting the problem of retirement as a complex social institution, in which longer life expectancies and earlier retirement have resulted in prolonged dependence on Social Security and other retirement benefits as well as loss of older workers' skills. These institutional difficulties are discussed further in Chapter 19.

## SOURCES OF INCOME IN RETIREMENT

Sources of income for the older population include savings, assets and investments, Social Security, private pensions, and, for a small percentage, a salary. The distribution of these income sources is illustrated in Figure 14-2. Mr.

Valdres and Mrs. Howard in the introductory vignettes demonstrate the diversity among older people in their reliance on these various income sources.

### Social Security

Social Security remains the heart of the retirement income system. Older people depend more heavily on Social Security for their income than on any other source. In 1994, 40 percent of all income received by older units (i.e., a married couple with one or both members aged 65 or older and living together, or a person aged 65 or older not living with a spouse) was from Social Security (see Figure 14-2). Social Security is received by approximately 95 percent of older people. Of those age 65 and over, 62 percent received at least half of their income from Social Security; this increases to 85 percent among those over age 85. The average monthly benefit for retired workers at the end of 1993 was $656 (Aleksa, 1994). Today, Social Security replaces, on average, 44 percent of preretirement earnings (National Academy on Aging, 1994).

Yet Social Security was never intended to provide an adequate retirement income, but

60%

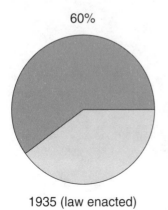

1935 (law enacted)

95%

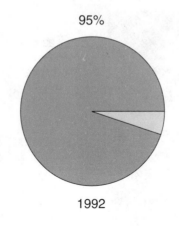

1992

**FIGURE 14–3 Percentage of Employees Covered by Social Security**
SOURCE: Aleksa, K., *Income among Older Americans in 1992.* Washington, DC: American Association of Retired Persons, Public Policy Institute, 1994, 1–4.

rather a floor of protection or the first tier of support. It was assumed that pensions and individual savings would also help support people in their later years. This assumption has not been borne out, as reflected in the proportionately lower income received by retirees from savings and private pensions. It has been estimated that, without Social Security, poverty rates among the older population would increase from 12 percent to 54 percent (Kingson, 1994). As an example of the effects of Social Security in alleviating poverty, the median income (in 1989 dollars) of families headed by persons age 65 and older increased from $13,620 in 1965 to $22,806 in 1989, representing a 67.4 percent increase compared to a 20 percent increase for younger families (Kingson, 1994; Schwenk, 1993). Not surprisingly, older individuals with the lowest income have Social Security as their sole income. Social Security provides 75 percent of the aggregate income of older households with less than $10,000 income compared to 31 percent of households at $30,000–$49,999 (Kingson, 1994).

The Social Security system is based on the concept of earned rights, rather than on the universal eligibility of all older persons. This means that it is not welfare, but rather a public trust into which all pay and all are guaranteed an income floor in old age or disability. In order to be insured, a worker retiring now must be age 62 or more and must have been employed consecutively for at least eight years or 34 quarters. The level of benefits received is based on a percentage of the retired worker's average monthly earnings that were subject to Social Security tax. Insured persons are eligible for full benefits at age 65; if they choose to retire at age 62, their monthly benefits are permanently reduced and are not increased when they reach age 65. Approximately 60 percent of all recipients currently receive such reduced benefits because they have retired even before the age of 62. As noted earlier, Social Security benefits may also be reduced for those who work after age 65. This "earnings test" has been strongly criticized as an unfair deterrent to older people's labor force participation. Limited income exceptions now exist (Crystal and Shea, 1990).

It is a myth that Social Security is a funded pension system in which retirees are merely paid back, with interest, the "contributions" which they made during their working years. Instead, it is a system whereby current workers support current retirees. In fact, Social Security—a "pay as you go system"—has been described as like a pipeline: taxes from today's workers flow in, are invested in special U.S. government bonds, and then flow out to current beneficiaries (Hardy and Hardy, 1991).

Because of the dramatic growth in the number of retirees and the consequent decline in number of workers, there is concern about the number of employees paying into the Social Security system for every 100 persons drawing

---

**OLDER PERSON LIVING ON SOCIAL SECURITY**

As an example of the difficulty of living on Social Security, a New York City woman wrote to the Older Women's League, "I will be 65 in February, but cannot afford to retire since my $500 a month Social Security income (which is all I will have in this world) will pay for rent, utilities and nothing else. It is not possible to move to cheaper quarters....I receive no assistance in paying for utilities....I have severe physical problems which preclude my being able to work for too much longer. I am an unmonied city dweller, but cannot even qualify for Medicaid."

*Source:The OWL Observer,* From the Mailbag, July/August 1984, p. 10.

---

benefits; this so-called dependency ratio dropped from 410 to 320 between 1970 and 1980, and may fall to as low as 200 by the year 2025. As a result, some policy makers have advocated policies to discourage early retirement; for example, the age of Social Security eligibility is to be increased from age 62 to 67 by the year 2027, as specified by the 1983 amendments. Despite concerns in the early 1980s that the fund might go bankrupt, it is projected to have a surplus until at least 2010 since the Social Security trust fund is taking in more money than it pays out. By the year 2020, however, the system is predicted to go into deficit (Hardy and Hardy, 1991). The extent to which concern about shifting dependency ratios and the deficit has fueled public perceptions of intergenerational inequity is discussed further in Chapter 19.

Since 1975, Social Security benefits have been automatically increased annually whenever the Consumer Price Index increases by 3 percent or more. This is known as the *cost of living adjustment,* or COLA. They have thus been protected from inflation. Since benefits are related to a worker's wage and employment history, women and ethnic minorities, with their pattern of intermittent or part-time work, tend to receive less than the average monthly benefit.

Women's Social Security payments may also be sharply reduced by widowhood or divorce. A widow may start to collect surviving dependents' benefits when she reaches age 60; however, she will lose about 28 percent of what she would have received if she had waited until age 65. But for each additional year after 60, a widow receives a larger percentage of Social Security benefits. And after age 65, she receives full benefits, even if she has been getting only 71 percent for the past four years. Widows and divorcees under age 60 who are not disabled and who do not have children under age 18 entitled to Social Security, or who are not responsible for disabled persons, cannot receive Social Security benefits. This group of women, who generally do not have a paid work history and do not qualify for any public benefits, are often referred to as *displaced homemakers.* Since the average age at widowhood is 56 years, many women face this "widow's

---

**DISPLACED HOMEMAKER**

Mrs. Kelly lost her husband over a year ago at the age of 56. Her daughter was 15 years old at the time. When the daughter turned 16 and was no longer considered a legal dependent, Mrs. Kelly's Social Security check stopped. Mrs. Kelly has no health insurance; she cannot work because she is caring for her 90-year-old mother. Nevertheless, she is too young for Social Security and Medicare benefits.

gap." A woman who is divorced after at least 10 years of marriage and who reaches retirement age may collect up to 50 percent of her ex-husband's retirement benefits, but only when he turns 62 and if she remains single. Because many widows or divorced women do not meet these criteria, a large percentage of single older women live in poverty or near-poverty conditions. These gender inequities will be discussed further in Chapter 18.

The Social Security payroll tax, now 7.65 percent on the first $53,400 of earnings, is a regressive tax (i.e., having the same effect on both the rich and the poor). This means that low-income workers, many of whom are women and ethnic minorities, pay a larger proportion of their monthly salary for the Social Security tax compared to higher-income workers. On the other hand, proportionately, lower-income workers benefit more from Social Security when they retire, receiving benefits equal to 90 percent of their working wages, while high-income workers' benefit are only 19 percent of their prior salary (Beedon, 1994). Some minority advocates contend that Social Security is discriminatory because ethnic minorities, as a group, pay more Social Security tax on the basis of low income and also have reduced total benefits because of lower average life expectancy than that of the general population. (In fact, because of this difference in life expectancy, many ethnic minorities do not live long enough to collect their first Social Security check!) On the other hand, Social Security's benefit structure is least generous to high-income contributors, who receive a smaller percentage of what their income was prior to retirement and who must now pay income tax on 50 percent of their Social Security benefits. Generally, however, high-income contributors do not need the floor of support provided by Social Security because they are covered by pensions and assets.

## Assets

Income from assets (e.g., savings, home equity, and personal property) comprised 23 percent of all income received by older people in 1990, and

was the second most important income source. However, it was unevenly distributed, with nearly 33 percent of the older units—typically the oldest-old, women, and ethnic minorities—reporting no asset income, and 26 percent of those with asset income reporting less than $500 a year. Only 33 percent of those with such income—typically married couple households—received more than $5,000 a year from this source (Radner, 1991; Taeuber, 1992). Older people's assets consist primarily of home equity, representing 40 to 50 percent of their net worth (National Academy on Aging, 1994; Radner, 1991). Currently, 76 percent of older people own their homes, although this percentage declines among ethnic minority elders (Schwenk, 1993). Yet 50 percent of older homeowners spend at least 45 percent of their incomes on property taxes, utilities, and maintenance (Quinn and Smeeding, 1994). Home equity therefore does not represent liquid wealth or cash and cannot be relied on to cover daily expenses. However, even though most older people with fixed incomes cannot depend on assets to meet current expenses, it is nevertheless true that their net worth tends to be greater than those under age 35 (National Academy on Aging, 1994).

## Earnings

Earnings are an important income source to the young-old, but decline in importance with age. Thus, individuals age 65 to 69 receive 30 percent of their income from earnings, compared with only 4 percent for those 80 years and older. Overall, current job earnings form 17 percent of the income of older units compared with 23 percent in 1978 (National Academy on Aging, 1994). This low percentage is consistent with the declining labor force participation among people age 65 and over.

## Pensions

While most jobholders are covered by Social Security, which is a *general public pension*, some employees are covered by *job-specific pensions*.

These are available only through a specific position of employment and are administered by a work organization, union, or private insurance company. Job-specific pensions include *public employee pensions* (for those who work for federal, state, or local governments) and *private pensions.* Since 1950, pension plans have increased from 25 to 50 percent among private sector wage and salary workers, and from 60 to 90 percent among civilian government workers, although only half of those eligible for benefits have had enough years of service to be fully vested in a plan and thus entitled to future benefits (National Academy on Aging, 1994). With the average annual pension income as $8,278 in 1992, most private pensions are intended to supplement Social Security, not be the sole source of income (Aleksa, 1994). Employee pensions provide approximately 18 percent of the older population's aggregate income. Overall, 66 percent of older units receive some income from public and/or private pension benefits; and 25 percent have income from private pensions only (Quinn and Smeeding, 1994).

Pension benefits are generally based on earnings or a combination of earnings and years of service. Eligibility age is usually between ages 60 and 65, although it ranges from ages 50 to 70. Only about 3 percent of pension plans provide for cost-of-living increases. Yet an annual inflation rate of 5 percent for 15 years can erode the real value of benefits by about one-half, making inflation the greatest threat to those dependent on private pensions. Federal policies support private pension programs by postponing taxation of pension benefits, allowing benefits to be invested and to generate earnings that are not taxed. Only when the pension is drawn is tax paid, after the money has produced many years of earnings.

Private pensions go to workers with long, continuous service in jobs that have such coverage. In general, these are higher-income, relatively skilled positions of 30 or more years concentrated among large, unionized settings or service and financial sectors. As a result, retirees who benefit from private pensions tend to be in the middle and upper income brackets, with the lowest-income older persons receiving, on average, only three percent of their income from pensions (Quinn and Smeeding, 1994). Pension coverage varies dramatically by class, race, and gender, being relatively low for women, ethnic minorities, and lower-income workers in small, nonunion plants and low-wage industries, such as retail sales and services and for retirees currently over age 65. These problems are compounded for women, who are more likely than men to be "in and out" of the labor force and therefore less likely to achieve the required length of service for vesting; this is a minimum of 5 years, although most employers require longer periods. Nonemployed women face an additional problem: most pension plans reduce benefits for those who elect to protect their spouses through survivors' benefits. In the past, many men have chosen higher monthly benefits rather than survivors' benefits; when they died, their wives were left without adequate financial protection.

The Employment Retirement Income Security Act (ERISA), enacted in 1974 to strengthen private pension systems, was the first comprehensive effort to regulate them. As a result, private pension plans must *vest* benefits (vesting refers to the amount of time a person must work on a job in order to acquire rights to the pension) in such a way that all covered workers are guaranteed a full pension upon retirement after 10 or 15 years with the company, regardless of whether or not they remain with that organization until retirement. This means that a person could work for one firm for 12 years, move to a second company until retirement at age 65, and then receive pensions from both based on years of service. Although vesting options increased under ERISA, portability (whereby pension contributions and rights with one organization can be transferred to another) remains low. This has been criticized for penalizing worker mobility and career changes. For example, an individual who serves 40 years with one company will receive a higher pension than one who spent 20 years with one firm and 20 with another.

ERISA also strengthened standards for financing, administering, and protecting pension plans, although during the recession of the 1990s, some major pension plans were discontinued. Tax-exempt individual retirement accounts (IRAs) were created for workers with pension coverage, and were made available to all workers in 1981, in an effort to increase personal savings for retirement. (Under the 1986 tax reform plan, employees with other private pensions no longer are able to use an IRA as a tax deduction.) Yet IRAs are not an option for most workers; they are used primarily by those earning $50,000 or more who have disposable income (Schulz, 1985). Lower-income workers generally cannot spare the money, and the tax benefit is considerably less for them. (This tax benefit is greatest at higher incomes because it is based on a tax deduction.) Ironically, the people who need retirement income the most generally cannot take advantage of IRAs. As with employer pension plans, the tax deferral of IRAs provides the equivalent of a long-term interest-free loan (e.g., tax shelter) to the predominantly high-income taxpayers who use IRAs. In sum, the equalizing effects of Social Security are outweighed by private pensions, asset income, IRAs, and other preferential tax treatment for a small percentage of wealthy older adults, resulting in greater economic inequality over time (Crystal and Shea, 1990).

## POVERTY AMONG OLD AND YOUNG

The economic position of older people has improved since the 1960s. In 1959, 35.2 percent of the population aged 65 and over fell below the official poverty line compared to 12.2 percent in 1990.* In contrast, the poverty figure was 10.8

percent for those aged 18 to 64, and 13.7 percent of all persons under age 65 (Holden, 1993). When those just above the poverty level are combined with those in poverty, nearly 20 percent of the older population lives in or close to poverty (Kassner, 1992; U.S. Government Accounting Office, 1993). What these figures do not reflect is that the federal poverty level for a single adult younger than age 65 is higher than for an older individual. The U.S. Bureau of the Census has assumed that the costs of food and other necessities are lower for older people, even though they spend proportionately more on housing, transportation, and health care than do younger groups (Schwenk, 1993).

If the same poverty standard were applied to the older population as to the other age groups, the poverty rate for older people would increase to over 15 percent (Quinn and Smeeding, 1994). At the other extreme, 5.6 percent of all households headed by an older person have incomes exceeding $50,000. The moderate- to high-income elders depend primarily upon assets, private pensions, and savings for their retirement income, not Social Security (Davis and Rowland, 1991). On a per capita basis, this amount is higher than that of well-off American households in any other age group. Another indicator of the older population's improved economic status is that people aged 50 and over hold one out of every two discretionary dollars, a fact that has particular relevance for marketing products to this segment of the population. The primary reasons for this differential are that today's older cohort has benefited economically from the strong performance of the economy in the 1950s and 1960s, accumulation of home equity, and expansion of Social Security and other pension protection.

The primary factors underlying these gains are improved and longer coverage by pensions, the 1972 increases in Social Security benefits, the 1975 automatic annual cost of living adjustments (COLAs) in Social Security, and implementation of the Supplemental Security Income program. An example of the dramatic impact of these

---

*Poverty is a measure of the adequacy of money income in relation to a minimal level of consumption—the poverty level. This level is fixed in real terms and adjusted for family size. The dollar values of the poverty levels are adjusted each year to reflect changes in the Consumer Price Index. In 1987, the official poverty line for an elderly individual was $5,701. This means that an individual whose weekly income fell below $109 was classified as officially poor, and *not* poor if that income were greater, even by only one dollar!

changes is that without Social Security, the poverty rate for the older population would be 55 percent (Davis and Rowland, 1991). Because of such changes, a widely held public perception is that older persons are better off financially than other age groups—a perception based, to some extent, on the reality of their improved condition. This perception is also fueled by the increase of poverty among children under age 18, making them the poorest age group. (In 1990, this rate was over 20 percent [Radner, 1991]).

It is true that when all sources of income are considered (including tax and in-kind benefits), fewer older families have subpoverty resources than younger families, but the distribution of income among older adults is extremely diverse. Similarly, a larger percentage of older families have economic resources just above the poverty line, and thus are *at-risk* of poverty or economically vulnerable. More likely than other age groups to be among the "near-poor," 28 percent of the older population have incomes below 150

percent of the poverty line (U.S. Senate Special Committee on Aging, 1992). Almost six in ten older people survive on less than $10,000 a year, with 93 percent of their income based upon Social Security and Supplemental Security Income (Davis and Rowland, 1991).

The overall poverty rates for older individuals hide the fact that rates range from 6 percent for persons in families headed by a male to nearly 50 percent for African American female-headed families to over 60 percent of African American females living alone (see Figure 14-4). Furthermore, cohorts continue to experience income loss as they age, and therefore economic deprivation, relative to younger cohorts (Smeeding, 1990). Many older persons never qualify for Social Security benefits because they were employed in occupations such as domestic work not covered by the system. Since retirement from the labor force can reduce individual incomes by one-third to one-half, most retirees must adjust their standard of living downward—at the same time their out-of-pocket spending for health care

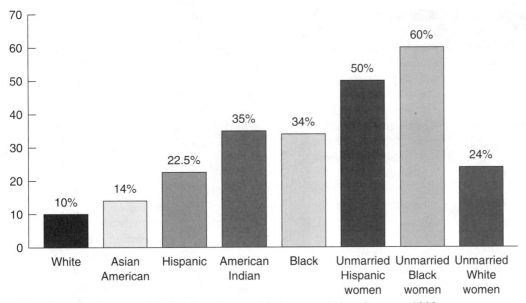

**FIGURE 14–4   Percent of Older Americans with Incomes below Poverty: 1990.**
SOURCE: U.S. Bureau of the Census, *Poverty in the United States: 1990.* Current Population reports, Series P–60, No. 175. U.S. Government Printing Office, Washington DC, 1991.

needs may increase (Estes, Gerard, and Clarke, 1984). Chapters 19 and 20 address this matter further.

The stereotype of the static nature of poverty, suggested by cross-sectional information, must be altered to take account of the fact that many older people move in and out of poverty over time. When such individual movements are identified, the risk of falling below the poverty line *at some time* during a specified period is more than double the highest average risk among older couples, and is raised by almost 30 percent for widows. For example, many women become poor for the first time in their lives after depleting their assets in order to qualify for the needs-based Medicaid program. For those who were not poor earlier in life, the high inflation of the 1970s eroded the value of many sources of their retirement income (Davis and Rowland, 1991). There are also many "hidden poor" among the older population, who are either institutionalized or living with relatives and thus not counted in official census statistics. Including these individuals in the total count would significantly raise the poverty rate among older people. In sum, more older people are at marginal levels of income and at greater risk of poverty than younger people; they are also more likely to be trapped in long-term poverty (Bould, Sanborn, and Reif, 1989).

The primary predictors of poverty in old age continue to be race, gender (female), no high school degree, divorced or widowed status, and nonmetropolitan living environment (McLaughlin and Jensen, 1993). Economic marginality is more pronounced among older women, those who live alone, ethnic minorities, and the old-old, with the lower poverty rates among the young-old partly due to their continuing to be employed and to the greater likelihood of their retiring with good pension plans (Bould, Sanborn, and Reif, 1989; McLaughlin and Jensen, 1993). Their economic hardships are often compounded by a lifetime of discrimination, by historical factors such as working at jobs with no pension or inadequate health insurance, and by recent stressful events such as loss of spouse or declining health. Mr. Valdres and Mrs. Clark in the introductory vignettes illustrate these elderly. Mr. Valdres worked as a migrant farm laborer and therefore relies on the minimum Social Security level for his income. Mrs. Clark, on the other hand, thought her savings would be adequate for her old age, but the cost of caring for her ill husband for 18 years left her penniless. Of all older people living alone, 24 percent are poor, compared to 14 percent of those living with others. When the poor and the near-poor are grouped together, 45 percent of older people living alone fall into this category. This increases with age, with nearly 50 percent of those age 85 and over either poor or near-poor (U.S. Senate Special Committee on Aging, 1992).

The "tweeners" are a group caught between upper-income and poor older people. Forming 20 percent of the older population, these economically insecure lower-income elders fall just above the poverty line. "Tweeners" are not well enough off to be financially secure but not poor enough to qualify for the means-tested safety net of Medicaid and SSI. Paradoxically, the only way that they can improve their economic well-being and qualify for Medicaid and SSI is to spend down (Smeeding, 1990).

Even older persons who have pensions may have marginal incomes. It is generally agreed that retirees must receive 75 percent of their pre-retirement income (adjusted for inflation) in order to maintain an adequate standard of living. Yet relatively few workers are enrolled in private pension programs that provide this replacement rate. Most people do not plan sufficiently for their retirement income, presuming that Social Security will be sufficient and failing to assess the impact of inflation and reduced income levels.

In addition, economic recessions, escalating health care costs, and inflation during the 1990s will reduce pension assets. Therefore, any policy reforms contemplated for the 1990s must assume that the economic status of the oldest-old will decline (Torres-Gil, 1992). Aging advocates maintain that any strategies to alleviate poverty among today's older Americans cannot rely on an improving labor market and must be immediate, such as improving levels of Social Security for those with low lifetime earnings and insuring that women and men have full access to benefits accrued by their spouses (McLaughlin and Jensen 1993).

As will be discussed in detail in Chapter 18, older women are among the poorest group in our society, particularly women living alone and those aged 85 and older. The risk of poverty among couples and single men has sharply fallen, leaving poverty in old age a characteristic primarily of single, frail women who have outlived their husbands. This is consistent with the feminization of poverty in general. Although women account for more than half of the older population, they comprise nearly three-quarters of the older poor. Over 14 percent of older women are poor, compared to 8 percent of older men; this rate increases to 19.7 percent among women age 85 and over, to 21 percent among widowed women, and to approximately 23 percent among women living alone and 26 percent of those divorced or separated (McLauglin and Jensen, 1993). Widows account for nearly 50 percent of all older poor, reflecting the loss of pension income and earnings often associated with the death of a wage-earner spouse. The median income of widowed women is four-fifths that of widowed men, since men are more likely to have

retained pensions or earned income after a spouse's death (U.S. Senate Special Committee on Aging, 1992). Even though there has been some decline in poverty among older women over the past 20 years (consistent with the improvement of the economic status of older people generally), their position relative to that of middle-aged women has still not improved, primarily because of lower retirement income than that of male counterparts. The primary reasons for these gaps are women's interrupted work histories related to family responsibilities and their resultant lower Social Security benefits, less likelihood of private pensions to supplement Social Security, lower wages, and fewer part-time work options.

African American and Hispanic elders of both sexes have substantially lower incomes than do their white counterparts, as shown in Figure 14–5. The median income of older African American and Hispanic men living alone is about a third below that of older white men living alone. Although the differences are less pronounced among women, the median incomes of older African American and Hispanic women are generally two-thirds to three-quarters those of white women. Minority women's slight economic advantage relative to that of their male peers stems from the higher rates of unemployment and unsteady work histories among minority males. Not surprisingly, the poverty rates among minority

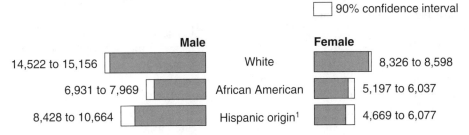

**FIGURE 14–5   Median Incomes in 1989 of Persons 65 Years and Over, by Sex and Race: March 1990 (in dollars)**

[1]Hispanic origin may be of any race.

SOURCE:  C. DeNavas and E. Welniak, U.S. Bureau of the Census, *Money Income of Households, Families, and Persons in the United States: 1990,* Current Population Reports, Series P–60, No. 174. U.S. Government Printing Office, Washington, DC, July 1991, table 26.

elders are higher than among whites. In 1980, the poverty rate among African American elders was more than triple—and among Hispanic elders more than double—the rate among white older people; 34 percent of older African Americans and 22.5 percent of older Hispanics were poor, compared to 10 percent of older whites. (Kassner, 1992; U.S. Bureau of the Census, 1991). Poverty rates are the highest among minority women living alone. Over 60 percent of older African American women not living with family have incomes below the poverty line; almost 70 percent of rural African American women live in poverty, making them the most economically deprived group in our society (U.S. Bureau of the Census, 1991). Disparities between ethnic minority groups are discussed further in Chapter 17.

In sum, despite the improved financial situation of the older population generally, large pockets of poverty and near-poverty exist, particularly among women, ethnic minorities, those over age 75, those who live alone, and those who live in rural areas. As a result, economic inequality is actually greater among older people than among other age groups.

## Public Assistance

Of the older population, 11 percent receive some type of public assistance, primarily in the form of Supplemental Security Income (SSI) and Medicaid (health insurance for the poor, regardless of age). The proportions are higher among ethnic minority older women.

SSI was established in 1974 to provide a minimum income for elders living on the margin of poverty. In contrast to Social Security, SSI does not require a history of covered employment contributions. Instead, eligibility is determined by a categorical requirement that the recipient be 65 years of age, blind, or disabled with limits on amount of monthly income and assets determining eligibility. SSI provides a subsistence income to over four million needy persons, 75 percent of whom are women age 75 and over. Yet only about 50 percent of the eligible older poor par-

ticipate in SSI. In 1994, the maximum federal benefit was $446 a month for an individual and $669 a month for a couple, or only 75 to 90 percent of the poverty level respectively (National Committee to Save Social Security and Medicare, 1994). Older people whose Social Security income is less than that amount can apply for a monthly SSI payment to bring them up to that income level. Nevertheless, the federal SSI benefits fall substantially below the poverty line. Even when states supplement federal benefits (the median state supplement is $36 a month), benefit levels remain low, so that SSI supplies only 14 percent of the income of poor older people (Kasper, 1988). Those who receive SSI may also qualify for foodstamps, but 26 percent of older recipients receive only the minimum food stamp benefit of $10 a month (Kassner, 1992).

Becoming eligible for SSI is a time-consuming and often demeaning process, requiring extensive documentation and the ability to deal with the complexity of conflicting criteria for benefits from SSI, Medicaid, and food stamps. As a result of the 1990 SSI Modernization Task Force, legislative efforts are underway to increase the program's low minimum payments, to liberalize eligibility requirements, and to reduce the red tape and complexity.

An additional limitation of SSI is that any gifts or contributions from family members for food, clothing, or housing are counted as income and can result in the older person's benefit being cut by up to one-third. For example, if a granddaughter takes her grandmother into her home or out to dinner, her grandmother's benefit can be cut. But it is not reduced if the grandmother lives in federal housing or eats at a soup kitchen. Such policies can serve to discourage family support for older SSI recipients.

Despite the increased reliance on public assistance programs and the growing public perception that older people are no longer needy, low income is still a substantial problem for older individuals, many of whom become "poor" or "near-poor" for the first time in their lives in old age. The distribution of income and assets among older persons is highly skewed, with the poorest one-fifth receiving 5.5 percent of the older population's total resources and the wealthiest one-fifth receiving 46 percent (Crystal and Shea, 1990). Although some older people are financially quite comfortable, many are not, particularly since reduced income is not necessarily accompanied by reduced needs or desires for goods and services. An additional problem is that older people spend a greater share of their income than younger people do on the basic necessities of food, utilities, and health care—areas particularly hard hit by inflation. Older adults are also less likely to have reserve funds to cover emergencies, such as catastrophic medical expenses. As a result, low-income elders are at risk of malnutrition, poorly heated and inadequate housing, neglect of medical needs, and increasing isolation.

## SUMMARY AND IMPLICATIONS

Although it is a relatively new phenomenon, retirement has become a normative expectation of old age in this country. Increasingly, Americans are leaving work in their early sixties and looking forward to two to three decades of leisure time in relatively good health. Not all retirement is desired; many older people would prefer the opportunity for part-time work. However, although flexible work opportunities for older people could be created, they rarely are, and the employment rate among older Americans is very low. In some cases, this is due to age discrimination; in other cases, it is due to mandatory retirement in the past and other public policies. Health status, the availability of pensions, and attitudes toward the job also influence the decision about when to retire.

Most retirees adjust well to this important transition, and are satisfied with the quality of their lives. Those with good health, higher status jobs, adequate income, and previously developed social networks and leisure interests are most likely to be satisfied. Preparation for the retirement transition is beneficial, but planning assistance is generally not available to those who need it most—workers who have less education, lower job status, and lower retirement incomes. Retirement preparation programs that do exist often address only financial needs, not health and lifestyle issues. Retirement by itself does not cause poor health or loss of identity and self-esteem. Unhappiness in this stage of life is more often due to poor health and low income.

Although a smaller percentage of older people have incomes below the poverty line than they did in the past, more older than younger people live at marginal economic levels. Social Security is the major source of retirement income for a large proportion of the older population, but it was never intended to be the only source. Those who depend on Social Security alone are the poorest older group. Private pensions tend to be small in relation to previous earnings, to be subject to attrition through inflation, and to go only to workers in large, unionized, or industrialized settings. Recent federal legislation has protected pension rights to some extent. Income from assets is distributed unequally among the older population, with a small number of older persons receiving sizable amounts from savings and investments, whereas the most common asset of older people is their home, which provides no immediate income. In addition to those elderly who are officially counted as living below the poverty line, many others live near this level, and many are "hidden" poor who live in nursing homes or with their families. Frail, unmarried women—and ethnic minority women especially—are the most likely to live in or near poverty. Public assistance programs, such as SSI and Medicaid, have not removed the very serious financial problems of the older poor.

The trends toward greater longevity, early retirement, low rates of labor force participation, and pockets of poverty among older women, ethnic minorities, and the old-old suggest that a growing problem for the United States is the increase in the relative size of an older population encouraged not to work. The increased segmentation of life into a period of full-time work and one of total or partial retirement is, to a great extent, a product of our present pension systems. The ending of mandatory retirement laws is a first step to a smoother mix of labor and leisure across life, but this does not address the underlying economic incentives for retirement inherent in U.S. pension systems. More basic and far-reaching changes are needed, including greater flexibility in the workplace—opportunities for part-time work and a gradual transition from full-time productive work to leisure activities and retirement—and policies to address levels of unemployment in the general population.

## REFERENCES

Achenbaum, W. A., and Morrison, M. H. Is unretirement unprecedented? In S. A. Bass, F. G. Caro, and Y-P Chen, (Eds.), *Achieving a productive aging society*. Westport, CT: Auburn House, 1993, 97–116.

Aleksa, K. *Income among older Americans in 1992*. Washington, DC: American Association of Retired Persons, 1994.

American Association of Retired Persons (AARP). *Life events, retirement preparation, and women's adjustment to retirement: A comparative study*. Washington, D.C.: AARP, 1984.

American Association of Retired Persons. *Business and older workers: Current perceptions and new directions for the 1990s*. Washington, D.C.: American Association of Retired Persons, 1989.

American Association of Retired Persons. *Work and retirement: Employees over 40 and their views*. Washington, D.C.: American Association of Retired Persons, 1986.

American Association of Retired Persons (AARP). *A profile of older Americans, 1990*. Washington, D.C.: AARP, 1991.

Atchley, R. *The sociology of retirement*. New York: Wiley/Schenkman, 1976.

Atchley, R. Retirement as a social institution. In R. H. Turner and J. F. Short (Eds.), *Annual Review of Sociology* (Vol. 8). Palo Alto, Calif.: Annual Reviews, 1982.

Atchley, R. C. *Aging: Continuity or change*. Belmont, Calif.: Wadsworth, 1983.

Atchley, R. and Miller, S., Types of elderly couples. In T. H. Brubaker (ed.), *Family relationships in later life*. Beverly Hills, Calif.: Sage, 1983, 77–90.

Bammel, L. L. B., and Bammel, G. Leisure and recreation. In J. E. Birren and K. W. Schaie (Eds.), *Handbook of the psychology of aging* (2d ed.). New York: Van Nostrand Reinhold, 1985.

Barth, M., McNaught, W., and Rizzi, P. Corporations and the aging workforce. In P. H. Mirvis (Ed.), *Building the competitive workforce*. NY: John Wiley & Sons, 1993.

Bartlett, D., and Steelar, J. The vanishing pensions: Will money be there when you retire? *The Seattle Times*, November 5, 1991, A–4.

Beedon, L. *Administering Social Security*. American Association of Retired Persons. Washington, D.C., 1994.

Belgrave, L. L. The effects of race differences in work history, work attitudes, economic resources and health on women's retirement. *Research on Aging*, 1988, *10*, 383–398.

Belgrave, L. L. Understanding women's retirement. *Generations*, Spring 1989, 99–152.

Belgrave, L., Haug, M. R., and Gomez, B. Gender and race differences in effects of health and pension and retirement before 65. *Comparative Gerontology*, 1987, *1*(3), 109–117.

Bossé, L., Aldwin, C., Leverson, M., and Workman-Daniel, K. How stressful is retirement? Findings from the normative aging study. *Journals of Gerontology*, 1991, *46*(1), 9–15.

Bossé, R., Aldwin, C. M., Levenson, M. R., Spiro, A., and Mroczek, D. Changes in social support after retirement: Longitudinal findings from the Normative Aging Study. *Journals of Gerontology*, 1993, *48*(4), 210–217.

Bossé, R., Aldwin, C. M., Levenson, M. R., and Ekerdt, D. J. Mental health differences among retirees and workers: Findings from the normative aging study. *Psychology and Aging*, 1987, *2*, 383–389.

Bould, S., Sanborn, B., and Reif, L. *Eighty-five plus: The oldest old*. Belmont, Calif.: Wadsworth, 1989.

Bureau of Labor Statistics. *Handbook of labor statistics*. Washington, D.C.: U.S. Government Printing Office, 1983.

Burkhauser, R. V., and Quinn, J. F. *Labor force participation of older workers: Background Paper No. 20*. Washington D.C.: U.S. Department of Labor, Commission on Workforce Quality and Labor Market Efficiency, 1989.

Butler, J. S., Anderson, K. H., and Burkhauser, R. V. Work and health and retirement: A competing risks model with semiparametric unobserved heterogeneity. *Review of Economics and Statistics*, 1989, 70, 46–53.

Calasanti, T. M. Participation in a dual economy and adjustment to retirement. *International Journal of Aging and Human Development*, 1988, 26, 13–27.

Calasanti, T., and Bonardo, A. Working "over-time": Economic restructuring and retirement of a class. *Sociological Quarterly*, 1993, 33(1), 135.

Campione, W. The married woman's retirement decision: A methodological comparison. *Journal of Gerontology*, 1987, 42(4), 381–386.

Caro, F. G., Bass, S. A., and Chen, Y-P. Introduction: Achieving a productive aging society. In S. A. Bass, F. G. Caro, and Y-P Chen (Eds.), *Achieving a productive aging society*, Westport, CT: Auburn House, 1993, 3-25.

Clark, R. L., Ghent, L., and Heeden, A. Retiree health insurance and pension coverage: Variations by firm characteristics. *Journals of Gerontology*, 1994, 49, 553–561.

Clark, R. L., and Sumner, D. Inflation and the real income of the elderly: Recent evidence and expectations for the future. *The Gerontologist*, 1985, 25, 146–152.

Clark, R. L. Income maintenance policies. In R. Binstock and L. George (Eds.), *Handbook of aging and the social sciences* (3d ed.). New York: Academic Press, 1990, 382–397.

Colsher, P., Dorfman, L., and Wallace, R. Specific health conditions and work: Retirement among the elderly. *Journal of Applied Gerontology*, 1988, 7(4), 485–503.

Commonwealth Fund, The. *The untapped resource: The final report of the Americans over 55 at work program*. New York: The Commonwealth Fund, 1993.

Commonwealth Fund Commission. *Old, alone and poor. A plan for reducing poverty among elderly people living alone*. Baltimore, Md.: Commonwealth Fund Commission, 1987.

Congressional Institute for the Future. *Tomorrow's elderly*. Washington, D.C.: Congressional Institute for the Future, 1984.

Crook, F. L., and Kramek, L. Measuring economic hardship among older Americans. *The Gerontologist*, 1986, 26, 38–48.

Crowley, J. Longitudinal effects of retirement on men's psychological and physical well being. In H. S. Parnes (Ed.), *Retirement among American men*. Lexington, MA: Heath, 1985.

Crystal, S., and Shea, D. Cumulative advantage, cumulative disadvantage, and inequality among elderly people. *The Gerontologist*, 1990, 30, 437–443.

Davis, K., and Rowland, D. Old and poor: Policy challenges in the 1990s, *Journal of Aging and Social Policy*, 1991, 2, 37–59.

Duncan, G. *Years of poverty, years of plenty: The changing economic fortunes of American workers and families*. Ann Arbor: University of Michigan, Institute for Social Research, 1984.

Eglit, H. Ageism in the work place: An elusive quarry. *Generations*, 1989, 2, 31–35.

Ekerdt, D. Why the notion persists that retirement harms health. *The Gerontologist*, 1987, 27(4), 454–457.

Ekerdt, D. J., Bossé, R., and Levkoff, S. An empirical test for phases of retirement: Findings from the Normative Aging Study. *Journal of Gerontology*, 1985, 40, 95–101.

Ekerdt, D., Bossé, R., and LoCastro, J. Claims that retirement improves health. *Journal of Gerontology*, 1983, 38, 231–236.

Ekerdt, D. J., and DeViney, S. Evidence for a pre-retirement process among older male workers. *Journals of Gerontology*, 1993, 48(2), 535–543.

Ekerdt, D. J., and Vinick, B. H. Marital complaints in husband working vs. husband retired couples. *Research on Aging*, 1991, 13(3), 364–382.

Estes, C., Gerard, L., and Clarke, A. Women and the economics of aging. *International Journal of Health Services*, 1984, 14, 55–68.

Feuerbach, E. and Erdwins, C. Women's retirement: The influence of work history. *Journal of Women and Aging*, 1994, 6(3), 69.

Fox, A. Income changes at and after Social Security benefit receipt: Evidence from the Retirement History Study. *Social Security Bulletin*, 1984, 47, 3–23.

George, L., Fillenbaum, G., and Palmore, E. Sex differences in the antecedents and consequences of retirement. *Journal of Gerontology*, 1984, 39, 364–371.

Gibson, R. C. Reconceptualizing retirement for black Americans. *The Gerontologist, 1987, 27,* 691–698.

Gibson, R. C. The subjective retirement of black Americans. *Journals of Gerontology, 1991, 46,* S204–209.

Government Accounting Office, *Elderly Americans: Health, housing and nutrition gaps between the poor and new poor.* (GAO/PEMD-92-29), 1993.

Grad, S. Income of the aged and nonaged, 1950–1982. *Social Security Bulletin, 1984, 47,* 3–17.

Grad, S. *Income of the population 65 and over, 1986.* Pub. No. 13-11871. Washington, D.C.: U.S. Department of Health and Human Services, Social Security Administration, 1988.

Hall, P. T., and Mirvis, H. *The new workplace and older workers.* Paper presented at a symposium of the National Planning Association/National Council on the Aging Joint Project on U.S. Competitiveness and the Aging American Workforce. Washington, D.C., 1993.

Hardy, D., and Hardy, C. *Social insecurity.* New York: Villard Books, 1991.

Hatch, L. R. Gender differences in orientation toward retirement from paid labor. *Gender and Society, 1992, 6(1),* 66.

Haug, M., Belgrave, L., and Jones, S. Partner's health and retirement adaptation of women and their husbands. *Journal of Women and Aging, 1992, 43(3),* 5–29.

Hayward, M., Grady, W., and McLaughlin, S. The retirement process among older women in the United States: Changes in the 1970s. *Research on Aging, 1988, 10(3),* 358–382.

Herz, D. E. Employment characteristics of older women, *Monthly Labor Review, 1988, 111,* 3–9.

Herzog, A. R., and House, J. S. Productive activities and aging well. *Generations,* Winter 1991, 49–54.

Herzog, A. R., Kahn, R. L., Morgan, J. N., Jackson, J. S., and Antonucci, T. C. Age differences in productive activities. *Journals of Gerontology, 1989, 44,* S129–S138.

Holden, K. C. Continuing limits on productive aging: The lesser rewards for working women. In S. A. Bass, F. G. Caro, and Y-P Chen (Eds.), *Achieving a productive aging society.* Westport, CT: Auburn House, 1993, 269–284.

Holden, K., Burkhauser, R., and Myers, D. Income transitions of older stages of life: The dynamics of poverty. *The Gerontologist, 1986, 26,* 292–297.

Hooker, K., and Ventis, D. Work ethic, daily activities, and retirement satisfaction. *Journal of Gerontology, 1984, 39,* 478–484.

Horn, J. C., and Meet, J. The vintage years. *Psychology Today, 1987, 21,* 76–84.

Howard, M. I. Employment of retired-worker women. *Social Security Bulletin, 1986, 49(3),* 4–18.

Jacobs, B. The elderly: How do they fare? In D. Besharov (Ed.) *Measuring poverty: Scientific controversy and political implications.* New York: Free Press, 1990.

Johnson, E., and Williamson, J. Retirement in the United States. In K. Markidas and C. Cooper (Eds.), *Retirement in industrialized societies.* New York: John Wiley & Sons, 1987, 9–41.

Kaspar, J. *Aging alone: Profiles and projections.* Baltimore, Md.: Commonwealth Fund Commission, 1988.

Kassner, E. *Falling through the safety net: Missed opportunities for America's elderly poor.* American Association of Retired Persons, Washington, D.C., 1992.

Keith, P. Work, retirement and well-being among unmarried men and women. *The Gerontologist, 1985, 25(4),* 410–416.

Kelly, J. R., and Steinkemp, M. W. Leisure in later life: Roles and identities. In N. J. Osgood (Ed.), *Life after work: Retirement, leisure, recreation and the elderly.* New York: Praeger, 1982, 268–292.

Kingson, E. Testing the boundaries of universality: What's mean? What's not? *The Gerontologist, 1994, 34(6),* 736–742.

Kingson, E., Hirshorn, B., and Harootyan, L. *The common stake: The interdependence of generations.* Washington, D.C., The Gerontological Society of America, 1986.

Kunkel, S. An extra eight hours a day. *Generations, 1989, 13(2),* 57–60.

Markey, J., and Parks, W. Occupational change: Pursuing a different kind of work. *Monthly Labor Review, 1989, 112,* 3–13.

Marsh, R. The income and resources of the elderly in 1978. *Social Security Bulletin, 1981, 44,* 3–11.

Matthews, A. M., and Brown, K. H. Retirement as a critical life event. *Research on Aging, 1987, 9,* 548–576.

McConnell, S. Retirement and employment. In D. Woodruff and J. Birren (Eds.), *Aging: Scientific perspectives and social issues* (2d ed.). Monterey, Calif.: Brooks Cole, 1983, 333–350.

McGuire, F. A., and Dottavio, D. Outdoor recreation participation across the lifespan: Abandonment, continuity and liberation. *International Journal of Aging and Human Development*, 1986–87, *24*, 87–100.

McLaughlin, D., and Jensen, C. Poverty among older Americans: The plight of non-metropolitan elders. *Journals of Gerontology*, 1993, *48*(2), 544–554.

Miller, M. *Suicide after sixty: The final alternative*. New York: Springer, 1979.

Minkler, M. Research on the health effects of retirement. *Journal of Health and Social Behavior*, 1981, *22*, 117–130.

Mor-Barak, M. E., Scharloch, A. E., Birba, L., and Sokolov, J. Employment, social networks, and health in the retirement years. *International Journal of Aging and Human Development*, 1992, 35 2 143–157.

Mor-Barak, M., and Tynan, M. Older workers and the workplace: A new challenge for occupational social work. *Social Work*, 1993, *38*(1), 45–55.

Morse, D. *The utilization of older workers* (Special Report No. 33). Washington, D.C.: National Commission for Manpower Policy, 1979.

Myers, D. A. Work after cessation of career job. *Journals of Gerontology*, 1991, *46*, S93–102.

National Academy on Aging. *Old age in the 21st century*. Syracuse, NY: Syracuse University, The Maxwell School, 1994.

National Center for Health Statistics, *National Health Interview Survey*, Supplement on Aging, 1984.

National Committee to Save Social Security and Medicare. *Supplemental Security Income*. Washington, D.C., 1994.

National Institute on Aging. *Health and Retirement Study*. Washington, D.C.: Press Release, June 17, 1993.

Olson, L, K. Aging policy: Who benefits? *Generations*, Fall 1984, 10–14.

*The OWL Observer*, From the mailbag, Washington, D.C.: The Older Women's League, July/August 1984, p. 10.

Palmore, E. B., Fillenbaum, G., and George, L. Consequences of retirement. *Journal of Gerontology*, 1984, *39*, 109–116.

Palmore, E. B., Barchett, B. M., Fillenbaum, G. G., George, L. K., and Wallman, L. M. *Retirement causes and consequences*. New York: Springer, 1985.

Parnes, H. *Work and retirement: A longitudinal study of men*. Cambridge, Mass.: MIT Press, 1981.

Parnes, H. S., and Sommers, D. G. Shunning retirement: Work experience of men in their seventies and early eighties. *Journals of Gerontology*, 1994, *49*(3), S117–S124.

Perkins, K. Psychosocial implications of women and retirement. *Social Work*, 1992, *37*(6), 526–527.

Pifer, A., and Bronte, L. *Our aging society: Paradox and promise*. New York: W. W. Norton, 1986.

Quinn, J. F., and Burkhauser, R. V. Work and retirement. In R. Binstock and L. George (Eds.), *Handbook of aging and the social sciences*. (3rd ed.) New York: Academic Press, 1990, 307–323.

Quinn, J. F., and Burkhauser, R. V. Labor market obstacles to aging productively. In S. A. Bass, F. G. Caro, and Y-P Chen (Eds.), *Achieving a productive aging society*. Westport, CT: Auburn House, 1993, 43–59.

Quinn, J. F., and Smeeding, T. M. Defying the averages: Poverty and well-being among older Americans. *Aging Today*, September/October, 1994, 9.

Radner, D. B. Changes in the incomes of age groups: 1984 to 1989. *Social Security Bulletin*, 1991, 54.

Ramirez, A. Making better use of older workers. *Fortune*, January 1989, 179–182.

Riddick, C. C. Life satisfaction for older female homemakers, retirees and workers. *Research on Aging*, 1985, *7*(3), 383–393.

Rix, S. (Ed.). *Older workers: How do they measure up? An overview of age differences in employee costs and performance*. Washington D.C.: American Association of Retired Persons, 1994.

Rones, P. Labor market problems of older workers. *Monthly Labor Review*, May 1983, 3–12.

Ruhm, C. J. Why older Americans stop working. *The Gerontologist*, 1989, *29*, 3, 294–299.

Schulz, J. H. *The economics of aging (3d ed.)*. Belmont, Calif.: Wadsworth, 1985.

Schulz, J. H. and Myles, J. Old age pensions: A comparative perspective. In R. Binstock and L. George (Eds.), *Handbook of aging and the social sciences* (3d ed.). New York: Academic Press, 1990, 398–419.

Schwenk, F. N. Changes in the economic status of America's elderly population during the last 50 years. *Family Economics Review*, 1993, *6*(1), 18–27.

Seccombe, K., and Lee, G. Gender differences in retirement satisfaction and its antecedents. *Research on Aging*, 1986, *8*, 426–440.

Sheppard, H. Work continuation vs. retirement: Reasons for continuing work. In R. Momis and S. Bass (Eds.), *Retirement reconsidered*. New York: Springer, 1988.

Smeeding, T. Economic status of the elderly. In R. Binstock and L. George (Eds.), *Handbook of aging and the social sciences* (3d ed.). New York: Academic Press, 1990, 362–381.

Soldo, B. America's elderly in the 1980s. *Population Bulletin*, 1980, *35*, 1–47.

Sterns, H., and McDaniel, M. Job performance and the older worker. In S. Rix (Ed.), *Older workers: How do they measure up?* Washington, D.C.: AARP, 1994, 27–51.

Straka, J. W. *The demand for older workers: The neglected side of a labor market*. Washington, D.C.: Social Security Administration, Office of Research and Statistics, 1992.

Streib, G., and Schneider, C. J. *Retirement in American society. Impact and process*. Ithaca, N.Y.: Cornell University Press, 1971.

Szinovacz, M. Retirement, couples and household work. In S. J. Bahi and E. T. Peterson (Eds.), *Aging and the family*. Lexington, Mass.: Lexington Press, 1989.

Taeuber, C. M. *Sixty-five plus in America*. Washington, D.C.: U.S. Department of Commerce, Bureau of the Census, 1992, 23–178.

Taylor, H., and Bass, R. *Productive aging: A survey of Americans age 55 and over*. New York: Louis Harris & Associates, 1992.

Taylor, R. J., and Chatters, L. M. Correlate of education, income and poverty among aged blacks. *The Gerontologist*, 1988, *28*, 435–441.

Torres-Gil, F. M. *The new aging: Politics and change in America*. New York: Auburn House, 1992.

Uhlenberg, P., and Salmon, M. G. Change in relative income of older women, 1960–1980. *The Gerontologist*, 1986, *26*, 164–170.

U.S. Bureau of the Census. *Poverty in the United States: 1990*. Current Population Reports, Series P-60, No. 175. U.S. Government Printing Office, Washington, D.C., 1991.

U.S. Department of Labor. *Labor workers' problems of older women*. Washington, D.C.: U.S. Department of Labor, January 1989.

U.S. Department of Labor, Bureau of Labor Statistics. *Employment and Earnings, 37*. Washington, D.C.: U.S. Department of Labor, 1989.

U.S. Department of Labor, Bureau of Labor Statistics, *Employment and Earnings, 37*, 1990.

U.S. Government Accounting Office. *Social Security—Sustained effort needed to improve management and prepare for the future*. Report to the Commissioner, Social Security Administration. GAO/HRD 94-22. October 1993.

U.S. Joint Economic Committee, Special Study on Economic Change. *Social Security and pensions: Programs of equity and security*. Washington, D.C.: U.S. Government Printing Office, 1980.

U.S. Senate Special Committee on Aging. *America in transition: An aging society* (1984–85 ed.). Washington, D.C.: U.S. Government Printing Office, 1985.

U.S. Senate Special Committee on Aging, *Aging America: Trends and projections*. Washington, D.C.: U.S. Department of Health and Human Services, 1992.

Villers Foundation. *On the other side of easy street: Myths and facts about the economics of old age*. Washington, D.C., 1987.

Ward, R. Occupational variation in the life course: Implications for later life. In N. Osgood (Ed.), *Life after work: Retirement, leisure, recreation and elderly*. New York: Praeger, 1982.

Zsembik, B., and Singer, A. The problem of defining retirement among minorities: The Mexican Americans. *The Gerontologist*, 1990, *30*, 749–757.

# CHAPTER 15

## CHANGING ROLES: COMMUNITY, ORGANIZATIONAL, AND POLITICAL

The living arrangements, neighborhoods, and socioeconomic status of adults, as well as their physical capacities, attitudes, skills, and values, all influence their social activity patterns. People's use of time and arenas of involvement vary with the opportunities provided by the environment and with each developmental phase in the life cycle. Young and middle-aged adults may feel that there is not enough time for all they want to do. Their days are crowded with task-oriented activities—employment, child care, and household maintenance. During middle age, people may idealize the free time of retirement, postponing travel or classes until they are retired and have "time for things like that." With retirement, the departure of children, and other role changes, most older adults experience discretion over their use of time, perhaps more than at any other point in their adult lives. The reality of nonwork time for retirees, however, may be quite different from their middle-age fantasies of "if only we had the time." Many retirees overestimate the extent and variety of activities they will pursue upon retirement. Poor health, re-

duced income, transportation difficulties, isolated living arrangements, and role changes all may disrupt and reduce these anticipated activities in old age. In fact, as discussed in Chapter 14, a growing percentage of older people wish they could have continued to work, at least on a part-time basis.

This chapter focuses on the activity patterns most common among older people in American society, including leisure pursuits, membership in community and interest associations, education, volunteering, religious participation and spirituality, and political involvement. Even with changes in their competence in physical health and physiological functioning, as described in earlier chapters, older people can stay active and maintain optimal quality of life by modifying their involvement in community and organizational activities, thereby reestablishing congruence between their needs and abilities and the demands of the social environment. For each of these forms of community and organizational involvement, the factors that influence the rates and patterns of participation, the functions of such participation, and gender and ethnic minority variations in activities are considered.

As noted in Chapter 14, there are a variety of ways in which older people can be active and productive, including unpaid work in the home, volunteer work, helping others, and acquiring training and skills to enhance their capacity to perform such tasks. Such activities, which tend not to decrease with age, can be viewed as productive or valuable as paid work and can enhance older people's physical and psychological well-being (Herzog and Morgan, 1992; Herzog et al., 1989; Danigelis and McIntosh, 1993). The concept of productive aging emphasizes the roles older people play in society as contrasted to successful aging, which focuses on individual physiological and psychological capacity and performance (Caro, Bass, and Chen, 1993). While there is disagreement about whether leisure activities per se should be considered productive aging (Bass et al., 1993), we would argue that such activities, particularly participation in voluntary associations, senior organizations and educational programs, can enhance older people's well-being and thus are consistent with a broad definition of productive aging. This chapter begins with a discussion of the types and functions of leisure for older people.

## VARIATIONS IN ACTIVITIES IN OLD AGE

As described in Chapter 4, there are widely different perspectives on participation in old age—from activity theory, which stresses the beneficial effects of continued involvement, to disengagement theory, which argues the appropriateness of withdrawal. These and other theoretical perspectives have addressed the questions: Does age bring a desire for increased social autonomy? Are older people content to disengage from society? Is daily activity essential to successful adjustment to aging? How is use of time related to life satisfaction and to feelings of competence toward the larger environment? These questions have long been topics of research and debate.

Although time is less fragmented upon retirement than it is at earlier life stages, there still are numerous constraints on how people choose to become involved in different social arenas. As identified in earlier chapters, the normal physical and psychological changes of aging, and any diseases that affect older persons, may limit their capacities to engage in certain activities and to maintain competence in relation to environmental demands. Cohort experiences and socialization to certain activities and values, gender and ethnic minority group memberships, and type of living arrangements (e.g., a retirement community or nursing home) may interact and result in certain activities being stratified by age. Some older individuals may not undertake particular activities because they feel they lack the skills, physical strength, or knowledge to do them, or that they are too old to undertake such activities. Atchley (1971) has suggested that if "activity competence" is not learned by middle age, it never will be. This implies that active and creative use of free time in youth is necessary to assume it in the later years. On the other hand, there are many instances of individuals successfully pursuing new activities, such as art, running, or skiing, for the first time in old age.

Nevertheless, past activity patterns and personality dynamics do shape the use of time. There appears to be continuity between leisure pursuits enjoyed at earlier and later stages of life, consistent with continuity theory (discussed in Chapter 4). Adults have been found to have a core of leisure activities that persists across the life course, although the specific means of carrying out such patterns may alter with age (Kelly, Steinkamp and Kelly, 1987). As people's interests crystallize over the life span, they generally become more selective about how they invest their time and energy.

## LEISURE PURSUITS

The term *leisure* evokes different reactions in people. For some, it signifies wasting time. For others, it is only the frenzied pursuit of "leisure activities" on the weekends that sustains them through the work week. People's reactions to the concept of leisure are clearly influenced by cultural values attached to work. In American culture, the Puritan work ethic has tended to instill a mistrust of nonproductive uses of time. Some implicit assumptions in our society have been that work is better than leisure; group activities are better than solitary ones; and active pursuits, such as sports, are better than contemplation or meditation. Because of American cultural values of productivity and hard work—values that are particularly strong for the current generation of older persons but that may be changing for future cohorts—many older people lack experience in satisfying nonwork activities at earlier phases in their lives.

Societal values regarding leisure are changing, however, with more legitimacy given to leisure throughout the life cycle, as evidenced by the growing number of classes and businesses that specialize in this area. For low-income or ethnic minority elders or for older people in developing countries, however, leisure may be a meaningless concept, if they have had to continue working or lack the resources for satisfying recreational time.

Independent of such social norms, leisure can be defined as any activity characterized by the absence of obligation that is inherently satisfying and has intrinsic meaning. Free time alone is not necessarily leisure. Instead, the critical variable is how a person defines tasks and situations to bring intrinsic pleasure (Bammel and Bammel, 1985). Accordingly, leisure implies feelings of freedom and pleasure. People who engage in sports, travel, or visits to museums and do not experience such feelings may still be at "work" rather than at "leisure" (Kelly, 1982; Kleiber and Kelly, 1980).

Disagreement regarding the value of leisure pursuits for older people is reflected in the gerontological literature. Most definitions of productive aging (Caro, Bass, and Chen, 1993; Herzog and Morgan, 1992, 1993; Danigelis and McIntosh, 1993) do not include activities of a personal, enrichment nature, which would exclude

some leisure activities (watching television, attending a concert, travel), but not others that are discussed in this chapter, such as volunteering and participation in senior organizations. An early perspective was that leisure roles cannot substitute for work roles, because they are not legitimated by societal norms. Since work is a dominant value in American society, it was argued that individuals cannot derive self-respect from leisure. It was also observed that older individuals, fearing the embarrassment of failing in a leisure activity, avoid leisure pursuits that are common to younger people (Miller, 1965), although this pattern may change with future cohorts who will be healthier and more active.

The counterargument is that leisure is neither demoralizing nor traumatizing to most older people. It is argued that leisure can replace the work role and provide personal satisfaction in later life, especially when the retired person has good health and an adequate income, and when retirement activities build upon preretirement skills and interests (Lawton, Moss, and Fulcomer, 1986–87). In fact, some gerontologists have suggested that leisure is central in maintaining a positive identity and self-concept in old age (Kelly, Steinkamp, and Kelly, 1987). Accordingly, activities that result in a sense of being valued and contributing to society have been found in many instances to be positively related to life satisfaction and mental well-being in retirement (Riddick and Stewart, 1994).

Another perspective is that retirement is legitimated in our work-oriented society by an ethic that esteems leisure that is earnest, occupied, and filled with activity—a "busy" ethic, which is consistent with the activity theory of aging (Ekerdt, 1986). For those with strong work values, work-like activities are probably important for achieving satisfaction in retirement (Hooker and Ventes, 1984). The prevalence of the "busy" ethic is reflected in the question commonly asked of retirees: What do you do to keep busy? "Keeping busy" and engaging in productive useful activities analogous to work are presumed to ease the adjustment to retirement by adapting retired life to prevailing societal norms, although the "busy" ethic is contrary to the definition of leisure as intrinsically satisfying.

Although there are wide variations, patterns of activity among older individuals have been identified. Most leisure time is not spent in public recreation programs developed specially for older persons. Compared to younger people, older people are more likely to engage in solitary and sedentary pursuits, such as watching television, visiting with family and friends, and reading; they are also less likely to participate in active sports, attend cultural events, travel, or visit theaters, parks, and libraries (Cutler and Hendricks, 1990). However, compared to a decade ago, older people today are choosing activities far more like those of people twenty years younger than themselves. Not surprisingly, residents of retirement communities have higher levels of leisure activity than do those living in dispersed housing (Cutler and Hendricks, 1990), and a wide range of leisure-oriented businesses, including group travel programs, are marketing services to them.

Leisure activities also vary by gender and socioeconomic status. Not surprisingly, higher-income older people tend to be more active in leisure pursuits than low-income elders (Riddick and Stewart, 1994). These differences in activities are attributable primarily to the costs of pursuing them, not necessarily to inherent differences in people of low and high socioeconomic status. Older men tend to do more household maintenance and paid work outside the home, while older women perform more housework, child care, volunteer work, and participate in more voluntary associations (Danigelis and McIntosh, 1993; Herzog et al., 1989). Less is known about how leisure pursuits vary among ethnic minority groups.

Several benefit programs are designed to reduce financial barriers to leisure. For instance, Golden Passports give older people reduced admission fees to national parks. Similar programs at the local or state level provide free admission to parks, museums, and cultural activities, and reduced prices from businesses and transportation. Older people may take courses on a tuition-free basis at many colleges and universities. And Elderhostel programs are an economical way to combine travel, learning, and socializing (Moody, 1993).

All older people spend considerable time in obligatory activities, such as housework, shopping, and personal care. As their health declines, they may devote even more time to these routine pursuits and become less involved in externally oriented activities such as community organizations, outdoor recreation and travel (Kelly, 1987; Lawton, Moss, and Fulcomer, 1986–87). For low-income older people, these routines may be their only options. When judged by younger persons or by middle-class standards, these obligatory activities may be viewed as "boring" or "nonproductive," yet the ability to perform these more mundane activities—personal care, cooking, puttering around the house, or sitting in quiet reflection—can be critical to maintaining older people's competence, self-esteem, and life satisfaction. Furthermore, these routines may represent realistic adjustments to declining energy levels and incomes (Bammel and Bammel, 1985). In fact, older people may need to accept less externally oriented activities in order to attain a sense of "ego integrity," as defined by Erikson (Kleiber and Kelly, 1980). Such routine leisure pursuits, consistent with the broader concept of productive aging, may thus reflect rational choices to develop ways of coping congruent with changes in environments and may also enhance quality of life.

## THE MEANING AND FUNCTIONS OF LEISURE FOR OLDER PEOPLE

Leisure activities have been classified in terms of the following psychological benefits perceived by older participants: companionship (e.g., playing cards or going dancing); compensation for past activities (e.g., picnicking instead of hiking) temporary disengagement (e.g., watching TV); comfortable solitude (e.g., reading); expressive solitude (e.g., knitting and crocheting); and expressive service (e.g., volunteer service, attending meetings of social groups) (Tinsley et al., 1985). Leisure activities also serve to help maintain ties with others and to provide new sources of personal meaning and competence to replace earlier sources that have been lost. A positive association has been found between leisure activities and a sense of well-being and a positive self-concept among older people. This relationship does not mean, however, that leisure activity itself creates well-being, since older people who are active also tend to be healthier and of higher socioeconomic status. In fact, it appears that the quality of interactions with others in leisure pursuits may be more salient than the number or frequency of interactions for life satisfaction and morale (Larson, Zuzanek, and Mannell, 1985; Kelly, Steinkamp, and Kelly, 1987; Cutler and Hendricks, 1990).

A challenge for those working with older people is to create leisure opportunities that participants perceive as meaningful and as contributing to their sense of satisfaction and well-being. Structured opportunities also need to maximize older people's skills and interests and be broadly inclusive, serving a culturally and economically diverse population. Such options may

Artistic pursuits can enhance quality of life in the later years.

be especially important for single older persons who lack daily companionship (Larson, Zuzanek, and Mannell, 1985).

Senior centers are one mechanism to provide such opportunities. These vary greatly in the type of services offered, which range from purely recreational events, to social action, to the delivery of social and health services, including health screening and illness prevention. In fact, the Older Americans Act identifies centers as preferred focal points for comprehensive, coordinated service delivery. Despite the range of activities, however, only about 15 percent of older persons participate in senior centers for several reasons (Krout, Cutler, and Coward, 1990; Krout, 1989). Individuals may be busy elsewhere, uninterested in the center's activities, in poor health, or without the necessary transportation. As noted in Chapter 13, people are more likely to participate in senior centers that are physically close to their homes. Also, some older people refuse to participate because they "don't want to be with only old people," and the low proportion of men in many centers may deter other men from taking part. Furthermore, some centers draw from a relatively narrow population, reaching primarily healthy, working- to lower-middle-class individuals with a "lifetime of joining clubs" who are attracted by opportunities for socializing and friendships. Nationwide, individuals who are generally less advantaged, but not the least advantaged, are most likely to participate in senior center activities (Krout, Cutler, and Coward, 1990). Those who participate tend to do so out of a desire for social interaction and have been invited by friends (Bazargan, Barbre, and Torres-Gil, 1992).

Senior centers face a number of programmatic challenges. One is that they have gotten "older" in the 1990s as their users have "aged in place" and the young-old have been less inclined to attend. However, participation declines after age 84 (Krout, 1989). Centers have been criticized for not doing more to reach older ethnic minorities and older people who are frail, low-income, or disabled. Although African American elders are slightly more likely than whites to attend centers, critics maintain that programs must change to be multicultural. Many communities with ethnic minority neighborhoods have established senior centers in these areas, and have successfully attracted diverse elders who would not otherwise participate. In contrast, some observers contend that targeting services to ethnic minorities, the disabled, and the poor would run counter to the universal nature of services under the Older Americans Act and could reduce the participation of those relatively more advantaged older people who currently attend centers (Krout, Cutler, and Coward, 1990; Ralston, 1991).

## MEMBERSHIP IN VOLUNTARY ASSOCIATIONS

Given the emphasis in our society on being active, productive, and a joiner, voluntary association membership is often assumed to be "good" for older people. Based on such assumptions, well-meaning professionals may go to considerable lengths to try to recruit older people to such associations, oftentimes without success. Overall, older people are less likely to belong to organizations than are younger people, but their reduced membership does not necessarily indicate a slackening of interest with age. Rather, membership is most closely tied to social class and is more characteristic of our society than of most other cultures. When socioeconomic status is taken into account, older people show considerable stability in their general level of voluntary association participation from middle age until their sixties (Cutler and Hendricks, 1990).

The kind of organizations in which older people participate varies by gender and ethnic minority status. Older women appear to be more active participants in voluntary associations than are older men (Danigelis and McIntosh, 1993). Women's multiple roles at earlier phases of the life span, such as volunteer work and participation in voluntary associations, has been found to

be positively related to health and occupying multiple roles in old age (Moen, Dempster-McClain, and Williams, 1992). Older African Americans have higher rates of organizational membership than do older whites or members of other ethnic minority groups, although for both blacks and whites, membership is most frequent among those with better health and higher income and education levels. Black and white elders differ in the types of associations they join; older blacks are especially likely to belong to church-related groups and social and recreational clubs; older whites frequently belong to nationality organizations and senior citizen clubs (Krout, Cutler, and Coward, 1990; Watts and Zarit, 1991). Hispanics participate in fraternal and service-oriented organizations, mutual aid societies, and "hometown" clubs. Some of these memberships are related to historical circumstances rather than to age or ethnic minority status per se.

Older persons who are active in community and interest organizations derive a variety of benefits. Socializing appears to be the primary reward, especially for people like Mrs. Howard in the introductory vignette. Because many organizations are age-graded, people interact with others similar in age and interests. These interactions often result in friendships, support, mutual exchanges of resources, and collective activity.

Consistent with the broader concept of productivity, voluntary associations can also serve to maintain the social integration of older people, countering losses in roles and in interactions with others (Cutler and Hendricks, 1990). Older people in voluntary organizations have been found to have higher morale than do nonmembers, although this may be attributed to their higher levels of health, income, and education, factors that have been found to contribute to well-being. When these other characteristics are taken into account, organizational membership is apparently unrelated to overall life satisfaction. If people join organizations primarily to "make the time pass," their membership is generally not central to their sense of well-being. In contrast, the most satisfied members of organizations are those who become involved in order to have new experiences, achieve something, be creative, and help others. Such members, in turn, participate actively through planning and leadership. Their responsibilities yield them more novel experiences and greater feelings of competence and creativity than is the case with those who participate in only social and recreational activities, such as card playing for pleasure and "passing the time" (Babchuk et al., 1979). Opportunities for more active participation are found in senior advocacy groups or in organizations such as advisory boards to Area Agencies on Aging where older people must, by charter, be in leadership roles. Thus, voluntary association membership appears to be more satisfying when it provides opportunities for active, intense involvement and significant leadership roles.

## VOLUNTEER WORK

With cutbacks in public funding, voluntary, service, and religious organizations increasingly rely upon volunteers to accomplish their missions, especially as more women, who used to volunteer as part of traditional homemaker roles, have entered the paid work force. Because Americans are retiring at younger ages and are in better health and better educated than earlier cohorts, they are likely to have the time, energy, and skills to contribute to society through volunteer work. Older persons have long played a critical role as volunteers in hospitals, senior centers, churches, and children's homes and schools. Such activity is consistent with the concept of productive aging, whereby older people produce valued goods and services, even though they are not paid. This kind of volunteering, similar to participation in voluntary associations, is more characteristic of American society than others.

Within the past twenty years, a number of public and private initiatives have been designed to expand community service by older persons.

One of the best known of the government-sponsored initiatives is the Foster Grandparent Program, which pairs seniors with disabled children; it has been found to be mutually beneficial to both. This mutual aid concept was extended to the Senior Companion Program, in which able-bodied seniors serve disabled older people. The Peace Corps has also increased its recruitment of older volunteers; over 4 percent of its volunteers in developing countries today are seniors. The Older American Volunteer Program of ACTION recruits older people to work with disadvantaged groups within the United States. One of the largest of the volunteer networks is the Retired Senior Volunteer Program (RSVP), which is part of the National Older Americans' Volunteer Program, authorized by the 1969 amendments to the Older Americans Act. RSVP has projects in schools, hospitals, adult and child day centers, and nursing homes.

Within the private sector, programs sponsored by the American Association of Retired Persons involve 8 percent of older volunteers, who are matched with jobs through a nationwide Volunteer Talent Bank (Chambré, 1993). Other private sector programs are the National and International Executive Services Corps of Retired Executives which permits retired executives to use their technical and financial expertise in consultant-type arrangements with companies in the United States and abroad and the Citizen Democracy Corps where retirees provide assistance to formerly Communist countries.

It is estimated that 40 percent of older people volunteer; even among those over age 75, nearly 30 percent are still active as volunteers—rates of involvement that are considerably higher than other age groups (Chambré, 1993; The Commonwealth Fund, 1993; Haygne, 1991; Herzog and Morgan, 1993). Among the older population, rates of volunteering are highest among those with higher income and education, a history of volunteering throughout their lives, and a broad range of interests along with a belief that they can make valuable contributions (Haygne, 1991; Herzog and Morgan, 1993).

Among older college graduates, for example, 66 percent volunteer (Chambré, 1993). The most frequent type of volunteer work is through religious organizations, followed by direct service such as tutoring, handiwork, raising money, serving on a board or committee, or assisting in an office, with about 40 percent of volunteers serving more than one organization. The average amount of time volunteered per week is 6.5 hours, but for some, volunteer work is equivalent to a full-time job (Caro et al., 1993; The Commonwealth Fund, 1993; Taylor and Bass, 1992).

As is the case generally in voluntary activities, women (especially widows) are more likely to volunteer than men, 27 percent and 25 percent respectively (The Commonwealth Fund, 1993). Although women generally view volunteering as a way to help others, men more frequently define it as a substitute for the worker role. Differences have also been noted among ethnic minorities. Volunteering as a way to help others through informal networks is frequent in ethnic minority communities, primarily through African American churches, and may represent a history of self-reliance and incorporating a lifetime of hard work into leisure experiences and services to others (Allen and Chin-Sang, 1990). Mutual aid (e.g., providing food and lodging to older persons) is common in American Indian communities. Volunteer activities among Pacific Asian elders are ethnically specific and reinforce the continuation of Pacific Asian value systems. Older Chinese, for example, often work through family associations or benevolent societies. Some Japanese elders participate in clubs, which are an extension of the "family helping itself" concept that is rooted in traditional Japanese culture. The Hispanic community has been found to emphasize self-help, mutual aid, neighborhood assistance, and advocacy for their older members (Height et al., 1981).

Volunteer programs serve two major social benefits: They provide individuals with meaningful social roles and they furnish organizations with experienced, reliable workers at minimal cost. In a national survey, 90 percent of older volunteers believe that their work contributes to their organization, and 71 percent are very satisfied with their lives compared to 58 percent of those who do not volunteer (The Commonwealth Fund, 1993). In a number of studies, volunteers have been found to rank higher in life satisfaction, enhanced physical and mental well-being, and a sense of accomplishment and feelings of usefulness (Fogelman, 1981; Hunter and Linn, 1981; Kasper, 1988). Contrary to the assumptions of activity theory, the desire to replace lost roles, such as the role of employee or spouse, is not a primary motivator for volunteers; in fact, older people are more likely to volunteer if they are married, involved in other organizations, and employed part-time while nonemployed older people tend to volunteer less (Chambré, 1993; Herzog and Morgan, 1993). For most retirees, volunteering is apparently not a work substitute (Chambré, 1984). Consistent with the continuity theory of aging, most older volunteers have volunteered earlier in their lives and have a sense of obligation to be productive (Caro et al., 1993). Volunteerism is part of an overall active lifestyle that unfolds in the formal arenas of work and organized activities, with their long-standing involvement either remaining constant or expanding as they age (Chambré, 1984; 1993; Marriot, 1991). Nevertheless, it is still possible to recruit new volunteers in old age, especially if volunteer assignments are perceived as meaningful and challenging (Caro et al., 1993). From the perspective of social exchange theory, volunteering may ensure valued social resources as a basis of exchange, primarily by assisting others rather than by being perceived as dependent.

The first vignette below illustrates how some older adults achieve life satisfaction by substituting volunteering for previous professions as teachers and mentors. The second vignette illustrates how volunteering can support older people in helping roles.

Volunteers clearly make a major social and financial contribution to communities and to the economy. The unpaid volunteer activities of older

---

## VOLUNTEERING AS A SUBSTITUTION FOR PAST ROLES

Ted was a teacher of 6th-grade science in an inner city public school for thirty-five years. When he retired at age 57, he began a successful second career selling real estate. Now at age 72, he continues to work on average two days per week. He enjoys the contact with people, and finds his work very different than teaching. Because he believes it is important to give back to his community, he also volunteers as a tutor in an after-school program run by his church for neighborhood "latchkey" kids.

---

Americans are estimated to be worth $17 billion per year, assuming hourly wages paid to workers with similar jobs (The Commonwealth Fund, 1993). Since they often save human service agencies and schools substantial money, there is ongoing debate about whether volunteers are exploited as "free labor" and a means to cut costs. Such debate is heightened when public social services are reduced and volunteers, frequently women, are expected to fill gaps in programs. For low-income older persons in particular, volunteering can be an unaffordable luxury. The National Council of Senior Citizens contends that many older volunteers need additional income and would prefer part-time paid work. The Council has taken a position against any program that asks older people to perform, on a volunteer basis, community service work for which younger people are paid.

A number of trends will influence the meaning and functions of volunteerism for older persons. Changing economic conditions may mean that fewer individuals can afford the additional costs of transportation, meals, and out-of-pocket expenses. With the increasing emphasis nationally on self-help and mutual aid, people may choose instead to become more active in neighborhood and community advocacy organizations that seek to empower individuals through solving problems. In the future, older people are likely to be more involved in advisory councils and commissions; in lobbying efforts, as legislative aides and interns; and in national senior organizations, such as those described later in this chapter. These volunteer and advocacy efforts will continue to face the challenge of developing ways to involve older people who are low-income, ethnic minorities, live alone, frail and disabled, or from areas without adequate public transportation.

## Educational Programs

Most educational programs have been oriented toward enrichment or practical personal assis-

---

## VOLUNTEERING AS A SOURCE OF SUPPORT

Mary, a homemaker and mother of four children, spent her early years being involved with Scouts, PTA, and teaching Sunday School. When her last child left home when she was 52, she felt "lost" because there was no one to "need" her in the same ways the children had. At 53, she began volunteering, answering the phone for a community center that served children and elders, and found a new role. When she was widowed at age 70, she increased the hours of volunteering to fill the lonely hours when she missed her husband. Since she has never driven, she takes the bus one day a week to the community center. Now at age 80, she was recently honored by the city at a special reception for her 8,000 hours of volunteer service.

tance in such areas as health and finances rather than education for new paid roles, and therefore have not necessarily supported older people moving into new productive roles (Caro et al., 1993). A primary reason for the limited role of education for productive aging is that higher education institutions have not viewed older learners as a priority. Even though 80 percent of the states have tuition-free, space available policies for older people, state legislators typically have provided little funding to support older adult programs. In addition, in times of fiscal constraint, older adult programs are often the first to be cut (Moody, 1993).

Fortunately, some creative late-life learning initiatives in higher education have developed which are constructed around images of productive aging, not of decline or need. One of the best known is Elderhostel, where older adults attend special seminars or institutes on campus throughout the country. Although over 200,000 older learners participate each year, few campuses enroll more than a few hundred Elderhostel students each year, in part because the program does not generate new sources of revenue for higher education. An example of effective marketing of higher education to older residents within a geographic area is Saddleback College's Emeritus Institute near the Leisure World retirement community in California. As a sign of its success, nearly 20 percent of the 21,000 student body are retired persons. Some gerontology certificate programs, such as the University of Massachusetts at Boston, are committed to preparing significant numbers of older people for roles as advocates and service providers. On a statewide level, the North Carolina legislature appropriated funds for a Center for Creative Retirement at the University of North Carolina at Asheville. This network of programs offers liberal arts education, peer learning groups, health promotion, training of older volunteers, intergenerational programming, and seniors' mentoring of younger undergraduates for career guidance. Moody (1993) classifies these programs as illustrative of the social investment model of adult education,

in which older people are viewed as both productive, active teachers and as learners. These programs are also characterized by strong links with the practice community which serves older adults, intergenerational opportunities, and models of peer learning. Community colleges, because of their accessibility, would be ideal settings in which to develop more educational programs that offer older adults a variety of ways to be productive. Programs for older learners represent an area in need of further development and funding, especially with the increase in healthy, active older people who seek new opportunities to contribute to society after retirement.

## Religious Participation, Religiousness, and Spirituality

Of the various options for organizational participation, the most common choice for older persons is religious affiliation.[*] After family and government, religious groups are an important source of instrumental support for older people (Blazer, 1991). Across the life span, church and synagogue attendance is lowest among those in their thirties, peaks in the late fifties to early sixties (with approximately 60 percent of this age group attending), and begins to decline in the late sixties or early seventies. Despite this slight decline, the rate of church or synagogue attendance for older people exceeds that of other age groups, with 50 percent of persons over age 65 attending church or synagogue in an average week and many more attending less frequently. Furthermore, people age 65 and over are the most likely of any age group to belong to church-affiliated groups and fraternal associations. In contrast to other types

---

[*]This discussion of religion and the elderly is limited to the broad cultural mainstream of American society. A multinational, multicultural review of religion is beyond the scope of this book. Since world religions differ greatly, the religious values, attitudes, and practices discussed here may have little generalization beyond our society to other major segments of the world.

of voluntary organizations, leadership positions in churches and synagogues tend to be concentrated among older people (Koenig, George, and Siegler, 1988; Worthington, 1989).

One reason for inconsistent empirical findings regarding the relationship between aging and religion is that rates of church attendance in themselves do not indicate the extent of religiosity among older persons (Hunsberger, 1985). Religious behaviors can be examined in terms of three factors: (1) participation in religious organizations, (2) the personal meaning of religion and private devotional activities within the home, and (3) the contribution of religion to individuals' adjustment to the aging process and their confrontation with death and dying. For many elders, religious behavior, defined broadly as encompassing trust and faith in God, prayer, and strength from God, is an effective way to cope with the losses they experience (Koenig, George, and Siegler, 1988). Declines in rates of religious participation after age 70 may reflect health and transportation difficulties more than lack of religiousness. In fact, while attendance at formal services declines with age, older individuals apparently compensate by an increase in internal religious practices through reading the Bible, listening to religious broadcasts, praying, or studying religion. Thus, some older people who appear to be disengaged from religious organizations may be fully engaged nonorganizationally, experiencing strong and meaningful subjective ties to religion (Stuckey, 1990).

Although religion appears to be very important to many older people, they probably also valued it when they were young. That is, contrary to popular stereotypes, we do not necessarily become more religious as we age. When the religious practices of older individuals are conceptualized to include patterns of belief, religious orientation, and stability of religious attitudes, rather than only activities within the formal association of the church, the importance of religion remains stable over time. Religious *beliefs,* as contrasted with church attendance, appear to be relatively stable from the late teens until age

60, and to *increase* thereafter (McFadden and Gerl, 1990).

Most surveys on religiousness share the limitations of cross-sectional research, as discussed in Chapter 2. That is, they do not attempt to measure the individual's past religious values and behaviors. The few longitudinal studies available suggest that cohort differences may be more important than the effects of age (Hunsberger, 1985). Thus, although religious convictions appear to become more salient over the years, this may be a generational phenomenon captured by the cross-sectional nature of most of the research. The current cohort of older persons, raised during a time of more widespread religious involvement, had their peak rates of attendance in the 1950s, when this country experienced a church revival. All cohorts, not only older people, have shown a decline in church or synagogue attendance since 1965, although this may be changing in the 1990s. There are also other possible effects of selective survival. Orthodox religious persons are less likely to smoke, drink alcohol excessively, and participate in other behaviors that have been linked to early death. The survival of the more religious may make the older population as a whole appear to be more orthodox in their beliefs than younger age groups.

Studies of religious activity have found both gender and ethnic minority differences. Consistent with patterns of involvement in other organizations, women, particularly African American women, have higher rates of church membership than do men (Stuckey, 1990). Religion also appears to be central to the lives of most older African Americans of both sexes and to be related to their life satisfaction, personal well-being, and sense of integration in the larger community (Walls and Zarit, 1991). The high esteem afforded African American elders in the church may partially underlie these positive associations. Historically, African Americans have had more autonomy in their religious lives than in their economic and political lives. The negative effects of life stress for older African Americans have been found to be offset by increased religious involvement, with use of prayer, other private religious activities and a cognitive reframing of the situation in positive terms (e.g., "I have been through a lot before and I'll get through this too") as effective coping mechanisms. For some African American caregivers, for example, the church and God are considered part of their informal system of support and respite (Krause and Tran, 1989; Wood and Parham, 1990; Wood and Wan, 1993). For African American elders, the church has also provided social services, such as in-home visitation, counseling and transportation (Walls and Zarit, 1991; Taylor and Chatters, 1991). Such instrumental support reflects the fact that the African American church has historically been responsible for improving the socioeconomic and political conditions of their parishioners (Gurin, Hatchett, and Jackson, 1989). In a study comparing Mexican-Americans and whites for two time periods, Mexican-Americans were found to be more religious as measured by church attendance, self-rated religiousness, and private prayer. Furthermore, these three factors were positively related to their life satisfaction (Markides, 1983).

Although the relationship between religious involvement and life satisfaction is not clear-cut, religious attitudes, beliefs, and participation have generally been found to be positively associated with well-being, happiness, a sense of usefulness, and morale. The strength of these relationships increases over time (Hunsberger, 1985; Koenig, George, and Siegler, 1988; Koenig, Kvale, and Ferrel, 1988). In fact, for some individuals age 75 and over, religion was second to health in its relationship to morale (Koenig, George, and Siegler, 1988). Across all religions, the more religiously devout are usually less afraid of death than the less devout (Spilka, Hood, and Gorosch, 1985). Accordingly, individuals for whom faith provides meaning experience greater feelings of internal control and a more positive self-concept (Kivett, 1979). It is unclear, however, whether religiousness itself is beneficial, or if the organizational aspects of the sense of belonging and social support are the determinants, since religious

participation is associated with other types of group involvement. Satisfaction, serenity, or acceptance of death may result not from faith or spirituality per se, but rather from participation in social networks and reference groups that offer support and security. Older people themselves list among the benefits of religion both the meaning it gives to life and the social interaction it affords (Stuckey, 1990; Walls and Zarit, 1991). Therefore, it is important to consider how social support in churches complements and interacts with religious beliefs and activities.

## The Value of Spiritual Well-Being

Spiritual well-being can be differentiated from organized religion and includes: (1) self-determined wisdom in which the individual tries to achieve stability in his or her environment; (2) self-transcendence or crossing a boundary beyond the self in which the individual adjusts to losses and rejects material security; (3) achievement of meaning and purpose for one's continued existence; and (4) acceptance of the wholeness of life (Blazer, 1991; Whitehead, 1981). According to this perspective, people can be spiritual without being religious in the sense of organized religion (Fischer, 1985). Listening to music, viewing a sunset or a painting, loving, and being loved can all be profound spiritual activities. It is believed that people can only be fully spiritual human beings if they find meaning in life generally or in specific daily events, such as working on a project (Missine, 1986). High levels of spirituality have been found to be associated with mental health indicators, such as purpose in life, self-esteem, and social skills (Paloutzian and Ellison, 1982). Spirituality has been identified as an important factor in an individual's perception of quality of life (irrespective of age or socioeconomic status) and in maintaining a healthy lifestyle (Levine, 1983). Spiritual well-being is related not only to the quality of life but also to the will to live. Some gerontologists and theologians maintain that the person who aims to enhance spiritual well-being and to find meaning in life will have a reason to live, despite losses associated with aging (Thorson, 1983). Mr. Mansfield, in the introduction to this section, illustrates the role of spirituality in helping older persons cope with tragic losses in their lives.

Aging has been characterized as a spiritual journey, in which the person aims to achieve integration across a number of areas of life—biological, psychological, social, and spiritual (Greenberg, 1985; Hyer, Jacob, and Pattison, 1987; Worthington, 1989). An ageless self, that is, a person who is not preoccupied or discouraged by his or her aging, has an identity that maintains continuity and is on a spiritual journey in time, despite age-related physical and social changes; for such an individual, being old per se is neither a central feature of the self nor the source of its meaning (Kaufman, 1986). Confronting negative images of aging, loss, and death is essential for psychological-spiritual growth and successful aging (Bianchi, 1982). In fact, dealing with loss has been viewed as one of aging's greatest spiritual challenges (Fischer, 1985). Autobiographical storytelling, journal keeping, and empathic interactions with others have been found to be useful in supporting older persons' spiritual integration (McFadden and Gerl, 1990).

The spiritual dimensions of health care have been examined. Because good health is seen as an indication that one's life is in harmony, illness may be viewed as having a spiritual dimension (Wood and Wan, 1993). Practitioners who view spiritual well-being as important to older people's physical and mental health have attempted to develop instruments to measure an individual's spiritual interests and resources, including his or her personal values, philosophy, and sense of purpose. Some health promotion screening tools include questions on the individual's spiritual or philosophic values, life goal-setting, and approach to answering questions, such as: What is the meaning of my life? How can I increase the quality of my life? Proponents of this approach advocate training health care providers to be sensitive to, and to ask questions about, spiritual

well-being in order to respond to older people's total needs (McSherry, 1983).

## Meeting Older People's Needs

The increasing recognition of elders' spiritual well-being among those who work with older people may be in part a reaction to organized religion's limited outreach and programming for older parishioners. In the past, most churches were oriented to serving relatively youthful families, through programs for children, teens, and young adults. Older parishioners were assumed to benefit from the same programs that serve the rest of the church membership. In recent years, however, churches have begun to recognize their older members' special needs and to develop ministries specifically to serve them.

Church programs for older members have grown at the national, regional, and local levels. These services include counseling, adult day care, advocacy, education, income maintenance, in-home services, nutrition services, retirement training, and transportation. A growing number of churches are developing housing programs, such as retirement homes and congregate care facilities, described in the previous chapter. Churches and synagogues are increasingly aware that ministry to older individuals must involve more than prayer; church-based advocacy and organizing are needed as well. With cutbacks in government services, churches are often faced with filling service gaps through volunteer chore programs, nutrition sites, and meals and home care for the homebound. As churches and synagogues are increasingly responding to older people's daily care needs, they have begun to co-sponsor programs with other religious organizations or with public agencies.

## POLITICAL PARTICIPATION

Another major arena of participation in American society is political life. Political acts range from voting, to participation in a political party

Older people are politically active both as voters and as volunteers.

or a political action group (e.g., organizations seeking to advance the interests of older persons), to running for or holding elective office. In an examination of older people's political behavior, three factors make any interpretation of the relationship between age and political behavior complex. These factors are *stages in the life cycle, cohort effects,* and *historical* or *period effects,* as discussed in Chapter 2.

Historical effects have influenced interpretations of older people's political behavior, particularly analyses of the extent of conservatism. Some early studies of political participation found older people to be more conservative than younger people, as measured by preference for the Republican party and voting behavior (Dobson, 1983; Campbell, 1962). Exit polls in the 1984 Presidential election concluded that approximately 60 percent of older individuals voted Republican (U.S. Senate Special Committee on Aging, 1985). Older people's apparent conservatism partially reflects the fact that people born and raised in different historical periods tend to have perspectives reflecting those times, in this instance, the historical effect of party realign-

ments in the late 1920s and 1930s. Before the New Deal of the 1930s and 40s, people entering the electorate identified with the Republican party to a disproportionate extent; they have voted Republican ever since, and form the majority of the population over age 65. The apparent association of Republicanism with age thus reflects generational differences, not the effects of aging per se (Hudson and Strate, 1985). Age differences in conservatism/liberalism are less a matter of people becoming more conservative than of their remaining the same, whereas successive generations entering the electorate since World War II have become comparatively more liberal, with more older people identifying with the Democratic party since the mid-1980s, as illustrated in Figure 15-1. For example, in the 1986 midterm elections for the House and the Senate and the 1992 Presidential election, more older people voted for Democrats than for Republicans; recent polling data show higher rates of Democratic party identification among older than among younger age groups (Stanley and Niemi, 1989; Statistical Abstracts of the United States, 1994). This shift may be due, in part, to more low-income and retired blue-collar people opposed to the fiscal conservatism of the Republican party, especially on issues such as pensions and health care. In fact, older persons are more likely to favor national health care reform than are younger people, in part because of the escalating costs of care. At the same time, increasing numbers of young people have identified with the conservative element of the Republican party since the 1980s.

As seen in earlier discussions of cross-sectional samples, it is misleading to look once at a group of individuals of various ages, compare their attitudes and reported behaviors, and maintain that differences based on age alone have been isolated. Conclusions about older people's political behavior and attitudes are thus limited by the cross-sectional nature of most research on these variables, which has not taken account of historical and cohort effects. In short, how a person thinks and acts politically can be traced

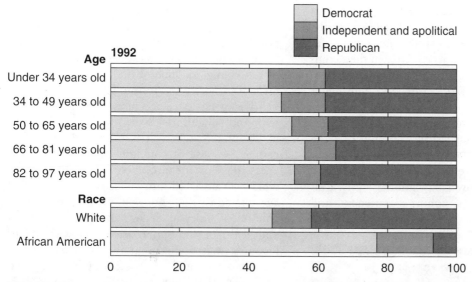

**FIGURE 15–1   1992 Political Party Identification of the Adult Population**
SOURCE: Chart prepared by U.S. Bureau of the Census.

largely to environmental and historical factors, not to that person's age (Jacobs, 1990).

Overall, individuals of all ages are not ideologically consistent in their issue-specific preferences (Hudson and Strate, 1985). Rather, age differences on particular issues may reflect the closeness of issues to people's lives; the further removed a political issue, the less age appears to affect attitudes toward it (Douglass, Cleveland, and Maddox, 1974). Furthermore, both older and younger people may hold beliefs on specific issues that contradict their views on more general principles. Within a heterogeneous group such as the older population—not only between younger and older generations—differences of opinion on any political issue are likely to equal or exceed variations between age groups (Hudson and Strate, 1985).

## Voting Behavior

Older Americans are somewhat more likely than younger adults to vote, although rates of electoral participation are low for all age groups in our society. Older people currently comprise 20 percent of the general electorate and nearly 70 percent of those who vote in presidential elections and 60 percent in Congressional election years (Statistical Abstract of the United States, 1994). The participation rate of older people in elections from 1980 through 1992 has been almost three times the rate of 18 to 20 year olds. Although voting participation declines for those age 75 and older, the 75-plus group was still more likely to vote in the last five presidential elections than those younger than age 35 (Statistical Abstracts of the United States, 1994).

In instances where voter turnout is lower among older people, factors other than aging are probably the cause, including gender, ethnic minority, education, and generational factors. For example, the voter turnout of ethnic minority groups is lower than that of whites. Only 51.5 percent of African American elders voted in the 1988 presidential election, while less than 50 percent of Hispanic elders regularly vote (U.S. Bureau of the Census, 1989). The political acculturation of ethnic minority groups also influences their participation. For example, Mexican American elders, historically fearful of deportation, have a more cautious, conservative approach to political involvement (Torres-Gil, 1976). On the other hand, a more recent study found that older African Americans who were active in their communities, had a strong sense of citizen duty, identified themselves as Democrats, and had higher levels of education were more likely to vote (Barzagan, Barbre, and Torres-Gil, 1992). These and earlier findings suggest that differences in the rates of political participation among older people of color do not reflect age or ethnic identity per se, but rather lower educational levels, feelings of powerlessness, cohort experiences, and real or perceived barriers to voting and other political activities.

In sum, when education, gender, and ethnic minority status are taken into account, political interest and activity actually increase with age. Older members of political parties tend to have more influence than do younger members because of their years of party involvement and their overrepresentation at nominating conventions and in public offices. The older electorate therefore has the potential to exert political influence substantially beyond what their numbers might suggest (Cutler, Pierce, and Steckenrider, 1984; Hudson and Strate, 1985).

## Senior Power

Research on "senior power" reflects an ongoing debate about whether age can serve as a catalyst for a viable political movement. In the model of interest group politics, social policy arises from the conflicts and accommodations of organized groups, each seeking to fulfill their interests (Torres-Gil, 1993). It is contended that older people can be a powerful political constituency in this process, because legislators and appointed officials are influenced by public opinion, especially by those who vote and are political party leaders as is the case with older people. Since the 1980s, older Americans have been portrayed by the media and by some policy makers as an organized group of "greedy geezers," acting as a monolithic bloc to achieve their interests (Binstock, 1993).

Those who believe that the elderly have benefited economically at the expense of younger age groups define the "tyranny of America's old," united to maintain old age benefits at the expense of the young, as "one of the most crucial issues facing U.S. society" (Preston, 1984; Smith, 1992).

This perspective of senior power is consistent with the subculture theory of aging, discussed in Chapter 4, where it is presumed that older people, because of common values and experiences, develop a shared political consciousness, which is translated into collective action on old age-related issues (Thomson, 1993). Since future cohorts of older adults will be better educated and healthier and may retire earlier with higher incomes, it is argued that they will have more resources essential to political power. It also presumes that older people in future will experience increasing pride, dignity, and shared consciousness about old age and thus define problems collectively (Cutler, 1982). From this perspective, age is assumed to become a more salient aspect of politics, even if all older persons and their organizations do not speak (or vote) with a unified political voice. It is argued that heterogeneity among the older population does not preclude age—as with gender and ethnic minority status—from exerting political influence (Cutler, 1983).

Admittedly, old-age advocacy groups enjoy a number of advantages in the political arena, including large, active memberships, policy information and expertise, and widespread public support and legitimacy as public benefit recipients (Day, 1993). "Senior citizens" have traditionally been one of the prime targets of campaign efforts focused on critical states with large blocs of electoral votes, because of their aggregate numerical importance and the relative ease with which they can be accessed through age-segregated housing and existing organizations and programs such as senior centers, AARP chapters, and congregate meal sites (Binstock, 1993).

The alternative argument, that older people do not constitute a significant age-based political force, has been advanced primarily by Hudson and Binstock (Hudson and Binstock, 1976; Hudson and Strate, 1985; Binstock, 1983) and more recently by Torres-Gil in his concepts of new aging and diversity (1992; 1993). Early critics of the aged as a subculture argue that the diversity of the older population precludes their having shared interests around which to coalesce. Most older people, especially the young-old, do not identify themselves as "aged," nor do they perceive their problems as stemming from their age. Nor are they captives of any single political philosophy, party, or mass organization. Therefore, according to this alternate position, age alone is not a relevant factor in predicting political behavior or age group consciousness based on differential access to resources (Streib, 1965). Since age-based consciousness is lacking, older people are unlikely to be swayed by politicians' appeals to the age vote, nor can they substantially influence social policy development (Binstock, 1983; Hudson and Strate, 1985).

The disunity that arises from their very diversity also places older people at a political disadvantage. Even though older adults can be mobilized for meetings with legislators or political rallies, it cannot be assumed that they necessarily act in a unified manner with regard to social policies. For example, contrary to widely held perceptions, older people are rarely unified toward issues affecting the young, such as school levies, and do not vote as a bloc against increasing property taxes to support public schools (Button and Rosenbaum, 1989). This example suggests that old-age related issues are not necessarily more important to them than other issues, partisan attachments, or the characteristics of specific candidates. In fact, recent studies indicate that older and younger people are more likely to form alliances along economic, racial, ethnic, and ideological lines than to unite horizontally on the basis of age (Day, 1990; Torres-Gil, 1993). The national organization, Generations United, represents one such vertical alliance across age groups.

Rather than a strong age cohort consciousness, there are increasing differences by socioeconomic class, race and ethnicity, gender and

religion among older people which affect political interests. An outcome of such diversity will be increased competition within an age cohort, with groups of older people developing alliances with younger groups with common concerns. The increased policy focus upon generational equity has served to undermine the cross-class strengths of alliances among senior organizations and counter the power of the senior lobby (Quadagno, 1990). For example, poor older people may work with younger welfare beneficiaries for universal health care coverage while upper-income older adults may be more interested in long-term care (Achenbaum, 1993; Torres-Gil, 1993). In the face of budget deficits, future subgroups of older people may become more politically organized, with political agendas different from most of today's senior organizations, especially around issues of means-testing and higher eligibility ages for benefits such as Social Security (Torres-Gil, 1993). For example, lower-income older people have a much greater stake in the maintenance and enhancement of Social Security, since it accounts for a much larger proportion of their income (Binstock, 1993). Accordingly, the failure of the 1988 Medicare Catastrophic Coverage Act illustrates the fragility of interest-group politics when upper middle-class older adults were asked to sustain a program that benefited primarily low-income older people.

At first glance, the number, variety, and strength of age-based national organizations appear to support the viewpoint that older people are a powerful political force. Age-based organizations are viewed as able to build memberships, conduct policy analyses, marshal grass-roots support, and utilize direct mail and political action. Conscious organizing of older individuals is not without historical precedent in this country. The first age-based politically oriented interest group grew out of the social and economic dislocations of the Depression. Called the Townsend Movement, after its founder, Dr. Francis E. Townsend, it began in California in 1933 and reached its peak in 1936, with 1 million members nationally. It proposed a tax on all business transactions to finance a $200/month pension for every pensioner over age 60. However, passage of the Social Security Act, in which groups of older people played a supporting but not a leading role, took away the Townsend Movement's momentum, and the organization died out in the 1940s. Most political divisions during the turbulent period of the Depression were class- and labor-based, rather than age-based; the Townsend Movement did demonstrate, however, that old age could be a short-term basis for organizing (Vinyard, 1982).

The McClain Movement, another early age-based organization, was initially part of the Ham and Eggs movement, which aimed to establish financial benefits for older persons through a referendum in the 1938 California elections. George McClain formed this group to exert political pressure on local legislatures to improve conditions for older people. McClain lost many of his followers after economic conditions improved in the 1940s. These early groups gave impetus to the passage of Social Security, but their greatest contribution was furnishing older people with a collective voice and identity (Torres-Gil, 1993). Organized interest groups representing older people did not reemerge until the 1950s and 1960s. Currently, over 1,000 separately organized groups for older adults exist at the local, state, and national levels, with at least 20 major national organizations involved in political action on behalf of older persons. In many ways, the diversity of the older population is reflected in the variety of organizations themselves, ranging from mass membership groups, non-membership staff organizations, and associations of professionals or service providers. Yet the very diversity of these groups reduces their potential to act together as a unified bloc. For example, the National Caucus for the Black Aged, the National Hispanic Council on Aging, and the National Indian Council on Aging have been created to address political inequities facing minority elders and may not act in concert with organizations, such as the American Association of Retired Persons (AARP), that represent primarily a white, middle-class constituency.

Three of the largest mass membership organizations are the National Council of Senior Citizens (NCSC), the National Association of Retired Federal Employees (NARFE), and the American Association of Retired Persons together with the National Retired Teachers' Association (AARP). Their combined membership represents a significant political force (Pratt, 1983). The National Council of Senior Citizens (NCSC) was developed by organized labor in the early 1960s with the objective of passing Medicare. Although anyone may join, most members of NCSC are former blue-collar workers who receive insurance and other tangible membership benefits. The National Association of Retired Federal Employees (NARFE) was also formed for a specific political purpose—the passage of the Federal Employees Pension Act in the 1920s. It has since concentrated on bread and butter issues for federal employees, such as labor/management relations, rather than broader political issues affecting older persons generally. NARFE is the smallest of these three national organizations, with its membership primarily in the Washington, D.C. area.

The best known and largest of these organizations is the American Association of Retired Persons (AARP), with a membership of over 34 million—half the nation's older population—nearly 50 lobbyists, and over 400,000 active volunteers. In fact, 13 percent of the United States public belongs to AARP. With an annual fee of only $8, members are attracted by the benefits of lower cost health insurance, credit cards, travel discounts, and mail order drugs, and by a myriad of programs related to retirement planning, crime prevention, housing, and widowhood. AARP's magazine, *Modern Maturity,* is the most widely circulated membership periodical in the world (Jacobs, 1990). In recent years, AARP has become increasingly active politically, particularly in terms of expanding public financing of long-term care, and it was instrumental in helping to end mandatory retirement based on age and in the initial passage of catastrophic health care legislation (which was later repealed) (Montgomery, 1989).

Four trade associations, one professional society, a confederation of social welfare agencies, and other organizations concerned with aging issues also exist at the national level. The trade associations are the American Association of Homes for the Aged, the American Nursing Home Association, the National Council of Health Care Services (consisting of commercial enterprises in the long-term care business, such as the nursing home subsidiary of Holiday Inns), and the National Association of State Units in Aging (NASUA), which is composed of administrators of state area agencies on aging. The emphasis of these associations is on obtaining federal funds and influencing the development of regulations for long-term care facilities and the delivery of public services. The professional association most active in aging policy issues, the Gerontological Society of America (GSA), is composed of professionals from many disciplines. The GSA has become active in public policy issues since the 1960s, primarily in efforts to influence the allocation of research and education funds.

The major confederation of social welfare agencies concerned with aging is the National Council on the Aging (NCOA), which encompasses almost 2,000 organized affiliates, including public and private health, social work, and community action agencies. It serves as technical consultant to organizations addressing problems facing older people.

Political momentum is also building in several organizations that began at the grass-roots level and now have a nationwide membership and enjoy national recognition. The Older Women's League (OWL), founded in 1981, brings together people concerned about issues affecting older women, especially health care and health insurance, Social Security, pensions, and caregiving. It has advocated for older women both in the federal policy-making process and within the programs of national associations, such as the GSA. Women activists within OWL may represent a trend away from the comparatively lower rates of past political participation among older women.

The Gray Panthers aim to form grass-roots intergenerational alliances around issues affecting all ages, but emphasize social action to solve problems faced by older people. The Gray Panthers is the most radical of these national organizations, emphasizing social change and "transcending" existing social values and structures. More than any other present-day senior group, the Gray Panthers has been the outgrowth of one person—its founding leader, the late Maggie Kuhn (Pratt, 1983).

The existence of these organizations is not necessarily an indication of the political power of

---

**POLITICAL ACTIVISM AND OLDER WOMEN**

Tish Sommers is an example of the increasing political activism of older women. Sommers, a long-time homemaker, learned about the vulnerability of older women when she was divorced at age 57. She found that newly single homemakers her age had a hard time getting benefits that people who have been employed take for granted. She coined the term *displaced homemaker* and built a force of women. They successfully lobbied for centers where displaced homemakers had job training during the late 1970s. In 1980, she and Laurie Shields founded the Older Women's League, a national organization that has grown to over 14,000 members and over 100 chapters. Her maxim always was "Don't agonize, organize." During the six years of organizing OWL, Sommers also fought a battle with cancer. Even at her death in 1986, she was still fighting, organizing groups nationally around the right to maintain control over the conditions of one's death.

older people, however. Binstock (1984, 1987) argues that these groups were organized on a short-term basis to promote specific pieces of legislation, not to intervene continually in the political process on issues affecting older people.

Those skeptical of the sustained political influence of organizations for older adults contend that their electoral potency and representativeness have not yet been tested and that political visibility is not the same as enhanced political influence (McKenzie, 1991). Even though these organizations actively participated in the passage of Medicare, Medicaid, Supplemental Security Income, and the Older Americans Act and the White House Conferences on Aging, these major legislative breakthroughs in the past 30 years have been largely engineered by Presidents and members of Congress, not by age-based organizations which instead played only a supportive role (Binstock, 1987; Heclo, 1988; Hudson and Strate, 1985). These legislative successes have also been attributed to legislators' belief that older people were worse off and more deserving than other groups, not to their political power. It is argued that their influence has been confined largely to minor changes and defense of current benefits, with minimal impact in the design and enactment of major old-age policies (Binstock, 1993). On certain issues, such as health care reform, the influence of organizations of older people has been shown to be limited relative to powerful interest groups such as the insurance, medical, and pharmaceutical industries (Day, 1993). Nevertheless, until recently, most politicians were not eager to offend age-based organizations and constituencies of older people. After higher-income older people organized to influence Congress to repeal the Medicare Catastrophic Coverage Act, no proposals concerning seniors got out of committees in the next Congressional election year. Whether older people do act as a unified bloc, many policy makers act as if there were a "politics of age" founded on cohort-based interest groups; even if older people cannot effect the passage of legislation, they can at least block changes in existing policies, especially when programs such as Social Security and

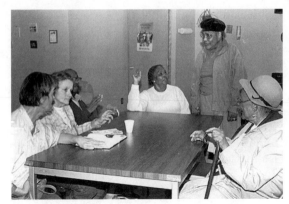

Many older people are active in clubs and community organizations.

Medicare are threatened (Day, 1990; Rauch, 1987; Torres-Gil, 1993). Perceptions of such influence then affect whether major changes in policies on aging are viewed as feasible (Binstock, 1993; Torres-Gil, 1993).

National age-based organizations have been subject to the criticism that they are biased toward the interests of middle and upper working-class older people. AARP, for example, has been criticized for advancing only the interests of its primarily middle-class membership and for recruiting members largely on the basis of selective incentives and direct member services (e.g., insurance, drug discounts, travel, etc.), not by appeals to changing existing policies to benefit lower-income older people (Hudson and Strate, 1985). However, in recent years, age-based organizations have made more effort not only to reach out to lower-income older persons, but also to collaborate with other groups, as reflected by the cross-age coalitions that have formed around health care reform and long-term care. In addition to national associations, a wide range of organizations at the local and state level have mobilized around intergenerational and cross-class issues, such as affordable public transportation, safe streets, and low-cost health care (Reitzes and Reitzes, 1991).

In sum, national organizations of elderly people have influenced a wide range of policies, even though they have not functioned consistently to deliver a unified bloc of votes, nor to change significantly the social and economic conditions faced by the most disadvantaged segments of older people. Age-based groups that will have the greatest influence in the future will be characterized by effective use of direct mail, fund-raising, ability to act on "red flag" issues such as Social Security benefits, direct services to members, use of the media, and lobbying at the federal and state levels (Torres-Gil, 1993). However, given limited public resources, such groups must also form alliances with other populations and age groups. Such intergenerational collaboration is further discussed in Chapter 19 with regard to influencing social policies.

## SUMMARY AND IMPLICATIONS

As earlier chapters have documented, changes in employment and parenting roles, income, and physical and sensory capacities often have detrimental social consequences for older adults. Nevertheless, there are arenas in which older people may still experience meaningful involvement and develop new opportunities and skills. Such participation is consistent with the broader definition of productive aging in which older individuals continue to contribute goods and services to society, even though not paid. This chapter has considered six of these arenas: leisure pursuits, voluntary association membership, volunteering, education, religious involvement, and political activity. The meaning and functions of participation in these arenas are obviously highly individualized. Participation may be a means to strengthen and build informal social networks, influence wider social policies, serve other persons, and substitute for role changes. The extent of involvement is influenced not by age alone, but also by a variety of other salient factors, including gender, ethnic minority status, health, socioeconomic status, and educational level. Because of the number of interacting variables, age-related patterns in participation are not clearly defined.

In general, there are some age-related differences in types of leisure pursuits; with increasing

age, people tend to engage in more sedentary, inner-directed, and routine pursuits in their homes than social activities or obligations outside the home. Changes in organizational participation and volunteering are less clearly age-related. Participation in voluntary associations stabilizes or declines only slightly with old age. Declines that do occur are likely to be associated with poor health, inadequate income, and transportation problems. Volunteering, which is higher among the older population than other age groups, tends to represent a life-long pattern of community service.

Past research on religious and political participation by older individuals has pointed inaccurately to declines in old age. Although formal religious participation, such as church or synagogue attendance, appears to diminish, other kinds of religious behavior, such as reading religious texts or listening to religious broadcasts, increase. Religious activity has been found to be an effective way of coping, particularly among ethnic minority elders. Spirituality has been differentiated from religion as a positive factor in older people's physical and mental well-being, and their quality of life.

Since the 1980s, voting by older people has increased. Declines in voting and political participation in the past may have been a function of low educational status or physical limitations, not of age per se. In fact, older persons' skills and experiences may be more valued in the political arena than in other spheres. The extent to which older people form a unified political bloc, that can influence politicians and public policy, remains subject to debate. Some argue that older adults form a subculture with a strong collective consciousness. Others point to the increasing diversity among the older population, where upper-income older people may organize to advance their interests at the expense of lower-income elders, as occurred with the Medicare Catastrophic Health Care legislation.

Most forms of organizational involvement appear to represent stability across the life course; the knowledge and skills necessary for a varied set of activities in old age are generally developed in early or middle adulthood and maintained into later life. On the other hand, preretirement patterns are not fixed; individuals can develop new interests and activities in later life, often with the assistance of senior centers, continuing education programs, or community or special interest organizations.

## REFERENCES

Achenbaum, W. A. Generational relations in historical context. In V. L. Bengtson and W. A. Achenbaum (Eds.), *The changing contract across generations.* New York: Aldine De Gruyter, 1993, 25–42.

Allen, K., and Chin-Sang, V. A lifetime of work: The context and meaning of leisure for aging black women. *The Gerontologist,* 1990, *30*(6), 734–740.

Atchley, R. Retirement and leisure participation: Continuity or crisis? *The Gerontologist,* 1971, *11,* 13–17.

Babchuk, N., Peters, G., Hoyt, D., and Kaiser, M. The voluntary associations of the aged. *Journal of Gerontology,* 1979, *34,* 579–587.

Bammel, L. L. B., and Bammel, G. Leisure and recreation. In J. E. Birren and K. W. Schaie (Eds.), *Handbook of the psychology of aging,* New York: Van Nostrand Reinhold, 1985, 848–863.

Bartlett, D., and Steeler, J. The vanishing pensions: Will money be there when you retire? *The Seattle Times,* November 5, 1991, A-4.

Bass, S. A., Caro, F. G., and Chen, Y-P. *Achieving a productive aging society.* Westport, Conn.: Auburn House, 1993.

Bazargan, M., Barbre, A., and Torres-Gil, F. Voting behavior among low-income black elderly: A multi-election perspective. *The Gerontologist,* 1992, *12*(5), 584–591.

Bengtson, V., and Chenbaun, A. (Ed.). *The changing contract across generations.* New York: Aldine de Gruyter, 1993.

Bianchi, E. *Aging as a spiritual journey.* New York: Crossroad, 1982.

Binstock, R. H. The aged as scapegoat. *The Gerontologist,* 1983, *23,* 136–143.

Binstock, R. H. Reframing the agenda of policies on aging. In M. Minkler and C. Estes (Eds.), *Readings in the political economy of aging.* Farmingdale, N. Y.: Baywood, 1984.

Binstock, R. H. The implications of population aging for American politics. Paper delivered at the annual meeting of the American Political Science Association, Chicago, September 1987.

Binstock, R. H. Older voters and the 1992 Presidential election. *The Gerontologist,* 1993, *32*(5), 601–606.

Binstock, R. H., Levin, M. A., and Weatherly, R. The political dilemmas of social intervention. In R. H. Binstock and E. Shanas (Eds.), *Handbook of aging and the social sciences* (2d ed.). New York: Van Nostrand Reinhold, 1985.

Blazer, D. Spirituality and aging well. *Generations,* Winter 1991, 61–65.

Button, J. W., and Rosenbaum, W. A. Seeing gray: School bond issues and the aging in Florida. *Research on Aging,* 1989 *11*(2), 158–173.

Campbell, A. Social and psychological determinants of voting behavior. In W. Donohue and C. Tibbits (Eds.), *Politics of age.* Ann Arbor: University of Michigan, 1962.

Caro, F. G., Bass, S. A., and Chen, Y-P. Introduction: Achieving a productive aging society. In S. A. Bass, F. G. Caro, and Y-P Chen (Eds.), *Achieving a productive aging society.* Westport, Conn.: Auburn House, 1993, 3–25.

Chambré, S. M. Is volunteering a substitute for role loss in old age? An empirical test of activity theory. *The Gerontologist,* 1984, *23,* 292–299.

Chambré, S. M. Volunteerism by elders: Past trends and future prospects. *The Gerontologist,* 1993, *33*(2), 221–228.

The Commonwealth Fund. *The untapped resource.* New York: The Commonwealth Fund, 1993.

Cuellar, J. B. El Senior Citizens Club: The older Mexican American in the voluntary association. In B. G. Myerhoff and A. Bimic (Eds.), *Life's career—aging: Cultural variations on growing old.* Beverly Hills: Sage Publications, 1978.

Cutler, N. Subjective age identification. In D. Mangen and W. Peterson (Eds.), *Research instruments in social gerontology.* Minneapolis: University of Minnesota Press, 1982.

Cutler, N. Age and political behavior. In D. Woodruff and J. Birren (Eds.), *Aging: Scientific perspectives and social issues* (2d ed.). New York: Van Nostrand Reinhold, 1983.

Cutler, N., Pierce, R., and Steckenrider, J. How golden is the future? *Generations,* Fall 1984, 38–43.

Cutler, S. J., and Hendricks, J. Leisure and time use across the life course. In R. Binstock and L.

George, (Eds.), *Aging and the social sciences* (3d ed.), New York: Academic Press, 1990.

Danigelis, N. C., and McIntosh, B. R. Resources and the productive activity of elders: Race and gender as contexts. *Journals of Gerontology,* 1993, *48*(4), S192–S203.

Day, C. L. *What older Americans think: Interest groups and aging policy.* N.J.: Princeton University Press, 1990.

Day, C. L. The organized elderly: Perilous, powerless, or progressive. *The Gerontologist,* 1993, *33*(3), 426–427.

Delloff, L. The WHCOA and WAA: Spiritual well-being gets lost. *Generations,* 1983, *8,* 8–10.

Dobson, D. The elderly as a political force. In W. Browne and L. K. Olson (Eds.), *Aging and public policy.* Westport, Conn.: Greenwood Press, 1983.

Douglass, E. B., Cleveland, W. P., and Maddox, G. Political attitudes, age and aging: A cohort analysis of archival data. *Journal of Gerontology,* 1974, *29,* 666–675.

Dye, D., Goodman, M., Roth, M., and Jensen, K. The older adult volunteer compared to the non-volunteer. *The Gerontologist,* 1973, *13,* 215–218.

Ekerdt, D. J. The busy ethic: Moral continuity between work and retirement. *The Gerontologist,* 1986, *26,* 239–244.

Ellison, G. W. Spiritual well-being: Conceptualization and measurement. *Journal of Psychology and Theology,* 1983, *11,* 330–340.

Ferrel, C., Koenig, H. G., and Kvale, J. N. Religion and well-being in later life. *The Gerontologist,* 1988, *28*(1), 18–28.

Fischer, K. *Winter grace. Spirituality for the later years.* New York: Paulist Press, 1985.

Fogelman, C. Being a volunteer: Some effects on older people, *Generations,* 1981, *4,* 24–25.

Foner, A., and Schwab, L. Work and retirement in a changing society. In M. W. Riley, B. Hess, and K. Bond (Eds.), *Aging and society: Selected reviews of recent research.* Hillsdale, N.J.: Lawrence Erlbaum Assoc., 1983.

Glenn, N. A. Aging and conservatism. *The Annals of the American Academy of Political and Social Science,* 1974, *CDXV,* 176–186.

Greenberg, J. Health and wellness: A conceptual differentiation. *Journal of School Health,* 1985, *55,* 403–406.

Greene, V. C., and Ondrich, J. J. Risk factors for nursing home admissions and exits: A discrete-time hazard function approach. *Journals of Gerontology,* 1990, *45,* S250–S258.

Gurin, P., Hatchett, S., and Jackson, J. S. *Hope and independence: Blacks' response to electoral and party politics.* New York: Russell Sage Foundation, 1989.

Hadaway, C. K. Life satisfaction and religion: A re-analysis. *Social Forces,* 1978, *57,* 636–643.

Hanssen, A., Nichols, M., Buckspan, L., Henderson, B., Helbig, T., and Zarit, S. Correlates of senior center participation. *The Gerontologist,* 1978, *18,* 193–200.

Haygne, H. V. Volunteers in the U.S.: Who donates the time? *Monthly Labor Review,* 1991, *114*(2), 17–23.

Heclo, H. Generational politics. In J. L. Palmer, T. Smeeding, and B. B. Torrey (Eds.), *The vulnerable.* Washington, D.C.: Urban Institute Press, 1988, 381–411.

Height, D., Toya, J., Kamekawa, L., and Maldonaldo, D. Senior volunteering in minority communities. *Generations,* 1981, *5,* 14–18.

Heisel, M. A., and Faulkner, A. O. Religiosity in an older Black population. *The Gerontologist,* 1982, *22,* 354–368.

Herzog, A. R., and Morgan, J. Age and gender differences in the value of productive activities. *Research on Aging,* 1992, *12*(2), 169–198.

Herzog, A. R., and Morgan, J. N. Formal volunteer work among older Americans. In S. A. Bass, F. G. Caro, and Y-P. Chen (Eds.), *Achieving a productive aging society,* Westport, Conn.: Auburn House, 1993, 119–142.

Herzog, A. R., Kahn, R., Morgan, J., Jackson, J., and Antonucci, T. Age differences in productive activities. *Journals of Gerontology,* 1989, 44, S129–S138.

Holstein, M. Women's lives, women's work: Productivity, gender, and aging. In S. A. Bass, F. G. Caro, and Y-P. Chen (Eds.), *Achieving a productive aging society.* Westport, Conn.: Auburn House, 1993, 235–248.

Hooker, K., and Ventes, D. Work ethic, daily activities and retirement satisfaction. *Journal of Gerontology,* 1984, *39,* 478–484.

Hudson, R. B., and Binstock, R. Political systems and aging. In R. Binstock and E. Shanas (Eds.), *Handbook of aging and the social sciences.* New York: Van Nostrand, 1976.

Hudson, R. B., and Strate, J. Aging and political systems. In R. Binstock and E. Shanas (Eds.), *Hand-*

book of aging and the social sciences (2d ed.). New York: Van Nostrand, 1985.

Hunsberger, B. Religion, age, life satisfaction, and perceived sources of religiousness: A study of older persons. *Journal of Gerontology*, 1985, *40*, 615–620.

Hunter, K., and Linn, M. Psychosocial differences between elderly volunteers and nonvolunteers. *Aging and Human Development*, 1981, *12*, 205–213.

Hyer, L., Jacob, M. R., and Pattison, E. M. Later life struggles: Psychological/spiritual convergence. *Journal of Pastoral Care*, 1987, 41, 2, 141–149.

Jacobs, G. Aging and politics. In R. H. Binstock and L. George (Eds.), *Handbook of Aging and the Social Sciences* (3d ed.). New York: Academic Press, 1990.

Kasper, J. *Aging alone: Profiles and projections*. Baltimore, Md.: Commonwealth Fund, 1988.

Kaufman, S. R. *The ageless self*. New York: New American Library, 1986.

Kelly, J. R. *Leisure*. Englewood Cliffs, N.J.: Prentice-Hall, 1982.

Kelly, J. R. *Peoria winter: Styles and resources in later life*. Lexington, Mass.: D. C. Heath, 1987.

Kelly, J. R., Steinkamp, M., and Kelly, J. Later life leisure: How they play in Peoria. *The Gerontologist*, 1986, *26*, 531–537.

Kelly, J. R., and Steinkamp, M. W. Leisure in later life: Roles and identities. In N. J. Osgood (Ed.), *Life after work: Retirement, leisure, recreation and the elderly*. New York: Praeger, 1982, 268–292.

Kelly, J. R., Steinkamp, M. W., and Kelly, J. Later life satisfaction: Does leisure contribute? *Leisure Sciences*, 1986, *9*, 189–200.

Kivett, V. Religious motivation in middle age: Correlates and implications. *Journal of Gerontology*, 1979, *34*, 106–115.

Kleiber, D., and Kelly, J. Leisure, socialization and the life cycle. In Seppo Iso-Ahola (Ed.), *Social psychological perspectives on leisure and recreation*. Springfield, Ill.: Charles C. Thomas, 1980.

Koenig, H. G., George, L. K., and Siegler, I. C. The use of religion and other emotion-regulating coping strategies among older adults. *The Gerontologist*, 1988, *28*, 303–310.

Koenig, H. G., Kvale, H., and Ferrel, C. Religion and well-being in later life. *The Gerontologist*, 1988, *28*, 18–28.

Krause, N., and Tran, V. T. Stress and religious involvement among older Blacks, *Journals of Gerontology*, 1989, *44*, S4–13.

Krout, J. Senior center activities and services: Findings from a national study. *Research on Aging*, 1985, *7*, 455–471.

Krout, J. *Senior centers in America*. Westport, Conn.: Greenwood, 1989.

Krout, J., Cutler, S. J., and Coward, R. T. Correlates of senior center participation: A national analysis. *The Gerontologist*, 1990, *30*, 72–79.

Larson, R., Zuzanek, J., and Mannell, R. Being alone versus being with people: Disengagement in the daily experience of older adults. *Journal of Gerontology*, 1985, *40*, 375–381.

Lawton, M. P., Moss, M., and Fulcomer, M. Objective and subjective uses of time by older people. *International Journal of Aging and Human Development*, 1986–87, *24*, 171–188.

Levin, J. S., and Taylor, R. J. Gender and age differences in religiosity among black Americans. *The Gerontologist*, 1993, *33*(1), 16–23.

Levine, S. The hidden health care system. *Medical Care*, 1983, *21*, 378.

Markides, K. S. Aging, religiosity and adjustment: A longitudinal analysis. *Journal of Gerontology*, 1983, *38*, 621–626.

Markides, K. S., Levin, J. S., and Ray, L. R. Religion, aging and life satisfaction: An eight-year, three-wave longitudinal study. *The Gerontologist*, 1987, *27*, 660–665.

Marriott Senior Living Services. *Marriott Seniors Volunteerism Study*. Washington, D.C.: Marriott Senior Living Services, 1991.

Mayers, R. S., and Souflee, F. Utilizing social support systems in the delivery of social services to the Mexican-American elderly. *The Journal of Applied Social Sciences*, 1990–91, *15*(1), 31–50.

McFadden, S., and Gerl, R. Approaches to understanding spirituality in the second half of life. *Generations*, Fall 1990, 35–38.

McGuire, F. A., and Dottavio, D. Outdoor recreation participation across the lifespan: Abandonment, continuity or liberation. *International Journal of Aging and Human Development*, 1986–87, *24*, 87–100.

McKenzie, R. The retreat of the elderly welfare state. *Wall Street Journal*, 1991, March 12, 29.

McSherry, E. The spiritual dimension of elder health care. *Generations*, 1983, *8*, 13–21.

Miller, S. The social dilemmas of the aging leisure participant. In A. Rose and W. Peterson (Eds.), *Older people and their social world.* Philadelphia: F. A. Davis, 1965.

Missine, L. Keynote presentation from the Conference on Religion, Spirituality, and Aging. American Society on Aging, 1986.

Moberg, D. Religiosity in old age. *The Gerontologist,* 1965, *5,* 78–87.

Moen, P., Dempster-McClain, D., and Williams, R. M. Jr. Successful aging: A life course perspective on women's multiple roles and health. *American Journal of Sociology,* 1992, 97(6), 1613.

Montgomery, R. As AARP grows, so does criticism of its priorities, *Kansas City Star,* November 18, 1989.

Moody, H. R. A strategy for productive aging: Education in later life. In S. A. Bass, F. G. Caro, and Y-P. Chen (Eds.), *Achieving a productive aging society,* Westport, Conn.: Auburn House, 1993, 221–231.

Moss, M., and Lawton, M. P. Time budgets of older people: A window on four lifestyles. *Journal of Gerontology,* 1982, 37, 115–123.

National Council of Silver Haired Legislatures (SHL). *Newsletter,* Hallendale, Fla.:SHL, 1986.

Neulinger, J. *The psychology of leisure: Recent approaches to the study of leisure.* Springfield, Ill.: Charles C. Thomas, 1974.

Palmore, E. The social factors in aging. In E. Busse and D. Blazer (Eds.), *Handbook of geriatric psychiatry.* New York: Van Nostrand Reinhold, 1980.

Paloutzian, R. F., and Ellison, C. W. Loneliness and quality of life measures: Measuring loneliness, spiritual well-being and their social and emotional correlates. In L. A. Peplau and D. Perlman (Eds.), *Loneliness: A sourcebook of current theory, research and therapy.* New York: Wiley Inter-Science, 1982.

Payne, B. P. Research and theoretical approaches to spirituality and aging. *Generations,* Fall 1990, 11–14.

Peterson, S., and Somet, A. The political behavior of older American blacks. *The Gerontologist,* 1993, 32(5), 592–600.

Pieper, H. Church membership and participation in church activities among the elderly. *Activities, adaptation and aging,* 1981, *1,* 23–29.

Preston, S. H. Children and the elderly in the United States. *Scientific American,* 1984, 251, 6, 44–49.

Quadagno, J. Generational equity and the politics of the welfare state. *Intergenerational Journal of Health Services,* 1990, 20, 631–649.

Ralston, P. Senior centers and minority elders: A critical review. *The Gerontologist,* 1991, *31,* 325–331.

Rauch, J. The politics of joy. *National Journal,* 1987, January 17, 125–130.

Reitzes, D. C., and Reitzes, D. C. Metro services in action: A case study of a citywide senior organization. *The Gerontologist,* 1991, *31,* 256–266.

Reynolds, D., and Kalish, R. Anticipation of futurity as a foundation of ethnicity and aging. *Journal of Gerontology,* 1974, *29,* 224–231.

Riddick, C., and Stewart, D. An examination of the life satisfaction and importance of leisure in the lives of older female retirees: A comparison of blacks to whites. *Journal of Leisure Research,* 1994, *26*(1), 75–87.

Smith, L. The tyranny of America's old. *Fortune, 125*(1), 1992, 68–72.

Soldo, B., and Agree, E. *America's elderly.* Washington, D.C.: Population Reference Bureau, 1988.

Spilka, B., Hood, R., and Gorosch, R. *The psychology of religion.* Englewood Cliffs, N.J.: Prentice Hall, 1985.

Stanley, H. W., and Niemi, R. G. *Vital statistics on American politics* (2d ed.). Washington, D.C.: C. Q. Press, 1989.

Statistical Abstract of the United States, 114th Edition, U.S. Department of Commerce, Bureau of the Census, Washington, D.C.: 1994.

Steinitz, L. Y. The local church as support for the elderly. *Journal of Gerontological Social Work,* 1981, 4, 42–53.

Streib, G. F. Are the aged a minority group? In A. W. Gouldner and S. M. Miller (Eds.), *Applied sociology.* New York: Free Press, 1965.

Stuckey, J. D. *The Sunday school class: The meaning of older women's participation in church.* Presented at the Annual Scientific Meeting of the Gerontological Society, Boston, Mass., November 1990.

Taylor, H., and Bass, R. *Productive aging: A survey of Americans age 55 and over.* New York: Louis Harris & Associates, 1992.

Taylor, R. J., and Chatters, L. M. Nonorganizational religious participation among elderly Black adults. *Journals of Gerontology,* 1991, *46,* S103–110.

Thomson, D. Generations, justice and the future of collective action. In P. Laslett and J. Fishkin (Eds.), *Philosophy, politics and society, Vol. VI, Relations between age groups and generations.* New Haven, Conn: Yale University Press, 1993.

Thorson, J. Spiritual well-being in the secular society. *Generations,* 1983, *8,* 10–11.

Tinsley, H., Teaff, J., Colbs, S., and Kaufman, N. A system of classifying leisure activities in terms of the psychological benefits of participation reported by older persons. *Journal of Gerontology,* 1985, *40,* 172–178.

Tinsley, H. E., Colbs, S., Teaff, J. I., and Kaufman, N. The relationship of age, gender, health, and economic status to the psychological benefits older persons report from participation in leisure activities. *Leisure Sciences,* 1987, *9,* 53–65.

Torres-Gil, F. Political behavior: A study of political attitudes and political participation among older Mexican Americans. Unpublished dissertation, Heller School, Brandeis University, 1976.

Torres-Gil, F. M. *The new aging: Politics and change in America.* Westport, Conn.: Auburn House, 1992.

Torres-Gil, F. M. Interest group politics: Generational changes in the politics of aging. In V. L. Bengtson and W. A. Achenbaum (Eds.), *The changing contract across generations.* New York: Aldine de Gruyter, 1993, 239–257.

U.S. Bureau of the Census. *Statistical abstract of the United States 1994, 114th Edition.* Washington, D.C.: U.S. Department of Commerce, Economic and Statistics Administration, September 1994.

U.S. Bureau of the Census. Voting and registration in the election of November 1988. Current Population Reports, Ser. P-20, No. 435. Washington, D.C.: U.S. Government Printing Office, 1989.

U.S. Senate Special Committee on Aging. *America in transition: An aging society.* Washington, D.C.: U.S. Government Printing Office, 1985.

Vinovskis, M. A. An historical perspective on support for schooling by different age cohorts. In V. L. Bengtson and W. A. Achenbaum (Eds.), *The changing contract across generations.* New York: Aldine De Gruyter, 1993, 45–65.

Vinyard, D. The rediscovery of the elderly. In B. Hess (Ed.), *Growing old in America* (2d ed.). New Brunswick, N.J.: Transaction Books, 1982.

Walls, C. T., and Zarit, S. Informal support from black churches and the well-being of elderly blacks. *The Gerontologist,* 1991, *31,* 490–495.

Weiner, A. I., and Hunt, S. C. Retirees' perception of work and leisure meanings. *The Gerontologist,* 1981, *21,* 444–448.

Whitehead, E. E. Religious images of aging. In C. LeFevre and P. LeFevre (Eds.), *Aging and the human spirit: A reader in religion and gerontology,* Chicago: Exploration Press, 1981, 156–167.

Wood, J. B., and Parham, I. A. Coping with perceived burden: Ethnic and cultural issues in Alzheimer's family caregiving. *Journal of Applied Gerontology,* 1990, *9,* 325–339.

Wood, J. B., and Wan, T. Ethnicity and minority issues in family caregiving to rural Black elders. In C. Barresi and D. Stull (Eds.), *Ethnic elderly and long-term care.* New York: Springer, 1993.

Worthington, E. L. Religious faith across the life span: Implications for counseling and research. *The Counseling Psychology,* 1989, *17,* 4, 555–612.

# CHAPTER 16

# DEATH, DYING, BEREAVEMENT, AND WIDOWHOOD

You have probably heard of people who "lost their will to live" or "died when they were ready." Such ideas are not simply superstitions. Similar to other topics addressed throughout this book, death involves an interaction of physiological, social, and psychological factors. The social context is illustrated by the fact that all cultures develop beliefs and practices regarding death in order to minimize its disruptive effects on the social structure. These cultural practices influence how members of society react to their own death and that of others. Although measures of death are physical, such as the absence of heart beat or brain waves, psychosocial factors can influence the biological event. For instance, terminally ill people have been found to die shortly after an important engagement, such as a child's wedding, a family reunion, or holiday, suggesting that their "will to live" prolonged life to that point (Kalish, 1984). How people approach their own death and that of others is closely related to personality styles, sense of competence, coping skills, and social supports, as discussed in Chapter 9.

This chapter examines age-related attitudes toward death in our culture; the dying process and its meaning to the dying person; the conditions for care of the dying; the concept of the right to die; the increasing ethical, medical, and legal issues raised by life-sustaining technologies; the legal options of advance directives available to individuals; the rituals of bereavement, grief, and mourning; and the experience of widowhood. Research on death and dying and professional interventions to support dying persons and their families are relatively recent and are a significant and growing area for gerontological research and practice; these interventions are discussed briefly here.

## THE CHANGING CONTEXT OF DYING

In our culture, dying is associated primarily with old age. Although, as we have seen, aging does not cause death, and younger people also die, there are a number of reasons for this association. The major factors are medical advances and the increase in life expectancy. In preindustrial societies, death rates were high in childhood and youth, and parents could expect that one-third to one-half of their children would die before the age of ten (Marshall, 1980). Now it is increasingly the old who die, making death predictable as a function of age. Death has thus come to be viewed as a timely event, the completion of the life cycle in old age. Others view death not only as the province of the old, but also as an unnatural event that is to be fought off as long as medically possible. At the end of a prolonged chronic illness, when medicine may care for but not cure the patient, dying may seem more unnatural than if the person had been allowed to die earlier in the progression of the illness. With expanded technological mastery over the conditions of dying, chronically ill people have often been kept alive long past the point at which they might have died naturally in the past. As noted by Callahan (1993), achieving a peaceful death is difficult because of the complexity in drawing a clear line between living and dying, which is partially a result of technology, and societal and professional ambivalence about whether to fight or accept death.

The surroundings in which death occurs have also changed with increased medical interventions. In preindustrial society, most people died at home, with the entire community often involved in rituals surrounding the death. Now over 80 percent of all deaths occur in institutions, generally in hospitals and nursing homes, with only small groups of relatives and friends present. This is the case even though most people express a preference to die at home surrounded by friends and family (Choice in Dying, 1994).

## Attitudes toward Death

More insulated from death than in the past, most people are uncomfortable with talking about it, especially the prospect of their own death. This discomfort is shown even in the euphemisms people use—"sleep, pass away, rest"—instead of the word *death* itself. Freud, in fact, recognized that although death was natural, undeniable, and unavoidable, people behaved as though it would occur only to others; that is, *they* will die, but not *me*. Fear and denial are natural and comforting responses to being unable to comprehend our own death and nonexistence (Thorson and Powell, 1988). Such fear has tended to make death a taboo topic in our society. Although in recent years death has become a more legitimate topic for scientific and social discussion, most people are more likely to talk about it on a rational, intellectual level than to discuss their own death (Kalish, 1985).

Whether people's fear of death is natural or learned is unclear. When asked what they fear most about death, respondents mention suffering and pain, loss of their body, punishment, loss of self-control, concern over an afterlife and the unknown, loneliness, the effect on survivors, and the destruction of the personality. In general, people fear the inability to predict what the future might bring and the process of dying, particularly the prospect of dying slowly and in pain, more than death itself (Marshall and Levy, 1990; Thorson and Powell, 1988). Yet, when questioned directly, people are more concerned with the death of close friends and family than with their own, and generally express an acceptance of death (Kalish and Reynolds, 1976; Kastenbaum and Aisenberg, 1976; Bengtson, Cuellar, and Ragan, 1977). Although the validity of responses to questions about one's own death is difficult to ascertain, it appears that most people both deny and accept the reality of dying. These ambivalent views reflect the basic paradox surrounding death, in which we recognize its universality, but cannot comprehend or imagine our own dying (Weisman, 1972).

## Variation by Age and Sex

Multiple factors, particularly age and gender, influence socioemotional responses to death, although more research is needed regarding such differences (Thorson and Powell, 1988). Attitudes toward death and dying do appear to differ by sex and age. In research utilizing metaphors for death, women fear death, especially pain and bodily decomposition, but are also more accepting of their own death, viewing it as peaceful, like a "compassionate mother" or an "understanding doctor." Men tend to perceive death as antagonistic, a "grinning butcher" or a "hangman with bloody hands" (Thorson and Powell, 1988; Keith, 1979). Compared to older men, older women are less negative about death (Kalish and Reynolds, 1976; Keith, 1979). In general, older people think and talk more about death and appear to be less afraid of their own death than are younger people (Stillion, 1985; Thorson and Powell, 1988; Kalish, 1985). A number of factors may explain this apparent paradox of a lessened fear of death in the face of its proximity. Having internalized society's views, older people may see their lives as having ever-decreasing social value, thereby lowering their own positive expectation of the future (Stillion, 1985). If they have lived past the age they expected to, they may view themselves as living on "borrowed time" (Kalish, 1985, 1982). A painless death tends to be viewed as preferable to deteriorating physically and mentally and being socially useless or a burden on family (Marshall, 1980). In addition, dealing with their friends' deaths, especially in age-segregated retirement communities or nursing homes, can help socialize older people toward an acceptance of their own. Experiencing deaths and other losses more frequently, they are more likely to think and talk about death on a regular basis than are younger people (Kalish, 1985) and to develop effective means of coping (Lund, 1993). If they achieve the developmental stage of ego integrity, as described in our discussion of Erikson in Chapter 9, and engage in life review, they are able to resolve conflicts and relieve anxiety, becoming more accepting of death as fair.

Older adults have also been found to react differently to perceptions of limited remaining time, and thus to death as an *organizer of time.* Compared to youth, older people confronting death may conclude that little of meaning can be

Attending funerals can help older people prepare for their own deaths.

accomplished because all activities will be short-lived and unfinished. Accordingly, many older people whose death is imminent make less effort than younger people to alter their way of life or to attempt to complete projects. Instead, they are more likely to turn inward to contemplation, reminiscence, reading, or spiritual activities (Kalish, 1985).

The awareness of one's mortality can stimulate a need for the "legitimization of biography," to find meaning in one's life and death. People who successfully achieve such legitimization experience a new freedom and relaxation about the future and tend to hold favorable attitudes toward death (Keith, 1982; Marshall, 1986). Many older people consider a sudden death to be more tragic than a slow one, desiring time to see loved ones, settle their affairs, and reminisce. Older people generally can accept the inevitability of their own death, even though they tend to be concerned about the death of relative to others (Keller, Sherry, and Piotrowski, 1984).

It is unclear whether variability in the acceptance of death is due to age or to cohort differences. For example, the current cohort of older people has fewer years of formal schooling than younger generations have, a factor that affects attitudes toward death. The interactive effects of other variables with age need to be further probed. For instance, in all age groups the most religious persons who have the greatest belief in an afterlife have less anxiety about dying (Feifel and Nagy, 1981). For the religious, death is the doorway to a better life. Similarly, people who are most confirmed in their lack of religious belief also express less fear about death. Those most fearful about death are the irregular church-goers, or those intermediate in their religiosity whose belief systems may be confused and uncertain (Downey, 1984; Kalish, 1985; Keller, Sherry, and Piotrowski, 1984). Religion apparently can either comfort or create anxiety about an afterlife, but it provides some individuals with one way to try to make sense of death (Marshall, 1980). Age is also a factor in how survivors react to death. Because the death of older people is often anticipated, it may be viewed as a "blessing" for someone whose "time has come" rather than as a tragic experience.

## Death as Loss

Researchers have also defined death as loss—loss of self, of all forms of sensory awareness, and of loved ones. Seven values lost through death have been identified:

1. Loss of ability to have experiences
2. Loss of control and the ability to predict subsequent events
3. Loss of body (and fear of what will happen to the body)
4. Loss of ability to care for dependents
5. Loss suffered by friends and family (e.g., causing grief to others)
6. Loss of opportunity to continue and plan projects
7. Loss of being in a relatively painless state

In an early study of attitudes about death, younger respondents cited causing grief to friends as their major anticipated concern, whereas those over age 40 chose the inability to care for dependents (Diggory and Rothman, 1961). In a later survey of a somewhat older and lower income sample, older respondents were less concerned about caring for dependents and causing grief to friends and relatives than were younger respondents (Kalish and Reynolds, 1976). One reason for this difference may be that older people are already experiencing "bereavement overload" through the increased frequency of family and friends' deaths, and thus are more aware of the reduced impact of their death on others (Kastenbaum, 1981). Loss of the ability to retain control over one's life can be especially poignant for an older dying person, particularly since concern with being in control tends to increase with age (Marshall and Levy, 1990). It is important to recognize that to an older person the meaning of threats to identity and the loss of the physical body may be very different from the meaning of a loss of self-control over how they die.

## THE DYING PROCESS

One of the most widely known frameworks for understanding the stages of the dying process has been advanced by Kübler-Ross (1969, 1981). According to Kübler-Ross, dying persons experience five stages in reaction to their death: (1) denial and isolation, (2) anger and resentment, (3) bargaining and an attempt to postpone, (4) depression and sense of loss, and (5) acceptance. Each of these stages represents a form of coping with the process of death.

Denial is initially a healthy buffer, but it can prevent dying persons from moving to subsequent stages if others are unwilling to talk with them about their concerns. In the second stage, anger ("Why me?") may be displaced on family or medical staff and can lead to withdrawal and avoidance. This stage may be the most difficult for caregivers to tolerate. In the bargaining stage, the dying person may try to make a deal with God to live long enough to attain some goal or to postpone death as a reward for good behavior. The fourth stage is depression, which represents a natural grieving process over the final separation of death. The dying person may withdraw from loved ones as a way to prepare for this separation. The final stage, acceptance, is achieved only if the dying person is able or allowed to express and deal with earlier feelings, such as anger and depression. The dying person thereby achieves a sense that personal tasks have been accomplished and the struggle is over. Rather than a happy stage, the acceptance phase is almost devoid of feelings, and should not be confused with wishing to die. Although Kübler-Ross cautioned that these stages were not invariant, immutable, or universal, she nevertheless implied that progression from one to the other is normal and adaptive; she encouraged health care providers to help their patients to advance through them; and she depicted the final stage as consummatory.

Kübler-Ross (1975) emphasizes that dying can be a time of growth. By accepting death's inevitability, dying persons can use life meaningfully and productively and come to terms with who they really are. Since the dying are "our best teachers," those who work with them can learn from them and emerge from such experiences with fewer anxieties about their own dying (Kübler-Ross, 1969).

The religious assumptions and allegations about life after death that are embedded in Kübler-Ross's writings have evoked scientific and theological criticism, and have often detracted from the importance of her work with dying patients (Fox, 1981). Also, since her findings were based on a sample of young and middle-aged adults, their generalizability to older individuals is limited. Nevertheless, although her work is controversial, Kübler-Ross has been a pioneering catalyst, increasing public awareness of death and the needs of the dying and their caregivers. Her framework should be viewed as a helpful cognitive grid or guideline of possible modes and ways of coping with death, not as a fixed sequence that determines a "good death." Empirical testing of the stage theory has produced mixed findings. Apathy, apprehension, and anticipation have been found as well as acceptance of death (Weisman and Kastenbaum,

1968). Moreover, any of these feelings and behaviors may occur at any time during the dying process, and the person may move back and forth between them, displaying several of the feelings simultaneously. Many patients remain at one of the first stages (denial or anger) and never pass through all five stages of the sequence.

Family members and health care providers must be cautious about implying that the dying person must follow Kübler-Ross's stages, and thus creating the illusion of control by naming phases. Instead, they should be open to the dying person's choice of whether and how to move through these stages (Kalish and Reynolds, 1976). In sum, subsequent studies have found that there is no "typical," unidirectional way to die through progressive stages. Instead, there may be an alternation between acceptance and denial, between understanding what is happening and magically disbelieving its reality (Fox, 1981; Schneidman, 1980; Kastenbaum, 1981, 1985). Consistent with the framework of dynamic interactions discussed throughout this book, the dying process is shaped by an individual's own personality and philosophy of life, by the specific illness, and by the social context (e.g., whether at home surrounded by family who encourage the expression of feelings, or isolated in a hospital).

## An Appropriate Death

Questions have also been raised about whether acceptance of death should be the goal of dying. The concept of an *appropriate death* has been suggested as an alternative goal for those working with the dying. An appropriate death means that the person has died as he or she wished to, which generally is consistent with past personality patterns and styles of coping. Permitting individuals an appropriate death allows them to maintain a sense of hopefulness—the positive anticipation of the future—which provides a sense of control or mastery (Kastenbaum, 1981). Dying people can sustain hope if they maintain their belief in "significant survival"—the belief in their lives that they have done "something worth doing and that others think so too."

In a good or appropriate death, the dying person is able to bring life to an orderly close, and the final stage of life contributes to personal growth (Levy and Gordon, 1987). Another hopeful perspective is to view death as a healthy companion to life (Kastenbaum, 1977). Most people try to maintain as much control over their dying as possible in order to render it meaningful. This involves completing unfinished business, such as saying farewell, making a will, funeral plans, and other arrangements for survivors after death (Marshall and Levy, 1990). Although an appropriate death is usually only partially obtained, those working with the dying can help them to exert such control by establishing an environment in which information and emotions can be shared.

# THE DYING TRAJECTORY FRAMEWORK

An alternative to the framework of stage theories is the concept of *dying trajectory,* or the perceived course of dying and expected time of death. The pace of a dying trajectory can be sudden or slow, regular or erratic, and it is usually shaped by the condition causing death (e.g., dying from lung cancer versus a heart attack) and by others' level of disclosure to the dying person (Marshall and Levy, 1990; Pattison, 1977). Most people with terminal conditions have an idea of how much longer they will live, and plan their lives within that interval. A *death crisis* in the dying trajectory is an unanticipated change in the amount of time remaining to live. The living-dying interval, which occurs between the death crisis and the actual time of death, is characterized by three phases. During the *acute phase,* the dying person expresses maximum anxiety or fear. At the *chronic phase* of dying, anxiety declines as the person faces death's reality, confronts questions about the dying process and the future, and enacts necessary rituals and preparations. The

*terminal phase* is characterized by the dying person's withdrawal (Glaser and Strauss, 1968). Just as Kübler-Ross's stages are not fixed or invariant for all people, not every individual goes through the trajectory of these three phases.

## Care of the Dying

Both frameworks just discussed—stages and trajectories—highlight the importance of giving attention to the ways in which care is provided to the dying. Although most dying people prefer to die at home, the common practice has been to hospitalize them, with most deaths occurring in nursing homes or hospitals.

In recent years, more training has been provided to health care providers who work with the dying. Medical professionals have become more open in talking about death with their patients as well as among themselves, and most now believe that dying persons have the right to know their condition and prognosis and to have some control over their death (Urofsky, 1993). Increasingly, the pursuit of a peaceful death is viewed as the proper end of medicine, although less agreement exists on how this is to be achieved, largely because of advances in medical technology. This breaking of "professional silence" is in part a reaction to external pressures, including patients who insist on being informed about their illnesses, and current public affirmations about the "right to know" and the "right to die."

The Dying Person's Bill of Rights, developed over 20 years ago, states that individuals have rights to treatment as living persons until death, to participate in decisions about their care, to be free from pain, to maintain their individuality, and to be cared for by sensitive and knowledgeable people. As discussed below, the right-to-die rather than to endure prolonged suffering through life extension is emphasized currently more than it was at the time the Dying Person's Bill of Rights was articulated. While controversy surrounds the use of life-sustaining technology, both sides would agree that the dying person's self-determination and right to be free from physical pain are essential to human care. As articulated by the Ethics Committee of the American Geriatrics Society in its position paper on the care of dying patients, dying persons should be provided with opportunities to make the circumstances of their dying consistent with their preferences and lifestyle. Palliative care of dying patients should focus on the relief of symptoms, not limited to pain, and be addressed by both pharmacologic and nonpharmacologic means (American Geriatrics Society, 1994). It is critical to establish conditions in which dying persons can be open about their concerns and reassured by others for expressing feelings, without necessarily being forced to be expressive. Individual needs and preferences for privacy, making decisions, and saying good-byes should be supported. The social support of friends and family, perhaps more than other interventions, can be a major source of strength and enhance the quality of their remaining days for older dying people.

**Hospice Care**   Another trend toward being more responsive to dying patients and their families has been the expansion of the hospice model of caring for the terminally ill. Hospice is a philosophy of caring and an array of services that can best be implemented through the home, although its principles can also be enacted as inpatient services for the terminally ill (Koff, 1981). As palliative care, hospice is dedicated to helping individuals who are beyond the curative power of medicine to remain in familiar environments that minimize pain, and to maintain personal dignity and control over the dying process. Assessment and coordination of the physical, psychosocial, and spiritual needs of patient and family are fundamental to the hospice approach. St. Christopher's Hospice, started by Dr. Cicely Saunders in Great Britain in 1967, was the first hospice; it is a self-contained facility with its own home-residential care.

The first hospice in the United States was developed in 1974 in New Haven, Connecticut, and now over 1,600 hospices exist in our coun-

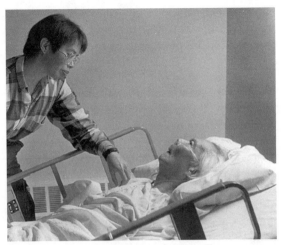

Families can be a major source of support for the dying person.

try. The majority of these provide in-home services for cancer patients (McCann and Enck, 1984). In 1986, Congress passed legislation making hospice a permanent Medicare benefit and granting a modest increase in reimbursement rates, although funding regulations are restrictive. Even though older people have been both providers and recipients of hospice care, there is some evidence that hospices have underserved the older population compared to other age groups (Kalish, 1985).

Both professional and lay providers contribute as an interdisciplinary team to hospice goals. For example, hospice workers advocate for providing dying persons with full and accurate information about their condition. Another important function is to develop supportive environments in which people can tell their life stories and find meaning in their deaths. Listening, touching the dying person, family involvement, and ritual celebration of special events such as birthdays and weddings are all emphasized by the staff (Levy, 1987). In addition, hospice staff work directly with family and friends to help them resolve their feelings, clarify expectations, and relate most effectively to the dying patient. Hospice workers also recognize the importance of bereavement counseling after the death, generally following up with support to grieving family members. In addition, hospice programs provide counseling and support to staff members to help prevent "burnout." Unfortunately, hospice models of care are still unavailable to many terminally ill persons, because of restrictive Medicare reimbursement mechanisms for in-patient care and lack of Medicaid funding for hospice benefits. Despite its over 20-year history, hospice remains essentially outside the mainstream of American medicine, with a separate philosophy, and therefore is limited in its overall impact on quality of care of dying persons (Callahan, 1993; Sachs, 1994).

Although it has many benefits, hospice is not always the best approach, since caring for a dying person at home can severely strain the resources of family and friends. Such burdens on families, discussed further in Chapter 20, have intensified with restrictions in public funding for home health care. A danger is that cost-containment objectives may take priority over the goals of quality care for the dying and their families (Aroskar, 1985). If the preference of most people to die at home is to be realized, more community-based programs to ease the strain on family caregivers must be developed.

**Psychotherapeutic Approaches** Due largely to Kübler-Ross's work, increased recognition has been given to the value of psychotherapy with dying persons. Until recently, psychotherapists have generally preferred to work with people presumed able to return to productive life, as discussed in Chapter 9. The focus of most psychotherapy with dying persons is to support the process of working through their denial and despair, thereby enabling them to live out their remaining months as fully as their disease allows. Even in the first interview, a therapist should strive to open the door for the dying person to communicate without fear and anxiety (Kübler-Ross, 1975). The process and satisfaction of personal growth, not a sense of accomplishment, are believed to be of therapeutic value in themselves.

Caring relationships with health care providers may also have therapeutic effects, even though formal psychotherapy is not involved (Kalish, 1982).

Although traditional medical treatments are generally used with dying patients, other more controversial approaches include faith-healing, acupuncture and meditation. Each of these treatments has its adherents and detractors, even within the medical profession. One controversial treatment that claims effectiveness, especially in healing cancer patients defined as terminally ill by their physicians, is the combined imagery, relaxation, and psychotherapy program developed by physician Carl Simonton (Simonton, Matthews-Simonton, and Creighton, 1978). The Simonton approach maintains that cancer patients have the power to get rid of the cancer; this emphasis on self-responsibility is assumed to marshall whatever will to live exists (Kalish, 1982). We have probably all heard anecdotes of cancer patients who practiced meditation and relaxation and lived well beyond their prognosis, again suggesting the complex interaction of psychological, social, and medical aspects of living and dying. Adherents of approaches that emphasize patient responsibility also recognize that when people have decided they are ready to die, they should be supported in that decision.

## THE RIGHT TO DIE

Along with increased attention to the ways in which people choose to die and the meanings they assign to their deaths, the right-to-die movement has grown in recent years, and has given rise to new debates regarding euthanasia, which, literally translated, means a "good death." Whether others have a right to help people die, and under what conditions, has been discussed throughout history, but recent debates about the complex ethical, social, and legal issues raised by euthanasia have intensified with increased medical advances used to prolong life. These issues revolve around three different types of patients:

the terminally ill who are conscious, the irreversibly comatose, and the brain-damaged or severely debilitated who have good chances for survival but are at a low level of existence (e.g., Alzheimer's patients).

## Passive Euthanasia
## (Voluntary Elective Death)

Euthanasia can be *passive (allowing death)* or *active (causing death)*. In *passive euthanasia*, treatment is withdrawn, and nothing is done to prolong the patient's life artificially. Suspension of medical interventions allows the preexisting process to take its course, but no active steps are taken to bring about death. In order to relieve pain, medications are sometimes given which may hasten death, but the object is to relieve suffering, not to bring about death. Withholding or withdrawing useless or unwanted medical treatments, or providing adequate pain relief, even if it hastens death, has been determined to be neither illegal nor unethical (Choice in Dying, 1994). The legal context for this is the 1990 U.S. Supreme Court case of *Cruzan v. Director, Missouri Department of Health,* which recognized the right of a competent patient to refuse unwanted medical care, including artificial nutrition and hydration, as a "liberty" interest, and therefore as constitutionally protected. While the Cruzan decision recognized this, the Court delegated regulation of this constitutional right to the states. Another indicator of the changing legal interpretations is the position of the American Medical Association (AMA). The 1984 statement on euthanasia by physicians presented two fundamental guidelines: the patient's role in decision-making is paramount, and a decrease in aggressive treatment of the hopelessly ill patient is advisable when treatment would only prolong a difficult and uncomfortable process of dying (Wanzer et al., 1984). A 1988 American Medical Association poll found that 80 to 90 percent of physicians agree that withholding and withdrawing nutrition and hydration are permissible in certain circumstances and that it is the physi-

cian's duty to initiate discussion of these issues with the patients and families (*New York Times,* 1988). In fact, in 1989, the American Medical Association adopted the position that, with informed consent, physicians could withhold or withdraw treatment from patients who are close to death. Consistent with this changing medical position is that over 80 percent of respondents in Gallup polls believe that ill patients should be able to request that doctors terminate treatment (KCR Communications Research, 1991).

In contrast to passive euthanasia where deliberate decisions are made about withholding or withdrawing treatment, there is also a form of euthanasia whereby older people may voluntarily make decisions that are equivalent to choosing to die by refusing extra help at home or by insisting on hospital discharge directly to their home, in spite of their need for skilled nursing care. When an older person commits suicide through the process of self-neglect, the effects of their decisions are subtle and gradual. If older people neglect their care needs or choose an inappropriate living situation because of impaired judgment, involuntary treatment laws can sometimes be used to move them to protected settings. If their "failure to care," however, is not immediately life-threatening, they usually have to be allowed to deteriorate to that point before being legally compelled to comply with treatment.

*Active euthanasia* refers to positive steps taken to bring about someone else's death, by administering a lethal injection or by some other means. Sometimes called mercy killing, active euthanasia is not legal in any state at this time, but its legality is being tested by several highly controversial court cases, voter initiatives, and state legislation. A subject of intense controversy is physician-assisted suicide or assisted suicide; this occurs when someone else provides the means by which an individual ends his or her life. For example, a physician may prescribe medication knowing that the individual intends to use it to commit suicide, but it is the individual who decides when and whether or not to take it (Choice in Dying, 1994). One of the states in which the legality of assisted suicide has been the focus of public attention is Michigan, where Dr. Jack Kevorkian, as of June 1995, had assisted 24 people to commit suicide. In the first case involving a woman with Alzheimer's disease, the court threw out the murder charges on the grounds that no law in Michigan prohibited assisting in a suicide. Subsequently, the legislature passed legislation in an effort to stop Dr. Kevorkian's activities. One case has been dismissed on the grounds that the law is unconstitutional, and others are pending. While controversial, Kevorkian's crusade to legalize active euthanasia has been functional in pushing the debate on physician-assisted suicide to the forefront of the American political scene.

The legal system's response to assisted suicide has varied widely. For example, in two different Florida cases where husbands assisted in the deaths of their terminally ill wives, one man was sentenced to 25 years in prison, while the other was not convicted. In Connecticut, a man who helped his dying father commit suicide by putting a plastic bag over his head was sentenced to two years' probation rather than prison because he was viewed as selflessly carrying out his father's wishes. In California, an older woman who had cared for her bed-bound husband for years and strangled him with a nylon stocking to end his suffering was not prosecuted.

The organization that has most actively attempted to change the law in order to legalize assisted suicide for the terminally ill is the Hemlock Society. Their popular publication, *Final Exit,* by their founder Derek Humphry, is a manual on nonviolent methods to commit suicide with prescription barbiturates to assure a gentle, peaceful death. The Hemlock Society distinguishes between "rational or responsible suicide" (i.e., the option of ending one's life for good and valid reasons) and suicide that is caused by a rejection of life because of emotional disturbance. Public opinion polls also reflect a growing acceptance of the idea of assisted suicide, especially among those who believe that to force people to endure prolonged pain is in-

humane and cruel. Advocates of physician-assisted suicide view the right to request assistance in dying as merely an extension of the individual's right to control the kind of treatment he or she receives when dying. Rejecting remote chances of recovery as a basis to justify prolonging life, they also discard the notion of any ethical difference between stopping treatment and assisting someone to die.

Citizen initiatives and recent state legislation also reflect increasing public support for physician-assisted suicide. As noted above, national surveys generally find growing support for the option of dying with a doctor's assistance (Choice in Dying, 1994; KCR Communications Research, 1991). *Compassion et al. v. Washington State* was the first case to challenge in a federal court the constitutionality of a state law on assisted suicide insofar as it applies to mentally competent, terminally ill patients seeking prescribed medications with which to hasten death. An initiative in Washington State to permit physician aid-in-dying was only narrowly defeated in 1992. Patients could request such assistance in writing at the time they want to die, as long as two witnesses would certify that the request is voluntary and two doctors would state that the patient would die within six months. However, four months after the initiative was defeated at the polls, the legislature passed a bill giving comatose and dying people the right to have food and water withdrawn (*Seattle Times,* 1992). In 1994, the federal district court ruled that the Washington State ban on physician-assisted suicide violates the patient's constitutional right to liberty, but this ruling did not protect physicians from prosecution if they assist in a terminally ill patient's suicide (Hudson, 1994).

Measure 16, passed by Oregon voters in 1994, would allow doctors to write a prescription of lethal drug doses for an aware, adult, terminally ill patient who asks, both orally and in writing, although doctors would not be compelled to comply with this request. A 15-day waiting period is required for the first oral request, and two witnesses are necessary for the written request along with agreement of a second doctor. The doctor must inform the patient about options, including pain control, and make sure that the request really is voluntary. At the end of this elaborate process, only the patient can decide whether and when to take fatal drugs and must do so him or herself. However, in response to a lawsuit that argued that the law does not provide adequate safeguards against undue influence, particularly in instances of depression, a federal judge blocked implementation of this citizen initiative that would have made Oregon the first entity in the world to legalize physician-assisted suicide (Egar, December 25, 1994). More recently, a federal judge refused to strike down the New York laws banning physician-assisted suicide, maintaining that the state has a legitimate interest in preserving life, a decision opposite to that of Washington State. Conflicting state rules make it likely that the issue will go to the U.S. Supreme Court. If successful at the Supreme Court, this challenge could invalidate all state laws which summarily prohibit assistance with suicide. Theses issues are also being debated internationally; in the Netherlands, for example, euthanasia is technically illegal, but doctors are exempt from prosecution if their actions have been carried out with the consent of both the patient and the family physician, the patient is "competent," and economic factors have not played a part in the decision (Gianelli, May 16, 1994).

Given the divided public and legal opinion about these emotionally charged issues, the medical community has extensively debated active euthanasia. In a March 1989 article in the *New England Journal of Medicine*, 10 of the 12 authors stated that "it is not immoral for a physician to assist in the rational suicide of a terminally ill person" (p. 848). In 1991, the *New England Journal of Medicine* published an account by Dr. Timothy Quill, in which he detailed his decision to assist a terminally ill cancer patient in taking her life by prescribing medication and telling her what would constitute a fatal dose (Quill, 1991). Attempts to prosecute

Dr. Quill failed. While some physicians felt that Dr. Quill had behaved responsibly and that he showed that active euthanasia could be an acceptable alternative to slow dying, others felt that he violated basic human values as well the trust inherent in the doctor-patient relationship (Choice in Dying, 1994). Those who argue against the legalization of assisted suicide view that a "right to die" could become a "duty to die" and be inappropriately applied to older adults and other dependent members of society. They fear that a law made to convey permission could become seen as prescriptive, with assisted suicide viewed as a solution no longer requiring careful scrutiny. The American Medical Association, in their opposition to physician-assisted suicide, urges the medical community to find better ways to control patients' pain as a humane alternative (McCormick, 1993). Given physicians' tendency to equate a patient's death with professional failure, they contend that "hopeless" patients may survive to lead meaningful lives and that relevant new medical discoveries may be made that would save lives.

## Legal Options regarding End-of-Life Care

While active euthanasia continues to be debated in courtrooms and the ballot box, all 50 states have laws authorizing the use of some type of *advance directive,* which refers to a patient's oral and written instructions about future medical care in the event of their inability to speak for themselves. Both federal and state laws govern the use of advance directives. The federal law, the Patient Self-Determination Act, requires health care facilities that receive Medicaid and Medicare funds to inform patients of their rights to execute advance directives regarding how they want to live or die.

The most frequently used type of advance directive is a *Living Will,* in which an individual's wishes about medical treatment are put in writing should he or she be unable to communicate at the end of life. Living Wills can direct physicians at hospitals to withhold life-sustaining procedures in the event of an irreversible terminal condition and can assist family members in making decisions when they are unable to consult a comatose or mentally incompetent relative. Such stipulations only apply to care in hospitals, although some states are now drafting laws that would exempt emergency medical technicians from liability for not resuscitating patients with legal do-not-resuscitate (DNR) medical directives (Gianelli, November 7, 1994). A 1991 Gallup Poll found that 75 percent of Americans approve of Living Wills, and more than 20 percent have a Living Will or Durable Power of Attorney for health care designation (Choice in Dying, 1994). The existence of a Living Will, however, does not mean that health care providers, oftentimes with conflicting beliefs, will always follow it, especially if there is no one to advocate for the dying individual. Or family members may later change their minds about adhering to a Living Will.

In situations where there is no Living Will, the family of an incompetent patient has had to go to court to obtain legal authority if they wish to refuse life support on the patient's behalf. This expensive and time-consuming process has been viewed as necessary where doctors and health care facilities are unwilling to make decisions to remove life-sustaining treatment because of the perceived risk of liability. To obviate this court process, 24 states and the District of Columbia have passed statutes governing *surrogate decision-making*. The surrogate has a duty to act according to the known wishes of the patient; if those wishes are not known, the surrogate must act according to the "best interest" of the patient. Such laws support the concept that the people closest to the patient are in the best position to know their wishes or to act in their best interest. Each state's law includes a prioritized list of people connected to the patient who are potential surrogates. The doctor must approach these individuals, in order of priority, to find someone who is willing to make decisions about life support (Choice in Dying, 1994).

Another type of advance directive is *durable power of attorney*, which authorizes someone to act in an individual's behalf with regard to property and financial matters, and a durable power of attorney for health care decisions specifically allows for a health care surrogate to interpret a person's Living Will. The individual does not relinquish control with a power of attorney since it is granted only for the financial matters specifically set forth in the relevant document. Durable means that the arrangement continues even when the person is incapacitated and unable to make his or her own medical decisions. A durable power of attorney agreement may be written either to go into effect upon its signing or only when the disability occurs. When the disability does occur, bills can continue to be paid and revenues can continue to be collected while other more permanent arrangements are being made, such as the appointment of a *conservator* or *guardian*.

*Conservatorship* also relates to control of financial matters. In this instance, the probate court appoints a person to care for an individual's property and finances because that person is unable to do so due to advanced age, mental weakness, or physical incapacity. Such a condition must be attested to by a physician. Once appointed, the conservator will be required to file an inventory of all the assets and to report annually all income and expenses. The old or disabled individual, however, loses actual control over his or her property and finances.

*Guardianship* is a legal tool that establishes control over a person's body as well as financial affairs. In a guardianship, the probate court appoints someone to care for the individual's person, property, and finances because of the individual's mental inability to care for him- or herself. The guardian has a responsibility for directing the individual's medical treatment, housing, personal needs, finances, and property. To establish the guardianship, a medical certificate from a physician must state that the individual is incapable of caring for him- or herself because of mental illness. As with conservatorships, the medical certificate required by the physician must be made not more than 10 days before the probate court hearing, so in this sense, guardianship cannot be arranged in advance of need. However, through a durable power of attorney, an individual may nominate someone he or she would like to act as guardian in the event that such a need develops. Since the guardian manages all the affairs of the individual, guardianship is generally considered a last resort because the process essentially eliminates an individual's legal rights.

Family members who are concerned about finances may move too quickly through these options. However, families and service providers should try, as long as possible, to respect the wishes of the older person with regard to living arrangements, legal will, and other financial decisions. In other words, the older person should be encouraged to exercise as much control as possible, to the extent that his or her cognitive status allows.

A wide range of organizations have been developed to educate the public, health care providers, and lawmakers regarding right-to-die issues and advance directive options. The largest of these is Choice in Dying, Inc., a national not-for-profit organization that was created in 1991 by a merger of the nation's two oldest organizations advocating the rights of dying patients, Concern for Dying and Society for the Right to Die. These two organizations pioneered patients'

rights to refuse unwanted life support and developed the first Living Will document in 1967. Choice in Dying has provided national leadership on Living Wills, guided the enactment of advance directives in all states and lobbied for the passage of the Patient Self-Determination Act. Their goal is to achieve full societal and legal support for the right of all individuals to make decisions regarding the nature and extent of life-sustaining measures, as well as the conditions under which dying occurs, and to have those decisions recognized and honored (Choice in Dying, 1994).

Societal cost-benefit criteria inevitably come into play in discussions of active and passive euthanasia. As society seeks to contain rising health and long-term care costs, physicians are subject to demands for financial restraint. While a significant proportion of the money spent on medical care in a person's lifetime goes to services received during the last years and months of life, even if such care were eliminated, the dollars saved would be insignificant in the larger context of national health care costs (Binstock, 1994). Nevertheless, given limited resources on a societal level, what appear to be huge expenditures to keep alive a comparatively small number of people can take resources away from medical needs of other populations (Callahan, 1986; 1993).

## ISSUES RAISED BY THE RIGHT TO DIE

Consider the case of a California couple, both home-bound and under the care of round-the-clock nurses. The wife had emphysema and was unable to walk, talk, or stand up straight without severe breathing difficulties. She was attached 24 hours a day to a machine that delivered oxygen to her through two nasal prongs. The husband, in the final stages of congestive heart disease, was subject to hallucinations and could not walk, read, hear clearly, get dressed, bathe himself, or control his bladder. If they had waited four months, they could have celebrated their fiftieth wedding anniversary, but

instead they chose, as they put it in their letters to their children, to "terminate their terminal illnesses." During the last year of their lives, they had discussed their plans with their children and grandchildren, written detailed letters describing their intentions and philosophies, and carefully studied manuals published by *right to die* societies. Their adult children believed that their parents, perceiving a painful and narrowed future, had availed themselves of their right to choose the dignity of death over the sanctity of life (Fadiman, 1984).

THE FOLLOWING IS AN EXAMPLE OF A LIVING WILL FOR THE
STATE OF FLORIDA. PLEASE CONTACT CHOICE IN DYING AT
(800) 989-WILL TO RECEIVE A FREE COPY OF
APPROPRIATE ADVANCE DIRECTIVES FOR YOUR STATE.

# FLORIDA LIVING WILL

**INSTRUCTIONS**

**PRINT THE DATE**

Declaration made this _____ day of _____, 19_____.

**PRINT YOUR
NAME**

I, _____, willfully
and voluntarily make known my desire that my dying not be artificially
prolonged under the circumstances set forth below, and I do hereby declare:

If at any time I have a terminal condition and if my attending or treating
physician and another consulting physician have determined that there is no
medical probability of my recovery from such condition, I direct that life-
prolonging procedures be withheld or withdrawn when the application of such
procedures would serve only to prolong artificially the process of dying, and
that I be permitted to die naturally with only the administration of medication
or the performance of any medical procedure deemed necessary to provide me
with comfort care or to alleviate pain.

It is my intention that this declaration be honored by my family and physician
as the final expression of my legal right to refuse medical or surgical treatment
and to accept the consequences for such refusal.

In the event that I have been determined to be unable to provide express and
informed consent regarding the withholding, withdrawal, or continuation of
life-prolonging procedures, I wish to designate, as my surrogate to carry out the
provisions of this declaration:

**PRINT THE
NAME, HOME
ADDRESS AND
TELEPHONE
NUMBER OF
YOUR
SURROGATE**

Name: _____

Address: _____

_____ Zip Code: _____

Phone: _____

© 1993
CHOICE IN DYING, INC.

**ADD PERSONAL INSTRUCTIONS (IF ANY)**

Additional instructions (optional):

I further affirm that this designation is not being made as a condition of treatment or admission to a health care facility. I will notify and send a copy of this document to the following persons other than my surrogate, so they may know who my surrogate is:

**PRINT THE NAMES AND ADDRESSES OF THOSE WHO YOU WANT TO KEEP COPIES OF THIS DOCUMENT**

Name: _____

Address: _____

Name: _____

Address: _____

**SIGN AND DATE THE DOCUMENT**

Signed: _____

Date: _____

**WITNESSING PROCEDURE**

**TWO WITNESSES MUST SIGN AND PRINT THEIR ADDRESSES**

Witness 1:

    Signed: _____

    Address: _____

Witness 2:

    Signed: _____

    Address: _____

© 1993
CHOICE IN DYING, INC.

*Courtesy of Choice In Dying*   11/93
200 Varick Street, New York, NY 10014  1-800-989-WILL

**PAGE 2**

Reprinted by permission of Choice In Dying.

Debates about cost benefits are clearly illustrated in decisions involving organ transplants. Should money be spent on such transplants to benefit a relatively few people, or should these people be permitted to die and our health resources focused on prevention and outreach? Rapid improvements in medical technology have not been matched by refinements in the law and the ethics of using those therapies. Euthanasia thus raises not only complex ethical and legal dilemmas, but also resource allocation issues that cannot be ignored. On a personal level, many dying people find that the medical technology that prolongs their lives may financially ruin their families. These issues, which will become more critical in the future with advancing medical technology, will be discussed further in our Epilogue.

## BEREAVEMENT, GRIEF, AND MOURNING RITUALS

Death affects the social structure through the person's survivors, who have social and emotional needs resulting from that death. Some studies have found that the intensity of these needs is reflected in the higher rates of suicide, hospitalization for psychiatric disorders, visits to physicians, and somatic complaints (Marshall, 1980; Kalish, 1982). Numerous epidemiological studies over the past 20 years reveal a higher mortality rate in the newly widowed, particularly among younger white male widowers. However, these studies failed to take account of other factors that may influence mortality in bereavement, such as length of illness in the deceased spouse, preexisting illness in the survivor, and socioeconomic and ethnic minority status (Parkes, Murray, and Fitzgerald, 1969; Jacobs and Ostfeld, 1977). High mortality rates may also reflect fatigue, self-neglect, or stress resulting both from caring for the dying person and from mourning (Kalish, 1982). More recent studies suggest that the resiliency and ability of the grieving spouse to cope effectively are often underestimated (Caserta and Lund, 1992; Lund, 1993).

The relationship between bereavement and suicide in the older population also requires further investigation. Although findings are inconsistent, the first six months of widowhood appear to be the most stressful, especially for older men who are more at risk of poor health, death, and suicide. To minimize these disruptive effects, older survivors, who, as we have seen in earlier chapters, frequently face multiple losses, need help from both formal and informal networks in dealing with their grief. Such efforts to be supportive must take account of cultural values and belief.

Bereavement refers to both the situation and the long-term process of adjusting to the death of someone with whom the person felt close (Lund, 1993). *Grief* is the complex emotional response to bereavement. *Bereavement* refers to the state of being deprived of a loved one by death. *Mourning* signifies culturally patterned expectations about the expression of grief. Grief reactions can include shock and disbelief, guilt, psychological numbness, depression, loneliness, fatigue, loss of appetite, sleeplessness, and anxiety about one's ability to reorganize and carry on with life (Kalish, 1982; Martocchio, 1985).

The grieving process may be assisted by reminiscence.

Although there appear to be clusters or phases of grief reactions, the progression is more like a roller coaster—with overlapping responses and wide individual variability—rather than orderly stages or a fixed or universal sequence (Lund, 1993). To expect grieving individuals to progress in some specified fashion is inappropriate, and can be potentially harmful to them (Martocchio, 1985). The highs and lows within broad phases can occur within minutes, days, months, or years, with grieving individuals moving back and forth among them. Even within the individual, there can be mixed reactions, with a person simultaneously experiencing anger, guilt, helplessness, and loneliness along with personal strength and pride in their coping (Lund, Caserta, and Dimond, 1993). Emotions change rapidly beginning with shock, numbness, and disbelief, followed by an all-encompassing sorrow. Early months following the loss are the most difficult, with early indicators serving as predictors of longer-term adjustment (Lund et al., 1993). In older adults, somatic illnesses tend to be associated with and intensify the reaction to loss at these early stages (Thompson et al., 1984).

An intermediate phase of grief often involves an idealization and searching for the presence of the deceased person, as well as an obsessional review in an attempt to find meaning for the death. Anger toward the deceased, toward God, and toward caregivers may also be experienced, as well as guilt and regrets for what survivors did not do or say. When the permanence of the loss is acknowledged and yearning ceases, anguish, disorganization, and despair often result. The grieving person tends to experience a sense of confusion, a feeling of aimlessness, a loss of motivation, confidence, and interest, and an inability to make decisions. These feelings may be exacerbated if the grieving person tries to live according to the expectations of others, including those of the deceased. Instead, successful adjustments tend to require active rather than passive coping strategies in which the individual finds his or her own best way to live with grief (Lund, 1993).

The final phase—reorganization and recovery—is marked by a resumption of routine activities and social relationships, and identification with the deceased. The ability to effectively communicate one's thoughts and feelings to others and to experience a reciprocal relationship between their self-esteem and learning new skills and competencies enhances the adjustment process (Lund, 1993).

Some people never fully resolve their loss and cease grieving, but learn to live with it (Lund, 1993). Unresolved grief may be misdiagnosed as illness, and may lead to depression, as described in Chapter 11. For most people, some of the pain of loss remains for a lifetime. Older adults' experiences with grief may be even more complex than other age groups' for several reasons. As noted in Chapter 9, they are more likely to experience unrelated, multiple losses over relatively brief periods, at a time when their coping capacities and environmental resources are often diminished. The cumulative effects of losses may be greater, especially if the older person has not resolved earlier losses, or interprets current losses as evidence of an inevitable continuing process (Freeman, 1984). Health care providers must be careful not to misdiagnose grief symptoms as physical illness, dementia, or hypochondriasis. Not surprisingly, loneliness has been found to be the greatest difficulty for older bereaved spouses, and cannot be managed simply by surrounding oneself with others (Lund et al., 1993).

Research findings are mixed regarding whether adjustment to bereavement is more difficult when death is sudden or unexpected. In comparison to the young, older people may be less affected negatively by a sudden death because they have rehearsed and planned for widowhood as a life stage task (Lund et al., 1993). As noted in Chapter 9 in the discussion of anticipatory coping, an expected death can allow survivors to prepare for the changes through "anticipatory grief," but it does not necessarily minimize the grief and emotional strain. However, some studies indicate that a longer period of anticipatory grief, through caring for an individual during a long period of chronic or terminal illness, can actually create barriers to successful adaptation, increasing the risk of post-mortem depression. Family members who experience the death as a relief from long-term demands of care may experience premature detachment, ambivalent and hostile feelings, guilt, depression, and a reduced ability to mourn publicly. Others have concluded that the adjustment process is similar whether the loss is expected or unexpected, although suddenness may make a difference early in the process of bereavement (Lund 1989).

Factors that have been found to help minimize grief are whether the death is viewed as natural, the degree to which relationships seem complete, and the presence of surviving confidants to provide emotional support (Carey, 1979–80). To work through grief successfully requires facing the pain and fully expressing the related feelings (Martocchio, 1985). In recent years, health care providers have recognized the importance of grief work, and view grieving as a natural healing process (Benoliel, 1985). Because of the cumulative impact of multiple losses, older adults especially may need assistance in grief resolution, perhaps through life review and encouragement of new risk-taking (Freeman, 1984). Unfortunately, most studies of bereavement have been based on case studies or retrospective studies during the early phase of grief. There are few well-controlled longitudinal studies of the bereavement process. An additional limitation is that few researchers have controlled for the effects of variables such as gender, ethnic minority status, age, social class, and education. Our understanding of the emotional components of bereavement is based largely on middle-aged, middle-class Caucasians, thereby limiting the cultural relevance of interventions to address the emotional aspects of grieving.

*Mourning* involves cultural assumptions about appropriate behavior during bereavement. Mourning rituals develop in every culture as a way to channel the normal expression of grief, to define the appropriate timing of bereavement, and to encourage support for the bereaved among family and friends. Professionals need to be sensitive to cultural and ethnic differences regarding the form and meaning of death and the burial of the dead. As Kastenbaum (1977) notes, the "death system" of cultural groups involves people (e.g., funeral directors, florists, and life insurance agents in Western society), places (funeral homes), objects (tombstones), times (Memorial Day), and symbols (black dress and funeral music). The major function of the death system is to help both the individual and society deal with the problems created by death. Grief rituals such as sorting and disposing of personal effects and visiting the grave site are important in working through the grief process (Bolton and Delpha, 1989).

The funeral, for example, serves as a rite of passage for the deceased and a focal point for the expression of the survivors' grief. Funerals also allow the family to demonstrate cohesion through sharing ritual, food, and drink, and thus minimize the disruptive effects of the death. Funerals and associated customs are more important in societies with a high mortality throughout the life cycle than in societies where death is predominantly confined to the old. Money donations instead of flowers, and cremations instead of land burial signal the development of new kinds of death rituals today. Contemporary funerals have been criticized for being costly, for exploiting people at a time when they are vulnerable, and for elaborate cosmetic restorations of the body. Legislation has been enacted recently to control some of the excesses of the funeral industry. Despite such criticisms, however, most people approve of traditional funerals; and some type of ceremony appears to make the death more real to the survivors and to offer a meaningful way to cope with the initial grief.

## WIDOWHOOD

A spouse's death may be the most stressful event that an older person will experience, altering one's self-concept to an "uncoupled identity" (Lund,

1993; Saunders, 1981). With the average age of widowhood at 56 years and the average life expectancy approaching 80, many women face over 20 years of widowhood. The proportion of widows among nonwhites is twice that among whites; nonwhite women are also widowed earlier (U.S. Senate Special Committee on Aging, 1988). This is a reflection of the shorter life expectancy of nonwhite men in our society, as discussed in Chapters 1 and 17.

Despite the stress, the course of spousal bereavement is often characterized by resiliency and effective coping which allows depression, loneliness, and sadness to be followed by feelings of pride, confidence, and personal growth. In fact, only 15 to 25 percent of bereaved spouses have long-term difficulties in coping and, contrary to early studies which identified an increase in physical symptoms and somatic illness among older widows (Parkes and Brown, 1972), the stress of bereavement does not necessarily negatively impact health (Caserta and Lund, 1992; Caserta, Lund, and Dimond, 1989; Lund, 1993; Lund, Caserta, and Dimond, 1986; McCrae and Costa, 1988; Norris and Murrell, 1987). It appears that the impact of widowhood can be attenuated through a number of complex social-psychological variables. These include the adequacy of the social support network, including closeness to children and having intimate friends, the individual's characteristic ways of coping with stress, and religious commitment. Other variables that appear to affect the degree of stress of widowhood are age, gender, and health status of the widowed person (Dimond, Lund, and Caserta, 1987; Goldberg, Comstock, and Harlow, 1988). Age by itself, however, has been found to have little effect on bereavement outcomes. Differences between younger and older widows can be explained by the relationship of age to employment status and income. Age is associated, however, with a greater need to learn new life skills, such as older women's mastering of financial management tasks.

It is unclear whether the stress of bereavement is greater for the young than for the old.

Although younger spouses have been found initially to manifest more intense grief, a reverse trend has been noted after 18 months, with older spouses showing exacerbated grief reactions. As noted earlier, older people are more likely to experience other losses simultaneously, or "bereavement overload" (Kastenbaum, 1991), which may intensify and prolong their grief. On the other hand, spousal bereavement in later life is an "on-time" event and older adults have had more opportunities to manage a variety of losses and to develop a variety of coping strategies (Lund, 1993).

Findings are mixed regarding the association between age and emotional response to bereavement. Some studies have found that older widows experience less psychological distress (for example, restlessness, sleep disturbance, and irritability) than do younger widows (Maddison and Viola, 1968; Parkes, 1964). Conflicting results have also been found regarding the value of anticipatory grieving in helping individuals adjust to a loss. For younger widowers, anticipatory grief tends to reduce the intensity of their bereavement (Carey, 1979–80; Marshall, 1980). As noted earlier, this is not always the case among older widowers studied, largely because of the lengthy chronic illness preceding the spouse's death.

## Gender Differences in Widowhood

Whether widowhood is more difficult for women or men is unclear. Certainly, coping or adaptation to widowhood is related to income. Adequate financial resources are necessary to maintain a sense of self-sufficiency and to continue participation in meaningful activities. Older widows are generally worse off than widowers in terms of finances, legal problems, and prospects for remarriage. Women who have been economically dependent on their husbands often find their incomes drastically reduced, especially if they do not yet qualify for Social Security or if their husbands had not chosen survivors' pension benefits. Insurance benefits, when they exist, tend to be exhausted within two years of the husband's death.

Financial hardships may be especially great for women who have been caring for a spouse during a long chronic illness or who have depleted their joint resources during the spouse's institutionalization. Furthermore, many older widows have few opportunities to augment their income through paid employment. As noted earlier, older women have limited chances of remarrying into an economically desirable situation. Consequently, 60 percent of all widows age 65 and over live alone or with nonrelatives, and only 25 percent of older widows report living reasonably free of financial worries. An estimated 40 percent of older widows live near or below the poverty line (Smeading, 1990). Although finding jobs for older widows has been suggested as a way to meet their economic needs, employment is not necessarily an appropriate adaptive strategy for them (Morgan, 1984).

Some women, however, do not depend on a man for economic or social support. Because women generally have more diverse, extensive friendship networks than men do, and because widowhood is prevalent in later life, many women form strong support networks with other widows. These friendship groups can compensate for the loss of a husband's companionship and ease the adjustment to living alone. Friends are of greatest support, in some instances more so than children, when they accept the widow's emotional ambivalence, do not offer advice, and respond to what she defines as her needs (Morgan, 1989; Roberto and Scott, 1986; Mutran and Reitzes, 1984; Lopata, 1973). Among women over age 70, two-thirds of whom are widowed, the married person is the unusual case, and the married individual has fewer friends than does the widow in the same age group (Blau, 1981).

Many widows have no interest in remarriage. Even among Lopata's (1973) classic study of widows with happy prior marriages, 36 percent said they would not marry again. Although many persons feel great loss with a spouse's death, for some who have been restricted in their

marriage or who faced long-term caregiving responsibilities, widowhood can bring relief and opportunities to develop new interests. In fact, for those in unhappy marriages who feel they cannot divorce, death may be the only acceptable separation.

Adjusting to the loss of a spouse is likely to be most difficult for women who are in poor health, have had few economic and social resources throughout their lives, and perceive themselves as dependent, and when the identity of wife is lost without the substitution of other viable roles and lifestyles (O'Bryant and Morgan, 1990; Ferraro, 1984). However, as the example below illustrates, older widows can learn to become more independent.

The importance of economic and social supports has been identified in societies throughout the Middle East, Asia, and the Pacific, as well as in various cultures within Canada and the United States. A closely related factor appears to be whether a gap exists between how a woman was socialized to be dependent upon a man and how she must now live more independently as a widow (Lopata, 1987). For example, Lopata (1973) found that widows who did not have their own friends or who had only couple-based friendships before their husband's death generally had difficulty forming new friendships and were left without satisfying roles. They also tended not to have access to social services. In our couples-oriented society, such women were lonely and isolated, and turned primarily to their children for emotional support. Friendships were thus the least frequent and the least deeply involving among the most disadvantaged, uneducated of the urban widows studied by Lopata. (Because more women have entered the workforce in the past 30 years, future cohorts of older women may be better prepared to live independently than the women in Lopata's early studies). Blau (1981) also found that lower-class women who did not share social activities with other women, outside of neighbors, were less likely to have a reserve of social options upon which to draw in widowhood. Whether widows have strong friendship networks thus appears to vary with socioeconomic class and ethnic minority status, with whether they had a social network and satisfying roles before their husband's death, and with the prevalence of widowhood among a person's own age, sex, and class peers. Hispanic and Asian American widows are more likely to live with others and thus to have more active support systems than do Caucasian widows or those from other ethnic minority groups (Bengtson, Rosenthal, and Burton, 1990).

A woman's change in status inevitably affects her relationship with her children and other relatives. Most widows move in with their children only as a "last resort," although their children may view them as "helpless" and urge them to make the move. Older widows tend to grow closer to their daughters through patterns of mutual assistance, but sons may provide instrumental support for mothers in their own homes. Nevertheless, although children provide both socioeconomic support and assistance with tasks, this may not necessarily reduce their widowed parents' loneliness. For example, interactions with an adult child are less reciprocal, while friends and neighbors are better suited for sharing leisure activities and providing companionship; such reciprocity tends to be associated with higher morale. What is clear is the importance of diverse social networks that include age generational peers, whether family or nonfamily (Blau, 1981; Mutran and Reitzes, 1984; Roberto and Scott, 1986; Morgan, 1989; Bengtson, Rosenthal and Burton, 1990).

Most research on widowhood has focused on women, inasmuch as there are five widows to every widower in our society. Less is known about the effects of widowhood on older men. Men more often complain of loneliness and appear to make slower emotional recoveries than do women. They may have more difficulty expressing their grief and adjusting to the loss than women do, because of their lower degree of involvement in family and friendship roles throughout life, their life-long patterns of restraining emotions, their limited prior housekeeping and cooking, and the greater likelihood of a double role loss of worker and spouse (Martin-Matthews, 1988; Wister and Strain, 1986). On the other hand, some men experience pride and positive self-esteem from mastering new housekeeping skills (Lund et al., 1993). Many men have depended on their wives for emotional support, household maintenance, and social planning. Given these factors, men appear to "need" remarriage more than women do, and perhaps have been socialized to move more quickly into restructuring their lives through remarriage (Hess and Soldo, 1985). Other studies have concluded that the impact of bereavement on older people's mental health is comparable for both men and women, and that with advancing age and increasing functional limitations, the similarities between widows and widowers become more striking than the differences (Bengtson, Rosenthal and Burton, 1990; Lund, 1989; Lund et al., 1993). Men, however, have been found to experience more medical problems (as

---

## DEVELOPING NEW ROLES IN WIDOWHOOD

Martha had always seen her role as wife and mother and left the paying of the bills and "business" aspects of family life to her husband. Her "job" was to keep the home a comfortable place for him and their daughter. When he died five years ago, she was 63. She felt ill-prepared to take on paying the bills and managing other financial mat-

ters. She sought the advice of her banker on the best way to set up a bookkeeping system. After paying the bills, ordering some appliances for the house, and taking care of the Medicare paperwork for the past few years, she now sees herself as being in the role of "manager" for herself, and is pleased with what she has learned.

measured by increased physicians' visits and use of medications) and to be at greater risk of mortality during the six months following their wife's death. Higher rates of illness may result from hormonal responses to the stress of loss, which can lead to depression of the body's immune system (Stephenson, 1985). Although widowhood may significantly impair older men's emotional and medical well-being, it is less likely to place men at an economic disadvantage. More research is needed on how men cope with the loss of their wives. Even less is known about how older men's experience of widowhood varies by social class or ethnic minority status.

Generally, widowhood increases social isolation for both men and women, with loneliness perceived as a major problem. In fact, for widowed persons generally, mental and physical impairments are higher than those for married persons of the same age (Barrett, 1978). Rates of chronic illness, suicide, and death tend to be even higher for those widowed persons, particularly for older men, without additional support systems, especially a confidant (Strain and Chappell, 1982; Maris, 1981; Helsing and Szklo, 1981).

In order to provide such support for persons coping with loneliness and isolation, mutual help groups and bereavement centers have been developed by both mental health professionals and lay organizations. Women are the most frequent participants. These widow-to-widow groups are based on the principle of bringing together people who have the common experience of widowhood and who can help each other identify solutions to shared concerns. They recognize that a widowed person generally accepts help from other widowed people more readily than from professionals or family members. Support groups thus can provide widows with effective role models and can help integrate them into a social network and enhance their sense of competence toward their environment (Caserta and Lund, 1993; Silverman, 1980). Similar groups also need to be developed for gay men and lesbian women who are coping with the loss of a partner. Recent studies have suggested that a widowed person's

sense of self-esteem, competence, and life satisfaction may be as or more important resources than the self-help intervention. One implication is that interventions should focus upon ways for the bereaved to draw upon and enhance their internal resources and to experience growth and development, not just serve as a forum to address the disruptive effects of the loss (Caserta and Lund, 1993). Clearly, more research is needed on group objectives and how support group dynamics and structure relate to specific adjustment outcomes.

## SUMMARY AND IMPLICATIONS

Although death and dying have been taboo topics for many people in our society, they have become more legitimate issues for scientific and social discussion in recent years. At the same time, there has been a growing emphasis on how professionals should work with the dying and their families, as well as a movement to permit death with dignity.

Two major frameworks have been advanced for understanding the dying process: the concept of stages of dying and the formulation of a dying trajectory. Both frameworks are only an inventory of possible sequences, not fixed steps.

Most people appear both to deny and to accept death, being better able to discuss others' deaths than their own and fearing a painful dying process more than the event of death itself. Different attitudes toward dying have been noted among the old and the young. Older people are less fearful and anxious about their death than younger people and would prefer a slow death that allows them time to prepare. Likewise, survivors tend to view an older person's death as less tragic than a younger individual's.

Professionals and family members can address the dying person's fears, minimize the pain of the dying process, and help the individual to attain a "good death." One of the major developments in this regard has been hospice care, a philosophy of caring that can be implemented in both home and institutional settings, and that provides people with more control over how they die and over the quality of their remaining days.

The movement for a right to a dignified death has prompted new debates about euthanasia. Both passive and active euthanasia raise complex moral and legal questions that have been only partially addressed by the passage of Living Will legislation and a growing number of judicial decisions. Economic issues are also at stake; as resources for health care become more scarce, questions about how much public money should be spent on maintaining chronically ill people are likely to intensify.

Regardless of how individuals die, their survivors experience grief and mourning. The intensity and duration of grief appear to vary by age and sex, although more research is needed regarding gender differences in reaction to loss of spouse and adjustment to widowhood.

By age 70, the majority of older women are widows; a much smaller number of older men become widowers, generally not until after age 85. The status of widowhood has negative consequences for many women in terms of increased legal difficulties, reduced finances, and few remarriage prospects. Although men are less economically disadvantaged by widowhood, they may be lonelier and have more difficulty adjusting than women do. For both men and women, social supports, particularly close friends or confidants, are important to physical and mental well-being during widowhood. In addition to mourning rituals to help widows and widowers cope with their grief, more support services, such as widows' support groups, are needed. Comprehensive and diverse service formats are essential, given the variety of grief responses, and interventions should be available early in the bereavement process and continue over relatively long periods of time to insure maximum effectiveness (Lund, 1989). Health and social service professionals can play a crucial role in developing services for the dying and their survivors that are sensitive to cultural, ethnic minority, sexual orientation, and gender differences.

## REFERENCES

Amenta, M. Hospice in the United States: Multiple models and varied programs. *Nursing Clinics of North America,* 1985, *20,* 269–279.

American Geriatrics Society. The care of dying patients: A position paper from the American Geriatrics Society. *Journal of the American Geriatrics Society,* 1994.

Angell, M. The right to die in dignity. *Newsweek,* July 23, 1990, 9.

Aroskar, M. Access to hospice: Ethical dimensions. *Nursing Clinics of North America,* 1985, *20,* 299–309.

Back, K. W. Metaphors as a test of personal philosophy of aging. *Sociological Focus,* 1971, *5,* 1–8.

Ball, J. F. Widows' grief: The impact of age and mode of death. *Omega,* 1977, *7,* 307–333.

Barbou, J. The dying person's Bill of Rights. *American Journal of Nursing,* 1975, 75–99.

Barrett, C. Sex differences in the experience of widowhood. Paper presented at the meetings of the American Psychological Association, 1978.

*Bartling* v. *Superior Court,* 163 Cal. App. 3d 186 (1984).

Bengtson, V., Cuellar, J., and Ragan, P. Stratum contrasts and similarities in attitudes toward death. *Journal of Gerontology,* 1977, *32,* 76–88.

Bengtson, V., Rosenthal, C., and Burton, L. Families and aging: Diversity and heterogeneity. In R. Binstock and L. George, (Eds.), *Handbook of aging and the social sciences* (3d ed.) New York: Academic Press, 1990.

Benoliel, J. Loss and terminal illness. *Nursing Clinics of North America,* 1985, *20,* 439–448.

Berardo, F. M. Survivorship and social isolation: The case of the aged widower. *Family Coordinator,* 1970, *19,* 11–25.

Binstock, R. B. Old-age-based rationing: From rhetoric to risk? *Generations,* Winter 1994, 37.

Blau, Z. S. *Aging in a changing society.* New York: Franklin Watts, 1981.

Bolton, C., and Delpha, C. J. The post-funeral ritual in bereavement counseling and grief work. *Journal of Gerontological Social Work,* 1989, *13,* 49–57.

Callahan, D. Health care in the aging society: A moral dilemma. In A. Pifer and L. Bronte, (Eds.), *Our aging society: Paradox and promise.* New York: W W Norton, 1986.

Callahan, D. *The troubled dream of life: Living with mortality.* New York: Simon and Schuster, 1993.

Carey, R. Weathering widowhood: Problems and adjustments of the widowed during the first year. *Omega*, 1979–80, *10*, 163–174.

Caserta, M. S. and Lund, D. A. Bereavement, stress and coping among older adults: Expectations versus the actual experience. *Omega*, 1992, *25*(1), 33–45.

Caserta, M. S. and Lund, D. A. Intrapersonal resources and the effectiveness of self-help groups to bereaved older adults. *The Gerontologist*, 1993, *33*(5), 619–629.

Caserta, M. S., Lund, D. A., and Dimond, M. Older widows' early bereavement adjustments. *Journal of Women & Aging*, 1989, *1*(4), 5–27.

Choice on Dying, Fact Sheets: National Advance Directive Campaign. New York: Choice on Dying, 1994.

Conrad, N. Spiritual support for the dying. *Nursing Clinics of North America*, 1985, *20*, 415–425.

Diggory, J. C., and Rothman, D. Z. Values destroyed by death. *Journal of Abnormal and Social Psychology*, 1961, *30*, 11–17.

Dimond, M., Lund, D. A., and Caserta, M. S. The role of social support in the first two years of bereavement in an elderly sample. *The Gerontologist*, 1987, *27*(5), 599–604.

Downey, A. Relationship of religiosity to death anxiety of middle-aged males. *Psychological Reports*, 1984, *54*, 811–822.

DuBois, P. *The hospice way of death*. New York: Human Sciences Press, 1980.

Egar, T. Suicide law placing Oregon on several uncharted paths. *The New York Times*, December 25, 1994, A1, A13.

Fadiman, A. The liberation of Lolly and Gronky. *Life Magazine*, 1984, 71–94.

Feifel, H., and Nagy, W. T. Another look at fear of death. *Journal of Consulting and Clinical Psychology*, 1981, *49*, 278–286.

Ferraro, K. F. Widowhood and social participation in later life: Isolation or compensation? *Research on Aging*, 1984, *6*, 451–468.

Fletcher, J. Elective death. In E. Fuller Torrey (Ed.), *Ethical issues in medicine*. Boston: Little Brown, 1968.

Fox, R. The sting of death in American society. *Social Science Review*, 1981, *49*, 42–59.

Freeman, E. Multiple losses in the elderly: An ecological approach. *Social Casework*, 1984, *65*, 287–296.

Fulton, R., and Gattesma, D. G. Anticipatory grief: A psychosocial concept reconsidered. *British Journal of Psychiatry*, 1980, *137*, 45–54.

Gallagher, D., Thompson, L., and Peterson, J. Psychosocial factors affecting adaptation to bereavement in the elderly. *International Journal of Aging and Human Development*, 1981–82, *14*, 79–95.

*The Gallup Report*. No. 235, April 1985, 29.

Germain, C. Nursing the dying: Implications of Kübler-Ross' stage theory. In R. Fox (Ed.), The social meaning of death. Special issue of *Annals of the American Academy of Political and Social Science*, 1980, *447*, 89–99.

Gianelli, D. Right-to-die debate turns to out-of-hospital DNR order. *American Medical News*, November 7, 1994, *37*(41), 3.

Gianelli, D. Suicide watch: Proposed "aid in dying" guidelines, Kevorkian acquittal fuel physician debate in Michigan. *American Medical News*, May 16, 1994, *37*(19), 1.

Glaser, B., and Strauss, A. *Time for dying*. Chicago: Aldine, 1968.

Goldberg, E. L., Comstock, G. W., and Harlow, S. D., Emotional problems and widowhood. *Journals of Gerontology*, 1988, *43*, S206–S208.

Haber, D., Tuttle, J., and Rogers, M. Attitudes about death in the nursing home: A research note. *Death Education*, 1981, *5*, 25–28.

Haug, M. Aging and the right to terminate medical treatment. *Journal of Gerontology*, 1978, *33*, 586–591.

Helsing, G., and Szklo, M. Mortality after bereavement. *American Journal of Epidemiology*, 1981, *114*, 41–52.

Henderson, M. Beyond the Living Will. *The Gerontologist*, 1990, *30*, 480–485.

Herriott, M., and Kiyak, H. A. Bereavement in old age: Implications for therapy and research. *Journal of Gerontological Social Work*, 1981, *3*, 15–43.

Hess, B., and Soldo, B. J. Husband and wife networks. In W. J. Sauer and R. T. Coward (Eds.), *Social support networks and the care of elderly: Theory, research and practice*, New York: Springer, 1985, 67–92.

Hinton, J. The influence of previous personality on reactions to having terminal cancer. *Omega*, 1975, *6*, 95–112.

Hudson, T. Court strikes down assisted suicide ban in Washington State. *Hospitals and Health Networks*, August 5, 1994, *68*(15), 180.

Jacobs, S., and Ostfeld, A. An epidemiological review of the mortality of bereavement. *Journal of Gerontology,* 1977, *28,* 359–362.

Kalish, R. Death. In G. L. Maddox (Ed.), *Encyclopedia of aging.* New York: Springer, 1981.

Kalish, R. Death and survivorship: The final transition. *Annals of the American Academy of Political and Social Sciences,* 1982, *464,* 163–173.

Kalish, R. *Death, grief, and caring relationships* (2d ed.). Monterey, Calif: Brooks Cole, 1984.

Kalish, R. The social context of death and dying. In R. Binstock and E. Shanas (Eds.), *Handbook of aging and the social sciences* (2d ed.). New York: Van Nostrand Reinhold, 1985.

Kalish, R., and Reynolds, D. *Death and ethnicity: A psychocultural study.* Los Angeles: University of Southern California Press, 1976.

Kastenbaum, R. *Death, society and human experience* (4th ed.). New York: Macmillan/Merrill, 1991.

Kastenbaum, R. Death, suicide and the older adult. *Suicide and Life-Threatening Behavior,* 1992, *22*(1), 1–14.

Kastenbaum, R. Dying and death: A life-span approach. In J. Birren and K. W. Schaie (Eds.), *Handbook of the psychology of aging.* New York: Van Nostrand Reinhold, 1985.

Kastenbaum, R., and Aisenberg, R. *The psychology of death: Concise edition.* New York: Springer, 1976.

KCR Communications Research. Survey conducted for the *Boston Globe* and the Harvard School of Public Health by Richard Knox, October 18–20, 1991.

Keith, P. Life changes and perceptions of life and death among older men and women. *Journal of Gerontology,* 1979, *34,* 870–878.

Keith, P. Perceptions of time remaining and distance from death. *Omega,* 1982, *12,* 307–318.

Keller, J. W., Sherry, D., and Piotrowski, C. Perspectives on death: A developmental study. *Journal of Psychology,* 116, 1984, 137–142.

Koff, T. H. *Hospice: A caring community.* Cambridge, Mass.: Winthrop Publishers, 1981.

Kübler-Ross, E. *On death and dying.* New York: Macmillan, 1969.

Kübler-Ross, E. (Ed.). *Death: The final stage of growth.* Englewood Cliffs, N.J.: Prentice-Hall, 1975.

Kübler-Ross, E. *Living with dying.* New York: Macmillan, 1981.

Lerner, M. When, why, and where people die. In O. Brimm et al. (Eds.), *The dying patient.* New York: Russell Sage, 1970.

Lesnoff-Caravaglia, G. *Values, ethics and aging.* New York: Human Sciences Press, 1985.

Levy, J. A. A life course perspective on hospice and the family. *Marriage and Family Review,* 1987, *11,* 39–64.

Levy, J. A., and Gordon, A. Stress and burnout in the social world of hospice. *Hospice Journal,* 1987, *3,* 29–51.

Lindemann, E. *Beyond grief: Studies in crisis intervention.* New York: Jason Aronson, 1979.

Lopata, H. Z. *Widowhood in an American city.* Cambridge, Mass.: Schenkman, 1973.

Lopata, H. Z. Widowhood: Societal factors in life-span disruptions and alternatives. In N. Datan and L. Ginsberg (Eds.), *Life-span developmental psychology: Normative life crises.* New York: Academic Press, 1975.

Lopata, H. Z. *Widows.* Durham, N.C.: Duke University Press, 1987.

Lopata, H. Z. *Women and widows.* New York: Elsevier, 1979.

Lubitz, J., and Prihoda, R. The use and costs of Medicare services in the last two years of life. *Health Care Review,* 1984, *5,* 329–334.

Lund, D. A. Conclusions about bereavement in later life and implications for interventions and future research. In D. Lund (Ed.), *Older bereaved spouses: Research with practical applications.* New York: Hemisphere, 1989, 221–232.

Lund, D. A. Widowhood: The coping response. In R. Kastenbaum (Ed.), *Encyclopedia of adult development.* Phoenix, AZ: Onyx Press, 1993, 537–541.

Lund, D. A., Caserta, M., and Dimond, M. The course of spousal bereavement in later life. In M. Stroebe, W. Stroebe, and R. Hanson (Eds.), *Handbook of bereavement.* Cambridge University Press, 1993, 240–254.

Lund, D. A., Caserta, M. S., and Dimond, M. F. Gender differences through two years of bereavement among the elderly. *The Gerontologist,* 1986, *26,* 314–320.

Maddison, D., and Viola, A. The health of widows in the year following bereavement. *Journal of Psychosomatic Research,* 1968, *12,* 297–306.

Malcolm, A. Plaintiff in death, but suit goes on. *The New York Times,* November 8, 1984.

Maris, R. *Pathways to suicide*. Baltimore, Md.: Johns Hopkins, 1981.

Marshall, V. *Last chapters: A sociology of aging and dying*. Monterey, Calif.: Brooks Cole, 1980.

Marshall, V. A sociological perspective on aging and dying. In V. Marshall, (Ed.), *Later life: The social psychology of aging*, Beverly Hills, Calif.: Sage, 1986, 125–146.

Marshall, V., and Levy, J. Aging and dying. In R. Binstock and L. George (Eds.), *Handbook of aging and the social sciences* (3d ed.). New York: Academic Press, 1990.

Martin-Matthews, A. Widowhood as an expectable life event. In V. Marshall (Ed.), *Aging in Canada: Social perspectives* (2d ed.). Markham, Ont.: Fitzhenry and Whiteside, 1988.

Martocchio, B. Grief and bereavement. *Nursing Clinics of North America*, 1985, *20*, 327–346.

McCall, N. Utilization and costs of Medicare services by beneficiaries in their last year of life. *Medical Care*, 1984, *22*, 329–342.

McCann, B., and Enck, R. Standards for hospice care: A JCAH hospice project overview. *Progress in Clinical and Biological Research*, 1984, *156*, 431–449.

McCormick, B. Continued opposition: House refuses to open door on physician-assisted suicide. *American Medical News*, December 20, 1993, *36*(47), 7.

McCrae, R. R., and Costa, P. T. Psychological resilience among widowed men and women: A 10-year follow-up of a national sample. *Journal of Social Issues*, 1988, *44*(3), 129–142.

Morgan, C. Continuity and change in the labor force activities of recently widowed women. *The Gerontologist*, 1984, *24*, 530–535.

Morgan, D. Adjusting to widowhood: Do social networks make it easier? *The Gerontologist*, 1989, *29*, 101–107.

Moseley, J. Alterations in comfort. *Nursing Clinics of North America*, 1985, *20*, 427–437.

Mutran, E., and Reitzes, D. C. Intergenerational support activities and well-being among the elderly: A convergence of exchange and symbolic interaction perspectives. *American Sociological Review*, 1984, *49*, 117–130.

*New York Times*, Doctors polled on life support. Sunday, June 5, 1988.

Norris, F. H., and Murrell, S. A. Older adult family stress and adaptation before and after bereavement. *Journal of Gerontology*, 1987, *42*, 606–612.

O'Bryant, S., and Morgan, C. Recent widows' kin support and orientations to self-sufficiency. *The Gerontologist*, 1991, *30*, 391–398.

Older Women's League. *Death and dying: Staying in control to the end of our lives*. Washington, D.C.: Older Women's League, 1986.

Ostheimer, J., and Ritt, L. Life and death: Current public attitudes. In N. Ostheimer and J. Ostheimer (Eds.), *Life or death—Who controls?* New York: Springer, 1976.

Owen, G., Fulton, R., and Markuson, E. Death at a distance: A study of family survivors. *Omega*, 1982–83, *13*, 191–225.

Parkes, C. M. Effects of bereavement on physical and mental health: A study of the medical records of widows. *British Medical Journal*, 1964, *2*, 274–279.

Parkes, C. M. 'Seeking' and 'finding' a lost object. *Social Science and Medicine*, 1970a, *4*, 187–201.

Parkes, C. M. The first year of bereavement. *Psychiatry*, 1970b, *33*, 444–467.

Parkes, C. M. Terminal care: Evaluation of an advisory domiciliary service at St. Christopher's House. *Postgraduate Medical Journal*, 1980, *56*, 685–689.

Parkes, C. M,, and Brown, R. J. Health after bereavement: A controlled study of young Boston widows and widowers. *Psychosomatic Medicine*, 1972, *34*, 449–461.

Parkes, C. M., Murray, B. B., and Fitzgerald, R. G. Broken heart: A statistical study of increased mortality among widows. *British Medical Journal*, 1969, *1*, 740–743.

Quill, T. Death and dignity: A case of individualized decision-making. *New England Journal of Medicine*, 1991, *324*(10), 691–694.

Rando, T. A. A comprehensive analysis of anticipatory grief: Perspectives, processes, promises and problems. In T. A. Rando (Ed.), *Loss and anticipatory grief*. Lexington, Mass.: D. C. Heath, 1986.

Roberto, K. A., and Scott, J. P. Confronting widowhood. *American Behavioral Scientist*, 1986, *29*, 497–511.

Robertson, J. *The rights of the critically ill*. Cambridge, Mass.: Ballinger, 1983.

Rowland, K. F. Environmental events predicting death for elderly. *Psychological Bulletin*, 1977, *84*, 349–372.

Sachs, G. A. Improving care of the dying. *Generations,* Winter 1994, 3.

Saunders, J. A process of bereavement resolution: Uncoupled identity. *Western Journal of Nursing Research,* 1981, *3,* 319–332.

Schulz, R. *The psychology of death, dying, and bereavement.* Reading, Mass.: Addison-Wesley, 1978.

Schwab, J. J., Chalmers, J. M., Conroy, S. J., Farris, P. B., and Markush, R. E. Studies in grief: A preliminary report. In B. Shoenberg, I. Gerber, A. Wiener, A. H. Kutscher, D. Peretz, and A. Carr (Eds.), *Psychosocial aspects of bereavement.* New York: Columbia University Press, 1975.

*Seattle Times,* "Death with dignity" bill approved by Senate, March 6, 1992, 1–B2.

Shanas, E., Townsend, P., Wedderburn, D., Friis, H., Milhoj, P., and Stehouwer, J. *Older people in three industrial societies.* New York: Atherton Press, 1968.

Silverman, P. *Helping each other in widowhood.* New York: Health Sciences Publishing, 1974.

Silverman, P. *Mutual help groups: Organization and development.* Beverly Hills, Calif : Sage, 1980.

Simonton, O. C., Matthews-Simonton, S., and Creighton, J. *Getting well again.* Los Angeles: Tercher, 1978.

Smeeding, T. Economic status of the elderly. In R. Binstock and L. George (Eds.), *Handbook of aging and the social sciences,* New York: Academic Press, 1990.

Sommers, T. On matters of life and death. *Gray Panther Network.* Summer 1985, 12.

Stephenson, J. S. *Death, grief and mourning: Individual and social realities.* New York: Free Press, 1985.

Stillion, J. *Death and the sexes.* Washington, D.C.: Hemisphere Publishing, 1985.

Strain, L. A., and Chappell, N. L. Confidants: Do they make a difference in quality of life? *Research on Aging, 1982,* 479–502.

Thompson, L., Breckenridge, J., Gallagher, D., and Peterson, J. "Effects of bereavement on self-perceptions of physical health in elderly widows and widowers. *Journal of Gerontology,* 1984, *39,* 309–314.

Thorson, J. A., and Powell, F. C. Elements of death anxiety and meanings of death. *Journal of Clinical Psychology,* 1988, *44,* 691–701.

U.S. Bureau of the Census. Marital status and living arrangements: March 1990. *Current Population Reports,* Series P-20, No. 450, Washington, D.C.: Government Printing Office, 1991.

U.S. Senate Special Committee on Aging. *Aging America: Trends and projections, 1987–1988.* Washington, D.C.: U.S. Department of Health and Human Services, 1988.

Wagner, K., and Lorion, R. Correlates of death anxiety in elderly persons. *Journal of Clinical Psychology,* 1984, *40,* 1235–1241.

Wanzer, S., Adelstein, J., Cranford, R., Federman, D., Hook, E., Moertel, C., Sofar, P., Stone, A., Taussig, H., and Vey Eys, J. The physician's responsibility toward hopelessly ill patients. *New England Journal of Medicine,* 1984, *310,* 955–959.

Ward, R. *The aging experience: An introduction to social gerontology.* New York: Harper and Row, 1984.

Wass, H., Christian, M., Myers, J., and Murphy, M., Jr. Similarities and dissimilarities in attitudes toward death in a population of older persons. *Omega,* 1979, *9,* 337–354.

Watson, W. H., and Maxwell, R. J. *Human aging and dying.* New York: St. Martin's Press, 1977.

Weisman, A. D. On dying and denying. New York: Behavioral Publications, 1972.

Weisman, A. D., and Kastenbaum, R. The psychological autopsy: A study of the terminal phase of life. *Community Mental Health Journal Monograph No. 4.* New York: Behavioral Publications, 1968.

Weisman, A. D., and Warden, J. W. Psychosocial analysis of cancer deaths. *Omega,* 1975, *6,* 61–75.

Wister, A. V., and Strain, L. Social support and well being: A comparison of older widows and widowers. *Canadian Journal on Aging,* 1986, *5,* 205–220.

Wrofsky, M. I. Letting go: Death, dying and the law. New York: Charles Scribner's Sons. 1993.

# CHAPTER 17

# POPULATIONS AT RISK: OLDER ETHNIC MINORITIES

**W**hen discussing the physiological, psychological, and social changes experienced by older people, there is a tendency to speak about them as if they were a homogeneous group. Yet, as illustrated throughout this book, the older population is more heterogeneous than any other. Two primary variables in this differentiation are *gender* and *ethnic minority status*. To be old and a member of an ethnic minority group, or to be an older woman, is to experience environments substantially different from those of a white male across the life span. It also means a higher risk of being unhealthy, poor, alone, and inadequately housed.

In fact, living alone places both women and ethnic minorities at greater risk of economic insecurity, poorer health status, and social isolation. As examples of the interaction of gender, ethnicity, living arrangements, and socioeconomic status, the poverty rate for women who live alone is five times greater than that for their peers who live with a partner. The income of African Americans and Hispanics who live alone is about 33 percent lower than that of older whites living alone. And older minority women who live alone form the poorest group in our society (Quinn and Smeeding, 1994).

Whereas relevant differences among older people arising from their gender and their ethnic minority status have been noted throughout this text, the next two chapters focus specifically on these factors because of their interactive effects with age and the resulting higher incidence of social problems. This chapter examines demographic changes and variations in socioeconomic status, health, and living arrangements among older ethnic minorities. The next chapter discusses similar variables among older women. In this sense, both older women and ethnic minorities are affected by changes in the environment that are not always congruent with their needs as they age. Each chapter begins by examining the relatively limited research on these groups, as compared with that on older white males, and concludes with a brief discussion of implications for the development of public policies and services for older ethnic minorities and women.

# DEFINING ETHNICITY

Ethnicity as discussed here involves three components: culture and an internalized common heritage which are not fully understood or shared by outsiders; social status; and support systems (Barresi and Stull, 1993). These components influence the way people feel about themselves and how they interact with their environments, resulting in particular patterns of adjustment to the experience of aging. Thus, ethnicity may produce differing responses to aging, even among older Americans who share common experiences with poverty and discrimination. By identifying the culturally conditioned beliefs and values in an older person's heritage, we can gain a better understanding of that person's attitudes and behaviors in the face of their own aging. For example, many Japanese-American elders emigrated from small farming villages where ancestor worship was practiced, reflecting the respect traditionally accorded older people. They have grown old in a country where youth is more highly valued than age, and thus may experience conflicts between the views they hold and those of their children.

Ethnicity can serve as an integrating force in passing through significant life changes; a buffer to the vicissitudes and stress of old age, especially when the environment encourages the expression of ethnicity; and a filter to the aging process, influencing beliefs, behaviors, and interactions with professionals. Given these various functions, it is important that social and health care providers understand ethnicity and how it influences health behaviors and beliefs, for example (Hopper, 1993; Krause, 1987; Markides, Liang, and Jackson, 1990).

Ethnicity may or may not encompass minority status, since there are older people in the United States who belong to white ethnic groups that are not necessarily social and cultural "minorities," as defined by the U.S. Congress as federally protected groups. Gutmann's (1979) work on immigrants from eastern, central, and southern Europe demonstrates that white ethnics may preserve the traditional practices of their culture, religion, or nationality and remain homogeneous and segregated within their own ethnic communities, but not necessarily experience prejudice, discrimination, or oppression.

## Who Are Ethnic Minority Older People?

For purposes of this chapter, ethnic minority elders include older people belonging to groups whose language and/or physical and cultural characteristics make them visible and identifiable, who have experienced differential and unequal treatment, who experience a common bond between group members, and who regard themselves as objects of collective discrimination and oppression by reason of their social class or race (Markides, Liang, and Jackson, 1990). Specifically, we examine the life conditions and adaptation to aging among people of color who are defined by the federal government as protected groups—African Americans, Hispanic Americans (including Mexican Americans/Chicanos, Puerto Ricans, Cubans, and Latin Americans), American Indians, and Pacific Asians (including Japanese, Chinese, Filipino, Korean, Guamanian, Samoan, other Pacific Islanders, and the newer immigrants from Southeast Asia). Their aging process and quality of life are inevitably affected by the experiences of a lifetime of racial discrimination. These populations of color are distinct from most European origin ethnic groups in the United States (Irish, Germans, Italians, etc.) which at some point have been sociological minorities, but today are generally considered part of the dominant group (Markides, Liang, and Jackson, 1990).

Although there are some recurring themes in analyses of ethnicity and older people, such as family structure and behavior, values about independence, and the evaluation of persons in terms of their material "productivity," variations within as well as among these groups must be kept in mind. Differences in immigration patterns, birthrates, region, social class, rural or urban location, gender, and acculturation level add to the intragroup variations. Hispanics, for example, who are defined by the U.S. Bureau of the Census as Spanish-speaking persons in the United States, incorporate groups from many different cultures, and include a high percentage of immigrants to the United States, particularly from Mexico. American Indian refers to the indigenous peoples of North America, including Indians, Eskimos, and Aleuts and over 500 recognized tribes, bands, or Alaskan Native villages; in recent years, the term *American Indian* has been used rather than *Native American*, which under certain federal legislation includes native Hawaiians, Samoans, and other Pacific Islanders (Kramer, 1992). African Americans differ from one another in terms of cultural background, socioeconomic status, and geographic location. Recent immigrants from Laos, Cambodia, and Vietnam have a higher proportion of older persons than do other Pacific Asian groups.

In summary, while our focus is on people of color who have experienced economic and racial discrimination, we also consider how ethnicity or cultural homogeneity influences the aging process. Hence, we use the term *ethnic minority older people* throughout this book. As referred to earlier, characteristics of *ethnic minorities* relevant to aging (Barresi and Stull, 1993; Cool, 1987) include the following:

- Each group has a special history.
- The special history has been accompanied by discrimination, resulting in fewer power resources.
- Sets of individuals interact and feel bonds of attachment to each other based on shared traits, such as religion, race, and nationality.
- Coping structures have developed.

Based on its unique history, each ethnic minority population developed its own methods of coping with the inevitable conflicts between traditional and adopted ways of life, leading to both vulnerabilities and strengths, including a source of self-esteem in the ways they adjust to aging.

Two distinct issues should be kept in mind in this discussion of ethnic minority elders: the unique historical calendar of life events and culture and their impact on lifestyles, many of which are positive, and the consequences of racism, ageism, discrimination, and prolonged poverty, most of which are negative.

As noted in Chapter 1, ethnic minorities form only 11 percent of the older U.S. population. But by the year 2020, it is projected that 22 percent of the older population will be nonwhite. Within each ethnic minority group, older people form a smaller percentage of the total ethnic minority population, as compared to the percentage of people age 65 and over within the white population, as illustrated in Table 17-1. The different age distributions of these groups reflect variations in their fertility, mortality, and immigration rates. A general trend is the growing presence of females in each of these populations, with older men more likely than older women to be married and less likely to be widowed or divorced—a pattern similar to that found among the older white population (U.S. Senate Special Committee on Aging, 1992).

Although small in size, ethnic minority populations are of increasing concern to gerontologists because of the disproportionately greater number of social problems they face, relative to whites. In addition, they are expected to increase at a proportionately higher rate than whites, as discussed in Chapter 1. For example, it has been predicted that the immigrant groups of the twentieth century—Hispanics, Asians, and Pacific Islanders—will redefine American culture in the twenty-first century (Torres-Gil, 1986). While immigrants are generally younger persons, many have brought or sent for their older parents and relatives, especially from countries experiencing political oppression (Barresi and Stull, 1993). An aging society will need to grapple with the cultural homogeneity of an older minority population and the cultural diversity of its younger minority populations, who will not form a significant portion of the older population until after the year 2015.

**TABLE 17–1    Distribution of the Older Population**

|  | % OF TOTAL POPULATION, 65+ | % OF THE ETHNIC MINORITY POPULATION, 65+ | MEDIAN AGE |
|---|---|---|---|
| Whites | 89.8 |  | 34.4 |
| African Americans | 8.0 | 7.9 | 28.4 |
| Asian Americans | 1.5 | 5.9 | 28.7 |
| American Indians | 0.4 | 5.2 | 23 |
| Hispanic Americans | 4.0* | 4.9 | 26.1 |

SOURCE: U.S. Bureau of the Census, 1993 Selected Population Tables.

*The sum of the specific percentages reported here will never round off to approximately 100 percent if a Hispanic percentage is included. The reason for this anomaly is that the U.S. Bureau of the Census does not treat the Hispanic category (which includes Mexicans, Venezuelans, and Latinos who self–designate themselves as being white) as one that is mutually exclusive from the racial categories. Thus, the Hispanic data are also included within each of the racial categories. Persons of Hispanic origin may be of any race, and represent 3 percent of the older population.

## Research History

*Ethnogerontology* is the newest and perhaps most underdeveloped field of social gerontology. It is the study of the causes, processes, and consequences of race, national origin, and culture on individual and population aging. A predominant concern has been the documentation of social inequities between dominant and minority aged (Jackson, 1985).

From 1940 to 1970, when both scholarly and political concern with older adults grew, little was written about the special circumstances of ethnic minority elders. In 1956, Tally and Kaplan first raised the question: Are the African American aged doubly jeopardized relative to their white counterparts? That is, do lifetime factors of economic and racial discrimination make adjusting to old age more difficult for African Americans (and other minorities) than for whites? As a result of such double jeopardy, do ethnic minorities experience lower life satisfaction (Cuellar and Weeks, 1980)? The *double jeopardy* hypothesis also raises the policy question of whether ethnic minority status alone constitutes a sufficient basis for targeting special services and policies.

A second but related position asserts that patterns of racial stratification and inequalities

have changed recently, and that African Americans' opportunities throughout their lives are related to their economic class position rather than to their minority group status. Social class rather than minority membership jeopardizes them. The multiple hierarchy stratification perspective encompasses both views, defining ethnic minority status as another source of inequality along with class, gender, and age itself (Bengtson, 1979). More recent studies have found that while ethnic minorities may experience increasing income and health disadvantages with age, they nevertheless display considerable strengths and experience higher levels of psychological well-being and emotional support from families, friends and neighbors than mainstream groups (Lubben and Becerra, 1987; Markides et al., 1990). Debates about double jeopardy, whether it exists and is related to socioeconomic status or to race per se, have been central in research and policy discussions in ethnogerontology. Ethnogerontologists now argue that double jeopardy should not be a central concept, because cross-sectional studies have rarely produced useful information about age changes as opposed to age differences (Gibson, 1989; Markides, Liang, and Jackson, 1990). They suggest that double jeopardy may be time-bound, resulting largely from major social and

Older women are often a source of strength in the African American community.

political changes in the status of minorities, not from racial differences. Determining the effects of ethnic minority group status on age changes in the later years thus requires more longitudinal studies.

A counterargument to the double jeopardy hypothesis is that age is a leveler of differences in life expectancy. This crossover effect, described in Chapter 1, refers to the fact that the life expectancies for African Americans, Pacific Asians, and American Indians after age 75 are actually greater than for whites, due to a combination of biological vigor, psychological strength, and resources for coping with stress, such as religious practices that link individuals to the community. Similarly, although their rate of chronic illness is higher, the death rate for African Americans age 85 and over is lower than for whites (Cool, 1987; Gibson, 1986; Markides, Liang, and Jackson, 1990). It has been suggested that the apparent racial crossover is due to enumerative errors, not

to health differences (Manton, 1982). Although the relative status and mortality risks of whites and nonwhites are still debated, the apparent racial crossover effect raises questions about the usefulness of chronological age as a measure of aging. What is conclusive is that tremendous variation occurs both across and within ethnic minority categories (Jackson, 1985).

The year 1971 marked a turning point in the recognition of the ethnic minority elders as a special area of study within gerontology. In that year, the National Caucus on the Black Aged was formed (later becoming the National Center and Caucus on the Black Aged), and a session on "Aging and the Aged Black" was held at the White House Conference on Aging. This conference was especially important from a policy perspective, because reports showed that twice as many of the ethnic minority older people live below the poverty level relative to whites. Therefore, the session highlighted the need for income and health care supports. Since 1971, the National Association for Spanish-speaking Elderly, the National Indian Council on Aging, and the National Pacific/Asian Resource Center on Aging have been established. The National Center and Caucus on the Black Aged is the most influential of these associations, which function as advocacy groups, and as research and academic centers.

The census has been the primary source of information for these organizations involved in planning services for ethnic minority elders. Census data, however, are criticized for undercounting minority subgroups, misclassifying individuals, or merging data about various nonwhite groups (Jackson, 1985). For example, the census data have often grouped people by race as "white," "black" or "other." In addition, research on minorities generally does not provide a breakdown of data by sex and studies on older women do not cross-classify data by minority status. In such instances, how racism and sexism interact to produce "gender-specific race effects" and race-specific gender effects" is not recognized (Gould, 1989).

Despite the recent growth and variety of research on ethnic minority older people, there are few definitive conclusions about this segment of society. It is a segment made up of many subgroups exhibiting a diversity of cultural patterns. Consequently, few generalizations can be made that are valid for this population as a whole. We turn next to a brief review of the life conditions of each of the four major ethnic minority groups. As we do so, keep in mind the low socioeconomic status and increased poverty among older minority populations, as shown in Figure 17–1.

## OLDER AFRICAN AMERICANS

Although African Americans form only about 8 percent of the total population aged 65 and over, they represent 36 percent of the low-income older population. In 1990, 33 percent of African American families headed by persons age 65 and over lived below the poverty line, more than three times the proportion of older white families. The incidence of poverty increases dramatically among households composed of unrelated African American individuals, especially females age 65 and over. The median income of African American males over 65 is approximately 60 percent of white men; that of African American women about 66 percent that of white women, with the proportion of older African American female-headed families in poverty increasing in the past decade (U.S. Senate Special Committee on Aging, 1992). Differences in education do not explain this gap in income between white and African American older people, which has not changed substantially in ten years. For example, poverty is almost as high among African American women who attended high school as among those with less than six years of schooling (Jackson, 1985). In fact, the short-term trend is toward a growing gap, as public income supports such as Supplemental Security Income are reduced.

As noted in Chapter 14, the primary reason for the lower socioeconomic status of older African Americans is their pattern of limited

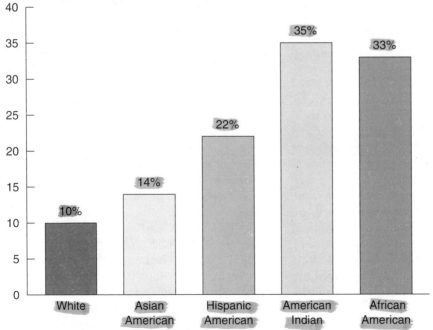

**FIGURE 17–1  Percentage of Older Americans with Incomes below Poverty**

employment opportunities and periods of unemployment throughout their lives as well as their concentration in low-paying, sporadic service jobs with few benefits, that were not covered by Social Security prior to the 1950s. Not only do African Americans accumulate less work experience, but they also are more likely to leave the work force earlier, frequently because of health problems. Out of economic necessity, however, they often return to work after retirement, creating the phenomenon of the "unretired/retired" (Gibson, 1989; Harper and Alexander, 1990). This pattern reduces not only their lifetime earnings, but also their Social Security and pension benefits. As a result, they are more likely to receive only the minimum Social Security benefits and less likely to receive pension income than are whites. Accordingly, more African Americans than white older persons rely on Supplemental Security Income (SSI). Some advocates have argued that African Americans should be eligible for Social Security earlier than whites because of their lifetime experiences with racism and their resultant lower life expectancy (Jackson, 1977).

The prevalence of chronic diseases has been estimated to be twice as high among African Americans as among whites, and the former more often perceive themselves as being in poor health than do their white counterparts (Barresi and Stull, 1993; Harper and Alexander, 1990). Older African Americans, for example, experience hypertension more frequently than do their white peers. As a result, deaths due to stroke are more common in older blacks, as are nonfatal strokes that often disrupt the older person's activities of daily living. Obesity is also a frequent health problem among African American women, which often leads to complications of hypertension and diabetes (Waller, 1989). Kidney failure, which may result from hypertension and diabetes, is more common in older African Americans, with the rate of diabetes mellitus among black women almost twice that among white women. They also experience more days of functional disability, (i.e., substantially reduced daily activities) and bed disability (i.e., being

confined to bed for at least half of the day) and at earlier ages than whites (Belgrave, Wykle, and Choi, 1993). Proportionately more African American older people are completely incapacitated and unable to carry on any major activity (e.g., paid employment, keeping house), although still residing in community-based households. They also appear to have less access to health care than their white counterparts, although they are more likely than whites to use hospital emergency rooms as a way to enter the health care system. An important predictor of health service utilization is the availability of health insurance. While 94 percent of older whites have Medicare and 73 percent have private insurance, the corresponding proportion of blacks is 87 percent and 42 percent respectively (Harper and Alexander, 1990). These factors combine to result in African American Medicare patients receiving worse care at hospitals than other acutely ill Medicare patients (Kahn, Pearson, and Harrison, 1994). At the same time, they are more likely to use self-care health practices, such as home remedies, lay consultations, and folk medicine that diverge from mainstream Western scientific medical concepts (Davis and McGadney, 1993; Hopper, 1993).

Black-white differences in mortality rates are notable for the three leading causes of death. Thus, while heart disease, cancer, and cerebrovascular accidents (strokes) are the leading causes of death for both races at age 65 and older, rates for African Americans are 5 percent, 17 percent, and 24 percent higher respectively for each of these conditions in 1988 (NCHS, 1992). However, due to the crossover phenomenon, the higher likelihood of death for blacks from these conditions occurs only until about age 85, when both black men and women begin to have a *lower* incidence of death (Gibson, 1994). African Americans have higher death rates for cancers of the lungs, prostate, and cervix than do other ethnic groups. Similarly, their five-year survival rate for cancer of the cervix, uterus, and esophagus is lower than for any other segment of the population. They have many of the risk factors for cancer, including inadequate access to and discontinuity of health care (especially preventive care), higher occupational and residential exposure to cancer-causing substances, higher rates of obesity (e.g., 60 percent of black women over age 45 are obese), higher prevalence of smoking, and less knowledge about cancer and its prevention (Baquet, 1988).

The socioeconomic disadvantages experienced by African Americans explain much of the variance in their utilization of health services, their health status, and mortality. As noted earlier, deaths in late life due to lifestyle and environmental hazards, including accidents and homicides among men, are much higher in blacks than in whites, except for those age 80 and over.

Despite their poor economic and health conditions, many older African Americans appear to have a greater sense of satisfaction in their lives than do their white counterparts, who have better living conditions. This difference has been explained in terms of the spiritual orientation of many African American people and the support of their extended families and of the church. Religion is important in the lives of many black elders for adaptation and support, and is related to feelings of well-being, self-esteem, and personal control. The church also provides a support network of spiritual help, companionship, advice, encouragement, and financial aid. Older African Americans tend to draw from a more varied pool of friends, fellow church members, and other associational contacts, and are more likely to use them interchangeably than are their white counterparts (Chatters and Taylor, 1989; George, 1988; Krause and Tran, 1989; Taylor, 1988; Taylor and Chatters, 1991; Wood and Parham, 1990; Wood and Wan, 1993). Studies that have found lower life satisfaction among blacks as compared to whites explain this as a result of the disparity between past aspirations and present economic circumstances (Krause, 1993).

The extent to which older African Americans are at the center of an extended family network has been the focus of considerable research (George, 1988; Hatch, 1991; Taylor, Chatters, and Mays, 1988). The proportion of African Americans who are married is lower than that of the white population, because of lower life expectancy for black men in particular. Almost 50 percent of African American women live alone, a higher proportion than that of their white counterparts or their black male peers. Similarly, rates of remarriage are lower than in other groups. One reason for these differences is that widowhood, separation, or divorce are more prevalent among older African Americans and are more likely to have occurred at an earlier age (Brown, 1990). In a national probability sample of African American elders, more than 42 percent in each of the three older cohorts reported that there were no members of their immediate family within their state, but 78 percent received considerable help from church members (Gibson and Jackson, 1987). In some instances, African American women active in church are more likely to turn to non-relatives in times of need than to their children, but these nonrelatives may be considered part of an extended family network (Hatch, 1991).

Although most older African Americans do not live in extended families, approximately 20 percent of them, compared to 12 percent of their white counterparts, live with some family member other than their spouse. Comparative studies depict older African Americans as having larger, more extended families than do whites, a higher frequency of family-based households, and higher levels of social support from their extended families, including friends, neighbors, and co-workers (George, 1988; Taylor, Chatters, and Mays, 1988). Accordingly, older African American women are more likely than white women to have family living with them in their homes. Most often, these are three-generation households, with older women providing financial assistance and care for grandchildren as well as children of other family members and friends. As noted in Chapter 12, an increasing number of African American women have primary responsibility for the care of grandchildren because of their adult children's substance abuse and financial problems (Minkler and Roe, 1993).

Although African Americans are more likely to receive help from children and grandchildren, and to take children into their homes, giving such intergenerational assistance is a function not just of race, but of age, marital and socioeconomic status, and health. Some researchers have pointed to such multigenerational households as an adaptation to poverty rather than as an indicator of a close, loving extended family (Multran, 1985). Rather than be viewed as a weakness associated with low income and joblessness, however, intergenerational households that develop out of financial necessity illustrate the resourcefulness of black families whose domestic networks expand and contract according to economic resources (Johnson and Barer, 1990). Even though socioeconomic factors are important in helping to explain race differences in intergenerational exchanges, there is strong adherence to norms of filial support and attitudes of respect toward elders among African Americans across social classes (Barresi and Stull, 1993).

Similar to whites, adult children remain a primary source of assistance and support of older African Americans (Harper and Alexander, 1990). For childless older adults, siblings are the most important kin tie. The creation of "fictive kin," including foster parents or children who function in the absence of blood relatives or when family relationships are unsatisfactory, is another source of loving support (George, 1988). In sum, African American elders appear to have a broader range—not just a larger number—of informal instrumental and emotional supports than is characteristic of Caucasian older people (Wood and Parham, 1990). Norms of reciprocity are strong and have evolved from a cooperative lifestyle that served as a survival mechanism in earlier times and that continues to be a source of support (Wood and Wan, 1993).

Studies of psychological and general well-being among African American elders have illustrated the benefits of social integration. Despite significant economic hardships, the majority of older blacks report high life satisfaction and happiness. The fact that this is most likely for those age 75 and over may reflect the decreasing demands of family and employment responsibilities in this oldest group, and the associated perception of no significant stressors affecting them. At the same time, however, older African Americans are more likely to report high levels of life satisfaction and happiness if they perceive their physical health to be good, which is consistent with other evidence of the link between physical and psychological health generally among the older population (Jackson, Chatters, and Neighbors, 1982). Thus, it appears that black elders who survive to age 75 *and* are in good health *and* are relieved of the burdens of family caregiving are most likely to experience life satisfaction. Indeed, older blacks seem to be more affected by stressors influencing members of their social networks, particularly children and grandchildren, than are older whites, who are more affected by personal financial strain (Krause, 1987).

Of all older people, African Americans are the least likely to enter a nursing home, with institutional care considered the last resort (Belgrave, Wykle, and Choi, 1993; Wood and Wan, 1993). As a result, only 3 percent of all African Americans age 65 and older and only 12 percent of those over age 85 are institutionalized, compared to 5 percent and 23 percent of their white counterparts respectively. African American nursing home residents have been found to be more limited than whites in their ability to carry out activities of daily living, and less often receiving the appropriate level of care (Belgrave, et al., 1993). Once admitted to a nursing home, older African Americans are less likely to be discharged, in large part because informal resources have been exhausted (Greene and Ondrich, 1990). Low rates of nursing home placement may reflect the lack of nursing homes in African American communities, inadequate income to pay for private nursing home care, the greater probability that an African American elder, dependent upon Medicaid, has fewer institutional options, and that some elders may turn to traditional folk medicine (Brown, 1990; Wood and Wan, 1993). Or they may be due to current or historical racist practices and procedures among medical providers and nursing home staff.

## OLDER HISPANIC AMERICANS

As noted in Chapter 1, Hispanic Americans are the largest ethnic minority population following African Americans, and since the term Hispanic represents Cubans, Mexicans, Puerto Ricans, and Latin Americans, they also are a highly diverse population, including native born, legal, and undocumented immigrants with varying lengths of residence in the United States. The greatest proportion (60 percent) are Mexican Americans or Chicanos, followed by Cuban Americans (14.5 percent) and Puerto Ricans (10.8 percent) followed by others (Lacayo, 1993). With a growing number of recent immigrants from El Salvador, Nicaragua, and Guatemala, each group within the Hispanic population has a unique cultural heritage, history, and dialect. The needs of Hispanic elders may be underestimated since many studies have not considered Hispanics as a separate group, but included them in both black and white ethnic categories. In addition, studies that include a Hispanic ethnic classification often fail to differentiate among the diverse Hispanic subgroups (Lacayo, 1993). Hispanics also age "faster" than whites, with 66 percent of a sample of older Mexican Americans viewing themselves as old beginning at or below 60 years of age (Espino, 1993). Such earlier functional aging can be attributed to harder working conditions, poor nutrition, and inadequate health care (Lacayo, 1993).

In terms of life expectancy, Hispanics appear to be in an intermediate position between Anglos and African Americans, which may be partially explained by poor economic and health status among the two largest subgroups of Hispanics—Mexican Americans and Puerto Ricans. Because Cuban American elders are generally more educated and have higher incomes than Mexican

Americans and Puerto Rican elders and because most research has focused on the latter two groups, the remainder of this discussion addresses Puerto Rican and Mexican American needs in particular.

Sociocultural factors underlie the poor economic and health status of Hispanics. More than any other group, they have retained their native language, partially because of geographic proximity to their home countries, combined with the availability of mass communication. In fact, it has been estimated that 40 percent of older Hispanics speak only Spanish. Although serving to preserve their cultural identity, their inability to speak English has been a major barrier to their education, employment, and utilization of social and health services (Cuellar, 1990; Lacayo, 1993). Another barrier has been encountered by those who entered the country illegally and thus have been unable to apply for Social Security, Medicare, or Medicaid. This legal barrier to eligibility, however, has recently been altered by changes in immigration laws for those who entered prior to 1982. On the other hand, the peak arrival of Latin Americans took place in the 1980s; immigrants arrived at a time when the United States was undergoing major economic and political changes and was less tolerant toward noncitizens. All these factors may partly explain why such large numbers of Mexican American and Puerto Rican elders have minimal education and work in unskilled, low-paying jobs with few benefits, particularly retirement pension benefits and income from annuities, or are unemployed. Three out of every five retirement dollars are Social Security or Supplemental Security Income for Hispanic elders, compared to two out of every five dollars for older whites (Miranda, 1990). Yet 19 percent receive neither Social Security nor pension income, and 8 percent have no public or private medical insurance (Lacayo, 1993). Mexican Americans and Puerto Ricans are also the most educationally deprived group in our society, with 31 percent of men and 31.5 percent of women having less than a fourth-grade education (Lacayo, 1993).

The foregoing employment and educational conditions contribute to the high rate of poverty among older Hispanic Americans. In 1990, 22 percent lived below the poverty level, compared to 10 percent of older whites; and approximately 33 percent, compared to 18 percent of older whites, hover just above the "near poverty" threshold at incomes below 125 percent of the poverty line. The median personal income of Hispanic men age 65 and over is about 65 percent of white males; for Hispanic women age 65 and over, the median income is 68 percent of white females (Lacayo, 1993).

The poverty of Hispanic Americans is undoubtedly a major factor in their generally poor health, with 85 percent of older Hispanics reporting at least one chronic condition and 45 percent reporting some limitation on activities of daily living (Cuellar, 1990; Espino, 1993). Physiological aging tends to precede chronological aging, with those in their late forties experiencing health disabilities typical of 65-year-old whites. Arthritis, high blood pressure, circulatory disorders, diabetes, cataracts, glaucoma, and heart disease are the most common health problems (Cuellar, 1990). Hispanic women have higher mortality rates from cervical cancer and cancer of the uterus than do white women. There are proportionately more Hispanic men to women over age 65 than among the white older population, but this is due to the higher mortality rate of Hispanic women at earlier ages, not to increases in longevity among Hispanic men. Given the high proportion of Hispanics who have been migrant farm workers, exposure to potentially harmful pesticides may put them at further risk of health problems.

Regardless of the foregoing statistics, Hispanics are the least likely among all groups of older adults to have a regular physician, to use hospitals frequently, to have private insurance coverage, to seek preventive care, or to access dental care (Miranda, 1990). Only 83 percent receive Medicare benefits compared to 96 percent of the older population generally (Kasper, 1988). Social and cultural barriers to health care,

such as mistrust of white medical providers, stigmas associated with receiving mental health services, reliance on folk medicine and religious healing, and structural factors such as less health insurance coverage and greater dissatisfaction with services, may partially underlie their underutilization of health care services and their greater negative perceptions of their health than whites have (Miranda, 1990). Difficulty in comprehending English is another important barrier, highlighting the need for bilingual and bicultural health care providers. Only about 3 percent are in nursing homes, with 10 percent of those over age 85 institutionalized, compared to 23 percent of oldest-old whites (Cuellar, 1990). Since families attempt to provide support as long as possible, when older Hispanics do enter nursing homes, they tend to be more physically and functionally impaired than their non-Hispanic white counterparts (Espino, 1993).

Historically, the extended family has been a major emotional support to older Hispanics, especially in rural areas. An early study of informal supports found that Hispanic elders had consistently higher levels of interaction and a greater potential for support from children than did either white or African American older adults, even controlling for gender, social class, and levels of functional ability (Cantor, 1979). Older Hispanics are more likely than whites to believe that older persons should be cared for in the community, and they are more than four times as likely as Anglos between the ages of 65 and 74, and more than two times as likely as those 74 years of age and older, to live with their adult children. Although patterns of intergenerational assistance are strong compared to Caucasian populations, more older Mexican Americans, for example, are reporting unfulfilled expectations of filial responsibility by their adult children (Markides, Boldt and Ray, 1986; Markides et al., 1990). Not surprisingly, how older parents evaluate their care from their adult children may differ from the objective reality (Markides et al., 1990). Widowed women over 75 are the most likely to live in extended family households (Cuellar, 1990). Those who live alone are generally inadequately housed, with the incidence of substandard housing substantially greater among Hispanics than among whites.

As a culture, Hispanics place a high value on family relations, believing particularly that the needs of the family as a whole or of individual family members should take precedence over one's own needs. However, the percentage in multigenerational families has declined in recent years. With their urbanization and greater acculturation, younger Hispanics are increasingly unable to meet their older parents' expectations and support an extended family in one location. Nevertheless, even when families are living apart, family members often still perform parental roles, assist with child care, advising, and decision-making, and serve as role models (Mayers and Souflee, 1990–91). For example, a study of three-generational Mexican-American families in San Antonio found strong intergenerational solidarity. Socioemotional help and advice were sought from elders by the young and vice versa. Caregiving during times of acute illness was provided primarily by daughters, as in other ethnic groups, but both the youngest and oldest respondents relied on women in the middle generation for caregiving when sick (Markides, Boldt, and Ray, 1986). Although families remain the most important system of support for their older members, it does appear that a division of labor is emerging between the family, which provides support and personal care, and public agencies, which provide financial assistance and medical care, along with churches and mutual aid, fraternal and self-help groups in the Hispanic community. These community-based groups provide outreach, advocacy, and information about resources, socialization opportunities, financial credit for services, and folk medicine. The supportive social and cultural context of neighborhood and community is congruent with the Hispanic's strong sense of peoplehood and cultural identity. Being part of "La Raza" encompasses a shared experience, history and sense of one's place in the world (Espino, 1993; Mayers and Souflee, 1990–91).

## OLDER AMERICAN INDIANS

As noted above, American Indian refers to indigenous people of North America (Kramer, 1992). Except for very general trends, less systematic data are available for American Indians than for the other ethnic minority groups discussed thus far. The two federal agencies responsible for collecting data, the Bureau of Indian Affairs and the Census Bureau, frequently have different estimates, making it difficult to generalize about American Indian older people. An additional complication in generalizing findings is that this population includes Indians, Eskimos, and Aleuts. There are nearly 500 federally recognized tribes and approximately 300 federally recognized reservations. Also, many urban Indians do not live on reservations, and therefore their conditions and needs are less visible (Kramer, 1992). Nearly 200 native languages are spoken, and there is a wide range of cultural traditions. More American Indian elders live in rural areas than do other minority older populations, with nearly 25 percent on reservations or in Alaskan Native villages. Over 50 percent are concentrated in Southwestern states, with the remainder in states along the Canadian border. Approximately one half of all Indians are under the age of 22 years, compared to approximately 30 years for the general population (Rhoades, 1990). While 13 percent of the American Indian population will enter the 65 plus age category compared to 19.5 percent of the U.S. population as a whole by the end of this century, the number of American Indians who are age 75 and over will at least double (Manson, 1993).

It has been estimated that up to 50 percent of older American Indians are poor, with per capita incomes that are 40 to 59 percent less than those of whites. While about 50 percent of older urban American Indians live with family members, their families are also more likely to be poor than their white counterparts (Kramer, 1992; Manson, 1993). As in other ethnic minority populations, the poverty of older American Indians tends to reflect lifelong patterns of unemployment, employment in jobs not covered by Social Security, especially on reservations, and poor working conditions. An additional factor is that historical circumstances and federal policies toward tribes have intensified the pattern of economic underdevelopment and impoverishment in "Indian country." The median income for this group is barely above the poverty threshold. In some areas, particularly in rural areas, as many as 75 percent of American Indians are unemployed, with 32 percent having incomes below federal poverty levels, compared with 10 percent of whites (Gould, 1989). For example, the proportion of rural Indian families with aged members that are below the poverty line is over twice that of average urban Indian families with a member age 65 and over (Manson and Callaway, 1990). Only about 50 percent of American Indian elders receive Social Security and Medicare benefits, and less than 40 percent receive Medicaid (Cook, 1990). By age 45, incomes have usually peaked among male American Indians, and decline thereafter. American Indian women are generally less educated than the men, and seldom earn even half the income of the men, putting them in a severely disadvantaged position. Another factor negatively affecting the socioeconomic and living conditions of American Indian women is that more than 50 percent of those age 60 and over are widowed. High unemployment and low income levels tend to result in the necessity of intergenerational living arrangements among the American Indian older people in order to share scarce irregular resources (Manson, 1993). Without government-sponsored social and health services, many older American Indians could not survive.

American Indians may have the poorest health of all Americans, due in part to poor housing conditions and greater isolation of American Indian communities (Barresi and Stull, 1993). Older American Indians have a higher incidence than whites of diabetes, hypertension, accidents, tuberculosis, heart disease, liver and kidney disease, strokes, influenza, pneumonia, hearing and visual impairments, and problems stemming from obesity, gall bladder, or arthritic ailments. In fact, nearly 75 percent suffer limitations in their ability to perform activities of daily living (Manson, 1995; Kramer, 1992). Although liver and kidney problems often result from lifelong problems with drinking, alcoholism generally takes its toll before old age. The death rate from alcoholism among American Indians is seven times higher than that of the United States generally, but alcohol-related deaths drop sharply among American Indians who have reached age 55 (Rhoades, 1990). Automobile accidents also take a disproportionately heavy toll on American Indian males (Manson, 1993).

Given these health problems, it is not surprising that on reservations, people appear to be old by 45 years of age, and in urban areas, by age 55. Accordingly, American Indians are less likely than non-Indians to define aging chronologically; instead, they frequently use social functioning and decline in physical activities to identify an elder. For example, in Los Angeles, the median age for those considered elders by the community is 58 years (Weibel-Orlando and Kramer, 1989). A significant barrier to publicly funded health services is that eligibility is typically based on chronological age.

Because of the importance of tribal sovereignty, many American Indians believe that health and social services are owed to them as a result of the transfer of land and derive from solemn agreements between sovereign nations. Despite this attitude, the majority of American Indian elders rarely see a physician, often because of living in isolated areas, lacking transportation, and not trusting non-Indian health professionals (Kramer, 1992). In addition, many prefer traditional health care from their tribal medicine people and resist using non-Indian medical resources. For traditional American Indians, medicine is holistic and wellness oriented. It focuses on behaviors and lifestyles through which harmony can be achieved in the physical, mental, spiritual, and personal aspects of one's role in the family, community and environment (Kramer, 1992; Manson, 1992). The Indian Health Service provides health care to those on reservations, and has developed health clinics for urban Indians. During the 1980s, very few urban older people sought such care generally because of the cost, transportation difficulties, or professionals' lack of sensitivity to Indians' ritual folk healing or cultural definitions of disease, although utilization of these clinics has increased in recent years. The most frequent services available include congregate meals and nutrition programs, community and senior centers, and tribal community health nurses who provide in-home care (Rhoades, 1990). As a whole however, urban American Indians are typically underserved by the federally funded network of services for older people (Kramer, 1992).

Another structural barrier to health care is that the Indian Health Service emphasizes services to youth and families and acute care rather than long-term care, such as skilled and intermediate care facilities. For example, the Indian Health Service operates only 10 reservation nursing homes as compared to 49 hospitals. This means that older American Indians who need nursing home care frequently have to go to facilities that are at a geographic distance and not oriented to Indian peoples. Such cultural and geographic barriers have resulted in a pattern of repeated short-term hospitalizations or revolving door admissions for chronic conditions (Manson, 1993). Accordingly, among those over 85 years of age, only 13 percent are in nursing homes, compared to 23 percent of whites (AARP, 1987).

American Indians perceive their physical and mental health to be poorer than white older adults do, and some studies have documented a higher incidence of suicide (National Indian Council on Aging, 1984). Research findings regarding the mental health of older American Indians are mixed, with some studies suggesting that those who maintain a tribal identity experience less stress than their white counterparts. As

they grow older, they appear to shift to a more passive relationship with their world, accepting age-related changes as a natural part of life and utilizing passive forbearance as a coping strategy (Kramer, 1992). This movement from active mastery to passive accommodative styles is consistent with Gutmann's findings for diverse cultures, described in Chapter 9. It is also an adaptation to the decreasing P-E congruence experienced by many ethnic minorities as they age. More recent studies have found that depression is a major mental health problem among American Indians, but difficult to diagnose because of cultural factors (Rhoades, 1990; Cook, 1990). American Indians' low utilization of mental health services is not necessarily a reflection of fewer mental health problems, but may represent greater barriers to treatment and less information about psychological and supportive services from their physicians (Kramer, 1992; Markides, 1986).

A factor that often creates adjustment problems is the degree to which older American Indians' lives are dictated by government bureaucratic policies. Unlike any other group in the United States, various tribes are sovereign nations and possess a distinct and special relationship with the U.S. Government, based largely, but not exclusively, on treaties agreed to by the two parties. Congress and the Bureau of Indian Affairs, not the individual states, largely determine daily practices on the reservations. Although the Bureau's regulations are intended to ensure basic support, it has been criticized for its inflexibility. American Indian advocates have accused the Bureau of expending 90 percent of its $3 billion-per-year budget on maintaining and supporting the bureaucracy, with only 10 percent actually going to services for Indian people (Cook, 1990). It has also been accused of denying traditional cultural values. As an example, land-grazing privileges were historically extended to all tribal members for as long as they desired; today, older American Indians must transfer their grazing rights to their heirs before they qualify for supplemental financial assistance. Although extra income may be welcome, the program serves to deprive the old of their traditional position within the tribal structure. The history of older American Indians and their relationship with the federal bureaucracy must be considered in efforts to develop culturally appropriate social and health services.

Historical and cultural factors also strongly influence the family relationships of American Indians. For them, family is the central institution and "honoring" and giving respect to elders and sharing family resources are an integral part of their ethos. American Indians' deep reverence for nature and belief in a supreme force, the importance of the clan, and a sense of individual autonomy as a key to group cohesiveness and lack of competition underlie their practices toward their elders. Historically, the old were accorded respect and fulfilled specified useful tribal roles, including that of the "wise elder" who instructs the young and assists with child care, especially for foster children and grandchildren. They also maintained responsibility for remembering and relating tribal philosophies, myths, and traditions, and served as religious and political advisors to tribal leaders. These relationships have changed, however, with the restructuring of American Indian life by the Bureau of Indian Affairs and by the increasing urbanization of native populations.

Despite these changes, many American Indian older people, particularly in rural settings, continue to live in an extended family. Approximately 66 percent of all American Indian elders live with family members (e.g., spouse, children, grandchildren, and foster children). American Indian older women are more likely to be married in their later years than are white women, although 55 percent are widowed. Some 25 percent of Indian older people care for at least one grandchild, and 67 percent live within five miles of relatives (Manson and Callaway, 1990). Given the cultural values and norms of intergenerational assistance, family caregivers may feel less anger and guilt toward relatives for whom they provide care, accepting such care as the reality of aging relatives (Kramer, 1992; Strong,

1984). This pattern of helping family members, combined with mistrust of governmental programs, partially underlies American Indians' comparatively low utilization of social and health services. These factors combine to put undue pressure on families to keep their elders at home, even though families may lack sufficient resources to do so (Kramer, 1992).

## PACIFIC ASIAN ELDERS

Pacific Asian elders consist mainly of three groups: immigrants who arrived during the turn of the century; children born to these immigrants; and older immigrants, primarily from Southeast Asia who entered the United States in the 1970s with their families, largely because of the Vietnam War. The Pacific Asian elders who were born in this country around the turn of the century or who came to the United States during the early 1900s share the experience of discrimination and isolation. Laws discriminating against Asians are numerous, ranging from the Chinese Exclusion Act of 1882, the Japanese Alien Land Law of 1913, the Executive Order of 1942 for the internment of 110,000 persons of Japanese ancestry, denial of citizenship to first-generation Asians in

Many elderly Asian Americans prefer reading newspapers from their native countries.

1922, the anti-miscegenation statute of 1935, and more recently, Public Law 95-507 excluding Asians as a protected minority under the definition of "socially and economically disadvantaged" (U.S. Commission on Civil Rights, 1979). Such legislation, combined with a history of prejudice and discrimination, has contributed to feelings of mistrust, injustice, powerlessness, and fear of government among many Pacific Asian elders, and thus a reluctance to utilize services.

Compared to other ethnic groups, the graying of Asian America is occurring at the fastest rate. In addition, there is considerable variability in the percentage of persons age 65 and older as well as the percentage of foreign-born within that age group. For example, of older immigrant groups, Filipino older people have the highest percentage of foreign-born (95.9 percent), compared with Chinese (80.9 percent), and Japanese (43.1 percent). Among new immigrants (Koreans, Thai) or refugees (Vietnamese, Laotians, and Cambodians), the percentage of foreign-born is even higher (Yee, Kim, Liu, and Wong, 1993).

The older Asians who immigrated prior to 1924 generally differ substantially in their occupational and educational background from those who came later. As a result of denial of property rights and discrimination against them for public jobs, most Asian older people who immigrated in the early part of the century are less educated and more economically deprived than many of their white counterparts. Older Pacific Asians have, on the average, 6 years of school, with the exception of the Japanese, who average 8.5 years. Many still speak only their native language. For example, only 1.4 percent of the foreign-born Chinese elders and less than 1 percent of the Japanese older people speak English (Kim, 1983). Their social worlds, therefore, have been limited to ethnic enclaves, such as Chinatown and Koreatown, where they have developed small retail and service businesses, mutual aid or benevolent societies, and recreational clubs.

While representing segregation from the general society, these ethnic enclaves are a center for leisure activities and for the delivery of services to Pacific Asian older people. These functions served by the closely knit community, however, will probably not exist for future generations of Pacific Asians, who have become more geographically and socially mobile.

Although Japanese-American older people tend to be economically better off than other ethnic minority groups, 14 percent of Pacific Asian elders live below the poverty level (Gould, 1989). The poverty rate may be even higher than that reflected in official statistics, since the number of employed adults, often self-employed as farmers or in small businesses, is greater than in other groups, thereby inflating "family" income. The poverty figures are high among female heads of households over age 75, ranging from 31.1 percent to 40.4 percent; and among Chinese and Filipino men living alone, the rate is 41 percent compared to 31 percent of their male peers in the general population (Liu, 1986). Many older Chinese and Filipinos have experienced a lifetime of low-paying jobs, often in self-employment, garment factories, service or farming work not covered by Social Security or other pensions. Filipino males, in particular, were concentrated in live-in domestic, migrant agricultural, or other unsettled work, often living in homogeneous male camps and failing both to gain an insured work history and to develop close ties with family and neighborhood.

As is the case with older Hispanics, many older Pacific Asians qualify for public financial supports, such as Supplemental Security Income, but do not apply. After years of living under discrimination and fear of deportation, they resist seeking help from a government bureaucracy. Their reluctance to seek nonfamilial assistance is also influenced by cultural and linguistic traditions emphasizing personal status and self-restraint. When unsure of others' social status, some older Pacific Asians avoid interaction with them. In the past, they turned to the benevolent societies and clubs in their tightly knit communities, as well as to their families. Yet many are caught between their cultural traditions of group and familial honor and the values of their adopted culture that stress independence and self-sufficiency, making them loath to turn to others for support.

Filipino Americans represent an example of how cultural values can create reluctance to utilize services. They are guided by values of both respect and shame. Respect includes listening to others, self-imposed restraints, loyalty to family, and unquestioning obedience to authority; shame involves fear of being left exposed, unprotected, and unaccepted. Filipino Americans are also very concerned with good relations or the avoidance of disagreement or conflict (Kim, 1990). Japanese American older people are more likely to value social interaction, hierarchical relationships, interdependency, and empathy—all characteristics that may not be present in the delivery of formal services in this country. Both situations illustrate the problem of lack of person-environment fit between the cultural values of many minority groups and the service system that is generally established by the larger society.

Compared to the national average, Pacific Asian groups show higher proportions of extended family arrangements, although the majority of Pacific Asian older adults live by themselves or with a spouse, not with children. Advancing age increases the probability of living alone (Manson, 1993). Some 2 percent over age 65, and 10 percent over age 85 are in nursing homes compared to 23 percent of whites. One of the major reasons for a relative decline in intergenerational living arrangements is acculturation of the elder's offspring into the larger society. For example, many Chinese older people prefer to remain in their ethnic communities rather than live with children who have moved to the suburbs or across the country.

Despite their strong commitment to family and filial responsibility, Chinese American elders generally live with their children only in cases of extreme poverty or poor health. Living with adult children may also be a function of their dependency on them for translation. Korean American older persons, for example, accept separation from their children as a way to promote the children's happiness and success. For first-generation Japanese, or Issei, a value that transcends that of family is group conscience, characterized by cohesiveness, strong pride, and identity through a devotion to and sense of mutuality among peer group members. This value has been preserved through the residential and occupational isolation of Japanese American elders from mainstream American culture. Even among the second generation (Nissei), the Japanese vision of Buddhism endures in the cherishing of filial devotion and the loving indulgence between young and old. The dependence of the aged and respect for elders who have greater life experience, knowledge, and wisdom are widely accepted values.

Although Pacific Asians represent tremendous diversity in terms of country of origin, degree of acculturation, and transcending values and religion, they all share the erosion of the law of primogeniture, or the relationship between aged parents and oldest son who provides care for them and, in turn, inherits their wealth. Nevertheless, compared with the majority culture, they place a high value on reciprocal exchanges between young and old and the prestige of being old, and seek outside help only in desperate circumstances. Any discussion of family care should take account of differences in culture, economic circumstances, and generation. A strain faced by many Pacific Asian families is the duality of cultures within families and the inevitable clashes when different generations have different languages, values, and ethos.

Traditional values also underlie this population's comparative underutilization of Medicare and Medicaid, and their reliance on non-Western medicine or family and friends to assist them with their health problems. It has been estimated that 33 percent of Pacific Asian elders have never seen a doctor or a dentist (Kim, 1990). What is unclear is whether this low utilization of health services is due to their having fewer chronic diseases than do their majority group peers, or to their reluctance to use formal Western health services.

Among Chinese American elders who value traditional healing practices, hospitals are seen as places to die, not to get well (Baker, 1990). Southeast Asian refugees' belief in the supernatural powers of ancestral and natural spirits is the cause of their low utilization of health care services. Some studies point to a sense of shame, particularly among Japanese-American older adults, about the use of public services as an indicator of dependency and inability to care for oneself (Ishizuka, 1978). But, when bilingual and bicultural personnel are used within service programs, some of this resistance to the use of services is overcome (Yip, 1981). Accordingly, Japanese American elder's low utilization of mental health services is due in large part to their definition of mental illness as stigma. Korean Americans tend to hold themselves and their families responsible for their problems rather than turn to others for assistance. Another barrier has been the myth held by some service providers that Pacific Asian older persons do not have problems and "take care of their own."

Information on the health of Pacific Asian older people is very limited, although it appears that they are in poorer health than the general population (Barresi and Stull, 1993). In Hawaii and California, life expectancies for older Japanese and Chinese are longer than those for the white population age 65 and over. This may be due to the higher incidence of most diseases, especially heart disease, hypertension, and strokes in whites compared with these two groups, although the rate of digestive system cancer is higher in Japanese Americans (Park, Yokoyama and Tokuyama, 1991). The incidence of strokes in Chinese and Japanese living in the United States is lower than in China and Japan. The relatively better health status of these two Pacific Asian groups may be due to their diet, with lower fat and higher carbohydrate intakes compared with whites, and lower obesity rates compared with other minority groups (Choi et al., 1990; Wright and Mindel, 1993). Less comparative research has been conducted on the health status and behaviors of other Pacific Asian groups.

The suicide rate among Chinese elders is three times as high as among their white peers; this has been attributed to the incongruities between the Chinese elder's values and the reality of their lives in an alien culture (Kim, 1990). Older Japanese males in California have been found to be hospitalized for schizophrenia more frequently than their white counterparts. However, since cultural factors influence the diagnosis of mental health problems, this finding may not necessarily reflect the mental health status of this population.

## IMPLICATIONS FOR SERVICE DELIVERY

Because it is important that gerontologists develop services responsive to ethnic minority older adults, we will briefly consider the implications of sociocultural factors for the delivery of social and health services. Several studies point to underutilization of services by ethnic minority elders, and to declining use of services in recent years (Fellin and Powell, 1988; Yeatts, Crow, and Folts, 1992). For example, Medicaid is not fully used by potentially eligible minority elders, even when they are aware of it. Underutilization of Medicaid has been attributed to lack of knowledge about the program, difficulties in applying, and an aversion to accepting publicly funded benefits. Other barriers to service utilization include:

- Cultural isolation, including language barriers
- Lack of services that are specifically oriented toward and operated by members of respective ethnic groups
- Stigma of utilizing services, especially mental health
- Nonminority staff who are not bilingual, who are insensitive to ethnic and cultural differences, and who serve meals that conflict with customary dietary preferences
- Lack of knowledge of services
- Geographic distance of services from minority neighborhoods

- Lack of transportation to services
- Ethnic minority elder's fear of doctors and hospitals, which may be related to present or historical acts of racism by medical providers
- Lack of trust and faith in the efficacy of health and social service professionals

Although some service providers have rationalized that ethnic minority older adults do not utilize formal services because they have their families' assistance, underutilization cannot be explained in terms of strong family support. In fact, a study of African American elders found that those aided by their families were also those who needed and used the greatest number of social services, which suggests their need for a variety of formal and informal supports (Mindel and Wright, 1982). Underutilization of in-home services may result more from services not being presented to ethnic minorities as a viable alternative to long-term care than to the existence of family supports. In fact, medical and psychosocial interventions that are culturally sensitive have been found to increase minority service utilization (Solomon, 1990).

The implication for practice is not whether ethnic minority elders need services, but rather how services can be designed to take account of inter- and intracultural and geographic differ-

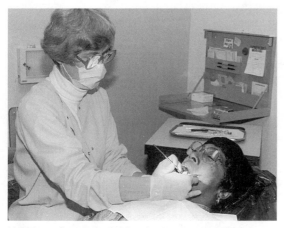

Health professionals need to be sensitive to cultural differences when caring for older patients.

ences. From this perspective, *preferential* consideration is needed to reduce social inequities between the elders of dominant and minority groups, along with *differential* consideration to take account of the diversity of needs and to increase the participation of various ethnic minority groups. Services are most likely to be used by ethnic minority older people under the following conditions:

1. Services should be located in the ethnic minority community, easily accessible, near complementary supports, and transportation should be provided.

2. Services should adhere to the cultural integrity of the ethnic minority group's lifestyle; for example, nutrition programs should include appropriate ethnic foods, and nursing homes should offer culturally appropriate recreation.

3. The organizational climate should be informal and personalized.

4. Staff should include bilingual, bicultural, and/or indigenous workers, or translators who are culturally sensitive and who use personalized outreach methods to establish trust and rapport. Medical and insurance forms, newsletters, and descriptions of services should be bilingual.

5. Ethnic minorities should be involved in both the planning and the delivery of services, so that programs are accountable to the community served.

6. Services should be advertised in ways to reach ethnic minorities, such as through minority-oriented television and radio programs and newspapers, and announcements made through churches, neighborhood organizations, civic and social clubs, other natural support systems, and influential persons as advocates. For example, black churches can be used to recruit more African American elderly to participate in the formal delivery of services as well as to coordinate and link with other agencies (Walls and Zarit, 1991).

7. Services should have a strong prevention and education component, with special efforts to enhance continuity of care.

Service providers should recognize and respect that many older ethnic minorities may adhere to traditional paradigms of health and illness and associated folk beliefs and behaviors that diverge from mainstream Western scientific medical concepts or they may combine these with orthodox or scientific treatments. As noted earlier, such folk treatments are often important in terms of psychological well-being (Hopper, 1993). Accordingly, current health promotion efforts aimed at older whites may not be appropriate for ethnic minorities. For example, social entities that play a key role in older African Americans' lives, such as the church and group leaders from the community, are more likely to change health beliefs and behaviors than traditional approaches to health promotion. The involvement of health promotion experts from the same culture may also help bridge the gap between cultural values and scientific knowledge about the causes and treatment of disease. This is particularly true for American Indian and Asian cultures, where traditional ways of treating disease are still widely practiced among older cohorts. Health promotion efforts that ignore traditional beliefs about harmony between the individual, nature, and the universe are more likely to fail in these cultures. For example, the Chinese believe that health represents a balance between Yin and Yang energy forces; certain foods are believed to bring about this balance. Because they also believe that the aging process predisposes people to Yin (or cold forces), older people avoid eating many cold foods such as leafy green vegetables (Yee and Weaver, 1994). Health promotion facilitators must recognize the basis for such avoidance if they are to encourage healthier diets among older Asians.

In sum, rather than a deficits model, in which interventions are developed to ameliorate personal or social problems, service providers should look for community strengths and use them to supplement and augment existing services (Mayers and Souflee, 1990–91). This also suggests the value of utilizing existing organizational structures, such as churches, to provide services and to link informal and formal sources of help (Wood and Wan, 1993).

Underlying such strategies are assumptions that the needs of ethnic minority elders are best understood by members of their own groups, that these elders should be treated as distinct populations, and that ethnic minorities should concentrate on the welfare of their own older members, rather than on the well-being of older people in general. These assumptions have led to demands by advocates for the minority aged that separate indigenous services be developed, that research and training programs give special attention to ethnic minorities, that ethnic minority practitioners be employed as service providers, and that federal regulations for aging programs include minority-specific statutes. These demands have been met in many communities, such as in Seattle with a special Asian Health Program that has both community-based and nursing home care, and in San Francisco with the On Lok program that provides comprehensive care for older Chinese and has been replicated in other ethnic communities.

The premises and strategies used by these minority advocates have been challenged, however. The extent to which ethnic minority professionals reflect the needs of their older members has been questioned, as well as whether ethnic minority issues are overemphasized. Critics of separate strategies advocate that ethnic minorities become involved in larger issues that affect all older persons, and that programs should be developed on the basis of need, regardless of ethnic minority status (Torres-Gil, 1982). This argument is supported by data that show the increased mobility and economic independence of younger minorities and their consequent upward and outward movement from formerly insulated ethnic communities. As younger members of ethnic minority groups move into the mainstream culture, the need for preferential services is assumed to decrease.

Others would argue, however, that even greater attention needs to be given to ethnic minorities in a period of growing competition for scarce resources. Two policy directions, decentralization and targeting services to the old-old, may, in fact, serve to exclude older members of minority groups, who are less able to influence decentralized decision making and less likely to reach advanced age. The persistently high unemployment among nonwhites across the life span, which will perpetuate major gaps in earnings, Social Security, and pension coverage in old age, suggests that strategies targeted to ethnic minority elders will continue to be necessary in the near future. During the current period of scarce resources, advocacy efforts are required to sustain the economic and social position of both minority and nonminority older people, suggesting the importance of collaborative efforts to ensure that low-income white and ethnic minority elders do not fall below the presumed "safety net" of services. In addition, more consideration needs to be given to improving the circumstances under which younger ethnic minorities will age, especially employment conditions, so that they will be better off when old. Such a perspective recognizes the need for cross-generational approaches to addressing environmental inequities.

## SUMMARY AND IMPLICATIONS

Although age is sometimes called the great equalizer, today's elders are a highly diverse group. As we have seen throughout this book, differences in income, health, and social supports significantly affect older adults' quality of life. An important source of this diversity is ethnic minority status. Ethnogerontology, or the study of the causes, processes, and consequences of race, national origin, and culture on individual and population aging, is the newest field of gerontology. One of the earliest debates in that field continues: whether ethnic minorities experience double jeopardy because of their race or whether age is a leveler of differences in income and life expectancy.

This chapter has reviewed the life situations of African Americans, Hispanic Americans,

American Indians, and Pacific Asian older people. Although there are variations among these groups, several common themes also emerge. For most ethnic minority older persons, their resources and status reflect social and economic discrimination experienced earlier in life. Many, especially those who migrated to the United States, experience cultural and language differences as well. They face shorter life expectancy and increased risks of poverty, malnutrition, substandard housing, and poor health. Social and health care assistance is of particular concern to ethnic minority elders. Cultural and language difficulties, physical isolation, and lower income, along with problems of service accessibility, underlie their underutilization of health and social services. Efforts must continue to modify such services to be more responsive to the particular needs of ethnic minority older adults.

In recent years, the older population has been growing faster among ethnic minorities than among whites—a trend that is expected to continue. Still, white elders outnumber their ethnic minority peers. The status of ethnic minority older people is not likely to improve greatly in the immediate future. The factors that largely determine the older population's quality of life—education, employment, income, and health—will not vary considerably among the ethnic minority population now approaching retirement age. This trend suggests the importance of targeting services to meet the needs of ethnic minority elders, although some minority aging advocates maintain that policies and programs should be directed toward improving the status of all older people. Efforts to increase opportunities for education and employment among younger minorities will be necessary to assure that the next generation will enjoy a higher quality of life than that of their predecessors.

## REFERENCES

Agree, E. M. *A portrait of older minorities*. Washington, D.C.: American Association of Retired Persons, Minority Affairs Initiative, 1987.

American Association of Retired Persons (AARP), *A profile of older Americans*, Washington, D.C.: AARP, 1987.

*American Indian elderly: A national profile*. Albuquerque, N.M.: National Indian Council on Aging, 1981.

Andersen, R. Access to medical care among the Hispanic population of the southwestern United States. *Journal of Health and Social Behavior*, 1981, *22*, 78–79.

Asociacion Nacional Pro Personas Mayores (ANPPM). *A national study to assess the service needs of the Hispanic elderly*. Los Angeles: Asociacion Nacional Pro Personas Mayores, 1980.

Baker, F. M. Ethnic minority issues: Differential diagnosis, medication, treatment and outcomes. In M. S. Harper (Ed.), *Minority aging*. DHHS Publication #HRS (P-DV-90-4), Washington, D.C.: U.S. Government Printing Office, 549–578.

Baquet, C. R. Cancer prevention and control in the Black population. In J. S. Jackson (Ed.), *The Black American elderly*. New York: Springer, 1988.

Barresi, C., and Stull, D. Ethnicity and long-term care: An overview. In C. Barresi and D. Stull (Eds.), *Ethnic elderly and long-term care*, New York: Springer, 1993, 3–22.

Beard, V. Health status of a successful Black aged population related to life satisfaction and self-concept. In W. Watson and Associates (Eds.), *Health in the Black aged*. Washington, D.C.: National Center on Black Aged, 1977.

Belgrave, L. L., Wykle, M. L., and Choi, J. M. Health, double jeopardy, and culture: The use of institutionalization by African-Americans. *The Gerontologist*, 1993, *33*(3), 379–385.

Bell, D., and Zellman, G. *Issues in service delivery to ethnic elderly*. Santa Monica, Calif.: Rand Corp., 1976.

Bengtson, V. L. Ethnicity and aging: Problems and issues in current social science inquiry. In D. E. Gelfand and A. J. Kutzik (Eds.), *Ethnicity and aging: Theory, research and policy*. New York: Springer, 1979, 9–31.

Bradshaw, B., and Foner, E. The mortality of Spanish-surnamed persons in Texas: 1969–1971. In F. D. Bean and W. P. Frisbie (Eds.), *The demography of racial and ethnic groups*. New York: Academic Press, 1979.

Brown, D. The Black elderly: Implications for the family. In M. S. Harper (Ed.), *Minority aging*. DHHS Publication #HRS (P-DV-90-4), Washington, D.C.: U.S. Government Printing Office.

Browne, C., and Onzuka-Anderson, R. Community support systems for the elderly in Hawaii. In D. S. Sanders and J. L. Fischer (Eds.), *Visions for the future: Social work and Pacific-Asian perspectives*. Honolulu: University of Hawaii, 1988.

Butler, R., and Lewis, M. *Aging and mental health*. St. Louis: Mosby, 1982.

Cantor, M. H. The informal support system of New York's inner city elderly: Is ethnicity a factor? In D. E. Gelfand and A. J. Kutzik (Eds.), *Ethnicity and aging: Theory, research and policy*. New York: Springer, 1979.

Cantor, M. H., Rosenthal, K., and Wilken, L. Social and family relationships of Black aged women in New York City. *Journal of Minority Aging*, 1979, *4*, 50–61.

Chatters, L., and Taylor, R. J. Age differences in religious participation among Black adults. *Journals of Gerontology*, 1989, *44*, S183–S189.

Choi, E. S., McGandy, R. B., Dallal, G. E., Russell, K. M., Jacob, R. A., Schaefer, E. J., and Sadowski, J. A. Prevalence of cardiovascular risk factors among elderly Chinese Americans. *Archives of Internal Medicine*, 1990, *150*, 413–418.

Cook, C. D. American Indian elderly and public policy issues. In M. S. Harper (Ed.), *Minority aging*. DHHS Publication #HRS (P-DV-90-4), Washington D.C.: U.S. Government Printing Office.

Cool, L. E. The effects of social class and ethnicity on the aging process. In D. Silverman (Ed.), *The elderly as modern pioneers*. Bloomington, Ind.: Indiana University Press, 1987.

Cuellar, J., Hispanic American aging: Geriatric educational curriculum development for selected health professions. In M. S. Harper (Ed.), *Minority aging*. DHHS Publication #HRS (P-DV-90-4), Washington D.C.: U.S. Government Printing Office, 1990.

Cuellar, J. *Minority elderly Americans: A prototype for area agencies on aging*. San Diego: Allied Home Health Association, 1980.

Cuellar, J., and Weeks, J. Minority elderly Americans: The assessment of needs and equitable receipt of public benefits as a prototype in area agencies on aging. Final Report. San Diego: Allied Home

Health Association, Grant AOA/DHHS 90-A-1667(01), 1980.

Curley, L. Curriculum development and American Indian elderly. In M. S. Harper (Ed.), *Minority aging.* DHHS Publication #HRS (P-DV-90-4), Washington D.C.: U.S. Government Printing Office, 1990.

Davis, D. Growing old Black. In J. S. Quodogne (Ed.), *Aging, the individual and society.* New York: St. Martin's Press, 1980.

Davis, L., and McGadney, B. Self-care practices of black elders. In C. Barresi and D. Stull (Eds.), *Ethnic elderly and long-term care.* New York: Springer, 1993, 73–86.

Employment and the elderly. *National Indian Council on Aging Quarterly,* Winter 1981, *1,* 2–4.

Espino, D. Hispanic elderly and long-term care: Implications for ethnically sensitive services. In C. Barresi and D. Stull (Eds.), *Ethnic elderly and long-term care.* New York: Springer, 1993, 101–112.

Fellin, P. A., and Powell, T. J. Mental health services and older adult minorities: An assessment. *The Gerontologist,* 1988, *28,* 442–447.

Gallego, D. The Mexican-American elderly: Familial and friendship support system . . . fact or fiction? Presented at the annual meeting of the Gerontological Society, San Diego, Calif., 1980.

George, L. K. Social participation in late life: Black-white differences. In J. S. Jackson (Ed.), *The Black American elderly.* New York: Springer, 1988.

Gibson, R. C. The age-by-race gap in health and mortality in the older population: A social science research agenda. *The Gerontologist,* 1994, *34,* 454–462.

Gibson, R. Outlook for the Black family. In A. Pifer and L. Bronte (Eds.), *Our aging society.* New York: W. W. Norton, 1986.

Gibson, R. Minority aging research: Opportunity and challenge. *Journals of Gerontology,* 1989, *44,* S52–53.

Gibson, R. C., and Jackson, J. S. The health, physical functioning and informal supports of the black elderly. *Milbank Quarterly,* 1987, *65,* 421–454.

Gould, K. H. A minority-feminist perspective on women and aging. *Journal of Women and Aging,* 1989, *1,* 195–216.

Gratton, B., and Wilson, V. Family support systems and the minority elderly: A cautionary analysis. *Journal of Gerontological Social Work,* 1988, *13,* 81–95.

Greene, V. L., and Ondrich, J. I. Risk factors for nursing home admissions and exits: A discrete-time hazard function approach. *Journal of Gerontology,* 1990, 45, 6, 250–258.

Gutmann, D. Use of informal and formal supports by white ethnic aged. In D. E. Gelfand and A. J. Kutzik (Eds.), *Ethnicity and aging: Theory, research and policy.* New York: Springer, 1979.

Harper, B. C. Some snapshots of death and dying among ethnic minorities. In R. C. Manuel (Ed.), *Minority aging: Sociological and social psychological issues.* Westport, Conn.: Greenwood Press, 1982.

Harper, M., and Alexander, C. Profile of the black elderly. In M. S. Harper (Ed.), *Minority aging.* DHHS Publication #HRS (P-DV-90-4), Washington D.C.: U.S. Government Printing Office, 1990.

Hatch, L. R. Informal support patterns of older African American and white women. *Research on Aging,* 1991, *13*(2), 144-170.

Hopper, S. V. The influence of ethnicity on the health of older women. *Clinics in Geriatric Medicine,* 1993, *9*(1), 231–259.

Ishikawa, W. *Pacific Asian elderly.* San Francisco: Hurron Resources Corp., 1978.

Ishizuka, K. C. *The elder Japanese.* San Diego: Campanile Press, 1978.

Jackson, J. J. The Black aging: A demographic overview. In R. Kalish (Ed.), *The later years.* Monterey, Calif.: Brooks/Cole, 1977.

Jackson, J. J. Race, national origin, ethnicity and aging. In E. Shanas and R. Binstock (Eds.), *Handbook of aging and the social sciences.* New York: Van Nostrand Reinhold, 1985.

Jackson, J. S. Death rates of aged Blacks and whites, 1964–1978. *The Black Scholar,* 1982, *13,* 36–48.

Jackson, J. S., Chatters, L. M., Neighbors, H. W. The mental health status of older Black Americans. *The Black Scholar,* 1982, *13,* 21–35.

Jaco, E. Social factors in mental disorders in Texas. *Social Problems,* 1957, *4,* 320–328.

Johnson, C., and Barer, B. Families and networks among older inner-city Blacks. *The Gerontologist,* 1990, *30,* 726–733.

Kahn, K., Pearson, M. L., and Harrison, E. R. Health care for black and poor hospitalized Medicare patients. *The Journal of the American Medical Association,* 1994, *271*(15), 1169–1174.

Kasper, J. *Aging alone: Profiles and projections.* Baltimore, Md.: The Commonwealth Fund Commission, 1988.

Keefe, S. E. Personal communities in the city: Support networks among Mexican-Americans and Anglo-Americans, *Urban Anthropology*, 1980, 9, 51–74.

Kim, P. Asian-American families and the elderly. In M. S. Harper (Ed.), *Minority aging*. DHHS Publication #HRS (P-DV-90-4), Washington, D.C.: U.S. Government Printing Office, 1990.

Kim, P. Demography of the Asian-Pacific elderly: Selected problems and implications. In R. L. McNeely and J. L. Colen (Eds.), *Aging in minority groups*. Beverly Hills: Sage, 1983.

Kramer, B. J. Cross-cultural medicine a decade later: Health and aging of urban American Indians. *The Western Journal of Medicine*, 1992, 157(3), 281–285.

Kramer, B. J. Urban American Indian aging. *Cross-Cultural Gerontology*, 1991, 6, 205–217.

Krause, N. Race differences in life satisfaction among aged men and women. *Journals of Gerontology*, 1993, 48(5), S235–S244.

Krause, N. Stress in racial differences in self-reported health among the elderly. *The Gerontologist*, 1987, 27, 72–76.

Krause, N., and Tran, T. V. Stress and religious involvement among older Blacks. *Journals of Gerontology*, 1989, 44, S4–S13.

Lacayo, C. G. Hispanic elderly: Policy issues in long-term care. In C. Barresi and D. Stull (Eds.), *Ethnic elderly and long-term care*, New York: Springer, 1993, 223-234.

Lacayo, C. G. *A national study to assess the service needs of the Hispanic elderly*. Los Angeles: Asociacion Nacional Pro Personas Mayores, 1980.

Levkoff, S., Pratt, C., Esperanza, R., and Tomina, S. *Minority elderly: An historical and cultural perspective*. Corvallis: Oregon State University, 1979.

Liu, W. T. Health services for the Asian elderly. *Research on Aging*, 1986, 8, 156–175.

Lubben, J. E., and Becerra, R. M. Social support among Black, Mexican and Chinese elderly. In E. E. Gelfand and C. H. Barresi (Eds.), *Ethnic dimensions of aging*, New York: Springer, 1987, 130–144.

Maldonado, D. The Chicano aged. In J. S. Quodagne (Ed.), *Aging, the individual and society*. New York: St. Martin's Press, 1980.

Manson, J. Long-term care of older American Indians: Challenges in the development of institutional services. In C. Barresi and D. Stull (Eds.), *Ethnic elderly and long-term care*. New York: Springer, 1993, 130–143.

Manson, S. M. *Problematic life situations: Cross-cultural variation in support mobilization among the elderly* (Grant No. 0090-AR-0067). Final report submitted to the Administration on Aging, 1984.

Manson, S. M. Long-term care in American Indian communities: Issues for planning and research. *The Gerontologist*, 1989, 29, 38–44.

Manson, S. M., *Older ethnic minorities and health care: Accommodating cultural diversity in clinical practice*. Unpublished data, 1991.

Manson, S. M., and Callaway, D. G. Health and aging among American Indians. In M. S. Harper (Ed.), *Minority aging*. DHHS Publication #HRS (P-DV-90-4), Washington D.C.: U.S. Government Printing Office, 1990.

Manton, K. Differential life expectancy: Possible explanations during the later years. In R. C. Manuel (Ed.), *Minority aging: Sociological and social psychological issues*. Westport, Conn.: Greenwood Press, 1982.

Markides, K. S. Minority status, aging and mental health. *International Journal of Aging and Human Development*, 1986, 23, 285–300.

Markides, K. S., and Martin, H. W. (with Gomez, E.). *Older Mexican Americans: A study in an urban barrio*. Monograph of the Center for Mexican American Studies, Austin: University of Texas Press, 1983.

Markides, K., Boldt, J. S., Ray, L. A. Sources of helping and intergenerational solidarity of Mexican-Americans. *Journal of Gerontology*, 1986, 41, 506–511.

Markides, K., Liang, J., and Jackson, J. Race, ethnicity and aging: Conceptual and methodological issues. In R. Binstock and L. George (Eds.), *Handbook of aging and the social sciences* (3d ed.). New York: Academic Press, 1990.

Mayers, R. S., and Souflee, L. Utilizing social support systems in the delivery of social services to the Mexican-American elderly. *The Journal of Applied Social Sciences*, Fall/Winter 1990–91, 15(1), 31–50.

McNeely, R. L., and Colen, J. L. *Aging in minority groups*. Beverly Hills, Calif.: Sage, 1983.

Mick, C. *A profile of American Indian nursing homes*. Reprint Series. Long-term Care Gerontology Center, University of Arizona, Tempe, Arizona, 1983.

Mindel, C. The elderly in minority families. In B. B. Hess and E. W. Markson (Eds.), *Growing old in America: New perspectives on old age* (3d ed.). New Brunswick, N.J.: Transaction, 1985.

Mindel, C., and Wright, R. Assessing the role of support systems among black and white elderly. Presented at the annual meeting of the Gerontological Society of America, San Diego, Calif., November 1980.

Mindel, C., and Wright, R. The use of health and social services by the minority elderly: The role of social support systems. *Journal of Gerontological Social Work,* 1982, *4,* 3–4.

Minkler, M., and Roe, K. *Grandmothers as caregivers.* Newbury Park, Calif.: Sage, 1993.

Minkler, M., and Roe, K. *Preliminary findings from the grandmother caregiver study of Oakland California.* Berkeley: University of California, 1991.

Miranda, M. Hispanic aging: An overview of issues and policy implications. In M. S. Harper (Ed.), *Minority aging.* DHHS Publication #HRS (P-DV-90-4), Washington D.C.: U.S. Government Printing Office, 1990.

Montiel, M. The social science myth of the Mexican-American family. *El Grito,* 1970, *2,* 56–63.

Moore, J. W. Mexican Americans. *The Gerontologist,* 1971, *11,* 30–35.

Multran, E. Intergenerational family support among blacks and whites: Responses to cultural or socioeconomic differences. *Journal of Gerontology,* 1985, *40,* 382–389.

Murdock, S. H., and Schwartz, D. F. Family structure and the use of agency services: An examination of patterns among Native Americans. *The Gerontologist,* 1978, *18,* 475–481.

Nathan, J. Public policy issues and the minority elderly. In M. S. Harper (Ed.), *Minority aging.* DHHS Publication #HRS (P-DV-90-4), Washington, D.C.: U.S. Government Printing Office, 1990.

National Caucus and Center on Black Aged. *The status of the Black elderly in the United States.* Washington, D.C.: U.S. Government Printing Office, 1987.

National Center for Health Statistics (NCHS). Current estimates from the National Health Interview Survey, 1988. *Vital and Health Statistics,* 1989, *10,* #173.

National Center for Health Statistics, *Health: United States, 1990.* Hyattsville, Md.: NCHS, 1992.

National Indian Council on Aging. Indians and Alaskan natives. In E. Palmore, *Handbook on the aged in the United States.* Westport, Conn.: Greenwood Press, 1984.

1981 White House Conference. Aging: The Indian issue. *National Indian Council on Aging Quarterly,* Autumn 1981, *1* (4).

Palmore, E. *Handbook on the aged in the United States.* Westport, Conn.: Greenwood Press, 1984.

Park, C. B., Yokoyama, E., and Tokuyama, G. H. Medical conditions at death in Hawaii. *Journal of Clinical Epidemiology,* 1991, *44,* 519–530.

Perry, C., and Johnson, C. Families and support networks among African-American oldest old. *International Journal of Aging and Human Development,* 1994, *38*(1), 41.

Quinn, J. F., and Smeeding T. M. Defying the averages: Poverty and well-being among older Americans. *Aging Today,* September/October 1994, *XV*(5), 9.

Rhoades, E. Profile of American Indians and Alaska natives. In M. S. Harper (Ed.), *Minority aging.* DHHS Publication #HRS (P-DV-90-4), Washington, D.C.: U.S. Government Printing Office, 1990.

Rhoades, E., Marshall, M., Attneave, C., Bjork, J., and Beiser, M. Impact of mental disorders upon elderly American Indians as reflected in visits to ambulatory care facilities. *Journal of the American Geriatrics Society,* 1980, *28,* 33–39.

Rubel, A. *Across the tracks: Mexican Americans in a Texas city.* Austin: University of Texas Press, 1966.

Sanchez, D., and Thomas, D. J. Dimensions of minority aging. In M. S. Harper (Ed.), *Minority aging.* DHHS Publication #HRS (P-DV-90-4), Washington, D.C.: U.S. Government Printing Office, 1990.

Slaughter, O., and Mignon, B. Service delivery and the Black aged: Identifying barriers to utilization of mental health services. In R. C. Manuel (Ed.), *Minority aging: Sociological and social psychological issues.* Westport, Conn.: Greenwood Press, 1982.

Soldo, B., and Agree, E. America's elderly. *Population Bulletin,* 1988, *43,* 1–46.

Soldo, B., and DaVita, C. *Profiles of tbc Black aged.* Washington, D.C.: Georgetown University Center for Population Studies, 1977.

Soldo, B., Sharma, M., and Campbell, R. T. Determinants of the community living arrangements of older unmarried women. *Journal of Gerontology,* 1984, *39,* 492–498.

Solomon, B. Counseling Black families of inner-city church sites. In H. E. Cheatham and J. B. Steward (Eds.), *Black families: Interdisciplinary perspectives*. London: Transaction Publishers, 1990, 33–48.

Sotomayer, M. The new immigrants: The undocumented and refugees. In M. S. Harper (Ed.), *Minority aging*. DHHS Publication #HRS (P-DV-90-4), Washington, D.C.: U.S. Government Printing Office, 1990.

Strong, C. Stress and caring for elderly relatives: Interpretations and coping strategies in an American Indian and white sample. *The Gerontologist*, 1984, *24*, 251–256.

Tally, T., and Kaplan, J. The Negro aged. *Gerontological Society Newsletter*, 1956, *3*.

Taylor, R. J. Aging and supportive relationships among black Americans. In J. S. Jackson, P. Newton, A. Ostfield, D. Savage, and E. Schneider (Eds.), *The Black American elderly: Research on physical and psychosocial health*. New York: Springer, 1988, 259–281.

Taylor, R. J., and Chatters, L. M. Nonorganizational religious participation among elderly Black adults. *Journals of Gerontology*, 1991, *46*, S103–S110.

Taylor, R. J., Chatters, L. M., and Mays, J. M. Parents, children, siblings, in-laws and non-kin as source of emergency assistance to Black Americans. *Family Relations*, 1988, *37*, 298–304.

Torres-Gil, F. The special interest concerns of the minority professional: An evolutionary process in affecting social policies for the minority aged. In R. C. Manuel (Ed.), *Minority aging: Sociological and social psychological issues*. Westport, Conn.: Greenwood Press, 1982.

Torres-Gil, F. Hispanics: A special challenge. In A. Pifer and L. Bronte (Eds.), *Our aging society*. New York: W. W. Norton, 1986.

U. S. Bureau of the Census. *Supplementary Reports, 1980 Census of Population. Age, sex, race and Spanish origin of the population by regions, divisions and states, 1980*. PC80-S1-1, Washington, D.C.: U.S. Government Printing Office, 1980.

U.S. Bureau of the Census. *Household and family characteristics*. Current Population Reports. Washington, D.C.: U.S. Government Printing Office, 1990.

U.S. Bureau of the Census. *Supplementary Reports, 1990 Census of Population. Age, sex, race and Spanish origin of the population by regions, divisions, and states*. Washington, D.C.: U.S. Government Printing Office, 1990.

U.S. Commission on Civil Rights. *Civil rights issues of Asian and Pacific Americans: Myths and realities*. Washington, D.C.: U.S. Commission on Civil Rights, 1979.

U.S. Department of Health and Human Services. *Characteristics of the Black elderly—1980*. Washington, D.C.: Administration on Aging, 1980.

U.S. Senate Special Committee on Aging. *Aging America: Trends and projections. 1990–91*. Washington, D.C.: U.S. Department of Health and Human Services, 1992.

Valle, R. The demography of Mexican-American aging. In R. L. McNeely and J. L. Colen (Eds.), *Aging in minority groups*. Beverly Hills, Calif.: Sage, 1983.

Waller, J. B. Challenges to the provision of health care to minority aged. First annual summer symposium—Geriatric Education Center of Michigan, Ann Arbor, Michigan, June 1989.

Walls, C., and Zarit, S. Informal support from Black churches and the well-being of elderly Blacks. *The Gerontologist*, 1991, *31*, 490–495.

Watson, W. Mental health of the minority aged: Selected correlates. In R. C. Manuel (Ed.), *Minority aging: Sociological and social psychological issues*. Westport, Conn.: Greenwood Press, 1982.

Weibel-Orlando, J., and Kramer, B. J. The urban American Indian elders outreach project. *Final Report of Administration on Aging demonstration project 90AMO1273*. County of Los Angeles Dept. of Community and Senior Citizens Services. Los Angeles, Calif., 1989.

Wesly-King, S. Service utilization and the minority elderly: A review. In R. L. McNeely and J. L. Colen (Eds.), *Aging in minority groups*. Beverly Hills, Calif.: Sage, 1983.

Williams, G. C. Warriors no more: A study of the American Indian elderly. In C. L. Fry (Ed.), *Aging in culture and society*. New York: J. E. Bergin Publishers, 1980.

Wood, J. B., and Parham, I. A. Coping with perceived burden: Ethnic and cultural issues in Alzheimer's family caregiving. *Journal of Applied Gerontology*, 1990, *9*, 325–339.

Wood, J. B., and Wan, T. Ethnicity and minority issues in family caregiving to rural black elders. In C.

Barresi and D. Stull (Eds.), *Ethnic elderly and long-term care.* New York: Springer, 1993, 39–56.

Wright, R., and Mindel, C. Economics, health and service use policies: Implications for long-term care of ethnic elderly. In C. Barresi and D. Stull (Eds.), *Ethnic elderly and long-term care.* New York: Springer, 1993, 247–263.

Yeatts, D. E., Crow, T., and Folts, E. Service use among low-income minority elderly: Strategies for overcoming barriers. *The Gerontologist,* 1992, *32*(1), 24–32.

Yee, B. W. K., and Weaver, G. D. Ethnic minorities and health promotion. *Generations,* 1994, *18*, 39–44.

Yee, E., Kim, K., Liu, W., and Wong, S-C. Functional abilities of Chinese and Korean elders in congre-gate housing. In C. Barresi and D. Stull (Eds.), *Ethnic elderly and long-term care.* New York: Springer, 1993, 87–100.

Yip, B. Accessibility of services for Pan-Asian elderly: Fact or fiction? In E. P. Stanford (Ed.), *Minority aging: Policy issues for the 80s.* San Diego: Campanile Press, 1981.

Young, J. *Aging in Los Angeles County: A needs assessment of service to older persons in planning service area 19 California.* Los Angeles: Los Angeles County Department of Senior Citizen Affairs and Clairmont Graduate School, Center for Applied Social Research, 1982.

# CHAPTER 18

## POPULATIONS AT RISK: OLDER WOMEN

Previous chapters have illustrated numerous areas in which women's experiences with aging differ from men's: in patterns of health and life expectancy, marital opportunities, social supports, employment, and retirement. We have devoted a separate chapter to elaborate on these differences, with attention to how personal and environmental factors interact vis-à-vis the special problems facing women in old age. The impact of social factors, particularly economic ones, on physiological and psychological variables is vividly illustrated in terms of women's daily lives. This chapter first reviews the economic conditions faced by older women, then their health and social status, and how these factors interact. The chapter concludes with a brief discussion of program and policy options to reduce older women's vulnerability to poverty, poor health, and social isolation, primarily through changes affecting their socioeconomic conditions.

## CONCERN FOR OLDER WOMEN'S NEEDS

A major reason for gerontological research and practice to take account of older women's special needs is that they form the fastest growing segment of our population. As noted in Chapter 1, the aging society is primarily a female one. Women represent 56 percent of the population aged 65 to 74 and 72 percent of those over age 85; also, they outnumber men age 65 and over by three to two and men age 85 and over by five to two, with differences in this ratio among ethnic minorities, as noted in Chapter 17 (Bass, Torres-Gil, and Kutza, 1991). Chapter 1 noted that these disproportionate ratios result from differences in life expectancy between women and men, which are due to a combination of biological factors, such as the genetic theory that the female's two X chromosomes make her physiologically more robust, and to lifestyle factors, such as women's greater likelihood of consulting doctors and their lower rates of smoking, problem drinking, and risk-taking. At age 65, women can expect to live about 19 more years, compared to 15 more years for men at the same age. At age 75, the comparable figures are 12 more years for women and 9 more years for men. Even at age 85, the life expectancy for females is 1.5 years more than that for males (National Center for Health Statistics, 1989).

Another reason to examine the status of older women separate from that of older men is that gender structures opportunities across the life course so that the processes of aging and the quality of life in old age are often very different for men and women (Levy, 1988; Holstein, 1993; Huyck, 1991). Research on women and aging increasingly recognizes that gender and age interact to affect the distribution of power, privilege, and social well-being of both men and women. As noted by feminist writers, as more women reach old age, age compounds a woman's already devalued status (Gottlieb, 1989; Holstein, 1993). Since gender and age are powerful systems of ranking, neither can be understood fully without reference to the other (Levy, 1988). Given this interaction, it is not surprising that the problems of aging are increasingly women's problems. Older

Many older women have overcome a wide range of obstacles and are remarkable survivors.

women are more likely than older men to be poor; to have inadequate retirement income; to be widowed, divorced, and alone; and to be caregivers to other relatives. Women are viewed as experiencing double jeopardy; they are discriminated against both for being old and for being female. For example, older women have been found to experience combined negative effects, greater than the effects of being either old or female alone, on objective indicators of mental health (Chappell and Haven, 1980). In addition, the emphasis on youth and beauty in our society, which traditionally values women for their sex appeal and ability to bear children, is particularly difficult for older women.

Despite their greater problems, many older women display resilience and innovativeness in the face of adversity. In terms of measures of subjective well-being, they do not appear to experience double jeopardy (Chappell and Haven, 1980). For example, women who live alone are not necessarily unhappy. On the average, women are less likely than men to die following a spouse's death (Martin-Matthews, 1987). Many older women are remarkable survivors, having developed skills to cope with discontinuities and losses through their lives. There is growing awareness of middle-aged and older women's capacity to move in new directions—to advance their education, to enter new occupations, and to combine marriage and care for dependents with employment and volunteer roles. The impact of advocacy groups, such as the Older Women's League, on federal legislation clearly illustrates older women's power as activists. It is predicted that today's middle-aged women, who are enacting more diverse roles than past cohorts, will reach old age with even greater role flexibility and skills in coping with complex, changing life experiences (Riley and Riley, 1986).

Given the predominance of older women, it might be supposed that they, rather than men, would be the major focus of social gerontology. Yet, older women were nearly invisible in social gerontological research until the mid-1970s. For example, they were not added to the Baltimore

Longitudinal Study (one of the major studies described in Chapters 2 and 6) until 1978, because it was assumed that women's hormonal cycles would affect the data (Leonard, 1991)! It was not until 1975 that the first older women's caucus met at the annual meetings of the Gerontological Society of America. The 1981 White House Conference on Aging was the first to sponsor a special committee on older women's concerns. Research on issues specific to women, such as menopause, breast cancer, hormone replacement therapy, and osteoporosis, has been relatively limited until the 1980s. In 1991, Congress directed the National Institutes of Health to establish an Office of Research on Women's Health to redress the insufficient attention that had been paid to women's health issues in the biomedical and behavioral research community. This directive should stop the practice of excluding women from major research studies and help to increase the research on diseases that primarily afflict women, such as breast cancer.

In recent years older women's resilience as well as their vulnerability to social, economic, and health problems have been increasingly recognized, primarily as the result of the educational and advocacy efforts of such interest groups as the Older Women's League (OWL). Although the women's movement of the 1970s tended to focus on issues specific to young women, recently younger feminists have aligned themselves with efforts to influence older women's economic and social situations. Women of all ages have become more aware of their interdependence as both the primary recipients and providers of long-term care, and of the potential power of age-integrated women's organizations. Young and old women are beginning to unite around issues of caregiving, for example, pressing for unpaid, job-guaranteed leave for the care of both dependent parents and newborn children through the Family and Medical Leave Act that was passed in 1992. Women are caregivers throughout their lives, whether as daughters, daughters-in-law, wives, mothers, or staff members within public social service agencies, nursing homes, and hospitals.

Their roles as unpaid caregivers and as underpaid employees are interconnected, and influence all aspects of their lives. Women's unpaid and under-valued work as family caregivers, along with their employment in low-status, low-paid jobs, result in economic insecurity in old age, with consequent negative effects on their health status and health and long-term care options.

## OLDER WOMEN'S ECONOMIC STATUS

As described in Chapter 14, women age 65 and over account for over 70 percent of the older poor population. They thus form one of the poorest groups in our society, with nearly 15 percent of them living in poverty compared to 8 percent of men, representing the feminization of poverty across the life span and into old age (Minkler and Stone, 1985); (AARP, 1991; U.S. Bureau of the Census, 1990). With less than one in ten women over age 65 currently in the labor force (Schwenk, 1992) the median annual income of older women is approximately 58 percent that of older men. Furthermore, older men were three times as likely as older women to be financially well off, with incomes of $20,000 or more (Kravitz, Pelaez, and Rothman, 1991), and this difference persists even with employed women. As an example, the median income of mid-life and older women working full-time in 1989 was less than two-thirds that of their male counterparts. While, on average, women's wages peak at age 44 before beginning to decline, men's median earnings continue to climb until age 55. Although older women have less education and employment experience than both men and younger women, these differences do not completely account for the wage gap. In 1989, for example, college-educated women earned only 92 percent of that earned by male high school graduates of the same age (Older Women's League, 1991).

Unmarried women living alone, ethnic minority women, and those aged 75 and over are especially likely to be poor. The poverty rate among unmarried older women living alone, for example, is about 25 percent compared to less than 6 percent of older married women or men, and seven out of ten poor older women live alone (Quinn and Smeeding, 1994). Nearly 66 percent of older African American women not living with family and 61 percent of older Hispanic women living alone have incomes below the poverty level (Taeuber, 1991). The greater likelihood that old women will be poor compared to their male counterparts tends to be true of most other industrialized societies. In addition, the poverty rate increases with age for all women age 75 and over, to nearly 52 percent of white women, 42 percent of Indian, Eskimo, and Aleut women, 40 percent of African American women, 37 percent of Mexican American and Puerto Rican women, and 37 percent of Asian and Pacific Islander women (Taeuber, 1991). These figures may not reveal the extent of poverty among single older women, primarily widows, who are not counted as poor, despite their low income, because they may live in a household headed by a younger person whose income is above the poverty line. When these hidden poor are taken into account,

over 55 percent of older women are estimated to be poor (Estes, 1985).

Gender differences in employment history, career interruptions, types of occupations, earnings, and retirement circumstances are all contributing factors to older women's higher rates of poverty (Hatch, 1990). A primary reason for their economic vulnerability is that most women of this current cohort aged 65 and over did not work consistently for pay, largely because they were socialized to marry, have children, and depend on their husbands for economic support. Their labor force participation rate was 9.7 percent in 1950, rose slightly in the 1950s, and then dropped to 7.8 percent in 1983. When they were employed, women tended to be concentrated in low-paying clerical or service positions without adequate pensions. Those who try to enter the labor market after age 40 are likely to encounter discrimination and a growing earnings gap from their male counterparts. Although older African American women were more likely to have been employed during their youth than their white counterparts, their rates of labor force participa-

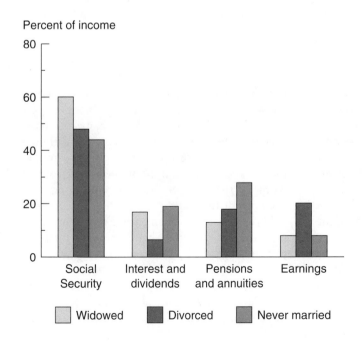

FIGURE 18–1    Sources of income of widowed, divorced, and never-married women 65 years or older who live alone, 1988–89

**TABLE 18–1    Sources and Distribution of Income among Older Women**

| Income source | AVERAGE INCOME[1] | | | PERCENT RECEIVING INCOME | | |
|---|---|---|---|---|---|---|
| | Widowed | Divorced | Never Married | Widowed | Divorced | Never Married |
| Before–tax income | $9,777 | $11,077 | $12,415 | 100 | 100 | 100 |
| Social Security and Railroad Retirement | 5,855 | 5,354 | 5,658 | 96 | 93 | 85 |
| Pensions and annuities | 1,272 | 2,033 | 3,429 | 26 | 33 | 45 |
| Interest and dividends | 1,648 | 629 | 2,340 | 37 | 35 | 51 |
| Earnings | 754 | 2,251 | 935 | 12 | 24 | 10 |
| Other | 248 | 810 | 53 | 19 | 32 | 6 |

[1]Calculated for all women 65 years or older living alone, with and without the income source.

tion throughout their lives were not significantly higher; and they were most likely to work in low-paying jobs (Rix, 1984). Generally dependent on men for both their income and their retirement benefits, most women of previous generations lacked the means to build up their economic security for old age.

A deleterious consequence of such dependency is that when women become widowed or divorced, they frequently lose their primary source of income. This vulnerability, resulting from the close interconnection between marital status and income level, has been described as being "only one man away from poverty" (Friends of the San Francisco Commission on the Status of Women, 1980). With over 60 percent of older women living without a spouse, many women face old age without pension income, particularly if their husbands did not select survivors' benefits.

In fact, the economic gap between married and widowed older women is increasing, especially among the oldest-old (Jacobs, 1991). The median income of widowed women was 76 percent that of widowed men in 1989, since men are more likely to retain pension or earned income after death of a spouse (U.S. Senate Special Committee on Aging, 1992). Of those eligible for

benefits, less than 60 percent of widows receive them in full, oftentimes because of misinformation about how to access these funds. Income level and marital status are thus inextricably linked, especially for old women without spouses (Vaughn, 1989).

At age 65, widows can receive full Social Security benefits based on their husband's earnings or their own, whichever is larger. However, because most women aged 60 and over are unemployed, the majority opt for reduced benefits at age 62, an amount about 28.5 percent lower than what she would have received if her husband had lived to retire at age 65 (Hatch, 1990). Widowed women receive an average of $5,855 or 60 percent of their income from Social Security (Schwenk, 1992). This monthly income is barely adequate, even for women who support only themselves and their homes. Widowhood has been found to reduce living standards by 18 percent, on average, and to push 10 percent of women whose incomes were above the poverty line prior to widowhood into poverty after it (Bound et al., 1991). In fact, a 1992 study found that the average income of widowed old women was lower than that of divorced or never-married women. This difference reflects several factors: widowed women are likely to have had their resources depleted by their husband's illness, are less likely than divorced women to have current earnings, and may not be receiving any of their husband's pension income if he retired before the 1984 Retirement Equity Act and did not select survivors' benefits (Schwenk, 1992). As noted by the late Tish Sommers, the first president of the Older Women's League, "Motherhood and apple pie may be sacred, but neither guarantees economic security in old age" (1975).

Older women are also not immune to the growing divorce rate; 16 percent of divorces occur among women age 45 and over, and 1.3 percent occur among those age 65 and above; these rates continue to increase (AARP, 1991). Older divorced women experience a lower standard of living than do widows, with the majority lacking alimony payments and less than 50 percent receiving property settlements (Uhlenberg, Cooney, and Boyd, 1990). Further compounding the problem for divorced women is the Social Security regulation that a marriage of less than nine years' duration does not allow for the payment of a divorced spouse's Social Security benefits. Upon retirement, divorced wives married for at least ten years are entitled to a benefit amount of 50 percent of their ex-husbands' benefits. However, they are not eligible until the former husband reaches age 62, regardless of whether he has retired. Divorced and separated women are more likely to be employed out of economic necessity than are married women. Remarriage tends to be the most effective route out of post-divorce poverty, but with increasing age and number of children, the rate of remarriage declines (MacLean, 1991). Women who in their youth cared for children and parents thus frequently find themselves alone and with less than subsistence income in old age. These dire economic conditions have prompted a number of proposals to ensure homemakers' economic security in old age, such as paying them Social Security or some other form of income, but none of these proposals has received widespread Congressional support. The likelihood of such endorsement in the future is small, considering current legislative efforts to reduce federal spending.

Although not all old women are poor, those who rely primarily on their own resources are likely to have fewer assets such as savings, to have lower lifetime earnings, to depend on Social Security as their sole source of income, and to receive low benefits as retirees or disabled workers. While 95 percent of women receive Social Security, only 38 percent have income from interest or dividends, 28 percent from pensions or annuities, and 13 percent from earnings (Schwenk, 1992). Even though they form 60 percent of Social Security beneficiaries, older women are three times more likely than their male peers to receive only the minimum benefits. Yet, a person who receives only Social Security income is seven times more likely to be poor than one who also has wage and salary income (Older Women's League, 1986; 1990).

A number of political, social, and economic factors underlie these low benefit levels. One factor that affects both men and women age 70 and over is that the Social Security program was not established until 1935; thus, there are relatively fewer years upon which to base benefits for the cohort of older people today. An additional handicap for women is that they are more likely than men to have interrupted their employment for marriage and childrearing. Women of the current older cohort generally worked until marriage or the birth of children, and then withdrew from the paid labor force, either permanently or until their children were grown. They often assumed their first full-time job on the average of five years later than male workers. Even after becoming employed, they are more likely than their male counterparts to leave jobs to assume caregiving responsibilities, either for older generations or for a spouse, and usually not by choice (Estes, Swan, and Associates, 1993).

The average woman now spends nearly one-half of her life fulfilling the role of family caregiver to dependents, leaving the paid labor force to provide care for 11.5 years compared to 1.3 years for her male counterparts (Older Women's

League, 1990). For many women, such disconti-nuities carry severe economic costs, since years of lower or no earnings reduce their Social Security benefits and minimize the likelihood of their re-ceiving a private pension. This is because pension systems benefit traditional male work patterns that are not disrupted by family care responsibil-ities. Homemakers have no individual eligibility and no credits to add to their employment cred-its, and cannot receive disability supports on their own, despite the economic value of their household labor to their families. If they left the workforce to care for a husband during his final illness, this amounts to early retirement, espe-cially given the low probability of re-employment among older workers. They have lost not only wages but also the opportunity to develop higher earnings profiles and subsequently greater retire-ment benefits (Levy, 1988; Schulz, 1988).

Another factor affecting Social Security ben-efits for women is that those who are employed tend to be concentrated in part-time, short-term, or irregular and poorly paid jobs (Arendell and Estes, 1991). Even when they have been em-ployed throughout their lives, most women have received inadequate salaries, generally in low-status service, clerical, and retail-sales jobs. As a result, they frequently find that their husband's Social Security benefits are higher than benefits based on their own work records. In such in-stances, women who have worked all their lives in low-paying jobs are not much better off at re-tirement than women who have never worked for pay outside the home. As an example, in 1970, women's total average retirement benefits were 70 percent of their male counterparts; in 1990, despite more women in the paid work force, the figure increased to only 73 percent (Older Women's League, 1990). Because of lower retirement benefits, older women may find them-selves forced to continue working well beyond the age at which they would choose to retire (Herz, 1988).

Older women who have never married may be in better financial condition than their di-vorced or widowed counterparts. Data from the

1988–89 Consumer Expenditure Surveys by the Bureau of the Census and the Bureau of Labor Statistics reveal that, among this sample of over 3,000 mostly white women, never married older women had an average annual income 26 percent greater than widowed women, and 12 percent greater than divorced women. They were also far more likely to derive their income from pensions and annuities, as well as from interest and divi-dends. This survey also found that never married women spent less on housing and health care than did widowed women, in spite of their com-parable ages (Schwenk, 1992).

Women are also less likely to have private pensions than men, both because of their con-centration in low-paying positions and their shorter work careers, and because mandatory pension laws were not in effect when many women of this cohort were employed (i.e., in the 1920's and 1930's). As discussed in Chapter 14, pension plans reward the long-term steady worker with high earnings and job stability, a pattern that tends to be more characteristic of men than of women who have interrupted their careers to marry, rear children, and perhaps care for older relatives. This continues to be the trend even among the current cohort of women. Over 40 percent of men are covered by private pen-sions, compared with fewer than 20 percent of women who have been employed (Older Women's League, 1995). Those women with pensions receive approximately half the benefit income of men because of salary differentials during their working years (Older Women's League, 1995). A woman whose family role re-sulted in economic dependence on her husband can benefit from his private pension only if he is covered by one, does not die before retirement age, stays married to her, and is willing to reduce his monthly benefits in order to provide her with a survivor annuity. Given the economic vicissi-tudes of aging, most older men choose higher monthly benefits rather than survivors' benefits. Such a choice can be detrimental to older women, since, as noted earlier, most wives out-live their husbands by an average of eight years.

Fortunately, pension provisions enacted by Congress in 1980 will benefit older women by shortening the time it takes to earn a pension and improving coverage for lower income workers, for those who begin work after age 60, and for those who continue to work after age 65. However, most of these provisions are effective for pension plans that began in January 1989, and thus do not affect the current cohort of old women. In addition, the federal laws designed to provide protection to spouses of private pension plans do not apply to state government pension plans. As a result, 26 states do not have a "spousal consent" requirement before a plan participant waives survivor benefits. Thus a wife may discover only after the death of her husband that she will no longer be entitled to pension benefits which were paid prior to her husband's death (AARP, 1994). Another limitation is that most policies to address women's special vulnerability as nonemployed or late entry workers have focused on improving the financial well-being of older women in danger of being impoverished, not old women who have been poor throughout life.

The economic outlook for women in the future remains bleak. One reason for this is that when middle-aged and older women are employed, they are more likely to hold the growing number of part-time and poorly paid jobs in the service sector (DeViney and O'Rand, 1988; Rodehaever, 1990). It is predicted that by the year 2020, poverty will remain widespread among old women living alone—those who are divorced, widowed, or never married—while Social Security and pension systems will have practically eroded poverty among old men and couples (Older Women's League, 1990). Older women without private pensions and whose Social Security income falls below the poverty line must rely on Supplemental Security Income (SSI). In fact, women comprise nearly 75 percent of older SSI recipients (Older Women's League, 1995). For those women who value economic self-sufficiency, dependency on the government for such support can be stigmatizing.

In summary, traditional family caregiving roles of women tend to result in discontinuous employment work histories. This pattern, combined with limited pension opportunities and lower Social Security benefits, produces a double jeopardy for women's economic status in old age. Unfortunately, most changes in Social Security and pension laws have improved the benefits of women as dependents rather than as employees. As discussed in the following section, the disadvantaged economic position of old women also increases their health risks.

## OLDER WOMEN'S HEALTH STATUS

As noted in Chapter 7, older people who are poor, represented primarily by women and ethnic minorities, tend to be less healthy than higher-income older adults. Their living conditions are not conducive to good health. Compared to their wealthier peers, they are more likely to be living alone, to have inadequate diets, to have less access to information about how to maintain their health, and to have fewer dental visits and physician contacts per year (Van Mering and O'Rand, 1981). Since older women, especially the divorced and widowed, predominate among the older poor, women's health status is more frequently harmed by the adverse conditions associated with poverty than is men's. In turn, the cost of poor health can deplete the limited resources of the low-income poor.

### Less Access to Health Insurance

Previous family and work patterns affect older women's access to adequate health care and health maintenance information. Specifically, the workplace determines such access through opportunities to enroll in group insurance plans. Most insurance systems exclude the occupation of homemaker, except as a dependent. As a result, older women who are never or sporadically employed generally have inadequate health insurance. Low-income divorced or widowed women, unable to rely on their husbands' insurance, are especially disadvantaged. Divorced women are about twice as likely to lack health insurance as married women, and are more likely than widows to be uninsured. Some 40 percent of all divorced women and 27 percent of all widows not in the labor force have no private health insurance (Older Women's League, 1986). Some uninsured women gamble on staying healthy until qualifying for Medicare coverage at age 65. Since the incidence of chronic diseases is higher among older women than among men, many women do not win this gamble. Yet they may not qualify for Medicaid. The late Tish Sommers, founder of the Older Women's League, represented this group of women. When she was diagnosed with cancer in her late fifties, she was too young to qualify for Medicare, too sick to obtain private insurance, and, as a divorcee, unable to turn to her former husband's insurance. Groups such as the Older Women's League have succeeded in advocating for conversion laws that require insurance companies to allow widowed and divorced women to remain in their spouse's group insurance for up to three years.

Even with adequate health insurance, older women spend 33 percent of their median annual income for out-of-pocket health care costs. It is estimated that, in 1986, Medicare paid for approximately 49 percent of the health care expenditures of older unmarried men, but only 33 percent of the expenditures of older single women (Older Women's League, 1987). (See Chapter 20 for a detailed discussion of the limitations of Medicare coverage that affect old women.)

Because of their lower socioeconomic status, older women are more likely than men to depend on Medicaid, forming over 60 percent of Medicaid recipients (Davis and Rowland, 1991). An insidious negative effect of this dependency is that health care providers, fearing financial losses, are often unwilling to accept Medicaid patients, making it difficult for older women to obtain adequate care. Male-female differences in longevity, marital status, and income are central

in assessing the impact of recent increases in Medicaid co-payments and deductibles. Women outnumber men two to one among frail elders, for whom health and long-term care use and costs are greatest. This means that, as Medicaid costs are shifted to the patient, more low-income frail women will be unable to afford health care. For example, co-payment provisions in Medicaid may force some women to choose between prescriptions and groceries, or between clinic visits and the bus fare to get there.

Women more than men would benefit from implementation of national health care reform that would guarantee universal access. The Women's Health Equity Act of 1991 was intended to give women's health issues the same resources and visibility as those that mostly affect men, but given their lower socioeconomic status, women will still be less likely to be insured than their male counterparts.

## Higher Incidence of Chronic Health Problems

Limited insurance options and greater dependence on Medicaid are especially problematic because 85 percent of old women have some kind of chronic disease or disability. As discussed in Chapter 7, older women experience arthritis, hypertension, strokes, diabetes, most digestive and urinary problems (except ulcer and hernia), incontinence, most types of orthopedic problems, and visual impairments more frequently than do older men.

Contrary to common perceptions that men are at higher risk of heart attacks than are women, cardiovascular disease is the number one killer for both men and women, although men do experience the symptoms of coronary heart disease at younger ages. And coronary heart disease kills five times as many women as breast cancer does. This is because, as noted in Chapter 7, women lose the advantage of protection from estrogen after menopause and have a longer life expectancy than do men after ages 45–55. Women also face health problems specifically associated with their reproductive functions, such as breast, cervical, and uterine cancers—all of which have increased in recent years—as well as high-risk complications from hysterectomies. Tragically, women over age 60 who are most at risk of cancers of the reproductive system are least likely to have annual pap smears (Older Women's League, 1987). In the past 25 years, the chances of a woman developing breast cancer have grown from 1 in 16 to 1 in 9, while prevention, diagnosis, and treatment have lagged. One fortunate change, taken by Congress in 1990, was to include mammography screening as a biennial Medicare benefit, but physicians frequently do not refer older women for mammography (Leonard, 1991). As noted in Chapter 7, although women suffer from more chronic health conditions, most of these are not life-threatening; they do, however, interfere with daily functioning and require frequent physician contacts.

For example, over 50 percent of women age 70 to 74 find it difficult or impossible to lift or carry 25 pounds, and 60 percent of women over age 65 have been screened out of random public physical fitness testing for reasons of health risk. This lack of basic strength increases the likelihood of falls (O'Brien and Vertinsky, 1991). Although men tend to experience fewer daily aches and pains than do women, when they do become ill, they are more likely to face life-threatening conditions and to require hospitalization. These differences in types of chronic health problems may be one reason why women live longer than men, even though they are less healthy (Manton, 1989). Male-female differences in death rates can also be attributed to immunity, environmental hazards, health habits and utilization of services, personality styles, and differences in reactions to and knowledge about disease and disability (Lewis, 1985).

Compared to their male counterparts, older women also experience more injuries and more days of restricted activity and bed disability. These measures are generally indicators of chronic disorders, such as high blood pressure and arthritis, although it may be that they reflect women's greater readiness to take curative action and spend more time in bed recuperating when they are ill. Among people aged 75 and over, gender differences in patterns of illness become even more striking, with women forming about 69 percent of nursing home residents (Older Women's League, 1987). There are, of course, several factors besides health status that may account for such differences. As discussed in Chapter 12, old men are more likely to be married, with wives to care for them at home instead of being placed in a nursing home. Women over age 75, on the other hand, have few available resources for home-based care, and are often unable to afford private home health services. In addition, as noted earlier, men who survive to age 75 and older are the healthiest and hardiest of their cohort.

## Osteoporosis

Of those older people with osteoporosis, 90 percent are women (Gambrell, 1987). As noted in Chapter 7, women begin losing bone mass between 30 and 35 years of age, resulting in a 35 percent reduction in their bone mineral content by 65 years of age and 50 percent by age 75, with a consequent increase in the risk of bone fracture. The higher incidence of hip fractures is one reason for the greater number of injuries and days of restricted activity among old women. Also, as noted in Chapter 7, many hip fractures are associated with postmenopausal osteoporosis, and up to 35 percent of these patients die within six months (Gambrell, 1987; Older Women's League, 1994). Most of these deaths result from post-operative complications, such as a pulmonary embolism, which occur more often among older women. The incidence of hip fractures in older women doubles every five years after the age of 60 (Gambrell, 1987). Although women who take estrogen for at least seven years between menopause and age 75 have been found to reduce their risk of fracture by half during that time, recent studies indicate little difference after age 75, the period when women are most at risk.

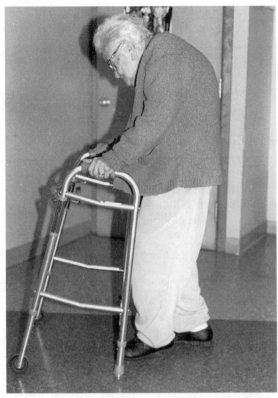

Osteoporosis can make movement difficult and painful.

The threat of hip fractures can create numerous fears among older women—of additional falls, further fractures, hospitalization, institutionalization, loss of independence, and death. As a result, an older woman's social world may become increasingly circumscribed, with accompanying feelings of isolation and loneliness. As for the expenses to society, the long-term care costs entailed by hip fractures are approximately $3.8 billion a year (Gambrell, 1987). The value of strategies that prevent falls and minimize injuries is increasingly recognized.

## Menopause

The physiological changes associated with menopause were discussed in Chapter 10. Social attitudes can make menopause troublesome as well, given that many of its associated discomforts result from society's tendency to view menopause as a disease, rather than as a normal biological process. Hence, many women anticipate that depression, loss of sexual desire and sexual attractiveness, and such signs of aging as wrinkled skin and weight gain are inevitable. Contrary to such expectations, menopause is not an illness or a deficiency. It can, however, be a major transition for many women. Menopausal symptoms thus provide another example of the interaction of normal physiological changes with psychological conditions and societal expectations.

The culturally prevalent model of menopause as a disease attributes changes to loss of estrogen. When thus defined as a "deficiency disease," a treatment implication is that estrogen must be replaced. Accordingly, the primary medical response to treating symptoms such as hot flashes has been hormone replacement therapy. When menopause is viewed as a normal life transition, however, lower estrogen levels among postmenopausal women can then be considered normal. Recently, many women have been using nonmedical approaches to minimize uncomfortable symptoms. These include hypnosis, biofeedback, relaxation techniques, exercise, support groups, herbal remedies, Vitamin E, and diets low in fats and preservatives and high in fiber and calcium.

Although the disease model of menopause links depression with the endocrine changes that occur, depression among postmenopausal women appears to be more closely associated with psychosocial variables, particularly changes in women's roles and relationships, than with physiological factors. Menopausal women who experience depression tend to have invested heavily in childrearing responsibilities and to lack supportive social networks, other satisfying roles, and skills for effectively coping with their role changes, although this is not always the case (Bart, 1981; Neugarten et al., 1968). Health care providers have often treated the symptoms of depression with drugs, or have assumed that middle-aged and older women were "too old" to benefit from therapeutic interventions. More recently, efforts have been made to provide women with ways of exerting control over their lives, such as assertiveness training, and to develop women's counseling and social support interventions as a means of combating depression. Such social support groups have been found to reduce women's feelings of isolation and to enhance their self-esteem and self-control.

## OLDER WOMEN'S SOCIAL STATUS

Older women's physical and mental health problems are frequently intensified by the greater likelihood of their living alone. For example, old women who live alone are more likely to be diagnosed as malnourished. This is not surprising when the social functions of eating are considered. The older person living alone may derive no pleasure from eating and may skip meals, subsisting instead on such snacks as tea and cookies. The high poverty rates among older women who live alone, as we have seen earlier in this chapter, may also account for their poor eating habits. Even mild nutritional deficiencies may produce disorientation, confusion, depression, and reduced ability to respond to stress. One result is that a person with few immediate social supports may be less likely to resist infections and viral diseases. Her ability to live in the community may thus be sharply curtailed.

Nearly 50 percent of older women (compared to 16 percent of older men) live alone for approximately one-third of their adult lives, primarily because of widowhood or divorce. Among widowed, divorced and never-married women, the percentage living alone increases to 68 percent (Schwenk, 1992). At the turn of the century, widows lived alone for 5 to 10 years; now, the average is 24 years alone at the same time that fewer adult children are available to provide care (Huckle, 1991). Women comprise 80 percent of the older population who live alone. In fact, only 33 percent of all women aged

65 and over live with their husbands, and only 20 percent live with other family members, generally a daughter (AARP, 1991). Among women aged 75 and over, the percentage living with their husbands drops to less than 25 percent, and the proportion living alone increases to over 50 percent, a rate at least twice that of their male counterparts (Kasper, 1988). However, older minority divorced and widowed women are more likely to live in extended family households. For example, African American and Mexican women often extend their households to include children and grandchildren, taking on child care and housekeeping responsibilities into old age (Choi, 1991).

### Widowhood

As discussed in Chapter 16, the average age of widowhood for women is 56 years; therefore, it is not surprising that 85 percent of all wives outlive their husbands. Because women generally marry men older than themselves, live longer than men, and, in their later years, seldom remarry after the deaths of their husbands, widowhood is a more common status for females than for males. Some 52 percent of women aged 65 and over are widowed, in contrast to 14 percent of men in this age group. This gap increases dramatically with age, with 73 percent of women over 80 years of age widowed. The expected years of widowhood are far more than the four-year difference in life expectancy between women and men at these ages. At age 65 a widow can anticipate living another 18 years, at age 70, 11 years and at age 85, another 9 years (Burkhauser, 1991). Moreover, this increased time living alone is accompanied by shrinking family size, with fewer children as potential caregivers (Huckle, 1991).

As noted previously, the primary negative consequence of widowhood is low socioeconomic status with over 30 percent of older widows living alone and in poverty. These economic conditions have numerous social implications; low-income women have fewer options to interact with others, fewer affordable and safe accommodations, and fewer resources to purchase in-home support services. The most negative consequence may be that older women's economic situation precludes continued independent living when health problems arise. Despite these objective disadvantages of widowhood, recent studies are challenging the stereotype of the "lonely widow," finding that widowhood does not necessarily produce the major, enduring negative emotional effects that typically have been reported (O'Bryant and Morgan, 1990; Hatch and Bulcroft, 1992).

## Divorce

Divorced women are even more vulnerable to social and economic problems. Compared to both their married and widowed peers, divorced women aged 65 and over have been found to have poorer health, higher mortality rates, and lower levels of life satisfaction. If divorced earlier in life, the disadvantages of having no financial support and often being employed in low-paying positions may have resulted in a lifetime of marginal economic security.

## Limited Opportunities to Remarry

Although remarriage may be viewed as a way to ensure economic security, older widowed and divorced women have fewer remarriage options than do their male peers. The primary obstacles to remarriage are the disproportionate number of women to men age 65 and over, and the cultural stigma against women marrying younger men. At age 65 and over, remarriage rates are 2 per 1,000 for unmarried women compared to 17 per 1,000 for unmarried men. Some 77 percent of men age 65 and older are married, compared to 41 percent of women (AARP, 1991). As noted earlier, with the ratio of 80-year-old women to men being three to one, the chances for remarriage decline drastically with age (Hess and Waring, 1983). These differences lead to differential needs for support in the face of failing health

(e.g., most older men are cared for by their wives, whereas most older women rely on their children, usually daughters, for help). As discussed in Chapter 13, women are the primary caregivers of older relatives. Increasingly, adult daughters who assist their widowed mothers are themselves in their sixties and seventies, and are faced with their own physical limitations. One consequence of this pattern is that older women may have to depend more on public support services. They are thus the primary informal providers of care as well as the major users of public services. As invisible laborers, women's work is essential to the health care system and to their relatives' long-term care, but it is not well supported by public policies.

In addition to having high rates of widowhood and increasing rates of divorce, the current cohort of old women had relatively high rates of remaining unmarried throughout their lives (approximately 8 percent for women now in their seventies and eighties), so that a cohort effect also may explain the large numbers of older women living without spouses. Another factor that increases the probability of being alone among this current cohort of older women is that approximately one in five has either been childless throughout her life or has survived her offspring (Hess and Waring, 1983).

It appears that widows without children tend to be more lonely and dissatisfied than widows who have adult children (Beckman and Houser, 1982). The absence of children and spouse also increases the chance of being placed in a nursing home. This suggests that women are more likely to be institutionalized for social rather than medical reasons, and may be inappropriately placed in a nursing home when alternative community supports might have permitted more independent lifestyles. As a result, women form over 70 percent of nursing home residents, with the majority of them widowed or single, often dependent on Medicaid and lacking family members to assist them either socially or financially. After age 85, one in four women, especially never-married and widowed women, are in nursing homes (Hess and Waring, 1983).

In general, older women have fewer economic but more social resources and richer, more intimate relationships than do older men. However, men tend to have larger non-kin networks, perhaps as a result of employment (Depner and Ingersoll, 1982; Goldberg, Kantrow, Kremen and Lauter, 1986; Keith, 1983; Kohen, 1983; Peters, Hoty, Babchuck, Kaiser, and Iijima, 1987). Widowed women, in particular, tend to have more frequent and intimate contacts with friends (Hatch and Bulcroft, 1992). Even when their friends die, women generally establish new relationships, exchanging affection and material assistance outside their families, although they may not feel that such relationships should be called upon to provide them with secure care. Instead, they value the mutuality of their friendships and do not want to become dependent upon friends (Rubenstein et al., 1991). Support groups for widows and family caregivers build on such reciprocal exchange relations among peers. With age, some women first become comfortable with being open about their lesbianism and their strong emotional bonds with other women, although they may face rejection from their adult children when they do so. One function of the affirmation of women's competencies by the women's movement has been to encourage them to support each other rather than depend on men, as evidenced by the growth of shared households, older women's support and advocacy groups, and intergenerational alliances.

## FUTURE DIRECTIONS

Since women's socioeconomic status compounds most of the problems they face in old age, fundamental changes are needed to remove inequities in the workplace, Social Security, and pension systems. Most such changes, however, will benefit future generations of older women, rather than the current cohort, which was socialized for work and family roles that no longer prevail. For

example, recent efforts in some states to assure that women and men earn equal pay for jobs of comparable economic worth and to remove other salary inequities may mean that future generations of old women will have retirement benefits based on a lifetime of more adequate earnings, and will have more experience in handling finances. Some businesses and government agencies have initiated more flexible work arrangements with full benefits, which will allow men and women to share employment and family responsibilities more equitably. When such options exist, women may have fewer years of zero earnings to be calculated into their Social Security benefits, and will be more likely to hold jobs covered by private pensions. Even so, it is predicted that 60 percent of women in the year 2030 will still have had five or more years of zero earnings averaged into the calculation of their Social Security benefits, widening the current gap between older women living alone and all other groups (Davis and Rowland, 1991). This is in large part due to the fact that despite three decades of legislation, women have not achieved equality in the work force. Women remain disproportionately in the secondary labor market, marked by low wages, few benefits, part-time employment, and

Women frequently provide emotional support within the multi-generational family.

little job security (Holstein, 1993). Even the entrance of more women into previously male-dominated positions has not resulted in a significant restructuring of the distribution of responsibilities within families, with women still responsible for the majority of child care and housework (Hochschild and Machung, 1989).

Changes in Social Security that would benefit women workers have been proposed by a number of federal studies and commissions. The current Social Security system is based on an outmoded model of lifelong marriage, in which one spouse is the paid worker, and the other is the homemaker. As the prior discussion of divorce and changing work patterns suggests, this model no longer accommodates the emerging diversity of employment and family roles. Nor for that matter has this model really represented the diversity of American families. The most commonly discussed remedy is earnings sharing, whereby each partner in marriage is entitled to a separate Social Security account, regardless of which spouse is employed in the paid labor force. Covered earnings would be divided between two spouses, with one-half credited to each spouse's account. Credits for homemaking, benefits for widows under age 62, full benefits for widows after age 65, and the option of collecting benefits as both worker and wife have also been discussed by senior citizen advocacy groups and by some legislators. Given the large federal deficit, the likelihood of any such changes being instituted in the next few years is small. Pension reforms have also been passed on the federal level that would increase by more than 20 percent the number of women covered by private pensions, by reducing the amount of time required for vesting. In the long run, changes are needed in society's view of work throughout the life cycle, so that men and women may share more equitably in caregiving and employment responsibilities. At the same time, employers must recognize that skills gained through homemaking and voluntary activity are legitimate and transferable to the marketplace. The ways in which women contribute to society through their caregiving, housekeeping responsi-bilities, and informal helping of others along with voluntarism also need to be recognized under a broad concept of productivity, rather than equating productivity only with paid work (Holstein, 1993).

An observable positive change in recent years is that more women of all ages are supporting one another, as illustrated by the intergenerational advocacy efforts of the Older Women's League and the National Action Forum for Women. Another promising change is the growth of social support groups among old women. Groups of older widows and women caregivers have been found to be effective in reducing women's isolation. They have encouraged group members to meet their own needs and have expanded women's awareness of public services to which they are entitled. This function of educating and politicizing older women has also helped many to see the societal causes of the difficulties that they have experienced as individuals. Awareness of external causes of their problems may also serve to bring together for common action women of diverse ages, ethnic backgrounds, socioeconomic classes, and sexual orientation. As women unite to work for change, they can make further progress in reducing the disadvantages of their economic and social position.

## SUMMARY AND IMPLICATIONS

Old women are the fastest growing segment of our population, making the aging society primarily female. In addition, the problems of aging are increasingly the problems of women. Threats to Social Security, inadequate health and long-term care, and insufficient pensions are issues for women of all ages. Increasingly, older women are not only the recipients of social and health services, but also are cared for by other women, who are unpaid daughters and daughters-in-law, or staff within public social services, nursing homes, and hospitals.

Women's family caregiving roles are interconnected with their economic, social, and health status. Women who devoted their lives to attending to the needs of children, spouses, or older relatives often face years of living alone on low or poverty level incomes, with inadequate health care, in substandard housing, and with little chance for employment to supplement their limited resources. Older women face more problems in old age, not only because they live longer than their male peers, but also because, as unpaid or underpaid caregivers with discontinuous employment histories, they have not accrued adequate retirement or health care benefits. If they have depended on their husbands for economic security, divorce or widowhood increases their risks of poverty. As one of the poorest groups in our society, women account for nearly three-fourths of the older poor. The incidence of problems associated with poverty increases dramatically for older women living alone, for ethnic minority women, and for those age 75 and over. Frequently outliving their children and husbands, they have no one to care for them and are more likely than their male counterparts to be in nursing homes.

On the other hand, many women show remarkable resilience in the face of adversity. Fortunately, the number of exceptions to patterns of economic deprivation and social isolation is growing. With their lifelong experiences of caring for others, for example, women tend to be skilled at forming and sustaining friendships with each other, which provide them with social support and intimacy. Recently, increasing attention has been paid to old women's capacity for change and to their strengths, largely because of efforts of advocacy groups such as the Older Women's League. Current efforts to improve the employment and educational opportunities available to younger women will undoubtedly mean improved economic, social, and health status for future generations of women.

## REFERENCES

American Association of Retired Persons (AARP). *Roundtable on older women in the work force.* Washington, D.C.: AARP, 1986.

American Association of Retired Persons (AARP). *A profile of older Americans, 1986.* Washington, D.C.: AARP, 1987.

American Association of Retired Persons (AARP). *America: Changing work force.* Washington, D.C.: AARP, 1988.

American Association of Retired Persons (AARP). *A profile of older Americans, 1990.* Washington, D.C.: AARP, 1991.

American Association of Retired Persons (AARP). *Falling short: A 50-state survey of spousal rights under state pension plans.* Washington, D.C.: AARP, 1994.

Arendell, T., and Estes, C. Older women in the post-Reagan era. In M. Minkler and C. Estes (Eds.), *Critical perspectives on aging: The political and moral economy of growing old.* Amityville, N.Y.: Baywood Publishing, 1991, 209–226.

Arendell, T., and Estes, C. Unsettled future: Older women—economics and health. *Feminist Issues,* 1987, Spring, 3–24.

Backman, L., and Houser, B. The consequences of childlessness on the social-psychological well-being of older women. *Journal of Gerontology,* 1982, 37, 243–250.

Bart, P. Mental health issues: Is the end of the curse a blessing? *Health issues of older women.* Stony Brook: State University of New York, 1981.

Bass, S., Torres-Gil, F., and Kutza, B. On the relationship between the diversity of the aging population and public policy. *Journal of Aging and Social Policy,* 1991, 2, 101–116.

Berk, M., and Taylor, A. Women and divorce: Health insurance coverage, utilization, and health care expenditures. *American Journal of Public Health,* 1984, 74, 1276–1278.

Bernstein, M. C. Forecasting women's retirement income: Cloudy and colder and 25 percent chance of poverty. In M. Fuller and C. Martin (Eds.), *The older woman: Lavender rose or gray panther.* Springfield, Ill.: Charles C. Thomas, 1980.

Bound, J., Duncan, G., Laren, D. S., and Oleinick, L. Poverty dynamics in widowhood. *Journals of Gerontology,* 1991, 46, S115–124.

Brody, E. Parent care as a normative family stress. *The Gerontologist,* 1985, 25, 19–30.

Burkhauser, R. V. How public policy increases the vulnerability of older widows. *Journal of Aging and Social Policy,* 1991, 2, 117–130.

Buskirk, E. R. Exercise, fitness and aging. In C. Bouchard, R. J. Shephard, T. Stephens, J. R. Sutton, and B. D. McPherson (Eds.), *Exercise, fitness and health*. Champaign, Ill.: Human Kinetics Publishers, 1990.

Carter, L. *Canada's health promotion survey*. Ottawa: Health and Welfare Canada, 1988.

Chappell, N. L., and Haven, B. Old and female: Testing the double jeopardy hypothesis. *The Sociological Quarterly*, 1980, *21*, 157–171.

Choi, N. Racial differences in the determinants of living arrangements of widowed and divorced elderly women. *The Gerontologist*, 1991, *31*, 496–504.

Coalition on Women and the Budget. *Inequality of sacrifice: The impact of the Reagan budget on women*, Washington, D.C.: National Women's Law Center, 1984.

Davis, K., and Rowland, D. Old and poor: Policy challenges in the 1990's. *Journal of Aging and Social Policy*, 1991, *2*, 37–59.

Depner, C., and Ingersoll, B. Employment status and social support: The experience of the mature woman. In M. Szinovacz (Ed.), *Women's retirement: Policy implications for recent research*. Beverly Hills, Sage, 1982, 61–76.

DeViney, S., and O'Rand, A. Gender-cohort succession and retirement among older men and women, 1951–1984. *Sociological Quarterly*, 1988, *29*(4), 525–540.

Estes, C. L. Older women and poverty. Presented at the annual meeting of the Western Gerontological Society, Denver, Colorado, March 1985.

Estes, C. L., Swan J., & Associates. *The long-term care crisis*. Newbury Park, Calif.: Sage Publications, 1993.

Friends of the San Francisco Commission on the Status of Women. *Womennews*, December 1980, 1.

Gambrell, R. D. Estrogen replacement therapy for the elderly woman. *Medical Aspects of Human Sexuality*, 1987, *21*(5), 81–93.

Goldberg, G., Kantrow, R., Kremen, E., and Lauter, L. Spouseless, childless elderly women and their social supports. *Social Work*, 1986, *31*(2), 104–112.

Gottlieb, N. Families, work, and the lives of older women. In J. D. Garner and S. Mercer (Eds.), *Women as they age: Challenge, opportunity, and triumph*. New York: Haworth Press, 1989, 217–244.

Hatch, L. R. Gender and work at midlife and beyond. *Generations*, 1990, *14*(3), 48–52.

Hatch, L., and Bulcroft, K. Contact with friends in later life: Disentangling the effects of gender and mental status. *Journal of Marriage and the Family*, 1992, *54*, 222–232.

Herz, D. Bureau of Labor Statistics. Employment characteristics of older women, 1987. *Monthly Labor Review* (September, 1988), 3.

Hess, B., and Waring, J. Family relationships of older women: A women's issue. In E. Markson (Ed.), *Older women*. Lexington, Mass.: Lexington Books, 1983.

Hochschild, A., and Machung, A. *The second shift: Inside the two-job marriage*. New York: Viking Press, 1989.

Holstein, M. Women's lives, women's work: Productivity, gender, and aging. In S. A. Bass, F. G. Caro, and Y-P Chen (Eds.), *Achieving a productive aging society*. Westport, Conn.: Auburn House, 1993, 235–248.

Huckle, P. *Tish Sommers, activist and the founder of the Older Women's League*. Knoxville: The University of Tennessee Press, 1991.

Huyck, M. *Understanding gender diversity in later life*. Paper presented at the Annual Convention of the American Psychological Association. San Francisco, Calif.: August 1991.

Jacobs, B. Public policy and poverty among the oldest old: Looking to 2040. *Journal of Aging and Social Policy*, 1991, *2*, 85–99.

Kasper, J. *Aging alone: Profiles and projections*. Baltimore, Md.: The Commonwealth Fund Commission, 1988.

Keith, P. M. A comparison of the resources of parents and childless men and women in very old age. *Family Relations*, 1983, *32*, 403–409.

Kohen, J. A. Old but not alone: Informal social supports among the elderly by marital status and sex. *The Gerontologist*, 1983, *23*, 57–63.

Kravitz, S., Pelaez, M., and Rothman, M. Delivering services to elders: Responsiveness to populations in need. In S. Bass, E. Kutza, and F. M. Torres-Gil (Eds.), *Diversity in aging*. Glenview, Ill.: Scott, Foresman & Co., 1991, 47–71.

Leonard, F. The curse. *The Owl Observer*, September/October, 1991, 7.

Lesnoff-Caravaglia, G. (Ed.), *The world of the older woman*. New York: Human Sciences Press, 1984.

Levy, J. A. Intersections of gender and aging. *The Sociological Quarterly,* 1988, *29*(4), 479–486.

Lewis, M. Older women and health. *Women and Health,* 1985, *10* (2–3), 1–16.

Luben, J., and Becerra, R. M. Social support among black, Mexican and Chinese elderly. In D. E. Gelford and C. H. Barreri (Eds.), *Ethnic dimensions of aging.* New York: Springer, 1987, 130–144.

MacLean, M. *Surviving divorce: Women's resources after separation.* New York: MacMillan, 1991.

Manton, K. G. Disability policy: Restoring socioeconomic independence. *The Milbank Quarterly,* 1989, *67*(2), 13–58.

Markson, E. *Older women.* Lexington, Mass.: Lexington Books, 1983.

Martin-Matthews, M. A. Widowhood as an expectable life event. In V. Marshall (ed.), *Aging in Canada,* Markham, Ont.: Fitzhenry and Whiteside, 1987.

Minkler, M., and Stone R. The feminization of poverty and older women. *The Gerontologist,* 1985, *25*(4), 351–357.

Nathan, S. The impact of poverty on the minority elderly: Implications for geriatric education. In Harper, M. S. (Ed.), *Minority aging,* DHHS Publication #HRS (P-DV-90-4). Washington, D.C.: U.S. Government Printing Office, 1990.

National Center for Health Statistics. *Health: United States.* DHHS Pub. No. (DHS) 88-1232, Public Health Service. Washington, D.C.: U.S. Government Printing Office, 1989.

Neugarten, B., Wood, V., Kraines, R., and Loomis, B. Women's attitudes toward the menopause. *Middle age and aging.* Chicago: University of Chicago Press, 1968.

O'Brien, S., and Vertinsky, P. Unfit survivors: Exercise as a resource for aging women. *The Gerontologist,* 1991, *31*, 347–348.

O'Bryant, S., and Morgan, C. Recent widows' kin support and orientations to self-sufficiency. *The Gerontologist,* 1990, *30*, 391–398.

Older Women's League. *Report on the status of midlife and older women in America.* Washington, D.C.: Older Women's League, 1986.

Older Women's League. *The picture of health for midlife and older women.* Washington, D.C.: Older Women's League, 1987.

Older Women's League. *Heading for hardship: Retirement income for American women in the next century.* Washington, D.C.: Older Women's League, 1990.

Older Women's League. *Paying for prejudice.* Washington, D.C.: Older Women's League, 1991.

Older Women's League. *The Path to Poverty: An Analysis of Women's Retirement Income.* Washington, D.C.: Older Women's League, 1995.

Older Women's League. *Status Report on Osteoporosis.* Washington, D.C., 1994.

O'Rand, A. M. Women. In E. Palmore (Ed.), *Handbook on the aged in the United States.* Westport, Conn.: Greenwood Press, 1984.

Peters, G., Hoty, D., Babchuck, N., Kaiser, M., and Iijima, Y. Primary group support systems of the aged. *Research on Aging,* 1987, *9,* 392–416.

Quinn, J. F., and Smeeding T. M. Defying the averages: Poverty and well-being among older Americans. *Aging Today,* September/October 1994, *XV*(5), 9.

Raphael, S., and Robinson, M. The older lesbian: Love relationships and friendship patterns. *Alternate Lifestyles,* 1980, *3* (2), 207–229.

Riley, M., and Riley, J. Longevity and social structure: The potential of the added years. In A. Pifer and L. Bronte (Eds.), *Our aging society: Paradox and promise.* New York: W. W. Norton, 1986.

Rix, S. *Older women: The economics of aging.* Washington, D.C.: Women's Research and Education Institute, 1984.

Roberto, K. A., and Scott, J. P. Confronting widowhood. *American Behavioral Scientist,* 1986, *29,* 497–511.

Rodehaever, D. Labor market progeria. *Generations,* Summer 1990, *14*(3), 53–59.

Rubenstein, R., Alexander, B., Goodman, M., and Lubovsky, M. Key relationships of never-married, childless older women: A cultural analysis. *Journals of Gerontology,* 1991, *46,* S270–277.

Schulz, J. *The economics of aging* (4th ed.). Belmont, Calif.: Wadsworth, 1988.

Schwenk, F. N. Income and Expenditures of older widowed, divorced, and never-married women who live alone. *Family Economics Review,* 1992, *5*(1), 2–8.

Scott, H. *Working your way to the bottom: The feminization of poverty.* London: Pandora Press, 1984.

Sommers, T. On growing old female: An interview with Tish Sommers. *Aging,* 1975, Nov.–Dec, 11.

Taeuber, C. Diversity: The dramatic reality. In S. Bass, E. Kutza, and F. M. Torres-Gil (Eds.),

*Diversity in aging.* Glenview, Il.: Scott, Foresman, 1991, 1–47.

Uhlenberg, P., Cooney, T., and Boyd, R. Divorce for women after midlife. *Journals of Gerontology,* 1990, *45,* S3–11.

U.S. Bureau of the Census. Social and economic characteristics of the older population. *Current population reports: Special studies.* Series P-25, No. 85, August 1979. Washington, D.C.: U.S. Government Printing Office.

U.S. Bureau of the Census. *Money income and poverty status in the United States: 1989 Current Population Survey.* Washington, D.C.: U.S. Department of Commerce, 1990.

U.S. Senate Special Committee on Aging. *America in transition: An aging society.* Washington, D.C.: U.S. Government Printing Office, 1985.

U.S. Senate Special Committee on Aging. *Aging America: Trends and projections, 1991 edition.* Washington, D.C.: U.S. Department of Health and Human Services, 1992.

U.S. Senate Special Committee on Aging. *Developments in aging: 1989* (Vol. I). Washington, D.C.: U.S. Government Printing Office, 1990.

Van Mering, G., and O'Rand, A. M. Aging, illness and the organization of health care: A sociocultural perspective. In C. L. Fry (Ed.), *Dimensions: Aging, culture and health.* New York: Praeger, 1981.

Vaughn, D. R. Development and evaluation of a survey based type of benefit classification for the Social Security program. *Social Security Bulletin,* 1989, *52,* 12–26.

Verbrugge, L. An epidemiological profile of older women. In M. Haug, A. Ford, and M. Sheafor (Eds.), *The physical and mental health of aged women.* New York: Springer, 1985.

Verbrugge, L. The twain meet: Empirical explanations of sex differences in health and mortality. *Journal of Health and Social Behavior,* 1989, *30,* 282–304.

Verbrugge, L. Pathway to health and death. In R. D. Apple (Ed.), *Women, health and medicine in America: A historical handbook.* New York and London: Garland Publishers, 1990.

Waldron, I. An analysis of causes of sex differences in mortality and morbidity. In W. R. Gove and G. M. Carpenter, (Eds.), *The fundamental connection between nature and nurture: A review of the evidence.* Lexington, Mass.: D. C. Heath, 1982.

# PART **Five**

# THE SOCIETAL CONTEXT OF AGING

The final section of this book examines aging and older people from the broader context of society. The values and beliefs that policy makers and voters hold toward a particular group or topic are often the basis on which policies are made. To the extent that these policies also are grounded in knowledge, they can aid the status of that group. On the other hand, policies that are based solely on stereotypes or generalizations about a segment of society may be inadequate and even harmful.

Throughout this book, we have reviewed the current state of knowledge about the physiological, psychological, and social aspects of aging. We have examined variations among older ethnic minority groups, between older men and women, and among other segments of the older population. The diversity in processes of aging has been emphasized. Differences in lifestyle, work patterns, and family and social experiences in earlier periods of life can have a significant impact on health and social functioning in old age. As a result, there are greater variations among the older population than among members of any other

segment of society. As Chapter 19 points out, increasingly, this diversity is a factor affecting the development of social policies and programs.

Some age-based programs such as Medicare are directed toward all people who fulfill age criteria, whereas others such as Supplemental Security Income (SSI) and food stamps are based on financial need. The eligibility criteria and services provided through these programs and policies are often determined by the prevailing social values and by those of the political party and presidential administration in power. These values, in turn, reflect society's attitudes toward older people, their contributions, and their responsibilities to society. For example, attitudes and values regarding older people's rights and needs, whether chronological age is an appropriate basis for services, and whether care of the aging population is a societal or individual responsibility, all influence the development of social, health and long-term care policies. The historical development of aging policy in the United States and changes in existing programs such as Social Security are also reviewed within

**487**

the context of societal changes that influence such values. One societal change examined in this section is the growing economic security of a proportion of the older population that, in turn, has fueled an attitude that they are financially better off than other age groups. Such an attitude also stereotypes older adults as being "all alike"; it overlooks both the economic and racial diversity among older people and that younger and older generations engage in reciprocal exchanges and share interests throughout life.

Health and long-term care policies toward older people also have evolved in response to society's values and expectations of responsibility and need. Chapter 20 describes these policies; the impact of demographic changes, especially the increased number of the oldest-old with multiple chronic illnesses; the growing need for long-term care for older persons, especially home and community-based long-term care; the rising costs of health and long-term care; and current attempts at cost containment. Innovative community-based services, such as respite and adult day health programs, have emerged in response to the escalating costs of hospital and nursing home care, but public funding for these programs is limited. The need for and obstacles to health care reform, including long-term care, are also discussed.

Finally, we examine in the Epilogue the implications of a changing older population upon future social, health and long-term care policy and programming. As noted throughout this book, society is undergoing major transitions regarding the role and perceptions of older people. Changes such as the termination of mandatory retirement, the growing numbers of older people desiring part-time work, and the increased proportions of workers covered by employer pension plans suggest that the cohort entering old age in the next few decades will be far different from previous ones. These changes will have a dramatic impact on society as a whole. Conversely, the tremendous technological advances in medicine raise hopes of a longer life but also questions about the quality of such extended years. Moreover, computers have revo-

lutionized society and will play an increasing role in older people's social and physical well-being. The following vignettes illustrate the impact of changing societal attitudes and policies regarding the older population upon individuals who have been raised in different eras.

### An Older Person Born at the Turn of the Century

Mr. O'Brien was born in 1910 in New York City. His parents had migrated to the United States from Ireland ten years earlier, in search of better employment opportunities for themselves and a better life for their children. One of Mr. O'Brien's brothers died during a flu epidemic while still in Ireland; a sister and brother who were born in New York died of measles. Mr. O'Brien and his three surviving siblings worked from the age of 12 in their parents' small grocery store. He could not continue his education beyond high school because his father's death of tuberculosis at age 45 left him in charge of the family store. Mr. O'Brien thought of signing up for the newly created Social Security program in 1940, but he was confident that he would not need any help from the government in his old age. The family grocery was supporting him and his wife quite well; he planned to work until the day he died, and besides, his family had all died in their forties and fifties anyway. He has been a heavy smoker all his life, just as his father had been. As he approaches his eighty-third birthday, however, Mr. O'Brien has been having second thoughts about old age. His emphysema and arthritis make it difficult for him to manage the store. He has had two heart attacks in the past ten years, both of which could have been fatal if it had not been for the skills of the emergency medical team and their sophisticated equipment in his local hospital. Mr. O'Brien's savings, which had seemed substantial a few years ago, now are dwindling as he pays for his wife's care in a nursing home and for his medications and doctor's care for his heart condition, emphysema, and arthritis. Despite these struggles, Mr. O'Brien is reluctant to seek assistance from the government or from his children and grandchildren. They, in turn, assume that Mr. O'Brien is financially independent because he still works part-time, and never seems to require help from anybody.

### An Individual Born in the Post-War Baby Boom

Ms. Smith was born in 1949, soon after WWII ended and her father returned from his military duty. Her father took advantage of the GI bill to complete his college education and purchase a home in one of the newly emerging suburbs around Chicago. As Ms. Smith grew up, her parents gave her all the advantages they had missed as children of the Depression: regular medical and dental check-ups, education in a private school, a weekly allowance, and a college trust fund. She completed college, obtained a Master's degree in business, and now holds a middle-level management position in a bank. She has already begun planning a "second career" by starting work on a Master's degree in systems analysis. Recognizing the value of health promotion at all ages, she has been a member of a health club for several years, participating in aerobic exercise classes and jogging every day. She has also encouraged her parents, now in their mid-seventies, to participate in health promotion activities in their local senior center. Her parents both receive pensions, are enrolled in Medicare Parts A and B, and have planned for the possibility of catastrophic illness by enrolling in a supplemental health in-

surance program. Ms. Smith has encouraged her parents to get on the waiting list of an excellent retirement community nearby, which includes a life contract for residential and nursing home care, should they ever need it. She is also considering some long-term investments that will support her if she needs long-term care or costly medical care as she herself reaches old age. In this way, both Ms. Smith and her parents are planning for an independent and, to the extent they can control it through prevention, a healthy old age.

These vignettes illustrate the changing social and economic status of older people today and in the future. The implications of these changes for the development of social, health and long-term care policy, as well as on individuals' planning for their own aging, are discussed in the remainder of this book.

# 19

# SOCIAL POLICIES TO ADDRESS SOCIAL PROBLEMS

A wide range of policies has been established within the past 30 years in efforts to improve the social, physical, and economic environments of older people described throughout this book. Approximately 50 major programs are directed specifically toward older persons, with another 200 affecting them indirectly. Prior to the 1960s, however, the United States lagged behind most European countries in its development of policy for its older citizens. Accordingly, the percentage of the Gross National Product spent and the extent of tax support for programs for the older population are greater in Europe than in the United States. For example, Social Security benefits were not awarded to retirees in the United States until 1940, whereas alternative Social Security systems were instituted in the nineteenth century in most Western European countries. The United States has slowly and cautiously accepted the concept of public responsibility for vulnerable persons.

Since the 1960s, however, federal spending for programs for older adults has rapidly expanded, resulting in what has been called the "graying of the federal budget." The growth in federal support is vividly shown through budgetary figures (see Figure 19.1). In 1960, only 13 percent of federal expenditures went to programs for older people compared to 32 percent in 1991 (Hardy and Hardy, 1991; U.S. Congress, 1994a). This represents, in real terms, over five times what was spent on older people 30 years earlier (U.S. Senate Special Committee on Aging, 1992).

Raising even greater public concern is that 47 percent of federal spending goes toward entitlement programs—those for which spending is determined by ongoing eligibility requirements and benefit levels rather than by annual Congressional appropriations. These programs—Social Security, Medicare, Medicaid, and civil service and military pensions—are growing so fast (see Figure 19–2) that it is predicted they will consume nearly all the federal tax revenues by 2012. (Binstock, 1993). The long-term increase in the share of the budget spent on the older population has occurred primarily because of legislative improvements in income protection, health

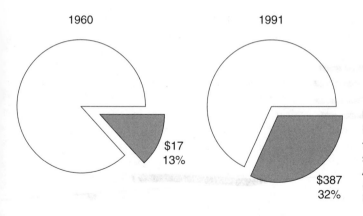

1960                    1991

$17
13%

$387
32%

**FIGURE 19–1    Changes in Percentage of
Federal Budget Entitlement Programs
for Older People (in billions of dollars)**
SOURCE:  U.S. Senate Special Committee on Aging,
*Aging America:Trends and Projections:1991 edition*
(Washington, D.C.: Department of Health and
Human Services, 1992).

insurance, and services enacted in the late 1960s
and early 1970s to reduce poverty among older
adults. At the same time, the focus of spending on
age-based programs has shifted. Retirement income has declined as a percent of federal spending, while health and long-term care spending has
increased. For example, Medicare, the fastest
growing entitlement program, has increased tenfold since its inception in 1965, and funds are expected to be exhausted early in the 21st century
(Rosenblatt, 1994).

It is important to recognize, however, that
when Social Security and Medicare are excluded
from these allocations, only about 4 percent of

the total federal budget is devoted to programs
that benefit older individuals. The growing percentage of allocations also masks the fact that
funded services are often fragmented, duplicated,
and inadequate in reaching those with the greatest need (Binstock, 1990). Without an integrated
and comprehensive public policy toward older
persons, the United States, despite growing allocations to age-based programs, is increasingly
faced with complex unresolved policy dilemmas.

This and the next chapter describe the social,
health and long-term care programs, processes,
and consequences of the "graying of America"
along with perceptions that older people have

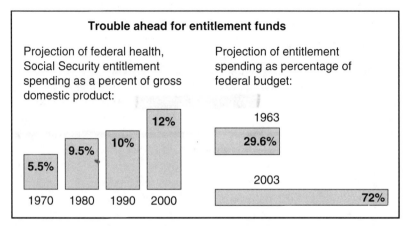

**Trouble ahead for entitlement funds**

Projection of federal health,
Social Security entitlement
spending as a percent of gross
domestic product:

5.5%    9.5%    10%    12%

1970    1980    1990    2000

Projection of entitlement
spending as percentage of
federal budget:

1963
29.6%

2003
72%

**FIGURE 19–2    Entitlement Spending at the National Level**
SOURCE:  *Bipartisan Commission on Entitlements and Tax Reform*

benefited at the expense of younger age groups. First, policy is defined, types of policies are differentiated, and factors that affect policy development are identified. The relatively slow development of policies for older persons prior to the 1960s is contrasted with the rapid expansion of programs in the 1970s and the federal budget cuts of the 1980s and 1990s. The policy impacts of the White House Conferences on Aging and of public perceptions about the "deservingness" of older persons are then reviewed. The two major programs that comprise the bulk of federal expenditures and thus shape public policy on old age are discussed in depth: first, Social Security and then in Chapter 20, Medicare and Medicaid. The development and coordination of direct social services, comprising less than 1 percent of federal expenditures for older people, are also described. Each chapter concludes with a discussion of policy dilemmas, which have numerous implications for future directions discussed in the Epilogue.

## VARIATIONS AMONG POLICIES AND PROGRAMS

*Policy* refers generally to the principles that govern action directed toward specific ends. It is within the purview of social policy not only to identify problems, but also to take action to ameliorate them. The development of policy thus implies change in both means and ends: changing situations, systems, practices, beliefs, or behaviors. The procedures governments develop for making such changes encompass planned interventions, bureaucratic structures for implementing interventions, and regulations governing the distribution of public funds. Policy for the older population reflects society's definition of what choices to make in meeting their needs and how to share such responsibilities between the public and private sectors. Each policy development serves to determine which older persons should receive what benefits, from which sources, and on what basis.

*Social programs* are the visible manifestations of policies. The implementation of the 1965

Older Americans Act, for example, resulted in programs, including senior centers, nutrition sites, homemaker and home health services, and adult day care. Some programs are designed specifically for older people, whereas others benefit them indirectly. Programs can be differentiated from each other in many ways; these dimensions are presented in Table 19-1 and described next.

**1.** *Eligibility criteria.* In some programs, eligibility for benefits depends on *age* alone (i.e., a person entitled to Medicare benefits at age 65), whereas in other programs, eligibility depends on *financial need* (i.e., a person's financial need entitles him or her to benefits, such as Medicaid, food stamps, and public housing). Although *age entitlement* programs are categorical and specifically for older persons, *need entitlement* programs affect all age populations that meet particular income criteria. Means-tested programs for low-income older and disabled persons, such as Supplemental Security Income, are examples of need entitlement programs.

Most programs for older adults are age entitlements, with the government automatically paying benefits to anyone who qualifies and is thereby "entitled" to the benefits. With about 60 percent of entitlement spending on programs for older persons, critics maintain that benefits will be less generous in the future, although maintained for current recipients (Binstock, 1993). In contrast, many programs for children are discretionary and means-based, which limits participation. This difference fuels ongoing debates about generational equity.

**2.** *Form of benefits.* Another variation is the form in which benefits are given—either *directly* or *indirectly through a cash transfer* or a *cash substitute.* Social Security benefits are a direct cash transfer, whereas tax policies that affect selected groups (e.g., personal income tax exemptions for older persons) are indirect cash transfers of funds from one segment of the population to another. An example of a direct cash substitute is vouchers for the restricted purchase of goods, such as food stamps and rent supple-

**Table 19–1    Dimensions Along Which Programs and Policies Vary**

|  | EXAMPLES |
|---|---|
| *Eligibility* | |
| On basis of age | Medicare |
| On basis of financial need | Supplemental Security Income |
|  | Medicaid |
| *Form of benefits* | |
| Cash | |
| Direct cash transfers | Social Security |
| Indirect cash transfers | Income tax exemption |
| Cash substitute | |
| Direct cash substitutes | Vouchers |
| Indirect cash substitutes | Medicare payments to service providers |
| *Method of financing* | |
| Contributory (earned rights) | Social Security |
| Noncontributory | Supplemental Security Income |
| *Universal or selective benefits* | |
| Universal—for all persons who belong to a particular category | Older Americans Act |
| Selective—determined on an individual basis | Food stamps |

ments. Medicare payments to health care providers, rather than directly to beneficiaries, are indirect cash substitutes.

3. *Method of financing.* Programs also vary in how they are financed. Social Security and Medicare are *contributory programs;* benefit entitlement is tied to a person's contributions to the system through his or her prior status as a paid worker across the life span. On the other hand, Supplemental Security Income (SSI) is a *noncontributory program* available to older persons who meet financial need criteria, regardless of their prior contributions through payroll taxes.

4. *Universal or selective benefits.* Programs differ according to whether they benefit populations on a universal or selective basis. Benefits from universal programs are available on the basis of social right to all persons belonging to a designated group. Eligibility for Medicare, the Old Age Survivors Insurance of Social Security, and the Older Americans Act is established by virtue of belonging to the older population. In contrast, *selective benefits* are determined individually. These include Supplementary Security Income, Medicaid, food stamps, and housing subsidies, which use economic need as a criterion. Whether or not aging services should be targeted to low-income elders and subsidized by higher-income older individuals is an ongoing debate. Not surprisingly, higher income older people do not necessarily agree that services should be targeted to low-income peers, as was illustrated when wealthier older people organized to repeal the "tax" on them under the Catastrophic Health Care legislation. Accordingly, public consensus does not exist on which approach to service delivery is best, as reflected in the following discussion of the factors, including ideology and values, that influence social policy (Torres-Gil, 1992).

## FACTORS AFFECTING THE DEVELOPMENT OF POLICIES

Despite the orderliness of these dimensions, the policy development process is not necessarily rational nor part of an overall plan. These approaches to the financing and delivery of aging services evolved in a very different time period when life expectancy was shorter and there was less concern about the federal deficit. A major characteristic of our public policy process is its shortsightedness—its general inability, because of annual budgetary cycles and the frequency of national elections, to deal with long-term economic and social trends, or to anticipate future consequences of policies established to meet today's needs or political imperatives. In an aging society, shortsightedness in policy development has resulted in a combination of programs, with separate entitlements and eligibility requirements added to a fragmented array of services. In fact, this can be so complex and confusing to older people and their families that it has spawned the growth of private case managers who are contracted by older persons or families to serve as "labyrinth guides" (Kane and Kane, 1990).

The complexity of the process of public policy formation for the older population is also magnified by the variety of societal factors influencing it. These factors include values and beliefs; economic, social, and governmental structures; the configuration of domestic and international problems; powerful interest groups and even random events or the chance appearance of charismatic political figures.

Two different sets of values have been played out in American social policies. In one, individual welfare is held to be essentially the person's responsibility within a free-market economy unfettered by government control. This belief in individual freedom and rights, self-determination, privacy and freedom from instruction is deeply rooted in our history and culture. As the legacy of our 19th-century past, the premise of private responsibility is currently widely embraced by many segments of our society and underlies many public policies. The second set of values assumes individual welfare to be the responsibility both of the individual and the community at large. Government intervention is necessary to compensate for the free market's failure to distribute goods and opportunities more equi-

tably, although given the belief in individual productivity and the competitiveness of the free market, some degree of income inequality is accepted as desirable. This emphasis on individual and family responsibility results in a "public burden" model of welfare, whereby older persons with disabilities are often viewed as a burden upon the state rather than as entitled to services as a matter of right. Accordingly, government performs a residual or "back up" role, supporting private efforts rather than taking a lead in promoting social welfare (Dalley, 1988). Even when government intervenes, such intervention is justified because of the failure of the market economy, the family, or the individual to provide for themselves or their relatives (Gill and Ingman, 1994; Kane and Kane, 1991; Walker, 1990). Accordingly, solutions tend to be patterned after private sector initiatives rather than socially widespread benefits.

Since the New Deal of the 1930s, policy has oscillated between these two value orientations as public mood and national administrations have shifted. Although Social Security was the first federal initiative to address the income needs of the older population, it succeeded largely because it was (and is today) an insurance plan for "deserving" elders who have contributed through their prior employment, not an income maintenance policy for all vulnerable citizens. The increasingly frequent debate about the nature and extent of public provisions versus the responsibility of individuals, families, and private philanthropy thus has moral overtones. Judgments about the relative worth of vulnerable populations that compete for a share of limited resources, and about the proper divisions between public and private responsibilities, are ultimately based on values (or preferences) held by individuals or groups. A major policy issue thus revolves around the question of whose values shape policy.

American *cultural values* of productivity, independence, and youthfulness, *public attitudes* toward governmental programs and toward older citizens, and *public perceptions* of older people as "deserving" have converged to create universal categorical programs that are limited to older persons, but available to *all* elders, regardless of their income. In contrast, policies that use income (e.g., means-testing) to determine if a person is "deserving" of services reflect our cultural bias toward productivity and independence; means-testing policies, such as Supplemental Security Income, determine the eligibility of low-income older persons for financial assistance and are often perceived as stigmatizing.

In the past, the American public tended to perceive older people as more deserving of assistance than other welfare recipients. Accordingly, Social Security and Medicare have generally been viewed as inviolate and not to be cut drastically. The passage of such otherwise unpopular programs as a national health insurance for older people (i.e., Medicare) and guaranteed income (i.e., Supplemental Security Income) can be partially explained by the fact that older persons have aroused public support. In addition, older people, viewed as a powerful and organized constituency, were more likely than children and low-income or homeless families to arouse a favorable response from politicians. As noted in Chapter 15, such catering to the senior vote also reflects the democratic pluralism or interest group politics used to advance one's interest in our political system, although older people are now less able to act as a unified bloc to influence legislation than in the past.

Society's technical and financial resources and current economic conditions (e.g., unemployment, inflation, and the deficit) also significantly influence policy development. Medicare and the Older Americans Act, for example, were passed during the 1960s and early 1970s. This was a period of economic growth and optimism, with government resources expanding under the so-called War on Poverty on behalf of both the younger poor and older people. Adverse economic conditions also can create a climate conducive to the passage of income maintenance policies. For instance, Social Security was enacted in part because the Great Depression dislodged the middle class from financial security and from their belief that older people who needed financial assistance were undeserving of aid. A strategy to increase the number of persons retiring at age 65 was also congruent with economic pressures to reduce widespread unemployment in the 1930s. With economic constraints, program cost factors were salient. For example, a public pension was assumed to cost less than reliance on local poorhouses, as had been the practice prior to the 1920s. Thus, a variety of economic and resource factors converged to create the necessary public and legislative support for a system of social insurance in the 1930s.

The influence of both economic resources and cultural values is also evident in the current public emphasis on fiscal austerity, private responsibility for the care of older persons, program cost-effectiveness and cost-containment, and targeting services to those most in need. Particularly under the Republican leadership's fiscal conservatism, the concept of states' rights and prerogatives has been emphasized, with the states assuming a stronger role in the development and financing of social programs. Unfortunately, this has resulted in increased variability among the states of eligibility criteria and benefits such as SSI. Periods of scarcity tend to produce limited and often punitive legislative responses, as occurred in the 1980s and is emerging again in the 1990s. As examples of the erosion of public support for universal age-based benefits, Medicare co-payments, deductibles, and Part B premiums have been increased, Social Security benefits for higher income older people are taxed, and conservative legislators propose cutting Medicare, Medicaid, and Social Security in order to reduce the federal deficit. The growing preoccupation with ways to reduce public expenditures has meant that more emphasis has been placed upon finding the most efficient and least expensive solutions, rather than having the criteria be one of equity and common well-being (Estes, Swan, and Associates, 1993).

## THE RESIDUAL AND INCREMENTAL NATURE OF POLICIES FOR THE OLDER POPULATION

These cultural values, economic conditions, and the consequent resource capability underlie the fact that American policy for older adults tends to be *categorical, residual,* and *incremental.* As noted previously, eligibility for categorical programs is determined by belonging to a particular age group. Residual and incremental policies assume that when the family or market economy does not adequately meet individual's needs, then social and health programs attend to emergency functions. In other words, programs are developed to respond incrementally to crisis conditions, not to prevent problems from arising or to attack their underlying causes. This contrasts with many other countries where national health and welfare policies represent a consensus that citizens are universally entitled to have certain needs met (Torres-Gil, 1992).

In her critique of this approach, Estes (1979, 1984, 1989, 1993) maintains that our conceptions of aging have socially constructed the major problems faced by older people and thereby have adversely influenced U.S. age-based policies. These conceptions, discussed as the political economy perspective in Chapter 4, are as follows:

1. Older individuals, not economic or social structural conditions, are defined as a "social problem."
2. Older people are seen as special and different, requiring separate programs.
3. The problems of older people are individually generated, best treated through medical services to individuals. This has resulted in the medicalization of aging and limited public funding for home and community-based social services.
4. The use of costly medical services is justified by characterizing old age as a period of inevitable physical decline and deficiency.
5. There is a growing perception that problems of older adults cannot be solved by national programs, but rather by initiatives of state and local governments, the private sector, or the individual.

According to Estes, these misconceptions have fostered a policy structure that assumes that treating individuals through services, not through guaranteed income, health care, or long-term care, can solve "the problem" of aging. Yet, our societal failure to develop a comprehensive, coordinated policy framework has served to reinforce older persons' marginality and to segregate them.

Whereas Estes contends that policies for older people are inadequate, others maintain that the older population is "busting the budget." Expenditures for older persons are seen as a primary reason for the growing federal budget deficit, and for the declining economic status of many younger people (Concord Coalition, 1993; Moody, 1990). This viewpoint has been fueled by the fact that Social Security is completely exempt and Medicare mostly exempt from automatic cuts of the 1985 Gramm-Rudman-Hollings legislation to reduce the federal deficit. In reality, however, the net contribution of Social Security and Medicare to the federal deficit has been nearly the same since 1980. There is widespread disagreement about the extent to which the deficit is due to excessive spending for entitlement programs, which "mortgage the future" of succeeding generations of Americans (Concord Coalition, 1993) or to spiraling interest rates, high unemployment, and shrinking real incomes. Within this context of the types of programs and factors affecting policy development, we turn now to the development of public policy for older persons in the United States.

## THE DEVELOPMENT OF POLICIES FOR OLDER PEOPLE

### 1930–1950

Prior to 1930, the United States had few social programs for older people; family, community, charity organizations, and local government (e.g.

county work farms) were expected to respond. Compared to European countries with similar levels of socioeconomic development, the United States was slower in implementing policies affecting the aging population. Factors such as the lower percentage of older persons in the population in the past, a strong belief in individual responsibility, and the free-market economy partially explain this slower pace. Table 19-2 traces the historical development of policy for older adults. The Social Security Act of 1935 was the first major policy enacted for older persons. Justified as a "pay as you go" system of financing, the act is based on an implicit guarantee of social insurance—that the succeeding generation

will provide for its older members through their Social Security contributions as employees. The original provisions of the act were intended to be only the beginning of a universal program covering all "major hazards" in life. The concept of the program in its entirety, including a nationwide program for preventing sickness and insuring security for children, was never realized, however.

After Social Security's passage, national interest in policies to benefit older persons subsided. One exception was President Truman's advocacy to expand Social Security benefits and to launch a national health insurance plan. His efforts for a national health insurance were

**TABLE 19–2   Major Historical Developments of Policies that Benefit Older People**

| | |
|---|---|
| 1935 | Social Security Act |
| 1950 | Amendments to assist states with health care costs |
| 1959 | Section 202 Direct Loan Program of the Housing Act |
| 1960 | Extension of Social Security benefits |
| | Advisory commissions on aging |
| 1961 | Senate Special Committee on Aging |
| 1961 | First White House Conference on Aging |
| 1965 | Medicare and Medicaid, Older Americans Act, establishment of Administration on Aging |
| 1971 | Second White House Conference on Aging |
| 1972 & 1977 | Social Security amendments |
| 1974 | Supplemental Security Income |
| 1974 | Title XX |
| 1974 | House Select Committee on Aging |
| 1974 | Change in mandatory retirement age |
| 1974 | Establishment of the National Institute on Aging |
| 1980 | Federal measures to control health care expenditures |
| 1981 | Third White House Conference on Aging |
| 1981 | Social Services Block Grant Program |
| 1986 | Elimination of mandatory retirement |
| 1987 | Nursing Home Reform Act |
| 1989–90 | Medicare Catastrophic Health Care Legislation passed, then repealed |
| 1995 | Fourth White House Conference on Aging |

opposed by organizations such as the American Medical Association. President Truman did succeed, however, in his push for an amendment to Social Security in 1950 to provide financial help to states that choose to pay partial health care costs for needy older persons. This amendment then became the basis for the establishment of Medicare in 1965. In the late 1950s, Social Security benefits were extended to farmers, self-employed persons, and some state and local government employees. In approximately half the states, advisory commissions on aging were formed; and in 1961, the Senate Special Committee on Aging and the first White House Conference on Aging were established.

## Program Expansion in the 1960s and 1970s

Since the 1960s, programs directed at the welfare of older people have rapidly evolved, including Medicare, Medicaid, the Older Americans Act, Supplemental Security Income (SSI), the Social Security Amendments of 1972 and 1977, Section 202 Housing, and Title XX social services legislation. The pervasiveness of "compassionate stereotypes," which assumed most older people to be deserving poor, frail, ill-housed, unable to keep up with inflation, and therefore in need of government assistance, undoubtedly influenced this rapid development (Binstock, 1990). This is an instance where policies are framed in terms of ageism (i.e., the same characteristics and status are attributed to a group labeled "the aged"). A negative consequence of "compassionate ageism," however, was a tendency to develop programs that obscured individual and subgroup differences among the older population. On the other hand, such stereotypes served to create a "permissive consensus" for government action on age-based services in the 1960s and 1970s, as illustrated by the discussion of programs that follows (Binstock, 1990).

The first White House Conference on Aging in 1961 was significant in highlighting older people's needs. Four years later, Medicare and the Older Americans Act were passed for which eligibility is determined by age, not by need. Although the Older Americans Act established the Administration on Aging at the federal level, as well as statewide area agencies to provide aging services, funding to implement these provisions was low. Therefore, one of the primary objectives of the 1971 White House Conference on Aging was strengthening the Older Americans Act. In 1972, Social Security benefits were expanded 20 percent, and the system of indexing benefits to take account of inflation ("cost of living adjustments" or COLA) was established. Additional funding was provided for the Older Americans Act in 1973. The 1970s witnessed more developments to improve older people's economic status: the creation of the Supplemental Security Income (SSI) programs, protection of private pensions, formation of the House Select Committee on Aging, increases in Social Security benefit levels and taxes, and the change in mandatory retirement from age 65 to age 70. (As noted in Chapter 14, mandatory retirement was later abolished for most jobs in 1986.) During this period of federal government expansion, more than 40 different national committees and subcommittees were involved in legislative efforts affecting older people (Binstock, 1990). As a result of the expansion of age-related programs, agencies, and benefits along with interest groups representing older people, individuals grew to expect that they would be entitled to receive certain benefits, such as Social Security and Medicare, based on age rather than on income or need.

A large constituency—including those older people who are not poor, frail, or inadequately housed—has benefited from the policy consensus built upon the "compassionate stereotype." In fact, Estes (1979) contends that human service professionals, such as administrators, medical personnel, and social service staff, gained from this program development more than did the older population most in need of services, thus creating a "service enterprise." Since old age constituencies have been viewed as relatively homogeneous (white, English-speaking and male), many older people with the greatest needs—women, ethnic minorities, and those living alone—have not always benefited from program improvements, as was described in Chapters 17 and 18.

## Program Reductions in the 1980s and 1990s

Although compassionate stereotypes about older people and a "permissive consensus" underlay the growth of age-entitlement programs in the 1960s and 1970s, the fiscal pressures and increasing concern about the younger age groups in the 1980s and 1990s have brought into question the size and structure of these programs. A new stereotype of older people as relatively well-off has resulted in their being scapegoated and blamed as "greedy geezers" who are responsible for the increasing poverty rates among younger age groups (Bengtson, 1993; Torres-Gil, 1992, 1993).

The impact of tax cuts, reductions in federal programs, the huge federal deficit, the Gramm-Rudman Act, and an overemphasis on economic growth prevented consideration of any large or bold programs for domestic spending in social and health care services during the Reagan years. At the same time, public perceptions of and support for aging programs varied widely. Senior advocates urged more funding, particularly for social services, and watched closely that Social Security not be cut. Concern over the future of Social Security was fueled by the near-term deficit facing the Social Security trust fund, and as a result, Social Security was amended in 1983 to address financing problems. As public scrutiny of the costs of Social Security, Medicare, and Medicaid grew, cost-efficiency measures were implemented, such as taxation on Social Security benefits and less generous cost of living increases.

During the 1980s, the political reality of the economic and social diversity of the aging population—that old age is not an accurate marker of economic status—became more apparent. The variability in distribution of income is reflected among three different groupings of older people: (1) those not eligible for Social Security, including both the lifelong underclass and the working poor who have interrupted employment histories, hourly wages without benefits, and few personal assets; (2) those who depend heavily on Social Security, small or no private pensions, and few assets except from their own home; and (3) those with generous private pensions, personal savings, and Social Security benefits. A number of policies passed in the 1980s recognized that the older population has differential capabilities for helping to finance public programs, so that both age and economic status are considered as eligibility criteria for old age benefit programs (Binstock, 1994). For example, the Social Security Reform Act of 1983 taxed Social Security benefits for higher-income recipients. The Tax Reform Act of 1986 provided tax credits on a sliding scale to very low-income older people and eliminated an extra person exemption previously available to older people. And programs funded under the Older Americans Act have been gradually targeted toward low-income people. Most recently, President Clinton's proposed health care reform would have differentiated among older people with respect to their economic status and ability to pay for Medicare and long-term care. These policy changes, combined with public perceptions that older people are better off than younger populations, reflect a transition from the legacy of a modern aging period (1930–1990) to a new period in which old age alone is not sufficient grounds for public benefits (Torres-Gil and Puccinelli, 1994).

## The Politics of Diversity and Deficit Spending in the 1990s

The growing federal deficit is profoundly affecting public policy development in the 1990s. To reduce the deficit, there are two major options—reductions in spending through program cutbacks, or revenue enhancement through higher taxes. National groups that cut across the political spectrum, such as the Bipartisan Commission on Entitlement and Tax Reform and the Concord Coalition, maintain that entitlement programs for older people are growing so fast that they will consume nearly all the federal tax revenues by the year 2012, leaving government with little money for anything else. Increasingly such groups argue that programs such as Social Security, Medicare, and Medicaid must be drastically curtailed through a "zero-deficit" plan in order to balance the federal budget by the year 2000. The fact that such programs are "under attack" reflects that older people are now less often perceived as a "politically sympathetic" and powerful group (Binstock, 1993, 1994; Peterson, 1993). At the same time, differences within the older population are becoming more evident, with subgroups of poor, minorities, women, and persons living alone likely to join political alliances that may compete with groups of more affluent elders. The "politics of diversity" may thus fragment the political influence of established aging organizations, further eroding support for universal programs (Bass, Torres-Gil, and Kutza, 1991; Torres-Gil, 1992).

This diversity, combined with the growing federal deficit, has resulted in a greater emphasis on private sector initiatives that can be supported by higher-income older adults. With more older people able to self-finance or privately insure against the social and health costs of later life, the base of support for high-quality government programs may erode. This could result in more limited services available to those elders without retirement plans and thus lead to increasing inequality among the older population generally. A policy challenge in the 1990s is to target policy responses to those who risk seriously declining income and those who have never had economic stability, while maintaining public support for the financing of quality universal programs (Bass, Torres-Gil, and Kutza, 1991). These complex issues set the framework for the 1995 White House Conference on Aging. Delegates at the 1995 Conference voted to maintain Social Security, the Older Americans Act, the nature of Med-

icaid and Medicare, and the advocacy functions under the Older Americans Act—all directions that conflict with the current Congress's emphasis on cutting entitlement programs as a way to reduce the federal deficit.

We next review the programs that account for the majority of federal expenditures: Social Security (OASDI) and Supplemental Security Income (SSI); tax provisions and private pensions that provide indirect benefits; social services through Title XX Block Grants and the "Aging Network" of the Older Americans Act; and, in Chapter 20, Medicare and Medicaid. As noted earlier, Social Security and health and long-term care represent the greatest percentage of federal funds expended on behalf of older persons, as illustrated in Figure 19–3.

## INCOME SECURITY PROGRAMS: SOCIAL SECURITY AND SUPPLEMENTAL SECURITY INCOME

### Social Security

As indicated earlier, the primary objective of the 1935 Social Security Act was to establish a system of income maintenance for older persons through individual insurance. A secondary purpose was to provide a basic level of protection for the most needy of the older population, initially through state plans for Old Age Insurance and, since 1974, through the federally funded Supplemental Security Income (SSI) program. A more recent objective has been to provide compensatory income to persons, regardless of age, who experience a sudden loss of income, such as widows, surviving children, and persons with disabilities.

To meet these objectives, Social Security has four separate "trust funds": Old Age and Survivors Insurance (OASI); Disability Insurance (DI); Hospital Insurance (HI), which is funded through Medicare; and revenues for the supplemental insurance portion of Medicare. This discussion focuses on the combined OASDI

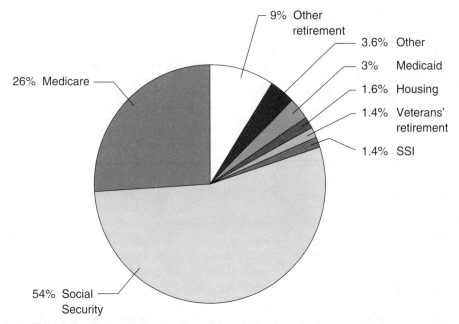

9% Other retirement

3.6% Other

3% Medicaid

1.6% Housing

1.4% Veterans' retirement

1.4% SSI

26% Medicare

54% Social Security

**FIGURE 19–3    Federal Outlays Benefiting Older People: Fiscal Year 1991**
SOURCE: U.S. Senate Special Committee on Aging, *Aging America: Trends and projections: 1991 edition* (Washington, D.C.: Department of Health and Human Services, 1992).

fund, of which programs for persons with disabilities are only 7 percent of the combined obligation. Funding for Medicare will be discussed in Chapter 20.

As described in Chapter 14, the Social Security system was based first on the concept of earned rights, rather than universal eligibility for all older persons. In fact, only 60 percent of the labor force was initially eligible to earn future benefits on the basis of the 1935 law. Coverage has since been expanded so that approximately 95 percent of the labor force is insured, reflecting nearly universal protection across socioeconomic classes (Aleksa, 1994). Social Security is thus distinguished by nearly universal coverage and wage-price indexing that protect recipients against economic changes over which they have no control. While Social Security provides a mechanism to pool resources and share the risk, no one is excluded no matter how "bad" a risk (Kingson, 1994). Therefore, it is unlike a private insurance or a welfare program (Kingson, 1994).

Contrary to public perceptions, Social Security was never intended to be the sole source of retirement income, but rather a minimum floor of protection. Social Security's average older recipients are paid 41 percent of their income at retirement, a figure that is projected to remain stable through the year 2040 (Cook and Barrett, 1989). Those at the lowest earning brackets receive about 79 percent, while the highest paid workers get 23 percent of their preretirement paychecks. Therefore, while higher-income workers receive higher benefit amounts, lower-income workers are assured a greater rate of return. This reflects Social Security's dual goals of social adequacy and individual equity, with benefits proportionate to what workers have paid into the system (Kingson, 1994). It is assumed that older people have other pensions and individual savings; nevertheless, a substantial percentage rely on Social Security for most or all of their retirement income; for example, Social Security provides 75 percent of the aggregate

Because of a sporadic work history, many older people cannot rely on Social Security.

income of older households with incomes of $10,000 or less (Kingson, 1994). In short, consistent with the conclusion of the 1982 National Commission on Social Security Reform, Social Security's nearly universal coverage and predictability of income make it the foundation of economic security for most retirees.

Social Security is financed through separate trust funds, revenues raised equally from the taxing of employees and employers, and income based on current tax revenues. This pay-as-you-go method of financing partially underlay the fiscal crisis faced by the system in the early 1980s, when the reserves were inadequate for projected benefits. A primary factor behind threats of bankruptcy was the economic recession; high unemployment and low productivity resulted in fewer taxes collected so that less money was available in the Social Security trust funds. Another structural factor was increases in longevity and the number of retired workers in

proportion to younger employees, with fewer workers paying into Social Security. This changing dependency ratio, discussed in Chapter 14, means that the ratio of taxpayers to beneficiaries is projected to drop from 3.2 to 1 in the early 1980s to 2.0 to 1 by 2030—a decline of over one-third. When Social Security was enacted, life expectancy was 61 years and the average recipient collected for 12 years, compared to 78 years and 19 years respectively now (Concord Coalition, 1993). Yet it was never intended that Social Security would support individuals for up to a third of their lives (Mathews, 1995). The most pessimistic interpretation of these shifts argues that "apocalyptic demography" will make it difficult for our nation to sustain all age-related benefits through the first half of the 21st century (Schneider and Guralnik, 1990; Wattenberg, 1987). An alternative view is that future benefits to older populations will not depend on the proportion of workers to retirees, but on whether the economy generates sufficient resources to be transferred and whether the political will to transfer them to older persons will be present (Binstock, 1994).

The short-term danger of bankruptcy was averted through remedial legislation passed in 1983, which resulted in benefit reductions and revenue increases. These reforms allowed the system to accumulate reserves, because the revenues from 110 million workers that finance the program exceed the benefits paid to 41 million retired beneficiaries (Concord Coalition, 1993). Because of such surplus in its trust funds, Social Security actually contributed to reducing the federal deficit, although this pattern was changed by legislation in 1990 (Hardy and Hardy, 1991). Despite such solvency, there is a long-range concern that the federal government debt is turning the surplus into paper savings. This concern stems from the fact that the Treasury Department borrows and then spends the Social Security reserves. In effect, it gives Social Security an IOU so that the reserves accumulated now may be consumed by deficits in later years. As described in Chapter 14, Social Security trust funds are predicted to remain solvent until approximately the year 2020, when the "outgo" will exceed current taxes, largely because of the aging of the "baby boom" generation (Beedon, 1994; Hardy and Hardy, 1991). Then the only way to repay the reserves in the future is for the federal government to raise taxes, increase borrowing, reduce benefits, or rely on economic growth.

As noted above, more bipartisan groups are calling for reduced spending, for example, through developing means to increase the labor force participation of older people, rolling back payroll taxes to the level of the early 1980s, or instituting a means-test which would reduce payments for higher-income beneficiaries (Quadagno, 1990). Means-testing is presented as morally imperative in order to preserve the American dream for younger generations, who currently perceive the monthly benefits for older retirees as increasing more rapidly than their income and who fear they will not receive a rate of return on their taxes comparable to that of many early recipients. This would mean abandoning the basic principles of social adequacy and the right of both rich and poor older people to Social Security benefits. Private schemes are also frequently proposed, such as making Social Security voluntary and relying upon private securities for retirement income— alternatives that would place workers at risk of their investments failing and losing disability and survivor insurance. Regardless of the extent of one's agreement with these proposals to alter Social Security, it is important to recognize that such changes are counter to the basic philosophy of a social insurance with universal eligibility, which has represented societal willingness to compensate those whose income has been destroyed or lowered by economic forces of the marketplace, regardless of the individual's actual contribution (Quadagno, 1990). As such, these proposed changes challenge the notion that governments subsidize programs that are deemed to be in the common good (Binstock, 1993). They also reflect a major shift from the past where Social Security (and Medicare) were viewed by policy-makers as "sacred entitlements," not to be

altered, even at the expense of other groups (Concord Coalition, 1993).

Despite the rhetoric of some national leaders to alter Social Security, the majority of the public, in national opinion polls, do not perceive that older people receive an inequitable amount of government benefits, nor that the programs provide benefits that are too costly (Bengtson and Murray, 1994). This may reflect recognition of how Social Security can also benefit younger family members by reducing their financial responsibility to their older relatives (Kingson, Hirshorn, and Cornman, 1986; Torres-Gil, 1992). There may be greater support for intergenerational transfer programs than the media and politicians typically portray, an issue discussed below related to the intergenerational equity framework.

## Supplemental Security Income

Supplemental Security Income (SSI) is the central income transfer for the older persons living on the margin of poverty. It is financed fully by the federal government under the Social Security Administration, although states may supplement the federal payment, which has resulted in variability in benefits among states. As noted in Chapter 14, SSI is intended to be a protective system or "safety net" for the least economically fortunate, but it has not eliminated poverty among older people. A primary reason for this is that SSI only brings needy individuals up to 75 percent of the poverty level and couples up to 90 percent, even where the state supplements the federal payment (Binstock, 1990). Nevertheless, relatively minor changes within the existing program could alleviate most poverty. For example, setting the SSI benefit at the poverty line would reduce the poverty rate for older persons living alone from 19 percent to 12 percent (Davis and Rowland, 1991).

Another limitation is that SSI reaches only half of those who are eligible (Miranda, 1990). Some eligible older people resist applying because of the perceived stigma of "welfare." Even more are unaware of SSI, believe that they would not be eligible, or are deterred by the complexity of the forms. Some states have formed SSI outreach coalitions to promote awareness of the program. The national SSI Modernization Project has recommended expanding outreach efforts, increasing SSI benefits to 100 percent of the poverty line, liberalizing asset tests to make it easier for people with limited assets to qualify, and allowing SSI beneficiaries to live in the home of a family member or friend without being penalized (SSI Modernization Project, 1992).

## PRIVATE PENSIONS AND INCOME TAX PROVISIONS

### Private Pensions

A smaller number of older persons receive a combination of government-supported public and/or private pensions in addition to their Social Security checks. As described in Chapter 14, 50 percent of the current labor force, primarily middle- and high-income workers, are covered by an employer-sponsored pension plan, which supplements Social Security. This translates into nearly 40 percent of older adults receiving some income from public or private pensions. It is expected that fewer than 50 percent of retirees early in the next century will have private pension income, a small increase from the current situation (U.S. Senate Special Committee on Aging, 1992).

The pension system tends to perpetuate systematic inequities across the life span by income, ethnic minority status, and sex, with lower-income workers, often women and ethnic minorities, least likely to be in jobs that are covered by pensions and to have attained the vesting requirements (e.g., ten years on the same job). In many respects, private pensions exaggerate the division of the work force into an advantaged and disadvantaged sector (Crystal and Shea, 1990), favoring white males in technical, professional, or managerial careers. Retired civil service, military veterans, and railroad employees,

for example, also receive cash benefits in addition to Social Security. This means that cash benefits from government-supported private savings plans and favorable tax policies accrue to those who are already relatively well-off, intensifying economic inequities over time.

Pension systems have not, however, been well funded in recent years. In the past 10 years, corporate contributions to pension plans have declined, and many businesses have instead used pension funds to pay for employee health care expenses. Defined benefit plans beneficial to employees have been terminated and replaced by contribution plans beneficial to employers. This "dipping into" pension funds occurred because the money that once went to pensions was used to pay the interest debt that resulted from the excessive borrowing typical in the 1980s (Bartlett and Steele, 1991).

### Income Tax Provisions

Pension plans are not the only "tax expenditures" related to aging. Some older individuals also benefit from extra tax deductions, and pay on average a smaller percent of their income in taxes. Many older people who file tax returns benefit from not paying a tax on Railroad Retirement and other government pensions. After these exclusions, however, less than 50 percent of the older population receive benefits from the other tax-preferenced items because their incomes are below the taxable level (Kutza, 1981). Wealthy older persons also benefit from double income tax exemptions, property tax reductions, and preferential treatment of the sale of a home (e.g., exemption from capital gains taxation for sale of a home after age 55). Tax provisions thus highlight the inequitable distribution of public benefits to older people. For example, the majority of tax benefits go to older individuals with incomes over $20,000, and only a small percent go to persons with incomes less than $5,000. Only the former group is able to deal with the economic hardships generally associated with old age by combining their private resources with these public tax benefit items, Social Security, and Medicare. In addition, this same group is more likely to have the resources to benefit disproportionately from senior citizen discounts for restaurants, transportation, theaters, and other businesses than those with limited incomes.

## SOCIAL SERVICES

Social service programs for older people have developed in response to needs unmet by income maintenance, health, and housing programs. Despite these developments, federal and state expenditures are primarily oriented toward medical care. Less than 1 percent of the older population's share of the federal budget is spent on social service programs (U.S. Senate Special Committee on Aging, 1990).

Funding for social services for older people derives from four federal sources: Medicare, Medicaid, amendments to the Social Security Act (Title XX), and the Older Americans Act of 1965. This section will focus on Title XX (of the Social Services Block Grants) and the Older Americans Act as the primary basis of social service funding.

Title XX was established in 1974 to provide social services to all age groups; entitlements are means-tested (e.g., by financial need), with most services to older persons going to those who

Nutrition sites are one of the most widely used services for the elderly.

receive SSI. In terms of the program classification system discussed earlier, Title XX is a universal program aimed at redressing needs. Because income is an eligibility criterion, the older people compete with a diverse group of Title XX recipients—primarily families with dependent children and persons who are blind or mentally and physically disabled.

Title XX services are viewed as basic life-sustaining, self-care services to compensate for losses in health and the capacity for self-maintenance. Homemaker and chore services, home-delivered meals, adult protective services, adult day care, foster care, and institutional or residential care services financed by Title XX have generally assured a minimum of support for vulnerable older people, but have not necessarily improved their overall quality of life.

Under the federal Omnibus Budget Reconciliation Act of 1981, Title XX was converted to the Social Services Block Grant program at the same time that federal funds allocated to the states were reduced on the average by 20 percent. The Social Services Block Grant program was one of the initial decentralization efforts emerging from the new federalism of the 1980s. Block grant funding increased the states' discretion in determining clients' needs and allocating Title XX funds among the diverse eligible groups. For example, national income eligibility guidelines aimed at targeting programs to needy persons were eliminated. Accordingly, the competition for funds increased along with variability in services between and within states. As a result, most states have allocated a greater percentage of block grant funds to children than to older persons. Limits to federal funding under decentralization, along with fiscal crises in most cities and states, have served to decrease revenues for social services under Title XX for older people at the same time that the demand for services has increased. As a result, competition for limited funds has increased, sometimes pitting the poor and their allied service providers against older groups.

The Older Americans Act (OAA) seeks to alter state and local priorities to ensure that older

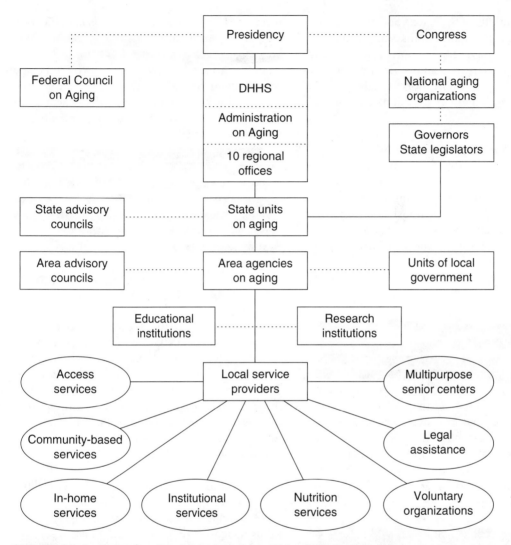

**FIGURE 19–4   Aging Services Network of the Older Americans Act**
SOURCE: Adapted from F. Torres-Gil, *The new aging: Politics and change in America* (New York: Auburn House, 1992).

people receive a proportionate share of social services allocations. Title III of the Older Americans Act is the single federal social service statute designed specifically for older people. Entitlements to services are universal, with the only eligibility criterion that one be over age 60, regardless of income or need. The OAA was to create a national network for the comprehensive planning, coordination, and delivery of aging

services. At the federal level, the Act charges the Administration on Aging (AOA), through the Commissioner on Aging, to oversee the activities of the Aging Network (i.e., the system of social services for older people) and to advocate for them nationally. The Federal Council on Aging is appointed by the President, and advises the President and the Commissioner on Aging.

The Older Americans Act also established State Units on Aging (SUAs). Each of these has a state advisory council to engage in statewide planning and advocacy on behalf of older persons' service needs. State Units on Aging designate local Area Agencies on Aging (AAAs) to develop and administer service plans within local areas. Approximately 700 Area Agencies on Aging operate at regional and local levels, and have advisory boards that include older persons. In addition to the federal, state, and local agencies responsible for planning and coordination, a fourth tier is composed of direct service providers in local communities. As described in Chapter 13, these include information and referral, case management, transportation, outreach, home-maker services, day care, nutrition education and congregate meals (e.g., hot meals at senior centers and home-delivered meals), legal services, respite care, senior centers, and part-time community service jobs. These services under OAA overlap with the goals and provisions of the Social Services Block Grants. Given the range of programs, the Act's relatively low level of funding ($900 million in 1992) requires it to target services to low-income, minority, rural or frail older adults.

Since participation rates in many OAA services have been highest among middle-income older individuals, proposals have been introduced for cost-sharing of services. This raises fears among OAA program staff that cost-sharing would introduce means-testing and stigmatize OAA programs as "welfare," thereby discouraging their use. However, by targeting services to low-income older people, an implicit means test is already being employed. Another concern is to increase minority participation in OAA programs through targeted outreach and increased recruitment of ethnic minority staff and board members.

Critics also contend that local and regional planning units have had limited influence on service agencies and have not reduced rates of institutionalization. They maintain that too much money has been spent on planning and coordi-

nating services that are becoming even scarcer so that the actual services delivered have not been improved. Another criticism, as noted earlier, is that the Older Americans Act has benefited professional gerontologists, through jobs and research funds, more than the older people who are studied and served by professionals (Minkler and Estes, 1984).

## POLICY DILEMMAS

### Age-Based Versus Needs-Based Programs

Ongoing debates about the need for *age-based programs* underlie most policy developments in the aging field. These debates highlight choices about whom to serve and how to restrict eligibility for program benefits. The major argument for age-based programs is that they are an efficient way to set a minimum floor of protection for beneficiaries, and are less stigmatizing than means-tested services. According to proponents

Gray Panthers are strong advocates for intergenerational programs.

of age-based programs, efficiency is enhanced by the fact that certain policies, such as Social Security, exclusively or predominantly affect older people. Accordingly, it is argued that age-based programs involve fewer eligibility disputes and are less administratively intrusive into applicants' lives.

Neugarten (1982; Neugarten and Neugarten, 1986), in particular, argues strongly against age-based services. She maintains that they reinforce the perception of "the old" as a problem, thereby stigmatizing older people and adding to age segregation. The Older Americans Act, for example, implicitly views anyone over age 60 as vulnerable and therefore needing services. Yet, as we have seen, many people over age 60 are in good health, have an adequate income, and therefore do not need services. The use of age as a criterion for benefits assumes that older people are homogeneous and different from other age groups, but Neugarten maintains that old age in itself does not constitute a basis for treatment different from that of other ages. Age has become a poor predictor of the timing of life events; of health, income, and family status; and therefore of people's interests and needs. Since age is not a useful indicator of changes within a person, it is an arbitrary criterion for service delivery. Instead, it is argued that economic and health needs, rather than age, should be the basis for selectively targeting services. For example, the need for services increases after age 75, when an individual's health and income also tend to decline. Yet universal age-based programs have benefited the young-old who are relatively healthy and in the top third of the income distribution, and have even further disadvantaged low-income and frail elders. Torres-Gil (1992) argues that with up to 25 percent of the population qualifying for age-related benefits, this approach has become politically and economically unfeasible. Proposals to take account of older people's socioeconomic status as a basis for eligibility for Social Security and Medicare are congruent with a needs-based approach. Some advocates for targeting service to older persons most at-risk favor a combination of categorical and group eligibility mechanisms. For example, a portion of Older Americans Act service moneys could be restricted for allocation to SSI and older Medicaid recipients, thereby reaching individuals with lowest incomes and presumably the most service needs. Given the increasing economic inequality within the older population, it can be argued that means-testing programs that comprise the "safety net" for the least well-off older adults, such as Supplemental Security Income and Medicaid, should be priorities for improvement. (Crystal and Shea, 1990).

## The Politics of Productivity Versus the Politics of Entitlement

Closely related to the ongoing debate about age-based versus needs-based programs is a more recent debate on the politics of productivity versus the politics of entitlement (Moody, 1990). The politics of entitlement is characterized as follows:

1. In a "failure model of old age," older people, solely because of their age, are defined as needy, worthy, and deserving of public support.
2. Issues are defined in terms of needs and rights.
3. The emphasis is on what older people deserve to receive as their right rather than what they can give.
4. Resources are transferred to the older population as a categorical group.
5. Other groups must pay for the benefits due the older population.

The politics of productivity is characterized this way:

1. The older population is increasingly diverse.
2. The implementation of new policies will require an expanding economy toward which older adults can contribute.
3. Older people are defined as a resource in an interdependent society and can contribute to

younger populations. Old age is a time for giving assistance and advice to the young.

4. "Investing in human resources" across the life span is essential to future economic growth to benefit all ages.

As we noted earlier, a growing number of national groups as well as members of Congress, particularly among the "New Right," are questioning entitlement programs for all age groups. While they point to the increased socioeconomic diversity of the older population, especially the growing middle class, as a rationale for means-testing, there is no agreement on how much to target resources in order to benefit those most at-risk, such as women and ethnic minorities. In other words, most advocates of changing entitlement programs appear to be motivated by fiscal goals, not by considerations of reducing status inequities within the older population.

## Intergenerational Inequity Framework

Closely related to the debate about both age-based entitlement programs and a politics of productivity is the argument that older persons are benefiting at the expense of younger age groups, who lack the political clout represented by senior organizations. The generational inequity debate began in 1984 with Samuel Preston's analysis of poverty rates among the young and old and public expenditures on behalf of older people; the old, who were perceived to be thriving, at the expense of children, as a result of expanded Social Security benefits and inflationary increases in real estate and home equity (Preston, 1984). This generated a rather simplistic picture of generational conflict, expounded in a growing number of newspaper and magazine editorials. It also resulted in the formation of groups such as Americans for Generational Equity (AGE), which later merged with the American Association of Boomers (AAB), and the National Taxpayers Union. These organizations maintain that the baby boom generation (e.g. those born between 1946 and 1964) will collec-

tively face a disastrous retirement, and its children will, in turn, be much more heavily burdened with the support of their parents than any other generation has been in our nation's history. They argue that policies and programs for older people have created "greedy geezers," who are selfish, concerned only with their own interests and with their share of the federal budget, and somehow responsible for the cutbacks in programs for other age groups, thereby contributing to the suffering of mothers and children (Chakravarty and Weisman, 1988). As evidence, they point to the fact that in 1990, federal and state governments spent more than $11,000 on every American age 65 and over, compared to $4,200 for each American under age 18 and at the same time that Social Security claimed more than 6 percent of the gross national product (Dickerson, March 19, 1993). Declining expenditures for national defense are also used to illustrate how the future of younger generations is being threatened by increased expenditures for programs benefiting older people.

Underlying their arguments is the assumption that our country faces significant distributional choices, especially related to Social Security and other retirement incentives, about how to pay the costs of an aging society (Moody, 1990). Policy questions then become framed in terms of competition and conflict between generations, creating a backlash against the gains experienced by the older population and furthering a destructive polarization between younger and older generations.

The themes of the backlash argument are:

- America's older citizens are now better off financially than is the population as a whole and are selfish and concerned only with personal pension and income benefits.
- Programs for older people are a major cause of current budget deficits, economic problems, and increases in poverty among children.
- Children are the most impoverished age group.

- Young adults—the group referred to as Generation X—now have a harder time making ends meet and face a far stiffer tax burden than their parents did when they were the same age.
- Younger people will not receive fair returns for their Social Security and Medicare investments.

Admittedly, high inflation, lack of real wage growth, and runaway housing costs in the early 1980s have hurt young adults who are struggling to start jobs and families and to buy a home. A slowing economy has collided with growing expectations about the good life, and long-term predictions are that the decline in the standard of living for the middle class will continue (Morris, 1989). This results primarily from larger societal conditions, such as the loss of U.S. industrial competitiveness and well-paid jobs, rather than from the cost of Social Security per se.

Similarly, the growing divorce rate has thrown millions of children into one-parent households and poverty. (The poverty rate among children is over 20 percent [Radner, 1991].) At the same time, older people are perceived as benefiting from generous entitlement programs which policy makers have been loath to cut. Another factor that feeds into the backlash is that old age benefits were cut only a small percentage compared to human resources spending for all other age groups in the 1980s.

As described in Chapter 14, the older population is financially better off than in the past. In many ways, the improved economic status of the older population actually represents a success story of government interventions rather than a basis for criticism. As noted in Chapter 14, 1 out of 3 older persons was poor in 1959, as compared to 1 out of 8 currently, an improvement that represents the effects of Medicaid and Medicare, reform in Social Security, and the Older Americans Act (Torres-Gil, 1992). Yet, beneath the appearance of a dramatic decline in poverty among the older population is the reality that many of those who "moved out" of poverty

have shifted from a few hundred dollars below the poverty line to a few hundred above it. In addition, the distribution of income among the older population is extremely diverse and the level of inequality among them is extraordinarily high. As we have seen in earlier chapters, large pockets of poverty and near poverty persist among older ethnic minorities and women, the oldest-old, and those older people living alone.

As noted in Chapter 14, older adults are also more likely than other age groups to be among the "near poor" and the "hidden poor." Federal budget cuts of means-tested programs (e.g., food stamps, subsidized housing, and Medicaid) have fallen primarily on low-income older persons who depend on multiple public benefits. The tax cuts and lessened inflation in the mid-1980s did not improve the low-income elder's economic status. Even when services are available, low-income older adults appear less likely to use them than are other groups (Cook and Kramek, 1986; Uehara, Geron, and Beeman, 1986). Finally, the safety net for low-income seniors is extremely weak. For example, the SSI benefit for a single person is only about 75 percent of the poverty line (Taeuber, 1990).

## Critique of the Inequity Framework

The intergenerational inequity framework that attempts to measure the relative hard times of one generation against the relative prosperity of another has been widely criticized by advocates for older people (Kingson, Hirshorn, and Harootyon, 1986). The major criticisms of this framework are as follows: Contrary to the pessimistic argument that society will not be able to provide for future generations of older people, the economy of the future, barring unforeseen disasters, will be able to support a mix of programs for all age groups. There is little real evidence of significant intergenerational conflict; instead, younger and older generations appear to recognize their interdependence and to support benefits to each other across the life span. For example, the Children's Defense Fund argues that funding for programs for the young should be increased at the cost of military spending, not at the expense of programs for the old. The American Association of Retired Persons agrees, and argues that older people's well-being contributes to the welfare of all other generations. Similarly, the public tends to be supportive of benefits for older generations (Bengtson and Murray, 1994).

On the other hand, some advocates for older adults are beginning to acknowledge that it is no longer realistic to proceed on the assumption that all benefits are sacrosanct, regardless of whether they are directed at those without significant need. It is counterproductive to oppose all measures imposed on financially better off older persons, such as treating part of Social Security as taxable income or subjecting Social Security and Medicare to means-testing. Yet the negative reaction of higher-income elders to paying the surtax for Catastrophic Health Care Insurance suggests that there are still many older adults who believe that services should be provided on the basis of age, not need.

The definition of fairness put forth by groups such as Americans for Generational Equity is narrow and misleading. Thus, the current preoccupation with conflict and inequity between generations "blinds us to inequities within age groups and throughout our society" (Nelson, 1989, p. 101). It also deters us from pursuing the goal of social justice for those most in need.

When fairness is equated with numerical equality, this assumes that the relative needs of children and older people for public funds are identical, and that equal expenditures are the equivalent of social justice. Even if needs and expenditures for each group were equal, this would not result in equal outcomes or social justice. By framing policy issues in terms of competition and conflict between generations, the intergenerational inequity perspective implies that public benefits to older individuals are a one-way flow from young to old, and that reciprocity between generations does not exist. It is true that younger generations are facing increased economic pressures. However, as noted earlier, rather than blame older adults, the role of federal deficits, slowed economic growth, and increasing housing costs needs to be recognized. By pitting young against old for the division of scarce resources, the intergenerational inequity framework assumes a "fixed pie," which can only be cut from the young or the old. In some instances, the intergenerational debate has become a convenient mechanism to justify shifting responsibility for all vulnerable groups to individuals, the private sector and local government (Quadagno, 1990). Accordingly, it overlooks other ways of increasing public resources through economic growth, increased tax revenues, or reduced defense spending.

## The Interdependence of Generations Framework

Consistent with social exchange theory, a continuing human dilemma is the "contract between generations." Typically, this has been defined between parents to children and children to aging parents. What is different today is the focus on relationships between age groups in society rather than individuals within the family. This shift from generations to age groups has increased the magnitude and complexity of the issues involved, so that it is no longer youth versus elders, but rather elders versus middle-aged and youth. Never before have so many individuals lived so long and never have there been so relatively few members of the younger generation to support them (Bengtson, 1993).

The interdependence of generations framework, advocated especially by the Gerontological Society of America, recognizes the changing societal and political context that, along with the increase in life expectancy and decreases in fertility, there are increased policy concerns about welfare costs and public expenditures that are targeted to various age groups (Bengtson, 1993). Within this larger context, public and private intergenerational transfers are viewed as central to social progress. A major way in which generations assist one another is through the family; for example, through care for children and dependent adults, financial support, gifts to children and grandchildren, and inheritances. Private intergenerational transfers are essential to meeting families' needs at various points over the life course and to transmitting legacies of the past (e.g., economic growth, culture, values, and knowledge). Transfers based on public policy (e.g., education, Social Security, and health care programs) also serve intergenerational goals. For example, Social Security benefits are distributed widely across all generations and protect against risks to families' economic well-being over the course of their lives. It is erroneous to think of Social Security as a one-way flow of resources from young to old. Instead, younger generations have at least two important stakes in Social Security: they will be served by it when they become old, and, as stated earlier, programs that support their older relatives' autonomy currently relieve them from financial responsibilities. Defining Social Security in terms of intergenerational conflicts also obscures the fact that it has been successful in reducing poverty (Quadango, 1990). Similarly, when it is recognized that long-term care can affect all age groups, particularly given the increase in the number of younger adults with AIDS or who are developmentally disabled or chronically mentally ill, then long-term care services can benefit all generations. Likewise, it is erroneous to think of education as a one-way flow to children, which the older population resists. Instead, older people have contributed to public education throughout their working careers, and, as noted in Chapter 15, the extent of support among them for school levies is higher than commonly assumed (Binstock, 1993). Such support reflects their recognition that older generations benefit directly and indirectly from education programs that increase workforce productivity.

The Gerontological Society's report on the interdependence of generations concluded:

A sufficiently broad policy framework for responding to the challenge of an aging society must include a concern for the long-term welfare of all age groups, an appreciation of policies that support the family as an institution, and an understanding of the significance of public and private investments in the human resources that will define the possibilities for the future (Kingson, Hirshorn, and Cornman, 1986, p. 28).

Along those lines, it has been argued that older people can be the vanguard of renewed efforts to ensure a decent standard of living for all Americans (Morris, 1989). This assumes that intergenerational competition can be reduced and the future needs of the older population effectively addressed by enhancing people's opportunities earlier in their lives. Similarly, a broadened welfare consensus could be fostered through an understanding of the life-course experiences that lead to problems in old age. This perspective of our common human vulnerability across the life course is not a new one. In fact, President Lyndon B. Johnson's charge to the 1968 Task Force Report on Older Americans was to determine the most important things to be done for the well-being of most older Americans. Since vulnerability in old age is the product of a life course of experiences, the Task Force concluded that the priority is to provide social and economic opportunities for the young and middle-aged (Binstock, 1990; Jacobs, 1991).

Within the framework of interdependence, other paradigms have been proposed as a way to conceptualize how the burdens and opportunities within our society can be fairly shared among generations. One paradigm is the concept of generational investment, in which age-based services and other social programs, such as public education, play an integral part in the system of reciprocal contributions that generations in any society make to one another. Programs such as Social Security and Medicare are mechanisms through which generations invest in one another and publicly administer returns to older cohorts for the investments made in the human capital of younger groups. As such, old-age benefits represent claims based on merit and social contributions and should not be subject to means testing (National Academy on Aging, 1994). The notion of processual justice also recognizes equity between age groups over time (Laslett and Fishkin, 1992).

Similar to the "politics of productivity" and the interdependence framework, Torres-Gil (1992, 1993) argues for a paradigm of "New Aging" in the post-1990s. The politics of the New Aging aims to identify how all generations can contribute to a new society, in contrast to a focus on serving the older population that has characterized the period from 1930 to 1990. He argues that our society must alter both our view of older adults to take account of their growing diversity and the manner in which we provide for them. With the increased heterogeneity of the older population, intergenerational conflict of old versus young cannot be assumed (Torres-Gil, 1992). While some tensions between young and old will remain, a more likely outcome is the politics of diversity, as noted earlier. There will be greater differences of political opinions among older people and between age cohorts, with more linkages based on political priorities, not age per se (Torres-Gil, 1992).

In the politics of the New Aging, advocacy and lobbying should be rechanneled from special interest issues toward politics to benefit all future generations. Likewise, age-segregated policies and programs should be abandoned; groups of older people should shift from the horizontal alliances that characterize interest group politics to new vertical alliances, representing common needs between aging and non-aging groups (Torres-Gil and Kmet, 1990). Previously underrepresented groups of older persons—minorities, women, rural residents—must establish alliances with non-aging groups. In fact, this has already started to occur. For example, Generations United has established a coalition of consumer, labor, children and senior groups, and AARP is establishing networks with minority populations. Not only should older adults be viewed as a resource able to contribute to the economy and

their own income security, but the young should also be educated for a long lifespan.

To address the problems of the disadvantaged under the interdependence framework of the New Aging requires an ideological consensus that government should help people in need, regardless of age. As we have seen in our earlier analysis of factors that affect policy development, such a consensus does not exist. Given this lack of consensus, some policy analysts argue that the real issue for the 1990s is not generational conflict or interdependence but rather the role of the public sector in caring for its vulnerable citizens and the relationship between the public and private sectors (Minkler and Estes, 1984; Estes, Swan, and Associates, 1993).

## WHO IS RESPONSIBLE?

As noted, many of these policy debates revolve around the division of responsibility between federal and state governments and the public and private sectors of family and business. Until recently, Social Security benefits, Medicare, Medicaid, SSI, and services under the Older Americans Act settled the question of responsibility for older citizens: It was to be a collective responsibility of the entire population, exercised through the national government. It was to be protection to which every older citizen was entitled, simply by virtue of age.

A growing view held by public officials since the 1980s is that the problems of older people and other disadvantaged groups cannot be solved with federal government policies and programs alone. Instead, solutions must come from state and local governments and from private sector and individual initiatives, such as advocacy, self-help, and family care. Individuals are assumed to be responsible for their own problems, and federal government interventions are considered to be too costly and to threaten national economic well-being by increasing the deficit. An anti-tax mentality, combined with growing public concern about the federal deficit, have resulted in legislative changes to reduce federal funds and to rely upon the states through block grants. These cuts are also justified by the assumption that the states can most efficiently and innovatively respond to local needs. A limitation of this decentralized approach, however, is that states, which have the fewest resources for supporting community services, are generally the least likely to respond to the needs of the most disadvantaged. As noted previously, with decentralization, there is little assurance of policy uniformity and of equity for powerless groups across different states. National initiatives that establish stable, uniformly administered federal policies are usually necessary to bring the states with the most limited expenditures up to a minimum standard.

Decentralization also makes it harder for older people to influence policy development, since they must address officials in hundreds of different state and local agencies. Block grants, for example, have few central directives, thus allowing the most well-organized and informed groups to influence the distribution of funds. Powerful interest groups, such as insurance companies, hospitals, and physicians, tend to have more political influence at the state level, with the low-income older people faring poorly under decentralization. Decentralization has also placed older people in competition with child welfare advocates, thereby fueling perceptions of intergenerational conflict (Minkler and Estes, 1984). Although decentralization can increase program responsiveness to a given area, broad inequities tend to result.

# REDUCTIONS IN GOVERNMENT SUPPORT

What is more important than federal–state relations, however, is the level of public spending. Although public spending has increased in terms of total dollars, it has declined when measured as a percentage of the gross national product or as government expenditures per capita, corrected for inflation. Economically disadvantaged older persons have been hurt the most by the budget cuts of the past 15 years.

Public spending levels are being reduced at the same time that private and local spheres are being expected to be more responsible for older people with chronic disabilities. Policy makers often assume that public programs reduce family involvement and that families could do more for their older relatives. However, as discussed in Chapter 12, the family has consistently played a major role in caring for older relatives. Family members may be providing all the support that they are able or willing to do, although such assistance is not necessarily financial. When resources become scarce, the family tends to be viewed as a cost-effective alternative to nursing home placement and to publicly funded social services. But as Chapter 12 illustrated, few public programs support families' caregiving efforts.

Not only is the family unable to carry expanded responsibilities, but the private nonprofit service sector cannot fill the gaps created by federal cuts. In fact, the 1986 federal tax law reduced incentives for corporate giving. In addition, private contributions traditionally have not been concentrated on social services, so that increased private giving would not automatically flow into areas most severely cut. Instead, both public and private funds are decreasing as the older population and their need for services increase.

In summary, rapid demographic and social changes mean that our society is faced with complex, difficult policy choices. It is increasingly apparent that the older population is not one constituency but several, in which race, gender, and socioeconomic class may be greater unifiers than age. A political agenda must be drafted that can unite different older constituencies—low-income, middle-class, and wealthy—as well as different age groupings with common needs. Lack of public resources in itself is not the primary barrier to action, however. For example, the cost of eliminating poverty among the older population is well within our societal resources, coming to approximately .06 percent of the Gross National Product (Davis and Rowland, 1991). The greater challenge is in framing the political consensus to ensure a minimal level of economic security and health for all Americans. Progress could be made in both areas largely by improving the basic income support of SSI and expanding Medicaid eligibility—changes that are possible within current budgetary restraints. Unfortunately, such gains are unlikely to occur without larger changes in our political structures and belief systems of democratic pluralism, states' rights, and individual freedom. Until then, Americans will continue to be personally generous, but reluctant to support income maintenance programs for an entire class of needy persons or a national health care system that is perceived to threaten individual choice.

## SUMMARY AND IMPLICATIONS

This chapter has reviewed federal programs that benefit older persons. Since 1960, age-specific spending has increased significantly, mostly through Medicare and Old Age Survivors Insurance of Social Security. In the past, such age entitlement programs have been based on cultural values and public attitudes that older people are deserving. However, the rapid expansion of these programs, combined with the improved economic status of the majority of older people, have created a growing public and political sentiment that such age-based entitlement programs must be reduced, perhaps through means-testing to minimize the benefits received by higher-income older adults. At the same time, older persons with the greatest needs, such as women, ethnic minorities, and those living alone, have not necessarily benefited from these entitlement programs.

The United States developed policies aimed at older populations more slowly than European countries. The Social Security Act of 1935 was the first major policy aimed at older people. Social Security was expanded slightly in 1950 to support partial health care costs through individual states. These changes led to the enactment of Medicare in 1965. Since then, there has been a significant growth in the number of programs aimed at improving the welfare of older people: the Older Americans Act, Supplemental Security Income, the Social Security Amendments of 1972 and 1977, and Title XX social services legislation. These programs have been strengthened by national forums such as the 1961 and 1971 White House Conferences on Aging. During the 1980s, however, there was a decline in these programs; allocations for homemaker, nutrition, chore services, adult day care, low-income energy assistance, respite, and volunteer programs such as Retired Senior Volunteer Programs all diminished. These cost-efficiency measures are based on a perception that the older population has greater financial security than younger age groups. The fiscal crisis faced by the Social Security system in the early 1980s fueled this stereotype through speculations that the growing number of older persons was primarily responsible for the crisis, and would drain the system before future generations could benefit from it. However, numerous structural factors were responsible for the problems; changes that have subsequently been made in this system assure its future viability, but only until approximately 2020.

The debate over age-based versus needs-based programs has also led to the emergence of organizations that have expounded arguments about older people benefiting at the expense of younger age groups. Yet, evidence for such inequities is weak; numerous other organizations such as the Children's Defense Fund and the Gerontological Society of America recognize generational interdependence and the importance of seeking increased public support for all ages through other sources. This framework, known as the *interdependence of generations,* assumes that assistance from young to old and old to young benefits all ages and supports the role of families across the life span.

In sum, the policy agenda for older people for the remainder of the twentieth century is full and complex. The current federal emphasis on fiscal austerity underlies all policy debates about how much the government should be expected to provide and for whom. Increasing public perceptions of older people as well-off, combined with decreased governmental resources, will undoubtedly affect the types of future programs and policies developed to meet older adults' income, housing, and social service needs. Older people are less likely to act as a unified bloc in support of age-based programs. Instead, the increased diversity of the older population suggests that there will be alliances formed between at-risk elders and other age groups. Consistent with the frameworks of interdependence and generational investment, such alliances may be able to develop policies that benefit both older people and future generations. Threatening such cross-age efforts, however, is the anti-tax mood of the public and the fiscal conservatism of the "New Right." These pressures suggest that advocates for older people will need to find new ways to address the complex needs created by increased life expectancy and diversity among the older population. A major challenge is the development and funding of home- and community-based forms of long-term care, the topic addressed next in Chapter 20.

## References

Aleksa, K., *Income among older Americans in 1992.* Washington, D.C.: American Association of Retired Persons, 1994.

Bartlett, D., and Steele, J. The vanishing pensions: Will money be there when you retire? *The Seattle Times,* November 5, 1991, A-4.

Bass, S., Torres-Gil, F. M., and Kutza, B. On the relationship between the diversity of the aging population and public policy. *Journal of Aging and Social Policy,* 1991, 2, 101–116.

Beedon, L. *Old age, survivors, and disability insurance trust funds: The short and long term.* Washington D.C.: AARP, Public Policy Institute, 1994.

Bengtson, V. L. Is the contract across generations changing? Effects of population aging on obligations and expectations across age groups. In V. L. Bengtson and W. A. Auchenbaum (Eds.), *The changing contract across generations.* New York: Aldine de Gruyter, 1993, 3–24.

Bengtson, V. L., and Murray, T. M. Justice across generations (and cohorts): Sociological perspectives on the life course and reciprocities over time. In L. Cohen (Ed.), *Justice across generations: What does it mean?* Washington, D.C.: American Association of Retired Persons, 1994.

Berry, J. Planning to the 21st Century. *Journal of Aging and Social Policy,* 1991, 2, 9–12.

Binstock, R. H. The aged as scapegoats. *The Gerontologist,* 1983, 23, 136–143.

Binstock, R. H. Changing criteria in old-age programs: The introduction of economic status and need for services. *The Gerontologist,* 1994, 34(6), 726–730.

Binstock, R. H. The deficit entitlements and policies on aging. *Gerontology News,* Washington, D.C.: Gerontological Society of America, February, 1993, 2.

Binstock, R. H. The oldest old: A fresh perspective on compassionate ageism revisited. *Milbank Memorial Fund Quarterly: Health and Society,* 1985, 63, 437–438.

Binstock, R. H. The politics and economics of aging and diversity. In S. Bass, E. Kutza, and F. M. Torres-Gil (Eds.), *Diversity in aging.* Glenview, Ill.: Scott, Foresman and Co., 1990.

Binstock, R. H. Reframing the agenda of policies on aging. In M. Minkler and C. Estes (Eds.), *Readings in the political economy of aging.* Farmingdale, N.Y.: Baywood, 1984.

Binstock, R. H. (Ed.) Will "generational accounting" doom the welfare state? *The Gerontologist,* 1993, 33(6), 812–819.

Chakravarty, S. N., and K. Weisman. Consuming our children? *Forbes,* 142 (Nov. 14, 1988), 222–232.

Clark, R. *The role of private pensions in maintaining living standards in retirement.* National Planning Association Report, No. 154, Washington, D.C., 1977.

Clark, R., and Menefee, J. Federal expenditures for the elderly: Past and future. *The Gerontologist,* 1981, 21, 134–142.

Concord Coalition. *The zero deficit plan: A plan for eliminating the federal budget deficit by the year 2000.* Washington, D.C.: The Concord Coalition, 1993.

Cook, F.L., and Barrett, E.J. *Social Security: What the public thinks.* Chicago: Northwestern University

Center for Urban Affairs and Policy Research, 1989.

Cook, F. L., and Kramek, L. Measuring economic hardship among older Americans. *The Gerontologist*, 1986, *26*, 38–48.

Crystal, S., and Shea, D. Cumulative advantage, cumulative disadvantage and inequality among older people. *The Gerontologist*, 1990, *30*, 432–443.

Dalley, G. *Ideologies of caring: Rethinking community and collectivism.* London: MacMillan Education, 1988.

Davis, K., and Rowland, D. Public policy issues for the 1990s. *Journal of Aging and Social Policy*, 1991, *2*, 39–60.

Dickerson, M. Younger generation: "Don't tread on me, Granny." *The Seattle Times*, Friday, March 19, 1993, A4.

Estes, C. L. *The aging enterprise.* San Francisco: Jossey-Bass, 1979.

Estes, C. L. Fiscal austerity and aging. In C. Estes, R. Newcomer, and Associates (Eds.), *Fiscal austerity and aging.* Beverly Hills, Calif.: Sage, 1983.

Estes, C. L. Austerity and aging: 1980 and beyond. In M. Minkler and C. Estes (Eds.), *Readings in the political economy of aging.* Farmingdale, N.Y.: Baywood, 1984.

Estes, C. L. Aging, health and social policy: Crisis and crossroads. *Journal of Aging and Social Policy*, 1989, *1*, 17–32.

Estes, C. L., Swan, J. H., & Associates. *The long-term care crisis.* Newbury Park, Calif.: Sage, 1993.

Gill, D. and Ingman, S. *Eldercare, distributive justice, and the welfare state: Retrenchment or expansion.* Albany, New York: State University of New York, 1994.

Giwirtzman, M. Remarks made on television by the chairman of the National Commission on Social Security, which were reported in the *Los Angeles Times* (December 6, 1982), 16.

Hardy, D. and Hardy, C. *Social Insecurity.* New York: Villard Books, 1991.

Hudson, R.B. The 'graying' of the federal budget and its consequences for old age policy. *The Gerontologist*, 1978, *18*, 428–440.

Hudson, R. B. Old-age politics in a period of change. In E. Borgatta and N. McCluskey (Eds.), *Aging and society: Current research and policy perspectives.* Beverly Hills, Calif.: Sage, 1980.

Hudson, R. B. The new politics of aging. *Generations*, 1984, *9*, 5–7.

Jacobs, B. Public policy and poverty among the oldest old: Looking to 2040. *Journal of Aging and Social Policy*, 1991, *2*, 85–99.

Kane, R. C., and Kane, R. A. Health care for older people: Organizational and policy issues. In R. Binstock and L. George (Eds.), *Aging and the social sciences* (3d ed.). New York: Academic Press, 1990.

Kane, R. C., and Kane, R. A. Long-term care in the United States and Canada: A question of will. In *North American look at economic security for the elderly*, edited by T. R. Marmor (Chair). Symposium conducted at Yale University, New Haven, Conn., 1991.

Kingson, E. Testing the boundaries of universality: What's mean? What's not? *The Gerontologist*, 1994, *34*(6), 736–742.

Kingson, E., Hirshorn, B., and Cornman, J. *Ties that bind: The interdependence of generations.* Washington, D.C.: Seven Locks Press, 1986.

Kingson, E., Hirshorn, B., and Harootyon, L. *The common stake: The interdependence of generations.* Washington, D.C.: The Gerontological Society of America, 1986.

Klemmack, D. L., and Roff, L. L. Predicting general comparative support for governments providing benefits to older persons. *The Gerontologist*, 1981, *21*, 592–599.

Kutza, E. *The benefits of old age: Social welfare policy for the elderly.* Chicago: University Press, 1981.

Kutza, E. Responding to diversity: Is American society capable? In S. Bass, E. Kutza, and F. M. Torres-Gil (Eds.), *Diversity in aging.* Glenview, Ill.: Scott, Foresman, and Co., 1990.

Kutza, E., and Zweibel, N. Age as a criterion for focusing public programs. In B. Neugarten (Ed.), *Age or need? Public policies for older people.* Beverly Hills, Calif.: Sage, 1982.

Laslett, P., and Fishkin, J. *Justice between age groups and generations.* New Haven, Conn.: Yale University Press, 1992.

Mathews, J. The retirement crisis. *The Seattle Times*, Friday, January 6, 1995, B5 (Special to *The Washington Post*).

Minkler, M. Introduction. In M. Minkler and C. Estes (Eds.), *Readings in the political economy of aging.* Farmingdale, N.Y.: Baywood, 1984.

Minkler, M., and Estes, C. L. (Eds.), *Readings in the political economy of aging.* Farmingdale, N.Y.: Baywood, 1984.

Miranda, M. Hispanic aging: An overview of issues and policy implications. In M. S. Harper (Ed.), *Minority aging.* DHHS Publication #HRS (P-DV-90-4), Washington, D.C.: U.S. Government Printing Office.

Moody, H. R. The politics of entitlement and the politics of productivity. In S. Bass, E. Kutza, and F. M. Torres-Gil (Eds.), *Diversity in Aging.* Glenview, Ill.: Scott, Foresman and Co., 1990.

Morgan, J.M. The redistribution of income of families and institutions and emergency hospital patterns. In G. Duncan and J. Morgan (Eds.), *Two thousand families—patterns of economic progress.* Ann Arbor: Institute for Social Research, 1983.

Morris, R. Challenges of aging in tomorrow's world: Will gerontology grow, stagnate or change? *The Gerontologist,* 1989, *29,* 494–501.

Nathan, S. The impact of poverty on the minority elderly. In M. S. Harper (Ed.), *Minority aging.* DHHS Publication #HRS (P-DV-90-4), Washington, D.C.: U.S. Government Printing Office.

National Academy on Aging. *Old age in the 21st century.* A report to the Assistant Secretary for Aging, U.S. Department of Health and Human Services. Syracuse University, Maxwell School of Citizenship and Public Affairs & The U.S. Administration on Aging, June 1994.

National Commission on Social Security Reform. *Report of the National Commission on Social Security Reform.* Washington, D.C.: U.S. Government Printing Office, 1983.

Nelson, C. T., and Feldman, A. M. *Estimating after-tax money income distribution using data from the March Current Population Survey.* U.S. Bureau of the Census, Current Population Survey, Special Publication Series P-23, No. 126, August 1983.

Nelson, G. Fair public-cost view must include direct, indirect spending. *The Aging Connection,* October/November 1989, *X,* 10.

Nelson, G. Tax expenditures for the elderly. *The Gerontologist,* 1983, *23,* 471–478.

Neugarten, B. Policy in the 1980s: Age or need entitlement. In B. Neugarten (Ed.), *Age or need: Public policies for older people.* Beverly Hills, Calif.: Sage, 1982.

Neugarten, B., and Neugarten, D. Changing meanings of age in the aging society. In A. Pifer and L. Bronte (Eds.), *Our aging society: Paradox and promise.* New York: W. W. Norton, 1986.

Olson, L. K. Aging policy: Who benefits? *Generations,* 1984, *9,* 10–14.

Palmer, J. L., and Sawhill, I. V. (Eds.), *The Reagan experiment.* Washington, D.C.: The Urban Institute, 1983.

Peterson, P. G. *Facing up: How to rescue the economy from crushing debt and restore the American Dream.* New York: Simon & Schuster, 1993.

Population Reference Bureau. *America in the 21st century: Social and economic support systems.* Washington, D.C.: Population Reference and the Population Resource Center, December 1990.

President's Task Force on Older Americans. *Report of the President's Task Force on Older Americans.* Washington, D.C.: Executive Office of the President of the United States, 1968.

Preston, S. H. Children and the elderly in the United States. *Scientific American,* 1984, *251,* 44–49.

Quadagno, J. Generational equity and the politics of the welfare state. *International Journal of Health Services,* 1990, *20*(4), 631–649.

Quinn, J. F., and Smeeding T. M. Defying the averages: Poverty and well-being among older Americans. *Aging Today,* September/October 1994, *XV*(5), 9.

Radner, D. B. Changes in the incomes of age groups: 1984 to 1989. *Social Security Bulletin,* 1991, 54.

Rosenblatt, R. Entitlement report targets spending on program benefits. *Aging Today,* San Francisco, Calif.: American Society on Aging, Sept./Oct. 1994, 1–2.

Schneider, E. C., and Guralnik, J. M. The aging of America: Impact on health care costs. *Journal of the American Medical Association,* 1990, *263,* 2335–2340.

SSI Modernization Project. *Supplemental Security Income modernization project: Final report of the experts.* Baltimore, Md.: Social Security Administration, 1992.

Taeuber, C. The dramatic reality. In S. Bass, E. Kutza, and F. M. Torres-Gil (Eds.), *Diversity in aging.* Glenview, Ill.: Scott, Foresman and Co., 1990.

Torres-Gil, F. M. *The new aging: Politics and change in America.* New York: Auburn House, 1992.

Torres-Gil, F. M., and Kmet, M. Elder leadership for a diverse America. In S. Bass, E. Kutza, and F. M. Torres-Gil (Eds.), *Diversity in aging.* Glenview, Ill.: Scott, Foresman and Co., 1990.

Torres-Gil, F., and Puccinelli, M. Mainstreaming gerontology in the policy arena. *The Gerontologist,* 1994, *34*(6), 749–752.

Uehara, E., Geron, S., and Beeman, S. The elderly poor in the Reagan era. *The Gerontologist,* 1986, *26,* 48–55.

Uhlenberg, P., and Salmon, M. G. Change in relative income of older women, 1960–80. *The Gerontologist,* 1986, *26,* 164–170.

U.S. Bureau of the Census. *Money income and poverty status of families and persons in the United States: 1984.* Advance Data from the March 1985 Current Population Survey. Current Population Report, Series P-60, No. 149, August 1985.

U.S. Congress, Congressional Budget Office. *Reducing the deficit: Spending and revenue options.* Washington, D.C.: U.S. Government Printing Office, 1994(a).

U.S. Congress, Congressional Budget Office. *The economic and budget outlook: Fiscal years 1995–1999.* Washington, D.C.: U.S. Government Printing Office, 1994(b).

U.S. House Select Committee on Aging. *Tomorrow's elderly: Issues for Congress.* Washington, D.C.: Congressional Institute for the Future, 1985.

U.S. House of Representatives, Select Committee on Aging. Working Documents. Washington, D.C.: U.S. Government Printing Office, 1991.

U.S. Senate Special Committee on Aging. *Aging America: Trends and projections, 1991 edition.* Washington, D.C.: U.S. Department of Health and Human Services, 1992.

U.S. Senate Special Committee on Aging, *Developments in aging: 1989, Vol 1.* Washington, D.C.: U.S. Government Printing Office, 1990.

Villers Foundation, *On the other side of Easy Street: Myths and facts about the economics of old age.* Washington, D.C.: Villers Foundation, 1987.

Walker, A. The economic "burden" of aging and the prospect of intergenerational conflict. *Aging and Society,* 1990, *10,* 377–396.

Wattenberg, B. J. *The birth dearth.* New York: Pharo's Books, 1987.

# CHAPTER 20

# HEALTH AND LONG-TERM CARE POLICY AND PROGRAMS

Throughout this book, we have examined the interplay of social, physiological, and psychological factors in how older people relate to their changing environments, and how health status affects this interaction. As noted earlier, technological advances, oriented toward cure, have created the paradox that while people are now living longer, they face serious, often debilitating or life-threatening disabilities that create the need for ongoing custodial care. Although disability per se in old age does not create dependency, growing numbers of older people, especially among the oldest-old, have multiple problems that result in physical and mental frailty and depend on the assistance of others as well as medical and non-medical services. This dependence is often intensified because of the interaction of age, race, gender, and poverty and because of changes in family structure that were described in Chapter 12. For example, the prevalence of limitations in daily activities increases to 56.8 percent among the oldest-old compared to 9.9 percent among the young old (Aday, 1993). As we have seen in earlier chapters, older persons

of color, women, and those who are low-income are more likely to have chronic disabilities that affect their ability to function (Leutz, Capitman, MacAdam, and Abraham, 1992).

It is this constellation of assistance and social services required to perform activities of daily living (ADLs)—bathing, dressing, toileting, eating, and transferring—and instrumental activities of daily living (IADLs)—shopping, cooking, and cleaning—combined with skilled care for medically related problems that constitute what is defined as *long-term care*. In addition to help with specific daily life tasks, people with cognitive impairments, such as Alzheimer's disease, may need nearly constant supervision. Such services may be delivered in an *institutional* setting, such as nursing homes or assisted living sites, which is the setting most people associate with long-term care. But such services are also delivered as *home- and community-based* long-term care. As described in Chapter 12, these services include those provided in *non-institutional community settings*, such as nutrition programs, senior centers, adult day care, respite, hospice, and transportation, and in a *person's home*, such as social work services, chore services, home-delivered meals, homemaker/home health aides, in-home respite, friendly visiting, and telephone reassurance. In most instances, these services are delivered directly to the older person but they may also serve to reduce demands upon family caregivers. For example, *respite*—a chance to be relieved of care responsibilities for a brief period of time—is one of the highest priorities among families who care for older members (Montgomery, 1989).

While the long-term care system also encompasses younger adults with AIDS, serious and persistent mental illness, and developmental disabilities, the focus of our discussion is on the structural and regulatory aspects of long-term care that affect older people. Because the current health care system emphasizes primary and acute care, long-term care is often perceived as a residual function to be undertaken when medical care has failed, rather than an essential and ongoing element of health care. Yet long-term care accounts for about 25 percent of all health care expenditures for older people. Since 25 to 33 percent of all persons age 65 and over are likely to be admitted to a nursing home during their lifetimes, the numbers needing nursing home care over the next 30 years have been projected to increase threefold. Of those admitted, 33 percent are discharged within three months to community settings (Gerety, 1994). In fact, two to three times as many older persons with disabilities are likely to receive long-term care at home as in nursing homes (National Academy on Aging, 1994). In a 1993 poll by the American Association of Retired Persons, 43 percent of respondents experienced a need in their immediate family for long-term care, but only a minority were confident that they could handle the costs of such care (AARP, 1993). Given the high incidence of chronic health needs in old age and the increasing numbers of older adults, it is not surprising that health care reform, including long-term care reform, is one of the most critical and controversial policy issues facing our nation.

We begin by examining the rising costs of health and long-term care and the factors that underlie these. Next, the public programs that fund long-term care—Medicare, Medicaid, Title XX, and the Older Americans Act—along with private insurance are described. This review highlights the major gap in long-term care: funding for home- and community-based care as opposed to the predominant mode—institutional care. Federal, state, and local demonstration efforts to reform health and long-term care are briefly described.

## HEALTH AND LONG-TERM CARE EXPENDITURES

Policy makers, service providers, and the general public are all concerned about the "crisis in health care." Total national expenditures for health care consume approximately 14 percent of the GNP or Gross National Product, (*Washington Post,* November 9, 1994). Services for older adults account for approximately 36 percent of these total health expenditures, with Medicaid and Medicare the fastest growing programs in the federal budget (Gerety, 1994). As noted by the former Director of the National Institute on Aging, T. Franklin Williams (1994), our society must deal with the fact that "the majority of all health care and related services will be needed by and provided to older persons and others with chronic conditions." The average expenditure for health services for persons age 65 and over is nearly four times the cost for those under age 65; this is largely attributable to older people's greater chronic disease needs and use of hospital and nursing home services as described above. As illustrated in Figure 20–1, federal and state governments in 1991 spent approximately $70 billion (through Medicare and Medicaid) to help provide long-term assistance (nursing home and home health care) to older people with chronic disabilities (NASHP, 1992). Most of this support—over 80 percent—went to institutional care.

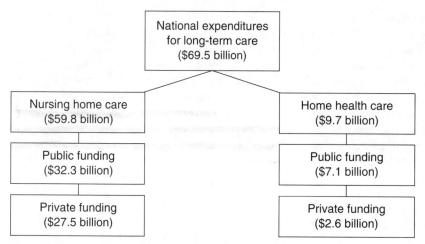

**FIGURE 20–1    Long-Term Care Funding (Calendar Year 1991)**
SOURCE: HCFA Office of the Actuary, April 1993

Prepared by: AARP Public Policy Institute

Although cost-containment changes in the private health care marketplace, especially through managed care, appear to have helped slow the rate of increase of medical costs, expenses are still rising faster than the national income. Medicare and Medicaid are expanding at several times the economic growth rate, adding to the pressure to cut spending on other programs or to raise taxes. Based on current trends, it is projected that spending on Medicare and Medicaid will consume 26.4 percent of the federal budget in the year 2003, up from 16.5 percent in 1994 (Jensen, 1994). While public expenditures for health and long-term care are rising, older individuals and their families are also paying more for care. Only 66 percent of the care costs of older people are covered by government funding (AARP, 1993). As mentioned earlier in this text, older Americans now spend a higher proportion (and more in actual dollars) of their incomes on health care than they did before Medicare and Medicaid were established three decades ago (or 23 percent versus 11 percent respectively) (AARP, 1994). As illustrated in Figure 20–2, out-of-pocket costs are incurred in utilizing physician, hospital, home health care, dental and vision services, prescription drugs, and durable medical equipment, typically through

the for-profit sector. Older people, on average, spend considerably more out-of-pocket than younger Americans because of their greater need for diverse health services described above, because Medicare benefits are often more limited than private insurance benefits, and because of higher premiums and cost-sharing required by Medicare.

With regard to long-term care and assistance with ADLs, families now provide 80 percent of all in-home care to older relatives residing outside of institutional settings. In most instances, older people and their families do not utilize formal services in order to remain in the community. In 1993, 66 percent of older individuals who received long-term care services at home had *only* unpaid services of family and friends; 20 percent utilized both paid and unpaid services, and 10 percent paid services only (See Figure 20–3; Families USA Foundation, 1994). This translates into older persons or their families financing about 55 percent of their long-term care costs (Hendricks and Hatch, 1993). In 1994, for example, 22 percent of out-of-pocket health costs for older adults went to home health care (AARP, 1994). Despite the escalating expenditures associated with health and long-term care, federal and state funds are not meeting the need of many

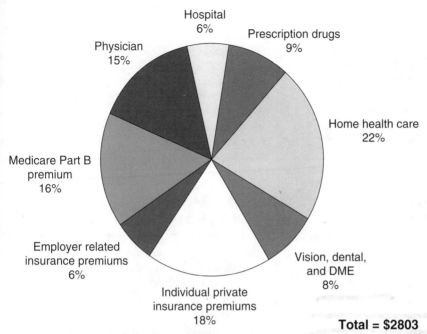

**FIGURE 20–2    Coming Up Short: Increasing Out-of-Pocket Health Spending by Older Americans**

Prepared by AARP/Public Policy Institute, April 1994.

DME = Durable Medical Equipment

frail elders to be able to remain in home and community-based settings and to reduce the burdens upon family caregivers, as is the case with Kay Ruggles and her daughter described below.

## Factors Underlying Growing Costs

A number of structural factors underlie these escalating costs. One is the success of modern medical care. While advances in medical science produce some cost-saving breakthroughs, they also make possible more sophisticated and expensive medical treatments. Declines in mortality earlier in the life cycle have, over time, resulted in a significant increase in disability and a growing need for medical interventions during the increased years of life expectancy that are spent in disability. This has created the paradox of the demographic imperative: the "high-tech" medical care that has contributed to expanded longevity is the same care that threatens the

provision of "low-tech, high-touch" community-based care and long-term care supportive services (Estes, Swan and Associates, 1993). Escalating health and long-term care costs are indicators that the United States can no longer afford to provide everything that medicine has to

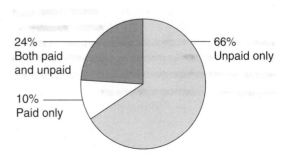

**FIGURE 20–3    Long-Term Care for the Older Population at Home, 1993**

SOURCE: Lewin-VHI analysis of National Long-Term Care Survey, updated to 1993.

---

### THE DILEMMAS OF HOME CARE

Kay Ruggles, age 87, suffers from severe osteoporosis and arthritis. Although she worries about falling, she wants to stay in her home as long as possible. Since she is not eligible for any publicly funded home care program, she must pay out of pocket for daily assistance with bathing, walking, and cooking. Her daughter is employed and has a family to care for, but tries to stay with her mother on weekends and assist her with the household chores. Because the cost of home care is so much greater than her income, Mrs. Ruggles' savings are dwindling. She and her daughter worry that she will have to go into a nursing home as a Medicaid patient as the only way to fund her care.

---

offer, which has raised complex moral, ethical, and legal questions about the nature and extent of care. In these debates, because of their rapid growth along with the public funding of a large portion of their care through Medicare and Medicaid, older people have often been "blamed" for escalating costs. Yet, contrary to media portrayals that medical costs in the last year of life escalate for the old-old, hospital and physician costs actually decline for those age 80 and over, although "custodial" or personal care costs are high (Cohen, 1994). Rather than population aging as the cause, escalating expenditures result, in large part, from the system of public financing, which is biased toward institutional care, and the lack of comprehensive, coordinated health and long-term care policy and programs that insure continuity of care.

Closely related to the success of medical technology in prolonging life is the conflict between the curative goals of medicine and the long-term care needs of older adults. As described in Chapter 7, U.S. health services, based on a biomedical model, have focused on curing acute illnesses rather than on caring for chronic diseases. As a result, there is a poor fit between the medical and related social service needs of the older population (e.g., long-term care needs) and the funding mechanisms, regulations, and fragmented services of the health care system. This poor fit has become even more pronounced in the past decade, as reimbursement rules have tightened to include primarily the medical aspects of care authorized by a physician, not social care necessary to perform ADLs (Chappell, 1990).

As we have seen in Chapter 19, underlying all these factors is a growing distrust of government and its ability to tackle health care reform, and a strong belief in the private sector, resulting in health and long-term care systems that encourage entrepreneurship and a market-driven approach to providing services (Moon, 1994). The shape of health care in the United States is largely determined by its method of payment. Although funding mechanisms are shifting with the growth of managed care, which aims to control the level of resources devoted to health care, the emphasis has been on the private provision of health services, without effective market control or uniform governmental regulation of expenditures. Instead, most health services are provided privately, and are financed by a mix of public programs, private insurance and direct patient payments. Patients have been largely free to choose the health care providers they prefer; in turn, physicians have been able to charge patients whatever they choose. Accordingly, prices in the health care sector—primarily in hospital costs and physician fees—have risen faster than the general inflation rate. These patterns are even more pronounced with regard to the "non-system" of long-term care, which begins with the assumption that individuals are financially responsible for costs until their assets and income have been exhausted, at which point welfare in the form of Medicaid takes over (Leutz et al., 1992).

In fact, critics of long-term care contend that there is less a system of long-term care than several ways to pay for it (Leutz et al., 1992). Acute and long-term care are, for the most part, two separate fragmented systems, with distinct caregivers, treatment settings, financing structures, and goals which create barriers and inefficiencies (Kane and Kane, 1994). Physicians are the primary care providers in acute care hospitals and outpatient settings, and Medicare, a federal entitlement program for acute care, covers most of the costs. Nursing staff and family members are the principal caregivers in nursing homes and home settings; Medicaid, a state-federal partnership of a welfare program, pays for a large percentage of institutional care (Kane and Kane, 1994). In the acute care setting, intensity of services drives costs, whereas in long-term care, duration of treatment is the driver. Although Medicare encourages speedy discharge of patients to nursing facilities, this nursing home care is so expensive and inadequately reimbursed that there is an incentive for providers to discharge residents back to hospitals. As noted by Vladeck (1994), the "irony with long-term care is that the better the care, the longer the individual lives and remains in the system accruing costs." The disjunction between the primary sources of funding and regulation—Medicaid and Medicare—is the greatest barrier to the integration of the two systems of care.

## MEDICARE

As a social insurance system, Medicare, or Title XVIII of the Social Security Act of 1965, is intended to provide financial protection against the cost of hospital, nursing home, and physician care for people age 65 and over. A value underlying Medicare is that older people are entitled to health care, which society has an obligation to provide. Medicare's focus on the older population also grew out of a compromise with the medical profession, which successfully opposed comprehensive health insurance for the general public. Yet Medicare was also viewed as the "first step" toward increasing access to health care for all age groups (Rubenstein, Marmor, Stone, Moon, and Harootyan, 1994). Despite Medicare's goal of financial protection, it covers less than 50 percent of the total health expenditures of older adults (U.S. Senate Committee on Aging, 1992).

The Medicare program has two basic components: Hospital Insurance (Part A) and Supplemental Medical Insurance (Part B). Part A, financed through the Social Security payroll tax, is available for all older persons who are eligible for Social Security. It pays for up to 90 days of hospital care and for a restricted amount of skilled nursing care and home health services. Recipients are responsible for their first day's hospital stay and for co-payments for hospital stays exceeding 60 days. When the 90 days of hospital care are used up, a patient has a "lifetime" reserve of 60 days. Part B, Supplemental Medical Insurance, is financed through general tax revenues paid by enrollees. Part B reimburses for some physician services, hospital outpatient services, home health care limited to certain types of health conditions and specific time periods, diagnostic laboratory and x-ray services and a variety of miscellaneous services. Part A covers 99 percent of the older population, compared to 97 percent who are covered by Part B.

Contrary to the assumption of many older persons that Medicare will cover their health care costs, it pays only 80 percent of the *allowable* charges, *not the actual amount* charged by health providers. The patient must pay the difference between "allowable" and "actual" charges, unless the physician accepts "assignment" and agrees to charge only what Medicare pays. Beneficiaries whose doctors do not accept Medicare assignment are responsible for the amount that their doctor charges above the Medicare-approved rate. Individuals with both Parts A and B must also pay an annual deductible and, in recent years, increasing co-payments. In fact, out-of-pocket expenditures for deductibles and copayments have increased

147 percent from 1980 to 1990, after adjusting for inflation (Jensen, 1994).

Although Medicare is a primary payer for hospital and physician services, its major limitation is its focus on *acute care*, whereby it either excludes or gives little coverage to significant long-term care expenses, such as nursing homes, preventive health measures, outpatient costs of prescriptions, mental health services, and custodial or non-medical services. Instead, 65 percent of Medicare dollars pay for hospital care, typically for catastrophic illness (Kane and Kane, 1990). Nursing home care is restricted to 100 days, with eligibility contingent on acute illness or injury, usually after hospitalization, and requiring co-payments. As a result, Medicare covers the expense of only 3 to 5 percent of the institutionalized older population (Gerety, 1994). Having believed that Medicare pays for long-term care, some older people only become aware of Medicare's limitations upon their first hospitalization or admission to a nursing home.

Despite the limitations on what Medicare will cover and the current policy focus on cost containment, expenditures, which are primarily associated with hospitals, have spiraled, making Medicare one of the fastest growing programs in the federal budget and a target for budget cuts (Rubenstein et al., 1994; Moon, 1994). For example, over the next seven years, Medicare is estimated to pay out $730 billion more than it collects (National Association of Social Workers, 1995). As noted earlier, these increases are due primarily to inflation in hospital costs and physician fees, not to the growth of the older population per se nor to their increased utilization of services in the last years of life (Cohen, 1994; Lee and Benjamin, 1989). Regardless of the specific causes, Medicare Part A (the Hospital Insurance Trust Fund) faces insolvency in the year 2002. (National Association of Social Workers, 1995).

In order to reduce incentives for physicians to provide more hospital-bed services under fee-for-service payment plans, a system of prospective payment (PPS) was instituted in 1983. Instead of reimbursing providers for each service

for each patient, the federal Health Care Financing Administration determines payment by the diagnostic category in which each patient is placed. These categories, which are used to classify patients by medical condition and thus set Medicare payments prior to the patient's admission, are called *diagnostic related groupings*, or DRGs. Under the prior cost-based reimbursement system, hospitals were paid more if they provided more and longer services, resulting in higher subsequent costs. With DRGs, a hospital is paid a fixed amount per admission. according to the diagnostic category. The rates for DRGs are, in turn, based on an expected length of stay for each condition. A hospital that keeps patients longer than needed, orders unnecessary tests, or provides care inefficiently must absorb the differential in cost between the care provided and the amount reimbursed by Medicare. Alternatively, hospitals that provide care at a cost below the established DRG can keep the difference.

Although findings are mixed, it appears that DRGs have resulted in increased pressures on nursing homes, families, and home health care agencies to provide care for patients who are discharged from hospitals on average two days earlier and sicker. These patients are in need of higher levels of post-hospital care than in the past. This has created 21 million more days of care annually that must be provided in the home or community (Binney, Estes, and Ingman, 1990). Since families and home health agencies often cannot provide these more complex and intensive levels of care, some studies have found that premature discharges have resulted in a "revolving door" pattern of more patients in and out of hospitals (Coulton, 1988; Estes, Wood, and Lee, 1988; Gaumer et al., 1989; Hing, 1989; Sager et al., 1989). On the other hand, findings of greater need for care and higher rates of mortality may be due, in part, to differences in risk factors, (e.g., the inpatient population is now older and sicker than before the prospective payment system), not because of shorter stays or declining quality of care (Hing, 1987; Leibson et al., 1990). As a whole, however, it does appear that admission to nursing homes and utilization of home health care have increased as a result of DRGs (Estes and Binney, 1988; Fitzgerald, Moore, and Dittus, 1988; Manton, Vertress, and Wrigley, 1990). This is partly because DRGs discourage the extra time required to make appropriate discharge plans and the use of ancillary personnel such as social workers except to expedite discharges from hospitals. An additional factor affecting the quality of community care available for older adults is that even though hospital discharges to home health care have risen 37 percent since the passage of DRGS, the rate of growth in community-based home health services for Medicare enrollees has slowed since the mid-1980s, largely as a result of inadequate reimbursement policies (Estes, Wood, and Lee, 1988).

Ironically, Medicare costs across the health care system as a whole have not declined since the passage of DRGs. This is because the prospective payment system has not altered Medicare's basic approach nor the structural arrangements that depend upon fee-for-service financing. Nor have DRGs reduced all the incentives for applying costly technologically oriented care (Estes, 1991). Costs have also increased because of increased federal oversight and regulatory control through hospital rate setting and the regulation of physician behavior. Other Medicare costs have grown as medical procedures have shifted to ambulatory settings and doctors' offices which are not restricted by the prospective payment system. At the same time, more stringent cost-sharing provisions associated with Medicare, through co-payments, deductibles and the Part B premium, have increased the financial burden on many elders and their families (Estes, 1991; Estes, Swan, and Associates, 1993; Fischer and Eustis, 1994).

In an effort to reduce costs associated with physician services, hospitalizations, and aftercare for acute illness, Congress passed the Medicare Catastrophic Health Care Act in 1988. This Act expanded acute care benefits for hospital stays, set a cap on yearly out-of-pocket expenses, provided protection against spousal impoverishment, and increased coverage in skilled nursing facilities and for home care. Such expanded coverage was to be financed by a mandatory supplemental premium. This surtax, ranging from $4 to $800 a year based on income, affected approximately 40 percent of the older population, specifically individuals with incomes over $30,000 or couples with incomes over $50,000 a year. Although the American Association of Retired Persons actively supported this legislation, none of its supporters anticipated the negative grassroots reaction among older persons nationwide. Many reacted against changes in the basic premise of Medicare financing: that higher-income older adults would pay a surtax for benefits serving primarily low-income older people, and that financing was entirely through a transfer of funds within older and disabled populations, not shared across populations. In addition, the legislation failed to address what most older people want—protection from the bankrupting costs of long-term care. In 1989, Congress voted to repeal the legislation, leaving many legislators wary of addressing additional policy changes affecting older persons.

The greatest gap in federal funding is home- and community-based care. With over 20 percent of nursing home placements estimated to be incongruent with older persons' needs, home care is widely advocated as an alternative to inappropriate institutionalization (Kane and Kane, 1990). Even older individuals who are in nursing homes may require home care at some point, since 25 to 45 percent of nursing home stays are less than three months, and 50 percent of these "short stayers" are able to return to live in the community (The Pepper Commission, 1990). Not only do most older people require home care, but they also prefer and tend to recover faster at home and may experience improvements in their quality of life (Kemper et al., 1987; Families USA Foundation, 1994).

Despite the need for home care, the availability of adequate home care services is limited for a number of reasons. First, Medicare only provides skilled nursing that is certified by a physician as necessary to rehabilitation from acute illness for homebound elders for 100 days or less. This means that an older person must have recently been hospitalized and be in need of physical therapy, speech therapy, or intermittent skilled nursing; must be restricted in their ability to leave home; and must have a doctor prescribe the care. This excludes from coverage the many people who need assistance with ADLs, but not skilled nursing or therapy and thus do not meet Medicare's restrictive eligibility criteria of "medically necessary" and potential for rehabilitation. In fact, most older people need about three times as many days of non-medical custodial care as they do days of medical services (Kane and Kane, 1990). Virtually none of the outpatient custodial or personal assistance (non-medical) services to older persons with chronic disabilities by non-physicians, such as visiting nurses, home health service providers, and home health aides, are covered. Consequently, spending for home care comprises only 3 percent of Medicare expenditures, and older people and their families pay directly for almost 75 percent of all non-institutional services such as home health care, homemaker services, and adult day care (Kane and Kane, 1990).

Recent changes have also affected the availability of home care services. Earlier hospital discharges have often meant that more technical care, such as intravenous therapy and ventilation therapy, must be delivered by families at the same time that public funding for home care has been cut and eligibility for services made more restrictive. Legislative changes have made it more difficult for Medicare patients to find home health agencies to service them. For example, the federal government has more strictly defined "medical necessity," which has resulted in an increased number of denials for Medicare-financed home health care. As a result, many home health agencies have dropped their Medicare certification, thereby reducing the pool of agencies available to Medicare beneficiaries. The growth that has

occurred in home care has been primarily within for-profit chains. This occurred in response to the 1980 and 1981 Omnibus Budget Reconciliation Acts, which eliminated the requirement for state licensure as a basis for reimbursing proprietary agencies. These regulatory changes served to stimulate competition for the provision and contracting out of services to proprietary agencies, which resulted in a decline in the proportion of home care provided by public and nonprofit agencies (Estes et al., 1993). As a result, more older persons and their families either have had to pay privately for home care or do without. With the cost of 24-hour home health care amounting to as much as $70,000 a year, such care is prohibitive for many people (Estes et al., 1993).

In sum, Medicare can be characterized as coverage that is broad but not deep: Every older American is covered, but they nevertheless remain vulnerable to long-term care expenses. And even covered services require substantial co-payments or costs shared by the older patient.

## MEDICAID

In contrast to Medicare, Medicaid is not a health insurance program for older people, but rather a federal and state means-tested welfare program of medical assistance for the categorically needy, regardless of age (e.g., to recipients of Aid to Families with Dependent Children and Supplemental Security Income). For example, participation in Supplemental Security Income, a federal-state program of public assistance to the older people and persons with disabilities, automatically triggers Medicaid eligibility. Although Medicaid is the principal health care insurance provided for the poor and is viewed as a "safety net" program, only 33 percent of poor older persons meet the stringent eligibility requirements (Kasper, 1988).

Medicaid, which was enacted in 1965, also differs from Medicare in that federal funds are administered locally through welfare departments. For some older people, this method of funding carries a stigma of welfare. Federal regulations require that all state Medicaid programs provide hospital inpatient care, physician services, skilled nursing facility care, laboratory and x-ray services, home health services, hospital outpatient care, family planning, rural health clinics, and early and periodic screening. In addition, some states provide other optional services, including intermediate care, prescription drugs outside the hospital, some dental services, and eyeglasses. Similar to Medicare, coverage for mental health and social services is limited. Given all these limitations, Medicaid, similar to Medicare, provides only 60 to 80 percent of daily health care charges, even though Medicaid public expenditures have grown more rapidly than inflation (Marsh, 1992). As with Medicare, the growth in federal and state expenditures is due primarily to price increases by health providers, not population growth or expansion of care.

Medicaid has become a highly visible target for federal and state cost-cutting. Because it forms a growing proportion of state budgets at the same time that federal funds allocated to states have declined, Medicaid benefits, eligibility, and utilization have been reduced at the state level and copayments have increased (Harrington, Estes, Lee, and Newcomer, 1986; The Pepper Commission, 1990). This has also meant that eligibility criteria and benefits, based on financial need, vary widely among states. Variability is especially great among states vis-à-vis access to "optional" benefits such as physical therapy and personal care. Such benefit reductions, however, fail to address the rising hospital and nursing home costs caused by price increases by health providers. Rather, Medicaid cuts have created a growing number of older adults who lack access to care and who are at risk of declining health status and increased mortality but who are not viewed as a vocal and powerful constituency by politicians (Meyer and Moon, 1988; National Association of Social Workers, 1995).

Older persons constitute a minority (approximately 13 percent) of the total users of Medicaid, yet they account for 40 percent of the total Medicaid expenditures (Waldo, Sonnefeld, McKusick, and Arnett, 1989; Wolfe, 1993). The predominant cause of this disproportionate rate of expenditures is that Medicaid is the primary public source for funding nursing home care. Nursing home costs account for about 45 percent of the total Medicaid expenditures and 68 percent of Medicaid funds spent on older people (Wolfe, 1993). While Medicare covers only care in skilled nursing facilities for patients with rehabilitative potential, Medicaid can cover both skilled care for rehabilitation and intermediate care of a more custodial nature. Nursing home expenditures are increasing at an average annual rate of 10 percent and form the fastest growing category of Medicaid expenditures. In contrast, only about 2 percent of Medicaid expenditures go to community-based home health services (Leutz et al., 1992). Medicaid's eligibility policies and benefit structure have created financial incentives to use nursing homes rather than community services, because home care benefits are limited and the income eligibility is higher for nursing home residents than for those categorically needy who are living in the community. Given the relatively small proportion of older people who are in nursing homes, Medicaid expenditures are thus concentrated on a very few individuals (Hendricks and Hatch, 1993).

From the perspective of increasing long-term care options, a positive development in 1981 was the passage of Section 2176 of the Omnibus Budget Reconciliation Act. This permits the waiver of Medicaid statutory requirements so that states can provide community-based alternatives to institutionalization. The waiver program specifies seven core services that have not been traditionally considered "medical," but which are necessary to keep people at home: case management, homemaker, home health aide, personal care, adult day care, rehabilitation, respite care, and other services approved by the federal government as "cost-effective." The primary criterion is that states must demonstrate that the costs of such home- and community-based services do not exceed the cost to Medicaid for care in institutions, and also that they serve to divert at-risk individuals from nursing home placement. Since the Medicaid waiver program assumes that home care is less expensive than placement in a nursing home or intermediate care facility, the target for benefits must meet the "but for" criterion; that is, the person would be in a Medicaid-financed institution, but for the services provided by the community care program.

Although 48 states have covered an array of health and social services under Section 2176, its cost containment goals mean that most states restrict the number of persons who can receive services and the scope of services provided. The waivers are optional, with the result that they are denied to many eligible individuals and the availability of community alternatives to institutional care has expanded only marginally. The Home and Community Based Care Program, under the 1990 Omnibus Budget Reconciliation Act, extends the waivers to incorporate community-based services as optional for individuals with severe physical or cognitive impairments who are eligible for Medicaid and who would otherwise require more costly institutional care (Lipson and Laudicina, 1991). Both programs are also constrained by their limited government funding relative to the extent of need (Leutz et al., 1992).

## Social Services Block Grants and the Older Americans Act

In addition to the limited allocations of Medicare and Medicaid for community-based services, Title XX Amendments to the Social Security Act (Social Services Block Grants) and Title III of the Older Americans Act provide limited funding for non-medical, custodial services for older people with disabilities.

As noted in Chapter 19, most services to older persons under Title XX go to those who receive Supplemental Security Income. Title XX services are viewed as necessary to carry out basic ADLs, and include homemaker and chore

services, home-delivered meals, adult protective services, adult day care, foster care, and institutional or residential care. With federal reductions in block grant funding to the states, competition for decreasing funds at the local level has increased. In 1989, states spent on average 21 percent of their block grant money on services to older people (Center on Elderly People Living Alone, 1994). Long-term care services funded under Title III of the Older Americans Act include information and referral, case management, transportation, homemaker, day care, nutrition education and congregate meals, respite care, and senior centers. In-home services are designed as a priority service for states. Since the primary eligibility criterion is age 60, OAA services may be provided without the restrictions of Medicare and the means test of Medicaid. However, services must be targeted to persons with the greatest social or economic need (AARP, 1994b).

Both programs are limited in their impact by the relatively small allocation of federal resources, with $1.2 billion appropriated to OAA in 1992 as compared to $15 billion for Medicaid (AARP, 1994b). Moreover, the Omnibus Budget Reconciliation Act, which intensified the tilt

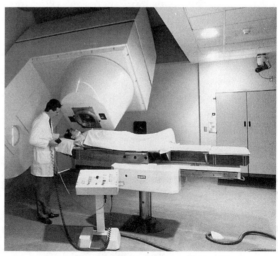

Advances in medical technology have raised the cost of health care while improving diagnosis and treatment capabilities.

toward medical services, reduced federal funds, and removed state matching funds and state reporting requirements for these programs (Berghold, Estes, and Villaneuva, 1990). Community agencies that relied heavily on Title XX funds tried to recover their losses by restructuring their programs toward the medical services reimbursed under Medicare. The programs most likely to be eliminated or reduced were homemaker, and chore and personal care services. These changes in the Social Services Block Grant and the Older Americans Act, along with those in Medicare and Medicaid, have reduced older adults' access to long-term care; this is particularly the case for low-income elders, thereby increasing gender and racial inequities in terms of access and availability of services. The general approach under both programs has been to give a few services to as many people as possible, which does not necessarily reach the most vulnerable older persons.

## PRIVATE INSURANCE

While the U.S. health and long-term care system is based on the assumption that individuals are first responsible for paying for their care, 37 million Americans or approximately 15 percent of the noninstitutionalized population lack insurance for hospital and doctor costs. A substantially greater number—over 200 million—have no insurance for long-term care (Corry, 1994). Among the older population, wide disparities exist in terms of their ability to purchase private supplemental and long-term care insurance.

For older adults who can afford more extensive coverage than Medicare provides, private "medigap" insurance is available. Over 70 percent of the older population have purchased some type of private supplemental insurance; of these, about 33 percent were able to obtain coverage through their former place of employment. This has meant unequal access to such insurance. The ability to afford private health insurance clearly varies widely by income. Of poor or near-

poor older persons, who suffer from more chronic illness and disability than do their higher-income peers, only 47 percent have private insurance, compared with 87 percent of high-income older adults. Also, less than 18 percent of elders of color have private Medigap coverage compared to 48 percent of poor older whites. And women are less likely to have had access to group health insurance through employment than their male counterparts. Only 20 percent of all retirees who lack private coverage are able to obtain Medicaid or other public health insurance, such as Veterans' Assistance (Folkemer, 1994).

Even those who carry supplemental coverage can suffer burdensome medical expenses if they are seriously ill, since Medicare does not cover the full costs of care. This burden was acknowledged by the 1988 passage of the Medicare Catastrophic Coverage Act, which was subsequently repealed. Few "medigap" policies pick up physician charges in excess of Medicare's allowable fees, nor do they ordinarily cover prescriptions, dental care, or nursing home care—all services essential to the long-term maintenance of the older population. As a result, supplemental private insurance plans cover, on average, only about 7 percent of older people's health care bills (Davis and Rowland, 1991).

As older adults have become more aware of the limits of public funding for long-term care, an increasing number of insurance companies are selling private long-term care insurance plans. Most policies cover nursing home care (at a range of $40–$120 a day), with home health and adult day care services usually reimbursed at 50–80 percent of the selected nursing home benefit. Yet less than one percent of older individuals with disabilities are covered by private insurance. The high premiums and co-payments mean that most policies are out of the financial reach of up to 20 percent of Americans age 55 to 79. Indeed, high-quality policies cost as much as $2500 annually when purchased at age 67 and $7700 for those age 79 (Wiener and Illston, 1994; Wiener, Illston, and Hanley, 1994). Accordingly, private insurance covers only about

2 percent of the nation's long-term care expenditures (Riley and Mollica, 1994; National Committee to Preserve Social Security and Medicare, 1993). Not surprisingly, women are less likely than men to be able to afford long-term care insurance and they spend a higher proportion of their income when they do, reflecting both gaps in coverage and their lower median income (Allen, 1993). Those individuals most likely to purchase and benefit from long-term care insurance are those with assets and a spouse to protect. Although such insurance is likely to become more affordable in the future, by the year 2018, only an estimated 20 percent of older people will be able to purchase private long-term care insurance. Even if private policies were to become more affordable, questions have been raised about the quality of these insurance plans (Wiener and Illston, 1994).

## Resultant Inequities

The system of financing health and long-term care—public funding that is biased toward institutional and acute care and private policies that are beyond the financial reach of low-income older Americans—has created a two-tier system of health care delivery: one level for those with private health insurance, Medicare or the means to pay for expensive medical treatment, including rising copayments and deductibles, and another for those forced to rely on Medicaid, Veterans' Assistance, or to do without health care altogether. Even with Medicare recipients, there are disparities. Older people who have Medicare only, many of whom may be near-poor, tend to have fewer doctor visits and hospital stays, and buy fewer drugs than those who can afford cost-sharing provisions and other private insurance. People between the ages of 60 and 65, who are too "young" for Medicare and are often no longer covered by job-related or other insurance, also fall between the cracks (Davis and Rowland, 1991). Not surprisingly, the proportion of income spent on health care increases as income decreases, as illustrated in Figure 20–4. Accordingly, the poor and near-poor spend over 30 percent of their income on health care, while the richest 20 percent of older families spend less than 15 percent (Smeeding, 1990).

Medicaid has been criticized for perpetuating class inequities, since about 25 percent of physicians refuse to take Medicaid patients, especially those with a high level of need because the fees allowed for reimbursement are generally below prevailing cost levels. Those who will accept Medicaid patients typically limit them to 20 percent of their load. Since the number of Medicaid beds in nursing homes is limited, Medicaid patients, typically older women and

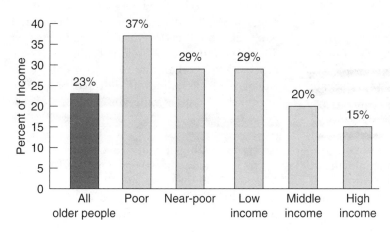

**FIGURE 20–4  Average Out-of-Pocket Health Costs as a Percent of Household Income by Poverty Status, 1994**

Poverty status definitions are: poor = family income below poverty line; near poor = family income between 100% and 125% of poverty line; low-income = family income over 125% to 200% of poverty line; middle-income = family income over 200% to 400% of poverty line; high-income = family income over 400% of poverty line.

SOURCE: AARP/PPI based on 1994 Urban Institute projections.

people of color, must often wait longer for placement than do private pay patients, and the homes available to them are frequently of lower quality. Individuals must spend-down their assets in order to be eligible for Medicaid; older persons who have been private-pay patients in a nursing home may find that the facility will no longer accept them after they have "spent down." Moreover, some 40 percent of the older population have incomes that are too high to be eligible for Medicaid, yet they typically lack the resources to pay out-of-pocket for long-term care. Those who fall in this "Medicaid gap" frequently receive inadequate medical care or must depend on families to provide care (Quadagno, Meyer, and Turner, 1991; Wiener, Illston, and Hanley, 1994).

Because only 25 percent of non-institutional care is publicly subsidized, inequities are even greater in terms of access to home care services. As noted above, most older people and their families either pay privately for home care or go without these services. Lack of access to home care is even greater for the 40 percent of low-income elders who fall just above the eligibility line for Medicaid, but who are nonetheless low-income (Leutz et al., 1992). Not surprisingly, older people and their families with higher incomes are able to purchase privately funded community care services, and private-paying clients receive more hours of home health care than do those who rely on public funds (Leutz et al., 1992; Kane, 1989). For example, older people with incomes 300 percent above the poverty line are nearly two and a half times more likely to use community services than elders at or below the poverty line (Coughlin, McBride, Perozek, and Liu, 1990). The affluent are also more likely to rely disproportionately for personal care services on home care aides, companions and attendants who are not affiliated with established organizations and whom they are able to recruit and pay independently. In contrast, older women and minorities had the lowest rates of utilization of private-pay community-based services (Leutz et al., 1992).

## HEALTH AND LONG-TERM CARE REFORMS

Given these gaps, national reform in health and long-term care has been widely debated in recent years. In some respects, the debates are not new, but rather more visible. In fact, since 1912, there have been efforts to create a program of access to health care for all Americans. In 1986, Wilbur Cohen, Assistant Secretary of Health, Education, and Welfare, predicted that major social legislation occurs in 30-year intervals, with Social Security (1935) followed by Medicare and Medicaid (1965) and national health care reform embracing universal coverage and continuity of care in 1995 (Brody, 1994). Yet the United States, along with South Africa, remain the only industrialized nations that do not provide some form of universal health coverage, regardless of ability to pay. Since the 1992 elections, health care reform has moved from academic debates to the legislative process, but one which ended in gridlock. In spite of escalating costs, growing numbers of uninsured citizens, and restrictive insurance policies, attempts to change the health care system created a clash between the goals of cost containment versus guaranteeing access to all, and ended without even modest changes in insurance industry practices (*The Seattle Times*, September 27, 1994). While the majority of Americans support health care reform in the abstract, they appear unwilling to accept less personal choice of doctors or hospitals, even if doing so would reduce health care costs or make universal coverage possible (Gill and Ingman, 1994). What ultimately killed health care reform, however, was the disproportionate influence of powerful special interest lobbies, particularly insurance companies and many small businesses, who in the 1994 Congressional debates spent at least $100 million to protect their financial interests and ways of doing business. Resistance to large-scale change in the health care system has grown since the Republican sweep in the November 1994 elections and health care reform is not mentioned in the "Contract with America."

Nevertheless, given the number of individuals who lack access to adequate care, the debate will undoubtedly continue, particularly at the state level, although perhaps in less visible forms and arenas. Central to such a debate is whether long-term care will be included in any health care package. As noted earlier, the current dichotomy between long-term care and acute care is not functional for either the older person or the formal and informal care providers, since acute and chronic disease and disability are frequently experienced concurrently. What is needed is a health care system that integrates acute and long-term care over the course of each individual's lifetime. Findings from four national surveys in 1993–94 show that bipartisan support for health care reform increases dramatically when long-term care coverage is included. Such support may signal recognition that the absence of a viable long-term care policy affects persons of all ages, classes, and racial and ethnic groups, since long-term care is the health crisis for which virtually every American is uninsured (Riley and Mollica, 1994). We turn now to a brief review of the history and status of long-term care legislation at the national level.

The first comprehensive long-term care legislation was introduced by Claude Pepper, who linked an initiative to fund long-term care in the home to the ill-fated catastrophic health care legislation in 1988. In 1990, the Pepper Commission recommended public funding of home, community, and nursing home care for seriously disabled Americans. In 1992, the Democratic leadership in the House and the Senate introduced bills for long-term care known as the Long Term Care Family Security Act. During the 1992 campaign, Bill Clinton was the first Presidential candidate to call for expanded public funding for home care services provided on a non-means-tested basis. Major national organizations concerned about long-term care, such as the National Committee to Preserve Social Security and Medicare and the Leadership Council of Aging Organizations, favor universal and comprehensive long-term care plans for disabled persons *of all ages,* with services encompassing institutional, home- and community-based care and personal assistance. In fact, this alliance between senior organizations, such as AARP, and groups serving other populations has been a positive development in the long-term care arena, despite the lack of a successful outcome. Of the major proposals that have been extensively debated by Congress, President Clinton's National Health Security Act was one of the few to offer new long-term care benefits.

Because of the visibility and scope of the President's plan, which set forth the principles of universal access, comprehensive health care benefits, and high-quality care, we briefly describe it rather than attempt a review of all the proposals introduced in the 103rd Congress. The President's plan would have achieved universal coverage through an employer-based financing approach supplemented with government subsidies for nonworkers. Employers' required payments would take the form of premium contributions of approximately 80 percent of the plan. Medicaid would have been eliminated as a separate program. Individuals would have received their insurance coverage by choosing among plans offered by a regional alliance of health plans. It was assumed that costs would be contained through "managed competition" among health care plans. Medicare would not have been changed, although prescription drug coverage would have been expanded and cost sharing would have been increased (Moon, 1994).

Although the President's plan focused on universal acute care coverage and cost controls, limits on Medicare would have helped to fund a new home and community services long-term care program (Brody, 1994). Eligibility would have been determined regardless of income or age on the basis of impairments in three or more of five activities of daily living due to physical, cognitive, or mental conditions, or other defined limitations in capacity. Proposed services were home- and community-based long-term care, adult day care, assisted living, case management, and cash payments to purchase assistance, rehabilitation, home modifications, personal care, and respite care. States would have had flexibility in developing individual service packages to fit the older recipients' needs. People with chronic disabilities were to be entitled to universal assessment and care planning, but government-financed services were to be provided on a funds-available basis only and states would have discretion about whether and how much long-term care service would be available (Wiener and Illston, 1994; Williams, 1994). As a capped entitlement program, the President's proposal differs sharply from open-ended entitlement programs such as Social Security. Although the President's proposal would have mandated that all states provide programs for the medically needy through Medicaid, this requirement was only for institutional care, not for home care. His proposal thus perpetuated the institutional bias inherent in the current Medicaid program and failed to assure comprehensiveness, integration, and continuity of long-term care.

While long-term care was debated at the national level, 35 states moved to develop their own long-term care packages. The primary goals of most state reforms have been to improve access to private health insurance and to assure universal access to coverage for people who are uninsured (Mollica, Riley, and Rydell, 1994). If federal health care reform remains in "gridlock," states will probably want and demand more flexibility under federal rules to develop their own plans. Other government programs addressing the needs of specific groups of older people are the Department of Veteran Affairs (VA) and the Indian Health Service. With a growing number of older patients, the VA has made comprehensive geriatric evaluation and management units an expected component of all VA medical centers and developed contracts with community nursing homes for additional care for eligible veterans (Williams, 1994). The Indian Health Service operates hospitals and community clinics for American Indian and Alaskan natives of all ages.

Model demonstration projects that seek to develop a continuum of services and test managed care continue to emerge locally. An area of rapid growth in terms of older consumers is Health Maintenance Organizations (HMOs), which provide an established package of services for a single capitated or limited rate. In the past, HMOs have served primarily younger, healthier populations because of the presumed higher costs associated with older patients (Moon, 1994). While older adults are still less likely to be in managed care systems than the rest of the population, approximately 7 percent of Medicare recipients have joined HMOs in the past year, largely in an effort to reduce their expenditures such as those required for Medigap insurance. In HMOs, care by a primary physician can often lead to better coordinated care than is possible when older people have more choice of physicians under Medicare (Eckholm, 1995). The federal government is also testing the effectiveness of Social Health Maintenance Organizations (SHMOs) in four demonstration sites. These prepaid health plans provide both acute medical and custodial care; services include all Medicare benefits for all members as well as home and community-based care, prescription drugs, and case management for members who are at risk of institutionalization. These demonstrations are testing whether comprehensive health services, linking acute and chronic care under an integrated financing scheme, can be provided at a cost that does not exceed the public costs of Medicare and Medicaid and can reduce nursing home placement.

As noted in Chapter 7, San Francisco's On Lok model of social care aims to integrate a full continuum of acute and chronic care into one agency and thus to prevent institutionalization. As a capitated system, On Lok is paid a flat amount for each person served, similar to the way that HMOs are paid. A comprehensive day health program is integrated with home care, including nursing, social work, meals, transportation, personal care, homemaker, and respite care. The Program for the All-Inclusive Care for the Elderly (PACE) is a ten-site federal demonstration project that aims to replicate the On Lok model and provide a comprehensive care package of primary, preventive, acute, and long-term care services to allow frail elders to live as independently as possible. Physicians, nurses, social workers, attendants, aides, and therapists coordinate their care under a system where rates are predetermined.

The rapid changes in the health care arena make predictions about future directions difficult, but clearly health care is moving from a system oriented toward acute care, independent providers, and fee for service insurance to one oriented toward chronic care, disability prevention, and managed care. Because of market changes and the growth of managed care, these patterns of consolidation and cost-saving in the delivery of health care will continue at the local level, even without the passage of national legislation to insure health care as a right, regardless of income or age. From the perspective of older people with chronic disabilities, it is important that any national health plan integrates preventive, acute, hospital, ambulatory and community-based and home care to insure continuity of care across the life span. In the short run, however, legislation at the federal level will be focused on ways to reduce Medicare and Medicaid expenditures and on block grant funding.

## SUMMARY AND IMPLICATIONS

The growing health and long-term care expenditures by both the federal and state governments and by older people and their families are a source of concern for most Americans. Escalating hospital and physician costs have placed enormous pressures on Medicare—the financing mechanism through which almost half of the funds for the elderly's care flows. The government's primary response to these Medicare costs has been cost-containment, especially through the diagnostic related groupings (DRGs), which provide financial incentives for shortening the hospital stays of Medicare patients and by greater deductibles and co-payments. For most older adults, Medicare fails to provide any protection against the costs of home- and community-based care. In fact, recent changes in Medicare funding have had the effect of reducing the availability of nonprofit home care agencies and meant that more older persons and their families have either had to pay privately for home care or do without. As the fastest growing portion of the federal budget, Medicare is under intense scrutiny, especially with the federal emphasis upon "balancing the budget."

While Medicare is the major payment source of hospital and physician care for older adults, but almost absent from nursing home financing, just the reverse applies to Medicaid. The largest portion of the Medicaid dollar goes to services needed by older persons, but not covered by Medicare—nursing home, custodial care, and prescription drugs. However, as Medicaid has been increasingly subject to cost-cutting measures at the state level, benefits have been reduced. For example, co-payments for health care services have increased as a way to reduce Medicaid spending, but this is a cost borne disproportionately by low-income elders. Another disadvantage for Medicaid recipients is that most nursing homes and doctors limit the number of Medicaid recipients they will accept. Although waivers by the federal government have allowed state funding of some community-based alternatives to institutionalization, Medicaid remains biased toward nursing home care. Other federal programs that fund community-based services are relatively limited in terms of the numbers of older people reached. Given the gaps in public funding for long-term care, a growing number of private companies are offering long-term care insurance options, but these are beyond the financial reach of most older people and fail to provide comprehensive home care benefits.

While there is widespread concern about the costs and gaps in public funding, there is little agreement about potential solutions. Since 1992, there has been increased visibility and legislative debate about health care reform, although most proposals have been oriented to acute care and not toward the greatest need of the older population for long-term care. President Clinton's health care reform bill did include a home and community services long-term care program, but was still oriented primarily toward institutional care. Although the prospects for a comprehensive health care reform bill that guarantees universal access along with cost containment are dim, many states, hospitals, and agencies have moved ahead with reforms that seek to provide a continuum of services and test managed (cost-limited) care. At the federal level, the emphasis in the near future will be on cutting Medicare and Medicaid to reduce the federal deficit and on incremental insurance reforms. However, as illustrated in earlier chapters, long-term care reform in the next decade will become an issue that Congress and the President cannot ignore because of the aging of the baby boomers and the continued growth of other vulnerable populations, such as older adults with developmental disabilities and chronic mental illness. Given the magnitude of both the need and the potential changes, it is not surprising that no other part of the health care system generates as much passionate debate as does long-term care (Wiener and Illston, 1994). How to meet the needs of growing populations with chronic disabilities will require creative solutions that integrate acute and long-term care. What is less clear is the balance that will be achieved between public and private financing for future solutions.

## REFERENCES

Aday, L. A. *At risk in America: The health and health care needs of vulnerable populations in the United States.* San Francisco, CA: Jossey-Bass, Inc. Publishers, 1993.

Allen, J. Caring, work and gender: Equity in an aging society. In J. Allen and A. Pifer (Eds.), *Women on the front lines: Meeting the challenge of an aging*

*America.* Washington, D.C.: The Urban Institute Press, 1993, 221–240.

American Association of Retired Persons (AARP). *A profile of older Americans, 1990.* Washington, D.C.: AARP, 1991.

American Association of Retired Persons. *Coming up short: Increasing out-of-pocket health spending by older Americans.* Washington, D.C.: American Association of Retired Persons, Public Policy Institute and The Urban Institute, April 1994a.

American Association of Retired Persons. *Home and community-based long-term care.* Washington, D.C.: American Association of Retired Persons, Public Policy Institute and Center on Elderly People Living Alone, 1994b.

American Association of Retired Persons. *Pollings on long-term care.* Washington, D.C.: AARP, 1993.

Applebaum, R. *A guide to the evaluation of long-term care case management programs.* Seattle: University of Washington, Institute on Aging, 1986.

Arling, G., Buhaug, H., Hagan, S., and Zimmerman, D. Medicaid spenddown among nursing home residents in Wisconsin. *The Gerontologist*, 1991, *31*, 174–182.

Avorn, J. Medicine: The life and death of Oliver Shay. In A. Pifer and L. Bronte (Eds.), *Our aging society: Paradox and promise.* New York: W. W. Norton, 1986.

Ball, R. Medicare: A strategy for protecting and improving it. *Generations*, 1985, *14*, 9–12.

Bergthold, C., and Estes, E. More or less? The impact of Medicare policy on home health care. Presented at meetings of the Gerontological Society of America, Chicago, November 1986.

Bergthold, L., Estes, C., and Villanueva, A. Public light and private dark: The privatization of home health services for the elderly in the U.S. *Home Health Care Services Quarterly*, 1990, *11*(3/4), 7–33.

Binney, E., and Estes, C. The retreat of the state and its transfer of responsibility: The intergenerational war. *International Journal of Health Services*, 1988, *18*(1), 83–96.

Binney, E., Estes, C., and Ingman, S. Medicalization, public policy and elderly: Social service in jeopardy? *Social Science and Medicine*, 1990, *30*, 761–771.

Binstock, R. H. The Clinton plan, Medicare integration, and old-age-based rationing—The need for public debate. *The Gerontologist,* 1994, *34*(5), 612–613.

Binstock, R. H. The politics and economics of aging and diversity. In S. Bass, E. Kutza, and F. M. Torres-Gil (Eds.), *Diversity in aging.* Glenview, Ill.: Scott, Foresman and Co., 1990.

Blair, S. N., Brill, P. A., and Kohe, H. W. Physical activity patterns in older individuals. In W. W. Spirdieso and H. M. Eckert (Eds.), *The academy papers: Physical activity and aging.* Champaign, Ill.: Human Kinetics Publishers, 1989.

Brickfield, C. Who will pay? *Generations,* 1986–87, *11,* 12–14.

Brody, S. A responsible geezer's analysis of the Clinton health proposal. *The Gerontologist,* 1994, *34*(5), 586–589.

Brown, E. R. Medicare and Medicaid: The process, values and limits of health care reforms. In M. Minkler and C. Estes (Eds.), *Readings in the political economy of aging.* Farmingdale, N.Y.: Baywood, 1984.

Butler, R. N. Politics versus policy in the health care debate. *The Gerontologist,* 1994 *34*(5), 614–615.

Callahan, D. Case management for the elderly: A panacea? *Journal of Aging and Social Policy,* 1989, *1*(1/2), 181–195.

Callahan, D. Health care in the aging society: A moral dilemma. In A. Pifer and L. Bronte (Eds.), *Our aging society: Paradox and promise.* New York: W. W. Norton, 1986.

Callahan, D. *Setting limits: Medical goals in an aging society.* New York: Simon and Schuster, 1987.

Capitman, J. Policy and program options in community-oriented long-term care. In P. M. Lawton (Ed.), *Annual Review of Gerontology and Geriatrics,* 1989, *9,* 357–388.

Center on Elderly People Living Alone. *The cost of long-term care.* Washington, D.C.: AARP, Public Policy Institute, May 1994.

Center on Elderly People Living Alone. *Home and community-based long-term care.* Washington, D.C.: AARP, Public Policy Institute, May 1994.

Chappell, N. Aging and social care. In R. Binstock and L. George (Eds.), *Aging and the social sciences.* New York: Academic Press, 1990.

Coalition on Women and the Budget. *Inequality of sacrifice: The impact of the Reagan budget on women.* Washington, D.C.: National Women's Law Center, 1983.

Cockburn, A. Health care: Sowing the seeds of revolution. *Gray Panther Network,* Spring 1986, 3–5.

Cohen, G. D. Health care reform and older adults: Introduction. *The Gerontologist,* 1994, *34*(5), 584–585.

Congressional Budget Office. *Veterans Administration health care: Planning for future years.* Washington, D.C.: U.S. Government Printing Office, 1984.

Corry, M. *Statement of the American Association of Retired Persons on Medicare and health care reform.* Washington, D.C.: American Association of Retired Persons, 1994.

Coughlin, T. A., McBride, T. D., Perozek, M., and Liu, K. *Home care for the disabled elderly: Predictors and expected costs.* Washington, D.C.: Urban Institute, 1990.

Coulton, C. Prospective payment requires increased attention to quality of post-hospital care. *Social Work in Health Care,* 1988, *13,* 19–31.

Coye, M. J. Health care for the uninsured. *Issues in Science and Technology,* Summer, 1991, 56–62.

Crystal, S. *America's old age crisis: Public policy and the two worlds of aging.* New York: Basic Books, 1982.

Davis, K. Paying the health-care bills of an aging population. In A. Pifer and L. Bronte (Eds.), *Our aging society: Paradox and promise.* New York: W. W. Norton, 1986.

Davis, K., and Rowland, D. Old and poor: Policy challenges in the 1990s. *Journal of Aging: Social Policy,* 1991, *2,* 37–59.

Dishman, R. K. Determinants of participation in physical activity. In C. Bouchord, R. J. Shephard, T. Stephens, J. R. Sutton, and B. D. McPherson (Eds.), *Exercise, fitness and health.* Champaign, Ill.: Human Kinetics Publishers, 1990.

Eckholm, E. An aging nation grapples with caring for the frail. *New York Times,* March 27, 1990.

Eckholm, E. H.M.O.'s are changing the face of Medicare. *New York Times National,* A1, January 11, 1995.

Eisdorfer, C., Kessler, D. A., and Spector, A. (Eds.), *Caring for the elderly: Reshaping health policy.* Baltimore: Johns Hopkins University Press, 1989.

Estes, C. Aging, health, and social policy. *Journal of Aging and Social Policy,* 1989, *1,* 17–32.

Estes, C. Austerity and aging: 1980 and beyond. In M. Minkler and C. Estes (Eds.), *Readings in the political economy of aging.* Farmingdale, N.Y.: Baywood, 1984.

Estes, C. Fiscal austerity and aging. In C. Estes, R. Newcomer, and Associates (Eds.), *Fiscal austerity and aging.* Beverly Hills, Calif.: Sage, 1983.

Estes, C. The Reagan legacy: Privatization, the welfare state and aging in the 1990s. In J. Myles and J. Quadagno (Eds.), *States, labor markets, and the future of old-age policy.* Philadelphia, PA: Temple University Press, 1991, 59–83.

Estes, C. L., and Binney, E. A. Toward a transformation of health and aging policy. *International Journal of Health Services,* 1988 18, 1, 69–82.

Estes, C., and Harrington, C. Future directions in long-term care. In C. Harrington, R. Newcomer, C. Estes, and Associates (Eds.), *Long-term care for the elderly: Public policy issues.* Beverly Hills, Calif.: Sage, 1985.

Estes, C., and Lee, P. Social, political and economic background of long-term care policy. In C. Harrington, R. Newcomer, C. Estes, and Associates (Eds.), *Long-term care of the elderly: Public policy issues.* Beverly Hills, Calif.: Sage, 1985.

Estes, C., Swan, J., and Associates. *The long term care crisis.* Newbury Park, Calif.: Sage Publications, 1993.

Estes, C., Wood, J. B., and Lee, P. R. *Organizational and community responses to Medicare policy.* San Francisco: Institute for Health and Aging, 1988.

Families USA Foundation. *Doing without: The sacrifices families make to provide home care.* Washington, D.C.: Families USA Foundation. July 1994.

Fischer, L., and Eustis, N. Care at home: Family caregivers and homecare workers. In E. Kahana; D. Biegel, and M. Wykle (Eds.), *Family caregiving across the lifespan.* Thousand Oaks, Calif.: Sage, 1994, 287–311.

Fitzgerald, J. F., Moore, P. S., and Dittus, R. S. The care of the elderly patients with hip fracture: Changes since implementation of the prospective payment system. *New England Journal of Medicine,* 1988, 29, 1392–97.

Folkemer, D. *State use of home and community-based services for the aged under Medicaid.* Washington, D.C.: American Association of Retired Persons, Public Policy Institute, 1994.

Fried, L. P., and Bush, T. L. Morbidity as a focus of preventive health care in the elderly. *Epidemiologic Review,* 1988, 10, 48–64.

Gaumer, G. L., Poggio, E. L., Coelen, C. G., Sennett, C. S., and Schmitz, R. J. Effects of state prospective reimbursement programs on hospital mortality. *Medical Care,* 1989, 27, 724–736.

Gerety, M. B. Health care reform from the view of a geriatrician. *The Gerontologist,* 1994, *34*(5), 590–597.

Gibson, R. M., Waldo, D. R., and Levit, K. R. National health expenditures, 1982. *Health Care Financing Review,* 1983, *5,* 1–31.

Gill, D., and Ingman, S. (Eds.) *Eldercare, distributive justice and the welfare state: Retrenchment or expansion.* Albany, New York: State University of New York, 1994.

Gosselin, P. G. Health reform in '95? Don't bet the house on it. *Boston Globe,* November 9, 1994.

Harrington, C. Alternatives to nursing home care. *Generations,* 1985, *9,* 43–46.

Harrington, C. Public policy and the nursing home industry. In M. Minkler and C. Estes (Eds.), *Readings in the political economy of aging.* Farmingdale, N.Y.: Baywood, 1984.

Harrington, C., Estes, C., Lee, P., and Newcomer, R. Effects of state Medicare policies on the aged. *The Gerontologist,* 1986, *26,* 626–663.

Harrington, C., Newcomer, R. J., and Estes, C. *Long term care of the elderly: Public policy issues.* Beverly Hills, Calif.: Sage, 1985.

Harrington, C., Newcomer, R. J., and Moore, T. G. Factors that contribute to Medicare HMO risk contract success. *Inquiry,* 1988, 251–262.

Harvard Medicare Project. Special report: The future of Medicare. *New England Journal of Medicine,* 1986, *314,* 722–728.

Health Care Financing Administration. *Health care financing: Program statistics.* Baltimore, Md.: U.S. Department of Health and Human Services, 1988.

Hendricks, J., and Hatch, L. R. Federal policy and family life of older Americans. In J. Hendricks and C. Rosenthal (Eds.), *The remainder of these days: Domestic policy and older families in the United States and Canada.* New York: Garland Publishing, 1993, 49–74.

Hendricks, J., and Rosenthal, C. J. *The remainder of their days: Domestic policy and older families in the United States and Canada.* New York: Garland Publishing, 1993.

Himmelstein, D., and Woolhandler, S. A national health program for the United States. *New*

*England Journal of Medicine,* 1989, *320,* 102–108.

Hing, E. Effects of the prospective payment systems on nursing homes. *Vital health statistics.* Hyattsville, Md.: National Center for Health Statistics, 1989.

Hing, E. *Use of nursing homes by the elderly: Preliminary data from the 1985 National Nursing Home Survey.* Hyattsville, Md.: Public Health Service, 1987.

Holt, S. The role of home care in long-term care. *Generations,* 1986–87, *11* (2), 9–11.

Iglehart, J. K. Medicare begins payment of hospitals. *New England Journal of Medicine,* 1983, *308*(23), 1428–1432,

Jackson, B., and Jensen, J. Home care tops consumers' list. *Modern Health Care,* 1984, 88–90.

Jacobs, B., and Abbott, S. Planning for wellness: A community-based approach. *Generations,* 1983, *7,* 57–59.

Jensen, D. *Elderly out-of-pocket health care expenditures, Part 2: Medicare-related liabilities 1980 to 1990.* Washington, D.C.: AARP, Public Policy Institute Issue Brief, March 1994.

Jones, A. Prospective payment: Curbing Medicare costs at patient's expense? *Generations,* 1984, *9,* 19–21.

Kane, R. A. The home care crisis of the nineties. *The Gerontologist,* 1989, *29,* 24–31.

Kane, R. A., and Kane, R. C. Long-term care: Variations on a quality assurance theme. *Inquiry,* 1988, *25,* 132–146.

Kane, R. C., and Kane, R. A. Health care for older people: Organizational and policy issues. In R. Binstock and L. George (Eds.), *Aging and the social sciences* (3d ed.). New York: Academic Press, 1990.

Kane, R. C., and Kane, R. A. Effects of the Clinton health reform on older persons and their families: A health care systems perspective. *The Gerontologist,* 1994, *34*(5), 598–605.

Kasper, J. *Aging alone: Profiles and projections.* Baltimore, Md.: The Commonwealth Fund, 1988.

Kemper, P., Applebaum, R., and Harrigan, M. Community care demonstrations: What have we learned? *Health Care Financing Review,* 1987(a), *8*(4), 87–100.

Kemper, P., Applebaum, R., and Harrigan, M. *A systematic comparison of community care demonstrations.* Special Report No. 45, Institute for Research on Poverty, University of Wisconsin, Madison. Reprint OM No. 88–0014, 1987(b).

Knight, B., and Walker, D. L. Toward a definition of alternatives to institutionalization for the frail elderly. *The Gerontologist,* 1985, *25,* 358–363.

Kutza E. Responding to diversity: Is American society capable? In S. Bass, E. Kutza, and F. M. Torres-Gil (Eds.), *Diversity in aging.* Glenview, Ill.: Scott, Foresman and Co., 1990.

Lave, J. Cost-containment policies in long-term care. *Inquiry,* 1985, *22,* 7–23.

Lee, P. R., and Benjamin, A. E. Health policy trends: Impact on the academic health center. In S. Andreapoulos and J. Hogness (Eds.), *Health care for an aging society.* New York: Churchill Livingstone, 1989.

Leibson, C., Naessens, J., Krishan, I., Campion, M., and Ballard, D. Disposition at discharge and 60-day mortality among elderly people following shorter hospital stays: A population-based comparison. *The Gerontologist,* 1990, *30,* 316–322.

Leonard, F. The legal observer. *The OWL Observer,* 1986, *5,* 219.

Leutz, W. N., Capitman, J. A., MacAdam, M., and Abrahams, R. *Care for frail elders: Developing community solutions,* Westport, Conn.: Auburn House, 1992.

Lipson, L., and Laudicina, S. S. *State home and community-based services for the aged under Medicaid: Waiver programs, optional services under the Medicaid state plan, and OBRA 1990 provisions for a new optional benefit.* Washington, D.C.: American Association of Retired Persons, Public Policy Institute, 1991.

Liu, K., and Manton, K. Nursing home length of stay and spenddown in Connecticut. *The Gerontologist,* 1991, *31,* 165–173.

Liu, K., Manton, K., and Liu, B. M. Home care expenses for the disabled, *Health Care Financing Review,* 1986, *7,* 33–49.

Lombardi, T. Nursing home without walls. *Generations,* 1986–87, *11,* 21–23.

Manton, K., Vertress, J., and Wrigley, J. Changes in health service use and mortality among U.S. elderly in 1980–86. *Journal of Aging and Health,* 1990, *2,* 131–156.

Marsh, D. *Families and mental illness.* New York: Praeger Publishers, 1992.

Mechanic, D. Health care and the elderly. *Annals of the American Academy of Political and Social Sciences*, 1989, *503*, 89–98.

Meiners, M. Long-term care insurance. *Generations*, 1985, *9*, 39–41.

Meiners, M., and Gollub, J. Long term care insurance: The edge of an emerging market. *Health Care Financial Management*, 1984, *38*, 58–62.

Meyer, J., and Moon, M. Health care spending on children and the elderly. In J. Palmer, T. Smeeding, and B. Torrey (Eds.), *The vulnerable*. Washington, D.C.: The Urban Institute Press, 1988.

Minkler, M. Blaming the aged victim: The politics of retrenchment in times of fiscal conservatism. In M. Minkler and C. Estes (Eds.), *Readings in the political economy of aging*. Farmingdale, N.Y.: Baywood, 1984.

Minkler, M., and Estes, C. *Readings in the political economy of aging*. Farmingdale, N.Y.: Baywood, 1984.

Mitchell, J., and Cromwell, J. Access to private physicians for public patients: Participation in Medicaid and Medicare. *Securing access to health care*. President's Commission for the Study of Ethical Problems in Medicine and Biomedical and Behavioral Research. Washington, D.C.: U.S. Government Printing Office, 1983.

Mollica, R. L., Riley, T., and Rydell, C. *The impact of health reform on vulnerable adults: Volume I*. Waltham, MA: Brandeis University Center for Vulnerable Populations, 1994.

Montgomery, R. Respite services for family caregivers. In M. D. Peterson and D. L. White (Eds.), *Health care of the elderly*, Newbury Park, Calif.: Sage, 1989.

Moon, M. Lessons from Medicare. *The Gerontologist*, 1994, *34*(5), 606–611.

Muse, D. N., and Sawyer, W. *The Medicare and Medicaid data book, 1981*. Washington, D.C.: U.S. Health Care Financing Administration, 1982.

Nassif, J. Z. The Social Health Maintenance Organization. *Caring*, 1986, *5*, 34–36.

Nassif, J. Z. There's still no place like home. *Generations*, 1986–87, *11*, 5–8.

Nathan, J. Public policy issues and the minority elderly. In *Minority aging*, Washington, D.C.: U.S. Public Health Service, 1990.

National Academy on Aging. *Old age in the 21st century: A report to the Assistant Secretary for Aging, U.S. Department of Health and Human Services, regarding his responsibilities in planning for the aging of the baby boom*. Maxwell School of Citizenship and Public Affairs, Syracuse University & the United States Administration on Aging, June 1994.

National Academy for State Health Policy (NASHP). *The status of America's vulnerable populations: A chartbook*. Portland, ME: Center for Vulnerable Populations, 1992.

National Association of Social Workers. *Health and mental health care in the 104th Congress*. Washington, D.C.: National Association of Social Workers, Office of Government Relations, 1995.

National Committee to Preserve Social Security and Medicare. *View point: Long term care*, April 1993.

Older Women's League. *Respite services bill*. Washington, D.C.: Older Women's League, 1985.

Olson, L. K. Aging policy: Who benefits? *Generations*, 1984, *10*, 10–14.

Ory, M., and Bond, K. *Aging and health care: Social science and policy perspectives*. London: Routledge, 1989.

Paringer, L. *The forgotten costs of long-term care*. Washington, D.C.: The Urban Institute, 1983.

The Pepper Commission (U.S. Bipartisan Commission on Comprehensive Health Care). *A call for action*. Washington, D.C.: U.S. Government Printing Office, 1990.

Pifer, A., and Bronte, L. *Our aging society: Paradox and promise*. New York: W. W. Norton, 1986.

President's Commission for the Study of Ethical Problems in Medicine and Biomedical and Behavioral Research. *Deciding to forego life-sustaining treatment*. Washington, D.C.: U.S. Government Printing Office, 1983.

Quadagno, J., Meyer, M., and Turner, J. Falling into the Medicaid gaps: The hidden long-term care dilemma. *The Gerontologist*, 1991, *31*, 521–526.

Riley, T., and Mollica, R. L. *The impact of health reform on vulnerable adults: Volume II. An analysis of national health reform proposals*. Waltham, MA: Brandeis University, Center for Vulnerable Populations, 1994.

Rivlin, A. M., and Wiener, J. M. *Caring for the disabled elderly*. Washington, D.C.: Brookings Institute, 1988.

Rubenstein, L. Z., Marmor, T. R., Stone, R., Moon, M., and Harootyan, L. K. Medicare: Challenges and future directions in a changing health care environment. *The Gerontologist,* 1994, *34*(5), 620–627.

Sager, M. A., Easterling, D. U., Kindig, D. A., and Anderson, O. W. Changes in the location of death after passage of Medicare's prospective payment system. *New England Journal of Medicine,* 1989, *320,* 433–439.

Samuelson, R. J. Busting the U.S. budget: The costs of an aging America. *National Journal,* 1983, *10,* 256–260.

Scitovsky, A. Medical costs in the last year of life. *Generations,* 1985, *9,* 27–29.

*Seattle Times.* Who killed health reform? Finger pointing begins. Associated Press, Tuesday, September 27, 1994, p. A-4.

Smeeding, T. Economic status of the elderly. In R. Binstock and L. George (Eds.), *Handbook of aging and the social sciences,* (3d ed.). New York: Academic Press, 1990.

Storey, J. R. *Older Americans in the Reagan era: Impact of federal policy changes.* Washington, D.C.: The Urban Institute Press, 1983.

Syme, S. L., and Berkman, L. F. Social class, susceptibility and sickness. *American Journal of Epidemiology,* 1976, *104,* 1–8.

Tolchin, M. Paying for long-term care: The struggle for lawmakers. *New York Times,* March 29, 1990, 1.

Torres-Gil, F. Hispanics: A special challenge. In A. Pifer and L. Bronte (Eds.), *Our aging society: Paradox and promise.* New York: W. W. Norton, 1986.

Torres-Gil, F., and Puccinelli, M. Mainstreaming gerontology in the policy arena. *The Gerontologist,* 1994, *34*(6), 749–752.

Trustees of the Federal Hospital Insurance Trust Fund and Trustees of the Federal Supplementary Medical Insurance Trust Fund. *1985 Annual Report.* Washington, D.C.: Department of Health and Human Services, 1985.

U.S. Commerce Clearing House. *Topical law reports, Medicare and Medicaid guide* (Vol. 3-A). Chicago: State charts, 1984.

U.S. Department of Health, Education, and Welfare. *Healthy people. The Surgeon General's Report on health promotion and disease prevention.* Public Health Service, Office of the Assistant Secretary for Health and Surgeon General, Washington, D.C., 1979.

U.S. General Accounting Office. *The elderly should benefit from expanded home health care, but increasing these services will not insure cost reductions.* Washington, D.C.: GAO/IPE, 83–1, 1982.

U.S. General Accounting Office. *Canadian health insurance's lessons for the United States.* Washington, D.C.: Superintendent of Documents, 1991.

U.S. Health Care Financing Administration (HCFA). *Medicare and Medicaid expenditures statistics.* Unpublished data. Baltimore, Md.: U.S. Department of Health and Human Services, 1982.

U.S. Health Care Financing Administration (HCFA). *National medical statistics: Fiscal years 1975 to 1982.* State 2082 Tables data tape. Baltimore, Md.: U.S. Department of Health and Human Services, 1984.

U.S. House of Representatives Committee on Ways and Means. *Background material on program under the jurisdiction of the committee on ways and means.* Washington, D.C.: U.S. Government Printing Office, 1983.

U.S. House of Representatives Special Committee on Aging. *Report on long-term care for Blue Cross and Blue Shield of Massachusetts,* 1985.

U.S. House Select Committee on Aging. *Long-term care and personal impoverishment: Seven in ten elderly living alone are at risk.* Comm. Pub. 100–631. Washington, D.C.: U.S. Government Printing Office, 1987.

U.S. Office of Management and Budget. *The budget of the United States government: Fiscal year 1981.* Washington, D.C.: U.S. Government Printing Office, 1980.

U.S. Senate Special Committee on Aging. *Developments on aging: 1981,* Part I. Washington, D.C.: U.S. Government Printing Office, 1982a.

U.S. Senate Special Committee on Aging. *The proposed fiscal year 1983 budget: What it means for older Americans.* Washington, D.C.: U.S. Government Printing Office, 1982b.

U.S. Senate Special Committee on Aging. *America in transition: An aging society.* Washington, D.C.: U.S. Government Printing Office, 1985a.

U.S. Senate Special Committee on Aging. *Aging reports,* Spring 1985b.

U.S. Senate Special Committee on Aging. *Aging America: Trends and projections, 1991 edition.* Washington, D.C.: U.S. Department of Health and Human Services, 1992.

U.S. Senate Special Committee on Aging. *Aging America: Trends and projections, 1987–88 edition*. Washington, D.C.: U.S. Department of Health and Human Services, 1988.

U.S. Senate Special Committee on Aging. *Developments in Aging: 1989*. Washington, D.C.: U.S. Government Printing Office, 1990.

Vladeck, B. Long-term care: What have we learned? Paper presented at the Western Gerontological Society Meeting on Health and Aging. San Francisco, November 1983.

Vladeck, B. *Unloving care: The nursing home tragedy.* New York: Basic Books, 1980.

Vladeck, B. Overview: The case for integration. Conference Proceedings, *Integrating acute and long-term care: Advancing the health care reform agenda*. AARP, Public Policy Institute, August 1994.

Waldo, D., and Lazenby, H. Demographic characteristics and health care use and expenditures by the aged in the U.S., 1977–1985. *Health Care Financing Review*, 1985, 6, 1–29.

Waldo, D., Sonnefeld, S., McKusick, D., and Arnett, R., Health expenditures by age group, 1977 and 1987. *Health Care Financing Review*, 1989, 10, 111–120.

Warshaw, G. Health promotion and aging: Preventive Health Services. *Surgeon General's workshop: Health Promotion and Aging, background papers*. Washington, D.C.: U.S. Government Printing Office, 1988.

Washington Post. Health costs slowing, but maybe not enough. *Washington Post*, November 9, 1994.

Weissert, W. G., Cready, C. M., and Powelak, J. E. Home and community care: Three decades of findings. In M. Peterson and D. White (Eds.), *Health care of the elderly*. Newbury Park, Calif.: Sage, 1989.

Whitcomb, M. Health care for the poor: A public-policy imperative. *New England Journal of Medicine*, 1986, *315*, 1220–1222.

Wiener, J., and Harris, K. Myths and realities: Why most of what everybody knows about long-term care is wrong. *The Brookings Review*, Fall 1990, 29–34.

Wiener, J., and Illston, L. Health care reform in the 1990s: Where does long-term care fit in? *The Gerontologist*, 1994, *34*(3), 402–408.

Wiener, J., Illston, L., and Hanley, R. *Sharing the burdens: Strategies for public and private long-term care insurance*. Washington, D.C.: The Brookings Institute, 1994.

Wilensky, G., and Berk, M. Medicare and the elderly poor. *Hearings on the future of Medicare*. Washington, D.C.: U.S. Senate Special Committee on Aging, April 13, 1983.

Williams, T. F. Integrating the needs of older Americans into the goals and structures of health care reform. *The Gerontologist*, 1994, *34*(5), 616–617.

Wolfe, J. *The coming health crisis: Who will pay for care for the aged in the 21st century*. Chicago: University of Chicago, 1993.

Wykle, M. L. Waking a sleeping giant: Considerations of health care reform. *The Gerontologist*, 1994, *34*(5), 618–619.

# E P I L O G U E

In Part I we emphasized the importance of studying social gerontology. Reasons for this included the need to better understand our own aging and that of our parents, grandparents and great grandparents; the significant increase in the proportion of older people, especially the oldest-old, in all countries; and historical developments that have dramatically changed the conditions of older people in society. Throughout the book, we have examined the physical and psychological status of people as they age, and how changes in these areas influence their social roles and behavior. Likewise, we have seen how societal changes interact with age-related changes in the individual. In this final section, we turn briefly to the future, to understand how future cohorts will differ from people who are currently age 65 and older, and to anticipate how existing policies will influence the social well-being and quality of life of the "future aged."

## TRENDS THAT WILL AFFECT AGING IN THE FUTURE

As noted throughout this text, the growth of the population over age 65, and the increased num-

bers who will survive to age 85 and beyond, provide a major challenge to society and to individuals themselves, as they anticipate living many more years after childrearing, education, and a career. The greatest increase in the aging population will occur early in the twenty-first century as the "baby boom" generation (those individuals born between 1946 and 1964) reaches old age and creates the "senior boom." Since this population is already alive, we can predict with considerable accuracy that 54 million people or approximately 20.2 percent of the U.S. population will be 65 and older in 2020, and people aged 55 to 65 will represent the largest subgroup of the population at that time. In that same period, the proportion over age 75 will increase from 42 percent to 50 percent of all older people (U.S. Bureau of the Census, 1991). Currently 3.5 million people in the United States are age 85 or older; it is estimated that these numbers will more than double by the year 2020. An even greater increase is expected in the population 100 years or older. Baby boomers will represent about 60 million of the projected 70 million people age 65 and over in 2030 (Day, 1994).

This future cohort of older people will differ from current cohorts in ways other than living longer. The era in which they were born and raised, their opportunities for education, their life expectancy, their health care, and their personal development were vastly different from those who were born between 1890 and 1920. The cohort born in the 1930s has been called the "good time" generation, since their prime working years occurred during the period of maximum earnings growth in the 1960s. Also, their home values soared during the inflation of the 1970s, and they have benefited from high real estate interest rates and the stock market boom of the early 1980s. Compared to earlier cohorts, this young-old group had a greater percentage of long-term, two-earner families, resulting in relatively higher private pension and Social Security benefits (Smeeding, 1990). Baby boomers are likely to enter old age in an even better economic position than pre-boom cohorts because of deferred marriages, reduced childbearing, and increased labor force participation of women into their 60's and 70's (Easterlin, Macdonald, and Macunovich, 1990).

In addition to economic conditions of their era, historical and political factors also shape people's experiences across the lifespan and in old age. In the United States and most other countries emerging from World War II and the Korean War, economic growth in the 1950s and 1960s appeared endless. Home ownership increased, especially in the newly developing suburbs and planned communities. Enrollment expanded in universities and colleges as the baby boomers reached college age. And advances in medicine and medical technology led to improvements in health care and reduced significantly the risks of mortality from major surgery and diseases, such as heart disease and cancer, that previously were assumed always to be fatal. With public resources seeming to be abundant, the federal government began to assume greater responsibility for the welfare of its citizens; pro-

grams to assist low-income families with children emerged in the 1960s (e.g., Aid to Families with Dependent Children and Head Start), as did low-interest loans to college students along with services to help older people maintain their health and social well-being (discussed in Chapters 19 and 20). More recently, however, with a less expansive economy, the trend has been toward a reduced role for government and an increased emphasis on individual responsibility and on the private sector and the family to provide services.

As noted in Chapter 19, social entitlement programs such as Social Security and AFDC are now subject to budget-cutting scrutiny and major changes in their goals and assumptions. Although it is clear that our country will not return to the levels of public spending characteristic of the 1960s, what is unclear is what the mix of public and private responsibility will be in the twenty-first century. We can predict, however, that the increasing rectangularization of the age pyramid will mean that older people will have to be more self-sufficient, and that proportionately fewer young persons will be available to care for frail elders.

By the year 2000, the single most important feature of the older population is that it will be primarily female and more than 50 percent of these women will be living alone (Paradise, 1993). It will also be a more ethnically and racially diverse population since minority populations are expected to comprise nearly half of the United States population by 2050. In fact, in many sections of the country, a "minority" population will be the majority, raising questions about the identity and meaning of "minority" and community (Cornman and Kingson, 1995; Day, 1994). Since the 1950s, the status of women and ethnic minorities has improved in the United States, although, as discussed in Chapters 17 and 18, older members of these populations have not necessarily benefited from improvements enjoyed by younger women and minorities. The passage of Civil Rights legislation, the women's movement, and increased demands from these segments of the population who were previously denied access to jobs and educational opportunities have resulted in more women and ethnic minorities completing college and obtaining professional degrees, entering the work force, and moving into higher-level positions. On the other hand, these gains have not necessarily been widely distributed. Women, for example, still are paid only about 70 cents for every dollar earned by their male counterparts, and they remain concentrated in secondary sector industries and traditionally female-oriented, lower-paying occupations. As described in Chapter 14, the rapidly growing number of low-income women as heads of single-parent households, commonly referred to as the *feminization of poverty,* suggests that a large segment of women may reach old age without the support of a spouse and with few economic resources. In fact, the Department of Labor projections identify five service occupations, dominated by women and characterized by low wages, as more likely to experience large-scale growth by the year 2000 than higher-paying occupations. Despite more women in the workforce, their earning profiles will continue to deteriorate and more mid-life and older women will be employed, out of economic necessity, for longer periods. Women over age 40 are predicted to comprise half of the work force (Smeeding, 1990), and 70 percent of baby boom women will outlive their husbands by 15 years, but on average will earn only two thirds of what their husbands earn (Older Women's League, 1990). Ethnic minorities among the baby boom cohort are, on average, poorer than their Euro-American counterparts and therefore will bring fewer financial resources and often poorer health to old age (Cornman and Kingson, 1995).

## Implications for the Future

What do these changes mean for the future of aging? What will life be like for the baby boomers when they become the senior boomers? Unfortunately, we do not have a crystal ball to predict the future with certainty. Some factors are well beyond the control of social gerontologists, including economic conditions, international conflicts, fatal diseases such as AIDS, and natural disasters. For example, as discussed in Chapter 7, the AIDS epidemic appears to affect only about 1 percent of the current cohort over age 65. However, it is unknown what the impact will be upon the future older population itself and upon health and long-term care systems from those baby boomers who have contracted the infection earlier in their lives. The onset of AIDS may occur when they are experiencing other age-related changes, given that the median interval between infection with HIV and onset is nearly ten years (Schmidt, 1989). Furthermore, the increased death rate as a result of AIDS among younger persons reduces even more the proportion of young available to support older people in the near future.

The number of multigenerational families will increase in the future.

There is, however, adequate knowledge about the baby boom generation to begin to speculate about the future. More of the future older population will be members of four- and five-generation families, although they probably will not be living together. Smaller family size may reduce the number of adult children and siblings available to provide support in times of illness or disability. These relationships will be further complicated by the growing number of divorces, step-families, gay and lesbian partners, and single parents. To what extent will younger members of "blended" families and those unrelated by blood but joined by years of sharing familial responsibilities assume the role of caregivers? Who will be responsible for the increasing numbers of never-married persons when they reach advanced old age if they can no longer care for themselves?

Another population that will require specialized care are older persons with developmental disabilities (e.g., cerebral palsy or Down syndrome). Earlier generations of people with developmental disabilities frequently did not survive until old age. As a result of improved health care, life expectancy for persons with Down syndrome has increased dramatically from 9 years in 1929 to 18.3 years in 1963, to 55 years today (Adlin, 1993). Now there are approximately 500,000 persons with developmental disabilities over age 65 and this population is projected to double by 2030. They may require services from agencies serving older adults and persons with developmental disabilities, as well as care by family members who may be among the old-old (Seltzer, 1989). What old age will be like for the growing number of adults who are chronically mentally ill or homeless is unknown and of concern to planners and policy makers. On the other hand, the typical older person in the future will be better educated and of higher socioeconomic status than the current cohort.

As noted in Chapter 1, the majority of future elders will be better educated. Because of the association between education, occupation, and income, those with high school and college degrees are likely to earn more during their lifetimes. The growing attention to the "mushrooming phenomenon of early retirement," promoted by the design of pensions, has created concern about the future costs of the older population and increased interest in special programs to encourage employment of older adults. These include efforts to encourage older workers to remain on the job, and for employers to retain and hire older workers, often in part-time and temporary positions (Schulz and Myles, 1990).

The economic "crunch" will come about 2010 when baby boomers begin to retire. In one decade, while the population grows by 2 percent, the number of retirees will swell by 30 percent. Instead of five Americans working to support one retiree, there will only be three. The possible scenarios that could result are: (1) the deficit will grow no matter how much other programs are cut, (2) those who are working will have to pay higher taxes, (3) retirees will receive lower benefits, or (4) a mandatory retirement age, older than the previous mandatory age of 65, will have to be re-established.

Despite current fears that the baby boom cohort will not benefit proportionately from Social Security, on average this cohort is likely to enter old age in a better economic position than did pre-boom cohorts. This is because of economic and demographic adjustments, such as deferred marriage, reduced childbearing, and increased labor force participation of wives, all of which have compensated for the baby-boomers' relatively lower wages in their earlier years (Easterlin et al., 1990). More individuals will have private pensions because of legislation during the past 25 years that requires larger employers to institute pension programs, although their pensions will not be large enough to sustain their preretirement standard of living.

Furthermore, the increased number of women and ethnic minorities in jobs with pension plans may make it easier for many people in these groups to enjoy their old age rather than experience it as a time of destitution and despair. A countering force, however, is that more women than men are in part-time jobs and in small businesses, which are not covered by pensions, so that it is unclear at this point to what extent the proportion of women covered by pensions will substantially grow.

Despite the increased number of women in the paid work force and the relatively greater affluence of younger women, older women in the future are predicted to remain significantly poorer than older men. When today's 25-year-old woman retires, after having been employed for as long as 35 years, she can expect to receive, on average, the same retirement benefits—adjusted only for inflation—that her mother received, even though she will have paid more into Social Security (Older Women's League, 1990).

More people over age 70 may choose to continue to be employed, preferably on a part-time basis, given the elimination of mandatory retirement, although the pattern of early retirement will probably persist. Most older people will undoubtedly be healthier, having had the advantages of medical technology, preventive medicine, health promotion programs, and widely available knowledge about ways of maintaining health. The difference in life expectancy between women and men may be narrowed by younger women's tendency to engage in riskier behaviors and life styles as well as the trend of more young men pursuing healthier lifestyles by avoiding smoking, limiting alcohol and fat intake, and increasing exercise levels (Ory and Warner, 1990). The projections of a healthier and wealthier older population have resulted in the growth of companies that offer products and services specifically geared to them. Popular periodicals such as *50 Plus* and *Mature Outlook* offer a prime medium for advertising these products. Yet the greatest purchasing power will probably be in the 50- to 64-year-old population, not among those over 65. In the remainder of the Epilogue, we examine some of the trends in family patterns, work and retirement, living arrangements, and health and long-term care that have significant implications for the future.

## Changing Family Relationships

The added years due to increased life expectancy serve to prolong a person's relationships to others—spouse, parents, offspring, friends—whose lives are also extended. For example, more than half of the children born in 1910 and who survived to age 50 had experienced the death of a parent or sibling by their early teens (Uhlenberg, 1980). In contrast, today the loss of parents is not expected until the second half of adulthood, and the death of a child is no longer an anticipated part of family life. For current generations of young women, the death of the mother may occur close to the daughter's retirement age. These changes mean that a growing proportion of parents and children will share such critical adulthood experiences as work, parenthood, and even retirement and widowhood. Similarly, grandparents may survive to experience many years of their grandchildren's adulthood.

Kinship networks in the future will become more complex, attenuated, and diffuse. We will see a growth of the verticalized or "beanpole family structure"; that is, an increasing number of living generations in a family accompanied by a decreasing number of family members within the same generation. Future cohorts of adult children will have a greater number of aging parents and grandparents to care for at the same time that they have fewer siblings to call on for assistance. As a result, kin networks will be top heavy (Bengtson, Rosenthal, and Burton, 1990).

Extending the number of years we can expect to live has also meant that more adult children are involved in caring for frail parents and grandparents, to the point that parent care is now a normative experience for adult children (Brody, 1985). Increased life expectancy has combined with reduced fertility, so that for the first time, women can expect to spend more years caring for an aged parent than for a dependent child (U.S. Senate Special Committee on Aging, 1992). These trends are likely to persist, given current patterns of reduced fertility, particularly the number of couples who are choosing not to have children, or delaying childbearing until their 30's or 40's. As a result, they may be caring for young children at the same time they are helping aging parents or parents-in-law. This phenomenon, more common among Caucasian families than among families of color, has also resulted in a larger-than-average age difference between each generation. This generational difference of 30 to 40 years may contribute to difficulties in building affective bonds across multiple generations due to different values or life orientations (George and Gold, 1991). Parallel to this phenomenon, however, is the age-condensed family where young women are bearing children in the teenage years. This may result in a blurring of roles and relationships (e.g., young grandmothers and great-grandmothers caring for grandchildren) and highly stressful situations (George and Gold, 1991; Minkler and Roe, 1993). It is noteworthy that a quarter of a million households in the United States that are headed by a person aged 65 or older receive Aid to Families with Dependent Children (Edelman, 1991).

The increase in longevity has also significantly changed grandparent-grandchildren roles. For example, we now anticipate that our grandparents will not die until our early adulthood, but until quite recently most grandparents did not live long enough to know their grandchildren well. Now, as more women have their first children anywhere from the early teens until their mid-40's, first-time grandparenthood occurs for persons ranging in age from 35 to 75.

Grandchildren encompass both infants and retirees, and grandparents include active middle-aged adults as well as frail, very old persons. For the first time in history, a woman can be both a granddaughter and a grandmother simultaneously. Additional complicating factors are that grandparents and grandchildren are often separated by geographic distance and by divorce and remarriage of the grandchildren's parents; this results in the two generations at the extremes rarely seeing each other. Given such diversity, what are grandparents' rights and obligations?

Without historical precedence, there are few clear culturally shared expectations about grandparent-grandchildren relationships.

As members of a person's social network survive longer, there is an increase in the complexity and the vertical links that cross generational lines of the networks. Individuals in a multigenerational family line interact in a much more complex set of family identities than is the case in a lineage with only two generations, those of parent and child. For example, who is responsible for a great-grandparent who falls and needs daily care: the grandparents who may themselves be frail, the parents who may both be employed, or grandchildren who are often still in school? Demarcations between generations are also becoming blurred. For example, active involvement in the daily demands of childrearing is now likely to be completed by the time women are grandmothers. However, two social trends that blur such demarcations are the growing number of single adolescent mothers, many of whom have substance abuse problems, and the high rates of divorce. In these instances, grandparents often assume many of the tasks of parenting (Minkler and Roe, 1993).

Two other demographic trends, in addition to the increase in longevity, have profoundly affected families. One is the decline in average family size, and the other is the smaller age difference common between a typical family's oldest and youngest child. Around the turn of the century, on the average, mothers bore 3.9 children, with as much as 15 years between the youngest and oldest child. From 1985 to 1988, the fertility rate decreased to a record low of 1.8 children, with a slight increase to 2.1 births per woman by 1992 (U.S. Bureau of the Census, 1992a). As more women postpone marriage and childbearing into their late thirties and early forties, these trends toward smaller families and toward childbearing compressed into fewer years of a woman's life will continue. Women will experience more years of the "empty nest," spending more years after parenting than during that phase. These changes suggest an increasing uniformity in childhood experiences and in parent-child relationships, factors that may affect future cohorts' caregiving experiences. For example, siblings who are closer in age and think of themselves as peers may be more likely to share caregiving tasks than to expect the oldest child or the unmarried daughter to be the primary caregiver—a pattern more common in large families in the past. On the other hand, with declining family size, combined with increases in the number of nonmarried persons and childless couples (the "truncated family"), the pool of potential caregivers is smaller, and this trend is likely to continue.

Another change with reduced fertility rates is that there are fewer individuals within each generation in which to invest emotionally. As a result, intergenerational relationships are not only more extensive, but also more emotionally intensive (Bengtson et al., 1990). As we saw in Chapter 12, parents remain invested in offspring for as long as they live. Adult children have a sense of obligation to their parents, and the family remains the major social support to older relatives. These family patterns will persist and perhaps even grow as the number of younger generations within a family increase, thereby distributing the responsibility across generations.

The widened gap between the mortality rates of men and women, which has produced a seven-year difference in the current life expectancy, is a third major demographic change that influences family relationships. Chapters 12 and 18 demonstrated that the world of the very old is a world of women, both in society and within families. Some five-generation families may include three generations of widows. Most older women are widows living alone; most older men live with their wives. Such differences in widowhood and remarriage mean that men are more likely to maintain horizontal, intragenerational ties, primarily through their wives, until the end of their lives. In contrast, women turn more to intergenerational relationships for help and support throughout their lives, especially in old age (Hagestad and Neugarten, 1985). Even though more women are

entering the marketplace traditionally dominated by men, they continue to place greater emphasis on interpersonal relationships. This, combined with the value placed by the women's movement on friendships and social support, suggests that women will continue to build diverse and extensive social networks to which they can turn in old age. For example, more older women in the future may choose to live with other women than do the women in today's older cohort, forming intergenerational households as a way to reduce housing costs and strengthen their support networks. Another factor that may contribute to this trend is the growing number of women who choose not to marry or who are lesbians. For these women, friends often represent a stronger social bond than relatives.

A social trend that interacts with these demographic changes is the increasing divorce rate. This increase may be inevitable in aging societies, because modern longevity makes marriage a greater long-term commitment than in the past. At the end of the nineteenth century, the average length of marriage until the time when one spouse died was about 28 years. In the late 1970s, it was over 43 years (Furstenberg et al., 1983). The chance of couples who married in the 1930s and 1940s reaching their golden wedding anniversary is less than 5 percent. In spite of increased life expectancy, no more couples reach this 50-year marker nowadays than did a century ago. But whereas before 1974, most marriages ended with death, after 1974, more marriages ended with divorce. As noted in Chapter 12, at least 50 percent of the people currently marrying (and entering old age around the year 2020) will divorce (Furstenberg, 1990). Among the 75 percent of men and 60 percent of women who remarry, more than 40 percent are estimated to divorce yet again (U.S. Bureau of the Census, 1992). On the other hand, with changing values about sexuality and increased understanding that age-related physiological changes generally do not impede sexual activity, more older people will enjoy intimate and sexual relationships through the last phase of life.

Trends in divorce and remarriage are shaping the life course and social networks of young and old but differentially affect men and women. For women, divorce reduces their standard of living and creates an uncertain financial future. The more resources (e.g., education and income) that a divorced woman has available, the less likely she is to remarry, whereas this is reversed for men (Furstenberg, 1990). Therefore, men and women who have divorced but not remarried will differ from today's population. Among women divorcing in the 1990s will be a number of resourceful individuals who will already have lived for many decades on their own as they face old age at the turn of the century (Hagestad, 1986). While they may experience financial struggles as single mothers, they also may be innovative and adept at coping with the changes that aging brings (Riley and Riley, 1986).

For men, the primary consequence of divorce is disruption of intergenerational family networks. Most common is reduced contact with and financial support for children, which also generally means less interaction between paternal grandparents and grandchildren. Children have always faced family disruptions, but now divorce is more common than death as the cause of disruption (Bulcroft and Bulcroft, 1991). It is estimated that more than 30 percent of all children under age 16 will experience the divorce of their parents. By the time children born in 1980 turn age 17, more than 80 percent of them will have spent some time living with only one parent, generally with the mother, because women represent 88 percent of all single-parent households in the United States (U.S. Bureau of the Census, 1992). Furthermore, among children whose parents remarry, nearly 40 percent will experience a second divorce (Furstenberg, 1990). A growing number of children, parents, and grandparents will thus devote substantial effort toward building reconstituted families and step-relationships, only to find them eventually dissolved. Recent trends in divorce and remarriage raise complex questions. How will children of divorce, remarriage, and redivorce approach relationships during their own adult years? What patterns of support will exist between aging parents and children in families disrupted by divorce?

As noted previously, women tend to develop larger and more diverse intergenerational networks, often with other women, than do men. Recent trends in marital disruption may further weaken men's involvement across generations, as suggested by the dramatic decline in number of years that men were involved with their children between 1960 and 1980, and the growing numbers of women who had primary childrearing responsibilities (Antonucci, 1985). Divorced fathers, for example, are less likely to keep in touch with their children or to name them as a source of support (Bulcroft and Bulcroft, 1991). Social values toward sexual equality have increased in recent years, but demographic and social changes have created very different family worlds for men and women. An increasing proportion of men have only tenuous vertical ties along generational lines, yet women have retained strong links to both young and old generations. What will be the relationships between aging fathers and their children with whom they have had only sporadic contact for many years? What sort of responsibility will adult children feel toward an aging father who never paid child support? Will the mother-daughter relationship become even more important as the mainstay of family cohesion? And how will these changes affect the development of policies regarding the care of frail elders?

At the same time that more women, both as single parents and as adult caregivers for parents and grandparents, are assuming more intergenerational responsibilities, their employment demands are expanding. The expectation and necessity for women to enter the paid work force has grown, without any significant diminution in women's family responsibilities, as evidenced by the fact that women devote as much time to household tasks as they did 50 years ago (Twigg and Atkin, 1994). Similarly, employment tends to reduce caregiving responsibilities for sons to their parents, but not for daughters (Foster and

Brizius, 1993; Kaye and Applegate, 1990). Such overload has been referred to as the "super-woman squeeze" (Friedan, 1981), or the "woman in the middle" (Brody, 1985). With the delay in the onset of morbidity and need for care among the old-old, caregivers of the future are likely to be among the young-old; and they will be more likely to remain in the work force, given improved health status, higher living standard expectations, a smaller pool of younger workers, and a lower likelihood of caring for young children at home. There are also more older women caring for adult children with AIDS. While this type of caregiving may last less than 2–3 years, it is a stressful, often emotionally and physically draining experience for the older parent. There is a great need for support programs and education for the caregivers regarding the transmission of the virus, preventive measures, and resources available (Allers, 1990).

As the number of women in the paid work force increases, traditional expectations about family caregiving can become an unbearable burden for women. Although such sex-based roles are slowly changing in terms of child care, the fact that women still assume primary care for children tempers any unrealistic expectations that men will soon become the primary caregivers of frail elders. Yet women who attempt to combine employment and care of persons with chronic disabilities often become physically and emotionally exhausted. A growing number of women are recognizing that they cannot "do it all," and are cutting back on employment responsibilities or turning to community agencies and other family members for assistance. For example, 12 percent of caregiving employees, usually women, have had to leave their jobs to become full-time caregivers (Older Women's League, 1989). Even if they remain employed, women are more likely to restrict their work schedules, reduce their hours, and miss opportunities for career development and job promotion.

At the same time that family caregivers are requesting more support, the current federal administration is expecting families to provide even more care as a cost-effective alternative to publicly supported services. Who will provide what care for older dependents is a volatile policy issue currently and for the future.

The private sector is, however, beginning to respond to the growing number of employees who have caregiving responsibilities, and elder care is a major employee benefit of the 1990s. It has been estimated that 25 percent of the workforce has elder care responsibilities, and that 38 percent of these caregivers have either missed or been late for work as a result (Anastas, Gibeau, and Larson, 1990; Sullivan and Gillmore, 1991). In recognition of the relationship between caregiving demands and productivity, a growing number of corporations such as IBM have initiated elder care referral and counseling services, especially for caregivers at a geographic distance. Other companies such as Travelers Insurance, AT&T, Stride-Rite, and Remington Products offer flexible hours and unpaid leave options for their employees who have caregiving responsibilities. Many universities have expanded their paid leave for child care to include care for frail older family members. Some universities such as the University of Pittsburgh have increased unpaid leave options for employees who are caregivers for seriously ill parents. The Stride-Rite corporation has even begun an on-site day care program for aged parents and young children of employees. Elder care services are increasingly provided by private case managers, who are nurses, social workers, psychologists, and gerontologists; they will locate services, visit regularly, and handle emergencies. However, their fees for an assessment range from $150 to $500, thereby limiting their service to a small proportion of family caregivers. These market-place initiatives will undoubtedly continue in the future as parental caregiving responsibilities increase. However, they are the exception, not the norm, and the trend toward cost cutting and reduction of employee benefits in many businesses may counteract such improvements.

## New Definitions of Work and Productivity

An imbalance has existed between a population of increasingly long-lived people and decreasing opportunities for them to participate in society (Riley and Riley, 1986). Perhaps the most striking area in which social and cultural structures lag behind demographic changes is in employment. Since 1900, the labor force participation of older people has been eroding, and the competence of older workers for productive performance has been consistently underrated. As work opportunities for the older population have declined, pressures have mounted for socially rewarding roles in retirement. Today, people find that they are spending over 20 percent of their adult lives in retirement, compared with only 3 percent in 1900 (U.S. Senate Special Committee on Aging, 1992). The trend toward early retirement, combined with increased longevity, means that retirement as a life stage will become even more protracted. As people begin to comprehend how much of the adult lifetime is spent in retirement, there is growing awareness that formal retirement does not end the need for involvement in the larger society. The concept of the "Third Age" has been developed by gerontologists at Fordham University to denote that stage in life which occurs after middle age but before the final stage, and is a time of continued involvement and development. This perspective emphasizes that with new understanding of the potential of older people, new public values regarding their opportunities and responsibilities are needed (Cornman and Kingson, 1995).

As members of successive cohorts retire at younger ages, are better educated, and perhaps healthier than their predecessors, it seems predictable that pressures from older people and from the public at large will modify existing work and retirement roles. Modifications in the workplace are already underway to offset the lag between changes in social structures and the recognition of older people's skills and productivity as well as to take account of the rapid growth among the older workforce, especially those ages 55 to 64. Another reason for develop-

ing incentives for older workers is the projected labor shortage among youth, particularly in the service sector. From 1993 to 2004, the population comprised of workers over age 40 will increase by over 28 million; aging of baby boomers will raise the median age of the labor force by 3 years. By 2005, there will be at least 5.9 million workers over age 55 in the labor force compared to an increase of less than .5 million over the past 15 years (Rix, 1994).

More companies are modifying the workplace in order to retain older workers in the labor force longer and to encourage multiple careers. To date, however, such workplace changes do not adequately meet the growing interest in part-time employment among many older people. These workplace modifications include both incentives to maintain the older workers' productivity and ways to ease the transition to retirement. They involve redesigning jobs (e.g., job sharing, flexible and part-time schedules, and conducting work at home) in order to accommodate older workers' needs and skills; providing retraining in the new technologies such as computers and robotics, counseling, and other support services for new careers; and offering additional forms of compensation such as health benefits or tax credits. Some companies, such as Travelers Insurance, have set up data banks of retiree skills for temporary employment and job sharing. Local and federal government agencies have developed programs to make use of retirees' skills in voluntary and paid employment. For example, the Small Business Administration's SCORE program (Senior Corps of Retired Executives) makes use of retired business executives as counselors for new businesses.

Other workplace options focus on easing the transition to retirement through retirement preparation programs. Retirement needs to be viewed not as a single and irreversible event, but as a process involving successive decisions. For example, IBM has a Retirement Education Assistance plan that provides tuition to employees and their spouses three years prior to retirement eligibility and two years after retirement; the plan aims to enable employees to develop new interests and prepare for new careers. Another model, common in some European countries and in Japan, is a "gliding out" plan of phased retirement that permits a gradual shift to a part-time schedule. Jobs can also be restructured, gradually allowing longer vacations, shorter work days, and more opportunities for community involvement during the pre-retirement working years. Volunteer opportunities that draw upon retirees' competence as well as provide them with chances to learn new skills can also blur the line between paid employment and retirement.

Other changes in occupational patterns are the increased number of people in their forties and fifties who are electing to move into second and even third careers. More organizations are allowing their employees opportunities for growth in their jobs by providing sabbaticals, extended vacations and leaves, retraining programs, and career development alternatives. Such adult education options benefit employees by allowing them to explore new careers and volunteer and leisure interests; this, in turn, can serve to prevent job burnout or boredom, so that early retirement is not perceived as the only viable option. These programs also benefit employers in organizations that are undergoing rapid technological changes, such as automobile manufacturing, where robotics and computerized assembly lines are already in place. By retraining their older, more experienced workers, such organizations can retain employees who have proven capable in the past.

A work-retirement continuum for a population with a longer lifespan will involve lifelong education and training. Changing social values about the "appropriate age" for education, employment, and retirement demand a reexamination of employment policies. The traditional linear life cycle of education for the young, employment for the middle aged, and retirement for the old are already undergoing major changes as more middle-aged and older persons enter college for the first time, or begin their studies for a graduate or professional degree. This phenomenon of

"a graying of the university" is evident in most academic settings. For example, since the *University of California Regents* v. *Bakke* decision in 1978, more and more persons over age 35 have entered professional schools. In 1985 more than 45 percent of college students were over age 25, while the average age of community college students was 38 (Dychtwald and Flower, 1989). From a developmental perspective, temporary "retirement" may be a more viable option for the young worker just starting a family, employment may be desirable for the teenager who is bored with school, and education may be attractive to the older person who can integrate his or her life experiences with academic content. Instead of the straight career trajectory traditionally followed in our society, movement in and out of the workforce, schooling, and family care may all need to be defined as legitimate options in a cyclic life plan (Dychtwald and Flower, 1989). Already we are seeing some markets geared specifically to the older learner.

Women have moved in and out of the workforce for years, largely because of assuming family responsibilities, but they have often been penalized for their discontinuous work patterns through lower salaries and retirement benefits. As noted earlier, this pattern will not change dramatically in the near future, given that women still earn only 70 cents for every dollar earned by men and still assume most of the caregiving of dependents. In fact, despite the increased number of women in the paid work force and the relatively greater economic affluence among younger women, older women in the future are predicted to remain significantly poorer than older men. However, with increasing numbers of career-oriented women who are committed to an ideology of shared family responsibilities, and with growing awareness of the possibility of two or three careers over the life course, movement in and out of the work force may come to be viewed as a legitimate alternative for both men and women. This may also encourage individuals to better integrate their work and family lives. Indeed, women and persons of color will account for over 60 percent of the projected labor force growth by the year 2000 (AARP, 1991).

There is disagreement, however, on the economy's ability to create such work alternatives. In the past decade, the U.S. economy has been characterized by lower growth in productivity, sharper competition from markets abroad, high inflation, and high unemployment. Few economists predict a return to the high growth rates of the 1950s and 1960s, when a rapidly expanding economy and low inflation provided jobs for almost all who wanted them, and improved retirement benefits for those who wanted to retire. There are also uncertainties about the potential impact of technological advances on job opportunities—whether these will produce new jobs or result in net job losses. Even so, some economists are predicting expansion for the economy toward the end of this century. Most of these jobs will be in the service sector (e.g., health and social services, food and recreation), rather than in production (e.g. assembly line jobs). What is certain, given the rapid growth of the older population, is that there will be greater labor market diversity among the older population and greater variations in the reasons for retirement, in the nonemployed by social class, and in economic well-being before and after retirement.

*Productive aging,* defined as activities that contribute to society in diverse ways, paid or unpaid, includes the opportunity to participate in the well-being of society even after retirement, in the form of volunteer work, informal assistance, and self-care. But society must provide flexible options for productive activity by older persons (Caro, Bass, and Chen, 1993; Herzog and House, 1991). The distinction between productive aging and *successful aging* (described in Chapter 9) is a focus on participating *roles* in the former concept, and on psychological and physiological *capacity* in the latter concept.

As noted in Chapters 7 and 9, there has been a growth in programs aimed at improving the physical and functional health as well as the cognitive abilities of older persons. However, there has been less emphasis on enhancing productive aging. Advocates of a productive aging society suggest that national policies and attitudes must be changed, including the development of a national consensus that encourages older persons to continue or create their own roles in society, opening doors to interested and capable elders; places a real value on unpaid volunteer and caregiving activities; takes practical steps such as publicly emphasizing that technology does not necessarily displace older workers; and provides settings where older people can use their talents more productively and in a more satisfying manner (Morris, 1993).

Such structural changes are a necessary first step, but our societal attitudes toward the productivity of older persons must also be altered. The meaning of productivity must be redefined to include more than employment. A more humanizing approach, consistent with the politics of productivity discussed in Chapter 19, is to ask how we can develop and use our human potential in old age as part of a productive society. The vitality of the older population must be recognized out of a need to involve their skills and wisdom, through both paid and unpaid positions, in the enrichment of our society (Butler and Gleason, 1985). Such fundamental redefinitions of old age and aging would move us beyond the artificially framed policy debates about young and old competing for scarce resources. They would also help to counteract the "new ageism" noted by Kalish (1979), and would serve, in the long run, to reduce the dependency, both real and perceived, of older persons. As suggested in Chapter 19, the interdependence of generations across the life span, when made explicit, can provide a future framework for policy and program development. Older people are becoming more aware of the creative and central roles that they can play in moving beyond their own needs and leaving a legacy for future generations—for example, through their active participation in environmental and energy issues. Likewise, intergenerational programs in schools, community centers, nursing homes, retirement facilities, and adult day care centers are growing.

Such programs serve to utilize older adults' skills, as well as provide children and youth with opportunities to interact with diverse older people; in other words, to build on the reciprocity that exists between generations. These cooperative, cross-age efforts may have the long-term effect of reducing ageism and competition among age groups, so that young and old work together to benefit the most needy in our society, regardless of age. Recently, we have seen such alliances between young and old form around the need for long-term care reform. Perhaps in the future it will be unnecessary to develop age-based social and health policies, but rather to establish programs that address special needs across the life span.

As noted in Chapter 19, with the shifting dependency ratio (e.g., more older people than younger people), intergenerational transfers to older people are disproportionately through Social Security pensions and other social programs. As populations age, the role of government in the distribution of income increases and that of the family tends to decline, even though most families are still very involved in their older relatives' care and support. A critical issue for the future is whether working age populations will accept this change and its consequences, particularly higher tax rates and growth of the federal deficit (Schulz and Myles, 1990). The "shift to the right" in recent elections and increasing attacks upon entitlement programs suggest that the basic concepts of social welfare and income maintenance are under attack.

In sum, among future cohorts, there will be a growing proportion of affluent older adults who will participate in the labor market or enjoy the pension benefits of their lifetime employment and who can pay through the private sector for most of the solutions to their needs. The extent to which the public sector will continue to focus on the needs of the economically vulnerable is unclear, given the increasingly more conservative political climate and the trend toward less federal support. And those in the middle, the "tweeners" who have too many resources to qualify for public programs, yet are unable to pay fully for their health and long-term care needs, will increase. In fact, it is the expansion of the tweeners that is predicted to create future intergenerational competition for scarce resources (Smeeding, 1990; Longino and Soldo, 1987).

## Leisure in Old Age

As noted in Chapter 15, the concept of leisure is difficult to define; some gerontologists equate it with retirement or describe it as absence of work. Others have defined it as unobligated discretionary time (Kabanoff, 1980) or free time for pleasurable passive or active pursuits (Caro et al., 1993). Still others differentiate leisure from recreation in that the former is unstructured but the latter is planned (Atchley, 1971). Traditionally, leisure pursuits and the leisure role have been relegated to the retirement years, so that the typical life trajectory consisted of education, employment, and childrearing, followed by leisure during retirement. According to this model of the life course, leisure opportunities are considered to be a reward for a lifetime of hard work and therefore are greater for affluent individuals and in societies with longer life expectancy and earlier retirement (Robinson, Coberly, and Paul, 1985). Accordingly, a leisure industry has developed, particularly in retirement communities, to meet the recreational needs of more affluent and healthy older adults. Think of the variety of social activities and recreational sports that are offered in many planned retirement communities. The growth of ski and running clubs as well as aerobic classes for older persons signals the increase in older people who recognize the health and psychological benefits of exercise.

Modifications in work patterns and organizational opportunities for career development, described in the previous section, suggest that definitions of leisure are also undergoing major changes. Employment and leisure are becoming less compartmentalized and more evenly distributed across the life span through modified work schedules, sabbaticals, job sharing, lifelong education, and phased retirement, as well as the increasing number of retirees who work part-time and engage in significant volunteer activities. This "blurring" of work and leisure is reinforced by increased organizational awareness of employee needs, such as on-the-job exercise and fitness programs, child care, staff training, and psychological counseling. To some extent, these factors are an outgrowth of the shift from the traditional work ethic to a more balanced view of employment and leisure in this society (Robinson, Coberly, and Paul, 1985). Therefore, it is not unrealistic to expect that future cohorts of elderly will view leisure in retirement merely as a continuation of their leisure activities during their younger years, and will not regard it as a new stage in life. Given that many people choose to retire earlier than in the past, and that life expectancy beyond age 65 continues to increase, future elders will benefit from the opportunity to adopt leisure activities in their preretirement years that can then be carried into the later years. Such integration of leisure throughout the life span will undoubtedly mean a smoother transition to retirement for many older people.

## Changes in Living Arrangements

The movement away from farms and city centers to the suburbs has also resulted in the graying of the suburbs, with many people who had moved to these areas after World War II reaching retirement. Older residents in these older suburbs have lower average incomes and lower home values than those in newer communities as seen in Chapter 13.

These trends will continue as the children of these migrants to the suburbs, who, in turn, built their homes in the suburbs and worked in nearby satellite communities, themselves age. Up until now, most health and social services, such as clinics, hospitals, senior centers, and nutrition sites, have been built near city centers with high concentrations of older people. Future cohorts will expect these services to be located closer to their homes in the suburbs, just as shopping centers, banks, and jobs have been moved outward from urban centers to these areas to accommodate the needs of this population. Think of the growing number of hospitals, nursing homes, and retirement communities that are being built in suburbs where 30 years ago family housing, shopping centers, and schools were the most prevalent type of construction, and where 20 years ago "business parks" and office buildings were being constructed.

The growth of the suburbs was a natural outcome of the increased automobile ownership among Americans after World War II. The dependence on private automobiles made it unnecessary for many suburban communities to provide mass transportation, even after the oil crisis of 1973. This reliance on a private car may be implicit in middle age and early old age. But what happens as the older person lives beyond age 80 in the suburbs and experiences increased problems with vision, hearing, and reaction time, to the point where he or she should give up driving? Unfortunately, the assumption that people will be willing and able to drive long distances in advanced old age prevails, even among developers of retirement communities. It is not unusual for such communities to be built in physically beautiful locations, but far from places served by

Institutions for older persons have become increasingly home-like and encourage continuity of previous lifestyles.

mass transportation and without provisions for vans or other group transport options.

These problems may be alleviated in the future, with the growth of community-based private and public programs that bring services to the older person's home (e.g., Meals on Wheels, chore-workers, and home health care, described in Chapter 13), as well as the increasing number of retirement communities that are self-contained. Many of these communities provide health and recreational services; even banking and shopping are nearby.

The residences of older adults who depend on community-based long-term care services will require structural modifications and communication and transportation systems to support older people's independence. Consistent with the person-environment model described in the Introduction and illustrated throughout this book, the home environment of older people can be modified to reduce the level of environmental press, enhance the aging person's level of competence and quality of life. For example, currently nearly 35 percent of individuals age 75 and older use at least one assistive device or have their home modified for accessibility. This proportion is expected to increase dramatically with newer cohorts of older persons (Emerman, 1994).

With the trends toward computerized home-based banking and shopping services, future cohorts may not need to leave their homes to obtain services. As more older people strive to remain independent, the market for home-based services will expand. Furthermore, programs such as Emergency Medical Services (911) and the Life Safety System or Lifeline Security Systems in retirement complexes, as well as Neighborhood Watch and programs by local utilities to watch over frail elders living alone, have offered a sense of safety for older people who choose to continue living in their own homes. These services will become even more critical in the future, as the proportion of older people living alone increases dramatically from 8.5 million in 1985 to an estimated 30 million in 2030 (Zedlewski et al., 1989). Not only will more older people be living

alone, but they will be even older and with more disabling conditions than current cohorts. In fact, it has been estimated that the demand for such services will increase by a factor of three or four between 1990 and 2030 (Zedlewski et al., 1989). These alternatives will continue to receive attention from future cohorts of older adults as technological advances make home-based care and security systems available to more older people. For example, robotics is a field that has significantly altered the workplace, and is beginning to be applied in the homes of persons with physical and sensory impairments. The National Association of Home Builders and private developers offer "Smart Houses," where computers and appliances can command each other and exchange feedback through advances in wiring. Computerized controls can improve the fuel efficiency of older people's homes, turn off unattended appliances, ensure even lighting on stairs and on floor surfaces, and provide a security system for an older person in a high crime area (Hiatt, 1988).

Voice-activated computer systems that are being used widely by individuals with physical disabilities can also serve to enhance the independence of older people with chronic diseases. For example, these new systems can help older persons suffering from severe arthritis to correspond with family and friends, or to "write" their life history. It may be possible to compensate for impaired vision by using audible information instead of visual displays. An example of the use of audible announcements for people with visual or memory impairments is an electric range that can announce: "The front right burner is on high heat" or "The oven temperature is 350 degrees."

Computer programs have also been developed to describe potential side effects of various medications and interactions among them. Although these programs are aimed at physicians, pharmacists, and other health professionals, it may be possible in the near future to buy such a program written in layman's language, type in the names and doses of medications one is taking, and then obtain a printout of potential side effects and special precautions. This would be particularly useful to the many older adults who are using numerous prescriptions and over-the-counter medications. Older people in Cleveland, Ohio can access from their home computers a health information computerized network, including individualized information on Alzheimer's disease and an "electronic support group." Computer dialing programs can be used to check daily on older people who live alone to make sure that they are safe. Although too costly to implement at present, it is technically possible to conduct remote monitoring between a patient's home and a local health care facility for such things as blood pressure and heart rate measures.

Another technological innovation that can help older persons continue to live independently is the Smart Cap, a tiny computer embodied in a prescription bottle cap. The cap beeps to remind the person to take the medication; it also counts how many pills were removed each day, and when. The system is connected via modem to the company that manufactures it, so a phone reminder can be made if the user forgets the medication that day. While the current cost of such a system is prohibitive for most older people, it offers great promise of improving medication adherence by future cohorts of elders.

Technology also can be used to enhance options for recreation and enrichment for older people. For example, computers are increasingly being used for leisure, such as games linked by telecommunication channels or books read on microchips. Interactive television, CD-ROM, and videodiscs, special TV programming, and open university via television can greatly expand the social worlds of homebound elders, and stimulate cognitive functions through active participation in learning. For example, Senior Net is a nationwide computer network that encourages discussion on diverse topics and offers hands-on classes in computer use. It is aimed at people age 55 and older. In addition to a small membership fee, users can attend local classes on computer

literacy, word processing, database management, spreadsheets, and newly emerging telecommunications systems.

Technological advances will also benefit younger family caregivers. As robotics and computer systems become more cost-effective and user-friendly, they will be used by frail older people who would otherwise need to rely on family or paid caregivers, or move to a nursing home. They may also be freer to use assisted living or other less intensive and less costly housing options if these facilities offer such technological assistance to their residents. Communication via FAX machines, video telephones, and electronic mail will also reduce the physical distance among older people and their families. These developments will be easier for future generations of elders to adopt, because they will have grown up with computers and rapid technological advances in their work and leisure. On the other hand, older people do not necessarily want technology that saves time or replaces activity, such as automatic tellers or shopping via television. As noted in Chapter 15, for many older adults, household tasks and shopping are not necessarily seen as onerous, but rather as interesting timefillers. Therefore, older people may be most interested in technology that makes life easier, safer, and improves their quality of life (Markle Foundation, 1989).

Although equipment will increasingly be used to supplement or replace personal assistance, there are financial barriers to the use of these technologies. Currently, third-party sources (private insurance, Medicare, Medicaid, Veterans Administration, or other private or public sources) cover about 50 percent of the assistive devices in use, with the rest paid by those in need or their families out-of-pocket. More than 75 percent of home accessibility features are paid for entirely by the user and family. The reason that older people most often give for not utilizing needed assistive devices is financial. Since reimbursement and regulatory issues are also a barrier to companies entering this marketplace, producers and consumers may share common goals in changing reimbursement mechanisms. Advocates for these new products and designs will also find support for their cause in federal legislation such as the Americans with Disabilities Act (ADA) which emphasizes the social desirability of increasing use of assistive technologies and accessible environmental design (Emerman, 1994).

The cost of maintaining their homes has represented another major deterrent for many older people who wish to remain independent. In response, numerous banks and mortgage companies offer reverse mortgage plans, described in Chapter 13. In effect, these programs buy the older person's home at current market values, while allowing the individual to remain in it and to have additional financial resources. Some banks offer low-interest home improvement loans to older people, thereby making the home easier to maintain and more attractive to future buyers.

Shared housing is another means of helping older people remain in their own homes, as discussed in Chapter 13. Community programs that match older homeowners with other elders, or with college students and younger working people who need housing, serve a useful function in making the cost of housing affordable to a wider cross-section of persons. These intergenerational programs also provide security for frail older people who need occasional assistance from their healthier peers or younger people, but who do not require the constant care of nursing homes. Future cohorts of elders may also continue the trends of their younger years by sharing housing with an unmarried companion. As society has become more accepting of unmarried couples and gay and lesbian partners living together, the advantages of such arrangements for older couples have become more evident. Thus, for example, sharing a home without marrying can reduce an older couple's expenses while they maintain their separate incomes from pensions and Social Security benefits. Most important, shared housing provides much-needed social companionship.

These trends suggest that more older people can and will remain independent in the commu-

nity. Nevertheless, there will continue to be a need for institutional care for the most disabled and frail older population. For example, it is estimated that the number of older people with four or more activity limitations will increase from 1.5 million currently to 4 million or more by 2030 (Zedlewski et al., 1989). Even with the expansion of home-based health care, it may not be possible for this segment of the population to remain in their own homes (see Figure E-1), but health providers and policy makers still must consider other options to home care and community-based nursing home placement. These include adult day health centers, day hospitals, cooperative care, and assisted living facilities for frail older people who do not need round-the-clock care.

## Health Care Delivery in the Future

As we have seen in earlier chapters, future cohorts of older people may cope with a longer lifetime of chronic diseases in different ways than previous generations have. The increasingly high costs of hospitalization and nursing homes have already resulted in the growth of various options in health and long-term care.

A major area of expansion is home health care provided by hospitals, private and nonprofit agencies, and local governments. These programs, described in Chapter 20, allow older people to remain as self-sufficient as possible in their homes—values that future generations may be more likely to hold because of their greater opportunities for choice. Adult day centers and adult day health programs also provide family members with respite from full-time caregiving for a chronically ill or demented older person. As noted in Chapter 20, however, funding for such options is limited. More comprehensive, coordinated in-home and community-based supportive services accessible to the older person are needed, along with changes in public financing of long-term care. What is unknown is the extent to which Medicare and Medicaid will be modified to cover more such programs in the future, or

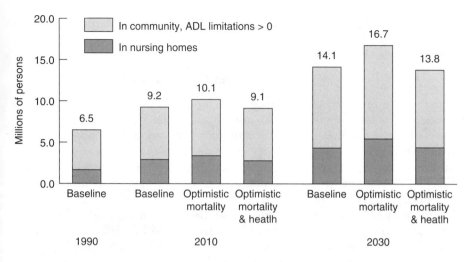

Key:

Baseline = Assumes that mortality rates will improve by .6 percent per year.

Optimistic mortality: Assumes that mortality rates will improve by 1.2 percent.

Optimistic & health: Assumes that disability rates will improve along with mortality rates improving by 1.2 percent per year.

**FIGURE E–1   Potential Need for Long-Term Care Services, Persons Over 65: 1990–2030**
SOURCE: Sheila Zedlewski, et al., *The Needs of the Elderly in the 21st Century*, (Washington, D.C.: The Urban Institute, 1989).

whether significant reform in health and long-term care will occur.

The growth in the number of hospitals, along with the surplus of physicians and an excess of hospital beds, has led to greater competition for older patients. At the same time, financial limitations on the provision of care have resulted in an increase in ambulatory services. Along with an increase in multi-hospital systems involving proprietary, nonprofit, and public hospitals, many hospitals have developed special geriatric units for both acute and chronic care (Lee and Benjamin, 1989). Some have established satellite clinics and provide health screening and foot care in senior centers and senior housing; others offer health education and health promotion activities for older persons and for family members of frail elders in hospital and in community settings. Still others provide emergency response systems, home health care, information and referral, and free transportation to the hospital for older patients. The number of hospitals with long-term care beds, or those planning to establish such beds or to convert acute care to long-term care beds, has also increased significantly.

A growing number of hospitals sponsor membership programs that provide a package of special services such as health screening, annual exams at reduced costs, telephone reassurance, and help with complex insurance forms. Such "health clubs" as Eldermed, Goldencare Plus, and Health Wise have sprung up around the country. Most are aimed at the financially better-off portion of the older population who have Medicare Parts A and B, *and* supplementary "medigap" insurance. They do not address the needs of uninsured people, nor do they generally reduce the cost of outpatient medical care or hospitalization. Many of these programs do, however, offer discounts on eyeglasses and medication. As competition among hospitals increases, these clubs may eventually lead to lower costs for older people.

Other developments in the health care industry may also reduce costs for future generations. Health maintenance organizations (HMOs), for example, have attracted a growing number of older persons as members by providing comprehensive health care at lower average costs than private hospitals and physicians can offer. These hospitals are also leading the way in preventive medicine and health promotion. Some existing private hospitals are converting to HMOs. Similarly, the increased number of alternative health care providers such as geriatric nurse practitioners offer older persons quality health services for chronic conditions without the high costs of traditional physician-based care. The growth of geriatric education in colleges of medicine, nursing, dentistry, social work, pharmacy, and in other areas such as nutrition and physical therapy suggest that a well-trained cadre of health care providers will become increasingly available to future older adults. These developments in hospital and community-based health services, combined with the increased number of health specialists training in geriatrics, offer hope for cost containment in the absence of national health care reform. They will also ensure improved quality of acute and chronic care for older people.

These changes will occur within the context of managed care which seeks to control health care costs through limiting resources, particularly through pressures on hospitals to cut costs by releasing patients sooner. These pressures have created demands for a new type of facility for the person who is too sick to go home, but is not sick enough for a hospital. As a result, subacute care facilities are growing, whereby nursing homes are becoming less like homes and more like hospitals, to provide stroke rehabilitation, cardiac care and intravenous feeding. This shift, however, does mean that in many facilities, spaces for Medicaid patients are being filled by higher paying Medicare patients (Fritz, 1995).

## Long-Term Care in the Future

Advances in long-term care for the chronically ill also offer future older persons the promise of greater options if they should ever need such care. Long-term care includes the array of community services that are needed on a continuing basis to enable people with chronic disabilities to maintain their physical, social, and psychological functioning, but these conditions do not generally require constant medical monitoring. Traditionally, such services have been provided by nursing homes, an alternative that has drained the resources of most older residents and their families. Currently, the possibility of long-term care for a chronic illness or functional limitation poses the greatest single threat to the economic security of all but the wealthiest of older Americans.

If disability rates remain what they are today, the number of older persons needing help with basic tasks is expected to double between 1990 and 2030, and the number of older individuals requiring nursing home care will more than triple. In addition, the use of high technology and new medical breakthroughs may continue                                    to extend the lives of people with disabilities of all ages (The Pepper Commission, 1990). Given these advances, it is not surprising that most American voters state that they want a government program of long-term care insurance across age groups, although many resist the tax increases inherent in such reform. Because of the limited help currently available in either our public programs or through the private sector to pay for potentially expensive long-term care, the need for a comprehensive, national long-term care policy, as well as for private long-term care insurance options, will grow. Private health insurance will probably change dramatically—at the same time that more public costs are shifted to local governments and the private sector. However, as noted in Chapter 20, American values of independence and private responsibility may deter the development of a publicly funded national health care plan that covers long-term care across the life span.

As one way to control costs, it is necessary to differentiate the problems of aging from the need for long-term care. For example, under comprehensive long-term care, losses in the areas of employment, income, and family should be compensated by job programs, volunteer opportunities, and options to participate in the community, while professionally oriented case-managed services should be reserved for those with physical or mental disabilities.

Current expectations that families should assume more responsibility for long-term care are unrealistic, because of cost and because of demographic and social trends that were discussed earlier. As noted, women, traditionally caregivers of older relatives, are now more likely to be employed than were previous generations; a typical life course of school, work, marriage, and caregiving no longer exists for most women. Yet few of our current or proposed programs adequately address the critical policy issue of the multiple demands on family caregivers. Geographic and occupational mobility may further reduce the family's ability to provide care, even though they may want to help their older relatives as much as possible. The problem of caring for elders with chronic illnesses is compounded by the reduction in federal assistance for the growing number of older veterans of U.S. wars. This group has traditionally received federal funding for health services as a means of recognizing their contributions to society. However, the Veterans Administration has raised the eligibility criteria for many health services as a means of cutting costs, thereby expecting families and the private sector to fill the gap. In sum, a major policy dilemma for the twenty-first century is: What should be the role of government, the private sector, and the family in meeting long-term care needs? Within these roles, what should be done to ensure the autonomy of the patient? These policy issues inevitably raise ethical dilem-

mas about the distribution of resources among various segments of society.

## Ethical Dilemmas

At the forefront of ethical dilemmas in an aging society is the issue of the prolongation of life at a time of escalating medical costs, increasing use of high-technology treatments, fears about rationing, and confusion over health care reform. As a society, we have valued finding cures for dreaded diseases and forestalling death as long as possible. Medical technology has made it possible to extend life expectancy, but not necessarily to assure quality of life. We are far from achieving the goal of "squaring the life expectancy course" where a healthy life is followed by a quick illness and death (Black and Levy, 1981; Fries, 1980). Many older people are now saved, often at considerable cost, from diseases that previously would have killed them, only to be guaranteed death from another disease at equally high or even higher costs. Medical professionals have been taught to spare no effort in keeping a patient alive, but increasingly both professionals and lay persons are questioning whether dying should be prolonged indefinitely when there is no possibility of recovery. Life-support systems, organ transplants, and other advances in medical technology have made it possible to prolong the life of the chronically and terminally ill, and have blurred definitions of when life ends. For example, technology now allows the transplantation of various human organs, and life can be prolonged by machines that keep the body functioning even if the conscious mind has died. But these advances have not necessarily ensured better quality of life.

The timing, place, and conditions of death are increasingly under medical control, although ambivalence remains about whether death should be fought or accepted (Callahan, 1993; Sachs, 1994). For almost any life-threatening condition, some interventions can now delay the moment of death, but not its inevitability. Doctors and nurses have always dealt with dying, but not until the present technical advances have they had so much power and responsibility to control how long life lasts and to determine when treatment is medically futile (Schneiderman, 1994). At the same time, technology has made it more difficult to draw a clear line between living and dying. As a result, these new medical capabilities demand a new set of ethics and practices. The field of *bioethics* was born out of the dilemmas that often confront health care providers, family members and patients regarding the introduction and withdrawal of invasive treatments, the patient's decision-making capacity to participate in treatment decisions, and the quality of the patient's life (Zuckerman, 1994).

At the core of these ethical issues is the question of who decides what for whom and thus issues of power and authority (Scofield, 1994). Decisions about whether and how to intervene in a terminal illness can be excruciating for doctors, nurses, family members, and older patients. At what point should efforts to prolong life be stopped, when the alternative is so final? How much suffering is "worth it" to stay alive? Which is more important: quality or quantity of life? And how do we measure or determine quality of life? Under what conditions and for which decisions should the wishes of the patient supersede those of his or her family members? What institutional mechanisms should be employed to resolve ethical conflicts? These decisions become even more complex when the older person is mentally incompetent, as in the case of Alzheimer's patients. Cross-cultural differences can also affect how patients, family members and health care providers interpret life-sustaining treatment (Michel, 1994).

There is increasing attention to establishing guidelines by which health professionals should withhold treatment (American Geriatrics Society, 1994), and health care facilities are now required to have the capacity to address such bioethical issues for patients, families, and staff, typically through ethics committees. As noted in Chapter 16, all 50 states now have laws authorizing the use of *advance directives*. These are supplemented

by a federal law, the Patient Self-Determination Act, which requires health care facilities that receive Medicare and Medicaid funds (i.e., most hospitals and nursing homes) to inform patients of their rights to complete advance directives stating how they wish to be treated in the case of a life and death situation. Nevertheless, these laws have not necessarily been successfully operationalized, suggesting that ethical issues surrounding the dying process cannot easily be legislated.

One result of the increased visibility of medicine and the media attention on bioethical issues is that more people know about their legal rights as patients and have thought about the personal moral principles that govern their individual choices. Accordingly, there is growing public support for individual determination regarding life-sustaining treatment, as evidenced by the increased number of people who have advanced directives such as living wills. As described in Chapter 16, many states have begun to grapple with the issue of physician-assisted suicide for mentally competent, terminally ill adults. Citizen initiatives and bills in state legislatures have increased the debate surrounding the "right to die" or "death with dignity." In most cases, the debate centers not on *if* such activity should be condoned but *under what circumstances* and what is meant by terminal and medical finality. As these arguments have reached federal and state courts, with mixed rulings, the likelihood has increased that a precedent-setting case will soon be filed with the U.S. Supreme Court. Even if the Supreme Court rules on this matter, it seems unlikely that the ethical arguments on either side of the issue will subside, much like the ongoing debates about abortion.

Such ethical considerations cannot be completely divorced from economic issues, since 38 percent of Medicare expenditures cover costs in the last year of life (Lubitz and Riley, 1993). With pressures mounting to reduce medical bills paid with public funds, interventions to extend life are increasingly questioned. Does the quality of life gained justify the enormous expenditures often entailed by such interventions? When public resources are scarce, questions become framed in terms of how benefits should be distributed among various groups in society. As we have seen, the intergenerational inequity perspective maintains that economic imbalances caused by the provision of health and long-term care for the older adults potentially threaten the welfare of younger generations and of society as a whole (Callahan, 1986, 1987). Yet studies to date suggest that the total savings achieved by denying high cost acute care to older people would have little impact on overall health care expenditures (National Academy on Aging, 1994). In fact, high-cost Medicare patients who die account annually for only 3.5 percent of Medicare expenditures (Binstock, 1994). Surrounding all such matters are issues of who should decide, in the aggregate and in individual instances, who receives what type of health care. Those who oppose "right to die" legislation fear that economic considerations will override compassionate concerns, with governments eventually requiring removal of life supports from older people as a way to control health care costs.

While expenditures to prolong the lives of older people are not as large a proportion of total health care costs as is commonly assumed, debates about the rationing of health care to older people have intensified, especially since the early 1980s when the Governor of Colorado suggested the removal of life supports from terminally ill older patients as a way to reduce costs. Critics of costly life-saving techniques for older adults, such as transplants, argue that with over 33 million people under age 65 without health care insurance and many more who cannot afford high-tech care, our health care system should first address such basic needs rather than spending disproportionate resources for expensive procedures for only a few. While these debates are often framed in terms of allocating scarce health care resources to the young, defined as an investment, versus the old, we have no accurate way of comparing the benefits of physical mobility allowed an older person by an expensive hip

replacement with those of an improved secondary education for a teenager, for example (Callahan, 1986). In contrast, in England, there is agreement among physicians, the public, and the government that equal access to labor-intensive services such as primary care, geriatric care, and home health services is more important than widespread access to high-technology services such as renal dialysis, coronary artery bypass surgery, or intensive care.

*Rationing* decisions tend to be made at a societal level, while decisions about whether treatment is *medically* futile are made at the patient's bedside. In other words, rationing specifically acknowledges that a treatment offers a benefit, but the issue is how to distribute beneficial but limited resources fairly, while medical futility signifies that a treatment offers no therapeutic benefit to a patient (Schneiderman, 1994). Some would argue that states already ration health care through physicians who refuse to treat Medicaid recipients. In fact, the state of Oregon is implementing a federally authorized policy experiment in which it operates with a fixed Medicaid budget and classifies specific categories of health care as not reimbursable (Binstock, 1994). Instead of spending Medicaid funds on costly transplants that can benefit relatively few patients, they are emphasizing the provision of basic health care to every poor person in the state and ranking diseases according to importance and insurability. Even if rationing is not formal policy, there is evidence to suggest that physicians sometimes ration the use of medical care to the oldest-old; one study of six major hospitals found that patients age 75 and older who entered a hospital with acute myocardial infarcts were 2.5 times less likely to be admitted to a coronary care unit (a more intensive and more costly hospital service) than were patients age 40 to 74 (Fleming, D'Agostino, and Selker, 1991). As doctors attempt to provide adequate care within the context of limited budgets such as capitated systems of care, they tend to be pressured by colleagues and administrators not to make available the same expensive tests and medical specialties as exist for younger patients, resulting in underservice for some older patients (Kane and Kane, 1994; Binstock, 1994). Debates about an equitable provision of services versus targeting life-saving interventions for a few will undoubtedly intensify in the future.

Ultimately, these decisions come down to how much our society values older people. Those who argue against rationing maintain that a major cost would be the destruction of moral barriers against placing any group of human beings in a category apart from humanity in general. If older people can be denied access to health care categorically, than that could happen to other groups as well. They argue that suggesting that older people are unworthy of lifesaving care starts us down the cliched "slippery slope." (Binstock, 1994, p. 40). Not only are the moral costs of rationing too great, but the potential contributions of older people to society are lost. They argue that alternatives other than rationing should be attempted as a way to contain health care costs. Former Surgeon General C. Everett Koop (1991, p. ix) maintained that "no matter what financial constraints, we must not let our economics guide our ethics, but must let our ethics guide our economics."

Others will continue to argue that given high and ever-escalating health care costs inherent in an aging and developed society, then we have to face difficult moral questions about the desirability of medical intervention, about the value we place on preserving and improving older adults' health, and about the comparative rights of different generations to the necessary resources of life (Callahan, 1986, 1987). They raise questions about how much we owe older people and why. What is our obligation to older populations in the face of health care needs and prerogatives of other age groups, especially when this presents costs to human welfare (McGregor, 1989)?

Ultimately, these larger ethical questions translate into daily practice dilemmas for those who are faced with the reality of caring for chronically ill and dying older people, as well as for children with acute medical needs in an era of diminishing resources of social and health services. As noted by Zuckerman, (1994), much of health care is carried out in settings where the need for timely, practical solutions outweighs the need for abstract philosophical debate about patients' ethical and legal rights. The question of who should control decisions about life and death will continue to be argued among doctors, families, and often lawyers. Conflicting pressures for change will likely give way to the creation of new norms, whereby more people will support the removal of life supports for the terminally ill and will want to have control over their own death.

As the older population continues to increase, the decisions regarding the allocation and withholding of health care to individuals will assume greater importance. These decisions must be made by an informed and humanistic society; they cannot be left to policy makers, physicians, and attorneys only. What many today consider to be medical or geriatric issues will increasingly influence the lives of most Americans, young and middle aged, not just the old (Avorn, 1986). For these reasons and consistent with the underlying assumptions of this book, it is important to understand the processes of aging, as well as the policies and services that affect the older population and how these policies are made, so that society as a whole can make informed choices. In the final section, we will review some of the many opportunities for careers in gerontology. Whether or not gerontology is chosen as a career, however, it is important for all of us to become informed about this field so that we can become better consumers, citizens, advocates, and caregivers to frail elders within our families and in our communities.

## Careers in Gerontology

One reason for studying social gerontology is to determine the types of career opportunities in this field. It should be clear by now that gerontology holds great promise for practitioners, re-

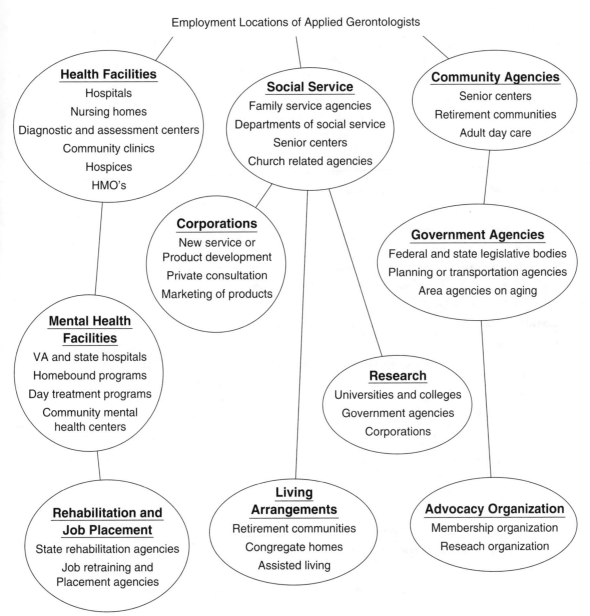

Employment Locations of Applied Gerontologists

**Health Facilities**
Hospitals
Nursing homes
Diagnostic and assessment centers
Community clinics
Hospices
HMO's

**Social Service**
Family service agencies
Departments of social service
Senior centers
Church related agencies

**Community Agencies**
Senior centers
Retirement communities
Adult day care

**Corporations**
New service or
Product development
Private consultation
Marketing of products

**Government Agencies**
Federal and state legislative bodies
Planning or transportation agencies
Area agencies on aging

**Mental Health Facilities**
VA and state hospitals
Homebound programs
Day treatment programs
Community mental
health centers

**Research**
Universities and colleges
Government agencies
Corporations

**Rehabilitation and Job Placement**
State rehabilitation agencies
Job retraining and
Placement agencies

**Living Arrangements**
Retirement communities
Congregate homes
Assisted living

**Advocacy Organization**
Membership organization
Reseach organization

**FIGURE E–2   Where Do Gerontologists Work? Employment Locations of Applied Gerontologists**
(Developed by M. Klein, University of Southern California: Used with permission of the author.)

searchers, and teachers in diverse aspects of the field. As we have seen throughout this book, specialists in geriatric health care will assume a greater role in helping the growing population of older people to maintain their quality of life, both in terms of treating chronic diseases and in

## FIGURE E–3    What Do Gerontologists Do?

1. *Direct Service*
   - Accesses client needs
   - Provides services directly to the older client and family
   - Coordinates services with other agencies and institutions
   - Works to assure that the older client and family receive appropriate services that are of a high quality
   - Evaluates and modifies the services needed
   - Conducts outreach to expand and enhance client base
   - Carries out advocacy on behalf of older persons

2. *Program Planning and Evaluation*
   - Identifies the needs of the community
   - Plans the programs and facilities
   - Determines the level and timing of funds required
   - Develops the staffing and management plans
   - Determines the evaluation plan for the program
   - Consults and coordinates with other agencies and programs

3. *Education and Training*
   - Plans and conducts educational programs for older persons, their caregivers and families
   - Plans and conducts continuing education programs for paraprofessionals and professionals interested in serving the elderly
   - Instructs preprofessionals
   - Intergenerational programs

4. *Administration and Policy*
   - Designs the structure, motivates and supervises the activities of staff members
   - Determines, monitors and modifies organizational expenditures
   - Coordinates activities within the organization and with outside organizations
   - Conducts analyses of current and proposed programs
   - Increases public awareness of needs and services

5. *Research*
   - Designs and carries out evaluations and academic studies to clarify aspects of aging and program interventions

preventing health problems. The increasing number of geriatric training programs in schools of medicine, nursing, dentistry, pharmacy, social work, and public health attest to the importance of this field. Specialists in geriatric nutrition and physical and occupational therapy will be in greater demand in the future as options expand in housing and long-term care. Attorneys with special training in medical ethics and aging will become critical members of the gerontological team. The increased interest in leisure activities in old age will call for more recreation specialists. Architects and planners will be urged to design housing that is sensitive to the needs of older people. Social workers and psychologists will be needed to work with older people and their families as counselors, advocates, support group facilitators, discharge planners, and case managers who coordinate services. Program planners, developers, and managers will have opportunities in a myriad of areas such as retirement housing, senior centers, adult day health programs, chore services, home health care, and respite care. There will even be opportunities for computer programmers and designers, as well as specialists in electronic communication, to design new products to help maintain older people's independence for as long as possible. In addition, there will be an ongoing need for low-tech workers, such as nursing aides and home health workers, who provide most of the personal daily long-term care services to older clients. This need must be addressed by better pay, training, and working conditions for these critically needed but low-paid workers (Morris, 1989; Older Women's League, 1988). Figure E-2 on page 567 illustrates the broad array of work settings for gerontologists. These range from government and community agencies to corporations and universities (Klein, 1994). These settings provide tremendous opportunities for significant contributions to improving the quality of life for older persons, as shown in Figure E-3 on page 568.

As noted throughout this book, more research is needed on the normal and pathological aspects of aging, and how age-related changes influence older people's social functioning. Researchers trained in sociology, psychology, economics, and political science must work with biologists, geneticists, nutritionists and others in the basic and clinical sciences to examine these important issues in aging.

In many ways, the field of gerontology is limited only by one's imagination. For those of you motivated and concerned about improving the quality of life for current and future generations of older people, we hope that the issues raised in this book will encourage you to join this exciting and challenging field.

## REFERENCES

Adlin, M. Health care issues. In E. Sutton, A. Factor, B. Hawkins, T. Heller, and G. Seltzer (Eds.) *Older adults with developmental disabilities,* Baltimore, MD: Paul H. Brookes Publishing Co., 1993, 49–60.

Allers, C. AIDS and the older adult. *The Gerontologist,* 1990, *30,* 405–410.

American Association of Retired Persons (AARP). *A profile of older Americans, 1990.* Washington, D.C.: AARP, 1991.

American Geriatrics Society. The care of dying patients: A position paper from the American Geriatrics Society. *Journal of the American Geriatrics Society,* 1994.

Anastas, J. W., Gibeau, J. L., and Larson, P. J. Working families and eldercare: A national perspective in an aging America. *Social Work,* 1990, *35,* 405–411.

Antonucci, T. Personal characteristics, social support and social behavior. In R. Binstock and E. Shanas (Eds.), *Handbook of aging and the social sciences* (2d ed.). New York: Van Nostrand and Reinhold, 1985.

Atchley, R. C. Retirement and leisure participation: Continuity or crisis? *The Gerontologist,* 1971, *2,* 13–17.

Avorn, J., Medicine: The life and death of Oliver Shay. In A. Pifer and L. Bronte (Eds.), *Our aging society: Paradox and promise.* New York: W. W. Norton, 1986.

Bengtson, V. C., Rosenthal, C. J., and Burton, C. Families and aging: Diversity and heterogeneity. In R. H. Binstock and L. George (Eds.), *Handbook of aging and the social sciences* (3d ed.). New York: Academic Press, 1990.

Binstock, R. H. Old-age-based rationing: From rhetoric to risk? *Generations,* 1994, 37–41.

Black, P., and Levy, E. Aging, natural death and the compression of morbidity: Another view. *New England Journal of Medicine,* 1981, *304,* 854–56.

Bulcroft, K. A., and Bulcroft, R. A. The timing of divorce effects on parent child relationships in later life. *Research on Aging,* 1991, *13,* 226–243.

Butler, R., and Gleason, H. *Productive aging: Enhancing vitality in later life.* New York: Springer, 1985.

Callahan, D. Health care in the aging society: A moral dilemma. In A. Pifer and L. Bronte (Eds.), *Our aging society: Paradox and promise.* New York: W. W. Norton, 1986.

Callahan, D. *Setting limits: Medical goals in an aging society.* New York: Simon and Schuster, 1987.

Callahan, D. *The troubled dream of life: Living with mortality.* New York: Simon & Schuster, 1993.

Caro, F. G., Bass, S. A., and Chen, Y. P. Introduction. In S. A. Bass, F. G. Caro and Y. P. Chen (Eds.), *Achieving a productive society.* Westport, Conn.: Auburn House, 1993.

Congressional Institute for the Future. *Tomorrow's elderly.* Washington, D.C., 1984.

Cornman, J. and Kingson, E. Trends, issues, perspectives and values for the aging of the baby boom cohorts. Background paper for the "Many faces of aging: Challenges for the future" Conference, Fordham University, New York, New York, March 30–31, 1995.

Day, J. Population projections of the United States by age, sex, race and Hispanic origin: 1992 to 2050. *Current Population Reports,* series P25, No. 1092, Washington, D.C.: United States Government Printing Office, 1992.

Dychtwald, K., and Flower, J. *Age wave: The challenges and opportunities of an aging America.* Los Angeles, Calif.: G. Tarcher, 1989.

Easterlin, R., Macdonald, C., and Macunovich, D. Retirement prospects of the baby boom generation: A different perspective. *The Gerontologist,* 1990, *30,* 776–783.

Edelman, M. W. Beyond Medicaid: Building a health care system for all ages. *Modern Maturity,* 1991, *34,* 9–12.

Emerman, J. Demand grows for technology that helps. *Aging Today.* September/October 1994, *XV* 11.

Family ties. *American Demographics,* 1986, *8,* 11–12.

Fleming, C., D'Agostino, R., and Selker, H. P. Is coronary care unit admission restricted for elderly patients? *American Journal of Public Health,* 1991, *81,* 1121–1125.

Foster, S. E., and Brizius, J. A. Caring too much? American women and the nation's caregiving crisis. In J. Allen and A. Pifer (Eds). *Women on the front lines: Meeting the challenge of an aging America.* Washington, D.C.: The Urban Institute Press, 1993, 47–73.

Friedan, B. *The second stage.* New York: Summit Books, 1981.

Fries, J. F. Aging, natural death, and the compression of morbidity. *The New England Journal of Medicine,* 1980, *303,* 130–135.

Fritz, M. Nursing homes chase big profits in subacute care. *The Seattle Times.* March 19, 1995, A4.

Furstenberg, F., Nord, C. W., Peterson, J. L., and Zill, N. The life course of children of divorce: Marital disruption and parental contact. *American Sociological Review,* 1983, *48,* 656–668.

Furstenberg, F. F., Jr. Divorce and the American family. *American Review of Sociology,* 1990, *16,* 379–403.

George, L. K., and Gold, D. T. Life course perspectives on intergenerational and generational connections. *Marriage and Family Review,* 1991, *16,* 1–2, 67.

Glick, P. Remarriage: Some recent changes and variations. *Journal of Family Issues,* 1980, *1,* 455–478.

Goldman, N., and Lord, G. Sex differences in life cycle measures of widowhood. *Demography,* 1983, *20,* 177–195.

Gordon, C., Gaitz, C. M., and Scott, J. Leisure and lives: Personal expressivity across the life span. In R. H. Binstock and E. Shanas (Eds.), *Handbook of aging and the social sciences* (1st ed.). New York: Van Nostrand Reinhold, 1976.

Hagestad, G. The family: Women and grandparents as kin-keepers. In A. Pifer and L. Bronte (Eds.), *Our aging society: Paradox and promise.* New York: W. W. Norton, 1986.

Hagestad, G., and Neugarten, B. Age and the life course. In E. Shanas and R. Binstock (Eds.), *Handbook of aging and the social sciences* (2d ed.). New York: Van Nostrand and Reinhold, 1985.

Haraven, T. Family time and historical time. *Daedalus,* Spring 1977, 57–70.

Hennon, C. B. Divorce and the elderly: A neglected area of research. In T. Brubaker (Ed.), *Family relationships in later life.* Beverly Hills, Calif.: Sage, 1983.

Herzog, A. R., and House, J. Productive activities: aging well. *Generations,* 1991, *15,* 49–54.

Hiatt, L. G. Smart houses for older people: General considerations. *International Journal of Technology and Aging,* 1988, *1,* 11–29.

Kabanoff, B. Work and nonwork: A review of models. *Psychological Bulletin,* 1980, *88,* 60–77.

Kalish, R. The new ageism and the failure models: A polemic. *The Gerontologist,* 1979, *19,* 398–402.

Kane, R. L., and Kane, R. A. Effects of the Clinton health reform on older persons and their families: A health care systems perspective. *Gerontologist,* 1994, *34,,* 598–606.

Kaye, L. W., and Applegate, J. S. *Men as caregivers to the elderly: Understanding and aiding unrecognized family support.* MA: Lexington Books, 1990.

Klein, M. Where do gerontologists work and what do gerontologists do? A model illustrating alternative careers in gerontology. Unpublished manuscript, University of Southern California: Andrus Gerontology Center, 1994.

Koop, C. E. Foreword In R. H. Binstock and S. G. Post (Eds.) *Too old for health care: Controversies in medicine, law, economics and ethics.* Baltimore, Md.: Johns Hopkins University Press, 1991, vii–x.

Lee, P. R., and Benjamin, A. E. Health policy trends: Impact on the academic health center. In S. Andreapoulos and J. Hogness (Eds.), *Health care for an aging society.* New York: Churchill Livingstone, 1989.

Longino, C., and Soldo, B. The graying of America: Implications of life extension for quality of life. In R. Ward and S. Tobin (Eds.), *Health in aging: Sociological issues and policy directions.* New York: Springer, 1987.

Lubitz, J. D., Riley, G. F. Trends in Medicare payments in the last year of life. *New England Journal of Medicine,* 1993, *328,* 1092–1096.

Markle Foundation, *Pioneers on the frontier of life: Aging in America,* New York: New York, 1989.

Matthews, J. The retirement crisis. *The Seattle Times,* January 6, 1995, B5 (Special to the Washington Post).

McGregor, M. Technology and the allocation of resources. *The New England Journal of Medicine,* 1989, *320,* 118–120.

Michel, V. Factoring ethnic and racial differences into bioethics decision making. *Generations,* 1994, *18,* 23–26.

Minkler, M., and Rose, K. *Grandmothers as caregivers: Raising children of the crack cocaine epidemic.* Newbury Park: Sage, 1993.

Morris, R. Challenges of aging in tomorrow's world: Will gerontology grow, stagnate, or change? *The Gerontologist,* 1989, *29,* 494–500.

Morris, R. Conclusion: Defining the place of the elderly in the twenty-first century. In S. A. Bass, F. G. Caro, and Y. P. Chen (Eds.), *Achieving a productive society.* Westport, CT: Auburn House, 1993.

National Center for Health Statistics. *Monthly Vital Statistics Report,* Vol. 32, No. 4. Hyattsville, Md.: Public Health Service, 1983.

New York Business Group on Health. *Employer support for employee caregivers.* New York: New York Business Group on Health, 1989.

Older Women's League. *OWL Observer,* Nov/Dec 1988, 7.

Older Women's League. *Failing America's caregivers: A status report on women who care.* Washington, D.C.: Older Women's League, 1989.

Older Women's League. *Heading for hardship: Retirement income for American women in the next century.* Washington, D.C.: Older Women's League, 1990.

Ory, M., and Warner, H. *Gender, health and longevity: Multidisciplinary perspectives.* New York: Springer, 1990.

Osgood, N. J. Work: Past, present and future. In N. J. Osgood (Ed.), *Life after work: Retirement, leisure, recreation, and the elderly.* New York: Praeger, 1982.

Paradise, S. Older never-married women: A cross-cultural investigation. *Women and Therapy,* 1993, *14,* 129.

The Pepper Commission (U.S. Bipartisan Commission on Comprehensive Health Care). *A call for action.* Washington, D.C.: U.S. Government Printing Office, 1990.

President's Commission for the Study of Ethical Problems in Medicine and Biomedical and Behavioral Research. *Deciding to forego life sustaining treatment.* Washington, D.C.: U.S. Government Printing Office, 1983.

Rice, D. P., and Feldman, J. J. Living longer in the United States: Demographic changes and health needs of the elderly. *Milbank Fund Memorial Quarterly/Health and Society,* 1983, *61,* 362–396.

Riley, M. W., and Riley, J. Longevity and social structure: The potential of the added years. In A. Pifer and L. Bronte (Eds.), *Our aging society: Paradox and promise.* New York: W. W. Norton, 1986.

Rix, S. *Older workers: How do they measure up? An overview of age differences on employee costs and performances.* Washington, D.C.: AARP, 1994.

Robinson, P. K., Coberly, S., and Paul, C. E. Work and retirement. In R. H. Binstock and E. Shanas (Eds.), *Handbook of aging and the social sciences* (2d ed.). New York: Van Nostrand Reinhold, 1985.

Sachs, G. A. Improving care of the dying. *Generations,* 1994, *18,* 19–22.

Schmidt, R. HIV and aging-related disorders. *Generations,* 1989, XIII, *13,* 6–15.

Schneider, E. L., and Brody, J. A. Aging, natural death, and the compression of morbidity: Another view. *New England Journal of Medicine,* 1983, *309,* 854–856.

Schneiderman, L. J. Medical futility and aging: Ethical implications. *Generations,* 1994, *18,* 61–65.

Schulz, J. H., and Myles, J. Old age pensions: A comparative perspective. In R. H. Binstock and L. George (Eds.), *Handbook of aging and the social sciences* (3d ed.). New York: Academic Press, 1990.

Scofield, G. R. Medical futility: Can we talk? *Generations,* 1994, *18,* 66–70.

Seltzer, M. Engaging two systems: The need for collaboration. Planning Paper presented at the Conference on Aging and Developmental Disabilities, University of Washington, Seattle, May 1989.

Smeeding, T. Nonmoney income and the elderly: The case of the "Tweeners." IRP Discussion Paper. Madison, Wis.: University of Wisconsin-Madison Institute for Research on Poverty, 1984.

Smeeding, T. Economic status of the elderly. In R. H. Binstock and L. George (Eds.), *Handbook of aging and the social sciences* (3d ed.). New York: Academic Press, 1990.

Spanier, G., and Glick, P. Paths to remarriage. *Journal of Divorce,* 1980, 283–298.

Sullivan, S., and Gilmore, J. Employers begin to accept eldercare as a business issue. *Personnel,* 1991 *68,* 3.

Twigg, J., and Atkin, K. *Carers perceived: Policy and practice in informal care.* Buckingham, UK: Open University Press, 1994.

Uhlenberg, P. Changing configurations of the life course. In T. Haraven (Ed.), *Transitions: The family and the life course in historical perspectives.* New York: Academic Press, 1978.

U.S. Bureau of the Census. *Current Population Survey,* March 1982, unpublished.

U.S. Bureau of the Census. 1980 and 1990 censuses of the population. *General Population Characteristics.* PC80-1-B1, Table 45. Washington, D.C.: Department of Commerce, 1991.

U.S. Bureau of the Census. *Population projections of the United States by age, sex, race and Hispanic origins: 1992–2050.* Current Population Reports, P-25, No. 1092. Washington, D.C.: U.S. Government Printing Office, 1992a.

U.S. Bureau of the Census. *Marital status and living arrangements: March 1992.* Current Population Reports, Series P-20, No. 468. Washington, D.C.: U.S. Government Printing Office, 1992b.

U.S. Senate Special Committee on Aging. *Aging America: Trends and projections, 1987–88 edition.* Washington, D.C.: U.S. Department of Health and Human Services, 1988.

U.S. Senate Special Committee on Aging. *Aging America: Trends and projections, 1991 edition.* Washington, D.C.: U.S. Department of Health and Human Services, 1992.

Verbrugge, L. Longer life but worsening health? Trends in health and mortality of middle-aged and older persons. *Milbank Memorial Fund Quarterly,* 1984, *62,* 475–519.

Wetle, T., Cwikel, J., and Levkoff, S. E. Geriatric medical decisions: Factors influencing the allocation of scarce resources and the decision to withhold treatment. *The Gerontologist,* 1988, *28,* 336–343.

Winsborough, H. A demographic approach to the life cycle. In K. W. Back (Ed.), *Life course: Integrative theories and exemplary populations.* Boulder, Co.: Westview Press, 1978.

Zedlewski, S. R., Barnes, R. O., Burt, M. K., McBride, T. D., and Meyer, J. A. *The needs of the elderly in the 21st century.* Final project report submitted to the AOA, Urban Institute, Washington, D.C., 1989.

Zuckerman, C. Clinical ethics in geriatric care settings. *Generations,* 1994, *18,* 9–12.

# INDEX

# PHOTO CREDITS